Continued on the back inside cover

SOCIAL PSYCHOLOGY

FOURTH CANADIAN EDITION

DAVID G. MYERS
Hope College

STEVEN J. SPENCER
University of Waterloo

CHRISTIAN JORDAN
Wilfrid Laurier University

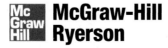

McGraw-Hill Ryerson

Toronto Montréal Burr Ridge, IL Dubuque, IA Madison, WI New York
San Francisco St. Louis Bangkok Bogotá Caracas Kuala Lumpur Lisbon London
Madrid Mexico City Milan New Delhi Santiago Seoul Singapore Sydney Taipei

The McGraw-Hill Companies

McGraw-Hill Ryerson

Social Psychology
Fourth Canadian Edition

ISBN-13: 978-0-07-076517-7
ISBN-10: 0-07-076517-0

1 2 3 4 5 6 7 8 9 10 TCP 0 9

Printed and bound in Canada.

Vice-President and Editor-in-Chief: Joanna Cotton
Publisher: Cara Yarzab
Marketing Manager: Michele Peach
Senior Developmental Editor: Denise Foote
Editorial Associate: Marina Seguin
Supervising Editor: Jessica Barnoski
Photo/Permission Research: Robyn Craig
Copy Editor: Erin Moore
Team Lead, Production: Paula Brown
Cover Design: Greg Devitt
Cover Image: Thomas Northcut/PhotoDisc/Getty Images
Interior Design: Greg Devitt
Page Layout: Bookman Typesetting Co. Inc.
Printer: Transcontinental Printing Group

Library and Archives Canada Cataloguing in Publication

Myers, David G
Social psychology / David G. Myers, Steven Spencer. — 4th Canadian ed.

Includes index.
ISBN 978-0-07-076517-7

1. Social psychology—Textbooks. I. Spencer, Steven J. II. Title.

HM1033.M947 2009 302 C2008-907881-0

ABOUT THE AUTHORS

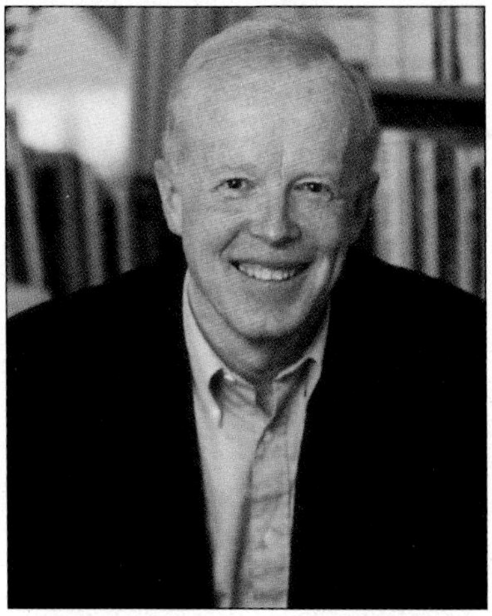

David G. Myers is the John Dirk Werkman Professor of Psychology at Michigan's Hope College, where he has been voted "Outstanding Professor" by students. Myers' love of teaching psychology is evident in his writing for the lay public. He has written for many magazines, including *Scientific American* and *Today's Education*. His 10 books include texts for Introductory and Social Psychology, and *The Pursuit of Happiness: Who Is Happy—and Why.*

Also an award-winning researcher, Dr. Myers received the Gordon Allport Prize from Division 9 of the American Psychological Association for his work on group polarization. His scientific articles have appeared in more than two dozen journals, including *Science, American Scientist, Psychological Bulletin,* and *Psychological Science*. He has served his discipline as consulting editor to the *Journal of Experimental Social Psychology* and the *Journal of Personality and Social Psychology.*

In his spare time he has chaired his city's Human Relations Commission, helped found a Community Action Centre that assists poverty-level families, and spoken to numerous collegiate and religious groups. David and Carol Myers are parents of two sons and a daughter.

Steven J. Spencer is an associate professor and chair of the social psychology division at the University of Waterloo. He teaches popular classes in Introductory Psychology, Social Psychology, and Social Cognition and is known for his lively lectures and engaging classroom demonstrations.

Dr. Spencer also maintains an active research program that investigates self-image maintenance processes, motivated social perception, and stereotyping. In particular, he has examined how threat to the self-concept can lead people to stereotype others and how being stereotyped by others can threaten people and undermine their performance on academic tasks. His work has been published in *Psychological Bulletin, Psychological Science,* the *Journal of Personality and Social Psychology, Personality and Social Psychology Bulletin,* and the *Journal of Experimental Social Psychology.* He serves his discipline as a consulting editor to the *Journal of Personality and Social Psychology* and as an associate editor to the *Journal of Experimental Social Psychology.*

In his spare time, he plays on an intramural basketball team organized by the graduate students in social psychology at the University of Waterloo, and enjoys spending time with his family. Steven and Shelley Spencer are the parents of two children, a daughter and a son.

Christian H. Jordan is an associate professor and graduate area coordinator of the social psychology division at Wilfrid Laurier University. He teaches lecture courses and seminars in Social Psychology and Research Methods at both the undergraduate and graduate levels.

Dr. Jordan is also an active researcher, studying implicit self-esteem and implicit attitudes—self-esteem and attitudes that come to mind spontaneously, like intuitions or gut feelings, but which may contradict our more reasoned evaluations of ourselves and the world. His work has been published in a number of scholarly handbooks and journals, including the *Journal of Personality and Social Psychology*, the *Personality and Social Psychology Bulletin*, *Self and Identity*, and the *Social and Personality Psychology Compass*. He has also written popular instructional pieces on how to effectively read journal articles and how to conduct and report persuasive psychology experiments.

In his spare time, he spends time with his family and friends, reads, listens to music, and exercises outdoors or at the gym. Christian and Lynne Jordan have a son, Grayson, and a daughter, Reilly, who they lost to leukemia.

BRIEF CONTENTS

TABLE OF CONTENTS

PREFACE

When I was asked to write this book, I was excited, but I also knew it would be a challenge. I was thrilled to be working with David Myers. He is known for his wonderful textbooks, which are solidly scientific and warmly human, factually rigorous, and intellectually provocative. His texts are simply the best. In addition, David is a fantastic friend, generous colleague, and one of my favourite undergraduate instructors—he was one of the readers on my honours thesis and has shaped my career from its very beginning. I knew him well and thought we could work well together. I expected that David would be a terrific mentor and he has more than exceeded my expectations.

In this edition, I also had the privilege of working with Christian Jordan. Christian is a fabulous writer, fantastic scholar, and a generous colleague. I first met Christian when he was an undergraduate and it was my great fortune to work with him while he was a graduate student. As Christian's career developed, I was hoping to bring him on as an author on this textbook and I could not be more pleased with the tremendous job he has done on this book.

I was very happy to have Christian along as we sought to meet the challenge of creating a comprehensive Canadian Social Psychology text. How does one select the material for inclusion in a "reasonably comprehensive" introduction to one's discipline—a text long enough to allow rich narrative (to weave a story) but crisp enough not to overwhelm? Further, what Canadian content will most capture the imaginations of Canadian students? We have sought to present theories and findings that are not too esoteric but capture the fundamental concepts of the field in scientifically rigorous manner. In doing so we have sought to balance classic findings with significant current Canadian research. We think you will find that as the book emphasizes the Canadian context, it also has a strong research focus presented in an understandable and engaging style.

ORGANIZATION

The book opens with a single chapter that includes our methods of inquiry. The chapter also warns students about how findings can seem obvious—once you know them—and how social psychologists' own values permeate the discipline. The intent is to give students just enough to prepare them for what follows.

The book then unfolds around its definition of social psychology: the scientific study of how people *think about* (Part One), *influence* (Part Two), and *relate to* (Part Three) one another.

Part One on *social thinking* examines how we view ourselves and others. It assesses the accuracy of our impressions, intuitions, and explanations, and examines the relation of our behaviour and our attitudes.

Part Two explores *social influence*. In this edition we now begin by discussing how social influence can shape attitudes—that is, how persuasion occurs. This structure allows instructors to focus on attitudes formation and change in a unit that covers both Chapters 4 and 5. We continue to examine social influence by examining the nature of conformity, group influence, and culture and language.

Part Three considers the attitudinal and behavioural manifestations of both negative and positive *social relations*. It flows from altruism to aggression and attraction to prejudice.

Applications of social psychology are both interwoven throughout every chapter and highlighted in the four concluding modules: **"Social Psychology in Conflict and Peacemaking,"** "**Social Psychology in the Clinic,**" "**Social Psychology in Court**," and "**Social Psychology and the Sustainable Future.**" These modules are not meant to be comprehensive treatments of these issues, but focus on interesting and engaging issues. They are meant to be included as supplements to the other chapters in the book when instructors want to emphasize these issues.

This book also has a multicultural emphasis that can be seen in Chapter 8's treatment of cultural influences, as well as in the inclusion of research from various cultures throughout the text. All authors are creatures of their cultures, and we are no exceptions. Yet by reading the world's social psychology literature, by corresponding with researchers worldwide, and by examining Canada's extensive research on the many cultures represented in this country, we have sought to present a multicultural text to a Canadian audience. The book's focus remains the *fundamental principles of social thinking, social influence, and social relations as revealed by careful empirical research*. However, hoping to broaden our awareness of the human family, we aim to illustrate these principles multiculturally.

To assist readers, we organize chapters into three or four readable-length sections. Each begins with a preview and ends with a summary that highlights the organization and key concepts.

In agreement with Thoreau's beliefs that "anything living is easily and naturally expressed in popular language," we have sought, paragraph by paragraph, to craft the most engaging and effective book possible. A bright, four-colour design complements the text revision and enhances the impact of the photos and figures. The definitions of key terms appear both in the margins and in the end-of-book Glossary.

HIGHLIGHTS OF THE FOURTH CANADIAN EDITION

- **Current Research**. The text's extensive references, more than 2700 in total, have been thoroughly updated to include the most cutting-edge research in social psychology. The latest findings on automatic processing, evolutionary psychology, video games and aggression, perceptions of media bias, counterarguments and attitude inoculation, culture and helping strangers, motivational sources of prejudice, and misperceptions of outgroups are just some of the examples of updated research in this new edition.
- **Additional Coverage of Culture**. Chapter 8, now titled "Culture and Language," has been revised extensively to reflect the burgeoning research literature on culture in social psychology. It has also been moved later in the text to allow more comprehensive treatment of social thinking and social influence. We also explore the impact of

culture on social relations, but leave more comprehensive coverage of these topics until later in the text. As this literature has grown and formed an important subfield in social psychology, it seemed comprehensive coverage of this topic in one chapter was necessary.

- **Additional Coverage of Gender**. Research on gender is evolving. Gender is now examined by a number of different researchers in a number of different contexts. As such, it seems that gender is less of a subfield of social psychology and more of a very important variable that is studied in many contexts. Given this evolution, gender is now covered throughout the book in many subsections.
- **Additional Coverage of Social Cognitive Neuroscience**. New developments in brain imaging and recording have provided a number of new insights in the field. These findings make a substantial contribution to a number of chapters.
- **Strong Pedagogy**. Readers benefit from features designed to engage interest while encouraging understanding of core concepts. Pedagogical elements include section previews; numerous photos, figures, and tables; a running glossary; Focus On boxes highlighting applied concepts; The Story Behind the Research vignettes written by leading researchers; a summary of each major section within the text; and an index printed on the inside covers highlighting coverage of concepts such as Culture, Ethics, Gender, Law and Justice, and Sexuality.
- **Relevant Examples**. Drawn from the arts, business, sports, and currents events, the text's examples appeal to students from a variety of majors and academic backgrounds.

WHAT'S NEW IN THE FOURTH CANADIAN EDITION

Key highlights of new and updated material in the Fourth Canadian Edition include:

CHAPTER 1: INTRODUCING SOCIAL PSYCHOLOGY

- Increased discussion of how values that vary across cultures can affect social psychology
- Expanded coverage of research methodology
- More detailed description of correlations and causal inference

CHAPTER 2: THE SELF IN A SOCIAL WORLD

- New organization that emphasizes the origin, organization, and functioning of the self
- Expanded research on the powers and perils of intuition
- New research on how goals function within the self-concept
- Includes new research on implicit self-esteem
- Expanded research on temporal self-appraisals
- New research on self-presentation and ego depletion

CHAPTER 3: SOCIAL BELIEFS AND JUDGMENTS

- Expanded coverage of research on priming
- Coverage of new research on the misinformation effect
- Covers new research on how lack of expertise can lead to confidence in one's judgments
- Covers new research on lack of attributional biases
- Expanded research on self-fulfilling prophecies

CHAPTER 4: BEHAVIOUR AND ATTITUDES

- New emphasis on implicit attitudes
- New research on the foot-in-the-door phenomenon on the Internet
- New research on dissonance and awareness
- New research on self-perception and body movements

CHAPTER 5: PERSUASION

- New organization that emphasizes dual process models of persuasion
- Coverage of new research on mimicry and persuasion
- Coverage of the latest research of the affect of cigarette warning labels on smoking in Canada
- Coverage of new research on fear and persuasion
- Coverage of new research on how aging affects the power of persuasive appeals and extremist positions
- Coverage of new research on attitude inoculation

CHAPTER 6: CONFORMITY

- Coverage of new research on implicit effect on conformity
- Coverage of new research on mimicry and conformity
- Coverage of new research on the liberating effects of conformity
- Coverage of new research on similarity and conformity
- Coverage of new research relating brain regions to conformity

CHAPTER 7: GROUP INFLUENCE

- New organization that emphasizes how group influences affect classic research on groups
- New emphasis on leadership
- New research on how friendship affects social loafing
- New research on antidotes to group think

CHAPTER 8: CULTURE AND LANGUAGE

- New section on culture and conformity
- New section on culture and persuasion

- New section on culture and group influence
- New section on multiculturalism in Canada
- New Focus On box describing the grassroots origins of bilingual education

CHAPTER 9: ALTRUISM: HELPING OTHERS

- New Focus On box describing how helping others can be a powerful source of happiness
- New research on gender and helping
- New research on attributions and helping
- New research on mood and helping
- New research on increasing helping

CHAPTER 10: AGGRESSION: HURTING OTHERS

- New research on motivations behind suicide bombers
- New research on testosterone and aggression
- New research on culture and aggression
- New research on weapons and aggression
- Updated research on video games and aggression

CHAPTER 11: ATTRACTION AND INTIMACY: LIKING AND LOVING OTHERS

- Updated research on the fundamental need to relate to others
- Expanded coverage of painful effects of ostracism and rejection by others
- Expanded coverage of similarity and attraction
- New research on gender differences and attraction
- Expanded coverage of self-esteem and attributions in relationships
- Expanded coverage of attachment processes in relationships
- New research on culture and relationships

CHAPTER 12: PREJUDICE: DISLIKING OTHERS

- Expands coverage on how the justice motive affects stereotyping and prejudice
- Expanded coverage of how attributions affect stereotyping and prejudice
- Updated research on stereotype threat
- Updated coverage on benevolent and hostile sexism
- New research on brain functioning and stereotypes and prejudice
- Expands coverage of the authoritarian personality and social dominance

MODULE A: SOCIAL PSYCHOLOGY IN CONFLICT AND PEACEMAKING

- New research on groups with intractable conflicts
- New research on arbitration
- New research on how simplistic thinking undermines peace building

MODULE B: SOCIAL PSYCHOLOGY IN THE CLINIC

- Updated research on difficulties with projective tests
- Expanded research on close relationships and health
- Updated research on realism in depression

MODULE C: SOCIAL PSYCHOLOGY IN COURT

- Updated research on how strong emotions affect eyewitness testimony
- Updated research on suggestive questioning and errors in memory
- Updated research on eyewitness lineups

MODULE D: SOCIAL PSYCHOLOGY AND THE SUSTAINABLE FUTURE

- Updated research on the threat of global warming
- Updated research on materialism and happiness

FEATURES

In addition to the authors' renowned engaging and personal writing style, which reflects their enthusiasm for the subject, *Social Psychology* also offers pedagogical elements designed to help students get the most out of the text.

SECTION PREVIEWS

These previews introduce each major section within a chapter, bringing forward the concepts and issues to be discussed in the ensuing pages.

SELF-SERVING BIAS: SEEING THE SELF POSITIVELY

As we process self-relevant information, a potent bias intrudes. We readily excuse our failures, accept credit for our successes, and in many ways see ourselves as better than average. Such self-enhancing perceptions enable most people to enjoy the benefits of high self-esteem, while occasionally suffering the perils of pride.

It is widely believed that most of us suffer low self-esteem. A generation ago, humanistic psychologist Carl Rogers (1958) concluded that most people he knew "despise themselves, regard themselves as worthless and unlovable." Many popularizers of humanistic psychology concur. "All of us have inferiority complexes," contends John Powell (1989). "Those who seem not to have such a complex are only pretending." As Groucho Marx (1960) lampooned, "I wouldn't want to belong to any club that would accept me as a member."

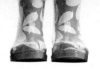

KEY TERMS

Every key concept is defined and placed in the margin to correspond to the term's use in the text. In addition, Key Terms are collected in the Glossary at the back of the text.

Social psychologists often venture into that ethical grey area when they design experiments that engage intense thoughts and emotions. Experiments need not have what Elliot Aronson, Marilynn Brewer, and Merrill Carlsmith (1985) call **mundane realism**. That is, laboratory behaviour (for example, delivering electric shocks as part of an experiment on aggression) need not be literally the same as everyday behaviour. For many researchers, that sort of realism is indeed mundane—not important. But the experiment *should* have **experimental realism**—it should absorb and involve the participants. Experimenters do not want their people consciously play-acting or ho-humming it; they want to engage real psychological processes. Forcing people to choose whether to give intense or mild electric shock to someone else can, for example, be a realistic measure of aggression. It functionally simulates real aggression.

Achieving experimental realism sometimes requires deceiving people with a plausible cover story. If the person in the next room actually is not receiving the shocks, the experimenter does not want the participants to know this. That would destroy the experimental realism. Thus, about one-third of social-psychological studies (though a decreasing number) have required deception (Korn & Nicks, 1993; Vitelli, 1988).

mundane realism
degree to which an experiment is superficially similar to everyday situations

experimental realism
degree to which an experiment absorbs and involves its participants

QUOTATIONS

Found throughout the text in the margins, quotations from philosophers, writers, and scientists highlight how social psychological concepts relate to many aspects of everyday society.

One problem with common sense, however, is that we invoke it *after* we know the facts. Events are far more "obvious" and predictable in hindsight than beforehand. Experiments reveal that when people learn the outcome of an experiment, that outcome suddenly seems unsurprising—certainly less surprising than it is to people who are simply told about the experimental procedure and the possible outcomes (Slovic & Fischhoff, 1977). People overestimate their ability to have foreseen the result. This happens especially when the result seems determined and not a mere product of chance (Hawkins & Hastie, 1990).

You perhaps experienced this phenomenon when reading Lazarsfeld's summary of findings. For Lazarsfeld went on to say, "Every one of these statements is the direct opposite of what was actually found." In reality, it was found that less-educated soldiers adapted more poorly. People from southern climates were not more likely than people from northern climates to adjust to tropical weather. Soldiers from city backgrounds were usually in better spirits than soldiers from rural backgrounds. And soldiers were actually more eager to come home after the fighting ended than while it was

"A first-rate theory predicts; a second-rate theory forbids; and a third-rate theory explains after the event."
Aleksander Isaakovich Kitaigorodskii

THE STORY BEHIND THE RESEARCH BOXES

In their own words, prominent social psychologists explain the motives and methods behind the studies conducted in their areas of expertise. These vignettes give students a first-hand account of studies cited in the text.

STORY BEHIND THE **RESEARCH**

Joseph Forgas
University of New South Wales, Sydney, Australia

We all know moody people, and I have often been struck by how their feelings seem to invade their thinking. It almost appears that their memories and judgments change with the colour of their mood. For some years now, I have been trying to understand how and why this mood infusion occurs.

One day while sitting in a restaurant, I noticed an odd couple at the next table—a beautiful young woman with an unattractive elderly man. As I found myself repeatedly wondering about this relationship, it occurred to me that the more I thought about them, the more opportunity there might be for my mood to infuse my thoughts. Testing this idea in the laboratory, we found that, indeed, mood had a greater effect on complex judgments of odd couples than on snap judgments of well-matched couples. Such findings have helped us to develop a theory that predicts when moodiness will infuse judgments.

FOCUS ON BOXES

In these boxes, a point–counterpoint approach to issues encourages student to apply the concepts of social psychology to their real-world experience.

FOCUS ON

SELF-SERVING BIAS—HOW DO I LOVE ME? LET ME COUNT THE WAYS

"The one thing that unites all human beings, regardless of age, gender, religion, economic status or ethnic background," notes Dave Barry (1998), "is that deep down inside, we all believe that we are above average drivers." We also believe we are above average on most any other subjective and desirable trait. Among the many faces of self-serving bias are these:

- *Intelligence.* Most people perceive themselves as more intelligent, better looking, and much less prejudiced than their average peer (Public Opinion, 1984; Wylie, 1979). When someone outperforms them, people tend to think of the other as a genius (Lassiter & Munhall, 2001).
- *Parental support.* Most adults believe they support their aging parents more than do their siblings (Lerner et al., 1991).

SUMMING UP

Found at the end of each major section within a chapter, this paragraph summarizes key concepts and draws connections between important issues.

SUMMING UP: SELF-CONCEPT

When we decide who we are and develop our self-concept one important source of information is our intuitions, which are curiously flawed. When powerful influences upon our behaviour are not so conspicuous that any observer could spot them, we, too, can miss them. The subtle implicit processes that control our behaviour may differ from our conscious explicit explanations of it.

A second important source of information that shapes our self-concepts is how we are viewed by others. The views of others are important building blocks of the self-concept although we heavily interpret these views as we define ourselves. Further whether we fit in and are seen positively by others forms an important basis of our self-esteem. How we compare to others and how our groups are viewed by others are two important ways that others shape our self-concepts.

KEY CONCEPTS INDEX

A valuable index of key concepts is printed on the text's inside covers. Topics organized under applied-concept headings such as Culture, Gender, Law and Justice, and Sexuality are keyed to page numbers within the text.

CONNECTIONS: APPLYING SOCIAL PSYCHOLOGY

From cover to cover, this book aims to expand our awareness, sharpen our thinking, and enable us to see connections among ideas. Although some readers of this book may become social psychologists, all should benefit from the power of social psychology's principles and analytic tools. Moreover, most readers can anticipate finding connections between their own interests and the ideas of social psychology, connections such as these:

COMPREHENSIVE SUPPORT

To help instructors and students meet today's teaching and learning challenges, *Social Psychology*, Fourth Canadian Edition, offers a complete, integrated supplements package.

SUPERIOR SERVICE

Service takes on a whole new meaning with McGraw-Hill Ryerson and *Social Psychology*. More than just bringing you the textbook, we have consistently raised the bar in terms of innovation and educational research. These investments in learning and the educational community have helped us to understand the needs of students and educators across the country and allowed us to foster the growth of truly innovative, integrated learning.

INTEGRATED LEARNING

Your Integrated Learning Sales Specialist is a McGraw-Hill Ryerson representative who has the experience, product knowledge, training, and support to help you assess and integrate any of our products, technology, and services into your course for optimum teaching and learning performance. Whether it's using our test bank software, helping your students improve their grades, or putting your entire course online, your *i*Learning Sales Specialist is there to help you do it. Contact your local *i*Learning Sales Specialist today to learn how to maximize all of McGraw-Hill Ryerson's resources!

*i*LEARNING SERVICES PROGRAM

McGraw-Hill Ryerson offers a unique *i*Services package designed for Canadian faculty. Our mission is to equip providers of higher education with superior tools and resources required for excellence in teaching. For additional information visit www.mcgrawhill.ca/highereducation/iservices.

TEACHING, TECHNOLOGY & LEARNING CONFERENCE SERIES

The educational environment has changed tremendously in recent years, and McGraw-Hill Ryerson continues to be committed to helping you acquire the skills you need to succeed in this new milieu. Our innovative Teaching, Technology & Learning Conference Series brings faculty together from across Canada with 3M Teaching Excellence award winners to share teaching and learning best practices in a collaborative and stimulating environment. Pre-conference workshops on general topics such as teaching large classes and technology integration are also offered. In addition, we will work with you at your own institution to customize workshops that best suit the needs of your faculty.

COURSESMART

CourseSmart brings together thousands of textbooks across hundreds of courses in an eTextbook format providing unique benefits to students and faculty. By purchasing an eTextbook, students can save up to 50 percent off the cost of a print textbook, reduce their impact on the environment, and gain access to powerful Web tools for learning including full text search, notes and highlighting, and e-mail tools for sharing notes between classmates. For faculty, CourseSmart provides instant access to review and compare textbooks and course materials in their discipline area without the time, cost, and environmental impact of mailing print exam copies. For further details contact your *i*Learning Sales Specialist or go to www.coursesmart.com.

INSTRUCTOR SUPPLEMENTS

*i*STUDY (www.istudypsychology.ca)

In partnership with Youthography, a Canadian youth research company, and hundreds of students from across Canada, McGraw-Hill Ryerson conducted extensive student research on student study habits, behaviours, and attitudes—we asked questions and listened . . . and we heard some things we didn't expect. We had two goals: to help faculty be more efficient in and out of the classroom by providing a study tool that would help them improve student engagement and to help students learn their course material and get better grades. Through this research, we gained a better understanding of how students study—and how we could make vast improvements to our current online study tools. The result is a study tool that students overwhelming said is *better* and there's *nothing else like it out there*. *i*Study really is the first study tool built by students for students. Getting better grades really is only a click away!

- **Study Plan:** An innovative tool that helps students customize their own learning experience. Students can diagnose their knowledge with pre- and post-tests and search contents of the entire learning package for content specific to the topic they're studying to add these resources to their study plan. Students told us the act of creating a study plan is how they actually study and that having the opportunity to have everything in one place, with the ability to search, customize and prioritize the class resources, was critical. No other publisher provides this type of tool and students told us without a doubt, the "Study Plan" feature is the most valuable tool they have used to help them study.
- **eText:** Now students can search the textbook online, too! When struggling with a concept or reviewing for an exam, students can conduct key word searches to quickly find the content they need.
- **Homework Assessment:** *i*Study assessment activities don't stop with students. There is material for instructors to leverage as well. For *Social Psychology,* this includes quizzes you can use in class, assign as homework, or add to exams.

ONLINE LEARNING CENTRE

The Online Learning Centre includes a password-protected Web site for instructors (www.mcgrawhill.ca/olc/myers) offering all the necessary instructor supplements:

- **Instructor's Manual:** Each chapter in the Instructor's Manual contains a chapter outline; a chapter summary; suggested classroom demonstration; and discussion questions.
- **Computerized Test Bank:** The Test Bank provides a variety of questions, including multiple-choice, true/false, and short answer. The multiple-choice and true/false questions include the answer as well as the page number in the main text where the material appears.
- **PowerPoint® Presentations:** These visual presentations, crafted for each chapter, include useful outlines, summaries, and visuals.

COURSE MANAGEMENT

Content cartridges are available for the course management systems WebCT and Blackboard. These platforms provide instructors with user-friendly, flexible teaching tools. Please contact your local McGraw-Hill Ryerson *i*Learning Sales Specialist for details.

STUDENT SUPPLEMENTS

i*Study *Social Psychology (www.istudypsychology.ca)
*i*Study was developed to help students master concepts and achieve better grades with all the learning tools they've come to expect, plus a lot more! Some of the key features include pre- and post-tests tied to the chapter learning objectives to assess mastery and monitor improvement, additional quizzing material, social psychology videos, and an eBook for easy reference. *i*Study offers the best, most convenient way to learn, interact, and succeed.

ONLINE LEARNING CENTRE

The Online Learning Centre for the text offers chapter outlines, multiple-choice quizzes, and other study tools. Visit www.mcgrawhill.ca/olc/myers.

IN APPRECIATION

I would like to thank the many people who helped me in writing this book. The following Canadian scholars provided thoughtful and thorough reviews, and their suggestions greatly improved this edition:

Delbert A. Brodie, *St. Thomas University*
Deborah Flynn, *Nipissing University*
Ken Fowler, *Memorial University of Newfoundland*
James Gibson, *University of Victoria*
Gerald Goldberg, *York University*
Gabriella Ilie, *University of Toronto Scarborough*
Linda Jessup, *University of Waterloo*
Christine Lomore, *St. Francis Xavier University*
Stephen B. Perrott, *Mount Saint Vincent University*
Jason Plaks, *University of Toronto St. George*
Stanley Sadava, *Brock University*
Saba Safdar, *University of Guelph*
Rodney Schmaltz, *University of Alberta*
Kelly Schwartz, *University of Calgary*
Monika Stelzl, *St. Thomas University*
Mahin Tavakoli, *Carleton University*
Warren Thorngate, *Carleton University*

I also want to thank the editorial staff at McGraw-Hill Ryerson for their excellent work. Nicole Lukach was instrumental in shaping the vision for the text. Denise Foote provided excellent editorial assistance by suggesting numerous revisions and countless editorial touches throughout the manuscript. Jessica Barnoski and Erin Moore also provided excellent help in guiding the book through the final changes needed for publication. Finally, I would like to thank my wife, Shelley, and my children, Emily and Jonathan, for their patience during the many evenings I was away from home while writing this book.

Steven J. Spencer
University of Waterloo
Waterloo, ON N2L 3G4
Canada
E-mail: sspencer@watarts.uwaterloo.ca

CHAPTER ONE

Introducing Social Psychology

What is social psychology: What does it try to do?

Major themes in social psychology
We construct our social reality
Our social intuitions are often powerful but sometimes perilous
Social influences shape our behaviour
Personal attitudes and dispositions also shape behaviour
Social behaviour is biologically rooted
Relating to others is a basic need
Social psychology's principles are applicable in everyday life

Social psychology and human values
Obvious ways in which values enter
Not-so-obvious ways in which values enter

I knew it all along: Is social psychology simply common sense?

Research methods: How does social psychology try to accomplish its goals?
Forming and testing hypotheses
Correlational research: Detecting natural associations
Experimental research: Searching for cause and effect
Generalizing from laboratory to life

There once was a man whose second wife was a vain and selfish woman. This woman had two daughters who were similarly vain and selfish. The man's own daughter, however, was sweet and kind. This sweet, kind daughter, whom we all know as Cinderella, learned early on that she had best do as she was told, accept insults, and not upstage her vain stepsisters.

But then, thanks to her fairy godmother, Cinderella was able to escape her situation and go to a grand ball, where she attracted a handsome prince. When the love-struck prince later encountered a homelier Cinderella back in her degrading home, he at first failed to recognize her.

Implausible? The folk tale demands that we accept the power of the situation. In one situation, playing one role in the presence of her oppressive stepmother, the meek and unattractive Cinderella was a different person from the charming and beautiful Cinderella whom the prince met. At home, she cowered. At the ball, Cinderella felt more beautiful and walked and talked and smiled as if she were.

WHAT IS SOCIAL PSYCHOLOGY: WHAT DOES IT TRY TO DO?

The French philosopher-novelist Jean-Paul Sartre (1946) would have had no problem accepting the Cinderella premise. We humans are "first of all beings in a situation," he believed. "We cannot be distinguished from our situations, for they form us and decide our possibilities" (pp. 59–60, paraphrased). **Social psychology** is a science that studies the influences of our situations, with special attention to how we view and affect one another. Said more precisely, it is the scientific study of how people think about, influence, and relate to one another (Figure 1–1).

Social psychology lies at psychologies boundaries with sociology. Compared with sociology (the study of people in groups and societies), social psychology focuses more on individuals with methods that more often use experimentation. Compared with personality psychology, social psychology focuses less on differences among individuals, and more on how individuals, in general, view and affect one another.

social psychology
the scientific study of how people think about, influence, and relate to one another

FIGURE 1–1

Social psychology is . . .

Social psychology is the scientific study of . . .

Social thinking	Social influence	Social relations
• How we perceive ourselves and others • What we believe • Judgments we make • Our attitudes	• Culture and biology • Pressures to conform • Persuasion • Groups of people	• Helping • Aggression • Attraction and intimacy • Prejudice

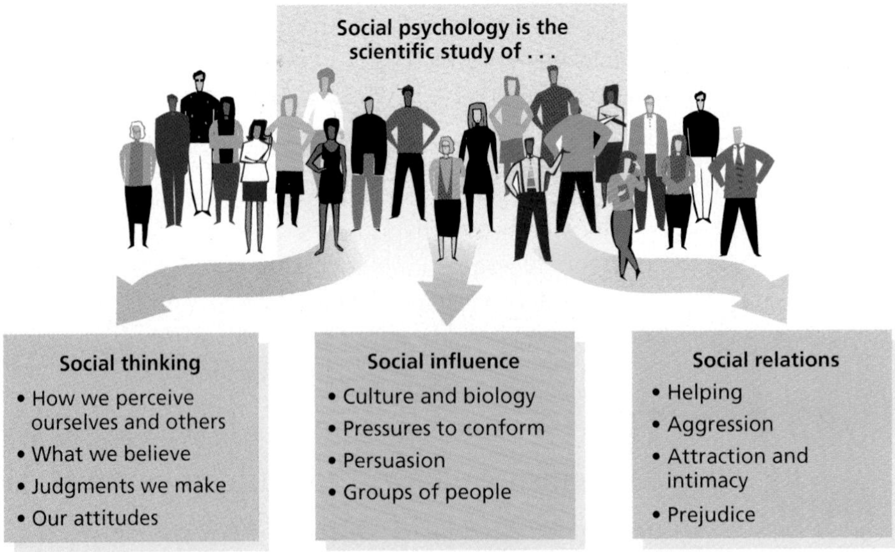

Social psychology is still a young science. The first social psychology experiments were barely more than a century ago (1898), and the first social psychology texts did not appear until just before and after 1900, in France, Italy, and Germany (Smith, 2005). Not until the 1930s did social psychology assume its current form. And not until the Second World War did it begin to emerge as the vibrant field it is today.

Social psychology studies our thinking, influence, and relationships by asking questions that have intrigued us all. Here are some examples:

How much of our social world is just in our heads?

As we will see in later chapters, our social behaviour varies not just with the objective situation, but with how we construe it. Social beliefs can be self-fulfilling. For example, happily married people will attribute their spouse's acid, "Can't you ever put that where it goes?" to something external ("He must have had a frustrating day"). Unhappily married people will attribute the same remark to a mean disposition ("Is he ever hostile!") and may therefore respond with a counterattack. Moreover, expecting hostility from their spouse, they may behave resentfully, thereby eliciting the hostility they expect.

Would you be cruel if ordered?

How did Nazi Germany conceive and implement the inconceivable slaughter of 6 million Jews? These evil acts occurred because thousands of people followed orders. They put the prisoners on trains, herded them into crowded showers, and poisoned them with gas. How could people engage in such horrific actions? Were these folks normal human beings? Stanley Milgram (1974) wondered. So he set up a situation where people were ordered to administer increasing

A memorial to Robert Dziekanski who died in Vancouver International Airport after he was tasered by authorities. He became confused and agitated after a long flight and could not understand authorities as they tried to deal with his behaviour. They followed protocol and shot him with a taser. Tragically he died. Could such an incident have been averted if rules allowed more flexible responding to altercations with authorities?

levels of electric shock to someone who was having difficulty learning a series of words. As we will see in Chapter 6, the experimental results were quite disturbing: nearly two-thirds of the participants fully complied.

To help? Or to help oneself?

As bags of cash tumbled from an armoured truck on a fall day in 1987, $2 million was scattered along a Toronto, Ontario, street. Some motorists who stopped to help returned $100,000. Judging from what disappeared, many more stopped to help themselves. When similar incidents occurred in San Francisco, California, and Columbus, Ohio, the results were the same: Passersby grabbed most of the money (Bowen, 1988).

Throughout this book, sources for information are cited parenthetically, and then fully provided in the reference section that begins on page 548.

What situations trigger people to be helpful or greedy? Do some cultural contexts—perhaps villages and small towns—breed greater helpfulness?

A common thread runs through these questions: They all deal with how people view and affect one another. And that is what social psychology is all about. Social psychologists study attitudes and beliefs, conformity and independence, love and hate.

MAJOR THEMES IN SOCIAL PSYCHOLOGY

What are social psychology's big lessons—its overarching themes? In many academic fields, the results of tens of thousands of studies, the conclusions of thousands of investigators, and the insights of hundreds of theorists can be boiled down to a few central ideas. Biology offers us principles such as natural selection and adaptation. Sociology builds on concepts such as social structure and organization. Music harnesses our ideas of rhythm, melody, and harmony.

What concepts are on social psychology's short list of central ideas? What themes, or fundamental principles, will be worth remembering long after you have forgotten most of the details? At a broad level the fundamental principles of social psychology can be captured by a classic statement by one of its founders, Kurt Lewin who said, "behaviour is a function of the person and the situation." From this general principle we developed a short list of "great ideas we ought never forget," each of which we will unpack in chapters to come (Figure 1–2).

WE CONSTRUCT OUR SOCIAL REALITY

We humans have an irresistible urge to explain behaviour, to attribute it to some cause, and therefore to make it seem orderly, predictable, and controllable. You and I may react differently to similar situations because we think differently. How we react to a friend's insult depends on whether we attribute it to hostility or to a bad day.

In a way, we are all intuitive scientists. We explain people's behaviour, usually with enough speed and accuracy to suit our daily needs. When someone's behaviour is consistent and distinctive, we attribute their behaviour to their personality. For example, if you observe someone who makes repeated snide comments, you may infer that person has a nasty disposition, and then you might try to avoid the person.

Our beliefs about ourselves also matter. Do we have an optimistic outlook? Do we see ourselves as in control of things? Do we view ourselves as relatively superior or inferior?

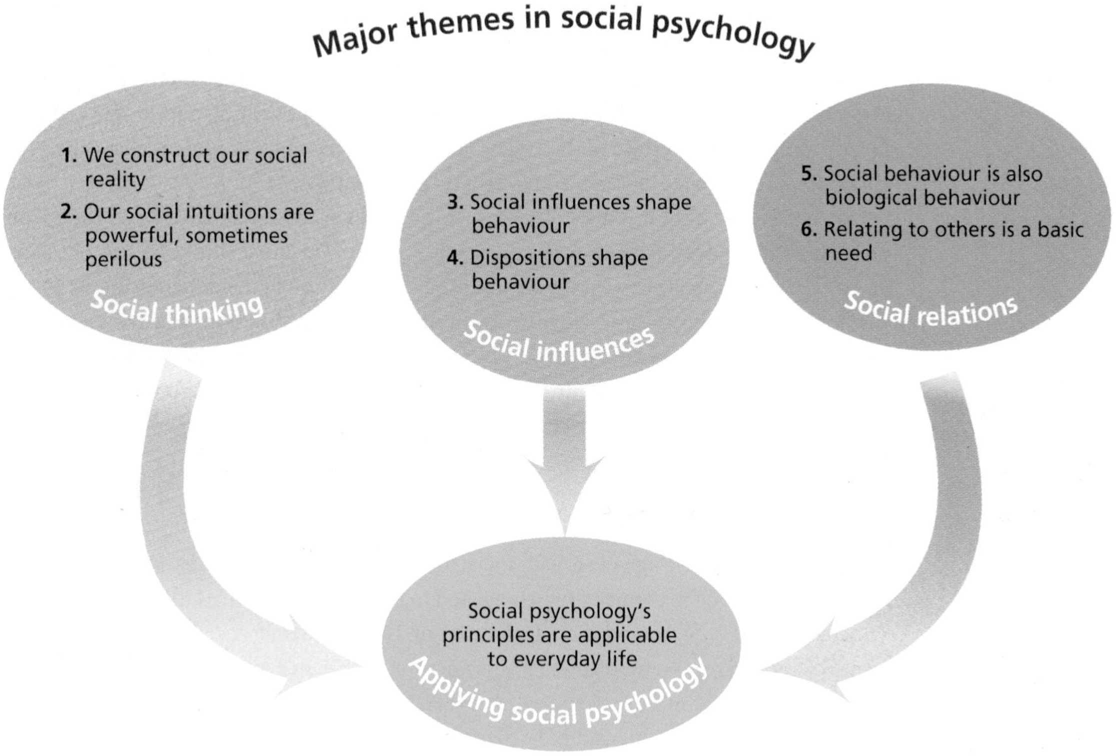
Major themes in social psychology
1. We construct our social reality
2. Our social intuitions are powerful, sometimes perilous
Social thinking
3. Social influences shape behaviour
4. Dispositions shape behaviour
Social influences
5. Social behaviour is also biological behaviour
6. Relating to others is a basic need
Social relations
Social psychology's principles are applicable to everyday life
Applying social psychology

FIGURE 1–2
Major themes in social psychology.

Our answers influence our emotions and actions. How we construe the world, and ourselves, matters.

OUR SOCIAL INTUITIONS ARE OFTEN POWERFUL BUT SOMETIMES PERILOUS

Our intuitions shape our fears (is flying dangerous?), impressions (can I trust him?), and relationships (does she like me?). Intuitions influence leaders in times of crisis, gamblers at the table, jurors in their assessments of guilt, and personnel directors when eyeing applicants. Such intuitions are commonplace.

Indeed, psychological science reveals a fascinating unconscious mind—an intuitive backstage mind—that Freud never told us about. More than we realized a decade or more ago, thinking occurs not onstage, but offstage, out of sight. As we will see, studies of "automatic processing," "implicit memory," "heuristics," "spontaneous trait inference," instant emotions, and nonverbal communication unveil our intuitive capacities. Thinking, memory, and attitudes all operate on two levels—one conscious and deliberate, the other unconscious and automatic. "Dual processing," today's researchers call it. We know more than we know we know.

Intuition is huge but intuition is also perilous. More than we realize, thinking occurs offscreen, with the results occasionally displayed on-screen. We misperceive others and we often fail to appreciate how our expectations shape our evaluations. Even our intuitions about ourselves often err. We intuitively trust our memories more than we should. We misread our own minds; in experiments, we deny being affected by things that do influence us. We mispredict our own feelings—how bad we'll feel a year from now if we lose our job or our romance breaks up, and how good we'll feel a year from now if we win our province's lottery. And we often mispredict our own future—when buying clothes, people approaching middle age will still buy snug ("I anticipate shedding a bit of weight"); rarely does anyone say, more realistically, "I'd better buy a relatively loose fit; people my age tend to put on weight").

So, our social intuitions are noteworthy for both their ineffable powers and their troublesome perils. Our lives are empowered by subterranean intuitive thinking and occasionally imperiled by predictable errors. By reminding us of intuition's gifts and alerting us to its pitfalls, social psychologists aim to fortify our thinking. In most situations, "fast and frugal" snap judgments serve us well enough. But in others, where accuracy matters—as when needing to fear the right things and spend our resources accordingly—we had best restrain our impulsive intuitions with critical thinking.

SOCIAL INFLUENCES SHAPE OUR BEHAVIOUR

We are, as Aristotle long ago observed, social animals. We speak and think in words we learned from others. We long to connect, to belong, and to be well thought of. Matthias Mehl and James Pennebaker (2003) quantified their University of Texas students' social behaviour by inviting them to wear microcassette recorders and microphones. Once every 12 minutes during their waking hours, the computer-operated recorder would imperceptibly record for 30 seconds. Although the observation period only covered weekdays (including class time), almost 30 percent of their time was spent talking. Relationships are a large part of being human.

As social creatures, we respond to our immediate contexts. Sometimes the power of a social situation leads us to act in ways that depart from our espoused attitudes. Indeed, powerful evil situations sometimes overwhelm good intentions, inducing people to agree with falsehoods or comply with cruelty. Under Nazi influence, many decent-seeming people became instruments of the Holocaust. Other situations may elicit great generosity and compassion. After the tsunami that struck much of Asia, people throughout the world gave generously to provide relief.

The power of the situation was also evident when Canadian officials gave in to the influence of pressures from the U.S. and supported the rendition of Maher Arar to Syria despite knowing that he would likely be tortured. Following the dramatic terrorist attacks in the U.S. on September 11, 2001, the situation powerfully swung concerns toward stopping terrorism and away from protecting individual rights. On a more positive note the ice storm in Quebec in 1998 brought together people from throughout Canada to clear trees and restore power. This situation brought out generosity and concern for others. Whether for good or ill this much is evident: Our situations matter.

Our cultures help define our situations. Our standards regarding promptness, frankness, and clothing vary with our cultural situation. Whether you equate female beauty with slimness or shapeliness likewise depends on when and where in the world you live. Whether you define social justice as equality (all receive the same) or as equity (those who earn more receive more) depends on whether your ideology has been shaped more by socialism or capitalism. Whether you tend to be expressive or reserved, casual or formal, hinges partly on your culture and ethnicity. Whether you focus primarily on yourself—your personal needs, desires, and morality—or on your family, clan, and communal groups, depends on how much you are a product of modern Western individualism. Social psychologist Hazel Markus (2005) sums it up: "People are, above all, malleable." Said differently, we adapt to our social context. *Our attitudes and behaviour are shaped by external forces.*

PERSONAL ATTITUDES AND DISPOSITIONS ALSO SHAPE BEHAVIOUR

Internal forces also matter. We are not passive tumbleweeds, merely blown this way and that by the social winds. Our inner attitudes affect our behaviour. Our political attitudes influence our voting behaviour. Our smoking attitudes influence our susceptibility to peer pressures to smoke. Our attitudes toward the poor influence our willingness to support them. (As we will see, attitudes also follow behaviour, which leads us to believe strongly in those things for which we have committed ourselves or suffered.)

Personality dispositions also affect behaviour. Facing the same situation, different people may react differently. Emerging from years of political imprisonment, one person exudes bitterness and seeks revenge. Another, such as South Africa's Nelson Mandela, seeks reconciliation and unity with onetime enemies. *Attitudes and personality influence behaviour.*

SOCIAL BEHAVIOUR IS BIOLOGICALLY ROOTED

Twenty-first-century social psychology is providing us with ever growing insights into our behaviour's biological foundations Many of our social behaviours reflect a deep biological wisdom.

Everyone who has taken introductory psychology knows that nature and nurture together form who we are. As the area of a field is determined by both its length and width, so do biology and experience together create us. If every psychological event (every thought, every emotion) is simultaneously a biological event, then we can also examine the neurobiology that underlies social behaviour. What brain areas enable our experiences of love and contempt, helping and aggression, perception and belief? How do brain, mind, and behaviour function together as one coordinated system? What does the timing of brain events reveal about how we process information? Such questions are asked by those in **social neuroscience** (Heatheron et al., 2004; Ochsner & Lieberman, 2001).

social neuroscience
an integration of biological and social perspectives that explores the neural and psychological bases of social and emotional behaviours

Social neuroscientists do not reduce complex social behaviours, such as helping and hurting, to simple neural or molecular mechanisms. Their point is this: To understand social behaviour, we must consider both under-the-skin (biological) and between-skins (social) influences. Mind and body are one grand system. Stress hormones affect how we feel and act; social ostracism elevates blood pressure. Social support strengthens the disease-fighting immune system. *We are bio-psycho-social organisms.* We reflect the interplay of our biological, psychological, and social influences. And that is why today's psychologists study behaviour from these different levels of analysis.

RELATING TO OTHERS IS A BASIC NEED

We want to fit in with others and our relationship with others can be an important source of stress and pain as well as joy and comfort. Kip Williams and his colleagues (Williams, 2002; Williams, Cheung & Choi, 2002; Williams & Zadro, 2001) have shown that feeling left out can have dramatic effects on how people feel about themselves. They had university students play a simple computer game in which each player was represented by a cartoon figure on the screen and the figures passed a ball to one another. When confederates of the experimenter passed the ball to one another and left the real participants out of the action, the participants felt miserable and reported steep drops in their self-esteem. Apparently, even university students can feel the pain that many school children experience when they are not included. Acts of aggression and prejudice inflict this sort of pain.

Of course, relating to others is not all pain. When others help, when we form romantic relationships, and when we promote harmony between groups, interpersonal relations can be an important source of joy and comfort. In fact, according to Mark Leary and Roy Baumeister, our relationships with others form the basis of our self-esteem (Leary & Baumeister, 2000). In fact, they argue that our self-esteem is nothing more than a reading of how accepted we feel by others. In this view, relating to others is a basic need that shapes all our social actions.

SOCIAL PSYCHOLOGY'S PRINCIPLES ARE APPLICABLE IN EVERYDAY LIFE

Social psychology has the potential to illuminate your life to make visible the subtle forces that guide your thinking and acting. And, as we will see, it offers many ideas about how to know ourselves better, how to win friends and influence people, how to transform closed fists into open arms.

"You can never foretell what any man [person] will do, but you can say with precision what an average number will be up to. Individuals may vary, but percentages remain constant."

Sherlock Holmes, in Sir Arthur Conan Doyle's *A Study in Scarlet*, 1887

Scholars are also applying social psychological insights to other disciplines. Principles of social thinking, social influence, and social relations have implications for human health and well-being, for judicial procedures and juror decisions in courtrooms, and for the encouragement of behaviours that will enable an environmentally sustainable human future.

As but one perspective on human existence, psychological science does not seek to engage life's ultimate questions: What is the meaning of human life? What should be our purpose? What is our ultimate destiny? But social psychology does give us a method for asking and answering some exceedingly interesting and important questions. *Social psychology is all about life—your life: your beliefs, your attitudes, your relationships.*

The rest of this chapter takes us inside social psychology. Let's first consider how social psychologists' own values influence their work in obvious and subtle ways. And let's focus on the chapter's biggest task: glimpsing how we do social psychology. How does it sleuth for explanations of social thinking, social influence, and social relations? And how might we use these analytical tools to think smarter?

SUMMING UP

Social psychology is the scientific study of how people think about, influence, and relate to one another. Social psychology tends to be more individualistic in its content and more experimental in its method than sociology. Compared to personality psychology, social psychology focuses less on differences among individuals and more on how people, in general, view and affect one another.

Social psychology is an environmental science; it reveals how the social environment influences behaviour. Its central themes concern:

- How we construe our social worlds
- How our social intuitions guide and sometimes deceive us
- How our social behaviour is shaped by other people, by our attitudes and personality, and by our biology
- How social psychology's principles apply to our everyday lives and to various other fields of study

SOCIAL PSYCHOLOGY AND HUMAN VALUES

Social psychologists' values penetrate their work in ways both obvious and subtle. What are such ways?

Social psychology is less a collection of findings than a set of strategies for answering questions. In science, as in courts of law, personal opinions are inadmissible. When ideas are put on trial, evidence determines the verdict. But are social psychologists really this objective? As human beings, don't our values—our personal convictions about what is desirable and how people ought to behave—seep into our work? And if they do, can social psychology really be scientific?

OBVIOUS WAYS IN WHICH VALUES ENTER

Values enter the picture with our choice of research topics. It was no accident that the study of prejudice flourished during the 1940s as fascism raged in Europe; that the 1950s, a time of look-alike fashions and rows of identical suburban homes, gave us studies of conformity; that the 1960s saw interest in aggression increase with riots and rising crime rates; that the 1970s feminist movement helped stimulate a wave of research on gender and sexism; that the 1980s offered a resurgence of attention to psychological aspects of the arms race; and that the 1990s were marked by heightened interest in how people respond to cultural diversity. These trends reflect the social concerns of their time. Social psychology reflects social history.

Values differ not only across time but also across cultures. In Europe, people take pride in their nationalities. The Scots are self-consciously distinct from the English, and the Austrians from the Germans. Consequently, Europe has given us a major theory of "social identity," whereas North American social psychologists have focused more on individuals—how one person thinks about others, is influenced by them, and relates to them (Fiske, 2004; Tajfel, 1981; Turner, 1984). Australian social psychologists have drawn theories and methods from both Europe and North America (Feather, 2005).

Values also influence the types of people attracted to various disciplines (Campbell, 1975; Moynihan, 1979). At your school, too, do the students attracted to the humanities, the natural sciences, and the social sciences noticeably differ? Do psychology and sociology attract people who are eager to challenge tradition, people who would rather shape the future than preserve the past?

Finally, values obviously enter the picture as the *object* of social-psychological analysis. Social psychologists investigate how values form, why they change, and how they influence attitudes and actions. None of this, however, tells us which values are "right."

culture
the enduring behaviours, ideas, attitudes, traditions, products, and institutions shared by a large group of people and transmitted from one generation to the next

social representations
socially shared beliefs. Widely held ideas and values, including our assumptions and cultural ideologies. Our social representations help us make sense of our world.

NOT-SO-OBVIOUS WAYS IN WHICH VALUES ENTER

We less often recognize the subtler ways in which value commitments masquerade as objective truth. Consider three not-so-obvious ways in which values enter social psychology and related areas.

The subjective aspects of science

Scientists and philosophers now agree: Science is not purely objective. Scientists do not simply read the book of nature. Rather, they interpret nature, using their own mental categories. In our daily lives, too, we view the world through the lens of our preconceptions.

"Science does not simply describe and explain nature; it is part of the interplay between nature and ourselves; it describes nature as exposed to our method of questioning."

Werner Heisenberg, *Physics and Philosophy*, 1958

While reading these words you have been unaware that you are also looking at your nose. Your mind blocks from awareness something that is there, if only you were predisposed to perceive it. This tendency to prejudge reality based on our expectations is a basic fact about the human mind.

Because scholars at work in any given area often share a common viewpoint or come from the same **culture**, their assumptions may go unchallenged. What we take for granted—the shared beliefs that European social psychologists call our **social representations** (Augoustinos & Innes, 1990; Moscovici, 1988; Pettifor, 1996)—are our most important but often most unexamined convictions. Social psychology has a history of questioning these convictions. In the early 1970s, social psychologists debated the approach, methods, and goals of research in what is sometimes called a crisis in confidence in the field (Gergen, 1973; Schlenker, 1974).

Sometimes, however, someone from outside the camp will also call attention to these assumptions. During the 1980s, feminists and Marxists exposed some of social psychology's unexamined assumptions. Feminist critics called attention to subtle biases—for example, the political conservatism of many scientists who favour a biological interpretation of gender differences in social behaviour (Unger, 1985). Marxist critics called attention to competitive, individualist biases—for example, the assumption that conformity is bad and that individual rewards are good. Marxists and feminists, of course, make their own assumptions, as critics of academic "political correctness" are fond of noting. Social psychologist Lee Jussim (2005), for example, argues that progressive social psychologists sometimes feel compelled to deny group differences and to assume that stereotypes of group differences are never rooted in reality but always in racism.

In Chapter 3 we will see more ways in which our preconceptions guide our interpretations. What's crucial for our behaviour is less the situation-as-it-is than the situation-as-we-construe-it.

Psychological concepts contain hidden values

Implicit in our understanding that psychology is not objective is the realization that psychologist' own values play an important part in the theories and judgments they support. Psychologists refer to people as mature or immature, as well-adjusted or poorly adjusted, as mentally healthy or mentally ill. They talk as if they were stating facts, when really they are *value judgments*. Here are some examples:

- *Defining the good life.* Values influence our idea of the best way to live our lives. The personality psychologist Abraham Maslow, for example, was known for his sensitive descriptions of "self-actualized" people—people who, with their needs for survival, safety, "belongingness," and self-esteem satisfied, go on to fulfill their human potential. Few readers noticed that Maslow himself, guided by his own values, selected the sample of self-actualized people he described. The resulting description of self-actualized personalities—as spontaneous, autonomous, mystical, and so forth—reflected Maslow's personal values. Had he begun with someone else's heroes—maybe Napoleon, Alexander the Great, and John D. Rockefeller—the resulting description of self-actualization would have differed (Smith, 1978).
- *Forming concepts.* Hidden values even seep into psychology's research-based concepts. Pretend you have taken a personality test and the psychologist, after scoring your answers, announces: "You scored high in self-esteem. You are low in anxiety. And you have exceptional ego-strength." "Ah," you think, "I suspected as much, but it feels good to know that." Now another psychologist gives you a similar test. For some peculiar reason, this test asks some of the same questions. Afterwards the psychologist informs you that you seem defensive, for you scored high in "repressiveness." "How could this be," you wonder, "the other psychologist said such nice things about me?" It could be because all these labels describe the same set of responses (a tendency to say nice things about oneself and not to acknowledge problems). Shall we call it high self-esteem or defensiveness? The label reflects a value judgment.
- *Naturalistic fallacy.* A seductive error for those who work in the social sciences is sliding from a description of *what is* into a prescription of *what ought to be*. Philosophers call this the **naturalistic fallacy**. The gulf between "is" and "ought," between scientific description and ethical prescription, remains as wide today as when philosopher David Hume pointed it out 200 years ago. No survey of human behaviour—say, of sexual practices—logically dictates what is "right" behaviour. If most people don't do something, that does not make it wrong. If most people do it, that does not make it right. We inject our values whenever we move from objective statements of fact to prescriptive statements of what ought to be.

naturalistic fallacy the error of defining what is good in terms of what is observable. For example: What's typical is normal; what's normal is good.

As these examples indicate, values lie hidden within our cultural definitions of mental health, our psychological advice for living, our concepts, and our psychological labels. Throughout this book we will call your attention to additional examples of hidden values. The point is never that the implicit values are necessarily bad. The point is that scientific interpretation, even

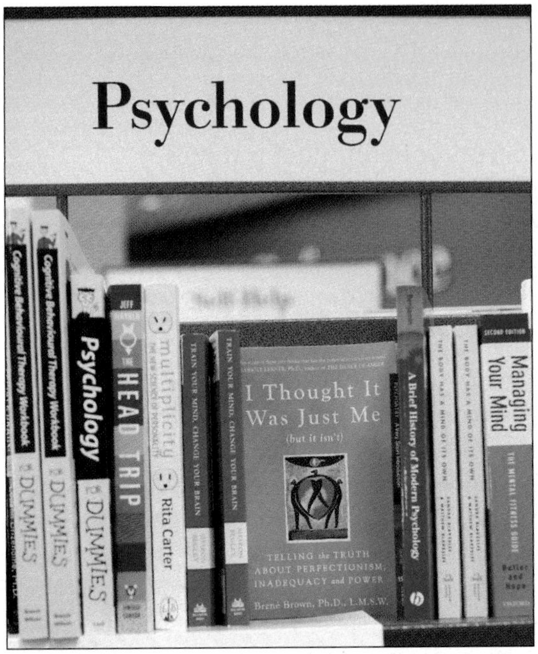

Hidden (and not-so-hidden) values seep into psychological advice. They permeate popular psychology books that offer guidance on living and loving.

at the level of labelling a phenomenon, is a human activity. It is therefore natural and inevitable that prior beliefs and values will influence what social psychologists think and write.

Should we dismiss science because it has its subjective side? Quite the contrary: The realization that human thinking always involves interpretation is precisely why we need researchers with varying biases to undertake scientific analysis. By constantly checking our beliefs against the facts, as best we know them, we check and retain our biases. Systematic observation and experimentation help us clean the lens through which we see reality.

STORY BEHIND THE RESEARCH

Fathali M. Moghaddam
Georgetown University

After being born in Iran and educated in England, I joined hundreds of thousands of Iranians returning home after the revolution of 1978. I soon found that my new Ph.D. ill-equipped me for work in a culture that was suspicious of Western psychology and demanding that my teaching and research reflect Iranian concerns and values. Through my experiences there, and subsequently with the United Nations Development Program, I became aware of the urgent need for a psychology that is appropriate to the poor and illiterate masses of Third World people. Believing that internationalizing psychology will benefit psychologists in all three worlds, I am now working to bridge the gap between social psychology in North America and other parts of the world and to educate psychologists for work in the Third World.

SUMMING UP

Social psychologists' values penetrate their work in obvious ways, such as their choice of research topics and the types of people who are attracted to various fields of study. Their values also penetrate in subtler ways, such as their hidden assumptions when forming concepts, choosing labels, defining reality, and giving advice. This penetration of values into science is not a reason to fault social psychology or any other science. That human thinking is seldom dispassionate is precisely why we need systematic observation and experimentation if we are to check our cherished ideas against reality.

I KNEW IT ALL ALONG: IS SOCIAL PSYCHOLOGY SIMPLY COMMON SENSE?

But do social psychology's theories provide new insight into the human condition? Or do they only describe the obvious?

Many of the conclusions presented in this book will probably have already occurred to you, for social psychology is all around you. We constantly observe people thinking about, influencing, and relating to one another. Much of our thinking aims to discern and explain relationships among social events. It pays to discern what that facial expression predicts, how to get someone to do something, or whether to regard another person as friend or foe. For centuries, philosophers, novelists, and poets have observed and commented on social behaviour, often with keen insight.

Does this mean that social psychology is only common sense in fancy words? We wouldn't have written this book if we thought so. Nevertheless, it must be acknowledged that social psychology faces two contradictory criticisms: first, that it is trivial because it documents the obvious; second that it is dangerous because its findings could be used to manipulate people.

We will explore the second criticism in Chapter 8. For the moment, let's examine the first objection.

Do social psychology and the other social sciences simply formalize what any amateur already knows intuitively? Writer Cullen Murphy (1990) thinks so: "Day after day social scientists go out into the world. Day after day they discover that people's behaviour is pretty much what you'd expect." Nearly a half-century earlier, historian Arthur Schlesinger, Jr. (1949) reacted with similar scorn to social scientists' studies of Second World War soldiers.

What were the findings? Another reviewer, Paul Lazarsfeld (1949), offered a sample with interpretive comments, a few of which we paraphrase:

1. Better-educated soldiers suffered more adjustment problems than did less-educated soldiers. (Intellectuals were less prepared for battle stresses than street-smart people.)
2. Soldiers from southern climates coped better with the hot South Sea Island weather than did northern soldiers. (People from southern climates are more accustomed to hot weather.)

3. Soldiers from rural backgrounds were usually in better spirits during their army life than soldiers from city backgrounds. (After all, they are more accustomed to hardships.)
4. Soldiers were more eager to return home during the fighting than they were after the German surrender. (You cannot blame people for not wanting to be killed.)

One problem with common sense, however, is that we invoke it *after* we know the facts. Events are far more "obvious" and predictable in hindsight than beforehand. Experiments reveal that when people learn the outcome of an experiment, that outcome suddenly seems unsurprising—certainly less surprising than it is to people who are simply told about the experimental procedure and the possible outcomes (Slovic & Fischhoff, 1977). People overestimate their ability to have foreseen the result. This happens especially when the result seems determined and not a mere product of chance (Hawkins & Hastie, 1990).

"A first-rate theory predicts; a second-rate theory forbids; and a third-rate theory explains after the event."

Aleksander Isaakovich Kitaigorodskii

You perhaps experienced this phenomenon when reading Lazarsfeld's summary of findings. For Lazarsfeld went on to say, "Every one of these statements is the direct opposite of what was actually found." In reality, it was found that less-educated soldiers adapted more poorly. People from southern climates were not more likely than people from northern climates to adjust to tropical weather. Soldiers from city backgrounds were usually in better spirits than soldiers from rural backgrounds. And soldiers were actually more eager to come home after the fighting ended than while it was still ongoing. "If we had mentioned the actual results of the investigation first [as Schlesinger experienced], the reader would have labelled these 'obvious' also."

Likewise, in everyday life we often do not expect something to happen until it does. We *then* suddenly see clearly the forces that brought it about and feel unsurprised. After the Quebec sovereignty vote of 1995, commentators—forgetting they had predicted a large win for the federalists—found the close vote unsurprising. It seems we often think we knew what we actually did not. As the philosopher-theologian Soren Kierkegaard put it, "Life is lived forwards, but understood backwards."

hindsight bias the tendency to exaggerate, *after* learning an outcome, one's ability to have foreseen how something turned out. Also known as the *I-knew-it-all-along phenomenon.*

If this **hindsight bias** (also called the I-knew-it-all-along phenomenon) is pervasive, you may now be feeling that you already knew about it. Indeed, almost any conceivable result of a psychological experiment can seem like common sense—*after* you know the result.

Here's how you can demonstrate the phenomenon. Give half a group one psychological finding and the other half the opposite result. For example, tell half as follows:

> Social psychologists have found that, whether choosing friends or falling in love, we are most attracted to people whose traits are different from our own. There seems to be wisdom in the old saying, "Opposites attract."

Tell the other half:

> Social psychologists have found that, whether choosing friends or falling in love, we are most attracted to people whose traits are similar to our own. There seems to be wisdom in the old saying, "Birds of a feather flock together."

Ask the people first to explain the result. Then ask them to say whether it is "surprising" or "not surprising." Virtually all will find whichever result they were given "not surprising."

Indeed, we can draw upon our stockpile of proverbs to make almost any result seem to make sense. If a social psychologist reports that separation intensifies romantic attraction, Joe Public responds, "You get paid for this? Everybody knows that 'absence makes the heart grow fonder.'" Should it turn out that separation weakens attraction, Judy Public may say, "My grandmother could have told you, 'Out of sight, out of mind.'"

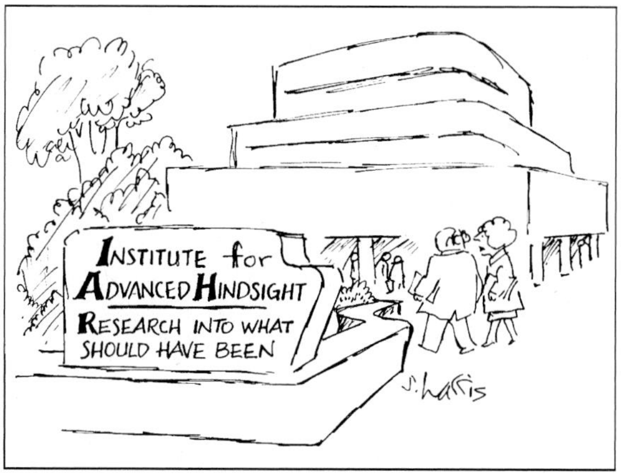

In hindsight, events seem obvious and predictable.

Karl Teigen (1986) must have had a few chuckles when he asked University of Leicester (England) students to evaluate actual proverbs and their opposites. When given the proverb, "Fear is stronger than love," most rated it as true. But so did students who were given its reversed form, "Love is stronger than fear." Likewise, the genuine proverb, "He that is fallen cannot help him who is down," was rated highly; but so too was, "He that is fallen can help him who is down." Our favourites, however, were the two highly rated proverbs: "Wise men make proverbs and fools repeat them" (authentic) and its made-up counterpart, "Fools make proverbs and wise men repeat them."

The hindsight bias creates a problem for many psychology students. Sometimes results are genuinely surprising (for example, that Olympic *bronze* medallists take more joy in their achievement than do silver medallists). More often, when you read the results of experiments in your textbooks, the material seems easy, even obvious. When you later take a multiple-choice test on which you must choose among several plausible conclusions, the task may become surprisingly difficult. "I don't know what happened," the befuddled student later moans. "I thought I knew the material." (A word to the wise: Beware of this phenomenon when studying for exams, lest you fool yourself into thinking that you know the material better than you do.)

So what do we conclude—that common sense is usually wrong? Sometimes it is. Until science dethroned the commonsense view, centuries of daily experience assured people that the sun revolved around the earth. Medical experience assured doctors that bleeding was an effective treatment for typhoid fever, until someone in the middle of the last century bothered to experiment—to divide patients into two groups, one bled, the other given mere bed rest.

"It is easy to be wise after the event."

Sherlock Holmes, in Arthur Conan Doyle's "The Problem of Thor Bridge"

Other times, conventional wisdom is right—or it falls on both sides of an issue: Does happiness come from knowing the truth or preserving illusions? From being with others or living in peaceful solitude? Opinions are a dime a dozen; no matter what we find, there will be someone who foresaw it. (Mark Twain jested that Adam was the only person who, when saying a good thing, knew that nobody had said it before.) But which of the many competing ideas best fit reality?

The point is not that common sense is predictably wrong. Rather, common sense usually is right *after the fact.* We therefore easily deceive ourselves into thinking that we know and knew more than we do and did. And this is precisely why we need science—to help us sift reality from illusion and genuine predictions from easy hindsight.

FOCUS ON

I KNEW IT ALL ALONG

Cullen Murphy (1990), managing editor of the *Atlantic*, faulted "sociology, psychology, and other social sciences for too often merely discerning the obvious or confirming the commonplace." His own casual survey of social science findings "turned up no ideas or conclusions that can't be found in *Bartlett's* or any other encyclopedia of quotations." Nevertheless, to sift through competing sayings, we need research. Consider some dueling proverbs:

Is it more true that . . .	*Or that . . .*
Too many cooks spoil the broth.	Two heads are better than one.
The pen is mightier than the sword.	Actions speak louder than words.
You can't teach an old dog new tricks.	You're never too old to learn.
Blood is thicker than water.	Many kinfolk, few friends.
He who hesitates is lost.	Look before you leap.
Forewarned is forearmed.	Don't cross the bridge until you come to it.

SUMMING UP

Social psychology is criticized for being trivial because it documents what seems obvious. Experiments, however, reveal that outcomes are more "obvious" *after* the facts are known. The hindsight bias (the *I-knew-it-all-along phenomenon*) often makes people overconfident about the validity of their judgments and predictions.

RESEARCH METHODS: HOW DOES SOCIAL PSYCHOLOGY TRY TO ACCOMPLISH ITS GOALS?

We have considered some of the intriguing questions social psychology seeks to answer. We have also seen the ways in which subjective, often unconscious processes influence the work that social psychologists do. Now let's consider the scientific methods that make social psychology a science.

In their quest for insight, social psychologists propose theories that organize their observations and imply testable hypotheses and practical predictions. To test a hypothesis, social psychologists may do research that predicts behaviour using correlational studies, often conducted in natural settings. Or they may seek to explain behaviour by conducting experiments that manipulate one or more factors under controlled conditions. Once they have conducted a research study, they explore ways to apply their findings to improve people's lives.

As we noted earlier, we are all amateur social psychologists. People-watching is a universal hobby—in parks, on the street, at school. As we observe people, we form ideas about how

humans think about, influence, and relate to one another. Professional social psychologists do the same, only more systematically (by forming theories) and painstakingly (often with experiments that create miniature social dramas to pin down cause and effect). And they have done it extensively, in 25 000 studies of 8 million people by one recent count (Richard et al., 2003).

"Nothing has such power to broaden the mind as the ability to investigate systematically and truly all that comes under thy observation in life."

Marcus Aurelius, *Meditations*

FORMING AND TESTING HYPOTHESES

We social psychologists have a hard time thinking of anything more fascinating than human existence. As we wrestle with human nature to pin down its secrets, we organize our ideas and findings into theories. A **theory** is *an integrated set of principles that explain and predict* observed events. Theories are a scientific shorthand.

In everyday conversation, "theory" often means "less than fact"—a middle rung on a confidence ladder from fact to theory to guess. Thus, people may, for example, dismiss Charles Darwin's theory of evolution as "just a theory." Indeed, notes Alan Leshner (2005), "Evolution *is* only a theory, but so is gravity." People often respond that gravity is a fact—but the *fact* is that your keys fall to the ground when dropped. Gravity is the *theoretical explanation* that accounts for such observed facts.

theory
an integrated set of principles that explain and predict observed events

To a scientist, facts and theories are apples and oranges. Facts are agreed-upon statements that we observe. Theories are ideas that summarize and explain facts. "Science is built up with facts, as a house is with stones," wrote French scientist Jules Henri Ponare, "but a collection of facts is no more a science than a heap of stones is a house.

Theories not only summarize, they also imply testable predictions, called **hypotheses**. Hypotheses serve several purposes. First, they allow us to *test* the theory on which they are based. By making specific predictions, a theory puts its money where its mouth is. Second, predictions give *direction* to research. Any scientific field will mature more rapidly if its researchers have a sense of direction. Theoretical predictions suggest new areas for research; they send investigators looking for things they might never have thought of. Third, the predictive feature of good theories can also make them *practical.* What, for example, would be of greater practical value today than a theory of aggression that would predict when to expect it and how to control it? As Kurt Lewin, one of modern social psychology's founders, declared, "There is nothing so practical as a good theory."

hypothesis
a testable proposition that describes a relationship that may exist between events

When testing our theories with specific hypotheses, however, we must always translate variables that are described at the theoretical level into the specific variables that we are going to observe. This process called *operationalization* is often as much an art as a science.

Consider how this works. Say we observe that people who loot, taunt, or attack others (i.e., exhibit extreme violence) often do so in crowds. We might therefore theorize that the presence of others in a crowd leads to extreme violence. Let's play with this idea for a moment. In order to test this hypothesis we need to translate our theoretical variable "crowd" into a meaningful example of it that we will observe. In this case maybe we would operationalize this variable as 20 strangers together in a relatively small room, even though this definition of crowd would probably be different from the crowds we originally observed. The crucial question for this study would be: does our operational variable of crowd represent what we mean theoretically by a crowd? The answer to that question determines whether our operational variable is a *valid* measure of our theoretical variable or not. If we can accept it as valid then we can go on to test our hypothesis. If we can't accept it as valid, then the proposed research will not tell us much about our theory and we should develop a new operationalization. What do you think of this operationalization of crowd? Could you do better? Good social psychology requires not only following the principles of science, but also developing tests of theories that creatively capture the essence of the theory being tested.

If we are going to test our hypothesis, however, we would also need to operationalize extreme violence. What if we asked individuals in "crowds" to administer punishing shocks to a hapless victim without knowing which one of the group was actually shocking the victim? Would these individuals administer stronger shocks than individuals acting alone, as our theory predicts? In this example, administering punishing shocks would be the operational variable of our concept of extreme violence. To be a good operationalization we would need to believe not only that it is a valid measure of violence, but we would also need to believe that by using this measure differences in violence could emerge and we would get basically the same results if we do the study over again. That is we would need to believe that it is a *reliable* measure. If this measure of violence sometimes showed violence and other times didn't, we might very well miss our effect.

When we test our theories we necessarily must make observations and when we make observations we have to decide what we are going to observe. This process of deciding on our observations, called operationalization, is how science puts its theories to test. A good operationalization captures the essence of the theoretical concept—that is, it is valid—and it does so sensitively and consistently—that is, reliably—so that tests of the theory can be observed.

You will note throughout the text, however, that quite regularly more than one theory can explain what we know about a given phenomenon. Not only must we test our own theory, science often proceeds by testing between two theories. How do we conclude that one theory is better than another? A good theory: (1) effectively summarizes a wide range of observations; and (2) makes clear predictions that we can use to (a) confirm or modify the theory, (b) generate new exploration, and (c) suggest practical application. When we discard theories, usually it's not because they have been proved false. Rather, like old cars, they get replaced by newer, better models.

field research research done in natural, real-life settings outside the laboratory

correlational research the study of the naturally occurring relationships among variables

experimental research studies that seek clues to cause-effect relationships by manipulating one or more factors (independent variables) while controlling others (holding them constant)

CORRELATIONAL RESEARCH: DETECTING NATURAL ASSOCIATIONS

Most of what you will learn about social-psychological research methods you will absorb as you read later chapters. But let us go backstage now and take a brief look at how social psychology is done. This glimpse behind the scenes will be just enough, we trust, for you to appreciate findings discussed later and to think critically about everyday social events.

Social-psychological research varies by location. It can take place in the laboratory (a controlled situation) or in the **field** (everyday situations). And it varies by method—being **correlational** (asking whether two or more factors are naturally associated) or **experimental** (manipulating some factor to see its effect on another). If you want to be a critical reader of psychological research reported in newspapers and magazines, it will pay to understand the difference between correlational and experimental research.

Using some real examples, let's first consider the advantages of correlational research (often involving important variables in natural settings) and the disadvantage (ambiguous interpretation of cause and effect). As we will see in Module B, today's psychologists are relating personal and social factors to human health. Among the researchers are Douglas Carroll at Glasgow Caledonian University and his colleagues, George Davey Smith and Paul Bennett (1994). In search of possible links between socioeconomic status and health, the researchers ventured into Glasgow's old graveyards. As a measure of health, they noted from grave markers the life spans of 843 individuals. As an indication of status, they measured the height of the pillars over the graves, reasoning that height reflected cost and therefore affluence. As Figure 1–3 shows, higher markers were related to longer lives, for both men and women.

Carroll and his colleagues explain how other researchers, using contemporary data, have confirmed the status-longevity correlation. Scottish postal-code regions having the least overcrowding and unemployment also have the greatest longevity. In contemporary Britain, occupational status correlates with longevity. One study followed 17 350 British civil service workers over 10 years. Compared to top-grade administrators, those at the professional-executive grade were 1.6 times more likely to die. Clerical workers were 2.2 times and labourers 2.7 times more likely to have died (Adler et al., 1993, 1994). Across times and places, the status-health correlation seems reliable.

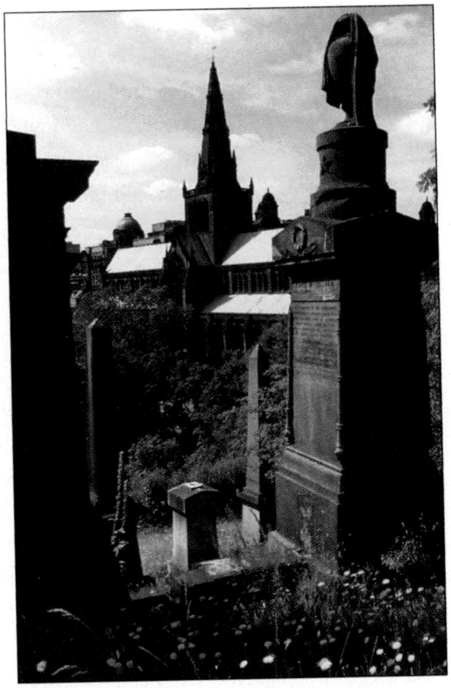

Commemorative markers in Glasgow Cathedral graveyard.

Correlation versus causation

The status-longevity question illustrates the most irresistible thinking error made by both amateur and professional social psychologists: When two factors like status and health go

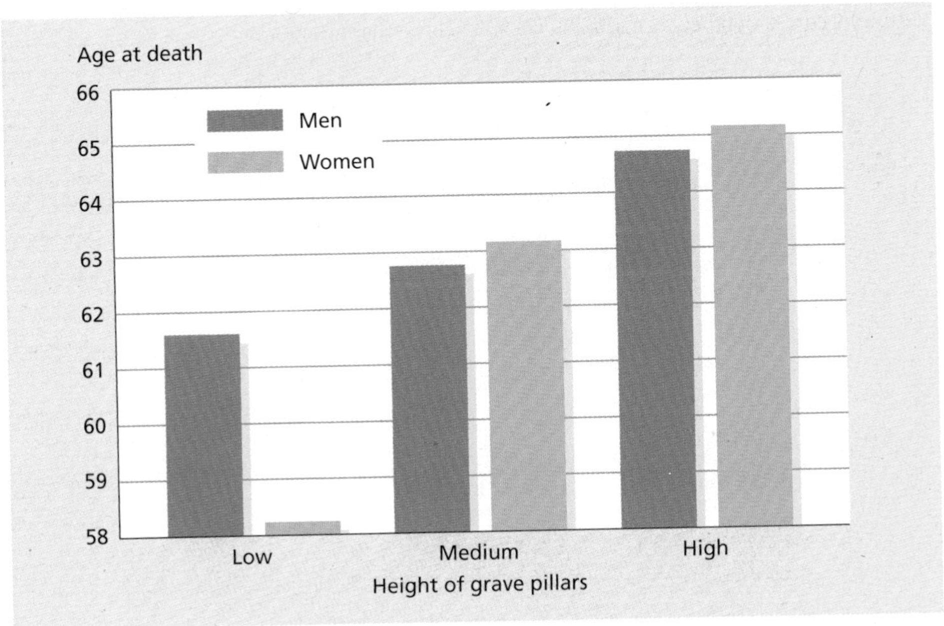

FIGURE 1–3

Status and longevity.

Tall grave pillars commemorated people who also tended to live longer.

together, it is terribly tempting to conclude that one is causing the other. Status, we might presume, somehow protects a person from health risks. Or might it be the other way around? Maybe health promotes vigour and success. Perhaps people who live longer accumulate more wealth (enabling them to have more expensive grave markers). Correlational research allows us to *predict,* but it cannot tell us whether changing one variable (such as social status) will *cause* changes in another (such as health).

The correlation-causation confusion is behind much muddled thinking in popular psychology. Consider another very real correlation—between self-esteem and academic achievement. Children with high self-esteem tend also to have high academic achievement. (As with any correlation, we can also state this the other way around: High achievers tend to have high self-esteem.) Why do you suppose this is (Figure 1–4)?

Some people believe a "healthy self-concept" contributes to achievement. Thus, boosting a child's self-image may also boost school achievement. But others, including psychologists William Damon (1995), Robyn Dawes (1994), Mark Leary (1998), and Martin Seligman (1994), doubt that self-esteem is really "the armor that protects kids" from underachievement (or drug abuse and delinquency). Perhaps it's the other way around: Perhaps problems and failures cause low self-esteem. Perhaps self-esteem often reflects the reality of how things are going for us. Perhaps self-esteem grows from hard-won achievements. Do well and you will feel good about yourself; goof off and fail and you will feel like a dolt. A study of 635 Norwegian schoolchildren suggests that a string of gold stars beside one's name on the spelling chart and constant praise from an admiring teacher can boost a child's self-esteem (Skaalvik & Hagtvet, 1990). Or perhaps, as in a recent study of nearly 6000 German seventh-graders, the traffic between self-esteem and academic achievement runs both ways (Trautwein et al., 2006).

It's also possible that self-esteem and achievement correlate because both are linked to underlying intelligence and family social status. That possibility was raised in two studies—one study of 1600 young men, another of 715 teenagers (Bachman & O'Malley, 1977; Maruyama et al., 1981). When the researchers statistically removed the effect of intelligence and family status, the correlation between self-esteem and achievement evaporated.

FIGURE 1–4

Correlation and causations.

When two variables correlate, any combination of three explanations is possible.

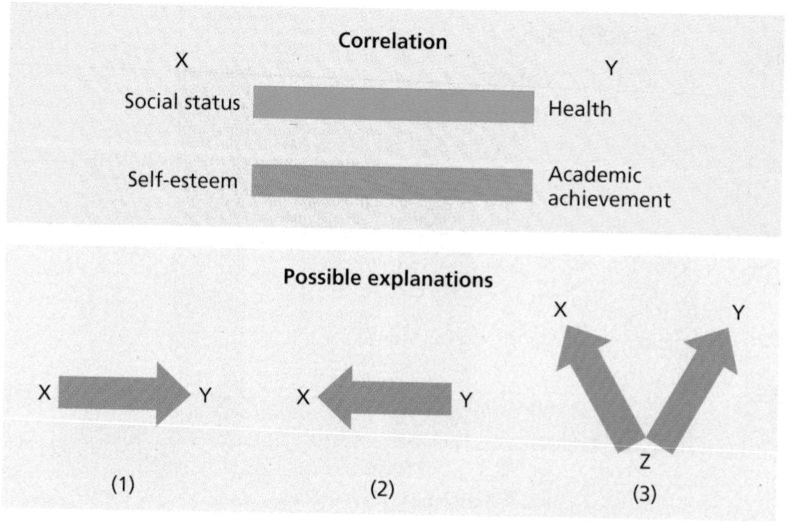

Correlations quantify, with a coefficient known as *r*, the degree of relationship between two factors—from −1.0 (as one factor score goes up, the other goes down) through 0 to +1.0 (the two factors' scores rise and fall together). Scores on self-esteem and depression tests correlate negatively (about −.6). The intelligence scores of identical twins correlate positively (about +.08). The strength of correlational research is that it tends to occur in real-world settings in which we can examine factors such as race, gender, and social status (factors that we cannot manipulate in the laboratory). Its great disadvantage lies in the ambiguity of the results. The point is so important that even if it fails to impress people the first 25 times they hear it, it is worth repeating a 26th time: *Knowing that two variables change together (correlate) enables us to predict one when we know the other, but correlation does not specify cause and effect.*

Researchers have found a modest but positive correlation between adolescents' preference for heavy metal music and their having attitudes favourable to premarital sex, pornography, Satanism, and drug and alcohol use (Landers, 1988). What are some possible explanations for this correlation?

When correlational research is extended over time it is called longitudinal research. Longitudinal research can begin to sort out cause and effect because we know that some things happen before others. Causes always happen before effects, so if we know that children almost always have a healthy positive self-image before they start to show more achievement than their peers, then we can rule out that it is achievement that causes a healthy positive self-image. Advanced statistical analyses can also help as they can *suggest* cause-effect relations. *Time-lagged* correlations reveal the *sequence* of events (for example, by indicating whether changed achievement more often precedes or follows changed self-esteem). Researchers can also use statistical techniques that extract the influence of "confounded" variables. Thus, the researchers just mentioned saw the correlation between self-esteem *and* achievement evaporate after extracting differences in intelligence and family status. (Among people of similar intelligence and family status, the self-esteem–achievement relationship was minimal.) The Scottish research team wondered whether the status-longevity relationship would survive their removing the effect of cigarette smoking, which is now much less common among those higher in status. It did, which suggested that some other factors, such as increased stress and decreased feelings of control, must also account for the greater mortality of the poor.

Survey research

How do we measure such variables as status and health? One way is by surveying representative samples of people. Survey researchers obtain a representative group by taking a **random sample**—*one in which every person in the population being studied has an equal chance of inclusion.* With this procedure any subgroup of people—red-haired people, for example—will tend to be represented in the survey to the extent that they are represented in the total population.

random sample
survey procedure in which every person in the population being studied has an equal chance of inclusion

It is an amazing fact that whether we survey people in a city or in a whole country, 1200 randomly selected participants will enable us to be 95 percent confident of describing the entire population with an error margin of 3 percentage points or less. Imagine a huge jar filled with beans, 50 percent red and 50 percent white. Randomly sample 1200 of these, and you will be 95 percent certain to draw out between 47 percent and 53 percent red beans—regardless of whether the jar contains 10 000 beans or 100 million beans. If we think of the red beans as supporters of one political party and the white beans as supporters of the other party, we can understand why polls taken just before national elections have diverged from election results by an average of less than 2 percent. As a few drops of blood can speak for the whole body, so can a random sample speak for a population.

Bear in mind that polls do not literally *predict* voting; they only *describe* public opinion as of the moment they are taken. Public opinion can shift. To evaluate surveys, we must also bear in mind three potentially biasing influences: unrepresentative samples, question wording, and response options.

Unrepresentative sample

Sample size is not all that matters in a survey; how closely the sample represents the population under study also matters. In 1984, columnist Ann Landers accepted a letter writer's challenge to poll her readers on the question of whether women find affection more important than sex. Her question: "Would you be content to be held close and treated tenderly and forget about 'the act'?" Of the more than 100 000 women who replied, 72 percent said yes. An avalanche of worldwide publicity followed. In response to critics, Landers (1985, p. 45) granted that "the sampling may not be representative of all American women. But it does provide honest—valuable—insights from a cross section of the public. This is because my column is read by people from every walk of life, approximately 70 million of them." Still, one wonders, are the 70 million readers representative of the entire population? And are the 1 in 700 readers who participated representative of the 699 in 700 who did not?

The importance of representativeness was effectively demonstrated in the 1936 U.S. presidential election, when a weekly news magazine, *Literary Digest,* mailed a postcard election poll to more than 10 million people. Among the more than 2 million returns, Alf Landon won by a landslide over Franklin D. Roosevelt. When the actual votes were counted a few days later, the results were the opposite—Roosevelt won in a landslide over Landon. The magazine had sent the poll only to people whose names it had obtained from telephone books and automobile registrations—thus omitting all those who could afford neither (Cleghorn, 1980).

Order of questions

Given a representative sample, we must also contend with other sources of bias, such as the order in which we ask questions. Asked whether "the Japanese government should be allowed to set limits on how much American industry can sell in Japan," most Americans answered no (Schuman & Ludwig, 1983). Simultaneously, two-thirds of an equivalent sample were answering yes to the same question because they were first asked whether "the American government should be allowed to set limits on how much Japanese industry can sell in the United States." Most of these people said the United States has the right to limit imports. To appear consistent, they then said that Japan should have the same right.

Response bias and social desirability

Consider, too, the dramatic effects of the response options. When Joop van der Plight and his coworkers (1987) asked English voters what percentage of Britain's energy they wished came from nuclear power, the average preference was 41 percent. They asked others what percentage they wished came from (1) nuclear, (2) coal, and (3) other sources. Their average preference for nuclear power was 21 percent.

It is not just the response options, however, that can bias people's responses. Sometimes people don't want to admit their true actions and beliefs either to the experimenter or sometimes even to themselves. Questions about prejudice often show very low levels of reported prejudice by the respondents. Yet systematic experiments demonstrate that prejudice is all too common. Why the difference in findings? People may not want to admit on a survey or even to themselves that they harbour some feelings of prejudice. This tendency for people to say what they want others to hear or what they want to believe about themselves is called *social desirability*. Recently social psychologists have developed new methods of measuring people's beliefs without them knowing that their beliefs are being measured. These *implicit measures* are often used when concerns about social desirability arise.

Wording of question

Given a representative sample, we must also contend with other sources of bias, such as the wording of questions. For example, one poll found that people favoured cutting "foreign aid" yet opposed cutting funding "to help hungry people in other nations" (Simon, 1996). Even subtle changes in the tone of a question can have large effects (Schuman & Kalton, 1985). Thus it is not surprising that politicians in Ottawa and Quebec have fought bitterly about the wording of referendum questions about Quebec sovereignty. Federalists have long charged that the Parti Québécois purposely has devised questions that are unclear and designed to elicit a "yes" vote in favour of sovereignty. In the 1995 election, Quebecers voted on the question, "Do you agree that Quebec should become sovereign, after having made a formal offer to Canada for a new economic and political partnership, within the scope of the Bill respecting the future of Quebec and the agreement signed on June 12, 1995?" Did this question affect the outcome of the election? It certainly might have because even when people say they feel strongly about an issue, a question's form and wording may affect their answer (Krosnick & Schuman, 1988).

Knowledge of the issues, however, can sometimes interact with the wording of the question to influence responses. Consider a study conducted by Darin Lehman at the University of British Columbia and his colleagues (Lehman et al., 1992). They had students read a number of newspaper clippings preceding a provincial election. The clippings were a mixed bag, some siding with the New Democratic Party (NDP), others siding with the Social Credit Party (SCP)—the two main rivals in the election. After the students had read the articles, Lehman and his colleagues asked the students in one condition to respond to a series of questions about how fair the articles were to the NDP. The students in the other condition were asked to

Survey researchers must be sensitive to subtle—and not so subtle—biases.

respond to nearly the same questions, except that they rated how fair the articles were to the SCP. So, the questions tended to lead students to see bias against one party over the other. Did the wording of the question affect all students equally? No. It primarily affected students who were less knowledgeable about the issues in the election. These students saw more bias against the NDP when the questions were about the NDP and more bias against the SCP when the questions were about the SCP. More knowledgeable students, on the other hand, were unaffected by the wording of the question.

EXPERIMENTAL RESEARCH: SEARCHING FOR CAUSE AND EFFECT

The difficulty of discerning cause and effect among naturally correlated events prompts most social psychologists to create laboratory simulations of everyday processes whenever this is feasible and ethical. These simulations are roughly similar to how aeronautical engineers work. They don't begin by observing how flying objects perform in a wide variety of natural environments. The variations in both atmospheric conditions and flying objects are so complex that they would surely find it difficult to organize and use such data to design better aircraft. Instead, they construct a simulated reality that is under their control—a wind tunnel. Then they can manipulate wind conditions and observe the precise effect of particular wind conditions on particular wing structures.

Control: Manipulating variables

independent variable the experimental factor that a researcher manipulates

Like aeronautical engineers, social psychologists experiment by constructing social situations that simulate important features of our daily lives. By varying just one or two factors at a time—called **independent variables**—the experimenter pinpoints how changes in these one or two things affect us. As the wind tunnel helps the aeronautical engineer discover principles of aerodynamics, so the experiment enables the social psychologist to discover principles of social thinking, social influence, and social relations. The ultimate aim of wind tunnel simulations is to understand and predict the flying characteristics of complex aircraft. Social psychologists experiment to understand and predict human behaviour.

Historically, social psychologists have used the experimental method in about three-fourths of their research studies (Higbee et al., 1982), and in two out of three studies the setting has been a research laboratory (Adair et al., 1985). To illustrate the laboratory experiment, consider two experiments that typify research from upcoming chapters on prejudice and aggression. Each suggests possible cause-effect explanations of correlational findings.

The first experiment concerns prejudice against people who are obese. People often perceive the obese as slow, lazy, and sloppy (Ryckman et al., 1989). Do such attitudes spawn discrimination? In hopes of finding out, Steven Gortmaker and his colleagues (1993) studied 370 obese 16- to 24-year-olds. When they restudied them seven years later, two-thirds of the women were still obese, and these women were less likely to be married and earning high salaries than a comparison group of some 5000 other women. Even after correcting for any differences in aptitude test scores, race, and parental income, the obese women's incomes were $7,000 a year below average.

Correcting for certain other factors makes it look like discrimination might explain the correlation between obesity and lower status, we can't be sure. (Can you think of other

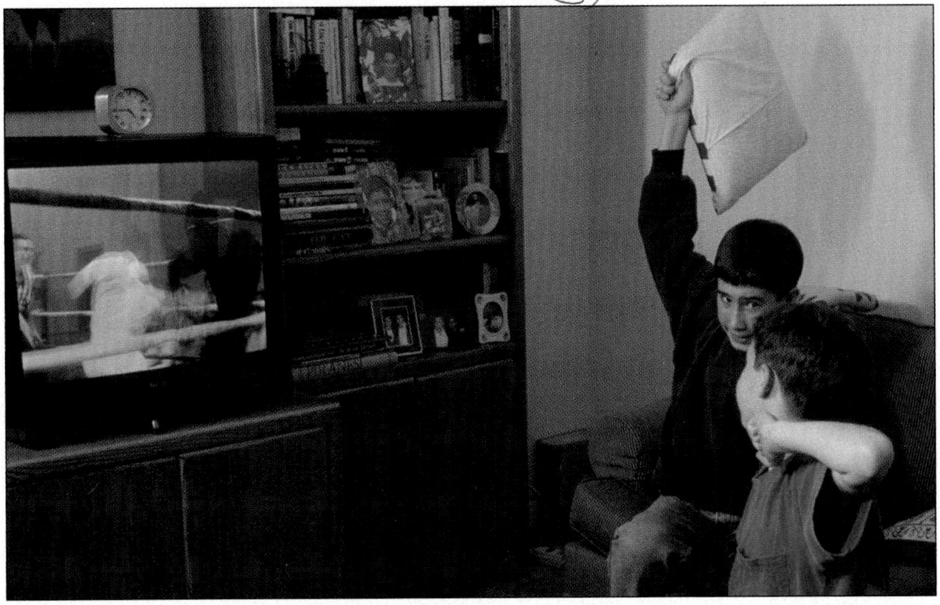

Does viewing violence on TV or in other media lead to imitation, especially among children? Experiments suggest that it does.

possibilities?) Enter social psychologists Mark Snyder and Julie Haugen (1994, 1995). They asked 76 University of Minnesota men students to have a getting-acquainted phone conversation with one of 76 women students. Each man was shown a photo *said* to picture his conversational partner. Half were shown an obese woman (not the actual partner); the other half were shown a normal-weight woman. In one part of the experiment, the men were asked to form an impression of the women's traits. Later analysis of just the women's side of the conversation revealed that, when women were being evaluated, they spoke less warmly and happily if they were presumed obese. Clearly, the men's beliefs induced them to behave in a way that led their supposedly obese partners to confirm the idea that such women are undesirable. Prejudice and discrimination were having an effect. Recalling the effect of the stepmother's attitudes, perhaps we should call this "the Cinderella effect."

As a second example of how an experiment can clarify causation, consider the correlation between television viewing and children's behaviour. Children who watch many violent television programs tend to be more aggressive than those who watch few. This suggests that children might be learning from what they see on the screen. But, as I hope you now recognize, this is a correlational finding. Figure 1-5 on p. 29 reminds us that there are two other cause-effect interpretations that do not implicate television as the cause of the children's aggression. (What are they?)

Social psychologists have therefore brought television viewing into the laboratory, where they control the amount of violence the children see. By exposing children to violent and nonviolent programs, researchers can observe how the amount of violence affects behaviour. Chris Boyatzis and his colleagues (1995) showed some elementary school children, but not others, an episode of the 1990s most popular—and violent—children's television program, *Power Rangers*. Immediately after viewing the episode, the viewers committed seven times as many aggressive acts per two-minute interval as the nonviewers. We call the observed aggressive acts the

dependent variable the variable being measured, so called because it may *depend* on manipulations of the independent variable

dependent variable. Such experiments indicate that television can be one cause of children's aggressive behaviour.

So far we have seen that the logic of experimentation is simple: By creating and controlling a miniature reality, we can vary one factor and then another and discover how these factors, separately or in combination, affect people. Now let's go a little deeper and see how an experiment is done.

Every social-psychological experiment has two essential ingredients. We have just considered one—*control.* We manipulate one or two independent variables while trying to hold everything else constant. The other ingredient is *random assignment.*

random assignment the process of assigning participants to the conditions of an experiment such that all persons have the same chance of being in a given condition. (Note the distinction between random *assignment* in experiments and random *sampling* in surveys. Random assignment helps us infer cause and effect. Random sampling helps us generalize to a population.)

Random assignment: The great equalizer

Recall that we were reluctant, on the basis of a correlation, to assume that obesity *caused* lower status (via discrimination) or that violence viewing *caused* aggressiveness (see Table 1–1 for more examples). A survey researcher might measure and statistically extract other possibly pertinent factors and see if the correlations survive. But one can never control for all the factors that might distinguish obese from nonobese, and violence viewers from nonviewers. Maybe violence viewers differ in education, culture, intelligence—or in dozens of ways the researcher hasn't considered.

In one fell swoop, **random assignment** eliminates all such extraneous factors. With random assignment, each person has an equal chance of viewing the violence or the nonviolence. Thus, the people in both groups would, in every conceivable way—family status, intelligence, education, initial aggressiveness—average about the same. Highly intelligent people, for example, are equally likely to appear in both groups. Because random assignment creates equivalent groups, any later aggression difference between the two groups must have something to do with the only way they differ—whether or not they viewed violence (Figure 1–5). And thanks to random assignment of the Minnesota students to the photo conditions, the women's behaviour *must* have been influenced by the men's beliefs about their obesity.

TABLE 1–1 Recognizing correlations and experimental research

	Can participants be randomly assigned to condition?	Independent variable	Dependent variable
Are early maturing children more confident?	No → Correlational		
Do students learn more in online or classroom courses?	Yes → Experimental	Take class online or in classroom	Learning
Do school grades predict vocational success?	No → Correlational		
Does playing violent video games increase aggressiveness?	Yes → Experimental	Play violent or nonviolent game	Aggressiveness
Do people find comedy funnier when alone or with others?	(you answer)		
Do higher-income people have higher self-esteem?	(you answer)		

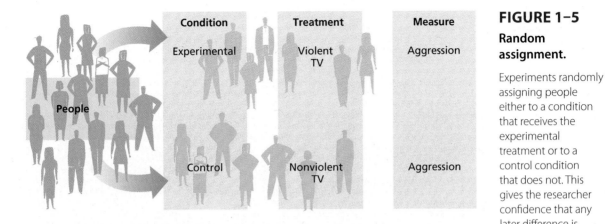

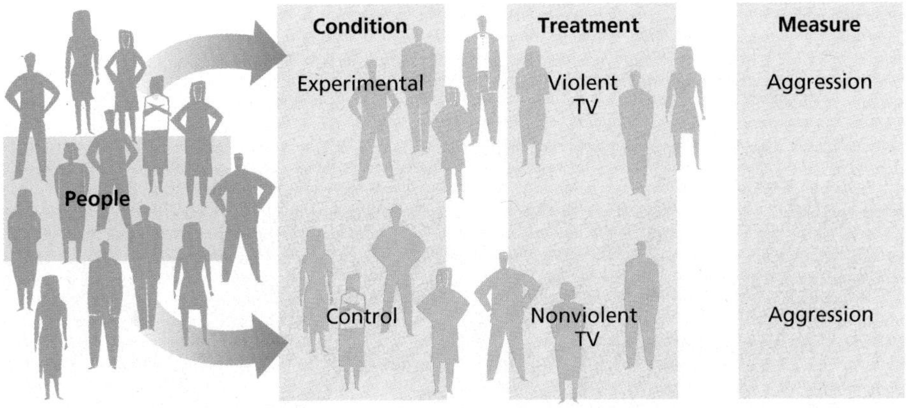

FIGURE 1–5
Random assignment.
Experiments randomly assigning people either to a condition that receives the experimental treatment or to a control condition that does not. This gives the researcher confidence that any later difference is somehow caused by the treatment.

The ethics of experimentation

Our television example illustrates why some experiments are ethically sensitive. Social psychologists would not, over long time periods, expose one group of children to brutal violence. Rather, they briefly alter people's social experience and note the effects. Sometimes the experimental treatment is a harmless, perhaps even enjoyable, experience to which people give their knowing consent. Sometimes, however, researchers find themselves operating in a grey area between the harmless and the risky.

Problems w/ experimental research)
1) Generalization
2) Experimenter Bias + Self Fulfilling Prophecy
3) Time & Ethical constraints.

Social psychologists often venture into that ethical grey area when they design experiments that engage intense thoughts and emotions. Experiments need not have what Elliot Aronson, Marilynn Brewer, and Merrill Carlsmith (1985) call **mundane realism**. That is, laboratory behaviour (for example, delivering electric shocks as part of an experiment on aggression) need not be literally the same as everyday behaviour. For many researchers, that sort of realism is indeed mundane—not important. But the experiment *should* have **experimental realism**—it should absorb and involve the participants. Experimenters do not want their people consciously play-acting or ho-humming it; they want to engage real psychological processes. Forcing people to choose whether to give intense or mild electric shock to someone else can, for example, be a realistic measure of aggression. It functionally simulates real aggression.

mundane realism degree to which an experiment is superficially similar to everyday situations

experimental realism degree to which an experiment absorbs and involves its participants

Achieving experimental realism sometimes requires deceiving people with a plausible cover story. If the person in the next room actually is not receiving the shocks, the experimenter does not want the participants to know this. That would destroy the experimental realism. Thus, about one-third of social-psychological studies (though a decreasing number) have required deception (Korn & Nicks, 1993; Vitelli, 1988).

Experimenters also seek to hide their predictions lest the participants, in their eagerness to be "good subjects," merely do what's expected or, in an ornery mood, do the opposite. In subtle ways, the experimenter's words, tone of voice, and gestures may call forth desired responses (Orhe, 1962). To minimize such **demand characteristics**—cues that seem to "demand" certain behaviour—experimenters typically standardize their instructions or even use a computer to present them.

demand characteristics cues in an experiment that tell the participant what behaviour is expected

Researchers often walk a tightrope in designing experiments that will be involving yet ethical. To believe that you are hurting someone, or to be subjected to strong social pressure

What influences occasionally trigger postgame violence among European soccer fans? Social psychologists have proposed hypotheses that have been tested with groups behaving under controlled conditions.

to see if it will change your opinion or behaviour, may be temporarily uncomfortable. Such experiments raise the age-old question of whether ends justify means. Do the insights gained justify deceiving and sometimes distressing people?

University ethics committees now review social-psychological research to ensure that it will treat people humanely. Ethical principles developed by major psychological organizations and government organizations such as Canada's tricouncil, which funds natural science, social science, humanities, and health research, urge investigators to:

informed consent an ethical principle requiring that research participants be told enough to enable them to choose whether they wish to participate

- Tell potential participants enough about the experiment to enable their **informed consent**.
- Be truthful. Use deception only if essential and justified by a significant purpose and if there is no alternative.
- Protect people from harm and significant discomfort.
- Treat information about the individual participants confidentially.
- Debrief participants. Fully explain the experiment afterward, including any deception. The only exception to this rule is when the feedback would be distressing, such as by making participants realize they have been stupid or cruel.

The experimenter should be sufficiently informative *and* considerate that people leave feeling at least as good about themselves as when they came in. Better yet, the participants should be repaid by having learned something about the nature of psychological inquiry. When treated respectfully, few participants mind being deceived (Christensen, 1988; Sharpe et al., 1992). Indeed, say social psychology's defenders, professors provoke far greater anxiety and distress by giving and returning course exams than researchers now do in their experiments.

GENERALIZING FROM LABORATORY TO LIFE

As the research on children, television, and violence illustrates, social psychology mixes everyday experience and laboratory analysis. Throughout this book we will do the same by drawing our data mostly from the laboratory and our illustrations mostly from life. Social psychology displays a healthy interplay between laboratory research and everyday life. Hunches gained from everyday experience often inspire laboratory research, which deepens our understanding of our experience.

This interplay appears in the children's television experiment. What people saw in everyday life suggested experimental research. Network and government policymakers, those with the power to make changes, are now aware of the results. This consistency of findings on television's effects—in the lab and in the field—is true of research in many other areas, including studies of helping, leadership style, depression, and achievement. The effects one finds in the lab have been mirrored by effects in the field. "The psychology laboratory has generally produced psychological truths rather than trivialities," note Craig Anderson and his colleagues (1999).

We need to be cautious, however, in generalizing from laboratory to life. Although the laboratory uncovers basic dynamics of human existence, it is still a simplified, controlled reality. It tells us what effect to expect of variable *X*, all other things being equal—which in real life they never are. Moreover, as you will see, the participants in many experiments are university students. Although this may help you identify with them, university students are hardly a random sample of all humanity. Would we get similar results with people of different ages, educational levels, and cultures? This is always an open question.

Nevertheless, we can distinguish between the *content* of people's thinking and acting (their attitudes, for example) and the *process* by which they think and act (for example, how attitudes affect actions and vice versa). The content varies more from culture to culture than does the process. People of different cultures may hold different opinions yet form them in similar ways. Consider:

- University students in Puerto Rico report greater loneliness than do collegians on the U.S. mainland. Yet in both cultures the ingredients of loneliness are much the same—shyness, uncertain purpose in life, low self-esteem (Jones et al., 1985).
- Ethnic groups differ in school achievement and delinquency, but the differences are "no more than skin deep," report David Rowe and his colleagues (1994). To the extent that family structure, peer influences, and parental education predict achievement or delinquency for one ethnic group, they do so for other groups.

Although our behaviours may differ, we are influenced by the same social forces. Beneath our surface diversity, we are more alike than different.

SUMMING UP

Social psychologists organize their ideas and findings into theories. A good theory will distill an array of facts into a much shorter list of predictive principles. We can use these predictions to confirm or modify the theory, to generate new research, and to suggest practical application.

Most social psychological research is either correlational or experimental. Correlational studies, sometimes conducted with systematic survey methods, discern the relationship between variables, such as between amount of education and amount of income. Knowing two things are naturally related is valuable information, but it seldom indicates what is causing what—or whether a third variable is involved.

When possible, social psychologists prefer to conduct experiments that explore cause and effect. By constructing a miniature reality that is under their control, experimenters can vary one thing and then another and discover how these things, separately or in combination, affect behaviour. We randomly assign participants to an experimental condition, which receives the experimental treatment, or to a control condition, which does not. We can then attribute any resulting difference between the two conditions to the independent variable (Figure 1-6).

In creating experiments, social psychologists sometimes stage situations that engage people's emotions. In doing so, they are obliged to follow professional ethical guidelines, such as obtaining people's informed consent, protecting them from harm, and fully disclosing afterwards any temporary deceptions. Laboratory experiments enable social psychologists to test ideas gleaned from life experience and then to apply the principles and findings back in the real world.

FIGURE 1-6 **Two methods of doing research: Correlational and experimental.**

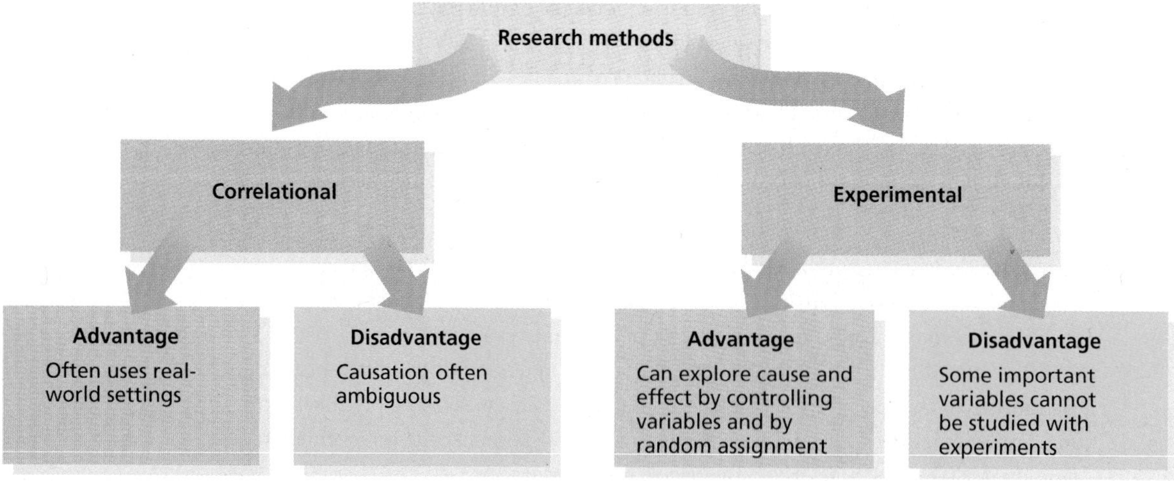

PART ONE

SOCIAL THINKING

This book unfolds around its definition of social psychology: the scientific study of how we *think about* (part one), *influence* (part two), and *relate to* (part three) one another.

These chapters on social thinking examine how we view ourselves and others. In varying ways, each chapter confronts an overriding question: How reasonable are our social attitudes, explanations, and beliefs? Are our impressions of ourselves and others generally accurate? How is our social thinking prone to bias and error, and how might we bring it closer to reality?

Chapter 2 explores the interplay between our sense of self and our social worlds. How do our social surroundings shape our self-identity? How does self-interest colour our social judgments and motivate our social behaviour?

Chapter 3 looks at the amazing and sometimes rather amusing ways in which we form beliefs about our social worlds. It also alerts us to some pitfalls of social thinking and suggests how to avoid them and think smarter.

Chapter 4 explores the links between attitudes and behaviours: Do our attitudes determine our behaviours? Do our behaviours determine our attitudes? Or does it work both ways?

"There are three things extremely hard, steel, a diamond, and to know one's self."

Benjamin Franklin

CHAPTER TWO

The Self in a Social World

Self-concept: Who am I?
Intuition: Looking within
Fitting in: Looking to others

Self-organization: How the self operates
At the centre of our worlds: Our sense of self
The self in action

Self-serving bias: Seeing the self positively
Evaluating the self
Explaining self-serving bias
Reflections on self-serving bias

Self-presentation: Looking good to others
False modesty
Self-handicapping
Impression management

Put yourself in the shoes of the students showing up for a simple experiment by Jacquie Vorauer from the University of Manitoba and Dale Miller from Princeton University

(1997). The experimenter explains to you and one other participant that the study explores students' experiences at the university. By a coin toss, the other participant is sent off to complete a questionnaire while you collect your thoughts before being interviewed. Fifteen minutes later, the experimenter gives you a peek at the other student's glum report:

> I guess I don't really feel like I have had very many positive academic experiences. . . . I've found a lot of the material very difficult. . . . The worst moment I can think of was my French final; I went completely blank at the start. . . . I haven't made many new friends since I got to Princeton. Mostly, I have to rely on the people that I knew before.

Now, it's your turn. Will you self-describe your personal experiences more negatively than had you just read (as other subjects did) a report of someone "doing well in my courses . . . . I have had some wonderful friendships and roommates. . . . I feel more socially accepted than I used to"? So it happened with the actual student subjects. The positivity of their self-presentations echoed those of the other student. Yet, remarkably, they did not recognize this social influence on their self-presentation. They were blind to the interplay between their social surroundings and their self-presentation.

This is but one of many examples of the subtle connections between what's happening in the world around us and what's going on in our heads. Some more examples:

- *Social surroundings shape how we think about ourselves* As individuals in a group of a different culture, race, or sex, we notice how we differ and how others are reacting to our difference. The only woman in an executive meeting or math class is likely to be acutely aware of her gender. One of the authors has noticed this phenomenon when volunteering at his children's school, where almost all the teachers are women. In the teacher's lounge, he is quite aware that he is the only male.
- *Self-interest colours our judgments about others and ourselves* We are not objective, dispassionate judges of events. When problems arise in a close relationship such as marriage, we usually attribute more responsibility to our partners than to ourselves. Few divorced people blame themselves. When things go *well* at home or work or play, we see ourselves as more responsible. In competing for prizes, scientists seldom underrate their own contributions. After Canadians Frederick Banting and John Macleod received a 1923 Nobel Prize for discovering insulin, they both thought the discovery was primarily their own. Banting claimed that Macleod, who headed the laboratory, had been more a hindrance than a help. Macleod omitted Banting's name in speeches about the discovery (Ross, 1981).
- *Looking good to others motivates our social behaviour* Our actions are often strategic. In hopes of making a positive impression, we spend billions on cosmetics and diet programs. Like politicians, we also monitor others' behaviour and expectations and adjust our behaviour accordingly. Concern for self-image drives much of our behaviour.

As these examples suggest, the traffic between self and society runs both ways. Your ideas and feelings about yourself affect how you interpret events, how you recall them, and how you respond to others. Others, in turn, help shape your sense of self (Figure 2–1).

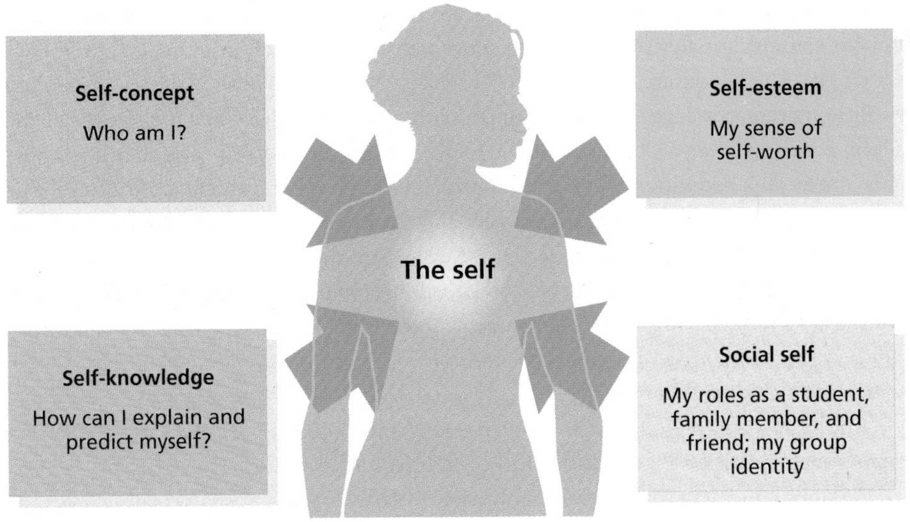

FIGURE 2–1
The self.

For these reasons, no topic in psychology is today more researched than the self. In 2008 the word "self" appeared in 15 073 book and article summaries in *PsychINFO (the online archive of psychological research)*—nine times the number in 1970. Our sense of self organizes our thoughts, feelings, and actions. We therefore begin our tour of social psychology with a look at *self-concept* (how we come to know ourselves) and at *the self in action* (how our sense of self drives our attitudes and actions).

SELF-CONCEPT: WHO AM I?

How do I come to know myself? How accurate is my self-knowledge? What determines my self-concept? In short, how do I know who I am?

self-concept
a person's answers to the question, "Who am I?"

INTUITION: LOOKING WITHIN

One answer to these questions that people sometimes give is that they "just know" who they are. By examining themselves and looking within themselves they believe they can develop an intuitive sense of who they are. Are our intuitions really the road to self-understanding? Should you as Steve Jobs (2005), the founder of Apple Computers, suggests, "have the courage to follow your heart and intuition?"

To answer this question let's begin by examining the power and perils of our intuitions.

Powers and perils of intuition

What are our powers of intuition—of immediately knowing something without reasoning or analysis? Advocates of "intuitive management" believe we should tune into our hunches. When judging others, they say, we should plug into the nonlogical smarts of our "right brain." When hiring, firing, and investing, we should listen to our premonitions. In making judgments, we should follow the example of *Star Wars*' Luke Skywalker by switching off our computer guidance systems and trusting the force within.

Are the intuitionists correct that important information is immediately available apart from our conscious analysis? Or are the skeptics right in saying that intuition is "our knowing we are right, whether we are or not"?

Priming research suggests that the unconscious indeed controls much of our behaviour. As John Bargh and Tanya Chartrand (1999) explain, "Most of a person's everyday life is determined not by their conscious intentions and deliberate choices but by mental processes that are put into motion by features of the environment and that operate outside of conscious awareness and guidance." When the light turns red, we react and hit the brake before consciously deciding to do so. Indeed, reflect Neil Macrae and Lucy Johnston (1998), "to be able to do just about anything at all (e.g., driving, dating, dancing), action initiation needs to be decoupled from the inefficient (i.e., slow, serial, resource consuming) workings of the conscious mind, otherwise inaction inevitably would prevail."

"The heart has its reasons which reason does not know," observed seventeenth-century philosopher-mathematician Blaise Pascal. Three centuries later, scientists have proved Pascal correct. We know more than we know we know. Studies of our unconscious information processing confirm our limited access to what's going on in our minds (Bargh, 1997; Greenwald & Banaji, 1995; Strack & Deutsch, 2004). Our thinking is partly **controlled** (reflective, deliberate, and conscious) and—more than most of us once supposed—partly **automatic** (impulsive, effortless, and without our awareness). Automatic, intuitive thinking occurs not "on-screen" but off-screen, out of sight, where reason does not go. Consider these examples of automatic thinking:

controlled processing "explicit" thinking that is deliberate, reflective, and conscious

automatic processing "implicit" thinking that is effortless, habitual, and without awareness, roughly corresponds to "intuition"

- *Schemas*—mental templates—intuitively guide our perceptions and interpretations of our experience. Whether we hear someone speaking of religious sects or sex depends not only on the word spoken but on how we automatically interpret the sound.
- *Emotional reactions* are often nearly instantaneous, before there is time for deliberate thinking. One neural shortcut takes information from the eye or ear to the brain's sensory switchboard (the thalamus) and out to its emotional control centre (the amygdala) before the thinking cortex has had any chance to intervene (LeDoux, 1994, 1996). Our ancestors who intuitively feared a sound in the bushes were usually fearing nothing, but they were more likely to survive to pass their genes down to us than their more deliberative cousins.
- Some things—facts, names, and past experiences—we remember explicitly (consciously). But other things—skills and conditioned dispositions—we remember *implicitly*, without consciously knowing and declaring that we know. It's true of us all, but most strikingly evident in people with brain damage who cannot form new explicit memories. One such person never could learn to recognize her physician, who would need to reintroduce himself with a handshake each day. One day the physician affixed a tack to his hand, causing the patient to jump with pain. When the physician next returned, he was still unrecognized (explicitly). But the patient, retaining an implicit memory, would not shake his hand (LeDoux, 1996).
- Equally dramatic are the cases of *blindsight*. Having lost a portion of the visual cortex to surgery or stroke, people may be functionally blind in part of their field of vision. Shown a series of sticks in the blind field, they report seeing nothing. After correctly guessing whether the sticks are vertical or horizontal, the patients are astounded when told, "You got them all right." Again, these people know more than they know they know.

- Although below our threshold for conscious awareness, subliminal stimuli may nevertheless have intriguing effects. For example, consider the following study conducted by McGill University's Mark Baldwin and his colleagues (1989). He had Catholic women read a sexually explicit passage and then subliminally flashed either a picture of the Pope frowning, a picture of a stranger frowning, or a blank screen. He then had the women rate themselves on a number of different dimensions of their self-concept. As you can see in Figure 2–2, he found that when the women were exposed to the frowning Pope they rated themselves more negatively than when they were exposed to the frowning stranger or the blank screen. This effect was particularly pronounced for those who reported higher levels of participation in their faith. Evidently, the subliminal priming of a disapproving Pope lowered these women's ratings of themselves.

So, many routine cognitive functions occur automatically, unintentionally, without awareness. Our minds function rather like big corporations. Our CEO—our controlled consciousness—attends to the most important, complex, or novel issues, while subordinates deal with routine affairs and matters requiring instant action. This delegation of resources enables us to react to many situations quickly and efficiently. The bottom line: Our brain knows much more than it tells us.

Intuitions about the self

The powers and perils of our intuitions demonstrate that much of our thinking occurs outside of our awareness and that our conscious thoughts often bear little resemblance to our unconscious thoughts that are controlling our behaviour. Do these findings hold for our intuitions about ourselves? Do our conscious explanations of our behaviours and our conscious understanding of who we are bear little resemblance to our unconscious thoughts and beliefs? Let's examine a number of studies that examine these issues.

Why did you choose your university? Why did you lash out at your roommate? Why did you fall in love with that special person? Sometimes we know. Sometimes we don't. Asked why

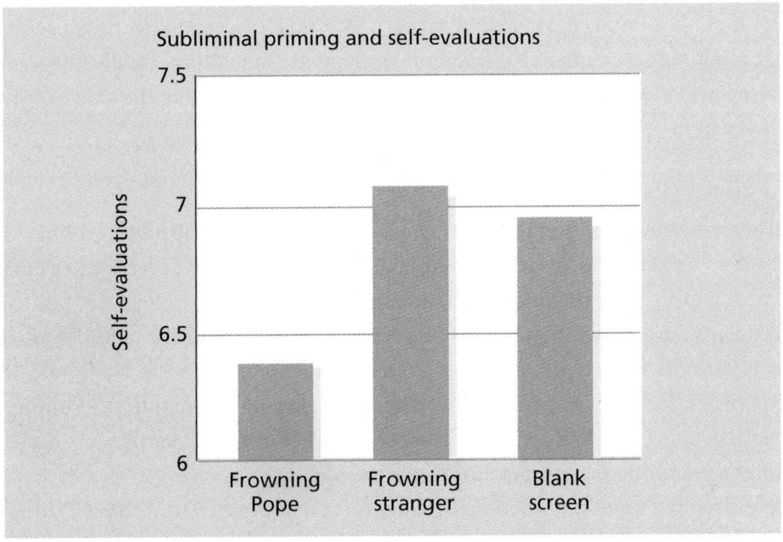

FIGURE 2–2

Subliminal priming and self-evaluations.

Catholic students primed with a subliminal picture of the Pope frowning rated themselves lower on a number of traits. (Data from Baldwin et al., 1989)

we have felt or acted as we have, we produce plausible answers. Yet, when causes are subtle, our self-explanations are often wrong. We may dismiss factors that matter and perceive others that don't as influential.

Richard Nisbett and Stanley Schachter (1966) demonstrated this by asking university students to take a series of electric shocks of steadily increasing intensity. Beforehand, some took a fake pill that, they were told, would produce heart palpitations, breathing irregularities, and butterflies in the stomach—the very typical reactions to being shocked. Nisbett and Schachter anticipated that people would attribute the shock symptoms to the pill and thus should tolerate more shock than people not given the pill. Indeed, the effect was enormous. People given the fake pill took four times as much shock. When asked why they withstood so much shock, they didn't mention the fake pill. When told the predicted pill effect, they granted that others might be influenced but denied its influence on them. "I didn't even think about the pill," was a typical reply.

"You don't know your own mind."

Jonathan Swift, *Polite Conversation*, 1738

Also thought provoking are studies in which people recorded their moods—every day for two or three months (Stone et al., 1985; Weiss & Brown, 1976; Wilson et al., 1982). They also recorded factors that might affect their moods: the day of the week, the weather, the amount they slept, and so forth. At the end of each study, the people judged how much each factor had affected their moods. Remarkably (given that their attention was being drawn to their daily moods), there was little relationship between their perceptions of how well a factor predicted their mood and how well it actually did so. These findings raise a disconcerting question: How much insight do we really have into what makes us happy or unhappy?

And how much insight do we have into our own freedom of will? As Daniel Wegner shows in *The Illusion of Conscious Will* (2002), people will *feel* that they have willed an action when their action-related thought precedes a behaviour that seems otherwise unexplainable. In one of Wegner's experiments, two people jointly control a computer mouse that glides over an "I-spy" board covered with little pictures. As the mouse roams, the participants hear the names of objects over headphones, and then stop on any picture they wish. Even when one person is a confederate who, on some trials, forces the mouse to a particular picture, the actual participants will typically perceive that they willed the mouse to the chosen picture. In this and other situations, the brain generates an intuition of personal efficacy. Other times, such as when dowsing for water or when one's arms raise under hypnotic suggestion, people misperceive that some external will is operating upon them. So, whether perceiving that they have (or have not) caused their actions, people sometimes err.

Predicting our behaviour

People also err when predicting their behaviour. If asked whether they would obey demands to deliver severe electric shocks or would hesitate to help a victim if several other people were present, people overwhelmingly deny their vulnerability to such influences. But as we will see, experiments have shown that many of us are vulnerable. Moreover, consider what Sidney Shrauger (1983) discovered when he had college students predict the likelihood that they would experience dozens of different events during the ensuing two months (becoming romantically involved, being sick, and so forth): Their self-predictions were hardly more accurate than predictions based on the average person's experience.

People also err frequently when predicting the fate of their relationships. Dating couples predict the longevity of their relationships through rose-coloured glasses. Focusing on the positives, lovers may feel sure they will always be lovers. Their friends and family often know better, report Tara MacDonald and Michael Ross (1997) from studies with University of Waterloo students. The less optimistic predictions of their parents and roommates tend to be more accurate. (Many a parent, having seen their child lunge confidently into an ill-fated relationship against all advice, nods yes.) In fact, the people who know you can probably predict your behaviour better than you can (for example, how nervous and chatty you will be when meeting someone new [Kenny, 1994]). So, how can you improve your self-predictions? The best advice is to consider your past behaviour in similar situations (Osberg & Shrauger, 1986, 1990). To predict your future, consider your past.

Nicholas Epley and David Dunning (2000) discovered that we can sometimes better predict people's behaviour by asking them to predict *others'* actions. Five weeks ahead of Cornell University's annual "Daffodil Days" charity event, Epley and Dunning asked students to predict whether they would buy at least one daffodil for charity, and also to predict what proportion of their fellow students would do so. More than four in five predicted they would buy a daffodil. But only 43 percent actually did, which was close to their prediction that 56 percent of others would buy one. In a laboratory game played for money, 84 percent predicted they would cooperate with another for their mutual gain, though only 61 percent did (again, close to their prediction of 64 percent cooperation by others.) If Lao-tzu was right that "He who knows others is learned. He who knows himself is enlightened," then most people, it would seem, are more learned than enlightened.

But do our intuitions always lead us astray? What if instead of deliberating about the right action we simply let time pass and allowed our automatic processes to influence our decisions. Ap Dijkersterhuis and his colleagues (2007) tested this idea. They had people make important decisions such as buying a home or a car and had them either make the decision right away, consciously deliberate on the decision noting the positives and negatives of each choice, or simply let time pass while they were occupied with other tasks. Their reasoning was that allowing time to pass without allowing people to actually think about the decision would allow the automatic or unconscious thought to influence the decision. They found that months later people were happiest with their decisions (both real world decisions and decisions in the lab) when they made the decision after a delay but without consciously deliberating on the decision. It seems that our unconscious intuitions might be better guides than we have previously thought.

Predicting our feelings

Many of life's big decisions involve predicting our future feelings. Would marrying this person lead to lifelong contentment? Would entering this profession make for satisfying work? Would going on this vacation produce a happy experience? Or would the likelier results be divorce, job burnout, and holiday disappointment?

Sometimes we know how we will feel—if we fail that exam, win that big game, or soothe our tensions with a half-hour jog. We know what exhilarates us, and what makes us anxious or bored. Other times we may mispredict our responses. Asked how they would feel if asked sexually harassing questions on a job interview, most women studied by Julie Woodzicka and Marianne LaFrance (2001) said they would feel angry. When actually asked such questions, however, women more often experienced fear. Studies of "affective forecasting" reveal that people nevertheless have greatest difficulty predicting the intensity and the duration of their future emotions

"When a feeling was there, they felt as if it would never go; when it was gone, they felt as if it had never been; when it returned, they felt as if it had never gone."

George MacDonald, *What's Mine's Mine*, 1886

(Wilson & Gilbert, 2003). People have mispredicted how they would feel some time after a romantic breakup, receiving a gift, losing an election, winning a game, and being insulted (Gilbert & Ebert, 2002; Loewenstein & Schkade 1999). Some examples:

- When male youths are shown sexually arousing photographs, then exposed to a passionate date scenario in which their date asks them to "stop," they admit that they might not stop. If not shown sexually arousing pictures first, they more often deny the possibility of being sexually aggressive. When not aroused, one easily mispredicts how one will feel and act when aroused—a phenomenon that leads to professions of love during lust, to unintended pregnancies, and to repeat offences among sex abusers who have sincerely vowed "never again."
- Hungry shoppers do more impulse buying ("Those doughnuts would be delicious!") than when shopping after scarfing a mega-sized blueberry muffin (Gilbert & Wilson, 2000). When hungry, one mispredicts how gross those deep-fried doughnuts will seem when sated. When stuffed, one mispredicts how yummy a doughnut might be with a late-night glass of milk.
- Only one in seven occasional smokers (of less than a cigarette per day) predicts they will be smoking in five years. But they underestimate the power of their drug cravings, for nearly half will still be smoking (Lynch & Bonnie, 1994).
- People overestimate how much their well-being would be affected by warmer winters, losing weight, more television channels, or more free time. Even extreme events, such as winning a provincial lottery or suffering a paralyzing accident, affect long-term happiness less than most people suppose.

impact bias overestimating the enduring impact of emotion-causing events

Our intuitive theory seems to be: We want. We get. We are happy. If that were true, this chapter would have fewer words. In reality, note Daniel Gilbert and Timothy Wilson (2000), we often "miswant." People who imagine an idyllic desert island holiday with sun, surf, and sand may be disappointed when they discover "how much they require daily structure, intellectual stimulation, or regular infusions of Pop Tarts." We think that if our candidate or team wins we will be delighted for a long while. But study after study reveals our vulnerability to **impact bias**—overestimating the enduring impact of emotion-causing events. Faster than we expect, the emotional traces of such good tidings evaporate.

Predicting behaviour, even one's own, is no easy matter, which may be why this visitor goes to a tarot card reader in hope of help.

Moreover, we are especially prone to impact bias after *negative* events. When people being tested for HIV predict how they will feel five weeks after getting the results, they expect to be feeling misery over bad news and elation over good news. Yet five weeks later, the bad news recipients are less distraught and the good news recipients are less elated than they anticipated (Sieff et al., 1999). And when Gilbert and his colleagues (1998) asked assistant professors to predict their happiness a few years after achieving tenure or not, most believed a favourable outcome was important for their future happiness. "Losing my job would crush my life's ambitions. It would be terrible." Yet when surveyed several years after the event, those denied tenure were about as happy as those who received it. Impact bias is important, say Wilson and Gilbert (2005), because people's "affective forecasts"—their predictions of their future emotions—influence their decisions. If people overestimate the intensity and duration of the pleasure they will gain from purchasing a new car or undergoing cosmetic surgery, then they may make ill-advised investments.

Let's make this personal. Gilbert and Wilson invite us to imagine how we might feel a year after losing our nondominant hands. Compared with today, how happy would you be?

Thinking about this, you perhaps focused on what the calamity would mean: no clapping, no shoe tying, no competitive basketball, no speedy keyboarding. Although you likely would forever regret the loss, your general happiness some time after the event would be influenced by "two things: (a) the event, and (b) everything else." In focusing on the negative event, we discount the importance of everything else that contributes to happiness and so overpredict our enduring misery. "Nothing that you focus on will make as much difference as you think," concur researchers David Schkade and Daniel Kahneman (1998). Notably, East Asians, who tend to think more holistically than Westerners—and so are more likely to consider many different factors when predicting their future feelings—are less susceptible to the impact bias (Lam et al., 2005). We will discuss these important differences in the self-concept of Easterners and Westerners in more detail in Chapter 8.

Moreover, say Wilson and Gilbert (2003), people neglect the speed and power of their psychological immune system, which includes their strategies for rationalizing, discounting, forgiving, and limiting emotional trauma. Being largely ignorant of our psychological immune system (a phenomenon Gilbert and Wilson call *immune neglect*), we accommodate to disabilities, romantic breakups, exam failures, tenure denials, and personal and team defeats more readily than we would expect. Ironically, Gilbert and his colleagues report (2004) major negative events (which activate our psychological defences) can be less enduringly distressing than minor irritations (which don't activate our defences). In other words, under most circumstances, we are remarkably resilient.

The wisdom and illusions of self-analysis

So, to a striking extent, our intuitions are often dead wrong about what has influenced us and what we will feel and do. But let's not overstate the case. When the causes of our behaviour are conspicuous and the correct explanation fits our intuition, our self-perceptions will be accurate (Gavanski & Hoffman, 1987). When the causes of behaviour are obvious to an observer, they are usually obvious to us as well.

As Chapter 3 will explore further, we are unaware of much that goes on in our minds. Studies of perception and memory show that we are more aware of the results of our thinking than its process. For example, we experience the results of our mind's unconscious workings when we set a mental clock to record the passage of time and to awaken us at an appointed hour, or when we somehow achieve a spontaneous creative insight after a problem has unconsciously "incubated." Creative scientists and artists, for example, often cannot report the thought processes that produced their insights.

Timothy Wilson (1985, 2002) offers a bold idea: The mental processes that *control* our social behaviour are distinct from the mental processes through which we explain our behaviour. Our rational explanations may therefore omit the gut-level attitudes that actually guide our behaviour. In nine experiments, Wilson and his coworkers (1989) found that expressed attitudes toward things or people usually predicted later behaviour reasonably well. If they first asked the participants to analyze their feelings, however, their attitude reports became useless. For example, dating couples' happiness with their relationship predicted whether they would still be dating several months later. But other participants first listed all the *reasons* they could think of why their relationship was good or bad before rating their happiness. After doing so, their attitude reports were useless in predicting the future of the relationship! Apparently the process of dissecting the relationship drew attention to easily verbalized factors that actually were less important than aspects of the relationship that were harder to verbalize. We are often "strangers to ourselves," says Wilson (2002).

"Self-contemplation is a curse that makes an old confusion worse."

Theodore Roethke, *The Collected Poems of Theodore Roethke*, 1975

In a later study, Wilson and his coworkers (1993) had people choose one of two art posters to take home. Those asked first to identify reasons for their choice preferred a humorous poster (whose positive features they could more easily verbalize). But a few weeks later, they were less satisfied with their choice than were those who just went by their gut feelings and generally chose the other poster. Compared with reasoned judgments of people with various facial attributes, gut-level reactions also are more consistent, report Gary Levine and colleagues (1996). First impressions can be telling.

dual attitudes differing implicit (automatic) and explicit (consciously controlled) attitudes toward the same object. Verbalized explicit attitudes may change with education and persuasion; implicit attitudes change slowly, with practice that forms new habits.

Such findings illustrate that we have a **dual attitude system**, say Wilson and his colleagues (2000). Our automatic *implicit* attitudes regarding someone or something often differ from our consciously controlled, *explicit* attitudes. From childhood, for example, we may retain a habitual, automatic fear or dislike of people for whom we now verbalize respect and appreciation. Although explicit attitudes may change with relative ease, notes Wilson, "implicit attitudes, like old habits, change more slowly." With repeated practice—acting on the new attitude—new habitual attitudes can, however, replace old ones.

Murray Millar and Abraham Tesser (1992) believe that Wilson overstates our ignorance of self. Their research suggests that, yes, drawing people's attention to reasons diminishes the usefulness of attitude reports in predicting behaviours that are driven by *feelings*. If, instead of having people analyze their romantic relationships, Wilson had first asked them to get more in touch with their feelings ("How do you feel when you are with and apart from your partner?"), the attitude reports might have been more insightful. Other behaviour domains—say, choosing which school to attend based on considerations of cost, career advancement, and so forth—seem more cognitively driven. For these, an analysis of reasons rather than feelings may be most useful. Although the heart has its reasons, sometimes the mind's own reasons are decisive.

This research on the limits of our self-knowledge has two practical implications. The first is for psychological inquiry. *Self-reports are often untrustworthy.* Errors in self-understanding limit the scientific usefulness of subjective personal reports.

The second implication is for our everyday lives. The sincerity with which people report and interpret their experiences is no guarantee of the validity of these reports. Personal testimonies are powerfully persuasive (as we will see in Module C, "Social Psychology in Court"). But they may also be wrong. Keeping this potential for error in mind can help us feel less intimidated by others and be less gullible.

FITTING IN: LOOKING TO OTHERS

As we try to answer the question, "Who am I?", maybe the answer isn't to be found so much by looking within our selves, but rather by looking at others. Several prominent theories and much research support the idea that how we are viewed by others and how we fit into our social groups are central to how we define ourselves. When people think well of us, it helps us think well of ourselves. Children whom others label as gifted, hard working, or helpful tend to incorporate such ideas into their self-concepts and behaviour (see Chapter 3). If minority students feel threatened by negative stereotypes of their academic ability, or if women feel threatened by low expectations for their math and science performance, they may "disidentify" with these realms. Rather than fight such prejudgments, they may identify their interests elsewhere (Steele, 1997).

The *looking-glass self* is how sociologist Charles H. Cooley (1902) described our using others as a mirror for perceiving ourselves. We see our reflection in how we appear to others, said Cooley. Fellow sociologist George Herbert Mead (1934) refined this concept, noting that what matters for our self-concept is not what others actually think of us, but the way we imagine they see us. Partly because most people feel freer to praise than criticize us, we may overestimate their appraisal, and our self-appraisals may become inflated.

Our ancestors' fate depended on what others thought of them. Their survival chances increased when protected by their group. Thus there was wisdom to their feeling shame and low self-esteem when perceiving their group's disapproval. As their heirs, we have a similar deep-seated need to belong (Mark Leary et al., 1995).

Social comparison

Not surprisingly given this theorizing, how we stack up compared to others is an important source of how we come to know who we are. Take, for example, a study conducted by Penelope Lockwood from the University of Toronto and Ziva Kunda from the University of Waterloo (Lockwood & Kunda, 1997). They exposed first-year or fourth-year accounting students to an article about a star accounting student who had won numerous awards, attained a very high grade average, and landed a spectacular job. For first-year students this role model represented an achievement they could hope to attain. If all went well, they too could have such a fantastic future. For fourth-year students, however, this role model did not present such hope. They knew all too well that at this point in their studies they would never measure up to such a superstar student. As you can see in Figure 2–3, such comparisons had strong effects on these

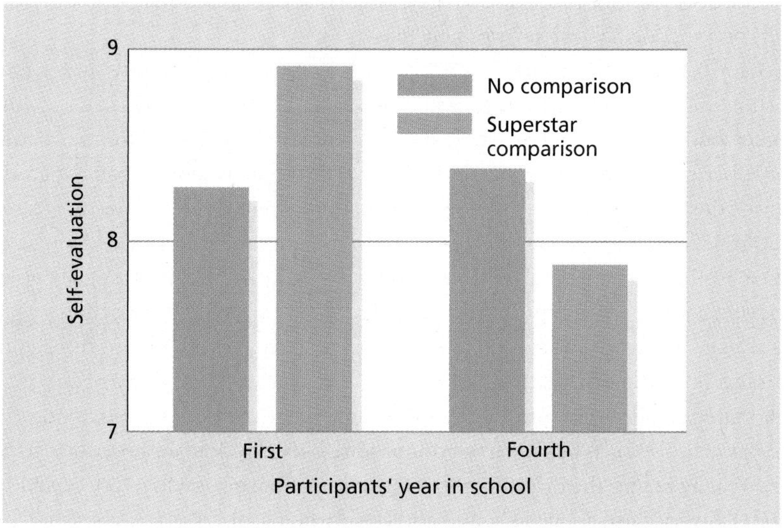

FIGURE 2–3

Social comparison and self-evaluation.

People are inspired by a role model if they can attain similar success but demoralized if they cannot. (Data from Lockwood & Kunda, 1997)

students' self- evaluations. When first- and fourth-year students did not compare to the superstar they had similar self-evaluations, but when they were exposed to the superstar, first-year students seemed inspired; their self-evaluations rose dramatically. Fourth-year students, on the other hand, seemed dejected; their self-evaluations dropped steeply. This research demonstrates the fundamental principle that our comparisons to others are a strong determinant of our self-views.

social comparison
evaluating one's abilities and opinions by comparing oneself to others

These **social comparisons** shape our identities as rich or poor, smart or dumb, tall or short: We compare ourselves with those around us and become conscious of how we differ. We then use others as a benchmark by which we can evaluate our performance and our beliefs. Social comparisons can profoundly affect our self-feelings. People who are concerned about their weight feel worse about themselves after just reading about a thin peer (Trottier, Polivy, & Herman, 2007).

Social comparison helps explain why students tend to have a higher academic self-concept if they attend a school with few exceptionally capable students (Marsh & Parker, 1984). After finishing secondary school near the top of their class, many academically confident students find their academic self-esteem threatened after entering big, selective universities where many students graduated near the top of their class. Given a little pond, a fish feels bigger.

self-esteem
a person's overall self-evaluation or sense of self-worth

Comparing ourselves to others in this way and seeing how we stack up to others is an important source of how we feel about ourselves. As Baumeister and Leary (1995) note **self-esteem**—our overall self-evaluation—is a psychological gauge by which we monitor and react to how others appraise us. Indeed our self-esteem tracks how we see ourselves on traits that we believe are valued by others. People believe that social acceptance often depends on easily observable traits, like physical appearance and social skills. Though people say they value communal traits, like kindness and understanding, they recognize that appearance is often what attracts others. And self-esteem corresponds more closely to such superficial traits than to communal qualities (Anthony, Holmes, & Wood, 2007). But self-esteem is also predicted by communal qualities for people whose roles make these qualities attractive to others. Our society values kindness and caring in women (more so than men) and in people in romantic relationships. For these individuals, self-esteem tracks communal qualities. Self-esteem thus depends on whether or not we believe we have traits that make us attractive to others, and not necessarily on the traits that we say we value most.

Abraham Tesser (1988) reports that a "self-esteem maintenance" motive predicts a variety of interesting findings, even friction among brothers and sisters. Do you have a sibling of the same gender who is close to you in age? If so, people probably compared the two of you as you grew up. Tesser presumes that people's perceiving one of you as more capable than the other will motivate the less able one to act in ways that maintain his or her self-esteem. (Tesser thinks the threat to self-esteem is greatest for an older child with a highly capable younger sibling.) Men with a brother with markedly different ability typically recall not getting along well with him; men with a similarly able brother are more likely to recall very little friction.

Self-esteem threats occur among friends, whose success can be more threatening than that of strangers (Zuckerman & Jost, 2001). And it can occur among married partners, too. Although shared interests are healthy, identical career goals may produce tension or jealousy (Clark & Bennett, 1992). When a partner outperforms us in a domain important to both our identities, we may reduce the threat by affirming our relationship, saying, "My capable partner, with whom I'm very close, is part of who I am" (Lockwood et al., 2004).

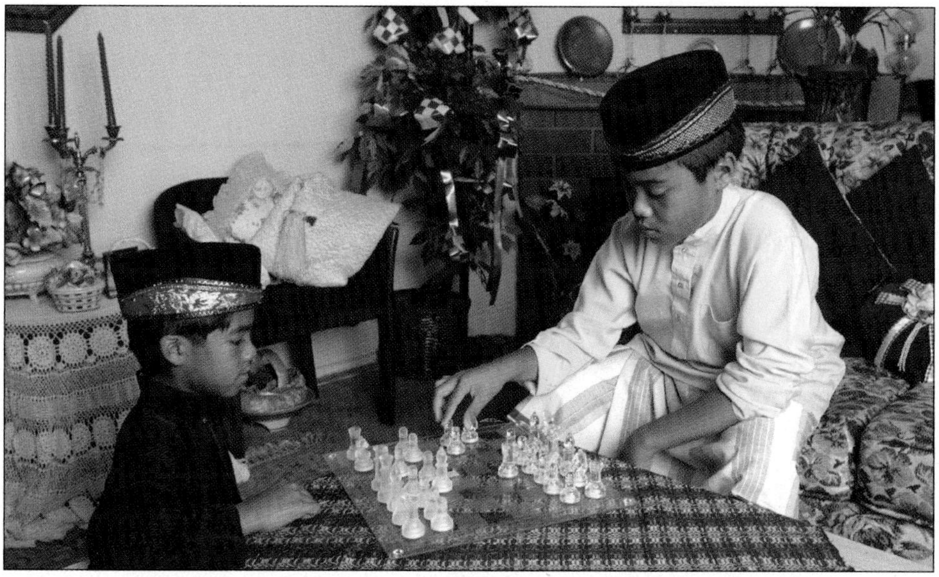

Among sibling relationships, the threat to self-esteem is greatest for an older child with a highly capable younger brother or sister.

Low self-esteem predicts increased risk of depression, drug abuse, and some forms of delinquency. For a low-self-esteem person, even public success can be aversive, by provoking anxiety that he or she will never live up to others' heightened expectations (Wood et al., 2005). (Have you ever done so well in a game, a recital, or a school exam that you worried about disappointing others on the next occasion?) High self-esteem fosters initiative, resilience, and pleasant feelings (Baumeister et al., 2003). Yet self-esteem can have a dark side as well. Teen males who engage in sexual activity at an "inappropriately young age" tend to have *higher* than average self-esteem. So do teen gang leaders, extreme ethnocentrists, and terrorists, notes Robyn Dawes (1994, 1998).

Finding their favourable self-esteem threatened, people often react by putting others down, sometimes with violence. A youth who develops a big ego, which then gets threatened or deflated by social rejection, is potentially dangerous. In one experiment, Todd Heatherton and Kathleen Vohs (2000) threatened some undergraduate men, but not those in a control condition, with a failure experience on an aptitude test. In response to the failure, only high-self-esteem men became considerably more antagonistic (Figure 2–4).

In another experiment, Brad Bushman and Roy Baumeister (1998) had 540 undergraduate volunteers write a paragraph, in response to which another supposed student gave them either praise ("great essay!") or stinging criticism ("one of the worst essays I have read!"). Then each essay writer played a reaction time game against the other student. When the opponent lost, the writer could assault him or her with noise of any intensity and for any duration. After criticism, the people with the biggest egos—those who agreed with "narcissistic" statements such as "I am more capable than other people"— were "exceptionally aggressive." They delivered three times the auditory torture of those with normal self-esteem. Wounded pride motivates retaliation.

"The enthusiastic claims of the self-esteem movement mostly range from fantasy to hogwash," says Baumeister (1996), who suspects he has "probably published more studies on self-esteem than anybody else." "The effects of self-esteem are small, limited, and not all good." High-self-esteem folks, he reports, are more likely to be obnoxious, to interrupt, and to talk at

FIGURE 2–4

When big egos get challenged.

When feeling threatened, only high-self-esteem people became significantly more antagonistic—arrogant, rude, and unfriendly. (Data from Heatherton & Vohs, 2000)

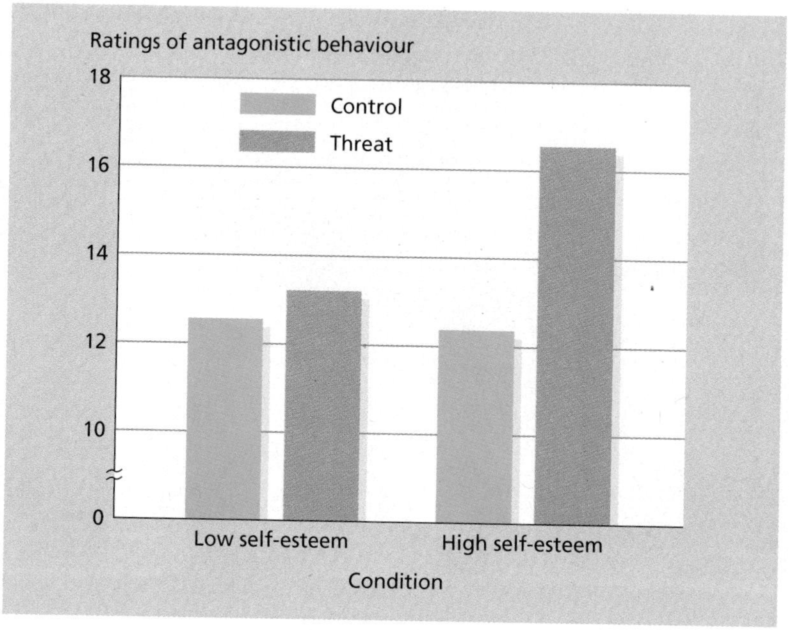

people rather than with them (in contrast to the more shy, modest, self-effacing folks with low self-esteem). "My conclusion is that self-control is worth 10 times as much as self-esteem."

Do the big egos of people who sometimes do bad things conceal inner insecurity and low self-esteem? Do assertive, narcissistic people actually have weak egos that are hidden by a self-inflating veneer? Many researchers have tried to find low self-esteem beneath such an outer crust. But studies of bullies, gang members, genocidal dictators, and obnoxious narcissists have turned up no sign of it. "Hitler had very high self-esteem," note Baumeister and his co-authors (2003).

What Baumeister and his colleagues call "the dark side of high self-esteem" exists in tension with the findings that people expressing low self-esteem are somewhat more vulnerable to assorted clinical problems, including anxiety, loneliness, and eating disorders. When feeling bad or threatened, they are more likely to view everything through dark glasses—to notice and remember others' worst behaviours and to think their partners don't love them (Murray et al., 1998, 2002; Ybarra, 1999).

Christian Jordan from Wilfrid Laurier University and his colleagues (2003, 2005) suggest that this tension may be more apparent than real. They suggest that not all high-self-esteem people are alike. New research indicates that self-esteem, like attitudes, comes in two forms—*explicit* (consciously controlled) and *implicit* (automatic or intuitive). Psychologists measure explicit self-esteem using questionnaires ("I feel I am a person of worth"), and measure implicit self-esteem with a variety of subtler measures, ranging from preference for the alphabet letters in one's name to computer-measured reaction times in classifying positive and negative words associated with oneself. Jordan and colleagues argue that when people have conscious views of themselves that are positive, but have low implicit self-esteem, they are likely to have fragile self-esteem. In several studies they found that people with such fragile high self-esteem are more narcissistic, favour their own group more, and discriminate more against Native-Canadians than other people. In similar experiments, Ian MacGregor and his colleagues (McGregor & Marigold, 2003; McGregor et al., 2005) found that York University students with defensive self-esteem responded to uncertainty by compensating with increased convictions in their political and social attitudes and by perceiving greater popularity for their views. In fact, when they feel threatened, people with low implicit self-esteem adopt more extreme views on controversial issues (like the war in Iraq and suicide bombing) and also believe that these views are more widely shared (McGregor & Jordan, 2007). Together this research suggests that some high-self-esteem people (those with negative implicit views of themselves) are prone to react defensively, whereas other high-self-esteem people (those with positive implicit views of themselves) are less likely to react in this way.

Unlike a fragile self-esteem, a secure self-esteem—one rooted more in feeling good about who one is than on grades, looks, money, or others' approval—is conducive to long-term well-being (Kernis, 2003; Schimel et al., 2001). Jennifer Crocker and her colleagues (2002, 2003, 2004, 2005) confirmed this in studies with University of Michigan students. Those whose self-worth was most fragile—most contingent on external sources—experienced more stress, anger, relationship problems, drug and alcohol use, and eating disorders than did those whose worth was rooted more on internal sources, such as personal virtues. Ironically, note Crocker and Lora Park (2004), those who pursue self-esteem, perhaps by seeking to become beautiful, rich, or popular, may lose sight of what really makes for quality of life. Moreover, if feeling good about ourselves is our goal, then we may become less open to criticism, more likely to blame than empathize with others, and more pressured to succeed at rather than simply to enjoy activities. Over time, such pursuit of self-esteem can fail to satisfy our deep needs for competence, relationship, and autonomy, note Crocker and Park. To focus less on one's self-image, and more on developing one's talents and relationships, eventually leads to greater well-being.

Social identity

Our self-concept—our sense of who we are—contains not just our personal identity (our sense of our personal attributes) but our **social identity**. The social definition of who you are—your race, religion, sex, academic major, and so forth—implies, too, a definition of who you are not.

social identity the "we" aspect of our self-concept. The part of our answer to "Who am I?" that comes from our group memberships. Examples: "I am Australian." "I am Catholic."

When we're part of a small group surrounded by a larger group, we are often conscious of our social identity; when our social group is the majority, we think less about it. As a solo female in a group of men, or as a solo Canadian in a group of Europeans, we are conscious of our uniqueness. To be a Black student on a mostly White campus, or a White student on a mostly Black campus, is to feel one's ethnic identity more keenly and to react accordingly. In Canada, most people identify themselves as "Canadian"—except in Quebec, where francophones are more likely to identify themselves as "Québécois" (Kalin & Berry, 1995).

In Britain, where the English outnumber the Scots 10 to 1, Scottish identity defines itself partly by differences with the English. "To be Scottish is, to some degree, to dislike or resent the English" (Meech & Kilborn, 1992). The English, as the majority, are less conscious of being not-Scottish. In the guest book of a Scottish hotel where one of the authors checked in recently, all the English guests reported "British" nationality, and all the Scots (who are equally British) reported their nationality as "Scottish."

SUMMING UP: SELF-CONCEPT

When we decide who we are and develop our self-concept one important source of information is our intuitions, which are curiously flawed. When powerful influences upon our behaviour are not so conspicuous that any observer could spot them, we, too, can miss them. The subtle implicit processes that control our behaviour may differ from our conscious explicit explanations of it.

A second important source of information that shapes our self-concepts is how we are viewed by others. The views of others are important building blocks of the self-concept although we heavily interpret these views as we define ourselves. Further whether we fit in and are seen positively by others forms an important basis of our self-esteem. How we compare to others and how our groups are viewed by others are two important ways that others shape our self-concepts.

SELF-ORGANIZATION: HOW THE SELF OPERATES

As people learn about themselves through looking within and looking without they gain a tremendous amount of information about themselves. In order to use and make sense of this information it needs to be organized. Bits of information that go with other bits need to develop connections in the brain and all those bits and connections need to be arranged so that the self-concept can influences people's thoughts and judgments. As we will see this organization of the self-concept has a strong influence on how the self operates.

AT THE CENTRE OF OUR WORLDS: OUR SENSE OF SELF

self-schema
beliefs about self that organize and guide the processing of self-relevant information

The elements of your self-concept, the specific beliefs by which you define yourself, are your **self-schemas** (Markus & Wurf, 1987). *Schemas* are mental templates by which we organize our worlds. Our *self*-schemas—our perceiving ourselves as athletic, overweight, smart, or whatever—powerfully affect, perceive, remember, and evaluate both other people and ourselves. If athletics is a central part of your self-concept (if being an athlete is one of your self-schemas), then you will tend to notice others' bodies and skills. You will quickly recall sports-related experiences. And you will welcome information that is consistent with your self-schema (Kihlstrom & Cantor, 1984). The self-schemas that make up our self-concepts help us organize and retrieve our experiences.

Self-reference

self-reference effect
the tendency to process efficiently and remember well information related to oneself

Consider how the self influences memory, a phenomenon known as the **self-reference effect**: *When information is relevant to our self-concepts, we process it quickly and remember it well* (Higgins & Bargh, 1987; Kuiper & Rogers, 1979; Symons & Johnson, 1997). If asked whether a specific word, such as "outgoing," describes us, we later remember that word better than if asked whether it describes someone else. If asked to compare ourselves with a character in a short story, we remember that character better. Two days after a conversation with someone, our recall is best for what the person said about us (Kahan & Johnson, 1992). Thus, memories

form around our primary interest: ourselves. When we think about something in relation to ourselves, we remember it better.

The self-reference effect illustrates a basic fact of life: Our sense of self is at the centre of our worlds. Because we tend to see ourselves on centre stage, we overestimate the extent to which others' behaviour is aimed at us. We often see ourselves as responsible for events in which we played only a small part (Fenigstein, 1984). When judging someone else's performance or behaviour, we often spontaneously compare it with our own (Dunning & Hayes, 1996). And if, while talking to one person, we overhear our name spoken by another in the room, our auditory radar instantly shifts our attention.

Possible selves

Our self-concepts include not only our self-schemas about who we currently are, they also include who we might become—our **possible selves**. Hazel Markus and her colleagues (Inglehart et al., 1989; Markus & Nurius, 1986) note that our possible selves include our visions of the self we dream of becoming—the rich self, the thin self, the passionately loved and loving self. They also include the self we fear becoming—the underemployed self, the unloved self, the academically failed self. Such possible selves motivate us with specific goals for a vision of the life we long for.

possible selves images of what we dream of or dread becoming in the future

Self-organization and self-esteem

Is self-esteem—our overall self-evaluation—the sum of all our self-schemas and possible selves? If we see ourselves as attractive, athletic, smart, and destined to be rich and loved, will we have high self-esteem? That's what psychologists assume when they suggest that to help people feel better about themselves, we should first make them feel more attractive, athletic, smarter, and so forth. This is especially so, Jennifer Crocker and Connie Wolfe (2001) argue, for the particular domains important to their self-esteem. "One person may have self-esteem that is highly contingent on doing well in school and being physically attractive, whereas another may have self-esteem that is contingent on being loved by God and adhering to moral standards." Thus the first person will feel high self-esteem when made to feel smart and good looking, the second person when made to feel moral.

But Jonathon Brown and Keith Dutton (1994) argue that this "bottom-up" view of self-esteem is not the whole story. The causal arrow, they believe, also goes the other way. People who value themselves in a general way—those with high self-esteem—are more likely then to value their looks, abilities, and so forth. They are like new parents who, loving their infant, delight in its fingers, toes, and hair: The parents do not first evaluate their infant's fingers or toes and then decide how much to value the whole baby.

To test their idea that global self-esteem affects specific self-perceptions ("top down"), Brown and Dutton introduced University of Washington students to a supposed trait called "integrative ability." They gave the students sets of three words—for example, "car," "swimming," "cue"—and challenged them to think of a word that linked the three words. (Hint: The word begins with p.) High-self-esteem people were more likely to report having this ability if told it was very important than if told it was useless. Feeling good about oneself in a general way, it seems, casts a rosy glow over one's specific self-schemas ("I have integrative ability") and possible selves.

THE SELF IN ACTION

So far we have considered what our self-concept is, how it develops, and how well we know ourselves. Now let's see why our self-concepts matter, by viewing the self in action.

Self-control

The self's action capacity has limits, note Roy Baumeister and his colleagues (1998; Muraven et al., 1998). People who exert self-control—by forcing themselves to eat radishes rather than chocolates, or by suppressing forbidden thoughts—subsequently quit faster when given unsolvable puzzles. People who try to control their emotions to an upsetting movie exhibit decreased physical stamina. Effortful self-control depletes our limited willpower reserves, it seems. Self-control operates like muscular strength, conclude Baumeister and Julia Exline (2000): Both are weaker after exertion, replenished with rest, and strengthened by exercise.

Nevertheless, our self-concept does influence our behaviour (Graziano et al., 1997). Given challenging tasks, people who imagine themselves as hardworking and successful outperform those who imagine themselves as failures (Ruvolo & Markus, 1992). Envision your positive possibilities and you become more likely to plan and enact a successful strategy. Perceived self-control matters.

Although exerting control over our thoughts and behaviours often seems like a difficult and demanding task, it need not always be so. Grainne Fitzsimons and John Bargh (2004) have shown that regulating our thoughts and actions in this way can at times become well learned and pursuing the goals that foster exerting control can become automatic. So for those who are on a diet long enough there is hope that avoiding a roommate's stash of candy can get easier over time and require less mental energy.

Self-determination

learned helplessness the hopelessness and resignation learned when a human or animal perceives no control over repeated bad events

The benefits of feelings of control also appear in animal research. Dogs taught that they cannot escape shocks while confined will learn a sense of helplessness. Later these dogs cower passively in other situations when they *could* escape punishment. Dogs that learn personal control (by escaping their first shocks successfully) adapt easily to a new situation. Researcher Martin Seligman (1975, 1991) notes similarities to this **learned helplessness** in human situations. Depressed or oppressed people, for example, become passive because they believe their efforts have no effect. Helpless dogs and depressed people both suffer paralysis of the will, passive resignation, even motionless apathy (Figure 2–5).

On the other hand, people benefit by training their self-control "muscles." That's the conclusion of studies by Megan Oaten and Ken Cheng (2006) at Sydney's Macquarie University. For example, students who were engaged in practising self-control by daily exercise, regular study, and time management became more capable of self-control in other settings, both in the laboratory and when taking exams.

Ellen Langer and Judith Rodin (1976) tested the importance of personal control by treating elderly patients in a high-rated nursing home in one of two ways. With one group the

FIGURE 2–5

Learned helplessness.

When animals and people experience uncontrollable bad events, they learn to feel helpless and resigned.

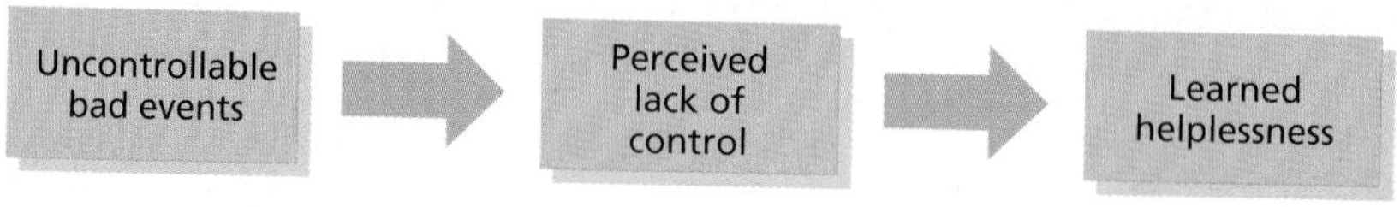

benevolent caregivers stressed "our responsibility to make this a home you can be proud of and happy in." They gave the passive patients their normal well-intentioned, sympathetic care. Three weeks later, most were rated by themselves, by interviewers, and by nurses as further debilitated. Langer and Rodin's other treatment promoted personal control. It stressed opportunities for choice, the possibilities for influencing nursing-home policy, and the person's responsibility "to make of your life whatever you want." These patients were given small decisions to make and responsibilities to fulfill. Over the ensuing three weeks, 93 percent of this group showed improved alertness, activity, and happiness.

Studies confirm that systems of governing or managing people that promote self-efficacy will indeed promote health and happiness (Deci & Ryan, 1987).

- University students who develop a sense of control over school gain a greater sense of control over their lives (Guay, Mageau, Vallerand, 2003).
- Prisoners given some control over their environments—by being able to move chairs, control TV sets, and switch the lights—experience less stress, exhibit fewer health problems, and commit less vandalism (Ruback et al., 1986; Wener et al., 1987).
- Workers given leeway in carrying out tasks and making decisions experience improved morale (Miller & Monge, 1986).
- Institutionalized residents allowed choice in such matters as what to eat for breakfast, when to go to a movie, whether to sleep late or get up early, may live longer and certainly are happier (Timko & Moos, 1989).
- Homeless shelter residents who perceive little choice in when to eat and sleep, and little control over their privacy, are more likely to have a passive, helpless attitude regarding finding housing and work (Burn, 1992).

"*This gives my confidence a real boost.*"

Confidence and feelings of self-efficacy grow from successes.

- In all countries studied, including Canada, people who perceive themselves as having free choice experience greater satisfaction with their lives. And countries where people experience more freedom have more satisfied citizens (Inglehart & Welzel, 2005).

Although this psychological research on perceived self-control is new, the emphasis on taking charge of one's life and realizing one's potential is not. The notion that "you can do it if you try hard enough" has permeated our culture. When we were little children most of us were taught the story about the Little Engine That Could. The cultural lesson is clear: If you try hard enough and keep a positive attitude you can achieve whatever you dream. The same lesson we find in many self-help books and videos.

"Argue for your limitations, and sure enough they're yours."

Richard Bach, *Illusions: Adventures of a Reluctant Messiah*, 1977

Research on self-control gives us greater confidence in traditional virtues such as perseverance and hope. A sense of self-control does not grow primarily by self-persuasion ("I think I can, I think I can") or by puffing people up like hot-air balloons ("You're terrific!). Its chief source is the experience of success. If your initial efforts to lose weight, stop smoking, or improve your grades succeed, your self-efficacy increases.

SUMMING UP: SELF-ORGANIZATION

Our sense of self helps organize our thoughts and actions. When we process information with reference to ourselves, we remember it well (a phenomenon called the *self-reference* effect). The elements of our self-concept are the specific *self-schemas* that guide our processing of self-relevant information and the *possible selves* that we dream of or dread.

Our self-esteem appears to be shaped by both top-down views of the self derived from our self-schemas and bottom processing of how we see ourselves. When the self is in action we see that the organization of the self can affect our sense of self-control and self-regulation

People who believe in their own competence and effectiveness cope better and achieve more than do those who have learned a helpless, pessimistic outlook.

SELF-SERVING BIAS: SEEING THE SELF POSITIVELY

As we process self-relevant information, a potent bias intrudes. We readily excuse our failures, accept credit for our successes, and in many ways see ourselves as better than average. Such self-enhancing perceptions enable most people to enjoy the benefits of high self-esteem, while occasionally suffering the perils of pride.

It is widely believed that most of us suffer low self-esteem. A generation ago, humanistic psychologist Carl Rogers (1958) concluded that most people he knew "despise themselves, regard themselves as worthless and unlovable." Many popularizers of humanistic psychology concur. "All of us have inferiority complexes," contends John Powell (1989). "Those who seem not to have such a complex are only pretending." As Groucho Marx (1960) lampooned, "I wouldn't want to belong to any club that would accept me as a member."

Actually, most of us have a good reputation with ourselves. In studies of self-esteem, even low-scoring people respond in the midrange of possible scores. (A low-self-esteem person responds to such statements as "I have good ideas" with a qualifying adjective, such as "somewhat" or "sometimes.") Moreover, one of social psychology's most provocative yet firmly established conclusions concerns the potency of **self-serving bias**.

The self-serving bias.

© Jean Sorensen.

EVALUATING THE SELF

When evaluating the self do we act as dispassionate observers or do we look to see ourselves in the most positive light possible? We do tend to view ourselves positively, but is this self-serving bias a simple inference from our beliefs about ourselves or is it a motivated bias? There is actually evidence that both types of processes occur. If a dispassionate observer had the same information about us that we have, they would often make the same inferences we make. Self-serving biases can be solely the result of our cognitive machinery.

Nevertheless, a motivational engine powers our cognitive machinery (Dunning, 1999; Kunda, 1990). We are not just cool, information-processing machines. We are motivated to see ourselves positive and adept at doing so.

Explanations for positive and negative events

Time and again, experimenters have found that people readily accept credit when told they have succeeded (attributing the success to their ability and effort), yet attribute failure to such external factors as bad luck or the problem's inherent "impossibility" (Whitley & Frieze, 1985; Campbell & Sedikides, 1999). Similarly, in explaining their victories, athletes commonly credit themselves, but they attribute losses to something else: bad breaks, bad referee calls, or the other team's super effort or dirty play (Grove et al., 1991; Lalonde, 1992; Mullen & Riordan, 1988). And how much responsibility do you suppose car drivers tend to accept for their accidents? On insurance forms, drivers have described their accidents in words such as these: "An invisible car came out of nowhere, struck my car and vanished," "As I reached an intersection, a hedge sprang up, obscuring my vision, and I did not see the other car," "A pedestrian hit me and went under my car" (*Toronto News*, 1977).

self-serving bias
the tendency to perceive oneself favourably

Situations that combine skill and chance (games, exams, job applications) are especially prone to the phenomenon: Winners can easily attribute their successes to their skill, while losers can attribute their losses to chance. When one wins at Scrabble, it's because of one's verbal dexterity; when one loses, it's because "Who could get anywhere with a Q but no U?" Politicians similarly tend to attribute their wins to themselves (hard work, constituent service, reputation, and strategy) and their losses to factors beyond their control (their district's party makeup, their opponent's name, political trends) (Kingdon, 1967). This phenomenon of **self-serving attributions** (attributing positive outcomes to oneself and negative outcomes to something else) is one of the most potent of human biases.

self-serving attributions
a form of self-serving bias; the tendency to attribute positive outcomes to oneself and negative outcomes to other factors

Self-serving attributions contribute to marital discord, worker dissatisfaction, and bargaining impasses (Kruger & Gilovich, 1999). Small wonder that divorced people usually blame their partner for the breakup (Gray & Silver, 1990), or that managers usually blame poor performance on workers' lack of ability or effort (Imai, 1994; Rice, 1985). (Workers are more likely to blame something external—inadequate supplies, excessive workload, difficult coworkers, or ambiguous assignments.) Small wonder, too, that people evaluate reward distributions such as pay raises as fairer when they receive more than most others rather than less (Diekmann et al., 1997).

Students also exhibit self-serving bias. After receiving an exam grade, those who do well tend to accept personal credit. They judge the exam to be a valid measure of their competence (Arkin & Maruyama, 1979; Briere & Vallerand, 1990; Davis & Stephan, 1980; Gilmor & Reid, 1979; Griffin et al., 1983). Those who do poorly are much more likely to criticize the exam.

Reading this research, we couldn't resist a satisfied "knew-it-all-along" feeling. But consider teachers' ways of explaining students' good and bad performances. When there is no need to feign modesty, those assigned the role of teacher tend to take credit for positive outcomes and blame failure on the student (Arkin et al., 1980; Davis, 1979). Teachers, it seems, are likely to think, "With my help, Maria graduated with honours. Despite all my help, Melinda flunked out."

Can we all be better than average?

Self-serving bias also appears when people compare themselves with others. If the sixth-century B.C. Chinese philosopher Lao-tzu was right that "at no time in the world will a man who is sane over-reach himself, over-spend himself, over-rate himself," then most of us are a little insane. For on most subjective and socially desirable dimensions, most people see themselves as better

STORY BEHIND THE RESEARCH

Michael Ross
University of Waterloo

Suppose that you have collaborated on a project with another student and that the two of you evaluated each other's contributions to the final product. You may be disappointed to discover that your partner is less impressed with the quality and extent of your contribution than you are. In the history of science, there are many examples of such disagreements; erstwhile friends and colleagues become bitter enemies as they contest each other's contributions to important discoveries. Sicoly and I suggested that individuals generally tend to accept more responsibility for a joint product than other contributors attribute to them. In many everyday activities, participants are unaware of their divergent views because they don't share their opinions with each other. After cleaning the kitchen, for example, spouses don't usually discuss how much each contributed to the cleanup. When such opinions are voiced, people are likely to be upset because they believe that the other person is not giving them sufficient credit. If the consequences are high (e.g., academic grades, job promotions, or Nobel prizes at stake), they may well assume that their partner is deliberately downgrading their contributions to enhance his or her own achievements. In our research, Sicoly and I showed that differences in assessments of responsibility are common in many everyday contests, and that contrasting judgments may reflect normal cognitive processes rather than deliberate deceit. Differences in judgment can result from honest evaluations of information that is differentially available to the two participants.

FOCUS ON

SELF-SERVING BIAS—HOW DO I LOVE ME? LET ME COUNT THE WAYS

"The one thing that unites all human beings, regardless of age, gender, religion, economic status or ethnic background," notes Dave Barry (1998), "is that deep down inside, we all believe that we are above average drivers." We also believe we are above average on most any other subjective and desirable trait. Among the many faces of self-serving bias are these:

- *Ethics.* Most businesspeople see themselves as more ethical than the average businessperson (Baumhart, 1968; Brenner & Molander, 1977). One national survey asked, "How would you rate your own morals and values on a scale from 1 to 100 (100 being perfect)?" Fifty percent of people rated themselves 90 or above; only 11 percent said 74 or less (Lovett, 1997).
- *Professional competence.* Ninety percent of business managers rate their performance as superior to their average peer (French, 1968). In Australia, 86 percent of people rate their job performance as above average, 1 percent as below average (Headey & Wearing, 1987). Most surgeons believe their patients' mortality rate to be lower than average (Gawande, 2002).
- *Virtues.* In the Netherlands, most high school students rate themselves as more honest, persistent, original, friendly, and reliable than the average high school student (Hoorens, 1993, 1995).
- *Intelligence.* Most people perceive themselves as more intelligent, better looking, and much less prejudiced than their average peer (Public Opinion, 1984; Wylie, 1979). When someone outperforms them, people tend to think of the other as a genius (Lassiter & Munhall, 2001).
- *Parental support.* Most adults believe they support their aging parents more than do their siblings (Lerner et al., 1991).
- *Health.* Los Angeles residents view themselves as healthier than most of their neighbours, and most university students believe they will outlive their actuarially predicted age of death by about 10 years (Larwood, 1978; C. R. Snyder, 1978).
- *Insight.* Others' words and deeds reveal their natures, we presume. Our private thoughts do the same. Thus, most of us believe we know and understand others better than they know and understand us. We also believe we know ourselves better than others know themselves (Pronin et al., 2001). Few university students see themselves as more naïve or more gullible than others; many more think they're less naïve and gullible (Levine, 2003).
- *Driving.* Most drivers—even most drivers who have been hospitalized for accidents—believe themselves to be safer and more skilled than the average driver (Guerin, 1994; McKenna & Myers, 1997; Svenson, 1981). Dave Barry got it right!

than the average person. Compared with people in general, most people see themselves as more ethical, more competent at their job, friendlier, more intelligent, better looking, less prejudiced, healthier, and even more insightful and less biased in their self-assessments (see "Focus on: Self-Serving Bias—How Do I Love Me? Let Me Count the Ways").

Every community, it seems, is like Garrison Keillor's fictional Lake Wobegon, where "all the women are strong, all the men are good-looking, and all the children are above average." Perhaps one reason for this optimism is that although 12 percent of people feel old for their age, many more—66 percent—think they are young for their age (Public Opinion, 1984). All of which calls to mind Freud's joke about the husband who told his wife, "If one of us should die, I think I would go live in Paris."

Michael Ross and Fiore Sicoly (1979) observed a marital version of self-serving bias. They found that young married Canadians usually felt they took more responsibility for such activities as cleaning the house and caring for the children than their spouses credited them for. In one survey, 91 percent of wives but only 76 percent of husbands credited the wife with doing most of the food shopping (Burros, 1988). In other studies, wives estimated they did proportionally more of the housework than their husbands credited them with (Bird, 1999; Fiebert, 1990). Every night, one of the authors and his wife used to pitch their laundry at the foot of their bedroom clothes hamper. In the morning, one of them would put it in the hamper. When the wife suggested that the author take more responsibility for this, he thought, "Huh? I already do it 75 percent of the time." So he asked her how often she thought she picked up the clothes. "Oh," she replied, "about 75 percent of the time."

Subjective behaviour dimensions (such as "disciplined") trigger greater self-serving bias than objective behavioural dimensions (such as "punctual"). Students are more likely to rate themselves superior in "moral goodness" than in "intelligence" (Allison et al., 1989; Van Lange, 1991). And community residents overwhelmingly see themselves as caring more than most others about the environment, about hunger, and about other social issues, though they don't see themselves as doing more, such as contributing time or money to those issues (White & Plous, 1995). Education doesn't eliminate self-serving bias; even social psychologists exhibit it, by believing themselves more ethical than most social psychologists (Van Lange et al., 1997).

Subjective qualities give us leeway in constructing our own definitions of success (Dunning et al., 1989, 1991). Rating my "athletic ability," I ponder my basketball play, not the agonizing weeks I spent as a Little League baseball player hiding in right field. Assessing my "leadership ability," I conjure up an image of a great leader whose style is similar to mine. By defining ambiguous criteria in our own terms, each of us can see ourselves as relatively successful. In one University Entrance Examination Board survey of 829 000 high school seniors, 0 percent rated themselves below average in "ability to get along with others" (a subjective, desirable trait), 60 percent rated themselves in the top 10 percent, and 25 percent saw themselves among the top 1 percent!

We also support our self-images by assigning importance to the things we're good at. Over a semester, those who ace an introductory computer science course come to place a higher value on being a computer-literate person in today's world. Those who do poorly are more likely to scorn computer geeks and to exclude computer skills as pertinent to their self-images (Hill et al., 1989).

People display one other ironic bias: Most people see themselves as freer from bias than most people (Ehrlinger et al., 2005; Pronin et al., 2002). Indeed, they even see themselves as less vulnerable to self-serving bias! They will admit to some bias in the abstract, and they see others as biased. But when asked about specific traits and behaviours, such as when rating their own ethics or likeability, they judge their self-assessments as untainted.

"Views of the future are so rosy that they would make Pollyanna blush."

Shelley E. Taylor, *Positive Illusions*, 1989

Unrealistic optimism

Optimism predisposes a positive approach to life. "The optimist," notes H. Jackson Brown (1990, p. 79), "goes to the window every morning and says, 'Good morning,

God.' The pessimist goes to the window and says, 'good god, morning.'" Many of us however, have what researcher Neil Weinstein (1980, 1982) terms "an unrealistic optimism about future life events." Partly because of their relative pessimism about others' fates (Shepperd, 2003), students perceive themselves as far more likely than their classmates to get a good job, draw a good salary, and own a home, and as far less likely to experience negative events, such as developing a drinking problem, having a heart attack before age 40, or being fired.

Linda Perloff (1987) notes how illusory optimism increases our vulnerability. Believing ourselves immune to misfortune, we do not take sensible precautions. In one survey, 137 marriage licence applicants accurately estimated that half of marriages end in divorce, yet most assessed their chance of divorce as zero percent (Baker & Emery, 1993). Sexually active undergraduate women who don't consistently use contraceptives perceive themselves, compared to other women at their university, as much less vulnerable to unwanted pregnancy (Burger & Burns, 1988). In Scotland, most older teens think they are much less likely than their peers to become infected by HIV (Abrams, 1991; Pryor & Reeder, 1993).

"O God, give us grace to accept with serenity the things that cannot be changed, courage to change the things which should be changed, and the wisdom to distinguish the one from the other."

Reinhold Niebuhr, "The Serenity Prayer," 1943

Those who cheerfully shun seat belts deny the effects of smoking, and stumble into ill-fated relationships remind us that blind optimism, like pride, may go before a fall. When gambling, optimists more than pessimists persist, even when piling up losses (Gibson & Sanbonmatsu, 2004). If those who deal in the stock market or in real estate perceive their business intuition to be superior to that of their competitors, they, too, may be in for severe disappointment. Even the seventeenth-century economist Adam Smith, a defender of human economic rationality, foresaw that people would overestimate their chances of gain. This "absurd presumption in their own good fortune," he said, arises from "the overweening conceit which the greater part of men have of their own abilities" (Spiegel, 1971, p. 243).

Optimism definitely beats pessimism in promoting self-efficacy, health, and well-being (Armor & Taylor, 1996). If our optimistic ancestors were more likely than their pessimistic neighbours to surmount challenges and survive, then small wonder that we are disposed to optimism (Haselton & Nettle, 2006). Yet a dash of realism can save us from the perils of unrealistic optimism. Self-doubt can energize students, most of whom—especially those destined for low grades—exhibit excess optimism about upcoming exams (Prohaska, 1994; Sparrell & Shrauger, 1984). (Such illusory optimism often disappears as the time approaches for receiving

Penthouse *publisher Bob Guccione, responding to a national survey revealing that 83 percent of adults reported zero or one sexual partner in the past year: "Positively, outrageously stupid and unbelievable. I would say five partners a year is the average for men."*

(Elmer-DeWitt, 1994)

the exam back—Shepperd et al., 1996.) Students who are overconfident tend to underprepare. Their equally able but more anxious peers, fearing that they are going to bomb on the upcoming exam, study furiously and get higher grades (Goodhart, 1986; Norem & Cantor, 1986; Showers & Ruben, 1987). The moral: Success in school and beyond requires enough optimism to sustain hope and enough pessimism to motivate concern.

false consensus effect the tendency to overestimate the commonality of one's opinions and one's undesirable or unsuccessful behaviours

False consensus and uniqueness

We have a curious tendency to further enhance our self-images by overestimating or underestimating the extent to which others think and act as we do. On matters of *opinion*, we find support for our positions by overestimating the extent to which others agree—a phenomenon called the **false consensus effect** (Krueger & Clement, 1994; Marks & Miller, 1987; Mullen & Goethals, 1990). Those who have favoured a Canadian referendum or supported New Zealand's National Party wishfully overestimated the extent to which others agree (Babad et al., 1992; Koestner, 1993). The sense we make of the world seems like common sense.

"I think few people have conventional family relationships."

Madonna, 2000

When we behave badly or fail in a task, we reassure ourselves by thinking that such lapses also are common. After one person lies to another, the liar begins to perceive the *other* person as dishonest (Sagarin et al., 1998). They guess that others think and act as they do: "I lie, but doesn't everyone?" If we cheat on our income taxes or smoke, we are likely to overestimate the number of other people who do likewise. If we feel sexual desire toward another, we may overestimate the other's reciprocal desire. Four recent studies illustrate:

- People who sneak a shower during a shower ban believe (more than nonbathers) lots of others are doing the same (Monin & Norton, 2003).
- Those thirsty after hard exercise imagine that lost hikers would become more bothered by thirst than by hunger. That's what 88 percent of thirsty post exercisers guessed in a study by Leaf Van Boven and George Lowenstein (2003), compared with 57 percent of people who were about to exercise.

Illusory optimism: Most couples marry feeling confident of long-term love. Actually, in individualistic cultures, new marriages often fail.

- As people's own lives change, they see the world changing. Protective new parents come to see the world as a more dangerous place. People who go on a diet judge food ads to be more prevalent (Eibach et al., 2003).
- People who harbour negative ideas about another racial group presume that many others also have negative stereotypes (Krueger, 1996). Thus our perceptions of others' stereotypes may reveal something of our own.

"Everybody says I'm plastic from head to toe. Can't stand next to a radiator or I'll melt. I had (breast) implants, but so has every single person in L.A" (Talbert, 1997).

Actress Pamela Lee

"We don't see things as they are," says the Talmud. "We see things as we are." False consensus may occur because we generalize from a limited sample, which prominently includes ourselves (Dawes, 1990). Lacking other information, why not "project" ourselves; why not impute our own knowledge to others and use our responses as a clue to their likely responses? Also, we're more likely to associate with people who share our attitudes and behaviours and then to judge the world from the people we know.

On matters of *ability* or when we behave well or successfully, a **false uniqueness effect** more often occurs (Goethals et al., 1991). We serve our self-image by seeing our talents and moral behaviours as relatively unusual. Thus those who drink heavily but use seat belts will *overestimate* (false consensus) the number of other heavy drinkers and *underestimate* (false uniqueness) the commonality of seat belt use (Suls et al., 1988). Thus we may see our failings as relatively normal and our virtues as less commonplace than they are.

false uniqueness effect
the tendency to underestimate the commonality of one's abilities and one's desirable or successful behaviours

Temporal comparison

Not only our comparisons with others, but also our comparisons with who we used to be and who we want to be can be potent sources of self-serving bias. These **temporal comparisons** with our past and future selves also portray the current self in a positive light.

temporal comparison
a comparison between how the self is viewed now and how the self was viewed in the past or how the self is expected to be viewed in the future

Anne Wilson from Wilfrid Laurier University and Mike Ross from the University of Waterloo (Wilson & Ross, 2001; Ross & Wilson, 2002) have studied temporal comparisons extensively. They have found that people maintain a positive view of themselves by disparaging their distant past selves and complimenting their recent past selves. For example, in one experiment Wilson and Ross had university students and their parents rate the students on a number of traits both as they currently were and as they were when they were 16. As can be seen in Figure 2–6, both students and their parents believed that they had improved significantly with time. This evidence would seem to indicate that people disparage their past selves and compliment their future selves, but it could also simply indicate a developmental trend—perhaps people just get better with time. Wilson and Ross (2001) conducted several other studies to rule out this possibility. They showed that while students perceive dramatic improvements in themselves, they do not perceive similar improvement in their acquaintances and siblings. In addition, when students rate themselves at the beginning of term and then retrospectively rate their beginning-of-term self at the end of term, they remember themselves as being much worse at the beginning of term than they rated themselves at the time, suggesting that students create an illusion of improvement that is more apparent than real.

Ross and Wilson (2002) also found that we perceive positive past selves as closer in time and negative past selves as more distant. In one study, they had students rate their social success in high school and later rate how psychologically distant high school seemed. Those who were popular in high school saw it as much more recent than those who were less popular, and the

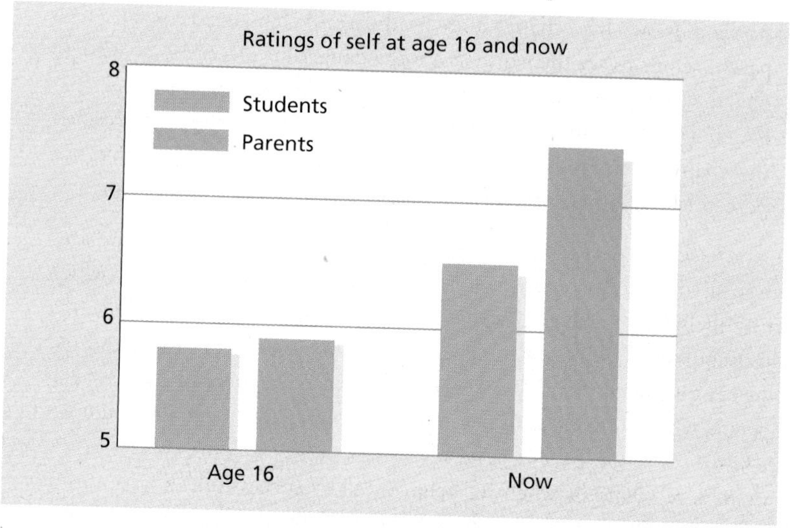

FIGURE 2–6

Both university students and their parents believe they have improved with time. (Wilson & Ross, 2001)

effect was especially strong for people high in self-esteem. As we will see later in this chapter, high-self-esteem people engage in a number of self-enhancing strategies more frequently than do low-self-esteem people. It seems that bringing positive selves closer and pushing away negative selves is one of those strategies. These high-self-esteem people seem to view their glory days as having just occurred, while their days as a geek are part of the ancient past.

To sum up, these tendencies toward self-serving attributions, self-congratulatory comparisons, illusory optimism, and false consensus for our failings are major sources of self-serving bias (Figure 2–7).

EXPLAINING SELF-SERVING BIAS

Why do people perceive themselves in self-enhancing ways? One explanation sees the self-serving bias as a by-product of how we process and remember information about ourselves.

FIGURE 2–7

How self-serving bias works.

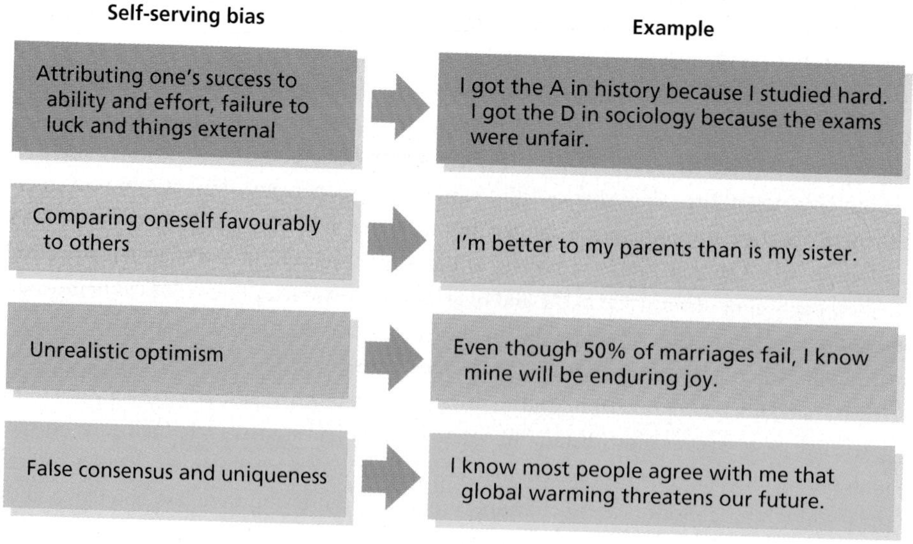

Comparing ourselves with others requires us to notice, assess, and recall their behaviour and ours. Thus, there are multiple opportunities for flaws in our information processing (Chambers & Wincdschitl, 2004). Recall the study in which married people gave themselves credit for doing more housework than their spouses did. Might this not be due, as Michael Ross and Fiore Sicoly (1979) believe, to our greater recall for what we've actively done and our lesser recall for what we've not done or merely observed others doing? I can easily picture myself picking up the laundry, but I am less aware of the times when I absentmindedly overlooked it.

"*I admit it does look very impressive. But you see nowadays everyone graduates in the top ten per cent of his class.*"

Can we all be better than average?

(William W. Haefeli, *Saturday Review*, 1/20/79). Reprinted with permission of General Media Magazines.

Are the biased perceptions, then, simply a perceptual error, an emotion-free glitch in how we process information? Or are self-serving *motives* also involved? It's now clear from research that we have multiple motives. Questing for self-knowledge, we're eager to assess our competence (Dunning, 1995). Questing for self-confirmation, we're eager to verify our self-conceptions (Sanitioso et al., 1990; Swann, 1996, 1997). Questing for self-affirmation, we're especially motivated to enhance our self-image (Sedikides, 1993). Self-esteem motivation helps power self-serving bias. As social psychologist Daniel Batson (2006) surmises, "The head is an extension of the heart."

REFLECTIONS ON SELF-SERVING BIAS

No doubt many readers are finding all this either depressing or contrary to their own occasional feelings of inadequacy. Even people who exhibit the self-serving bias may feel inferior to specific individuals, especially those who are a step or two higher on the ladder of success, attractiveness, or skill. And not everyone operates with a self-serving bias. Some people *do* suffer from low self-esteem.

> "Narcissism, like selfishness, is an overcompensation for the basic lack of self-love."
>
> Erich Fromm, *Escape from Freedom*, 1941

In experiments, people whose self-esteem is temporarily bruised—say by being told they did miserably on an intelligence test—are more likely to disparage others (Beauregard & Dunning, 1998). Those whose egos have recently been wounded also are more prone to self-serving explanations of success or failure than are those whose egos have recently received a boost (McCarrey et al., 1982). So threats to self-esteem may provoke self-protective defensiveness. When they feel unaffirmed, people may offer self-affirming boasts, excuses, and put-downs of others (Fein & Spencer, 1997). More generally, people who are down on themselves tend also to be down on others (Wills, 1981). Mockery says as much about the mocker as the one who is mocked.

The self-serving bias as adaptive

Self-esteem has its dark side, but also its bright side. When good things happen, high- more than low-self-esteem people tend to savour and sustain the good feelings (Wood et al., 2003). "Believing one has more talents and positive qualities than one's peers allows one to feel good about oneself and to enter the stressful circumstances of daily life with the resources conferred by a positive sense of self," note Shelley Taylor and her co-researchers (2003).

Self-serving bias and its accompanying excuses also help protect people from depression (Snyder & Higgins, 1988). Nondepressed people excuse their failures on laboratory tasks or perceive themselves as being more in control than they are. Depressed people's self-appraisals are more accurate: sadder but wiser. (More on this in Module B.)

Self-serving bias additionally helps buffer stress. Bonnano and colleagues (2005) assessed the emotional resiliency of workers who escaped the World Trade Center or its environs on September 11, 2001. They found that those who displayed self-enhancing tendencies were the most resilient.

In their "terror management theory," Jeff Greenberg, Sheldon Solomon, and Tom Pyszczynski (1997) propose another reason why positive self-esteem is adaptive—it buffers anxiety, including anxiety related to our certain death. In childhood we learn that when we meet the standards taught us by our parents, we are loved and protected; when we don't, love and protection may be withdrawn. We therefore come to associate viewing ourselves as good with feeling secure. Greenberg and colleagues argue that positive self-esteem—viewing oneself as good and secure—even protects us from feeling terror over our eventual death. Their research shows that reminding people of their mortality (say, by writing a short essay on dying) motivates them to affirm their self-worth. Moreover, when facing threats, increased self-esteem leads to decreased anxiety.

As this new research on depression and anxiety suggests, there may be some practical wisdom in self-serving perceptions. It may be strategic to believe we are smarter, stronger, and more socially successful than we are. Cheaters may give a more convincing display of honesty if they believe themselves honourable. Belief in our superiority can also motivate us to achieve—creating a self-fulfilling prophecy—and can sustain a sense of hope in difficult times.

Self-serving pride in group settings can become especially dangerous.

"Then we're in agreement. There's nothing rotten in Denmark. Something is rotten everywhere else."

The self-serving bias as maladaptive

Although self-serving pride may help protect us from depression, it can at times be maladaptive. People who blame others for their social difficulties are often unhappier than people who can acknowledge their mistakes (C. A. Anderson et al., 1983; Newman & Langer, 1981; Peterson et al., 1981).

Research by Barry Schlenker (1976; Schlenker & Miller, 1977a, 1977b) has also shown how self-serving perceptions can poison a group. As a rock band guitarist during his college days, Schlenker noted that "rock band members typically overestimated their contributions to a group's success and underestimated their contributions to failure. I saw many good bands disintegrate from the problems caused by these self-glorifying tendencies." In his later life as a University of Florida social psychologist, Schlenker explored group members' self-serving perceptions. In nine experiments, he had people work together on some task. He then falsely informed them that their group had done either well or poorly. In every one of these studies, the members of successful groups claimed more responsibility for their group's performance than did members of groups that supposedly failed at the task.

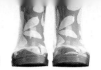

If most group members believe they are underpaid and underappreciated relative to their better-than-average contributions, disharmony and envy are likely. College presidents and academic deans will readily recognize the phenomenon. Ninety percent or more of college faculty members rate themselves as superior to their average colleague (Blackburn et al., 1980; Cross, 1977). It is therefore inevitable that when merit salary raises are announced and half receive an average raise or less, many will feel themselves victims of injustice.

"Victory finds a hundred fathers but defeat is an orphan."

Count Galeazzo Ciano, *The Ciano Diaries*, 1938

Self-serving biases also inflate people's judgments of their groups. When groups are comparable, most people consider their own group superior (Codol, 1976; Jourden & Heath, 1996; Taylor & Doria, 1981). Thus,

- most university sorority members perceive those in their sorority as far less likely to be conceited and snobby than those in other sororities (Biernat et al., 1996).
- 53 percent of Dutch adults rate their marriage or partnership as better than that of most others; only 1 percent rate it as worse than most (Buunk & van der Eijnden, 1997).
- most corporation presidents and production managers overpredict their own firms' productivity and growth (Kidd & Morgan, 1969; Larwood & Whittaker, 1977).

That people see themselves with a favourable bias is hardly new—the tragic flaw portrayed in ancient Greek drama was hubris, or pride. Like the subjects of our experiments, the Greek tragic figures were not self-consciously evil; they merely thought too highly of themselves. In literature, the pitfalls of pride are portrayed again and again. In theology, pride has long been first among the "seven deadly sins."

If pride is akin to the self-serving bias, then what is humility? Is it self-contempt? Or can we be self-affirming and self-accepting without a self-serving bias? To paraphrase the English scholar-writer C. S. Lewis, humility is not handsome people trying to believe they are ugly and clever people trying to believe they are fools. False modesty can actually be a cover for pride in one's better-than-average humility. (James Friedrich [1996] reports that most students congratulate themselves on being better than average at not thinking themselves better than average!) True humility is more like self-forgetfulness than false modesty. It leaves people free to rejoice in their special talents and, with the same honesty, to recognize others.

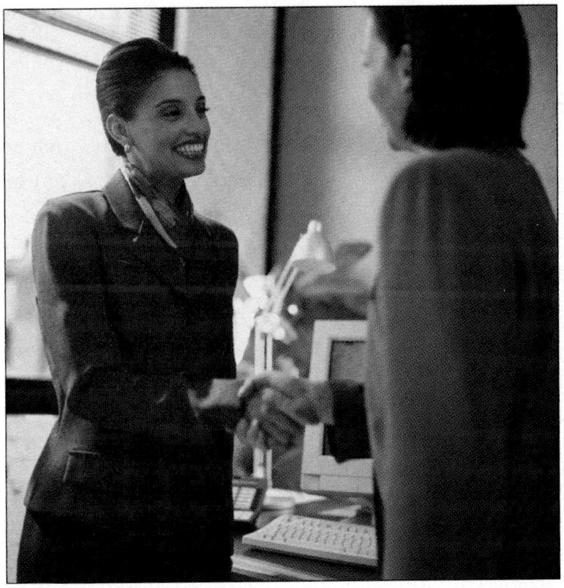
After just one brief conversation with a prospective employee, interviewers are prone to overconfidence in their intuitive judgments.

SUMMING UP: SELF-SERVING BIAS

Contrary to the presumption that most people suffer from feelings of inferiority, researchers consistently find that most people exhibit a *self-serving bias*. In experiments and everyday life we often blame failures on the situation while taking credit for successes. We typically rate ourselves as better than average on subjective, desirable traits and abilities. Believing in ourselves, we exhibit unrealistic optimism about our futures. And we overestimate the commonality of our opinions and foibles (*false consensus*) while underestimating the commonality of our abilities and virtues (*false uniqueness*). We also remember ourselves in the past and project ourselves into the future in ways that portray a positive image of the current self. Self-serving bias can be adaptive in that it allows us to savour the good things that happen in our lives. When bad things happen, however, self-serving bias can have the maladaptive effect of causing us to blame others or feel cheated out of something we "deserved."

SELF-PRESENTATION: LOOKING GOOD TO OTHERS

We humans seem motivated not only to perceive ourselves in self-enhancing ways but also to present ourselves to others in desired ways. How might our tactics of "impression management" lead to false modesty or to self-defeating behaviour?

So far we have seen that the self is at the centre of our social worlds, that self-esteem and self-efficacy pay dividends, and that self-serving pride biases self-evaluations. But are self-enhancing expressions always sincere? Do people have the same feelings privately as they express publicly? Or are they just putting on a positive face even while living with self-doubt?

FALSE MODESTY

There is indeed evidence that people sometimes present a different self than they feel. The clearest example, however, is not false pride but false modesty. Perhaps you have by now recalled times when someone was not self-praising but self-disparaging. Such put-downs can be subtly self-serving, for often they elicit reassurance. "I felt like a fool" may trigger a friend to say, "You did fine!" Even a remark such as "I wish I weren't so ugly" may elicit at least a "Come now. I know a couple of people who are uglier than you."

There is another reason people disparage themselves and praise others. Think of the coach who, before the big game, extols the opponent's strength. Is the coach utterly sincere? When coaches publicly exalt their opponents, they convey an image of modesty and good sportsmanship and set the stage for a favourable evaluation no matter what the outcome. A win becomes a praiseworthy achievement; a loss is attributable to the opponent's "great defence." Modesty, said the seventeenth-century philosopher Francis Bacon, is but one of the "arts of ostentation." Thus, Robert Gould, Paul Brounstein, and Harold Sigall (1977) found that, in a laboratory contest, their students similarly aggrandized their anticipated opponent, but only when the assessment was made publicly. Anonymously, they credited their future opponent with much less ability.

False modesty also appears in people's autobiographical accounts of their achievements. At awards ceremonies, honorees graciously thank others for their support. Upon receiving an Academy Award, Maureen Stapleton thanked "my family, my children, my friends, and everyone I have ever met in my entire life." Does such generous sharing of credit contradict the common finding that people readily attribute success to their own effort and competence?

To find out, Roy Baumeister and Stacey Ilko (1995) invited students to write a description of "an important success experience." Those whom they asked to sign their names and who anticipated reading their story to others often acknowledged the help or emotional support they had received. Those who wrote anonymously rarely made such mentions; rather, they portrayed themselves achieving their successes on their own. To Baumeister and Ilko, these results suggest "shallow gratitude"—superficial gratitude offered to *appear* humble, while "in the privacy of their own minds" the subjects credited themselves.

> *"Humility is often but a trick whereby pride abases itself only to exalt itself later."*
>
> La Rochefoucauld, *Maxims*, 1665

SELF-HANDICAPPING

Sometimes people sabotage their chances for success by creating impediments that make success less likely. Far from being deliberately self-destructive, such behaviours typically have a self-protective aim (Arkin et al., 1986; Baumeister & Scher, 1988; Rhodewalt, 1987): "I'm really not a failure—I would have done well except for this problem."

Why would people handicap themselves with self-defeating behaviour? Recall that we eagerly protect our self-images by attributing failures to external factors. Can you see why, *fearing failure*, people might handicap themselves by partying half the night before a job interview or playing video games instead of studying before a big exam? When self-image is tied up with performance, it can be more self-deflating to try hard and fail than to procrastinate and have a ready excuse. If we fail while working under a handicap, we can cling to a sense of competence; if we succeed under such conditions, it can only boost our self-image. Handicaps protect both self-esteem and public image by allowing us to attribute failures to something temporary or external ("I was feeling sick"; "I was out too late the night before") rather than to lack of talent or ability.

This analysis of **self-handicapping**, proposed by Steven Berglas and Edward Jones (1978), has been confirmed. One experiment was said to concern "drugs and intellectual performance." Imagine yourself in the position of their participants. You guess answers to some difficult aptitude questions and then are told, "Yours was one of the best scores seen to date!" Feeling incredibly lucky, you are then offered a choice between two drugs before answering more of these items. One drug will aid intellectual performance and the other will inhibit it. Which drug do you want? Most students wanted the drug that would supposedly disrupt their thinking and thus provide a handy excuse for anticipated poorer performance.

self-handicapping protecting one's self-image with behaviours that create a handy excuse for later failure

Researchers have documented other ways in which people self-handicap. Fearing failure, people will:

- Reduce their preparation for important individual athletic events (Rhodewalt et al., 1984).
- Give their opponent an advantage (Shepperd & Arkin, 1991).

self-presentation the act of expressing oneself and behaving in ways designed to create a favourable impression or an impression that corresponds to one's ideals

- Perform poorly at the beginning of a task in order not to create unreachable expectations (Baumgardner & Brownlee, 1987).
- Not try as hard as they could during a tough, ego-involving task (Hormuth, 1986; Pyszczynski & Greenberg, 1987; Riggs, 1992; Turner & Pratkanis, 1993).

IMPRESSION MANAGEMENT

Self-serving bias, false modesty, and self-handicapping reveal the depth of our concern for self-image. To varying degrees, we are continually managing the impressions we create. Whether we wish to impress, to intimidate, or to seem helpless, we are social animals, playing to an audience.

"With no attempt there can be no failure; with no failure no humiliation."

William James, *Principles of Psychology*, 1890

"Public opinion is always more tyrannical towards those who obviously fear it than towards those who feel indifferent to it."

Bertrand Russell, *The Conquest of Happiness*, 1930

"It is not, therefore, necessary for a prince to have all the desirable qualities . . . but it is very necessary to seem to have them."

Niccolo Machiavelli, 1469–1527

Self-presentation refers to our wanting to present a desired image both to an external audience (other people) and to an internal audience (ourselves). We work at managing the impressions we create. We excuse, justify, or apologize as necessary to shore up our self-esteem and verify our self-images (Schlenker & Weigold, 1992). In familiar situations, this happens without conscious effort. In unfamiliar situations, perhaps at a party with people we would like to impress or in conversation with someone of the other sex, we are acutely self-conscious of the impressions we are creating and we are therefore less modest than when among friends who know us well (Leary et al., 1994; Tice et al., 1995). Preparing to present ourselves in a photograph, we may even try out different faces in a mirror. We do so even though active self-presentation depletes energy, which often leads to diminished effectiveness—for example, to less persistence on a tedious experimental task or more difficulty stifling emotional expressions (Vohs et al., 2005).

Given our concern for self-presentation, it's no wonder, say self-presentation researchers, that people will self-handicap when failure might make them look bad (Arkin & Baumgardner, 1985). It's no wonder that people take health risks—tanning their skin with wrinkle- and cancer-causing radiation; becoming anorexic; failing to obtain and use condoms; yielding to peer pressures to smoke, get drunk, and do drugs (Leary et al., 1994). It's no wonder that people express more modesty when their self-flattery is vulnerable to being debunked, perhaps by experts who will be scrutinizing their self-evaluations (Arkin et al., 1980; Riess et al., 1981; Weary et al., 1982). Professor Smith will express less confidence in the significance of her work when presenting it to professional colleagues than when presenting to students.

For some people, conscious self-presentation is a way of life. They continually monitor their own behaviour and note how others react, then adjust their social performance to gain a desired effect. Those who score high on a scale of **self-monitoring** tendency (who, for example, agree that "I tend to be what people expect me to be") act like social chameleons—they adjust their behaviour in response to external situations (Snyder, 1987). Having attuned their behaviour to the situation, they are more likely to espouse attitudes they don't really hold (Zanna & Olson, 1982). Being conscious of others, they are less likely to act on their own attitudes. As Mark Leary (2004) observed, the self they know often differs from the self they show.

self-monitoring being attuned to the way one presents oneself in social situations and adjusting one's performance to create the desired impression

Those who score low in self-monitoring care less about what others think. They are more internally guided and thus more likely to talk and act as they feel and believe (McCann & Hancock, 1983). For example, if asked to list their thoughts about gay couples, they simply express what they think, regardless of the attitudes of their anticipated audience (Klein et al., 2004). As you might imagine, someone who is extremely low in self-monitoring could come across as an insensitive boor, whereas extremely high self-monitoring could result in dishonest behaviour worthy of a con artist. Most of us fall somewhere between those two extremes.

In Asian countries, self-presentation is restrained. Children learn to identify themselves with their groups.

Presenting oneself in ways that create a desired impression is a very delicate matter. People want to be seen as able, but also as modest and honest (Carlston & Shovar, 1983). Modesty creates a good impression, and unsolicited boasting creates a bad impression (Forsyth et al., 1981; Holtgraves & Srull, 1989; Schlenker & Leary, 1982). Thus, the false modesty phenomenon: We often display less self-esteem than we privately feel (Miller & Schlenker, 1985). But when we have obviously done extremely well, false disclaimers ("I did well, but it's no big deal") may come across as feigned humility. To make good impressions—as modest yet competent—requires social skill.

Self-presented modesty is greatest in cultures that value self-restraint, such as those of China and Japan (Heine & Lehman, 1995, 1997; Lee & Seligman, 1997; Markus & Kitayama, 1991; Wu & Tsseng, 1985). In China and Japan, people exhibit less self-serving bias. Unlike Westerners, who (as we have seen in this chapter) tend to take credit for successes and attribute failures to the situation, Japanese children learn to share credit for success and to accept responsibility for failures. "When I fail, it's my fault, not my group's" is a typical Japanese attitude (Anderson, 1999).

Despite such self-presentational concerns, people worldwide are privately self-enhancing. Self-serving bias has been noted among Dutch high-school and university students, Belgian basketball players, Indian Hindus, Japanese drivers, Israeli and Singaporean schoolchildren, Australian students and workers, Chinese students, Hong Kong sports writers, and French people of all ages (Codol, 1976; de Vries & van Knippenberg, 1987; Falbo et al., 1997; Feather, 1983; Hagiwara, 1983; Hallahan et al., 1997; Jain, 1990; Liebrand et al., 1986; Lefebvre, 1979; Murphy-Berman & Sharma, 1986; and Ruzzene & Noller, 1986, respectively).

"If an American is hit on the head by a ball at the ballpark, he sues. If a Japanese person is hit on the head he says, 'It's my honor. It's my fault. I shouldn't have been standing there.'"

Japanese bar-association official Koji Yanase, explaining why there are half as many lawyers in his country as in the Greater Washington area alone, *Newsweek*, February 26, 1996

SUMMING UP: SELF-PRESENTATION

As social animals, we adjust our words and actions to suit our audiences. To varying degrees, we *self-monitor;* we note our performance and adjust it to create a desired impression. Such *impression management* tactics explain examples of false modesty, in which people put themselves down, extol future competitors, or publicly credit others when privately they credit themselves. Sometimes people will even *self-handicap* with self-defeating behaviours that protect self-esteem by providing excuses for failure. Self-presentation refers to our wanting to present a favourable image both to an external audience (other people) and to an internal audience (ourselves). With regard to an external audience, those who score high on a scale of self-monitoring adjust their behaviour to each situation, whereas those low in self-monitoring may do so little social adjusting that they seem insensitive.

The Water
is
RISING

CHAPTER THREE

Social Beliefs and Judgments

Hurricane Katrina's 2005 devastation left in its wake television images of largely poor and Black victims stranded for days in New Orleans' Superdome and convention centre amid chaos and without food and water. Although television journalists had no trouble driving into New Orleans to record the images of pleading people, government agencies mysteriously failed to deliver relief supplies and evacuation buses.

Days later, after dozens of deaths and bodies left lying in the streets, relief came and public attention shifted to "the blame game." To what should we attribute the delayed relief? To bumbling local officials? To an uncaring president who stayed on holidays as the hurricane struck? Was it simply a matter of prejudice? Would the government response have been faster if most victims had been White?

In the summer of 1972, Canada played a landmark hockey series with the former Soviet Union. The Canadian team was made up of veterans who had all played for years in the physically aggressive National Hockey League (NHL). The Soviet team played in a style that was less physically aggressive and demanded precision passing.

After the fourth game in the series the Soviet media roundly criticized the "goons" from Canada, who, from their perspective, were dirty players using brute force when confronted with the superior skill of the Soviets. From this point in the series the officiating was much tighter, with most of the penalties going against Canada. The Canadian media saw the change in officiating as the Soviets' attempt to steal the series—the Soviets had picked the referees.

Were the media in each country right to attribute the players' and referees' actions to evil intent? Or was each act an understandable response to the situation? Was the Canadians' style of play shaped by years in the NHL? Were the referees simply trying to keep the contest under control?

This chapter addresses these and other issues:

- To what do we attribute others' behaviour?
- How do we perceive and recall our social worlds?
- What are the ways we judge each other?
- When do we tend to fulfill someone's expectations of us?

PERCEIVING OUR SOCIAL WORLDS

Striking research reveals the extent to which our assumptions and prejudgments can bias our perceptions, interpretations, and recall.

Chapter 1 noted a significant fact about the human mind: that our preconceptions guide how we perceive and interpret information. We construe the world through theory-tinted glasses. "Sure, preconceptions matter," people will agree; yet, they fail to realize how great the effect is.

Let's consider some provocative experiments. The first group of experiments examines how *pre*dispositions and *pre*judgments affect how we perceive and interpret information. The second group plants a judgment in people's minds after they have been given information to study how after-the-fact ideas bias recall. The overarching point: We respond not to reality as it is but to reality as we construe it.

PRIMING

Even before we attend to the world around us, unattended stimuli can subtly predispose how we will interpret and recall events. Imagine yourself, during an experiment, wearing earphones and concentrating on ambiguous spoken sentences such as "We stood by the bank." When a pertinent word (*river* or *money*) is simultaneously sent to your other ear, you don't consciously hear it. Yet the word "primes" your interpretation of the sentence (Baars & McGovern, 1994).

Our memory system is a web of associations, and **priming** is the awakening or activating of certain associations. Priming experiments reveal how one thought, even without awareness, can influence another thought, or even an action. In an experiment, John Bargh and his colleagues (1996) asked people to complete a sentence containing words such as "old," "wise," and "retired." Shortly afterward, they observed these people walking more slowly to the elevator than did those not primed with aging-related words. Moreover, the slow walkers had no awareness of their walking speed or of having just viewed words that primed aging. Such priming can affect not only arcane behaviours like walking speed but also our goals to achieve and to get along with others (Fitzsimons & Bargh, 2005).

priming activating particular associations in memory

Often our thinking and acting are primed by events of which we are unaware. Rob Holland and his colleagues (2005) observed that Dutch students exposed to the scent of an all-purpose cleaner were quicker to identify cleaning-related words. In follow-up experiments, other students exposed to a cleaning scent recalled more cleaning-related activities when describing their day's activities and even kept their desks cleaner while eating a crumbly cookie. Moreover, all these effects occurred without the participants' conscious awareness of the scent and its influence.

Priming experiments have their counterparts in everyday life:

- Watching a scary movie alone at home can prime our thinking, by activating emotions that, without our realizing it, cause us to interpret furnace noises as a possible intruder.
- Depressed moods, as this chapter explains later, prime negative associations. But put people in a *good* mood and suddenly their past seems more wonderful, their future brighter.
- For many psychology students, reading about psychological disorders primes how they interpret their own anxieties and gloomy moods. Reading about disease symptoms similarly primes medical students to worry about their congestion, fever, or headache.

In a host of studies, priming effects surface even when the stimuli are presented subliminally—too briefly to be perceived consciously. What's out of sight may not be completely out of mind. An electric shock that is too slight to be felt may increase the perceived intensity of a later shock. An imperceptibly flashed word, "bread," may prime people to detect a related word such as "butter" more quickly than an unrelated word such as "bottle" or "bubble." A subliminal colour name facilitates speedier identification when the colour appears on the computer screen, whereas an unseen wrong name delays colour identification (Epley et al., 1999; Merikle et al., 2001). In each case, an invisible image or word primes a response to a later task.

Studies of how implanted ideas and images can prime our interpretations and recall illustrates one of this book's take-home lessons from twenty-first-century social psychology: *Much of our social information processing is automatic*. It is unintentional, out of sight, and without awareness.

PERCEIVING AND INTERPRETING EVENTS

Despite some startling and oft-confirmed biases and logical flaws in how we perceive and understand one another, we're mostly accurate (Jussim, 2005). Our first impressions of one another are more often right than wrong, and the better we know people, the more accurately we can read their minds and feelings. But on occasion our prejudgments err. The effects of prejudgments and expectations are standard fare for psychology's introductory course. Consider this phrase:

A
BIRD
IN THE
THE HAND

"As I am, so I see."

Ralph Waldo Emerson, *Essays*

"Once you have a belief, it influences how you perceive all other relevant information. Once you see a country as hostile, you are likely to interpret ambiguous actions on their part as signifying their hostility."

Political scientist Robert Jervis (1985)

Did you notice anything wrong with it? There is more to perception than meets the eye. The same is true of social perception. Because social perceptions are very much in the eye of the beholder, even a simple stimulus may strike two people quite differently. Saying that Stephen Harper is "an okay prime minister" may sound like a put-down to those who ardently admire him and as positively biased to those who regard him with contempt. When social information is subject to multiple interpretations, preconceptions matter (Hilton & von Hippel, 1990). We see here an echo of a lesson we learned in Chapter 2. Ways of thinking or *schemas* guide not only our interpretations of our self, but also our understanding of others.

An experiment by Robert Vallone, Lee Ross, and Mark Lepper (1985) reveals just how powerful preconceptions can be. They showed pro-Israeli and pro-Arab students six network news segments describing the 1982 killing of civilian refugees at two camps in Lebanon. As Figure 3–1 illustrates, each group perceived the networks as hostile to its side.

The phenomenon is commonplace: Sports fans perceive referees as partial to the other side. Presidential candidates and their supporters nearly always view the media as unsympathetic to their cause. But it's not just sports fans and politicians. People everywhere perceive media and mediators as biased against their position. "There is no subject about which people are less objective than objectivity," noted one media commentator (Poniewozik, 2003). Indeed, people's perceptions of bias can be used to assess their attitudes (Saucier & Miller, 2003). Tell me where you see bias, and you will tell me your attitudes.

Our assumptions about the world can even make contradictory evidence seem supportive. For example, Ross and Lepper assisted Charles Lord (1979) in asking students to evaluate the results of two supposedly new research studies. Half the students favoured capital punishment and half opposed it. One study confirmed and the other disconfirmed the students' beliefs about the deterrence effect of the death penalty. The results: Both proponents and opponents of capital punishment readily accepted evidence that confirmed their belief but were sharply critical of disconfirming evidence. Showing the two sides an *identical* body of mixed evidence had therefore not lessened their disagreement but *increased* it.

"Of course I care about how you imagined I thought you perceived I wanted you to feel."

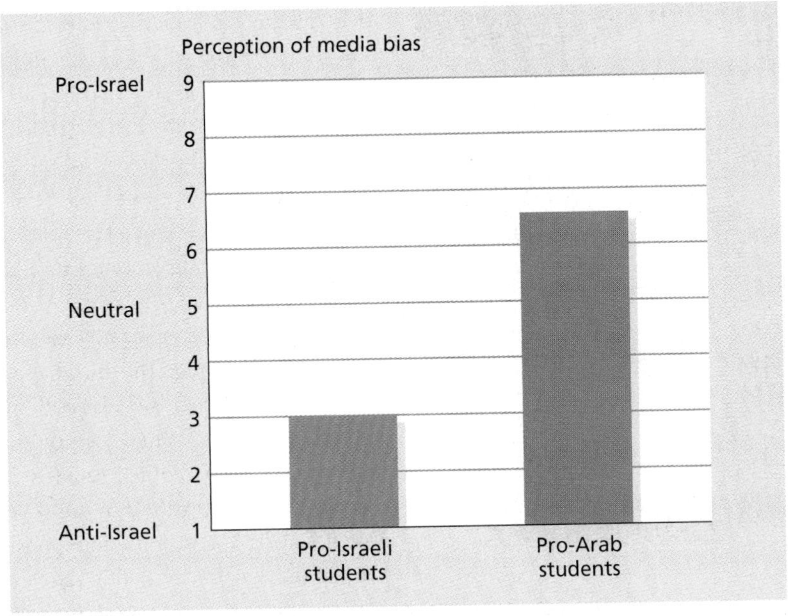

FIGURE 3–1

Pro-Israeli and pro-Arab students who viewed network news descriptions of the "Beirut massacre" believed the coverage was biased against their point of view. (Data from Vallone, Ross & Lepper, 1985)

Is this why, in politics, religion, and science, ambiguous information often fuels conflict? When political debates have no clear-cut winner they mostly reinforce predebate opinions. In one study of three different series of debates, by nearly a 10 to 1 margin, those who already favoured one candidate over the others perceived their candidate as having won (Kinder & Sears, 1985). Not only do people think their candidate won, but they report becoming even more supportive of them after the debate (Munro et al., 1997). It seems people can perceive and interpret the identical arguments quite differently. Given the same mixed information, opposing people can each assimilate it to their views and find their views strengthened.

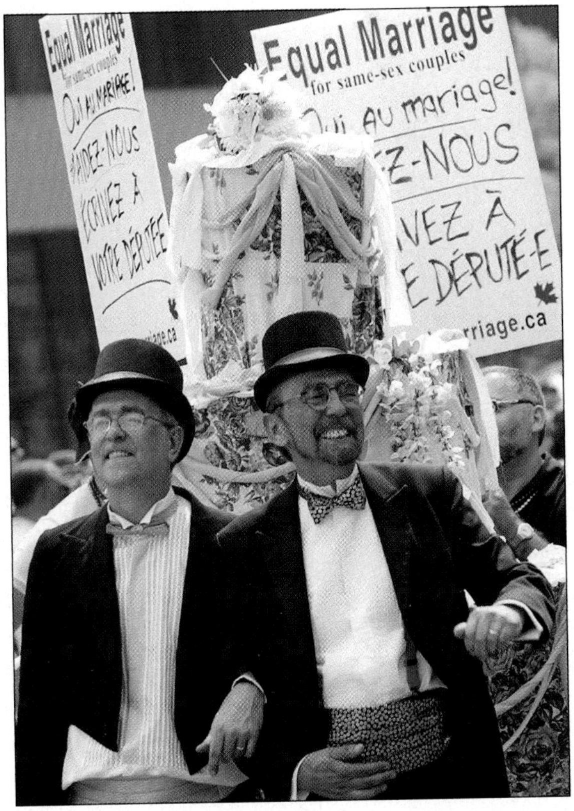

Supporters of a particular candidate or cause tend to see the media as favouring the other side.

Other experiments have manipulated preconceptions with astonishing effects on how people interpret and recall what they observe. Myron Rothbart and Pamela Birrell (1977) had students assess the facial expression of the man shown in Figure 3–2. Those told he was a Gestapo leader responsible for barbaric medical experiments on concentration camp inmates during the Second World War intuitively judged his expression as cruel. (Can you see that barely suppressed sneer?) Those told he was a leader in the anti-Nazi underground movement whose courage saved thousands of Jewish lives judged his facial expression as warm and kind. (Just look at those caring eyes and that almost smiling mouth.)

Filmmakers can control people's perceptions of emotion by manipulating the setting in which they see a face.

FIGURE 3–2

Judge for yourself: Is this person's expression cruel or kind? If told he was a Nazi, would your reading of his face differ?

They call this the "Kulechov effect," after a Russian film director who would skillfully guide viewers' inferences by manipulating their assumptions. Kulechov demonstrated the phenomenon by creating three short films that presented identical footage of the face of an actor with a neutral expression after viewers had first been shown one of three scenes: a dead woman, a dish of soup, or a girl playing. As a result, in the first film, the actor seemed sad, in the second thoughtful, and in the third happy.

Construal processes also colour others' perceptions of us. When we say something good or bad about another, people will tend to associate that trait with us, report Lynda Mae, Donal Carlston, and John Skowronski (1999; Carlston & Skowronski, 2005)—a phenomenon they call *spontaneous trait transference.* If we go around talking about others being gossipy, people may then unconsciously associate "gossip" with us. Call someone a jerk and folks may later construe *you* as one. Describe someone as sensitive, loving, and compassionate, and you may seem more so. There is, it appears, intuitive wisdom in the childhood taunt, "I'm rubber, you're glue; what you say bounces off me and sticks to you."

"The error of our eye directs our mind: What error leads must err."

Shakespeare, Troilus and Cressida, 1601–1602

"We hear and apprehend only what we already half know."

Henry David Thoreau, 1817–1862

The bottom line: There is an objective reality out there, but we view it through the spectacles of our beliefs, attitudes, and values. This is one reason our beliefs and schemas are so important; they shape our interpretation of everything else.

BELIEF PERSEVERANCE

Imagine a babysitter who decides, during an evening with a crying infant, that bottle feeding produces colicky babies: "Come to think of it, cow's milk obviously better suits calves than babies." If the infant turns out to be suffering a high fever, will the sitter nevertheless persist in believing that bottle feeding causes colic (Ross & Anderson, 1982)? To find out, Lee Ross, Craig Anderson, and their colleagues planted a falsehood in people's minds and then tried to discredit it.

belief perseverance persistence of one's initial conceptions, as when the basis for one's belief is discredited but an explanation of why the belief might be true survives

Their experiments reveal that it is surprisingly difficult to demolish a falsehood, once the person conjures up a rationale for it. Each experiment first implanted a belief, either by proclaiming it was true or by showing the participants some anecdotal evidence. Then the participants were asked to explain *why* it is true. Finally, the researchers totally discredited the initial information by telling the person the truth: The information was manufactured for the experiment, and half the people in the experiment had received opposite information. Nevertheless, the new belief survived about 75 percent intact, presumably because the participants still retained their invented explanations for the belief. This phenomenon, named **belief perseverance**, shows that beliefs can take on a life of their own and survive the discrediting of the evidence that inspired them.

For instance, Anderson, Lepper, and Ross (1980) asked people to decide whether people who take risks make good or bad firefighters. One group considered a risk-prone person who was a successful firefighter and a cautious person who was an unsuccessful one. The other group considered cases suggesting the opposite conclusion. After forming their theory that risk-prone people make better or worse firefighters, the individuals wrote explanations for it—for example, that risk-prone people are brave or that cautious people are careful. Once formed, each explanation could exist independently of the information that initially created the belief. When that information was discredited, the people still held their self-generated explanations and therefore continued to believe that risk-prone people really *do* make better or worse firefighters.

Do people who take risks make the best firefighters? Or the worst?

These experiments also show that the more we examine our theories and explain how they *might* be true, the more closed we become to information that challenges our belief. Once we consider why an accused person might be guilty, why someone of whom we have a negative first impression acts that way, or why a favoured stock might rise in value, our explanations may survive challenging evidence to the contrary (Davies, 1997; Jelalian & Miller, 1984).

The evidence is compelling: Our beliefs and expectations powerfully affect how we mentally construct events. Usually we benefit from our preconceptions, just as scientists benefit from creating theories that guide them in noticing and interpreting events. But the benefits sometimes entail a cost; we become prisoners of our own thought patterns. Thus the "canals" that were so often seen on Mars turned out to be the product of intelligent life—an intelligence on earth's side of the telescope. As another example, Germans, who widely believed that the introduction of the Euro currency led to increased prices, overestimated such price increases when comparing actual restaurant menus—the prior menu with German marks and a new one with Euro prices (Traut-Mattausch et al., 2004). As an old Chinese proverb says, "Two-thirds of what we see is behind our eyes."

"No one denies that new evidence can change people's beliefs. Children do eventually renounce their belief in Santa Claus. Our contention is simply that such changes generally occur slowly, and that more compelling evidence is often required to alter a belief than to create it."

Lee Ross & Mark Lepper (1980)

Belief perseverance may have important consequences, as Stephan Lewandowsky and his international collaborators (2005) discovered when they explored implanted and discredited information about the Iraq war that began in 2003. As the war unfolded, the Western media reported and repeated several claims—for example, that Iraqi forces executed coalition prisoners of war—that later were shown false and were retracted. Alas, having accepted the information, which fit their pre-existing assumptions, Americans tended to retain the belief (unlike Germans and Australians, who tended to be more predisposed to question the war's rationale).

Is there a remedy for belief perseverance? There is: *Explain the opposite.* Charles Lord, Mark Lepper, and Elizabeth Preston (1984) repeated the capital punishment study described earlier and added two variations. First, they asked some of their subjects when evaluating the evidence to be *"as objective* and *unbiased* as possible." It was to no avail; whether for or against capital punishment, those who received this plea made evaluations as biased as those who did not.

The researchers asked a third group of subjects to consider the opposite—to ask themselves "whether you would have made the same high or low evaluations had exactly the same study produced results on the *other* side of the issue." After imagining an opposite finding, these people were much less biased in their evaluations of the evidence for and against their views. In his experiments, Craig Anderson (1982; Anderson & Sechler, 1986) consistently found that explaining why an opposite theory might be true—why a cautious rather than a risk-taking person might be a better firefighter—reduces or eliminates belief perseverance. Indeed, explaining *any* alternative outcome, not just the opposite, drives people to ponder various possibilities (Hirt & Markman, 1995).

CONSTRUCTING MEMORIES

Do you agree or disagree with this statement?

> Memory can be likened to a storage chest in the brain into which we deposit material and from which we can withdraw it later if needed. Occasionally, something is lost from the "chest," and then we say we have forgotten.

About 85 percent of university students agree (Lamal, 1979). As one magazine ad put it, "Science has proven the accumulated experience of a lifetime is preserved perfectly in your mind."

Actually, psychological research has proved the opposite. Many memories are not copies of experiences that remain on deposit in a memory bank. Rather, we construct memories at the time of withdrawal, for memory involves backward reasoning. It infers what must have been, given what we now believe or know. Like a paleontologist inferring the appearance of a dinosaur from bone fragments, we reconstruct our distant past by using our current feelings and expectations to combine fragments of information (Hirt, 1990; Ross & Buehler, 1994). Thus we can easily (though unconsciously) revise our memories to suit our current knowledge. When one of the authors' sons complained, "The June issue of *Cricket* never came," and was then shown where it was, he delightedly responded, "Oh good, I knew I'd gotten it."

"Memory isn't like reading a book: it's more like writing a book from fragmentary notes."

John F. Kihlstrom, 1994

When an experimenter or a therapist manipulates people's presumptions about our past, a sizeable fraction will construct false memories. Asked to vividly imagine a childhood time when they ran, tripped, fell, and stuck their hand through a window, or a time when they knocked over a punch bowl at a wedding, about one-fourth will later recall the fictitious event as something that actually happened (Garry et al., 1996; Hyman et al., 1995, 1996; Loftus & Pickerell, 1995). In its search for truth, the mind sometimes constructs a falsehood.

In experiments involving more than 20 000 people, Elizabeth Loftus (2003) and her colleagues have revealed our tendency to construct memories. In the typical experiment, people witness an event, receive misleading information about it (or not), and then take a memory test. The repeated finding is the **misinformation effect**. People incorporate the misinformation into their memories: They recall a yield sign as a stop sign, hammers as screwdrivers, *Vogue* magazine as *Mademoiselle,* Dr. Henderson as "Dr. Davidson," breakfast cereal as eggs, and a clean-shaven man as a fellow with a moustache. Suggested misinformation may even produce false memories of supposed child sexual abuse, argues Loftus.

misinformation effect incorporating "misinformation" into one's memory of the event, after witnessing an event and receiving misleading information about it

This process affects our recall of social as well as physical events. Jack Croxton and his colleagues (1984) had students spend 15 minutes talking with someone. Those later informed that this person reported liking them recalled the person's behaviour as relaxed, comfortable, and happy. Those informed that the person disliked them recalled the person as nervous, uncomfortable, and not so happy.

Reconstructing past attitudes

Five years ago, how did you feel about nuclear power? About Stéphane Dion or Stephen Harper? About your parents? If your attitudes have changed, do you know the extent of the change?

Experimenters have tried to answer such questions, and the results have been unnerving. People whose attitudes have changed often insist that they have always felt much as they now feel. Daryl Bem and Keith McConnell (1970) conducted a survey to test these ideas among students at their university. Buried in it was a question concerning student control over the university curriculum. A week later the students agreed to write an essay opposing student control. After doing so, their attitudes shifted toward greater opposition to student control. When asked to recall how they had answered the question before writing the essay, they "remembered" holding the opinion that they *now* held and denied that the experiment had affected them. After observing students similarly denying their former attitudes, researchers D. R. Wixon and James Laird (1976) commented, "The speed, magnitude, and certainty" with which the students revised their own histories "was striking." As George Vaillant (1977, p. 197) noted after following some adults for a period of time, "It is all too common for caterpillars to become butterflies and then to maintain that in their youth they had been little butterflies. Maturation makes liars of us all."

"A man should never be ashamed to own that he has been in the wrong, which is but saying, in other words, that he is wiser today than he was yesterday."

Jonathan Swift, *Thoughts on Various Subjects*, 1711

The construction of positive memories does brighten our recollections. Terence Mitchell, Leigh Thompson, and their colleagues (1994, 1997) report that people often exhibit *rosy retrospection*—they *recall* mildly pleasant events more favourably than they experienced them. University students on a three-week bike trip, older adults on a guided tour of Austria, and undergraduates on vacation all report enjoying their experiences as they have them. But they later recall such experiences even more fondly, minimizing the unpleasant or boring aspects and remembering the high points. Thus, the pleasant times during which one of the authors has sojourned in Scotland he now (back in his office facing deadlines and interruptions) romanticizes as pure bliss. With any positive experience, some of the pleasure resides in the anticipation, some in the actual experience, and some in the rosy retrospection.

"Travel is glamorous only in retrospect."

Paul Theroux, in *The Observer*

Cathy McFarland and Michael Ross (1985) found that we also revise our recollections of other people as our relationships with them change. They had university students rate their steady dating partners. Two months later, they rated them again. Students who were more in love than ever had a tendency to recall love at first sight. Those who had broken up were more likely to recall having recognized the partner as somewhat selfish and bad-tempered.

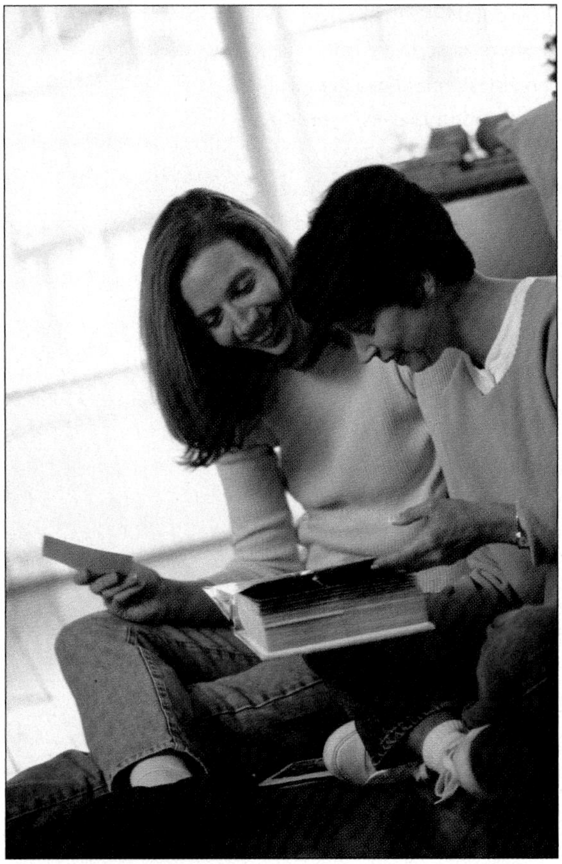

Unlike photos, memories get reconstructed when withdrawn from the memory bank.

Diane Holmberg and John Holmes (1994) discovered the same phenomenon among 373 newlywed couples, most of whom reported being very happy. When resurveyed two years later, those whose marriages had soured recalled that things had always been bad. The results are "frightening," say Holmberg and Holmes: "Such biases can lead to a dangerous downward spiral. The worse your current view of your partner is, the worse your memories are, which only further confirms your negative attitudes."

It's not that we are totally unaware of how we used to feel, just that when memories are hazy, current feelings guide our recall. Parents of every generation bemoan the values of the next generation, partly because they misrecall their youthful values as being closer to their current values.

Reconstructing past behaviour

Memory construction enables us to revise our own histories. Hartmuk Blank and his colleagues (2003) showed as much when inviting University of Leipzig students, after a surprising German election outcome, to recall their voting predictions from two months previous. The students demonstrated hindsight bias, by misrecalling their predictions as closer to the actual results.

Our memories reconstruct other sorts of past behaviours as well. Michael Ross, Cathy McFarland, and Garth Fletcher (1981) exposed some students to a message convincing them of the desirability of toothbrushing. Later, in a supposedly different experiment, these students recalled brushing their teeth more often during the preceding two weeks than did students who had not heard the message. Likewise, projecting from surveys, people report smoking many fewer cigarettes than are actually sold (Hall, 1985). And they recall casting more votes than were actually recorded (Census Bureau, 1993).

"Vanity plays lurid tricks with our memory."

Novelist Joseph Conrad, 1857–1924

Social psychologist Anthony Greenwald (1980) noted the similarity of such findings to happenings in George Orwell's novel *1984*—in which it was "necessary to remember that events happened in the desired manner." Indeed, argued Greenwald, we all have "totalitarian egos" that revise the past to suit our present views. Thus, we underreport bad behaviour and overreport good behaviour.

Sometimes our present view is that we've improved—in which case we may misrecall our past as more unlike the present than it actually was. This tendency resolves a puzzling pair of consistent findings: Those who participate in psychotherapy and self-improvement programs for weight control, antismoking, and exercise show only modest improvement on average. Yet they often claim considerable benefit (Myers, 2004). Michael Conway and Michael Ross (1985, 1986) explain why: Having expended so much time, effort, and money on self-improvement, people may think, "I may not be perfect now, but I was worse before; this did me a lot of good."

SUMMING UP: PERCEIVING OUR SOCIAL WORLDS

Our schemas and preconceptions strongly influence how we interpret and remember events. In a phenomenon called priming, people's prejudgments have striking effects on how they perceive and interpret information. Other experiments have planted judgments or false ideas in people's minds *after* they have been given information. These experiments reveal that as before-the-fact judgments bias our perceptions and interpretations, so after-the-fact judgments bias our recall. Far from being a repository for facts about the past, our memories are actually formed when we retrieve them, and subject to strong influence by the attitudes and feelings we hold at the time of retrieval.

JUDGING OUR SOCIAL WORLDS

As we have already noted, our cognitive mechanisms are efficient and adaptive, yet error-prone. Usually they serve us well, but sometimes clinicians misjudge patients, employers misjudge employees, people of one race misjudge people of another, and spouses misjudge their mates. The results are misdiagnoses, labour strife, prejudices, and divorces. So, how—and how well—do we make intuitive social judgments?

When historians describe social psychology's first century, they will surely record the last 30 years as the era of social cognition. By drawing upon advances in cognitive psychology—in how people perceive, represent, and remember events—social psychologists have shed welcome light on how we form impressions. Let's look at what this research reveals of the marvels and mistakes of our social judgments.

JUDGMENTAL OVERCONFIDENCE

So far we have seen that our cognitive systems process a vast amount of information efficiently and automatically. But our adaptive efficiency has a trade-off; as we interpret our experiences and construct memories, our automatic intuitions often err. Usually, we are unaware of our flaws. The "intellectual conceit" evident in judgments of past knowledge ("I knew it all along") extends to estimates of current knowledge and predictions of future behaviour. Although we know we've messed up in the past, our expectations for the future—how well we'll meet deadlines, manage relationships, follow an exercise routine—are vastly more positive (Ross & Newby-Clark, 1998). Even thinking of realistic obstacles to future exercising did not dissuade University of Guelph students from predicting that they would exercise more in the coming month (Newby-Clark, 2005).

overconfidence phenomenon the tendency to be more confident than correct—to overestimate the accuracy of one's beliefs

To explore this **overconfidence phenomenon**, Daniel Kahneman and Amos Tversky (1979) gave people factual questions and asked them to fill in the blanks, as in the following: "I feel 98 percent certain that the air distance between New Delhi and Beijing is more than _____ miles but less than _____ miles." Most subjects were overconfident: About 30 percent of the time, the correct answers lay outside the range they felt 98 percent confident about.

To find out whether overconfidence extends to social judgments, David Dunning and his associates (1990) created a little game show. They asked students to guess a stranger's answers to a series of questions, such as "Would you prepare for a difficult exam alone or with others?" and "Would you rate your lecture notes as neat or messy?" Knowing the type but not the actual questions, the subjects first interviewed their target person about background, hobbies, academic interests, aspirations, astrological sign—anything they thought might be helpful. Then, while the targets privately answered 20 of the two-choice questions, the interviewers predicted their target's answers and rated their own confidence in the predictions.

The interviewers guessed right 63 percent of the time, beating chance by 13 percent. But, on average, they *felt* 75 percent sure of their predictions. When guessing their own roommates' responses, they were 68 percent correct and 78 percent confident. Moreover, the most confident people were most likely to be *over*confident. Studies reveal a similar meagre correlation between self-confidence and accuracy in discerning whether someone is telling the truth (DePaulo et al., 1997). People also are markedly overconfident when estimating such things as the sexual history of their dating partner or the activity preferences of their roommates (Swann & Gill, 1997).

The air distance between New Delhi and Beijing is 2500 miles (4022 kilometres).

Ironically, incompetence feeds overconfidence. It takes competence to recognize what competence is, note Justin Kruger and David Dunning (1999). Students who score at the bottom on tests of grammar, humour, and logic are most prone to overestimating their gifts at such. Those who don't know what good logic or grammar is are often unaware that they lack it. Those who don't know what good logic or grammar is are often unaware that they lack it. If you make a list of all the words you can form out of the letters in "psychology," you may feel brilliant—but then stupid when a friend starts naming the ones you missed. Deanna Caputo and Dunning (2005) recreated this phenomenon in experiments, confirming that our ignorance of our ignorance sustains our self-confidence. Follow-up studies indicate that this "ignorance of one's incompetence" occurs mostly on relatively easy-seeming tasks, such as forming words out of "psychology." On really hard tasks, poor performers more often appreciate their lack of skill (Burson et al., 2006).

STORY BEHIND THE RESEARCH

Roger Buehler
Wilfrid Laurier University

As a graduate student, I noticed something peculiar about my work-related predictions. Most evenings I would stuff my briefcase with work to complete at home and then return the following day with much of it untouched. Yet each time I packed that briefcase I was sure my plans were realistic. In my Ph.D. dissertation and subsequent research (conducted with Dale Griffin and Michael Ross) I have addressed two related questions: Why do people often underestimate how long it will take to finish tasks? Why don't people learn from past experience and adjust their estimates accordingly? The findings suggest that people's unwarranted optimism stems in part from a desire to finish projects promptly and in part from the thought processes that they naturally engage in to generate predictions. People tend to focus narrowly on their plans for completing the task at hand and consequently dismiss other valuable sources of information, such as how long similar tasks have taken in the past. These research insights have, unfortunately, had little impact on my own predictions and I'm still lugging around an overweight briefcase.

This ignorance of one's own incompetence helps explain Dunning's (2005) startling conclusion from employee assessment studies that "what others see in us . . . tends to be more highly correlated with objective outcomes than what we see in ourselves." In one study, participants watched someone walk into a room, sit, read a weather report, and walk out (Borkenau & Liebler, 1993). Based on nothing more than that, their estimate of the person's intelligence correlated with the person's intelligence score (.30) about as well as did the person's own self-estimate (.32)! If ignorance can beget false confidence, then—yikes!—where, we may ask, are you and I unknowingly deficient?

In Chapter 2 we noted how poorly people overestimate their long-term emotional responses to good and bad happenings. Are people better at predicting their own behaviour? To find out, Robert Vallone and his colleagues (1990) had university students predict in September whether they would drop a course, declare a major, elect to live off campus next year, and so forth. Although the students felt, on average, 84 percent sure of these self-predictions, they were wrong nearly twice as often as they expected to be. Even when feeling 100 percent sure of their predictions, they erred 15 percent of the time. People may often give too much weight to their current intentions when predicting their future behaviour (Koehler & Poon, 2006). When University of Waterloo students predicted whether they would donate blood, they relied heavily on their intentions to do so. But their intentions did not so strongly predict their actual donations. The students failed to appreciate how much their busy schedules, looming deadlines, or simple forgetfulness would get in the way of their donating blood.

In estimating their chances for success on a task, such as a major exam, people's confidence runs highest when removed in time from "the moment of truth." By exam day, the possibility of failure looms larger and confidence typically drops (Gilovich et al., 1993). Roger Buehler and his colleagues (1994, 2002, 2003, 2005) report that most students also confidently underestimate how long it will take them to complete papers and other major assignments, even group projects for which they discuss likely completion times with other group members. They are not alone:

- Planners routinely underestimate the time and expense of projects. In 1969, Montreal Mayor Jean Drapeau proudly announced that a $120-million stadium with a retractable roof would be built for the 1976 Olympics. The roof was completed in 1989 and cost $120 million by itself.
- Investment experts market their services with the confident presumption that they can beat the stock market average, forgetting that for every stockbroker or buyer saying "Sell!" at a given price there is another saying "Buy!" A stock's price is the balance point between these mutually confident judgments. Thus, incredible as it may seem, economist Burton Malkiel (1985, 1995) reports that mutual fund portfolios selected by investment analysts have not outperformed randomly selected stocks.
- Overconfident decision makers can wreak havoc. It was a confident Adolf Hitler who from 1939 to 1945 waged war against the rest of Europe. In 1812 it was a confident James Madison who led the newly formed United States into a war to take over Upper Canada. It was a confident George W. Bush who proclaimed that peaceful democracy would soon prevail in a liberated Iraq, with its alleged weapons of mass destruction newly destroyed.

What produces overconfidence? Why does experience not lead us to a more realistic self-appraisal? There are several reasons (Klayman & Ha, 1987; Sanbomatsu et al., 1993; Skov &

> *"When you know a thing, to hold that you know it; and when you do not know a thing, to allow that you do not know it; this is knowledge."*
>
> Confucius, *Analects*

Sherman, 1986). For one thing, people tend to recall their mistaken judgments as times when they were *almost* right. Phillip Tetlock (1998, 1999) observed this after inviting various academic and government experts to project—from their viewpoint in the late 1980s—the future governance of the Soviet Union, South Africa, and Canada. Five years later communism collapsed, South Africa had become a multiracial democracy, and Canada continued undivided. Experts who had felt more than 80 percent confident were right in predicting these turns of events less than 40 percent of the time. Yet, reflecting on their judgments, those who erred believed they were still basically right. I was "almost right," said many. "The hardliners almost succeeded in their coup attempt against Gorbachev." "The Québécois separatists almost won the secessionist referendum." "But for the coincidence of de Klerk and Mandela, there would have been a lot bloodier transition to black majority rule in South Africa." Among political experts—and stock market forecasters, mental health workers, and sports prognosticators—overconfidence is hard to dislodge.

Confirmation bias

People also tend not to seek information that might disprove what they believe. P. C. Wason (1960) demonstrated this, as you can, by giving people a sequence of three numbers—2, 4, 6 —that conformed to a rule he had in mind (the rule was simply *any three ascending numbers*). To enable the people to discover the rule, Wason invited each person to generate sets of three numbers. Each time, Wason told the person whether or not the set conformed to his rule. When they were sure they had discovered the rule, the people were to stop and announce it.

The result? Seldom right but never in doubt: 23 of the 29 people convinced themselves of a wrong rule. They typically formed some erroneous belief about the rule (for example, counting by twos) and then searched for *confirming* evidence (for example, by testing 8, 10, 12) rather than attempting to *disconfirm* their hunches. We are eager to verify our beliefs but less inclined to seek evidence that might disprove them. We call this phenomenon the **confirmation bias**.

confirmation bias a tendency to search for information that confirms one's preconceptions

Our preference for confirming information helps explain why our self-images are so remarkably stable. In several experiments, William Swann and Stephen Read (1981; Swann et al., 1992a, 1992b, 1994) discovered that students seek, elicit, and recall feedback that confirms their beliefs about themselves. People seek as friends and spouses those who bolster their own self views—even if they think poorly of themselves (Swann et al., 1991, 1992, 2000). Swann and Read liken this *self-verification* to how someone with a domineering self-image might behave at a party. Upon arriving the person *seeks* those guests whom she knows acknowledge her dominance. In conversation she then presents her views in ways that *elicit* the respect she expects. After the party, she has trouble recalling conversations in which her influence was minimal and more easily *recalls* her persuasiveness in the conversations that she dominated. Thus her experience at the party confirms her self-image.

Remedies for overconfidence

What lessons can we draw from research on overconfidence? One lesson is to be careful about other people's dogmatic statements. Even when people seem sure they are right, they may be wrong. Confidence and competence need not coincide.

Three techniques have successfully reduced the overconfidence bias. One is prompt feedback (Lichtenstein & Fischhoff, 1980). In everyday life, weather forecasters and those who set the odds in horse racing both receive clear, daily feedback. Experts in both groups, therefore, do quite well at estimating their probable accuracy (Fischhoff, 1982).

To reduce "planning fallacy" overconfidence, people can be asked to "unpack" a task—to break it into its subcomponents—and estimate the time required for each. Justin Kruger and Matt Evans (2004) report that doing so leads to more realistic estimates of completion time. When people think about why an idea *might* be true it begins to seem true (Koehler, 1991). Thus, a third way to reduce overconfidence is to get people to think of one good reason *why their judgments might be wrong:* force them to consider disconfirming information (Koriat et al., 1980). Managers might foster more realistic judgments by insisting that all proposals and recommendations include reasons why they might not work.

Still, we should be careful not to undermine people's self-confidence to a point where they spend too much time in self-analysis or where self-doubts begin to cripple decisiveness. In times when their wisdom is needed, those lacking self-confidence may shrink from speaking up or making tough decisions. *Over*confidence can cost us, but realistic self-confidence is adaptive.

HEURISTICS: MENTAL SHORTCUTS

With precious little time to process so much information, our cognitive system specializes in mental shortcuts. With remarkable ease, we form impressions, make judgments, and invent explanations. We do so by using **heuristics**—simple, efficient thinking strategies. In many situations, our snap generalizations—"That's dangerous!"—are adaptive. Their speed promotes our survival. The biological purpose of thinking is less to make us right than to keep us alive. In some situations, however, haste makes error.

heuristics
a thinking strategy that enables quick, efficient judgments

Representativeness heuristic

A panel of psychologists interviewed a sample of 30 engineers and 70 lawyers and summarized their impressions in thumbnail descriptions. The following description has been drawn at random from the sample of 30 engineers and 70 lawyers:

> Twice divorced, Frank spends most of his free time hanging around the country club. His clubhouse bar conversations often centre on his regrets at having tried to follow his esteemed father's footsteps. The long hours he had spent at academic drudgery would have been better invested in learning how to be less quarrelsome in his relations with other people.

Question: What is the probability that Frank is a lawyer rather than an engineer?

Asked to guess Frank's occupation, more than 80 percent of students surmised he was one of the lawyers (Fischhoff & Bar-Hillel, 1984). Fair enough. But how do you suppose their estimates changed when the sample description was changed to say that 70 percent were engineers? Not in the slightest. The students took no account of the base rate of engineers and lawyers; in their minds Frank was more *representative* of lawyers, and that was all that seemed to matter.

representativeness heuristic
the tendency to presume, sometimes despite contrary odds, that someone or something belongs to a particular group if resembling (representing) a typical member

To judge something by intuitively comparing it to our mental representation of a category is to use the **representativeness heuristic.** *Heuristics* are simple, efficient thinking strategies—implicit rules of thumb. Like most heuristics, representativeness usually is a reasonable guide to reality. But not always. Consider Linda, who is 31, single, outspoken, and very bright. She majored in philosophy in college. As a student she was deeply concerned with discrimination and other social issues, and she participated in antinuclear demonstrations. Based on this description, would you say it is more likely that

a. Linda is a bank teller.
b. Linda is a bank teller and active in the feminist movement.

Most people think *b* is more likely, partly because Linda better *represents* their image of feminists. Consider: Is there a better chance that Linda is *both* a bank teller *and* a feminist than that she's a bank teller (whether feminist or not)? As Amos Tversky and Daniel Kahneman (1983) remind us, the conjunction of two events can't be more likely than either event alone.

The availability heuristic

Consider: Do more people live in Iraq or in Tanzania? (See p. 87.)

You probably answered in terms of how readily Iraqis and Tanzanians come to mind. If examples are readily *available* in our memory—as Iraqis tend to be—then we presume that the event is commonplace. Usually it is, so we are often well served by this cognitive rule, called the **availability heuristic**.

availability heuristic a cognitive rule that judges the likelihood of things in terms of their availability in memory. If instances of something come readily to mind, we presume it to be commonplace.

But sometimes the rule deludes us. If people hear a list of famous people of one sex (Avril Lavigne, Venus Williams, Hillary Clinton) intermixed with an equal size list of unfamous people of the other sex (Donald Scarr, William Wood, Mel Jasper), the famous names will later be more cognitively available. Most people will therefore recall having heard more (in this instance) women's names (McKelvie, 1995, 1997; Tversky & Kahneman, 1973). Vivid, easy-to-imagine events, such as diseases with easy-to-picture symptoms, may likewise seem more likely than harder-to-picture events (MacLeod & Campbell, 1992; Sherman et al., 1985). Even fictional happenings in novels, television, and movies leave images that later penetrate our judgments (Gerrig & Prentice, 1991; Green et al., 2002). The more absorbed and "transported" the reader ("I could easily picture the events"), the more the story affects the reader's later beliefs (Diekman et al., 2000). Readers who are captivated by romance novels, for example, may gain readily available sexual scripts that influence their own sexual attitudes and behaviours.

In one clever experiment that demonstrates the availability hueristic Norbert Schwarz and his colleagues (1991) had students list either 12 times they had been assertive or six times they had been assertive. For most students it was easy to come up with six times they were assertive, but hard to come up with 12 times they were assertive. The students then rated how assertive they were. Those who listed six times they were assertive reported being more assertive than those who listed 12 times they were assertive. It seems that easily thinking about being assertive had more influence on the students and the number of instances that they thought about.

Our use of the availability heuristic highlights a basic principle of social thinking: People are slow to deduce particular instances from a general truth, but they are remarkably quick to infer general truth from a vivid instance. No wonder that after hearing and reading stories of rapes, robberies, and beatings, 9 out of 10 Canadians overestimate—usually by a considerable margin—the percentage of crimes that involve violence (Doob & Roberts, 1988). And no wonder South Africans, after a series of headline-grabbing gangland robberies and slayings,

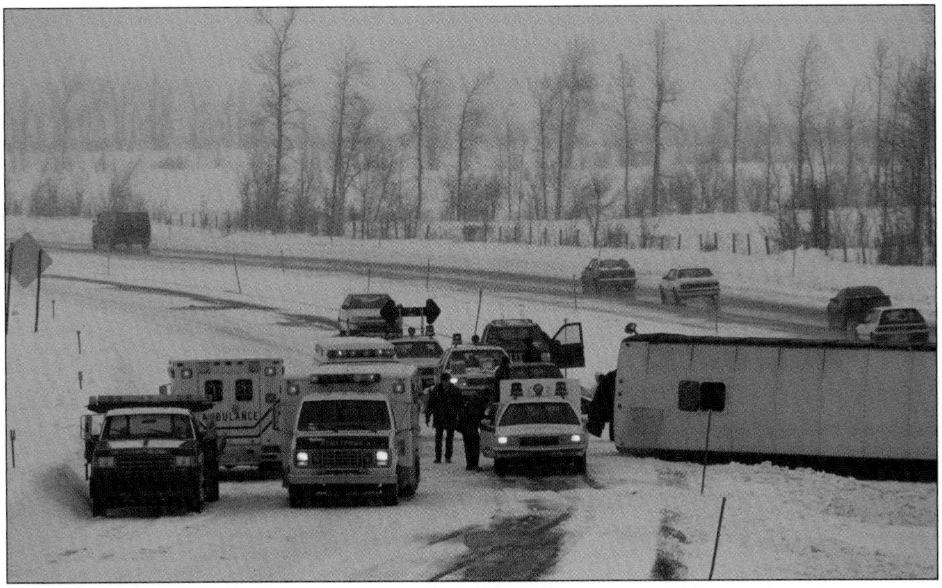

Although car crashes are the most common form of commuter injury, people often are more nervous about flying and tend to exaggerate the risk associated with plane travel.

estimated that violent crime had almost doubled between 1998 and 2004, when actually it had decreased substantially (Wines, 2005).

The availability heuristic explains why powerful anecdotes are often more compelling than statistical information and why perceived risk is therefore often badly out of joint with real risks (Allison et al., 1992). Because news footage of airplane crashes is a readily available memory for most of us, we often suppose we are more at risk travelling in commercial airplanes than in cars. Actually, from 2000 to 2002, U.S. travellers were 39.5 times more likely to die in a car crash than on a commercial flight covering the same distance (National Safety Council, 2005). For most air travellers, the most dangerous part of the journey is the drive to the airport.

Answer to Question: Tanzania's 37 million people greatly outnumber Iraq's 26 million. Most people, having more vivid images of Iraqis, guess wrong.

COUNTERFACTUAL THINKING

Easily imagined (cognitively available) events also influence our experiences of guilt, regret, frustration, and relief. If our team loses (or wins) a big game by one point, we can easily imagine how the game might have gone the other way, and thus we feel greater regret (or relief). Imagining worse alternatives helps us feel better. Imagining better alternatives, and pondering what we might do differently next time, helps us prepare to do better in the future (Boninger et al., 1994; Roese, 1994).

During the 1992 Olympics, bronze medallists (for whom an easily imagined alternative was finishing without a medal) exhibited more joy than silver medallists (who could more easily imagine having won the gold) (Medvec et al., 1995). Similarly, the higher a student's score within a grade category such as B+, the *worse* they feel (Medvec & Savitsky, 1997). The B+ student who misses an A– by a point feels worse than the B+ student who actually did worse and just made a B+ by a point.

Such **counterfactual thinking**—*mentally simulating what might have been*—occurs when we can easily picture an alternative outcome (Kahneman & Miller, 1986; Gavanski & Wells,

counterfactual thinking imagining alternative scenarios and outcomes that might have happened, but didn't

1989; Mandel & Lehman, 1996; Roese, 1997; Roese & Olson, 1993). If we barely miss a plane or bus, we imagine making it *if only* we had left at our usual time, taken our usual route, not paused to talk. If we change an exam answer, then get it wrong, we inevitably think, "If only . . ." and will vow next time to trust our immediate intuition—although, contrary to student lore, answer changes are more often from incorrect to correct (Kruger et al., 2005).

Counterfactual thinking underlies our feelings of luck. When we have barely escaped a bad event—avoiding defeat with a last-minute goal or standing nearest a falling icicle—we easily imagine a negative counterfactual (losing, being hit) and therefore feel "good luck" (Teigen et al., 1999). "Bad luck," on the other hand, refers to bad events that did happen but might not have.

The more significant the event, the more intense the counterfactual thinking. Bereaved people who have lost a spouse or child in a vehicle accident, or a child to sudden infant death syndrome, commonly report replaying and undoing the event (Davis et al., 1995, 1996). One individual, having lost his wife, daughter, and mother in a head-on collision with a drunk driver, reported that "For months I turned the events of that day over and over in my mind. I kept reliving the day, changing the order of events so that the accident wouldn't occur" (Sittser, 1994).

Across Asian and Western cultures most people, however, live with less regret over things done than over things they failed to do, such as, "I wish I had been more serious in college" or "I should have told my father I loved him before he died" (Gilovich & Medvec, 1994; Gilovich et al., 2003; Savitsky et al., 1997). In one survey of adults, the most common regret was not taking their education more seriously (Kinnier & Metha, 1989). Would we live with less regret if we dared more often to reach beyond our comfort zone—to venture out, risking failure, but at least having tried?

ILLUSORY THINKING

Another influence on everyday thinking is our search for order in random events, a tendency that can lead us down all sorts of wrong paths.

Illusory correlation

illusory correlation perception of a relationship where none exists, or perception of a stronger relationship than actually exists

It's easy to see a correlation where none exists. When we expect significant relationships, we easily associate random events, perceiving an **illusory correlation**. William Ward and Herbert Jenkins (1965) showed people the results of a hypothetical 50-day cloud-seeding experiment. They told their subjects which of the 50 days the clouds had been seeded and which days it rained. This information was nothing more than a random mix of results: Sometimes it rained after seeding; sometimes it didn't. People nevertheless became convinced—in conformity with their ideas about the effects of cloud seeding—that they really had observed a relationship between cloud seeding and rain.

Other experiments confirm that people easily misperceive random events as confirming their beliefs (Crocker, 1981; Jennings et al., 1982; Trolier & Hamilton, 1986). If we believe a correlation exists, we are more likely to notice and recall confirming instances. If we believe that premonitions correlate with events, we notice and remember the joint occurrence of the premonition and the event's later occurrence. We seldom notice or remember all the times unusual events do not coincide. If, after we think about a friend, the friend calls us, we notice and remember this coincidence. We don't notice all the times we think of a friend without any ensuing call, or receive a call from a friend about whom we've not been thinking.

"I see men ordinarily more eager to discover a reason for things than to find out whether the things are so."

French essayist Montaigne, 1533–1592

Illusion of control

Our tendency to perceive random events as related feeds an **illusion of control**—*the idea that chance events are subject to our influence.* This is what keeps gamblers going and what makes the rest of us do all sorts of unlikely things.

Gambling

Ellen Langer (1977) demonstrated the illusion of control with experiments on gambling. Compared to those given an assigned lottery number, people who chose their own number demanded four times as much money when asked about selling their ticket. When playing a game of chance against an awkward and nervous person, they bet significantly more than when playing against a dapper, confident opponent. In these and other ways, more than 50 experiments have consistently found people acting as if they can predict or control chance events (Presson & Benassi, 1996).

illusion of control perception of uncontrollable events as subject to one's control or as more controllable than they are

Observations of real-life gamblers confirm these experimental findings. Dice players may throw softly for low numbers and hard for high numbers (Henslin, 1967). The gambling industry thrives on gamblers' illusions. Gamblers attribute wins to their skill and foresight. Losses become "near misses" or "flukes"—perhaps (for the sports gambler) a bad call by the referee or a freakish bounce of the ball (Gilovich & Douglas, 1986).

Regression toward the average

Tversky and Kahneman (1974) noted another way by which an illusion of control may arise: We fail to recognize the statistical phenomenon of **regression toward the average**. Because exam scores fluctuate partly by chance, most students who get extremely high scores on an exam will get lower scores on the next exam. Because their first score is at the ceiling, their second score is more likely to fall back ("regress") toward their own average than to push the ceiling even higher. (This is why a student who does consistently good work, even if never the best, will sometimes end a course at the top of the class.) Conversely, the lowest-scoring students on the first exam are likely to improve. If those who scored lowest go for tutoring after the first exam, the tutors are likely to feel effective when the student improves, even if the tutoring had no effect.

regression toward the average the statistical tendency for extreme scores or extreme behaviour to return toward one's average

Indeed, when things reach a low point, we will try anything, and whatever we try—going to a psychotherapist, starting a new diet-exercise plan, reading a self-help book—is more likely to be followed by improvement than by further deterioration. Sometimes we recognize that events are not likely to continue at an unusually good or bad extreme. Experience has taught us that when everything is going great, something will go wrong, and that when life is dealing us terrible blows, we can usually look forward to things getting better. Often, though, we fail to recognize this regression effect. We puzzle at why baseball's rookie-of-the-year often has a more ordinary second year—did he become overconfident? Self-conscious? We forget that exceptional performance tends to regress toward normality.

By simulating the consequences of using praise and punishment, Paul Schaffner (1985) invited students to train an imaginary fourth-grade boy, "Harold," to come to school by 8:30

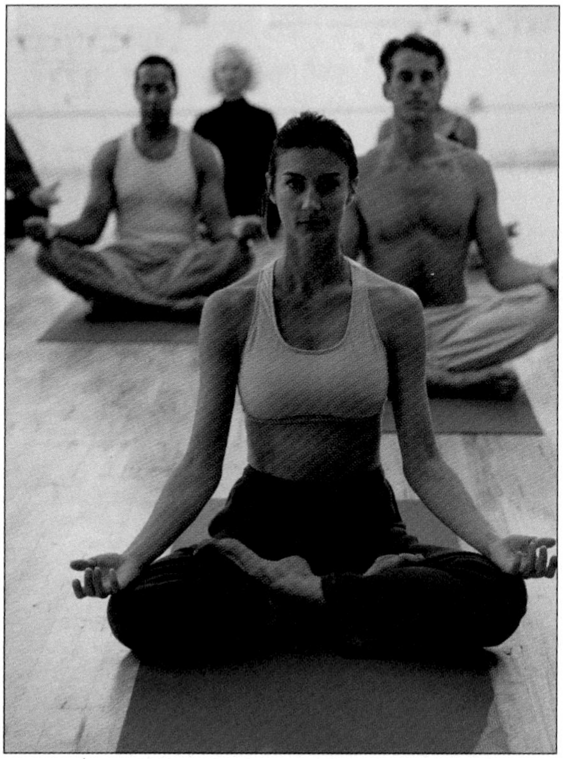

Regression to the average: When we are at an extremely low point, anything we try, like meditation or yoga, will usually seem effective as we return to our more usual state.

each morning. For each school day of a three-week period, a computer displayed Harold's arrival time, which was always between 8:20 and 8:40. The subjects would then select a response to Harold, ranging from strong praise to strong reprimand. As you might expect, they usually praised Harold when he arrived before 8:30 and reprimanded him when he arrived after 8:30. Because Schaffner had programmed the computer to display a random sequence of arrival times, Harold's arrival time tended to improve (to regress toward 8:30) after being reprimanded. For example, if Harold arrived at 8:39, he was almost sure to be reprimanded, and his randomly selected next-day arrival time was likely to be earlier than 8:39. Thus, *even though their reprimands were having no effect,* most subjects ended the experiment believing that their reprimands had been effective.

This experiment demonstrates Tversky and Kahneman's provocative conclusion: Nature operates in such a way that we often feel punished for rewarding others and rewarded for punishing them. In actuality, as every student of psychology knows, positive reinforcement for doing things right is usually more effective and has fewer negative side effects.

MOOD AND JUDGMENT

Social judgment involves efficient, though fallible, information processing. It also involves our feelings: Our moods infuse our judgments. We are not cool computing machines, we are emotional creatures. The extent to which feeling infuses cognition appears in new studies comparing happy and sad individuals (Myers, 1993, 2000). Unhappy people—especially those bereaved or depressed—tend to be more self-focused and brooding. A depressed mood motivates intense thinking—a search for information that makes one's environment more understandable and controllable (Weary & Edwards, 1994).

Happy people, by contrast, are more trusting, more loving, more responsive. If made temporarily happy by receiving a small gift while mall-shopping, they will report, a few moments later on an unrelated survey, that their cars and TV sets are working beautifully—better, if you took their word for it, than those belonging to folks who didn't receive a gift.

Moods pervade our thinking. To West Germans enjoying their team's World Cup soccer victory (Schwarz et al., 1987) and to Australians emerging from a heartwarming movie (Forgas & Moylan, 1987), people seem good-hearted, life seems wonderful. After (but not before) a 1990 football game between rivals Alabama and Auburn, victorious Alabama fans deemed war less likely and potentially devastating than did the gloomier Auburn fans (Schweitzer et al., 1992). In a happy mood, the world seems friendlier, decisions are easier, good news more readily comes to mind (Johnson & Tversky, 1983; Isen & Means, 1983; Stone & Glass, 1986).

Let a mood turn gloomy, however, and thoughts switch onto a different track. Off come the rose-coloured glasses; on come the dark glasses. Now the bad mood primes our recollections of negative events (Bower, 1987; Johnson & Magaro, 1987). Our relationships seem to sour. Our self-image takes a dive. Our hopes for the future dim. Other people's behaviour seems more sinister (Brown & Taylor, 1986; Esses, 1989; Mayer & Salovey, 1987).

University of New South Wales social psychologist Joseph Forgas (1999) had often been struck by how moody people's "feelings seem to invade their thinking. It almost appears that their memories and judgments change with the color of their mood." To understand this "mood infusion" he began to experiment. Imagine yourself in one such study. Using hypnosis, Forgas and his colleagues (1984) put you in a good or bad mood and then have you watch a videotape (made the day before) of yourself talking with someone. If made to feel happy, you feel pleased with what you see, and you are able to detect many instances of your poise, interest, and social skill. If you've been put in a bad mood, viewing the same tape seems to reveal a quite different you—one who is frequently stiff, nervous, and inarticulate (Figure 3–3). Given how your mood colours your judgments, you feel relieved at how things brighten when the experimenter switches you to a happy mood before leaving the experiment. Curiously, note Michael Ross and Garth Fletcher (1985), we don't attribute our changing perceptions to our mood shifts. Rather, the world really seems different.

Our moods colour how we see our worlds partly by bringing to mind past experiences associated with the mood. In a bad mood we have more depressing thoughts. Mood-related thoughts may distract us from complex thinking about something else. Thus, when emotionally aroused—when angry or even in a very good mood—we become more likely to make snap judgments and evaluate others based on stereotypes (Bodenhausen et al., 1994; Paulhus & Lim, 1994). But if our attention is drawn to our moods, we may "correct" our judgments. People in a foul mood had less flattering views of another person than did people in a happy mood, unless they first attended to their moods. In that case, mood had little impact on impressions of the other person (McFarland, White & Newth, 2006). It seems that if we acknowledge our moods, we can keep them from biasing our judgments.

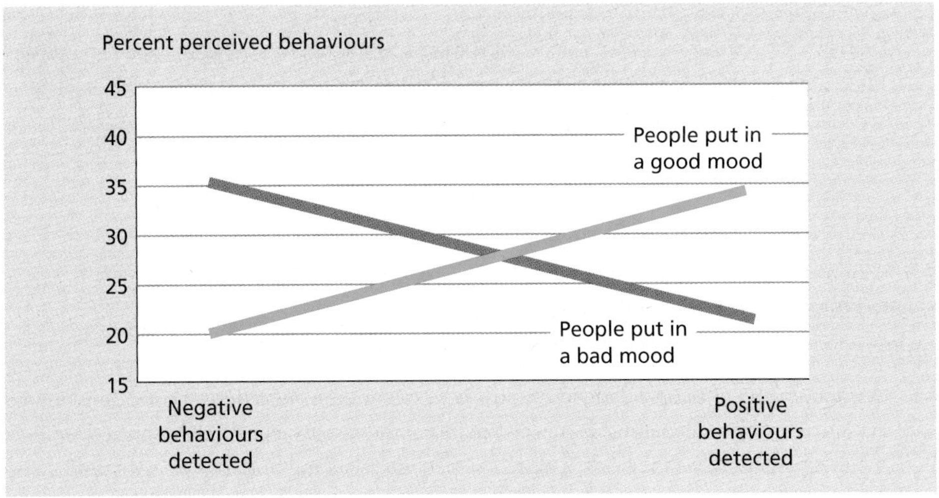

FIGURE 3–3

A temporary good or bad mood strongly influenced people's ratings of their videotaped behaviour. Those in a bad mood detected far fewer positive behaviours. (Forgas et al., 1984)

STORY BEHIND THE RESEARCH

Joseph Forgas
University of New South Wales, Sydney, Australia

We all know moody people, and I have often been struck by how their feelings seem to invade their thinking. It almost appears that their memories and judgments change with the colour of their mood. For some years now, I have been trying to understand how and why this mood infusion occurs.

One day while sitting in a restaurant, I noticed an odd couple at the next table—a beautiful young woman with an unattractive elderly man. As I found myself repeatedly wondering about this relationship, it occurred to me that the more I thought about them, the more opportunity there might be for my mood to infuse my thoughts. Testing this idea in the laboratory, we found that, indeed, mood had a greater effect on complex judgments of odd couples than on snap judgments of well-matched couples. Such findings have helped us to develop a theory that predicts when moodiness will infuse judgments.

SUMMING UP: JUDGING OUR SOCIAL WORLDS

When we examine our judgments of others, we see four ways in which these judgments are often biased.

First, we often overestimate our judgments. This "overconfidence phenomenon" stems partly from the much greater ease with which we can imagine why we might be right than why we might be wrong. Moreover, people are much more likely to search for information that can confirm their beliefs than information that can disconfirm them.

Second, when given compelling anecdotes or even useless information, we often ignore useful information. This is partly due to the later ease of recall ("availability") of vivid information.

Third, we are often swayed by illusions of correlation and personal control. It is tempting to perceive correlations where none exist ("illusory correlation") and to think we can predict or control chance events (the "illusion of control").

Finally, moods infuse judgments. Good and bad moods trigger memories of experiences associated with those moods. Moods colour our interpretation of current experiences. And by distracting us, moods can also influence how deeply or superficially we think when making judgments.

EXPLAINING OUR SOCIAL WORLDS

People make it their business to explain other people, and social psychologists make it their business to explain people's explanations. So, how—and how accurately—do people explain others' behaviour? Attribution theory suggests some answers.

Our judgments of people depend on how we explain their behaviour. Depending on our explanation, we may judge killing as murder, manslaughter, self-defence, or heroism. Depending on our explanation, we may view a homeless person as lacking initiative or as victimized by job and social assistance cutbacks. Depending on our explanation, we may attribute someone's friendly behaviour as genuine warmth or ingratiation.

ATTRIBUTING CAUSALITY: TO THE PERSON OR THE SITUATION?

We endlessly analyze and discuss why things happen as they do, especially when we experience something negative or unexpected (Bohner et al., 1988; Weiner, 1985). If worker productivity declines, do we assume the workers are getting lazier? Or has their workplace become less efficient? Does a young boy who hits his classmates have a hostile personality? Or is he responding to relentless teasing? Amy Holtzworth-Munroe and Neil Jacobson (1985, 1988) report that married people often analyze their partners' behaviours, especially their negative behaviours. Cold hostility is more likely than a warm hug to leave the partner wondering "why?" Spouses' answers correlate with their marriage satisfaction. Those in unhappy relationships typically offer distress-maintaining explanations for negative acts ("she was late because she doesn't care about me"). Happy couples more often externalize ("she was late because of heavy traffic"). With positive partner behaviour their explanations similarly work either to maintain distress ("he brought me flowers because he wants sex") or to enhance the relationship ("he brought me flowers to show he loves me") (Gelinas et al., 1995; Hewstone & Fincham, 1996; Weiner, 1995).

Antonia Abbey (1987, 1991) and her colleagues have repeatedly found that men are more likely than women to attribute a woman's friendliness to mild sexual interest. This misreading of warmth as a sexual come-on—an example of **misattribution**—can lead to behaviour that women regard as sexual harassment (Johnson et al., 1991; Pryor et al., 1997; Saal et al., 1989). Many believe women are flattered by repeated requests for dates, which women more often see as harassing (Rotundo et al., 2001). Misattribution is especially likely when men are in positions of power. The boss may misinterpret a subordinate woman's submissive or friendly behaviour and, full of himself, may see women only in sexual terms (Bargh & Raymond, 1995). Men can easily overestimate the sexual significance of a woman's courtesy smile (Nelson & LeBoeuf, 2002). What Jane intends as "just a smile" may give John the wrong idea.

misattribution mistakenly attributing a behaviour to the wrong cause

Such misattributions help explain the greater sexual assertiveness exhibited by men across the world and the greater tendency of men in various cultures, from Boston to Bangalore, to justify rape by arguing that the victim consented or implied consent (Kanekar & Nazareth, 1988; Muehlenhard, 1988; Shotland, 1989). Women more often judge the same behaviour as meriting conviction and a stiff sentence (Schutte & Hosch, 1997). Misattributions also help

To what should we attribute this student's sleepiness? To lack of sleep? To boredom? Whether we make internal or external attributions depends on whether we notice her consistently sleeping in this and other classes, and on whether other students react as she does to this particular class.

attribution theory the theory of how people explain others' behaviour—for example, by attributing it either to internal dispositions (enduring traits, motives, and attitudes) or to external situations

dispositional attribution attributing behaviour to the person's disposition and traits

situational attribution attributing behaviour to the environment

explain why the 23 percent of American women who say they have been forced into unwanted sexual behaviour is eight times the 3 percent of American men who say they have ever forced a woman into a sexual act (Laumann et al., 1994).

Attribution theory analyzes how we explain people's behaviour. The variations of attribution theory share some common assumptions. As Daniel Gilbert and Patrick Malone (1995) explain, each "construes the human skin as a special boundary that separates one set of 'causal forces' from another. On the sunny side of the epidermis are the external or situational forces that press inward upon the person, and on the meaty side are the internal or personal forces that exert pressure outward. Sometimes these forces press in conjunction, sometimes in opposition, and their dynamic interplay manifests itself as observable behavior."

Fritz Heider (1958), widely regarded as attribution theory's originator, analyzed the "commonsense psychology" by which people explain everyday events. Heider concluded that people tend to attribute someone's behaviour to *internal* causes (for example, the person's disposition) or *external* causes (for example, something about the person's situation). A teacher may wonder whether a child's underachievement is due to lack of motivation and ability (a **dispositional attribution**) or to physical and social circumstances (a **situational attribution**). Some people are more inclined to attribute behaviour to stable personality; others tend more to attribute behaviour to situations (Bastian & Haslam, 2006; Robins et al., 2004).

Inferring traits

Edward Jones and Keith Davis (1965) noted that we often infer that other people's actions are indicative of their intentions and dispositions. If I observe Rick making a sarcastic comment to Linda, I infer that Rick is a hostile person. Jones and Davis's "theory of correspondent inferences" specifies the conditions under which such attributions are most likely. For example, normal or expected behaviour tells us less about the person than does unusual behaviour. If Samantha is sarcastic in a job interview, where a person would normally be pleasant, this tells us more about Samantha than if she is sarcastic with her siblings.

The ease with which we infer traits is remarkable. In one set of experiments James Uleman (1989) gave students statements to remember, like "The librarian carries the old woman's groceries across the street." The students would instantly, unintentionally, and unconsciously infer a trait. When later they were helped to recall the sentence, the most valuable clue word was not "books" (to cue librarian) or "bags" (to cue groceries) but "helpful"—the inferred trait that we suspect you, too, spontaneously attributed to the librarian.

We tend to attribute someone's behaviour or the outcome of an event either to internal (dispositional) or external (situational) causes.

"So! If it's good, it's Mister Coffee. If it's bad, it's me."

Commonsense attributions

As these examples suggest, attributions often are rational. In testimony to the reasonable ways in which we explain behaviour, attribution theorist Harold Kelley (1973) described how we use information about "consistency," "distinctiveness," and "consensus" (Figure 3-4). When explaining why Edgar is having trouble with his computer, most people use information concerning *consistency* (Is Edgar usually unable to get his computer to work?), *distinctiveness* (Does Edgar have trouble with other computers, or only this

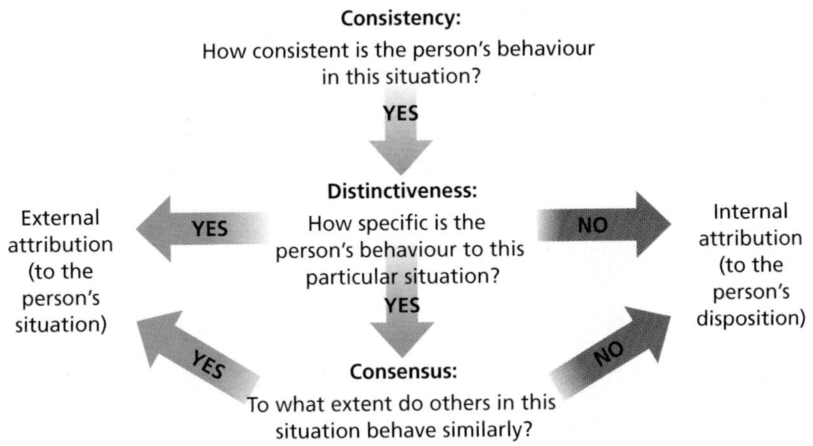
Consistency:
How consistent is the person's behaviour in this situation?
YES
Distinctiveness:
How specific is the person's behaviour to this particular situation?
YES
Consensus:
To what extent do others in this situation behave similarly?
External attribution (to the person's situation)
Internal attribution (to the person's disposition)
YES
NO
YES
NO

FIGURE 3–4

Harold Kelley's theory of attributions.

Three factors—consistency, distinctiveness, and consensus—influence whether we attribute someone's behaviour to internal or external causes. Try creating your own examples such as: If Mary and many others criticize Steve (with consensus), and if Mary isn't critical of others (high distinctiveness), then we make an external attribution (it's something about Steve). If Mary alone (low consensus) criticizes Steve, and if she criticizes lots of other people, too (low distinctiveness), then we are drawn to an internal attribution (it's something about Mary).

one?), and *consensus* (Do other people have similar problems with this make of computer?). If we learn that Edgar alone consistently has trouble with this and other computers, we likely will attribute the troubles to Edgar, not to defects in this computer.

So our commonsense psychology often explains behaviour logically. But Kelley also found people often discount a contributing cause of behaviour if other plausible causes are already known. If we can specify one or two reasons a student might have done poorly on an exam, we may ignore or discount other possibilities (McClure, 1998).

THE FUNDAMENTAL ATTRIBUTION ERROR

Social psychology's most important lesson concerns the influence of our social environment. At any moment, our internal state, and therefore what we say and do, depends on the situation, as well as on what we bring to the situation. In experiments, a slight difference between two situations sometimes greatly affects how people respond. We have seen this when teaching classes at both 8:30 A.M. and 7:00 P.M. Silent stares would greet us at 8:30; at 7:00 one of the authors had to break up a party. In each situation some individuals were more talkative than others, but the difference between the two situations exceeded the individual differences.

Attribution researchers have found that we often fail to appreciate this important lesson. When explaining someone's behaviour, we underestimate the impact of the situation and overestimate the extent to which it reflects the individual's traits and attitudes. Thus, even knowing the effect of the time of day on classroom conversation, we found it terribly tempting to assume that the people in the 7:00 P.M. class were more extroverted than the "silent types" who come at 8:30 A.M.

fundamental attribution error the tendency for observers to underestimate situational influences and overestimate dispositional influences on others' behaviour. (Also called *correspondence bias*, because we so often see behaviour as corresponding to a disposition.)

This discounting of the situation, dubbed by Lee Ross (1977) as the **fundamental attribution error**, appears in many experiments. In the first such study, Edward Jones and Victor Harris (1967) had students read debaters' speeches supporting or attacking Cuba's leader, Fidel Castro. When the position taken was said to have been chosen by the debater, the students logically enough assumed it reflected the person's own attitude. But what happened when the students were told that the debate coach had assigned the position? People who are merely feigning a position write stronger statements than you'd expect (Allison et al., 1993; Miller et al., 1990). Thus, even knowing that the debater had been told to take a pro-Castro position did

FIGURE 3–5

The fundamental attribution error.

When people read a debate speech supporting or attacking Fidel Castro, they attributed corresponding attitudes to the speech writer, even when the debate coach assigned the writer's position.

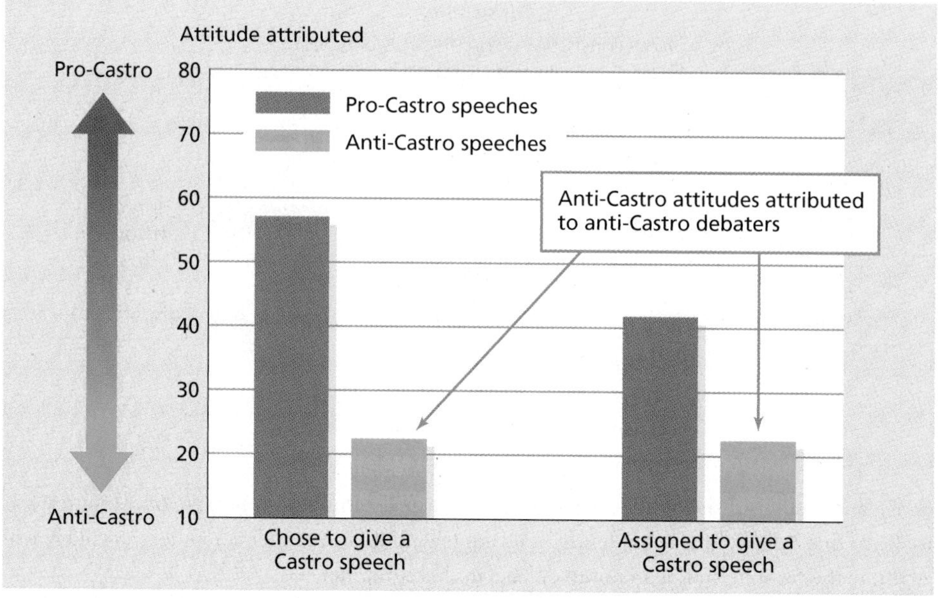

not prevent students' inferring that the debater in fact had some pro-Castro leanings (Figure 3–5 above). People seemed to think, "Yeah, I know he was assigned that position, but to some extent I think he really believes it."

The error is so irresistible that even when people know they are causing someone else's behaviour, they still underestimate external influences. If subjects dictate an opinion that someone else must then express, they still tend to see the person as actually holding that opinion (Gilbert & Jones, 1986). If subjects are asked to be either self-enhancing or self-deprecating during an interview, they are very aware of why they are acting so. But they are *un*aware of their effect on another person. If Juan acts modestly, his naive partner Bob is likely to exhibit modesty as well. Juan will easily understand his own behaviour, but he will think that poor Bob suffers low self-esteem (Baumeister et al., 1988). In short, we tend to presume that others *are* the way they act. Observing Cinderella cowering in her oppressive home, people infer she is meek; dancing with her at the ball, the prince sees a suave and glamorous person.

People often attribute keen intelligence to those, such as teachers and quiz show hosts, who test others' knowledge.

The discounting of social constraints was further evident in a thought-provoking experiment by Lee Ross and his collaborators (Ross et al., 1977). The experiment recreated Ross's first-hand experience of moving from graduate student to professor. His doctoral oral exam had proved a humbling experience as his apparently brilliant professors quizzed him on topics they specialized in. Six months later, *Dr.* Ross was himself an examiner, now able to ask penetrating questions on *his* favourite topics. Ross's hapless student later confessed to feeling exactly as Ross had a half-year before—dissatisfied with his ignorance and impressed with the apparent brilliance of the examiners.

In the experiment, with Teresa Amabile and Julia Steinmetz, Ross set up a simulated quiz game. He randomly assigned some students to play the role of questioner, some to play the role of contestant, and others to observe. The researchers invited the questioners to make up difficult questions that would demonstrate their wealth of knowledge. It's fun to imagine the questions: "Where are the clearest waters for scuba diving in Canada?" "What is the seventh book in the Old Testament?" "Which has the longer coastline, Europe or Africa?" If even these few questions have you feeling a little uninformed, then you will appreciate the results of this experiment.*

Everyone had to know that the questioner would have the advantage. Yet both contestants and observers (but not the questioners) came to the erroneous conclusion that the questioners *really were* more knowledgeable than the contestants (Figure 3–6). Follow-up research shows that these misimpressions are hardly a reflection of low social intelligence. If anything, intelligent and socially competent people are *more* likely to make the attribution error (Block & Funder, 1986).

In real life, those with social power usually initiate and control conversations, which often leads underlings to overestimate their knowledge and intelligence. Medical doctors, for example, are often presumed to be experts on all sorts of questions unrelated to medicine. Similarly, students often overestimate the brilliance of their teachers. (As in the experiment, teachers are

*Tobermorey, Ontario, has the clearest waters in Canada. The seventh Old Testament book is Judges. Although the African continent is more than double the area of Europe, Europe's coastline is longer. (It is more convoluted, with lots of harbours and inlets, a geographical fact that contributed to its role in the history of maritime trade.)

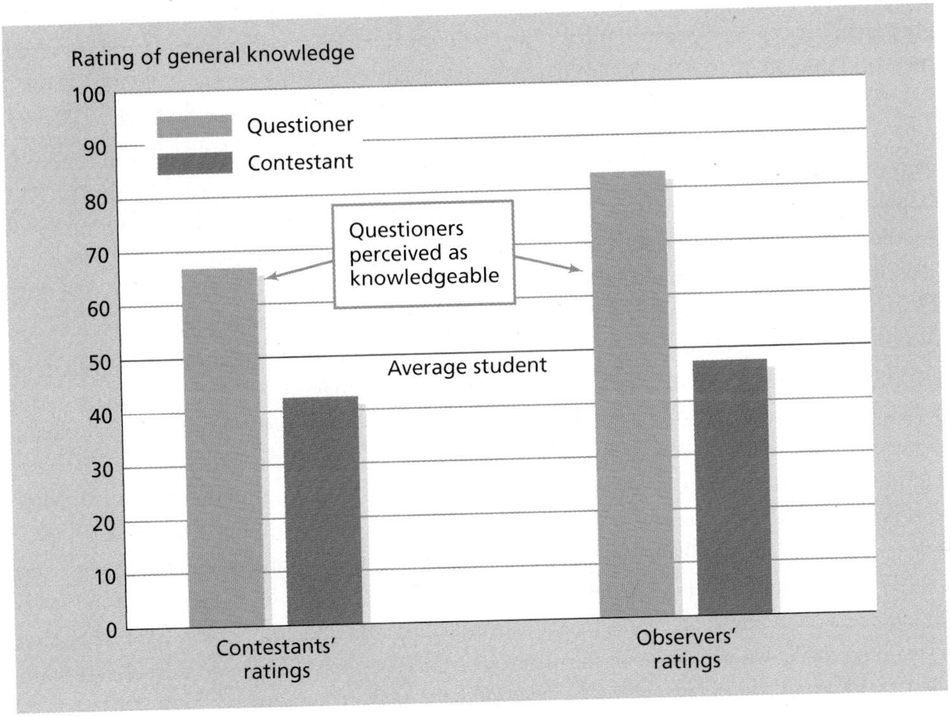

FIGURE 3–6

Both contestants and observers of a simulated quiz game assumed that a person who had been randomly assigned the role of questioner was far more knowledgeable than the contestant. Actually the assigned roles of questioner and contestant simply made the questioner seem more knowledgeable. The failure to appreciate this illustrates the fundamental attribution error. (Data from Ross, Amabile, & Steinmetz, 1977) questioners on subjects of their special expertise.) When some of these students later become teachers, they are usually amazed to discover that teachers are not so brilliant after all.

To illustrate the fundamental attribution error, most of us need look no further than our own experience. Determined to make some new friends, Bev plasters a smile on her face and anxiously plunges into a party. Everyone else seems quite relaxed and happy as they laugh and talk with one another. Bev wonders to herself, "Why is everyone always so at ease in groups like this while I'm feeling shy and tense?" Actually, everyone else is feeling nervous, too, and making the same attribution error in assuming that Bev and the others *are* as they *appear*—confidently convivial.

WHY DO WE MAKE THE ATTRIBUTION ERROR?

So far we have seen a bias in the way we explain other people's behaviour: We often ignore powerful situational determinants. Why do we tend to underestimate the situational determinants of others' behaviour but not of our own?

Perspective and situational awareness

An actor–observer difference

Attribution theorists point out that we have a different perspective when observing others than when acting (Jones & Nisbett, 1971; Jones, 1976). When we act, the environment commands our attention. When we watch another person act, that *person* occupies the centre of our attention and the situation becomes relatively invisible. To use the perceptual analogy of figure and ground, the person is the figure that stands out from the surrounding environmental ground. So the person seems to cause whatever happens. If this theory is true, what might we expect if the perspectives were reversed? What if we could see ourselves as others see us and if we saw the world through their eyes? Shouldn't this eliminate or reverse the typical attribution error?

See if you can predict the result of a clever experiment conducted by Michael Storms (1973). Picture yourself as a subject in Storms's experiment. You are seated facing another student with whom you are to talk for a few minutes. Beside you is a TV camera that shares your view of the other student. Facing you from alongside the other student are an observer and another TV camera. Afterwards, both you and the observer judge whether your behaviour was caused more by your personal characteristics or by the situation.

Question: Which of you—participant or observer—will attribute the least importance to the situation? Storms found it was the observer (another demonstration of the fundamental attribution tendency). What if we reverse points of view by having you and the observer each watch the videotape recorded from the other's perspective? (You now view yourself, while the observer views what you were seeing while you were being videotaped.) This reverses the attributions: The observer now attributes your behaviour mostly to the situation you faced, while you now attribute it to your person. *Remembering* an experience from an observer's perspective—by "seeing" oneself from the outside—has the same effect (Frank & Gilovich, 1989).

From his analysis of 173 studies, Bertram Malle (2007) concludes that the actor–observer difference is often minimal. People typically exhibit empathy when they observe someone after explaining their own behaviour in the same situation. It's when one person misbehaves while another observes that the two will offer strikingly different attributions.

The camera perspective bias

In some experiments, people viewed a videotape of a suspect confessing during a police interview. If they viewed the confession through a camera focused on the suspect, they perceived the confession as genuine. If they viewed it through a camera focused on the detective, they perceived it as more coerced (Lassiter & Irvine, 1986). The camera perspective influenced people's guilt judgments even when the judge instructed them not to allow it to (Lassiter et al., 2005). In courtrooms, most confession videotapes focus on the confessor. As we might expect, note Daniel Lassiter and Kimberly Dudley (1991), such tapes yield a nearly 100-percent conviction rate when played by prosecutors. Aware of this research, reports Lassiter, New Zealand has made it a national policy that police interrogations are filmed with equal focus on the officer and the suspect, such as by filming them with side profiles of both.

Perspectives change with time

As the once-visible person recedes in their memory, observers often give more and more credit to the situation. Immediately after hearing someone argue an assigned position, people assume that's how the person really felt. A week later they are much more likely to credit the situational constraints (Burger, 1991). The day after a major election, Jerry Burger and Julie Pavelich (1994) asked voters why the election turned out the way it did. Most attributed the outcome to the candidates' personal traits and positions (the winner was likeable; the loser had poor ideas). When they asked the same voters the same question a year later, only a third attributed the verdict to the candidates. More people now credited the circumstances, such as the mood of the electorate and the nature of the economy.

Let's make this personal: Are you generally quiet, talkative, or does it depend on the situation? "Depends on the situation" is a common answer. But when asked to describe a friend—or to describe what they were like five years ago—people more often ascribe trait descriptions. When recalling our past, we become like observers of someone else, note researchers Emily Pronin and Lee Ross (2006). For most of us, the "old you" is someone other than today's "real you."

Self-awareness

Circumstances can also shift our perspective on ourselves. Seeing ourselves on television redirects our attention to ourselves. Seeing ourselves in a mirror, hearing our tape-recorded voices, having our pictures taken, or filling out biographical questionnaires similarly focus our attention inward, making us *self*-conscious instead of *situation*-conscious. Looking back on ill-fated relationships that once seemed like the unsinkable *Titanic*, people can see the icebergs (Berscheid, 1999).

Robert Wicklund, Shelley Duval, and their collaborators have explored the effects of **self-awareness** (Duval & Wicklund, 1972; Silvia & Duval, 2001). When our attention focuses on ourselves, we attribute more responsibility to ourselves. Allan Fenigstein and Charles Carver (1978) demonstrated this by having students imagine themselves in hypothetical situations. Those who were made self-conscious by thinking they were hearing their own heartbeats while pondering the situation saw themselves as more responsible for the imaginary outcome than did those who thought they were just hearing extraneous noises.

self-awareness
a self-conscious state in which attention focuses on oneself. It makes people more sensitive to their own attitudes and dispositions.

Some people are typically quite self-conscious. In experiments, people who report themselves as privately self-conscious (who agree with statements such as "I'm generally attentive to my inner feelings") behave similarly to people whose attention has been self-focused with a mirror (Carver & Scheier, 1978). Thus, people whose attention focuses on themselves—either briefly during an experiment or because they are self-conscious persons—view themselves more as observers typically do; they attribute their behaviour more to internal factors and less to the situation.

All these experiments point to a reason for the attribution error: *We find causes where we look for them.* To see this in your own experience, consider: Would you say your social psychology instructor is a quiet or a talkative person?

Our guess is you inferred that he or she is fairly outgoing. But consider the situation further: Your attention focuses on your instructor while he or she behaves in a public context that demands speaking. The instructor also observes his or her own behaviour in many different situations—in the classroom, in meetings, at home. "Me talkative?" your instructor might say. "Well, it all depends on the situation. When I'm in class or with good friends, I'm rather outgoing. But at conventions and in unfamiliar situations I feel and act rather shy." Because we are acutely aware of how our behaviour varies with the situation, we see ourselves as more variable than other people (Baxter & Goldberg, 1987; Kammer, 1982; Sande et al., 1988). "Nigel is uptight, Fiona is relaxed. With me it varies."

HOW FUNDAMENTAL IS THE FUNDAMENTAL ATTRIBUTION ERROR?

Like most provocative ideas, the presumption that we're all prone to a fundamental attribution error has its critics. Granted, say some, there is an attribution *bias.* But in any given instance, this may or may not produce an "error," just as parents who are biased to believe their child does not use drugs may or may not be correct (Harvey et al., 1981). We can be biased to believe what is true. Moreover, some everyday circumstances, such as being in church or on a job interview, are like the experiments we have been considering: As actors realize better than observers, the circumstances involve clear constraints. Hence the attribution error. But in other settings—in one's room, at a park—people exhibit their individuality. In such settings, people may see their own behaviour as *less* constrained than do observers (Monson & Snyder, 1977; Quattrone, 1982; Robins et al., 1996). So it's an overstatement to say that at all times and in all settings observers underestimate situational influences. For this reason, many social psychologists follow Edward Jones in referring to the fundamental attribution error—seeing behaviour as corresponding to an inner disposition—as the *correspondence bias.*

Nevertheless, experiments reveal that the bias occurs even when we are aware of the situational forces—when we know that an assigned debate position is not a good basis for inferring someone's real attitudes (Croxton & Morrow, 1984; Croxton & Miller, 1987; Reeder et al., 1989) or that the questioners' role in the quiz game gives the questioners an advantage (Johnson et al., 1984). It is sobering to think that we can know about a social process that distorts our thinking and still be susceptible to it. Perhaps that's because it takes more mental effort to assess social effects on someone's behaviour than merely to attribute it to a disposition (Gilbert et al., 1988, 1992; Webster, 1993). It's as if the busy person thinks, "This isn't a very good basis for making a judgment, but it's easy and all I've got time to look at."

Culture also has a strong influence on the fundamental attribution error. In cultures that emphasize collectivism as opposed to individualism the fundamental attribution error is less likely to emerge and more easily overcome. We will return to this issue in Chapter 8.

The fundamental attribution error: People are biased to assume that people's behaviour corresponds to their inner dispositions. Such assumptions are sometimes, but not always, correct. Some weekend bikers are weekday professionals.

In many ways, this is adaptive (psychologists generally assume that even our biases serve a purpose, or else nature would have rejected rather than selected those who exhibit them). Attributing behaviour to dispositions rather than to situations is not only efficient, it often does little harm. For one thing, our dispositions often lead us to choose our situations. If bankers dress conservatively, note Daniel Gilbert and Patrick Malone (1995), that may reflect not only their profession's demands but also the conservative person's choice of a profession. Assume that the banker really is more conservative than the artist and you are likely right. Some situations really are of our own making. Moreover, when we experience people only in a single role—as a banker, teacher, or grandmother—we can predict their behaviour equally well whether attributing it to their role or to their disposition. It's only when we experience a person in a new situation that our disposition-based predictions may go astray.

The attribution error is, however, *fundamental* because it colours our explanations in basic and important ways. Researchers in Britain, India, Australia, and the United States have found, for example, that people's attributions predict their attitudes toward the poor and unemployed (Feather, 1983; Furnham, 1982; Pandey et al., 1982; Wagstaff, 1983; Zucker & Weiner, 1993). Those who attribute poverty and unemployment to personal dispositions ("They're just lazy and undeserving") tend to adopt political positions unsympathetic to such people (Figure 3–7). Their views differ from those who make external attributions ("If you or I were to live with the same overcrowding, poor education, and discrimination, would we be any better off?"). French investigators Jean-Leon Beauvois and Nicole Dubois (1988) report that "relatively privileged" middle-class people are more likely than less advantaged people to assume that people's behaviours have internal explanations. (Those who

"Most poor people are not lazy. . . . They catch the early bus. . . . They raise other people's children. . . . They clean the streets. No, no, they're not lazy."

The Reverend Jesse Jackson, address to the Democratic National Convention, July 1988

FIGURE 3–7

Attributions and reactions.

How we explain someone's negative behaviour determines how we feel about it.

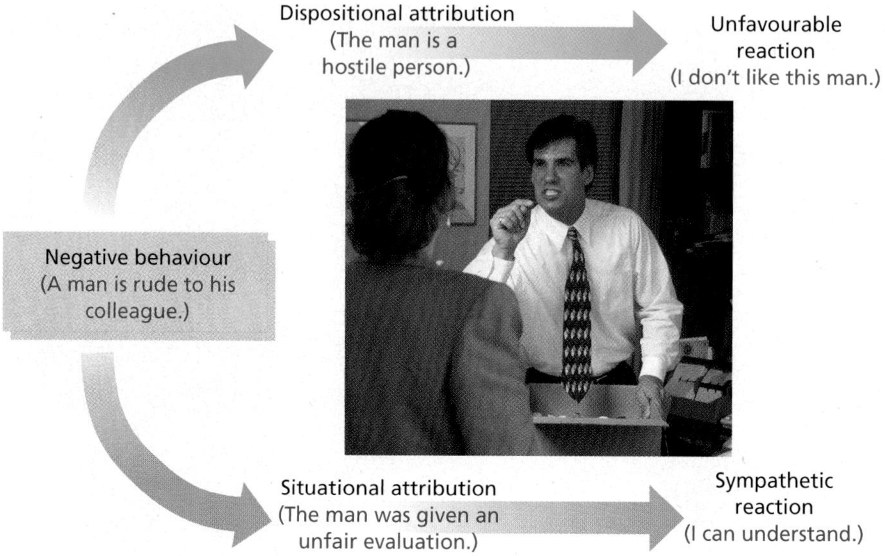

have made it tend to assume that you get what you deserve.) This is also called *situational attribution*—when behaviour is attributed to the environment.

WHY WE STUDY ATTRIBUTION ERRORS

This chapter, like the one before, explains some foibles and fallacies in our social thinking. Reading these may make it seem, as one of our students put it, that "social psychologists get their kicks out of playing tricks on people." Actually, the experiments are not designed to demonstrate "what fools these mortals be" (although some of the experiments *are* amusing); their purpose is to reveal how we think about ourselves and others.

If our capacity for illusion and self-deception is shocking, remember that our modes of thought are generally adaptive. Illusory thinking is often a by-product of our mind's strategies for simplifying complex information. It parallels our perceptual mechanisms, which generally give us a useful image of the world, but sometimes lead us astray.

A second reason for focusing on biases such as the fundamental attribution error is humanitarian. One of social psychology's "great humanizing messages," note Thomas Gilovich and Richard Eibach (2001), is that people should not always be blamed for their problems. "Failure, disability, and misfortune are more often than people are willing to acknowledge the product of real environmental causes."

A third reason for focusing on the biases is that we are mostly unaware of them and can benefit from greater awareness. As with other biases, such as the self-serving bias (Chapter 2), people see themselves as less susceptible than others to attribution errors (Pronin et al., 2004). Our hunch is that you will find more surprises, more challenges, and more benefit in an analysis of errors and biases than you would in a string of testimonies to the human capacity for logic and intellectual achievement. That is also why world literature so often portrays pride and other human failings. Social psychology aims to expose us to fallacies in our thinking in the hope that we will become more rational, more in touch with reality. The hope is not in vain:

Psychology students explain behaviour less simplistically than equally able natural science students (Fletcher et al., 1986).

SUMMING UP: EXPLAINING OUR SOCIAL WORLDS

Attribution theory involves how we explain people's behaviour. When will we attribute someone's behaviour to a person's disposition and when to the situation? By and large we make reasonable attributions. When explaining other people's behaviour, however, we often commit the *fundamental attribution error* (also called *correspondence bias*). We attribute their behaviour so much to their inner traits and attitudes that we discount situational constraints, even when these are obvious. We make this attribution error partly because when we watch someone act, that *person* is the focus of our attention and the situation is relatively invisible. When *we* act, our attention is usually on what we are reacting to—the situation is more visible.

EXPECTATIONS OF OUR SOCIAL WORLD

Having considered how we explain and judge others—efficiently, adaptively, but sometimes wrongly—we conclude by pondering the effects of our social judgments. Do our beliefs about social reality matter? Do they change reality?

Our social beliefs and judgments matter because they have effects. They influence how we feel and act, and by so doing may generate their own reality. When our ideas lead us to act in ways that produce their apparent confirmation, they have become what sociologist Robert Merton (1948) termed **self-fulfilling prophecies**—false beliefs that lead to their own fulfillment. If, led to believe that their bank is about to crash, its customers race to withdraw their money, their false perceptions may create reality, noted Merton. If people are led to believe that stocks are about to soar, they will indeed.

self-fulfilling prophecy a belief that leads to its own fulfillment

In his well-known studies of "experimenter bias," Robert Rosenthal (1985) found that research participants sometimes live up to what is expected of them. In one study, experimenters asked individuals to judge the success of people in various photographs. The experimenters read the same instructions to all their participants and showed them the same photos. Nevertheless, experimenters led to expect high ratings obtained higher ratings than did those who expected their participants to see the photographed people as failures. Even more startling—and controversial—are reports that teachers' beliefs about their students similarly serve as self-fulfilling prophecies. If a teacher believes a student is good at math, will the student do well in the class? Let's examine this.

TEACHER EXPECTATIONS AND STUDENT PERFORMANCE

Teachers do have higher expectations for some students than for others. Perhaps you have detected this after having a brother or sister precede you in school, after receiving a label such as "gifted" or "learning disabled," or after being tracked with "high-ability" or "average-ability" students. Perhaps conversation in the teachers' lounge sent your reputation ahead of you, or your new teacher scrutinized your school file or discovered your family's social status. Do such teacher expectations affect student performance? It's clear that teachers' evaluations *correlate* with student achievement: Teachers think well of students who do well. That's mostly because teachers accurately perceive their students' abilities and achievements (Jussim, 2005).

But are teachers' evaluations ever a *cause* as well as a consequence of student performance? One correlational study of 4300 British schoolchildren by William Crano and Phyllis Mellon (1978) suggested yes. Not only is high performance followed by higher teacher evaluations, but the reverse is true as well.

Could we test this "teacher-expectations effect" experimentally? Pretend we gave a teacher the impression that Dana, Sally, Todd, and Manuel—four randomly selected students—are unusually capable. Will the teacher give special treatment to these four and elicit superior performance from them? In a now famous experiment, Rosenthal and Lenore Jacobson (1968) reported precisely that. Randomly selected children in an elementary school who were said (on the basis of a fictitious test) to be on the verge of a dramatic intellectual spurt did then spurt ahead in IQ score.

This dramatic result seemed to suggest that the school problems of "disadvantaged" children might reflect their teachers' low expectations. The findings were soon publicized in the media as well as in many university textbooks in psychology and education. However, further analysis—which was not as highly publicized—revealed the teacher-expectations effect to be not so powerful and reliable as this initial study had led many people to believe (Spitz, 1999). By Rosenthal's own count, in only about 4 in 10 of the 448 published experiments do expectations significantly affect performance (Rosenthal, 1991, 2002). Low expectations do not doom a capable child, nor do high expectations magically transform a slow learner into a valedictorian. Human nature is not so pliable.

To judge a teacher or professor's overall warmth and enthusiasm also takes but a thin slice of behaviour—mere seconds.

Ambady & Rosenthal, 1992, 1993

High expectations do seem to give a boost to low achievers, for whom a teacher's positive attitude may be a hope-giving breath of fresh air (Madon et al., 1997). How are such expectations transmitted? Rosenthal and other investigators report that teachers look, smile, and nod more at "high-potential students." Teachers also may teach more to their "gifted" students, set higher goals for them, call on them more, and give them more time to answer (Cooper, 1983; Harris & Rosenthal, 1985, 1986; Jussim, 1986).

In one study, Elisha Babad, Frank Bernieri, and Rosenthal (1991) videotaped teachers talking to, or about, unseen students for whom they held high or low expectations. A random 10-second clip of either the teacher's voice or face was enough to tell viewers—both children and adults—whether this was a good or poor student and how much the teacher liked the student. (You read that right: 10 seconds.) Although teachers may think they can conceal their feelings, students are acutely sensitive to teachers' facial expressions and body movements (Figure 3–8).

Reading the experiments on teacher expectations makes one wonder about the effect of *students'* expectations on their teachers. You no doubt begin many of your courses having heard "Professor Smith is interesting" and "Professor Jones is a bore." Robert Feldman and Thomas Prohaska (1979; Feldman & Theiss, 1982) found that such expectations can affect both student and teacher. Students in a learning experiment who expected to be taught by a competent teacher perceived their teacher (who was unaware of their expectations) as more competent and interesting than did students with low expectations. Furthermore, the students actually learned

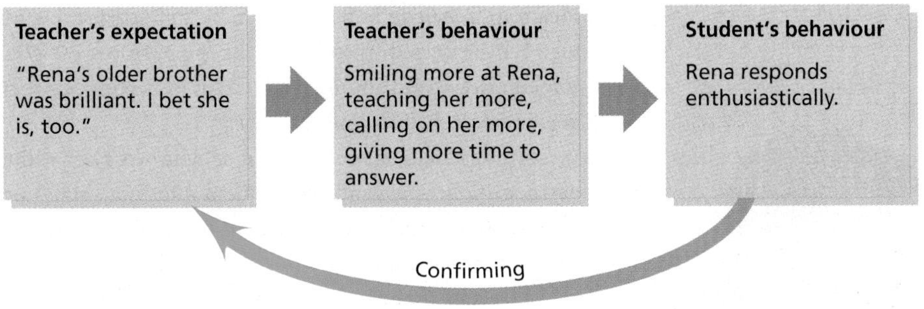
Teacher's expectation
"Rena's older brother was brilliant. I bet she is, too."
Teacher's behaviour
Smiling more at Rena, teaching her more, calling on her more, giving more time to answer.
Student's behaviour
Rena responds enthusiastically.
Confirming

FIGURE 3–8
Self-fulfilling prophecies.

Teacher expectations can become self-fulfilling prophecies.

more. In a follow-up experiment, Feldman and Prohaska videotaped teachers and had observers later rate their performance. Teachers were judged most capable when assigned a student who nonverbally conveyed positive expectations.

To see whether such effects might also occur in actual classrooms, a research team led by David Jamieson (1987) experimented with four Ontario high-school classes taught by a newly transferred teacher. During individual interviews they told students in two of the classes that both other students and the research team rated the teacher very highly. Compared to the control classes, whose expectations they did not raise, the students given positive expectations paid better attention during class. At the end of the teaching unit, they also got better grades and rated the teacher as clearer in her teaching. The attitudes that a class has toward its teacher are as important, it seems, as the teacher's attitude toward the students.

GETTING FROM OTHERS WHAT WE EXPECT

So the expectations of experimenters and teachers, though usually reasonably accurate assessments, occasionally act as self-fulfilling prophecies. How general is this effect? Do we get from others what we expect of them? Studies show that self-fulfilling prophecies also operate in work settings (with managers who have high or low expectations), in courtrooms (as judges instruct juries), and in simulated police contexts (as interrogators with guilty or innocent expectations interrogate and pressure suspects) (Kassin et al., 2003; Rosenthal, 2003).

Do self-fulfilling prophecies colour our personal relationships? There are times when negative expectations of someone lead us to be extra nice to that person, which induces them to be nice in return—thus *dis*confirming our expectations. But a more common finding in studies of social interaction is that, yes, we do to some extent get what we expect (Olson et al., 1996).

In laboratory games, hostility nearly always begets hostility: People who *perceive* their opponents as noncooperative will readily induce them to *be* noncooperative (Kelley & Stahelski, 1970). Each party's perception of the other as aggressive, resentful, and vindictive induces the other to display these behaviours in self-defence, thus creating a vicious self-perpetuating circle. Whether a husband expects his wife to be in a bad mood or in a warm, loving mood may affect how he relates to her, thereby inducing her to confirm his belief.

So do intimate relationships prosper when partners idealize one another? Are positive illusions of the other's virtues self-fulfilling? Or are they more often self-defeating, by creating expectations that can't be met? Among University of Waterloo dating couples followed by Sandra Murray and her associates (1996, 2000), positive ideals of one's partner were good omens.

What we believe about someone can lead us to treat the person in ways that create a self-fulfilling prophecy. Consider this in the context of Internet dating and email exchange with strangers.

Idealization helped buffer conflict, bolster satisfaction, and turn self-perceived frogs into princes or princesses. When someone loves and admires us, it helps us become more the person he or she imagines us to be.

Among married couples, those who worry that their partner doesn't love and accept them interpret slight hurts as rejections, which motivate them to devalue the partner and distance themselves. Those who presume their partner's love and acceptance respond less defensively and even may be closer to their partner (Murray et al., 2003). Love helps create its presumed reality.

Several experiments conducted by Mark Snyder (1984) show how, once formed, erroneous beliefs about the social world can induce others to confirm those beliefs, a phenomenon called **behavioural confirmation**. In a now-classic study, Snyder, Elizabeth Tanke, and Ellen Berscheid (1977) had male students talk on the telephone with women they thought (from having been shown a picture) were either attractive or unattractive. Analysis of just the women's comments during the conversations revealed that the supposedly attractive women spoke more warmly than the supposedly unattractive women. The men's erroneous beliefs had become a self-fulfilling prophecy by leading them to act in a way that influenced the women to fulfill their stereotype that beautiful people are desirable people.

Behavioural confirmation also occurs as people interact with partners holding mistaken beliefs. People who are believed lonely behave less sociably (Rotenberg et al., 2002). Men who are believed sexist behave less favourably toward women (Pinel, 2002). Job interviewees who are believed to be warm behave more warmly.

behavioural confirmation a type of self-fulfilling prophecy whereby people's social expectations lead them to act in ways that cause others to confirm their expectations

Imagine yourself as one of the 60 young men or 60 young women in an experiment by Robert Ridge and Jeffrey Reber (2002). Each man is to interview one of the women to assess her suitability for a teaching assistant position. Before doing so, he is told either that she feels attracted to him (based on his answers to a biographical questionnaire) or not attracted. (Imagine being told that someone you were about to meet reported considerable interest in getting to know you and in dating you, or none whatsoever.) The result was behavioural confirmation: Applicants believed to feel an attraction exhibited more flirtatiousness (and without being aware of doing so). This process may be one of the roots of sexual harassment, Ridge and Reber believe. If a woman's behaviour seems to confirm a man's beliefs, he may then escalate his overtures until they become sufficiently overt for the woman to recognize and interpret them as inappropriate or harassing.

Expectations influence children's behaviour, too. After observing the amount of litter in three classrooms, Richard Miller and his colleagues (1975) had the teacher and others repeatedly tell one class that they should be neat and tidy. This persuasion increased the amount of litter placed in wastebaskets from 15 to 45 percent, but only temporarily. Another class, which also had been placing only 15 percent of its litter in wastebaskets, was repeatedly congratulated for being so neat and tidy. After eight days of hearing this, and still two weeks later, these children were fulfilling the expectation by putting more than 80 percent of their litter in wastebaskets. Repeatedly tell children they are hard-working and kind (rather than lazy and mean), and they may live up to their label.

These experiments help us understand how social beliefs, such as stereotypes about people with disabilities or about people of a particular race or sex, may be self-confirming. We help construct our own social realities. How others treat us reflects how we and others have treated them.

As with every social phenomenon, the tendency to confirm others' expectations has its limits. Expectations often predict behaviour simply because they are accurate (Jussim, 1993).

SUMMING UP: EXPECTATIONS OF OUR SOCIAL WORLDS

Our beliefs sometimes take on a life of their own. Usually, our beliefs about others have a basis in reality. But studies of experimenter bias and teacher expectations show that an erroneous belief that certain people are unusually capable (or incapable) can lead teachers and researchers to give those people special treatment. This may elicit superior (or inferior) performance and, therefore, seem to confirm an assumption that is actually false. Similarly, in everyday life we often get "behavioural confirmation" of what we expect. Told that someone we are about to meet is intelligent and attractive, we may come away impressed with just how intelligent and attractive he or she is.

CONCLUSIONS

Social cognition studies reveal that our information-processing powers are impressive for their efficiency and adaptiveness ("in apprehension how like a god!" exclaimed Shakespeare's Hamlet), yet vulnerable to predictable errors and misjudgments ("headpiece filled with straw," said T. S. Eliot). What practical lessons, and what insights into human nature, can we take home from this research?

We have reviewed some reasons why people sometimes come to believe what may be untrue. We cannot easily dismiss these experiments: Most of their participants were intelligent people, mostly students at leading universities. Moreover, these predictable distortions and biases occurred even when payment for right answers motivated people to think optimally. As one researcher concluded, the illusions "have a persistent quality not unlike that of perceptual illusions" (Slovic, 1972).

Research in cognitive social psychology thus mirrors the mixed review given humanity in literature, philosophy, and religion. Many research psychologists have spent lifetimes exploring the awesome capacities of the human mind. We are smart enough to have cracked our own genetic code, to have invented talking computers, to have sent people to the moon. Three cheers for human reason.

Well, two cheers—because the mind's premium on efficient judgment makes our intuition more vulnerable to misjudgment than we suspect. With remarkable ease, we form and sustain false beliefs. Led by our preconceptions, overconfident, persuaded by vivid anecdotes, perceiving correlations and control even where none may exist, we construct our social beliefs and then influence others to confirm them. "The naked intellect," observed novelist Madeline L'Engle, "is an extraordinarily inaccurate instrument."

But have these experiments just been intellectual tricks played on hapless participants, thus making them look worse than they are? Richard Nisbett and Lee Ross (1980) contend that, if anything, laboratory procedures overestimate our intuitive powers. The experiments usually present people with clear evidence and warn them that their reasoning ability is being tested. Seldom does life say to us: "Here is some evidence. Now put on your intellectual Sunday best and answer these questions."

"In creating these problems, we didn't set out to fool people. All our problems fooled us, too."

Amos Tversky (1985)

Often our everyday failings are inconsequential, but not always so. False impressions, interpretations, and beliefs can produce serious consequences. Even small biases can have profound social effects when we are making important social judgments: Why are so many people homeless? Unhappy? Homicidal? Does my friend love me or my money? Cognitive biases even creep into sophisticated scientific thinking. Apparently human nature has not changed in the 3000 years since the Psalmist noted that "no one can see his own errors."

Is this too cynical? Leonard Martin and Ralph Erber (2005) invite us to imagine that an intelligent being swooped down just for a moment and begged for information that would help it understand the human species. When you hand it this social psychology text, the alien says, "thank you" and zooms back off into space. After (I'd like to presume) resolving your remorse over giving up this book, how would you feel about having offered social psychology's analysis? Joachim Krueger and David Funder (2003a, 2003b) wouldn't feel too good. Social psychology's preoccupation with human foibles needs balancing with "a more positive view of human nature," they argue.

Fellow social psychologist Lee Jussim (2005) agrees, adding, "Despite the oft-demonstrated existence of a slew of logical flaws and systematic biases in lay judgment and social perception, such as the fundamental attribution error, false consensus, over-reliance on imperfect heuristics, self-serving biases, etc., people's perceptions of one another are surprisingly (though rarely perfectly) accurate." The elegant analyses of the imperfections of our thinking are themselves a tribute to human wisdom. (Were one to argue that all human thought is illusory, the assertion would be self-refuting, for it, too, would be but an illusion. It would be logically equivalent to contending "All generalizations are false, including this one.")

As medical science assumes that any given body organ serves a function, so behavioural scientists find it useful to assume that our modes of thought and behaviour are generally adaptive (Funder, 1987; Kruglanski & Ajzen, 1983; Swann, 1984). The rules of thought that produce false beliefs and striking deficiencies in our statistical intuition usually serve us well. Frequently, the errors are a by-product of our mental shortcuts that simplify the complex information we receive.

Nobel laureate psychologist Herbert Simon (1957) was among the modern researchers who first described the bounds of human reason. Simon contends that to cope with reality, we simplify it. Consider the complexity of a chess game: The number of possible games is greater than the number of particles in the universe. How do we cope? We adopt some simplifying rules of thumb—heuristics. These heuristics sometimes lead us to defeat. But they do enable us to make efficient snap judgments.

Illusory thinking can likewise spring from useful heuristics that aid our survival. The belief in our power to control events helps maintain hope and effort. If things are sometimes subject to control and sometimes not, we maximize our outcomes by positive thinking. Optimism pays dividends. We might even say that our beliefs are like scientific theories—sometimes in error yet useful as generalizations. As Susan Fiske (1992) says, "Thinking is for doing."

"The spirit of liberty is the spirit which is not too sure that it is right; the spirit of liberty is the spirit which seeks to understand the minds of other men and women; the spirit of liberty is the spirit which weighs their interests alongside its own without bias."

Learned Hand,
The Spirit of Liberty, 1952

As we constantly seek to improve our theories, might we not also work to reduce error in our social thinking? In school, math teachers teach, teach, and teach until the mind is finally trained to process numerical information accurately and automatically. We assume that such ability does not come naturally; otherwise, why bother with the years of training? Research psychologist Robyn Dawes (1980)—who is dismayed that "study after study has shown [that] people have very limited abilities to process information on a conscious level, particularly social information"—suggests that we should also teach, teach, and teach how to process social information.

Richard Nisbett and Lee Ross (1980) believe that education could indeed reduce our vulnerability to certain types of error. They propose that:

- We train people to recognize likely sources of error in their own social intuition.
- We set up statistics courses geared to everyday problems of logic and social judgment. Given such training, people do in fact reason better about everyday events (Lehman et al., 1988; Nisbett et al., 1987).
- We make such teaching more effective by richly illustrating it with concrete, vivid anecdotes and examples from everyday life.
- We teach memorable and useful slogans, such as: "It's an empirical question." Or "Which hat did you draw that sample out of?" Or "You can lie with statistics, but a well-chosen example does the job better."

SUMMING UP

Research on social beliefs and judgments reveals how we form and sustain beliefs that usually serve us well, but sometimes lead us astray. A balanced social psychology will therefore appreciate both the powers and perils of social thinking.

CHAPTER FOUR

Behaviour and Attitudes

How well do our attitudes predict our behaviour?
Are we all hypocrites?
When attitudes predict behaviour

When does our behaviour affect our attitudes?
Role playing
When saying becomes believing
The foot-in-the-door phenomenon
Evil and moral acts
Social movements

Why does our behaviour affect our attitudes?
Self-presentation: Impression management
Self-justification: Cognitive dissonance
Self-perception
Comparing the theories

Each year throughout the industrialized world, the tobacco industry kills some 2 million of its best customers (Peto et al., 1992). Given present trends, estimates a 1994 World Health

Attitudes and actions: Many sports events, which glorify health and physical prowess, are sponsored by manufacturers of products like cigarettes, which are dangerous to health.

Organization report, *half a billion* people alive today will be killed by tobacco. Although quick assisted suicide may be illegal, slow-motion suicide assisted by the tobacco industry is not.

People wonder: With the tobacco industry responsible for fatalities equal to 14 loaded and crashed jumbo jets a day (not including those in the expanding but hard to count developing world market), how do tobacco company executives live with themselves? At one of the world's two largest tobacco advertisers, upper-level executives—mostly intelligent, family-oriented, community-minded people—resent being called "mass murderers." They were less than pleased when one government official (Koop, 1997) called them "a sleazy bunch of people who misled us, deceived us and lied to us for three decades." Moreover, they defend smokers' right to choose. "Is it an addiction issue?" asks one vice-president. "I don't believe it. People do all sorts of things to express their individuality and to protest against society. And smoking is one of them, and not the worst" (Rosenblatt, 1994).

Social psychologists wonder: Do such statements reflect privately held attitudes? If this executive really thinks smoking is a comparatively healthy expression of individuality, how are such attitudes internalized? Or do his statements reflect social pressure to say things he doesn't believe?

When people question someone's attitude, they refer to beliefs and feelings related to a person or event and the resulting behaviour. Taken together, favourable or unfavourable evaluative reactions—whether exhibited in beliefs, feelings, or inclinations to act—define a person's **attitude** toward something (Olson & Zanna, 1993). Attitudes are an efficient way to size up the world. When we have to respond quickly to something, how we feel about it can guide how we react (Bassili & Roy, 1998; Breckler & Wiggins, 1989; Sanbonmatsu & Fazio, 1990). For example, a person who believes a particular ethnic group is lazy and aggressive may feel dislike for such people and therefore intend to act in a discriminatory manner. When assessing attitudes, we tap one of these three dimensions. You can remember them as the ABCs of attitudes: affect (feelings), behaviour (intention), and cognition (thoughts).

attitude
a favourable or unfavourable evaluative reaction toward something or someone, exhibited in one's beliefs, feelings, or intended behaviour

The study of attitudes is close to the heart of social psychology and historically was one of its first concerns. Researchers wondered: How much do our attitudes affect our actions?

HOW WELL DO OUR ATTITUDES PREDICT OUR BEHAVIOUR?

To what extent, and under what conditions, do attitudes drive our outward actions? Why were social psychologists at first surprised by a seemingly small connection between attitudes and actions?

What is the relationship between what we are (on the inside) and what we do (on the outside)? Philosophers, theologians, and educators have long speculated about the connection between thought and action, character and conduct, private word and public deed. The prevailing assumption, which underlies most teaching, counselling, and child rearing, has been that our private beliefs and feelings determine our public behaviour. So if we want to alter the way people act, we need to change their hearts and minds.

"The ancestor of every action is a thought."

Ralph Waldo Emerson, *Essays, First Series*, 1841

ARE WE ALL HYPOCRITES?

In the beginning, social psychologists agreed: To know people's attitudes is to predict their actions. But in 1964, Leon Festinger—judged by some to have been social psychology's most important contributor (Gerard, 1994)—concluded the evidence did *not* show that changing attitudes changes behaviour. Festinger believed the attitude–behaviour relation works the other way around, with our behaviour as the horse and our attitudes as the cart. As Robert Abelson (1972) put it, we are "very well trained and very good at finding reasons for what we do, but not very good at doing what we find reasons for."

A further blow to the supposed power of attitudes came in 1969, when social psychologist Allan Wicker reviewed several dozen research studies covering a wide variety of people, attitudes, and behaviours, and offered a shocking conclusion: People's expressed attitudes hardly predicted their varying behaviours. Student attitudes toward cheating bore little relation to the likelihood of their actually cheating. Attitudes toward the church were only modestly linked with church attendance on any given Sunday. Self-described racial attitudes provided little clue to behaviours in actual situations.

An example of the disjuncture between attitudes and actions is what Daniel Batson and his colleagues (1997, 1999) call "moral hypocrisy" (appearing moral without being so). Their

STORY BEHIND THE RESEARCH

James T. Olson
University of Western Ontario

I began studying attitudes while I was a graduate student working with Mark Zanna. Initially, I was most interested in the consequences of attitudes, rather than attitude formation or change. For example, Mark and I investigated the effects of attitudes on behaviour (attitude–behaviour consistency) and memory (selective learning). I then became interested in self-perception processes—the tendency for people to make inferences about their attitudes from their behaviours. More recently, my research has turned to issues concerning the nature and origins of attitudes, such as the functions of attitudes, the effects of attitude accessibility, the relation between attitudes and values, and the heritability of attitudes. I have been extremely fortunate to work with many outstanding graduate students at the University of Western Ontario, including Carolyn Hafer, Douglas Hazelwood, Gregory Maio, and Neal Roese, whose thinking has helped to shape my work.

studies presented their university with an appealing task (where the participant could earn raffle tickets toward a $30 prize) and a dull task with no positive consequences. The students had to assign themselves to one and a supposed second participant to the other. Only 1 in 20 believed that assigning the positive task to themselves was the most moral thing to do, yet 80 percent did so. In follow-up experiments on moral hypocrisy, participants were given coins they could flip privately if they wished. Even if they chose to flip, 90 percent assigned themselves to the positive task! Was this because they could specify the consequences of heads and tails after the coin toss? In yet another experiment, Batson put a sticker on each side of the coin, indicating what the flip outcome would signify. Still, 24 of 28 people who made the toss assigned themselves to the positive task. When morality and greed were put on a collision course, greed won.

If people don't play the same game that they talk, it's little wonder that attempts to change behaviour by changing attitudes often fail. Warnings about the dangers of smoking only minimally affect those who already smoke. Increasing public awareness of the desensitizing and brutalizing effects of a prolonged diet of television violence has stimulated many people to voice a desire for less violent programming—yet they still watch media murder as much as ever. Sex education programs have often influenced *attitudes* towards abstinence and condom use without affecting long-term abstinence and condom use *behaviours*. We are it seems at base all hypocrites.

"It may be desirable to abandon the attitude concept."

Allan Wicker, 1971

All in all, the developing picture of what controls behaviour emphasized external social influences, such as others' behaviour and expectations, and played down internal factors, such as attitudes and personality. The original thesis that attitudes determine actions was countered during the 1960s by the antithesis that attitudes determine virtually nothing.

Thesis. Antithesis. Is there a synthesis? The surprising finding that what people *say* often differs from what they *do* sent social psychologists scurrying to find out why. Surely, we reasoned, convictions and feelings *must* sometimes make a difference.

Indeed. In fact, what we are about to explain now seems so obvious that we wonder why most social psychologists (ourselves included) were not thinking this way before the early 1970s. We must remind ourselves that truth never seems obvious until it is known.

WHEN ATTITUDES PREDICT BEHAVIOUR

The reason—now obvious—why our behaviour and our expressed attitudes differ is because both are subject to other influences. Many other influences. One social psychologist counted 40 separate factors that complicate their relationship (Triandis, 1982; see also Kraus, 1995). But if we could just neutralize the other influences on behaviour—make all other things equal—might attitudes accurately predict behaviours?

When social influences on what we say are minimal

Unlike a physician measuring heart rate, social psychologists never get a direct reading on attitudes. Rather, we measure *expressed* attitudes. Like other behaviours, expressions are subject to outside influences. This was vividly demonstrated when politicians once overwhelmingly passed a salary increase for themselves in an off-the-record vote, then moments later overwhelmingly defeated the same bill on a roll-call vote. Fear of criticism had distorted the true sentiment on the roll-call vote. We sometimes say what we think others want to hear.

Today's social psychologists have some clever means at their disposal for subtly assessing attitudes. One is to measure facial muscle responses to statements (Cacioppo & Petty, 1981). Do the facial muscles reveal a microsmile or a microfrown?

Another method offers a *bogus pipeline* to the heart. It wires people to a fake lie detector, which the participants are told is real. The researchers show them how well it displays their (previously obtained) attitudes, and then ask them new questions. In one study, students admitted more prejudice when hooked up (Sigall & Page, 1971). No wonder people who are first persuaded that lie detectors work may then admit the truth—in which case, the lie detector worked! (Note the irony of deceiving people to elicit truthfulness.)

Yet another subtle attitude measure, the *implicit association test (IAT)*, uses reaction times to measure how quickly people associate concepts (Greenwald et al., 2002, 2003). One can, for example, measure implicit racial attitudes by assessing whether White people take longer to associate positive words with Black rather than White faces. Across 126 studies, implicit attitudes measured by the IAT have correlated, on average, a modest .24 with explicit self-reported attitudes (Hofmann et al., 2005).

When others influences on behaviour are minimal

On any occasion, it's not only our inner attitudes that guide us but also the situation we face. As Chapters 5 to 8 will illustrate again and again, social influences can be enormous—enormous enough to induce people to violate their deepest convictions. Before Jesus' crucifixion, his disciple Peter denied ever knowing him. Government aides may go along with actions they know are wrong. Prisoners of war may lie to placate their captors. So, would *averaging* many occasions enable us to detect more clearly the impact of our attitudes? Predicting people's behaviour is like predicting a baseball or cricket player's hitting. The outcome of any particular time at bat is nearly impossible to predict, because it is affected not only by the batter but also by what the pitcher throws and by chance factors. When we aggregate many times at bat, we neutralize these complicating factors. Knowing the players, we can predict their approximate batting *averages*.

To use a research example, people's general attitude toward religion poorly predicts whether they will go to worship next weekend (because the weather, the preacher, how one is feeling, and so forth also influence attendance). But religious attitudes predict quite well the total quantity of religious behaviours over time (Fishbein & Ajzen, 1974; Kahle & Berman, 1979). The findings define a *principle of aggregation:* The effects of an attitude on behaviour become more apparent when we look at a person's aggregate or average behaviour rather than at isolated acts.

"Do I contradict myself? Very well then I contradict myself. (I am large, I contain multitudes.)"

Walt Whitman, *Song of Myself*, 1855

When attitudes specific to behaviour are examined

Other conditions further improve the predictive accuracy of attitudes. As Icek Ajzen and Martin Fishbein (1977; Ajzen, 1982) point out, when the measured attitude is general—say, an attitude toward Asians—and the behaviour is very specific—say, a decision whether to help a particular Asian couple—we should not expect a close correspondence between words and actions. Indeed, report Fishbein and Ajzen, in 26 out of 27 such research studies, attitudes did not predict behaviour. But attitudes *did* predict behaviour in all 26 studies they could find in which the measured attitude was directly pertinent to the situation. Thus, attitudes toward the general concept of "health fitness" poorly predict specific exercise and dietary practices. Whether people jog is more likely to depend on their opinions about the costs and benefits of *jogging* (Figure 4–1).

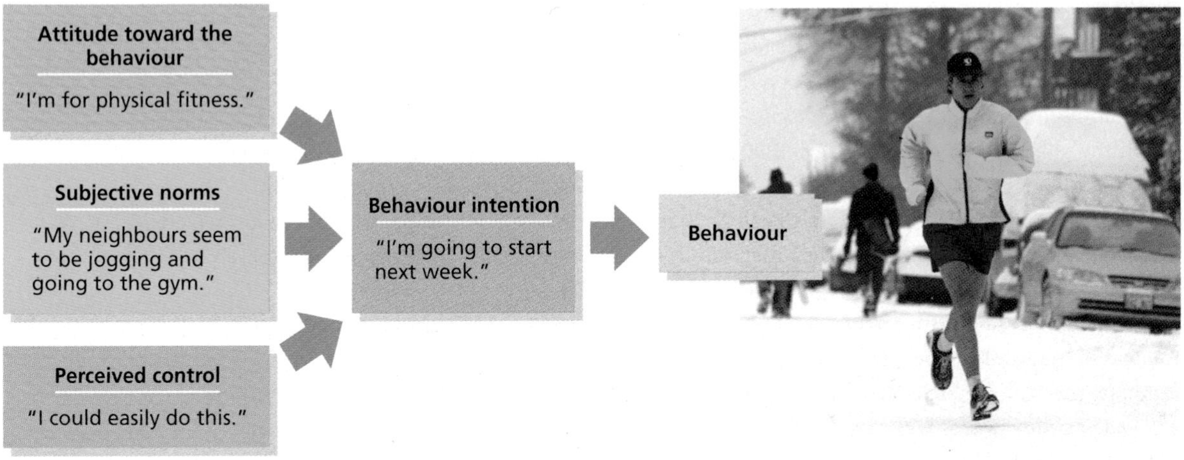

FIGURE 4–1

The theory of planned behaviour.

Içek Ajzen, working with Martin Fishbein, has shown that one's (a) attitudes, (b) perceived social norms, and (c) feelings of control together determine one's intentions, which guide behaviour.

Compared to their general attitudes toward a healthy lifestyle, people's specific attitudes regarding jogging predict their jogging behaviour much better.

Further studies—more than 700 in all—confirmed that specific, relevant attitudes *do* predict behaviour (Bassili, 1995; Six & Eckes, 1996; Wallace et al., 2004). For example, attitudes toward condoms strongly predict condom use (Albarracin et al., 2001). And attitudes toward recycling (but not general attitudes toward environmental issues) predict participation in recycling (Oskamp, 1991). To change health habits through persuasion, we had best alter people's attitudes toward specific practices (Olson & Zanna, 1981; Ajzen & Timko, 1986; Courneya, 1995).

So far we have seen two conditions under which attitudes will predict behaviour: (1) When we minimize other influences on our attitude statements and our behaviour, and (2) when the attitude is specifically relevant to the observed behaviour. There is a third condition: An attitude predicts behaviour better when it is potent.

When attitudes are powerful

Much of our behaviour is automatic. We act out familiar scripts, without reflecting on what we're doing. We respond to people we meet in the hall with an automatic "Hi." We answer the restaurant cashier's question, "How was your meal?" by saying, "Fine," even if we found it tasteless. Such mindless reaction is adaptive. It frees our minds to work on other things. As the philosopher Alfred North Whitehead argued, "Civilization advances by extending the number of operations which we can perform without thinking about them." But when we are on automatic pilot, our attitudes are dormant.

Bringing attitudes to mind

In novel situations our behaviour is less automatic; lacking a script, we think before we act. If they are prompted to think about their attitudes before acting, will people be truer to themselves? Mark Snyder and William Swann (1976) wanted to find out. So two weeks after 120 of their students indicated their attitudes toward affirmative-action employment policies, Snyder and Swann invited them to act as jurors in a sex-discrimination court case. Only if they first induced the students to remember their attitudes—by giving them "a few minutes to organize your thoughts and views on the affirmative-action issue"—did attitudes predict verdicts.

Similarly, people who take a few moments to review their past behaviour express attitudes that better predict their future behaviour (Zanna et al., 1981). Our attitudes guide our behaviour if we think about them.

Self-conscious people usually are in touch with their attitudes (Miller & Grush, 1986). This suggests another way to induce people to focus on their inner convictions: Make them self-conscious, perhaps by having them act in front of a mirror (Carver & Scheier, 1981). Maybe you can recall suddenly being acutely aware of yourself upon entering a room with a large mirror. Making people self-aware in this way promotes consistency between words and deeds (Gibbons, 1978; Froming et al., 1982).

"Thinking is easy, acting difficult, and to put one's thoughts into action, the most difficult thing in the world."

German poet Goethe, 1749–1832

Edward Diener and Mark Wallbom (1976) noted that nearly all university students *say* that cheating is morally wrong. But will they follow the advice of Shakespeare's Polonius, "To thine own self be true"? Diener and Wallbom set students to work on an anagram-solving task (said to predict IQ) and told them to stop when a bell in the room sounded. Left alone, 71 percent cheated by working past the bell. Among students made self-aware—by working in front of a mirror while hearing their tape-recorded voices—only 7 percent cheated. It makes one wonder: Would eye-level mirrors in stores make people more conscious of their attitudes about stealing?

Remember Batson's studies of moral hypocrisy described on pp. 113–114? In a later experiment, Batson and his colleagues (1999) found that mirrors did bring behaviour into line with espoused moral attitudes. When people flipped a coin while facing a mirror, the coin flip became scrupulously fair. Exactly half of the self-conscious participants assigned the other person to the positive task.

"Without doubt it is a delightful harmony when doing and saying go together."

Montaigne, *Essays*, 1588

The power of attitudes forged through experience

Finally, we acquire attitudes in a manner that makes them sometimes potent, sometimes not. An extensive series of experiments by Russell Fazio and Mark Zanna (1981) shows that when attitudes arise from experience, they are far more likely to endure and to guide actions. They conducted one of their studies with the unwitting help of their university. A housing shortage forced the university to assign some first-year students to several weeks on cots in dormitory lounges while others basked in the relative luxury of permanent rooms.

When questioned by Dennis Regan and Fazio (1977), students in both groups had equally negative attitudes about the housing situation and how the administration was dealing with it. Given opportunities to act on their attitudes—to sign a petition and solicit other signatures, to join a committee to investigate the situation, to write a letter—only those whose attitudes grew from direct experience with the temporary housing acted. Moreover, compared to attitudes formed passively, those forged in the fire of experience are more thoughtful, more certain, more stable, more resistant to attack, more accessible, and more emotionally charged (Millar & Millar, 1996; Sherman et al., 1983; Watts, 1967; Wu & Shaffer, 1987). And when the emotional and belief components of an attitude are consistent, the attitude moves behaviour—as strong attitudes do (Chaiken et al., 1995).

To summarize, our attitudes predict our actions if

- Other influences are minimized
- The attitude is specific to the action
- The attitude is potent—because something reminds us of it, or because we gained it in a manner that makes it strong

"It is easier to preach virtue than to practice it."

La Rochefoucauld, *Maxims*, 1665

SUMMING UP: HOW WELL DO OUR ATTITUDES PREDICT OUR BEHAVIOUR?

How do our inner attitudes relate to our external actions? Social psychologists agree that attitudes and actions feed each other. Popular wisdom stresses the impact of attitudes on action. Surprisingly, attitudes—usually assessed as feelings toward some object or person—are often poor predictors of actions. Moreover, changing people's attitudes typically fails to produce much change in their behaviour. These findings sent social psychologists scurrying to find out why we so often fail to play the game we talk. The answer: Our expressions of attitudes and our behaviours are each subject to many influences.

Our attitudes *will* predict our behaviour (1) if these "other influences" are minimized, (2) if the attitude corresponds very closely to the predicted behaviour (as in voting studies), and (3) if the attitude is potent (because something reminds us of it, or because we acquired it by direct experience). Thus there *is* a connection between what we think and feel and what we do, but in many situations that connection is weaker than we think.

WHEN DOES OUR BEHAVIOUR AFFECT OUR ATTITUDES?

If social psychology has taught us anything during the last 25 years, it is that we are likely not only to think ourselves into a way of acting but also to act ourselves into a way of thinking. What lines of evidence support this assertion?

Now we turn to the more startling idea that behaviour determines attitudes. It's true that we sometimes stand up for what we believe, but it's also true that we come to believe in what we stand up for. Social-psychological theories inspired much of the research that underlies this conclusion. Instead of beginning with these theories, we think it more interesting to first present the wide-ranging evidence that behaviour affects attitudes. This way you can play theorist as you read. Speculate *why* actions affect attitudes, and then compare your ideas with the explanations proposed by social psychologists.

> "Thought is the child of Action."
>
> Benjamin Disraeli, *Vivian Grey*, 1826

Consider the following incidents, each based on actual happenings:

- Sarah is hypnotized and told to take off her shoes when a book drops on the floor. Fifteen minutes later a book drops, and Sarah quietly slips out of her loafers. "Sarah," asks the hypnotist, "why did you take off your shoes?" "Well . . . my feet are hot and tired," Sarah replies. "It has been a long day." The act produces the idea.
- George has electrodes temporarily implanted in the brain region that controls his head movements. When neurosurgeon José Delgado (1973) stimulates the electrode by remote control, George always turns his head. Unaware of the remote stimulation, he offers a reasonable explanation for it: "I'm looking for my slipper." "I heard a noise." "I'm restless." "I was looking under the bed."
- Carol's severe seizures were relieved by surgically separating her two brain hemispheres. Now, in an experiment, psychologist Michael Gazzaniga (1985) flashes a picture of a nude woman to the left half of Carol's field of vision and thus to her

nonverbal right brain hemisphere. A sheepish smile spreads over her face, and she begins chuckling. Asked why, she invents—and apparently believes—a plausible explanation: "Oh—that funny machine." Frank, another split-brain patient, has the word "smile" flashed to his nonverbal right hemisphere. He obliges and forces a smile. Asked why, he explains, "This experiment is very funny."

The mental after-effects of our behaviour indeed appear in a rich variety of social situations: *Our attitudes follow our behaviour.* The following examples will illustrate the power of self-persuasion.

role
a set of norms that define how people in a given social position ought to behave

"No man, for any considerable period, can wear one face to himself and another to the multitude without finally getting bewildered as to which may be true."

Nathaniel Hawthorne, 1850

ROLE PLAYING

The word **role** is borrowed from the theatre and, as in the theatre, refers to *actions expected of those who occupy a particular social position.* When stepping into a new social role, we must perform its actions, even if we feel phony. But our unease seldom lasts.

Think of a time when you stepped into some new role—perhaps your first days on a job, or at university, or in a sorority or fraternity. That first week on campus, for example, you may have been supersensitive to your new social situation and tried valiantly to act appropriately and root out your high-school behaviour. At such times we feel self-conscious. We observe our new speech and actions because they aren't natural to us. Then one day an amazing thing happens: We notice that our sorority enthusiasm or our pseudo-intellectual talk no longer feels forced. The role has begun to fit as comfortably as our old jeans and T-shirt.

In one study, university men volunteered to spend time in a simulated prison constructed in the psychology department by Philip Zimbardo (1971). Zimbardo, like so many others, wondered whether prison brutality is a product of evil prisoners and malicious guards or whether the institutional roles of guard and prisoner would embitter and harden even compassionate people. Do the people make the place violent? Or does the place make the people violent?

By a flip of a coin, he designated some students as guards. He gave them uniforms, billy clubs, and whistles and instructed them to enforce the rules. The other half, the prisoners, were locked in cells and made to wear humiliating outfits. After a jovial first day of "playing" their roles, the guards and prisoners, and even the experimenters, got caught up in the situation. The guards began to disparage the prisoners, and some devised cruel and degrading routines. The prisoners broke down, rebelled, or became apathetic. There developed, reported Zimbardo (1972), a "growing confusion between reality and illusion, between role-playing and self-identity. . . . This prison which we had created . . . was absorbing us as creatures of its own reality." Observing the emerging social pathology, Zimbardo was forced to call off the planned two-week simulation after only six days.

Images from the Abu Ghraib prison in Iraq bore an eerie similarity to the Stanford prison experiment. U.S. soldiers acting as prison guards engaged in brutal and demeaning treatment of their Iraqi prisoners. Most soldiers sat by and watched

After the degradation of Iraqi prisoners by some U.S. military personnel, Philip Zimbardo (2004a, 2004b) noted "direct and sad parallels between similar behaviour of the 'guards' in the Stanford Prison Experiment." Such behaviour, he contends, is attributable to a toxic situation that can make good people into perpetrators of evil. "It's not that we put bad apples in a good barrel. We put good apples in a bad barrel. The barrel corrupts anything that it touches."

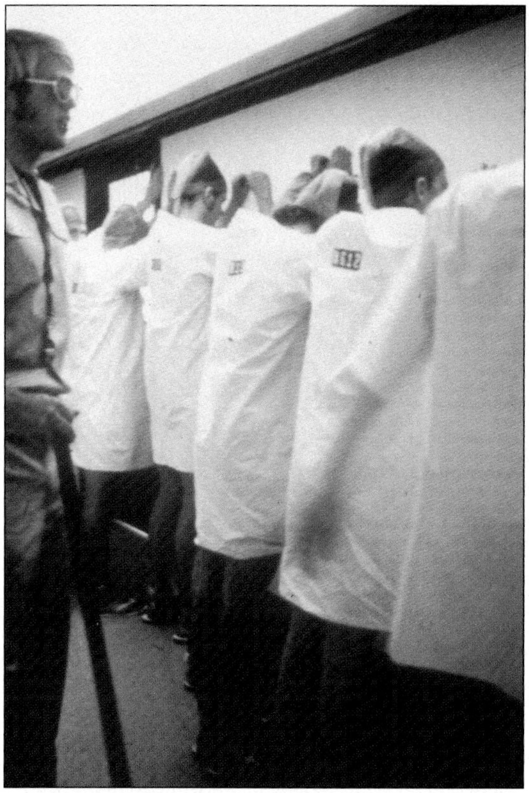

Guards and prisoners in a prison simulation quickly absorbed the roles they played.

the atrocities occur without raising a warning or trying to stop them. This reaction too resembled the Stanford prison experiment. The role of prison guard brought out hostility in some, but an even more common result of the role seems to be that it prevents intervening even to help those who are clearly in need.

The deeper lesson of role-playing studies concerns how what is unreal (an artificial role) can evolve into what is real. In a new career, as teacher, soldier, or businessperson, we act a role that shapes our attitudes.

Gender roles

One prominent role given to us by our society is our gender. Early on we are socialized into gender roles. Gender socialization, it has been said, gives girls "roots" and boys "wings." In Caldecott Award children's books over the last half-century, girls have four times more often than boys been shown using household objects (such as broom, sewing needle, or pots and pans), and boys have five times more often than girls been shown using production objects (such as pitchfork, plough, or gun) (Crabb & Bielawski, 1994). The adult result: "Everywhere," reports the United Nations (1991), women do most household work. And "everywhere, cooking and dishwashing are the least shared household chores." Such behaviour expectations for males and females define **gender roles**.

In an experiment with undergraduate women, Mark Zanna and Susan Pack (1975) showed the impact of gender role expectations. The women answered a questionnaire on which they described themselves to a tall, unattached, senior man they expected to meet. Those led to believe his ideal woman was home-oriented and deferential to her husband presented themselves as more traditionally feminine than did women expecting to meet a man who liked strong, ambitious women. Moreover, given a problem-solving test, those expecting to meet the nonsexist man behaved more intelligently: They solved 18 percent more problems than those expecting to meet the man with the traditional views. This adapting of themselves to fit the man's image was much less pronounced if the man was less desirable—a short, already attached freshman. In a companion experiment by Dean Morier and Cara Seroy (1994), men similarly adapted their self-presentations to meet desirable women's gender role expectations. Clearly our gender roles can shape our actions.

"My whole personality changed during the time I was doing the part."

Ian Charleson on his role as serene and devout Olympic hero Eric Liddell in *Chariots of Fire*

gender role
a set of behaviour expectations (norms) for males and females

WHEN SAYING BECOMES BELIEVING

People often adapt what they say to please their listeners. They are quicker to tell people good news than bad, and they adjust their message toward the listener's position (Manis et al., 1974; Tesser et al., 1972; Tetlock, 1983). When induced to give spoken or written support to something they doubt, people will often feel bad about the deceit. Nevertheless, they begin to believe what they are saying—*provided* they weren't bribed or coerced into doing so. When there is

"That was a fine report, Barbara. But since the sexes speak different languages, I probably didn't understand a word of it."

Do you ever present one self to members of your own sex and a different self to members of the other sex?

Canadian husbands do 67 percent of the maintenance and repairs around the home, but only 27 percent of the meal preparation and cleanup, and only 23 percent of the housecleaning.

Statistics Canada, 1998

no compelling external explanation for one's words, saying becomes believing (Klaas, 1978).

Tory Higgins and his colleagues (Higgins & Rholes, 1978; Higgins & McCann, 1984) illustrated how saying becomes believing. They had university students read a personality description of someone and then summarize it for someone else who was believed either to like or to dislike this person. The students wrote a more

STORY BEHIND THE RESEARCH

Mark Zanna
University of Waterloo

When I began my career at Princeton in 1970, the first group of female undergraduates had just enrolled at this formerly all-male bastion. These pioneers were incredibly bright and very ambitious. Indeed, the majority intended to become doctors, lawyers, or professors! It was Susan Pack's intuition that, despite the great capabilities and high achievement motivation of her female peers, they still "acted dumb" when confronted with the typical attractive, though chauvinistic, Princeton male.

Susan's undergraduate honours thesis, designed to test this notion, demonstrated that Princeton females "acted dumb" or "acted smart" depending, in part, on whether they believed an attractive Princeton male held chauvinistic or liberated attitudes about women. I wonder: Would these results hold today at Princeton? At other colleges? Would males, too, act to fulfill the gender stereotypes of attractive females?

positive description when the recipient liked the person, and, having said positive things, then liked the person more themselves. Asked to recall what they had read, they remembered the description as being more positive than it was. In short, it seems that we are prone to adjust our messages to our listeners, and having done so, to believe the altered message.

THE FOOT-IN-THE-DOOR PHENOMENON

Most of us can recall times when, after agreeing to help out with a project or an organization, we ended up more involved than we ever intended, vowing that in the future we would say no to such requests. How does this happen? Experiments suggest that if you want people to do a big favour for you, one technique is to get them to do a small favour first. In the best-known demonstration of this **foot-in-the-door phenomenon**, researchers posing as safety-drive volunteers asked people to permit the installation of a huge, poorly lettered "Drive Carefully" sign in their front yards. Only 17 percent consented. Others were first approached with a small request: Would they display a 7.5-centimetre "Be a safe driver" window sign? Nearly all readily agreed. When approached two weeks later to allow the large, ugly sign in their front yards, 76 percent consented (Freedman & Fraser, 1966). One project helper who went from house to house later recalled that, not knowing who had been previously visited, "I was simply stunned at how easy it was to convince some people and how impossible to convince others" (Ornstein, 1991).

foot-in-the-door phenomenon
the tendency for people who have first agreed to a small request to comply later with a larger request

Other researchers have confirmed the foot-in-the-door phenomenon with altruistic behaviours.

- Patricia Pliner and her collaborators (1974) found 46 percent of Toronto suburbanites willing to give to the Cancer Society when approached directly. Others, asked a day ahead to wear a lapel pin publicizing the drive (which all agreed to do), were nearly twice as likely to donate.
- Angela Lipsitz and others (1989) report that ending blood-drive reminder calls with "We'll count on seeing you then, OK? [pause for response]" increased the show-up rate from 62 to 81 percent.
- In Internet chat rooms, Paul Markey and his colleagues (2002) requested help ("I can't get my email to work. Is there any way I can get you to send me an email?). Help increased—from 2 to 16 percent—by including a smaller prior request ("I am new to this whole computer thing. Is there any way you can tell me how to look at someone's profile?).
- Nicols Gueguen and Celine Jacob (2001) tripled the rate of French Internet users contributing to a child land-mine victims organization (from 1.6 to 4.9 percent) by first inviting them to sign a petition against land mines.

low-ball technique
a tactic for getting people to agree to something. People who agree to an initial request will often still comply when the requester ups the ante. People who receive only the costly request are less likely to comply with it.

Note that in these experiments the initial compliance—signing a petition, wearing a lapel pin, stating one's intention—was voluntary. We will see again and again that when people commit themselves to public behaviours *and* perceive these acts to be their own doing, they come to believe more strongly in what they have done.

"You will easily find folk to do favors if you cultivate those who have done them."

Publilius Syrus, 42 B.C.

Robert Cialdini [chal-DEE-nee] and his collaborators (1978) demonstrated a variation of the foot-in-the-door phenomenon by experimenting with the **low-ball technique**, a tactic reportedly used by some car dealers. After the customer agrees to buy a new car because of its great price and begins completing the sales forms,

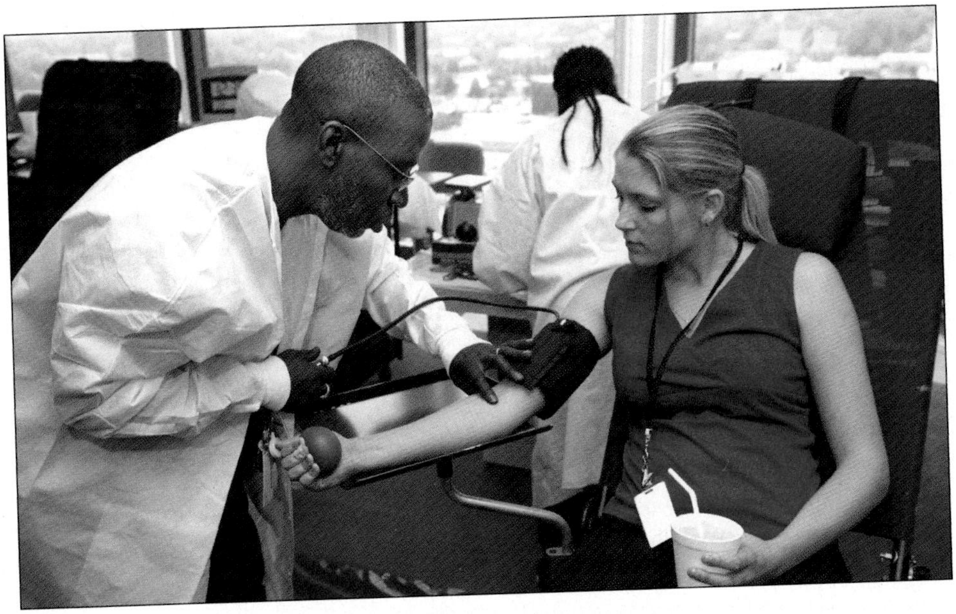

A foot in the door. To get people to donate blood or money, it often helps to first elicit a smaller commitment to the same cause.

the salesperson removes the price advantage by charging for options the customer thought were included or by checking with a boss who disallows the deal because, "We'd be losing money." Folklore has it that more customers now stick with the higher-priced purchase than would have agreed to it at the outset.

Cialdini and his collaborators found that this technique indeed works. When they invited introductory psychology students to participate in an experiment at 7:00 A.M., only 24 percent showed up. But if the students first agreed to participate without knowing the time and only then were asked to participate at 7:00 A.M., 53 percent came.

Marketing researchers and salespeople have found that the principle works even when we are aware of a profit motive (Cialdini, 1988). A harmless initial commitment—returning a card for more information and a gift, agreeing to listen to an investment possibility—often moves us toward a larger commitment. Salespeople may exploit the power of small commitments when trying to bind people to purchase agreements. Many places now have laws that allow customers of door-to-door salespeople a few days to think over their purchases and cancel. To combat the effect of these laws, many companies use what the sales-training program of one encyclopedia

The low-ball technique. The *Born Loser* reprinted by permission of Newspaper Enterprise Association, Inc.

company calls "a very important psychological aid in preventing customers from backing out of their contracts" (Cialdini, 1988, p. 78). They simply have the customer, rather than the salesperson, fill out the agreement. Having written it themselves, people usually live up to their commitment.

The foot-in-the-door phenomenon is well worth learning about. Someone trying to seduce us—financially, politically, or sexually—usually will try to create a momentum of compliance. Before agreeing to a small request, think about what may follow.

EVIL AND MORAL ACTS

The attitudes-follow-behaviour principle works with more immoral acts as well. Evil sometimes results from gradually escalating commitments. A trifling evil act can make a worse act easier. Evil acts gnaw at the actor's moral sensitivity. To paraphrase La Rochefoucauld's *Maxims* (1665), it is not as difficult to find a person who has never succumbed to a given temptation as to find a person who has succumbed only once. After telling a "white lie" and thinking, "Well, that wasn't so bad," the person may go on to tell a bigger lie.

"Our self-definitions are not constructed in our heads; they are forged by our deeds."

Robert McAfee Brown, *Creative Dislocation—The Movement of Grace*, 1980

Cruel acts can even corrode the consciences of those who perform them. Harming an innocent victim—by uttering hurtful comments or delivering electric shocks—typically leads aggressors to disparage their victims, thus helping them justify their behaviour (Berscheid et al., 1968; Davis & Jones, 1960; Glass, 1964). We tend not only to hurt those we dislike but to dislike those we hurt. In studies establishing this, people would justify an action especially when coaxed, not coerced, into it. When we voluntarily agree to do a deed, we take more responsibility for it.

The phenomenon appears in wartime, as soldiers denigrate their enemies with dehumanizing nicknames. It also appears in peacetime. A group that holds another in slavery will likely come to perceive the slaves as having traits that justify their oppression. Actions and

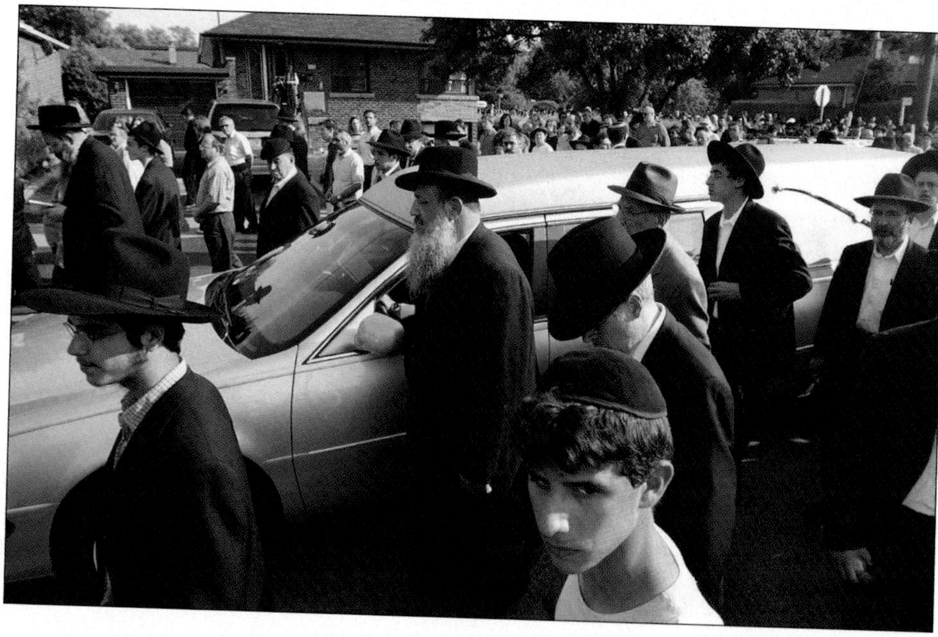

Mourners walk with the hearse carrying murder victim David Rosenzweig following his funeral service at Toronto in July 2002. Rosenzweig was the victim of an alleged hate crime. Acts like this can compound fear or even breed more prejudice.

attitudes feed one another, sometimes to the point of moral numbness. The more one harms another and adjusts one's attitudes, the easier harm-doing becomes. Conscience mutates.

Evil acts shape the self, but, thankfully, so do moral acts. Character, it is said, is reflected in what we do when we think no one is looking. Researchers have tested character by giving children temptations when it seems no one is watching. Consider what happens when children resist the temptation. They internalize the conscientious act *if* the deterrent is strong enough to elicit the desired *behaviour* yet mild enough to leave them with a sense of *choice*. In a dramatic experiment, Jonathan Freedman (1965) introduced elementary school children to an enticing battery-controlled robot, instructing them not to play with it while he was out of the room. Freedman used a severe threat with half the children and a mild threat with the others. Both were sufficient to deter the children.

Several weeks later a different researcher, with no apparent relation to the earlier events, left each child to play in the same room with the same toys. Of the 18 children who had been given the severe threat, 14 now freely played with the robot; but two-thirds of those who had been given the mild deterrent still resisted playing with it. Having earlier made a conscious choice *not* to play with the toy, the mildly deterred children apparently internalized their decision. This new attitude controlled their subsequent action. Thus, moral action, especially when chosen rather than coerced, affects moral thinking.

If moral action feeds moral attitudes, can laws and rules that require moral conduct lead to genuine moral beliefs? Elliot Aronson (1992) has argued that such change is possible. His argument runs like this: If we wait for the heart to change—through preaching and teaching—we will wait a long time. But if we legislate moral action, we can, under the right conditions, indirectly affect heartfelt attitudes.

The idea runs counter to the presumption that "you can't legislate morality." Yet attitude change has, in fact, followed changes in the laws. Consider some of the following:

- In the 1980s and 1990s many governments began requiring the use of seat belts by all people riding in automobiles. Initially, these laws were seen as burdensome and were opposed by many. But over time seat belt use has risen dramatically, and now most people in these jurisdictions favour mandatory seat belt laws.
- In 1954 the Supreme Court of the United States ruled that schools segregated by race were inherently unfair and that such schools were required to desegregate. Since that decision the percentage of Whites in the U.S. favouring integrated schools has more than doubled and now includes nearly everyone.
- In the 1970s many National Hockey League players did not wear helmets. Older players saw this as a measure of toughness. But in the 1980s, almost all bantam and junior hockey leagues required players to wear helmets. Now all players in the NHL wear helmets and see them as an important safety measure. Having grown up with helmets, they now believe they are useful.

"We do not love people so much for the good they have done us, as for the good we have done them."

Leo Tolstoy, *War and Peace*, 1867–1869

Do laws always lead to the adoption of consistent attitudes? Almost certainly not. There are times when it is true that "you can't legislate morality." But research in social psychology confirms that under the right conditions people's attitudes follow their behaviours even when these behaviours are required. For example, experiments demonstrate that positive behaviour toward someone fosters liking for that person.

Doing a favour for an experimenter or another subject, or tutoring a student, usually increases liking of the person helped (Blanchard & Cook, 1976). It is a lesson worth remembering: If you wish to love someone more, act as if you do.

SOCIAL MOVEMENTS

We have now seen that a society's laws and, therefore, its behaviour, can have a strong influence on people's behaviour. And a danger lies in the possibility of employing the same idea for political socialization on a mass scale. For many Germans during the 1930s, participation in Nazi rallies, wearing uniforms, demonstrating, and especially the public greeting "Heil Hitler" established a profound inconsistency between behaviour and belief. Historian Richard Grunberger (1971) reports that for those who had their doubts about Hitler, "The 'German greeting' was a powerful conditioning device. Having once decided to intone it as an outward token of conformity, many experienced schizophrenic discomfort at the contradiction between their words and their feelings. Prevented from saying what they believed, they tried to establish their psychic equilibrium by consciously making themselves believe what they said" (p. 27).

The practice is not limited to totalitarian regimes. Political rituals—the daily flag salute by schoolchildren, singing the national anthem—use public conformity to build a private belief in patriotism. Steven Spencer was amazed at the strong sense of being a Canadian that his son developed in junior kindergarten. Before school his son had virtually no identity as a Canadian, but after three weeks of singing *O Canada* on Mondays he was Canadian through and through. Observers noted how the civil rights marches of the 1960s strengthened the demonstrators' commitments. Their actions expressed an idea whose time had come and drove that idea more deeply into their hearts. The 1980s' move toward gender-inclusive language has similarly strengthened inclusive attitudes.

"One does what one is; one becomes what one does."

Robert Musil, *Kleine Prosa*, 1930

Many people assume that most social indoctrination comes through *brainwashing,* a term coined to describe what happened to prisoners of war (POWs) during the 1950s' Korean War. Actually, the Chinese "thought-control" program, developed to re-educate the Chinese populace into communism, was not nearly as irresistible as this term suggests. But the results still were disconcerting. Hundreds of prisoners cooperated

Celebrating Canada Day: Patriotic actions strengthen patriotic attitudes.

with their captors. Twenty-one chose to remain after being granted permission to return to the United States. And many of those who did return came home believing "although communism won't work in America, I think it's a good thing for Asia" (Segal, 1954).

Edgar Schein (1956) interviewed many of the POWs during their journey home and reported that the captors' methods included a gradual escalation of demands. The Chinese always started with trivial requests and gradually worked up to more significant ones. "Thus after a prisoner had once been 'trained' to speak or write out trivia, statements on more important issues were demanded." Moreover, they always expected active participation, be it just copying something or participating in group discussions, writing self-criticism, or uttering public confessions. Once a prisoner had spoken or written a statement, he felt an inner need to make his beliefs consistent with his acts. This often drove prisoners to persuade themselves of what they had done. The "start-small-and-build" tactic was an effective application of the foot-in-the-door technique, as it continues to be today in the socialization of terrorists and torturers (Chapter 6).

Now let me ask you, before reading further, to play theorist. Ask yourself: Why in these studies and real-life examples did attitudes follow behaviour? Why might playing a role or making a speech influence how *you* feel about something?

> *"You can use small commitments to manipulate a person's self-image; you can use them to turn citizens into 'public servants,' prospects into 'customers,' prisoners into 'collaborators.'"*
>
> Robert Cialdini, *Influence*, 1988

SUMMING UP: WHEN DOES OUR BEHAVIOUR AFFECT OUR ATTITUDES?

The attitude–action relation also works in the reverse direction: We are likely not only to think ourselves into action but also to act ourselves into a way of thinking. When we act, we amplify the idea underlying what we have done, especially when we feel responsible for it. Many streams of evidence converge on this principle. The actions prescribed by social roles mould the attitudes of the role players.

Similarly, what we say or write can strongly influence attitudes that we subsequently hold. Research on the foot-in-the-door phenomenon reveals that committing a small act later makes people more willing to do a larger one. Actions also affect our moral attitudes: That which we have done we tend to justify as right.

In addition, our political behaviours help shape our social consciousness: We not only stand up for what we believe, we also believe in what we have stood up for. Political and social movement may legislate behaviour to lead to attitude change on a mass scale.

WHY DOES OUR BEHAVIOUR AFFECT OUR ATTITUDES?

What theories help explain the attitudes-follow-behaviour phenomenon? How does the contest between these competing ideas illustrate the process of scientific explanation?

We have seen that several streams of evidence merge to form a river: the effect of actions on attitudes. Do these observations contain any clues to *why* action affects attitude? Social psychology's detectives suspect three possible sources. *Self-presentation theory* assumes that

Self-presentation theory assumes that our behaviour aims to create desired impressions.

for strategic reasons we express attitudes that make us appear consistent. *Cognitive dissonance theory* assumes that to reduce discomfort, we *justify* our actions to ourselves. *Self-perception theory* assumes that our actions are *self-revealing* (when uncertain about our feelings or beliefs, we look to our behaviour, much as anyone else would). Let's examine each.

SELF-PRESENTATION: IMPRESSION MANAGEMENT

The first explanation began as a simple idea, which you may recall from Chapter 2. Who among us does not care what people think? We spend countless dollars on clothes, diets, cosmetics, even plastic surgery—all because we worry about what others think of us. To make a good impression is often to gain social and material rewards, to feel better about ourselves, even to become more secure in our social identities (Leary, 1994).

No one wants to look foolishly inconsistent. To avoid seeming so, we express attitudes that match our actions. To *appear* consistent, we may pretend attitudes we don't really believe in. Even if it means displaying a little insincerity or hypocrisy, it can pay to manage the impression one is making. Or so *self-presentation theory* suggests.

Does our eagerness to *appear* consistent explain why expressed attitudes shift toward consistency with behaviour? To some extent, yes—people exhibit a much smaller attitude change when a bogus pipeline inhibits trying to make a good impression (Paulhus, 1982; Tedeschi et al., 1987).

But there is more to the attitude changes we have reviewed than self-presentation, for people express their changed attitudes even to someone who doesn't know how they have behaved. Two other theories explain why people sometimes internalize their self-presentations as genuine attitude changes.

cognitive dissonance
tension that arises when one is simultaneously aware of two inconsistent cognitions. For example, dissonance may occur when we realize that we have, with little justification, acted contrary to our attitudes or made a decision favouring one alternative despite reasons favouring another.

SELF-JUSTIFICATION: COGNITIVE DISSONANCE

One theory is that our attitudes change because we are motivated to maintain consistency among our cognitions. This is the implication of Leon Festinger's (1957) **cognitive dissonance theory**. The theory is simple, but its range of application is enormous. It assumes *we feel tension ("dissonance") when two simultaneously accessible thoughts or beliefs ("cognitions") are psychologically inconsistent*—as when we decide to say or do something we have mixed feelings about.

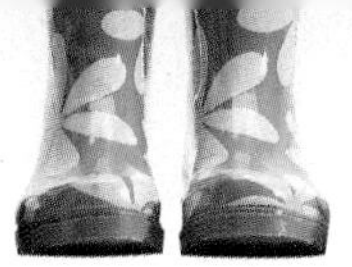

Festinger argued that to reduce this unpleasant arousal, we often adjust our thinking. This simple idea, and some surprising predictions derived from it, have spawned more than 2000 studies (Cooper, 1999).

Dissonance theory pertains mostly to discrepancies between behaviour and attitudes. We are aware of both. Thus, if we sense some inconsistency, perhaps some hypocrisy, we feel pressure for change. That helps explain why, in a British survey, half of cigarette smokers therefore disagreed with the near-consensus among nonsmokers that smoking is "really as dangerous as people say" (Eiser et al., 1979) and why the perception of risk among those who have quit declines after relapsing (Gibbons et al., 1997).

So if we can persuade others to adopt a *new* attitude, their behaviour should change accordingly; that's common sense. Or if we can induce people to behave differently, their attitude should change (that's the self-persuasion effect we have been reviewing). But cognitive dissonance theory offers several surprising predictions. See if you can anticipate them.

Insufficient justification

Imagine you are a subject in a famous experiment staged by the creative Festinger and his student, J. Merrill Carlsmith (1959). For an hour, you are required to perform dull tasks, such as turning wooden knobs again and again. After you finish, the experimenter (Carlsmith) explains that the study concerns how expectations affect performance. The next subject, waiting outside, must be led to expect an interesting experiment. The seemingly distraught experimenter, whom Festinger had spent hours coaching until he became extremely convincing, explains that the assistant who usually creates this expectation couldn't make this session. Wringing his hands, he pleads, "Could you fill in and do this?"

"A foolish consistency is the hobgoblin of little minds."

Ralph Waldo Emerson, "Self-Reliance," 1841

It's for science and you are being paid, so you agree to tell the next subject (who is actually the experimenter's real assistant) what a delightful experience you have just had. "Really?" responds the supposed subject. "A friend of mine was in this experiment a week ago, and she said it was boring." "Oh, no," you respond, "it's really very interesting. You get good exercise while turning some knobs. I'm sure you'll enjoy it." Finally, someone else who is studying how people react to experiments has you complete a questionnaire that asks how much you actually enjoyed your knob-turning experience.

Now for the prediction: Under which condition are you most likely to believe your little lie and say the experiment was indeed interesting? When paid $1 for doing so, as some of the

STORY BEHIND THE RESEARCH

Following a 1934 earthquake in India, there were rumours outside the disaster zone of worse disasters to follow. It occurred to me that these rumours might be "anxiety-justifying"—cognitions that would justify their lingering fears. From that germ of an idea, I developed my theory of dissonance reduction—making your view of the world fit with how you feel or what you've done.

Leon Festinger 1920–1989

subjects were? Or when paid a then-generous $20, as others were? Contrary to the common notion that big rewards produce big effects, Festinger and Carlsmith made an outrageous prediction: Those paid just $1 (hardly sufficient justification for a lie) would be most likely to adjust their attitudes to their actions. Having **insufficient justification** for their action, they would experience more discomfort (dissonance) and thus be more motivated to believe in what they had done. Those paid $20 had sufficient justification for what they did and hence should have experienced less dissonance. As Figure 4–2 shows, the results fit this intriguing prediction.*

insufficient justification effect
reduction of dissonance by internally justifying one's behaviour when external justification is "insufficient"

In dozens of later experiments, the attitudes-follow-behaviour effect was strongest when people felt some *choice* and when their action had foreseeable *consequences*. One experiment had people read disparaging lawyer jokes into a recorder (for example, "How can you tell when a lawyer is lying? His lips are moving"). The reading produced more negative attitudes toward lawyers when it was a chosen rather than coerced activity (Hobden & Olson, 1994). Other experiments have engaged people to write an essay for a measly $1.50 or so. When the essay argues something they don't believe in—say, a tuition increase—the underpaid writers begin to feel somewhat greater sympathy with the policy. Advocating a policy favourable to another race may improve your attitudes not only toward the policy but toward the race. This is especially so if something makes you face the inconsistency or if you think important people will actually read an essay with your name on it (Leippe & Eisenstadt, 1994; Leippe & Elkin, 1987). Feeling responsible for statements you have made, you will now believe them more strongly. Pretense becomes reality.

*There is a seldom-reported final aspect of this 1950s experiment. Imagine yourself finally back with the experimenter, who is truthfully explaining the whole study. Not only do you learn that you've been duped, but the experimenter asks for the $20 back. Do you comply? Festinger and Carlsmith note that all their student subjects willingly reached into their pockets and gave back the money. This is a foretaste of some quite amazing observations on compliance and conformity discussed in Chapter 6. As we will see, when the social situation makes clear demands, people usually respond accordingly.

FIGURE 4–2

Insufficient justification.

Dissonance theory predicts that when our actions are not fully explained by external rewards or coercion, we will experience dissonance, which we can reduce by believing what we have done. (Data from Festinger & Carlsmith, 1959)

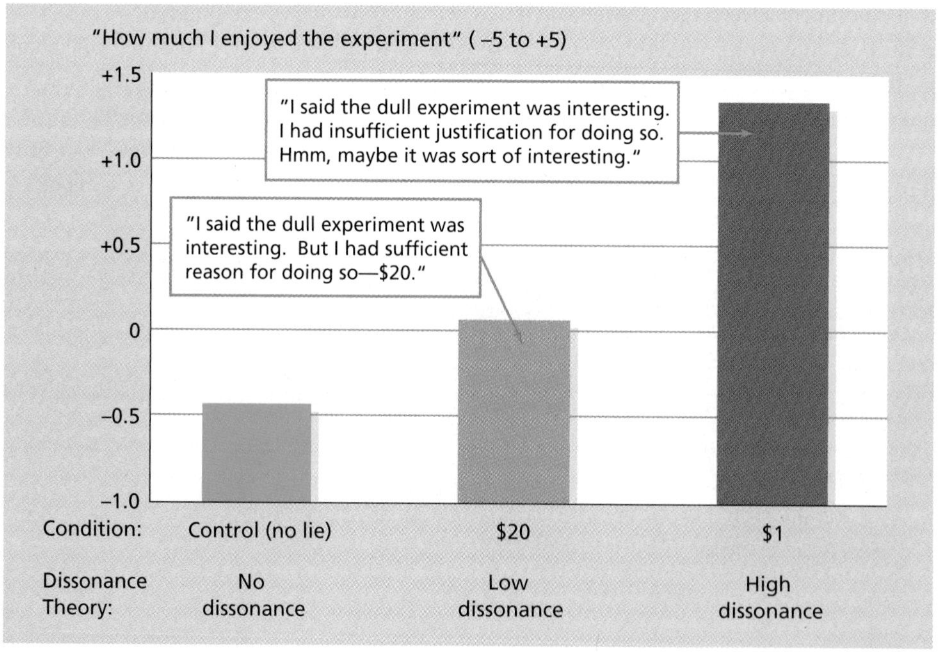

Earlier we noted how the insufficient justification principle works with punishments. Children were more likely to internalize a request not to play with an attractive toy if given a mild threat that insufficiently justified their compliance. When a parent says, "Clean up your room, Johnny, or I'll knock your block off," Johnny won't need to internally justify cleaning his room. The severe threat is justification enough.

Note that cognitive dissonance theory focuses on what *induces* a desired action, rather than the relative effectiveness of rewards and punishments administered *after* the act. It aims to have Johnny say, "I am cleaning up my room because I want a clean room," rather than, "I am cleaning up my room because my parents will kill me if I don't." The principle: We accept responsibility for our behaviour if we have chosen it without obvious pressure and incentives.

These implications of dissonance theory have led some to view it as an integration of humanistic and scientific perspectives. Authoritarian management will be effective, the theory predicts, only when the authority is present—because people are unlikely to internalize forced behaviour. Bree, a formerly enslaved talking horse in C. S. Lewis's *The Horse and His Boy* (1974), observes that "One of the worst results of being a slave and being forced to do things is that when there is no one to force you any more you find you have almost lost the power of forcing yourself" (p. 193). Dissonance theory insists that encouragement and inducement should be enough to elicit the desired action. But it suggests that managers, teachers, and parents should use only enough incentive to elicit the desired behaviour.

Dissonance after decisions

The emphasis on perceived choice and responsibility implies that *decisions* produce dissonance. When faced with an important decision—what university to attend, whom to date, which job to accept—we are sometimes torn between two equally attractive alternatives. Perhaps you can recall a time when, having committed yourself, you become painfully aware of dissonant cognitions—the desirable features of what you had rejected and the undesirable features of what you had chosen. If you decided to live on campus, you may have realized you were forgoing the

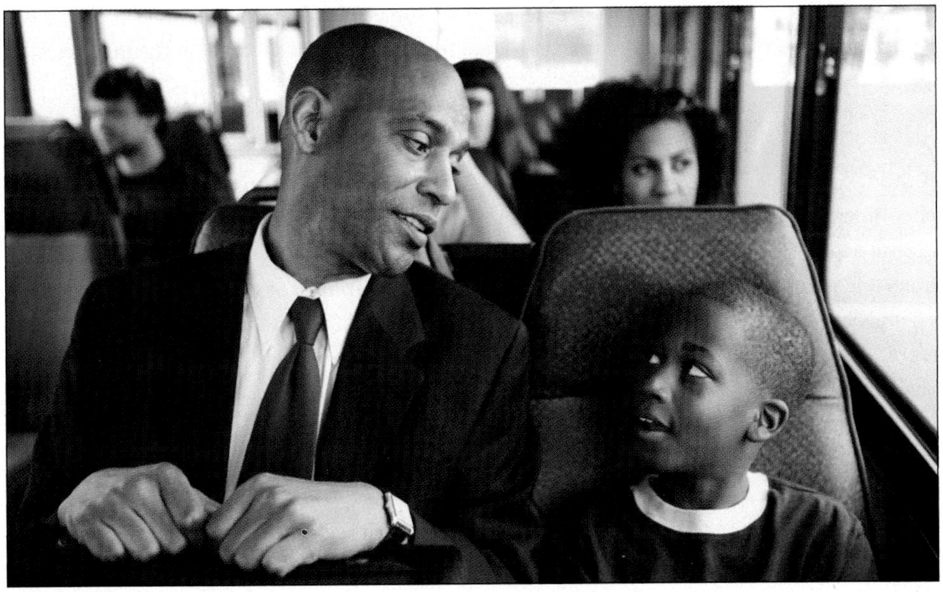

Dissonance theory suggests that parents should aim to elicit desired behaviour noncoercively, thus motivating children to internalize the appropriate attitudes.

spaciousness and freedom of an apartment in favour of cramped, noisy dorm quarters. If you elected to live off campus, you may have realized that your decision meant physical separation from campus and friends and having to cook for yourself.

After making important decisions, we usually reduce dissonance by upgrading the chosen alternative and downgrading the unchosen option. In the first published dissonance experiment (1956), Jack Brehm had women rate eight products, such as a toaster, a radio, and a hair dryer. Brehm then showed the women two objects they had rated closely and told them they could have whichever they chose. Later, when rerating the eight objects, the women increased their evaluations of the item they had chosen and decreased their evaluations of the rejected item. It seems that after we have made our choice, the grass does *not* then grow greener on the other side of the fence.

With simple decisions, this deciding-becomes-believing effect can breed overconfidence (Blanton et al., 2001): "What I have decided must be right." The effect can occur very quickly. Robert Knox and James Inkster (1968) found that bettors at a Vancouver racetrack who had just put down their money on a horse felt more optimistic about their bet than did those who were about to bet. In the few moments that intervened between standing in line and walking away from the betting window, nothing had changed—except the decisive action and the person's feelings about it. Contestants in carnival games of chance feel more confident of winning right after agreeing to play than right before. And voters indicate more esteem and confidence in a candidate just after voting than just before (Younger et al., 1977).

> *"Every time you make a choice you are turning the central part of you, the part of you that chooses, into something a little different from what it was before."*
>
> C. S. Lewis, *Mere Christianity*, 1943

These experiments and examples suggest that, once made, decisions grow their own self-justifying legs of support. Often, these new legs are strong enough that when one leg is pulled away—perhaps the original one—the decision does not collapse. Alison decides to take a trip home if it can be done for an airfare under $400. It can, so she makes her reservation and begins to think of additional reasons why she is glad she is going. When she goes to buy the tickets, however, she learns there has been a fare increase to $475. No matter, she is now determined to go. As when being low-balled by a car dealer, it never occurs to people, reports Robert Cialdini (1984, p. 103), "that those additional reasons might never have existed had the choice not been made in the first place."

SELF-PERCEPTION

Although dissonance theory has inspired much research, an even simpler theory explains its phenomena. Consider how we make inferences about other people's attitudes. We see how a person acts in a particular situation, and then we attribute the behaviour either to the person's traits and attitudes or to environmental forces. If we see parents coercing their little Susie into saying, "I'm sorry," we attribute Susie's reluctant behaviour to the situation, not to her personal regret. If we see Susie apologizing with no apparent inducement, we attribute the apology to Susie herself.

self-perception theory the theory that when unsure of our attitudes, we infer them much as would someone observing us—by looking at our behaviour and the circumstances under which it occurs

Self-perception theory (proposed by Daryl Bem, 1972) assumes that we make similar inferences when we observe our own behaviour. When our attitudes are weak or ambiguous, we are in the position of someone observing us from the outside. We discern people's attitudes by looking closely at their actions when they are free to act as they please. We similarly discern our

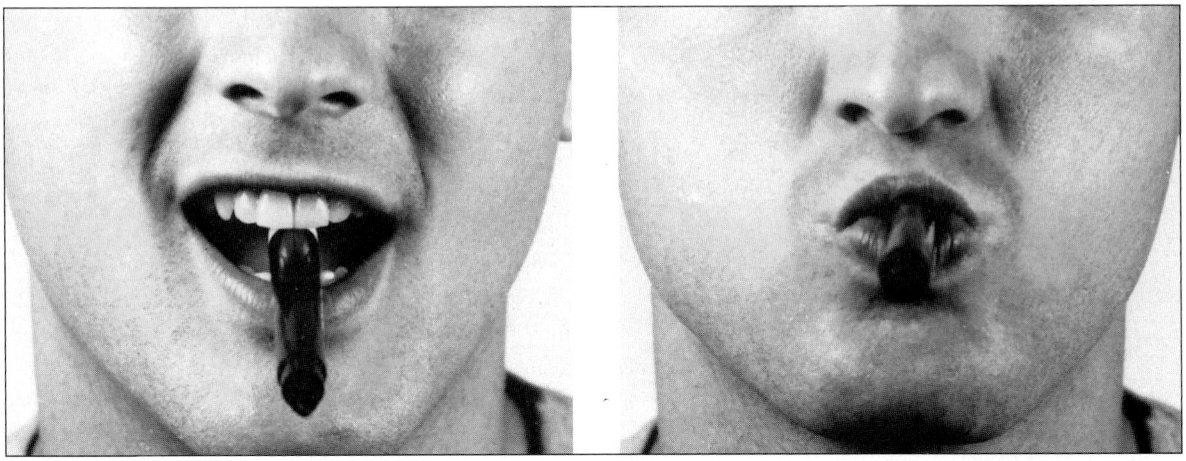

According to German psychologist Fritz Strack and colleagues (1988), people find cartoons funnier while holding a pen with their teeth using a smiling muscle) than while holding it with their lips (using muscles incompatible with smiling).

own attitudes. Hearing yourself talk informs you of your attitudes; seeing your actions provides clues to how strong your beliefs are. This is especially so when you can't easily attribute your behaviour to external constraints. The acts we freely commit are self-revealing (Figure 4–3).

William James proposed a similar explanation for emotion a century ago. We infer our emotions, he suggested, by observing our bodies and our behaviours. A stimulus such as a growling bear confronts a woman in the forest. She tenses, her heartbeat increases, adrenalin flows, and she runs away. Observing all this, she then experiences fear. Before big lectures one of the authors often wakes before dawn and is unable to get back to sleep. Noting his wakefulness, he concludes that he must be anxious.

FIGURE 4–3

Attitudes follow behaviour.

Why do actions affect attitudes?

Self-presentation
(impression management)
I look like a cool smoker.
Self-justification
(cognitive dissonance)
I know smoking is bad for me.
Ah . . . I've been waiting all day for this.
Oh well . . . the statistics aren't as awful as they say. Anyway, I'm very healthy. I won't get sick.
Self-perception
(self-observation)
Here I am smoking again. I must like smoking.

Expressions and attitude

You may be skeptical of the self-perception effect. We were when we first heard it. Experiments on the effects of facial expressions, however, suggest a way for you to experience it. When James Laird (1974, 1984; Duclos et al., 1989) induced university students to frown while attaching electrodes to their faces—"contract these muscles," "pull your brows together"—they reported feeling angry. It's more fun to try out Laird's other finding: Those induced to make a smiling face felt happier and found cartoons more humorous.

"Self-knowledge is best learned, not by contemplation, but action."

Goethe, 1749–1832

We have all experienced this phenomenon. We're feeling crabby, but then the phone rings or someone comes to the door and elicits from us warm, polite behaviour. "How's everything?" "Just fine, thanks. How are things with you?" "Oh, not bad. . . ." If our feelings are not intense, this warm behaviour may change our whole attitude. It's tough to smile and feel grouchy. When Miss Universe parades her smile, she may, after all, be helping herself feel happy. As Rodgers and Hammerstein reminded us, when we are afraid it may help to "whistle a happy tune." Going through the motions can trigger the emotions.

Even your gait can affect how you feel. When you get up from reading this chapter, walk for a minute taking short, shuffling steps, with eyes downcast. It's a great way to feel depressed. "Sit all day in a moping posture, sigh, and reply to everything with a dismal voice, and your melancholy lingers," noted William James (1890, p. 463). Want to feel better? Walk for a minute taking long strides with your arms swinging and your eyes straight ahead. Can you, like the participants in an experiment by Sara Snodgrass (1986), feel the difference?

"I can watch myself and my actions, just like an outsider."

Anne Frank, *The Diary of a Young Girl*, 1947

If our expressions influence our feelings, then would imitating others' expressions help us know what they are feeling? An experiment by Katherine Burns Vaughan and John Lanzetta (1981) suggests it would. They asked students to observe someone receiving electric shock. They told some of the observers to make a pained expression whenever the shock came on. If, as Freud and others supposed, expressing an emotion allows us to discharge it, then the pained expression should be inwardly calming (Cacioppo et al., 1991). Actually, compared to other students who did not act out the expressions, these grimacing students perspired *more* and had a faster heart rate whenever they saw the person shocked. Acting out the person's emotion apparently enabled the observers to feel more empathy. The implication: To sense how other people are feeling, let your own face mirror their expressions.

Actually, you hardly need try. Observing others' faces, postures, and voices, we naturally and unconsciously mimic their moment-to-moment reactions (Hatfield et al., 1992). We synchronize our movements, postures, and tones of voice with theirs. Doing so helps us tune in to what they're feeling. It also makes for "emotional contagion," helping explain why it's fun to be around happy people and depressing to be around depressed people (see Module B).

Our facial expressions also influence our attitudes. In a clever experiment, Gary Wells and Richard Petty (1980) had University of Alberta students "test headphone sets" by making either vertical or horizontal head movements while listening to a radio editorial. Who most agreed with the editorial? Those who had been nodding their heads up and down. Why? Wells and Petty surmised that positive thoughts are compatible with vertical nodding and incompatible with horizontal motion. Try it yourself when listening to someone: Do you feel more agreeable when nodding rather than shaking your head?

This assumes you are not in Bulgaria—where an abrupt vertical head nod signifies not yes, but "no."

At the University of Cologne, Thomas Mussweiler (2006) likewise discovered that stereotyped actions feed stereotyped thinking. In one clever experiment, he induced some people to move about in the portly manner of an obese person—by having them wear a life vest and putting weights on their wrists and ankles—and then give their impression of someone described on paper. Those whose movements simulated obesity, more than those in a control condition, perceived the person (described on paper) as exhibiting traits (friendliness, sluggishness, unhealthiness) that people often perceive in obese people. In follow-up experiments, people induced to move slowly, as an elderly person might, ascribed more elderly stereotypic traits to a target person. Doing influenced thinking.

"The free expression by outward signs of emotion intensifies it. On the other hand, the repression as far as possible, of all outward signs softens our emotions."

Charles Darwin, *The Expression of the Emotions in Man and Animals*, 1897

Overjustification and intrinsic motivations

Recall the insufficient justification effect—the *smallest* incentive that will get people to do something is usually the most effective in getting them to like the activity and keep on doing it. Cognitive dissonance theory offers one explanation for this: When external inducements are insufficient to justify our behaviour, we reduce dissonance by justifying the behaviour internally.

Self-perception theory offers another explanation: People explain their behaviour by noting the conditions under which it occurs. Imagine hearing someone proclaim the wisdom of a tuition increase after being paid $20 to do so. Surely the statement would seem less sincere than if you thought the person was expressing those opinions for no pay. Perhaps we make similar inferences when observing ourselves.

Self-perception theory goes even a step further. Contrary to the notion that rewards always increase motivation, it suggests that unnecessary rewards sometimes have a hidden cost. Rewarding people for doing what they already enjoy may lead them to attribute their doing it to the reward, thus undermining their self-perception that they do it because they like it. Experiments by Edward Deci and Richard Ryan (1991, 1997), by Mark Lepper and David Greene (1979), and by Ann Boggiano and her colleagues (1985, 1987) confirm this **overjustification effect**. Pay people for playing with puzzles, and they will later play with the puzzles less than those who play without being paid; promise children a reward for doing what they intrinsically enjoy (for example, playing with magic markers) and you will turn their play into work (Figure 4–4).

overjustification effect the result of bribing people to do what they already like doing; they may then see their action as externally controlled rather than intrinsically appealing

A folk tale illustrates the overjustification effect. An old man lived alone on a street where boys played noisily every afternoon. The din annoyed him, so one day he called the boys to his door. He told them he loved the cheerful sound of children's voices and promised them each 50

Natural mimicry and emotional contagion. People in sync, like these volunteers videotaped during a study by Frank Bernieri and colleagues (1994), feel more rapport with each other.

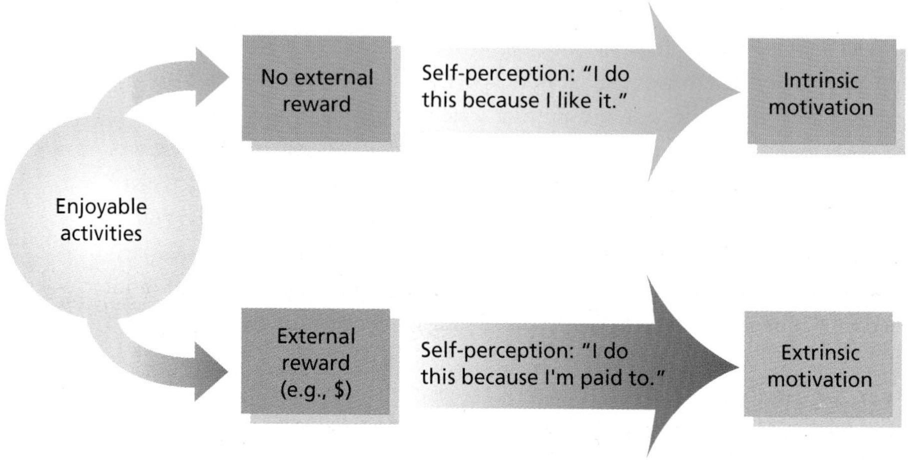

FIGURE 4–4

Intrinsic and extrinsic motivation.

When people do something they enjoy, without reward or coercion, they attribute their behaviour to their love of the activity. External rewards undermine intrinsic motivation by leading people to attribute their behaviour to the incentive.

cents if they would return the next day. Next afternoon the youngsters raced back and played more lustily than ever. The old man paid them and promised another reward the next day. Again they returned, whooping it up, and the man again paid them; this time 25 cents. The following day they got only 15 cents, and the man explained that his meagre resources were being exhausted. "Please, though, would you come to play for 10 cents tomorrow?" The disappointed boys told the man they would not be back. It wasn't worth the effort, they said, to play all afternoon at his house for only 10 cents.

As self-perception theory implies, an *unanticipated* reward does *not* diminish intrinsic interest, because people can still attribute their action to their own motivation (Bradley & Mannell, 1984; Tang & Hall, 1994). (It's like the heroine who, having fallen in love with the woodcutter, now learns that he's really a prince.) And if compliments for a good job make us feel more competent and successful, this can actually *increase* our intrinsic motivation. When rightly administered, rewards may also boost creativity (Eisenberger et al., 1999, 2001, 2003).

The overjustification effect occurs when someone offers an unnecessary reward beforehand in an obvious effort to control behaviour. What matters is what a reward implies: Rewards and praise that inform people of their achievements (that make them feel, "I'm very good at this") boost intrinsic motivation. Rewards that seek to control people and lead them to believe it was the reward that caused their effort ("I did it for the money") diminish the intrinsic appeal of an enjoyable task (Freedman et al., 1992; Rosenfeld et al., 1980; Sansone, 1986).

How then can we cultivate people's enjoyment of tasks that are not intrinsically appealing? Young Maria may find her first piano lessons frustrating. Toshi may not have an intrinsic love of fifth-grade science. Sandra may not look forward to making those first sales calls. In such cases, the parent, teacher, or manager should probably use some incentives to coax the desired behaviour (Boggiano & Ruble, 1985; Workman & Williams, 1980). After the person complies, suggest an intrinsic reason for doing so: "I knew you'd share your toys because you're a generous person."

If we provide students with *just enough* justification to perform a learning task and use rewards and labels to help them feel competent, we may enhance their enjoyment and their eagerness to pursue the subject on their own. When there is too much justification—as happens in classrooms where teachers dictate behaviour and use rewards to control the children—child-driven learning may diminish (Deci & Ryan, 1985, 1991). One of the authors' sons eagerly consumed six or eight library books a week—until his library started a reading club that promised a party to those who read 10 books in three months. Three weeks later he began checking out only one or two books during his weekly visit. Why? "Because you only need to read 10 books, you know."

COMPARING THE THEORIES

We have seen one explanation of why our actions *seem* to affect our attitudes (self-presentation theory). And we have seen two explanations of why our actions *genuinely* affect our attitudes: (1) The dissonance-theory assumption that we justify our behaviour to reduce our internal discomfort, and (2) the self-perception theory assumption that we observe our behaviour and make reasonable inferences about our attitudes, as we do when observing other people.

The last two explanations seem to contradict one another. Which is right? It's difficult to find a definitive test. In most instances they make the same predictions, and we can bend each theory to accommodate most of the findings we have considered (Greenwald, 1975). Daryl Bem (1972), the self-perception theorist, even suggested it boils down to a matter of loyalties and esthetics. This illustrates the subjectivity of scientific theorizing (see Chapter 1). Neither dissonance theory nor self-perception theory has been handed to us by nature. Both are products of human imagination—creative attempts to simplify and explain what we've observed.

It is not unusual in science to find that a principle, such as "attitudes follow behaviour," is predictable from more than one theory. Physicist Richard Feynman (1967) marvelled that "one of the amazing characteristics of nature" is the "wide range of beautiful ways" in which we can describe it: "I do not understand the reason why it is that the correct laws of physics seem to be expressible in such a tremendous variety of ways" (pp. 53–55). Like different roads leading to the same place, different sets of assumptions can lead to the same principle. If anything, this *strengthens* our confidence in the principle. It becomes credible not only because of the data supporting it but also because it rests on more than one theoretical pillar.

Dissonance as arousal

Can we say that one of our theories is better? On one key point, strong support has emerged for dissonance theory. Recall that dissonance is, by definition, *an aroused state of uncomfortable tension*. To reduce this tension, we supposedly change our attitudes. Self-perception theory says nothing about tension being aroused when our actions and attitudes are not in harmony. It assumes merely that when our attitudes are weak to begin with, we will use our behaviour and its circumstances as a clue to those attitudes (like the person who said, "How do I know how I feel until I hear what I say?").

Are conditions that supposedly produce dissonance (for example, making decisions or acting contrary to one's attitudes) actually uncomfortably arousing? Clearly yes, considering the classic study by the University of Waterloo's Mark Zanna and Princeton University's Joel Cooper (1974). They had students write an essay banning all speakers on campus, a view with which all the students disagreed. Half the students were told that they had no choice but to write the essay, while the other half were given the illusion that they chose to write the essay. Thus far, the study is just a replication of many previous dissonance studies, but Zanna and Cooper added a simple manipulation that helped establish arousal as central to the experience

Sally Forth reprinted with special permission of King Features Syndicate.

of dissonance. They had all the students take a pill (actually filled with powdered milk) at the beginning of the experiment. One-third of the students were told that the pill would make them feel aroused, one-third were told that it would make them feel relaxed, and one-third were given no information about the effects of the pill. Zanna and Cooper reasoned that if students thought the pill would make them feel aroused, when they experienced the arousal from the cognitive dissonance they were feeling they would blame the arousal on the pill and would not change their attitude. As you can see in Figure 4–5 the results of the experiment supported this reasoning. When students thought the pill would be arousing, students who had high and low choice to write the essay did not differ in their attitudes. When they were given no information about the pill students showed the typical dissonance pattern of attitude change—students who were given the illusion of choice to write the essay changed their attitudes more than students who were given no choice to write it. Finally, the students who were told the pill would be relaxing showed an especially large amount of attitude change. These results demonstrate that feeling aroused is a central part of the experience of cognitive dissonance and that people must attribute this arousal to their own actions before they engage in self-justifying attitude change.

self-affirmation theory a theory that people often experience self-image threat after engaging in an undesirable behaviour, they compensate for this threat by affirming another aspect of the self. Threaten people's self-concept in one domain, and they will compensate either by refocusing or by doing good deeds in some other domain.

There is a reason why "volunteering" to say or do undesirable things is arousing, suggests Claude Steele (1988). According to the **self-affirmation theory**, such acts are embarrassing. They make us feel foolish. They threaten our sense of personal competence and goodness. Justifying our actions and decisions is therefore self-affirming; it maintains our sense of integrity and self-worth.

So what do you suppose happens if, after committing a self-contradictory act, we offer people some other way to reaffirm their sense of self-worth, such as by doing a good deed? In several experiments Steele found that, with their self-concepts secure, people (especially those who came to the experiments with strong self-concepts) felt much less need to justify their acts (Steele, Spencer & Lynch, 1993). People with secure and stable high self-esteem also engage in less self-justification (Holland et al., 2002; Jordan, Spencer, Zanna & Correl, 2003).

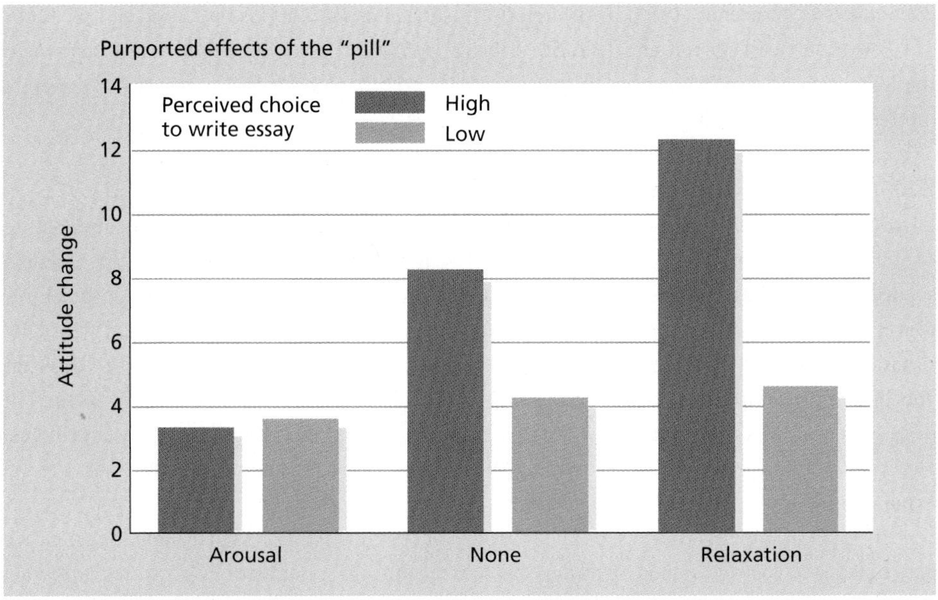

FIGURE 4–5

Dissonance and the pill.

When people attributed their arousal to a pill they had taken, they did not change their attitudes, demonstrating the role of dissonance in attitude change. (Data from Zanna & Cooper, 1974)

So dissonance conditions do indeed arouse tension, especially when they threaten positive feelings of self-worth. (In the study of relapsed smokers, it was those with high self-esteem who especially downplayed the risks.) But is this arousal necessary for the attitudes-follow-behaviour effect? Steele and his colleagues (1981) believe the answer is yes. When drinking alcohol reduces dissonance-produced arousal, the attitudes-follow-behaviour effect disappears. In one of their experiments, they induced students to write an essay favouring a big tuition increase. The students reduced their resulting dissonance by softening their anti-tuition attitudes—*unless* after writing the unpleasant essay they drank alcohol, supposedly as part of a beer- or vodka-tasting experiment.

Nearly five decades after Festinger first proposed his theory, social psychologists continue to study and debate alternative views of what causes dissonance. Some say Festinger was right to think that merely behaving *inconsistently* with one's attitudes—say, writing privately that one liked a foul-tasting drink and being simultaneously aware of the inconsistency—is enough to provoke some attitude change (Harmon-Jones et al., 1996; Johnson et al., 1995; McGregor et al., 1998). In fact, in studies with people suffering amnesia—and thus with an inability to explicitly remember their behaviour—attitudes still changed following behaviour (Lieberman et al., 2001). (This startling result suggests that there's more to the effect than conscious self-justification. Unconscious processing also seems to be at work.) Others argue that the crucial inconsistency is between one's behaviour and one's self-concept (Prislin

People rarely internalize coerced behaviour.

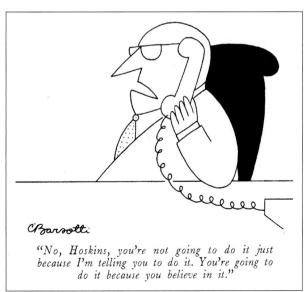

"No, Hoskins, you're not going to do it just because I'm telling you to do it. You're going to do it because you believe in it."

& Pool, 1996; Stone et al., 1999). Although the dust has not settled, this much is clear, say Richard Petty, Duane Wegener, and Leandre Fabrigar (1997): "Dissonance theory has captivated the imagination of social psychologists as virtually no other, and it has continued to generate interesting new research."

Self-perceiving when not self-contradicting

Dissonance procedures are uncomfortably arousing, which leads to self-persuasion after acting contrary to one's attitudes. But dissonance theory cannot explain all the findings. When people argue a position that is in line with their opinion, although a step or two beyond it, procedures that usually eliminate arousal do not eliminate attitude change (Fazio et al., 1977, 1979). Dissonance theory also does not explain the overjustification effect, since being paid to do what you like to do should not arouse great tension. And what about situations where the action does not contradict any attitude—when, for example, people are induced to smile or grimace. Here, too, there should be no dissonance. For these cases, self-perception theory has a ready explanation.

In short, it appears that dissonance theory successfully explains what happens when we act contrary to clearly defined attitudes: We feel tension, so we adjust our attitudes to reduce it. Dissonance theory, then, explains attitude *change.* In situations where our attitudes are not well formed, self-perception theory explains attitude *formation.* As we act and reflect, we develop a more readily accessible attitude to guide our future behaviour (Fazio, 1987; Roese & Olson, 1994).

SUMMING UP: WHY DOES OUR BEHAVIOUR AFFECT OUR ATTITUDES?

Three competing theories explain *why* our actions affect our attitude reports. *Self-presentation theory* assumes that people, especially those who self-monitor their behaviour hoping to create a good impression, will adapt their attitude reports to *appear* consistent with their actions. The available evidence confirms that people do adjust their attitude statements out of concern for what other people will think. But it also shows that some genuine attitude change occurs.

Two theories propose that our actions trigger genuine attitude change. *Dissonance theory* explains this attitude change by assuming that we feel tension after acting contrary to our attitudes or making a difficult decision. To reduce this arousal, we internally justify our behaviour. Dissonance theory further proposes that the less external justification we have for an undesirable action, the more we feel responsible for it, and thus the more dissonance arises and the more attitudes change.

Self-perception theory assumes that when our attitudes are weak, we simply observe our behaviour and its circumstances and infer our attitudes. One interesting implication of self-perception theory is the "overjustification effect": Rewarding people to do what they like doing anyway can turn their pleasure into drudgery (if the reward leads them to attribute their behaviour to the reward). Evidence supports predictions from both theories, suggesting that each describes what happens under certain conditions.

PART TWO

SOCIAL INFLUENCE

So far we have considered mostly "within-the-skin" phenomena—how we think about one another. Now we consider "between-skins" happenings—how we influence and relate to one another. Therefore, in Chapters 5 through 8 we probe social psychology's central concern: the powers of social influence.

What are these unseen social forces that push and pull us? How powerful are they? Research on social influence helps illuminate the invisible strings by which our social worlds move us about. This part reveals these subtle powers, especially the principles of persuasion (Chapter 5), the forces of social conformity (Chapter 6), the consequences of participation in groups (Chapter 7), the cultural sources of attitudes and behaviour (Chapter 8), and how all these influences operate together in everyday situations.

Seeing these influences, we may better understand why people feel and act as they do. And we may ourselves become less vulnerable to unwanted manipulation and more adept at pulling our own strings.

Jugend dient dem Führer
ALLE ZEHNJÄHRIGEN IN DIE HJ.

CHAPTER FIVE

Persuasion

Joseph Goebbels, Germany's minister of "popular enlightenment" and propaganda from 1933 to 1945, understood the power of **persuasion**. Given control of publications, radio programs,

persuasion the process by which a message induces change in beliefs, attitudes, or behaviours

motion pictures, and the arts, he undertook to persuade Germans to accept Nazi ideology in general and anti-Semitism in particular. His colleague Julius Streicher published a weekly anti-Semitic newspaper, *Der Stürmer,* with a circulation of 500 000 and the only paper read cover to cover by Adolf Hitler. Streicher also published anti-Semitic children's books and, with Goebbels, spoke at the mass rallies that became a part of the Nazi propaganda machine.

How effective were Goebbels, Streicher, and other Nazi propagandists? Did they, as the Allies alleged at Streicher's Nuremberg trial, "inject poison into the minds of millions and millions" (Bytwerk, 1976)?

Most Germans were not persuaded to feel raging hatred for the Jews. But many were. Others became sympathetic to measures such as firing Jewish university professors, boycotting Jewish-owned businesses, and, eventually, sending Jews to concentration camps. Most other Germans became either sufficiently uncertain or sufficiently intimidated to condone the regime's massive genocidal program, or at least to allow it to happen. Without the complicity of millions of people, there would have been no Holocaust (Goldhagen, 1996).

The powers of persuasion were more recently apparent in differences between Canadian and U.S. citizens over the war in Iraq. Surveys shortly before the war, for example, revealed that Canadians opposed military action against Iraq by about two to one, while Americans favoured it by the same margin (Burkholder, 2003; Moore, 2003; Pew, 2003). Once the war began, support for the war rose, for a time, to more than three to one in the U.S. (Newport et al., 2003). Except for Israel, people surveyed in all other countries were opposed to the attack.

Without taking sides regarding the wisdom of the war—that debate we can leave to history—we can observe that the huge rift between Americans and citizens of other countries is a sign of persuasion at work. What persuaded most Americans to favour the war? What persuaded most people elsewhere to oppose it?

Attitudes were being shaped, at least in part, by persuasive messages in the U.S. media that led half of the people in the U.S. to believe that Saddam Hussein was directly involved in the 9/11 attacks and four in five to falsely believe that weapons of mass destruction would be found (Duffy, 2003; Gallup, 2003; Newport et al., 2003). Sociologist James Davison Hunter (2002) notes that culture-shaping usually occurs top-down, as cultural elites control the dissemination of information and ideas. Thus, people in the U.S. and people elsewhere learned about and watched a different war (della Cava, 2003; Friedman, 2003; Goldsmith, 2003; Krugman, 2003; Tomorrow, 2003). Depending on the country where you lived and the media available to you, you may have witnessed "America's liberation of Iraq" or "America's invasion of Iraq," or read headlines as divergent as "Tense Standoff Between Troops and Iraqis Erupts in Bloodshed" (ambiguous passive voice headline of *Los Angeles Times*) or "U.S. Troops Fire on Iraqis; 13 Reported Dead" (active voice headline of the same incident by the CBC).

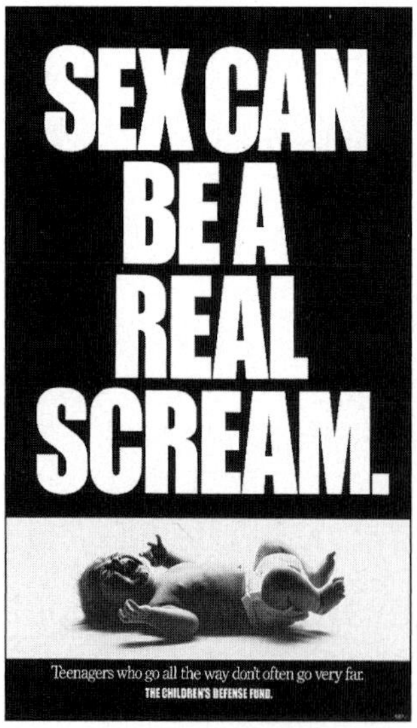

Teenage pregnancy has social consequences for both parent and child. How persuasive is this message in addressing the problem?

In the view of many Americans, the other nations' media combined a pervasive anti-U.S. bias with a blindness to the threat posed by Saddam Hussein. To many people elsewhere, the "embedded" U.S. media were biased in favour of the military. Regardless of where bias lay or whose perspective was better informed, this much seems clear: Depending on where they lived, people were given (and discussed and believed) somewhat differing information. Persuasion matters.

Persuasive forces also have been harnessed to promote healthier living. Thanks partly to health promotion campaigns, the Canadian Centre on Substance Abuse reports that the Canadian smoking rate has plunged to 27 percent, barely more than half the rate of 30 years ago. And the rate of 17- and 18-year-old high-school students in Ontario that abstain from drinking beer has increased—from 8.3 percent in 1981 to 22.2 percent in 1993. More than at any time in recent decades, health- and safety-conscious educated adults are shunning cigarettes and beer.

As these examples show, efforts to persuade are sometimes diabolical, sometimes controversial, and sometimes beneficial. Persuasion is neither inherently good nor bad. It is usually the content of the message that elicits judgments of good or bad. The bad we call "propaganda." The good we call "education." Education is more factually based and less coercive than propaganda. Yet generally we call it "education" when we believe it, "propaganda" when we don't (Lumsden et al., 1980). In the last decade, North Americans' support for gay rights and gay civil unions or marriage has significantly increased (Myers & Scanzoni, 2005). Some people view such attitude change as reflecting "education," others as reflecting "propaganda."

Our opinions have to come from somewhere. Persuasion—whether it be education or propaganda—is therefore inevitable. Indeed, persuasion is everywhere—at the heart of politics, marketing, courtship, parenting, negotiation, evangelism, and courtroom decision making. Social psychologists therefore seek to understand what leads to effective, long-lasting attitude change. What factors affect persuasion? And how, as persuaders, can we most effectively "educate" others?

> *"Speech has power. Words do not fade. What starts out as a sound ends in a deed."*
>
> Rabbi Abraham Heschel, 1961

> *"A fanatic is one who can't change his mind and won't change the subject."*
>
> Winston Churchill, 1954

> *"Remember that to change thy mind and to follow him that sets thee right, is to be none the less a free agent."*
>
> Marcus Aurelius Antoninus, *Meditations*, viii. 16, 121–180

> *"To swallow and follow, whether old doctrine or new propaganda, is a weakness still dominating the human mind."*
>
> Charlotte Perkins Gilman, *Human Work*, 1904

WHAT PATHS LEAD TO PERSUASION?

When people try to persuade others, they can try to use good arguments and convince people that if they really think through the issues they will become persuaded to change their minds. At the opposite extreme they can try to change people's minds without having them think about this issue at all. Perhaps the best way to convince people that something is good is just to associate it with something positive. Think of your favourite television ad. Most people like TV ads because they are funny or contain captivating images. Such ads can be effective ways to sell products, even if they have few—if any—convincing arguments.

In the 1940s and 1950s, Carl Hovland and his colleagues (1949) at Yale University studied the barriers that can prevent a message from being persuasive. They approached their task

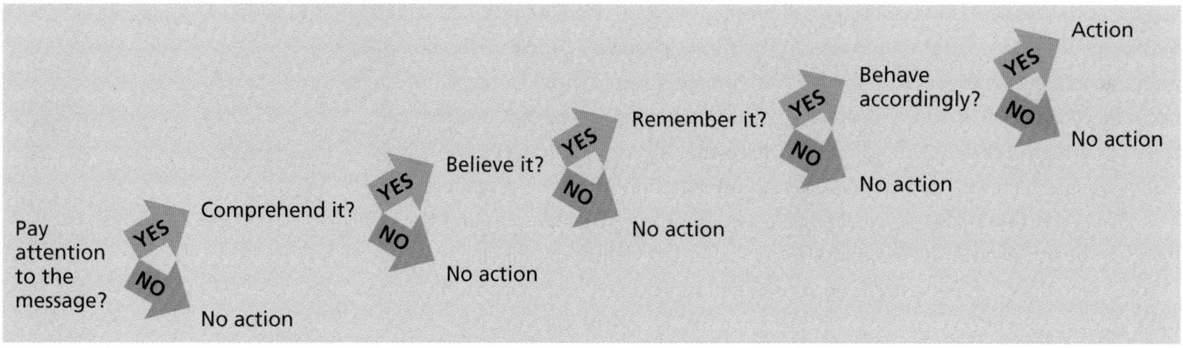

FIGURE 5–1

To elicit action, a persuasive message must clear several hurdles. What is crucial is not so much remembering the message itself as remembering one's own thoughts in response. (From W. J. McGuire, "An Information-Processing Model of Advertising Effectiveness," *Behavioral and Management Sciences in Marketing,* edited by H. L. Davis and A. J. Silk, 1978. Copyright © 1978. Reprinted by permission of John Wiley & Sons, Inc.)

carefully, varying factors related to the communicator, the content of the message, the channel of communication, and the audience. As shown in Figure 5–1 above, they believed persuasion entailed clearing several hurdles. Any factors that help people clear the hurdles in the persuasion process increase the likelihood of persuasion. For example, if an attractive source increases your attention to a message, then the message should have a better chance of persuading you. The Yale group's approach to studying persuasion provides us with a good understanding of when persuasion is likely to occur.

Researchers at Ohio State University then suggested that people's thoughts in response to persuasive messages also matter. If a message is clear but unconvincing, then you will easily counterargue the message and won't be persuaded. If the message offers convincing arguments, then your thoughts will be more favourable and you will most likely be persuaded. This "cognitive response" approach helps us to understand why persuasion occurs more in some situations than in others. If you live in North America, advertisers spend about $500 annually trying to influence you.

central route to persuasion occurs when interested people focus on the arguments and respond with favourable thoughts

THE CENTRAL ROUTE

Richard Petty and John Cacioppo (1986; Petty & Wegener, 1999) and Alice Eagly and Shelly Chaiken (1993, 1998) theorized that persuasion is likely to occur via one of two routes. When people are motivated and able to think systematically about an issue, they are likely to take the **central route to persuasion**—focusing on the arguments. If those arguments are strong and compelling, persuasion is likely. If the message only contains weak arguments, thoughtful people will notice that the arguments aren't very compelling and will counterargue.

peripheral route to persuasion occurs when people are influenced by incidental cues, such as a speaker's attractiveness

THE PERIPHERAL ROUTE

But sometimes the strength of the arguments doesn't matter. Sometimes we're not all that motivated or able to think carefully. If we're distracted, uninvolved, or just plain busy, we may not take the time to think carefully about the message content. Rather than noticing whether the arguments are particularly compelling, we might follow the **peripheral route to persuasion**—focusing on cues that trigger acceptance without much thinking—the aura around the persuasive appeal. When people are distracted or not motivated to think, easily understood familiar statements are more persuasive than novel statements with the same meaning. Thus, for uninvolved or distracted people, "Don't put all your eggs in one basket" has more impact than "Don't risk everything on a single venture" (Howard, 1997).

Smart advertisers adapt ads to their consumers' thinking. They do so for good reason, given how much of consumers' behaviour—such as one's spontaneous decision, while shopping, to pick up some ice cream of a particular brand—is made unthinkingly (Dijksterhuis et al., 2005). Billboards and television commercials—media that consumers are only able to take in for brief amounts of time—typically use visual images as peripheral cues. Our opinions regarding products such as food and drink, cigarettes, and clothing are often based more on feelings than on logic. Ads for such products often use visual peripheral cues. Instead of providing arguments in favour of smoking, cigarette ads associate the product with images of beauty and pleasure. So do beer ads that promote Molson's Canadian with symbols of what is and is not Canadian. On the other hand, computer ads, which interested, logical consumers may pore over for some time, seldom feature Hollywood stars or great athletes; instead they offer customers information on competitive features and prices.

"All effective propaganda must be limited to a very few points and must harp on these in slogans until the last member of the public understands."

Adolf Hitler, *Mein Kampf*

DIFFERENT ROUTES FOR DIFFERENT PURPOSES

The ultimate goal of the advertiser, the preacher, and even the teacher is not just to have people pay attention to the message and move on. Typically, the goal involves some sort of behaviour change. Are both routes to persuasion equally likely to fulfill this goal? Petty and his colleagues (1995) note how central route processing can lead to more enduring change than does the peripheral route.

Thus, the central route is more likely to lead to attitude and behaviour changes that "stick," whereas the peripheral route may lead merely to superficial and temporary attitude change. As sex educators know, changing attitudes is easier than changing behaviour. Studies assessing the effectiveness of abstinence education find some increases in attitudes supporting abstinence but little long-term impact on sexual behaviour (Hauser, 2005). Likewise, HIV-prevention education tends to have more effect on attitudes toward condoms than on condom use (Albarracin et al., 2003). In both cases, changing behaviour as well as attitudes seems to require people's actively processing and rehearsing their own convictions.

None of us has the time to thoughtfully analyze all issues. Often we take the peripheral route, by using simple rule-of-thumb heuristics, such as "trust the experts" or "long messages are credible" (Chaiken & Maheswaran, 1994). Residents of one of the authors' community recently voted on a complicated issue involving the legal ownership of its local hospital. The author didn't have the time or interest to study this question himself (he had this book to write). But he noted that referendum supporters were all people he either liked or regarded as experts. So he used a simple heuristic—friends and experts can be trusted—and voted accordingly. We all make snap judgments using other rule-of-thumb heuristics: If a speaker is articulate and appealing, has apparently good motives, and has several arguments (or better, if the different arguments come from different sources), we usually take the easy peripheral route and accept the message without much thought (Figure 5–2).

"Attitude changes are stronger the more they are based on issue-relevant thinking."

Richard Petty and Duane Wegener (1998)

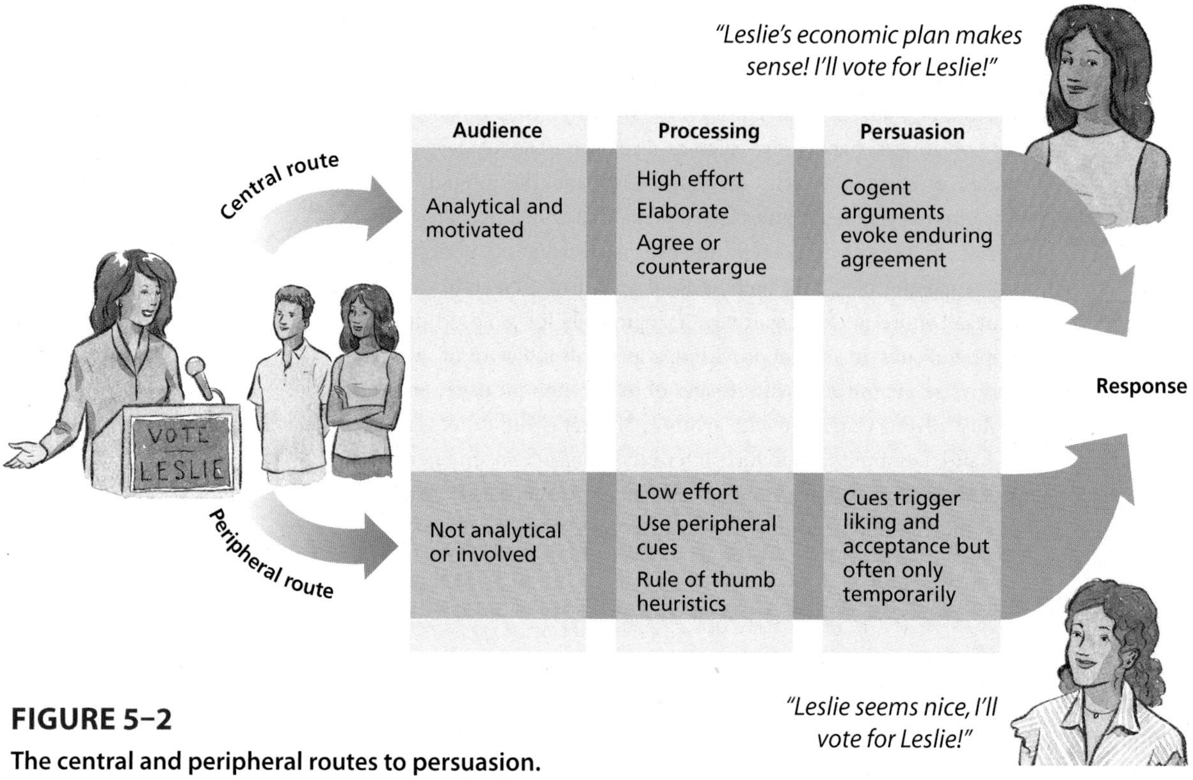

FIGURE 5–2

The central and peripheral routes to persuasion.

Computer ads typically take the central route, by assuming their audience wants to systematically compare features and prices. Soft-drink ads usually take the peripheral route, by merely associating their product with glamour, pleasure, and good moods. Central route processing more often produces enduring attitude change.

SUMMING UP: WHAT PATHS LEAD TO PERSUASION?

Sometimes persuasion occurs as people focus on arguments and respond with favourable thoughts. Such systematic, or "central route," persuasion occurs when people are naturally analytical or involved in the issue. When issues don't engage systematic thinking, persuasion may occur through a faster "peripheral route" as people use heuristics or incidental cues to make snap judgments. Central route persuasion, being more thoughtful and less superficial, is more durable and more likely to influence behaviour.

WHAT ARE THE ELEMENTS OF PERSUASION?

Among the primary ingredients of persuasion explored by social psychologists are these four: (1) the communicator, (2) the message, (3) how the message is communicated, and (4) the audience. In other words, who says what by what means to whom? How do these factors affect the likelihood that we will take either the central or peripheral route to persuasion?

WHO SAYS? THE COMMUNICATOR

Imagine the following scene: I. M. Wright, a hockey fan who was the "goon" on his junior hockey team, is watching a sports program. One sportswriter complains about a vicious hit she saw recently and says, "This guy meant to hurt the other player and he never got suspended. It's awful. This kind of thing should be stopped. . . ." Angered, Mr. Wright mutters to his wife, "I'm sick of these people who know nothing about hockey trying to ruin it. Good hits are just part of the game." Later in the program the same sportswriter complains about Canadian fans that were booing players from an opposing country. She remarks that she felt it "was a disgrace," and that it made her feel ashamed to be Canadian. Mr. Wright chimes in and says, "Where did they find this woman? She should learn to support her country and her fellow countrymen."

Now switch the scene. Imagine Mr. Wright hearing these statements from Don Cherry on *Coach's Corner* describing a vicious hit by Swedish player Peter Forsberg on Canadian star Brendan Shanahan or describing his dismay when Canadian fans booed Canadian-born Brett Hull. Do you think Mr. Wright would react differently?

Social psychologists have found that who is saying something affects how an audience receives it. In one experiment, when the Socialist and Liberal leaders in the Dutch parliament argued identical positions using the same words, each was most effective with members of his own party (Wiegman, 1985). It's not just the central message that matters, but also who says it. What, then, makes one communicator more persuasive than another?

Credibility

Any of us would find a statement about the benefits of exercise more believable if it came from a scientific journal rather than from a tabloid newspaper. But the effects of source **credibility** (perceived expertise and trustworthiness) diminish after a month or so. If a credible person's message is persuasive, its impact may fade as its source is forgotten or dissociated from the message. The impact of a noncredible person may correspondingly *increase* over time if people remember the message better than the reason for discounting it (Cook & Flay, 1978; Gruder et al., 1978; Pratkanis et al., 1988). This delayed persuasion, after people forget the source or its connection with the message, is called the **sleeper effect**.

credibility
believability. A credible communicator is perceived as both expert and trustworthy.

sleeper effect
a delayed impact of a message; occurs when we remember the message but forget a reason for discounting it

Perceived expertise

How does one become "expert"? One way is to begin by saying things the audience agrees with, which makes one seem smart. Another is to be introduced as someone who is knowledgeable on the topic. A message about toothbrushing from "Dr. James Rundle of the Canadian Dental Association" is much more convincing than the same message from "Jim Rundle, a local high-school student who did a project with some of his classmates on dental hygiene" (Olson & Cal, 1984). After more than a decade studying high-school marijuana use, researchers concluded that scare messages from unreliable sources did not affect marijuana use during the 1960s and 1970s. However, from a credible source, scientific reports of the biological and psychological results of long-term marijuana use "can play an important role in reducing . . . drug use" (Bachman et al., 1988).

"Believe an expert."

Virgil, *Aeneid*

Another way to appear credible is to speak confidently. Bonnie Erickson and her collaborators (1978) had students evaluate courtroom testimony given in the straightforward manner or in a more hesitant manner. For example:

Effective persuaders know how to convey a message effectively.

"If I seem excited, Mr. Bolling, it's only because I know that I can make you a very rich man."

QUESTION: Approximately how long did you stay there before the ambulance arrived?

ANSWER: [*Straightforward*] Twenty minutes. Long enough to help get Mrs. David straightened out.

[*Hesitating*] Oh, it seems like it was about uh, 20 minutes. Just long enough to help my friend Mrs. David, you know, get straightened out.

The students found the straightforward witnesses much more competent and credible.

Perceived trustworthiness

Speech style also affects a speaker's apparent trustworthiness. Gordon Hemsley and Anthony Doob (1978) found that if, while testifying, videotaped witnesses looked their questioner straight in the eye instead of gazing downward, they impressed people as more believable.

Trustworthiness is also higher if the audience believes the communicator is not trying to persuade them. In an experimental version of what later became the "hidden-camera" method of television advertising, Elaine Hatfield and Leon Festinger (Walster & Festinger, 1962) had some undergraduates eavesdrop on graduate students' conversations. (What they actually heard was a tape recording.) When the conversational topic was relevant to the eavesdroppers (having to do with campus regulations), the speakers had more influence if the listeners presumed the speakers were unaware of the eavesdropping. After all, if people don't know someone's listening, why would they be less than fully honest?

We also perceive as sincere those who argue against their own self-interest. Alice Eagly, Wendy Wood, and Shelly Chaiken (1978) presented students with a speech attacking a company's pollution of a river. When they said the speech was given by a political candidate with a business background or to an audience of company supporters, it seemed unbiased and was persuasive. When the same antibusiness speech was supposedly given to environmentalists by a pro-environment politician, listeners could attribute the politician's arguments to personal bias or to the audience. Being willing to suffer for one's beliefs—which Gandhi, Martin Luther King, Jr., and other great leaders have done—also helps convince people of one's sincerity (Knight & Weiss, 1980).

Norman Miller and his colleagues (1976) found that trustworthiness and credibility increase when people talk fast. People who listened to tape-recorded messages rated fast speakers (about 190 words per minute) as more objective, intelligent, and knowledgeable than slow speakers (about 110 words per minute). They also found the more rapid speakers more persuasive.

Some television ads are obviously constructed to make the communicator appear both expert and trustworthy. Drug companies peddle pain relievers using a speaker in a white lab coat, who declares confidently that most doctors recommend their ingredient (which is merely aspirin). Given such peripheral cues, people who don't care enough to analyze the evidence may reflexively infer the product's value. Other ads seem not to use the credibility principle. Is Alex Trebek really a trustworthy expert on insurance companies?

Attractiveness and liking

Most people deny that endorsements by star athletes and entertainers affect them. Everyone knows that stars are seldom knowledgeable about the products. Besides, we know the intent is to persuade us: we don't just accidentally eavesdrop on Don Cherry and Tie Domi buying subs. Such ads are based on another characteristic of an effective communicator: **attractiveness**. We may think we are not influenced by attractiveness or likeability, but researchers have found otherwise. We're more likely to respond to those we like, a phenomenon well known to those organizing charitable solicitations, candy sales, and Tupperware parties. Even a mere fleeting conversation with someone is enough to increase our liking for that person, and our responsiveness to his or her influence (Burger et al., 2001). Our liking may open us up to the communicator's arguments (central route persuasion), or it may trigger positive associations when we see the product later (peripheral route persuasion). As with credibility, the liking begets persuasion principle suggests applications (see Table 5–1).

attractiveness having qualities that appeal to an audience. An appealing communicator (often someone similar to the audience) is most persuasive on matters of subjective preference.

Attractiveness varies in several ways. *Physical appeal* is one. Arguments, especially emotional ones, are often more influential when they come from people we consider beautiful (Chaiken, 1979; Dion & Stein, 1978; Pallak et al., 1983).

TABLE 5–1 Six persuasion principles

In his book *Influence: Science and Practice*, persuasion researcher Robert Cialdini (2000) illustrates six principles that underlie human relationships and human influence.

Principle	Application
Authority: People defer to credible experts.	Establish your expertise; identify problems you have solved and people you have served.
Liking: People respond more affirmatively to those they like.	Win friends and influence people. Create bonds based on similar interests, praise freely.
Social proof: People allow the example of others to validate how to think, feel, and act.	Use "peer power"—have respected others lead the way.
Reciprocity: People feel obliged to repay in kind what they've received.	Be generous with your time and resources. What goes around, comes around.
Consistency: People tend to honour their public commitments.	Have others write or voice their intentions. Don't say "Please do this by. . . ." Instead, elicit a"yes" by asking.
Scarcity: People prize what's scarce.	Highlight genuinely exclusive information or opportunities.

Similarity is another. As Chapter 11 will emphasize, we tend to like people who are like us. We also are influenced by them, a fact that has been harnessed by a successful antismoking campaign that features youth appealing to other youth through ads that challenge the tobacco industry about its destructiveness and its marketing practices (Krisberg, 2004). People who act as we do, subtly mimicking our postures, are likewise more influential (Bailenson & Yee, 2005).

Another example: Theodore Dembroski, Thomas Lasater, and Albert Ramirez (1978) gave Black junior high students a taped appeal for proper dental care. When a dentist assessed the cleanliness of their teeth the next day, those who heard the appeal from a Black dentist had cleaner teeth. As a general rule, people respond better to a message that comes from someone in their group (Van Knippenberg & Wilke, 1992; Wilder, 1990).

Is similarity more important than credibility? Sometimes yes, sometimes no. Timothy Brock (1965) found paint store customers more influenced by the testimony of an ordinary person who had recently bought the same amount of paint they planned to buy than by an expert who had recently purchased 20 times as much. On the other hand, recall that when discussing dental hygiene, a leading dentist (a dissimilar but expert source) was more persuasive than a student (a similar but inexpert source).

Such seemingly contradictory findings bring out the detective in the scientist. They suggest that an undiscovered factor is at work—that similarity is more important given factor X, and credibility is more important given the absence of factor X. Factor X, as George Goethals and Erick Nelson (1973) discovered, is whether the topic is one of *subjective preference* or *objective reality.* When the choice concerns matters of personal value, taste, or way of life, *similar* communicators have the most influence. But on judgments of *fact*—Does Sydney have less rainfall than London?—confirmation of belief by a *dissimilar* person does more to boost confidence. A dissimilar person provides a more independent judgment.

WHAT IS SAID? THE MESSAGE CONTENT

It matters not only who says something, but *what* that person says. If you were to help organize an appeal to get people to vote for school taxes, or to stop smoking, or to give money to world hunger relief, you might wonder how to concoct a recipe for central route persuasion. Common sense could lead you to either side of these questions:

- Is a purely logical message more persuasive—or one that arouses emotion?
- Will you get more opinion change by advocating a position only slightly discrepant from the listeners' existing opinions? Or by advocating an extreme point of view?
- Should the message express your side only, or should it acknowledge and refute the opposing views?
- If people are to present both sides—say, in successive talks at a community meeting—is there an advantage to going first or last?

Let's take these questions one at a time.

Reason versus emotion

Suppose you were campaigning in support of world hunger relief. Would it be best to itemize your arguments and cite an array of impressive statistics? Or would you be more effective presenting an emotional approach—say, the compelling story of one starving child? Of course, an argument can be both reasonable and emotional. You can marry passion and logic. Still, which is more influential—reason or emotion? Was Shakespeare's Lysander right: "The will of man is by his reason sway'd"? Or was Lord Chesterfield's advice wiser: "Address yourself generally to the senses, to the heart, and to the weaknesses of mankind, but rarely to their reason"?

The answer: It depends on the audience. Well-educated or analytical people are more responsive to rational appeals than are less educated or less analytical people (Cacioppo et al., 1983, 1996; Hovland et al., 1949). Thoughtful, involved audiences travel the central route; they are most responsive to reasoned arguments. Disinterested audiences travel the peripheral route; they are more affected by how much they like the communicator (Chaiken, 1980; Petty et al., 1981).

It also depends on how people's attitudes were formed. When people's initial attitudes are formed primarily through emotion they are more persuaded by later emotional appeals; when their initial attitudes are formed primarily through reason, they are more persuaded by later intellectual arguments (Edwards, 1990; Fabrigar & Petty, 1999). New emotions may sway an emotion-based attitude. But to change an information-based attitude, more information may be needed.

Attractive communicators—such as Jacques Villeneuve at the height of his Formula One racing success in the late 90s—wearing a number of company logos often trigger peripheral route persuasion. We associate their message or product with our good feelings toward the communicator, and we approve and believe.

The effect of good feelings

Messages also become more persuasive through association with good feelings. Irving Janis and his colleagues (1965; Dabbs & Janis, 1965) found that students were more convinced by persuasive messages if they were allowed to enjoy peanuts and Pepsi while reading them (Figure 5–3). Similarly, Mark Galizio and Clyde Hendrick (1972) found that students were more persuaded by folk-song lyrics accompanied by pleasant guitar music than by unaccompanied lyrics. Those who like conducting business over sumptuous lunches with soft background music can celebrate these results.

> "The truth is always the strongest argument."
>
> Sophocles, *Phaedra*

Advertising research, as in one study of the persuasiveness of 168 television commercials (Agres, 1987), reveals that the most effective ads invoke both reasons ("You'll get whiter whites with Detergent X") and emotions ("Choosy mothers choose Jif").

> "Opinion is ultimately determined by the feelings and not by the intellect."
>
> Herbert Spencer, *Social Statics*, 1851

Good feelings often enhance persuasion, partly by enhancing positive thinking—if people are motivated to think—and partly by linking good feelings with the message (Petty et al., 1993). As noted in Chapter 3, in a good mood, people view the world through rose-coloured glasses. But they also make faster, more impulsive decisions; they rely more on peripheral cues (Bodenhausen, 1993; Schwarz et al., 1991). Unhappy people ruminate more before reacting, so they are less easily swayed by weak arguments. Thus, if you can't make a strong case, it's a smart idea

FIGURE 5–3

People who snacked as they read were more persuaded than those who read without snacking. (Data from Janis, Kaye, & Kirschner, 1965)

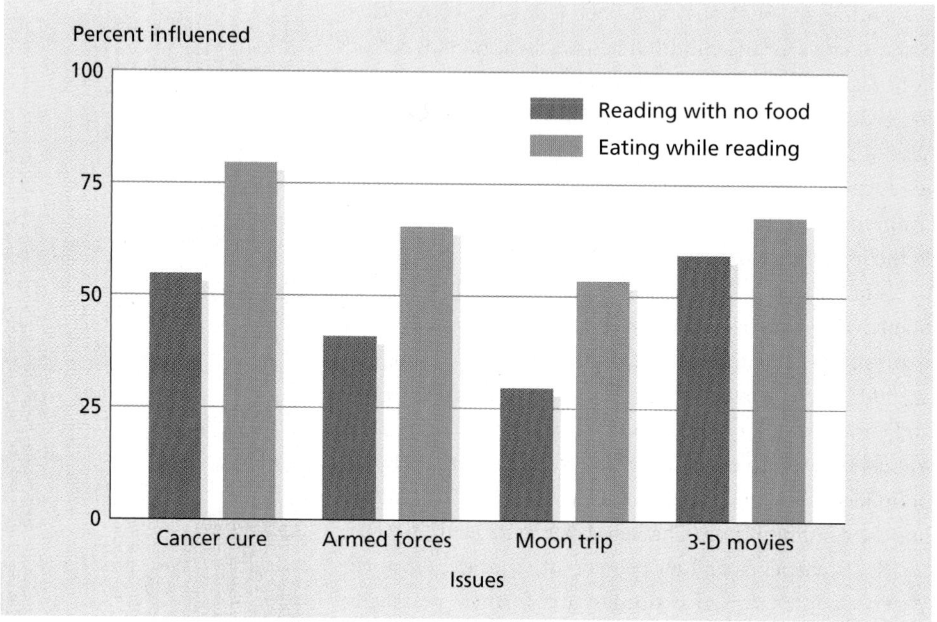

to put your audience in a good mood and hope they'll feel good about your message without thinking too much about it.

The effect of arousing fear

Messages also can be effective by evoking negative emotions. When trying to convince people to cut down on smoking, brush their teeth more often, get a tetanus shot, or drive carefully, a fear-arousing message can be potent (Muller & Johnson, 1990). By requiring cigarette makers to include graphic warning labels depicting the hazards of smoking on each pack of cigarettes, the Canadian government is counting on the fact that showing cigarette smokers the horrible things that can happen to people who smoke adds to persuasiveness (Newman, 2001). And the warning labels appear to be effective: compared to smokers in countries like the U.S. that have less prominent warnings on cigarette packs, Canadian smokers are more likely to have stopped from having a cigarette because of the warning labels, think more about the risks of smoking, and have increased intentions to quit smoking (Hammond et al., 2007).

But how much fear should you arouse? Should you evoke just a little fear, lest people become so frightened that they tune out your painful message? Or should you try to scare the daylights out of them? Experiments by Howard Leventhal (1970) and his collaborators and by Ronald Rogers and his collaborators (Robberson & Rogers, 1988) show that, often, the more frightened people are, the more they respond.

The effectiveness of fear-arousing communications is being applied in ads discouraging not only smoking, but also drinking and driving, and risky sexual behaviours. When Claude Levy-Leboyer (1988) found that attitudes toward alcohol and drinking habits among French youth were effectively changed by fear-arousing pictures, the French government incorporated this kind of information in its TV spots.

"If the jury had been sequestered in a nicer hotel, this would probably never have happened."

Good feelings help create positive attitudes.

Fear-arousing communications are increasing people's detection behaviours, such as getting mammograms, doing breast or testicular self-exams, and checking for signs of skin cancer. Sara Banks, Peter Salovey, and their colleagues (1995) had women aged 40–66 who had not obtained mammograms view an educational video on mammography. Of those who received a positively framed message (emphasizing that getting a mammogram can save your life through early detection), only half got a mammogram within 12 months. Of those who received a fear-framed message (emphasizing that not getting a mammogram can cost you your life), two-thirds got a mammogram within 12 months. Anxiety-creating health messages about, say, the risks of high cholesterol can increase people's intentions to eat a low fat, low cholesterol diet (Millar & Millar, 1996). To have one's fears aroused is to become more intensely interested in information about a disease, and in ways to prevent it (Das et al., 2003; Ruiter et al., 2001). Fear-framed messages

Canadian cigarette warnings, sampled here, use fear-arousal.

work better when trying to prevent a bad outcome (such as cancer) than when trying to promote a good outcome (such as fitness) (Lee & Aaker, 2004).

Playing on fear won't always make a message more potent, though. Many people who have been made afraid of AIDS are *not* abstaining or using condoms. Many people who have been made to fear an early death from smoking continue to smoke. When the fear pertains to a pleasurable activity, notes Elliot Aronson (1997), the result often is not behavioural change but denial. People may engage in denial because, when they aren't told how to avoid the danger, frightening messages can be overwhelming (Leventhal, 1970; Rogers & Mewborn, 1976).

For that reason, fear-arousing messages are more effective if you lead people not only to fear the severity and likelihood of a threatened event but also to perceive a solution and feel capable of implementing it (Maddux & Rogers, 1983). Many ads aimed at reducing sexual risks aim both to arouse fear—"AIDS kills"—and to offer a protective strategy: abstain or wear a condom or save sex for a committed relationship. During the 1980s, fear of AIDS did persuade many men to alter their behaviour. One study of 5000 gay men found that as the AIDS crisis mushroomed between 1984 and 1986, the number saying they were celibate or monogamous rose from 14 to 39 percent (Fineberg, 1988).

"If those who have studied the art of writing are in accord on any one point, it is on this: the surest way to arouse and hold the attention of the reader is by being specific, definite, and concrete."

William Strunk and E. B. White, *The Elements of Style*, 1979

Vivid propaganda often exploits fears. Streicher's *Der Stürmer* aroused fear with hundreds upon hundreds of unsubstantiated anecdotes about Jews who were said to have ground rats to make hash, seduced non-Jewish women, and cheated families out of their life savings. Streicher's appeals, like most Nazi propaganda, were emotional, not logical. The appeals also gave clear, specific instructions on how to combat "the danger": They listed Jewish businesses so readers would avoid them, encouraged readers to submit for publication the names of Germans who patronized Jewish shops and professionals, and directed readers to compile lists of Jews in their area (Bytwerk & Brooks, 1980).

Discrepancy

Picture the following scene: Wanda arrives home on spring vacation and hopes to convert her portly, middle-aged father to her new "health-fitness lifestyle." She runs 8 kilometres a day. Her father says his idea of exercise is "channel surfing." Wanda thinks, "Would I be more likely to get Dad off his duff by urging him to try a modest exercise program, say a daily walk, or by trying to get him involved in something strenuous, say a program of calisthenics and running? Maybe if I asked him to take up a rigorous exercise program he would compromise and at least take up something worthwhile. But then again maybe he'd think I'm crazy and do nothing."

Like Wanda, social psychologists can reason either way. Disagreement produces discomfort, and discomfort prompts people to change their opinions. (Recall from Chapter 4 the effects of dissonance.) So perhaps greater disagreement will produce more change. But then again, a communicator who proclaims an uncomfortable message may be discredited. People who disagree with conclusions drawn by a newscaster rate the newscaster as more biased, inaccurate, and untrustworthy. People are more open to conclusions within their range of acceptability (Liberman & Chaiken, 1992; Zanna, 1993). So perhaps greater disagreement will produce *less* change.

Elliot Aronson, Judith Turner, and Merrill Carlsmith (1963) reasoned that a *credible source*—one hard to discount—would elicit considerable opinion change when advocating a position *greatly discrepant* from the recipient's. Sure enough, when credible T. S. Eliot was said to have highly praised a disliked poem, people changed their opinion more than when he gave it faint praise. But when Agnes Stearns, a lowly university student, evaluated a disliked poem, high praise was no more persuasive than faint praise. Thus, as Figure 5–4 shows, discrepancy and credibility *interact:* The effect of a large versus small discrepancy depends on whether the communicator is credible.

So the answer to Wanda's question—"Should I argue an extreme position?"—is "It depends." Is Wanda in her adoring father's eyes a highly prestigious, authoritative source? If so, Wanda should push for a complete fitness program. If not, Wanda would be wise to make a more modest appeal.

The answer also depends on how involved her father is in the issue. Deeply involved people tend to accept only a narrow range of views. To them, a moderately discrepant message may seem foolishly radical, especially if the message argues an opposing view rather than being a more extreme version of a view with which they already agree (Maio et al., 1996; Pallak et al., 1972; Petty & Cacioppo, 1979; Rhine & Severance, 1970). If Wanda's father has not yet thought or cared much about exercise, she can probably take a more extreme position than if he is strongly committed to not exercising. So, *if you are a credible authority and your audience isn't much concerned with your issue, go for it:* Advocate a discrepant view.

One-sided versus two-sided appeals

Persuaders face another practical issue: how to deal with opposing arguments. Once again, common sense offers no clear answer. Acknowledging the opposing arguments might confuse the audience and weaken the case. On the other hand, a message might seem fairer and be more disarming if it recognizes the opposition's arguments.

Carol Werner and her colleagues (2002) showed the disarming power of a simple two-sided message in experimental messages that promoted aluminum can recycling. Signs added to wastebaskets in a classroom said, for example, "No Aluminum Cans Please!!!!! Use the Recycler Located on the First Floor, Near the Entrance." When a final persuasive message

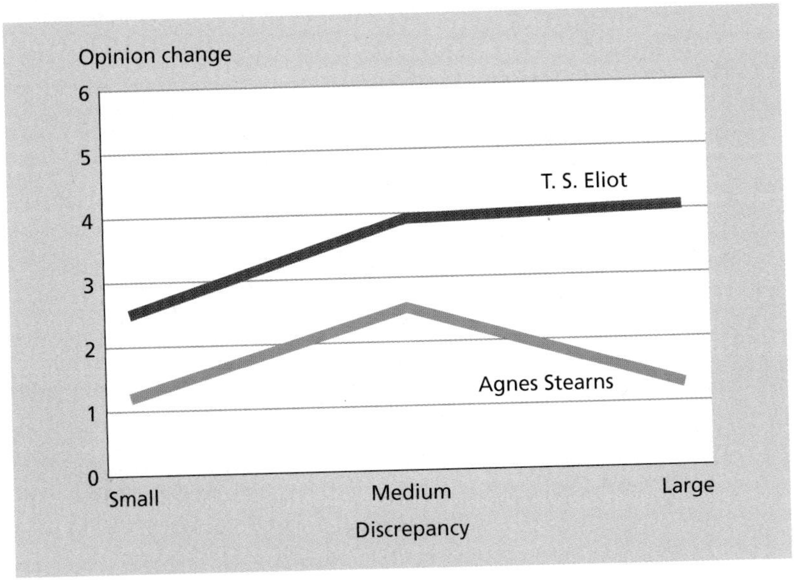

FIGURE 5–4

Discrepancy interacts with communicator credibility.

Only a highly credible communicator maintains effectiveness when arguing an extreme position. (Data from Aronson, Turner & Carlsmith, 1963)

acknowledged and responded to the main counterargument—"It May Be Inconvenient. But It Is Important!!!!!!!!!!"—recycling reached 80 percent (double the rate before any message, and more than in other message conditions).

After Germany's defeat in the Second World War, the Allies did not want soldiers to relax and think that the still ongoing war with Japan would become easy. So social psychologist Carl Hovland and his colleagues (1949) designed two radio broadcasts arguing that the war in the Pacific would last at least two more years. One broadcast was one-sided; it did not acknowledge the existence of contradictory arguments, such as the advantage of fighting only one enemy instead of two. The other broadcast was two-sided; it mentioned and responded to the opposing arguments. As Figure 5–5 illustrates, the effectiveness of the message depended on the listener. A one-sided appeal was most effective with those who already agreed. An appeal that acknowledged opposing arguments worked better with those who disagreed.

Experiments also revealed that a two-sided presentation is more persuasive and enduring if people are (or will be) aware of opposing arguments (Jones & Brehm, 1970; Lumsdaine & Janis, 1953). In simulated trials, a defence case becomes more credible when the defence brings up damaging evidence before the prosecution does (Williams et al., 1993). Apparently, a one-sided message stimulates an informed audience to think of counterarguments and to view the communicator as biased. Thus, a political candidate speaking to a politically informed group would indeed be wise to respond to the opposition. So *if your audience will be exposed to opposing views, offer a two-sided appeal.*

This interaction effect typifies persuasion research. For optimists, positive persuasion works best ("The new plan reduces tuition in exchange for part-time university service"). For pessimists, negative persuasion is more effective ("All students will have to work part-time for the university, lest they pay exorbitant tuition fees."). We might wish that persuasion variables had simple effects. (It would make this an easier chapter to study.) Alas, most variables, note Richard Petty and Duane Wegener (1998), "have complex effects—increasing persuasion in some situations and decreasing it in others."

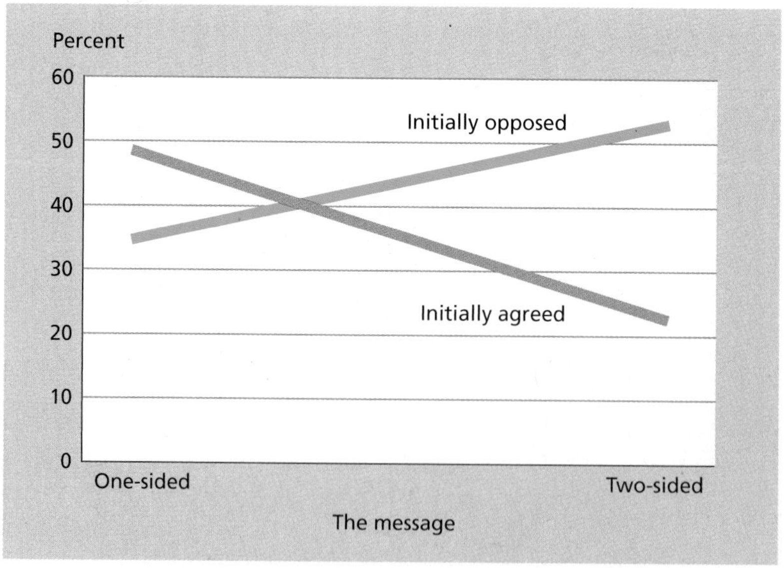

FIGURE 5–5

The interaction of initial opinion with one- versus two-sidedness.

After Germany's defeat in the Second World War, Allied soldiers skeptical of a message suggesting Japan's strength were more persuaded by a two-sided communication. Soldiers initially agreeing with the message were strengthened more by a one-sided message. (Data from Howland, Lumsdaine & Sheffield, 1949)

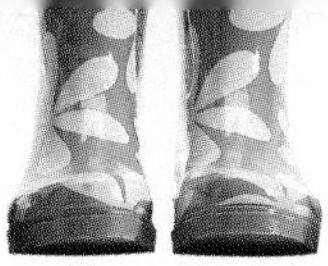

As students and scientists we cherish "Occam's razor"—seeking the simplest possible principles. But if human reality is complex, well, our principles will need to have some complexity as well.

> *"Opponents fancy they refute us when they repeat their own opinion and pay no attention to ours."*
>
> Goethe, *Maxims and Reflections*, early nineteenth century

Primacy versus recency

Imagine yourself a consultant to a prominent politician who must soon debate another prominent politician regarding a proposed arms limitation treaty. Three weeks before the vote, each politician is to appear on the nightly news and present a prepared statement. By the flip of a coin, your side receives the choice of whether to speak first or last. Knowing that you are a former social psychology student, everyone looks to you for advice.

You mentally scan your old books and lecture notes. Would first be best? People's preconceptions control their interpretations. Moreover, a belief, once formed, is difficult to discredit. So going first could give people ideas that would favourably bias how they would perceive and interpret the second speech. Besides, people may pay most attention to what comes first. But then again, people remember recent things best. Might it really be more effective to speak last?

Your first line of reasoning predicts what is most common, a **primacy effect**: Information presented early is most persuasive. First impressions *are* important. For example, can you sense a difference between these two descriptions?

primacy effect other things being equal, information presented first usually has the most influence

- John is intelligent, industrious, impulsive, critical, stubborn, and envious.
- John is envious, stubborn, critical, impulsive, industrious, and intelligent.

When Solomon Asch (1946) gave these sentences to university students, those who read the adjectives in the intelligent-to-envious order rated the person more positively than did those given the envious-to-intelligent order. The earlier information seemed to colour their interpretation of the later information, producing the primacy effect.

A similar effect occurs in experiments where people succeed on a guessing task 50 percent of the time. Those whose successes come early seem more able than those whose successes come mostly after early failures (Jones et al., 1968; Langer & Roth, 1975; McAndrew, 1981). A curious primacy effect also appears in political polls and in election voting: Candidates benefit from being listed first on the ballot (Moore, 2004). As another example, Norman Miller and Donald Campbell (1959) gave university students a condensed transcript from an actual civil trial. They placed the plaintiff's testimony and arguments in one block, those for the defence in another. The students read both blocks. When they returned a week later to declare their opinions, most sided with the information they had read first.

What about the opposite possibility? Would our better memory for the most recent information we've received ever create a **recency effect**? We have all experienced what the book of Proverbs observed: "The one who first states a case seems right, until the other comes and cross-examines." We know from our experience (as well as from memory experiments) that today's events can temporarily outweigh significant past events. To test this, Miller and Campbell gave another group of students one block of testimony to read. A week later the researchers had them read the second block and then immediately state their opinions. Now the results were just the reverse—a recency effect. Apparently the first block of arguments, being a week old, had largely faded from memory.

recency effect information presented last sometimes has the most influence. Recency effects are less common than primacy effects.

FIGURE 5–6

Primacy effect versus recency effect.

When two persuasive messages are back to back and the audience then responds at some later time, the first message has the advantage (primacy effect). When the two messages are separated in time and the audience responds soon after the second message, the second message has the advantage (recency effect).

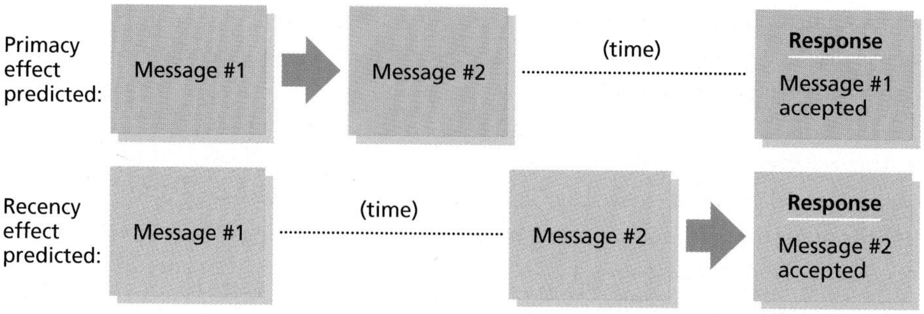

Forgetting creates the recency effect (1) when enough time separates the two messages *and* (2) when the audience commits itself soon after the second message. When the two messages are back to back, followed by a time gap, a primacy effect usually occurs (Figure 5–6 above). This is especially so when the first message stimulates thinking (Haugtvedt & Wegener, 1994). So what advice would you now give to the political debater?

HOW IS IT SAID? THE CHANNEL OF COMMUNICATION

For persuasion to occur there must be communication. And for communication to occur there must be a **channel of communication**: a face-to-face appeal, a written sign or document, a TV or radio advertisement.

channel of communication the way the message is delivered—whether face to face, in writing, on film, or in some other way

Commonsense psychology places faith in the power of written words. How do we try to get people out to a campus event? We post notices. How do we get drivers to slow down and keep their eyes on the road? We put "Drive Carefully" messages on billboards. How do we discourage students from dropping garbage on campus? We post anti-litter messages on campus bulletin boards and in mailboxes.

Active experience or passive reception?

Are spoken appeals more persuasive? Not necessarily. Those of us who do public speaking, as teachers or persuaders, become so easily enamoured of our spoken words that we are tempted to overestimate their power. Ask university students what aspect of their school experience has been most valuable or what they remember from their first year, and few, we are sad to say, recall the brilliant lectures that we faculty remember giving.

Thomas Crawford (1974) and his associates tested the impact of the spoken word by going to the homes of people from 12 churches shortly before and after they heard sermons opposing racial bigotry and injustice. When asked during the second interview whether they had heard or read anything about racial prejudice or discrimination since the previous interview, only 10 percent recalled the sermons spontaneously. When the remaining 90 percent were asked directly whether their priest had "talked about prejudice or discrimination in the last couple of weeks," more than 30 percent denied hearing such a sermon. The end result: the sermons left racial attitudes unaffected.

When you stop to think about it, an effective preacher has many hurdles to surmount. As Figure 5-1 showed, a persuasive speaker must deliver a message that not only gets attention but also is understandable, convincing, memorable, and compelling. A carefully thought-out appeal must consider each of those steps in the persuasion process.

Consider another well-intentioned effort. At one university a weeklong anti-litter campaign urged students with slogans such as, "Let's clean up our trash." Posters using such slogans were displayed in prominent places across campus, and flyers using the slogans were placed in students' mailboxes each morning. The day before the campaign began, social psychologist Raymond Paloutzian (1979) placed litter near a trash can along a well-travelled sidewalk. Then he stepped back to record the behaviour of 180 passersby. No one picked up anything. On the last day of the campaign he repeated the test with 180 more passersby. Did the pedestrians now race one another in their zeal to comply with the appeals? Hardly. Only two of the 180 picked up the trash.

Passively received appeals, however, are not always futile. One drugstore sells two brands of Aspirin, one heavily advertised and one unadvertised. Apart from slight differences in how fast each tablet crumbles in your mouth, any pharmacist will tell you the two brands are identical. Aspirin is Aspirin. Our bodies cannot tell the difference. But our pocketbooks can. The advertised brand sells for three times the price of the unadvertised brand.

Although currently banned, cigarette advertising was once common. This photo shows models practising the "correct" pucker and blow technique for a 1950s TV ad.

With such power, can the media help a wealthy political candidate buy an election? In political elections, those who spend the most usually get the most votes (Grush, 1980; opensecrets.org, 2005). Advertising exposure helps make an unfamiliar candidate into a familiar one. As we will see in Chapter 11, mere exposure to unfamiliar stimuli breeds liking. Moreover, *mere repetition* can make things believable. People rate trivial statements like "Mercury has a higher boiling point than copper" as more truthful if they read and rated them a week before.

Researcher Hal Arkes (1990) views such findings as "scary." As political manipulators know, believable lies can displace hard truths. Repeated clichés can cover complex realities. Even repeatedly saying that a consumer claim ("Shark cartilage is good for arthritis") is false can, when the discounting is presented amid other true and *false* claims, lead older adults to later misremember it as *true* (Skurnik et al., 2005). As they forget the discounting, their lingering familiarity with the claim can make it seem believable.

In study after study, most people agree that mass media influence attitudes—other people's attitudes, but not their own.

Duck et al., 1995

Mere repetition of a statement also serves to increase its fluency—the ease with which it spills off our tongue—which increases believability (McGlone & Tofighbakhsh, 2000). Other factors, such as rhyming, also increase fluency, and believability. "Haste makes waste" may say essentially the same thing as "rushing causes mistakes," but it seems more true. Whatever makes for fluency (familiarity, rhyming) also makes for credibility.

Because passively received appeals are sometimes effective and sometimes not, can we specify in advance the topics on which a persuasive appeal will be successful? There is a simple rule: Persuasion *decreases* as the significance and familiarity of the issue *increase*. On minor issues, such as which brand of Aspirin to buy, it's easy to demonstrate the media's power. On more familiar and important issues, such as whether the federal government is doing enough to meet Canada's Kyoto Accord targets for reduced environmental pollution, persuading people is like trying to push a piano uphill. It is not impossible, but one shove won't do it.

As we saw in Chapter 4, active experience also strengthens attitudes. When we act, we amplify the idea behind what we've done, especially when we feel responsible. What is more, attitudes more often endure and influence our behaviour when rooted in our own experience. Compared with attitudes formed passively, experience-based attitudes are more confident, more stable, and less vulnerable to attack. These principles are evident in many studies which show that the most effective HIV-prevention interventions not only give people information but also give them behavioural training, such as by practising assertiveness in refusing sex and using protection (Albarracin et al., 2005).

Personal versus media influence

Persuasion studies demonstrate that the major influence on us is not the media but our contact with people. Modern selling strategies seek to harness the power of word-of-mouth personal influence through "viral marketing," "creating a buzz," and "seeding" sales (Walker, 2004). The *Harry Potter* series was not expected to be a best seller (*Harry Potter and the Philosopher's Stone* had a first printing of 500 copies) until kids talking to other kids made it so.

> *"You do realize, you will never make a fortune out of writing children's books?"*
>
> J. K. Rowling's literary agent before the release of *Harry Potter and the Philosopher's Stone*

Two classic field experiments illustrate the strength of personal influence. Some years ago, Samuel Eldersveld and Richard Dodge (1954) studied political persuasion in a local election. They divided citizens intending not to vote for a revision of the city charter into three groups. Of those exposed only to what they saw and heard in the mass media, 19 percent changed their minds and voted in favour of the revision on election day. Of a second group, who received four mailings in support of the revision, 45 percent voted for it. Among people in a third group, who were visited personally and given the appeal face-to-face, 75 percent cast their votes for the revision.

In another field experiment, a research team led by John Farquhar and Nathan Maccoby (1977; Maccoby & Alexander, 1980; Maccoby, 1980) tried to reduce the frequency of heart disease among middle-aged adults in three small California cities. To check the relative effectiveness of personal and media influence, they interviewed and medically examined some 1200 people before the project began and at the end of each of the following three years. Residents of Tracy, California, received no persuasive appeals other than those occurring in their regular media. In Gilroy, California, a two-year multimedia campaign used TV, radio, newspapers, and direct mail to teach people about coronary risk and what they could do to reduce it. In Watsonville, California, this media campaign was supplemented by personal contacts with two-thirds of those whose blood pressure, weight, and age put them in a high-risk group. Using behaviour-modification principles, the researchers helped people set specific goals and reinforced their successes.

As Figure 5–7 shows, after one, two, and three years the high-risk people in Tracy (the control town) were about as much at risk as before. High-risk people in Gilroy, which was deluged

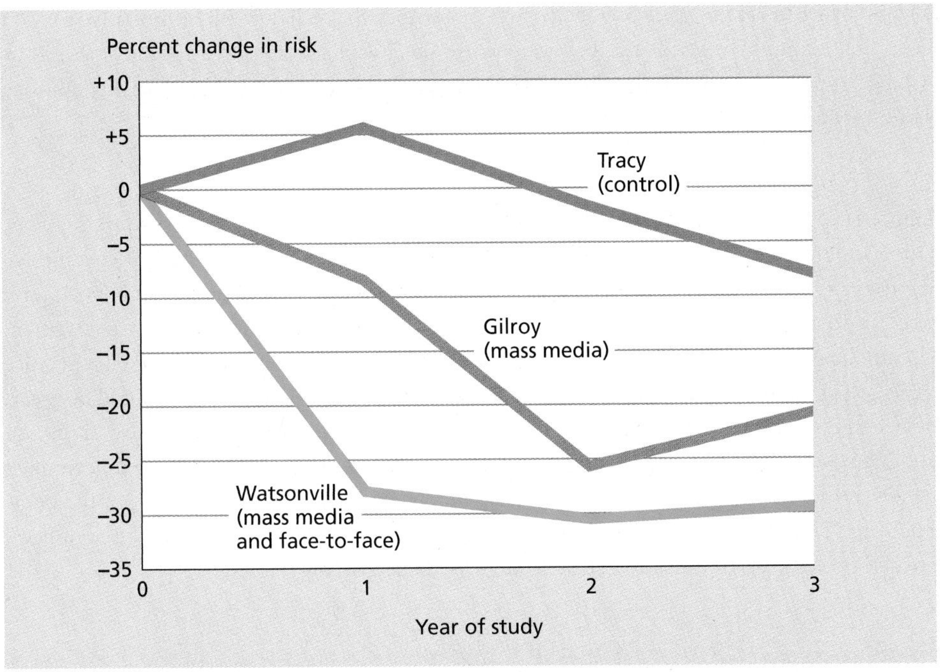

FIGURE 5–7
Percentage change from baseline (0) in coronary risk after one, two, or three years of health education. (Data from Maccoby, 1980)

with media appeals, improved their health habits and were now somewhat less at risk. Those in Watsonville, who also received the personal contacts, changed most.

Do you recognize the potency of personal influence in your own experience? In retrospect, most university students say they have learned more from their friends and other students than from contact with books or professors. Educational researchers have confirmed the students' intuition: Out-of-class personal relationships powerfully influence how students mature during university (Astin, 1972; Wilson et al., 1975).

Media influence: The two-step flow

Although face-to-face influence is usually greater than media influence, we should not underestimate the media's power. Those who personally influence our opinions must get their ideas somewhere, and often their sources are the media. Elihu Katz (1957) observed that much of the media's effects operate in a **two-step flow of communication**: from media to opinion leaders to the rank and file. In any large group, it is these *opinion leaders* and trendsetters—"the influentials"—that marketers and politicians seek to woo (Keller & Berry, 2003). Opinion leaders are individuals perceived as experts. They may include talk show hosts and editorial columnists; doctors, teachers, and scientists; and people in all walks of life who have made it their business to absorb information and to inform their friends and family. If a father wants to evaluate computer equipment, he may defer to the opinions of his son, who gets many of his ideas from the printed page. Sell the son, and you sell the father too.

two-step flow of communication
the process by which media influence often occurs through opinion leaders, who in turn influence others

The two-step flow model reminds us that media influences penetrate the culture in subtle ways. Even if the media had little direct effect on people's attitudes, they could still have a big indirect effect. Those rare children who grow up without watching television do not grow up beyond television's influence. Unless they live as hermits, they will join in TV-imitative play on the school ground. They will ask their parents for the TV-related toys their friends have. They will beg or demand to watch their friend's favourite programs. Parents can just say no, but they cannot switch off television's influence.

Comparing media

Lumping together all media, from mass mailings to television to podcasting, oversimplifies. Studies comparing different media find that the more lifelike the medium, the more persuasive its message. Thus the order of persuasiveness seems to be: live, videotaped, audiotaped, and written. To add to the complexity, messages are best *comprehended* and *recalled* when written. Comprehension is one of the first steps in the persuasion process. So Shelly Chaiken and Alice Eagly (1978) reasoned that if a message is difficult to comprehend, persuasion should be greatest when the message is written. They gave students easy or difficult messages in writing, on audiotape, or videotape. Figure 5–8 displays their results: Difficult messages were indeed most persuasive when written, easy messages when videotaped. By drawing attention to the communicator and away from the message itself, the TV medium also draws attention to peripheral cues, such as the communicator's attractiveness (Chaiken & Eagly, 1983).

TO WHOM IS IT SAID? THE AUDIENCE

People's traits often don't predict their response to social influence. A particular trait may enhance one step in the persuasion process (Figure 5–1) but work against another. Take self-esteem. People with low self-esteem are often slow to comprehend a message and therefore hard to persuade. Those with high self-esteem may comprehend yet remain confident of their own opinions; thus self-esteem alone won't directly predict persuadability. The conclusion: People with moderate self-esteem are the easiest to influence (Rhodes & Wood, 1992).

Let's also consider two other characteristics of those who receive a message: their age and their thoughtfulness.

FIGURE 5–8

Easy-to-understand messages are most persuasive when videotaped. Difficult messages are most persuasive when written. Thus the difficulty of the message interacts with the medium to determine persuasiveness. (Data from Chaiken & Eagly, 1978)

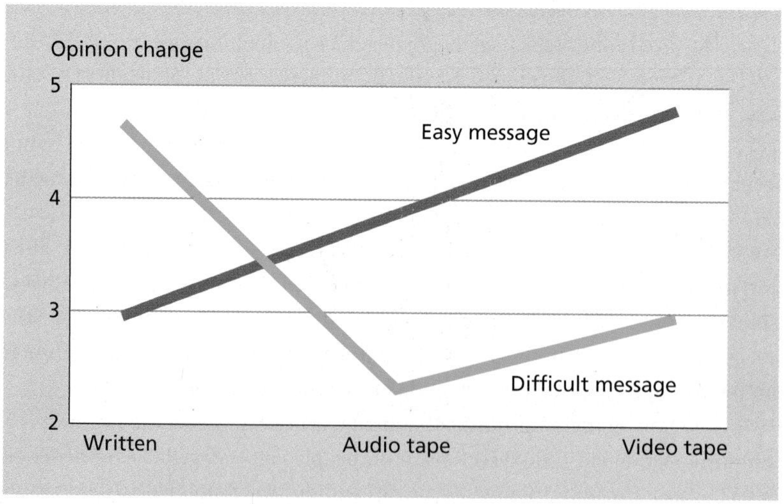

STORY BEHIND THE RESEARCH

Shelley Chaiken
New York University

My interest in studying persuasion was spurred when my graduate adviser, Alice Eagly, pointed me to William McGuire's analysis of media effects. McGuire reasoned that different factors might affect someone's *comprehending* a persuasive argument and their *yielding* to it. This took me back to my preteen experience watching John F. Kennedy demolish (or so I thought) Richard Nixon during their presidential debates. Yet, I later learned, the perception that Kennedy "won" may have been stronger among people who *viewed* the debates than among people who only *heard* them or *read* them. Had my verdict been influenced more than I'd imagined by my hero's attractive appearance and bearing?

My master's thesis research (Figure 5–8) confirmed that the medium of communication indeed matters. Moreover, this led to the idea that people sometimes process messages *heuristically*, basing judgments on extrinsic factors such as the communicator's likeability or attractiveness. I like to take credit for this idea, but it's high time I thanked Alice Eagly, Bill McGuire, and President Kennedy for their input.

How old are they?

People today tend to have different social and political attitudes depending on their age. There are two explanations for the difference. One is a *life cycle explanation:* Attitudes change (for example, become more conservative) as people grow older. The other is a *generational explanation:* Attitudes do *not* change; older people largely hold onto the attitudes they adopted when they were young. Because these attitudes are different from those now being adopted by young people today, a generation gap develops.

The evidence mostly supports the generational explanation. In surveying and resurveying groups of younger and older people over several years, the attitudes of older people usually change less than do those of young people. As David Sears (1979, 1986) puts it, researchers have "almost invariably found generational rather than life cycle effects."

The teens and early twenties are important formative years (Krosnick & Alwin, 1989; Arnett, 2000). Attitudes are changeable during that time and the attitudes formed then tend to stabilize through middle adulthood. Young people might therefore be advised to choose their social influences—the groups they join, the media they imbibe, the roles they adopt—carefully.

A striking example: During the late 1930s and early 1940s, students at one small prestigious school—women from privileged, conservative families—encountered a free-spirited environment led by a left-leaning young faculty. One of those faculties, social psychologist Theodore Newcomb, later denied the faculty was trying to make "good little liberals" out of its students. Nevertheless, they succeeded. The students became much more liberal than was typical of those from their social backgrounds. Moreover, attitudes formed at the school endured. A half-century later, the women, now in their seventies, voted for liberal candidates by a 3 to 1 margin in the 1984 national election, while other university-educated women in their seventies were voting for conservative candidates by a 3 to 1 margin (Alwin et al., 1991). The views embraced at an impressionable time had survived a lifetime of wider experience.

Adolescent and early-adulthood experiences are formative partly because they make deep and lasting impressions. When Howard Schuman and Jacqueline Scott (1989) asked people to name the one or two most important world events of the previous half-century, most recalled events from their teens or early twenties. For those who experienced the Great Depression or the Second World War as 16- to 24-year-olds, those events overshadowed more recent events that were imprinted on the minds of those who experienced them as 16- to 24-year-olds. We may therefore expect that for today's young adults the memorable turning points in world history will be events such as the September 11, 2001 terrorist attacks and Canada's military presence in Afghanistan.

That is not to say that older adults are inflexible. Studies conducted by Norval Glenn in 1980 and 1981 found that most people in their fifities and sixties had more liberal sexual and racial attitudes than they had in their thirties and forties. Given the "sexual revolution" that began in the 1960s and became mainstream in the 1970s, these middle-aged people had apparently changed with the times. Few of us are utterly uninfluenced by changing cultural norms. Moreover, research by Penny Visser and Jon Krosnick (1998) suggests that elderly adults, near the end of the life cycle, may again become more susceptible to attitude change, perhaps because of the decline in the strength of their attitudes.

What are they thinking?

In central route persuasion, what's crucial is not the message but the responses it evokes in a person's mind. Our minds are not sponges that soak up whatever pours over them. If the message summons favourable thoughts, it persuades us. If it provokes us to think of contrary arguments, we remain unpersuaded.

Forewarned is forearmed—If you care enough to counterargue

What circumstances breed counterarguing? One is a warning that someone is going to try to persuade you. If you had to tell your family that you wanted to drop out of school, you would likely anticipate their pleading with you to stay. So you might develop a list of arguments to counter every conceivable argument they might make.

Jonathan Freedman and David Sears (1965) demonstrated the difficulty of their trying to persuade you under such circumstances. They warned one group of high schoolers that they were going to hear a talk: "Why Teenagers Should Not Be Allowed to Drive." Those forewarned did not budge in their opinions. Others, not forewarned, did budge. In courtrooms, too, defence attorneys sometimes forewarn juries about prosecution evidence to come. With mock juries, such "stealing thunder" neutralizes its impact (Dolnik et al., 2003).

Distraction disarms counterarguing

Verbal persuasion is also enhanced by distracting people with something that attracts their attention just enough to inhibit counterarguing (Festinger & Maccoby, 1964; Keating & Brock, 1974; Osterhouse & Brock, 1970). Political ads often use this technique. The words promote the candidate, and the visual images keep us occupied so we don't analyze the words. Distraction is especially effective when the message is simple (Harkins & Petty, 1981; Regan & Cheng,

1973). Sometimes, though, distraction precludes our processing an ad. That helps explain why ads viewed during violent or sexual TV programs are so often unremembered and ineffective (Bushman, 2005; Bushman & Bonacci, 2002).

need for cognition the motivation to think and analyze. Assessed by agreement with items such as "The notion of thinking abstractly is appealing to me" and disagreement with items such as "I only think as hard as I have to."

Uninvolved audiences use peripheral cues

Recall the two routes to persuasion—the central route of systematic thinking and the peripheral route of heuristic cues. Like the road through town, the central route has starts and stops as the mind analyzes arguments and formulates responses. Like the highway around town, the peripheral route zips people to their destination. Analytical people—those with a high **need for cognition**—enjoy thinking carefully and prefer central routes (Cacioppo et al., 1996). People who like to conserve their mental resources—those with a low need for cognition—are quicker to respond to such peripheral cues as the communicator's attractiveness and the pleasantness of the surroundings.

But the issue matters, too. All of us struggle actively with issues that involve us while making snap judgments about things that matter little (Johnson & Eagly, 1990; Maio & Olson, 1990). The more we think about an issue the more we take the central route. Consider the following study conducted by Queen's University's Leandre Fabrigar and his colleagues (1998). They made some students think a lot about their attitudes toward vegetarianism by asking them a lot of questions about it; others were only asked about their views once. As you can see in Figure 5–9 those who had thought a lot about their views were persuaded by strong arguments about vegetarianism but were uninfluenced by weak arguments. But for people who had not thought much about the topic, the strength of the arguments did not matter.

"To be forewarned and therefore forearmed . . . is eminently rational if our belief is true; but if our belief is a delusion, this same forewarning and forearming would obviously be the method whereby the delusion rendered itself incurable."

C. S. Lewis, *Screwtape Proposes a Toast*, 1965

This simple theory—that *what we think in response to a message is crucial*, especially if we are motivated and able to think about it—has generated many predictions, most of which have been confirmed by Petty, Cacioppo, and others (Axsom et al., 1987; Hafer et al., 1996; Harkins & Petty, 1987; Leippe & Elkin, 1987). Many experiments have explored ways to stimulate people's thinking—by

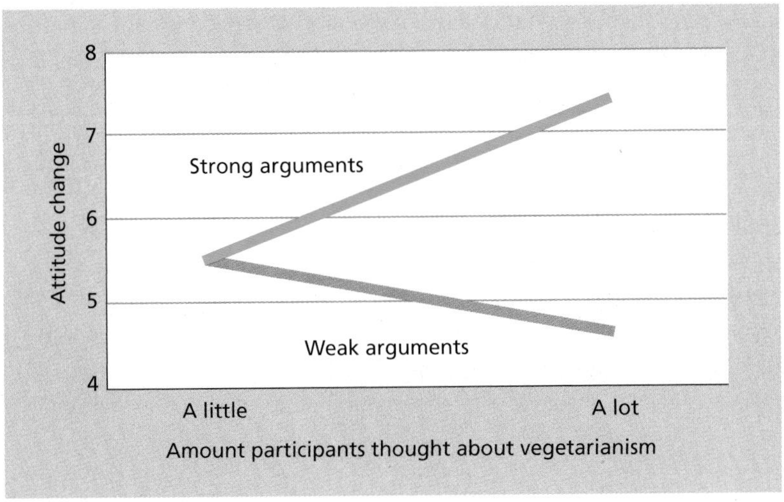

FIGURE 5–9

Attitude accessibility and persuasion.

When people's attitudes are accessible they process information through the central route, but when their attitudes are less accessible they process information through the peripheral route. (Data from Fabrigar et al., 1998)

using *rhetorical questions;* by presenting *multiple speakers* (for example, having three speakers each give one argument instead of one speaker giving three); by making people *feel responsible* for evaluating or passing along the message; by *repeating* the message; and by getting people's *undistracted attention.* The consistent finding with each of these techniques: *Stimulating thinking makes strong messages more persuasive and* (because of counterarguing) *weak messages less persuasive.*

The theory also has practical implications. Effective communicators care not only about their images and their messages but also about how their audience is likely to react. How they will react depends not only on their interest in the issue but also on their dispositions—their analytical inclinations, their tolerance for uncertainty, their need to be true to themselves (Cacioppo et al., 1996; Kruglanski et al., 1993; Snyder & DeBono, 1987; Sorrentino et al., 1988). The best instructors tend to get students to think actively. They ask rhetorical questions, provide intriguing examples, and challenge students with difficult problems. All these techniques are likely to foster processing information through the central route to persuasion. In classes where the instruction is less engaging you can provide your own central processing. If you think about the material and elaborate on the arguments you are likely to do better in the course.

SUMMING UP: WHAT ARE THE ELEMENTS OF PERSUASION?

What makes persuasion effective? Researchers have explored four factors: the communicator (who says it), the message (what is said), the channel (how is it said), and the audience (to whom is it said).

Credible communicators are perceived as trustworthy experts. People who speak unhesitatingly, who talk fast, and who look listeners straight in the eye seem more credible. So are people who argue against their own self-interest. An attractive communicator also is effective on matters of taste and personal values.

The message itself persuades; associating it with good feelings makes it more convincing. People often make quicker, less reflective judgments while in good moods. Fear-arousing messages can also be effective, especially if recipients can take protective action.

How discrepant a message should be from an audience's existing opinions depends on the communicator's credibility. And whether a one- or a two-sided message is most persuasive depends on whether the audience already agrees with the message, is unaware of opposing arguments, and is unlikely later to consider the opposition.

When two sides of an issue are included, the primacy effect results in the first message being more persuasive. If a time gap separates the presentations, the effect of the result will likely be a recency effect in which the second message prevails.

Another important consideration is *how* the message is communicated. Usually face-to-face appeals work best. Print media can be effective for complex messages. And the mass media can be effective when the issue is minor or unfamiliar.

Finally, it matters *who* receives the message. What does the audience think while receiving a message? Do they think favourable thoughts? Do they counterargue? Were they forewarned? The age of the audience makes a difference; young people's attitudes are more subject to change.

EXTREME PERSUASION: HOW DO CULTS INDOCTRINATE?

What persuasion and group influence principles are harnessed by New Religious movements ("cults")?

On March 22, 1997, Marshall Herff Applewhite and 37 of his disciples decided the time had come to shed their bodies—mere "containers"—and be whisked up to a UFO trailing Haley-Bopp Comet, en route to heaven's gate. So they put themselves to sleep by mixing phenobarbital into pudding or applesauce, washing it down with vodka, and then fixing plastic bags over their heads so they would suffocate in their slumber. On that same day, a cottage in the French-Canadian village of St. Casimir exploded in an inferno, consuming five people—the latest of 74 members of the Order of the Solar Temple to have committed suicide in Canada, Switzerland, and France. All were hoping to be transported to the star Sirius, nine light-years away.

The question on many minds: What persuades people to leave behind their former beliefs and join these mental chain gangs? Shall we attribute their strange behaviours to strange personalities? Or do their experiences illustrate the common dynamics of social influence and persuasion?

Bear two things in mind: First, this is hindsight analysis. It uses persuasion principles as categories for explaining, after the fact, a troubling social phenomenon. Second, explaining *why* people believe something says nothing about the *truth* of their beliefs. That is a logically separate issue. A psychology of religion might tell us *why* a theist believes in God and an atheist disbelieves, but it cannot tell us who is right. Explaining either belief does not change its validity. So if someone tries to discount your beliefs by saying, "You just believe that because . . . ," you might recall Archbishop William Temple's reply to a questioner who challenged: "Well, of course, Archbishop, the point is that you believe what you believe because of the way you were brought up." To which the archbishop replied: "That is as it may be. But the fact remains that you believe I believe what I believe because of the way I was brought up, because of the way you were brought up."

In recent decades, several **cults**—which some social scientists prefer to call New Religious movements—have gained much publicity: Sun Myung Moon's Unification Church, Jim Jones's People's Temple, David Koresh's Branch Davidians, and Marshall Applewhite's Heaven's Gate. Sun Myung Moon's mixture of Christianity, anticommunism, and glorification of Moon himself as a new messiah attracted a worldwide following. In response to Moon's declaration, "What I wish must be your wish," many committed themselves and their incomes to the Unification Church.

cult (also called New Religious movement) a group typically characterized by (1) the distinctive ritual of its devotion to a god or a person, (2) isolation from the surrounding "evil" culture, and (3) a charismatic leader. (A sect, by contrast, is a spinoff from a major religion.)

In 1978 in Guyana, 914 followers of the Reverend Jones, who had followed him there from San Francisco, shocked the world when they died by following his order to down a strawberry drink laced with tranquilizers, painkillers, and a lethal dose of cyanide.

In 1993, high-school dropout David Koresh used his talent for memorizing Scripture and mesmerizing people to seize control of a faction of a sect called the Branch Davidians. Over time, members were gradually relieved of their bank accounts and possessions. Koresh also persuaded the men to live celibately while he slept with their wives and daughters, and he convinced his 19 "wives" that they should bear his children. Under siege after a shootout that killed six members and four federal agents, Koresh told his followers they would soon die and go with him straight to heaven. Federal agents rammed the compound with tanks, hoping to inject tear gas, but by the end of the assault, 86 people were consumed in a fire that engulfed the compound.

Marshall Applewhite was not similarly tempted to command sexual favours. Having been fired from two music teaching jobs for affairs with students, he sought sexless devotion by castration, as had seven of the other 17 Heaven's Gate men who died with him (Chua-Eoan, 1997; Gardner, 1997). While in a psychiatric hospital in 1971, Applewhite had linked up with nurse and astrology dabbler Bonnie Lu Nettles, who gave the intense and charismatic Applewhite a cosmological vision of a route to "the next level." Preaching with passion, he persuaded his followers to renounce families, sex, drugs, and personal money with promises of a spaceship voyage to salvation.

How could such things happen? What persuaded these people to give such total allegiance? Shall we make disposition explanations—by blaming the victims? Shall we dismiss them as gullible or unbalanced? Or can familiar principles of conformity, compliance, dissonance, persuasion, and group influence explain their behaviour—putting them on common ground with the rest of us who in our own ways are shaped by such forces?

ATTITUDES FOLLOW BEHAVIOUR

As Chapter 4 showed over and again, people usually internalize commitments made voluntarily, publicly, and repeatedly. Cult leaders seem to know this.

Compliance breeds acceptance

New converts soon learn that membership is no trivial matter. They are quickly made active members of the team. Rituals within the cult community, and public canvassing and fundraising, strengthen the initiates' identities as members. As those in social-psychological experiments come to believe in what they bear witness to (Aronson & Mills, 1959; Gerard & Mathewson, 1966), so cult initiates become committed advocates. The greater the personal commitment, the more the need to justify it.

The foot-in-the-door phenomenon

How are people induced to make such a drastic life change? Seldom by an abrupt, conscious decision. One does not just decide, "I'm through with mainstream religion. I'm gonna find a cult." Nor do cult recruiters approach people on the street with, "Hi. I'm a Moonie. Care to join us?" Rather, the recruitment strategy exploits the foot-in-the-door principle. Unification Church recruiters, for example, would invite people to a dinner and then to a weekend of warm fellowship and discussions of philosophies of life. At the weekend retreat, they encouraged the attenders to join them in songs, activities, and discussion. Potential converts were then urged to sign up for longer training retreats. Eventually the activities became more arduous, culminating in having recruits solicit contributions and attempt to convert others.

Once into the cult, converts find that monetary offerings are at first voluntary, then mandatory. Jim Jones eventually inaugurated a required 10-percent-of-income contribution, which soon increased to 25 percent. Finally, he ordered members to turn over to him everything they owned. Workloads also became progressively more demanding. Former cult member Grace Stoen recalls the gradual progress:

> Nothing was ever done drastically. That's how Jim Jones got away with so much. You slowly gave up things and slowly had to put up with more, but it was always done very gradually. It was amazing, because you would sit up sometimes and say, wow, I really have given up a lot. I really am putting up with a lot. But he did it so slowly that you figured, I've made it this far, what the hell is the difference? (Conway & Siegelman, 1979, p. 236)

PERSUASIVE ELEMENTS

We can also analyze cult persuasion using the factors discussed in this chapter (and summarized in Figure 5–10): *Who* (the communicator) said *what* (the message) to *whom* (the audience)?

"You go home without me, Irene. I'm going to join this man's cult."

Hundreds of thousands of people in recent years have been recruited by members of some 2500 religious cults, but seldom through an abrupt decision.

The communicator

Successful cults have a charismatic leader—someone who attracts and directs the members. As in experiments on persuasion, a credible communicator is someone the audience perceives as expert and trustworthy—for example, as "Father" Moon.

Jim Jones used "psychic readings" to establish his credibility. Newcomers were asked to identify themselves as they entered the church before services. Then one of his aides would call the person's home and say, "Hi. We're doing a survey, and we'd like to ask you some questions." During the service, one ex-member recalled, Jones would call out the person's name and say

> Have you ever seen me before? Well, you live in such and such a place, your phone number is such and such, and in your living room you've got this, that, and the other, and on your sofa you've got such and such a pillow. . . . Now do you remember me ever being in your house? (Conway & Siegelman, 1979, p. 234)

Trust is another aspect of credibility. Cult researcher Margaret Singer (1979) noted that middle-class Caucasian youths are more vulnerable because they are more trusting. They lack the "street smarts" of lower-class youths (who know how to resist a hustle) and the wariness of

FIGURE 5–10

Variables known to affect the impact of persuasive communications.

In real life, these variables may interact; the effect of one may depend on the level of another.

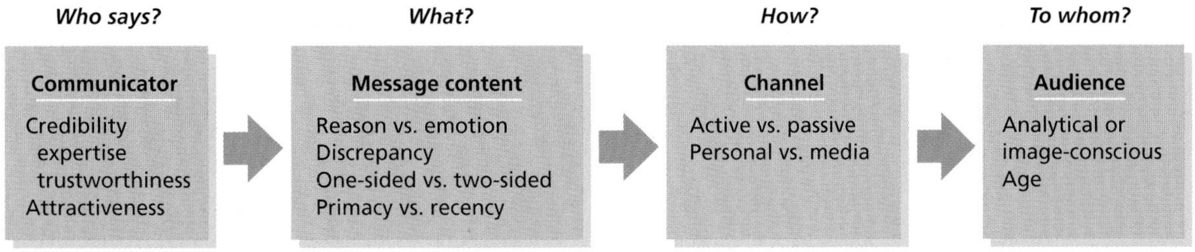

upper-class youths (who have been warned of kidnappers since childhood). Many cult members have been recruited by friends or relatives, people they trust (Stark & Bainbridge, 1980).

The message

The vivid, emotional messages and the warmth and acceptance with which the group showers them can be strikingly appealing: Trust the master, join the family; we have the answer, the "one way." The message echoes through channels as varied as lectures, small-group discussions, and direct social pressure.

The audience

Recruits are often young—people under 25 and still at that comparatively open age before attitudes and values stabilize. Some, such as the followers of Jim Jones, are less educated people who like the simplicity of the message and find it difficult to counterargue. But most are educated, middle-class people who, taken by the ideals, overlook the contradictions in those who profess selflessness and practise greed, who pretend concern and behave indifferently.

Potential converts often are at a turning point in their lives, facing a personal crisis, or vacationing or living away from home. They have needs; the cult offers them an answer (Singer, 1979; Lofland & Stark, 1965). Gail Maeder joined Heaven's Gate after her T-shirt shop had failed. David Moore joined when he was 19, just out of high school, and searching for direction. Times of social and economic upheaval are especially conducive to an ayatollah or a "father" who can make apparent simple sense out of the confusion (O'Dea, 1968; Sales, 1972).

Most of those who have carried out suicide bombings in the Middle East (and other places such as Bali, Madrid, and London) were, likewise, young men at the transition between adolescence and maturity. Like cult recruits, they come under the influence of authoritative, religiously oriented communicators who indoctrinate them into seeing themselves as "living martyrs" whose fleeting moment of self-destruction will be their portal into bliss and heroism. To help ensure their overcoming the will to survive, each candidate makes public commitments—creating a will, writing goodbye letters, making a farewell video—that create a psychological point of no return (Kruglanski & Grolec de Zavala, 2005). All this typically transpires in the relative isolation of small cells, with group influences that fan hatred for the enemy.

GROUP EFFECTS

Cults also illustrate the upcoming theme of Chapter 7: the power of a group to shape members' views and behaviour. The cult typically separates members from their previous social support systems and isolates them with other cultists. There may then occur what Rodney Stark and William Bainbridge (1980) call a "social implosion": External ties weaken until the group collapses inward socially, each person engaging only with other group members. Cut off from families and former friends, they lose access to counterarguments. The group now offers identity and defines reality. Because the cult frowns on or punishes disagreements, the apparent consensus helps eliminate any lingering doubts. Moreover, stress and emotional arousal narrow attention, making people "more susceptible to poorly supported arguments, social pressure, and the temptation to derogate nongroup members" (Baron, 2000).

Marshall Applewhite and Bonnie Nettles (who died of cancer in 1985) at first formed their own group of two, reinforcing each other's aberrant thinking—a phenomenon that psychiatrists call *folie à deux* (French for "insanity of two"). As others joined them, the group's social isolation facilitated more peculiar thinking. As conspiracy theory Internet discussion groups illustrate (Heaven's Gate was skilled in Internet recruiting), virtual groups can likewise foster paranoia.

These techniques—increasing behavioural commitments, persuasion, and group isolation—do not, however, have unlimited power. The Unification Church has successfully recruited fewer than 1 in 10 people who attend its workshops (Ennis & Verrilli, 1989). Most who joined Heaven's Gate had left before that fateful day. David Koresh ruled with a mix of persuasion, intimidation, and violence. As Jim Jones made his demands more extreme, he, too, increasingly had to control people with intimidation. He used threats of harm to those who fled the community, beatings for noncompliance, and drugs to neutralize disagreeable members. By the end, he was as much an arm twister as a mind bender.

Some of these cult influence techniques bear similarities to techniques used by more benign, widely accepted groups. Fraternity and sorority members have reported that the initial "love bombing" of potential cult recruits is not unlike their own "rush" period. Members lavish prospective pledges with attention and make them feel special. During the pledge period, new members are somewhat isolated, cut off from old friends who did not pledge. They spend time studying the history and rules of their new group. They suffer and commit time on its behalf. They are expected to comply with all its demands. Not surprisingly, the result is usually a committed new member.

Much the same is true of some therapeutic communities for recovering drug and alcohol abusers. Zealous self-help groups form a cohesive "social cocoon," have intense beliefs, and exert a profound influence on members' behaviour (Galanter, 1989, 1990).

Another constructive use of persuasion is in counselling and psychotherapy, which social-counselling psychologist Stanley Strong views "as a branch of applied social psychology" (1978, p. 101). Like Strong, psychiatrist Jerome Frank (1974, 1982) recognized years ago that it takes persuasion to change self-defeating attitudes and behaviours. Frank noted that

Military training creates cohesion and commitment through some of the same tactics used by cult leaders.

the psychotherapy setting, like cults and zealous self-help groups, provides (1) a supportive, confiding social relationship, (2) an offer of expertise and hope, (3) a special rationale or myth that explains one's difficulties and offers a new perspective, and (4) a set of rituals and learning experiences that promises a new sense of peace and happiness.

We chose the examples of fraternities, sororities, self-help groups, and psychotherapy not to disparage them but to illustrate two concluding observations. First, if we attribute New Religious movements to the leader's mystical force or to the followers' peculiar weaknesses, we may delude ourselves into thinking we are immune to social control techniques. In truth, our own groups—and countless political leaders, educators and other persuaders—successfully use many of these tactics on us. Between education and indoctrination, enlightenment and propaganda, conversion and coercion, therapy and mind control, there is but a blurry line.

Second, the fact that Jim Jones abused the power of persuasion does not mean persuasion is intrinsically bad. Nuclear power enables us to light up homes or wipe out cities. Sexual power enables us to express and celebrate committed love or exploit people for selfish gratification. Similarly, persuasive power enables us to enlighten or deceive. Knowing that these powers can be harnessed for evil purposes should alert us, as scientists and citizens, to guard against their immoral use. But the powers themselves are neither inherently evil nor inherently good; how we use them determines whether their effect is destructive or constructive. Condemning persuasion because of deceit is like condemning eating because of gluttony.

SUMMING UP: EXTREME PERSUASION: HOW DO CULTS INDOCRINATE?

The successes of religious cults provide an opportunity to see powerful persuasion processes at work. It appears that their success has resulted from three general techniques: eliciting behavioural commitments (as described in Chapter 4); applying principles of effective persuasion (this chapter); and isolating members in like-minded groups (to be discussed in Chapter 7).

HOW CAN PERSUASION BE RESISTED?

Having perused the "weapons of influence," we consider, finally, some tactics for resisting influence. How might we prepare people to resist unwanted persuasion?

Martial arts trainers devote as much time teaching defensive blocks, deflections, and parries as they do teaching attack. "On the social influence battlefield," note Brad Sagarin and his colleagues (2002), researchers have focused more on persuasive attack than on defence. Being persuaded comes naturally, Daniel Gilbert and his colleagues (1990, 1993) report. It is easier to accept persuasive messages than to doubt them. To *understand* an assertion (say, that lead pencils are a health hazard) is to *believe* it—at least temporarily, until one actively undoes the initial, automatic acceptance. If a distracting event prevents the undoing, the acceptance lingers.

Still, blessed with logic, information, and motivation, we do resist falsehoods. If, because of an aura of credibility, the repair person's uniform and the doctor's title have intimidated us into unquestioning agreement, we can rethink our habitual responses to authority. We can seek more information before committing time or money. We can question what we don't understand.

STRENGTHENING PERSONAL COMMITMENT

The next chapter presents another way to resist: Before encountering others' judgments, make a public commitment to your position. Having stood up for your convictions, you will become less susceptible (or should we say less "open"?) to what others have to say. In mock civil trials, straw polls of jurors can foster a hardening of expressed positions, leading to more deadlocks (Davis et al., 1993).

Challenging beliefs

How might we stimulate people to commit themselves? From his experiments, Charles Kiesler (1971) offers one possible way: Mildly attack their position. Kiesler found that when committed people were attacked strongly enough to cause them to react, but not so strongly as to overwhelm them, they became even more committed. Kiesler explained: "When you attack committed people and your attack is of inadequate strength, you drive them to even more extreme behaviours in defense of their previous commitment" (p. 88). Perhaps you can recall a time when this happened in an argument, as those involved escalated their rhetoric, committing themselves to increasingly extreme positions.

Developing counterarguments

There is a second reason a mild attack might build resistance. Like inoculations against disease, even weak arguments will prompt counterarguments, which are then available for a stronger attack. William McGuire (1964) documented this in a series of experiments. McGuire wondered: Could we inoculate people against persuasion much as we inoculate them against a virus? Is there such a thing as **attitude inoculation**? Could we take people raised in a "germ-free ideological environment"—people who hold some unquestioned belief—and stimulate their mental defences? And would subjecting them to a small dose of belief-threatening material inoculate them against later persuasion?

attitude inoculation exposing people to weak attacks on their attitudes so that when stronger attacks come, they will have refutations available

That is what McGuire did. First, he found some cultural truisms, such as, "It's a good idea to brush your teeth after every meal if at all possible." He then showed that people were vulnerable to a massive, credible assault on these truisms (for example, prestigious authorities were said to have discovered that too much toothbrushing can damage one's gums). If, however,

A "poison parasite" ad.

before having their belief attacked, they were "immunized" by first receiving a small challenge to their belief, *and* if they read or wrote an essay in refutation of this mild attack, then they were better able to resist the powerful attack.

Robert Cialdini and his colleagues (2003) agree that appropriate counterarguments are a great way to resist persuasion but wondered how to bring them to mind in response to an opponent's ads. The answer, they suggest, is a "poison parasite" defence—one that combines a poison (strong counterarguments) with a parasite (retrieval cues that bring those arguments to mind when seeing the opponent's ads). In their studies, participants who viewed a familiar political ad were least persuaded by it when they had earlier seen counterarguments overlaid on a replica of the ad. Seeing the ad again thus also brought to mind the puncturing counterarguments. Antismoking ads have effectively done this, for example, by re-creating a "Marlboro Man" commercial set in the rugged outdoors but now showing a coughing, decrepit cowboy.

REAL-LIFE APPLICATIONS: INOCULATION PROGRAMS

Could attitude inoculation indeed prepare people to resist unwanted persuasion? Applied research on smoking prevention and consumer education offers encouraging answers.

Inoculating children against peer pressure to smoke

In a demonstration of how laboratory research findings can lead to practical application, a research team led by Alfred McAlister (1980) had high-school students "inoculate" seventh graders against peer pressures to smoke. The seventh graders were taught to respond to advertisements implying that liberated women smoke by saying, "She's not really liberated if she is hooked on tobacco." They also acted in role plays; after being called "chicken" for not taking a cigarette, they answered with statements like, "I'd be a real chicken if I smoked just to impress you." After several of these sessions during the seventh and eighth grades, the inoculated students were half as likely to begin smoking as uninoculated students at another junior high school that had an identical parental smoking rate (Figure 5–11).

Other research teams have confirmed that such inoculation procedures, sometimes supplemented by other life skill training, reduce teen smoking (Botvin et al., 1995; Evans et al., 1984; Flay et al., 1985). Most new efforts emphasize strategies for resisting social pressure. One study exposed sixth to eighth graders to antismoking films or to information about smoking, together with role plays of student-generated ways of refusing a cigarette (Hirschman & Leventhal, 1989). A year and a half later 31 percent of those who watched the antismoking films had taken up smoking. Among those who role-played refusing, only 19 percent had begun smoking.

Antismoking and drug education programs apply other persuasion principles, too. They use attractive peers to communicate information. They trigger the students' own cognitive processing ("Here's something you might want to think about"). They get the students to make a public commitment (by making a rational decision about smoking and then announcing it, along with their reasoning, to their classmates). Some of these smoking-prevention programs require only two to six hours of class, using prepared printed materials or videotapes. Today any school district or teacher wishing to use the social-psychological approach to smoking prevention can do so easily, inexpensively, and with the hope of significant reductions in future smoking rates and associated health costs.

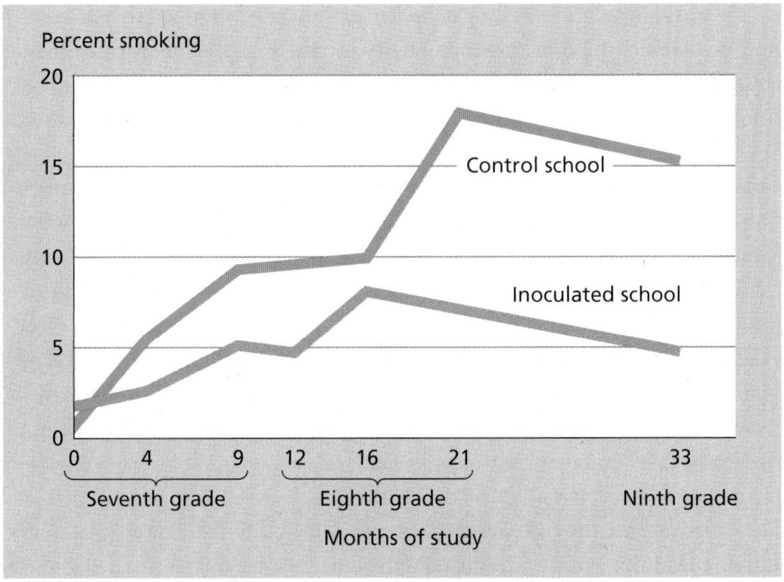

FIGURE 5–11

The percentage of cigarette smokers at an "inoculated" junior high school was much less than at a matched control school using a more typical smoking education program. (Data from McAlister et al., 1980; Telch et al., 1981)

Inoculating children against the influence of advertising

Belgium, Denmark, Greece, Ireland, Italy, and Sweden all restrict advertising that targets children, and other European countries have been discussing doing the same (McGuire, 2002). Advertising to children is prohibited by law in Quebec, and regulated in other provinces by guidelines set forth in The Broadcast Code for Advertising to Children. Nevertheless, in North America, notes Robert Levine in *The Power of Persuasion: How We're Bought and Sold*, the average child sees over 10 000 commercials a year. "Two decades ago," he notes, "children drank twice as much milk as soda. Thanks to advertising the ratio is now reversed" (2003, p. 16).

Smokers often develop an "initial brand choice" in their teens, said a 1981 report from researchers at Philip Morris, a major player in the $11.2-billion spent annually on tobacco advertising and promotions (FTC, 2003). "Today's teenager is tomorrow's potential regular customer, and the overwhelming majority of smokers first begin to smoke while still in their teens" (Libhtblau, 2003). That explains why some cigarette and smokeless tobacco companies aggressively market to university students, by advertising, by sponsoring parties, and by offering free cigarettes (usually in situations where students are also drinking), all as part of their $12.5-billion marketing of nicotine to "entry level" smokers (Farrell, 2005).

Hoping to restrain advertisers' influence, researchers have studied how to immunize young children against the effects of television commercials. Their research was prompted partly by studies showing that children, especially those under eight years old, (1) have trouble distinguishing commercials from programs and fail to grasp their persuasive intent, (2) trust television advertising rather indiscriminately, and (3) desire and badger their parents for advertised products (Adler et al., 1980; Feshbach, 1980; Palmer & Dorr, 1980). Children, it seems, are an advertiser's dream: gullible, vulnerable, an easy sell.

"In general, my children refuse to eat anything that hasn't danced on television."

Erma Bombeck

Armed with this data, citizens' groups have given the advertisers of such products a chewing out (Moody, 1980): "When a sophisticated advertiser spends millions to sell unsophisticated, trusting children an unhealthy product, this can only be called exploitation. No wonder the consumption of dairy products has declined since the start of television, while soft-drink consumption has almost doubled." In "Mothers' Statement to Advertisers" (Motherhood Project, 2001), a broad coalition of American women echoed this outrage:

> For us, our children are priceless gifts. For you, our children are customers, and childhood is a "market segment" to be exploited. . . . The line between meeting and creating consumer needs and desire is increasingly being crossed, as your battery of highly trained and creative experts study, analyze, persuade, and manipulate our children. . . . The driving messages are "You deserve a break today," "Have it your way," "Follow your instincts. Obey your thirst," "Just Do It," "No Boundaries," "Got the Urge?" These [exemplify] the dominant message of advertising and marketing: that life is about selfishness, instant gratification, and materialism.

On the other side are the commercial interests. They claim that ads allow parents to teach their children consumer skills and, more important, finance children's television programs. Government agencies that oversee the media are often stuck in the middle, pushed by research findings and political pressures while trying to decide whether to place new constraints on TV ads aimed at young children.

Meanwhile, researchers have wondered whether children can be taught to resist deceptive ads. In one such effort, a team of investigators led by Norma Feshbach (1980; Cohen, 1980) gave small groups of elementary schoolchildren three half-hour lessons in analyzing commercials. The children were inoculated by viewing ads and discussing them. For example, after viewing a toy ad, they were immediately given the toy and challenged to make it do what they had just seen in the commercial. Such experiences helped breed a more realistic understanding of commercials.

Consumer advocates worry that inoculation may be insufficient. Better to clean the air than to wear a gas mask. It is no surprise, then, that parents resent it when advertisers market products to children, then place them on lower store shelves where kids will see them, pick them up, nag and whine until sometimes wearing the parent down. For that reason, urges the "Mothers' Code for Advertisers," there should be no advertising in schools, no targeting children under eight, no product placement in movies and programs targeting children and adolescents, and no ads directed at children and adolescents "that promote an ethic of selfishness and a focus on instant gratification" (Motherhood Project, 2001).

IMPLICATIONS

The best way to build resistance to brainwashing isn't to reinforce one's current beliefs. If parents are worried that their children could become members of a cult, they might better teach their children about the various cults and prepare them to counter persuasive appeals.

For the same reason, religious educators should be wary of creating a "germ-free ideological environment" in their churches and schools. An attack, if refuted, is more likely to solidify one's position than to undermine it, particularly if the threatening material can be examined

Children are the advertiser's dream. Researchers have therefore studied ways to inoculate children against the 20 000 or so ads they see each year, many as they are glued to a TV set.

with like-minded others (Visser & Mirabile, 2004). Cults apply this principle by forewarning members of how families and friends will attack the cult's beliefs. When the expected challenge comes, the member is armed with counterarguments.

Another implication is that, for the persuader, an ineffective appeal can be worse than none. Can you see why? Those who reject an appeal are inoculated against further appeals. Consider an experiment in which Susan Darley and Joel Cooper (1972) invited students to write essays advocating a strict dress code. Because this was against the students' own positions and the essays were to be published, all chose *not* to write the essay—even those offered money to do so. After turning down the money, they became even more extreme and confident in their anti-dress-code opinions. Having made an overt decision against the dress code, they became even more resistant to it. Those who have rejected initial appeals to quit smoking may likewise become immune to further appeals. Ineffective persuasion, by stimulating the listener's defences, may be counterproductive. It may "harden the heart" against later appeals.

SUMMING UP: HOW CAN PERSUASION BE RESISTED?

How do people resist persuasion? A prior public commitment to one's own position, stimulated perhaps by a mild attack on the position, breeds resistance to later persuasion. A mild attack can also serve as an inoculation, stimulating one to develop counterarguments that will then be available if and when a strong attack comes. This implies, paradoxically, that one way to strengthen existing attitudes is to challenge them, though the challenge must not be so strong as to overwhelm them.

CHAPTER SIX

Conformity

You have surely experienced the phenomenon: As a controversial speaker or music concert finishes, the admiring fans near the front stand to applaud. The approving folks just behind them follow their example and join the standing ovation. Now the wave of people standing reaches people who, unprompted, would merely be giving polite applause from their comfortable seats. Seated among them, part of you wants to stay seated ("this speaker doesn't represent my views at all"). But as the wave of standing people sweeps by, will you alone stay seated? It's not easy, being a minority of one.

Such scenes of conformity raise this chapter's questions:

- Why, given the diversity of individuals in large groups, is their behaviour so often uniform?
- Under what circumstances do people conform?
- Are certain people more likely than others to conform?
- Who resists the pressure to conform?
- Is conformity as bad as my image of a docile "herd" implies? Should I instead be describing their "group solidarity" and "social sensitivity"?

WHAT IS CONFORMITY?

Let us take the last question first. Is conformity good or bad? This is a question that has no scientific answer, but, assuming the values most of us share, conformity is at times bad (when it leads someone to drink and drive or to join in racist behaviour), at times good (when it inhibits people from cutting in front of us in a theatre line), and at times inconsequential (when it disposes tennis players to wear white).

The word *conformity* does carry a negative value judgment. How would you feel if you overheard someone describing you as a "real conformist"? I suspect you would feel hurt, because you are probably from a Western culture that doesn't prize submitting to peer pressure. Hence North American and European social psychologists, reflecting their individualistic cultures, give it negative labels (conformity, submission, compliance) rather than positive ones (communal sensitivity, responsiveness, cooperative team play).

"The social pressures community brings to bear are a mainstay of our moral values."

Amitai Etzioni, *The Spirit of Community*, 1993

In Japan, going along with others is a sign not of weakness but of tolerance, self-control, and maturity (Markus & Kitayama, 1994). "Everywhere in Japan," observed Lance Morrow (1983), "one senses an intricate serenity that comes to a people who know exactly what to expect from each other."

"The race of men, while sheep in credulity, are wolves for conformity."

Carl Van Doren, *Why I Am an Unbeliever*

The moral: We choose labels to suit our values and judgments. In retrospect, some have viewed legislators who cast unpopular votes against ballistic missile defence "independent" and "inner-directed" and those who cast unpopular votes against the Kyoto Protocol as "reactionary" and "self-centred." Labels both describe and evaluate, and they are inescapable. We cannot discuss the topics of this chapter without labels. So let us be clear on the meanings of the following labels: conformity, obedience, compliance, and acceptance.

Conformity is not just acting as other people act; it is also being affected by how they act. It is acting differently from the way you would act alone. Thus **conformity** is a change in behaviour or belief to accord with others. When, as part of a crowd, you rise to cheer a game-winning goal, are you conforming? When, along with millions of others, you drink milk or coffee, are you conforming? When you and everyone else agree that women look better with longer hair

conformity
a change in behaviour or belief to accord with others

than with crewcuts, are you conforming? Maybe, maybe not. The key is whether your behaviour and beliefs would be the same apart from the group. Would you rise to cheer the goal if you were the only fan in the stands?

"Whatever crushes individuality is despotism, by whatever name it may be called."

John Stuart Mill, *On Liberty,* 1859

There are several varieties of conformity (Nail et al., 2000). Consider three: compliance, obedience, and acceptance. Sometimes we conform to an expectation or request without really believing in what we are doing. We put on the necktie or dress, though we dislike doing so. This outward conformity is **compliance**. We comply primarily to reap a reward or avoid a punishment. If our compliance is to an explicit command, we call it **obedience**.

Sometimes we genuinely believe in what the group has persuaded us to do. We may join millions of others in drinking milk because we are convinced that milk is nutritious. This sincere, inward conformity is called **acceptance**. Acceptance sometimes follows compliance. As Chapter 4 emphasized, attitudes follow behaviour. Unless we feel no responsibility for our behaviour, we usually become sympathetic to what we have stood up for.

compliance
conformity that involves publicly acting in accord with social pressure while privately disagreeing

obedience
acting in accord with a direct order

acceptance
conformity that involves both acting and believing in accord with social pressure

WHAT ARE THE CLASSIC CONFORMITY AND OBEDIENCE STUDIES?

How have social psychologists studied conformity in the laboratory? What do their results reveal about the potency of social forces and the nature of evil?

Researchers who study conformity construct miniature social worlds—laboratory microcultures that simplify and simulate important features of everyday social influence. Some of these studies revealed such startling findings that they have been widely replicated and widely reported by other researchers, earning them the name of "classic" experiments. We will consider three, each of which provides a method for studying conformity—and plenty of food for thought.

SHERIF'S STUDIES OF NORM FORMATION

The first of the three classics bridges between Chapter 8's focus on culture's power to create and perpetuate arbitrary norms and this chapter's focus on conformity. Muzafer Sherif (1935, 1937) wondered whether it was possible to observe the emergence of a social norm in the laboratory. Like biologists seeking to isolate a virus so they can then experiment with it, Sherif wanted to isolate and then experiment with the social phenomenon of norm formation.

As a participant in one of Sherif's experiments, you might find yourself seated in a dark room. Five metres in front of you a pinpoint of light appears. At first, nothing happens. Then for a few seconds it moves erratically and finally disappears. Now you must guess how far it moved. The dark room gives you no way to judge distance, so you offer an uncertain "15 centimetres." The experimenter repeats the procedure. This time you say "25 centimetres." With further repetitions, your estimates continue to average about 20 centimetres.

The next day you return, joined by two others who the day before had the same experience. When the light goes off for the first time, the other two people offer their best guesses from the day before. "Five centimetres" says one. "Two centimetres," says the other. A bit taken aback, you nevertheless say "15 centimetres." With successive repetitions of this group experience, both on this day and for the next two days, will your responses change? The men whom Sherif tested changed their estimates markedly. As Figure 6–1 illustrates, a group norm typically emerged. (The norm was false. Why? The light never moved! Sherif had taken advantage of an optical illusion called the **autokinetic phenomenon**.)

autokinetic phenomenon
self (*auto*) motion (*kinetic*). The apparent movement of a stationary point of light in the dark. Perhaps you have experienced this when thinking you have spotted a moving satellite in the sky, only to realize later that it was merely an isolated star.

Sherif and others have used this technique to answer questions about people's suggestibility. When people were retested alone a year later, would their estimates again diverge or would they continue to follow the group norm? Remarkably, they continued to support the group norm (Rohrer et al., 1954). (Does this suggest compliance or acceptance?)

Struck by culture's seeming power to perpetuate false beliefs, Robert Jacobs and Donald Campbell (1961) studied the transmission of false beliefs. Using the autokinetic phenomenon, they had a **confederate** give an inflated estimate of how far the light moved. The confederate then left the experiment and was replaced by another real subject who was in turn replaced by a still newer member. The inflated illusion persisted (although less and less strongly) for five generations of participants. These people had become "unwitting conspirators in perpetuating a cultural fraud." The lesson of these experiments: Our views of reality are not ours alone.

confederate
an accomplice of the experimenter

In everyday life the results of suggestibility are sometimes amusing. One person coughs, laughs, or yawns, and others are soon doing the same. Comedy show laugh tracks capitalize on our suggestibility. Laugh tracks work especially well when we presume that the laughing audience is made up of folks like us—other students at the same university for participants in one study by Michael Platow and colleagues (2004)—rather than a group that's unlike us. Just being around happy people can help us feel happier, a phenomenon that Peter Totterdell and his colleagues (1998) call "mood linkage." In their studies of British nurses and accountants, people within the same work groups tended to share up and down moods.

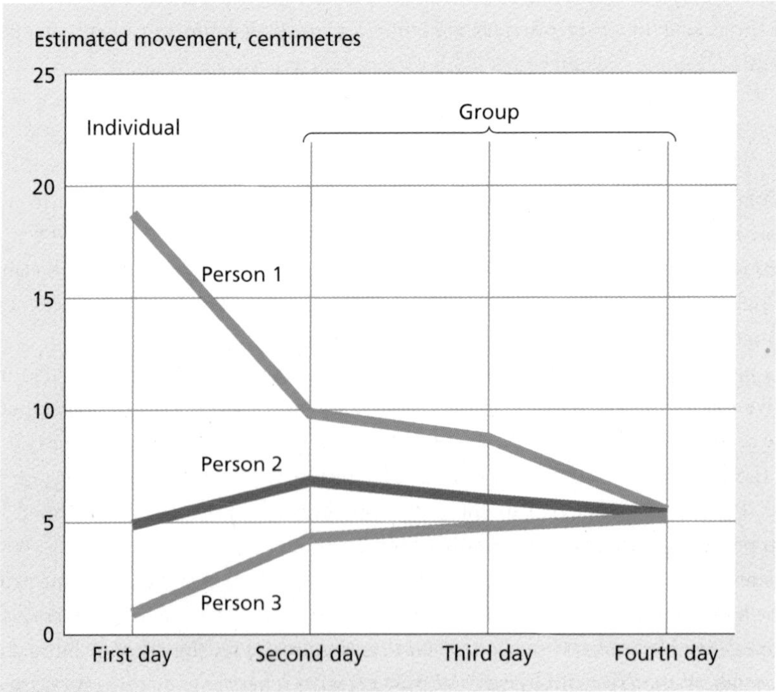

FIGURE 6–1
A sample group from Sherif's study of norm formation.
Three individuals converge as they give repeated estimates of the apparent movement of a point of light. (Data from Sherif & Sherif, 1969, p. 209)

Another form of social contagion is what Tanya Chartrand and John Bargh (1999) call "the chameleon effect." Picture yourself in one of their experiments, working alongside a confederate who occasionally either rubbed her face or shook her foot. Would you—like their participants—be more likely to rub your face when with a face-rubbing person and shake your foot when with a foot-shaking person? If so, it would quite likely be an automatic behaviour, done without any conscious intention to conform, and it would incline you to feel what the other feels (Neumann & Strack, 2000). An experiment in the Netherlands by Rick van Baaren and his colleagues (2004) indicates that your mimicry would also incline the other to like you and be helpful to you and to others. People become more likely to help pick up dropped pens for someone whose behaviour has mimicked their own. Being mimicked seems to enhance social bonds, which even leads to donating more money to a charity.

Authorities may impose public compliance, but private acceptance is another matter.

Suggestibility can also occur on a large scale. In late March 1954, one newspaper reported damage to car windshields in a city 125 kilometres to the north. On the morning of April 14, similar windshield damage was reported 105 kilometres away and later that day only 70 kilometres away. By nightfall, the windshield-pitting agent had reached the city itself. Before the end of April 15, the police department had received complaints of damage to more than 3000 windshields (Medalia & Larsen, 1958). That evening the mayor called on the federal government for help.

David Myers was an 11-year-old at the time. He recalls searching the family car's windshield, frightened by the explanation that an H-bomb test was raining fallout on his city. On April 16, however, the newspapers hinted that the real culprit might be mass suggestibility. After April 17 there were no more complaints. Later analysis of the pitted windshields concluded that the cause was ordinary road damage. Why did people notice this only after April 14? Given the suggestion, they had looked carefully *at* their windshields instead of *through* them.

"Why doth one man's yawning make another yawn?"

Robert Burton, *Anatomy of Melancholy*, 1621

Suggestibility is not always so amusing. Hijackings, UFO sightings, and even suicides tend to come in waves. Shortly after the 1774 publication of *The Sorrows of Young Werther*, Johann Wolfgang von Goethe's first novel, young European men started dressing in yellow trousers and blue jackets, as had Goethe's protagonist, a young man named Werther. Although the fashion epidemic triggered by the book was amusing, another apparent effect was less amusing and led to the book's banning in several areas. In the novel, Werther commits suicide with a pistol after being rejected by the woman whose heart he failed to win; after the book's publication, reports began accumulating of young men imitating Werther's desperate act.

Two centuries later, sociologist David Phillips confirmed such imitative suicidal behaviour and described it as "the Werther effect." Phillips and his colleagues (1985, 1989) discovered that suicides, as well as fatal auto accidents and private airplane crashes (which sometimes disguise suicides), increase after well-publicized suicides. For example, following Marilyn Monroe's August 6, 1962, suicide, there were 200 more August suicides than normal. Moreover, the increase happens only in areas where the suicide story is publicized. The more publicity, the greater the increase in later fatalities.

Although not all studies have found the copycat suicide phenomenon, it has surfaced in Germany, in a London psychiatric unit that experienced 14 patient suicides in one year, and in one high school that, within 18 days, suffered 2 suicides, 7 suicide attempts, and 23 students reporting suicidal thoughts (Joiner, 1999; Jonas, 1992). In both Germany and the United States, suicide rates rise slightly following fictional suicides on soap operas, and, ironically, even after serious dramas that focus on the suicide problem (Gould & Shaffer, 1986).

ASCH'S STUDIES OF GROUP PRESSURE

Participants in Sherif's darkened-room autokinetic experiments faced an ambiguous reality. Consider a less ambiguous perceptual problem faced by a young boy named Solomon Asch (1907–1996). While attending the traditional Jewish seder at Passover, Asch recalled,

> I asked my uncle, who was sitting next to me, why the door was being opened. He replied, "The prophet Elijah visits this evening every Jewish home and takes a sip of wine from the cup reserved for him."
>
> I was amazed at this news and repeated, "Does he really come? Does he really take a sip?"
>
> My uncle said, "If you watch very closely, when the door is opened you will see—you watch the cup—you will see that the wine will go down a little."
>
> And that's what happened. My eyes were riveted upon the cup of wine. I was determined to see whether there would be a change. And to me it seemed—it was tantalizing, and of course, it was hard to be absolutely sure—that indeed something was happening at the rim of the cup, and the wine did go down a little. (quoted by Aron & Aron, 1989, p. 27)

Years later, social psychologist Asch recreated his boyhood experience in his laboratory. Imagine yourself as one of Asch's volunteer subjects. You are seated sixth in a row of seven people. After explaining that you will be taking part in a study of perceptual judgments, the experimenter asks you to say which of the three lines in Figure 6–2 matches the standard line. You can easily see that it's line 2. So it's no surprise when the five people responding before you all say "line 2."

The next comparison proves as easy, and you settle in for what seems a simple test. But the third trial startles you. Although the correct answer seems just as clear-cut, the first person gives a wrong answer. When the second person gives the same wrong answer, you sit up in your chair and stare at the cards. The third person agrees with the first two. Your jaw drops; you start to perspire. "What is this?" you ask yourself. "Are they blind? Or am I?" The fourth and fifth people agree with the others. Then the experimenter looks at you. Now you are experiencing an epistemological dilemma: "How am I to know what is true? Is it what my peers tell me or what my eyes tell me?"

Dozens of university students experienced this conflict during Asch's experiments. Those in a control condition who answered alone were correct more than 99 percent of the time. Asch wondered: If several others (confederates coached by the experimenter) gave identical wrong answers, would people declare what they would otherwise have denied? Although some people never conformed, three-quarters did so at least once. All told, 37 percent of the responses were conforming (or should we say "*trusting* of others"?). Of course, that means 63 percent of the time people did not conform. The experiments show that most people "tell the truth even when others do not," note Bert Hodges and Ann Geyer (2006). Despite the independence shown by many of his subjects, Asch's (1955) feelings about the conformity were as clear as the correct answers to his questions: "That reasonably intelligent and well-meaning young people are willing to call white black is a matter of concern. It raises questions about our ways of education and about the values that guide our conduct."

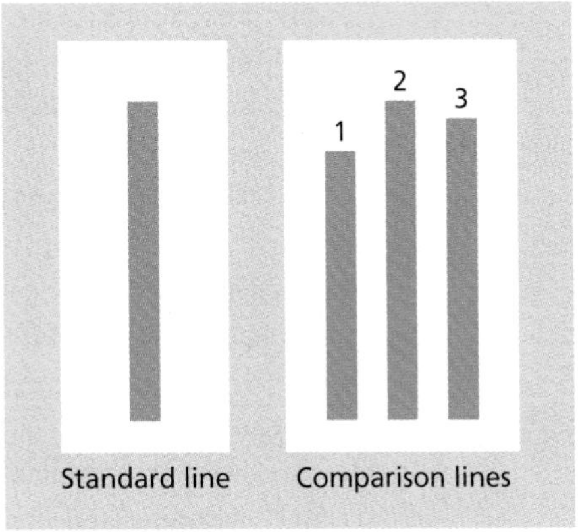

FIGURE 6–2

Sample comparison from Solomon Asch's conformity procedure.

The participants judged which of three comparison lines matched the standard.

"He who sees the truth, let him proclaim it, without asking who is for it or who is against it."

Henry George, *The Irish Land Question*, 1881

In one of Asch's conformity experiments (top), subject number 6 experienced uneasiness and conflict after hearing five people before him give a wrong answer.

Ethical note: *Professional ethics usually dictate explaining the experiment afterwards (see Chapter 1). Pretend you were an experimenter who had just finished a session with a conforming participant. Could you explain the deception without making the person feel gullible and dumb?*

"It is too easy to go over to the majority."

Seneca, *Epistulae ad Lucilium*

Asch's procedure became the standard for hundreds of later experiments. These experiments lack what Chapter 1 called the "mundane realism" of everyday conformity, but they do have "experimental realism." People become emotionally involved in the experience. The Sherif and Asch results are startling because they involve no obvious pressure to conform—there are no rewards for "team play," no punishments for individuality.

If people are this compliant in response to such minimal pressure, how much more compliant will they be if they are directly coerced? Could someone force an average North American to perform cruel acts? We would have guessed not: Their humane, democratic, individualistic values would make them resist such pressure. Besides, the easy verbal pronouncements of these experiments are a giant step away from actually harming someone; we would never yield to coercion to hurt another. Or would we? Social psychologist Stanley Milgram wondered.

MILGRAM'S OBEDIENCE STUDIES

Milgram's (1965, 1974) studies on what happens when the demands of authority clash with the demands of conscience have become social psychology's most famous and controversial studies. "Perhaps more than any other empirical contributions in the history of social science," notes Lee Ross (1988), "they have become part of our society's shared intellectual legacy—that small body of historical incidents, biblical parables, and classic literature that serious thinkers feel free to draw on when they debate about human nature or contemplate human history." Although you may therefore recall a mention of this research in a prior course, let's go backstage and examine the studies in depth.

Here is the scene staged by Milgram, a creative artist who wrote stories and stage plays: Two men come to the psychology laboratory to participate in a study of learning and memory. A stern experimenter in a grey technician's coat explains that this is a pioneering study of the effect of punishment on learning. The experiment requires one of them to teach a list of word pairs to the other and to punish errors by delivering shocks of increasing intensity. To assign the roles, they draw slips out of a hat. One of the men, a mild-mannered, 47-year-old accountant who is the experimenter's confederate, pretends that his slip says "learner" and is ushered into an adjacent room. The "teacher" (who has come in response to a newspaper ad) takes a mild sample shock and then looks on as the experimenter straps the learner into a chair and attaches an electrode to his wrist.

Teacher and experimenter then return to the main room where the teacher takes his place before a "shock generator" with switches ranging from 15 to 450 volts in 15-volt increments. The switches are labelled "Slight Shock," "Very Strong Shock," "Danger: Severe Shock," and so forth. Under the 435- and 450-volt switches appears "XXX." The experimenter tells the teacher to "move one level higher on the shock generator" each time the learner gives a wrong answer. With each flick of a switch, lights flash, relay switches click, and an electric buzz sounds.

If the participant complies with the experimenter's requests, he hears the learner grunt at 75, 90, and 105 volts. At 120 volts the learner shouts that the shocks are painful. And at 150 volts he cries out, "Experimenter, get me out of here! I won't be in the experiment anymore! I refuse to go on!" By 270 volts his protests have become screams of agony, and he continues to

insist to be let out. At 300 and 315 volts he screams his refusal to answer. After 330 volts he falls silent. In answer to the "teacher's" inquiries and pleas to end the experiment, the experimenter states that the nonresponses should be treated as wrong answers. To keep the participant going, he uses four verbal prods:

Prod 1: Please continue (*or* Please go on).
Prod 2: The experiment requires that you continue.
Prod 3: It is absolutely essential that you continue.
Prod 4: You have no other choice; you *must* go on.

How far would you go? Milgram described the study to 110 psychiatrists, university students, and middle-class adults. People in all three groups guessed that they would disobey by about 135 volts, which perhaps isn't surprising. But they also said that they thought *other* people would disobey by 200 volts and virtually no one expected anyone to proceed to XXX on the shock panel (Milgram, 1963; Kaufman & Kooman, 1967). (The psychiatrists guessed about one in a thousand.)

But when Milgram conducted the study with 40 men—a vocational mix of 20- to 50-year-olds—26 of them (65 percent) went all the way to 450 volts. In fact, all who reached 450 volts complied with a command to *continue* the procedure until, after two further trials, the experimenter called a halt.

Having expected a low rate of obedience, and with plans to replicate the study in Germany and assess the culture difference, Milgram was disturbed (A. Milgram, 2000). So instead of going to Germany, Milgram next made the learner's protests even more compelling. As the learner was strapped into the chair, the teacher heard him mention his "slight heart condition" and heard the experimenter's reassurance that "although the shocks may be painful, they cause no permanent tissue damage." The learner's anguished protests (see Table 6–1) were to little avail; of 40 new men in this study, 25 (63 percent) fully complied with the experimenter's demands (Figure 6–3).

TABLE 6–1 The learner's schedule of protests in Milgram's "heart disturbance" studies

75 volts	Ugh
90 volts	Ugh
105 volts	Ugh! (*Louder*)
120 volts	Ugh! Hey, this really hurts.
135 volts	Ugh!!
150 volts	Ugh!!! Experimenter! That's all. Get me out of here. I told you I had heart trouble. My heart's starting to bother me now. Get me out of here, please. My heart's starting to bother me. I refuse to go on. Let me out.
165 volts	Ugh! Let me out! (*Shouting*)
180 volts	Ugh! I can't stand the pain. Let me out of here! (*Shouting*)
195 volts	Ugh! Let me out of here. Let me out of here. My heart's bothering me. Let me out of here! You have no right to keep me here! Let me out! Let me out of here! Let me out! Let me out of here! My heart's bothering me. Let me out! Let me out!
210 volts	Ugh! Experimenter! Get me out of here. I've had enough. I won't be in the experiment any more.

Continued

TABLE 6–1 Continued

225 volts	Ugh!
240 volts	Ugh!
255 volts	Ugh! Get me out of here.
270 volts	*(Agonized scream)* Let me out of here. Let me out of here. Let me out of here. Let me out. Do you hear? Let me out of here.
285 volts	*(Agonized scream)*
300 volts	*(Agonized scream)* I absolutely refuse to answer any more. Get me out of here. You can't hold me here. Get me out. Get me out of here.
315 volts	*(Intensely agonized scream)* I told you I refuse to answer. I'm no longer part of this experiment.
330 volts	*(Intense and prolonged agonized scream)* Let me out of here. Let me out of here. My heart's bothering me. Let me out. I tell you. *(Hysterically)* Let me out of here. Let me out of here. You have no right to hold me here. Let me out! Let me out! Let me out! Let me out of here! Let me out! Let me out!

Source: *From Obedience to Authority* by Stanley Milgram. New York: Harper & Row, 1974, pp. 56–57.

The ethics of Milgram's studies

The obedience of his subjects disturbed Milgram. The procedures he used disturbed many social psychologists (Miller, 1986; Stam et al., 1998). The "learner" in these studies actually received no shock (he disengaged himself from the electric chair and turned on a tape recorder that delivered the protests). Nevertheless, some critics said that Milgram did to his participants

FIGURE 6–3

The Milgram obedience study.

Percentage of subjects complying despite the learner's cries of protest and failure to respond. (Milgram, 1965)

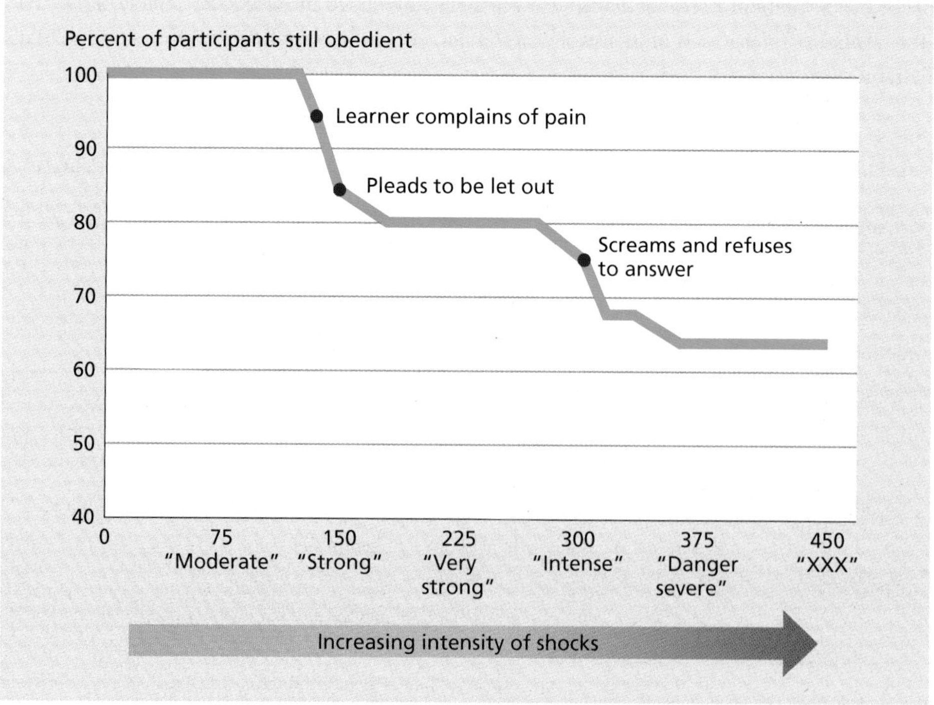

what they did to their victims: He stressed them against their will. Indeed, many of the "teachers" did experience agony. They sweated, trembled, stuttered, bit their lips, groaned, or even broke into uncontrollable nervous laughter. A *New York Times* reviewer complained that the cruelty inflicted by the studies "upon their unwitting subjects is surpassed only by the cruelty that they elicit from them" (Marcus, 1974).

Critics also argued that the participants' self-concepts may have been altered. One participant's wife told him, "You can call yourself Eichmann" (referring to Nazi death camp administrator Adolf Eichmann). CBS television depicted the results and controversy in a two-hour dramatization starring William Shatner of *Star Trek* fame as Milgram. "A world of evil so terrifying no one dares penetrate its secret. Until Now!" declared a *TV Guide* ad for the program (Elms, 1995).

In his own defence, Milgram pointed to the lessons taught by his nearly two dozen studies with a diverse sample of more than 1000 participants. He also reminded critics of the support he received from the participants after the deception was revealed and the study explained. When surveyed afterwards, 84 percent said they were glad to have participated; only 1 percent regretted volunteering. A year later, a psychiatrist interviewed 40 of those who had suffered most and concluded that, despite the temporary stress, none was harmed.

The ethical controversy was "terribly overblown," Milgram believed:

> There is less consequence to subjects in this experiment from the standpoint of effects on self-esteem, than to university students who take ordinary course examinations, and who do not get the grades they want. . . . It seems that [in giving exams] we are quite prepared to accept stress, tension, and consequences for self-esteem. But in regard to the process of generating new knowledge, how little tolerance we show. (quoted by Blass, 1996)

WHAT BREEDS OBEDIENCE?

Milgram did more than reveal the extent to which people will obey an authority; he also examined the conditions that breed obedience. In further studies, he varied the social conditions and got compliance ranging from 0 to 93 percent fully obedient. The determining factors were these four: the victim's emotional distance, the authority's closeness and legitimacy, whether or not the authority is institutionalized, and the liberating effects of a disobedient fellow participant.

The victim's distance

Milgram's participants acted with greatest obedience and least compassion when the "learners" could not be seen (and could not see them). When the victim was remote and the "teachers" heard no complaints, nearly all obeyed calmly to the end. When the learner was in the same room, "only" 40 percent obeyed to 450 volts. Full compliance dropped to a still-astonishing 30 percent when teachers were required to force the learner's hand into contact with a shock plate.

In everyday life, too, it is easiest to abuse someone who is distant or depersonalized. People who might never be cruel to someone in person may be downright nasty when posting comments aimed at anonymous people on Internet discussion boards. Throughout history, executioners have often depersonalized those being executed by placing hoods over their heads. The ethics of war allow one to bomb a helpless village from 13 000 metres but not to shoot an

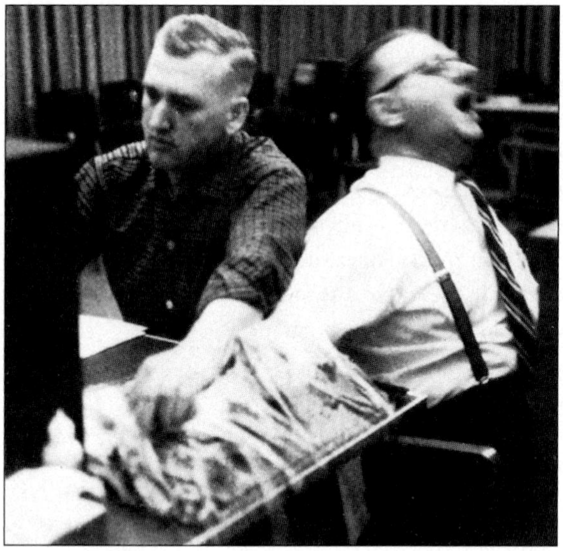

An obedient subject in Milgram's "touch" condition forces the victim's hand onto the shock plate. Usually, however, "teachers" were more merciful to victims who were this close to them.

equally helpless villager. In combat with an enemy they can see, many soldiers either do not fire or do not aim. Such disobedience is rare among those given orders to kill with the more distant artillery or aircraft weapons (Padgett, 1989).

As the Holocaust began, some Germans, under orders, used machine-guns or rifles to kill men, women, and children standing before them. But others could not bring themselves to do so, and some who did were left shaken by the experience of face-to-face killing. That led Heinrich Himmler, the Nazi "architect of genocide," to devise a "more humane" killing, one that would visually separate the killers and their victims. The solution was the construction of concrete gas chambers, where the killers would not see or hear the human consequences of their horror (Russell & Gregory, 2005).

On the positive side, people act most compassionately toward those who are personalized. This is why appeals for the unborn or the hungry are nearly always personalized with a compelling photograph or description. Perhaps even more compelling is an ultrasound picture of one's own developing fetus. When queried by John Lydon and Christine Dunkel-Schetter (1994), expectant women expressed more commitment to their pregnancy if they had earlier seen an ultrasound picture of their fetus that clearly displayed body parts.

Imagine you had the power to prevent either a tidal wave that would kill 25 000 people in Pakistan, a crash that would kill 250 people at your local airport, or a car accident that would kill a close friend. Which would you prevent?

Closeness and legitimacy of the authority

The physical presence of the experimenter also affected obedience. When Milgram gave the commands by telephone, full obedience dropped to 21 percent (although many lied and said they were obeying). Other studies confirm that when the one making the request is physically close, compliance increases. Given a light touch on the arm, people are more likely to lend a dime, sign a petition, or sample a new pizza (Kleinke, 1977; Smith et al., 1982; Willis & Hamm, 1980).

The authority, however, must be perceived as legitimate. In another twist on the basic study, the experimenter received a rigged telephone call that required him to leave the laboratory. He said that since the equipment recorded data automatically, the "teacher" should just go ahead. After the experimenter left, another person who had been assigned a clerical role (actually a second confederate) assumed command. The clerk "decided" that the shock should be increased one level for each wrong answer and instructed the teacher accordingly. Now 80 percent of the teachers refused to comply fully. The confederate, feigning disgust at this defiance, sat down in front of the shock generator and tried to take over the teacher's role. At this point most of the defiant participants protested. Some tried to unplug the generator. One large man lifted the zealous confederate from his chair and threw him across the room. This rebellion against an illegitimate authority contrasted sharply with the deferential politeness usually shown the experimenter.

It also contrasts with the behaviour of hospital nurses who in one study were called by an unknown physician and ordered to administer an obvious overdose of a drug (Hofling et al., 1966). The researchers told one group of nurses and nursing students about the experiment and asked how they would react. Nearly all said they would not have given the medication as ordered. One explained that she would have replied, "I'm sorry, sir, but I am not authorized to give any medication without a written order, especially one so large over the usual dose and one that I'm unfamiliar with. If it were possible, I would be glad to do it, but this is against hospital policy and my own ethical standards." Nevertheless, when 22 other nurses were actually given the phoned-in overdose order, all but one obeyed without delay (until being intercepted on their way to the patient). Although not all nurses are so compliant (Krackow & Blass, 1995; Rank & Jacobson, 1977), these nurses were following a familiar script: Doctor (a legitimate authority) orders; nurse obeys.

Compliance with legitimate authority was also apparent in the strange case of the "rectal earache" (Cohen & Davis, 1981). A doctor ordered ear drops given to a patient suffering infection in the right ear. On the prescription, the doctor abbreviated "place in right ear" as "place in *R ear*." Reading the order, the compliant nurse put the required drops in the compliant patient's rectum.

Institutional authority

If the prestige of the authority is important, then perhaps the institutional prestige of Yale University, where the studies were conducted legitimized the commands. In post-study interviews, many participants volunteered that had it not been for Yale's reputation, they would not have obeyed. To see whether this was true, Milgram moved the study to Bridgeport, Connecticut. He set himself up in a modest commercial building as the "Research Associates of Bridgeport." When the usual "heart disturbance" study was run with the same personnel, what percentage of the men do you suppose fully obeyed? Although the obedience rate (48 percent) was still remarkably high, it was significantly lower than the 65 percent Yale rate.

Given orders, most soldiers will torch people's homes or kill—behaviours that in other contexts they would consider immoral.

The liberating effects of group influence

These classic experiments give us a negative view of conformity. But conformity can also be constructive. The heroic figures who rushed into the flaming World Trade Center towers were "incredibly brave," note Susan Fiske and her colleagues (2004), but they were also "partly obeying their superiors, partly conforming to extraordinary group loyalty." Consider too, the occasional liberating effect of conformity. Perhaps you can recall a time you felt justifiably angry at an unfair teacher, or with someone's offensive behaviour, but you hesitated to object. Then one or two others objected, and you followed their example. Milgram captured this liberating effect of conformity by placing the teacher with two confederates who were to help conduct the procedure. During the study, both defied the experimenter, who then ordered the real subject to continue alone. Did he? No. Ninety percent liberated themselves by conforming to the defiant confederates.

REFLECTIONS ON THE CLASSIC STUDIES

The common response to Milgram's results is to note their counterparts in recent history: the "I was only following orders" defences of Adolf Eichmann in Nazi Germany; of Lieutenant William Calley, who in 1968 directed the unprovoked slaughter of hundreds of Vietnamese in the village of My Lai; and of the "ethnic cleansing" occurring more recently in Iraq, Rwanda, Bosnia, and the Sudan.

Soldiers are trained to obey superiors. Thus one participant in the My Lai massacre recalled:

> [Lieutenant Calley] told me to start shooting. So I started shooting, I poured about four clips into the group. . . . They were begging and saying, "No, no." And the mothers were hugging their children and. . . . Well, we kept right on firing. They was waving their arms and begging. (Wallace, 1969)

The "safe" scientific contexts of the obedience studies differ from the wartime contexts. Moreover, much of the mockery and brutality of war and genocide goes beyond obedience (Miller, 2004). Some of those who implemented the Holocaust were "willing executioners" who hardly needed to be commanded to kill (Goldhagen, 1996).

"If the commander-in-chief tells this lieutenant colonel to go stand in the corner and sit on his head, I will do so."

Oliver North, 1987

The obedience studies also differ from the other conformity studies in the strength of the social pressure: Obedience is explicitly commanded. Without the coercion, people did not act cruelly. Yet both the Asch and Milgram studies share certain commonalities. They show how compliance can take precedence over moral sense. They succeeded in pressuring people to go against their own conscience. They did more than teach us an academic lesson; they sensitized us to moral conflicts in our own lives. And they illustrate and affirm some familiar social psychological principles: the link between behaviour and attitudes, the power of the situation, and the strength of the fundamental attribution error.

Behaviour and attitudes

In Chapter 4 we noted that attitudes fail to determine behaviour when external influences override inner convictions. These experiments vividly illustrate this principle. When responding

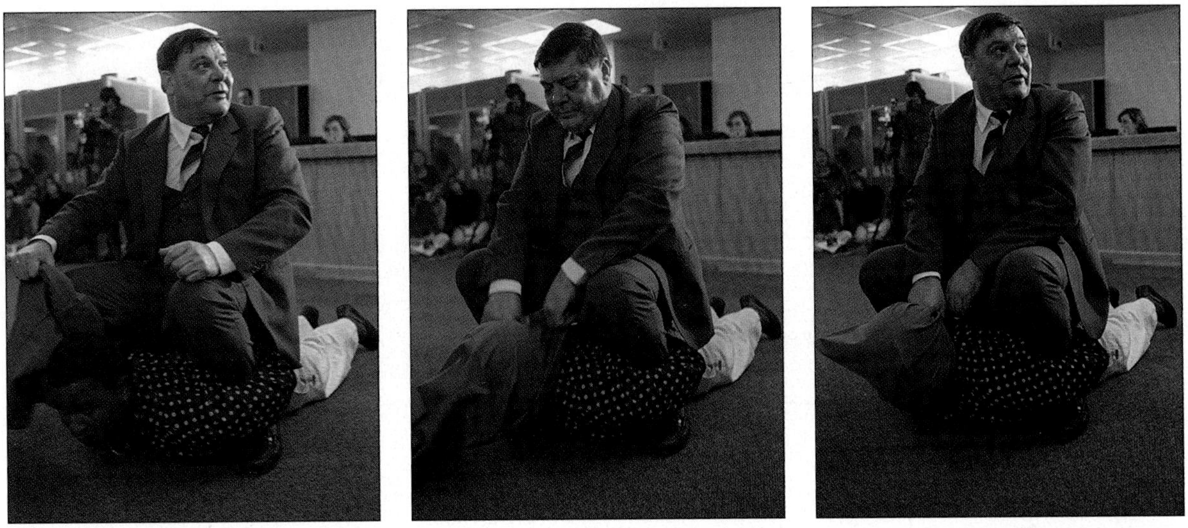

"Maybe I was too patriotic" So said ex-torturer Jeffrey Benzien, shown here demonstrating the "wet bag" technique to South Africa's Truth and Reconciliation Commission. He would place a cloth over victims' heads, bringing them to the terrifying brink of asphyxiation over and over again. Such terror by the former security police, who routinely denied such acts, were used to get an accused person to disclose, for example, where guns were hidden. "I did terrible things," Benzien admitted with apologies to his victims, though he claimed only to be following orders.

alone, Asch's subjects nearly always gave the correct answer. It was another matter when they stood alone against a group.

In the obedience studies, a powerful social pressure (the experimenter's commands) overcame a weaker one (the remote victim's pleas). Torn between the pleas of the victim and the orders of the experimenter, between the desire to avoid doing harm and the desire to be a good participant, a surprising number chose to obey.

Why were the participants unable to disengage themselves? How had they become trapped? Imagine yourself as the teacher in yet another version of Milgram's study, one he never conducted. Assume that when the learner gives the first wrong answer, the experimenter asks you to zap him with 330 volts. After flicking the switch, you hear the learner scream, complain of a heart disturbance, and plead for mercy. Do you continue?

I think not. Recall the step-by-step entrapment of the foot-in-the-door phenomenon (Chapter 4) as we compare this hypothetical experiment to what Milgram's subjects experienced. Their first commitment was mild—15 volts—and it elicited no protest. You, too, would agree to do that much. By the time they delivered 75 volts and heard the learner's first groan, they already had complied five times. On the next trial the experimenter asked them to commit an act only slightly more extreme than what they had already repeatedly committed. By the time they delivered 330 volts, the participants had complied 22 times and reduced some of their dissonance. They were therefore in a different psychological state from that of someone beginning the experiment at that point. As we saw in Chapter 4, external behaviour and internal disposition can feed one another, sometimes in an escalating spiral. Thus, reported Milgram (1974, p. 10):

> Many subjects harshly devalue the victim *as a consequence* of acting against him. Such comments as "He was so stupid and stubborn he deserved to get shocked," were common. Once having acted against the victim, these subjects found it necessary to view him as an unworthy individual, whose punishment was made inevitable by his own deficiencies of intellect and character.

STORY BEHIND THE RESEARCH

While working for Solomon E. Asch, I wondered whether his conformity experiments could be made more humanly significant. First, I imagined an experiment similar to Asch's except that the group induced the person to deliver shocks to a protesting victim. But a control was needed to see how much shock a person would give in the absence of group pressure. Someone, presumably the experimenter, would have to instruct the subject to give the shocks. But now a new question arose: Just how far would a person go when ordered to administer such shocks? In my mind, the issue had shifted to the willingness of people to comply with destructive orders. It was an exciting moment for me. I realized that this simple question was both humanly important and capable of being precisely answered.

The laboratory procedure gave scientific expression to a more general concern about authority, a concern forced upon members of my generation, in particular upon Jews such as myself, by the atrocities of the Second World War. The impact of the Holocaust on my own psyche energized my interest in obedience and shaped the particular form in which it was examined.

Stanley Milgram (1933–1984)
City University of New York

Abridged from the original for this book and from Milgram, 1977, with permission of Alexandra Milgram.

During the early 1970s, Greece's military junta used this "blame-the-victim" process to train torturers (Haritos-Fatouros, 1988; Staub, 1989). In Greece, as in the training of SS officers in Nazi Germany, the military selected candidates based on their respect for and submission to authority. But such tendencies alone do not a torturer make. Thus they would first assign the trainee to guard prisoners, then to participate in arrest squads, then to hit prisoners, then to observe torture, and only then to practise it. Step by step, an obedient but otherwise decent person evolved into an agent of cruelty. Compliance bred acceptance.

"Men's actions are too strong for them. Show me a man who has acted and who has not been the victim and slave of his action."

Ralph Waldo Emerson, *Representative Men*: Goethe, 1850

As a Holocaust survivor, University of Massachusetts social psychologist Ervin Staub knows too well the forces that can transform citizens into agents of death. From his study of human genocide across the world, Staub (2003) shows where this process can lead. Too often, criticism produces contempt, which licenses cruelty, which, when justified, leads to brutality, then killing, then systematic killing. Evolving attitudes both follow and justify actions. Staub's disturbing conclusion: "Human beings have the capacity to come to experience killing other people as nothing extraordinary" (1989, p. 13).

Humans also have a capacity for heroism. During the Holocaust, the French village of Le Chambon sheltered 5000 Jews and other refugees destined for deportation to Germany. These people were mostly Protestants, whose own authorities, their pastors, had taught them to "resist whenever our adversaries will demand of us obedience contrary to the orders of the Gospel" (Rochat, 1993; Rochat & Modigliani, 1995). Ordered to divulge the sheltered Jews, the head pastor modelled disobedience: "I don't know of Jews, I only know of human beings." Without knowing how terrible the war would be or how much they would suffer, the resisters made an initial commitment and then—supported by their beliefs, by their own authorities, and by one another—remained defiant to the war's end. Here and elsewhere, the ultimate response to Nazi occupation usually came early. The first acts of compliance or resistance bred attitudes that influenced behaviour, which strengthened attitudes. Initial helping heightened commitment, leading to more helping.

The power of the situation

This chapter's most important lesson—that immediate situational forces are powerful—reveal the strength of the social context. To feel this for yourself, imagine violating some minor norms: standing up in the middle of a class; singing out loud in a restaurant; greeting some distinguished senior professors by their first names; playing golf in a suit. In trying to break with social constraints, we suddenly realize how strong they are.

The students in a recent experiment found it surprisingly difficult to violate the norm of being "nice" rather than confrontational. Participants imagined themselves discussing with three others whom to select for survival on a desert island. They were asked to imagine one of the others, a man, injecting three sexist comments, such as "I think we need more women on the island to keep the men satisfied." How would they react to such sexist remarks? Only 5 percent predicted they would ignore each of the comments or wait to see how others reacted. But when Janet Swim and Lauri Hyers (1998) engaged other students in discussions where such comments were actually made by a male confederate, 56 percent (not 5 percent) said nothing. This once again demonstrates the power of normative pressures and how hard it is to predict behaviour, even our own behaviour. In another example, in 1994, two soldiers in the Canadian Airborne Regiment tortured and killed Shidane Arone, a Somali teenager who was caught stealing from their camp in Somalia. An inquiry into Arone's death suggested that 16 people passed through the area where he was tortured and that his screams could be heard throughout the camp, yet no one intervened. The Canadian public was outraged: They had prided their military as peacekeepers and did not believe that such atrocity could happen on its watch.

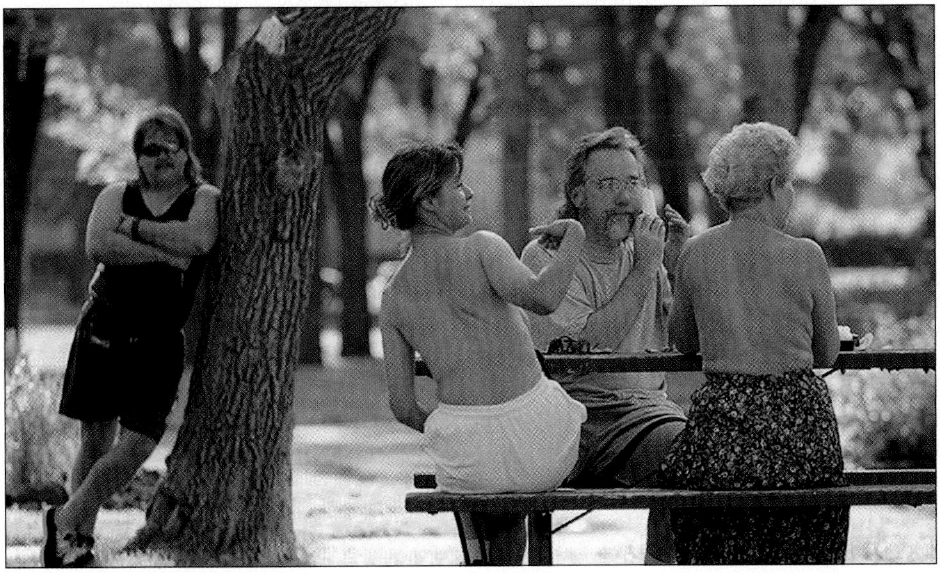

Even in an individualistic culture, few of us have the desire to rebel against society's clearest norms. The two women shown were the only participants in a topless parade in Winnipeg.

Milgram's studies also offer a lesson about evil. According to what we see in horror movies and suspense novels, evil results from a few bad apples, a few depraved killers. In real life we similarly think of Hitler's extermination of Jews, of Saddam Hussein's extermination of Kurds, of Osama bin Laden's plotting terror. But evil also results from social forces—from the heat, humidity, and disease that help make a whole barrel of apples go bad. The U.S. military police, whose abuse of Iraqi prisoners at Abu Ghraib prison horrified the world, were under stress, taunted by many of those they had come to save, angered by comrades' deaths, overdue to return home, and under lax supervision—an evil situation that produced evil behaviour (Fiske et al., 2004). Similar conditions prevailed in Somalia when Canadian soldiers turned a blind eye to Shidane Arone's murder. Situations can induce ordinary people to capitulate to cruelty.

This is especially true when, as happens often in complex societies, the most terrible evil evolves from a sequence of small evils. German civil servants surprised Nazi leaders with their willingness to handle the paperwork of the Holocaust. They were not killing Jews, of course; they were merely pushing paper (Silver & Geller, 1978). When fragmented, evil becomes easier. Milgram studied this compartmentalization of evil by involving yet another 40 men more indirectly. Rather than trigger the shock, they had only to administer the learning test. Now, 37 of the 40 fully complied.

So it is in our everyday lives: The drift toward evil usually comes in small increments, without any conscious intent to do evil. Procrastination involves a similar unintended drift, toward self-harm (Sabini & Silver, 1982). A student knows the deadline for a term paper weeks ahead. Each diversion from work on the paper—a video game here, a TV program there—seems harmless enough. Yet gradually the student veers toward not doing the paper without ever consciously deciding not to do it.

The fundamental attribution error

Why do the results of these classic experiments so often startle people? Is it not because we expect people to act in accord with their dispositions? It doesn't surprise us when a surly person is nasty, but we expect those with pleasant dispositions to be kind. Bad people do bad things; good people do good things.

"The assaulting quality of the Milgram experiment is really a valuable attack on the denial and indifference of all of us. Whatever upset follows facing the truth, we must eventually face up to the fact that so many of us are, in fact, available to be genociders or their assistants."

Israel W. Charny, Executive Director, International Conference on the Holocaust and Genocide, 1982

When you read about Milgram's studies, what impressions did you form of the subjects? Most people attribute negative qualities to them. When told about one or two of the obedient subjects, people judge them to be aggressive, cold, and unappealing—even after learning that their behaviour was typical (Miller et al., 1973). Cruelty, we presume, is inflicted by the cruel at heart.

Günter Bierbrauer (1979) tried to eliminate this underestimation of social forces (the fundamental attribution error). He had university students observe a vivid re-enactment of the experiment or play the role of obedient teacher themselves. They still predicted that their friends would, in a repeat of Milgram's study, be only minimally compliant. Bierbrauer concluded that although social scientists accumulate evidence that our behaviour is a product of our social histories and current environments, most people continue to believe that people's inner qualities reveal themselves—that only good people do good and that only evil people do evil.

It is tempting to assume that Eichmann and the Auschwitz death camp commanders were uncivilized monsters. Indeed, their evil was fuelled by virulent anti-Semitism. And the social situation alone does not explain why, in the same neighbourhood or death camp, some personalities displayed vicious cruelty and others heroic kindness. Still, the commanders would not have stood out to us as monsters. After a hard day's work, they would relax by listening to Beethoven and Schubert. Like most other Nazis, Eichmann himself was outwardly indistinguishable from common people with ordinary jobs (Arendt, 1963). Or consider the German police battalion responsible for shooting nearly 40 000 Jews in Poland, many of them women, children, and elderly people who were shot in the back of the head, gruesomely spraying their brains. Christopher Browning (1992) portrays the "normality" of these men. Like the many, many others who ravaged Europe's Jewish ghettos, operated the deportation trains, and administered the death camps (Goldhagen, 1996), they were not Nazis, SS members, or racial fanatics. They were labourers, salesmen, clerks, and artisans—family men who were too old for military service, but who, when directly ordered to kill, were unable to refuse.

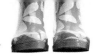

As Milgram noted (1974, p. 6): "The most fundamental lesson of our study is that ordinary people, simply doing their jobs, and without any particular hostility on their part, can become agents in a terrible destructive process." Perhaps then, we should be more wary of political leaders whose charming dispositions lull us into supposing they would never do evil. Under the sway of evil forces, even nice people are sometimes corrupted as they construct moral rationalizations for immoral behaviour (Tsang, 2002). So it is that ordinary soldiers will follow orders to shoot defenseless civilians, ordinary employees will follow instructions to produce and distribute degrading products, and ordinary group members will heed commands to brutally haze initiates.

"Eichmann did not hate Jews, and that made it worse, to have no feelings. To make Eichmann appear a monster renders him less dangerous than he was. If you kill a monster you can go to bed and sleep, for there aren't many of them. But if Eichmann was normality, then this is a far more dangerous situation."

Hannah Arendt, *Eichmann in Jerusalem*, 1963

So, does a situational analysis of harm-doing exonerate harm-doers? Does it absolve them of responsibility? In laypeople's minds, the answer is to some extent yes, notes Arthur Miller (2006). But the psychologists who study the roots of evil insist otherwise. To explain is not to excuse. To understand is not to forgive. You can forgive someone whose behaviour you don't understand, and you can understand someone whom you do not forgive. Moreover, adds James Waller (2002), "When we understand the ordinariness of extraordinary evil, we will be less surprised by evil, less likely to be unwitting contributors to evil, and perhaps better equipped to forestall evil."

Finally, a comment on the experimental method used in conformity research (see synopsis, Table 6–2): Conformity situations in the laboratory differ from those in everyday life. How

TABLE 6–2 Summary of classic obedience studies

Topic	Researcher	Method	Real-Life Example
Norm formation	Sherif	Assessing suggestibility regarding seeming movement of light	Interpreting events differently after hearing from others; appreciating a tasty food that others love
Conformity	Asch	Agreement with others' obviously wrong perceptual judgments	Doing as others do; fads such as tattoos
Obedience	Milgram	Complying with commands to shock another	Soldiers or employees following questionable orders

often are we asked to judge line lengths or administer shock? As combustion is similar for a burning match and a forest fire, so we assume that psychological processes in the laboratory and in everyday life are similar (Milgram, 1974). We must be careful in generalizing from the simplicity of a burning match to the complexity of a forest fire. Yet controlled experiments on burning matches can give us insights into combustion that we cannot gain by observing forest fires. So, too, the social-psychological experiment offers insights into behaviour not readily revealed in everyday life. The experimental situation is unique, but so is every social situation. By testing with a variety of unique tasks, and by repeating experiments in different times and places, researchers probe for the common principles that lie beneath the surface diversity.

The classic conformity studies answered some questions but raised others: (1) Sometimes people conform; sometimes they do not. When do they? (2) Why do people conform? Why don't they ignore the group and "to their own selves be true?" (3) Is there a type of person who is likely to conform? Let's take these questions one at a time.

SUMMING UP

Three classic sets of experiments illustrate how researchers have studied conformity.

Muzafer Sherif observed that others' judgments influenced people's estimates of the movement of a point of light that actually did not move. Norms for "proper" answers emerged and survived both over long periods of time and through succeeding generations of research participants.

Solomon Asch had people listen to others' judgments of which of three comparison lines was equal to a standard line and then make the same judgment themselves. When the others unanimously gave a wrong answer, the subjects conformed 37 percent of the time.

Stanley Milgram's obedience studies elicited an extreme form of compliance. Under optimum conditions—a legitimate, close-at-hand commander, a remote victim, and no one else to exemplify disobedience—65 percent of his adult male subjects fully obeyed instructions to deliver what were supposedly traumatizing electric shocks to a screaming innocent victim in an adjacent room.

These classic studies expose the potency of several phenomena. Behaviour and attitudes are mutually reinforcing, enabling a small act of evil to foster the attitude that leads to a larger evil act. The power of the situation is seen when good people, faced with dire circumstances, commit reprehensible acts (although dire situations may produce heroism in others). The fundamental attribution error leads us to think that evil is committed by people who are bad and that good is done by good people, and to discount situational forces that induce people to conform to falsehoods or capitulate to cruelty.

WHAT PREDICTS CONFORMITY?

Some situations trigger much conformity, others little conformity. If you want to produce maximum conformity, what conditions would you choose?

Social psychologists wondered: If even Asch's noncoercive, unambiguous situation could elicit a 37-percent conformity rate, would other settings produce even more? Researchers soon discovered that conformity did grow if the judgments were difficult or if the subjects felt incompetent. The more insecure we are about our judgments, the more influenced we are by others.

Group attributes also mattered. Conformity is highest when the group has three or more people and is cohesive, unanimous, and high in status. Conformity is also highest when the response is public and made without prior commitment. Let's look at each of these conditions.

GROUP SIZE

In laboratory experiments a group need not be large to have a large effect. Asch and other researchers found that three to five people will elicit much more conformity than just one or two. Increasing the number of people beyond five yields diminishing returns (Gerard et al., 1968; Rosenberg, 1961). In a field experiment, Milgram and his colleagues (1969) had 1, 2, 3, 5, 10, or 15 people pause on a busy sidewalk and look up. As Figure 6–4 shows, the percentage of passersby who also looked up increased as the number looking up increased from one to five persons.

The way the group is "packaged" also makes a difference. Researcher David Wilder (1977) gave students a jury case. Before giving their own judgments, the students watched videotapes of four confederates giving their judgments. When presented as two independent groups of two people, the participants conformed more than when the four confederates presented their judgments as a single group. Similarly, two groups of three people elicited more conformity than one group of six, and three groups of two people elicited even more. Evidently, the agreement of several small groups makes a position more credible.

UNANIMITY

Imagine yourself in a conformity experiment where all but one of the people responding before you give the same wrong answer. Would the example of this one nonconforming confederate be as liberating as it was for the subjects in Milgram's obedience experiment? Several experiments reveal that someone who punctures a group's unanimity deflates its social power (Allen

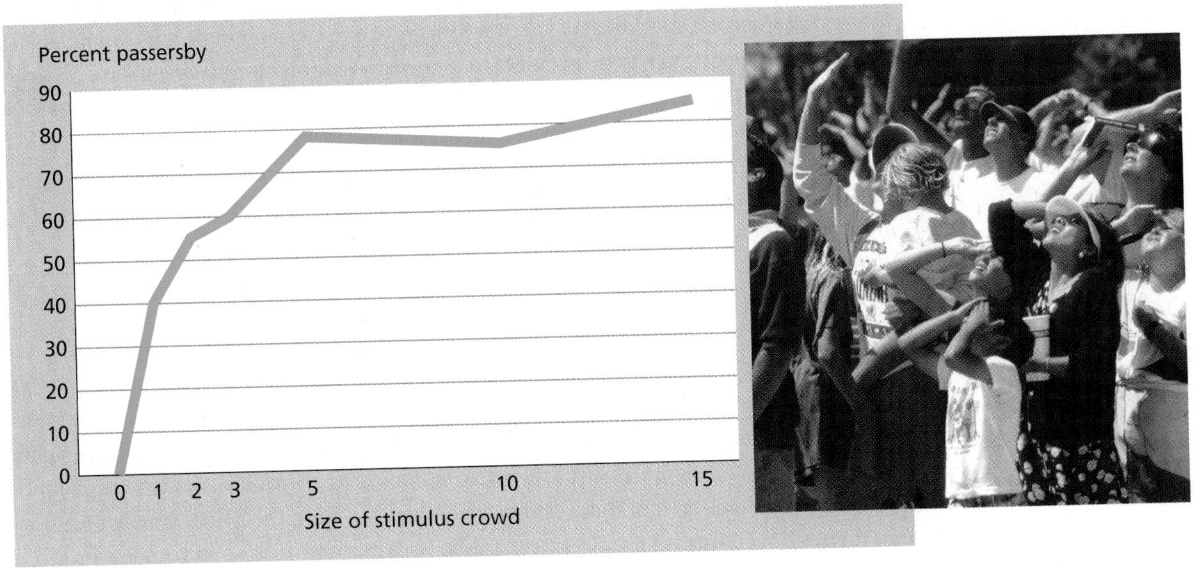

FIGURE 6–4

Group size and conformity.

The percentage of passersby who imitated a group looking upward increased as group size increased to five persons. (Data from Milgram, Bickman & Berkowitz, 1969)

FIGURE 6–5

The effect of unanimity on conformity.

When someone giving correct answers punctures the group's unanimity, subjects conform only one-fourth as often. (Data from Asch, 1955)

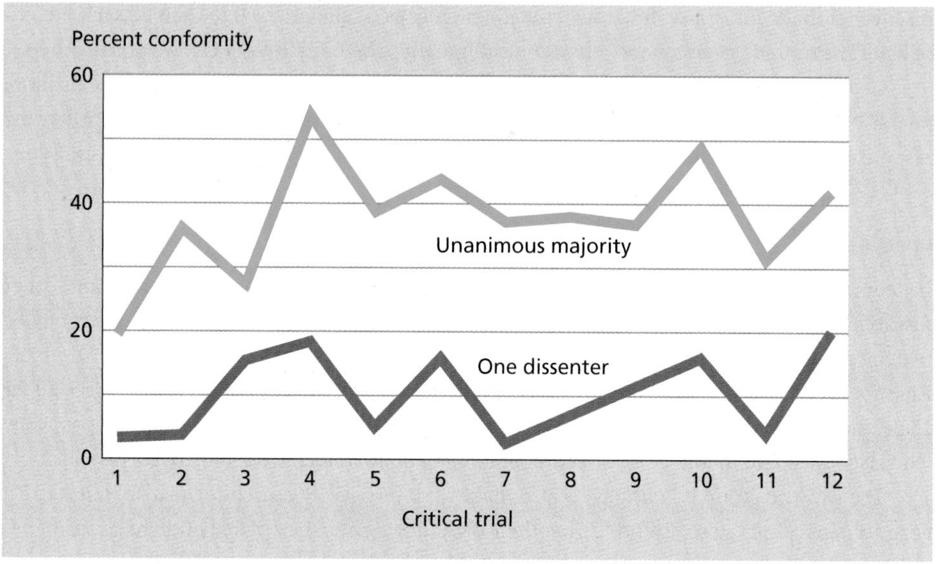

& Levine, 1969; Asch, 1955; Morris & Miller, 1975). As Figure 6–5 above illustrates, subjects will nearly always voice their convictions if just one other person has also differed from the majority. The subjects in such experiments often later say they felt warm toward and close to their nonconforming ally. Yet they deny that the ally influenced them: "I would have answered just the same if he weren't there."

"My opinion, my conviction, gains infinitely in strength and success, the moment a second mind has adopted it."

Novalis, Fragment

It's difficult to be a minority of one; few juries are hung because of one dissenting juror. These experiments teach the practical lesson that it is easier to stand up for something if you can find someone else to stand up with you. Many religious groups recognize this. Following the example of Jesus, who sent his disciples out in pairs, Jehovah's Witnesses send two missionaries into a neighbourhood together. The support of the one comrade greatly increases a person's social courage.

Observing someone else's dissent—even when it is wrong—can increase our own independence. Charlan Nemeth and Cynthia Chiles (1988) discovered this after having people observe a lone individual in a group of four misjudge blue stimuli as green. Although the dissenter was wrong, observing him enabled the observers to exhibit their own form of independence. In a follow-up experiment, 76 percent of the time they correctly labelled red slides "red" even when everyone else was calling them "orange." Participants who had no opportunity to observe the "green" dissenter conformed 70 percent of the time.

COHESION

cohesiveness
a "we feeling"—the extent to which members of a group are bound together, such as by attraction for one another

A minority opinion from someone outside the groups we identify with—from someone at another university or of a different religion—sways us less than the same minority opinion from someone within our group (Clark & Maass, 1988). A heterosexual arguing for gay rights would sway heterosexuals more effectively than a homosexual would. People even comply more readily with requests from those said to share their birthday, their first name, or features of their fingerprint (Burger et al., 2004; Silvia, 2005). The more **cohesive** a group is, the more power it gains over its members. In university sororities, for example, friends tend to share binge-eating tendencies, especially as they grow closer (Crandall, 1988).

In experiments, too, group members who feel attracted to the group are more responsive to its influence (Berkowitz, 1954; Boldt, 1976; Lott & Lott, 1961; Sakurai, 1975). They do not like disagreeing with other group members. Fearing rejection by those they like, they allow them a certain power. In his *Essay Concerning Human Understanding,* the seventeenth-century philosopher John Locke recognized the cohesiveness factor: "Nor is there one in ten thousand who is stiff and insensible enough to bear up under the constant dislike and condemnation of his own club."

As Chapter 11 (Attraction) will document, we tend to like others who are similar to ourselves. So, as we might expect, people tend to align their opinions with those of people like themselves. For example, they express more favourable opinions toward a piece of music after observing the liking of someone akin to themselves. And they express more negative opinions when the music is liked by someone unlike themselves (Hilmert et al., 2006).

STATUS

As you might suspect, higher-status people tend to have more impact (Driskell & Mullen, 1990). Junior group members—even junior social psychologists—acknowledge more conformity to their group than do senior group members (Jetten et al., 2006). Studies of jaywalking behaviour, conducted with the unwitting aid of nearly 24 000 pedestrians, reveal that the baseline jaywalking rate of 25 percent decreases to 17 percent in the presence of a nonjaywalking confederate and increases to 44 percent in the presence of another jaywalker (Mullen et al., 1990). The nonjaywalker best discourages jaywalking when well dressed. Clothes seem to "make the person" in Australia, too. Michael Walker, Susan Harriman, and Stuart Costello (1980) found that Sydney pedestrians were more compliant when approached by a well-dressed survey taker than one who was poorly dressed.

A cohesive group.

The entire parliament fell dead silent. For the first time since anyone could remember, one of the members voted "aye."

Milgram (1974) reports that in his obedience studies people of lower status accepted the experimenter's commands more readily than people of higher status. After delivering 450 volts, one participant, a 37-year-old welder, turned to the experimenter and deferentially asked, "Where do we go from here, Professor?" (p. 46). Another participant, a divinity school professor who disobeyed at 150 volts, said: "I don't understand why the experiment is placed above this person's life," and plied the experimenter with questions about "the ethics of this thing" (p. 48).

PUBLIC RESPONSE

One of the first questions researchers sought to answer was this: Would people conform more in their public responses than in their private opinions? Or would they wobble more in their private opinions but be unwilling to conform publicly, lest they appear wishy-washy? The answer is now clear: In experiments, people conform more when they must respond publicly in front of others rather than writing their answer privately. Asch's participants, after hearing others respond, were less influenced by group pressure if they could write an answer that only the experimenter would see. It is much easier to stand up for what we believe in the privacy of the voting booth than before a group.

NO PRIOR COMMITMENT

In 1980, Genuine Risk became the second filly ever to win the Kentucky Derby. In her next race, the Preakness, she came off the last turn gaining on the leader, Codex, a colt. As they came out of the turn neck and neck, Codex moved sideways toward Genuine Risk, causing her to hesitate and giving him a narrow victory. Had Codex brushed Genuine Risk? Had his jockey even whipped Genuine Risk in the face? The race referees huddled. After a brief deliberation they judged that no foul had occurred and confirmed Codex as the winner. The decision caused an uproar. Televised instant replays showed that Codex had indeed brushed Genuine Risk, the sentimental favourite. A protest was filed. The officials reconsidered their decision, but they did not change it.

"If you worry about missing the boat—remember the Titanic*."*

Anonymous

"Those who never retract their opinions love themselves more than they love truth."

Joubert, *Pensées*

Did their declared judgment immediately after the race affect officials' openness toward reaching a different decision later? We will never know for sure. We can, however, put people through a laboratory version of this event—with and without the immediate commitment—and observe whether the commitment makes a difference. Again, imagine yourself in an Asch-type experiment. The experimenter displays the lines and asks you to respond first. After you have given your judgment and then heard everyone else disagree, the experimenter offers you an opportunity to reconsider. In the face of group pressure, do you now back down?

People almost never do (Deutsch & Gerard, 1955). Once having made a public commitment, they stick to it. At most, they will change their judgments in later situations (Saltzstein & Sandberg, 1979). We may therefore expect that judges of diving or gymnastic competition, for example, will seldom change their ratings after seeing the other judges' ratings, although they might adjust their later performance ratings.

Did Codex brush against Genuine Risk? Once race referees publicly announced their decision, no amount of evidence could budge them.

"All right! Have it your own way. It was a ball."

Prior commitment: Once they commit themselves to a position, people seldom yield to social pressure. Real umpires and referees rarely reverse their initial judgments.

Prior commitments restrain persuasion, too. When simulated juries make decisions, hung verdicts are more likely in cases when jurors are polled by a show of hands rather than by secret ballot (Kerr & MacCoun, 1985). Making a public commitment makes people hesitant to back down. Smart persuaders know this. Salespeople ask questions that prompt us to make statements for, rather than against, what they are marketing. Environmentalists ask people to commit themselves to recycling, energy conservation, or bus riding—and find that behaviour then changes more than when environmental appeals are heard without inviting a commitment (Katzev & Wang, 1994).

SUMMING UP: WHAT PREDICTS CONFORMITY?

Using conformity testing procedures, experimenters have explored the circumstances that produce conformity. Certain situations appear to be especially powerful. For example, conformity is affected by the characteristics of the group: People conform most when faced with the unanimous reports of three or more people, or groups, model the behaviour or belief. Conformity is reduced if the model behaviour or belief is not unanimous. Conformity is enhanced by group cohesion. The higher the status of those modelling the behaviour or belief, the greater likelihood of conformity. People also conform most when their responses are public (in the presence of the group). A prior commitment to a certain behaviour or belief increases the likelihood that a person will stick with that commitment rather than conform.

WHY CONFORM?

"Do you see yonder cloud that's almost in the shape of a camel?" asks Shakespeare's Hamlet of Polonius. "Tis like a camel indeed," replies Polonius. "Methinks it is a weasel," says Hamlet a moment later. "It is backed like a weasel," acknowledges Polonius. "Or like a whale?" wonders Hamlet. "Very like a whale," agrees Polonius. Question: Why does Polonius so readily agree with Hamlet every time he changes his mind?

While attending a lecture at a German university, as the lecturer finished, one of the authors lifted his hands to join in the clapping. But rather than clap, the other people began rapping the tables with their knuckles. What did this mean? Did they disapprove of the speech? Surely, not everyone would be so openly rude. Nor did their faces express displeasure. No, the author decided, this must be a German ovation. Whereupon, he added his knuckles to the chorus.

What prompted this conformity? There are two possibilities: A person may bow to the group (a) to be accepted and avoid rejection or (b) to obtain important information. Morton Deutsch and Harold Gerard (1955) named these two possibilities **normative influence** and **informational influence**. The first springs from our desire to be liked, and the second from our desire to be right.

normative influence
conformity based on a person's desire to fulfill others' expectations, often to gain acceptance

informational influence
conformity that results from accepting evidence about reality provided by other people

Normative influence is "going along with the crowd" to avoid rejection, to stay in people's good graces, or to gain their approval. In the laboratory and in everyday life, groups often reject those who consistently deviate (Miller & Anderson, 1979; Schachter, 1951). This is especially so when dissent is not just "within the family" but when one's group is engaged with another group (Matheson et al., 2003). It's socially permissible for members of a parliament to disagree with their country's war plans during the internal debate before a war. But once the conflict has begun, there is far more pressure to "support the troops."

As most of us know, social rejection is painful; when we deviate from group norms, we often pay an emotional price. Gerard (1999) recalls that in one of his conformity experiments an initially friendly participant became upset, asked to leave the room, and returned looking

> sick and visibly shaken. I became worried and suggested that we discontinue the session. He absolutely refused to stop and continued through all 36 trials, not yielding to the others on a single trial. After the experiment was over and I explained the subterfuge to him, his entire body relaxed and he sighed with relief. Colour returned to his face. I asked him why he had left the room. "To vomit," he said. He did not yield, but at what a price! He wanted so much to be accepted and liked by the others and was afraid he would not be because he had stood his ground against them. There you have normative pressure operating with a vengeance.

Sometimes the high price of deviation compels people to support what they do not believe in or at least to suppress their disagreement.

Informational influence, on the other hand, leads people to privately accept others' influence. When reality is ambiguous, as it was for subjects in the autokinetic situation, other people can be a valuable source of information. The participant may reason, "I can't tell how far the light is moving. But this guy seems to know."

Normative influence: Newly elected politicians often dream of changing the system. Then, seeking to climb within the system, normative influences compel them to comply with its social rules.

To discover what the brain is doing when people experience an Asch-type conformity experiment, a neuroscience team put participants in a functional magnetic resonance imaging (fMRI) brain scanner while having them answer perceptual questions after hearing others' responses (Berns et al., 2005). (The task involved mentally rotating a figure to find its match among several possibilities.) When the participants conformed to a wrong answer, the brain regions dedicated to perception (and not conscious decision-making brain regions) became active. And when they went *against* the group, brain regions associated with emotion became active. These results suggested that when people conform, their perceptions were genuinely influenced.

So concern for *social image* produces *normative influence*. The desire to be *correct* produces *informational influence*. In day-to-day life, normative and informational influence often occur together. Normative influence can also cause people to construct reasons that justify their conformity. For example, consider the following studies by University of British Columbia's Dale Griffin and Wilfrid Laurier University's Roger Buehler (1993, 1994). Participants in these studies read about a character named Robert who had to make a decision to go to medical school (a safe decision, sure to provide financial stability) or pursue his life's dream of attending a music conservatory (a risky decision). They were told that most people thought Robert should go to one school or the other. As you can see in Figure 6–6, those who conformed to this group standard changed their perceptions of acceptable risk for Robert. Those who conformed to the recommendation that he go to medical school thought he should only consider the music conservatory if he was sure of success; those who conformed to the recommendation that he go to the music conservatory thought he should do so even if success was only a remote possibility. Participants also changed their construal of the situation after they conformed or dissented, in ways that justified their decision. Those who conformed to a recommendation that Robert go to the music conservatory, for example, thought the "success" he hoped for was "international fame," rather than simply a career with a "local symphony orchestra." Those who dissented had the opposite interpretation. Thus, the act of dissenting or conforming—driven by normative influence—led participants to interpret the situation quite differently.

Conformity experiments have sometimes isolated either normative or informational influence. Conformity is greater when people respond before a group; this surely reflects normative influence (because subjects receive the same information whether they respond publicly or privately). On the other hand, conformity is greater when participants feel incompetent, when the task is difficult, and when the subjects care about being right—all signs of informational influence.

"Do as most do and men will speak well of thee."

Thomas Fuller, *Gnomologia*

FIGURE 6–6

Changing our beliefs after we conform.

Sometimes we change what we say if the basis of our beliefs is a result of our conformity. (Data from Buehler & Griffin, 1994)

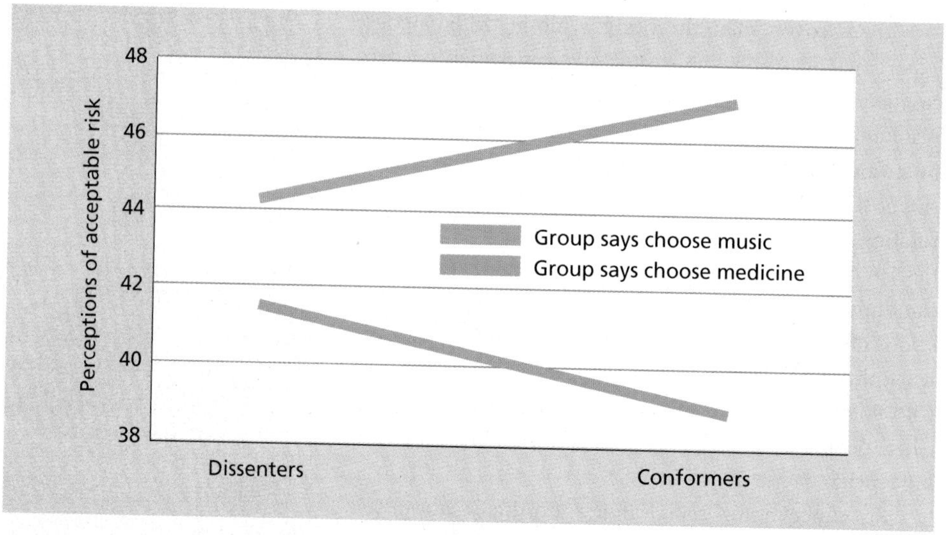

SUMMING UP: WHY CONFORM?

Experiments reveal two reasons people conform. *Normative influence* results from a person's desire for acceptance: We want to be liked. The tendency to conform more when responding publicly reflects normative influence. *Informational influence* results from others' providing evidence about reality. The tendency to conform more on difficult decision-making tasks reflects informational influence: We want to be right.

WHO CONFORMS?

Conformity varies not only with situations but also with persons. How much so? And in what social contexts do personality traits shine through?

Are some people generally more susceptible (or, should we say, more open) to social influence? Among your friends, can you identify some who are "conformists" and others who are "independent"? We suspect that most of us can. Researchers are exploring several areas in their search for the conformer. Let us look briefly at two: personality and culture.

PERSONALITY

During the late 1960s and 1970s, researchers observed only weak connections between personal characteristics with social behaviours such as conformity (Mischel, 1968). In contrast to the demonstrable power of situational factors, personality scores were poor predictors of individuals' behaviour. If you wanted to know how conforming or aggressive or helpful someone was going to be, it seemed you were better off knowing the details of the situation than the person's psychological test scores. As Milgram (1974) concluded: "I am certain that there is a complex personality basis to obedience and disobedience. But I know we have not found it" (p. 205).

Personality effects loom larger when we note people's differing reactions to the same situation, as when one person reacts with terror and another with delight to a roller coaster ride.

During the 1980s, the idea that personal dispositions make little difference prompted personality researchers to pinpoint the circumstances under which traits *do* predict behaviour. Their research affirms a principle that we met in Chapter 4: While internal factors (attitudes, traits) seldom precisely predict a specific action, they better predict a person's *average* behaviour across many situations (Epstein, 1980; Rushton et al., 1983). An analogy may help: Just as your response to a single test item is hard to predict, so is your behaviour in a single situation. And just as your total score across the many items of a test is more predictable, so is your total conformity (or outgoingness or aggressiveness) across many situations.

Personality also predicts behaviour better when social influences are weak. Milgram's obedience studies created "strong" situations; their clear-cut demands made it difficult for personality differences to operate. Even so, Milgram's participants differed widely in how obedient they were, and there is good reason to suspect that sometimes his participants' hostility, respect for authority, and concern for meeting expectations affected their obedience (Blass, 1990, 1991). And in "weaker" situations—as when two strangers sit in a waiting room with no cues to guide their behaviour—individual personalities are even freer to shine (Ickes et al., 1982; Monson et al., 1982).

It is interesting to note how the pendulum of professional opinion swings. Without discounting the undeniable power of social forces, the pendulum is now swinging back toward an appreciation of individual personality and its genetic predispositions. Like the attitude researchers we considered earlier, personality researchers are clarifying and reaffirming the connection between who we are and what we do. Thanks to their efforts, virtually every social psychologist today would agree with pioneering theorist Kurt Lewin's (1936) dictum: "Every psychological event depends upon the state of the person and at the same time on the environment, although their relative importance is different in different cases" (p. 12).

"I don't want to get adjusted to this world."

Woody Guthrie

CULTURE

Does cultural background help predict how conforming people will be? Indeed it does. We will review these findings in more detail in Chapter 8, but the basic finding is that although people in all cultures respond to conformity pressure, specific cultures feel these pressures more keenly than others. Conformity creates a powerful situation, but culture shapes the extent of that power.

SUMMING UP: WHO CONFORMS?

The question "Who conforms?" has produced few definitive answers. Global personality scores are poor predictors of specific acts of conformity but better predictors of average conformity. Trait effects are strongest in "weak" situations where social forces do not overwhelm individual differences. Although conformity and obedience are universal, culture socializes people to be more or less socially responsive.

DO WE EVER WANT TO BE DIFFERENT?

Will people ever actively resist social pressure? When compelled to do A will they instead do Z? What would motivate such anticonformity?

"To do just the opposite is also a form of imitation."

Lichtenberg, *Aphorismen*, 1764–1799

This chapter emphasizes the power of social forces. It is therefore fitting that we conclude by again reminding ourselves of the power of the person. We are not just billiard balls moving where pushed. We may act according to our own values, independently of the forces that push on us. Knowing that someone is trying to coerce us may even prompt us to react in the *opposite* direction.

REACTANCE

Individuals value their sense of freedom and self-efficacy (Baer et al., 1980). When social pressure becomes so blatant that it threatens their sense of freedom, they often rebel. Think of Romeo and Juliet, whose love was intensified by their families' opposition. Or think of children asserting their freedom and independence by doing the opposite of what their parents ask. Savvy parents therefore offer their children choices instead of commands: "It's time to clean up: Do you want a bath or a shower?"

reactance
a motive to protect or restore one's sense of freedom. Reactance arises when someone threatens our freedom of action.

The theory of psychological **reactance**—that people do indeed act to protect their sense of freedom—is supported by experiments showing that attempts to restrict a person's freedom often produce an anticonformity "boomerang effect" (Brehm & Brehm, 1981; Nail et al., 2000). After today's Western university women give thought to how traditional culture expects women to behave, they become *less* likely to exhibit traditional feminine modesty (Cialdini et al., 1998).

Reactance may contribute to underage drinking. A survey of 18- to 24-year-olds by the Canadian Centre on Substance Abuse (1997) revealed that 77 percent of those who were *underage* had been drunk in the last year, but only 69 percent of those who were legally allowed to drink had been drunk. Likewise, 21.5 percent of underage drinkers, but only 17 percent of legal

Reactance

NON SEQUITUR © 1997 Wiley. Dist. by Universal Press Syndicate.

drinkers, report that their drinking has caused personal problems in their life. They suspect this reflects a reactance against the restriction.

ATTRIBUTIONS FOR CONSENSUS

Reactance is driven by an emotional desire to maintain personal freedom. But people may also resist social pressure for more purely cognitive reasons. As we have seen, conformity can result from informational influence. If most people hold a particular attitude or make a particular decision, we may believe it is the most sensible choice. But what if we perceive that others were coerced? Their consensus, in this case, is less informative; their choice is not necessarily more sensible. Will we still go along with the crowd? Probably not. The attributions we make for others' consensus determine, in part, whether we follow their lead.

In a series of studies demonstrating this, University of British Columbia students imagined they were on a committee deciding which computer networking system a company would

Reactance at work? Underage students have been found to be less often abstinent and more often drinking to excess than students over the legal drinking age.

adopt (Conway & Schaller, 2005). They cast their vote after hearing that the rest of the committee preferred one option, WobbleNet. If that was all they knew, participants conformed and supported WobbleNet themselves. But what if they also knew that the company's president ordered the committee to choose WobbleNet? Now, participants faced pressure from both the group *and* an authority figure. Unsurprisingly, they conformed. But here's the twist: If, before they cast their vote, the president stepped down, they no longer conformed. Participants attributed the groups' consensus to the coercive power of the president. Once that pressure was removed, they were far less likely to conform to the group itself.

ASSERTING UNIQUENESS

Imagine a world of complete conformity where there were no differences among people. Would such a world be a happy place? If nonconformity can create discomfort, can sameness create comfort?

People feel uncomfortable when they appear too different from others. But, at least in Western cultures, they also feel uncomfortable when they appear exactly like everyone else. Marilyn Brewer (1991) has described this motive to not feel either too different or too similar to others as a drive for optimal distinctiveness. Experiments by C. R. Snyder and Howard Fromkin (1980) are consistent with this motive, people feel better when they see themselves as moderately unique. Moreover, they act in ways that will assert their individuality. In one experiment, Snyder (1980) led university students to believe that their "10 most important attitudes" were either distinct from or nearly identical to the attitudes of 10 000 other students. When they then participated in a conformity experiment, those deprived of their feeling of uniqueness were most likely to assert their individuality by nonconformity. For those of us in Western cultures, our distinctiveness is central to our identity (Vignoles et al., 2000).

"When I'm in America, I have no doubt I'm a Jew, but I have strong doubts about whether I'm really an American. And when I get to Israel, I know I'm an American, but I have strong doubts about whether I'm a Jew."

Leslie Fiedler, *Fiedler on the Roof*, 1991

Seeing oneself as unique also appears in people's "spontaneous self-concepts." William McGuire and his colleagues (McGuire & Padawer-Singer, 1978; McGuire et al., 1979) report that when children are invited to "tell us about yourself," they are most likely to mention their distinctive attributes. Foreign-born children are more likely than others to mention their birthplace. Redheads are more likely than black- and brown-haired children to volunteer their hair colour. Light and heavy children are the most likely to refer to their body weight. Minority children are the most likely to mention their race.

Likewise we become more keenly aware of our gender when we are with people of the other gender (Cota & Dion, 1986). When one of the authors recently attended a Psychological Association meeting with 10 others—all women as it happened—he immediately was aware of his gender. As the group took a break at the end of the second day, he joked that the line would be short at his bathroom, triggering the woman sitting next to him to notice what hadn't crossed her mind—the group's gender makeup.

The principle, says McGuire, is that "one is conscious of oneself insofar as, and in the ways that, one is different." Thus, "If I am a Black woman in a group of White women, I tend to think of myself as a Black; if I move to a group of Black men, my blackness loses salience and I become more conscious of being a woman" (McGuire et al., 1978). This insight helps us understand why White people who grow up amid non-White people tend to have a strong White identity, and why any minority group tends to be conscious of its distinctiveness and how the surrounding culture relates to it (Knowles & Peng, 2005). The majority group, being less conscious of race, may see the minority group as hypersensitive. When occasionally living in Scotland, where David Myers' accent marks him as a foreigner, he is conscious of his national identity and sensitive to how others react to it.

Asserting our uniqueness. While not wishing to be greatly deviant, most of us express our distinctiveness through our personal styles and dress.

When the people of two cultures are nearly identical, they still will notice their differences, however small. Even trivial distinctions may provoke scorn and conflict. Jonathan Swift satirized the phenomenon in *Gulliver's Travels* with the Little-Endians war against the Big-Endians. Their difference: The Little-Endians preferred to break their eggs on the small end, the Big-Endians on the large end. On a world scale, the differences may not seem great between Scots and English, Hutus and Tutus, Serbs and Croatians, or Catholic and Protestant Northern Irelanders. But small differences can mean big conflicts (Rothbart & Taylor, 1992). Rivalry is often most intense when the other group most closely resembles your own.

"There are no exceptions to the rule that everybody likes to be an exception to the rule."

Malcolm Forbes, *Forbes Magazine*

So, although we do not like being greatly deviant, we are, ironically, all alike in wanting to feel distinctive and noticing how we are distinctive. But as research on self-serving bias (Chapter 2) makes clear, it is not just any kind of distinctiveness we seek but distinctiveness in the right direction. Our quest is not merely to be different from the average, but better than average.

SUMMING UP: DO WE EVER WANT TO BE DIFFERENT?

Social psychology's emphasis on the power of social pressure must be joined by a complementary emphasis on the power of the person. We are not puppets. When social coercion becomes blatant, people often experience *reactance*—a motivation to defy the coercion in order to maintain their sense of freedom.

We are not comfortable being too different from a group, but neither do we want to appear the same as everyone else. Thus, we act in ways that preserve our sense of uniqueness and individuality. In a group, we are most conscious of how we differ from the others.

CHAPTER SEVEN

Group Influence

What is a group?

Social facilitation: How are we affected by the presence of others?
The mere presence of others
Crowding: The presence of many others
Why are we aroused in the presence of others?

Social loafing: Do individuals exert less effort in a group?
Many hands make light work
Social loafing in everyday life

Deindividuation: When do people lose their sense of self in groups?
Doing together what we would not do alone
Diminished self-awareness

Group polarization: Do groups intensify our opinions?
The case of the "risky shift"
Do groups intensify opinions?
Explaining polarization

Groupthink: Do groups hinder or assist good decisions?
Symptoms of groupthink
Critiquing the concept of groupthink
Preventing groupthink
Group problem solving

Leadership: How do leaders shape the group's actions?
Task leadership and social leadership
Transactional leadership
Transformational leadership

The influence of the minority: How do individuals influence the group?
Consistency
Self-confidence
Defections from the majority

Tawna is nearing the end of her daily run. Her mind prods her to keep going; her body begs her to just walk home. She compromises and slowly jogs home. The next day conditions are identical, except that two friends run with her. Tawna runs her route two minutes faster. She wonders, "Did I run better merely because Gail and Rachel went along? Would I always run better in a group?"

At almost every turn, we are involved in groups. Our world contains not only 6.5 billion individuals but also 200 nation-states, 4 million local communities, 20 million economic organizations, and hundreds of millions of other formal and informal groups—couples having dinner, housemates hanging out, clubs planning activities. How do these groups influence individuals?

Group interactions often have more dramatic effects. Intellectual university students hang out with other intellectuals, accentuating one another's intellectual interests. Deviant youth hang out with other deviant youth, amplifying one another's antisocial tendencies. But *how* do groups affect attitudes? And what influences lead groups to smart and dumb decisions?

Individuals influence their groups. As the 1957 movie *12 Angry Men* opens, 12 wary murder trial jurors file into the jury room. It is a hot day. The tired jurors are close to agreement and eager for a quick verdict convicting a teenage boy of knifing his father. But one maverick, played by Henry Fonda, refuses to vote guilty. As the heated deliberation proceeds, the jurors one by one change their verdicts until consensus is reached: "Not guilty." In real trials, a lone individual seldom sways the entire group. Yet, history is made by minorities that sway majorities. What helps make a minority—or an effective leader—persuasive?

We will examine these intriguing phenomena of group influence one at a time. But first things first: What is a group and why do groups exist?

WHAT IS A GROUP?

The answer to the question seems self-evident—until several people compare their definitions. Are jogging partners a group? Are airplane passengers a group? Is a group a set of people who identify with one another, who sense they belong together? Is a group those who share common goals and rely on one another? Does a group form when individuals become organized? When their relationships with one another continue over time? These are among the social psychological definitions of a group (McGrath, 1984).

Group dynamics expert Marvin Shaw (1981) argues that all groups have one thing in common: Their members interact. He therefore defines a **group** as two or more people who interact and influence one another. Moreover, notes Australian National University social psychologist John Turner (1987), groups perceive themselves as "us" in contrast to "them." So jogging companions are indeed a group. Groups may exist for a number of reasons—to meet a need to belong, to provide information, to supply rewards, to accomplish goals.

group
two or more people who, for longer than a few moments, interact with and influence one another and perceive one another as "us"

By Shaw's definition, the passengers on a routine airplane flight would *not* be a group. Although physically together, they are more a collection of individuals than an interacting group.

But the distinction between simple collective behaviour among unrelated individuals on a plane and the more influential group behaviour among interacting individuals sometimes blurs. People who are merely in one another's presence do sometimes influence one another. Moreover, they may perceive themselves as, say, "us" fans in contrast with "them" who root for the other team.

In this chapter we consider three examples of such collective influence: *social facilitation*, *social loafing*, and *deindividuation*. These three phenomena can occur with minimal interaction (in what we call "minimal group situations"), but they also influence people's behaviour while interacting. Then we will consider three examples of social influence in interacting groups: *group polarization*, *groupthink*, and *minority influence*.

SUMMING UP: WHAT IS A GROUP?

A group exists when two or more people interact for more than a few moments, affect one another in some way, and think of themselves as "us."

SOCIAL FACILITATION: HOW ARE WE AFFECTED BY THE PRESENCE OF OTHERS?

Let's begin with social psychology's most elementary question: Are we affected by the mere presence of another person? "Mere presence" means people are not competing, do not reward or punish, and in fact do nothing except be present as a passive audience or as ***coactors****. Would the mere presence of others affect a person's jogging, eating, typing, or exam performance? The search for the answer is a scientific mystery story.*

coactors a group of people working simultaneously and individually on a noncompetitive task

THE MERE PRESENCE OF OTHERS

A century ago, Norman Triplett (1898), a psychologist interested in bicycle racing, noticed that cyclists' times were faster when racing together than when racing alone against the clock. Before he peddled his hunch (that the presence of others boosts performance), Triplett conducted one of social psychology's early laboratory experiments. Children told to wind string on a fishing reel as rapidly as possible wound faster when they worked with coactors than when they worked alone.

Ensuing experiments found that others' presence also improves the speed with which people do simple multiplication problems and cross out designated letters. It also improves the accuracy with which people perform simple motor tasks, such as keeping a metal stick in contact with a dime-sized disk on a moving turntable (F. W. Allport, 1920; Dashiell, 1930; Travis, 1925). This **social-facilitation** effect, as it came to be called, also occurs with animals. In the presence of others of their species, ants excavate more sand and chickens eat more grain (Bayer, 1929; Chen, 1937). In the presence of other sexually active rat pairs, mating rats exhibit heightened sexual activity (Larsson, 1956).

social facilitation (1) original meaning—the tendency of people to perform simple or well-learned tasks better when others are present; (2) current meaning—the strengthening of dominant (prevalent, likely) responses owing to the presence of others

But wait: Other studies revealed that on some tasks the presence of others *hinders* performance. In the presence of others, cockroaches, parakeets, and green finches learn mazes more

Social facilitation: The motivating presence of a coactor or audience strengthens well-learned responses.

slowly (Allee & Masure, 1936; Gates & Allee, 1933; Klopfer, 1958). This disruptive effect also occurs with people. Others' presence diminishes efficiency at learning nonsense syllables, completing a maze, and performing complex multiplication problems (Dashiell, 1930; Pessin, 1933; Pessin & Husband, 1933).

Saying that the presence of others sometimes facilitates performance and sometimes hinders it is about as satisfying as a weather forecast predicting that it might be sunny but then again it might rain. By 1940, research activity in this area had ground to a halt. It lay dormant for 25 years until awakened by the touch of a new idea.

Social psychologist Robert Zajonc (pronounced *Zy-ence,* rhymes with *science*) wondered whether these seemingly contradictory findings could be reconciled. As often happens at creative moments in science, Zajonc (1965) used one field of research to illuminate another. In this case the illumination came from a well-established principle in experimental psychology: Arousal enhances whatever response tendency is dominant. Increased arousal enhances performance on easy tasks for which the most likely—"dominant"—response is the correct one. People solve easy anagrams, such as *akec,* fastest when they are anxious. On complex tasks, for which the correct answer is not dominant, increased arousal promotes *incorrect* responding. On harder anagrams people do worse when anxious.

Could this principle solve the mystery of social facilitation? It seemed reasonable to assume what evidence now confirms—that others' presence will arouse or energize people (Mullen et al., 1997). (Most of us can recall feeling more tense or excited before an audience.) If social arousal facilitates dominant responses, it should boost performance on easy tasks and hurt performance on difficult tasks. Now the confusing results made sense. Winding fishing reels, doing simple multiplication problems, and eating were all easy tasks for which the responses were well learned or naturally dominant. And sure enough, having others around boosted performance. Learning new material, doing a maze, and solving complex math problems were more difficult tasks for which the correct responses were initially less probable. And sure enough, the presence of others increased the number of *incorrect* responses on these tasks. The same general rule—*arousal facilitates dominant responses*—worked in both cases (see Figure 7–1). Suddenly, what had looked like contradictory results no longer seemed contradictory.

"Mere social contact begets . . . a stimulation of the animal spirits that heightens the efficiency of each individual workman."

Karl Marx, *Das Kapital,* 1867

Zajonc's solution, so simple and elegant, left other social psychologists thinking what Thomas H. Huxley thought after first reading Darwin's *Origin of the Species:* "How extremely stupid not to have thought of that!" It seemed obvious—once Zajonc had pointed it out. Perhaps, however, the pieces appeared to merge so neatly only because we viewed them through the spectacles of hindsight. Would the solution survive direct experimental tests?

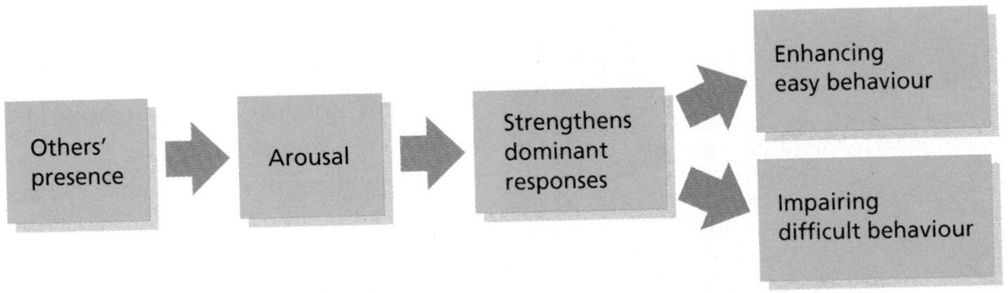

FIGURE 7-1

The effects of social arousal.

Robert Zajonc reconciled apparently conflicting findings by proposing that arousal from others' presence strengthens dominant responses (the correct responses only on easy or well-learned tasks).

After almost 300 studies conducted with the help of more than 25 000 volunteer subjects, it has survived (Bond & Titus, 1983; Guerin, 1993, 1999). Social arousal facilitates dominant responses, whether right or wrong. For example, Peter Hunt and Joseph Hillery (1973) found that in the presence of others, students took less time to learn a simple maze and more time to learn a complex one (just as the cockroaches do). And James Michaels and his collaborators (1982) found that good pool players (who had made 71 percent of their shots while being unobtrusively observed) did even better (80 percent) when four observers came up to watch them play. Poor shooters (who had previously averaged 36 percent) did even worse (25 percent) when closely observed.

"Discovery consists of seeing what everybody has seen and thinking what nobody has thought."

Albert Axent-Gyorgyi, *The Scientist Speculates*

Athletes perform well-practised skills, which helps explain why they often perform best when energized by the responses of a supportive crowd. Studies of more than 80 000 university and professional athletic events in Canada, the United States, and Great Britain reveal that home teams win about 6 in 10 games (somewhat fewer for baseball and football, somewhat more for basketball and soccer—see Table 7-1). The home advantage may, however, also stem from the players' familiarity with their home environment, less travel fatigue, feelings of dominance derived from territorial control, or increased team identity when cheered by fans (Zillmann & Paulus, 1993).

CROWDING: THE PRESENCE OF MANY OTHERS

So people do respond to others' presence. But does the presence of observers always arouse people? In times of stress, a comrade can be comforting. But with others present, people perspire more, breathe faster, tense their muscles more, and have higher blood pressure and a faster heart rate (Geen & Gange, 1983; Moore & Baron, 1983). Even a supportive audience may

TABLE 7-1 Home advantage in major team sports

Sport	Games Studied	Winning Percentage
baseball	135 665	54.3%
football	2592	57.3
hockey	4322	61.1
basketball	13 596	64.4
soccer	37 202	69.0

Data from Courneya & Carron (1992), except for major league baseball, 1900 to 1992, from Schlenker et al. (1995).

A good house is a full house, as James Maas's Cornell University introductory psychology students experienced in this 2000-seat auditorium. If the class had 100 students meeting in this large space, it would feel much less energized.

elicit poorer performance on challenging tasks (Butler & Baumeister, 1998). Having your family at your first piano recital likely won't boost your performance.

The effect of other people increases with their number (Jackson & Latané, 1981; Knowles, 1983). Sometimes the arousal and self-conscious attention created by a large audience interferes even with well-learned, automatic behaviours, such as speaking. Given extreme pressure, we're vulnerable to choking. Stutterers tend to stutter more in front of larger audiences than when speaking to just one or two people (Mullen, 1986).

Being *in* a crowd also intensifies positive or negative reactions. When they sit close together, friendly people are liked even more, and *un*friendly people are *dis*liked even more (Schiffenbauer & Schiavo, 1976; Storms & Thomas, 1977). In experiments with Columbia University students and with Ontario Science Centre visitors, Jonathan Freedman and his coworkers (1980) had an accomplice listen to a humorous tape or watch a movie with other subjects. When all sat close together, the accomplice could more readily induce them to laugh and clap. As theatre directors and sports fans know, and as researchers have confirmed, a "good house" is a full house (Agnew & Carron, 1994; Aiello et al., 1983; Worchel & Brown, 1984).

Heightened arousal in crowded homes also tends to increase stress. Crowding produces less distress in homes divided into many spaces, however, enabling people to withdraw in privacy.

(Evans et al., 1996)

Perhaps you've noticed that a class of 35 students feels warmer and livelier in a room that seats just 35 than when spread around a room that seats 100. This occurs partly because when others are close by, we are more likely to notice and join in their laughter or clapping. But crowding also enhances arousal, as Gary Evans (1979) found. He tested 10-person groups, either in a room 7 by 10 metres or in one 3 by 4 metres. Compared to those in the large room, those densely packed had higher pulse rates and blood pressure (indicating arousal). Though their performance on simple tasks did not suffer, on difficult tasks they made more errors. In a study of university students in India, Dinesh Nagar and Janak Pandey (1987) similarly found that crowding hampered performance only on complex tasks, such as solving difficult anagrams. So, crowding enhances arousal, which facilitates dominant responses.

WHY ARE WE AROUSED IN THE PRESENCE OF OTHERS?

What you do well, you will be energized to do best in front of others (unless you become hyperaroused and self-conscious). What you find difficult may seem impossible in the same circumstances. What is it about other people that creates arousal? There is evidence to support three possible factors (Aiello & Douthitt, 2001): evaluation apprehension, distraction, and mere presence.

Evaluation apprehension

Nickolas Cottrell surmised that observers make us apprehensive because we wonder how they are evaluating us. To test whether **evaluation apprehension** exists, Cottrell and his associates (1968) examined social facilitation for the pronunciation of nonsense syllables and well learned easy to pronounce syllables. In this "mere presence" condition they blindfolded observers, supposedly in preparation for a perception experiment. In contrast to the effect of the watching audience, the mere presence of these blindfolded people did *not* boost well-practised responses.

evaluation apprehension concern for how others are evaluating us

Other experiments confirmed Cottrell's conclusion: The enhancement of dominant responses is strongest when people think they are being evaluated. In one experiment, joggers on a jogging path sped up as they came upon a woman seated on the grass—*if* she was facing them rather than sitting with her back turned (Worringham & Messick, 1983).

Evaluation apprehension also helps explain:

- Why people perform best when their coactor is slightly superior (Seta, 1982)
- Why arousal lessens when a high-status group is diluted by adding people whose opinions don't matter to us (Seta & Seta, 1992)
- Why people who worry most about others' evaluations are the ones most affected by their presence (Gastorf et al., 1980; Geen & Gange, 1983)
- Why social-facilitation effects are greatest when the others are unfamiliar and hard to keep an eye on (Guerin & Innes, 1982)

The self-consciousness we feel when being evaluated can also interfere with behaviours that we perform best automatically (Mullen & Baumeister, 1987). If self-conscious basketball players analyze their body movements while shooting critical free throws, they are more likely to miss.

Driven by distraction

Glenn Sanders, Robert Baron, and Danny Moore (1978; Baron, 1986) carried evaluation apprehension a step further. They theorized that when people wonder how coactors are doing or how an audience is reacting, they get distracted. This *conflict* between paying attention to others and paying attention to the task overloads the cognitive system, causing arousal. Evidence that people are indeed "driven by distraction" comes from experiments that produce social facilitation not just by the presence of another person but even by a nonhuman distraction, such as bursts of light (Sanders, 1981a, 1981b).

Mere presence

Zajonc, however, believes that the mere presence of others, that is simply having other people around, produces some arousal even without evaluation apprehension or arousing distraction. He notes that even animals as lowly as cockroaches show social facilitation effects. This finding hints at an innate social arousal mechanism common to much of the zoological world. (Animals probably are not consciously worrying about how other animals are evaluating them.) At the human level, most joggers feel energized when jogging with someone else, even one who neither competes nor evaluates.

This is a good time to remind ourselves of the purpose of a theory. As we noted in Chapter 1, a good theory is a scientific shorthand: It simplifies and summarizes a variety of observations. Social-facilitation theory does this well. It is a simple summary of many research findings. A good theory also offers clear predictions that (1) help confirm or modify the theory, (2) guide new exploration, and (3) suggest practical application. Social-facilitation theory has definitely generated the first two types of prediction: (1) The basics of the theory (that the presence of others is arousing and that this social arousal enhances dominant responses) have been confirmed, and (2) the theory has brought new life to a long dormant field of research.

Are there (3) some practical applications? We can make some educated guesses. Many new office buildings have replaced private offices with large, open areas divided by low partitions. Might the resulting awareness of others' presence help boost the performance of well-learned tasks, but disrupt creative thinking on complex tasks? Can you think of other possible applications?

SUMMING UP: SOCIAL FACILITATION: HOW ARE WE AFFECTED BY THE PRESENCE OF OTHERS?

Social psychology's most elementary issue concerns the mere presence of others. Some early experiments on this question found that performance improved with observers or coactors present. Others found that the presence of others can hurt performance. Robert Zajonc reconciled these findings by applying a well-known principle from experimental psychology: Arousal facilitates dominant responses. Because the presence of others is arousing, the presence of observers or coactors boosts performance on easy tasks (for which the correct response is dominant) and hinders performance on difficult tasks (for which incorrect responses are dominant).

But why are we aroused by others' presence? Experiments suggest that the arousal stems partly from "evaluation apprehension" and partly from a conflict between paying attention to others and concentrating on the task. Other experiments, including some with animals, suggest that the presence of others can be arousing even when we are not evaluated or distracted.

SOCIAL LOAFING: DO INDIVIDUALS EXERT LESS EFFORT IN A GROUP?

In a team tug-of-war, will eight people on a side exert as much force as the sum of their best efforts in individual tugs of war? If not, why not? And what level of individual effort can we expect from members of work groups?

Social facilitation usually occurs when people work toward individual goals and when their efforts, whether winding fishing reels or solving math problems, can be individually evaluated. These situations parallel some everyday work situations, but not those where people cooperatively pool their efforts toward a common goal and where individuals are not accountable for their efforts. A team tug-of-war provides one such example. Organizational fundraising—pooling candy sale proceeds to pay for the class trip—provides another. So does a class project where all get the same grade. On such "additive tasks"—tasks where the group's achievement depends on the sum of the individual efforts—will team spirit boost productivity?

Will bricklayers lay bricks faster when working as a team than when working alone? One way to attack such questions is with laboratory simulations.

MANY HANDS MAKE LIGHT WORK

Nearly a century ago, French engineer Max Ringelmann (reported by Kravitz & Martin, 1986) found that the collective effort of such teams was but half the sum of the individual efforts. This suggests, contrary to the common notion "in unity there is strength," that group members may actually be *less* motivated when performing additive tasks. Maybe, though, poor performance stemmed from poor coordination—people pulling a rope in slightly different directions at slightly different times. A group of researchers led by Alan Ingham (1974) cleverly eliminated this problem by making individuals think others were pulling with them, when in fact they were pulling alone. Blindfolded participants assigned the first position in the apparatus shown in Figure 7–2 and told to "pull as hard as you can" pulled 18 percent harder when they knew they were pulling alone than when they believed that behind them two to five people were also pulling.

Researchers Bibb Latané, Kipling Williams, and Stephen Harkins (1979; Harkins et al., 1980) kept their ears open for other ways to investigate this phenomenon, which they labelled **social loafing**. They observed that the noise produced by six people shouting or clapping "as loud as you can" was less than three times that produced by one person alone. Like the tug-of-war task, however, noisemaking is vulnerable to group inefficiency. So Latané and his associates followed Ingham's example by leading their participants to believe others were shouting or clapping with them, when in fact they were doing so alone.

social loafing the tendency for people to exert less effort when they pool their efforts toward a common goal than when they are individually accountable

Their method was to blindfold six people, seat them in a semicircle, and have them put on headphones, over which they were blasted with the sound of people shouting or clapping. People could not hear their own shouting or clapping, much less that of others. On various trials they were instructed to shout or clap either alone or along with the group. People who were told about this experiment guessed the subjects would shout louder when with others,

FIGURE 7–2

The rope-pulling apparatus.

People in the first position pulled less hard when they thought people behind them were also pulling. (Data from Ingham, Levinger, Graves & Peckham, 1974) (Photo by Alan G. Ingham)

because they would be less inhibited (Harkins, 1981). The actual result? Social loafing: When the participants believed five others were also either shouting or clapping, they produced one-third less noise than when they thought themselves alone. Social loafing occurred even when the subjects were high-school cheerleaders who believed themselves to be cheering together or alone (Hardy & Latané, 1986).

Curiously, those who clapped both alone and in groups did not view themselves as loafing; they perceived themselves as clapping equally in both situations. This parallels what happens when students work on group projects for a shared grade. Williams reports that all agree loafing occurs—but no one admits to doing the loafing.

John Sweeney (1973), a political scientist interested in the policy implications of social loafing, obtained similar results. Students pumped exercise bicycles more energetically (as measured by electrical output) when they knew they were being individually monitored than when they thought their output was being pooled with that of other riders. In the group condition, people were tempted to **free-ride** on the group effort.

free riders
people who benefit from the group but give little in return

In this and some 160 other studies (Karau & Williams, 1993, and Figure 7–3), we see a twist on one of the psychological forces that makes for social facilitation: evaluation apprehension. In the social loafing experiments, individuals believe they are evaluated only when they act alone. The group situation (rope pulling, shouting, and so forth) *decreases* evaluation apprehension. When people are not accountable and cannot evaluate their own efforts, responsibility is diffused across all group members (Harkins & Jackson, 1985; Kerr & Bruun, 1981). By contrast, the social-facilitation experiments *increased* exposure to evaluation. When made the centre of attention, people self-consciously monitor their behaviour (Mullen & Baumeister, 1987). So the principle is the same: When being observed *increases* evaluation concerns, social facilitation occurs; when being lost in a crowd *decreases* evaluation concerns, social loafing occurs (Figure 7–4).

To motivate group members, one strategy is to make individual performance identifiable. Some football coaches do this by individually filming and evaluating each player. Williams

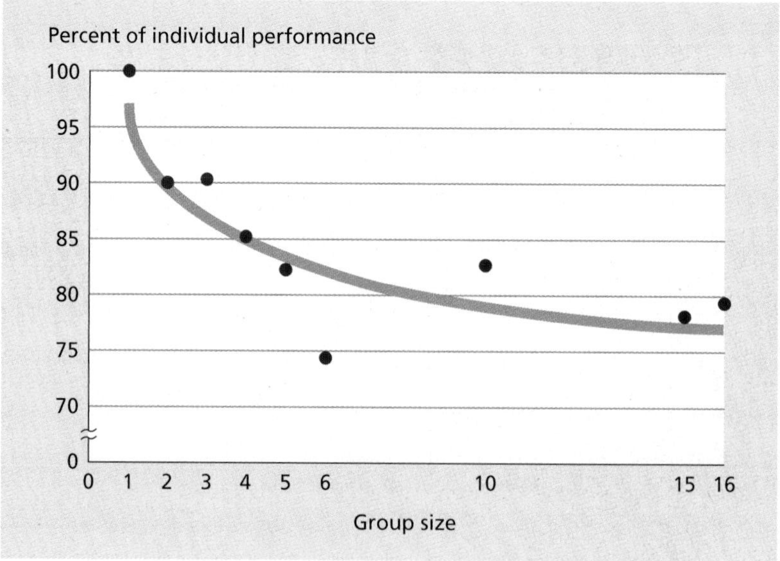

FIGURE 7–3

Effort decreases as group size increases.

A statistical digest of 49 studies, involving more than 4000 participants, revealed that effort decreases (loafing increases) as the size of the group increases. Each dot represents the aggregate data from one of these studies. (From Williams et al., 1992)

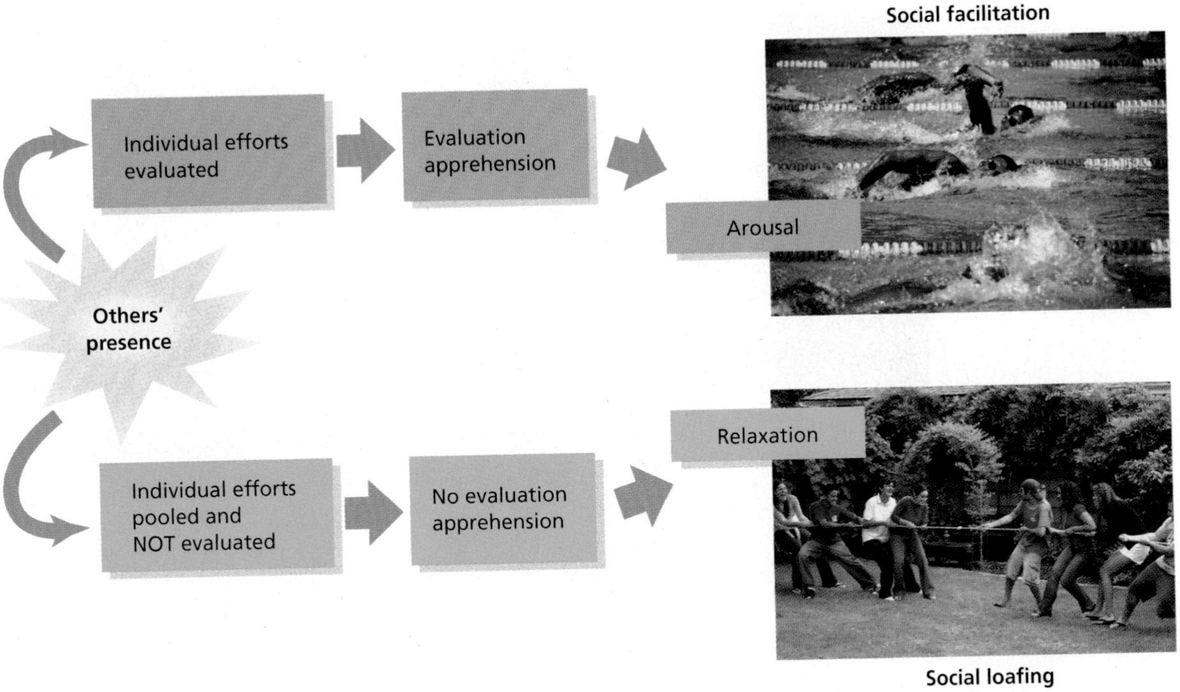

FIGURE 7-4

Social facilitation or social loafing?

When individuals cannot be evaluated or held accountable, loafing becomes more likely. An individual swimmer is evaluated on her ability to win the race. In tug of war, no single person on the team is held accountable, so any one member might relax or loaf.

and his colleagues (1981) had group members wear individual microphones while engaged in group shouting. Whether in a group or not, people exert more effort when their outputs are individually identifiable: University swim team members swim faster in intrasquad relay races when someone monitors and announces their individual times (Williams et al., 1989).

SOCIAL LOAFING IN EVERYDAY LIFE

How widespread is social loafing? In the laboratory, the phenomenon occurs not only among people who are pulling ropes, cycling, shouting, and clapping but also among those who are pumping water or air, evaluating poems or editorials, producing ideas, typing, and detecting signals. Do these results generalize to everyday worker productivity?

In one small experiment, assembly-line workers produced 16 percent more product when their individual output was identified, even though they knew their pay would not be affected (Faulkner & Williams, 1996). And consider: a key job in a pickle factory is picking the right-size dill-pickle halves off the conveyor belt and stuffing them in jars. Unfortunately, workers are tempted to stuff any size pickle in, because their output is not identifiable (the jars go into a common hopper before reaching the quality-control section). Williams, Harkins, and Latané (1981) note that research on social loafing suggests "making individual production identifiable, and raises the question: 'How many pickles could a pickle packer pack if pickle packers were only paid for properly packed pickles?'"

But surely collective effort does not always lead to slacking off. Sometimes the goal is so compelling and maximum output from everyone is so essential that team spirit maintains or

People usually give reduced effort when working in a group, but when group members are highly committed to one another and the success of the group—like these rowers for the Canadian National Team—such social loafing may not occur.

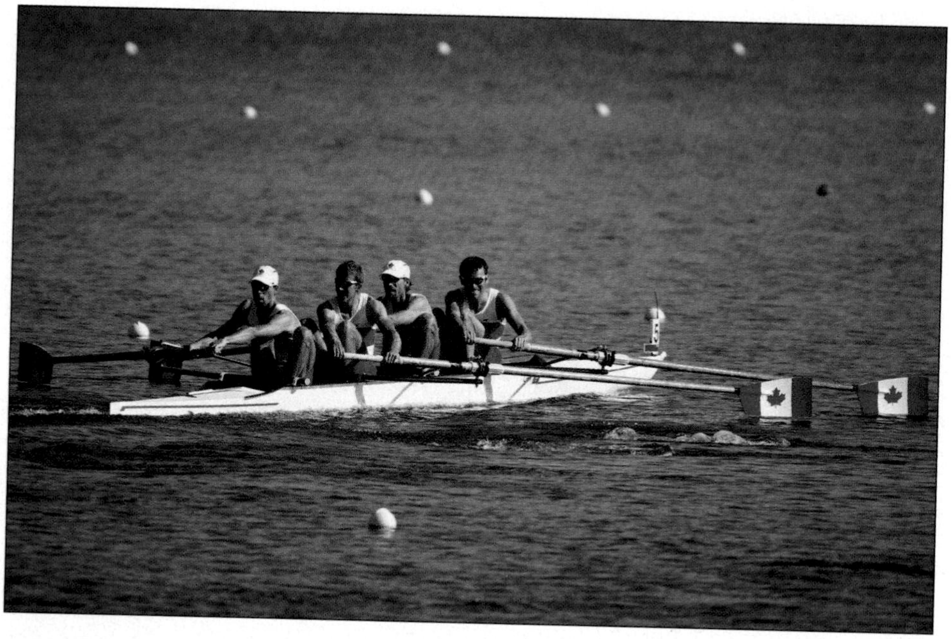

intensifies effort. In an Olympic crew race, will the individual rowers in a four-person crew pull their oars with less effort than those in a one- or two-person crew?

The evidence assures us they will not. People in groups loaf less when the task is *challenging, appealing,* or *involving* (Karau & Williams, 1993). On challenging tasks, people may perceive their efforts as indispensable (Harkins & Petty, 1982; Kerr, 1983; Kerr & Bruun, 1983). When people see others in their group as unreliable or as unable to contribute much, they work harder (Vancouver et al., 1991; Williams & Karau, 1991). Adding incentives or challenging a group to strive for certain standards also promotes collective effort (Harkins & Szymanski, 1989; Shepperd & Wright, 1989). When groups believe high effort will enable performance that will bring rewards—think of staff with stock options in a dot-com startup business—their members will work hard (Shepperd & Taylor, 1999).

Groups also loaf less when their members are *friends* or identified with their group rather than strangers (Davis & Greenlees, 1992; Karau & Williams, 1997; Worchel et al., 1998). Even just expecting to interact with someone again serves to increase efforts on team projects (Groenenboom et al., 2001). Collaborate on a class project with others whom you will be seeing often and you will probably feel more motivated that you would if you never expect to see them again. Latané notes that Israel's communal kibbutz farms have actually outproduced Israel's noncollective farms (Leon, 1969). Cohesiveness intensifies effort.

Some of these findings parallel those from studies of everyday work groups. When groups are given challenging objectives, when they are rewarded for group success, and when there is a spirit of commitment to the "team," group members work hard (Hackman, 1986). Keeping work groups small and forming them with equally competent people can also help members feel that their contributions are indispensable (Comer, 1995). So while social loafing is a common occurrence when group members work collectively and without individual accountability, many hands need not always make light work.

SUMMING UP: SOCIAL LOAFING: DO INDIVIDUALS EXERT LESS EFFORT IN A GROUP?

Social-facilitation researchers study people's performance on tasks where they can be individually evaluated. In many work situations people pool their efforts, however, and work toward a common goal without individual accountability. Group members often work less hard when performing such "additive tasks." This finding parallels everyday situations where diffused responsibility tempts individual group members to free-ride on the group's effort. People may, however, put forth more effort in a group when the goal is important, rewards are significant, and team spirit exists.

DEINDIVIDUATION: WHEN DO PEOPLE LOSE THEIR SENSE OF SELF IN GROUPS?

Group situations may cause people to lose self-awareness, with resulting loss of individuality and self-restraint. What circumstances trigger such "deindividuation"?

In the spring of 1993, soldiers from the Canadian Airborne Regiment were stationed in the remote town of Belet Huen, Somalia. On March 4 some soldiers shot two young Somalis for stealing supplies and killed one of the young men with a point-blank shot to the head. A few days later they captured, tortured, and killed a 16-year-old Somali named Shidane Arone. Pictures of the torture eventually made their way back to Canada, shocking the nation into a prolonged discussion of the state of the military and group violence. People wondered: Where

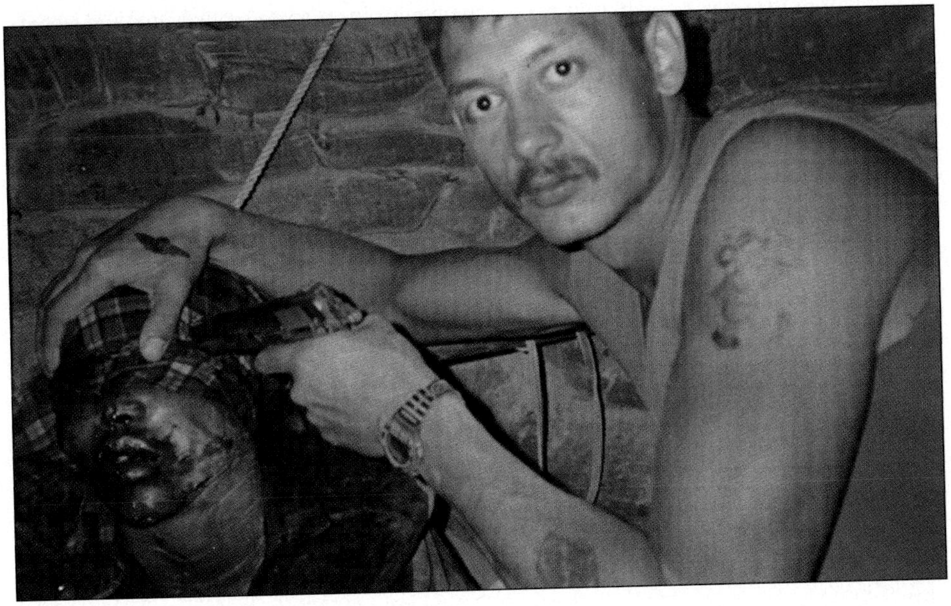

The beating of 16-year-old Shidane Arone by Canadian soldiers in Somalia made people wonder: How do group situations release people from normal restraints?

was the soldiers' humanity? What had happened to standards of military conduct? What could cause such behaviour?

DOING TOGETHER WHAT WE WOULD NOT DO ALONE

Social facilitation experiments show that groups can arouse people. Social loafing experiments show that groups can diffuse responsibility. When arousal and diffused responsibility combine and normal inhibitions diminish, the results may be startling. Acts may range from a mild lessening of restraint (throwing food in the dining hall, snarling at a referee, screaming during a rock concert) to impulsive self-gratification (group vandalism, orgies, thefts) to destructive social explosions (police brutality, riots, mass suicide).

These unrestrained behaviours have something in common: They are somehow provoked by the power of a group. Groups can generate a sense of excitement, of being caught up in something bigger than one's self. It is hard to imagine a single rock fan screaming deliriously at a private rock concert, or a single fan setting multiple cars on fire after a championship win. In certain kinds of group situations people are more likely to abandon normal restraints, to lose their sense of individual responsibility, to become what Leon Festinger, Albert Pepitone, and Theodore Newcomb (1952) labelled **deindividuated**. What circumstances elicit this psychological state?

deindividuation
loss of self-awareness and evaluation apprehension; occurs in group situations that foster anonymity and draw attention away from the individual

Group size

A group has the power not only to arouse its members but also to render them unidentifiable. The snarling crowd hides the snarling hockey fan. A mob enables its members to believe they will not be prosecuted; they perceive the action as the *group's*. Rioters, made faceless by the mob, are freed to loot. In an analysis of 21 instances in which crowds were present as someone threatened to jump from a building or bridge, Leon Mann (1981) found that when the crowd was small and exposed by daylight, people usually did not try to bait the person. But when a large crowd or the cover of night gave people anonymity, the crowd usually baited and jeered.

"A mob is a society of bodies voluntarily bereaving themselves of reason."

Ralph Waldo Emerson, "Compensation," *Essays, First Series*, 1841

From sports crowds to rioters, evaluation apprehension plummets. And because "everyone is doing it," all can attribute their behaviour to the situation rather than to their own choices.

Philip Zimbardo (1970) speculated that the mere immensity of crowded cities produces anonymity and thus norms that permit vandalism. He purchased two 10-year-old cars and left them with the hoods up and licence plates removed, one on a street near the old Bronx campus of New York University and one near the Stanford University campus in Palo Alto, California, a much smaller city. In New York the first auto strippers arrived within 10 minutes; they took the battery and radiator. After three days and 23 incidents of theft and vandalism (by neatly dressed white people), the car was reduced to a battered, useless hulk of metal. By contrast, the only person observed to touch the Palo Alto car in over a week was a passerby who lowered the hood when it began to rain.

Physical anonymity

How can we be sure that the crucial difference between the Bronx and Palo Alto is greater anonymity in the Bronx? We can't. But we can experiment with anonymity to see if it actually lessens inhibitions. In one creative experiment, Zimbardo (1970) dressed women in identical white coats and hoods, rather like Ku Klux Klan members (Figure 7–5). Asked to deliver electric shocks to a woman, they pressed the shock button twice as long as did women who were visible and wearing large name tags.

The Internet offers similar anonymity. The anonymity offered by chat rooms, newsgroups, and listservs also has been observed to foster higher levels of hostile, uninhibited "flaming" behaviour than observed in face-to-face conversations (Douglas & McGarty, 2001).

Testing the phenomenon on the streets, Patricia Ellison, John Govern, and their colleagues (1995) had a confederate driver stop at a red light and wait for 12 seconds whenever she was followed by a convertible or 4x4 vehicle. While enduring the wait she recorded any horn-honking (a mild aggressive act) by the car behind. Compared to drivers of convertibles and 4x4s with the top down, those who were relatively anonymous (with the top up) honked one-third sooner, twice as often, and for nearly twice as long.

A research team led by Ed Diener (1976) cleverly demonstrated the effect both of being in a group *and* of being physically anonymous. At Halloween, they observed 1352 children trick-or-treating. As the children, either alone or in groups, approached 1 of 27 homes scattered throughout the city, an experimenter greeted them warmly, invited them to "take *one* of the candies," and then left the room. Hidden observers noted that, compared to solo children, those in groups were more than twice as likely to take extra candy. Also, compared to children who had been asked their names and where they lived, those left anonymous were also more than twice as likely to transgress. As Figure 7–6 shows, the transgression rate thus varied dramatically with the situation. When deindividuated by group immersion combined with anonymity, most children stole extra candy.

"The use of self-control is like the use of brakes on a train. It is useful when you find yourself going in the wrong direction, but merely harmful when the direction is right."

Bertrand Russell, *Marriage and Morals*

These experiments make us wonder about the effect of wearing uniforms. Preparing for battle, warriors in some tribal cultures (like rabid fans of some sports teams) depersonalize themselves with body and face paints or special masks. After the battle, some cultures kill, torture, or mutilate any remaining enemies; other cultures take prisoners alive. Robert Watson (1973) scrutinized anthropological files and discovered that the cultures with depersonalized warriors were also the cultures that brutalized the enemy. The uniformed Canadian soldiers who tortured and killed Shidane Arone were angered and

FIGURE 7–5

Anonymous women delivered more shock to helpless victims than did identifiable women.

FIGURE 7–6

Children were more likely to transgress by taking extra Halloween candy when in a group, when anonymous, and, especially, when deindividuated by the combination of group immersion and anonymity. (Data from Diener et al., 1976)

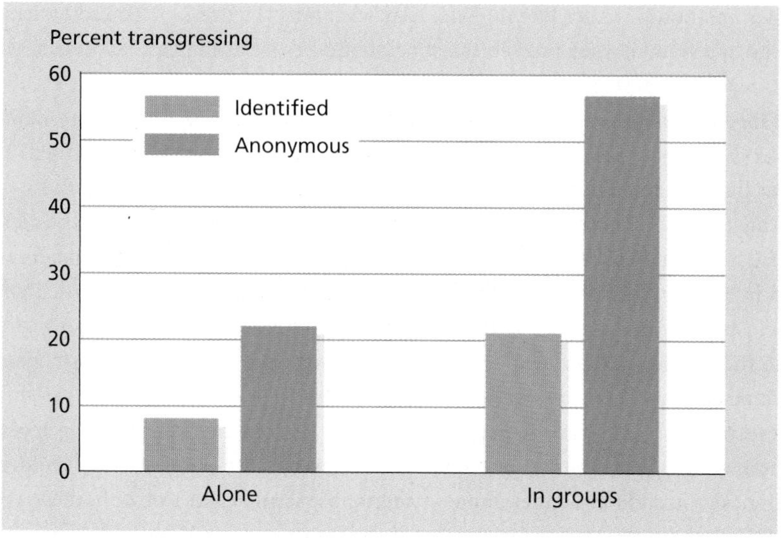

aroused by their frustrating mission and the brutal desert heat, and enjoying one another's camaraderie they were unaware that outsiders would view their actions. Thus, forgetting their normal standards, they were swept away by the situation. In Northern Ireland, 206 of 500 violent attacks studied by Andrew Silke (2003) were conducted by attackers who wore masks, hoods, or other face disguises. Compared with undisguised attackers, these anonymous attackers inflicted more serious injuries, attacked more people, and committed more vandalism.

Does becoming physically anonymous *always* unleash our worst impulses? Fortunately, no. For one thing, the situations in which some of these experiments took place had clear antisocial cues. Robert Johnson and Leslie Downing (1979) point out that the Klan-like outfits worn by Zimbardo's subjects may have encouraged hostility. In an experiment, they had women put on nurses' uniforms before deciding how much shock someone should receive. When those

Deindividuated English soccer fans after a 1985 riot that killed 39 people. The soccer hooligans are often likeable as individuals, reported one journalist who ran with them for eight years, but in a crowd they become demonic (Buford, 1992).

s' uniforms were made anonymous, they became *less* aggressive in administering shocks than when their names and personal identities were stressed. From their analysis of 60 deindividuation studies, Tom Postmes and Russell Spears (1998; Reicher et al., 1995) conclude that being anonymous makes one less self-conscious, and more responsive to cues present in the situation, whether negative (Klan uniforms) or positive (nurses' uniforms).

Arousing and distracting activities

Aggressive outbursts by large crowds are often preceded by minor actions that arouse and divert people's attention. Group shouting, chanting, clapping, or dancing serve both to hype people up and to reduce self-consciousness. One cult observer recalls how the "choo-choo" chant helped deindividuate:

> All the brothers and sisters joined hands and chanted with increasing intensity, choo-choo-choo, Choo-choo-choo, CHOO-CHOO-CHOO! YEA! YEA! POWW!!! The act made us a group, as though in some strange way we had all experienced something important together. The power of the choo-choo frightened me, but it made me feel more comfortable and there was something very relaxing about building up the energy and releasing it. (Zimbardo et al., 1977, p. 186)

Ed Diener's experiments (1976, 1979) have shown that such activities as throwing rocks and group singing can set the stage for more disinhibited behaviour. There is a self-reinforcing pleasure in doing an impulsive act while observing others doing it also. When we see others act as we are acting, we think they feel as we do, which reinforces our own feelings (Orive, 1984). Moreover, impulsive group action absorbs our attention. When we yell at the referee, we are not thinking about our values; we are reacting to the immediate situation. Later, when we stop to think about what we have done or said, we sometimes feel chagrined. Sometimes. At other times we seek deindividuating group experiences—dances, worship experiences, group encounters—where we can enjoy intense positive feelings and feel close to others.

> *"Attending a service in the Gothic cathedral, we have the sensation of being enclosed and steeped in an integral universe, and of losing a prickly sense of self in the community of worshippers."*
>
> Yi-Fu Tuan, 1982

DIMINISHED SELF-AWARENESS

Group experiences that diminish self-consciousness tend to disconnect behaviour from attitudes. Experiments by Ed Diener (1980) and Steven Prentice-Dunn and Ronald Rogers (1980, 1989) reveal that unselfconscious, deindividuated people are less restrained, less self-regulated, more likely to act without thinking about their own values, more responsive to the situation. These findings complement and reinforce the experiments on *self-awareness* considered in Chapter 3.

Self-awareness is the opposite of deindividuation. Those made self-aware, say by acting in front of a mirror or TV camera, exhibit *increased* self-control, and their actions more clearly reflect their attitudes. In front of a mirror, people taste-testing cream cheese varieties eat less of the high-fat alternative (Sentyrz & Bushman, 1997).

People made self-aware are also less likely to cheat (Beaman et al., 1979; Diener & Wallbom, 1976). So are those who generally have a strong sense of themselves as distinct and independent (Nadler et al., 1982). People who are self-conscious, or who are temporarily made so, exhibit greater consistency between their words outside a situation and their deeds in it.

We can apply those findings to many situations in everyday life. Circumstances that decrease self-awareness, as alcohol consumption does, therefore increase deindividuation (Hull et al., 1983). And deindividuation decreases in circumstances that increase self-awareness: mirrors and cameras, small towns, bright lights, large name tags, undistracted quiet, individual clothes and houses (Ickes et al., 1978). When a teenager leaves for a party, a parent's parting advice could well be this: "Have fun, and remember who you are." In other words, enjoy being with the group, but be self-aware; maintain your personal identity; be wary of deindividuated.

SUMMING UP: DEINDIVIDUATION: WHEN DO PEOPLE LOSE THEIR SENSE OF SELF IN GROUPS?

When high levels of social arousal combine with diffused responsibility, people may abandon their normal restraints and lose their sense of individuality. Such deindividuation is especially likely when people are in a large group, are physically anonymous, and are aroused and distracted. The resulting diminished self-awareness and self-restraint tend to increase people's responsiveness to the immediate situation, be it negative or positive.

GROUP POLARIZATION: DO GROUPS INTENSIFY OUR OPINIONS?

Many conflicts grow as people on both sides talk mostly with like-minded others. Does such interaction amplify pre-existing attitudes? If so, why?

Which effects—good or bad—does group interaction more often have? Police brutality and mob violence demonstrate its destructive potential. Yet support-group leaders, management consultants, and educational theorists proclaim its benefits. And social and religious movements urge their members to strengthen their identities by fellowship with like-minded others.

From studies of people in small groups, a principle emerges that helps explain both destructive and constructive outcomes: Group discussion often strengthens members' initial inclinations (good or bad). The unfolding of this research on "group polarization" illustrates the process of inquiry—how an interesting discovery often leads researchers to hasty and erroneous conclusions, which ultimately get replaced with more accurate conclusions.

THE CASE OF THE "RISKY SHIFT"

A research literature of more than 300 studies began with a surprising finding by James Stoner (1961). For his master's thesis in industrial management, Stoner compared risk taking by individuals and groups. To test the commonly held belief that groups are more cautious than individuals, Stoner posed decision dilemmas faced by fictional characters. The participant's task was to advise the imagined character how much risk to take. Put yourself in the participant's shoes: What advice would you give the character in this situation?

Helen is a writer who is said to have considerable creative talent but who so far has been earning a comfortable living by writing cheap westerns. Recently she has come up with an idea for a potentially significant novel. If it could be written and accepted, it might have considerable literary impact and be a big boost to her career. On the other hand, if she cannot work out her idea or if the novel is a flop, she will have expended considerable time and energy without remuneration.

Imagine that you are advising Helen. Please check the *lowest* probability that you would consider acceptable for Helen to attempt to write the novel.

Helen should attempt to write the novel if the chances that the novel will be a success are at least

________ 1 in 10

________ 2 in 10

________ 3 in 10

________ 4 in 10

________ 5 in 10

________ 6 in 10

________ 7 in 10

________ 8 in 10

________ 9 in 10

________ 10 in 10 (Place a check here if you think Helen should attempt the novel only if it is certain that the novel will be a success.)

After making your decision, guess what this book's average reader would advise.

Having marked their advice on a dozen such items, five or so individuals would then discuss and reach agreement on each item. How do you think the group decisions compared to the average decision before the discussions? Would the groups be likely to take greater risks? Be more cautious? Stay the same?

To everyone's amazement, the group decisions were usually riskier. Dubbed the "risky shift phenomenon," this finding set off a wave of investigation into group risk taking. The studies revealed that this effect occurs not only when a group decides by consensus; after a brief discussion, individuals, too, will alter their decisions. What is more, researchers successfully repeated Stoner's finding with people of varying ages and occupations in a dozen different nations.

During discussion, opinions converged. Curiously, however, the point toward which they converged was usually a lower (riskier) number than their initial average. Here was a delightful puzzle. The small risky shift effect was reliable, unexpected, and without any immediately obvious explanation. What group influences produce such an effect? And how widespread is it? Do discussions in juries, business committees, and military organizations also promote risk taking?

After several years of study and speculation about group risk taking, we became aware that the risky shift was not universal. We could write decision dilemmas on which people became more *cautious* after discussion. One of these featured "Roger," a young married man with two school-age children and a secure but low-paying job. Roger can afford life's necessities but few of its luxuries. He hears that the stock of a relatively unknown company may soon triple in

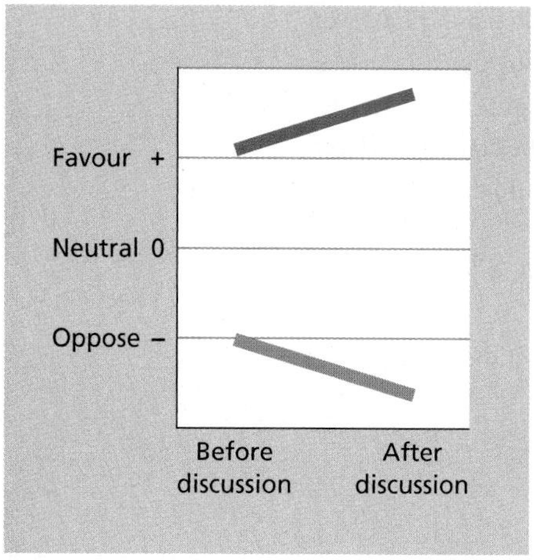

FIGURE 7–7

Group polarization.

The group-polarization hypothesis predicts that discussion will strengthen an attitude shared by group members. If people initially tend to favour something (say, risk on a life dilemma question), they tend to favour it even more after discussion. If they tend to oppose something, they tend to oppose it even more after discussion.

value if its new product is favourably received or decline considerably if it does not sell. Roger has no savings. To invest in the company, he is considering selling his life insurance policy.

Can you see a general principle that predicts both the tendency to give riskier advice after discussing Helen's situation and more cautious advice after discussing Roger's? If you are like most people, you would advise Helen to take greater risk than Roger, even before talking with others. It turns out there is a strong tendency for discussion to accentuate these initial leanings; groups discussing the "Roger" dilemma became more risk-averse than they were before discussion.

DO GROUPS INTENSIFY OPINIONS?

Realize that this group phenomenon was not a consistent shift to risk, but rather a tendency for group discussion to *enhance* the individuals' initial leanings. This idea led investigators to propose what Serge Moscovici and Marisa Zavalloni (1969) called a **group polarization** phenomenon: *Discussion typically strengthens the average inclination of group members.*

group polarization group-produced enhancement of members' pre-existing tendencies; a strengthening of the members' *average* tendency, not a split within the group

Group polarization experiments

This new view of the changes induced by group discussion prompted experimenters to have people discuss statements that most of them favoured or most of them opposed. Would talking in groups enhance their initial inclinations as it did with the decision dilemmas? That's what the group polarization hypothesis predicts (Figure 7–7 above).

Dozens of studies confirm group polarization. Moscovici and Zavalloni (1969) observed that discussion enhanced French students' initially positive attitude toward their premier and negative attitude toward Americans. Mititoshi Isozaki (1984) found that Japanese university students gave more pronounced judgments of "guilty" after discussing a traffic case. Markus Brauer and his coworkers (2001) found that French students' dislike for certain other people was exacerbated after discussing their shared negative impressions. And Glen Whyte (1993) reports that groups exacerbate the "too much invested to quit" phenomenon that has cost many businesses huge sums of money. Canadian business students imagined themselves having to decide whether to invest more money in the hope of preventing losses in various failing projects (for example, whether to make a high-risk loan to protect an earlier investment). They exhibited the typical effect: Seventy-two percent reinvested money they would seldom have invested if they were considering it as a new investment on its own merits. When making the same decision in groups, 94 percent opted for reinvestment.

Another research strategy has been to pick issues on which opinions are divided and then isolate people who hold the same view. Does discussion with like-minded people strengthen shared views? Does it magnify the attitude gap that separates the two sides?

George Bishop and David Myers wondered. So they set up groups of relatively prejudiced and unprejudiced high-school students and asked them to respond—before and after discussion—to issues involving racial attitudes, such as property rights versus open housing (Myers

& Bishop, 1970). They found that the discussions among like-minded students did indeed increase the initial gap between the two groups (Figure 7–8).

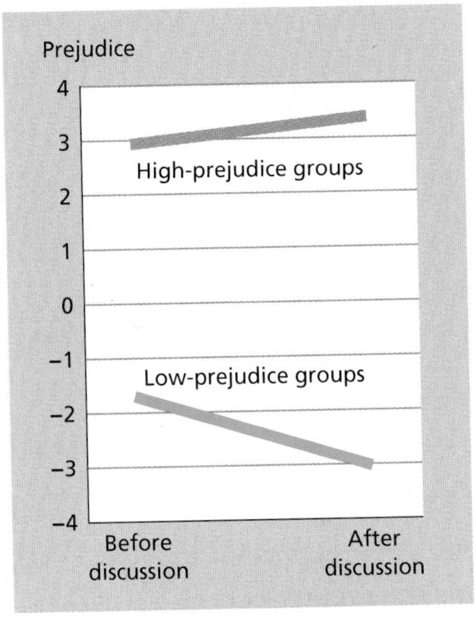

FIGURE 7–8

Discussion increased polarization between homogeneous groups of high- and low-prejudice high-school students. Talking over racial issues increased prejudice in a high-prejudice group and decreased it in a low-prejudice group. (Data from Myers & Bishop, 1970)

Group polarization in everyday life

People mostly associate with others whose attitudes are similar to their own (Chapter 11). (Look at your own circle of friends.) So, does everyday group interaction with like-minded friends intensify shared attitudes?

Group polarization in schools. One real-life parallel to the laboratory phenomenon is what education researchers have called the "accentuation phenomenon": Over time, initial differences among groups of university students become accentuated. If the students at university X are initially more intellectual than the students at university Y, that gap is likely to grow during university. Likewise, compared to fraternity and sorority members, independents tend to have more liberal political attitudes, a difference that grows with time in university (Pascarella & Terenzini, 1991). Researchers believe this results partly from group members reinforcing shared inclinations.

Group polarization in communities. Polarization also occurs in communities. During community conflicts, like-minded people associate increasingly with one another, amplifying their shared tendencies. Gang hostility emerges from a process of mutual reinforcement within neighbourhood gangs, whose members share attributes and hostilities (Cartwright, 1975). If, on your block, "a second out-of-control 15-year-old moves in," surmises David Lykken (1997), "the mischief they get into as a team is likely to be more than merely double what the first would do on his own. . . . A gang is more dangerous than the sum of its individual parts." Indeed, "unsupervised peer groups" are "the strongest predictor" of a neighbourhood's crime victimization rate, report Bonita Veysey and Steven Messner (1999). Moreover, experimental interventions that group young offenders with other young offenders actually—no surprise to any group polarization researcher—increase the rate of problem behaviour (Dishion et al., 1999).

Group polarization on the Internet. Email, blogs, and electronic chat rooms offer a potential new medium for group interaction. At myspace.com, for example, there are (as this edition goes to press) tens of thousands of groups of kindred spirits discussing, music, cars, politics, religion, hobbies, and you name it. The Internet's countless virtual groups enable peacemakers and neo-Nazis, geeks and goths, conspiracy theorists and cancer survivors to isolate themselves with one another and find support for their shared concerns, interests, and suspicions (Gerstenfeld, 2003; McKenna & Bargh, 1998, 2000; Sunstein, 2001). Without the nonverbal nuances of face-to-face contact, will such discussions produce group polarization? Will peacemakers become more pacifistic and militia members more terror prone? Email, search engines, and chat rooms "make it much easier for small groups to rally like-minded people, crystallize diffuse hatreds, and mobilize lethal force," observes Robert Wright (2003).

EXPLAINING POLARIZATION

Why do groups adopt stances that are more exaggerated than the average opinions of their individual members? Researchers hoped that solving the mystery of group polarization might provide some insights. Solving small puzzles sometimes provides clues for solving larger ones.

Among several proposed theories of group polarization, two survived scientific scrutiny. One deals with the arguments presented during a discussion, the other with how members of a group view themselves vis-à-vis the other members. The first idea is an example of what Chapter 6 called *informational influence* (influence that results from accepting evidence about reality). The second is an example of *normative influence* (influence based on a person's desire to be accepted or admired by others).

In two trials, South African courts reduced sentences after learning how social-psychological phenomena, including deindividuation and group polarization, led crowd members to commit murderous acts (Colman, 1991). Would you agree that courts should consider social-psychological phenomena as possible extenuating circumstances?

Informational influence

According to the best-supported explanation, group discussion elicits a pooling of ideas, most of which favour the dominant viewpoint. Ideas that were common knowledge to group members will often be brought up in discussion or, even if unmentioned, will jointly influence their discussion (Gigone & Hastie, 1993; Larson et al., 1994; Stasser, 1991). Other ideas may include persuasive arguments that some group members had not previously considered. When discussing Helen the writer, someone may say, "Helen should go for it, because she has little to lose. If her novel flops, she can always go back to writing cheap westerns." Such statements often entangle information about the person's *arguments* with cues concerning the person's *position* on the issue. But when people hear relevant arguments without learning the specific stands other people assume, they still shift their positions (Burnstein & Vinokur, 1977; Hinsz et al., 1997). *Arguments,* in and of themselves, matter.

But there's more to attitude change than merely hearing someone else's arguments. *Active participation* in discussion produces more attitude change than does passive listening. Participants and observers hear the same ideas, but when

Animal gangs. The pack is more than the sum of the wolves.

participants put them into their own words, the verbal commitment magnifies the impact. The more group members repeat one another's ideas, the more they rehearse and validate them (Brauer et al., 1995).

This illustrates a point made in Chapter 5: People's minds are not just blank tablets for persuaders to write on. In central route persuasion, what people *think* in response to a message is crucial. Indeed, just thinking about an issue for a couple of minutes can strengthen opinions (Tesser et al., 1995). (Perhaps you can recall your feelings becoming polarized as you merely ruminated about someone you disliked, or liked.) Even just *expecting* to discuss an issue with an equally expert person holding an opposing view can motivate people to marshal their arguments and thus to adopt a more extreme position (Fitzpatrick & Eagly, 1981).

Normative influence

A second explanation of polarization involves comparison with others. As Leon Festinger (1954) argued in his influential theory of **social comparison**, it is human nature to want to evaluate our abilities and opinions, something we can do by comparing our views with others'. We are most persuaded by people in our "reference groups"—groups we identify with (Abrams et al., 1990; Hogg et al., 1990). Moreover, wanting people to like us, we may express stronger opinions after discovering that others share our views.

social comparison
evaluating one's abilities and opinions by comparing oneself to others

Robert Baron and his colleagues (1996) explored the polarizing effect of having one's views socially corroborated. In one experiment, they asked dental clinic patients whether they considered the dental chair "comfortable" or "uncomfortable." Then the patients rated the chair on a +50 to −50 scale. Before making this rating, some subjects heard the experimenter ask: "By the way, Dr. X, what did the last patient say?" The dentist always echoed whatever response the patient had just made. Compared to subjects who did not hear their opinion corroborated, those who did gave decidedly more extreme ratings.

Perhaps you have been in the situation where you have wanted to go out with someone, but you were afraid to make the first move. You wait and watch, but the other person doesn't seem to be expressing any interest in you, so you think that he or she would probably reject you. But have you ever stopped to think that the other person might be doing the same thing you are. University of Manitoba researchers Jacquie Vorauer and Rebecca Ratner (1996) have shown that such reactions make it difficult for people to start up relationships.

Dale Miller and Cathy McFarland (1987) bottled a similar phenomenon in a laboratory experiment. They asked people to read an incomprehensible article and to seek help if they ran into "any really serious problems in understanding the paper." Although none of the subjects sought help, they presumed *other* subjects would not be similarly restrained by fear of embarrassment. They wrongly inferred that people who didn't seek help didn't need any. To overcome such **pluralistic ignorance**, someone must break the ice and enable others to reveal and reinforce their shared reactions.

pluralistic ignorance
a false impression of how other people are thinking, feeling, or responding

When we ask people (as we asked you earlier) to predict how others would respond to items such as the "Helen" dilemma, they typically exhibit pluralistic ignorance: They don't realize how much others support the socially preferred tendency (in this case, writing the novel). A typical person will advise writing the novel even if its chance of success is only 4 in 10, but estimate that most other people would require 5 or 6 in 10. When the discussion begins, most people discover they are not outshining the others as they had supposed. In fact, some others are ahead of them, having taken an even stronger position for writing the novel. No longer restrained by a misperceived group norm, they are liberated to voice their preferences more strongly.

This social comparison theory prompted experiments that exposed people to others' positions but not to their arguments. This is roughly the experience we have when reading the results of an opinion poll. When people learn others' positions—without discussion—will they adjust their responses to maintain a socially favourable position? When people have made no prior commitment to a particular response, seeing others' responses *does* stimulate a small polarization (Goethals & Zanna, 1979; Sanders & Baron, 1977). (See Figure 7–9 for an example.) This polarization from mere social comparison is usually less than that produced by a lively discussion. Still, it's surprising that, instead of simply conforming to the group average, people often go it one better. Are people "one-upping" the observed norm to differentiate themselves from the group? Is this another example of our need to feel unique (Chapter 6)?

This finding is reminiscent of the self-serving bias (Chapter 2): People tend to view themselves as better-than-average embodiments of socially desirable traits and attitudes.

Group polarization research illustrates the complexity of social-psychological inquiry. As much as we like our explanations of a phenomenon to be simple, one explanation seldom accounts for all the data. Because people are complex, more than one factor frequently influences an outcome. In group discussions, persuasive arguments predominate on issues that have a factual element ("Is she guilty of the crime?"). Social comparison sways responses on value-laden judgments ("How long a sentence should she serve?") (Kaplan, 1989). On the many issues that have both factual and value-laden aspects, the two factors work together. Discovering that others share one's feelings (social comparison) unleashes arguments (informational influence) supporting what everyone secretly favours.

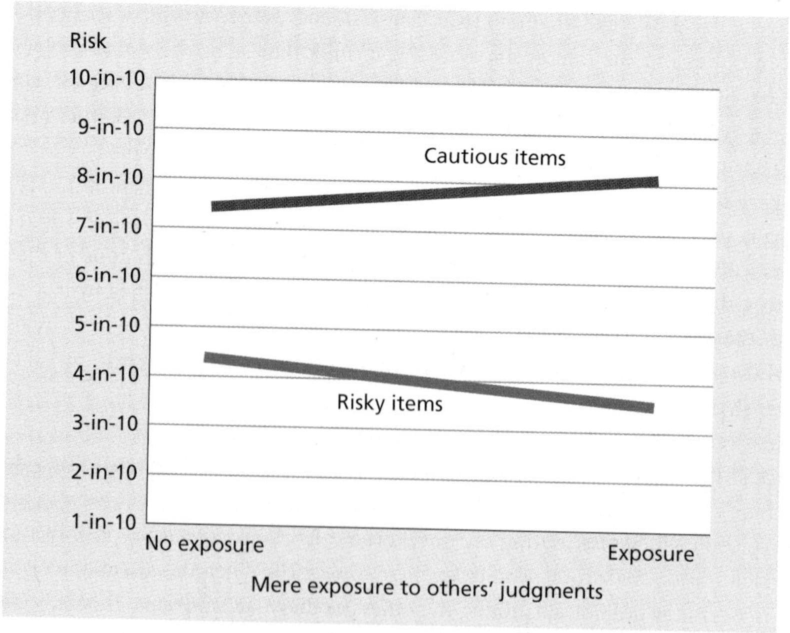

FIGURE 7–9

On "risky" dilemma items (such as the case of Helen), mere exposure to others' judgments enhanced individuals' risk-prone tendencies. On "cautious" dilemma items (such as the case of Roger), exposure to others' judgments enhanced their cautiousness. (Data from Myers, 1978)

SUMMING UP: GROUP POLARIZATION: DO GROUPS INTENSIFY OUR OPINIONS?

Potentially positive and negative results arise from group discussion. While trying to understand the curious finding that group discussion enhanced risk taking, investigators discovered that discussion actually tends to strengthen whatever is the initially dominant point of view, whether risky or cautious.

In everyday situations, too, group interaction tends to intensify opinions. This group polarization phenomenon provided a window through which researchers could observe group influence. Experiments confirmed two group influences: informational and normative. The information gleaned from a discussion mostly favours the initially preferred alternative, thus reinforcing support for it. Moreover, people may go further out on the limb when, after comparing positions, they discover surprising support for their initial inclinations.

GROUPTHINK: DO GROUPS HINDER OR ASSIST GOOD DECISIONS?

When do group influences hinder smart decisions? When do groups promote good decisions, and how can we lead groups to make optimal decisions?

Do the social psychological phenomena we have been considering in these first seven chapters occur in sophisticated groups like corporate boards where people are professionals and know each other well? Is there likely to be self-justification? Self-serving bias? A cohesive "we feeling" provoking conformity and rejection of dissent? Public commitment producing

Groupthink on a titanic scale. Despite four messages of possible icebergs ahead and the lookout person's unheeded plea for binoculars, Captain Edward Smith—a directive and respected leader—kept his ship sailing at full speed into the night. There was an illusion of invulnerability ("God Himself could not sink this ship," the captain had said). There was conformity pressure (crew mates chided the lookout for not being able to use his naked eye and dismissed his misgivings). And there was mindguarding (a *Titanic* telegraph operator failed to pass the last and most complete iceberg warning to Captain Smith).

resistance to change? Group polarization? Social psychologist Irving Janis (1971, 1982) wondered whether such phenomena might help explain good and bad decisions made by a number of leaders and their advisers. In particular he analyzed the decision making procedures that led to several major fiascos. Although Janis did not analyze it, the sinking of the *Titanic*—the worst seafaring accident in history—provides a compelling example of the type of disasters Janis analyzed.

We will try to give an accurate account of this tragedy, but the particulars of the disaster will probably always be a bit of a mystery. Most of you have probably seen the movie *Titanic* written and directed by Canadian James Cameron, as it was the most widely seen movie of all-time, but there are many accounts and it is often hard to sort out the truth. The playwright George Bernard Shaw and mystery writer Sir Arthur Conan Doyle, creator of the Sherlock Holmes character, fought bitterly back and forth about many of the details in the years after the shipwreck. Sherlock himself might not have been able to completely solve all the mysteries of this disaster. Nevertheless, here are some of the basic facts that are not in dispute.

On April 10, 1912, the *Titanic* left Southampton, England, on her maiden voyage across the Atlantic Ocean. At the time the *Titanic* was the largest and most fabulous ship in the world. It was as tall as an 11-storey building, as long as eight football fields, and weighed 1000 tonnes more than any other ship. It had a double hull system that made many believe the ship was unsinkable. It was the pride of the White Star line of ships that owned it. The ship was cruising briskly across the Atlantic when on Sunday, April 12 they received several messages that a group of icebergs was ahead. At least four of these messages reached the captain and at least one of these messages reached the president of the cruise line, who was aboard the ship. Despite these warnings the ship did not slow down. At about 11:40 P.M. one of the lookouts saw an iceberg straight ahead and sounded the warning. The first officer, who was at the helm, swung the ship to the port but only fast enough to avoid hitting the iceberg head-on. The ice tore a huge gash in the side of the ship. It took the crew some time, but not a great deal of time, to know the extent of the damage—by 12:15 A.M. they knew the ship was going to sink. Lifeboats were lowered and filled, or sadly only partially filled, with passengers, and distress calls were sent out to other ships. One sad fact was that the *Titanic* had only 20 lifeboats, which was not even enough for half of the passengers. The ship finally went under at 2:20 A.M. Only 705 people survived the shipwreck; at least twice those many died. The exact number is one of those facts that is in dispute. The estimates range between 1490 and 1635.

Janis believed that such tragedies could be traced to the tendency of decision-making groups to suppress dissent in the interests of group harmony, a phenomenon he called **groupthink**. In work groups, camaraderie boosts productivity (Mullen & Copper, 1994). Moreover, team spirit is good for morale. But when making decisions, close-knit groups may pay a price. Janis believed that the soil from which groupthink sprouts includes an amiable, cohesive group, relative isolation of the group from dissenting viewpoints, and a directive leader who signals what decision he or she favours. When deciding what to do with the threat of the icebergs ahead there is little doubt that Captain Edward J. Smith, the senior captain of the cruise line who had served for 38 years, was a strong and directive leader and he and his crew enjoyed a strong *esprit de corps*. As one source (Lord, 1955) put it, Smith was "worshipped by crew and passenger alike. . . . They loved everything about him." It is also clear that in the middle of the Atlantic they were isolated from other points of view. It is quite possible that groupthink may have influenced their decision making. Let's see if they displayed the symptoms of groupthink.

groupthink
"The mode of thinking that persons engage in when concurrence-seeking becomes so dominant in a cohesive in-group that it tends to override realistic appraisal of alternative courses of action."—Irving Janis (1971)

SYMPTOMS OF GROUPTHINK

From historical records and the memoirs of participants and observers, Janis identified eight groupthink symptoms. These symptoms are a collective form of dissonance reduction that surface as group members try to maintain the positive group feeling when facing a threat (Turner et al., 1992, 1994).

The first two groupthink symptoms lead group members to *overestimate their group's might and right:*

- **An illusion of invulnerability:** There is little question that Capt. Smith and his crew had developed an illusion that nothing bad could happen to them or their ship. Five years before the crash it was clear that Capt. Smith believed a disaster with loss of life could not happen to one of his ships, saying, "I cannot conceive of any vital disaster happening . . . . Modern shipbuilding has gone beyond that" (Marshall, 1912). As the ship departed from Southampton, one of the crew members expressed a view that seemed to be widespread. When asked if the *Titanic* was really unsinkable, he replied, "God Himself could not sink this ship" (Lord, 1955).
- **Unquestioned belief in the group's morality:** Group members assume the inherent morality of their group and ignore ethical and moral issues. Looking back on the tragedy of the *Titanic* it is clear that they should have had more lifeboats aboard the vessel, and sadly this would not have been difficult. But the builders of the ship and especially the president of the cruise line decided they were not needed.

Group members also become *closed-minded:*

- **Rationalization:** The group discounts challenges by collectively justifying their decisions. The officers on the *Titanic* knew they were in the vicinity of icebergs, but went on at full speed. In one critical conversation at 9:00 P.M. the second officer and Capt. Smith discussed how they should handle the ship. Both knew that they were in the vicinity of icebergs, but Capt. Smith remarked that it was an exceptionally clear night and therefore they did not need to slow down (Davie, 1986).
- **Stereotyped view of opponent:** One of the most controversial stories surrounding the *Titanic* is whether the ship was trying to break a speed record in crossing the Atlantic. You may recall that the movie *Titanic* portrayed the president of the cruise line as pressuring the captain to break a speed record. This story has been suggested several times and believed by many—even though the president of the cruise line, who survived, vehemently denied it. One reason the story is believable to some is that the shipping business was intensely competitive in the early 1900s and cruise lines had very derogatory views of others. These stereotyped views of their opponents might well have led Capt. Smith and his crew to ignore the warnings from other ships.

Self-censorship contributes to an illusion of unanimity.

Finally, the group suffers from *pressures toward uniformity:*

- **Conformity pressure:** Group members rebuff those who raised doubts about the group's assumptions and plans, at times not by argument but by ridicule. When Fredrick Fleet—the lookout who eventually saw the iceberg—complained that the crew did not have binoculars he was chided by his colleagues for not being able to use his naked eye.
- **Self-censorship:** Since disagreements are often uncomfortable and the groups seem in consensus, members often withhold or discount their misgivings. Despite Fleet's belief that he needed a pair of binoculars for his task as a lookout, he did not suggest that they pick up a new pair at the next port. He was at a loss to describe his failure to do so. He maintained until his dying day that if he had had a pair of binoculars he would have seen the iceberg soon enough to avoid hitting it.
- **Illusion of unanimity:** Self-censorship and pressure not to puncture the consensus create an illusion of unanimity. What is more, the apparent consensus confirms the group's decision. Did none of the experienced crew on the *Titanic* think they should slow down? It seems likely that the apparent unanimity about the decision to go full speed ahead was merely an illusion. This sort of illusion has been seen in other groups as well. Albert Speer (1971), an adviser to Hitler, described the atmosphere around Hitler as one where pressure to conform suppressed all deviance. The absence of dissent created the illusion of unanimity:

> In normal circumstances people who turn their backs on reality are soon set straight by the mockery and criticism of those around them, which makes them aware that they have lost credibility. In the Third Reich there were no such correctives, especially for those who belonged to the upper stratum. On the contrary, every self-deception was multiplied as in a hall of distorting mirrors, becoming a repeatedly confirmed picture of a fantastical dream world which no longer bore any relationship to the grim outside world. In those mirrors I could see nothing but my own face reproduced many times over. No external factors disturbed the uniformity of hundreds of unchanging faces, all mine. (p. 379)

People "are never so likely to settle a question rightly as when they discuss it freely."

John Stuart Mill, *On Liberty*, 1859

- **Mindguards:** Some members protect the group from information that would call into question the effectiveness or the morality of its decisions. The telegraph operator on the *Titanic* provided a compelling example of this symptom. After receiving several warning messages about icebergs, he failed to take down the final and most complete message about the iceberg that was struck and he failed to pass this message to the captain. Thus the operator deprived Capt. Smith of the latest information that would challenge his decision to go full steam ahead.

Groupthink symptoms can produce a failure to seek and discuss contrary information and alternative possibilities. When a leader promotes an idea and when a group insulates itself from dissenting views, groupthink may produce defective decisions (McCauley, 1989).

The management of the Walkerton, Ontario, water crisis in May 2000 by Stan Koebel, who ran the water treatment plant, shows many of the symptoms of groupthink. Koebel and his employees certainly showed an illusion of invulnerability. They believed that the water in Walkerton had always been safe and that little needed to be done to ensure its safety. They viewed the new chlorinator that they never installed as unnecessary. Koebel even continued to drink tap water long after people began getting sick and he knew the water tested positive for E. coli. The men at the water plant also engaged in massive rationalization. Even though they knew the water tested positive for contaminants, they continued to believe for days that the water was not what was making people sick. Self-censorship was also an important part of the group's response. Frank Koebel (Stan's brother) testified in the inquiry into the crisis that he knew the failure to chlorinate the water and to take proper samples could lead to problems, but he never raised his objections to his brother. Finally, the group clearly employed mindguards by failing to report the results of the tainted water to the Ministry of Environment and the Officer of Health.

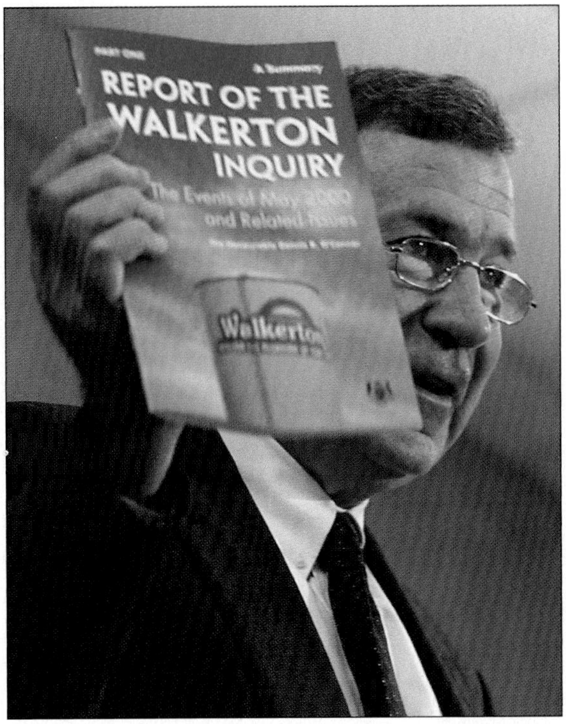

Groupthink in action: the contaminated water tragedy in Walkerton, Ontario.

CRITIQUING THE CONCEPT OF GROUPTHINK

Although Janis's ideas and observations have received enormous attention, some researchers are skeptical (Fuller & Aldag, 1998; Hart, 1989). The evidence was retrospective, so Janis could pick supporting cases. Follow-up experiments suggested that directive leadership is indeed associated with poorer decisions (Granstrom & Stiwne, 1998; McCauley, 1998). Groups do prefer supporting over challenging information (Schulz-Hardt et al., 2000). When members look to a group for acceptance, approval, and social identity, they may suppress disagreeable thoughts (Hogg & Hains, 1998; Turner & Pratkanis, 1997).

"Truth springs from argument amongst friends."

Philosopher David Hume, 1711–1776

Yet friendships need not breed groupthink (Esser, 1998; Mullen et al., 1994). Secure, highly cohesive groups (say, a married couple) can provide members with freedom to disagree. The norms of a cohesive group can favour consensus (which can lead to groupthink) or critical analysis, which prevents it (Postmes et al., 2001). When academic colleagues in a close-knit department share their draft manuscripts with one another they *want* critique: "Do what you can to save me from my own mistakes." In a free-spirited atmosphere, cohesion can enhance effective teamwork, too.

"There was a serious flaw in the decision-making process."

Report of the Presidential Commission on the Space Shuttle *Challenger* Accident, 1986

Moreover, when Philip Tetlock and his colleagues (1992) looked at a broader sample of historical episodes, it became clear that even good group procedures sometimes yield ill-fated decisions. As Jimmy Carter and his advisers plotted their humiliating attempt to rescue hostages in Iran in 1980, they welcomed different views and realistically considered the perils. But for a helicopter problem the rescue might have succeeded. (Carter later reflected that had he sent in one more helicopter he believed they would have succeeded.) To reword Mister Rogers, sometimes good groups do bad things.

Reflecting on the critiques of groupthink, Paul Paulus (1998) reminds us of Leon Festinger's (1987) observation that only an untestable theory is unchanging. "If a theory is at all testable, it will not remain unchanged. It has to change. All theories are wrong." Thus, said Festinger, we shouldn't ask whether a theory is right or wrong, but rather "how much of the empirical realm can it handle and how must it be modified." Irving Janis, having tested and modified his own theory before his death in 1990, would surely have welcomed others continuing to reshape it. For in science that is how we grope our way toward truth, by testing our ideas against reality, revising them, and then testing them some more.

PREVENTING GROUPTHINK

Flawed group dynamics help explain many failed decisions; sometimes too many cooks always spoil the broth. But given open leadership, a cohesive team spirit can improve decisions. Sometimes two or more heads are better than one.

In search of conditions that breed good decisions, Janis also analyzed two seemingly successful ventures: the formulation of the Marshall Plan for getting Europe back on its feet after the Second World War and the handling of the former U.S.S.R.'s attempts to install missile bases in Cuba in 1962. Janis's (1982) recommendations for preventing groupthink incorporate many of the effective group procedures used in both cases:

- Be impartial—do not endorse any position.
- Encourage critical evaluation; assign a "devil's advocate." Better yet, welcome the input of a genuine critic, which does even more to stimulate original thinking and to open a group to opposing views, report Charlan Nemeth and her colleagues (2001a, 2001b).
- Occasionally subdivide the group, and then reunite to air differences.
- Welcome critiques from outside experts and associates.
- Before implementing, call a "second-chance" meeting to air any lingering doubts.

Some of these practical principles for improved group dynamics are now being taught to airline flight crews. Training programs, called crew resource management, developed from the realization that flight crew mistakes contribute to more than two-thirds of plane accidents. Having two or three people in the cockpit should increase the odds that someone will notice a problem or see its solution—if the information is shared. Sometimes, however, groupthink pressures lead to conformity or self-censorship.

On the night of September 2, 1998, Swiss Air flight 111 crashed just off of Peggy's Cove, Nova Scotia, killing all 229 people on board. The crash appears to have occurred because faulty wiring led to a fire in the cockpit. Several stories in the media reported that the two pilots were at odds in how to respond to the fire. These reports suggested that the co-pilot wanted to forget about procedure and land the plane immediately. The pilot, on the other hand, was allegedly firm in his insistence that they follow the standard procedure, and was so busy with a checklist that he was not able to discuss a plan of action with the co-pilot. Could these faulty group dynamics have played a role in the crash? We do not even know if the media reports are accurate, but faulty group dynamics have been linked to other crashes (Helmrich, 1997).

Effective group dynamics enabled the crew of a disabled Denver to Chicago United flight to devise a technique for steering by adjusting relative power from its two remaining engines, enabling the survival of most passengers. Recognizing the importance of cockpit group dynamics, airlines now provide crew management training and seek pilots who are capable of functioning as team members.

But not always. In 1989, a three-person crew facing a similar problem responded as a model team to imminent disaster. The crew, which had been trained in crew resource management, faced the disintegration of the centre engine, severing lines to the rudder and ailerons needed to manoeuvre the plane. In the 34 minutes before crash-landing just short of the airport runway, the crew had to devise a strategy for bringing the plane under control, assessing damage, choosing a landing site, and preparing the crew and passengers for the crash. Minute-by-minute analysis of the cockpit conversation revealed intense interaction—31 communications per minute (one per second at its peak). In these minutes the crew members recruited a fourth pilot who was flying as a passenger, prioritized their work, and kept one another aware of unfolding events and decisions. Junior crew members freely suggested alternatives and the captain responded with appropriate commands. Bursts of social conversation provided emotional support, enabling the crew to cope with the extreme stress, and to save the lives of 185 of the 296 people on board.

"Two forecasters will come up with a forecast that is more accurate than either would have come up with working alone."

Joel N. Myers President, AccuWeather, 1997

GROUP PROBLEM SOLVING

Not every group decision is flawed by groupthink. Under some conditions two or more heads *are* better than one. Patrick Laughlin and John Adamopoulos (1980, 1996; Laughlin et al., 2003) have shown this with various intellectual tasks. Consider one of their analogy problems:

Assertion is to *disproved* as *action* is to

a. *hindered*
b. *opposed*
c. *illegal*
d. *precipitate*
e. *thwarted*

STORY BEHIND THE RESEARCH

A NOBEL PRIZE: TWO MINDS ARE BETTER THAN ONE

Daniel Kahneman
Princeton University
Nobel Laureate, 2002

In the spring of 1969, Amos Tversky, my younger colleague at the Hebrew University of Jerusalem, and I met over lunch and shared our own recurrent errors of judgment. From there were born our studies of human intuition.

I had enjoyed collaboration before, but this was magical. Amos was very smart, and also very funny. We could spend hours of solid work in continuous mirth. His work was always characterized by confidence and by a crisp elegance, and it was a joy to find those characteristics now attached to my ideas as well. As we were writing our first paper, I was conscious of how much better it was than the more hesitant piece I would have written by myself.

All our ideas were jointly owned. We did almost all the work on our joint projects while physically together, including the drafting of questionnaires and papers. Our principle was to discuss every disagreement until it had been resolved to our mutual satisfaction.

Some of the greatest joys of our collaboration—and probably much of its success—came from our ability to elaborate on each other's nascent thoughts: If I expressed a half-formed idea, I knew that Amos would be there to understand it, probably more clearly than I did, and that if it had merit, he would see it.

Amos and I shared the wonder of together owning a goose that could lay golden eggs—a joint mind that was better than our separate minds. We were a team, and we remained in that mode for well over a decade. The Nobel Prize was awarded for work that we produced during that period of intense collaboration.

Most university students miss this question when answering alone, but answer correctly (thwarted) after discussion. Moreover, Laughlin finds that if but two members of a six-person group are initially correct, two-thirds of the time they convince all the others. If but one person is correct, this "minority of one" almost three-fourths of the time fails to convince the group.

Dell Warnick and Glenn Sanders (1980) and Verlin Hinsz (1990) confirmed that several heads can be better than one when they studied the accuracy of eyewitness reports of a videotaped crime or job interview. Groups of eyewitnesses gave accounts that were much more accurate than those provided by the average isolated individual. Several heads critiquing each other can also allow the group to avoid some forms of cognitive bias and produce some higher-quality ideas (McGlynn et al., 1995; Wright et al., 1990).

Brainstorming with computer communication allows creative ideas to flow freely (Gallupe et al., 1994). But contrary to the popular idea that face-to-face brainstorming generates more creative ideas than do the same people working alone, researchers agree it isn't so (Paulus et al., 1995, 1997, 1998, 2000; Stroebe & Diehl, 1994). People *feel* more productive when generating ideas in groups (partly because people disproportionately credit themselves for the ideas that come out). But time and again researchers have found that people working alone usually will generate *more* good ideas than will the same people in a group. Large brainstorming groups are especially inefficient, causing some individuals to free-ride on others' efforts or to feel apprehensive about voicing oddball ideas. As John Watson and Francis Crick demonstrated in discovering DNA, challenging two-person conversations can more effectively engage creative thinking. Psychologists Daniel Kahneman and the late Amos Tversky similarly collaborated in their exploration of intuition and its influence on economic decision making (see Chapter 3 and "The Story Behind the Research: A Nobel Prize: Two Minds are Better than One" on the previous page).

However, Vincent Brown and Paul Paulus (2002) have identified three ways to enhance group brainstorming:

- **Combine group and solitary brainstorming.** Their data suggest using group brainstorming followed by solo brainstorming rather than the reverse order or either alone. With new categories primed by the group brainstorming, individuals' ideas can continue flowing without being impeded by the group context that only allows one person to speak at a time.
- **Have group members interact by writing.** Another way to take advantage of group priming, without being impeded by the one-at-a-time rule, is to have group members write and read, rather than speak and listen. Brown and Paulus describe this process of passing notes and adding ideas, which has everyone active at once, as "brainwriting."
- **Incorporate electronic brainstorming.** There is a potentially more efficient way to avoid the verbal traffic jams of traditional group brainstorming in larger groups: Let individuals produce and read ideas on networked computers.

SUMMING UP: GROUPTHINK: DO GROUPS HINDER OR ASSIST GOOD DECISIONS?

Analysis of the decisions that led to several international fiascos indicates that group desire for harmony can override realistic appraisal of contrary views. This is especially true when group members strongly desire unity, when they are isolated from opposing ideas, and when the leader signals what he or she wants from the group.

Symptomatic of this overriding concern for harmony, labelled "groupthink," are (1) an illusion of invulnerability, (2) rationalization, (3) unquestioned belief in the group's morality, (4) stereotyped views of the opposition, (5) pressure to conform, (6) self-censorship of misgivings, (7) an illusion of unanimity, and (8) "mindguards" who protect the group from unpleasant information. Critics have noted that some aspects of Janis's groupthink model (such as directive leadership) seem more implicated in flawed decisions than others (such as cohesiveness).

Both in experiments and in actual history, however, groups sometimes decide wisely. These cases suggest remedies for groupthink. By seeking information from all sides and improving the evaluation of possible alternatives, a group can benefit from its members' combined insights.

Research on group problem solving suggests that groups can be more accurate than individuals; groups also generate more and better ideas if the group is small or if, in a large group, individual brainstorming follows the group session.

LEADERSHIP: HOW DO LEADERS SHAPE THE GROUP'S ACTIONS?

In 1910, the Norwegians and English engaged in an epic race to the South Pole. The Norwegians, effectively led by Roald Amundsen, made it. The English, ineptly led by Robert Falcon Scott, did not; Scott and three team members died. Some coaches move from team to team, transforming losers into winners each time. For example, Scotty Bowman has led three different teams to Stanley Cup championships.

TASK LEADERSHIP AND SOCIAL LEADERSHIP

leadership
the process by which certain group members motivate and guide the group

Some leaders are formally appointed or elected; others emerge informally as the group interacts. What makes for good **leadership** often depends on the situation—the best person to lead the engineering team may not make the best leader of the sales force. Some people excel at *task leadership*—at organizing work, setting standards, and focusing on goal attainment. Others excel at *social leadership*—at building teamwork, mediating conflicts, and being supportive.

Task leaders often have a directive style—one that can work well if the leader is bright enough to give good orders (Fiedler, 1987). Being goal oriented, such leaders also keep the group's attention and effort focused on its mission. Experiments show that the combination of specific, challenging goals and periodic progress reports helps motivate high achievement (Locke & Latham, 1990). Task leaders also can effectively keep poorly functioning groups under control. Thus task leaders seem to get the most out of very high achieving and very low achieving groups.

Women more often than men have a democratic leadership style.

(Eagly & Johnson, 1990)

Social leaders often have a democratic style—one that delegates authority, welcomes input from team members, and, as we have seen, helps prevent groupthink. Many experiments reveal that such leadership is good for morale. Group members usually feel more satisfied when they participate in making decisions (Spector, 1986; Vanderslice et al., 1987). Given control over their tasks, workers also become more motivated to achieve (Burger, 1987). People who value good group feeling and take pride in achievement therefore thrive under democratic leadership (Lortie-Lussier et al., 1989).

Democratic leadership can be seen in the move by many businesses toward participative management, a management style common in Sweden and Japan (Naylor, 1990; Sundstrom et al., 1990). Ironically, a major influence on this "Japanese-style" management was social psychologist Kurt Lewin. In laboratory and factory experiments, Lewin and his students demonstrated the benefits of inviting workers to participate in decision making. Shortly before the Second World War, Lewin visited Japan and explained his findings to industrial and academic leaders (Nisbett & Ross, 1991). Japan's collectivist culture provided a receptive audience for Lewin's ideas about teamwork. Eventually, his influence circled back to North America.

TRANSACTIONAL LEADERSHIP

The once-popular "great person" theory of leadership—that all great leaders share certain traits—has fallen into disrepute. Effective leadership styles, we now know, vary with the situations. People who know what they are doing may resent task leadership, while those who don't

Participative management, illustrated in this "quality circle," requires democratic rather than autocratic leaders.

may welcome it. Recently, however, social psychologists have again wondered if there might be qualities that mark a good leader in many situations (Hogan et al., 1994). British social psychologists Peter Smith and Monir Tayeb (1989) report that studies done in India, Taiwan, and Iran have found that the most effective supervisors in coal mines, banks, and government offices score high on tests of *both* task and social leadership. They are actively concerned with how work is progressing *and* sensitive to the needs of their subordinates.

These transactional leaders (Hollander, 1985) focus on getting to know their subordinates and listening carefully. They seek to fulfill the subordinates' needs but maintain high expectation for how subordinates will perform. Such leaders who allow people to express their opinions both learn from others and receive strong support from their followers (Tyler, Rasinski & Spodick, 1985).

TRANSFORMATIONAL LEADERSHIP

Studies also reveal that many effective leaders of laboratory groups, work teams, and large corporations exhibit the behaviours that help make a minority view persuasive. Such leaders engender trust by *consistently* sticking to their goals. And they often exude a *self-confident* charisma that kindles the allegiance of their followers (Bennis, 1984; House & Singh, 1987). Charismatic leaders typically have a compelling *vision* of some desired state of affairs, an ability to *communicate* this to others in clear and simple language, and enough optimism and faith in their group to *inspire* others to follow.

In one analysis of 50 Dutch companies, the highest morale was at firms with chief executives who most inspired their colleagues "to transcend their own self-interests for the sake of the collective" (de Hoogh et al., 2004). Leadership of this kind—transformational leadership—motivates others to identify with and commit themselves to the group's mission. Transformational leaders—many of whom are charismatic, energetic, self-confident extraverts—articulate high standards, inspire people to share their vision, and offer personal attention (Bono & Judge,

2004). In organizations, the frequent result of such leadership is a more engaged, trusting, and effective workforce (Turner et al., 2002).

To be sure, groups also influence their leaders. Sometimes those at the front of the herd have simply sensed where it is already heading. Political candidates know how to read the opinion polls. A leader who deviates too radically from the group's standards may be rejected. Smart leaders usually remain with the majority and spend their influence prudently. Nevertheless, effective individual leaders can sometimes exhibit a type of minority influence by mobilizing and guiding their group's energy.

In rare circumstances, the right traits matched with the right situation yield history-making greatness, notes Dean Keith Simonton (1994). To have a Winston Churchill or a Margaret Thatcher, a Pierre Trudeau or a Karl Marx, a Napoleon or an Adolf Hitler, a Wilfrid Laurier or a Martin Luther King, Jr., takes the right person in the right place at the right time. When an apt combination of intelligence, skill, determination, self-confidence, and social charisma meets a rare opportunity, the result is sometimes a championship, a Nobel Prize, or a social revolution.

SUMMING UP: LEADERSHIP: HOW DO LEADERS SHAPE THE GROUP'S ACTIONS?

Some leader focus more on tasks and other leaders focus more on the social functioning of the group. Leaders who focus on tasks are often most effective for very high and very low functioning groups.

Some leaders, however, combine social and task leadership by listening to followers and seeking to meet their needs, but at the same time holding them to high standards for performance. These transactional leaders are often very effective.

Other leaders gain a following through their charisma and by offering personal attention. These transformational leaders inspire people to make self-sacrifices for the sake of the group and can lead others to be committed and engaged at the task at hand.

THE INFLUENCE OF THE MINORITY: HOW DO INDIVIDUALS INFLUENCE THE GROUP?

Groups influence individuals, but when—and how—do individuals influence their groups? And what defines effective leadership?

Each chapter in this social influence unit concludes with a reminder of our power as individuals. We have seen that

- cultural situations mould us, but we also help create and choose these situations;
- pressures to conform sometimes overwhelm our better judgment, but blatant pressure can motivate us to assert our individuality and freedom;
- persuasive forces are indeed powerful, but we can resist persuasion by making public commitments and by anticipating persuasive appeals.

This chapter has emphasized group influences on the individual, so we conclude by seeing how individuals can influence their groups.

At the beginning of most social movements, a small minority will sometimes sway, and then even become, the majority. "All history," wrote Ralph Waldo Emerson, "is a record of the power of minorities, and of minorities of one." For good or bad, minorities of one often have a huge impact. Think of Copernicus, Hitler, Galileo, and Pol Pot. In Canadian history, the Meech Lake Accord might well have been ratified as part of the Constitution if not for the efforts of Elijah Harper, a member of the Manitoba legislature. Technological history is also made by innovative minorities. As Robert Fulton developed his steamboat—"Fulton's Folly"—he endured constant derision: "Never did a single encouraging remark, a bright hope, a warm wish, cross my path" (Cantril & Bumstead, 1960).

"Minority influence" refers to minority opinions, not to ethnic minorities.

What makes a minority persuasive? What might the crew of the *Titanic* have done to convince Captain Smith that the ship needed to slow down? Experiments initiated by Serge Moscovici in Paris have identified several determinants of minority influence: consistency, self-confidence, defection.

CONSISTENCY

More influential than a minority that wavers is a minority that sticks to its position. Moscovici and his associates (1969, 1985) have found that if a minority consistently judges blue slides as green, members of the majority will occasionally agree. But if the minority wavers, saying "blue" to one-third of the blue slides and "green" to the rest, virtually no one in the majority will ever agree with "green."

"If the single man plant himself indomitably on his instincts, and there abide, the huge world will come round to him."

Ralph Waldo Emerson, *Nature, Address, and Lectures: The American Scholar*, 1849

Experiments show—and experience confirms—that nonconformity, especially persistent nonconformity, is often painful (Levine, 1989). That helps explain a *minority slowness effect*—a tendency for people with minority views to express them less quickly than people in the majority (Bassili, 2003). If you set out to be Emerson's minority of one, prepare yourself for ridicule—especially when you argue an issue that's personally relevant to the majority and when the group wants to settle an issue by reaching consensus (Kameda & Sugimori, 1993; Kruglanski & Webster, 1991; Trost et al., 1992). People may attribute your dissent to psychological peculiarities (Papastamou & Mugny, 1990). When Charlan Nemeth (1979) planted a minority of two within a simulated jury and had them oppose the majority's opinions, the duo was inevitably disliked. Nevertheless, the majority acknowledged that the persistence of the two did more than anything else to make them rethink their positions.

In so doing, a minority may stimulate creative thinking (Martin, 1996; Mucchi-Faina et al., 1991; Peterson & Nemeth, 1996). With dissent from within one's own group, people take in more information, think about it in new ways, and often make better decisions. Believing that one need not win friends to influence people, Nemeth quotes Oscar Wilde: "We dislike arguments of any kind; they are always vulgar, and often convincing."

A persistent minority is influential, even if not popular, partly because it soon becomes the focus of debate (Schachter, 1951). Being the centre of conversation allows one to contribute a disproportionate number of arguments. And Nemeth reports that in experiments on minority influence, as in the studies dealing with group polarization, the position supported by the most arguments usually wins. Talkative group members are usually influential (Mullen et al., 1989).

SELF-CONFIDENCE

Consistency and persistence convey self-confidence. Furthermore, Nemeth and Joel Wachtler (1974) reported that any behaviour by a minority that conveys self-confidence—for example, taking the head seat at the table—tends to raise self-doubts among the majority. By being firm and forceful, the minority's apparent self-assurance may prompt the majority to reconsider its position. This is especially so on matters of opinion rather than fact. In her research at Italy's University of Padova, Anne Maass and her colleagues (1996) report that minorities are less persuasive regarding fact ("from which country does Italy import most of its raw oil?") than regarding attitude ("from which country should Italy import most of its raw oil?").

DEFECTIONS FROM THE MAJORITY

A persistent minority punctures any illusion of unanimity. When a minority consistently doubts the majority wisdom, majority members become freer to express their own doubts and may even switch to the minority position. John Levine (1989) found that a minority person who had defected from the majority was more persuasive than a consistent minority voice. In her jury-simulation experiments, Nemeth found that once defections begin, others often soon follow, initiating a snowball effect.

Are these factors that strengthen minority influence unique to minorities? Sharon Wolf and Bibb Latané (1985; Wolf, 1987) and Russell Clark (1995) believe not. They argue that the same social forces work for both majorities and minorities. Informational and normative influence fuels both group polarization and minority influence. And if consistency, self-confidence, and defections from the other side strengthen the minority, such variables also strengthen a majority. The social impact of any position depends on the strength, immediacy, and number of those who support it. Minorities have less influence than majorities simply because they are smaller.

Anne Maass and Russell Clark (1984, 1986) agree with Moscovici, however, that minorities are more likely to convert people to *accepting* their views. And from their analyses of how groups evolve over time, John Levine and Richard Moreland (1985) conclude that new recruits to a group exert a different type of minority influence than do longtime members. Newcomers exert influence through the attention they receive and the group awareness they trigger in the old-timers. Established members feel freer to dissent and to exert leadership.

There is a delightful irony in this new emphasis on how individuals can influence the group. Until recently, the idea that the minority could sway the majority was itself a minority view in social psychology. Nevertheless, by arguing consistently and forcefully, Moscovici, Nemeth, Maass, Clark, and others have convinced the majority of group influence researchers that minority influence is a phenomenon worthy of study. And the way that several of these minority influence researchers came by their interests should, perhaps, not surprise us. Anne Maass (1998) became interested in how minorities could effect social change after growing up in post-war Germany and hearing her grandmother's personal accounts of fascism. Charlan

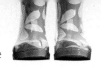

Nemeth (1999) developed her interest while she was a visiting professor in Europe "working with Henri Tajfel and Serge Moscovici. The three of us were 'outsiders'—I am American Roman Catholic female in Europe, they having survived World War II as Eastern European Jews. Sensitivity to the value and the struggles of the minority perspective came to dominate our work."

SUMMING UP: THE INFLUENCE OF THE MINORITY: HOW DO INDIVIDUALS INFLUENCE THE GROUP?

Although majority viewpoints often prevail, sometimes a minority can influence and even overturn a majority position. Even if the majority does not adopt the minority's views, the minority's speaking up can increase the majority's self-doubts and prompt it to consider other alternatives, often leading to better, more creative decisions.

In experiments, a minority is most influential when consistent and persistent in its views, when its actions convey self-confidence, and after it begins to elicit some defections from the majority.

CHAPTER EIGHT

Culture and Language

How are we influenced by human nature and cultural diversity?
Evolution and behaviour
Culture and behaviour
Social roles

How does culture shape our social thinking?
Culture and the self
Culture and reasoning: Holistic versus analytical reasoning
Culture and cognitive dissonance

How does culture impact social influence?
Culture and emotional expression
Culture and persuasion
Culture and conformity
Culture and group behaviour

How are social relations affected by culture?
Culture and aggression
Culture and relationships
Multiculturalism and intergroup relations

How do language and culture influence one another?
Language *and* culture
Bilingualism and language education

Conclusions
Biology and culture
The power of the situation and the person

Approaching earth from light-years away, alien scientists assigned to study the species *Homo sapiens* can hardly contain their excitement. Their plan: to observe, then abduct two randomly sampled humans for a week of study. Their first subject, Jan, is a verbally combative Toronto trial lawyer who grew up in Saskatchewan but moved east seeking an "urban lifestyle." After an affair and a divorce, Jan is enjoying a second marriage. Friends describe Jan as an independent thinker who is self-confident, competitive, and somewhat domineering.

Their second subject, Tomoko, lives with a spouse and their two children in a rural Japanese village, a walk from the homes of both their parents. Tomoko is proud of being a good child, loyal spouse, and protective parent. Friends describe Tomoko as kind, gentle, respectful, sensitive, and supportive of Tomoko's extended family.

From their small sample of two people of differing genders and cultures, what might our alien scientists conclude about human nature? Would they wonder whether both are actually of the same species? Or would they be struck by deeper similarities beneath the surface differences?

The questions faced by our alien scientists are those faced by today's earth-bound scientists: How do we humans differ? How are we alike? These questions are central to a world where social diversity has become, as historian Arthur Schlesinger (1991) said, "the explosive problem of our times." In a world ripped apart by ethnic, cultural, and gender differences, how can we learn to accept our diversity, value our cultural identity, and recognize the extent of our human kinship? So let's step back for a look at the evolutionary and cultural perspectives, and then see how each might help us understand gender similarities and differences.

HOW ARE WE INFLUENCED BY HUMAN NATURE AND CULTURAL DIVERSITY?

In viewing human similarities and differences, two perspectives dominate current thinking: an evolutionary perspective, emphasizing human kinship, and a cultural perspective, emphasizing human diversity. Nearly everyone agrees that we need both: Our genes design an adaptive human brain—a hard drive that receives the culture's software.

In many important ways, Jan and Tomoko are more alike than different. As members of one great family with common ancestors, they share not only a common biology but common behaviour tendencies. Each perceives the world, feels thirst, and develops language through identical mechanisms. Jan and Tomoko both prefer sweet tastes to sour and divide the visual spectrum into similar colours. They and their kin across the globe all know how to read one another's frowns and smiles.

Jan and Tomoko—and all of us everywhere—are intensely social creatures. We join groups, conform, and recognize distinctions of social status. We return favours, punish offences, and grieve a child's death. As children, beginning at about eight months of age, we fear strangers, and as adults we favour members of our own groups. Confronted by those with dissimilar attitudes or attributes, we react warily or negatively. Anthropologist Donald Brown (1991, 2000) has, in fact, identified several hundred such universal behaviour and language patterns. To sample among just those beginning with "v," all human societies have verbs, violence, visiting, and vowels.

Our alien scientists could drop in anywhere and find humans conversing and arguing, laughing and crying, singing and worshipping. Everywhere, humans prefer living with

others—in families and communal groups—to living alone. Everywhere, the family dramas that entertain us—from Greek tragedies to Chinese fiction to Mexican soap operas—portray similar plots (Dutton, 2006). Ditto adventure stories in which strong and courageous men, supported by wise old people, overcome evil to the delight of beautiful women or threatened children. Such commonalities define our shared human nature. We indeed are all kin beneath the skin.

EVOLUTION AND BEHAVIOUR

The universal behaviours that define human nature arise from our biological similarity. Some 100 000 to 200 000 years ago, most anthropologists believe, we humans were all Africans (Shipman, 2003). Feeling the urge to "be fruitful and multiply, and fill the earth," and driven by climate change and the availability of food many of our ancestors migrated across Africa to Asia, Europe, the Australian subcontinent and, eventually, the Americas. As they adapted to their new environments, these early humans developed differences that, measured on anthropological scales, are relatively recent and superficial. For example, those who stayed in Africa had darker skin pigment—what psychologist Steven Pinker (2002) calls "sunscreen for the tropics"—and those who went far north of the equator developed lighter skins capable of synthesizing vitamin D in less direct sunlight. Still, historically, we all are Africans.

Indeed, we were Africans recently enough that "there has not been much time to accumulate many new versions of the genes," notes Steven Pinker (2002, p. 143). And, indeed, biologists who have studied our genes, have found that we humans—even humans as seemingly different as Jan and Tomoko—are strikingly similar, like members of one tribe. We may be more numerous than chimpanzees, but chimps are more genetically varied.

To explain the traits of our species, and all species, the British naturalist Charles Darwin (1859) proposed an evolutionary process. As organisms vary, nature selects those best equipped to survive and reproduce in particular environments. Genes that produced traits that increased the odds of leaving descendants became more abundant. In the snowy Arctic environment, for example, polar bear genes programming a thick coat of camouflaging white fur have won the genetic competition and now predominate. This process of **natural selection**, long an organizing principle of biology, has recently become an important principle for psychology as well.

Evolutionary psychology studies how natural selection predisposes not just adaptive physical traits suited to particular contexts—polar bears' coats, bats' sonar, humans' colour vision—but also psychological traits and social behaviours that enhance the preservation and spread of one's genes (Buss, 2005). We humans are the way we are, say evolutionary psychologists, because nature selected those who had our traits—those who, for example, preferred the sweet taste of nutritious, energy-providing foods and who disliked bitter or sour flavours of foods that are toxic. Those who lacked such preferences were less likely to survive to contribute their genes to posterity.

As mobile gene machines, we carry the legacy of our ancestors' adaptive preferences. We long for whatever helped them survive, reproduce, and nurture their offspring to survive and reproduce. "The purpose of the heart is to pump blood," notes evolutionary psychologist David Barash (2003). "The brain's purpose," he adds, is to direct our organs and our behaviour "in a way that maximizes our evolutionary success. That's it."

natural selection the evolutionary process by which nature selects traits that best enable organisms to survive and reproduce in particular environmental niches

evolutionary psychology the study of the evolution of behaviour using principles of natural selection

The evolutionary perspective highlights our universal human nature. We not only maintain certain food preferences, we also share answers to social questions such as: Whom should I trust, and fear? Whom should I help? When, and with whom, should I mate? Who may dominate me, and whom may I control? Evolutionary psychologists contend that our emotional and behavioural answers to those questions are the same answers that worked for our ancestors.

"Psychology will be based on a new foundation."

Charles Darwin, *The Origin of Species*, 1859

Because these social tasks are common to people everywhere, humans everywhere tend to agree on the answers. For example, all humans rank others by authority and status. And all have ideas about economic justice (Fiske, 1992). Evolutionary psychologists highlight these universal characteristics that are handed down from our ancestors. Cultures, however, provide the specific rules for working out the elements of social life.

CULTURE AND BEHAVIOUR

Perhaps our most important similarity, the hallmark of our species, is our capacity to learn and adapt. Evolution may have prepared us to live creatively in a changing world and to adapt to environments from equatorial jungles to arctic icefields. Compared to bees, birds, and bulldogs, nature has us on a looser genetic leash. Ironically, it is our shared human biology that enables our cultural diversity. It enables those in one **culture** to value promptness, welcome frankness, and accept premarital sex, whereas those in another culture do not (Figure 8–1). As social psychologist Roy Baumeister (2005, p. 29) observes, "Evolution made us for culture. (See "Focus On: The Cultural Animal.")

culture the enduring behaviours, ideas, attitudes, and traditions shared by a large group of people and transmitted from one generation to the next

Evolutionary psychology incorporates environmental influences. It recognizes the nature and nurture interact in forming us. Genes are not fixed blueprints; their expression depends on the environment. One study of New Zealand young adults revealed a gene variation that put

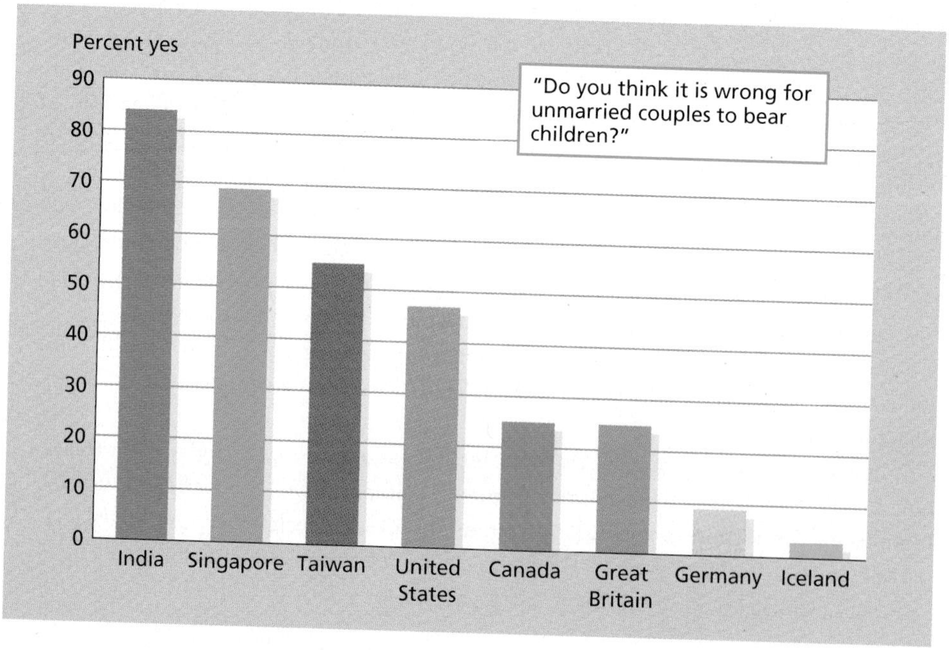

FIGURE 8–1

Culture matters.

These responses to a 1997 World Gallup survey illustrate our cultural diversity. (Gallup & Lindsay, 1999)

FOCUS ON

THE CULTURAL ANIMAL

We are, said Aristotle, the social animal. We humans have at least one thing in common with wolves and bees: We flourish by organizing ourselves into groups and working together.

But more that that, notes Roy Baumeister, we are—as he labels us in the title of his 2005 book—*The Cultural Animal* (Oxford University Press, 2005). Humans more than other animals harness the power of culture to make life better. "Culture is a better way of being social," he writes. We have culture to thank for our communication through language, our driving safely on one side of the road, our eating fruit in winter, and our use of money to pay for our cars and fruit. Culture facilitates our survival and reproduction, and nature has blessed us with a brain that, like no other, enables culture. Other animals show rudiments of culture and language. Monkeys have been observed to learn new food-washing techniques, which then are passed across future generations. And chimps exhibit a modest capacity for language. But no species can accumulate progress across generations as smartly as humans. Your nineteenth-century ancestors had no cars, no indoor plumbing, no electricity, no air conditioning, no Internet, no iPods, and no Post-it notes—all things for which you can thank culture. Intelligence enables innovation, and culture enables dissemination—the transmission of information and innovation across time and place.

The division of labor is "another huge and powerful advantage of culture," notes Baumeister. Few of us kill or grow food or build shelter, yet nearly everyone reading this book enjoys food and shelter. Indeed, books themselves are a tribute to the division of labor enabled by culture. Although only one lucky person gets his name on this book's cover, the product is actually the work of a coordinated team of scores of researchers, reviewers, assistants, and editors. And books and other new media then become part of the dissemination of knowledge, which is a powerful engine of progress.

"Culture is what is special about human beings," concludes Baumeister. "Culture helps us to become something much more than the sum of our talents, efforts, and other individual blessings. In that sense, culture is the greatest blessing of all. . . . Alone we would be but cunning brutes, at the mercy of our surroundings. Together we can sustain a system that enables us to make life progressively better for ourselves, our children, and those who come after."

people at risk for depression, but only if they had also experienced major life stresses such as a marital breakup (Caspi et al., 2003). Neither the stress nor the gene alone produced depression, but the two interacting did.

We humans have been selected not only for big brains and biceps but also for social competence. We come prepared to learn language and to cooperate in securing food, caring for young, and protecting ourselves. Nature therefore predisposes us to learn whatever culture we are born into (Fiske et al., 1998). The cultural perspective, while acknowledging that all behaviour requires our evolved genes, highlights human adaptability. People's "natures are alike," said Confucius, "it is their habits that carry them far apart." And far apart we still are, notes world culture researchers Ronal Inglehart and Christian Welzel (2005). Despite increasing education, "we are not moving toward a uniform global culture: cultural convergence is not taking place. A society's cultural heritage is remarkably enduring" (p. 46).

Cultural diversity

The diversity of our languages, customs, and expressive behaviours suggests that much of our behaviour is socially programmed, not hardwired. The genetic leash is indeed long. As sociologist Ian Robertson (1987) has noted:

> Americans eat oysters but not snails. The French eat snails but not locusts. The Zulus eat locusts but not fish. The Jews eat fish but not pork. The Hindus eat pork but not beef. The Russians eat beef but not snakes. The Chinese eat snakes but not people. The Jalé of New Guinea find people delicious. (p. 67)

If we all lived as homogeneous ethnic groups in separate regions of the world, as some people still do, cultural diversity would be less relevant. In Japan, where there are 127 million people, of whom 126 million are Japanese, internal cultural differences are minimal compared with those found in Toronto, where dozens of ethnic groups coexist.

Increasingly, cultural diversity surrounds us. More and more we live in a global village, connected to our fellow villagers by telecommunications, jumbo jets, and international trade. The mingling of cultures is nothing new. From Shakespeare's *Antony and Cleopatra* to Verdi's *Aida* to Forster's *A Passage to India*, the arts and literature have reflected the fascinating interplay of cultures. In our own day, an unknown pundit has said nothing typifies globalization like the death of Princess Diana. "An English princess with an Egyptian boyfriend crashes in a French tunnel, driving a German car with a Dutch engine, driven by a Belgian who was high on Scotch whiskey, followed closely by Italian paparazzi on Japanese motorcycles, and gets treated by an American doctor using medicines from Brazil." Cultural diversity exists within nations, too. As those from the Middle East, North Ireland, and the Balkans know well, conflicts stemming from cultural differences are longstanding. Cultural conflicts have been described as "the AIDS of international politics—lying dormant for years, then flaring up to destroy countries" (*Economist,* 1991).

Confronting another culture is sometimes a startling experience. North American males may feel uncomfortable when Middle Eastern heads of state greet their head of state with a kiss on the cheek. A German student, accustomed to speaking rarely to "Herr Professor," considers it strange that at our institutions most faculty office doors are open and students stop by freely. An Iranian student on her first visit to a North American McDonald's restaurant fumbles around in her paper bag looking for the eating utensils until she sees the other customers eating their French fries with, of all things, their hands. In many areas of the globe our best manners are a serious breach of etiquette. Foreigners visiting Japan often struggle to master the rules of the social game—when to take their shoes off, how to pour the tea, when to give and open gifts, how to act toward someone higher or lower in the social hierarchy.

Cultures mix. As this moose from Chinatown in Toronto illustrates, immigration and globalization are bringing once-distant cultures together.

Migration and refugee evacuations are mixing cultures more than ever. "East is East and West is West, and never the twain shall meet," wrote the nineteenth-century British author Rudyard Kipling.

But today, East and West, and North and South, meet all the time. Italy is home to many Albanians, Germany to Turks, England to Pakistanis and West Indians, and the result is both new friendship and surging hate crimes. For Canadians, Americans, and Australians, too, one's country is more and more a mingling of cultures. One in six Canadians is an immigrant. As we work, play, and live with people from diverse cultural backgrounds, it helps to understand how our cultures influence us and to appreciate important ways in which cultures differ. In a world divided by wars, genuine peace requires respect for both differences and similarities.

"Women kiss women good night. Men kiss women good night. But men do not kiss men good night—especially in Armonk."

Although some norms are universal, every culture has its own norms—rules for accepted and expected social behaviour.

Norms: Expected behaviour

As etiquette rules illustrate, all cultures have their accepted ideas about appropriate behaviour. We often view these social expectations, or **norms**, as a negative force that imprisons people in a blind effort to perpetuate tradition. Norms do restrain and control us—so successfully and so subtly that we hardly sense their existence. Like fish in the ocean, we are so immersed in our culture that we must leap out of it to understand it. "When we see other Dutch people behaving in what foreigners would call a Dutch way," note Dutch psychologists Willem Koomen and Anton Dijker (1997), "we often do not realize that the behaviour is typically Dutch."

There is no better way to learn the norms of our culture than to visit another culture and see that its members do things *that* way, whereas we do them *this* way. Norms can be arbitrary and confining. Is it right that mothers are criticized more often than fathers for too little involvement at home and too much on the job (Deutsch & Saxon, 1998)? Just as a play moves smoothly when the actors know their lines, however, so social behaviour occurs smoothly when people know what to expect. Norms grease the social machinery. In unfamiliar situations, when the norms may be unclear, we monitor others' behaviour and adjust our own accordingly. In familiar situations, our words and acts come effortlessly.

norms
rules for accepted and expected behaviour. Norms *prescribe* "proper" behaviour. (In a different sense of the word, norms also *describe* what most others do—what is *normal*.)

Cultural similarity

Thanks to human adaptability, cultures differ. Yet beneath the veneer of cultural differences, cross-cultural psychologists see "an essential universality" (Lonner, 1989). As members of one species, the processes that underlie our differing behaviours are much the same everywhere. At ages 4 to 5, for example, children across the world begin to exhibit a "theory of mind" that enables them to infer what others are thinking (Norenzayan & Heine, 2005). If they witness a toy being moved while another child isn't looking, they become able—no matter their culture—to infer that the other child will think it still is where it was.

Although norms vary by culture, humans do hold some norms in common. Best known is the taboo against incest: Parents are not to have sexual relations with their children, nor siblings with one another. Although the taboo apparently is violated more often than psychologists once

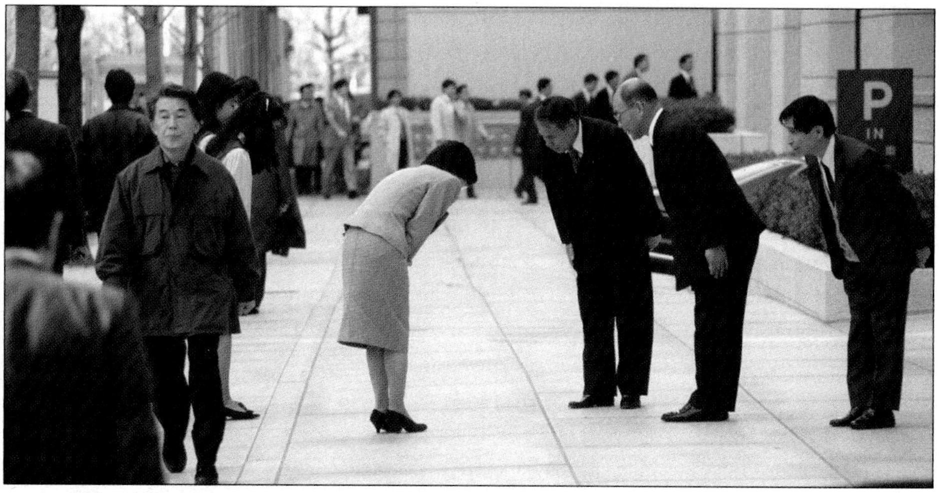

Norms—rules for accepted and expected behaviour—vary by culture.

believed, the norm is still universal. Every society disapproves of incest. Given the biological penalties for inbreeding, evolutionary psychologists can easily understand why people everywhere are predisposed against incest.

People everywhere also have some common norms for friendship. From studies conducted in Britain, Italy, Hong Kong, and Japan, Michael Argyle and Monika Henderson (1985) noted several cultural variations in the norms that define the role of friend (in Japan it's especially important not to embarrass a friend with public criticism). But there are also some apparently universal norms: Respect the friend's privacy, make eye contact while talking, don't divulge things said in confidence. These are among the rules of the friendship game. Break them and the game is over.

"I am confident that [if] modern psychology had developed in, let us say, India, the psychologists there would have discovered most of the principles discovered by the Westerners."

Cross-cultural psychologist John E. Williams (1993)

Around the world, people tend to describe others as more or less stable, outgoing, open, agreeable, and conscientious (John & Srivastava, 1999; McCrae & Costa, 1999). If a test specifies where you stand on these "Big Five" personality dimensions, it pretty well describes your personality, no matter where you live. Likewise, say Hong Kong social psychologists Kwok Leung and Michael Harris Bond (2004), there are five universal dimensions of social beliefs. In each of the 38 countries they studied, people vary in the extent to which they endorse and apply these social understandings in their daily lives: cynicism, social complexity, reward for application, spirituality, and fate control (Figure 8–2). People's adherence to these social beliefs appears to guide their living. Those who espouse cynicism express lower life satisfaction and favour assertive influence tactics and right-wing politics. Those who espouse reward for application are inclined to invest themselves in studying, planning, and competing.

Roger Brown (1965, 1987; Kroger & Wood, 1992) noticed another universal norm. Everywhere—in 27 languages studied to date—people not only form status hierarchies, they also talk to higher-status people in the respectful way they often talk to strangers. And they talk to lower-status people in the more familiar, first name way they speak to friends. Patients call their physician "Dr. So and So"; the physician often replies using their first name. Students and professors typically address one another in a similar nonmutual way.

"Look, everyone here loves vanilla, right? So let's start there."

Despite the enormous cultural variation in norms, we humans do hold some norms in common.

Most languages have two forms of the English pronoun "you": a respectful form and a familiar form (for example, *Sie* and *du* in German, *vous* and *tu* in French, *usted* and *tu* in Spanish). People typically use the familiar form with intimates and subordinates (not only with close friends and family members but also in speaking to children and dogs). A German child receives a boost when strangers begin addressing the child as "Sie" instead of "du."

This first aspect of Brown's universal norm—that forms of address communicate not only social distance but also social status—correlates with a second aspect: Advances in intimacy are usually suggested by the higher-status person. In Europe, where most twosomes begin a relationship with the polite, formal "you" and may eventually progress to the more intimate "you," someone obviously has to initiate the increased intimacy. Who do you suppose does so? On some congenial occasion, the elder, or richer, or more distinguished of the two may say, "Why don't we say du to one another?"

The Big Five Social Beliefs	Sample Questionnaire Item
Cynicism	"Powerful people tend to exploit others."
Social complexity	"One has to deal with matters according to the specific circumstances."
Reward for application	"One will succeed if he/she really tries."
Spirituality	"Religious faith contributes to good mental health."
Fate control	"Fate determines one's success and failures."

FIGURE 8–2
Leung and Bond's universal social belief dimensions.

This norm extends beyond language to every type of advance in intimacy. It is more acceptable to borrow a pen from or put a hand on the shoulder of one's intimates and subordinates than to behave in such a casual way with strangers or superiors. Similarly, the presidents of our universities invite faculty to their homes before faculty members reciprocate. In general, then, the higher-status person is the pacesetter in the progression toward intimacy.

So, some norms are culture-specific, others are universal. The force of culture appears in varying norms, and also in the roles that people play. Cultures everywhere influence people by engaging them in playing certain roles. Chapter 4 illustrated a powerful phenomenon: Playing a role often leads people to internalize their behaviour. Acting becomes believing. So let's consider how roles vary within and across cultures.

SOCIAL ROLES

All the world's a stage,
And all the men and women merely players:
They have their exits and their entrances;
And one man in his time plays many parts.
William Shakespeare

Role theorists assume, as did William Shakespeare, that social life is like acting on a theatrical stage, with all its scenes, masks, and scripts. Like the role of Jaques, who speaks these lines in *As You Like It,* social roles, such as parent, student, and friend, outlast those who play them. And, as Jaques says, these roles allow some freedom of interpretation to those who act them out; great performances are defined by the way the role is played. Some aspects of any role *must* be performed, however. A student must at least show up for exams, turn in papers, and maintain some minimum grade point average. Some roles (student, healer, mother, father) exist in all cultures, yet (as we will see) vary with culture.

When only a few norms are associated with a social category (for example, sidewalk pedestrians should keep to the right and not jaywalk), we do not regard the position as a social role. It takes a whole cluster of norms to define a role. We could readily generate a long list of norms prescribing our activities as professors or as fathers. Although we may acquire our particular images by violating the least important norms (e.g., rarely arriving early for anything), violating our role's most important norms (failing to meet our classes, abusing our children) could lead to our being fired or divorced.

Roles have powerful effects. In Chapter 4, we noted that we tend to absorb our roles. On a first date or on a new job, we may act the role self-consciously. As we internalize the role, self-consciousness subsides. What felt awkward now feels genuine.

This is the experience of many refugees, immigrants, missionaries, aid workers, and international students and executives. After arriving in a new country, it takes time to learn how to talk and act appropriately in the new context. Once adapted, the almost universal experience of those who repatriate back to their home country is re-entry distress (Sussman, 2000). Home sweet home is no longer quite so sweet. In ways one may not have been aware, one's behaviour,

Stephen Reid, serving his sentence for bank robbery (left), and with his wife, author Susan Musgrave (right).

values, and identity will have shifted to accommodate the role of citizen in a different place. One must reacculturate before being back in sync.

"Nowhere is social psychology further apart from public consciousness," noted Philip Brickman (1978), "than in its understanding of how things become real for people." Take the case of Stephen Reid. In the 1970s, Reid was part of the notorious group of bank robbers called the "Stop Watch Gang." They robbed over 100 banks, stealing more than $15 million. Reid was eventually arrested and while in prison he wrote the highly regarded novel, *Jackrabbit Parole.* Award-winning Canadian poet Susan Musgrave edited the book and asked Reid to marry her. They were married and when he was released they raised two children. By all accounts Reid was a happy and devoted husband and father. He was fond of saying, "My criminal career ended the day I began writing."

Sadly this was not to be. In 1998, Reid began using drugs and became addicted. On June 9, 1999, he robbed a Victoria bank, shot at a police officer, and held an elderly couple hostage. If Reid had been a bank robber all along and only pretended to be a good family man, people could have more easily understood his actions. What they could not understand was that he could really be a bank robber, then really a devoted husband and father, and then really a bank robber again. Could such a thing happen to you or me?

Yes and no. Our actions depend not only on the social situation but also on our dispositions. Reid may have had a predisposition to drug abuse, which probably played a role in his criminal activities. You might well have responded differently. Nevertheless, some social situations can move most "normal" people to behave in "abnormal" ways. This is clear from experiments that put well-intentioned people in a bad situation to see whether good or evil prevails. To a dismaying extent, evil wins. Nice guys often don't finish nice.

SUMMING UP: HOW ARE WE INFLUENCED BY HUMAN NATURE AND CULTURAL DIVERSITY?

How are we humans alike, how do we differ—and why? Evolutionary psychologists study how natural selection favours traits that promote the perpetuation of one's genes. Although part of evolution's legacy is our human capacity to learn and adapt (and therefore to differ from one another), the evolutionary perspective highlights the kinship that results from our shared human nature.

The cultural perspective highlights human diversity—the behaviours, ideas, and traditions that help define a group and that are transmitted across generations. The remarkably wide diversity of attitudes and behaviours from one culture to another indicates the extent to which we are the products of cultural norms and roles.

Yet cross-cultural psychologists also seek to identify the "essential universality" of all people. For example, despite their differences, cultures share some norms in common. One apparently universal norm concerns how people of unequal status relate to one another.

All cultures assign people to social roles. Playing a cultural role often leads people to internalize their behaviour. Switching roles can therefore change our perspective.

HOW DOES CULTURE SHAPE OUR THINKING?

One of the most profound ways that culture influences us is by shaping the way we think about ourselves and our world. The very way that we see or do not see inconsistencies in our selves, in our world, and between our thoughts and actions are powerfully shaped by culture.

CULTURE AND THE SELF

Wherever we go, whomever we are with, we are also with ourselves. The self is a constant in our social experience. As we learned in Chapter 2 there are certainly times when the self takes centre stage (e.g., the spot light effect) and times when its influence fades (e.g., during deindividuation), but there is little question that the self powerfully shapes our thinking. If the self has such influence on our thinking and if culture shapes the self, then one of the important ways that cultures influences our thinking is through the self concept.

Individualist and collectivist selves

individualism
the concept of giving priority to one's own goals over group goals and defining one's identity in terms of personal attributes rather than group identifications

How would you complete this "I am ___" statement? Would you give information about your personal traits, such as "I am honest," "I am tall," or "I am outgoing"? Or would you also describe your social identity, such as "I am a Pisces," "I am a MacDonald," or "I am a Muslim"?

For some people, especially those in industrialized Western cultures, **individualism** prevails. Identity is pretty much self-contained. Adolescence is a time of separating from parents, becoming self-reliant, and defining one's personal, *independent self.* Uprooted and placed in a foreign land, one's identity—as a unique individual with particular abilities, traits, values, and dreams—would remain intact. The psychology of Western cultures assumes that your life will be enriched by defining your possible selves and believing in your power of personal control. Western literature, from the *Iliad* to *The Adventures of Huckleberry Finn,* celebrates the self-reliant individual more than the person who fulfills others' expectations. Movie plots feature rugged heroes who buck the establishment. Songs proclaim, "I Did It My Way" and "I Gotta Be Me," and revere "The Greatest Love of All"—loving oneself (Schoeneman, 1994). Individualism flourishes when people experience affluence, mobility, urbanism, and mass media (Freeman, 1997; Marshall, 1997; Triandis, 1994).

collectivism giving priority to the goals of one's groups (often one's extended family or work group) and defining one's identity accordingly

Most cultures native to Asia, Africa, and Central and South America place a greater value on **collectivism**. They nurture what Shinobu Kitayama and Hazel Markus (1995) call the *interdependent self.* People are more self-critical and have less need for positive self-regard (Heine et al., 1999). Identity is defined more in relation to others. Malaysians, Indians, Japanese, and traditional Kenyans such as the Maasai, for example, are much more likely than Australians, Americans, and the British to complete the "I am" statement with their group identities (Kanagawa et al., 2001; Ma & Schoeneman, 1997). When speaking, people using the languages of collectivist countries say "I" less often (Kashima & Kashima, 1998, 2003). A person might say "Went to the movie" rather than "I went to the movie," with the subject made clear by the grammar or context.

> *"One needs to cultivate the spirits of sacrificing the* little me *to achieve the benefits of the* big me."
>
> Chinese saying

Pigeonholing cultures as solely individualist or collectivist oversimplifies, because with any culture individualism varies from person to person (Oyserman et al., 2002a, b). There are individualist Chinese and collectivist Americans, and most of us sometimes behave communally, sometimes individualistically (Bandura, 2004a). Individualism-collectivism also varies across a country's regions and political views. Conservatives tend to be economic individualists ("don't tax or regulate me") and moral collectivists ("do legislate against immorality"). Liberals tend to be economic collectivists and moral individualists. Despite individual and subcultural variations, researchers continue to regard individualism and collectivism as genuine cultural variables (Schimmak et al., 2005).

In his book *The Geography of Thought* (2003), social psychologist Richard Nisbett contends that collectivism results not only in social relations that differ from the more individualist West but also in differing ways of thinking. Consider: Which two—of a panda, a monkey, and a banana—go together? Perhaps a monkey and panda, because they both fit the category "animal"? Asians more often than Americans see relationships: monkey eats banana. When shown an animated underwater scene (Figure 8–3), Japanese spontaneously recalled 60 percent more background features than did Americans, and they spoke of more relationships (the frog beside the plant). Americans attend more to the focal object, such as a single big fish and attend less to the surroundings (Nisbett, 2003). Shinobu Kitayama and his colleagues (2003) also found Japanese to be more responsive to the perceptual context. Shown the stimulus in Figure 8–4 and asked to draw in a smaller empty box a similarly proportioned line, they did so more accurately than did Americans. Asked to draw a

FIGURE 8–3

Asian and Western thinking.

When shown an underwater scene, Asians often describe the environment and the relationships among the fish. Americans attend more to a single big fish. (Nisbett, 2003)

line of the same absolute length, Americans more accurately ignored the context and drew an identical line. Nisbett concludes from such studies that East Asians think more holistically—perceiving and thinking about objects and people in relationship to one another and to their environment.

With an *inter*dependent self one has a greater sense of belonging. Uprooted and cut off from family, colleagues, and loyal friends, interdependent people would lose the social connections that define who they are. They have not one self but many selves: self-with-parents, self-at-work, self-with-friends (Cross et al., 1992). As Figure 8–5 and Table 8–1 suggest, the interdependent self is embedded in social memberships. Conversation is less direct and more polite (Holtgraves, 1997). The goal of social life is not so much to enhance one's individual self as to harmonize with and support one's communities. The individualized latté—"decaf, single shot, skinny, extra hot"—that seems just right at a North American espresso shop would seem a bit weird in Seoul, note Heejung Kim and Hazel Markus (1999). In Korea, people place less value on expressing their uniqueness and more on tradition and shared practices (Choi & Choi, 2002). Korean advertisements less often highlight personal choice and freedom and more often feature people together (Markus, 2001).

The original stimulus

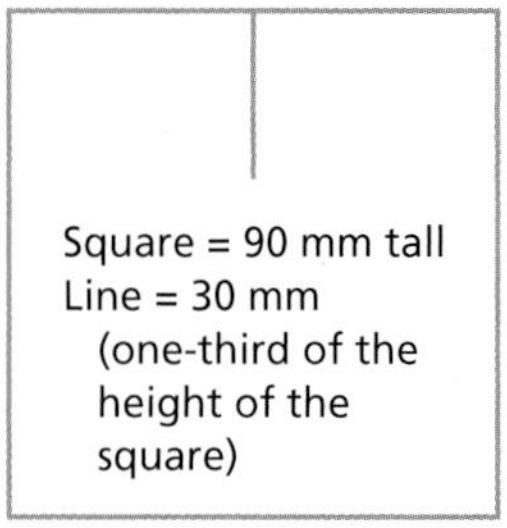

FIGURE 8–4

Perceiving in different cultures.

Shinobu Kitayama and his colleagues (2003) showed people a stimulus such as above, then asked them to reproduce, in a smaller or larger box, a line of the same length or of the same proportion relative to the box. American students were most accurate when drawing same-length lines; Japanese students when drawing same-proportion lines.

Self-esteem and culture

Self-esteem in collectivist cultures correlates closely with "what others think of me and my group." Self-concept is malleable (context-specific) rather than stable (enduring across situations). In one study, four in five Canadian students but only one in three Chinese and Japanese students agreed that "the beliefs that you hold about who you are (your inner self) remain the same across different activity domains" (Tafarodi et al., 2004).

For those in individualistic cultures self-esteem is more personal and less relational. Threaten our *personal* identity and we'll feel angrier and gloomier than when someone threatens our collective identity (Gaertner et al., 1999). Unlike Japanese who persist more on tasks when they are failing (not wanting to fall short of others' expectations), people in individualistic countries persist more when succeeding, because success elevates self-esteem (Heine et al., 2001). Western individualists like to make comparisons with others to boost their self-esteem. Asian collectivists make comparisons (often upward, with those doing better) in ways that

FIGURE 8–5

Self-construal as independent or interdependent.

The independent self acknowledges relationships with others. But the interdependent self is more deeply embedded in others. (Markus & Kitayama, 1991)

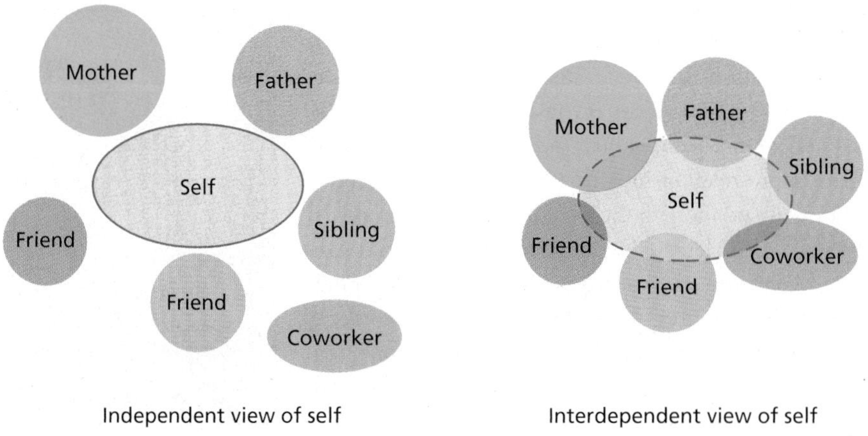

TABLE 8–1 Self-concept: Independent or interdependent

	Independent	Interdependent
Identity is	Personal, defined by individual traits and goals	Social, defined by connections with others
What matters	Me—personal achievement and fulfillment; my rights and liberties	We—group goals and solidarity; our social responsibilities and relationships
Disapproves of	Conformity	Egotism
Illustrative motto	"To thine own self be true"	"No one is an island"
Cultures that support	Individualistic Western	Collectivistic Asian and developing world

facilitate self-improvement (White & Lehman, 2005). Self-esteem among some collectivist cultures is also more balanced. As Julie Spencer-Rodgers and her colleagues (Spencer-Rodgers, Peng, Wang & Hou, 2004) have shown, Chinese students' self-evaluations are not negative rather they are characterized by both positive and negative views that are not necessarily resolved. In contrast, North American students' self-evaluations are more neatly resolved to reflect positive views of the self.

Would these preferences for exclusively positive information among North Americans and the preference for more balanced information among Asians extend to what role models they find motivating? Penelope Lockwood, Tara Marshall, and Pam Sadler (2005) addressed this question by examining how Asian Canadians and European Canadians responded to role models who were doing better or worse than themselves. European Canadians were inspired to be like those doing better, whereas Asian Canadians were motivated to avoid the mistakes of those who did worse.

So when, do you suppose, are university students in collectivist Japan and individualist United States most likely to report positive emotions such as happiness and elation? For Japanese students, report Shinobu Kitayama and Hazel Markus (2000), happiness comes with positive social engagement—with feeling close, friendly, and respectful. For American students, it more often comes with disengaged emotions—with feeling effective, superior, and proud. Conflict in collectivist cultures often is between groups; individualist cultures breed more crime and divorce between individuals (Triandis, 2000).

Hidden (and not-so-hidden) values seep into psychological advice. They permeate popular psychology books that offer guidance on living and loving.

When Kitayama (1999), after 10 years of teaching and researching in the United States, visited his Japanese alma mater, Kyoto University, graduate students were "astounded" when he explained the Western idea of the independent self. "I persisted in explaining this Western notion of self-concept—one that my American students understood intuitively—and finally began to persuade them that, indeed, many Americans do have such a disconnected notion of self. Still, one of them, sighing deeply, said at the end, 'Could this *really* be true?'"

When East continues to meet West—as happens, for example, thanks to Western influences in urban Japan and to Japanese exchange students visiting Western countries—does the self-concept become more individualized? Are the Japanese, for example, influenced when exposed to a Western bombardment of promotions based on individual achievement rather than seniority, with admonitions to "believe in one's own possibilities," and with movies in which the heroic individual police officer catches the crook *despite* others' interference? They seem to be, report Steven Heine and his co-researchers. Personal self-esteem increased among Japanese exchange students after spending seven months at the University of British Columbia. Individual self-esteem is also higher among long-term Asian immigrants to Canada than among more recent immigrants (and than among those living in Asia).

CULTURE AND REASONING: HOLISTIC VERSUS ANALYTICAL REASONING

Culture shapes not only the way we think about ourselves, but also the way we think about and perceive the world. In interpreting the world, we often have to make sense of events that at first blush make no sense at all. Consider the following two incidents:

holistic reasoning reasoning that emphasizes considering all possible influences and balancing competing forces

analytical reasoning reasoning that emphasizes the proper use of rules and that contradictory statements cannot be true

- On October 31, 1991, Gang Lu, a Chinese graduate student studying physics in North America, entered his department and shot his adviser, several students, and then himself. Having recently lost an award competition, and an appeal of that decision handled by his adviser, he was unable to find a job.
- On November 14, 1991, Thomas McIlvane, a postal worker of Irish descent, entered his office and shot his supervisor, several coworkers, and then himself. Having recently lost his job, and an appeal of that decision handled by his supervisor, he was unable to find a new job.

The similarities of these two events are striking. Not only did they happen just two weeks apart, but the circumstances of these tragic events are remarkably similar. Why did these men commit these awful murders?

Michael Morris and Kaiping Peng (1994) wondered how people would answer this question, and particularly whether Chinese and American students would answer this question differently. They presented students with a description of one of the cases and asked them to evaluate a number of possible causes for the tragedy. Regardless of the ethnicity of the assailant, American students emphasized personal causes (he was mentally unbalanced; he had personality problems). Chinese students emphasized situational causes (American movies that glorify revenge; the failure of the adviser or supervisor to respond to the assailant). Other studies confirm that people from Western cultures are more likely than people from Eastern cultures to prefer personal rather than situational explanations for others' behaviour (Choi & Nisbett, 1998; Choi, Nisbett & Norenzayan, 1999; Miller, 1984).

Given these differences in reasoning, it is not surprising that cultures also influence our attributions (Ickes, 1980; Watson, 1982). A Western worldview predisposes people to assume that people, not situations, cause events. Internal explanations are more socially approved

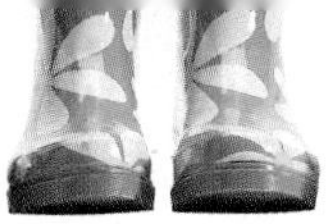

STORY BEHIND THE RESEARCH

Hazel Rose Markus
Stanford University

Shinobu Kitayama
University of Michigan

We began our collaboration by wondering out loud. Shinobu wondered why American life was so weird. Hazel countered with anecdotes about the strangeness of Japan. Cultural psychology is about making the strange familiar and the familiar strange. Our shared cultural encounters astonished us and convinced us that when it comes to psychological functioning, place matters.

After weeks of lecturing in Japan to students with a good command of English, Hazel wondered why the students did not say anything—no questions, no comments. She assured students she was interested in ideas that were different from hers, so why was there no response? Where were the arguments, debates, and signs of critical thinking? Even if she asked a straightforward question, "Where is the best noodle shop?" the answer was invariably an audible intake of air followed by, "It depends." Didn't Japanese students have preferences, ideas, opinions, and attitudes? What is inside a head if it isn't these things? How could you know someone if she didn't tell you what she was thinking?

Shinobu was curious about why students shouldn't just listen to a lecture and why American students felt the need to be constantly interrupting each other and talking over each other and the professor. Why did the comments and questions reveal strong emotions and have a competitive edge? What was the point of this arguing? Why did intelligence seem to be associated with getting the best of another person, even within a class where people knew each other well?

Shinobu expressed his amazement at American hosts who bombard their guests with choices. Do you want wine or beer, or soft drinks or juice, or coffee or tea? Why burden the guest with trivial decisions? Surely the host knew what would be good refreshment on this occasion and could just provide something appropriate and good.

Choice as a burden? Hazel wondered if this could be the key to one particularly humiliating experience in Japan. A group of eight was in a French restaurant, and everyone was following the universal restaurant script and was studying the menu. The waiter approached and stood nearby. Hazel announced her choice of appetizer and entrée. Next was a tense conversation among the Japanese host and the Japanese guests. When the meal was served, it was not what she had ordered. Everyone at the table was served the same meal. This was deeply disturbing. If you can't choose your own dinner, how could it be enjoyable? What was the point of the menu if everybody is served the same meal?

Could a sense of sameness be a good or a desirable feeling in Japan? When Hazel walked around the grounds of a temple in Kyoto, there was a fork in the path and a sign that read: "ordinary path." Who would want to take the ordinary path? Where was the special, less travelled path? Choosing the non-ordinary path may be an obvious course for Americans, but in this case it led to the temple dump outside the temple grounds. The ordinary path did not denote the dull and unchallenging way, but meant the appropriate and the good way.

These exchanges inspired our experimental studies and remind us that there are ways of life beyond the ones that each of us knows best. So far, most of psychology has been produced by psychologists in middle-class European American settings studying middle-class European American respondents. In other sociocultural contexts, there can be different ideas and practices about how to be a person and how to live a meaningful life, and these differences have an influence on psychological functioning. It is this realization that fuels our continuing interest in collaboration and in cultural psychology.

Culture influences attribution. Who is to blame for employees making unauthorized financial trades—the individual or the organization?

(Jellison & Green, 1981). "You can do it!" we are assured by the pop psychology of positive-thinking Western culture. You get what you deserve and you deserve what you get.

As children grow up in Western culture, they learn to explain behaviour in terms of the other's personal characteristics (Rholes et al., 1990; Ross, 1981). As a first-grader, one of my sons brought home an example. He unscrambled the words "gate the sleeve caught Tom on his" into "The gate caught Tom on his sleeve." His teacher, applying the Western cultural assumptions of the curriculum materials, marked this wrong. The "right" answer located the cause within Tom: "Tom caught his sleeve on the gate."

The fundamental attribution error occurs across all cultures studied (Krull et al., 1999). Yet people in Eastern Asian cultures are somewhat more sensitive to the importance of situations. Thus, when aware of the social context, they are less inclined to assume that others' behaviour corresponds to their traits (Choi et al., 1999; Farwell & Weiner, 2000; Masuda & Kitayama, 2004).

Some languages promote external attributions. Instead of "I was late," Spanish idiom allows one to say, "The clock caused me to be late." In collectivist cultures, people less often perceive others in terms of personal dispositions (Lee et al., 1996; Zebrowitz-McArthur, 1988). They are less likely to spontaneously interpret a behaviour as reflecting an inner trait (Newman, 1993). When told of someone's actions, Hindus in India are less likely than Americans to offer dispositional explanations ("She is kind") and more likely to offer situational explanations ("Her friends were with her") (Miller, 1984).

Does this mean that people from Eastern cultures think that people are inconsistent from one situation to the next and that they do not have an enduring personality? Apparently not. Ara Norenzayan from the University of British Columbia and his colleagues (Norenzayan, Nisbett & Choi, 2002) gave American and Chinese students a number of simple behavioural descriptions such as:

> Suppose you observed two people, A and B, being asked to participate in a blood donation drive and saw that A volunteers more hours than B collecting blood. What do you suppose is the probability that, being approached by a homeless person asking money to buy food, A gives more money than B?

Both Chinese and American students greatly overestimated the correlation between behaviour in one context and in another, thinking the correlation would be quite high ($r = .66$) when research actually suggests it is quite low ($r = .10$). So, it seems that people from both Eastern and Western cultures recognize that people have stable dispositions and distinct personalities.

Why then do people from Eastern cultures make more situational attributions? If they believe that people have stable personalities why don't they make attributions to these personalities? The answer to these questions seems to be that people from Eastern cultures perceive the world more holistically and less analytically than people from Western cultures (Nisbett, Peng, Choi & Norenzayan, 2001; Peng & Nisbett, 1999). In seeing the world more holistically, Easterners are more sensitive to social constraints in the situation and therefore are more likely to see the situation as a cause of a particular behaviour (Choi & Nisbett, 1998). This does not mean, however, that people from Eastern cultures do not see personality as an important cause of behaviour. When the situation is not salient, Easterners see personality as just as potent a cause of behaviour as Westerners do. Easterners and Westerners alike see other people as having coherent, enduring personalities.

The tendency to see the world holistically in Eastern cultures and analytically in Western cultures seems rooted in the cultures' histories and philosophies. Eastern cultures have been heavily influenced by Chinese philosophy that emphasizes cyclical change and the interrelationship of all aspects of the world. These ideas are captured in the relationship between yin and yang: When the yin reaches its extreme it becomes yang; when yang reaches its extreme it becomes yin. The pure yin is hidden from the pure yang, and the pure yang is hidden from the pure yin (Ji, Nisbett & Su, 2001). Reasoning is holistic—it emphasizes all of the relevant influences and finds a balance between competing forces. For example, a rock is a part of the mountain on which it is found. Its formation in the heart of the mountain and its eventual breakdown into pebbles must be understood in understanding the rock.

In contrast, Western cultures have been heavily influenced by Greek philosophy that emphasizes linear change, logical analysis, and the isolation of elements into discrete categories. Reasoning is analytical—it emphasizes the proper use of rules and principles, including the understanding that contradictory truths cannot both be true (e.g., an object cannot be a rock and at the same time not be a rock) and the belief that things are what they are (e.g., a rock is a rock).

Peng and Nisbett (1999) argue that such differences in reasoning lie at the heart of differences in cultural understanding. In a series of studies they showed that Chinese students prefer proverbs, solutions, and even scientific findings that emphasize the integration of competing claims to truth much more than American students. For example, Chinese students preferred the proverb, "Too humble is half proud," which seems to contradict the meaning of the word "humble." Li-Jun Ji from Queen's University and her colleagues have extended this research by examining how such holistic versus analytical reasoning affects people's judgments about change. They presented Asian and North American students with a number of scenarios such as, "Two kids are fighting at kindergarten. How likely is it that they will become lovers some day?" Asian students consistently predicted that people were more likely to change than did North American students.

To date, the research on cultural differences in reasoning has focused primarily on differences between people in Eastern and Western cultures. The few studies that have examined reasoning in other cultures and subcultures mostly examined people's reasoning capacity and have found few cultural differences (Bickersteth & Das, 1981; Cropley & Cardey, 1975; Macarthur, 1973). Human brains seem to share a remarkably similar capacity for reasoning. The cultural differences suggest that culture can shape in what direction this capacity is channelled.

CULTURE AND COGNITIVE DISSONANCE

Do differences in individualism and collectivism lead to differences in the experience of cognitive dissonance? Recall from Chapter 4 that after people make difficult decisions they tend to emphasize the good aspects of the item that they chose and the bad aspects of the item they did not choose. But does this finding arise out of our desire to individualistically claim that we make good choices?

Steve Heine and Darrin Lehman (1999) from the University of British Columbia thought so. They had Canadian students from UBC and Japanese exchange students complete a typical dissonance experiment. All the students were asked to rate a number of compact discs (CDs), and then were given a choice between two of the CDs as a reward for being in the experiment. Previous studies conducted in individualistic cultures have shown that when people are given such a choice and then rate the CDs again, their ratings of the CD they chose become more positive and their ratings of the CD they did not choose become more negative. Heine and Lehman (1999) found this exact pattern among their Canadian participants. Apparently, Canadians protected their individualistic self-concepts by seeing their choices as good choices. But what about the Japanese participants, did they protect themselves by justifying their choices? No. Showing no evidence of the typical pattern, they rated the CDs the same regardless of what choice they had made.

Does this mean that people who have a collectivistic self-concept do not experience cognitive dissonance? Etsuko Hoshino-Browne and her colleagues (Hoshino-Browne, Spencer, Zanna & Zanna, 2004) thought they would experience dissonance if their collectivist self-concepts were threatened. They tested this idea by modifying the typical dissonance experiment. They had University of Waterloo students born in Canada or Kyoto University students from Japan make a choice for themselves or for a close friend. They reasoned that when Canadians made a choice for themselves their individualistic self-concept would be threatened, but when Japanese made a choice for a friend their collectivistic self-concept would be threatened. Consistent with this reasoning they found that Canadian students justified the choices they made for themselves, but not the choices they made for their friends, whereas Japanese students justified the choices they made for their friends, but not the choices they made for themselves.

These studies suggest that culture can shape the experience of cognitive dissonance. Having an individualistic versus a collectivistic self-concept will affect when and how people experience cognitive dissonance. They also suggest, however, that the experience of feeling cognitive dissonance may be shared across many cultures.

SUMMING UP: HOW DOES CULTURE SHAPE OUR THINKING?

Culture shapes our sense of self. Some people, especially in individualistic Western cultures, assume an independent sense of self in which they define themselves in terms of traits that make them distinct from others. Others, often in Asian and developing world cultures, assume a more interdependent sense of self in which they define themselves in terms of their important relationships and roles. Such difference in self-concept can shape the way that people experience cognitive dissonance.

Eastern cultures tend to reason holistically, Western cultures analytically. These differences in reasoning style are reflected in differing explanations of behaviour, preferences for descriptions of truth, perceptions of change, and attributions. People from Eastern cultures are more likely to see behaviour as being the result of situational constraints than are people from Western cultures, even though people from both cultures view personality as an important cause of behaviour. In addition, Eastern cultures more than Western cultures accept contradiction and predict that people will change.

Culture can shape people's experience of cognitive dissonance. Decisions that people make for themselves seem less likely to provoke cognitive dissonance among people with a collectivist self-concept. In contrast, decisions that people make for others are less likely to provoke cognitive dissonance among people from an individualistic culture.

HOW DOES CULTURE IMPACT SOCIAL INFLUENCE?

Throughout this section of the book we have examined how people influence one another. Do people everywhere influence one another in the same ways or does culture influence the ways that people influence one another? Let's look at both the similar ways that people influence one another and the way such influence differs across cultures.

CULTURE AND EMOTIONAL EXPRESSION

When people smile in different parts of the world, does this always mean the same thing? Are there parts of the world where a frown means that people are happy? There might be good reason to think so. Some of our expressions and gestures mean very different things in different parts of the world. Years ago, Otto Klineberg (1938) noted that in Chinese literature people clap their hands to express disappointment and laugh a great "Ho-Ho" to express anger. Such differences can lead to embarrassing misunderstandings. You can imagine the miscommunication that might result if a North American made the "A-OK" gesture in Brazil, where it has a very different sexual meaning.

But do facial expressions have different meanings in different parts of the world? It turns out that they do not. Look at the six faces in Figure 8–6. If you are like most people, you will be able to identify the emotional expression on each face. Two research teams, one led by Paul Ekman and Wallace Friesen (1975, 1987, 1994) and the other led by Carrol Izard (1977, 1994) showed similar pictures to people in different parts of the world and asked them to guess the emotion behind the expression. It turns out a smile is a smile the world over, and the same is true for all of these expressions (Elfendbein & Ambady, 2002). Nowhere do people frown when they are happy. Despite some cross-cultural variation (Russell, 1994, 1995) people also share many similarities in how they categorize emotions. It seems that our biology has provided all of us with the same set of emotional expressions.

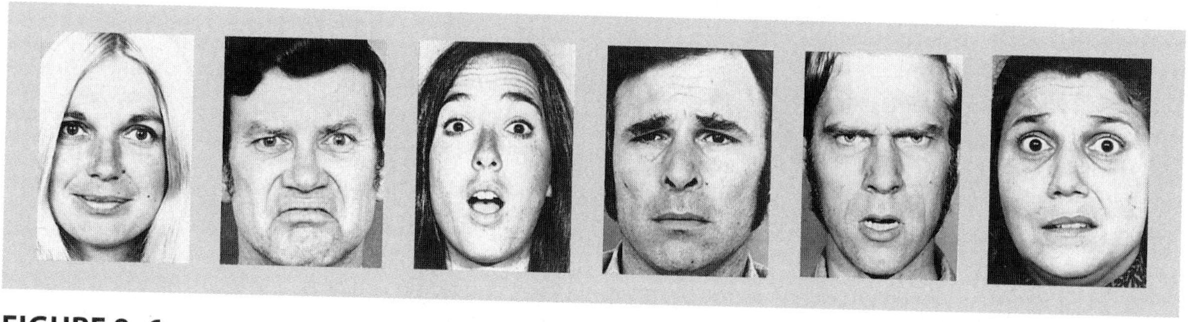

FIGURE 8–6

Is the perception of facial expressions culturally specific or universal?

What emotions do you see in these faces? Which face expresses anger? Happiness? Sadness? Disgust? Surprise? Fear? The answers are in the margin on page 281. (Ekman, 1973)

Although all cultures share a common language of facial expressions, cultures differ in how intensely people express emotions. In individualistic cultures the display of emotions tends to be more intense and prolonged than in collectivist cultures. While watching a gory horror movie, North Americans grimace whether they are alone or with others. Asians, in contrast, tailor their emotional expressions to fit in with those around them. To preserve social harmony they rarely and only briefly display negative or self-aggrandizing emotions (Markus & Kitayama, 1991; Matsumoto & Ekman, 1989; Matsumoto, Kudoh, Scherer & Wallbot, 1988).

Culture also affects the way that facial expressions are perceived. Studies by Takahiko Matsuda from the University of Alberta and his colleagues (Matsuda et al., 2008) have demonstrated that when people interpret the emotion behind a facial expression of others, Japanese people are more likely to take the expressions of all the people in the scene into account, whereas North Americans are more likely to focus solely on the expressions of the central character. Culture can also affect the way people perceive more ambiguous facial expressions. Dov Cohen and Alex Gunz (2002) compared Canadian- and Asian-born University of Waterloo students. They first induced one of six moods (e.g., anger, sadness, shame) by having people remember a time when they had experienced that mood. Once in their assigned mood, the people evaluated ambiguous facial expressions by guessing the mood of a person in a picture. Students born in Canada projected their own feelings onto the ambiguous faces. If they were angry, they thought the other person was angry; if they were sad, they thought the other person was sad. Students born in Asia had a very different reaction. They projected the complementary emotion to what they were feeling onto the ambiguous face. If they were feeling sad, they thought the ambiguous face was showing sympathy; if they were feeling shame, they thought the ambiguous face was showing disgust. Cohen and Gunz argue that such reactions result from and reinforce the collective nature of Asian communities.

In our facial expressions—and our interpretations of others' faces—we see biological and cultural factors working together. There are universally recognized facial expressions, yet culture shapes when and how these facial expressions are made and how they are interpreted.

So far we have examined cultural similarities and differences in how people express emotions. Does culture also shape the way we feel emotions and how we respond to our environment? Again, there are important similarities and differences. In a study of 37 countries on six continents, Klaus Scherer (1997) had people think of situations that made them feel different emotions. He found similarities in how people rated the situations that produced each emotion. For example, people from all countries rated situations that made them sad as being unpleasant, as blocking their goals, as caused by the situation, and as being difficult.

Scherer also noted cultural differences. For example, people from African countries tended to see immorality and unfairness as a larger component of anger, sadness, disgust, shame, and guilt. People from Latin American countries saw self-consistency as playing a smaller role in shame and guilt, and immorality as playing a smaller role in anger, sadness, and disgust.

Culture not only shapes our understanding of emotion, it also provides a framework through which we can interpret situations. For example, Shinobu Kitayama and his colleagues (2000) found that different activities predicted "good feelings" in the United States and Japan. In the U.S., good feelings were associated with isolated, disengaged feelings and actions. In Japan, good feelings were associated with interpersonally engaged—friendly—feelings that occur when interacting with others.

CULTURE AND PERSUASION

In Chapter 5, we examined how persuasive appeals can shape people's attitudes, but does culture shape the sort of persuasive appeals that are likely to be effective? Han and Shavitt (1994) have found that in Korea ads are more likely to emphasize the interpersonal benefits of products, whereas in North America ads are more likely to emphasize the personal benefits of products, and the content of these ads also affects how persuasive they are. In Korea ads that emphasize individual benefits such as personal success and personal benefits of products were less persuasive than ads that emphasized family or group benefits. The opposite was true in North America. Ads that emphasized individual benefits were more persuasive than ads that emphasized interpersonal benefits.

As we saw in Chapter 5, when people process persuasive appeals they sometime process them carefully and thoughtfully and sometimes process without much thought. When people process information thoughtfully the content of the message primarily determines people's reactions to the persuasive appeal—people are persuaded by good arguments and not persuaded by bad arguments. When people process information less thoughtfully, however, many subtle factors influence the persuasiveness of a message including the attractiveness of the communicator, the mood people are in, and the number of arguments (as opposed to the quality of the arguments) that are made. Does this basic model of persuasion hold across cultures?

Research by Jennifer Aacker and her colleagues (Aacker, 2000; Aacker & Maheswaran, 1997; Aacker & Patti, 1998; Aacker & Sengupta, 2000) suggests that the basic model of persuasion is similar across cultures. When people process information carefully the quality of the arguments that are made is the primary influence on whether an appeal is persuasive. When people process information less carefully, however, subtle factors influence the persuasiveness of a message, and it is at this point that cultural differences matter. The subtle cues that influence persuasive appeals when people process information less carefully vary across cultures.

A good example of such a cue is the influence of information about what most people do—what social psychologist call consensus information. In individualistic Western cultures people rarely pay attention to such consensus information. If one wants to shape a unique sense of self then what other people typically do hardly matters. In collectivistic Eastern cultures, however, fitting in with others is a central concern. In these cultures consensus information seems to be a cue that has a large effect on the persuasiveness of a message (Aacker & Maheswaran, 1997).

CULTURE AND CONFORMITY

Does cultural background predict how conforming people will be? Indeed it does. James Whittaker and Robert Meade (1967) repeated Asch's conformity experiment in several countries and found similar conformity rates in most—31 percent in Lebanon, 32 percent in Hong Kong, 34 percent in Brazil—but 51 percent among the Bantu of Zimbabwe, a tribe with strong sanctions on nonconformity. When Milgram (1961) used a different conformity procedure to compare Norwegian and French students, he consistently found the French students to be less conforming. An analysis by Rob Bond and Peter Smith (1996) of 133 studies in 17 countries showed how cultural values influence conformity. Compared with people in individualistic countries, those in collectivistic countries (in which harmony is prized and connections help define the self) are most responsive to others' influence

When researchers repeated Milgram's obedience experiments in Australia, Austria, Germany, Italy, Jordan, South Africa, and Spain how do you think the results compared to the original studies? The obedience rates were similar, or even higher—85 percent in Munich, Germany for example (Blass, 2000).

Cultures may change, however. Replications of Asch's experiment with university students in Britain, Canada, and the United States sometimes trigger less conformity than Asch observed decades earlier (Lalancette & Standing, 1990; Larsen, 1974, 1990; Nicholson et al., 1985; Perrin & Spencer, 1981). So conformity and obedience are universal phenomena, yet they vary across cultures and eras.

When immigrants come to a new country they can feel especially strong pressure to conform to the norms of their new society and perhaps especially so when their differences from the new society are highlighted. Romin Tafordi from the University of Toronto and his colleagues (Taforodi, Kang & Milne, 2002) tested this idea by having children of Chinese immigrants to Canada rate their preferences for abstract art either in front of a mirror (which presumably highlighted their ethnicity and potential differences from the dominant culture) or not. When in front of the mirror the Chinese Canadians made ratings that were more similar to what supposed European Canadians made, but they did not do so when the mirror was not present. Suggesting that the Chinese Canadians felt pressure to conform to the norms of Canadian society.

CULTURE AND GROUP BEHAVIOUR

Examining the impact of culture on group behaviour would seem like a natural step for social psychologists interested in culture. After all, many descriptions of culture emphasize the different ways that people from different cultures view groups versus individuals. To this point, however, little research has examined how culture affects group behaviour. Perhaps this is because some group behaviours seem poor candidates to display group differences. For example, research on social facilitation has demonstrated that social facilitation occurs not just in humans but in many different types of animals and even among insects. Such a phenomenon that appears to be deeply rooted in biology might not seem to be a likely candidate to vary by culture.

The impact of one aspect of group behaviour, however, has been studied extensively—social loafing. This research began by assessing the agricultural output in former communist countries. On their collective farms under communism, Russian peasants worked one field one day, another field the next, with little responsibility for any given plot. For their own use, they were given small private plots. One analysis found that the private plots occupied 1 percent of the agricultural land, yet produced 27 percent of the Soviet farm output (H. Smith, 1976). In communist Hungary, private plots accounted for only 13 percent of the farmland but produced one-third of the output (Spivak, 1979). When China began allowing farmers to sell food grown in excess of that owned to the state, food production jumped 8 percent per year—2.5 times the annual increase in the preceding 26 years (Church, 1986).

What about collectivist cultures under noncommunist regimes? Latane and his colleagues (Gabrenya et al., 1985) repeated the sound-production experiments described in Chapter 7 in Japan, Thailand, Taiwan, India, and Malaysia. Their findings? Social loafing was evident in all those countries too. Seventeen later studies in Asia reveal that people in collectivist cultures do, however, exhibit less social loafing than do people in individualist cultures (Karau & Williams, 1993; Kugihara, 1999). The nature of the group also seems to make a great deal of difference to whether social loafing occurs among collectivists. One study (Early, 1993) found that Chinese, Americans, and Israelis all showed social loafing when working with an outgroup member, but the Chinese and Israelis actually worked harder in the presence of ingroup members than when alone. Thus the Americans worked hardest when alone, but the Chinese and Israelis worked hardest when they were with other ingroup members.

SUMMING UP: HOW DOES CULTURE IMPACT SOCIAL INFLUENCE?

There are important similarities and differences in the expression and experience of emotion. People throughout the world see the same basic emotions in facial expressions, yet culture shapes the intensity and duration of facial expressions. Culture also shapes the emotions that people read into ambiguous expressions. Although people throughout the world view many of the same situations as producing specific emotions, culture shapes how people respond to specific situations.

Persuasive appeals that are tailored to the culture in which they are presented also seem to have much greater impact. It seems that advertisers have already learned this lesson well as ads in different cultures reflect as well as shape the culture.

There is strong evidence for conformity in many cultures. It seems that conformity occurs everywhere, but culture does seem to affect the strength of conformity effects.

Research on social loafing has shown that people across the globe loaf when working with strangers when their individual output is not monitored, but people from collectivist cultures in general seem to show a bit less social loafing and may even produce extra when working with ingroup members.

HOW ARE SOCIAL RELATIONS AFFECTED BY CULTURE?

Culture can also shape how we relate to one another. It can affect whether we hurt one another and whether we love one another. Let's examine how culture affects aggression and relationships, and intergroup relations.

CULTURE AND AGGRESSION

All cultures have norms that govern who gets resources and how resources are distributed (Bond, 2004). Violating these norms is often seen as an aggressive attack against the social order that can and should be punished with further violence. In this way, culture can provide the context for facilitating and inhibiting aggression.

An excellent example of how culture can shape aggressive reactions can be seen in a series of studies conducted by Dov Cohen and his colleagues (Cohen, 1998; Cohen & Nisbett, 1997; Cohen et al., 1996). They examined how men from the southern United States respond differently than northerners to threats to their honour. They argue that the rough-and-tumble settlement of the South led to a culture in which men had to stand up for themselves and defend their honour in order to protect their possessions, their families, and themselves. One by-product of this culture is that it requires that men respond to challenges to their honour with violence if necessary.

One of these studies (Cohen et al., 1996) examined the reactions of men from the northern or southern U.S. to an insult. In the narrow corridor on the way to the experiment a research assistant bumped the participants and insulted them with a vulgar epithet. This insult had very little effect on the northerners, but the southerners reacted with anger. They were more physiologically aroused, and they gave stronger shocks to a confederate in another study. In short, the southerners reacted to the insult by defending their honour. Such defence of one's honour helps explain why the South's murder rate is almost twice as high as it is in the rest of the United States (Cohen & Nisbett, 1997).

Cohen and his colleagues believe that a culture of honour is likely to emerge wherever people view violence as the only way to defend their hearth and home. They argue that many countries in the Mediterranean and Latin America also show aspects of a culture of honour.

That a frontier spirit can spur individualism is perhaps most strongly demonstrated in a typically collectivistic culture. In Japan the island of Hokkaido was settled primarily as a frontier outpost. Shinobu Kitayama and his colleagues have found that residents of this island showed much stronger individualism than is typically seen in Japan (Kitayama, Ishii, Imada, Takemura & Ramaswamy, 2006).

CULTURE AND RELATIONSHIPS

Do friendships and intimate relationships differ across cultures? In one sense they do not. Close friendships and intimate relations are a common aspect of all cultures, but culture can shape the way these relationships unfold.

University of Toronto social psychologist Glen Adams (2005) provides an intriguing example of how culture can influence relationships. He examined how people understood enemies in North America and West Africa. In North America, people see enemies as members of their outgroups and typically do not think that any of their friends could also be enemies. West Africans, however, see such views as somewhat quaint and naïve. They too recognize that outgroup members may well be enemies, but they are much more likely to recognize that their friends may actually not have their best interests at heart—that in fact they may be secret enemies. North Americans often think of such views as expressing paranoia, but is this really so? Research by Abe Tesser (1988) demonstrates that people will undermine a friend's performance more than a stranger's performance when their friend might outperform them on a task. West Africa's history of slave trading and colonialization may well have prepared West Africans to recognize that our friends can often be our worst enemies.

Individualism and collectivism can also shape the way we form intimate relationships. Young-ok Yum (2004) has examined how people from Hong Kong and Hawaii (collectivistic cultures) and people from the U.S. (an individualistic culture) form dating relationships. People from Hong Kong and Hawaii are more likely to develop a style of relationship that accommodates for the other's needs in the relationship, whereas people from the U.S. are more likely to develop a style of relationship that emphasizes meeting one's own needs in the relationship. Interestingly, people who are bicultural individuals (who identify with both Eastern and Western cultures) are the most likely to accommodate for the needs of others in the relationship.

Thus it seems that culture can shape our thoughts and actions as we engage in relationships.

Answers to Figure 8–6:
1. Happiness;
2. Disgust;
3. Surprise;
4. Sadness;
5. Anger;
6. Fear.

MULTICULTURALISM AND INTERGROUP RELATIONS

Canadians have traditionally championed the value of multiculturalism in which all groups are appreciated and valued for their culture and tradition by the group as a whole. We contrast this value with the emphasis on assimilation or a melting pot that is often seen in the United States, in which all members of society are encouraged to adopt a similar outlook.

The difference between the two countries can be seen in their policies about language. In the U.S. there is only one official language (English), and despite the fact that many people speak other languages, there is great opposition to education in any language other than English. In Canada, there are two official languages (English and French) and education is actively promoted in both languages as well as encouraged in others.

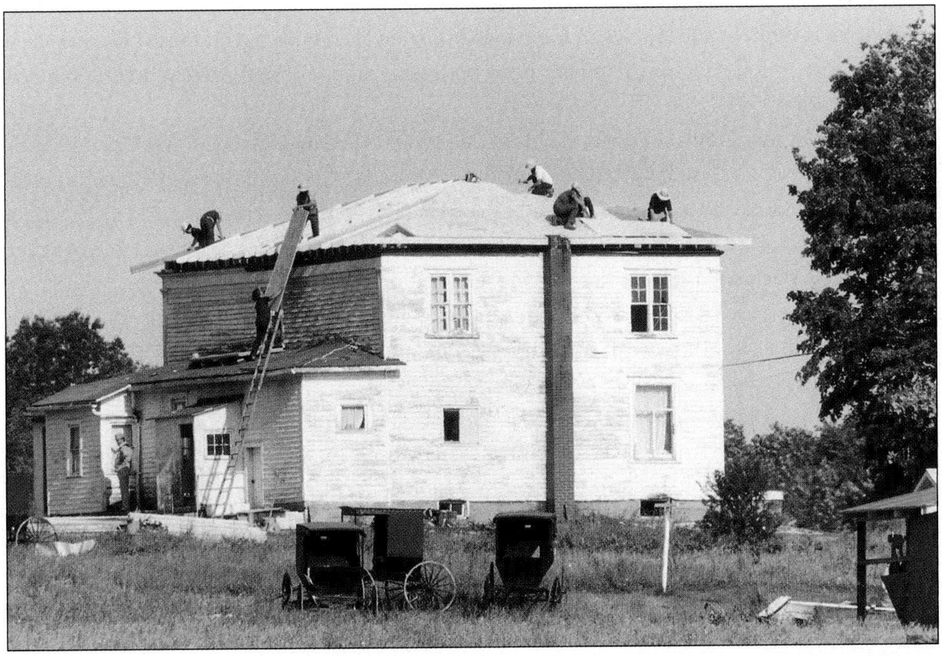

Cooperation and peace. Researchers have identified more than 40 peaceful societies—societies where people live with no, or virtually no, recorded instances of violence. An analysis of 25 of these societies, including the Amish shown here, reveals that most base their world views on cooperation rather than competition (Bonta, 1997).

Has Canada always sought the ideals of multiculturalism? No, at times the official policy has been assimilation. One example of this policy is the establishment of residential schools for First Nations children throughout most of twentieth-century Canada. Looking back, it seems clear that the goal of these schools was to assimilate First Nations children into "mainstream" or White Canadian society. First Nations children were separated from their communities and families and raised in White Canadian communities to learn White Canadian ways.

How can we and Canadian society actively promote multiculturalism? Social psychology has powerful answers to this question including promoting intergroup contact and cooperation.

Contact

Might putting two conflicting individuals or groups into close contact enable them to know and like each other? Or might it cause them to act on prejudices, escalating the conflict? There are reasons to think that either reaction could occur. In Chapter 11, we will see that proximity—and the accompanying interaction, anticipation of interaction, and mere exposure—boosts liking. On the other hand, we saw in Chapter 3 how negative expectations can colour people's judgments and can even create self-fulfilling prophecies, leading people to evaluate others negatively and bring out their worst. Such competing predictions are just the sort of puzzle that excites the scientist's detective spirit.

The original hypothesis, labelled the contact hypothesis by Gordon Allport (1954), was that contact between members of groups in conflict would lead to friendlier relations and a reduction in prejudiced attitudes. This hypothesis has been examined in hundreds of studies and the results of these investigations have enabled researchers to tell an interesting detective story.

Does contact improve intergroup relations?

A bird's-eye view of the studies suggests that contact improves intergroup relations. In comprehensive reviews of the studies that have investigated the contact hypothesis, there is clear evidence that contact does promote harmony between groups (Brown & Hewstone, 2005; Pettigrew & Tropp, 2006).

Studies in numerous countries including Canada, Germany, Pakistan, the United States, France, England, and Holland have found that increased contact between members of ethnic groups tends to be associated with better relations between groups (Brown, Vivian & Hewstone, 1999; Hamberger & Hewstone, 1997; Kalin & Berry, 1982; Pettigrew, 1997; Wagner, Hewstone & Machleit, 1989). Likewise, anti-gay feelings are lower among people who know gays personally (Herek, 1993). Additional studies of attitudes toward the elderly, the mentally ill, AIDS patients, and those with disabilities confirm that contact often predicts positive attitudes (Pettigrew, 1998).

In a painstakingly complete analysis of these studies, Linda Tropp and Thomas Pettigrew (2005a; Pettigrew and Tropp, 2006) assembled data from 516 studies of 250 000 people in 38 nations. In 94 percent of the studies, *increased contact predicted decreased prejudice.* This is especially true for majority group attitudes toward minorities (Tropp & Pettigrew, 2005b). So although it seemed reasonable that contact could promote or hinder intergroup relations, the evidence is clear that most of the time contact improves intergroup relations. Allport's original hypothesis has received overwhelming support.

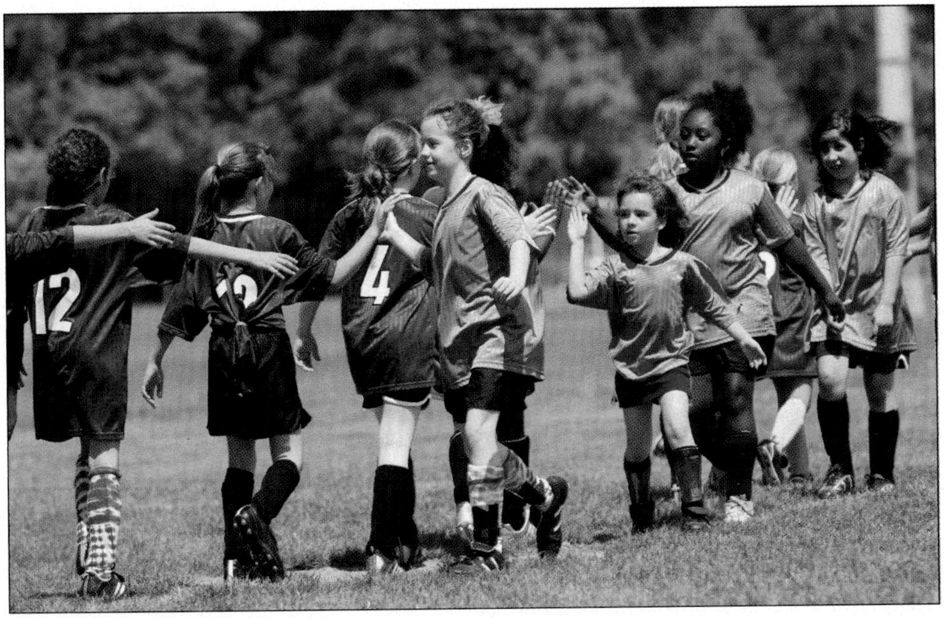

Interracial cooperation—on athletic teams, in class projects and extracurricular activities—melts differences and improves racial attitudes.

Cooperation

Although the evidence is overwhelming that contact can improve intergroup relations, it is sometimes not enough to overcome all the problems that exist between groups. For example, in one set of classic studies Muzafer Sherif (1966) brought boys to a summer camp and had them compete to the point that each group (the Eagles and the Rattlers) came to strongly dislike the members of the other group. Simply stopping the competition between the groups and bringing them together for noncompetitive activities, such as watching movies, shooting off fireworks, and eating was not enough. By this time, their hostility was so strong that what contact provided was the opportunity for taunts and attacks. When an Eagle was bumped by a Rattler, his fellow Eagles urged him to "brush off the dirt." Obviously, contact between the two groups had hardly promoted their social integration.

Given entrenched hostility, how can positive intergroup relations be established? Sherif brought the Eagles and the Rattlers together by having them cooperate on a number of activities in which both groups wanted to achieve a goal, but needed the other group's help to achieve it. Together, they were fighting for a common cause, striving toward a shared goal.

Superordinate goals

Such goals compelling for all in a group and requiring cooperative effort are called **superordinate goals**. To promote harmony among his warring campers, the specific goals that Sherif introduced included a problem with the camp water supply, necessitating their cooperation to restore the water; an opportunity to rent a movie, one expensive enough to require the joint resources of both groups, they again cooperated. When a truck "broke down" on a camping trip, a staff member casually left the tug-of-war rope nearby, prompting one boy to suggest that they all pull the truck to get it started. When it started, a backslapping celebration ensued over their victorious "tug-of-war against the truck."

superordinate goal a shared goal that necessitates cooperative effort; a goal that overrides people's differences from one another

After working together to achieve such superordinate goals, the boys ate together and enjoyed themselves around a campfire. Friendships sprouted across group lines. Hostilities plummeted (Figure 8–7). On the last day, the boys decided to travel home together on one bus. During the trip they no longer sat by groups. As the bus approached home, they, as one, spontaneously sang together and then bade their friends farewell. With isolation and competition, Sherif made strangers into bitter enemies. With superordinate goals, he made enemies into friends.

Are Sherif's experiments mere child's play? Or can pulling together to achieve superordinate goals be similarly beneficial with adults in conflict? Robert Blake and Jane Mouton (1979) wondered. So in a series of two-week experiments involving more than 1000 executives in 150 different groups, they recreated the essential features of the situation experienced by the Eagles and the Rattlers. Each group first engaged in activities by itself, then competed with another group, and then cooperated with the other group in working toward jointly chosen superordinate goals. Their results provided "unequivocal evidence that adult reactions parallel those of Sherif's younger subjects."

Extending these findings, Samuel Gaertner, John Dovidio, and their collaborators (1993, 1998) report that working cooperatively has especially favourable effects under conditions that lead people to define a new, inclusive group that dissolves their former subgroups. Old feelings of bias against another group diminish when members of the two groups sit alternately around a table (rather than on opposite sides), give their new group a single name, and then work together under conditions that foster a good mood. "Us" and "them" become "we." To combat Germany, Italy, and Japan during the Second World War, Canada, France, the United States, and England, along with other nations, formed one united group named the Allies. So long as the superordinate goal of defeating a common enemy lasted, so did supportive ties between these countries.

FIGURE 8–7

After competition, the Eagles and the Rattlers rated each other unfavourably. After they worked cooperatively to achieve superordinate goals, hostility dropped sharply. (Data from Sherif, 1966, p. 84)

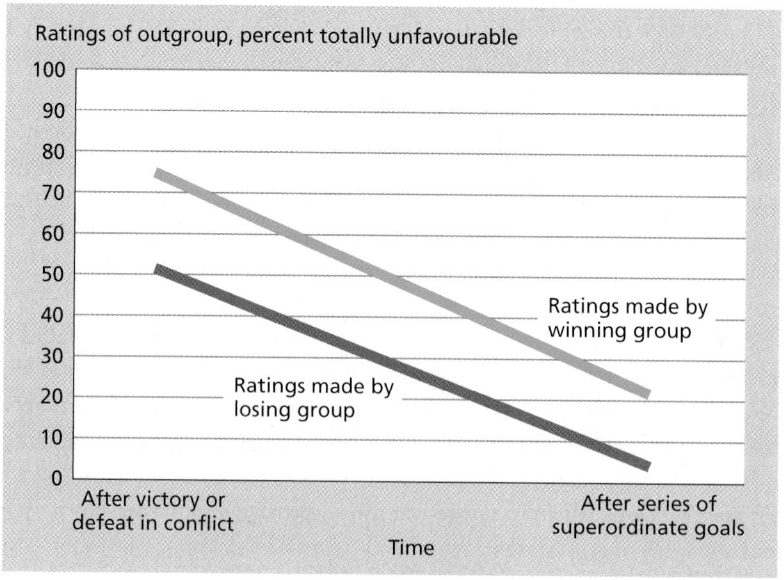

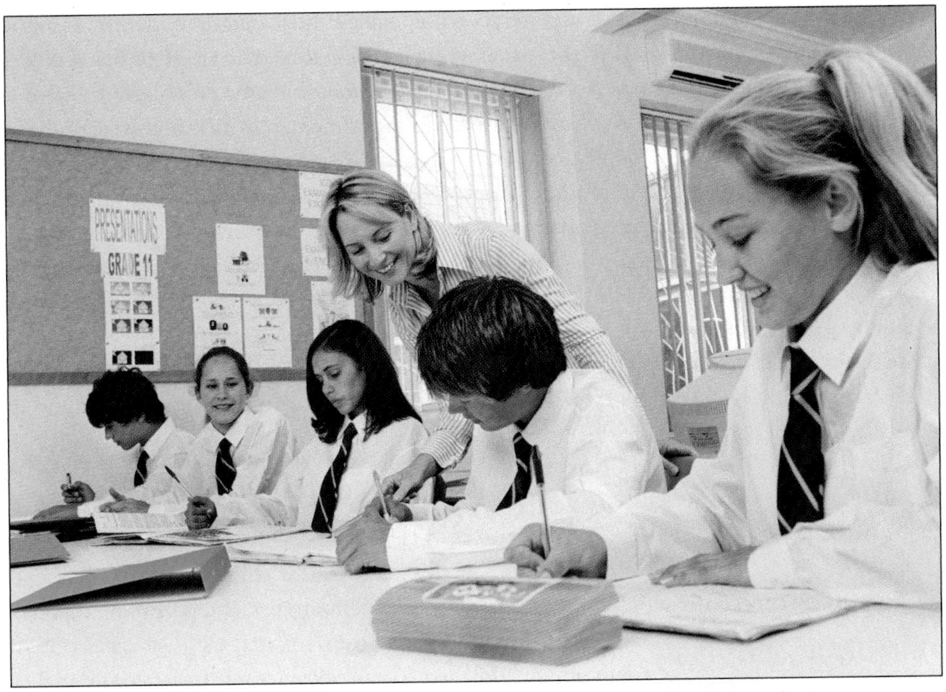

Promoting "common identity." The common European practice of school uniforms—used in many Canadian schools as well—aims to change "us" and "them" to "we."

The cooperative efforts by the Eagles and the Rattlers ended in success. Would the same harmony have emerged if the water had remained off, the movie unaffordable, the truck still stalled? Likely not. In experiments with University of Virginia students, Stephen Worchel and his associates (1977, 1978, 1980) confirmed that *successful* cooperation between two groups boosts their attraction for one another. If previously conflicting groups *fail* in a cooperative effort, however, *and* if conditions allow them to attribute their failure to each other, the conflict may worsen. Sherif's groups were already feeling hostile to one another. Thus, failure to raise sufficient funds for the movie might have been attributed to the one group's "stinginess" and "selfishness." This would have exacerbated rather than alleviated their conflict.

Generalizing positive attitudes

Given cooperative contacts with those from another group, will we generalize? If we come to like people in another group, will we generalize this positive attitude to the whole outgroup? As Northern Ireland's Catholic and Protestant farmers cooperate in agricultural pursuits, can we expect them to become more accepting of all Protestants (or Catholics)? The answer appears to be yes if

- we see others in our group modelling friendships with outgroup members (Wright et al., 1997),
- we perceive the others as representative of their group rather than atypical (Desforges et al., 1997), and
- we think of them not just as individuals but as having a different group identity than our own (Vivian et al., 1997; Pettigrew, 1998).

Initially, we will be most likely to interact with people if their outgroup identity is minimized—if we see them as essentially like us rather than feeling threatened by their being different. But if our liking is to generalize, their group identity must at some point become salient. An effective sequence was neatly illustrated by one experiment in which highly prejudiced White participants operated an imaginary railway system over 40 sessions with two supposed other participants, one Black, one White (Cook, 1984). As they shared successes and failures and won bonus money, the White participants came to like their new friends. To enhance generalization, the Black confederate, once rapport was established, told of a personal experience with racial discrimination, which the other White confederate lamented. By the end of the lengthy experiment, the subjects not only genuinely liked their Black partner, they expressed more positive racial attitudes than did control subjects not given the experience. So, generalizing from positive interracial experiences may be enhanced by initially minimizing group diversity, then acknowledging it, then transcending it.

A difficult balancing act. These ethnically conscious French Canadians—supporting Bill 101, "live French in Quebec"—may or may not also feel strongly Canadian. As countries become more ethnically diverse, people debate how we can build societies that are both plural and unified.

Group and superordinate identities

In everyday life, we often reconcile dual identities (Gaertner et al., 1998; Hewstone, 1996; Huo et al., 1996). We acknowledge our subgroup identity (as parent or child) and then transcend it (sensing our superordinate identity as a family). Blended families and corporate mergers leave us mindful of who we were, and who we are. Pride in our ethnic heritage need not displace our larger communal or national identity. Subgroup identity and social cohesion can co-exist.

Many in our society see themselves as Canadians and as members of another culture. This sense of identifying with both the ethnic culture and the larger culture is what researcher Jean Phinney (1990) calls a "bicultural" identity. Ujjal Dosanjh, British Columbia's and Canada's first Indo-Canadian premier (and as this book goes to print MP), is an excellent example of someone who seems to have such an identity, and it seems to have played a crucial role in his political career. He grew up in a highly political family. His grandfather was jailed and his uncle was killed in India's fight for independence. His father was a member of Mahatma Gandhi's Congress party. So it comes as little surprise that he pursued a career in politics, but he sees his Indian heritage as playing a critical role in his politics. "All around me has been politics and activism," Dosanjh says. "I have been a political animal most of my life. There's no question the fact that I am an Indo-Canadian has led me to do certain things in life that others might not have done."

Forming such a bicultural identity is not always easy. Many people feel a tension between the two identities, and not all people identify with both their culture of origin and the larger culture. Ethnically conscious Asians living in England may or may not also feel strongly British (Hutnik, 1985). French Canadians who identify with their ethnic roots may or may not also feel strongly Canadian (Driedger, 1975). Hispanic Americans who retain a strong sense of their "Cubanness" (or of their Mexican or Puerto Rican heritage) may or may not feel strongly American (Roger et al., 1991). When people find the larger culture as uninviting and unfriendly they are more likely to remain solely identified with their culture of origin.

Nevertheless, with time, identification with a new culture often grows. Second-generation Chinese immigrants to Australia feel their Chinese identity somewhat less keenly, and their new national identity more strongly than do immigrants who were born in China (Rosenthal & Feldman, 1992). Often, however, the *grand*children of immigrants feel more comfortable identifying with their ethnicity (Triandis, 1994).

Researchers have wondered whether pride in one's group competes with identification with the larger culture. We evaluate ourselves to a large extent in terms of our group memberships (Tajfel & Turner, 1976). Seeing our own group (our school, our employer, our family, our race, our nation) as good helps us feel good about ourselves. A positive ethnic identity can therefore contribute to positive self-esteem. So can a positive social identity among those who have assimilated into the mainstream culture. "Marginal" people, who have neither an ethnic nor a mainstream identity (Table 8–2), often have low self-esteem. Bicultural people, who affirm both identities, typically have a strongly positive self-concept (Phinney, 1990). Often, they alternate between their two cultures, adapting their language and behaviour to whichever group they are with (LaFromboise et al., 1993).

Taken to an extreme, group pride becomes destructive tribalism. Preoccupation with diversity may counter the "universalism" that is basic to nonviolent conflict resolution strategies (Mayton, et al., 1996). By seeking to understand, appreciate, and protect all people, universalists such as Gandhi, Martin Luther King, Jr., and Nelson Mandela advocate peaceful routes to justice.

By forging national identities with unifying ideals, immigrant countries such as Canada and Australia have avoided ethnic wars. Here, Irish and Italians, Swedes and Scots, Asians and Africans seldom kill in defence of their ethnic identities. Nevertheless, even in Canada we struggle between separation and wholeness, between people's pride in their distinct heritage and unity as one nation, between acknowledging the reality of diversity and questing for shared values. These tensions pose a very real and urgent challenge for our society as we try to develop and foster a truly multicultural nation.

TABLE 8–2 Ethnic and cultural identity

	Identification with Ethnic Group	
Identification with Majority Group	**Strong**	**Weak**
Strong	Bicultural	Assimilated
Weak	Separated	Marginal

SUMMING UP: HOW ARE SOCIAL RELATIONS AFFECTED BY CULTURE?

In all cultures people must divide resources and form relationships. These tasks are part of the human experience. Yet culture shapes the way we complete these tasks. Men in the southern U.S. respond to challenges to their honour with threats of violence and actual violence. People from West Africa recognize that their friends may also be their enemies, and people from collectivist cultures make more accommodation in their interpersonal relationships.

Multiculturalism as a basis of positive intergroup relations has been an important value for Canadians over the last quarter century. In order to achieve this goal Canadians must strive for cooperative contacts between groups that are characterized by the pursuit of superordinate goals. In this way positive relations between members of different groups can generalize to positive feelings about the group as a whole.

HOW DO LANGUAGE AND CULTURE INFLUENCE ONE ANOTHER?

Intimately related and often intertwined with culture is language. Culture may find its expression in language, but language can be a potent force that shapes culture as well.

LANGUAGE *AND* CULTURE

Benjamin Lee Whorf (1956) proposed that, "Language itself shapes a man's basic ideas." Whorf's controversial hypothesis that language shapes reality finds its strongest support when we compare the thoughts of bilingual people in the different languages they speak. To those who speak two dissimilar languages, it seems obvious that they think differently in each of their languages (Brown, 1986). For example, Japanese has many words for interpersonal emotions such as sympathy that have no counterpart in English (Markus & Kitayama, 1991). Many bilingual individuals even report that they have a different sense of self, depending on which language they use (Matsumoto, 1994).

Micheal Ross, Elaine Xun, and Anne Wilson (2002) tested these ideas by having University of Waterloo students who were born in China describe themselves in Chinese or English. When describing themselves in English, their self-descriptions were no different from Canadians born in Canada—they made more positive than negative self-statements, they showed more positive than negative mood, and they reported relatively high self-esteem. When they responded in Chinese, however, they made more collective self-statements, reported more agreement with Chinese cultural values, and reported roughly equal positive and negative self-statements and similar levels of positive and negative mood. This study provides compelling evidence that language can shape the way that people see themselves.

BILINGUALISM AND LANGUAGE EDUCATION

Canada has long been the leader in the study of bilingualism, and Canadian studies on bilingualism have provided a rationale for two official languages and extensive language education.

In the 1960s, Wallace Lambert from McGill University began to examine bilingualism as a way to address the disparities between French and English Canadians in Quebec (Lambert, 1992). Contrary to the popular notions of the time, he found that bilinguals outperformed monolinguals on intelligence tests and showed greater "mental flexibility" and a "more diversified structure of mental abilities" (Pearl & Lambert, 1962). Subsequent research in cultures from Africa to Switzerland and with languages from Chinese to Hebrew has generally supported this bilingual advantage (Balkan, 1970; Ben-Zeev, 1977; Ianco-Worrall, 1972; Torrence, Gowan, Wu & Alioti, 1970; Winsler, Diaz, Espinosa & Rodriguez, 1999).

Buoyed by this research, Lambert and his colleagues (Genesee, 1978, 1987; Lambert & Tucker, 1972; Swain, 1974) began a bold social experiment: a program of French immersion classes for the children of English Canadians. These programs begin schooling with all instruction exclusively in French through grade two, and then gradually specific subject matter is taught in English so that by grades five and six 50 percent of the instruction is in English and 50 percent is in French. The effects of these programs were dramatic. Immersion students develop functional bilingualism to a level that cannot be duplicated with other teaching strategies. They do so without any detriment to their language skills in English or to other content areas of the curriculum. Immersion students also develop a deeper appreciation for French Canadians and their culture. The experiment was a success: Language education could improve students' skills and help ease the tension between French and English Canadians.

The research also led to two important practical questions: Could adults learn a second language as easily as children? Would second language learning have the same benefits for linguistic minorities as it had for the English-language majority? The first question did not have as simple an answer. Based on research that suggests there is an early critical period for language development, many researchers reasoned that early training in a second language would be superior (Brown, 1973; Chomsky, 1959; Curtis, 1977). Others questioned these ideas, suggesting that there was no advantage to learning a language at a younger age (MacNamara, 1973; McLaughlin, 1977). As in most such disputes, additional evidence helped sort out the conflicting ideas. On the whole, younger children do seem to learn a language more easily than adults. For example, immigrants who arrive in a new country as children master the new language more completely than immigrants who arrive as teenagers or adults (Johnson & Newport, 1991; Johnson, Shenkman, Newport & Medin, 1996). In addition, immersion programs that begin in high school do not seem to have the same positive effects as early immersion programs (Marsh, Hau & Kong, 2000). It seems children have an advantage in learning a second language, particularly in developing its accent and grammar.

Learning a second language seems to have different implications for majority and minority linguistic groups in a culture. Lambert and Taylor (1984) make an important distinction between additive and subtractive bilingualism. When an English Canadian learns to speak French, there is little worry that this will lead to the eventual elimination of English as a language in Canada. For English Canadians, learning French is a form of additive bilingualism. The situation is very different for other groups. Consider the Inuit. For the Inuit, learning English or French raises the realistic possibility that their heritage language (Inuktitut) and even their culture may whither and die. Such second language learning is a form of subtractive bilingualism. Don Taylor, Stephen Wright, and their colleagues (Louis & Taylor, 2001; Wright

FOCUS ON

THE GRASSROOTS ORIGINS OF FRENCH IMMERSION INSTRUCTION IN CANADA

Although French immersion instruction has taken hold throughout much of Canada, it had a humble beginning in Quebec. In 1965 a group of English-speaking parents approached the school board in St. Lambert, Quebec and sought to have their students educated in French. They hoped that their children could learn French at school and speak English at home and in this way be bilingual. They saw such language skills as a major benefit when their children would enter the labour market in later life. At the time English-speaking children were educated in English and French-speaking children were educated in French, but the parents in St. Lambert were successful in lobbying the school board to have the children educated in French.

In a great example of what social psychologists call "Action Research" (in which the effects of theoretically meaningful variables are examined as they transported to the real world), Warren Lambert learned about these parents' efforts and sought to study the impact of French immersion on these students' learning. The grassroots efforts of these parents to offer their children a different and better education in this way formed the beginning of important studies on the impact of language education on children's success.

& Taylor, 1995; Wright, Taylor & Macarthur, 2000) have examined second language learning in the Inuit and have found clear evidence of subtractive bilingualism. Inuit children who are instructed exclusively in English or French have lower self-esteem, less pride in their culture, and lower Inuktitut proficiency. Early instruction in Inuktitut reversed these negative trends. It seems that training in one's heritage language can negate the detrimental effects of subtractive bilingualism.

SUMMING UP: HOW DO LANGUAGE AND CULTURE INFLUENCE ONE ANOTHER?

Language and culture both shape and influence one another. Language can even shape the way that people think about themselves. Bilingual education in Canada has provided a dramatic example of this influence. French language immersion by English Canadians has led to substantially increased learning of French and increased respect for French-Canadian culture. This type of language instruction seems to work best when it occurs among young children. In addition, second language learning seems to pose important problems for linguistic minorities. Subtractive bilingualism, in which bilingualism is gained at the expense of one's heritage language and respect for one's culture, is a clear danger for linguistic minorities.

CONCLUSIONS

Biology and culture do not exist in isolation, because culture works upon what is biologically given. How, then, do biology and culture interact? And how do our individual personalities interact with our situations?

BIOLOGY AND CULTURE

We needn't think of evolution and culture as competitors. Cultural norms subtly but powerfully affect our attitudes and behaviour, but they don't do so independent of biology. Everything social and psychological is ultimately biological. If others' expectations influence us, that is part of our biological programming. Moreover, what our biological heritage initiates, culture may accentuate. If genes and hormones predispose males to be more physically aggressive than females, culture may amplify this difference through norms that expect males to be tough and females to be the kinder, gentler sex.

Biology and culture may also **interact**. Today's genetic science indicates how experience uses genes to change the brain (Quartz & Sejnowski, 2002). Environmental stimuli can turn on genes that produce new brain cell branching receptors. Visual experience turns on genes that develop the brain's visual area. Parental touch turns on genes that help offspring cope with future stressful events. Genes don't just constrain us, they respond adaptively to our experiences.

interaction
the effect of one factor (such as biology) depends on another factor (such as environment)

THE POWER OF THE SITUATION AND THE PERSON

"There are trivial truths and great truths," declared the physicist Niels Bohr. "The opposite of a trivial truth is plainly false. The opposite of a great truth is also true." Each chapter in this unit on social influence teaches a great truth: *the power of the social situation*. This great truth about the power of external pressures would sufficiently explain our behaviour if we were passive, like tumbleweeds. But unlike tumbleweeds, we are not just blown here and there by the environment. We act; we react. We respond, and we get responses. We can resist the social situation and sometimes even change it. Thus each of these "social influence" chapters concludes by calling attention to the opposite of the great truth: *the power of the person*.

Perhaps stressing the power of culture leaves you somewhat uncomfortable. Most of us resent any suggestion that external forces determine our behaviour; we see ourselves as free beings, as the originators of our actions (well, at least of our good actions). We sense that believing in social determinism can lead to what philosopher Jean-Paul Sartre called "bad faith"—evading responsibility by blaming something or someone for one's fate.

Food for thought: If Bohr's statement is a great truth, what is its opposite?

Actually, social control (the power of the situation) and personal control (the power of the person) no more compete with one another than do biological and cultural explanations. Social and personal explanations of our social behaviour are both valid, for at any moment we are both the creatures and the creators of our social worlds. We may well be the products of our genes and environment. But it is also true that the future is coming, and it is our job to decide where it is going. Our choices today determine our environment tomorrow.

Social situations do profoundly influence individuals. But individuals also influence the social situation. The two *interact.* Asking whether external situations or inner dispositions (or culture or evolution) determine behaviour is like asking whether length or width determines the area of a field.

The interaction occurs in at least three ways (Snyder & Ickes, 1985):

- *A given social situation often affects different people differently.* Because our minds do not see reality identically, each of us responds to a situation as we construe it. And some people are more sensitive and responsive to social situations than others (Snyder, 1983). The Japanese, for example, are more responsive to social expectations than the British (Argyle et al., 1978).
- *People choose their situations* (Ickes et al., 1997). Given a choice, sociable people elect situations that evoke social interaction. When you chose your university, you were also choosing to expose yourself to a specific set of social influences. Ardent political liberals are unlikely to settle in rural Alberta and join the Chamber of Commerce. They are more likely to live in Toronto and join Greenpeace—in other words, to choose a social world that reinforces their inclinations.
- *People create their situations.* Recall again that our preconceptions can be self-fulfilling: If we expect someone to be extraverted, hostile, feminine, or sexy, our actions toward the person may induce the very behaviour we expect. What, after all, makes a social situation but the people in it? A liberal environment is created by liberals. What takes place in the sorority is created by the members. The social environment is not like the weather—something that just happens to us. It is more like our homes—something we make for ourselves.

"The words of truth are always paradoxical."

Lao-tzu, *The Simple Way*

SUMMING UP

Biological and cultural explanations need not be contradictory. Indeed, they interact. Biological factors operate within a cultural context, and culture builds on a biological foundation.

The great truth about the power of social influence is but half the truth if separated from its complementary truth: the power of the person. Persons and situations interact in at least three ways. First, individuals vary in how they interpret and react to a given situation. Second, people choose many of the situations that influence them. Third, people help create their social situations.

PART THREE

SOCIAL RELATIONS

Social psychology is the scientific study of how people think about, influence, and relate to one another. Having explored how we think about (Part One) and influence (Part Two) one another, we now consider social psychology's third facet—how we relate to one another. Our feelings and actions toward people are sometimes negative, sometimes positive. Chapters 9, "Altruism," and 10, "Aggression," examine why and when we help and hurt one another. Then in Chapters 11, "Attraction and Intimacy," and 12, "Prejudice," we explore why and when we love and hate one another.

CHAPTER NINE

Altruism: Helping Others

Why do we help?
Social exchange
Social norms
Evolutionary psychology
Comparing and evaluating theories of altruism

When will we help?
Number of bystanders
Helping when someone else does
Time pressures
Similarity

Who helps? Personality traits

How can we increase helping?
Reduce ambiguity, increase responsibility
Guilt and concern for self-image
Socializing altruism

Helping comes in many forms, most strikingly in heroic, caring acts. Hearing the rumble of an approaching subway train, Everett Sanderson leapt down onto the tracks and raced toward the approaching headlights to rescue Michelle De Jesus, a four-year-old who had fallen from the platform.

Three seconds before the train would have run her over, Sanderson flung Michelle into the crowd above. As the train roared in, he himself failed in his first effort to jump back to the platform. At the last instant, bystanders pulled him to safety (Young, 1977). On November 12, 1999, Rohan Wilson saw smoke and flames spewing out of an Edmonton, Alberta, apartment building. He quickly called 911 and then climbed up the outside of the building to a balcony where three children were stranded. He brought them down to safety and then climbed to another balcony and saved a pregnant woman. When asked if he was a hero, he said, "Someone needed help, I hope someone would do the same for me if I was in that position." On a hillside in Jerusalem, 800 trees form a simple line, the Avenue of the Righteous. Beneath each tree is a plaque with the name of a European Christian who gave refuge to one or more Jews during the Nazi Holocaust. These "righteous Gentiles" knew that if the refugees were discovered, Nazi policy dictated that both host and refugee would suffer a common fate. Many did (Hellman, 1980; Wiesel, 1985).

Less dramatic acts of comforting, caring, and helping abound: Without asking anything in return, people offer directions, donate money, give blood, volunteer time. Why, and when, will people perform altruistic acts? And what can be done to lessen indifference and increase altruism? These are this chapter's primary questions.

altruism
a motive to increase another's welfare without conscious regard for one's self-interests

Altruism is selfishness in reverse. An altruistic person is concerned and helpful even when no benefits are offered or expected in return. Jesus' parable of the Good Samaritan provides the classic illustration:

> A man was going down from Jerusalem to Jericho, and fell into the hands of robbers, who stripped him, beat him, and went away, leaving him half dead. Now by chance a priest was going down that road; and when he saw him, he passed by on the other side. So likewise a Levite, when he came to the place and saw him, passed by on the other side. But a Samaritan while traveling came near him; and when he saw him, he was moved with pity. He went to him and bandaged his wounds, having poured oil and wine on them. Then he put him on his own animal, brought him to an inn, and took care of him. The next day he took out two denarii, gave them to the innkeeper, and said, "Take care of him; and when I come back, I will repay you whatever more you spend." (Luke 10:30–35)

The Samaritan illustrates pure altruism. Filled with compassion, he gives a total stranger time, energy, and money while expecting neither repayment nor appreciation.

WHY DO WE HELP?

To study altruistic acts, social psychologists examine the conditions under which people perform such deeds. Before looking at what the experiments reveal, let's consider what motivates altruism. Three complementary theories offer some answers.

SOCIAL EXCHANGE

Several theories of helping agree that, in the long run, helping benefits the giver as well as the receiver. One explanation assumes that human interactions are guided by a "social economics." We exchange not only material goods and money but also *social* goods—love, services, information, status (Foa & Foa, 1975). In doing so, we use a "minimax" strategy—minimize costs, maximize rewards. **Social-exchange theory** does not contend that we consciously monitor costs and rewards, only that such considerations predict our behaviour.

social-exchange theory
the theory that human interactions are transactions that aim to maximize one's rewards and minimize one's costs

Suppose your campus is having a blood drive and someone asks you to participate. Might you not weigh the *costs* of donating (needle prick, time, fatigue) versus those of not donating (guilt, disapproval)? Might you not also weigh the *benefits* of donating (feeling good about helping someone, free refreshments) versus those of not donating (saving the time, discomfort, and anxiety)? According to social-exchange theory—and to studies of blood donors by Jane Allyn Piliavin, Dorcas Evans, and Peter Callero (1982)—such subtle calculations precede decisions to help or not. As if needing an excuse for their compassion people will donate more money to a charity when offered a product, such as candy or candles. Even when they don't want (and would never go buy) the product, it defines a social exchange (Holmes et al., 1997). We will examine social exchange by comparing helping as disguised self-interest and empathy as a genuine source of altruism.

Rewards

Rewards that motivate helping may be external or internal. When businesses donate money to improve their corporate images or when someone offers another a ride hoping to receive appreciation or friendship, the reward is external. We give to get. Thus we are most eager to help someone attractive to us, someone whose approval we desire (Krebs, 1970; Unger, 1979).

Rewards may also be internal. Helping also increases our sense of self-worth. Nearly all blood donors in Jane Piliavin's research agreed that giving blood "makes you feel good about yourself" and "gives you a feeling of self-satisfaction." This helps explain why people far from home will leave tips for waiters and do kindnesses for strangers whom they will never see again.

The positive effect of helping on feelings of self-worth is one explanation for why so many people feel good after doing good. One month-long study of 85 couples found that giving emotional support to one's partner was positive for the giver; giving support boosted the giver's mood (Gleason et al., 2003). Piliavin (2003) and Susan Anderson (1998) point to dozens of studies showing that youth engaged in community service projects, school-based "service learning," or tutoring children develop social skills and positive social values. They are at markedly less risk for committing criminal offences, becoming pregnant, or dropping out of school and are more likely to become engaged citizens. Volunteering likewise benefits the morale and even the health of adults. Those who do good tend to do well.

> *"Men do not value a good deed unless it brings a reward."*
>
> Ovid, *Epistulae ex Ponto*

This cost-benefit analysis can seem demeaning. In defence of the theory, however, is it not a credit to humanity that we can derive pleasure from helping others? That much of our behaviour is not antisocial but "prosocial"? That we can find fulfillment in the giving of love? How much worse if we gained pleasure only by serving ourselves.

STORY BEHIND THE RESEARCH

Dennis Krebs
Simon Fraser University

At age 14, I was traumatized when my family moved from Vancouver, B.C., to California. I fell from president of my junior high school to an object of social ridicule because of my clothes, accent, and behaviour. The skills I had acquired boxing soon generated a quite different reputation from the one I enjoyed in Canada. I sank lower and lower until, after several bouts with the law and several visits to juvenile detention homes, I was arrested for driving under the influence of drugs. I escaped from jail, hitchhiked to a logging camp in Oregon, and eventually made my way back to British Columbia. I was admitted to university on probation, graduated at the top of my class, won a Woodrow Wilson Fellowship, and was accepted at Harvard.

Concerned about my record in California, I turned myself in and suffered through the ensuing publicity. I was pardoned, in large part because of the tremendous support I received from many people. I attended Harvard, where, after three years, I was hired as an assistant professor. Eventually, I returned to British Columbia to chair the Psychology Department at Simon Fraser University. Though it makes me somewhat uncomfortable, I disclose this history as a way of encouraging people with two strikes against them to remain in the game. A great deal of the energy I have invested in understanding morality has stemmed from a need to understand why I went wrong, and my interest in altruism has been fuelled by the generosity of those who helped me overcome my past. I'm now working on a theory of self-deception.

"True," some readers may reply. "Still, doesn't social-exchange theory imply that a helpful act is never truly altruistic—that we merely *call* it 'altruistic' when its rewards are inconspicuous? If we help the screaming woman so we can gain social approval, relieve our distress, or boost our self-image, is it really altruistic?" This is reminiscent of B. F. Skinner's (1971) analysis of altruism. We credit people for their good deeds, said Skinner, only when we can't explain them. We attribute their behaviour to their inner dispositions only when we lack external explanations. When the external causes are obvious, we credit the causes, not the person.

There is, however, a weakness in social-exchange theory: It easily degenerates into explaining-by-naming. If someone volunteers for the Big Sister tutor program, it is tempting to "explain" her compassionate action by the satisfaction it brings her. But such after-the-fact naming of rewards creates a circular explanation: "Why did she volunteer?" "Because of the inner rewards." "How do you know there are inner rewards?" "Why else would she have volunteered?" Because of this flaw, **egoism**—the idea that self-interest motivates all behaviour—has fallen into disrepute among researchers. Egoism's ultimate goal is to increase one's own welfare; altruism's ultimate goal is to increase another's welfare.

egoism a motive (supposedly underlying all behaviour) to increase one's own welfare. The opposite of *altruism,* which aims to increase another's welfare.

To escape the circularity, we must define the rewards and costs independently of the helping behaviour. If social approval motivates helping, then in experiments we should find that when approval follows helping, helping increases. And it does (Staub, 1978).

Internal rewards

So far, we have considered external rewards for helping. We also need to consider internal factors, such as the helper's feelings and expectations.

The benefits of helping include internal self-rewards. Near someone in distress, we may feel distress. A woman's scream outside your window arouses and distresses you. If you cannot reduce your arousal by interpreting the scream as a playful shriek, then you may investigate or give aid, thereby reducing your distress (Piliavin & Piliavin, 1973). Altruism researcher Dennis Krebs (1975) found that university men whose physiological responses and self-reports revealed the most arousal in response to another's distress also gave the most help to the person.

Guilt

Distress is not the only negative emotion we act to reduce. Throughout recorded history, guilt has been a painful emotion, so painful that cultures have institutionalized ways to relieve it: animal and human sacrifices, offerings of grain and money, penitent behaviour, confession, denial. In ancient Israel, the sins of the people were periodically laid on a "scapegoat" animal that was then led into the wilderness to carry away the people's guilt.

To examine the consequences of guilt, social psychologists have induced people to transgress: to lie, to deliver shock, to knock over a table loaded with alphabetized cards, to break a machine, to cheat. Afterwards, the guilt-laden participants may be offered a way to relieve their guilt: by confessing, by disparaging the one harmed, or by doing a good deed to offset the bad one. The results are remarkably consistent: People will do whatever can be done to expunge the guilt and restore their self-image.

Picture yourself as a participant in one such experiment conducted with university students by David McMillen and James Austin (1971). You and another student, each seeking to earn credit toward a course requirement, arrive for the experiment. Soon after, a confederate enters, portraying himself as a previous subject looking for a lost book. He strikes up a conversation in which he mentions that the experiment involves taking a multiple-choice test, for which most of the correct answers are "B." After the accomplice departs, the experimenter arrives, explains the experiment, and then asks, "Have either of you been in this experiment before or heard anything about it?"

Would you lie? The behaviour of those who have gone before you in this experiment—100 percent of whom told the little lie—suggests that you would. After you have taken the test (without receiving any feedback on it), the experimenter says: "You are free to leave. However, if you have some spare time, I could use your help in scoring some questionnaires." Assuming you have told the lie, do you think you would now be more willing to volunteer some time? Judging from the results, the answer again is yes. On average, those who had not been induced to lie volunteered only two minutes of time. Those who had lied were apparently eager to redeem their self-image; on average they offered a whopping 63 minutes. One moral of this experiment was well expressed by a 7-year-old girl, who, in one of our own experiments, wrote: "Don't Lie or youl Live with gilt" (and you will feel a need to relieve it).

Our eagerness to do good after doing bad reflects both our need to reduce *private* guilt and restore our shaken self-image and our desire to reclaim a positive *public* image. We are more likely to redeem ourselves with helpful behaviour when other people know about our misdeeds (Carlsmith & Gross, 1969). But even when our guilt is private, we act to reduce it. Dennis

Regan and his associates (1972) demonstrated this in a shopping centre. They led women to think they had broken a camera. A few moments later a confederate, carrying a shopping bag with candy spilling out, crossed paths with each woman. Compared to women not put on the guilt trip—only 15 percent of whom bothered to alert the confederate to the spillage—nearly four times as many of the guilt-laden women did so. The guilt-laden women had no need to redeem themselves in the confederate's eyes. Their helpfulness offered relief from their private guilt feelings. It redeemed their self-image. Other ways of relieving guilt—as by confession—reduce guilt-induced helping (Carlsmith et al., 1968).

"Open confession is good for the soul."

Old Scottish proverb

All in all, guilt leads to much good. By motivating people to confess, apologize, help, and avoid repeated harm, it boosts sensitivity and sustains close relationships.

Among adults, the inner rewards of altruism—feeling good about oneself after donating blood or helping pick up someone's dropped materials—can offset other negative moods as well (Cialdini, Kenrick & Baumann, 1981; Williamson & Clark, 1989). Thus, when an adult is in a guilty, a sad, or an otherwise negative mood, a helpful deed (or any other mood improving experience) helps neutralize the bad feelings.

Exceptions to the feel bad–do good scenario

Among well-socialized adults, should we always expect to find the "feel bad–do good" phenomenon? One negative mood, anger, produces anything but compassion (as we will see in Chapter 10). Another exception is depression, which is characterized by brooding self-concern (Carlson & Miller, 1987; Wood et al., 1990). Yet another exception is profound grief. People who suffer the loss of a spouse or a child, whether through death or separation, often undergo a period of intense self-preoccupation, a state that makes it difficult to be giving (Aderman & Berkowitz, 1983; Gibbons & Wicklund, 1982).

In a powerfully involving laboratory simulation of self-focused grief, William Thompson, Claudia Cowan, and David Rosenhan (1980) had Stanford University students privately listen to a taped description of a person (whom they were to imagine was their best friend of the other sex) dying of cancer. The experiment focused some subjects' attention on their own worry and grief:

> He (she) could die and you would lose him, never be able to talk to him again. Or worse, he could die slowly. You would know every minute could be your last time together. For months you would have to be cheerful for him while you were sad. You would have to watch him die in pieces, until the last piece finally went, and you would be alone.

For others, it focused their attention on the friend:

> He spends his time lying in bed, waiting those interminable hours, just waiting and hoping for something to happen. Anything. He tells you that it's not knowing that is the hardest.

The researchers report that regardless of which tape the participants heard, they were profoundly moved and sobered by the experience, yet not the least regretful of participating

(although some participants who listened to a boring control condition tape were regretful). Did their mood affect their helpfulness? When immediately thereafter they were given a chance to anonymously help a graduate student with her research, 25 percent of those whose attention had been self-focused helped. Of those whose attention was other-focused, 83 percent helped. The two groups were equally touched. But only the other-focused participants found helping someone especially rewarding. In short, the feel bad–do good effect occurs with people whose attention is on others, people for whom altruism is therefore rewarding (Barnett et al., 1980; McMillen et al., 1977). If not self-preoccupied by depression or grief, sad people are sensitive, helpful people.

Feel good, do good

Are happy people unhelpful? Quite the contrary. There are few more consistent findings in the entire literature of psychology: Happy people are helpful people. This effect occurs with both children and adults, regardless of whether the good mood comes from a success, from thinking happy thoughts, or from any of several other positive experiences (Salovey et al., 1991). One woman recalled her experience after falling in love:

> At the office, I could hardly keep from shouting out how deliriously happy I felt. The work was easy; things that had annoyed me on previous occasions were taken in stride. And I had strong impulses to help others; I wanted to share my joy. When Mary's typewriter broke down, I virtually sprang to my feet to assist. Mary! My former "enemy"! (Tennov, 1979, p. 22)

In experiments the one helped may be someone seeking a donation, an experimenter seeking help with paperwork, or a woman who drops papers. For example, in Opole, Poland, Dariusz Dolinski and Richard Nawrat (1998) found that a positive mood of relief can dramatically boost helping. Imagine yourself as one of their unwitting subjects. After illegally parking your car for a few moments, you return to discover what looks like a ticket under your windshield wiper (where parking tickets are placed). Groaning inwardly, you pick up the apparent ticket, and then are much relieved to discover it is only an ad (or a blood drive appeal). Moments later, a university student approaches you and asks you to spend 15 minutes answering questions—to "help me complete my M.A. thesis." Would your positive, relieved mood make you more likely to help? Indeed, 62 percent of people whose fear had just turned to relief willingly agreed. This was nearly double the number who did so when no ticket-like paper was left or when it was left on the car door (a location not associated with a ticket).

"It's curious how, when you're in love, you yearn to go about doing acts of kindness to everybody."

P. G. Wodehouse, *The Mating Season*, 1949

In another experiment, Alice Isen, Margaret Clark, and Mark Schwartz (1976) had a confederate, who had supposedly spent her last dime on a wrong number, call people who had received a free sample of stationery 0 to 20 minutes earlier. As Figure 9–1 shows, their willingness to relay the phone message rose during the five minutes afterwards. Then, as the good mood wore off, helpfulness dropped.

If sad people are sometimes extra helpful, how can it be that happy people are also helpful? Experiments reveal that several factors are at work (Carlson et al., 1988; Schaller & Cialdini, 1990). Helping softens a bad mood and sustains a good mood. A positive mood is, in turn, conducive to positive thoughts and positive self-esteem, which predispose us to positive behaviour

FIGURE 9–1

Percentage of those willing to relay a phone message 0 to 20 minutes after receiving a free sample.

Of control subjects who did not receive a gift, only 10 percent helped. (Data from Isen et al., 1976)

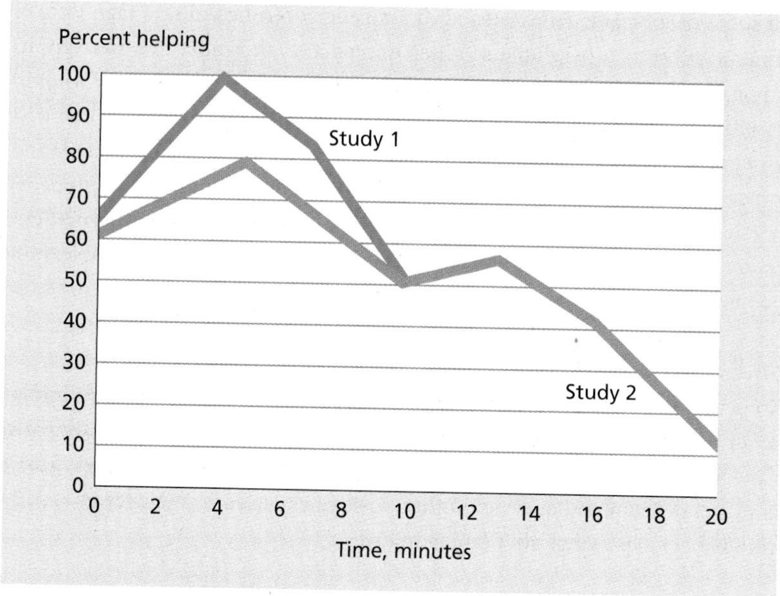

(Berkowitz, 1987; Cunningham et al., 1990; Isen et al., 1978). In a good mood—after being given a gift or while feeling the warm glow of success—people are more likely to have positive thoughts and to have positive associations with being helpful. Positive thinkers are likely to be positive actors.

SOCIAL NORMS

Often we help others not because we have consciously calculated that such behaviour is in our self-interest but simply because something tells us we *ought* to. We ought to help a new neighbour move in. We ought to turn off a parked car's lights. We ought to return the wallet we found. We ought to protect our combat buddies from harm. Norms (as you may recall from Chapter 5) are social expectations. They *prescribe* proper behaviour, the *oughts* of our lives. Researchers studying helping behaviour have identified two social norms that motivate altruism: the reciprocity norm and the social-responsibility norm.

"There is no duty more indispensable than that of returning a kindness."

Cicero

The reciprocity norm

Sociologist Alvin Gouldner (1960) contended that one universal moral code is a **norm of reciprocity**: *To those who help us, we should return help, not harm.* Gouldner believed this norm is as universal as the incest taboo. We "invest" in others and expect dividends. Mail surveys and solicitations sometimes include a little gift of money or individualized address labels, assuming some people will reciprocate the favour. Politicians know that the one who gives a favour can later expect a favour in return. The reciprocity norm even applies with marriage. Sometimes one may give more than one receives. But in the long run, the exchange should balance out. In all such interactions, to receive without giving in return violates the reciprocity norm.

reciprocity norm an expectation that people will help, not hurt, those who have helped them

FOCUS ON

MONEY, HAPPINESS, AND HELPING

Imagine that you won a million dollars in the lottery. How would you spend it? Do you think that spending the money would make you happy? If you are like most people you probably thought about buying some nice things for yourself with the money. Recent research by University of British Columbia researcher Elizabeth Dunn and her colleagues (Dunn, Aknin & Norton, 2008), however, suggests one of the common ways that we mispredict our future emotional reactions is that we think that spending money on ourselves will make us happy, when it usually does not. In contrast, we think that spending money on other people will bring us little joy when in fact spending money on others usually makes us quite happy.

To test the impact of spending money on oneself versus others, Dunn and her colleagues gave students an envelope with a fresh new bill (either a 5 or a 20) and told them either to spend the money on a gift for themselves or spend the money on a gift for someone else or a charitable donation. Later that evening they called the students and asked them how happy they were. Students who spent the money on themselves (regardless of the amount they spent) were less happy than those who spent money on others. These experimental findings mirror what is seen in correlational data as well. When people make more money on average this only has a small effect on their happiness, but if they spend money on others—regardless of how much they make—they tend to be a lot happier.

This line of research is a dramatic example of how the internal rewards for helping others can have a larger impact on happiness than even a powerful external reward like money.

Reciprocity within social networks helps define the "social capital"—the supportive connections, information flow, trust, and cooperative actions—that keep a community healthy. Keeping an eye on each other's homes is social capital in action.

The norm operates most effectively as people respond publicly to deeds earlier done to them. In laboratory games as in everyday life, fleeting one-shot encounters produce greater selfishness than sustained relationships. But even when people respond anonymously, they sometimes do the right thing and repay the good done to them. In one experiment, Mark Whatley and his colleagues (1999) found that more university students willingly made a pledge to the charity of someone who had previously bought them some candy (Figure 9–2).

When people cannot reciprocate, they may feel threatened and demeaned by accepting aid. Thus, proud, high self-esteem people are often reluctant to seek help (Nadler & Fisher, 1986). Receiving unsolicited help can take one's self-esteem down a notch (Schneider et al., 1996; Shell & Eisenberg, 1992). Studies show this can happen to beneficiaries of affirmative action, especially when affirmative action fails to affirm the person's competence and chances for future success (Pratkanis & Turner, 1996).

"A language's syntax and vocabulary are not determined by our biological nature (otherwise, there could not be a multitude of tongues), but are products of human culture. Likewise, moral norms are not determined by biological processes, but by cultural traditions and principles that are products of human history."

Francisco Ayala, *The Difference of Being Human*, 1995

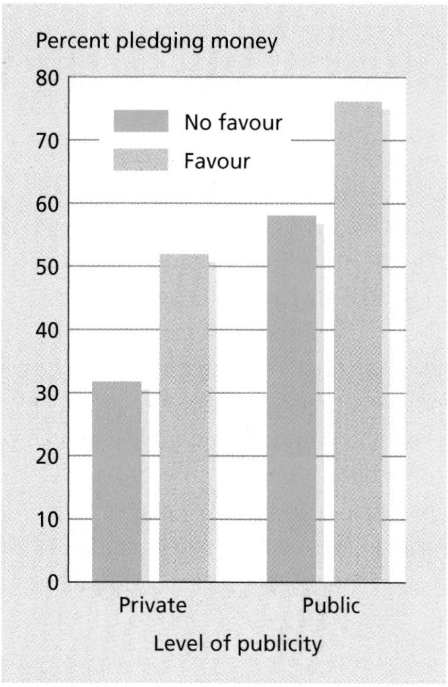

FIGURE 9–2

Private and public reciprocation of a favour.

People were more willing to pledge to an experimental confederate's charity if the confederate had done a small favour for them earlier, especially when their reciprocation was made known to the confederate. (Whatley et al., 1999)

The social-responsibility norm

The reciprocity norm reminds us to balance giving and receiving in social relations. If the only norm was reciprocity, however, the Samaritan would not have been the Good Samaritan. In the parable, Jesus obviously had something more humanitarian in mind, something explicit in another of his teachings: "If you love those who love you [the reciprocity norm], what right have you to claim any credit? . . . I say to you, Love your enemies" (Matthew 5:46, 44).

With people who clearly are dependent and unable to reciprocate—children, the severely impoverished and disabled, and others perceived as unable to return as much as they receive—another social norm motivates our helping. The belief that people should help those who need help, without regard to future exchanges, is the **norm of social responsibility** (Berkowitz, 1972b; Schwartz, 1975). The norm motivates people to retrieve a dropped book for a person on crutches. In India, a relatively collectivist culture, people support the social-responsibility norm more strongly than in the individualist West (Miller et al., 1990). They voice an obligation to help even when the need is not life-threatening or the needy person is outside their family circle.

Experiments show that even when helpers remain anonymous and have no expectation of any reward, they often help needy people (Harrel, 1994; Shotland & Stebbins, 1983). However, they usually apply the social-responsibility norm selectively to those whose need appears not to be due to their own negligence. Especially among political conservatives (Skitka & Tetlock, 1993), the norm seems to be: Give people what they deserve. If they are victims of circumstance, like natural disaster, then by all means be generous. If they seem to have created their own problems, by laziness, immorality, or lack of foresight, then they should get what they deserve. Responses are thus closely tied to *attributions*. If we attribute the need to an uncontrollable predicament, we help. If we attribute the need to the person's choices, fairness does not require us to help; we say it's the person's own fault (Weiner, 1980).

The key, say Udo Rudolph and colleagues (2004) from their review of more than three dozen pertinent studies, is whether your attributions evoke sympathy, which in turn motivates helping.

Imagine yourself as one of the students in a study by Richard Barnes, William Ickes, and Robert Kidd (1979). You receive a call from a "Tony Freeman" who explains that he is in your introductory psychology class. He says that he needs help for the upcoming exam and that he has gotten your name from the class roster. "I don't know. I just don't seem to take good notes in there," Tony explains. "I know I can, but sometimes I just don't feel like it, so most of the notes I have aren't very good to study with." How sympathetic would you feel toward Tony? How much of a sacrifice would you make to lend him your notes? If you are like the students in this experiment, you would probably be much less inclined to help than if Tony had just explained that his troubles were beyond his control. Thus, the social-responsibility norm compels us to help those most in need and those most deserving.

social-responsibility norm
an expectation that people will help those dependent upon them

EVOLUTIONARY PSYCHOLOGY

The third explanation of altruism comes from evolutionary theory. As you may recall from Chapter 8, evolutionary psychology contends that the essence of life is gene survival. Our genes drive us in ways that have maximized their chance of survival. When our ancestors died, their genes lived on, predisposing us to behave in ways that will spread them into the future.

As suggested by the title of Richard Dawkins' (1976) popular book *The Selfish Gene,* evolutionary psychology offers a humbling human image—one that psychologist Donald Campbell (1975a, 1975b) called a biological reaffirmation of a deep, self-serving "original sin." Genes that predispose individuals to selflessly promote strangers' welfare would not survive in the evolutionary competition. Genetic selfishness should, however, predispose us toward two specific types of selfless or even self-sacrificial altruism: kin protection and reciprocity.

> *"Fallen heroes do not have children. If self-sacrifice results in fewer descendants, the genes that allow heroes to be created can be expected to disappear gradually from the population."*
>
> E. O. Wilson, *On Human Nature,* 1978

Kin protection

Our genes dispose us to care for relatives in whom they reside. Thus one form of self-sacrifice that *would* increase gene survival is devotion to one's children. Parents who put their children's welfare ahead of their own are more likely to pass their genes on than parents who neglect their children. As evolutionary psychologist David Barash (1979, p. 153) has said, "Genes help themselves by being nice to themselves, even if they are enclosed in different bodies." Although evolution favours altruism toward one's children, children have less at stake in the survival of their parents' genes. Thus, parents are generally more devoted to their children than their children are to them.

Other relatives share genes in proportion to their biological closeness. You share one-half of your genes with your brothers and sisters, one-eighth with your cousins. **Kin selection**—favouritism toward those who share our genes—led the evolutionary biologist J. B. S. Haldane to jest that while he would not give up his life for his brother, he would sacrifice himself for *three* brothers—or for nine cousins. Haldane would not have been surprised that, compared to fraternal twins, genetically identical twins are noticeably more mutually supportive (Segal, 1984). In one laboratory game experiment, identical twins were half again as likely to cooperate with their twin for a shared gain when playing for money (Segal & Hershberger, 1999).

> **kin selection** the idea that evolution has selected altruism toward one's close relatives to enhance the survival of mutually shared genes

The point is not that we calculate genetic relatedness before helping but that nature programs us to care about close relatives. The Carnegie medal for heroism is seldom awarded for saving an immediate family member. When Carlos Rogers of the Toronto Raptors NBA basketball team volunteered to end his career and donate a kidney to his sister (who died before she received it), people applauded his self-sacrificial love. But such acts for close kin are not totally unexpected. What we do not expect (and therefore honour) is the altruism of those who, like our subway hero Everett Sanderson, risk themselves to save a stranger.

We share common genes with many besides our relatives. Blue-eyed people share particular genes with other blue-eyed people, for example. How do we detect the people in which copies of our genes occur most abundantly? As the blue-eyes example suggests, one clue lies in physical similarities (Rushton et al., 1984). Also, in evolutionary history genes were shared more with neighbours than with foreigners. Are we therefore biologically biased to act more altruistically toward those similar to us and those who live near us? In the aftermath of natural disasters and other life-and-death situations, the order of who gets helped would not surprise an evolutionary psychologist: the young before the old, family members before friends, neighbours before strangers (Burnstein et al., 1994; Form & Nosow, 1958). Helping stays close to home.

Some evolutionary psychologists say we can also expect ethnic ingroup favouritism—the root of countless historical and contemporary conflicts (Rushton, 1991). E. O. Wilson (1978) noted that kin selection is "the enemy of civilization. If human beings are to a large extent guided . . . to favour their own relatives and tribe, only a limited amount of global harmony is possible" (p. 167).

"Morality governs our actions toward others in much the same way that gravity governs the motions of the planets: its strength is in inverse proportion to the square of the distance between them."

James Q. Wilson, *"The Universal Aspiration,"* 1993

Reciprocity

Genetic self-interest also predicts reciprocity. An organism helps another, biologist Robert Trivers argues, because it expects help in return (Binham, 1980). The giver expects later to be the getter, whereas failure to reciprocate is punished: The cheat, the turncoat, and the traitor are universally despised.

Reciprocity works best in small, isolated groups, groups in which one will often see the people for whom one does favours. If a vampire bat has gone a day or two without food—it can't go much more than 60 hours without starving to death—it asks a well-fed nestmate to regurgitate food for a meal (Wilkinson, 1990). The donor bat does so willingly, losing fewer hours till starvation than the recipient gains. But such favours occur only among familiar nestmates who share in the give and take. Those who always take and never give, and those who have no relationship with the donor bat, go hungry. It pays to have friends.

For similar reasons, reciprocity is stronger in the remote Cook Islands of the South Pacific than in New York City (Barash, 1979, p. 160). Small schools, towns, churches, work teams, and dorms are all conducive to a community spirit in which people care for each other. Compared to people in small-town or rural environments, those in big cities are less willing to relay a phone message, less likely to mail "lost" letters, less cooperative with survey interviewers, less helpful to a lost child, and less willing to do small favours (Hedge & Yousif, 1992; Steblay, 1987).

If individual self-interest inevitably wins in genetic competition, then why does nonreciprocal altruism toward strangers occur? What caused Mother Teresa to act as she did? What causes soldiers to throw themselves on grenades? One answer, initially favoured by Darwin (then discounted by selfish gene theorists but now back again) is group selection: Groups of altruists survive better than groups of nonaltruists (Krebs, 1998; Sober & Wilson, 1998). This is most dramatically evident with the social insects, who function like cells in a body. Bees and ants will labour sacrificially for their colony's survival. To a much lesser extent, humans exhibit ingroup loyalty, by sacrificing to support "us" sometimes against "them."

Donald Campbell's (1975) answer is that human societies evolved ethical and religious rules that serve as brakes on the biological bias toward self-interest. Commandments such as "Love your neighbour" admonish us to balance self-concern with concern for the group, and so contribute to the survival of the group. Richard Dawkins (1976) offered a similar conclusion: "Let us try to *teach* generosity and altruism, because we are born selfish. Let us understand what our selfish genes are up to, because we may then at least have the chance to upset their designs, something no other species has ever aspired to" (p. 3).

COMPARING AND EVALUATING THEORIES OF ALTRUISM

By now you have perhaps noticed similarities among the social-exchange, social norm, and evolutionary views of altruism. As Table 9–1 shows, each proposes two types of prosocial behaviour: a tit-for-tat reciprocal exchange and a more unconditional helpfulness. They do so at three complementary levels of explanation. If the evolutionary view is correct, then our genetic predispositions *should* manifest themselves in psychological and sociological phenomena.

Each theory appeals to logic. Yet each is vulnerable to charges of being speculative and after the fact. When we start with a known effect (the give and take of everyday life) and explain it by conjecturing a social-exchange process, a "reciprocity norm," or an evolutionary origin, we might be merely explaining-by-naming. The argument that a behaviour occurs because of its survival function is hard to disprove. With hindsight, it's easy to think it had to be that way. If we can explain any conceivable behaviour after the fact as the result of a social exchange, a norm, or natural selection, then we cannot disprove the theories. Each theory's task is therefore to generate predictions that enable us to test it.

TABLE 9–1 Comparing theories of altruism

		How Is Altruism Explained?	
Theory	**Level of Explanation**	**Mutual "Altruism"**	**Intrinsic Altruism**
social norms	sociological	reciprocity norm	social-responsibility norm
social exchange	psychological	external rewards for helping	distress → inner rewards for helping
evolutionary	biological	reciprocity	kin selection

STORY BEHIND THE RESEARCH

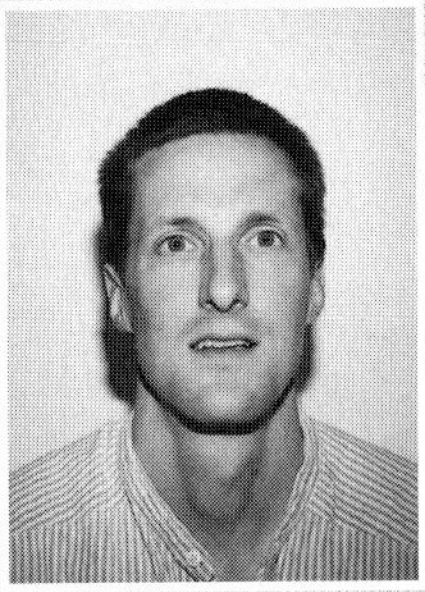

Mark Schaller
University of British Columbia

The reasons why people do things aren't always what they seem. For instance, the things I'll tell you shortly may imply that my motive for going to graduate school was to study interesting questions about helping behaviour. It's more likely, though, that I went to graduate school because I didn't fancy having to find a job in the real world. Before going to graduate school, I heard about research suggesting that the emotional experience of empathy leads to a truly altruistic motive to help others. I didn't buy it. Neither did Bob Cialdini, and so I chose to go work with him.

We conducted several studies supporting the hypothesis that the alleged altruistic motive to help is actually a mood-management motive in disguise. So even when people feel empathic toward someone else, they may help that person for selfish, not selfless, motives. Of course, these motives may not account fully for the effects of empathy on helping behaviour. Recently I've been thinking that some of the effects on helping may be so automated that they may not be driven by motives and goals at all, even though they appear to be. After all, the reasons why people do things aren't always what they seem.

An effective theory also provides a coherent scheme for summarizing a variety of observations. On this criterion, the three altruism theories get higher marks. Each offers us a broad perspective from which we can understand both enduring commitments and spontaneous help.

Genuine altruism

Are life-saving heroes, everyday blood donors, and relief workers *ever* motivated by an ultimate goal of selfless concern for another? Or is their ultimate goal always some form of self-benefit, such as relief from distress or avoidance of guilt?

Philosophers have debated this question for centuries. Consider the case of Rohan Wilson that was described at the beginning of the chapter. He risked his life to save three young children and a pregnant woman. But do we really know that this was a selfless act of concern? Perhaps he only helped because he would not have been able to live with himself if he did not. Or maybe he helped because he expected the praise and accolades he received. The skeptic can always see a hidden motive of self-interest in even the most heroic acts. We can all be skeptical of some acts of helping. Take as an example corporate donations to charity. John Cleghorn (2000), the chairman and CEO of Royal Bank noted that in 1999 his bank gave over $25 million to charity. Yet even he had to admit that, "In some cases the line between marketing and philanthropic activities has become increasingly blurred." So do people help so they just won't feel bad, and do companies give to charities only to increase their bottom lines? Until recently, psychologists have generally argued that self-interest is behind most instances of helping.

Psychologist Daniel Batson (2001), however, theorizes that our willingness to help is influenced by both self-serving *and* selfless considerations (Figure 9–3). Distress over someone's

"Are you all right, Mister? Is there anything I can do?"
"Young man, you're the only one who bothered to stop! I'm a millionaire and I'm going to give you five thousand dollars!"

We never know what benefits may come from helping someone in distress.

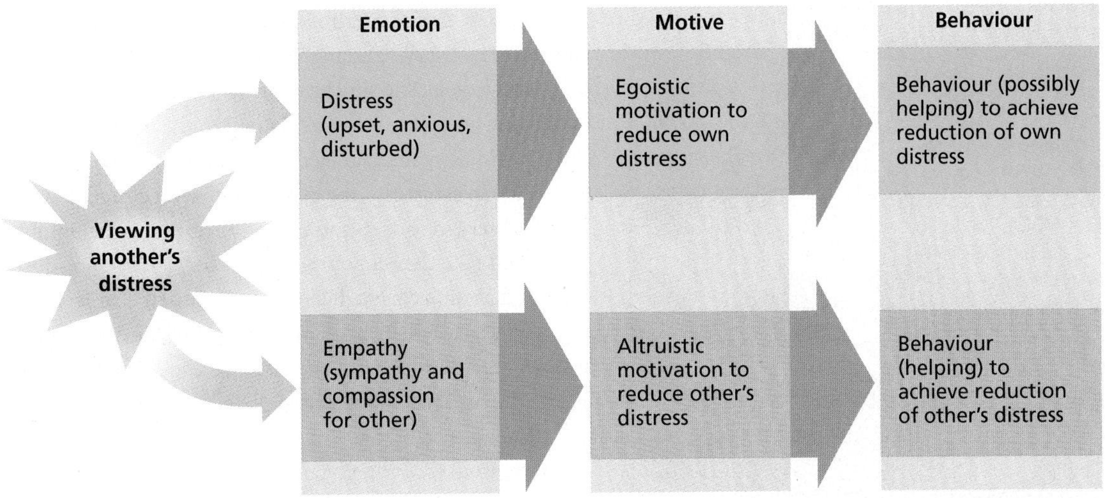

FIGURE 9–3

Egoistic and altruistic routes to helping.

Viewing another's distress can evoke a mixture of self-focused distress and other-focused empathy. Researchers agree that distress triggers egoistic motives. But they debate whether empathy can trigger a pure altruistic motive. (Adapted from Batson, Fultz & Schoenrade, 1987)

suffering motivates us to relieve our upset, either by escaping the distressing situation (like the priest and Levite) or by helping (like the Samaritan). But especially when we feel attached to someone, report Batson and his colleagues, we also feel **empathy**. Loving parents suffer when their children suffer and rejoice over their children's joys—an empathy lacking in child abusers and other perpetrators of cruelty (Miller & Eisenberg, 1988). We also feel empathy for those we identify with. In September 1997, millions of people who never came within 80 kilometres of Princess Diana (but who felt like they knew her after hundreds of tabloid stories and 44 *People* magazine cover articles) wept for her and her motherless sons (after shedding no tears for the nearly 1 million faceless Rwandans murdered or dead in squalid refugee camps since 1994).

When feeling empathy we focus not so much on our own distress as on the sufferer. Genuine sympathy and compassion motivate us to help the person for his or her own sake. Such empathy comes naturally. Even day-old infants cry more when they hear another infant cry (Hoffman, 1981). In hospital nurseries, one baby's crying sometimes evokes a chorus of crying. We come, it seems, hard-wired for empathy.

Often distress and empathy together motivate responses to a crisis (Gordon & Mentzel, 1990). In 1983, people watched on television as an Australian bushfire wiped out hundreds of homes near Melbourne. Afterwards, Paul Amato (1986) studied donations of money and goods. He found that those who felt angry or indifferent gave less than those who felt either distressed (shocked and sickened) or empathic (sympathetic and worried for the victims). Children's generosity, too, varies with their capacity for distress and empathy. George Knight and his Arizona State University co-researchers (1994) found that some 6- to 9-year-olds more than others reported feeling sorry when others were sad or being picked on. After watching a video of a burned girl, these sympathetic children were also the most generous when given a chance to contribute some of their research earnings to a children's burn unit.

empathy the vicarious experience of another's feeling; putting oneself in another's shoes

To separate egoistic distress reduction from altruistic empathy, Batson's research group conducted studies that aroused feelings of empathy. Then the researchers noted whether the aroused people would reduce their own distress by escaping the situation or whether they would go out of their way to aid the person. The results were consistent: Their empathy aroused, they usually helped.

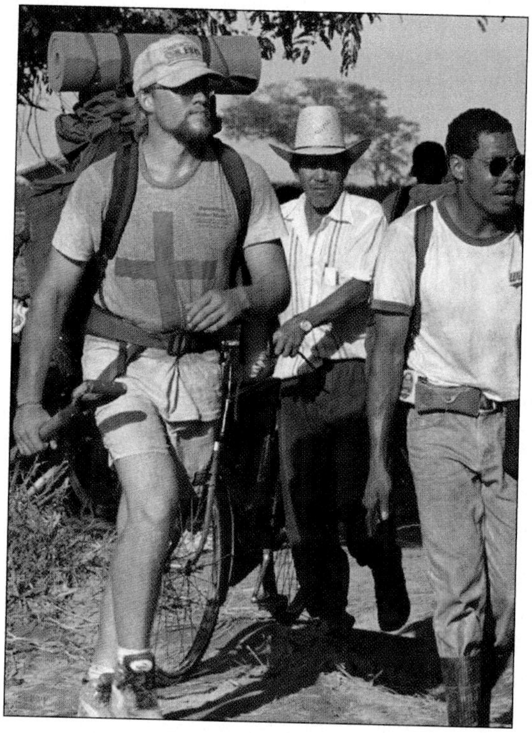

Might genuine empathy motivate a humanitarian aid worker to travel from British Columbia to Honduras to help in a medical clinic? Daniel Batson believes yes.

In one of these experiments, Batson and his associates (1981) had women observe a young woman suffering while she supposedly received electric shocks. During a pause in the experiment, the obviously upset victim explained to the experimenter that a childhood fall against an electric fence left her acutely sensitive to shocks. In sympathy, the experimenter suggested that perhaps the observer (the actual subject in this experiment) might trade places and take the remaining shocks for her. Previously, half of these actual subjects had been led to believe the suffering person was a kindred spirit on matters of values and interests (thus arousing their empathy). Some also were led to believe that their part in the experiment was completed, so that in any case they were done observing the woman's suffering. Nevertheless, their empathy aroused, virtually all these student observers willingly offered to substitute for the victim.

Is this pure altruism? Mark Schaller and Robert Cialdini (1988) doubted it. Feeling empathy for a sufferer makes one sad, they noted. In one of their experiments they led people to believe that their sadness was going to be relieved by a different sort of mood-boosting experience—listening to a comedy tape. Under such conditions, people who felt empathy were not especially helpful. Schaller and Cialdini concluded that if we feel empathy but know that something else will make us feel better, we aren't so likely to help. Also, remembering that our self-identity is collective as well as personal, Cialdini and his colleagues (1997) found that we are good to others when we are so bonded with them that we see something of ourselves in them.

Other findings suggest that genuine altruism may exist:

"How selfish soever man may be supposed, there are evidently some principles in his nature, which interest him in the fortune of others, and render their happiness necessary to him, though he derives nothing from it except the pleasure of seeing it."

Adam Smith, *The Theory of Moral Sentiments*, 1759

- Empathy produces helping even toward members of rival groups (Batson et al., 1997), but only when people believe the other will receive the needed help (Dovidio et al., 1990).
- With their empathy aroused, people will help even when they believe no one will know about their helping. Their concern continues until someone *has* helped (Fultz et al., 1986). If their efforts to help are unsuccessful, they feel bad even if the failure is not their fault (Batson & Weeks, 1996).
- People will sometimes persist in wanting to help a suffering person even when they believe their distressed mood has been temporarily frozen by a "mood-fixing" drug (Schroeder et al., 1988).

So everyone agrees that some helpful acts are either obviously egoistic (done to gain rewards or avoid punishment) or subtly egoistic (done to relieve inner distress). Is there a third type of helpfulness—an altruism that aims simply to increase another's welfare (producing happiness for oneself merely as a by-product)? Is empathy-based helping a source of such altruism? Cialdini (1991) and his colleagues Mark Schaller and Jim Fultz still doubt it. They note that no experiment rules out all possible egoistic explanations for helpfulness.

However, after some 25 experiments testing egoism versus empathy, Batson (2001) and others (Dovidio, 1991; Staub, 1991) believe that sometimes people *do* focus on others' welfare, not on their own. Batson, a former philosophy and theology student, had begun his research feeling "excited to think that if we could ascertain whether people's concerned reactions were genuine, and not simply a subtle form of selfishness, then we could shed new light on a basic issue regarding human nature" (1999a). Two decades later he believes he has his answer. Genuine "empathy-induced altruism is part of human nature" (1999b). And that, says Batson, raises the hope—confirmed by research—that inducing empathy might improve attitudes toward stigmatized people—people with AIDS, the homeless, the imprisoned, and other minorities.

SUMMING UP: WHY DO WE HELP?

Three theories explain altruistic behaviour. The *social-exchange theory* assumes that helping, like other social behaviours, is motivated by a desire to maximize rewards, which may be external or internal. Thus after wrongdoing, people often become more willing to offer help. Sad people also tend to be helpful. Finally there is a striking feel good–do good effect: Happy people are helpful people.

Social norms also mandate helping. The reciprocity norm stimulates us to return help, not harm, to those who have helped us. The social-responsibility norm beckons us to help needy people, even if they cannot reciprocate, as long as they are deserving.

Evolutionary psychology assumes two types of altruism: devotion to kin and reciprocity. Most evolutionary psychologists, however, believe that the genes of selfish individuals are more likely to survive than the genes of self-sacrificing individuals and that society must therefore teach altruism.

WHEN WILL WE HELP?

What circumstances prompt people to help, or not to help? How and why is helping influenced by the number and behaviour of other bystanders?

On March 13, 1964, bar manager Kitty Genovese is set upon by a knife-wielding rapist as she returns to her apartment house at 3:00 A.M. Her screams of terror and pleas for help—"Oh my God, he stabbed me! Please help me! Please help me!"—arouse 38 of her neighbours. Many come to their windows and see her plight while she struggles for 35 minutes to escape her attacker. Not until her attacker departs does anyone so much as call the police. Soon after, she dies.

Why had Genovese's neighbours not come to her aid? Were they callous? Indifferent? Apathetic? If so, there are many such people. Consider:

- Andrew Mormille is knifed in the stomach as he rides the subway home. After his attackers leave the car, 11 other riders watch the young man bleed to death.
- An 18-year-old switchboard operator, working alone, is sexually assaulted. She momentarily escapes and runs naked and bleeding to the street and screams for help. Forty pedestrians watch as the rapist tries to drag her back inside. Fortunately, two police officers happen by and arrest the assailant.

- Eleanor Bradley trips and breaks her leg while shopping. Dazed and in pain, she pleads for help. For 40 minutes the stream of shoppers simply parts and flows around her. Finally, a cab driver helps her to a doctor (Darley & Latané, 1968).

What is shocking is not that in these cases some people failed to help but that in each of these groups (of 38, 11, 40, and 100s) almost 100 percent of those involved failed to respond. Why? In the same or similar situations, would we react as they did?

Social psychologists were curious and concerned about bystanders' lack of involvement during such events as the Kitty Genovese rape-murder. So they undertook experiments to identify when people will help in an emergency.

NUMBER OF BYSTANDERS

Bystander passivity during emergencies has prompted social commentators to lament people's "alienation," "apathy," "indifference," and "unconscious sadistic impulses." By attributing the nonintervention to the bystanders' dispositions, we can reassure ourselves that as caring people, we *would* have helped. But were the bystanders such inhuman characters?

Social psychologists Bibb Latané and John Darley (1970) were unconvinced. So they staged ingenious emergencies and found that a single situational factor—the presence of other bystanders—greatly decreased intervention. By 1980 some four dozen experiments had compared help given by bystanders who perceived themselves to be either alone or with others. In about 90 percent of these comparisons, involving nearly 6000 people, lone bystanders were more likely to help (Latané & Nida, 1981).

Sometimes, the victim was actually less likely to get help when many people were around. When Latané, James Dabbs (1975), and 145 collaborators "accidentally" dropped coins or pencils during 1497 elevator rides, they were helped 40 percent of the time when one other person was on the elevator and less than 20 percent of the time when there were six passengers.

Why? Latané and Darley surmised that as the number of bystanders increases, any given bystander is less likely to *notice* the incident, less likely to *interpret* the incident as a problem or emergency, and less likely to *assume responsibility* for taking action (Figure 9–4).

FIGURE 9–4

Latané and Darley's decision tree.

Only one path up the tree leads to helping. At each fork of the path, the presence of other bystanders may divert a person down a branch toward not helping. (Adapted from Darley & Latané, 1968)

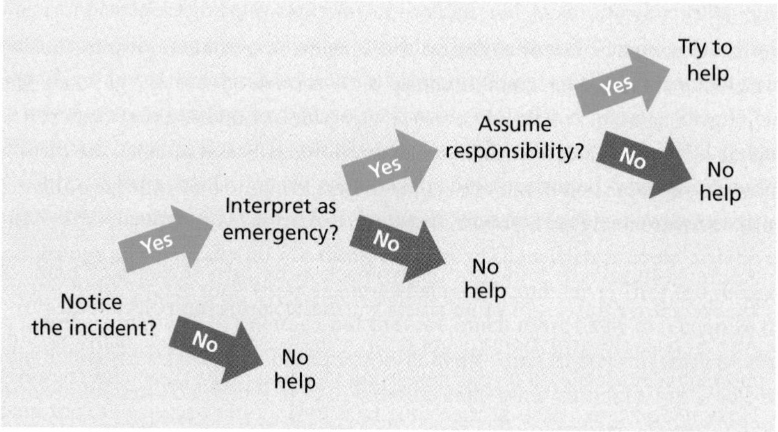

Noticing

Twenty minutes after Eleanor Bradley has fallen and broken her leg on a crowded city sidewalk, you come along. Your eyes are on the backs of the pedestrians in front of you (it is bad manners to stare at those you pass) and your private thoughts are on the day's events. Would you therefore be less likely to notice the injured woman than if the sidewalk were virtually deserted?

To find out, Latané and Darley (1968) had men fill out a questionnaire in a room, either by themselves or with two strangers. While they were working (and being observed through a one-way mirror), there was a staged emergency: Smoke poured into the room through a wall vent. Solitary students, who often glanced idly about the room while working, noticed the smoke almost immediately—usually in less than five seconds. Those in groups kept their eyes on their work. It typically took them about 20 seconds to *notice* the smoke.

Interpreting

Once we notice an ambiguous event, we must interpret it. Put yourself in the room filling with smoke. Though worried, you don't want to embarrass yourself by getting flustered. You glance at the others. They look calm, indifferent. Assuming everything must be okay, you shrug it off and go back to work. Then one of the others notices the smoke and, noting your apparent unconcern, reacts similarly. This is yet another example of informational influence (Chapter 6). Each person uses others' behaviour as clues to reality.

The misinterpretations are fed by what Thomas Gilovich, Kenneth Savitsky, and Victoria Husted Medvec (1997) call an *illusion of transparency*—a tendency to overestimate others' ability to "read" our internal states. More than we usually suppose, our disgust, our deceit, and our alarm is opaque. Keenly aware of our emotions, we presume they leak out and that others see right through us. Sometimes others do. But often we keep our cool quite effectively. The result is what Chapter 7 called "pluralistic ignorance"—ignorance that others are thinking and feeling what we are. Thus, in emergencies, each person may think "I'm very concerned," but perceive others as looking not alarmed—"so maybe it's not an emergency."

So it happened in the actual experiment. When those working alone noticed the smoke, they usually hesitated a moment, then got up, walked over to the vent, felt, sniffed, and waved at the smoke, hesitated again, and then went to report it. In dramatic contrast, those in groups of three did not move. Among the 24 men in eight groups, only one person reported the smoke within the first four minutes (Figure 9–5). By the end of the six-minute experiment, the smoke was so thick it was obscuring the men's vision and they were rubbing their eyes and coughing. Still, in only three of the eight groups did even a single person leave to report the problem.

Equally interesting, the group's passivity affected its members' interpretations. What caused the smoke? "A leak in the air conditioning," "Chemistry labs in the building," "Steam pipes," "Truth gas." They offered many explanations. Not one said, "Fire." The group members, in serving as nonresponsive models, influenced each other's interpretation.

That experimental dilemma parallels dilemmas each of us faces. Are the shrieks outside merely playful antics or the desperate screams of someone being assaulted? Is the boys' scuffling a friendly tussle or a vicious fight? Is the person slumped in the doorway sleeping, high on drugs, or seriously ill, perhaps in a diabetic coma? That surely was the question confronting those who passed by Sidney Brookins (Goleman, 1993; AP, 1993). Brookins, who had suffered a concussion when beaten, died after lying near the door to his apartment house for two days.

FIGURE 9–5

The smoke-filled room experiment.

Smoke pouring into the testing room was much more likely to be reported by individuals working alone than by three-person groups. (Data from Latané & Darley, 1968)

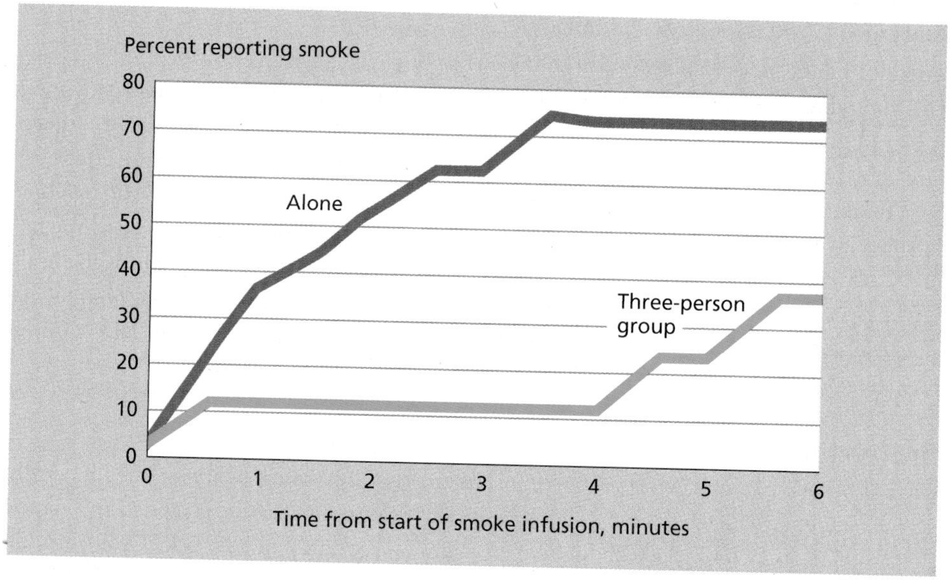

bystander effect
the finding that a person is less likely to provide help when there are other bystanders

That may also have been the question for those who in 2003 watched Brandon Vedas overdose and die online. As his life ebbed, his audience, which was left to wonder whether he was putting on an act, failed to decipher available clues to his whereabouts and to contact police (Nichols, 2003).

Unlike the smoke-filled-room experiment, however, each of these everyday situations involves danger to passersby. To see if the same **bystander effect** occurs in such situations, Latané and Judith Rodin (1969) staged an experiment around a woman in distress. A female researcher set men to work on a questionnaire and then left through a curtained doorway to work in an adjacent office. Four minutes later she could be heard (from a tape recorder) climbing on a chair to reach some papers. This was followed by a scream and a loud crash as the chair collapsed and she fell to the floor. "Oh, my God, my foot . . . I . . . I . . . can't move it," she sobbed. "Oh . . . my ankle . . . I . . . can't get this . . . thing . . . off me." Only after two minutes of moaning did she manage to make it out her office door.

Interpretations matter. Is this man locked out of his car or is he a burglar? Our answer affects how we respond.

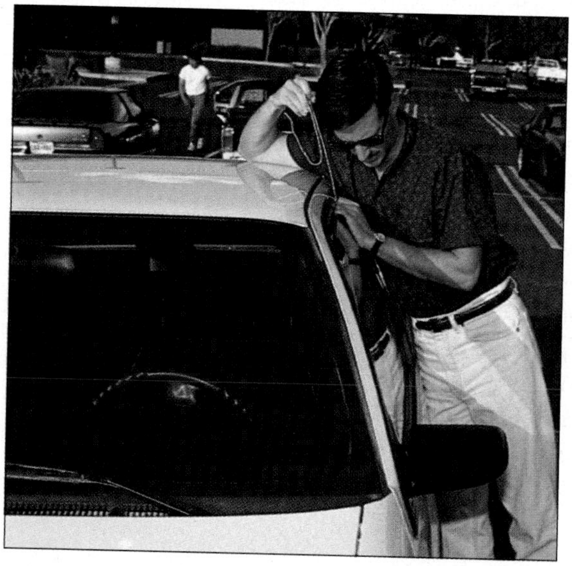

Seventy percent of those alone when they overheard the "accident" came into the room or called out to offer help. Among pairs of strangers confronting the emergency, only 40 percent of the time did either person offer help. Those who did nothing apparently interpreted the situation as a nonemergency. "A mild sprain," said some. "I didn't want to embarrass her," explained others. This again demonstrates the bystander effect: As the number of people known to be aware of an emergency increases, any given person becomes *less* likely to help. For the victim, there is therefore no safety in numbers.

People's interpretations also affect their reactions to street crimes. In staging physical fights between a man and a woman, Lance Shotland and Margaret Straw (1976) found that bystanders intervened 65 percent of the time when the woman shouted, "Get away from me; I don't know you," but only 19 percent of the time when she shouted, "Get away from me; I don't know why I ever married you." People seemed to think it wasn't their business when the woman was married to the attacker. Spouse abuse, it seems, just doesn't trigger as much concern as stranger abuse.

Harold Takooshian and Herzel Bodinger (1982) suspected that interpretations could also affect bystanders' reactions to burglaries. When they staged hundreds of car burglaries in 18 cities (using a coat hanger to gain access to a valuable object, such as a TV set or fur coat), they were astonished. Fewer than 1 in 10 passersby so much as questioned their activity. Many people noticed and even stopped to stare, snicker, or offer help. Some apparently interpreted the "burglar" as the car's owner.

Assuming responsibility

Failing to notice and misinterpretation is not the bystander effect's only cause. Even when a shabby 14-year-old was the "burglar," when someone simultaneously broke into two adjacent cars, or when onlookers saw a different person breaking into the car than had just gotten out of it, Takooshian and Bodinger report there still was virtually no intervention. And what about those times when an emergency is obvious? Those who saw and heard Kitty Genovese's pleas for help correctly interpreted what was happening. But the lights and silhouetted figures in neighbouring windows told them that others were also watching. This diffused the responsibility for action.

Few of us have observed a murder. But all of us have at times been slower to react to a need when others were present. Passing a stranded motorist on a highway, we are less likely to offer help than on a country road. To explore bystander inaction in clear emergencies, Darley and Latané (1968) simulated the Genovese drama. They placed people in separate rooms from which the participants would hear a victim crying for help. To create this situation, Darley and Latané asked some students to discuss their problems with university life over a laboratory intercom. They told the students that to guarantee their anonymity, no one would be visible, nor would the experimenter eavesdrop. During the ensuing discussion, the participants heard one person, when the experimenter turned his microphone on, lapse into an epileptic seizure. With increasing intensity and speech difficulty, he pleaded for someone to help.

Responsibility diffusion. The nine paparazzi photographers on the scene immediately after the Princess Diana car accident all had cellphones. With one exception, none called for help. Their almost unanimous explanation was that they assumed "someone else" had already called (Sancton, 1997).

Of those led to believe they were the only listener, 85 percent left their room to seek help. Of those who believed four others also overheard the victim, only 31 percent went for help. Were those who didn't respond apathetic and indifferent? When the experimenter came in to end the experiment, she did not find this response. Most immediately expressed concern. Many had trembling hands and sweating palms. They believed an emergency had occurred but were undecided whether to act.

After the smoke-filled room, the woman-in-distress, and the seizure experiments, Latané and Darley asked the participants whether the presence of others had influenced

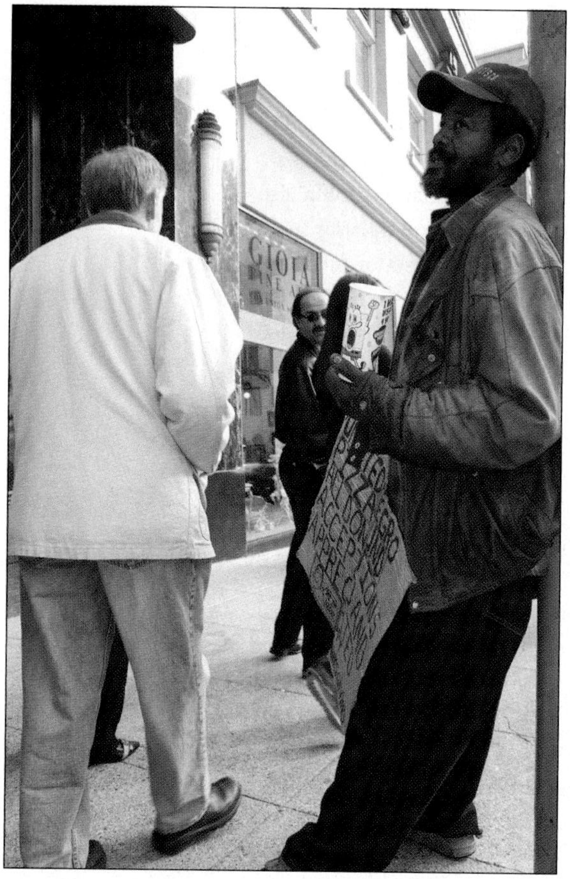

Compassion fatigue helps explain why those seeking help receive fewer responses from city people than from country people.

them. We know the others had a dramatic effect. Yet the participants almost invariably denied the influence. The typical reply? "I was aware of the others, but I would have reacted just the same if they weren't there." This response reinforces a familiar point: We often do not know why we do what we do. That is why experiments such as these are revealing. A survey of uninvolved bystanders following a real emergency would have left the bystander effect hidden.

Further experiments revealed situations in which others' presence sometimes does *not* inhibit people from offering help. Irving Piliavin and his colleagues (1969) staged an emergency in a laboratory on wheels, the unwitting subjects being 4450 riders of the subway. On each of 103 occasions, a confederate entered a subway car and stood in the centre next to a pole. After the train pulled out of the station, he staggered, then collapsed. When the victim carried a cane, one or more bystanders almost always promptly offered help. Even when the victim carried a bottle and smelled of liquor, he was often promptly offered aid—aid that was especially prompt when several male bystanders were close by. Why? Did the presence of other passengers provide a sense of security to those who helped? Was it because the situation was unambiguous? (The passengers couldn't help noticing and realizing what was happening.)

To test this latter possibility, Linda Solomon, Henry Solomon, and Ronald Stone (1978) conducted experiments in which people either saw and heard someone's distress, as in the subway experiment, or only heard it, as in the woman-in-distress experiment (leaving the situation more open to interpretation). When the emergencies were very clear, those in groups were only slightly less likely to help than were those alone. When the emergencies were somewhat ambiguous, however, the subjects in groups were far less likely to help than were solitary bystanders.

Most people who live in large cities are seldom alone in public places, which helps account for why city people often are less helpful than country people. "Compassion fatigue" and "sensory overload" from encountering so many people in need further restrain helping in large cities across the world (Yousif & Korte, 1995). This explains what happened when Robert LeVine and colleagues (1994) approached several thousand people in 36 cities, dropping an unnoticed pen, asking for change, simulating a blind person needing help at a corner, and so forth. The bigger and more densely populated the city, the less likely people were to help.

Levine and his collaborators (2001, 2003) found that willingness to help strangers also varies around the world (Figure 9-6). People in economically advanced countries tended to offer

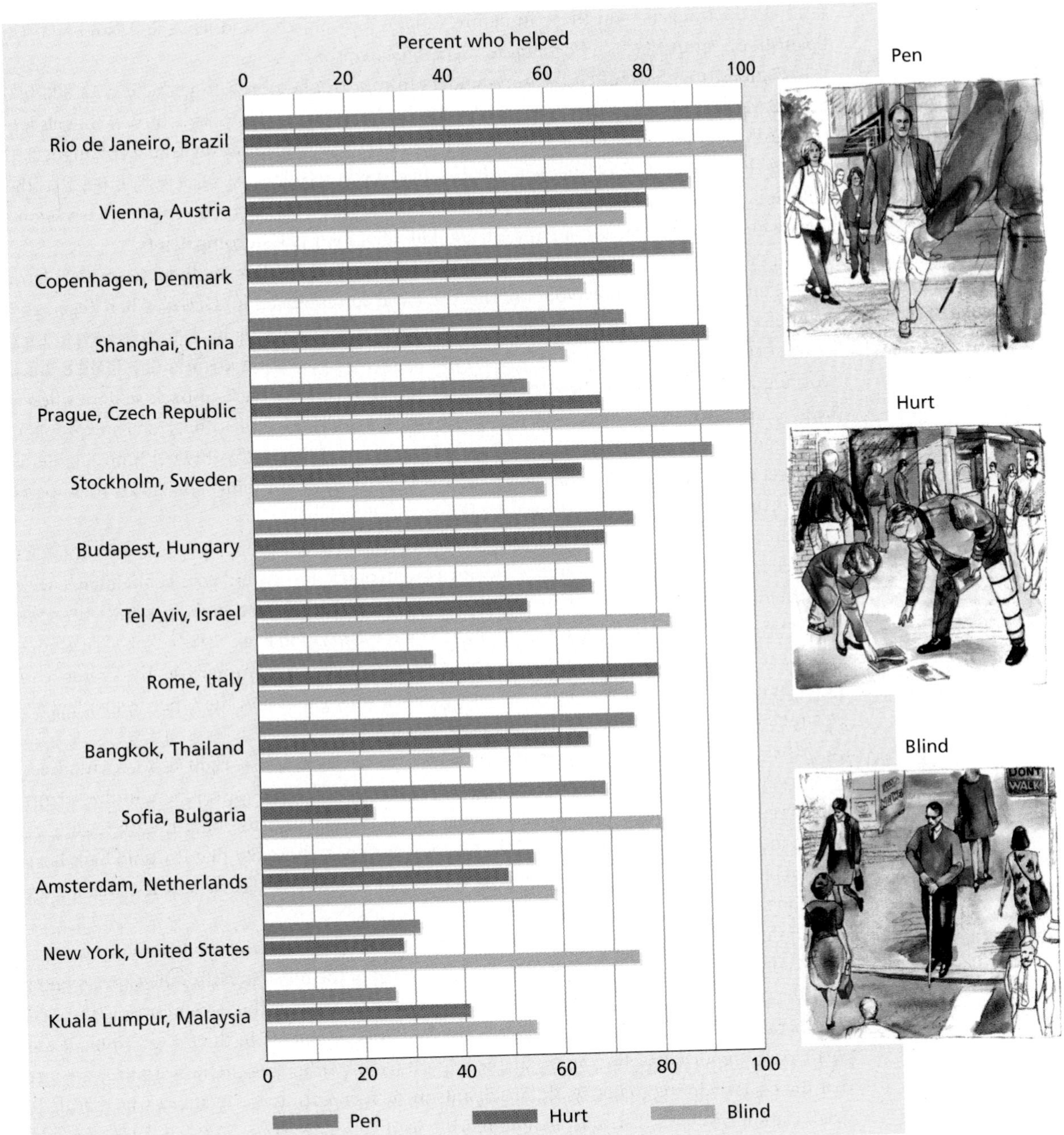

FIGURE 9–6

A world of difference in helping strangers.

To compare helping in different cities and cultures, Robert Levine and his collaborators would "accidentally" drop a pen, drop magazines while limping with an apparently injured leg, or feign blindness when approaching an intersection as the light turned green. Those dropping a pen in Rio were, for example, four times more likely to be helped than those doing so in New York City or Kuala Lumpur. (This is a sample of data from 14 countries.) (Adapted from R. V. Levine (2003). "The kindness of strangers." *American Scientist*, 91, 226–233) *less* help to strangers, and those in cultures marked by amiable and agreeable "simpatia" (in Spanish) or "simpatico" (in Portuguese) were *more* helpful.

Nations, too, have often been bystanders to catastrophes, even to genocide. As 800 000 people were murdered in Rwanda, we all stood by. "With many potential actors, each feels less responsible," notes Ervin Staub (1997). "It's not our responsibility," say the leaders of unaffected nations. Psychologist Peter Suedfeld (2000)—like Staub, a Holocaust survivor—notes that the diffusion of responsibility also helps explain "why the vast majority of European citizens stood idly by during the persecution, removal, and killing of their Jewish compatriots."

In the subway experiment, the passengers sat face-to-face, allowing them to see the alarm on one another's faces. To explore the effect of facial communication, Darley, Allan Teger, and Lawrence Lewis (1973) had people working either face-to-face or back-to-back when they heard a crash in the adjacent room as several metal screens fell on a workman. Unlike those working alone, who almost always offered help, pairs working back-to-back seldom offered help. A person working face-to-face with a partner could notice the other's facial expression and know that the person had also observed the event. Apparently, this led both people to interpret the situation as an emergency and to feel some responsibility to act, for these pairs were virtually as likely to give aid as were those working alone.

Finally, all the experiments we have considered involved groups of strangers. Imagine yourself facing any of these emergencies with a group of friends. Would your acquaintance with the other bystanders make a difference? Experiments conducted in several cities and across the world reveal that the answer is yes (Rutkowski et al., 1983; Yinon et al., 1982). Cohesive groups are *less* inhibited about helping than are solitary individuals. To summarize: The presence of other bystanders inhibits helping *if* the emergency is *ambiguous* and the other bystanders are *strangers* who *cannot easily read one another's reactions.*

These experiments raise again the issue of research ethics. Is it right to force hundreds of subway riders to witness someone's apparent collapse? Were the researchers in the seizure experiment ethical when they forced people to decide whether to abort the discussion to report the problem? Would you object to being in such a study? Note that it would have been impossible to get your "informed consent"; doing so would have destroyed the cover for the experiment.

In defence of the researchers, they were always careful to debrief the laboratory participants. After explaining the seizure experiment, probably the most stressful, the experimenter gave the participants a questionnaire. One hundred percent said the deception was justified and that they would be willing to take part in similar experiments in the future. None of the participants reported feeling angry at the experimenter. Other researchers similarly report that the overwhelming majority of participants in such experiments say afterwards that their participation was both instructive and ethically justified (Schwartz & Gottlieb, 1981). In field experiments, such as the one in the subway car, an accomplice assisted the victim if no one else did, thus reassuring bystanders that the problem was being dealt with.

Remember that the social psychologist has a twofold ethical obligation: to protect the participants and to enhance human welfare by discovering influences upon human behaviour. Such discoveries can alert us to unwanted influences and show us how we might exert positive

influences. The ethical principle seems to be thus: After protecting participants' welfare, social psychologists fulfill their responsibility to society by doing such research.

HELPING WHEN SOMEONE ELSE DOES

If aggressive models can heighten aggression (Chapter 10) and if unresponsive models can heighten nonresponding, then will helpful models promote helping? Imagine hearing a crash followed by sobs and moans. If another bystander said: "Uh oh. This is an emergency! We've got to do something," would this stimulate others to help?

The evidence is clear: Prosocial models do promote altruism. Some examples:

> *"We are, in truth, more than half what we are by imitation. The great point is, to choose good models and to study them with care."*
>
> Lord Chesterfield, *Letters*, January 18, 1750

- James Bryan and Mary Ann Test (1967) found that in one field study drivers were more likely to offer help to a female driver with a flat tire if a quarter-mile (0.4-kilometre) earlier they witnessed someone helping another woman change a tire.
- In another experiment, Bryan and Test observed that Christmas shoppers were more likely to drop money in a Salvation Army kettle if they had just seen someone else do the same.
- Philippe Rushton and Anne Campbell (1977) found British adults more willing to donate blood if they were approached after observing a confederate consent to donating.
- A glimpse of extraordinary human kindness and charity—such as we gave you in the examples of heroic altruism at this chapter's outset—often triggers what Jonathan Haidt (2003) calls *elevation*, "a distinctive feeling in the chest of warmth and expansion" that may provoke chills, tears, and throat clenching and that often inspires people to become more self-giving.

Models sometimes contradict in practice what they preach. Parents may tell their children, "Do as I say, not as I do." Experiments show that children learn moral judgments from both what they hear preached and what they see practised (Rice & Grusec, 1975; Rushton, 1975). When exposed to hypocrites, they imitate: They do what the model does and say what the model says.

TIME PRESSURES

Darley and Batson (1973) discerned another determinant of helping in the Good Samaritan parable. The priest and the Levite were both busy, important people, probably hurrying to their duties. The lowly Samaritan surely was less pressed for time. To see whether people in a hurry would behave as the priest and Levite did, Darley and Batson cleverly staged the situation described in the parable.

After collecting their thoughts prior to recording a brief extemporaneous talk (which, for half the participants, was on the Good Samaritan parable), theological seminary students were directed to a recording studio in an adjacent building. En route, they passed a man sitting slumped in a doorway, head down, coughing and groaning. Some of the students had been sent off nonchalantly:

"It will be a few minutes before they're ready for you, but you might as well head on over." Of these, almost two-thirds stopped to offer help. Others were told, "Oh, you're late. They were expecting you a few minutes ago . . . so you'd better hurry." Of these, only 10 percent offered help.

Reflecting on these findings, Darley and Batson remarked:

> A person not in a hurry may stop and offer help to a person in distress. A person in a hurry is likely to keep going. Ironically, he is likely to keep going even if he is hurrying to speak on the parable of the Good Samaritan, thus inadvertently confirming the point of the parable. (Indeed, on several occasions, a seminary student going to give his talk on the parable of the Good Samaritan literally stepped over the victim as he hurried on his way!)

Are we being unfair to the seminary students, who were, after all, hurrying to *help* the experimenter? Perhaps they keenly felt the social-responsibility norm but found it pulling them two ways—toward the experimenter and toward the victim. In another enactment of the Good Samaritan situation, Batson and his associates (1978) directed 40 university students to an experiment in another building. Half were told they were late; half knew they had plenty of time. Half thought their participation was vitally important to the experimenter; half thought it was not essential. The results: Those on their way to an unimportant appointment usually stopped to help. But people seldom stopped to help if, like the White Rabbit in *Alice's Adventures in Wonderland,* they were late for a very important date.

Can we conclude that those who were rushed were callous? Did the seminarians notice the victim's distress and then consciously choose to ignore it? No. In their hurry, they never fully grasped the situation. Harried, preoccupied, rushing to meet a deadline, they simply did not take time to tune in to the person in need.

SIMILARITY

Because similarity is conducive to liking, and liking is conducive to helping, we are more empathic and helpful toward those similar to us (Miller et al., 2001). This similarity bias applies to both dress and beliefs. Tim Emswiller and his fellow researchers (1971) had confederates, dressed either conservatively or in counterculture garb, approach "conservative" or "hip" students seeking money for a phone call. Fewer than half the students did the favour for those dressed differently than themselves. Two-thirds did so for those dressed similarly. Likewise, Scottish shoppers in a more antigay era were less willing to make change for someone if the person wore a T-shirt with a pro-gay slogan (Gray et al., 1991).

No face is more familiar than one's own. That explains why, when Lisa DeBruine (2002) had McMaster University students play an interactive game with a supposed other player, they were more trusting and generous when the other person's pictured face had some features of their own morphed into it (Figure 9–7). In me I trust. Even just sharing a birthday, a first name, or a fingerprint pattern leads people to respond more to a request for help (Burger et al., 2004).

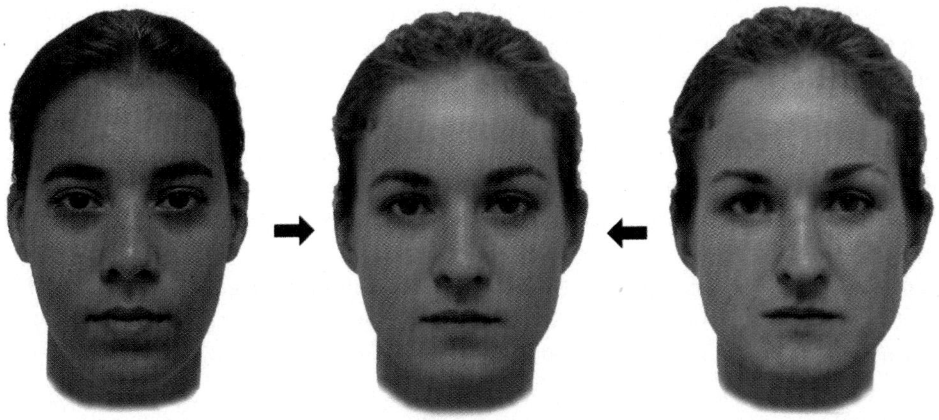

FIGURE 9–7

Similarity breeds cooperation.

Lisa DeBruine (2002) morphed participants' faces (left) with strangers' faces (right) to make the composite centre faces—toward whom the participants were more generous than toward the stranger.

SUMMING UP: WHEN WILL WE HELP?

Several situational influences work to inhibit or to encourage altruism. As the number of bystanders at an emergency increases, any given bystander is (1) less likely to notice the incident, (2) less likely to interpret it as an emergency, and (3) less likely to assume responsibility.

When are people most likely to help? After observing someone else helping and when not hurried. We tend to help those whom we perceive as being similar to us.

WHO HELPS? PERSONALITY TRAITS

We have considered internal influences on the decision to help (such as guilt and mood) and external influences as well (such as social norms, number of bystanders, time pressure, and similarity). We also need to consider the helper's personality.

Surely some traits must distinguish the Mother Teresa types. Faced with identical situations, some people will respond helpfully, others won't bother. Who are the likely helpers?

For many years social psychologists were unable to discover a single personality trait that predicted altruistic behaviour with anything close to the predictive power of the situation, guilt, and mood factors. Modest relationships were found between helping and certain personality variables, such as need for social approval. But by and large, the personality tests were unable to identify the helpers. Studies of rescuers of Jews in Nazi Europe reveal a similar conclusion: Although the social context clearly influenced willingness to help, there was no definable set of altruistic personality traits (Darley, 1995).

"There are . . . reasons why personality should be rather unimportant in determining people's reactions to the emergency. For one thing, the situational forces affecting a person's decision are so strong."

Bibb Latané and John Darley (1970, p. 115)

If that has a familiar ring, it could be from a similar conclusion by conformity researchers (Chapter 6): Conformity, too, seemed more influenced by the situation than by measurable personality traits. Perhaps, though, you recall from Chapter 2 that who we are does affect what we do. Attitude and trait measures seldom predict a *specific* act, which is what most experiments on altruism measure, in contrast to the lifelong altruism of a Mother Teresa. But they better predict average behaviour across many situations more accurately.

Personality researchers have responded to the challenge. First, they have found individual differences in helpfulness and shown that these differences persist over time and are noticed by one's peers (Hampson, 1984; Rushton et al., 1981). Second, they are gathering clues to the network of traits that predispose a person to helpfulness. Those high in emotionality, empathy, and self-efficacy are most likely to be concerned and helpful (Bierhoff et al., 1991; Eisenberg et al., 1991; Tice & Baumeister, 1985). Third, personality influences how particular people react to particular situations (Carlo et al., 1991; Romer et al., 1986; Wilson & Petruska, 1984). High self-monitoring people, being attuned to other people's expectations, are especially helpful *if* they think helpfulness will be socially rewarded (White & Gerstein, 1987). Others' opinions matter less to internally guided, low self-monitoring people.

This interaction of person and situation also appears in the 172 studies that have compared the helpfulness of nearly 50 000 male and female subjects. After analyzing these results, Alice Eagly and Maureen Crowley (1986) reported that when faced with potentially dangerous situations in which strangers need help (such as with a flat tire or a fall in a subway), men more often help. (Eagly and Crowley also report that among 6767 individuals who have received the Carnegie medal for heroism in saving human life, 90 percent have been men.) But in safer situations, such as volunteering to help with an experiment or spend time with children with developmental disabilities, women are slightly more likely to help. They also have been as likely as, or more likely than, men to risk death as Holocaust rescuers, to donate a kidney, and to volunteer with aid agencies (Becker & Eagly, 2004). Thus, the gender difference interacts with (depends on) the situation.

SUMMING UP: WHO HELPS? PERSONALITY TRAITS

Evidence indicates that some people are consistently more helpful than others, but the effect of personality (and gender as well) may depend on the situation.

HOW CAN WE INCREASE HELPING?

To increase helping, we can reverse the factors that inhibit helping. Or we can teach altruistic norms and socialize people to see themselves as helpful.

As social scientists, our goal is to understand human behaviour, thus also suggesting ways to improve it. We therefore wonder how we might apply insights from research to increase altruism. One way to promote altruism is to reverse those factors that inhibit it. Given that hurried, preoccupied people are less likely to help, can we think of ways to encourage them to slow down and turn their attention outward? If the presence of others diminishes each bystander's sense of responsibility, how can we enhance responsibility?

REDUCE AMBIGUITY, INCREASE RESPONSIBILITY

If Latané and Darley's decision tree (Figure 9–4) describes the dilemmas bystanders face, then assisting people to interpret an incident correctly and to assume responsibility should increase their involvement. Leonard Bickman and his colleagues (1975, 1977, 1979) tested this presumption in a series of experiments on crime reporting. In each, supermarket or bookstore shoppers witnessed a shoplifting. Some witnesses had seen signs that attempted to sensitize them to shoplifting and to inform them how to report it. But the signs had little effect. Other witnesses heard a bystander interpret the incident: "Say, look at her. She's shoplifting. She put that into her purse." (The bystander then left to look for a lost child.) Still others heard this person add, "We saw it. We should report it. It's our responsibility." Both face-to-face comments substantially boosted reporting of the crime.

The potency of personal influence is no longer in doubt. Robert Foss (1978) surveyed several hundred blood donors and found that neophyte donors, unlike veterans, were usually there at someone's personal invitation. Leonard Jason and his collaborators (1984) confirmed that personal appeals for blood donation are much more effective than posters and media announcements—*if* the personal appeals come from friends. Nonverbal appeals can also be effective when they are personalized. Mark Snyder and his coworkers (1974) found that hitch-hikers doubled the number of ride offers by looking drivers straight in the eye. A personal approach, as the author's panhandler knew, makes one feel less anonymous, more responsible.

Henry Solomon and Linda Solomon (1978; Solomon et al., 1981) explored ways to reduce anonymity. They found that bystanders who had identified themselves to one another—by name, age, and so forth—were more likely to offer aid to a sick person than were anonymous bystanders. Similarly, when a female experimenter caught the eye of another shopper and gave her a warm smile prior to stepping on an elevator, that shopper was far more likely than other shoppers to offer help when the experimenter later said, "Damn. I've left my glasses. Can anyone tell me what floor the umbrellas are on?" Even a trivial momentary conversation with someone ("Excuse me, aren't you Suzie Spear's sister?" "No, I'm not") dramatically increased the person's later helpfulness.

Helpfulness also increases when one expects to meet the victim and other witnesses again. Using a laboratory intercom system, Jody Gottlieb and Charles Carver (1980) led students to believe they were discussing problems of university living with other students. (Actually, the other discussants were tape-recorded.) When one of the supposed fellow discussants had a choking fit and cried out for help, she was helped most quickly by subjects who believed they would soon be meeting the discussants face-to-face. In short, anything that personalizes bystanders—a personal request, eye contact, stating one's name, anticipation of interaction—increases willingness to help.

Personal treatment makes bystanders more self-aware and therefore more attuned to their own altruistic ideals. Recall from earlier chapters that people made self-aware by acting in front of a mirror or TV camera exhibit increased consistency between attitudes and actions. By contrast, "deindividuated" people are less responsible. Thus, circumstances that promote self-awareness—name tags, being watched and evaluated, undistracted quiet—should also increase helping. Shelley Duval, Virginia Duval, and Robert Neely (1979) confirmed this. They showed some women their own image on a TV screen or had them complete a biographical questionnaire just before giving them a chance to contribute time and money to people in need. Those made self-aware contributed more. Similarly, pedestrians who have just had their picture taken by someone became more likely to help another pedestrian pick up dropped envelopes (Hoover et al., 1983). Self-aware people more often put their ideals into practice.

GUILT AND CONCERN FOR SELF-IMAGE

Earlier we noted that people who feel guilty will act to reduce guilt and restore their self-worth. Can heightening people's awareness of their transgressions therefore increase desire to help? A research team led by Richard Katzev (1978) wondered. So when visitors to an art museum disobeyed a "Please do not touch" sign, experimenters reprimanded some of them: "Please don't touch the objects. If everyone touches them, they will deteriorate." Likewise, when visitors to a zoo fed unauthorized food to the bears, some of them were admonished with, "Hey, don't feed unauthorized food to the animals. Don't you know it could hurt them?" In both cases, 58 percent of the now guilt-laden subjects shortly thereafter offered help to another experimenter who had "accidentally" dropped something. Of those not reprimanded, only one-third helped. Guilt-laden people are helpful people.

door-in-the-face technique a strategy for gaining a concession. After someone first turns down a large request (the door-in-the-face), the same requester counteroffers with a more reasonable request.

People also care about their public image. When Robert Cialdini and his colleagues (1975) asked some of their university students to chaperone delinquent children on a zoo trip, only 32 percent agreed to do so. With other students the questioner first made a very large request—that the students commit two years as volunteer counsellors to delinquent children. After getting the **door-in-the-face** in response to this request (all refused), the questioner then counteroffered with the chaperoning request, saying, in effect, "Okay, if you won't do that, would you do just this much?" With this technique, nearly twice as many—56 percent—agreed to help.

Cialdini and David Schroeder (1976) offer another practical way to trigger concern for self-image: Ask for a contribution so small that it's hard to say no without feeling like a Scrooge. Cialdini (1995) discovered this when a United Way canvasser came to his door. As she solicited his contribution, he was mentally preparing his refusal—until she said magic words that demolished his financial excuse: "Even a penny will help." "I had been neatly finessed into compliance," recalled Cialdini. "And there was another interesting feature of our exchange as well. When I stopped coughing (I really had choked on my attempted rejection), I gave her *not* the penny she had mentioned but the amount I usually allot to legitimate charity solicitors. At that, she thanked me, smiled innocently, and moved on."

Door-in-the-face technique.

Was Cialdini's response atypical? To find out, he and Schroeder had a solicitor approach suburbanites. When the solicitor said he or she was collecting money for the cancer society, 29 percent contributed an average of $1.44 each. When the solicitor added, "Even a penny will help," 50 percent contributed an average of $1.54 each. When James Weyant (1984) repeated this experiment, he found similar results: The "even a penny will help" boosted the number contributing from 39 to 57 percent. And when 6000 people were solicited by mail for the cancer society, those asked for small amounts were more likely to give—and gave no less on average—than those asked for larger amounts (Weyant & Smith, 1987). When approaching previous donors, bigger requests (within reason) do elicit bigger donations (Doob & McLaughlin, 1989). But with door-to-door solicitation, there is more success with requests for small contributions, which are difficult to turn down and still allow the person to maintain an altruistic self-image.

Labelling people as helpful can also strengthen a helpful self-image. After they had made a charitable contribution, Robert Kraut (1973) told women, "You are a generous person." Two weeks later, these women were more willing than those not so labelled to contribute to a different charity.

SOCIALIZING ALTRUISM

If we can learn altruism, then how might we teach it? Here are three ways.

Teaching moral inclusion

Rescuers of Jews in Nazi Europe, relief workers in foreign countries, and volunteers at homeless shelters share at least one thing in common: They include people who differ from them within the human circle to which their moral values and rules of justice apply. These people are *morally inclusive,* as illustrated by one rescuer who faked a pregnancy on behalf of a pregnant hidden Jew—thus including the soon-to-be-born child within the circle of her own children's identities (Fogelman, 1994).

"We consider humankind our family."

Parliament of the World Religions, *Towards a Global Ethic,* 1993

Moral exclusion—omitting certain people from one's circle of moral concern—has the opposite effect. It justifies all sorts of harm, from discrimination to genocide (Opotow, 1990; Staub, 1990; Tyler & Lind, 1990). Exploitation or cruelty becomes acceptable, even appropriate, toward those we regard as undeserving or as nonpersons. The Nazis excluded Jews from their moral community; so does anyone who participates in enslavement, death squads, or torture. To a lesser extent, moral exclusion describes any of us who concentrate our concerns, favours, and financial inheritance on "our people" (for example, our children) to the exclusion of others.

moral exclusion
the perception of certain individuals or groups as outside the boundary within which one applies moral values and rules of fairness. Moral *inclusion* is regarding others as within one's circle of moral concern.

A first step toward socializing altruism is therefore to counter the natural ingroup bias favouring kin and tribe by broadening the range of people whose well-being concerns us. Daniel Batson (1983) notes how religious teachings do this. They extend the reach of kin-linked altruism by urging "brotherly and sisterly" love toward all "children of God" in the whole human "family." If everyone is part of our family, then everyone has a moral claim on us. The boundaries between "we" and "they" fade. Nurturing children to have a secure sense of self also helps, by enabling them to accept social diversity without feeling threatened (Deutsch, 1990). (See Figure 9–8.)

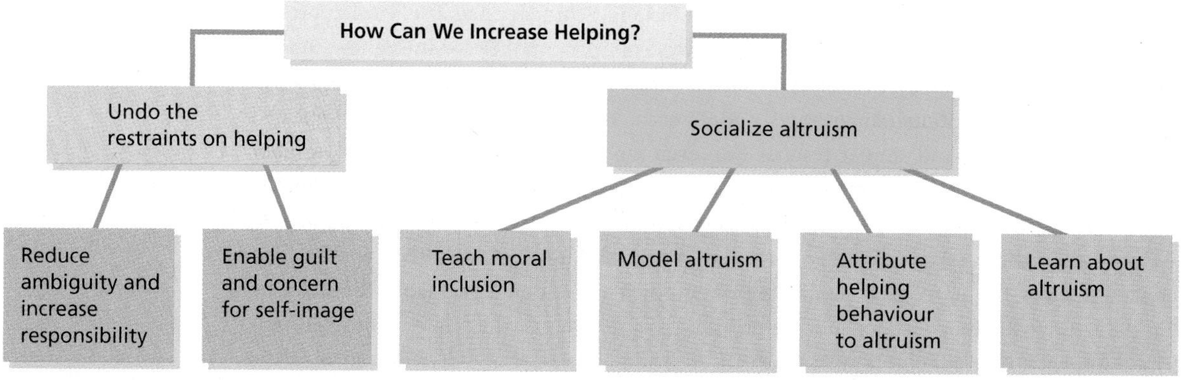

FIGURE 9–8
Practical ways to increase helping.

Modelling altruism

Earlier we learned that when we see unresponsive bystanders, we, too, are unlikely to help. If we see or read about someone helping, we are more likely to offer assistance. It's better, find Robert Cialdini and his coworkers (2003), *not* to publicize rampant tax cheating, littering, and teen drinking, and instead to emphasize—to define a norm of—people's widespread honesty, cleanliness, and abstinence. In one experiment, they asked visitors not to remove petrified wood from along the paths of the U.S. Petrified Forest National Park. Some were also told that "past visitors have removed the petrified wood." Other people who were told that "past visitors have left the petrified wood" in order to preserve the park were much less likely to pick up samples placed along a path. Perhaps norms for generosity could also be cultivated by simply including a new line on tax forms that requires people to compute—and thus to know—their annual donations as a percentage of income (Ayres & Nalebuff, 2003). People know and sometimes discuss their tipping percentage, for which there are well-defined norms, but usually not their charity.

Princess Diana earned the admiration of millions by modelling moral inclusiveness—reaching out to lepers, hugging AIDS patients, visiting sick children.

Modelling effects were also apparent within the families of European Christians who risked their lives to rescue Jews in the 1930s and 1940s and of the civil rights activists of the late 1950s. In both cases these exceptional altruists had warm and close relationships with at least one parent who was, similarly, a strong "moralist" or committed to humanitarian causes (London, 1970; Oliner & Oliner, 1988; Rosenhan, 1970). Their family—and often their friends and church—had taught them the norm of helping and caring for others. This "prosocial value orientation" led them to include people from other groups in their circle of moral concern and to feel responsible for others' welfare (Staub, 1989, 1991, 1992).

Do television's positive models promote helping, much as its aggressive portrayals promote aggression? Prosocial TV models have actually had even greater effects than antisocial models. Susan Hearold (1986) statistically combined 108 comparisons of prosocial programs with neutral

programs or no program. She found that, on average, "If the viewer watched prosocial programs instead of neutral programs, he would [at least temporarily] be elevated from the 50th to the 74th percentile in prosocial behaviour—typically altruism."

In one such study, researchers Lynette Friedrich and Aletha Stein (1973; Stein & Friedrich, 1972) showed preschool children *Mister Rogers' Neighborhood* episodes each day for four weeks as part of their nursery school program. (*Mister Rogers* aims to enhance young children's social and emotional development.) During this viewing period, children from less educated homes became more cooperative, helpful, and likely to state their feelings. In a follow-up study, kindergartners who viewed four *Mister Rogers* programs were able to state its prosocial content, both on a test and in puppet play (Friedrich & Stein, 1975; also Coates et al., 1976).

Attributing helpful behaviour to altruistic motives

Another clue to socializing altruism comes from research on the **overjustification effect**: When the justification for an act is more than sufficient, the person may attribute the act to the extrinsic justification rather than to an inner motive. Rewarding people for doing what they would do anyway therefore undermines intrinsic motivation. We can state the principle positively: By providing people with just enough justification to prompt a good deed (weaning them from bribes and threats when possible), we may increase their pleasure in doing such deeds on their own.

overjustification effect the result of bribing people to do what they already like doing; they may then see their action as externally controlled rather than intrinsically appealing

Daniel Batson and his associates (1978, 1979) put the overjustification phenomenon to work. In several experiments, they found that University of Kansas students felt most altruistic after they agreed to help someone without payment or implied social pressure. When pay had been offered or social pressures were present, people felt less altruistic after helping.

In another experiment, the researchers led students to attribute a helpful act to compliance ("I guess we really don't have a choice") or to compassion ("The guy really needs help"). Later, when the students were asked to volunteer their time to a local service agency, 25 percent of those who had been led to perceive their previous helpfulness as mere compliance now volunteered; of those led to see themselves as compassionate, 60 percent volunteered. The moral? When people wonder, "Why am I helping?" it's best if the circumstances enable them to answer, "Because help was needed, and I am a caring, giving, helpful person."

As you may recall from Chapter 4, rewards undermine intrinsic motivation when they function as controlling bribes. An unanticipated compliment, however, can make people feel competent and worthy. When Joe is coerced with, "If you quit being chicken and give blood, we'll win the fraternity prize for most donations," he isn't likely to attribute his donation to altruism. When Jocelyn is rewarded with, "That's terrific that you'd choose to take an hour out of such a busy week to give blood," she's more likely to walk away with an altruistic self-image—and thus to contribute again (Piliavin et al., 1982; Thomas & Batson, 1981; Thomas et al., 1981).

To predispose more people to help in situations where most don't, it can also pay to induce a tentative positive commitment, from which people may infer their own helpfulness. Delia Cioffi and Randy Garner (1998) observed that only about 5 percent of students responded to a campus blood drive after receiving an email announcement a week ahead. They asked other students to reply to the announcement with a "yes," "if you think you probably will donate." Of these, 29 percent did reply and the actual donation rate was 8 percent. They asked a third group to reply with a "no" if they did *not* anticipate donating. Now 71 percent implied they might give (by not replying). Imagine yourself in this third group. Might you have decided not to say no because, after all, you *are* a caring person so there's a chance you might give. And might that thought have opened you to persuasion as you encountered campus posters and flyers during the ensuing week? That apparently is what happened, because 12 percent of these students—more than twice the normal rate—showed up to offer their blood.

Inferring that one is a helpful person seems also to have happened when Dariusz Dolinski (2000) stopped pedestrians on the streets of Wroclaw, Poland, and asked them for directions to a nonexistent "Zubrzyckiego Street" or to an illegible address. Everyone tried unsuccessfully to help. After doing so, about two-thirds (twice the number of those not given the opportunity to try to help) agreed when asked by someone 100 metres further down the road to watch their heavy bag or bicycle for five minutes. On a larger scale, "service learning" and volunteer programs woven into a school curriculum have been shown to increase later citizen involvement, social responsibility, cooperation, and leadership (Andersen, 1998; Putnam, 2000). Attitudes follow behaviour. Helpful actions therefore promote the self-perception that one is caring and helpful, which in turn promotes further helping.

Learning about altruism

Researchers have found another way to boost altruism, one that provides a happy conclusion to this chapter. Some social psychologists worry that as people become more aware of social psychology's findings, their behaviour may change, thus invalidating the findings (Gergen, 1982). Will learning about the factors that inhibit altruism reduce their influence? Sometimes, such "enlightenment" is not our problem but one of our goals.

Experiments with university students by Arthur Beaman and his colleagues (1978) revealed that once people understand why the presence of bystanders inhibits helping, they become more likely to help in group situations. The researchers used a lecture to inform some students how bystander inaction can affect the interpretation of an emergency and feelings of responsibility. Other students heard either a different lecture or no lecture at all. Two weeks later, as part of a different experiment in a different location, the participants found themselves walking (with an unresponsive confederate) past someone slumped over or past a person sprawled beneath a bicycle. Of those who had not heard the helping lecture, a fourth paused to offer help; twice as many of those "enlightened" did so. Having read this chapter, you, too, have perhaps changed. As you come to understand what influences people's responses, will your attitudes and your behaviour be the same?

SUMMING UP: HOW CAN WE INCREASE HELPING?

Research suggests that we can enhance helpfulness in two ways. First, reverse those factors that inhibit helping. We can take steps to reduce the ambiguity of an emergency situation or to increase feelings of responsibility. We can even use reprimands or the door-in-the face technique to evoke guilt feelings or a concern for self-image.

Second, we can teach altruism. Research into television's portrayals of prosocial models shows the medium's power to teach positive behaviour. Children who view helpful behaviour tend to act helpfully.

If we want to coax altruistic behaviour from people, we should remember the overjustification effect: When we coerce good deeds, intrinsic love of the activity often diminishes. If we provide people with enough justification for them to decide to do good, but not much more, they will attribute their behaviour to their own altruistic motivation and henceforth be more willing to help. Learning about altruism, as you have done, can also prepare people to perceive and respond to other's needs.

POLICE

CHAPTER TEN

Aggression: Hurting Others

What is aggression?

What are some theories of aggression?
Aggression as a biological phenomenon
Aggression as response to frustration
Aggression as learned social behaviour

What are some influences on aggression?
Aversive incidents
Arousal
Aggression cues
Media influences: Pornography and sexual violence
Media influences: Television
Media influences: Video games
Group influences

How can aggression be reduced?
Catharsis?
A social learning approach

Although Woody Allen's prediction that "by 1990 kidnapping will be the dominant mode of social interaction" went unfulfilled, the years since have hardly been serene. The horror of 9/11 may have been the most dramatic violence, but in terms of human lives, it was not the most catastrophic. About the same time, the human carnage from tribal warfare in the Congo was claiming an estimated 3 million lives, some hacked to death with machetes, many others dying of starvation and disease after fleeing in terror from their villages (Sengupta, 2003). In neighbouring Rwanda, where some 750 000 people—including half the Tutsi population—were slaughtered in the genocidal summer of 1994, understood this human capacity for carnage (Staub, 1999). So are the people of the Sudan's Darfur region, as their country's government and its proxy force, the Janjaweed militias, carried out a terror campaign that by the end of 2005 had killed over 400 000 people and driven more than 2.5 million from their homes.

"Every gun that is made, every warship launched, every rocket fired signifies, in the final sense, a theft from those who hunger and are not fed, those who are cold and are not clothed."

President Dwight Eisenhower, Speech to the American Society of Newspaper Editors, 1953

Such hatred and destruction are hardly peculiar to the recent history of Africa. Worldwide, more than $2 billion per day is spent on arms and armies—$2 billion that could feed, educate, and protect the environment of the world's impoverished millions. During the last century, 250 wars killed 110 million people, enough to populate a "nation of the dead" with more than the combined population of France, Belgium, the Netherlands, Denmark, Finland, Norway, and Sweden (Sivard, 1996) (see Figure 10–1). The tolls came not only from the world wars, but also from genocides, including the 1915 to 1923 genocide of Armenians by the Ottoman Empire, the 1971 Pakistani genocide of 3 million Bangladeshis, and the 1.5 million Cambodians murdered in a reign of terror starting in 1975 (Sternberg, 2003). As Hitler's genocide of millions of Jews, Stalin's genocide of millions of Russians, Mao's genocide of millions of Chinese, and the genocide of millions of Native Americans from the time of Columbus through the nineteenth century make plain, the human potential for extraordinary cruelty crosses the globe.

FIGURE 10–1

The bloodiest century.

Twentieth-century humanity was the most educated, and homicidal, in history (data from Renner, 1999). Adding in genocides and human-made famines, there were approximately 182 million "deaths by mass unpleasantness." (White, 2000)

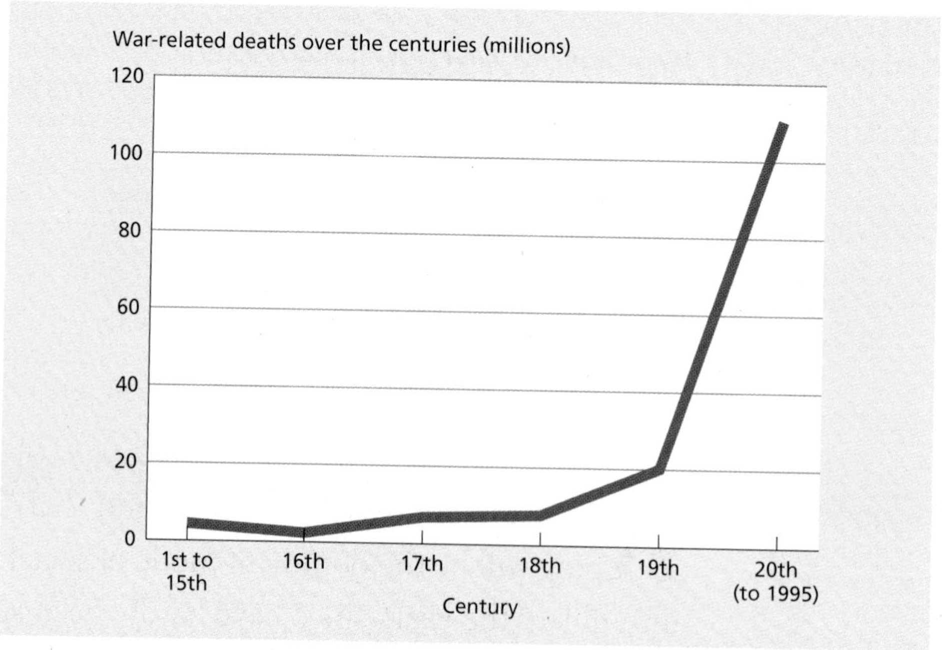

Are we like the mythical Minotaur, half human, half beast? What explains that midsummer day in 1941 when the non-Jewish half of the Polish town of Jebwabne murdered the other half in a macabre frenzy of violence, leaving only a dozen or so survivors among the 1600 Jews (Gross, 2001)? What explains such monstrous behaviour? In this chapter we ask four more-specific questions:

- Is aggression biologically predisposed, or do we learn it?
- What circumstances prompt hostile outbursts?
- Do the media influence aggression?
- How might we reduce aggression?

First, however, we need to clarify this term "aggression."

"Is there any way of delivering mankind from the menace of war?"

Albert Einstein,
letter to Sigmund Freud, 1932

WHAT IS AGGRESSION?

The original Thugs, members of a criminal fraternity in northern India, were aggressing when between 1550 and 1850 they strangled more than 2 million people, and claimed to do so in the service of the goddess Kali. But people also use "aggressive" to describe a dynamic salesperson. Social psychologists distinguish such self-assured, energetic, go-getting behaviour from behaviour that hurts, harms, or destroys. The former is assertiveness, the latter aggression.

For our discussion in this chapter, we will define **aggression** as *physical or verbal behaviour intended to cause harm.* This definition excludes unintentional harm, such as auto accidents or sidewalk collisions; it also excludes actions that may involve pain as an unavoidable side effect of helping someone, such as dental treatments or—in the extreme—assisted suicide. It includes kicks and slaps, threats and insults, even gossipy or snide "digs"; and decisions, during experiments, about how much to hurt someone, such as how much electric shock to impose. It also includes destroying property, lying, and other behaviour whose goal is to hurt.

aggression
physical or verbal behaviour intended to hurt someone

This definition covers two distinct types of aggression. Animals exhibit *social* aggression, characterized by displays of rage, and *silent* aggression, as when a predator stalks its prey. Social and silent aggressions involve separate brain regions. In humans, psychologists label the two types "hostile" and "instrumental" aggression. **Hostile aggression** springs from anger; its goal is to injure. **Instrumental aggression** aims to injure too—but only as a means to some other end.

hostile aggression
aggression driven by anger and performed as an end in itself

instrumental aggression
aggression that is a means to some other end

Most terrorism is instrumental aggression. "What nearly all suicide terrorist campaigns have in common is a specific secular and strategic goal," concludes Robert Pape (2003) after studying all suicide bombings from 1980 to 2001. That goal is "to compel liberal democracies to withdraw military forces from territory that the terrorists consider to be their homeland." Terrorism is rarely committed by someone with a psychological pathology, note Arie Kruglanski and Shira Fishman (2006). Rather, it is a strategic tool used during conflict.

Most wars are instrumental aggression. In 2003, U.S. and British leaders justified attacking Iraq not as a hostile effort to kill Iraqis but as an instrumental act of liberation and of self-defence against presumed weapons of mass destruction. Hostile aggression is "hot"; instrumental aggression is "cool."

Most murders, however, are hostile aggression. Approximately half of murders erupt from arguments, while others result from romantic triangles, or from brawls while under the influence of alcohol or narcotics (Ash, 1999). Such murders are impulsive, emotional outbursts—which helps explain why data from 110 nations show that enforcing the death penalty has not resulted in fewer homicides (Costanzo, 1998; Wilkes, 1987). Some murders and many other violent acts of retribution and sexual coercion, however, are instrumental (Felson, 2000). Most of Chicago's more than 1000 murders carried out by organized crime during the prohibition era and the years following were cool and calculated.

Given the extreme behaviours that characterize aggression, studying it ethically in the laboratory is a major challenge. In such experiments researchers have to use their ingenuity to develop measures that capture a clear intent to hurt others without actually allowing anyone to be hurt. Solving this problem is often difficult, so pay attention to the way researchers have addressed this issue throughout the rest of the chapter.

WHAT ARE SOME THEORIES OF AGGRESSION?

In analyzing causes of hostile and instrumental aggression, social psychologists have focused on three big ideas: (1) There is a biologically rooted aggressive drive; (2) aggression is a natural response to frustration; and (3) aggressive behaviour is learned.

AGGRESSION AS A BIOLOGICAL PHENOMENON

instinctive behaviour an innate, unlearned behaviour pattern exhibited by all members of a species

Philosophers have long debated whether our human nature is fundamentally that of a benign, contented "noble savage" or that of a brute. The first view, argued by the eighteenth-century French philosopher Jean-Jacques Rousseau (1712–1778), blames society, not human nature, for social evils. The second, associated with the English philosopher Thomas Hobbes (1588–1679), sees society's laws as necessary to restrain and control the human brute. In this century, the "brutish" view—that aggressive drive is inborn and thus inevitable—was argued by Sigmund Freud in Vienna and Konrad Lorenz in Germany.

"Our behaviour toward each other is the strangest, most unpredictable, and most unaccountable of all the phenomena with which we are obliged to live. In all of nature, there is nothing so threatening to humanity as humanity itself."

Lewis Thomas (1981)

Instinct theory and evolutionary psychology

Freud speculated that human aggression springs from a self-destructive impulse. It redirects toward others the energy of a primitive death urge (the "death instinct"). Lorenz, an animal behaviour expert, saw aggression as adaptive rather than self-destructive. Both agreed that aggressive energy is **instinctual** (unlearned and universal). If not discharged, it supposedly builds up until it explodes or until an appropriate stimulus "releases" it, like a mouse releasing a mousetrap.

The idea that aggression is an instinct collapsed as the list of supposed human instincts grew to include nearly every conceivable human behaviour. Nearly 6000 supposed instincts were enumerated in one 1924 survey of social science books (Barash, 1979). What the social scientists had tried to do was *explain* social behaviour by *naming* it. It's tempting to play this explaining-by-naming game: "Why do sheep stay together?" "Because of their herd instinct." "How do you know they have a herd instinct?" "Just look at them: They're always together!"

Instinct theory also fails to account for the variation in aggressiveness, from person to person and culture to culture. How would a shared human instinct for aggression explain the difference between the peaceful Iroquois before White invaders came and the hostile Iroquois after the invasion (Hornstein, 1976)? Although aggression *is* biologically influenced, the human propensity to aggress does not qualify as instinctive behaviour.

Our distant ancestors did, however, find aggression adaptive, note evolutionary psychologists David Buss and Todd Shackelford (1997). Aggressive behaviour was a strategy for gaining resources, defending against attack, intimidating or eliminating male rivals for females, and deterring mates from sexual infidelity. The adaptive value of aggression, Buss and Schackelford believe, helps explain the relatively high levels of male–male aggression across human history. "This does not imply . . . that men have an 'aggression instinct' in the sense of some pent-up energy that must be released. Rather, men have inherited from their successful ancestors psychological mechanisms" that improve their odds of contributing their genes to future generations.

A nineteenth-century engraving of Spanish warriors conquering Montezuma's Indian empire.

Neural influences

Because aggression is a complex behaviour, no one spot in the brain controls it. But researchers have found neural systems in both animals and humans that facilitate aggression. When the scientists activate these areas in the brain, hostility increases; when they deactivate them, hostility decreases. Docile animals can thus be provoked into rage, and raging animals into submission.

In one experiment, researchers placed an electrode in an aggression-inhibiting area of a domineering monkey's brain. A smaller monkey, given a button that activated the electrode, learned to push it every time the tyrant monkey became intimidating. Brain activation works with humans, too. After receiving painless electrical stimulation in her amygdala (a part of the brain core), one woman became enraged and smashed her guitar against the wall, barely missing her psychiatrist's head (Moyer, 1976, 1983).

Does this mean that violent people's brains are in some way abnormal? To find out, Adrian Raine and his colleagues (1998, 2000) used brain scans to measure brain activity in murderers and to measure the amount of grey matter in men with antisocial conduct disorder. They found that the prefrontal cortex, which acts like an emergency brake on deeper brain areas involved in aggressive behaviour, was 14 percent less active than normal in murderers (excluding those who had been abused by their parents) and 15 percent smaller in the antisocial men. As other studies of murderers and death-row inmates confirm, abnormal brains can contribute to abnormally aggressive behaviour (Davidson et al., 2000; Lewis, 1998; Pincus, 2001).

Genetic influences

Heredity influences the neural system's sensitivity to aggressive cues. It has long been known that animals of many species can be bred for aggressiveness. Sometimes this is done for practical purposes (the breeding of guard dogs). Sometimes, breeding is done for research. Finnish

"Of course, we'll never actually use it against a potential enemy, but it will allow us to negotiate from a position of strength."
John Ruge

Humanity has armed its capacity for destruction without comparably arming its capacity for the inhibition of aggression.

Reprinted with permission of General Media Magazines.

psychologist Kirsti Lagerspetz (1979) took normal albino mice and bred the most aggressive ones together and the least aggressive ones. After repeating the procedure for 26 generations, she had one set of fierce mice and one set of placid mice.

Aggressiveness similarly varies among primates and humans (Asher, 1987; Olweus, 1979). Our temperaments—how intense and reactive we are—are partly brought with us into the world, influenced by our sympathetic nervous system's reactivity (Kagan, 1989). A person's temperament, observed in infancy, usually endures (Larsen & Diener, 1987; Wilson & Matheny, 1986). A child who is nonaggressive at age 8 will very likely still be a nonaggressive person at age 48 (Huesmann et al., 2003). Thus, identical twins, when asked separately, are more likely than fraternal twins to agree on whether they have "a violent temper" or have gotten in fights (Rushton et al., 1986; Rowe et al., 1999). Of convicted criminals who are twins, fully half of their identical twins (but only one in five fraternal twins) also have criminal records (Raine, 1993).

Long-term studies following several hundred New Zealand children reveal that the recipe for aggressive behaviour combines a gene that alters neurotransmitter balance with childhood maltreatment (Caspi et al., 2002; Moffitt et al., 2003). Neither "bad" genes nor a "bad" environment alone predispose later aggressiveness and antisocial behaviour; rather, genes predispose some children to be more sensitive and responsive to maltreatment. Nature and nurture interact.

Biochemical influences

Blood chemistry also influences neural sensitivity to aggressive stimulation.

Alcohol

Both laboratory experiments and police data indicate that alcohol unleashes aggression when people are provoked (Bushman & Cooper, 1990; Bushman, 1993; Taylor & Chermack, 1993). Violent people are more likely (1) to drink, and (2) to become aggressive when intoxicated (White et al., 1993). Consider:

- In experiments, when asked to think back on relationship conflicts, intoxicated people administer stronger shocks and feel angrier than do sober people (MacDonald et al., 2000).
- In 65 percent of homicides and 55 percent of in-home fights and assaults, the assailant and/or the victim had been drinking (American Psychological Association, 1993).
- If spouse-battering alcoholics cease their problem drinking after treatment, their violent behaviour typically ceases as well (Murphy & O'Farrell, 1996).

Alcohol enhances aggressiveness by reducing people's self-awareness, and by reducing their ability to consider consequences, and by people's mentally associating alcohol with aggression (Bartholow & Heinz, 2006; Ito et al., 1996; Steele & Southwick, 1985). Alcohol deindividuates, and it disinhibits.

Testosterone

Hormonal influences appear much stronger in lower animals than in humans. But human aggressiveness does correlate with the male sex hormone, testosterone. Consider:

- Drugs that diminish testosterone levels in violent human males will subdue their aggressive tendencies (Dabbs, et al., 2002).
- After people reach age 25, their testosterone and rates of violent crime decrease together.
- Testosterone levels tend to be higher among prisoners convicted of planned and unprovoked violent crimes than of nonviolent crimes (Dabbs, 1992; Dabbs et al., 1995, 1997, 2001).
- Among the normal range of teen boys and adult men, those with high testosterone levels are more prone to delinquency, hard drug use, and aggressive responses to provocation (Archer, 1991; Dabbs & Morris, 1990; Olweus et al., 1988).
- After handling a gun, people's testosterone levels rise, and the more their testosterone rises the more they seek to inflict pain on someone else (Kleinsmith et al., 2006).

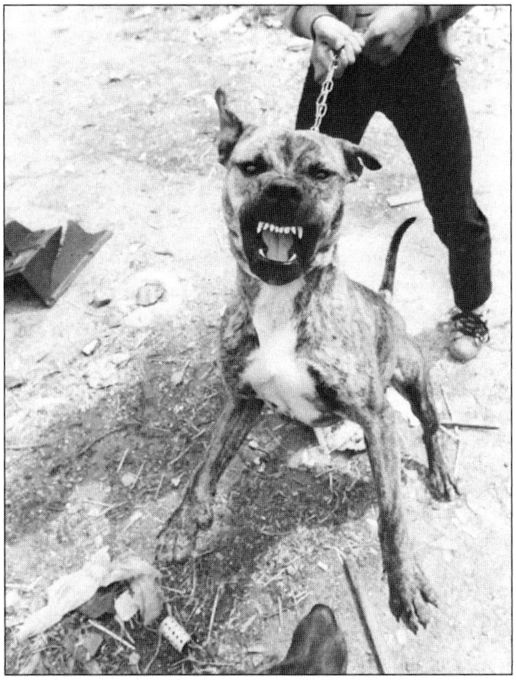

Genes predispose the pit bull's aggressiveness.

Testosterone, said James Dabbs (2000), "is a small molecule with large effects." Injecting a man with testosterone won't automatically make him aggressive, yet men with low testosterone are somewhat less likely to react aggressively when provoked (Geen, 1998). Testosterone is roughly like battery power. Only if the battery levels are very low will things noticeably slow down.

Question: Some violent sex offenders, wishing to free themselves of persistent, damaging impulses and to reduce their prison terms, have requested castration, an operation that is less invasive than a hysterectomy. Should their requests be granted? If so, and if they are deemed no longer at risk of sexual violence, should their prison terms be reduced or eliminated?

Low serotonin

Another culprit often found at the scene of violence is a low level of the neurotransmitter serotonin, for which the impulse-controlling frontal lobes have many receptors. In both primates and humans, low serotonin is often found among violence-prone children and adults (Bernhardt, 1997; Mehlman, 1994; Wright, 1995). Moreover, lowering people's serotonin levels in the laboratory increases their response to aversive events and willingness to deliver supposed electric shocks.

Biology and behaviour interact

It is important to remember that the traffic between testosterone, serotonin, and behaviour flows both ways. Testosterone, for example, may facilitate dominance and aggressiveness, but dominating or defeating behaviour also boosts testosterone levels (Gladue et al., 1989). After a World Cup soccer match or a big basketball game between archrivals, testosterone levels rise in the winning fans and fall in the losing fans (Bernhardt et al., 1998). That, plus celebration-related drinking, probably explains the finding of Cardiff University researchers that fans of winning rather than losing soccer and rugby teams commit more postgame assaults (Sivarajasingham et al., 2005).

So, neural, genetic, and biochemical influences predispose some people to react aggressively to conflict and provocation. But is aggression so much a part of human nature that it makes peace unattainable? The International Council of Psychologists has joined other organizations in unanimously endorsing a statement on violence developed by scientists from a dozen nations (Adams, 1991): "It is scientifically incorrect [to say that] war or any other violent behaviour is genetically programmed into our human nature [or that] war is caused by 'instinct' or any single motivation." Thus there are, as we will see, ways to reduce human aggression.

AGGRESSION AS RESPONSE TO FRUSTRATION

It is a warm evening. Tired and thirsty after two hours of studying, you borrow some change from a friend and head for the nearest soft-drink machine. As the machine devours the change, you can almost taste the cold, refreshing cola. But when you push the button, nothing happens. You push it again. Then you flip the coin return button. Still nothing. Again, you hit the buttons. You slam the machine. Alas, no money and no drink. You stomp back to your studies, empty-handed and short-changed. Should your roommate beware? Are you now more likely to say or do something hurtful?

frustration–aggression theory the theory that frustration triggers a readiness to aggress

frustration the blocking of goal-directed behaviour

One of the first psychological theories of aggression, the popular **frustration–aggression theory**, answers yes. "Frustration always leads to some form of aggression," said John Dollard and his colleagues (1939, p. 1). **Frustration** is anything (such as the malfunctioning vending machine) that *blocks our attaining a goal.* Frustration grows when our motivation to achieve a goal is very strong, when we expected gratification, and when the blocking is complete. When Rupert Brown and his colleagues (2001) surveyed British ferry passengers heading to France, they found much higher aggressive attitudes on a day when French fishing boats blockaded the port, preventing their travel. Blocked from obtaining their goal, the passengers became more likely (in responding to various vignettes) to agree with an insult toward a French person who had spilled coffee.

As Figure 10–2 suggests, the aggressive energy need not explode directly against its source. We learn to inhibit direct retaliation, especially when others might disapprove or punish;

FIGURE 10–2

The classic frustration–aggression theory.

Frustration creates a motive to aggress. Fear of punishment or disapproval for aggressing against the source of frustration may cause the aggressive drive to be displaced against some other target or even redirected against oneself. (Based on Dollard et al., 1939, and Miller, 1941)

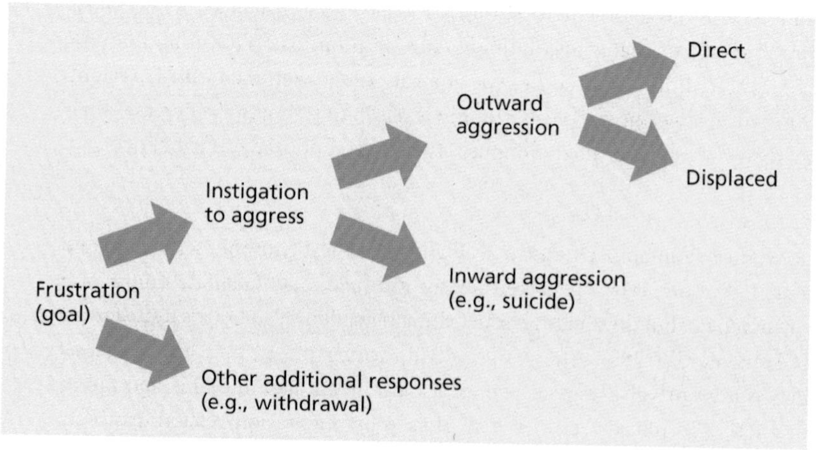

instead we *displace* our hostilities to safer targets. **Displacement** occurs in the old anecdote about a man who, humiliated by his boss, berates his wife, who yells at their son, who kicks the dog, which bites the mail carrier. In experiments and real life, displaced aggression is most likely when the target shares some similarity to the instigator and does some minor irritating act that unleashes the displaced aggression (Marcus-Newhall et al., 2000; Pedersen et al., 2000). When a person is harbouring anger, even a trivial offence—one that would normally produce no response—may elicit an explosive overreaction.

displacement the redirection of aggression to a target other than the source of the frustration. Generally, the new target is a safer or more socially acceptable target.

In one experiment, Eduardo Vasquez and his co-researchers (2005) provoked some university students (but not others) by having an experimenter insult their performance on an anagram-solving test. Shortly afterward, the students had to decide how long another supposed student should be required to immerse his or her hand in painful cold water while completing a task. When the supposed student committed a trivial offence—by giving a mild insult—the previously provoked participants responded punitively, by recommending a longer cold-water treatment than did the unprovoked participants. This phenomenon of displaced aggression helps us understand, notes Vasquez, why a previously provoked and still-angry person might respond to mild highway offences with road rage, or react to spousal criticism with spouse abuse.

Frustration-aggression theory revised

Laboratory tests of the frustration-aggression theory produced mixed results: Sometimes frustration increased aggressiveness, sometimes not. For example, if the frustration was understandable—if, as in one experiment by Eugene Burnstein and Philip Worchel (1962), a confederate disrupted a group's problem solving because his hearing aid malfunctioned (rather than just because he paid no attention)—then frustration led to irritation, but not aggression. Similarly, if someone frustrates us, we are less likely to respond aggressively if that person apologizes, accepts responsibility, or otherwise tries to make amends (Eaton & Struthers, 2006).

Leonard Berkowitz (1978, 1989) realized that the original theory overstated the frustration-aggression connection, so he revised it. Berkowitz theorized that frustration produces *anger*, an emotional readiness to aggress. Anger arises when someone who frustrates us could have chosen to act otherwise (Averill, 1983; Weiner, 1981). A frustrated person is especially likely to lash out when aggressive cues pull the cork, releasing bottled-up anger. Sometimes the cork will blow without such cues. But, as we will see, cues associated with aggression amplify aggression (Carlson et al., 1990).

Note that frustration-aggression theory is designed to explain hostile aggression, not instrumental aggression.

Terrorists understand the anger-inducing effect of their actions. Social psychologists Clark McCauley (2004) and Richard Wagner (2006) note that terrorists sometimes aim to commit an act that will induce a strong and angry enemy to overreact, producing effects that ultimately serve the terrorists' interests.

Is frustration the same as deprivation?

Picture someone feeling extremely frustrated—economically, sexually, or politically.

My hunch is that you are imagining someone economically, sexually, or politically deprived. And with good reason: When communities experience small increases in job layoffs, violence rates rise (Catalano et al., 1997). As American unemployment declined sharply during the mid-1990s, so did violent crime.

"I would say a person is deprived if he lacks a goal object people generally regard as attractive or desirable, but is frustrated only when he had been anticipating the pleasure to be gotten from this object and then cannot fulfill this expectation."

Leonard Berkowitz (1972)

But frustration may be unrelated to deprivation. The most sexually frustrated people are probably not celibate. The most economically frustrated people are probably not the impoverished residents of Jamaican shantytowns. When economic misery was everywhere during the 1930s depression, violent crime was not notably high. Likewise, Palestinian suicide bombers have not been the most deprived Palestinians; they are mostly middle class (Krueger & Maleckova, 2003; Pettigrew, 2003). So, too, were the 9/11 terrorists, who were professionally trained and world-travelled. Collective humiliation and antagonism feed terrorism far more than does absolute deprivation.

It seems that frustration is in the eye of the beholder. Objective reality may have little to do with people's experience of frustration, but even irrational frustration can lead to devastating violence.

Marc Lepine was a young man who wanted to be an engineer from the time he was a boy, but he was unable to get into a program to study engineering. He blamed his frustration on women and feminists in particular, who he felt were denying him his lifelong dream. On December 6, 1989, his frustration broke out into horrifying aggression. He took a semi-automatic rifle and went to the École Polytechnique de Montréal, the engineering school he had always wanted to attend. He entered one classroom and ordered the women to line up on one side. He opened fire, shooting them all at close range. He entered another classroom and did the same. He prowled the hallways killing any women he could find. In the end, he killed 14 women before turning the gun on himself. A full understanding of Marc Lepine's actions may never be possible, but it seems clear that his attainments in life fell far short of his expectations. And it seems plausible that this gap between his achievements and his aspirations may have fuelled his frustration and contributed to this tragedy.

This sort of frustration can explain revolutions as well. The political scientist–social psychologist team of Ivo and Rosaline Feierabend (1968, 1972) applied the frustration-aggression theory in a study of political instability within 84 nations. When people in rapidly modernizing nations become urbanized and literacy improves, they become more aware of material improvements. Since affluence usually diffuses slowly, however, the increasing gap between aspirations and achievements intensifies frustration. As deprivation diminishes, expectations outstrip reality so that frustration and political aggression may escalate.

"Evils which are patiently endured when they seem inevitable become intolerable when once the idea of escape from them is suggested."

Alexis de Tocqueville, 1856

The point is not that actual deprivation and social injustice are irrelevant to social unrest, but that *frustration arises from the gap between expectations and attainments.* When your expectations are fulfilled by your attainments, and when your desires are reachable at your income, you feel satisfied rather than frustrated (Solberg et al., 2002).

Relative deprivation

relative deprivation the perception that one is less well off than others to whom one compares oneself

Frustration is often compounded when we compare ourselves to others. Workers' feelings of well-being depend on whether their compensation is equitable compared to others in their line of work (Yuchtman, 1976). A salary raise for a city's police officers, while temporarily lifting their morale, may deflate that of the firefighters. Especially in people with shaky self-esteem, this kind of "upward comparison" can cause feelings of **relative deprivation** (Collins, 1996; Wood, 1989).

STORY BEHIND THE RESEARCH

For the last 25+ years, I have been exploring the psychology of perceived prejudice and discrimination from the "victim" or target's perspective. When I began this work in the early 1970s, little systematic or definitive research on the topic existed. Most research on prejudice concerned the bigot and ignored the target of the bigot's negative attitudes and behaviour. I felt, then as now, that there was an equally important story to be told about how people who experience prejudice and discrimination from others respond to these experiences.

I began with the assumption that perceived discrimination was vital for understanding the psychology of oppressed groups. My research has indicated that perceived discrimination is a social stressor and produces negative effect, but it also prompts perceivers to identify more closely with the positive aspects of their membership groups (as a likely response to stress). Perceived discrimination also has complex effects on self-esteem.

My more recent studies document the stressfulness of perceived discrimination by oppressed group members in the real social world rather than the artificial laboratory, and explore conditions under which they will take corrective action in response. This research shows that collective deprivation consistently predicts militancy better than "egotistic" or personal deprivation.

Ken Dion
University of Toronto

Such feelings, called relative deprivation, predict the reactions to perceived inequities by minority groups in Canada (Dion, 1985; Kawakami & Dion, 1993, 1995). They also explain why women who make less than men working in the same occupations feel underpaid only if they compare themselves with male rather than female colleagues (Bylsma & Major, 1994; Zanna et al., 1987). And it explains why East Germans revolted against their communist regime: They had a higher standard of living than some Western European countries, but a frustratingly lower one than their West German neighbours (Baron et al., 1992).

The term *relative deprivation* was coined by researchers studying the satisfaction felt by soldiers in the Second World War (Merton & Kitt, 1950; Stouffer et al., 1949). Ironically, those in the air corps felt *more* frustrated about their own rate of promotion than those in the military police, for whom promotions were slower. The air corps' promotion rate was rapid, and most air corps personnel probably perceived themselves as better than the average air corps member (the self-serving bias). Thus, their aspirations soared higher than their achievements. The result? Frustration.

One possible source of such frustration today is the affluence depicted in television programs and commercials. In cultures where television is a universal appliance, it helps turn absolute deprivation (lacking what others have) into relative deprivation (feeling deprived). Karen Hennigan and her coworkers (1982) analyzed crime rates in several cities around the time television was introduced. In 34 cities where television ownership became widespread in 1951, the 1951 larceny theft rate (for crimes such as shoplifting and bicycle stealing) took an observable

"A house may be large or small; as long as the surrounding houses are equally small, it satisfies all social demands for a dwelling. But let a palace arise beside the little house, and it shrinks from a little house into a hut."

Karl Marx

"Women's discontent increases in exact proportion to her development."

Elizabeth Cady Stanton, 1815–1902, American suffragette

jump. In 34 other cities, where a government freeze had delayed the introduction of television until 1955, a similar jump in the theft rate occurred—in 1955.

AGGRESSION AS LEARNED SOCIAL BEHAVIOUR

Theories of aggression based on instinct and frustration assume that hostile urges erupt from inner emotions, which naturally "push" aggression from within. Social psychologists contend that learning also "pulls" aggression out of us.

Frustration-triggered aggression sometimes appears as road rage.

The rewards of aggression

By experience and by observing others, we learn that aggression often pays. Experiments have transformed animals from docile creatures into ferocious fighters. Severe defeats, on the other hand, create submissiveness (Ginsburg & Allee, 1942; Kahn, 1951; Scott & Marston, 1953).

People, too, can learn the rewards of aggression. A child whose aggressive acts successfully intimidate other children will likely become increasingly aggressive (Patterson et al, 1967). Aggressive hockey players—the ones sent most often to the penalty box for rough play—score more goals than nonaggressive players (McCarthy & Kelly, 1978a, 1978b). Canadian teenage hockey players whose fathers applaud physically aggressive play show the most aggressive attitudes and style of play (Ennis & Zanna, 1991). In these cases, aggression is instrumental in achieving certain rewards.

The same is true of terrorist acts, which enable powerless people to garner widespread attention. "The primary targets of suicide-bombing attacks are not those who are injured but those who are made to witness it through media coverage," note Paul Marsden and Sharon Attia (2005). Terrorism's purpose is, with the help of media amplification, to terrorize. "Kill one, frighten ten thousand," asserts an ancient Chinese proverb. Deprived of what Margaret Thatcher called "the oxygen of publicity," terrorism would surely diminish, concluded Jeffrey Rubin (1986). It's like the 1970s incidents of naked spectators "streaking" onto football fields for a few seconds of television exposure. Once the networks decided to ignore the incidents, the phenomenon ended.

Observational learning

social learning theory the theory that we learn social behaviour by observing and imitating and by being rewarded and punished

Albert Bandura (1997) proposed a **social learning theory** of aggression. He believes that we learn aggression not only by experiencing its payoffs but also by observing others. As with most social behaviours, we acquire aggression by watching others act and noting the consequences.

Picture this scene from one of Bandura's experiments (Bandura et al., 1961). A preschool child is put to work on an interesting art activity. An adult is in another part of the room, where there are Tinker Toys, a mallet, and a big, inflated "Bobo" doll. After a minute of working with the Tinker Toys, the adult gets up and for almost 10 minutes attacks the inflated doll. She pounds it with the mallet, kicks it, and throws it, all the while yelling, "Sock him in the nose. . . . Knock him down. . . . Kick him."

After observing this outburst, the child goes to a different room with many very attractive toys. But after two minutes the experimenter interrupts, saying these are her best toys and she must "save them for the other children." The frustrated child now goes into another room with various toys for aggressive and nonaggressive play, two of which are a Bobo doll and a mallet.

Seldom did children not exposed to the aggressive adult model display any aggressive play or talk. Although frustrated, they nevertheless played calmly. Those who had observed the aggressive adult were many times more likely to pick up the mallet and lash out at the doll. Watching the adult's aggressive behaviour lowered their inhibitions. Moreover, the children often reproduced the model's acts and said her words. Observing aggressive behaviour had both lowered their inhibitions and taught them ways to aggress.

Bandura (1979) believes that everyday life exposes us to aggressive models in the family, in one's subculture, and, as we will see, in the mass media.

The family

Physically aggressive children tend to have physically punitive parents, who disciplined them by modelling aggression with screaming, slapping, and beating (Patterson et al., 1982). These parents often had parents who were themselves physically punitive (Bandura & Walters, 1959; Straus & Gelles, 1980). Such punitive behaviour may escalate into abuse, and although most abused children do not become criminals or abusive parents, 30 percent do later abuse their own children—four times the general population rate (Kaufman & Zigler, 1987; Widom, 1989). Violence often begets violence.

Family influence also appears in higher violence rates in cultures and in families with absentee fathers (Triandis, 1994). One large study reports that 70 percent of juveniles in detention did not grow up with two parents (Beck et al., 1988). Two-parent families differ not only in increased care and positive discipline by fathers but also in lesser poverty and greater educational achievement. The correlation between parental absence (usually father absence) and violence holds across races, income levels, education, and locations (Staub, 1996; Zill, 1988). In one British study that has followed more than 10 000 children for 33 years since birth in 1958, the risk of problems such as aggressive behaviour increased following a parental breakup during middle childhood (Cherlin et al., 1998).

The correlation also appears over time. In the Canada of 1960, less than 7 percent of children did not live with two parents and only 3653 juveniles were arrested for violent crime.

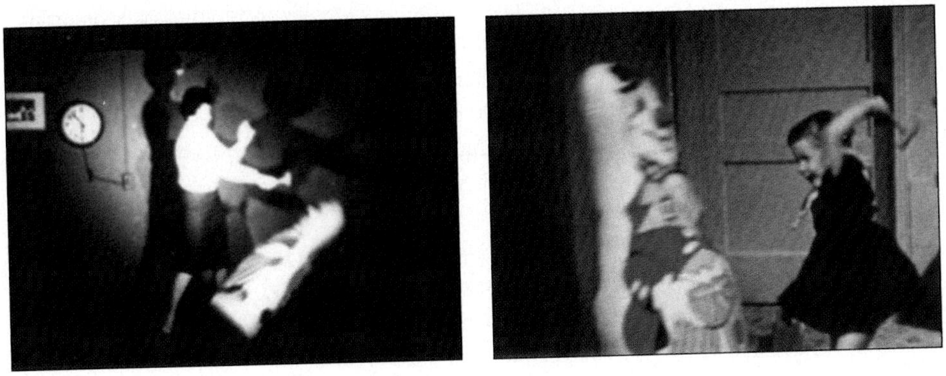

Monkey see, monkey do. In Bandura's famous experiment, children exposed to an adult's aggression against a Bobo doll were likely to reproduce the observed aggression.

In 1996, 19 percent of children did not live with two parents, and a similar-sized juvenile population produced more than 22 500 arrests for violent crime. The point is not that children from father-absent homes are likely to become delinquent or violent; in fact, nurtured by a caring mother and extended family, most such children thrive. The point is also not that father absence causes violence; we don't know that it does. The point is simply that there is a correlation: Where and when fathers are absent, the violence risk increases.

The culture

The social environment outside the home also provides models. In communities where "macho" images are admired, aggression is readily transmitted to new generations (Cartwright, 1975; Short, 1969). The violent subculture of teenage gangs, for instance, provides its junior members with aggressive models. Among adolescents, those who have observed gun violence are at doubled risk for violent behaviour (Bingenheimer et al., 2005).

The broader culture also matters. Show social psychologists a man from a nondemocratic culture that is economically underdeveloped, that has great economic inequality, that prepares men to be warriors and has engaged in war, and they will show you someone who is predisposed to aggressive behaviour (Bond, 2003).

Research reviewed in Chapter 8 by Richard Nisbett (1990, 1993) and Dov Cohen (1996, 1998) that demonstrates that Whites in the southern U.S. are more likely to commit and approve of violence to protect health and home than Whites in the northern U.S. provides another potent example of the effects of subculture on violence. Southerners also more strongly support wars and favour spanking (thus modelling violence in social relations).

People learn aggressive responses both by experience and by observing aggressive models. But when will aggressive responses actually occur? Bandura (1979) contends that aggressive acts are motivated by a variety of aversive experiences—frustration, pain, insults. Such experiences arouse us emotionally. But whether we act aggressively depends on the consequences we anticipate. Aggression is most likely when we are aroused *and* it seems safe and rewarding to aggress.

SUMMING UP: WHAT ARE SOME THEORIES OF AGGRESSION?

Aggression (defined as verbal or physical behaviour intended to cause harm) manifests itself in two forms: *hostile aggression,* which springs from emotions such as anger and intends to injure, and *instrumental aggression,* which is a means to some other end.

There are three broad theories of aggression. The *instinct view,* most commonly associated with Sigmund Freud and Konrad Lorenz, contended that aggressive energy will accumulate from within, like water accumulating behind a dam. Although the available evidence offers little support for this view, aggression *is* biologically influenced by heredity, blood chemistry, and the brain.

According to the second view, *frustration* causes anger and hostility. Given aggressive cues, this anger may provoke aggression. Frustration stems not from deprivation itself but from the gap between expectations and achievements.

The *social learning* view presents aggression as learned behaviour. By experience and by observing others' success, we sometimes learn that aggression pays. Social learning enables family and subculture influences on aggression, as well as media influences (which we will discuss in the next section).

WHAT ARE SOME INFLUENCES ON AGGRESSION?

Under what conditions do we aggress? In the previous section, we examined some theories of aggression. Now we dig deeper and examine some specific influences: aversive incidents, arousal, aggression cues, the media, and the group context.

AVERSIVE INCIDENTS

Recipes for aggression often include not only frustration but some type of aversive experience: pain, uncomfortable heat, an attack, or overcrowding.

Pain

Researcher Nathan Azrin (1967) was doing experiments with laboratory rats in a cage wire to deliver shocks to the animals' feet. Azrin wanted to know if switching off the foot shocks would reinforce two rats' positive interactions with each other. Azrin planned to turn on the shock and then, once the rats approached each other, cut off the pain. To his great surprise, the experiment proved impossible. As soon as the rats felt pain, they attacked each other, before the experimenter could switch off the shock. The greater the shock (and pain) the more violent the attack.

Is this true of rats alone? The researchers found that with a wide variety of species, the cruelty the animals imposed on each other matched zap for zap the cruelty imposed on them. As Azrin (1967) explained, the pain-attack response occurred

> in many different strains of rats. Then we found that shock produced attack when pairs of the following species were caged together: some kinds of mice, hamsters, opossums, raccoons, marmosets, foxes, nutria, cats, snapping turtles, squirrel monkeys, ferrets, red squirrels, bantam roosters, alligators, crayfish, amphiuma (an amphibian), and several species of snakes including the boa constrictor, rattlesnake, brown rat-snake, cottonmouth, copperhead, and black snake. The shock-attack reaction was clearly present in many very different kinds of creatures. In all the species in which shock produced attack it was fast and consistent, in the same "push-button" manner as with the rats.

Today's ethical guidelines restrict researchers' use of painful stimuli.

The animals were not choosy about their targets. They would attack animals of their own species and also those of a different species, or stuffed dolls, or even tennis balls.

The researchers also varied the source of pain. They found that not just shocks induce attack; intense heat and "psychological pain"—for example, suddenly not rewarding hungry pigeons that have been trained to expect a grain reward after pecking at a disk—brought the same reaction as shocks. "Psychological pain" is, of course, what we call frustration.

Pain heightens aggressiveness in humans, also. Many of us can recall such a reaction after stubbing a toe or suffering a headache. Leonard Berkowitz and his associates demonstrated this by having students hold one hand in lukewarm water or painfully cold water. Those whose hands were submerged in the cold water reported feeling more irritable and more annoyed, and they were more willing to blast another person with unpleasant noise. In view of such results, Berkowitz (1983, 1989) proposed that aversive stimulation rather than frustration is the basic

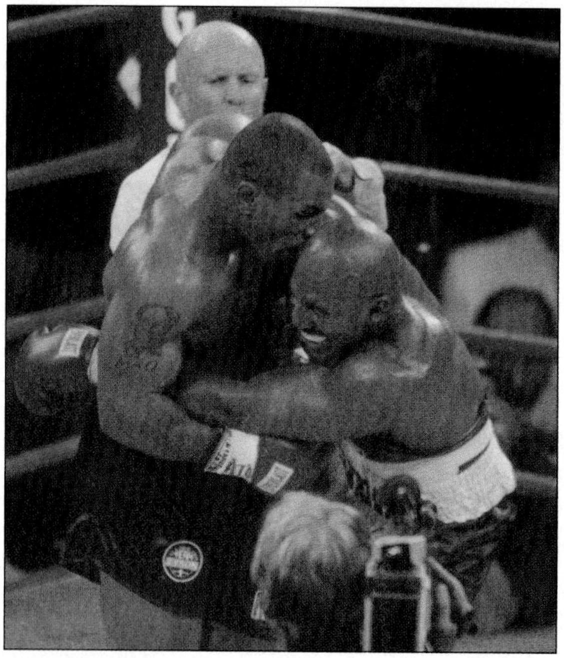

Pain attack. Frustrated after losing the first two rounds of his 1997 heavyweight championship fight with Evander Holyfield, and feeling pain from an accidental head butt, Mike Tyson reacts by biting off part of Holyfield's ear.

trigger of hostile aggression. Frustration is certainly one important type of unpleasantness. But any aversive event, whether a dashed expectation, a personal insult, or physical pain, can incite an emotional outburst. Even the torment of a depressed state increases the likelihood of hostile aggressive behaviour.

Heat

People have theorized for centuries about the effect of climate on human action. Hippocrates (ca. 460–377 B.C.), compared the civilized Greece of his day to the savagery in the region further north (what is now Germany and Switzerland), and decided that northern Europe's harsh climate was to blame. Later, the English attributed their "superior" culture to *England's* ideal climate. French thinkers proclaimed the same for France. Because climate remains relatively steady while cultural traits change over time, the climate theory of culture obviously has limited validity.

Temporary climate variations can, however, affect behaviour. Offensive odours, cigarette smoke, and air pollution have all been linked with aggressive behaviour (Rotton & Frey, 1985). But the most-studied environmental irritant is heat. William Griffitt (1970; Griffitt & Veitch, 1971) found that compared to students who answered questionnaires in a room with a normal temperature, those who did so in an uncomfortably hot room (over 32°C/90°F) reported feeling more tired and aggressive and expressed more hostility toward a stranger. Follow-up experiments revealed that heat also triggers retaliative actions (Bell, 1980; Rule et al., 1987).

Does uncomfortable heat increase aggression in the real world as well as in the laboratory? Consider:

- In hot weather, drivers without air conditioning are more likely to honk at a stalled car (Kenrick & MacFarlane, 1986).
- During the 1986 to 1988 major league baseball seasons, the number of batters hit by a pitch was two-thirds greater for games played at 32°C and above than for games played below 27°C (Reifman et al., 1991). Pitchers weren't wilder on hot days—they had no more walks or wild pitches. They just clobbered more batters.
- Riots occurring in 79 cities between 1967 and 1971 were more likely on hot than on cool days; none of them happened in winter.
- Studies in six cities have found that when the weather is hot, violent crimes are more likely (Anderson & Anderson, 1984; Cohn, 1993; Cotton, 1981, 1986; Harries & Stadler, 1988; Rotton & Frey, 1985).
- Across the northen hemisphere, it is not only hotter days that have more violent crimes, but also hotter seasons of the year, hotter summers, hotter years, hotter cities, and hotter regions (Anderson & Anderson, 1998, 2000). Anderson and his colleagues predict that if a 4-degree-Fahrenheit (about 2°C) global warming occurs, the United States alone will annually see at least 50 000 more serious assaults.

Do these findings show that heat discomfort directly fuels aggressiveness? Although the conclusion appears plausible, these *correlations* between temperature and aggression don't prove it. People certainly could be more irritable in hot, sticky weather. And in the laboratory, hot temperatures do increase arousal and hostile thoughts and feelings (Anderson et al., 1995). There may be other contributing factors, however. Maybe hot summer evenings drive people into the streets. There, other group influence factors may well take over. Then again (researchers are debating this), maybe there comes a point where stifling heat suppresses violence (Bell, 2005; Bushman et al., 2005a, 2005b; Cohn & Rotton, 2005).

"I pray thee, good Mercutio, let's retire; The day is hot, the Capulets abroad, And, if we meet, we shall not 'scape a brawl, For now, these hot days, is the mad blood stirring."

Shakespeare, *Romeo and Juliet*

Attacks

Being attacked or insulted by another is especially conducive to aggression. Experiments in several labs around the globe by Stuart Taylor (Taylor & Pisano, 1971), Harold Dengerink (Dengerink & Myers, 1977), and Kennichi Ohbuchi and Toshihiro Kambara (1985) confirm that intentional attacks breed retaliatory attacks. In most of these experiments one person competes with another in a reaction-time contest. After each test trial, the winner chooses how much shock to give the loser. Actually, each subject is playing a programmed opponent, who steadily escalates the amount of shock. Do the real subjects respond charitably? Hardly. Extracting "an eye for an eye" is the more likely response.

AROUSAL

So far we have seen that various aversive stimulations can arouse anger. Do other types of arousal, such as those that accompany exercise or sexual excitement, have a similar effect? Imagine that Tawna, having just finished a stimulating short run, comes home to discover that her date for the evening has called and left word that he has made other plans. Will Tawna more likely explode in fury after her run than if she discovered the same message after awakening from a nap? Or, having just exercised, will her aggressive tendencies be exorcised? To discover an answer, let's examine some intriguing research on how we interpret and label our bodily states.

In a famous experiment, Stanley Schachter and Jerome Singer (1962) found we can experience an aroused bodily state in different ways. They aroused men by injecting adrenalin. The drug produced body flushing, heart palpitation, and more rapid breathing. When forewarned that the drug would produce these effects, the men felt little emotion, even when waiting with either a hostile or a euphoric person. Of course, they could readily attribute their bodily sensations to the drug. Schachter and Singer led another group of men to believe the drug produced no such side effects. Then they, too, were placed in the company of a hostile or euphoric person. How did they feel and act? Angered when with the hostile person; amused when with the person who was euphoric. The principle seemed to be: *A given state of bodily arousal feeds one emotion or another, depending on how the person interprets and labels the arousal.*

Other experiments indicate that arousal is not as emotionally undifferentiated as Schachter believed. Yet being physically stirred up does intensify just about any emotion (Reisenzein, 1983). For example, Paul Biner (1991) reports that people find radio static unpleasant, *especially* when they are aroused by bright lighting. And Dolf Zillmann (1988), Jennings Bryant, and their collaborators found that people who have just pumped an exercise bike or watched a film of a Beatles rock concert find it easy to misattribute their arousal to a provocation. They then retaliate with heightened aggression. Although common sense might lead us to assume that Tawna's run would have drained her aggressive tensions, enabling her to accept bad news calmly, these studies show that arousal feeds emotions.

Sexual arousal and other forms of arousal, such as anger, can therefore amplify one another (Zillmann, 1989). Love is never so passionate as after a fight or a fright. In the laboratory, erotic stimuli are more arousing to people who have just been frightened. The arousal of a roller-coaster ride may similarly spill over into romantic feelings for one's partner.

A frustrating, hot, crowded, or insulting situation heightens arousal. When it does, the arousal, combined with hostile thoughts and feelings, may form a recipe for aggressive behaviour (Figure 10–3). In March, 2004, the Vancouver Canuck's Todd Bertuzzi, angered by an earlier attack to his captain in a hockey game, viciously sucker-punched the Colorado Avalanche's Steve Moore from behind, rendering him unconscious with three broken vertebrae and a concussion.

AGGRESSION CUES

As we noted when considering the frustration-aggression hypothesis, violence is more likely when aggressive cues release pent-up anger. Leonard Berkowitz (1968, 1981, 1995) and others have found that the sight of a weapon is such a cue. In one experiment, children who had just played with toy guns became more willing to knock down another child's blocks. In another, angered University of Wisconsin men gave more electric shocks to their tormenter when a rifle and a revolver (supposedly left over from a previous experiment) were nearby than when

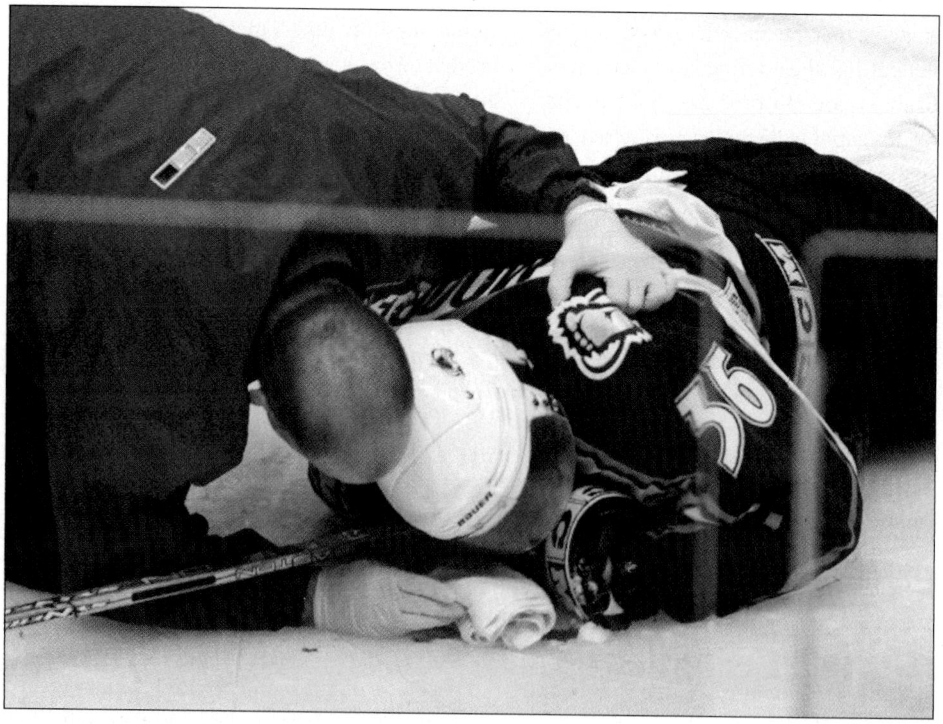

The NHL's Steve Moore collapsed on the ice after being hit by Todd Bertuzzi in March 2004. Bertuzzi's captain had taken a hard hit earlier in the season and it appears the attack on Moore was retaliatory.

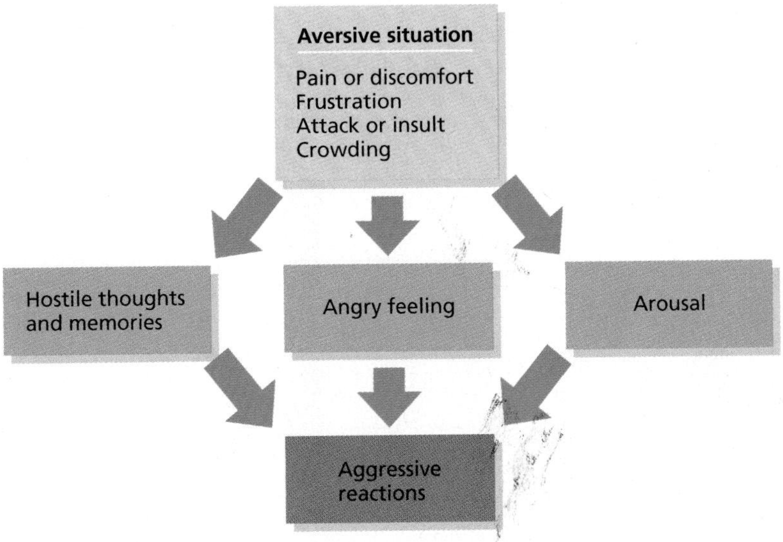

FIGURE 10–3

Elements of hostile aggression.

An aversive situation can trigger aggression by provoking hostile cognitions, hostile feelings, and arousal. These reactions make us more likely to perceive harmful intent and to react aggressively. (Simplified from Anderson, Deuser & DeNeve, 1995)

badminton racquets had been left behind (Berkowitz & LePage, 1967). Guns prime hostile thoughts and punitive judgments (Anderson et al., 1998; Dienstbier et al., 1998). What's within sight is within mind. This is especially so when a weapon is perceived as an instrument of violence rather than a recreational item. For hunters, for example, seeing a hunting rifle does not prime aggressive thoughts, though it does for nonhunters (Bartholow et al., 2004).

Berkowitz was not surprised that in the United States, a country with some 200 million privately owned guns, half of all murders are committed with handguns, or that handguns in homes are far more likely to kill household members than intruders. "Guns not only permit violence," he reported, "they can stimulate it as well. The finger pulls the trigger, but the trigger may also be pulling the finger."

Berkowitz is also not surprised that countries that ban handguns have lower murder rates. Compared to the United States, Britain has one-fourth as many people and one-sixteenth as many murders. The United States has 10 000 handgun homicides a year; Australia has about a dozen, Britain two dozen, and Canada 100. Vancouver, British Columbia, and Seattle, Washington, have similar populations, climates, economies, and rates of criminal activity and assault—except that Vancouver, which carefully restricts handgun ownership, has had one-fifth as many handgun murders as Seattle and thus a 40-percent lower overall murder rate (Sloan et al., 1988). Not only does Canada have a much lower murder rate than the U.S., the difference in the percentage of murders that occur by the use of a gun is striking. As you can see in Figure 10–4, Americans are more than twice as likely as Canadians to use guns when they commit murder.

Changes in gun laws do seem to affect murder rates. For example, when Washington, D.C., adopted a law restricting handgun possession, the numbers of gun-related murders dropped about 25 percent. No changes occurred in other methods of murder, nor did adjacent areas outside the reach of this law experience any such declines (Loftin et al., 1991).

Researchers also have examined risks of violence in homes with and without guns. This is controversial research, because such homes may differ in many ways. One study compared gun owners and nonowners of the same sex, race, age, and neighbourhood. The ironic and tragic

FIGURE 10–4

A comparison of weapons used to commit murder in Canada and the United States in 1996. (Data from Statistics Canada Uniform Crime Report and U.S. Federal Bureau of Investigation Uniform Crime Report)

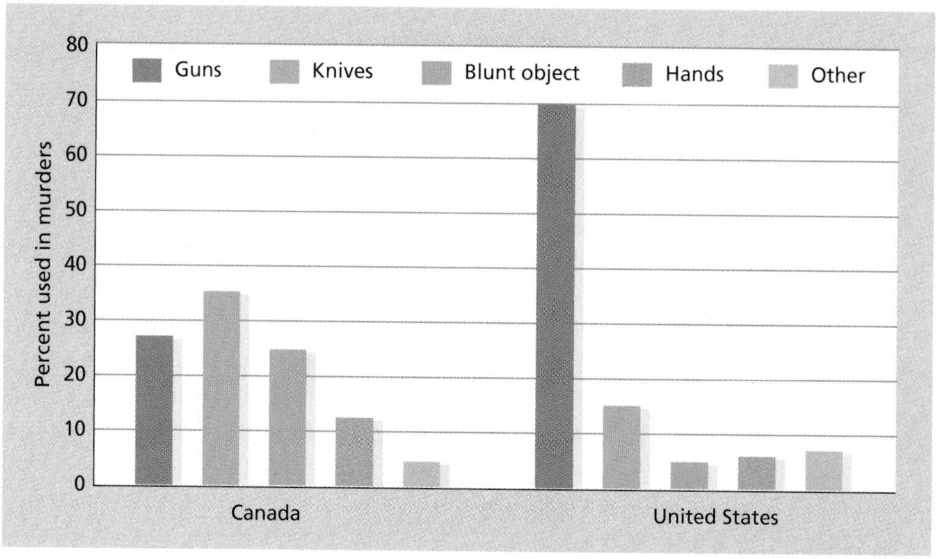

result was that those who kept a gun in the home (often for protection) were 2.7 times more likely to be murdered—nearly always by a family member or close acquaintance (Kellermann, 1993, 1997). Another study found that the risk of suicide in homes with guns was five times as high as in homes without them (Taubes, 1992). A newer study found a slightly weaker, but still significant, link between guns and homicide or suicide. Compared with others of the same gender, age, and race, people with guns at home were 41 percent as likely to be homicide victims and 3.4 times as likely to die of suicide (Wiebe, 2003). A gun in the home has often meant the difference between a fight and a funeral, or between suffering and suicide.

Is violent crime rising? Perceptions of increased crime can trigger gun purchases, but these guns are more likely to be used against a household member than as intended—against an intruder or attacker. Countries with fewer guns have lower murder rates.

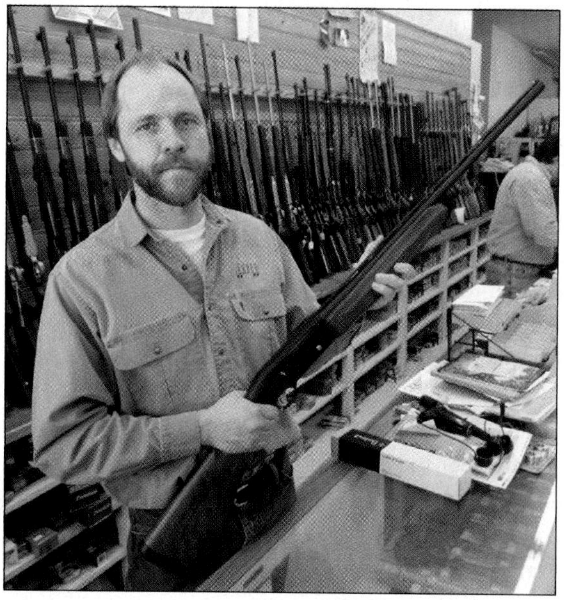

Guns not only serve as aggression cues, they also put psychological distance between aggressor and victim. As Milgram's obedience studies taught us, remoteness from the victim facilitates cruelty. A knife can kill someone, but a knife attack is more difficult than pulling a trigger from a distance.

MEDIA INFLUENCES: PORNOGRAPHY AND SEXUAL VIOLENCE

The substantial increase in reported violent crime, especially among juveniles, between 1960 and 1990, prompted social psychologists to wonder: Why the change? What social forces have caused the mushrooming violence?

Alcohol contributes to aggression, but alcohol use has not appreciably changed since 1960 (McAneny, 1994). Similarly, other biological factors (testosterone, genes, neurotransmitters) influence aggression but had not undergone any major change. Might the surging violence instead be fuelled by the growth in individualism and materialism? By the growing gap between the powerful rich and the powerless poor? By the decline in two-parent families and the increase in father absence? By the media's increasing modelling of unrestrained sexuality and violence?

The last question arises because increased rates of criminal violence, including sexual coercion, coincided with increases in media mayhem and sexual suggestion. Is the historical correlation a coincidence? To find out, researchers have explored the social consequences of pornography (which *Webster's* defines as erotic depictions intended to excite sexual arousal) and the effects of modelling violence in movies and on television.

Social-psychological research on pornography has focused mostly on depictions of sexual violence. A typical sexually violent episode finds a man forcing himself on a woman. She at first resists and tries to fight off her attacker. Gradually she becomes sexually aroused, and her resistance melts. By the end she is in ecstasy, pleading for more. We have all viewed or read nonpornographic versions of this sequence: She resists, he persists. Dashing man grabs and forcibly kisses protesting woman. Within moments, the arms that were pushing him away are clutching him tight, her resistance overwhelmed by her unleashed passion. In *Gone with the Wind,* Scarlett O'Hara is carried to bed protesting and kicking, and wakes up singing.

Social psychologists report that viewing such fictional scenes of a man overpowering and arousing a woman can distort one's perceptions of how women actually respond to sexual coercion and increase men's aggression against women, at least in laboratory settings.

Distorted perceptions of sexual reality

Does viewing sexual violence reinforce the myth that some women would welcome sexual assault—that "no doesn't really mean no"? To find out, Neil Malamuth and James Check (1981) showed University of Manitoba men either two nonsexual movies or two movies depicting a man sexually overcoming a woman. A week later, when surveyed by a different experimenter, those who saw the films with mild sexual violence were more accepting of violence against women.

"Pornography that portrays sexual aggression as pleasurable for the victim increases the acceptance of the use of coercion in sexual relations."

Social science consensus at Surgeon General's Workshop on Pornography and Public Health (Koop, 1987)

Other studies confirm that exposure to pornography increases acceptance of the rape myth (Oddone-Paolucci et al., 2000). For example, while spending three evenings watching sexually violent movies, male viewers in an experiment by Charles Mullin and Daniel Linz (1995) also became progressively less bothered by the raping and slashing. Compared with others not exposed to the films, they also, three days later, expressed less sympathy for domestic violence victims, and they rated the victims' injuries as less severe. In fact, said researchers Edward Donnerstein, Daniel Linz, and Steven Penrod (1987), what better way for an evil character to get people to react calmly to the torture and mutilation of women than to show a gradually escalating series of such films?

Note that the sexual message (that many women enjoy being "taken") was subtle and unlikely to elicit counterarguing. Given frequent media images of women's resistance melting in the arms of a forceful man, we shouldn't be surprised that even women often believe that some *other* woman might enjoy being sexually overpowered—though virtually none think it of themselves (Malamuth et al., 1980).

Repeated exposure to erotic films featuring quick, uncommitted sex also tends to
- *decrease attraction for one's partner*
- *increase acceptance of extramarital sex and of women's sexual submission to men*
- *increase men's perceiving women in sexual terms*

Meyers (2000)

Aggression against women

Correlational studies

Evidence also suggests that pornography, particularly violent pornography, may contribute to men's actual aggression toward women. Correlational studies raise that possibility. John Court (1985) noted that across the world, as pornography became more widely available during the 1960s and 1970s, the rate of reported rapes sharply increased—except in countries and areas where pornography was controlled. (The examples that counter this trend—such as Japan, where violent pornography is available but the rape rate is low—remind us that other factors are also important.) In Hawaii, the number of reported rapes rose ninefold between 1960 and 1974, dropped when restraints on pornography were temporarily imposed, and rose again when the restraints were lifted.

In another correlational study, Larry Baron and Murray Straus (1984) discovered that the sales of sexually explicit magazines (such as *Hustler* and *Playboy*) correlated with rape rates, even after controlling for a number of factors, such as the percentage of young males in each area. The areas that sold the most magazines had the most rapes, and those that sold the fewest magazines had the fewest rapes.

When interviewed, Canadian sexual offenders commonly acknowledge pornography use. For example, William Marshall (1989) reported that Ontario rapists

Was the use of pornography by Paul Bernardo (a.k.a. Paul Teale, in whose house police found pornographic tapes) merely a symptom of his derangement or a cause? Could the viewing of pornography actually have pushed him over the edge and led him to begin raping and murdering young girls? Notorious serial killer Ted Bundy saw such a role for pornography in his own life. On the eve of his execution he argued, "The most damaging kinds of pornography [involve] sexual violence. Like an addiction, you keep craving something that is harder, harder, something which, which gives you a greater sense of excitement. Until you reach a point where the pornography only goes so far, you reach that jumping off point where you begin to wonder if maybe actually doing it would give you that which is beyond just reading it or looking at it."

and child molesters used pornography much more than men who were not sexual offenders. Another study also reports considerable exposure to pornography among serial killers, and among most child sex abusers (Bennett, 1991; Ressler et al., 1988).

Experimental studies

Although limited to the sorts of short-term behaviours that can be studied in the laboratory, controlled experiments reveal what correlational studies cannot: cause and effect. A consensus statement by 21 leading social scientists sums up the results: "Exposure to violent pornography increases punitive behaviour toward women" (Koop, 1987). One of these social scientists, Edward Donnerstein (1980), had shown 120 men a neutral, an erotic, or an aggressive-erotic (rape) film. Then, the men, supposedly as part of another experiment, "taught" a male or female confederate some nonsense syllables by choosing how much shock to administer for incorrect answers. The men who had watched the rape film administered markedly stronger shocks (Figure 10–5), especially when angered and with a female victim.

If the ethics of conducting such experiments trouble you, rest assured that these researchers appreciate the controversial and powerful experience they are giving participants. Only after giving their knowing consent do people participate. Moreover, after the experiment researchers debunk any myths the film communicated. One hopes that such debriefing sufficiently offsets the vivid image of a supposedly euphoric rape victim. Judging from studies with University of Manitoba and Winnipeg students by James Check and Neil Malamuth (1984; Malamuth & Check, 1984), it does. Those who read erotic rape stories and were then fully debriefed became *less* accepting of the "women-enjoy-rape" myth than students who had not seen the film.

Justification for this experimentation is not only scientific but also humanitarian.

- In one careful survey, 22 percent of women reported having been forced by a man to do something sexual (Laumann et al., 1994).

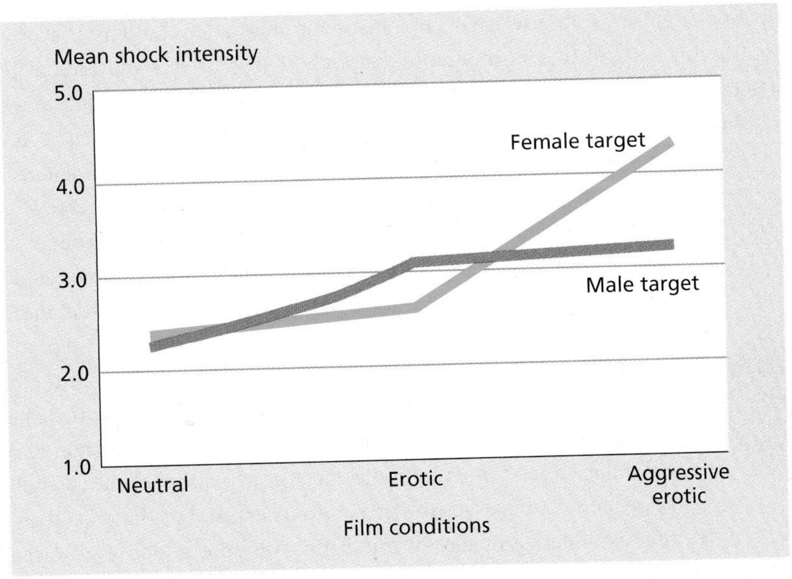

FIGURE 10–5

After viewing an aggressive-erotic film, university and college men delivered stronger shocks than before, especially to a woman. (Data from Donnerstein, 1980)

TABLE 10–1 **Reported rape experiences in five countries**

Country	Sample of Women	Completed & Attempted Rape
Canada	national sample at 95 colleges and universities	23% rape or sexual assault
New Zealand	convenience sample of psychology students	25%
United Kingdom	convenience sample at 22 universities	19%
United States	representative sample at 32 colleges and universities	28%
Seoul, Korea	adult women	22%

Source: Studies reported by Koss, Heise, and Russo (1994).

"What we're trying to do is raise the level of awareness of violence against women and pornography to at least the level of racist and Ku Klux Klan literature."

Gloria Steinem (1988)

- In another, 18 percent of women reported an experience that met the definition of rape (Tjaden & Thoennes, 2000). Six times in seven the perpetrator was someone they knew.
- Surveys in other industrialized countries produce similar results (Table 10–1 above). Three in four stranger rapes and nearly all acquaintance rapes went unreported to police. Thus the official rape rate *greatly* underestimates the actual rape rate.

Women are most at risk when encountering men who exhibit the promiscuous behaviour and hostile attitudes pornography cultivates (Figure 10–6).

Media awareness education

As most Germans quietly tolerated the degrading anti-Semitic images that fed the Holocaust, so most people today tolerate media images of women that feed sexual harassment, abuse, and rape. Should such portrayals that demean or violate women be restrained by law?

In the contest of individual versus collective rights, people in most Western nations side with individual rights. As an alternative to censorship, many psychologists favour "media awareness training." Recall that pornography researchers have successfully resensitized and educated participants to women's actual responses to sexual violence. Could educators similarly promote critical viewing skills? By sensitizing people to the view of women that predominates in pornography and to issues of sexual harassment and violence, it should be possible to counter the myth that women enjoy being coerced. "Our utopian and perhaps naive hope," say Edward Donnerstein, Daniel Linz, and Steven Penrod (1987, p. 196), "is that in the end the truth revealed through good science will prevail and the public will be convinced that these images not only demean those portrayed but also those who view them."

Is such a hope naive? Consider: Without banning cigarettes, the number of Canadian smokers dropped from 48 percent in 1972 to 27 percent in 1994. Without censoring racism, once-common media images of Blacks as childlike, superstitious buffoons have nearly disappeared. As public consciousness changed, scriptwriters, producers, and media executives decided that exploitative images of minorities were not good. More recently they have decided that drugs are not glamorous, as many films and songs from

FIGURE 10–6

Sexually aggressive men.

Men who sexually coerce women often combine a history of impersonal sex with hostile masculinity. (Neil Malamuth, 1996, 2003)

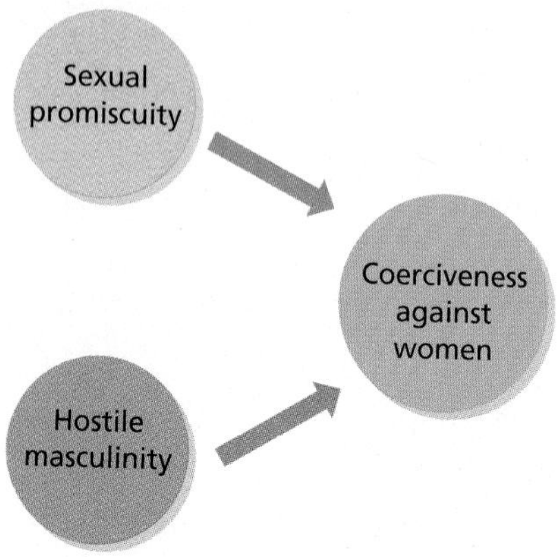

the 1960s and 1970s implied, but dangerous—and high-school seniors' marijuana use during the previous month dropped from 37 percent in 1979 to 11 percent in 1992, before rebounding to 22 percent in 1996 as the cultural antidrug voice softened and drug use became reglamourized in some music and films (Johnston, 1996). Will we one day look back with embarrassment on the time when movies entertained people with scenes of exploitation, mutilation, and sexual coercion?

MEDIA INFLUENCES: TELEVISION

We have seen that watching an aggressive model attack a Bobo doll can unleash children's aggressive urges and teach them new ways to aggress. And we have seen that after viewing movies depicting sexual violence, many angry men will act more violently toward women. Does television have any similar effects?

Consider these few facts about watching television. In 1945, the Gallup poll asked, "Do you know what television is?" (Gallup, 1972, p. 551). Today, in much of the industrialized world, 98 percent of households have a TV set, more than have bathtubs or telephones. Most homes have more than one set, which helps explain why parents' reports of what their children watch minimally correlate with children's reports of what they watch (Donnerstein, 1998). With MTV in 140 countries and CNN spanning the globe, television is creating a global culture (Stern, 1999).

In the average home, the set is on seven hours a day, with individual household members averaging three to four hours. Women watch more than men, non-Whites more than Whites, preschoolers and retired people more than those in school or working, and the less educated more than the highly educated. For the most part, these facts characterize people in most industrialized countries (Murray & Kippax, 1979).

During all those hours, what social behaviours are modelled? From 1994 to 1997, bleary-eyed employees of the National Television Violence Study (1997) have analyzed some 10 000 programs from the major networks and cable channels. Their findings? Six in 10 programs contain violence ("physically compelling action that threatens to hurt or kill, or actual hurting or killing"). What does it add up to? By the end of elementary school, the average child views some 8000 TV murders and 100 000 other violent acts (Huston et al., 1992). Reflecting on his 22 years of cruelty counting, media researcher George Gerbner (1994) lamented: "Humankind has had more bloodthirsty eras but none as filled with *images* of violence as the present. We are awash in a tide of violent representations the world has never seen . . . drenching every home with graphic scenes of expertly choreographed brutality."

Does prime-time crime stimulate the behaviour it depicts? Or, as viewers vicariously participate in aggressive acts, do the shows drain off aggressive energy? The latter idea, a variation on the **catharsis** hypothesis, maintains that watching violent drama enables people to release their pent-up hostilities. Defenders of the media cite this theory frequently and remind us that violence predates television. In an imaginary debate with one of television's critics, the medium's defender might argue, "Television played no role in the genocides of Jews and Native Americans. Television just reflects and caters to our tastes." "Agreed," responds the critic, "but it's also true that during the TV age, reported violent crime has increased several times faster than the population rate. Surely you don't mean the popular arts are mere passive reflections, without any power to influence public consciousness." The defender replies: "The violence

catharsis emotional release. The catharsis view of aggression is that aggressive drive is reduced when one "releases" aggressive energy, either by acting aggressively or by fantasizing aggression.

"One of television's great contributions is that it brought murder back into the home where it belongs. Seeing a murder on television can be good therapy. It can help work off one's antagonisms."

Alfred Hitchcock

epidemic results from many factors. TV may even reduce aggression by keeping people off the streets and by offering them a harmless opportunity to vent their aggression."

Studies of television viewing and aggression aim to identify effects more subtle and pervasive than the occasional "copy-cat" murders that capture public attention. They ask: How does television affect viewers' *behaviour?* Viewers' *thinking?*

Television's effects on behaviour

Do viewers imitate violent models? Examples abound of people re-enacting television crimes. In one survey of 208 prison convicts, 9 of 10 admitted that they learned new criminal tricks by watching crime programs. And 4 out of 10 said they had attempted specific crimes seen on television *(TV Guide,* 1977).

Correlating TV viewing and behaviour

Crime stories are not scientific evidence. Researchers therefore use correlational and experimental studies to examine the effects of viewing violence. One technique, commonly used with schoolchildren, asks whether their TV watching predicts their aggressiveness. The frequent result: The more violent the content of the child's TV viewing, the more aggressive the child (Eron, 1987; Kuntsche et al., 2006; Turner et al., 1986). The relationship is modest but consistently found in North America, Europe, and Australia. British girls who most often view programs that model gossiping, backbiting, and social exclusion also more often display such behaviour (Coyne & Archer, 2005).

So can we conclude that a diet of violent TV fuels aggression? Perhaps you are already thinking that because this is a correlational study, the cause-effect relation could also work in the opposite direction. Maybe aggressive children prefer aggressive programs. Or maybe some underlying third factor, such as lower intelligence, predisposes some children both to prefer aggressive programs and aggressive behaviour.

Researchers have developed two ways to test these alternative explanations. They test the "hidden third factor" explanation by statistically pulling out the influence of some of these possible factors. For example, British researcher William Belson (1978; Muson, 1978) studied 1565 London boys. Compared to those who watched little violence, those who watched a great deal (especially realistic rather than cartoon violence) admitted to 50 percent more violent acts during the preceding six months (for example, vandalizing a public telephone). Belson also examined 22 likely third factors, such as family size. The heavy and light viewers still differed after equating them with respect to potential third factors. So Belson surmised that the heavy viewers were indeed more violent *because* of their TV exposure.

Similarly, Leonard Eron and Rowell Huesmann (1980, 1985) found that violence viewing among 875 eight-year-olds correlated with aggressiveness even after statistically pulling out several obvious possible third factors. Moreover, when they restudied these individuals as 19-year-olds, they discovered that viewing violence at age 8 modestly predicted aggressiveness at age 19, but that aggressiveness at age 8 did *not* predict viewing violence at age 19. Aggression followed viewing, not the reverse. They confirmed these findings in follow-up studies of 758 Chicago-area and 220 Finnish youngsters (Huesmann et al., 1984). Moreover by age 30, those who had watched the most violence in childhood were more likely to have been convicted of a serious crime.

Follow-up studies have confirmed these findings in various ways, including these:

- Correlating 8-year-olds' violence viewing with their later likelihood of adult spouse abuse (Huesmann et al., 1984, 2003)
- Correlating adolescents' violence viewing with their later likelihood of assault, robbery, and threats of injury (Johnson et al., 2002)
- Correlating elementary schoolchildren's violent media exposure with how often they got into fights when restudied two to six months later (Gentile et al., 2004)

"I rarely turn down an invitation to speak to a PTA meeting or other civic groups in order to warn parents and other caretakers that they must control their children's viewing habits."

Leonard Eron (1985)

In all these studies, the investigators were careful to adjust for likely "third factors" such as preexisting lower intelligence or hostility.

Another fact to ponder: Where television goes, increased violence follows. Even murder rates increase when and where television comes. In Canada, the homicide rate doubled between 1957 and 1974 as violent television spread. In census regions where television came later, the homicide rate jumped later, too. In South Africa, where television was not introduced until 1975, a similar near doubling of the homicide rate did not begin until after 1975 (Centerwall, 1989). And in a closely studied rural Canadian town where television came late, playground aggression doubled soon after (Williams, 1986).

Notice that these studies illustrate how researchers are now using correlational findings to *suggest* cause and effect. Yet an infinite number of possible third factors could be creating a merely coincidental relation between viewing violence and aggression. Fortunately, however, the experimental method can control these extraneous factors. If we randomly assign some children to watch a violent film and others a nonviolent film, any later aggression difference between the two groups will be due to the only factor that distinguishes them: what they watched.

TV viewing experiments

The pioneering experiments by Albert Bandura and Richard Walters (1963) sometimes had young children view the adult pounding the inflated doll on film instead of observing it live—with much the same effect. Then Leonard Berkowitz and Russell Geen (1966) found that angered university students who viewed a violent film acted more aggressively than did similarly angered students who viewed nonaggressive films. These laboratory experiments, coupled with growing public concern, were sufficient to prompt the researchers to conduct more than 50 new research studies during the early 1970s. By and large, these studies confirmed that viewing violence amplifies aggression (Anderson & Bushman, 2002; Bushman & Anderson, 2001).

For example, research teams led by Ross Parke (1977) and Jacques Leyens (1975) showed institutionalized delinquent boys a series of either aggressive or nonaggressive commercial films. Their consistent finding: "Exposure to movie violence . . . led to an increase in viewer aggression." Compared to the week preceding the film series, physical attacks increased sharply in cottages where boys were viewing violent films. Dolf Zillmann and James Weaver (1999) similarly exposed

"Then shall we simply allow our children to listen to any story anyone happens to make up, and so receive into their minds ideas often the very opposite of those we shall think they ought to have when they are grown up?"

Plato, *The Republic*

STORY BEHIND THE RESEARCH

Jacques-Philippe Leyens
Universite catholique de Louvain, Louvain-la-Neuve

At the University of Louvain when I studied for my Ph.D. there was no social psychologist. But at a summer school organized by the newly founded European Association of Experimental Social Psychology, and later during two years of postdoctoral research on aggression with Leonard Berkowitz and Ross Parke at the University of Wisconsin, I learned what experimental social psychology really was about.

After returning to Belgium, I conducted the experiment on viewing violent or nonviolent movies with 12- to 18-year-old boys who were at an institution in a small village on the Belgian–French border. The boys liked this study, because their access to TV had been restricted to news, sports, and cultural programs they didn't care about. Although the data showed that viewing violence increased everyday aggression, the boys, the counsellors, and the management were undisturbed by the results. When I presented the results to a NATO conference, the French newspaper *Le Monde* reported the story. Then a tabloid newspaper called, hoping for a story about a child who knifed his roommate after watching *The Dirty Dozen*. Although the results of one experiment are never so dramatic, experiments can alert us to corrosive forces that, over time, may indeed affect society.

men and women, on four consecutive days, to violent or nonviolent feature films. When participating in a different project on the fifth day, those exposed to the violent films were more hostile to the research assistant.

> *"There is absolutely no doubt that higher levels of viewing violence on television are correlated with increased acceptance of aggressive attitudes and increased aggressive behaviour."*
>
> American Psychological Association Commission on Violence and Youth, 1993

The aggression provoked in these experiments is not assault and battery; it's more on the scale of a shove in the lunch line, a cruel comment, a threatening gesture. Nevertheless, the convergence of evidence is striking. "The irrefutable conclusion," said one commission of psychologists on youth violence, is "that viewing violence increases violence." This is especially so among people with aggressive tendencies and when, in the violent depiction, an attractive person commits justified, realistic violence that goes unpunished and that shows no pain or harm (Bushman, 1995; Donnerstein, 1998).

All in all, conclude researchers Brad Bushman and Craig Anderson (2001), violence viewing's effect on aggression surpasses the effect of passive smoking on lung cancer, calcium intake on bone mass, and homework on academic achievement. As with smoking and cancer, not everyone shows the effect—other factors matter as well. Media executives have discounted the evidence. But the evidence is now "overwhelming," say Bushman and Anderson: "Exposure to media violence causes significant increases in aggression." The research base is large, the methods diverse, and the overall findings consistent, echo a taskforce of leading media violence researchers (Anderson et al., 2003). "Our indepth review. . . reveals unequivocal evidence that exposure to media violence can increase the likelihood of aggressive and violent behaviour in both immediate and long-term contexts."

Why does TV viewing affect behaviour?

Given the convergence of correlational and experimental evidence, researchers have explored *why* viewing violence has this effect. Consider three possibilities (Geen & Thomas, 1986). One is that it's not the violent content itself that causes social violence but the *arousal* it produces (Mueller et al., 1983; Zillmann, 1989). As we noted earlier, arousal tends to spill over: One type of arousal energizes other behaviours.

Other research shows that viewing violence *disinhibits*. In Bandura's experiment, the adult's punching the Bobo doll seemed to legitimate such outbursts and to lower the children's inhibitions. Viewing violence primes the viewer for aggressive behaviour by activating violence-related thoughts (Berkowitz, 1984; Bushman & Geen, 1990; Josephson, 1987). Listening to music with sexually violent lyrics seems to have a similar effect (Barongan & Hall, 1995; Johnson et al., 1995; Pritchard, 1998).

Media portrayals also evoke *imitation*. The children in Bandura's experiments re-enacted the specific behaviours they had witnessed. The commercial television industry is hard-pressed to dispute that television leads viewers to imitate what they have seen: Its advertisers model consumption. Are media executives right, however, to argue that TV merely holds a mirror to a violent society? That art imitates life? And that the "reel" world therefore shows us the real world? Actually, on TV programs, acts of assault outnumber affectionate acts 4 to 1. In other ways as well, television models an unreal world.

But there is good news here, too. If the ways of relating and problem solving modelled on television do trigger imitation, especially among young viewers, then modelling **prosocial behaviour** should be socially beneficial. Chapter 9 explored how television's subtle influence can indeed teach children positive lessons in behaviour.

prosocial behaviour positive, constructive, helpful social behaviour; the opposite of antisocial behaviour

Television's effects on thinking

We have focused on television's effect on behaviour, but researchers have also examined the cognitive effects of viewing violence: Does prolonged viewing desensitize us to cruelty? Does it give us mental scripts for how to act? Does it distort perceptions of reality? Does it prime aggressive thoughts?

Desensitization

Repeat an emotion-arousing stimulus, such as an obscene word, over and over. What happens? From introductory psychology you may recall that the emotional response will "extinguish." After witnessing thousands of acts of cruelty, there is good reason to expect a similar emotional numbing. The most common response might well become, "Doesn't bother me at all." Such a response is precisely what Victor Cline and his colleagues (1973) observed when they measured the physiological arousal of 121 boys who watched a brutal boxing match. Compared to boys who watched little television, the responses of those who watched habitually were more a shrug than a concern.

"All television is educational. The question is, what is it teaching?"

Nicholas Johnson, Former Commissioner, Federal Communications Commission, 1978

Of course, these boys might differ in ways other than television viewing. But in experiments on the effects of viewing sexual violence, similar desensitization—a sort of psychic numbness—occurs among young men who view slasher films. Moreover, experiments by Ronald Drabman and Margaret Thomas (1974, 1975, 1976) confirmed that such viewing breeds a more blasé reaction when later viewing the film of a brawl or when actually observing two children fighting. In one survey of 5456 middle-school students, exposure to movies with brutality was widespread (Sargent et al., 2002). Such viewing patterns help explain why, despite the portrayals of extreme violence (or, should we say, *because* of it), youth surveys show that the percentage of 13- to 17-year-olds feeling there was too much movie violence has declined, from 42 percent in 1977 to 27 percent in 2003.

Social scripts

social script culturally provided mental instructions for how to act in various situations

When we find ourselves in new situations, uncertain how to act, we often rely on **social scripts**—culturally provided mental instructions for how to act. After so many action films, youngsters may acquire a script that is played when they face real-life conflicts. Challenged, they may "act like a man" by intimidating or eliminating the threat. Likewise, after viewing multiple sexual innuendoes and acts in most prime-time TV hours—mostly involving impulsive or short-term relationships—youths may acquire sexual scripts they later enact in real-life relationships (Kunkel et al., 2001; Sapolsky & Taberlet, 1991). Thus, the more sexual content that adolescents view (even when controlling for other predictors of early sexual activity), the more likely they are to perceive their peers as sexually active, to develop sexually permissive attitudes, and to experience early intercourse (Escobar-Chaves et al., 2005; Martino et al., 2005).

Altered perceptions

Does television's fictional world also mould our conceptions of the real world? George Gerbner and his associates (1979, 1994) suspect this is television's most potent effect. Their surveys of both adolescents and adults show that heavy viewers (four hours a day or more) are more likely than light viewers (two hours or fewer) to exaggerate the frequency of violence in the world around them and to fear being personally assaulted. Similar feelings of vulnerability have been expressed by South African women after viewing violence against women (Reid & Finchilescu, 1995). One survey of 7- to 11-year-old children found that heavy viewers were more likely than light viewers to admit fears "that somebody bad might get into your house" or that "when you go outside, somebody might hurt you" (Peterson & Zill, 1981).

"The more fully that any given generation was exposed to television in its formative years, the lower its civic engagement [its rate of voting, joining, meeting, giving, and volunteering]."

Robert Putnam, *Bowling Alone* (2000)

Cognitive priming

Evidence also reveals that watching violent videos primes networks of aggressive-related ideas (Bushman, 1998). After viewing violence, people offer more hostile explanations for others' behaviour (was the shove intentional?), interpret spoken homonyms with the more aggressive meaning (interpreting "punch" as a hit rather than a drink), and recognize aggressive words more quickly.

Perhaps, though, television's biggest effect relates not to its quality but to its quantity. Compared with more active recreation, TV watching sucks people's energy and dampens their moods (Kubey & Csikszentmihaly, 2002). Moreover, TV annually replaces in people's lives a thousand or more hours of other activities. Canadian adolescents who watch a lot of TV tend to be less physically active (Koezuka et al., 2006). If, like most others, you have spent a thousand-plus hours per year watching TV, think how you might have used that time if there were no television. What difference would that have made in who you are today? In seeking to explain the post-1960 decline in civic activities and organizational memberships, Robert Putnam (2000) reported that every added hour a day spent watching TV competes with civic participation. Television steals time from club meetings, volunteering, church activity, and political engagement.

MEDIA INFLUENCES: VIDEO GAMES

"The scientific debate over *whether* media violence has an effect is basically over," contend Douglas Gentile and Craig Anderson (2003). Researchers are now shifting their attention to video games, which have exploded in popularity and are exploding with increasing brutality. Educational research shows that "video games are excellent teaching tools," note Gentile and Anderson. "If health video games can successfully teach health behaviours, and flight simulator video games can teach people how to fly, then what should we expect violent murder-simulating games to teach?"

(Dan Perkins/THIS MODERN WORLD)

People who watch many hours of television see the world as a dangerous place.

Reprinted with permission of Dan Perkins.

The games kids play

In 2007, the video game industry celebrated its 35th birthday. Since the first video game in 1972 we have moved from electronic Ping-Pong to splatter games (Anderson, 2004; Gentile & Anderson, 2003). By the turn of the century, some 200 million games a year were being purchased, and the average girl was playing six hours a week and the average boy 12 hours (Gentile et al., 2004). Today's mass-murder simulators are not obscure games. In one survey of fourth graders, 59 percent of girls and 73 percent of boys reported their favourite games as violent ones (Anderson, 2003, 2004). Games rated "M" (mature) are supposedly intended for sale only to those 17 and older but often get marketed to those younger. The U.S. Federal Trade Commission found that in four out of five attempts, underage children could easily purchase them (Pereira, 2003).

In the popular *Grand Theft Auto: San Andreas* video game, youth are invited to play psychopath, notes Gentile (2004). "You can run down pedestrians with the car, you can do carjackings, you can do drive-by shootings, you can run down to the red-light district, pick up a prostitute, have sex with her in your car, and then kill her to get your money back." In effective 3D graphics, you can knock people over, stomp on them until they cough up blood, and watch them die. And as new research by Susan Persky and James Blascovich (2005) demonstrates, virtual-reality games promise even more realism, engagement, and impact.

> *"We had an internal rule that we wouldn't allow violence against people."*
>
> Nolan Bushnell, Atari founder

Effects of the games kids play

Concerns about violent video games heightened after teens enacted the horrific violence they had so often played on-screen in school shootings. People wondered: What do youth learn from endless hours of role-play attacking and dismembering people?

Most smokers don't die of lung cancer. Most abused children don't become abusive. And most people who spend hundreds of hours rehearsing human slaughter live gentle lives. This enables video game defenders, like tobacco and TV interests, to say their products are harmless.

"There is absolutely no evidence, none, that playing a violent game leads to aggressive behavior," contended Doug Lowenstein (2000), president of the Interactive Digital Software Association. Gentile and Anderson nevertheless offer some reasons why violent game playing *might* have a more toxic effect than watching violent television. With game playing, players

- identify with, and play the role of, a violent character.
- actively rehearse violence, not just passively watch it.
- engage in the whole sequence of enacting violence—selecting victims, acquiring weapons and ammunition, stalking the victim, aiming the weapon, pulling the trigger.
- are engaged with continual violence and threats of attack.
- repeat violent behaviours over and over.
- are rewarded for effective aggression.

For such reasons, military organizations often prepare soldiers to fire in combat (which many in the Second World War reportedly were hesitant to do) by engaging them with attack simulation games.

But what does the available research actually find? Craig Anderson (2003, 2004; Anderson et al., 2004) offers statistical digests of three dozen available studies that reveal five consistent effects. Playing violent video games, more than playing nonviolent games

- **increases arousal**—heart rate and blood pressure rise.
- **increases aggressive thinking**—for example, Brad Bushman and Anderson (2002) found that after playing games such as *Duke Nukem* and *Mortal Kombat*, university students became more likely to guess that a man whose car was just rear-ended would respond aggressively, by using abusive language, kicking out a window, or starting a fight.
- **increases aggressive feelings**—frustration levels rise, as does expressed hostility.
- **increases aggressive behaviours**—after violent game play, children and youth play more aggressively with their peers, get into more arguments with their teachers, and participate in more fights. The effect occurs inside and outside of the laboratory, across self-reports, teacher reports, and parent reports, and for reasons illustrated in Figure 10–7. Is this merely because naturally hostile kids are drawn to such games? No, even when controlling for personality and temperament, exposure to video-game violence desensitizes people to cruelty and increases aggressive behaviour (Bartholow et al., 2005). Moreover, observe Douglas Gentile and his co-researchers (2004) from a study of young adolescents, even among those who scored low in hostility, the percent of heavy violent gamers who got into fights was ten times the 4 percent involved in fights among their nongaming counterparts. And after they start playing the violent games, previously nonhostile kids become more likely to have fights.
- **decreases prosocial behaviours**—after violent video game playing, people become slower to help a person whimpering in the hallway outside and slower to offer help to peers. On a later monetary decision-making task, they become more likely to exploit rather than to trust and cooperate with a partner (Sheese & Graziano, 2005). They also, as revealed by decreased brain activity associated with emotion, become desensitized to violence (Bartholow et al., 2006).

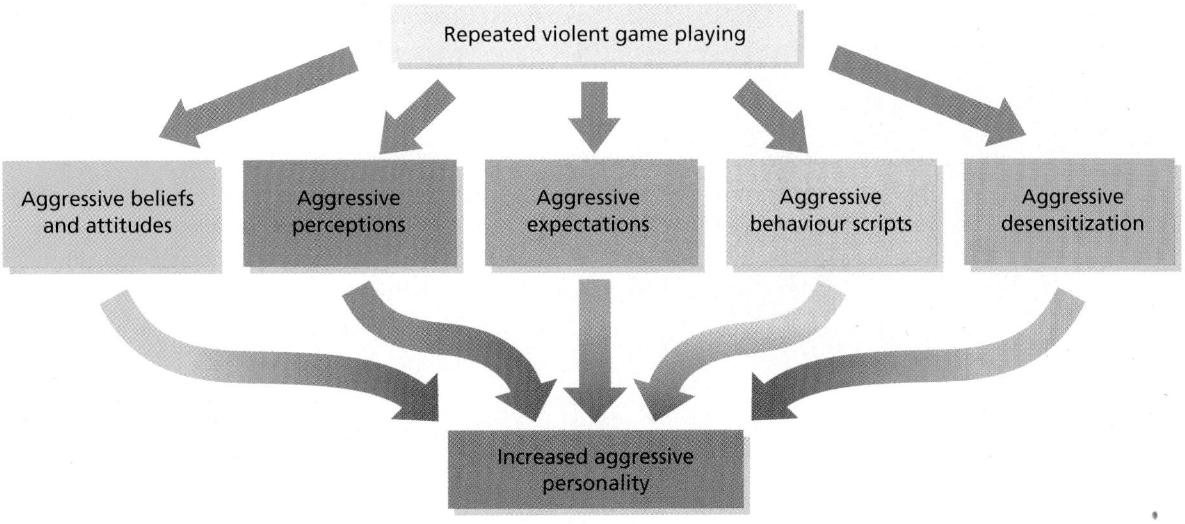

FIGURE 10–7

Violent video game influences on aggressive tendencies.

(Adapted from Craig A. Anderson & Brad J. Bushman, 2001)

Moreover, the more violent the games played, the bigger the effects. Video games *have* become more violent, which helps explain why newer studies find the biggest effects. Although much remains to be learned, these studies indicate that, contrary to the catharsis hypothesis, practising violence breeds rather than releases violence.

As a concerned scientist, Anderson (2003, 2004) therefore encourages parents to discover what their kids are ingesting and to ensure that their media diet, as least in their own home, is healthy. Parents may not be able to control what their child watches, plays, and eats in someone else's home, but they can oversee consumption in their own home and provide increased time for alternative activities. Networking with other parents can build a kid-friendly neighbourhood. And schools can help by providing media awareness education.

GROUP INFLUENCES

We have considered what provokes *individuals* to aggress. If frustrations, insults, and aggressive models heighten the aggressive tendencies of isolated people, then such factors are likely to prompt the same reaction in groups. As a riot begins, aggressive acts often spread rapidly after the "trigger" example of one antagonistic person. Seeing looters freely helping themselves to TV sets, normally law-abiding bystanders may drop their moral inhibitions and imitate.

> "The worst barbarity of war is that it forces men collectively to commit acts against which individually they would revolt with their whole being."
>
> Ellen Key, *War, Peace, and the Future*, 1916

Groups can amplify aggressive reactions partly by diffusing responsibility. Decisions to attack in war typically are made by strategists remote from the front lines. They give orders, but others carry them out. Does such distancing make it easier to recommend aggression?

Jacquelin Gaebelein and Anthony Mander (1978) simulated this situation in the laboratory. They asked their university student participants to *shock* someone or to *advise* someone how much shock to administer. When the recipient was innocent of any provocation, as are most victims of mass aggression, the advisers

Social contagion. When 17 juvenile, orphaned male bull elephants were relocated during the mid-1990s to a South African park, they became an out-of-control adolescent gang and killed 40 white rhinoceros. When, in 1998, concerned park officials relocated six older, stronger bull elephants into their midst, the rampaging soon quieted down (Slotow et al., 2000). One of these dominant bulls, at right, faces down several of the juveniles.

recommended more shock than given by the front-line participants, who felt more directly responsible for any hurt.

Diffusion of responsibility increases not only with distance but with numbers. (Recall from Chapter 7 the phenomenon of deindividuation.) When Brian Mullen (1986) analyzed information from 60 lynchings that occurred between 1899 and 1946, he made an interesting discovery: The greater the number of people in a lynch mob, the more vicious the murder and mutilation.

Through social "contagion," groups magnify aggressive tendencies, much as they polarize other tendencies. Examples are youth gangs, soccer fans, rapacious soldiers, urban rioters, and what Scandinavians call "mobbing"—schoolchildren in groups repeatedly harassing or attacking an insecure, weak schoolmate (Lagerspetz et al., 1982). Mobbing is a group activity.

Youths sharing antisocial tendencies and lacking close family bonds and expectations of academic success may find social identity in a gang. As group identity develops, conformity pressures and deindividuation increase (Staub, 1996). Self-identity diminishes as members give themselves over to the group, often feeling a satisfying oneness with the others. The frequent result is social contagion—group-fed arousal, disinhibition, and polarization. As gang expert Arnold Goldstein (1994) observed, until gang members marry out, age out, get a job, go to prison, or die, they hang out. They define their turf, display their colours, challenge rivals, and sometimes commit delinquent acts and fight over drugs, territory, honour, girls, or insults.

The twentieth-century massacres that claimed more than 150 million lives were "not the sums of individual actions," notes Robert Zajonc (2000). *"Genocide is not the plural of homicide."* Massacres are *social* phenomena fed by "moral imperatives"—a collective mentality (including images, rhetoric, and ideology) that mobilizes a group or a culture for extraordinary actions. The massacres of Rwanda's Tutsis, of Europe's Jews, and of North America's native population were collective phenomena requiring widespread support, organization, and participation. Before launching the genocidal initiative, Rwanda's Hutu government and business leaders bought and distributed 2 million Chinese machetes.

Experiments in Israel by Yoram Jaffe and Yoel Yinon (1979) confirm that groups can amplify aggressive tendencies. In one, university men angered by a supposed fellow subject retaliated with decisions to give much stronger shocks when in groups than when alone. In another experiment (Jaffe et al., 1981), people decided, either alone or in groups, how much punishing shock to give someone for incorrect answers on a task. As Figure 10–8 shows, individuals gave progressively more of the assumed shock as the experiment proceeded, and group decision making magnified this individual tendency. When circumstances provoke an individual's aggressive reaction, the addition of group interaction will often amplify it.

Aggression studies provide an apt opportunity to ask how well social psychology's laboratory findings generalize to everyday life. Do the circumstances that trigger someone's delivering electric shock or allocate hot sauce really tell us anything about the circumstances that trigger verbal abuse or a punch in the face? Craig Anderson and Brad Bushman (1997; Bushman & Anderson, 1998) note that social psychologists have studied aggression in both the laboratory

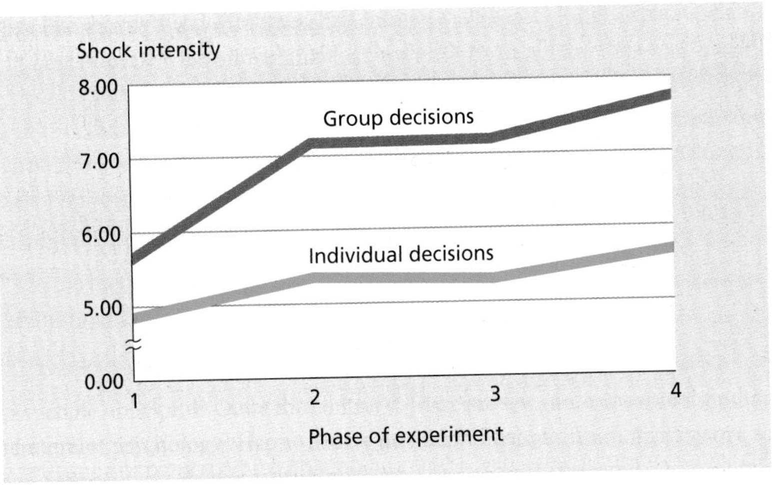

FIGURE 10–8

Group-enhanced aggression.

When individuals chose how much shock to administer as punishment for wrong answers, they escalated the shock level as the experiment proceeded. Group decision making further polarized this tendency. (Data from Jaffe et al., 1981)

and everyday worlds, and the findings are strikingly consistent. In both contexts, increased aggression is predicted by

- male actors,
- aggressive or Type A personalities,
- alcohol use,
- violence viewing,
- anonymity,
- provocation,
- the presence of weapons, and
- group interaction.

The laboratory allows us to test and revise theories under controlled conditions. Real-world events inspire ideas and provide the venue for applying our theories. Aggression research illustrates that an interplay between studies in the controlled lab and the complex real world advances psychology's contribution to human welfare. Hunches gained from everyday experience inspire theories, which stimulate laboratory research, which then deepens our understanding and our ability to apply psychology to real problems.

SUMMING UP: WHAT ARE SOME INFLUENCES ON AGGRESSION?

Many factors exert influence on aggression. One factor is aversive experiences, which include not only frustrations but also discomfort, pain, and personal attacks, both physical and verbal. Arousal from almost any source, even physical exercise or sexual stimulation, can be transformed into anger. Aggressive cues, such as the presence of a gun, increase the likelihood of aggressive behaviour.

Television portrays considerable violence. Correlational and experimental studies converge on the conclusion that viewing violence (1) breeds a modest increase in aggressive behaviour, especially in people who are provoked, and (2) desensitizes viewers to aggression and alters their perceptions of reality. These two findings parallel the results of research on the effects of viewing violent pornography, which can increase men's aggression against women and distort their perceptions of women's responses to sexual coercion. Repeatedly playing violent video games may even more greatly increase aggressive thinking, feelings, and behaviour.

Much aggression is committed by groups. Circumstances that provoke individuals may also provoke groups. By diffusing responsibility and polarizing actions, group situations amplify aggressive reactions.

HOW CAN AGGRESSION BE REDUCED?

We have examined instinct, frustration-aggression, and social learning theories of aggression, and we have scrutinized influences on aggression. How, then, can we reduce aggression? Do theory and research suggest ways to control aggression?

CATHARSIS?

"Youngsters should be taught to vent their anger." So advised Ann Landers (1969). If a person "bottles up his rage, we have to find an outlet. We have to give him an opportunity of letting off steam." So asserted the prominent psychiatrist Fritz Perls (1973). Both statements assume the "hydraulic model"—accumulated aggressive energy that, like dammed-up water, needs a release.

The concept of catharsis is usually credited to Aristotle. Although Aristotle actually said nothing about aggression, he did argue that we can purge emotions by experiencing them and that viewing the classic tragedies therefore enabled a catharsis ("purgation") of pity and fear. To have an emotion excited, he believed, is to have that emotion released (Butcher, 1951). The catharsis hypothesis has been extended to include the emotional release supposedly obtained not only by observing drama but also through recalling and reliving past events, through expressing emotions, and through our actions.

Assuming that aggressive action or fantasy drains pent-up aggression, some therapists and group leaders encourage people to ventilate suppressed aggression by acting it out—by whopping one another with foam bats or beating a bed with a tennis racquet while screaming. If led to believe that catharsis effectively vents emotions, people will react more aggressively to an insult as a way to improve their mood (Bushman et al., 2001). Some psychologists, believing that catharsis is therapeutic, advise parents to encourage children's release of emotional tension through aggressive play. Many people have also bought the catharsis idea, as reflected in their nearly 2 to 1 agreement with the statement, "Sexual materials provide an outlet for bottled-up impulses" (Niemi et al., 1989). But other surveys reveal that most people also agree, "Sexual materials lead people to commit rape." So is the catharsis approach valid or not?

Actually, notes researcher Brad Bushman (2002), "Venting to reduce anger is like using gasoline to put out a fire." Consider, if viewing erotica provides an outlet for sexual impulses, then people should afterwards experience diminished sexual desire and men should be less likely to view and treat women as sexual objects. But experiments show the opposite is true

effects of media violence. Wondering if the TV networks would ever "face the facts and change their programming," Eron and Huesmann (1984) taught 170 children that television portrays the world unrealistically, that aggression is less common and effective than TV suggests, and that aggressive behaviour is undesirable. (Drawing upon attitude research, Eron and Huesmann encouraged children to draw these inferences themselves and to attribute their expressed criticisms of television to their own convictions.) When restudied two years later, these children were less influenced by TV violence than were untrained children. In a more recent study, Stanford University used 18 classroom lessons to persuade children to simply reduce their TV watching and video game playing (Robinson et al., 2001). They did—their TV viewing by a third—and their aggressive behaviour at school dropped 25 percent compared to children in a control school.

Aggressive stimuli also trigger aggression. This suggests reducing the availability of weapons such as handguns. Jamaica in 1974 implemented a sweeping anticrime program that included strict gun control and censorship of gun scenes from television and movies (Diener & Crandall, 1979). In the following year, robberies dropped 25 percent, nonfatal shootings 37 percent. In Sweden, the toy industry has discontinued the sale of war toys. The Swedish Information Service (1980) states the national attitude: "Playing at war means learning to settle disputes by violent means."

Suggestions such as these can help us minimize aggression. But given the complexity of aggression's causes and the difficulty of controlling them, who can feel the optimism expressed by Andrew Carnegie's forecast that in the twentieth century, "To kill a man will be considered as disgusting as we in this day consider it disgusting to eat one." Since Carnegie uttered those words in 1900, some 200 million human beings have been killed. It is a sad irony that although today we understand human aggression better than ever before, humanity's inhumanity is hardly diminished. Nevertheless, cultures can change. "The Vikings slaughtered and plundered," notes Natalie Angier. "Their descendants in Sweden haven't fought a war in nearly 200 years."

SUMMING UP: HOW CAN AGGRESSION BE REDUCED?

How can we minimize aggression? Contrary to the catharsis hypothesis, expressing aggression more often breeds than reduces further aggression. The social learning approach suggests controlling aggression by counteracting the factors that provoke it—by reducing aversive stimulation, by rewarding and modelling nonaggression, and by eliciting reactions incompatible with aggression.

CHAPTER ELEVEN

Attraction and Intimacy: Liking and Loving Others

What leads to friendship and attraction?
Proximity
Physical attractiveness
Similarity versus complementarity
Liking those who like us
Relationship rewards

What is love?
Passionate love
Companionate love

What enables close relationships?
Attachment
Positive illusions
Equity
Self-disclosure

How do relationships end?
Divorce
The detachment process

Our lifelong dependence on one another puts relationships at the core of our existence. In your beginning there very likely was an attraction—the attraction between a particular

need to belong a motivation to bond with others in relationships that provide ongoing, positive interactions

man and a particular woman to which we each owe our existence. Aristotle called humans "the social animal." Indeed, we have what today's social psychologists call a **need to belong**—to connect with others in enduring, close relationships.

Social psychologists Roy Baumeister and Mark Leary (1995) illustrate the power of social attractions bred by our need to belong.

- For our ancestors, mutual attachments enabled group survival. When hunting game or erecting shelter, 10 hands were better than two.
- For a woman and a man, the bonds of love can lead to children, whose survival chances are boosted by the nurturing of two bonded parents who support each other.
- For children and their caregivers, social attachments enhance survival. Unexplainably separated from one another, parent and toddler may each panic, until reunited in a tight embrace. Reared under extreme neglect or in institutions without belonging to anybody, children become anxious creatures (Carlson, 1995).
- For university students, relationships consume much of life. How much of your waking life is spent talking with people? One sampling of 10 000 tape recordings of half-minute slices of students' waking hours (using belt-worn recorders) found them talking to someone 28 percent of the time—and that doesn't count the time they spent listening to someone (Mehl & Pennebaker, 2003).
- For people everywhere (no matter their sexual orientation), actual and hoped-for close relationships can dominate thinking and emotions. Finding a supportive soulmate in whom we can confide, we feel accepted and prized. Falling in love, we feel [illegible] on cosmetics, clothes, and diets. Even people who seem unconcerned with pleasing others relish being accepted (Carvallo & Gabriel, 2006).
- Exiled, imprisoned, or in solitary confinement, people ache for their own people and places. Rejected, we are at risk for depression (Nolan et al., 2003). Time goes slower and life seems less meaningful (Twenge et al., 2003).
- For the jilted, the widowed, and the sojourner in a strange place, the loss of social bonds triggers pain, anger, or withdrawal. Losing a close relationship, adults feel jealous, lonely, distraught, or bereaved, as well as more mindful of death and the fragility of life (Simpson, 1987; Strachman & Schimel, 2006).
- Reminders of death in turn heighten our need to belong, to be with others and hold close those we love (Mikulincer et al., 2003; Wisman & Koole, 2003). Facing the terror of 9/11, millions of Americans called and connected with loved ones. Likewise, the shocking death of a classmate, coworker, or family member brings people together, their differences no longer mattering.

We are indeed social animals. We need to belong. As Module A confirms, when we do belong—when we feel supported by close, intimate relationships—we tend to be healthier and happier.

At Australia's University of New South Wales, Kipling Williams (2002) explored what happens when our need to belong is thwarted by *ostracism* (acts of excluding or ignoring). Humans in all cultures, whether in schools, workplaces, or homes, use ostracism to regulate social behaviour. Some of us know what it is like to be shunned—to be avoided, met with

The architecture of friendship. People who live in close proximity, as do these university students, are more likely to become good friends.

averted eyes, or given the silent treatment. People (women especially) respond to ostracism with depressed mood, anxiety, hurt feelings, efforts to restore relationship, and eventual withdrawal. The silent treatment is "emotional abuse" and "a terrible, terrible weapon to use" say those who have experienced it from a family member or coworker. In experiments, people who are left out of a simple game of ball tossing feel deflated and stressed.

Sometimes deflation turns nasty. In several studies, Jean Twenge and her collaborators (2001, 2002; Baumeister et al., 2002) gave some people an experience of being socially included. Others experienced exclusion: They were either told (based on a personality test) that they "were likely to end up alone later in life" or that others whom they'd met didn't want them in their group. Those led to feel excluded became not only more likely to engage in self-defeating behaviours, such as underperforming on an aptitude test, but also less able to regulate their behaviour (they drank less of a healthy but bad-tasting drink and ate more unhealthy but good-tasting cookies). And they became more likely to disparage or deliver a blast of noise to someone who had insulted them. If a small laboratory experience could produce such aggression, noted the researchers, one wonders what aggressive tendencies "might arise from a series of important rejections or chronic exclusion."

Williams and his colleagues (2000) were surprised to discover that even "cyberostracism" by faceless people whom one will never meet takes a toll. (Perhaps you have experienced this when feeling ignored in a chat room or when your email is not answered.) The researchers had 1486 participants from 62 countries play a Web-based game of throwing a flying disc with two others (actually computer-generated fellow players). Those ostracized by the other players experienced poorer moods and became more likely to conform to others' wrong judgments on a subsequent perceptual task. They also, in a follow-up experiment, exhibited heightened activity in a brain cortex area that also is activated in response to physical pain (Figure 11–1). Other evidence, collected by Geoff MacDonald of the University of Toronto and Mark Leary of Duke University, confirms the convergence of social and physical pain in humans and other animals (MacDonald & Leary, 2005). Ostracism, it seems, is a real pain.

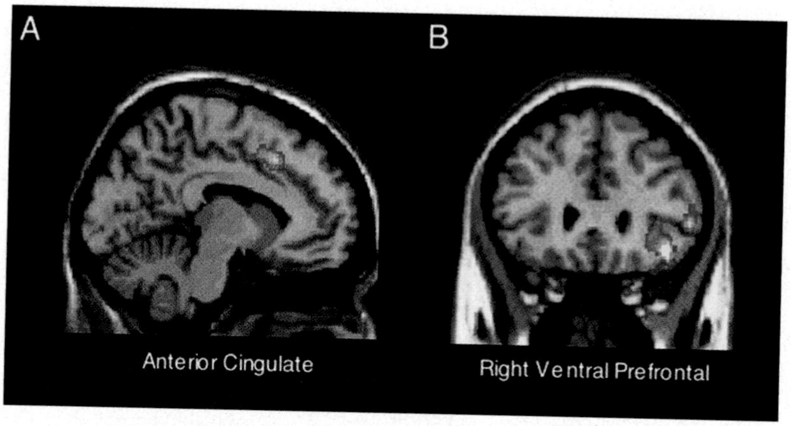

FIGURE 11–1

The pain of rejection.

Naomi Eisenberger, Matthew Lieberman, and Kipling Williams (2003) report that social ostracism evokes a brain response similar to that triggered by physical pain.

Williams and four of his colleagues (2000) even found ostracism stressful when each of them was ignored for an agreed-upon day by the unresponsive four others. Contrary to their expectations that this would be a laughter-filled role-playing game, the simulated ostracism disrupted work, interfered with pleasant social functioning, and "caused temporary concern, anxiety, paranoia, and general fragility of spirit." To thwart our deep need to belong is to unsettle our life.

Roy Baumeister (2005) finds a silver lining in the rejection research. When recently [illegible] experience a safe opportunity to make a new friend, they "seem willing and even eager to take it." And at a societal level, notes Baumeister, meeting the need to belong should pay dividends.

> My colleagues in sociology have pointed out that minority groups who feel excluded show many of the same patterns that our laboratory manipulations elicit: high rates of aggression and antisocial behaviour, decreased willingness to cooperate and obey rules, poorer intellectual performance, more self-destructive acts, short-term focus, and the like. Possibly, if we can promote a more inclusive society in which more people feel themselves to be accepted as valued members, some of these tragic patterns could be reduced.

WHAT LEADS TO FRIENDSHIP AND ATTRACTION?

What factors nurture liking and loving? Let's start with those that help initiate attraction: proximity, physical attractiveness, similarity, and feeling liked.

What predisposes one person to like, or to love, another? Few questions about human nature arouse greater interest. The ways affections flourish and fade form the stuff and fluff of soap operas, popular music, novels, and much of our everyday conversation.

So much has been written about liking and loving that almost every conceivable explanation—and its opposite—has already been proposed. For most people—and for you—what factors nurture liking and loving? Does absence make the heart grow fonder? Or is someone who is out of sight also out of mind? Is it likes that attract? Or opposites? How much do good

looks matter? What has fostered your close relationships? Let's start with those factors that help a friendship begin and then consider those that sustain and deepen a relationship, thus satisfying our need to belong.

"I cannot tell how my ankles bend, nor whence the cause of my faintest wish, nor the cause of the friendship I emit, nor the cause of the friendship I take again."

Walt Whitman, *Song of Myself*, 1855

PROXIMITY

One of the most powerful predictors of whether any two people are friends is sheer **proximity**. Proximity can also breed hostility; most assaults and murders involve people living close together. But far more often, proximity kindles liking. Though it may seem trivial to those pondering the mysterious origins of romantic love, sociologists have found that most people marry someone who lives in the same neighbourhood, or works at the same company or job, or sits in the same class (Bossard, 1932; Burr, 1973; Clarke, 1952; Katz & Hill, 1958). Look around. If you marry, it will likely be to someone who has lived or worked or studied within walking distance.

proximity geographical nearness. Proximity (more precisely, "functional distance") powerfully predicts liking.

Interaction

Actually, it is not geographical distance that is critical but "functional distance"—how often people's paths cross. We frequently become friends with those who use the same entrances, parking lots, and recreation areas. Randomly assigned university roommates, who of course can hardly avoid frequent interaction, are far more likely to become good friends than enemies (Newcomb, 1961). At the university where one of us teaches, the men and women once lived on opposite sides of the campus. They understandably bemoaned the lack of cross-sex friendships. Now that they occupy different areas of the same dormitories and share common sidewalks, lounges, and laundry facilities, cross-sex friendships are far more frequent. Interaction enables people to explore their similarities, to sense one another's liking, and to perceive themselves as a social unit (Arkin et al., 1980).

So if you're new in town and want to make friends, try to get an apartment near the mailboxes, an office desk near the coffee pot, a parking spot near the main buildings. Such is the architecture of friendship.

"When I'm not near the one I love, I love the one I'm near."

E. Y. Harburg, *Finian's Rainbow*, London: Chappell Music, 1947

The chance nature of such contacts helps explain a surprising finding. Consider: If you had an identical twin who became engaged to someone, wouldn't you (being in so many ways similar to your twin) expect to share your twin's attraction to this person? But no, report researchers David Lykken and Auke Tellegen (1993); only half of identical twins recall really liking their twin's selection, and only 5 percent said, "I could have fallen for my twin's fiancée." Romantic love is often rather like ducklings' imprinting, in which ducklings bond to whoever is near, surmised Lykken and Tellegen. With repeated exposure to someone, our infatuation may fix on almost anyone who has roughly similar characteristics and who reciprocates our affection.

Why does proximity breed liking? One factor is availability; obviously there are fewer opportunities to get to know someone who attends a different school or lives in another town. But there is more to it than that. Most people like their roommates, or those one door away, better than those two doors away. Those just a few doors away, or even a floor below, hardly live at an inconvenient distance. Moreover, those close by are potential enemies as well as friends. So why does proximity encourage affection more often than animosity?

Anticipation of interaction

Not only does proximity enable people to discover commonalities and exchange rewards, but merely *anticipating* interaction boosts liking. John Darley and Ellen Berscheid (1967) discovered this when they gave women ambiguous information about two other women, one of whom they expected to talk with intimately. Asked how much they liked each one, the women preferred the person they expected to meet. Expecting to date someone similarly boosts liking (Berscheid et al., 1976).

The phenomenon is adaptive. Anticipatory liking—expecting that someone will be pleasant and compatible—increases the chance of a rewarding relationship (Klein & Kunda, 1992; Knight & Vallacher, 1981; Miller & Marks, 1982). It's a good thing that we are biased to like those we often see, for our lives are filled with relationships with people whom we may not have chosen but with whom we need to have continuing interactions—roommates, siblings, grandparents, teachers, classmates, coworkers. Liking such people is surely conducive to better relationships with them, which in turn makes for happier, more productive living.

Mere exposure

Proximity leads to liking not only because it enables interaction and anticipatory liking but also for another reason: More than 200 experiments reveal that, contrary to an old proverb, familiarity does not breed contempt. Rather, it fosters fondness (Bornstein, 1989, 1999). **Mere exposure** to all sorts of novel stimuli—nonsense syllables, Chinese calligraphy characters, musical selections, faces—boosts people's ratings of them. Do the supposed Turkish words *nansoma, saricik,* and *afworbu* mean something better or something worse than the words *iktitaf, biwojni,* and *kadirga*? Students tested by Robert Zajonc (1968, 1970) preferred whichever of these words they had seen most frequently. The more times they had seen a meaningless word or a Chinese ideograph, the more likely they were to say it meant something good. This can make for a good class demonstration. Periodically flash certain nonsense words on a screen. By the end of the semester, students will rate those "words" more positively than other nonsense words they have never before seen.

mere-exposure effect the tendency for novel stimuli to be liked more or rated more positively after the rater has been repeatedly exposed to them

Feeling close to those close by. People often become attached to, and sometimes fall in love with, familiar coworkers.

Or consider: What are your favourite letters of the alphabet? People of differing nationalities, languages, and ages prefer the letters appearing in their own names and those that frequently appear in their own languages (Hoorens et al., 1990, 1993; Kitayama & Karasawa, 1997; Nuttin, 1987). French students rate capital *W*, the least frequent letter in French, as their least favourite letter. Japanese students not only prefer letters from their names, but numbers corresponding to their birth dates. This "name letter effect" reflects more than mere exposure, however—see the Focus On box titled "Liking Things Associated with Oneself" on p. 378.

The mere-exposure effect violates the commonsense prediction of *decreased* interest in repeatedly heard music or tasted foods (Kahneman & Snell, 1992). But unless the repetitions are incessant ("Even the best song becomes tiresome if heard too often," says a Korean proverb), liking usually increases. When completed in 1889, the Eiffel Tower in Paris was mocked as grotesque (Harrison, 1977). Today it is the beloved symbol of Paris. At its premiere in 1913, Stravinsky's *Rite of Spring* was vehemently condemned by critics and the public alike; today it is a classic admired the world over.

Do visitors to the Louvre in Paris really adore the *Mona Lisa* for the artistry it displays, or are they simply delighted to find a familiar face? It might be both: To know her is to like her. Eddie Harmon-Jones and John Allen (2001) explored this phenomenon experimentally. When they showed people a woman's face, their cheek (smiling) muscle typically became more active with repeated viewings. Mere exposure breeds pleasant feelings.

Zajonc and his coworkers, William Kunst-Wilson and Richard Moreland, reported that even exposure without awareness leads to liking (Kunst-Wilson & Zajonc, 1980; Moreland & Zajonc, 1977; Wilson, 1979). In fact, mere exposure has an even stronger effect when people perceive stimuli without awareness (Bornstein & D'Agostino, 1992). In one experiment, women students using headphones listened in one ear to a prose passage. They also repeated the words out loud and compared them to a written version to check for errors. Meanwhile, brief, novel melodies played in the other ear. This procedure focused attention on the verbal material and away from the tunes. Later, when the women heard the tunes interspersed among similar ones not previously played, they did not recognize them. Nevertheless, they *liked best* the tunes they had previously heard.

Note that conscious judgments about the stimuli in these experiments provided fewer clues to what people had heard or seen than did their instant feelings. You can probably recall immediately liking or disliking something or someone without consciously knowing why. Zajonc (1980) argues that emotions are often more instantaneous, more primitive, than thinking.

The mere-exposure effect has "enormous adaptive significance," notes Zajonc (1998). It is a "hard-wired" phenomenon that predisposes our attractions and attachments, and that helped our ancestors categorize things and people as either familiar and safe, or unfamiliar and possibly dangerous. The mere-exposure effect colours our evaluations of others: We like familiar people (Swap, 1977). It works the other way around too: People we like (for example, smiling rather than unsmiling strangers) seem more familiar (Garcia-Marques et al., 2004).

The phenomenon's negative side, as we will note in Chapter 12, is our wariness of the unfamiliar—which may explain the automatic, unconscious prejudice people often feel when confronting those who are different. Fearful or prejudicial feelings are not always expressions of stereotyped beliefs; sometimes the beliefs arise later as justifications for intuitive feelings.

We even like ourselves better when we are the way we're used to seeing ourselves. In a delightful experiment, Theodore Mita, Marshall Dermer, and Jeffrey Knight (1977)

FOCUS ON

LIKING THINGS ASSOCIATED WITH ONESELF

We humans love to feel good about ourselves, and generally we do. Not only are we prone to self-serving bias (Chapter 2), we exhibit what Brett Pelham, Matthew Mirenberg, and John Jones (2002) call *implicit egotism*: We like what we associate with ourselves.

That includes the letters of our name, but also the people, places, and things that we unconsciously connect with ourselves (Jones et al., 2002; Koole et al., 2001). If a stranger's face is morphed to include features of our own, we like the new face better (DeBruine, 2004). We are also more attracted to people whose arbitrary experimental code number resembles our birth date, and we are even disproportionately likely to marry someone whose first or last name resembles our own, such as by starting with the same letter (Jones et al., 2004).

Such preferences appear to subtly influence other major life decisions, including our locations and careers, report Pelham and his colleagues. Philadelphia, being larger than Jacksonville, has 2.2 times as many men named Jack. But it has 10.4 times as many people named Philip. Likewise, Virginia Beach has a disproportionate number of people named Virginia.

Does this merely reflect the influence of one's place when naming one's baby? Are people in Georgia, for example, more likely to name their babies George or Georgia? That may be so, but it doesn't explain why states tend to have a relative excess of people whose *last* names are similar to the state names. California, for example, has a disproportionate number of people whose names begin with Cali (as in Califano). Likewise, major Canadian cities tend to have larger-than-expected numbers of people whose last names overlap with the city names. Toronto has a marked excess of people whose names begin with Tor.

Moreover, women named "Georgia" are disproportionately likely to *move* to Georgia, as do Virginias to Virginia. Such mobility could help explain why St. Louis has a 49 percent excess (relative to the national proportion) of men named Louis, and why people named Hill, Park, Beach, Lake, or Rock are disproportionately likely to live in cities with names such as Park City that include their names. "People are attracted to places that resemble their names," surmise Pelham, Mirenberg, and Jones.

Weirder yet—I am not making this up—people seem to prefer careers related to their names. Across the United States, Jerry, Dennis, and Walter are equally popular names (0.42 percent of people carry each of these names). Yet America's dentists are almost twice as likely to be named Dennis as Jerry or Walter. There also are 2.5 times as many dentists named Denise as there are with the equally popular names, Beverly or Tammy. People named George or Geoffrey are overrepresented among geoscientists (geologists, geophysicists, and geochemists). And people may even prefer brand names that start with their initials—Tim, more than Harry, prefers Timex (Hodson & Olson, 2005).

photographed women students and later showed each one her actual picture along with a mirror image of it. Asked which picture they liked better, most preferred the mirror image—the image they were used to seeing. (No wonder our photographs never look quite right.) When close friends of the subjects were shown the same two pictures, they preferred the true picture—the image *they* were used to seeing.

Advertisers and politicians exploit this phenomenon. When people have no strong feelings about a product or a candidate, repetition alone can increase sales or votes (McCullough & Ostrom, 1974; Winter, 1973). After endless repetition of a commercial, shoppers often have an unthinking, automatic, favourable response to the product. If candidates are relatively unknown, those with the most media exposure usually win (Patterson, 1980; Schaffner et al., 1981). Political strategists who understand the mere-exposure effect have replaced reasoned argument with brief ads that hammer home a candidate's name and sound-bite message.

PHYSICAL ATTRACTIVENESS

What do (or did) you look for in a potential date? Sincerity? Good looks? Character? Conversational ability? Sophisticated, intelligent people are unconcerned with such superficial qualities as good looks; they know "beauty is only skin deep" and "you can't judge a book by its cover." At least they know that's how they *ought* to feel. As Cicero counselled, "Resist appearance."

The belief that looks are unimportant may be another instance of how we deny real influences on us, for there is now a file cabinet full of research studies showing that appearance *does* matter. The consistency and pervasiveness of this effect is astonishing. Good looks are a great asset.

> *"We should look to the mind, and not to the outward appearances."*
>
> Aesop, *Fables*

> *"Personal beauty is a greater recommendation than any letter of introduction."*
>
> Aristotle, *Diogenes Laertius*

Attractiveness and dating

Like it or not, a young woman's physical attractiveness is a moderately good predictor of how frequently she dates, and a young man's attractiveness is a modestly good predictor of how frequently he dates (Berscheid et al., 1971; Krebs & Adinolfi, 1975; Reis et al., 1980, 1982; Walster et al., 1966). Moreover, women more than men say they would prefer a mate who's homely and warm over one who's attractive and cold (Fletcher et al., 2004). Does this imply, as many have surmised, that women are better at following Cicero's advice? Or that nothing has changed since 1930, when the English philosopher Bertrand Russell wrote, "On the whole women tend to love men for their character while men tend to love women for their appearance." Or does it merely reflect the fact that men more often do the inviting? If women were to indicate their preferences among various men, would looks be as important to them as men?

To see whether men are indeed more influenced by looks, researchers have provided male and female students with various pieces of information about someone of the other sex, including the person's picture. Or they have briefly introduced a man and a woman and later asked each about their interest in dating the other. In such experiments, men do put somewhat more value on opposite-sex physical attractiveness (Feingold, 1990, 1991; Sprecher et al., 1994). Perhaps sensing this, women worry more about their appearance and constitute nearly 90 percent of cosmetic surgery patients (Crowley, 1996; Dion et al., 1990). But women, too, respond to a man's looks.

In one ambitious study, Elaine Hatfield and her coworkers (1966) matched 752 first-year students for a "Welcome Week" computer dance. The researchers gave each student personality and aptitude tests but then matched the couples randomly. On the night of the dance, the couples danced and talked for two and a half hours and then took a brief intermission to evaluate their dates. How well did the personality and aptitude tests predict attraction? Did people like someone better who was high in self-esteem, or low in anxiety, or different from themselves in outgoingness? The researchers examined a long list of possibilities. But as far as they could determine, only one thing mattered: how physically attractive the person was (as previously rated by the researchers). The more attractive a woman was, the more he liked her and wanted to date her again. And the more attractive the man was, the more she liked him and wanted to date him again. Pretty pleases.

But notice that in this experiment there were no differences between men and women in how much attractiveness affected their desire to see their partner again; both men and women preferred the attractive partner. Recently Paul Eastwick and Eli Finkel (2008) examined whether men and women differ in the strength of the preference for attractive partners. They ask men and women who were about to engage in speeding dating, in which they engage in a number of short conversations with potential partners, about what they were looking for in an ideal partner. Consistent with past research men reported that they were more interested in the attractiveness of their partner than women. Did these preferences for an ideal partner predict the partner they thought was ideal? Interestingly no. When evaluating which partner they wanted to see again after speed dating men and women were equally affected by their partners' attractiveness.

"If you would marry wisely, marry your equal."

Ovid, 43 B.C.–A.D. 17

The matching phenomenon

matching phenomenon the tendency for men and women to choose as partners those who are a "good match" in attractiveness and other traits

Not everyone can end up paired with someone stunningly attractive. So how do people pair off? Judging from research by Bernard Murstein (1986) and others, they get real. They pair off with people who are about as attractive as they are. Several studies have found a strong correspondence between the attractiveness of husbands and wives, of dating partners, and even of those within particular fraternities (Feingold, 1988). People tend to select as friends and especially to marry those who are a "good match" not only to their level of intelligence but also to their level of attractiveness.

Experiments confirm this **matching phenomenon**. When choosing whom to approach, knowing the other is free to say yes or no, people usually approach someone whose attractiveness roughly matches (or not too greatly exceeds) their own (Berscheid et al., 1971; Huston, 1973; Stroebe et al., 1971). Good physical matches may also be conducive to good relationships,

DILBERT reprinted by permission of United Feature Syndicate, Inc.

as Gregory White (1980) found in a study of dating couples. Those who were most similar in physical attractiveness were most likely, nine months later, to have fallen more deeply in love.

Perhaps this research prompts you to think of happy couples who are not equally attractive. In such cases, the less attractive person often has compensating qualities. Each partner brings assets to the social marketplace, and the value of the respective assets creates an equitable match. Personal advertisements exhibit this exchange of assets (Cicerello & Sheehan, 1995; Koestner & Wheeler, 1988; Rajecki et al., 1991). Men typically offer wealth or status and seek youth and attractiveness; women more often do the reverse: "Attractive, bright woman, 26, slender, seeks warm, professional male." Moreover, men who advertise their income and education, and women who advertise their youth and looks, receive more responses to their ads (Baize & Schroeder, 1995). The asset-matching process helps explain why beautiful young women often marry older men of higher social status (Elder, 1969).

The physical-attractiveness stereotype

Does the attractiveness effect spring entirely from sexual attractiveness? Clearly not, as Vicky Houston and Ray Bull (1994) discovered when they used a makeup artist to give an accomplice an apparently scarred, bruised, or birthmarked face. When riding on a Glasgow commuter rail line, people of *both* sexes avoided sitting next to the accomplice when she appeared facially disfigured. Moreover, much as adults are biased toward attractive adults, young children are biased toward attractive children (Dion, 1973; Dion & Berscheid, 1974; Langlois et al., 2000). To judge from how long they gaze at someone, even 3-month-old infants prefer attractive faces (Langlois et al., 1987).

> *"Love is often nothing but a favourable exchange between two people who get the most of what they can expect, considering their value on the personality market."*
>
> Erich Fromm, *The Sane Society*, 1955

Adults show a similar bias when judging children. Margaret Clifford and Elaine Hatfield (Clifford & Walster, 1973) gave grade five teachers identical information about a boy or girl, but with the photograph of an attractive or unattractive child attached. The teachers perceived the attractive child as more intelligent and successful in school. Think of yourself as a playground supervisor having to discipline an unruly child. Might you, like the women studied by Karen Dion (1972), show less warmth and tact to an unattractive child? The sad truth is that most of us assume that homely children are less able and socially competent than their beautiful peers.

What is more, we assume that beautiful people possess certain desirable traits. Other things being equal, we guess beautiful people are happier, sexually warmer, and more outgoing, intelligent, and successful—though not more honest or concerned for others (Eagly et al., 1991; Feingold, 1992; Jackson et al., 1995).

Added together, the findings define a **physical-attractiveness stereotype**: *What is beautiful is good*. Children learn the stereotype quite early—and one of the ways they learn it is through stories told to them by adults. Snow White and Cinderella are beautiful—and kind. The witch and the stepsisters are ugly—and wicked. "If you want to be loved by somebody who isn't already in your family, it doesn't hurt to be beautiful," surmised one 8-year-old girl. Or as one kindergarten girl put it when asked what it means to be pretty, "It's like to be a princess. Everybody loves you" (Dion, 1979). Think of the public's widespread admiration of Princess Diana and criticism of Prince Charles' second wife, the former Camilla Parker-Bowles.

physical-attractiveness stereotype the presumption that physically attractive people possess other socially desirable traits as well: What is beautiful is good

If physical attractiveness is this important, then permanently changing people's attractiveness should change the way others react to them. But is it ethical to alter someone's looks? Such manipulations are performed millions of times a year by plastic surgeons and orthodontists. With teeth and nose straightened, hair replaced and dyed, face lifted, fat liposuctioned, and breasts enlarged, lifted, or reduced, most self-dissatisfied people do express satisfaction with the results of their procedures, though some unhappy patients seek out repeat procedures (Honigman et al., 2004).

"Even virtue is fairer in a fair body."

Virgil, *Aeneid*

To examine the effect of such alterations, Michael Kalick (1977) had students rate their impressions of eight women based on profile photographs taken before or after cosmetic surgery. Not only did they judge the women as more physically attractive after the surgery but also as kinder, more sensitive, more sexually warm and responsive, more likeable, and so on.

First impressions

To say that attractiveness is important, other things being equal, is not to say that physical appearance always outranks other qualities. Some people more than others judge people by their looks (Livingston, 2001). Moreover, attractiveness probably most affects first impressions. But first impressions are important—and are becoming more so as societies become increasingly mobile and urbanized and as contacts with people become more fleeting (Berscheid, 1981).

Though interviewers may deny it, attractiveness and grooming affect first impressions in job interviews (Cash & Janda, 1984; Mack & Rainey, 1990; Marvelle & Green, 1980). This helps explain why attractive people and tall people have more prestigious jobs and make more money (Engemann & Owyang, 2003; Persico et al., 2004). Patricia Roszell and her colleagues (1990) looked at the incomes of a national sample of Canadians whom interviewers had rated on a 1 (homely) to 5 (strikingly attractive) scale. They found that for each additional scale unit of rated attractiveness, people earned, on average, an additional $1,988 annually. Irene Hanson Frieze and her associates (1991) did the same analysis with 737 MBA graduates after rating them on a similar 1 to 5 scale using student yearbook photos. For each additional scale unit of rated attractiveness, men earned an added $2,600 and women earned an added $2,150.

The speed with which first impressions form and their influence on thinking helps explain why pretty prospers. Even a .013 second exposure—too brief to actually discern a face—is enough to enable people to guess a face's attractiveness (Olson & Marchuetz, 2005). Moreover, when categorizing subsequent words as either good or bad, an attractive face predisposes people to categorize good words faster. Pretty is perceived promptly and primes positive processing.

Is the "beautiful is good" stereotype accurate?

Do beautiful people indeed have desirable traits? Or was Leo Tolstoy correct when he wrote that it's "a strange illusion . . . to suppose that beauty is goodness"? There is some truth to the stereotype. Attractive children and young adults are somewhat more relaxed, outgoing, and socially polished (Feingold, 1992; Langlois et al., 2000). William Goldman and Philip Lewis (1977) demonstrated this by having 60 men call and talk for five minutes with each of three women students. Afterwards the men and women rated the most attractive of their unseen telephone partners as somewhat more socially skillful and likeable. Physically attractive individuals tend also to be more popular, more outgoing, and more gender-typed—more traditionally masculine if male, more feminine if female (Langlois et al., 1996).

These small average differences between attractive and unattractive people probably result from self-fulfilling prophecies. Attractive people are valued and favoured, and so may develop

STORY BEHIND THE RESEARCH

Ellen Berscheid
University of Minnesota

I vividly remember the afternoon I began to appreciate the far-reaching implications of physical attractiveness. Graduate student Karen Dion (now a professor at the University of Toronto) learned that some researchers at our Institute of Child Development had collected popularity ratings from nursery school children and taken a photo of each child. Although teachers and caregivers of children had persuaded us that "all children are beautiful" and no physical-attractiveness discriminations could be made, Dion suggested we instruct some people to rate each child's looks and correlate these with popularity. After doing so, we realized our long shot had hit home: Attractive children were popular children. Indeed, the effect was far more potent than we and others had assumed, with a host of implications that investigators are still tracing.

more social self-confidence. (Recall from Chapter 2 an experiment in which men evoked a warm response from unseen women they *thought* were attractive.) By that analysis, what's crucial to your social skill is not how you look but how people treat you and how you feel about yourself—whether you accept yourself, like yourself, feel comfortable with yourself.

Who is attractive?

We have described attractiveness as if it were an objective quality like height, which some people have more of, some less. Strictly speaking, attractiveness is whatever the people of any given place and time find attractive. This, of course, varies. The beauty standards by which Miss Universe is judged hardly apply to the whole planet. People in various places and times have pierced noses, lengthened necks, dyed hair, painted skin, gorged themselves to become voluptuous, starved to become thin, and bound themselves with leather garments to make their breasts seem small—or used silicone and padded bras to make them seem big. For cultures with scarce resources and for poor or hungry people, plumpness seems attractive; for cultures and individuals with abundant resources, beauty more often equals slimness (Nelson & Morrison, 2005).

Despite such variations, there remains "strong agreement both within and across cultures about who is and who is not attractive," notes Judith Langlois and her colleagues (2000).

To be really attractive is, ironically, to be perfectly average (Rhodes, 2006). Research teams led by Judith Langlois and Lorri Roggman (1990, 1994) at the University of Texas and Anthony Little and David Perrett (2002), working with Ian Penton-Voak at the University of St. Andrews, have digitized multiple faces and averaged them using a computer. Inevitably, people find the composite faces more appealing than almost all the actual faces. As this suggests, attractive faces are also perceived as more alike than unattractive faces (Potter et al., 2006). There are more ways to be homely than beautiful. See Figure 11–2.

Computer averaged faces tend also to be perfectly symmetrical—another characteristic of strikingly attractive people (Gangestad & Thornhill, 1997; Grammer & Thornhill, 1994; Shackelford & Larsen, 1997). A University of Western Australia research team led by Gillian Rhodes (1999, 2006) and by Ian Penton-Voak (2001) has shown that if you could merge either half of

FIGURE 11-2

Who's the fairest of them all?

Each year's selection of "Miss Germany" provides one country's answer. A University of Regensburg student research team, working with a German television channel, offered an alternative. Christof Braun and his compatriots (Gruendl, 2005) photographed the twenty-two 2002 "Queen of Beauty" finalists, without makeup and with hair tied back, and then created a "Virtual Miss Germany" that was the blended composite of them all. When adults in a local shopping mall were shown the finalists and the Virtual Miss Germany, they easily rated Virtual Miss Germany as the most attractive of them all. Although the winning real Miss Germany may have been disappointed by the news that everyone preferred her virtual competitor to herself, she can reassure herself that she will never meet her virtual competitor.

your face with its mirror image—thus forming a perfectly symmetrical new face—you would boost your looks. Averaging a number of such attractive, symmetrical faces produces an even better looking face.

Evolution and attraction

Psychologists working from the evolutionary perspective explain the human preference for attractive partners in terms of reproductive strategy (Chapter 8). They assume that beauty signals biologically important information: health, youth, and fertility. Over time, men who preferred fertile-looking women outreproduced those who were as happy to mate with post-menopausal females. They also assume evolution predisposes women to favour male traits that signify an ability to provide and protect resources. That, David Buss (1989) believes, explains why the males he studied in 37 cultures—from Australia to Zambia—did indeed prefer youthful female characteristics that signify reproductive capacity. It also explains why physically attractive females tend to marry high-status males, and why men compete with such determination to display status by achieving fame and fortune. In screening potential mates, report Norman Li and his follow researchers (2002), men require a modicum of physical attractiveness, women require status and resources, and both welcome kindness and intelligence.

Evolutionary psychologists have also explored men's and women's responses to other cues to reproductive success. Judging from glamour models and beauty pageant winners, men everywhere have felt most attracted to women whose waists are 30 percent narrower than their hips—a shape associated with peak sexual fertility (Singh, 1993, 1995; Singh & Young, 1995; Streeter & McBurney, 2003). Circumstances that reduce a woman's fertility—malnutrition, pregnancy, menopause—also change her shape.

When judging males as potential marriage partners, women too, prefer a male waist-to-hip ratio suggesting health and vigour, and during ovulation they show heightened preference for men with masculinized features (Gangstead et al., 2004; Macrae et al., 2002). This makes evolutionary sense, notes Jared Diamond (1996): A muscular hunk was more likely than a scrawny fellow to gather food, build houses, and defeat rivals. But today's women prefer men with high incomes even more (Singh, 1995).

So, in every culture the beauty business is a big and growing business. Asians, Britons, Germans, and North Americans are all seeking cosmetic surgery in rapidly increasing numbers (Wall, 2002). In the United States and Canada, for example, 11.9 million cosmetic procedures such as liposuction, breast augmentation, and Botox injections were performed in 2004 (ASAPS, 2005). Modern, affluent people with cracked or discoloured teeth fix them. More and more, so do people with wrinkles and flab.

We are, evolutionary psychologists suggest, driven by primal attractions. Like eating and breathing, attraction and mating are too important to leave to the whims of culture.

Social comparison

Although our mating psychology has wisdom, attraction is not all hardwired. What's attractive to you also depends on your comparison standards.

Douglas Kenrick and Sara Gutierres (1980) had male confederates interrupt men in their dormitory rooms and explain, "We have a friend coming to town this week and we want to fix him up with a date, but we can't decide whether to fix him up with her or not, so we decided to conduct a survey. . . . We want you to give us your vote on how attractive you think she is . . . on a scale of 1 to 7." Shown a picture of an average young woman, those who had just been watching *Charlie's Angels* (a television show featuring three beautiful women) rated her less attractive than those who hadn't.

Laboratory experiments confirm this "contrast effect." To men who have recently been gazing at centrefolds, average women or even their own wives seem less attractive (Kenrick et al., 1989). Viewing pornographic films simulating passionate sex similarly decreases satisfaction with one's own partner (Zillmann, 1989). Being sexually aroused may temporarily make a person of the other sex seem more attractive. But the lingering effect of exposure to perfect "10s," or of unrealistic sexual depictions, is to make one's own partner seem less appealing—more like a "6" than an "8."

"Love is only a dirty trick played on us to achieve a continuation of the species."

Novelist W. Somerset Maugham, 1874–1965

It works the same way with our self-perceptions. After viewing a superattractive person of the same sex, people rate themselves as being *less* attractive than after viewing a homely person (Brown et al., 1992; Thornton & Maurice, 1997). This appears especially true for women. Men's self-rated desirability is also deflated by exposure to more dominant, successful men. Thanks to modern media, we may see in an hour "dozens of individuals who are more attractive and more successful than any of our ancestors would have seen in a year, or even a lifetime," note Sara Gutierres and her co-researchers (1999). Such extraordinary comparison standards trick us into devaluing our potential mates and ourselves and spending billions and billions on cosmetics, diet aids, and plastic surgery. But even after another 11.9 million annual cosmetic procedures, there may be no net gain in human satisfaction. If others get their teeth straightened, capped, and whitened and you don't, the social comparison may leave you more dissatisfied with your normal, natural teeth than you would have been if you were surrounded by peers whose teeth were also natural.

The attractiveness of those we love

Let's conclude our discussion of attractiveness on an upbeat note. First, a 17-year-old girl's facial attractiveness is a surprisingly weak predictor of her attractiveness at ages 30 and 50. Sometimes an average-looking adolescent becomes a quite attractive middle-aged adult (Zebrowitz et al., 1993, 1998).

"Do I love you because you are beautiful, or are you beautiful because I love you?"

Prince Charming, in Rodgers & Hammerstein's *Cinderella*

Second, not only do we perceive attractive people as likeable, we also perceive likeable people as attractive. Perhaps you can recall individuals who, as you grew to like them, became more attractive. Their physical imperfections were no longer so noticeable. Alan Gross and Christine Crofton (1977) had students view someone's photograph after reading a favourable or unfavourable description of the person's personality. Those portrayed as warm, helpful, and considerate also *looked* more attractive. It may be true, then, that "handsome is as handsome does." Discovering someone's similarities to us also makes the person seem more attractive (Beaman & Klentz, 1983; Klentz et al., 1987).

Standards of beauty differ from culture to culture. Yet some people are considered attractive throughout most of the world.

Moreover, love sees loveliness: The more in love a woman is with a man, the more physically attractive she finds him (Price et al., 1974). And the more in love people are, the *less* attractive they find all others of the opposite sex (Johnson & Rusbult, 1989; Simpson et al., 1990). John Lydon and his colleagues (1999) found this is especially true for people who are committed to their relationships. They recruited McGill University students and alumni who varied in their level of commitment to their relationships. These participants then rated an attractive, "single and not currently involved" member of the opposite sex who was apparently also a participant in the study. This attractive person was said to have been matched with them either randomly by a computer (a moderate threat to their relationship) or because he or she thought the participant was attractive (a more serious threat). As you can see in Figure 11–3, when people were threatened at the same level as they were committed, they saw the competition as less attractive. It seems that people modulate how attractive they find others in a way that maintains their close relationships. Beauty really *is*, to some extent, in the eye of the beholder.

"Can two walk together except they be agreed?"

Amos 3:3

SIMILARITY VERSUS COMPLEMENTARITY

From our discussion so far, one might surmise Leo Tolstoy was entirely correct: "Love depends . . . on frequent meetings, and on the style in which the hair is done up, and on the colour and cut of the dress." As people get to know one another, however, other factors influence whether acquaintance develops into friendship.

Do birds of a feather flock together?

Of this much we may be sure: Birds that flock together are of a feather. Friends, engaged couples, and spouses are far more likely than people randomly paired to share common attitudes,

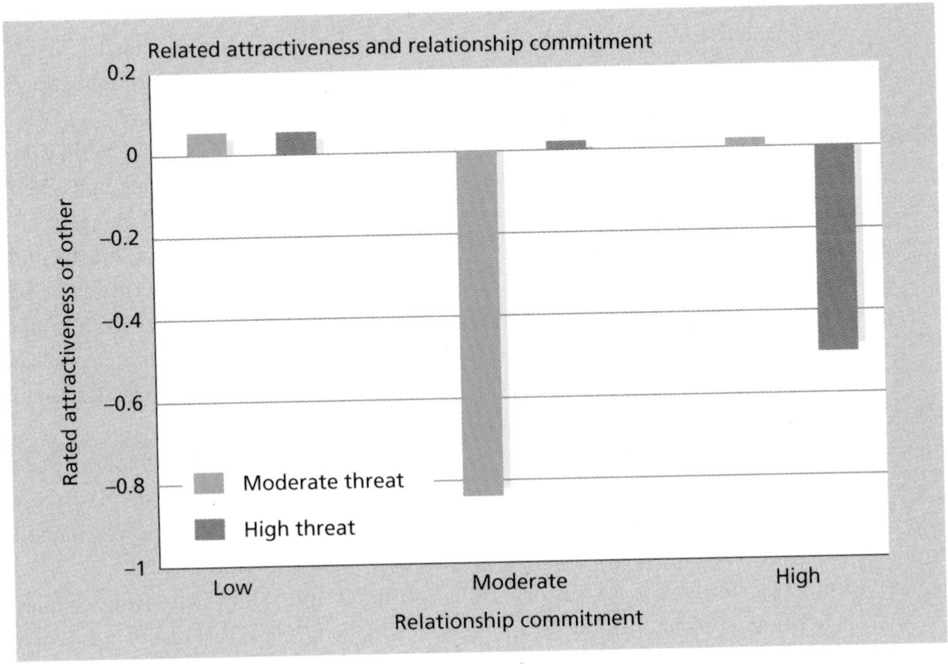

FIGURE 11–3

Related attractiveness and relationship commitment.

When people's relationships are threatened by an attractive member of the opposite sex, they rate this person as less attractive if the threat posed by the person matches their level of commitment.

Henry James's description of novelist George Eliot (the pen name of Mary Ann Evans): "She is magnificently ugly—deliciously hideous. She has a low forehead, a dull grey eye, a vast pendulous nose, a huge mouth, full of uneven teeth, and a chin and jaw-bone qui n'en finissent pas. . . . Now in this vast ugliness resides a most powerful beauty which, in a very few minutes, steals forth and charms the mind, so that you end as I ended, in falling in love with her."

beliefs, and values. Furthermore, the greater the similarity between husband and wife, the happier they are and the less likely they are to divorce (Byrne, 1971; Caspi & Herbener, 1990). Such correlational findings are intriguing. But cause and effect remain an enigma. Does similarity lead to liking? Or does liking lead to similarity?

Likeness begets liking

To discern cause and effect, we experiment. Imagine that at a campus party Laura gets involved in a long discussion of politics, religion, and personal likes and dislikes with Les and Larry. She and Les discover they agree on almost everything, she and Larry on few things. Afterwards, she reflects: "Les is really intelligent . . . and so likeable. I hope we meet again." In experiments, Donn Byrne (1971) and his colleagues captured the essence of Laura's experience. Over and over again they found that the more similar someone's attitudes are to your own, the more likeable you will find the person. Likeness produces liking not only for college and university students but also for children and the elderly, for people of various occupations, and for those in various cultures. When others think as we do, we not only appreciate their attitudes but also make positive inferences about their character (Montoya & Horton, 2004).

The likeness-leads-to-liking effect has been tested in real-life situations by noting who comes to like whom.

- William Griffitt and Russell Veitch (1974) compressed the getting-to-know-you process by confining 13 unacquainted men in a fallout shelter. (The men were paid volunteers.) Knowing the men's opinions on various issues, the researchers could predict with better-than-chance accuracy those each man would most like and most dislike.
- At two of Hong Kong's universities, Royce Lee and Michael Bond (1996) found that roommate friendships flourished over a six-month period when roommates shared values and personality traits, but more so when they perceived their roommates as similar. As so often happens, reality matters, but perception matters more.
- People like not only those who think as they do, but also those who act as they do. Subtle mimicry fosters fondness. Have you noticed that when someone nods their head as you do and echoes your thoughts, you feel a certain rapport and liking? That's a common experience, report Rick van Baaren and his colleagues (2003a, 2003b), and one result is higher tips for Dutch restaurant servers who mimic their customers by merely repeating their order. Moreover, people who are primed to affiliate with someone become more likely to mimic—for example, to unwittingly shake their foot or touch their face when the other does. Mimicry increases rapport, note Jessica Lakin and Tanya Chartrand (2003), and desire for rapport increases mimicry.
- When Peter Buston and Stephen Emlen (2003) surveyed nearly 1000 college-age people, they found that the desire for similar mates far outweighed the desire for beautiful mates. Attractive people sought attractive mates. Wealthy people wanted mates with money. Family-oriented people desired family-oriented mates.
- Studies of newlyweds reveal that similar attitudes and values help bring couples together and predict their satisfaction (Luo & Klohnen, 2005). That reality is the basis

of one psychologist-founded Internet dating site, which claims to match singles using the similarities that mark happy couples (Carter & Snow, 2004; Warren, 2005).

So similarity breeds content. Birds of a feather *do* flock together. Surely you have noticed this upon discovering a special someone who shares your ideas, values, and desires, a soulmate who likes the same music, the same activities, even the same foods you do.

"And they are friends who have come to regard the same things as good and the same things as evil, they who are friends of the same people, and they who are the enemies of the same people. . . . We like those who resemble us, and are engaged in the same pursuits."

Aristotle, *Rhetoric*

Dissimilarity breeds dislike

We have a bias—the false consensus bias—toward assuming that others share our attitudes. When we discover that someone does not, we may dislike the person. If those dissimilar attitudes pertain to our strong moral convictions, we dislike and distance ourselves from them all the more (Skitka et al., 2005). People in one political party often are not so much fond of fellow party members as they are disdainful of the opposition (Hoyle, 1993; Rosenbaum, 1986).

In general, dissimilar attitudes depress liking more than similar attitudes enhance it (Singh et al., 1999, 2000). Within their own groups, where they expect similarity, people find it especially hard to like someone with dissimilar views (Chen & Kenrick, 2002). That perhaps explains why dating partners and roommates become more similar over time in their emotional responses to events and in their attitudes (Anderson et al., 2003; Davis & Rusbult, 2001). "Attitude alignment" helps promote and sustain close relationships, a phenomenon that can lead partners to overestimate their attitude similarities (Kenny & Acitelli, 2001; Murray et al., 2002).

Whether people perceive those of another race as similar or dissimilar influences their racial attitudes. Wherever one group of people regards another as "other"—as creatures who speak differently, live differently, and think differently—the potential for conflict is high. In fact, except for intimate relationships such as dating, the perception of like minds seems more important for attraction than like skins. Most Whites have expressed more liking for, and willingness to work with, a like-minded Black than a dissimilarly minded White (Insko et al., 1983; Rokeach, 1968). The more that Whites presume that Blacks support their values, the more positive their racial attitudes (Biernat et al., 1996). Likewise, the more Montreal residents perceived a Canadian ethnic group as similar to themselves, the more willing they were to associate with its members (Osbeck et al., 1996).

"Cultural racism" persists, argues James Jones (1988), because cultural differences are a fact of life. Black culture tends to be present-oriented, spontaneously expressive, spiritual, and emotionally driven. White culture tends to be more future-oriented, materialistic, and achievement-driven. Rather than trying to eliminate such differences, says Jones, we might better appreciate what they "contribute to the cultural fabric of a multicultural society." There are

The most appealing people are those most like us.

"Actually, Lou, I think it was more than just my being in the right place at the right time. I think it was my being the right race, the right religion, the right sex, the right socioeconomic group, having the right accent, the right clothes, going to the right schools . . ."

situations in which expressiveness is advantageous and situations in which future orientation is advantageous. Each culture has much to learn from the other. In countries such as Canada, Britain, and the United States, where migration and different birthrates make for growing diversity, educating people to respect and enjoy those who differ is a major challenge. Given increasing cultural diversity and given our natural wariness of differences, this may in fact be the major social challenge of our time.

Do opposites attract?

Are we not also attracted to people who are in some ways *different* from ourselves, in ways that complement our own characteristics? Researchers have explored this question by comparing not only friends' and spouses' attitudes and beliefs but also their age, religion, race, smoking behaviour, economic level, education, height, intelligence, and appearance. In all these ways and more, similarity still prevails (Buss, 1985; Kandel, 1978). Smart birds flock together. So do rich birds, Protestant birds, tall birds, pretty birds.

Still we resist: Are we not attracted to people whose needs and personalities complement our own? Would a sadist and a masochist find true love? Even the *Reader's Digest* has told us that "opposites attract. . . . Socializers pair with loners, novelty-lovers with those who dislike change, free spenders with scrimpers, risk-takers with the very cautious" (Jacoby, 1986). Sociologist Robert Winch (1958) reasoned that the needs of someone who is outgoing and domineering would naturally complement those of someone who is shy and submissive. The logic seems compelling, and most of us can think of couples who view their differences as complementary: "My husband and I are perfect for each other. I'm Aquarius—a decisive person. He's Libra—can't make decisions. But he's always happy to go along with arrangements I make."

Given the idea's persuasiveness, the inability of researchers to confirm it is astonishing. For example, most people feel attracted to expressive, outgoing people (Friedman et al., 1988). Would this be especially so when one is down in the dumps? Do depressed people seek those whose gaiety will cheer them up? To the contrary, it is *non*depressed people who most prefer the company of happy people (Locke & Horowitz, 1990; Rosenblatt & Greenberg, 1988, 1991; Wenzlaff & Prohaska, 1989). When you're feeling blue, another's bubbly personality can be aggravating. The contrast effect that makes average people feel homely in the company of beautiful people also makes sad people more conscious of their misery in the company of cheerful people.

complementarity the popularly supposed tendency, in a relationship between two people, for each to complete what is missing in the other

Some **complementarity** may evolve as a relationship progresses (even a relationship between identical twins). Yet people seem slightly more prone to like and to marry those whose needs and personalities are *similar* (Botwin et al., 1997; Buss, 1984; Fishbein & Thelen, 1981a, 1981b; Nias, 1979). Perhaps we shall yet discover some ways (other than heterosexuality) in which differences commonly breed liking. Dominance/submissiveness may be one such way (Dryer & Horowitz, 1997). And we tend not to feel attracted to those who show our own worst traits (Schimel et al., 2000). But researcher David Buss (1985) doubts complementarity: "The tendency of opposites to marry, or mate . . . has never been reliably demonstrated, with the single exception of sex."

LIKING THOSE WHO LIKE US

Liking is usually mutual. Proximity and attractiveness influence our initial attraction to someone, and similarity influences longer-term attraction as well. If we have a deep need to belong

Like ethnic minorities elsewhere, Muslims living in France have encountered hostility. Here, protestors react against the law forbidding the wearing of veils in schools.

and to feel liked and accepted, would we not also take a liking to those who like us? Are the best friendships mutual admiration societies? Indeed, one person's liking for another does predict the other's liking in return (Kenny & Nasby, 1980). Liking is usually mutual.

But does one person's liking another *cause* the other to return the appreciation? People's reports of how they fell in love suggest yes (Aron et al., 1989). Discovering that an appealing someone really likes you seems to awaken romantic feelings. Experiments confirm it: Those told that certain others like or admire them usually feel a reciprocal affection (Berscheid & Walster, 1978).

"The average man is more interested in a woman who is interested in him than he is in a woman with beautiful legs."

Actress Marlene Dietrich (1901–1992)

And consider this finding by Ellen Berscheid and her colleagues (1969): People like even better another student who says eight positive things about them than one who says seven positive things and one negative thing. We are sensitive to the slightest hint of criticism. Writer Larry L. King speaks for many in noting, "I have discovered over the years that good reviews strangely fail to make the author feel as good as bad reviews make him feel bad."

Whether we are judging ourselves or others, negative information carries more weight because, being less usual, it grabs more attention (Yzerbyt & Leyens, 1991). People's votes are more influenced by their impressions of candidates' weaknesses than by their impressions of strengths (Klein, 1991), a phenomenon that has not been lost on those who design negative campaigns.

That we like those we perceive as liking us was recognized long ago. Observers from the ancient philosopher Hecato ("If you wish to be loved, love") to Ralph Waldo Emerson ("The only way to have a friend is to be one") to Dale Carnegie ("Dole out praise lavishly") anticipated the findings. What they did not anticipate was the precise conditions under which the principle works.

"Well—and I'm not just saying this because you're my husband—it stinks."

Attribution

As we've seen, flattery *will* get you somewhere. But not everywhere. If praise clearly violates what we know is true—if someone says, "Your hair looks great," when we haven't washed it in days—we may lose respect for the flatterer and wonder whether the compliment springs from ulterior motives (Shrauger, 1975). Thus we often perceive criticism to be more sincere than praise (Coleman et al., 1987).

Laboratory experiments reveal something we've noted in previous chapters: Our reactions depend on our attributions. Do we attribute the flattery to **ingratiation**—to a self-serving strategy? Is the person trying to get us to buy something, to acquiesce sexually, to do a favour? If so, both the flatterer and the praise lose appeal (Gordon, 1996; Jones, 1964). But if there is no apparent ulterior motive, then we warmly receive both flattery and flatterer.

ingratiation
the use of strategies, such as flattery, by which people seek to gain another's favour

Some people embrace compliments more readily than do others, however. People with low self-esteem focus narrowly on the literal meaning of compliments—to them, "You have a nice smile," means just that (Marigold et al., 2007). People with high self-esteem, in contrast, attribute more abstract significance to compliments—that their partner is attentive, values and cares for them—and feel more secure in their relationships. It's not that low self-esteem people can't derive the same benefit from compliments; they do if they are directed to consider what compliments mean for their relationship. Everyone feels more secure and valued if they attribute compliments to caring and affection. People with low self-esteem, it seems, just need more encouragement to do so.

How we explain our own actions also matters. Clive Seligman, Russell Fazio, and Mark Zanna (1980) paid undergraduate dating couples to indicate "why you go out with your girl friend/boy friend." They asked some to rank seven intrinsic reasons, such as "I go with _____ because we always have a good time together" and "because we share the same interests and concerns." Others ranked possible extrinsic reasons: "because my friends think more highly of me since I began seeing her/him" and "because she/he knows a lot of important people." Asked later to respond to a "Love Scale," those whose attention had been drawn to possible extrinsic reasons for their relationships expressed less love for their partners and saw marriage as a less likely possibility than did those made aware of possible intrinsic reasons. (Sensitive to ethical concerns, the researchers debriefed all the participants afterwards and confirmed that the experiment had no long-term effects on the participants' relationships.)

Self-esteem and attraction

Elaine Hatfield (Walster, 1965) wondered if another's approval is especially rewarding after we have been deprived of approval, much as eating is most powerfully rewarding after fasting. To test this idea, she gave some women either very favourable or very unfavourable analyses of their personalities, affirming some and wounding others. Then she asked them to evaluate several people, including an attractive male confederate who just before the experiment had struck up a warm conversation with each woman and had asked each for a date. (Not one turned him

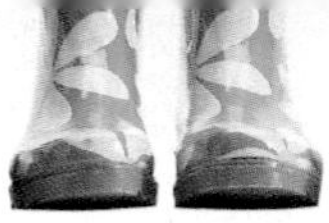

down.) Which women do you suppose most liked the man? It was those whose self-esteem had been temporarily shattered and who were presumably hungry for social approval. (After this experiment Dr. Hatfield spent almost an hour explaining the experiment and talking with each woman. She reports that in the end, none remained disturbed by the temporary ego blow or the broken date.)

This helps explain why people sometimes fall passionately in love on the rebound, after an ego-bruising rejection. Unfortunately, however, low self-esteem individuals tend to underestimate how much their partner appreciates them. They also have less generous views of their partner and are therefore less happy with the relationship (Murray et al., 2000). If you feel down about yourself, you will likely feel pessimistic about your relationships. Feel good about yourself and you're more likely to feel confident of your dating partner or spouse's regard. Accordingly, when low self-esteem people are focused on their own strengths, they feel more secure in their relationships (Murray et al., 2005). Somewhat ironically, however, they also feel more secure when they learn about mild faults in their *partner*. Because they generally see their partner as better than them and "out of their league," discovering a shortcoming in their partner can reassure them that their partner won't abandon them.

Gaining another's esteem

If approval that comes after disapproval is powerfully rewarding, then would we most like someone who liked us after initially disliking us? Or would we most like someone who liked us from the start (and therefore gave us more total approval)? Ray is in a small discussion class with his roommate's cousin, Sophia. After the first week of classes, Ray learns via his "pipeline" that Sophia thinks him rather shallow. As the semester progresses, however, he learns that Sophia's opinion of him is steadily rising; gradually she comes to view him as bright, thoughtful, and charming. Would Ray like Sophia more if she had thought well of him from the beginning? If Ray is simply counting the number of approving comments he receives, then the answer will be yes: He would like Sophia better had she consistently praised him. But if after her initial disapproval, Sophia's rewards become more potent, Rey then might like her better than if she had been consistently affirming.

"Hatred which is entirely conquered by love passes into love, and love on that account is greater than if it had not been preceded by hatred."

Benedict Spinoza, *Ethics*

To see which is most often true, Elliot Aronson and Darwyn Linder (1965) captured the essence of Ray's experience in a clever experiment. They "allowed" 80 women to overhear a sequence of evaluations of themselves by another woman. Some women heard consistently positive things about themselves, some consistently negative. Others heard evaluations that changed either from negative to positive (like Sophia's evaluations of Ray) or from positive to negative. In this and other experiments, the target person was well liked when the subject experienced a *gain* in the other's esteem, especially when the gain occurred gradually and reversed the earlier criticism (Aronson & Mettee, 1974; Clore et al., 1975). Perhaps Jan's nice words have more credibility coming after her not-so-nice words. Or perhaps after being withheld, they are especially gratifying.

Aronson speculated that constant approval can lose value. When a husband says for the five-hundredth time, "Gee, honey, you look great," the words carry far less impact than were he now to say, "Gee, honey, you look awful in that dress." A loved one you've doted upon is hard to reward but easy to hurt. This suggests that an open, honest relationship—one where people enjoy one another's esteem and acceptance yet are honest—is more likely to offer continuing rewards than one dulled by the suppression of unpleasant emotions, one in which people try only, as Dale Carnegie advised, to "lavish praise." Aronson (1988) put it this way:

> As a relationship ripens toward greater intimacy, what becomes increasingly important is authenticity—our ability to give up trying to make a good impression and begin to reveal things about ourselves that are honest even if unsavory. . . . If two people are genuinely fond of each other, they will have a more satisfying and exciting relationship over a longer period of time if they are able to express both positive and negative feelings than if they are completely "nice" to each other at all times. (p. 323)

In most social interactions, we self-censor our negative feelings. Thus, note William Swann and his colleagues (1991), some people receive no corrective feedback. Living in a world of pleasant illusion, they continue to act in ways that alienate their would-be friends. A true friend is one who can let us in on bad news.

"It takes your enemy and your friend, working together, to hurt you to the heart; the enemy to slander you and the friend to get the news to you."

Mark Twain, *Pudd'nhead Wilson's New Calender*, 1897

Someone who really loves us will be honest with us but will also tend to see us through rose-coloured glasses. When Sandra Murray and her colleagues (1996) studied dating and married couples from the University of Waterloo, they found that the happiest were those who idealized one another; they even saw their partners more positively than their partners saw themselves. When we're in love, we're biased to find those we love not only physically attractive, but socially attractive as well. Moreover, these relationship illusions were not only related to relationship satisfaction—they predicted it too. Those who had illusions, but were initially dissatisfied, became satisfied over time (Murray & Holmes, 1997).

RELATIONSHIP REWARDS

"No one is perfect until you fall in love with them."

Andy Rooney

Asked why they are friends with someone or why they were attracted to their partners, most people can readily answer. "I like Carol because she's warm, witty, and well-read." What such explanations leave out—and what social psychologists believe is most important—is ourselves. Attraction involves the one who is attracted as well as the attractor. Thus a more psychologically accurate answer might be, "I like Carol because of how I feel when I'm with her." We are attracted to those *we* find it satisfying and gratifying to be with. Attraction is in the eye (and brain) of the beholder.

reward theory of attraction the theory that we like those whose behaviour is rewarding to us or whom we associate with rewarding events

The point can be expressed as a simple **reward theory of attraction**: *Those who reward us, or whom we associate with rewards, we like.* If a relationship gives us more rewards than costs, we will like it and will wish it to continue. This will be especially true if the relationship is more profitable than alternative relationships (Burgess & Huston, 1979; Kelley, 1979; Rusbult, 1980). Mutual attraction flourishes when each meets the other's unmet needs (Byers & Wang, 2004). In his 1665 book of *Maxims*, La Rochefoucauld conjectured, "Friendship is a scheme for the mutual exchange of personal advantages and favours whereby self-esteem may profit."

We not only like people who are rewarding to be with; we also, according to the second version of the reward principle, like those we *associate* with good feelings. According to theorists Donn Byrne and Gerald Clore (1970), Albert Lott and Bernice Lott (1974), and Jan DeHouwer and colleagues (2001), conditioning creates positive feelings toward things and people linked with rewarding events. When, after a strenuous week, we relax in front of a fire, enjoying good food, drink, and music, we will likely feel a special warmth toward those around us. We are less likely to take a liking to someone we meet while suffering a splitting headache.

Pawel Lewicki (1985) tested this liking-by-association principle. In one experiment, University of Warsaw students were virtually 50–50 in choosing which of two pictured women (A or B in Figure 11–4) looked friendlier. Other students, having interacted with a warm, friendly experimenter who resembled woman A, chose woman A, by a 6 to 1 margin. In a follow-up study, the experimenter acted *un*friendly toward half the subjects. When these subjects later had to turn in their data to one of two women, they nearly always *avoided* the one who resembled the experimenter. (Perhaps you can recall a time when you reacted positively or negatively to someone who reminded you of someone else.)

Other experiments confirm this phenomenon of liking—and disliking—by association. In one, university students who evaluated strangers in a pleasant room liked them better than those who evaluated them in an uncomfortably hot room (Griffitt, 1970). In another, people evaluated photographs of other people while in either an elegant, sumptuously furnished room or in a shabby, dirty room (Maslow & Mintz, 1956). Again, the warm feelings evoked by the elegant surroundings transferred to the people being rated. Elaine Hatfield and William Walster (1978) found a practical tip in these research studies: "Romantic dinners, trips to the theatre, evenings at home together, and vacations never stop being important. . . . If your relationship is to survive, it's important that you both continue to associate your relationship with good things."

This simple theory of attraction—we like those who reward us and those we associate with rewards—helps us understand why people everywhere feel attracted to those who are warm,

FIGURE 11–4

Liking by association.

After interacting with a friendly experimenter, people preferred someone who looked like her (Person A) to one who didn't (Person B). After interacting with an unfriendly experimenter, people avoided the woman who resembled her (Lewicki, 1985).

Experimenter Person A Person B

Our liking and disliking of people is influenced by the events with which they are associated.

trustworthy, and responsive (Fletcher et al., 1999; Regan, 1998; Wojciszke et al., 1998). The reward theory also helps explain some of the influences on attraction:

- *Proximity* is rewarding. It costs less time and effort to receive friendship's benefits with someone who lives or works close by.
- We like *attractive* people because we perceive that they offer other desirable traits and because we benefit by associating with them.
- If others have *similar* opinions, we feel rewarded because we presume that they like us in return. Moreover, those who share our views help validate them. We especially like people if we have successfully converted them to our way of thinking (Lombardo et al., 1972; Riordan, 1980; Sigall, 1970).
- We like to be liked and love to be loved. Thus, liking is usually mutual. We like those who like us.

SUMMING UP: WHAT LEADS TO FRIENDSHIP AND ATTRACTION?

The best predictor of whether any two people are friends is their sheer *proximity* to one another. Proximity is conducive to repeated exposure and interaction, which enables us to discover similarities and to feel one another's liking.

A second determinant of initial attraction is *physical attractiveness.* Both in laboratory studies and in field experiments involving blind dates, university students tend to prefer attractive people. In everyday life, however, people tend actually to choose and marry someone whose attractiveness roughly matches their own (or someone who, if less attractive, has other compensating qualities). Positive attributions about attractive people define a physical-attractiveness stereotype—an assumption that what is beautiful is good.

Liking for another is greatly aided by *similarity* of attitudes, beliefs, and values. Likeness leads to liking; opposites rarely attract. We are also likely to develop friendships with people who *like us.*

A simple principle helps explain these influences upon our attractions to one another: We like people whose behaviour we find rewarding or whom we have associated with rewarding events.

WHAT IS LOVE?

What is this thing called "love"? Can passionate love endure? If not, what can replace it?

Loving is more complex than liking and thus more difficult to measure, more perplexing to study. People yearn for it, live for it, die for it. Yet only in the last couple of decades has loving become a serious topic in social psychology.

Most attraction researchers have studied what is most easily studied—responses during brief encounters between strangers. The influences on our initial liking of another—proximity, attractiveness, similarity, being liked, and other rewarding traits—also influence our long-term, close relationships. The impressions that dating couples quickly form of each other therefore provide a clue to their long-term future (Berg, 1984; Berg & McQuinn, 1986). Indeed, if North American romances flourished *randomly,* without regard to proximity and similarity, then most Catholics (being a minority) would marry Protestants, most Blacks would marry Whites, and college graduates would be as apt to marry high-school dropouts as fellow graduates.

So first impressions are important. Nevertheless, long-term loving is not merely an intensification of initial liking. Social psychologists have therefore shifted their attention from the mild attraction experienced during first encounters to the study of enduring, close relationships.

PASSIONATE LOVE

The first step in scientifically studying romantic love, as in studying any variable, is to decide how to define and measure it. We have ways to measure aggression, altruism, prejudice, and liking—but how do we measure love?

"How do I love thee? Let me count the ways," wrote Elizabeth Barrett Browning. Social scientists have counted various ways. Psychologist Robert Sternberg (1998) views love as a triangle consisting of three components: passion, intimacy, and commitment (Figure 11–5). Drawing from ancient philosophy and literature, sociologist John Alan Lee (1988) and psychologists Clyde Hendrick and Susan Hendrick (1993, 2003) identify three primary love styles—*eros* (self-disclosing passion), *ludus* (uncommitted game playing), and *storge* (friendship)—which, like the primary colours, combine to form secondary love styles. Some love styles, notably eros, predict high relationship satisfaction; others, such as ludus, predict low satisfaction.

Some elements are common to all loving relationships: mutual understanding, giving and receiving support, enjoying the loved one's company. Some elements are distinctive. If we experience passionate love, we express it physically, we expect the relationship to be exclusive,

FIGURE 11–5

Robert Sternberg's (1988) conception of kinds of loving as combinations of three basic components of love.

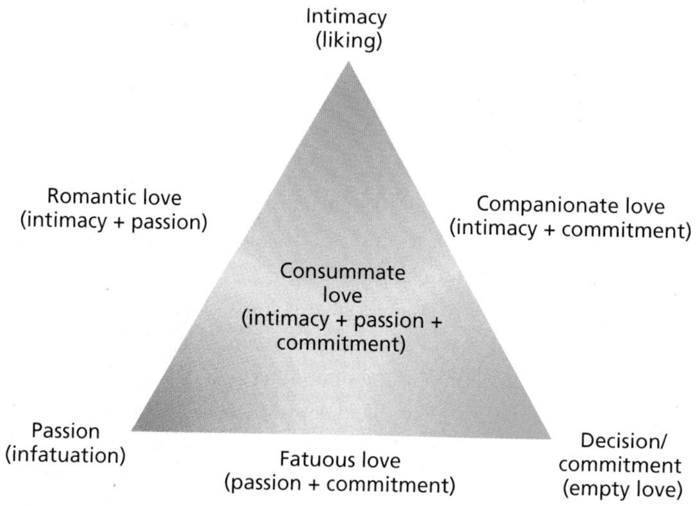

and we are intensely fascinated with our partner. You can see it in our eyes. Zick Rubin confirmed this. He administered his Love Scale to hundreds of dating couples. Later, from behind a one-way mirror in a laboratory waiting room, he clocked eye contact among "weak-love" and "strong-love" couples. His result will not surprise you: The strong-love couples gave themselves away by gazing long into one another's eyes.

passionate love a state of intense longing for union with another. Passionate lovers are absorbed in one another, feel ecstatic at attaining their partner's love, and are disconsolate on losing it.

Passionate love is emotional, exciting, intense. Elaine Hatfield (1988) defines it as *"a state of intense longing for union with another"* (p. 193). If reciprocated, one feels fulfilled and joyous; if not, one feels empty or despairing. Like other forms of emotional excitement, passionate love involves a mix of elation and gloom, tingling exhilaration and dejected misery.

Passionate love is what you feel when you not only love someone, you are "in love" with him or her. As Sarah Meyers and Ellen Berscheid (1997) note, we understand that someone who says, "I love you, but I'm not in love with you" means to say, "I like you. I care about you. I think you're marvellous. But I don't feel sexually attracted to you." I feel *storge* (friendship love) but not *eros* (passion).

A theory of passionate love

To explain passionate love, Hatfield notes that a given state of arousal can be steered into any of several emotions, depending on how we attribute the arousal. An emotion involves both body and mind—both arousal and how we interpret and label that arousal. Imagine yourself with pounding heart and trembling hands: Are you experiencing fear, anxiety, joy? Physiologically, one emotion is quite similar to another. You may therefore experience the arousal as joy if you are in a euphoric situation, anger if your environment is hostile, and passionate love if the situation is romantic. In this view, passionate love is the psychological experience of being biologically aroused by someone we find attractive.

If indeed passion is a revved-up state that's labelled "love," then whatever revs one up should intensify feelings of love. In several experiments, university and college men aroused sexually by reading or viewing erotic materials had a heightened response to a woman—for example, by scoring much higher on Rubin's Love Scale when describing their girlfriend (Carducci et al., 1978; Dermer & Pyszczynski, 1978; Stephan et al., 1971). Proponents of the **two-factor theory of emotion** argue that when the revved-up men responded to a woman, they easily misattributed some of their arousal to her.

According to this theory, being aroused by *any* source should intensify passionate feelings—providing the mind is free to attribute some of the arousal to a romantic stimulus. Donald Dutton and Arthur Aron (1974, 1989) invited University of British Columbia men to participate in a learning experiment. After meeting their attractive female partners, some were frightened with the news that they would be suffering some "quite painful" electric shocks. Before the experiment was to begin, the researcher gave a brief questionnaire "to get some information on your present feelings and reactions, since these often influence performance on the learning task." Asked how much they would like to date and kiss their female partners, the aroused (frightened) men expressed more intense attraction toward the women.

"When in doubt, Sis, you've got to listen to your heart. If it's going thump, thump, thump, slow and steady, you've got the wrong guy."

Does this phenomenon occur outside the laboratory? Dutton and Aron (1974) had an attractive young woman approach individual young men as they crossed a narrow, wobbly, 150-metre-long suspension walkway hanging 75 metres above British Columbia's rocky Capilano River. The woman asked each man to help her fill out a class questionnaire. When he had finished, she scribbled her name and phone number and invited him to call if he wanted to hear more about the project. Most accepted the phone number, and half who did so called. By contrast, men approached by the woman on a low, solid bridge, and men approached on the high bridge by a *male* interviewer, rarely called. Once again, physical arousal accentuated romantic responses.

two-factor theory of emotion
arousal × its label = emotion

Scary movies, roller-coaster rides, and physical exercise have the same effect (Cohen et al., 1989; White & Kight, 1984). The effect holds true with married couples, too. Those who do exciting things together report the best relationships. And after doing an arousing rather than a mundane laboratory task (roughly the equivalent of a three-legged race on their hands and knees), couples also reported higher satisfaction with their overall relationship (Aron et al., 2000). Adrenalin makes the heart grow fonder. As this suggests, passionate love is a biological as well as a psychological phenomenon. Research by Aron and his colleagues (2005) indicates that passionate love engages dopamine-rich brain areas associated with reward (see Figure 11–6).

"The 'adrenaline' associated with a wide variety of highs can spill over and make passion more passionate. (Sort of a 'Better loving through chemistry' phenomenon.)"

Elaine Hatfield and Richard Rapson (1987)

Variations in love: Culture and gender

There is always a temptation to assume that most others share our feelings and ideas. We assume, for example, that love is a precondition for marriage. Most cultures—89 percent in one analysis of 166 cultures—do have a concept of romantic love, as reflected in flirtation or couples running off together (Jankowiak & Fischer,

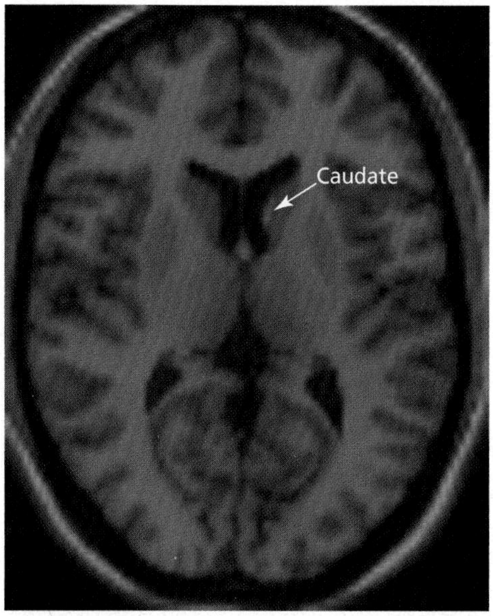

FIGURE 11–6

Love is in the brain.

MRI scans from young adults intensely in love revealed areas, such as the caudate nucleus, which became more active when gazing at the loved-one's photo (but not when gazing at the photo of another acquaintance). (Aron et al., 2005)

1992). But in some cultures, notably those practising arranged marriages, love tends to follow rather than to precede marriage.

Do males and females differ in how they experience passionate love? Studies of men and women falling in and out of love reveal some surprises. Most people, including the writer of the following letter to a newspaper advice columnist, suppose that women fall in love more readily:

> Dear Dr. Brothers:
> Do you think it's effeminate for a 19-year-old guy to fall in love so hard it's like the whole world's turned around? I think I'm really crazy because this has happened several times now and love just seems to hit me on the head from nowhere. . . . My father says this is the way girls fall in love and that it doesn't happen this way with guys—at least it's not supposed to. I can't change how I am in this way but it kind of worries me.—P.T. (quoted by Dion & Dion, 1985)

P.T. would be reassured by the repeated finding that it is actually *men* who tend to fall more readily in love (Dion & Dion, 1985; Peplau & Gordon, 1985). Men also seem to fall out of love more slowly and are less likely than women to break up a premarital romance. Once in love, however, women are typically as emotionally involved as their partners, or more so. They are more likely to report feeling euphoric and "giddy and carefree," as if they were "floating on a cloud." Women are also somewhat more likely than men to focus on the intimacy of the friendship and on their concern for their partner. Men are more likely than women to think about the playful and physical aspects of the relationship (Hendrick & Hendrick, 1995).

STORY BEHIND THE RESEARCH

For a number of years, I have been studying the social/developmental psychology of physical attractiveness. There is now considerable evidence that attractiveness affects judgments and evaluations of others. More recently, I've been interested in whether cultural values are related to the occurrence and/or strength of stereotyping based on attractiveness. Are there culture-related differences in the impact of physical attractiveness on evaluations of others?

This question reflects my more general research interest in the cultural context of attraction and interpersonal relationships. Increasingly, the importance of cultural perspectives is being acknowledged by social psychologists, as well as researchers in other areas of psychology—a promising trend within the field.

Karen Dion
University of Toronto

COMPANIONATE LOVE

companionate love
the affection we feel for those with whom our lives are deeply intertwined

Although passionate love burns hot, it inevitably simmers down. The longer a relationship endures, the fewer its emotional ups and downs (Berscheid et al., 1989). The high of romance may be sustained for a few months, even a couple of years. But no high lasts forever. "When you're in love it's the most glorious two-and-a-half days of your life," jests comedian Richard Lewis. The novelty, the intense absorption in the other, the thrill of the romance, the giddy "floating on a cloud" feeling, fades. After two years of marriage, spouses express affection about half as often as when they were newlyweds (Huston & Chorost, 1994). About four years after marriage, the divorce rate peaks in cultures worldwide (Fisher, 1994). If a close relationship is to endure, it will settle to a steadier but still warm afterglow that Hatfield calls **companionate love**.

Unlike the wild emotions of passionate love, companionate love is lower key; it's a deep, affectionate attachment. And it is just as real. Nisa, a !Kung San woman of the African Kalahari Desert, explains: "When two people are first together, their hearts are on fire and their passion is very great. After a while, the fire cools and that's how it stays. They continue to love each other, but it's in a different way—warm and dependable" (Shostak, 1981).

The flow and ebb of romantic love follows the pattern of addictions to coffee, alcohol, and other drugs. At first, a drug gives a big kick, perhaps a high. With repetition, opponent emotions gain strength and tolerance develops. An amount that once was highly stimulating no longer gives a thrill. Stopping the substance, however, does not return you to where you started. Rather, it triggers withdrawal symptoms—malaise, depression, the blahs. The same often happens in love. The passionate high is fated to become lukewarm. The no-longer-romantic relationship becomes taken for granted—until it ends. Then the jilted lover, the widower, the

"When two people are under the influence of the most violent, most insane, most delusive, and most transient of passions, they are required to swear that they will remain in that excited, abnormal, and exhausting condition continuously until death do them part."

George Bernard Shaw

Unlike passionate love, companionate love can last a lifetime.

divorcee, are surprised at how empty life now seems without the person they long ago stopped feeling passionately attached to. Having focused on what was not working, they stopped noticing what was (Carlson & Hatfield, 1992).

The cooling of passionate love over time and the growing importance of other factors, such as shared values, can be seen in the feelings of those who enter arranged versus love-based marriages in India. Usha Gupta and Pushpa Singh (1982) asked 50 couples in Jaipur, India, to complete a love scale. They found that those who married for love reported diminishing feelings of love after a five-year newlywed period. By contrast, those in arranged marriages reported *more* love if their marriage was five or more years old (Figure 11–7).

The cooling of intense romantic love often triggers a period of disillusion, especially among those who regard such love as essential both for a marriage and for its continuation. Jeffry Simpson, Bruce Campbell, and Ellen Berscheid (1986) suspect "the sharp rise in the divorce rate in the past two decades is linked, at least in part, to the growing importance of intense positive emotional experiences (e.g., romantic love) in people's lives, experiences that may be particularly difficult to sustain over time." Compared to North Americans, Asians tend to focus less on personal feelings and more on the practical aspects of social attachments (Dion & Dion, 1988; Sprecher et al., 1994). Thus, they are less vulnerable to disillusionment. Asians are also less prone to the self-focused individualism that in the long run can undermine a relationship and lead to divorce (Dion & Dion, 1991, 1996; Triandis et al., 1988).

"Grow old along with me! The best is yet to be.

Robert Browning

The decline in intense mutual fascination may be natural and adaptive for species survival. The result of passionate love frequently is children, whose survival is aided by the parents' waning obsession with one another (Kenrick & Trost, 1987). Nevertheless, for those married more

FIGURE 11–7

Romantic love between partners in arranged or love marriages in Jaipur, India.

(Data from Gupta & Singh, 1982)

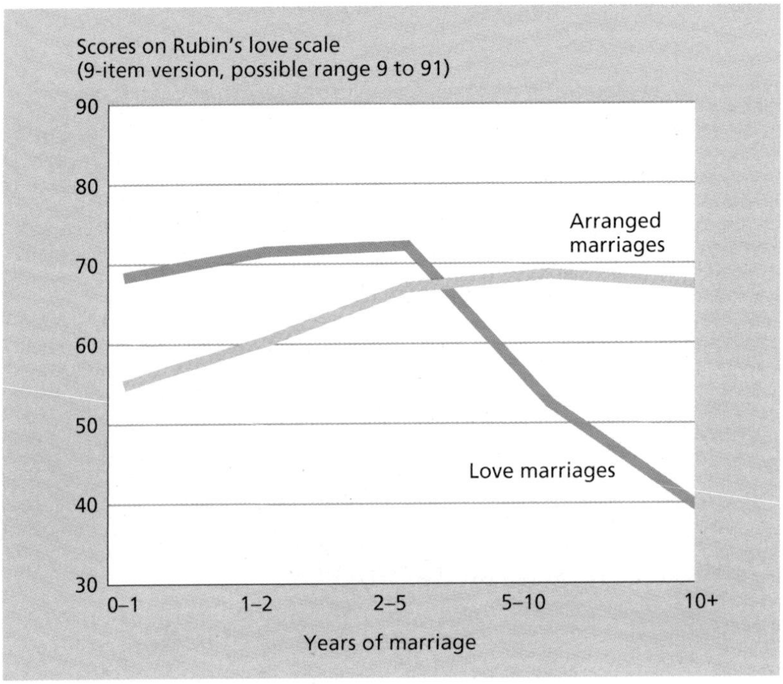

than 20 years, some of the lost romantic feeling is often renewed as the family nest empties and the parents are once again free to focus their attention on each other (Hatfield & Sprecher, 1986). "No man or woman really knows what love is until they have been married a quarter of a century," said Mark Twain. If the relationship has been intimate and mutually rewarding, companionate love rooted in a rich history of shared experiences deepens.

SUMMING UP: WHAT IS LOVE?

Researchers have characterized love as having components of friendship, passion, and committed game playing. Passionate love is experienced as a bewildering confusion of ecstasy and anxiety, elation and pain. The two-factor theory of emotion suggests that in a romantic context arousal from any source, even painful experiences, can be steered into passion. In the best of relationships, the initial romantic high settles to a steadier, more affectionate relationship called *companionate love.*

WHAT ENABLES CLOSE RELATIONSHIPS?

What factors influence the ups and downs of our close relationships? We consider several: attachment styles, equity, and self-disclosure.

ATTACHMENT

Love is a biological imperative. We are, in our roots, social creatures, destined to bond with others. Our need to belong is adaptive, as we noted at this chapter's beginning. Cooperation promoted our species' survival. In solo combat, our ancestors were not the toughest predators. But as hunter-gatherers, and in fending off predators, they gained strength from numbers. Because group dwellers survived and reproduced, we today carry genes that predispose such bonds.

Our infant dependency strengthens our human bonds. Soon after birth we exhibit various social responses—love, fear, anger. But the first and greatest of these is love. As babies, we almost immediately prefer familiar faces and voices. We coo and smile when our parents give us attention. By eight months, we crawl after mother or father and typically let out a wail when separated from them. Reunited, we cling. By keeping infants close to their caregivers, social attachment serves as a powerful survival impulse.

Deprived of familiar attachments, sometimes under conditions of extreme neglect, children may become withdrawn, frightened, silent. After studying the mental health of homeless children for the World Health Organization, psychiatrist John Bowlby (1980, p. 442) reflected, "Intimate attachments to other human beings are the hub around which a person's life revolves, not only when he is an infant or a toddler or a schoolchild but throughout his adolescence and his years of maturity as well, and on into old age. From these intimate attachments a person draws his strength and enjoyment of life."

Researchers have compared the nature of attachment and love in various close relationships—between parents and children, same-sex friends, and spouses or lovers (Davis, 1985; Maxwell, 1985; Sternberg & Grajek, 1984). Some elements are common to all loving attachments: mutual understanding, giving and receiving support, valuing and enjoying being with the loved one. Passionate love is, however, spiced with some added features: physical affection, an expectation of exclusiveness, and an intense fascination with the loved one.

Passionate love is not just for lovers. The intense love of parent and infant for each other qualifies as a form of passionate love, even to the point of engaging brain areas akin to those enabling passionate romantic love. Phillip Shaver and his coworkers (1988) note that year-old infants display a passionate attachment to their parents. Much like young adult lovers, they welcome physical affection, feel distress when separated, express intense affection when reunited, and take great pleasure in the significant other's attention and approval. Knowing that infants vary in their styles of relating to caregivers, Shaver and Cindy Hazan (1993, 1994) wondered whether infant attachment styles might carry over to adult relationships.

Attachment styles

secure attachment
attachments rooted in trust and marked by intimacy

About 7 in 10 infants, and nearly that many adults, exhibit **secure attachment** (Baldwin et al., 1996; Jones & Cunningham, 1996; Mickelson et al., 1997). When placed as infants in a strange situation (usually a laboratory playroom), they play comfortably in their mother's presence, happily exploring this strange environment. If she leaves, they get distressed; when she returns, they run to her, hold her, then relax and return to exploring and playing (Ainsworth, 1973, 1979). This trusting attachment style, many researchers believe, forms a working model of intimacy—a blueprint for one's adult intimate relationships, in which underlying trust sustains relationships through times of conflict (Miller & Rempel, 2004). Secure adults find it easy to get close to others and don't fret about getting too dependent or being abandoned. As lovers, they enjoy sexuality within the context of a continuing relationship. And their relationships tend to be satisfying and enduring (Feeney, 1996; Feeney & Noller, 1990; Keelan, Dion & Dion, 1998; Simpson et al., 1992).

Kim Bartholomew and Leonard Horowitz (1991) proposed an influential attachment model that classifies people's attachment styles according to their images of self (positive or negative) and of others (positive or negative). Secure people have a positive image of both self and others. They sense their own worth and lovability, and expect that others will accept and respond to their love.

preoccupied attachment
attachments marked by a sense of one's own unworthiness and anxiety, ambivalence, and possessiveness

People with the **preoccupied attachment** style (also called *anxious-ambivalent*) have positive expectations of others but a sense of their own unworthiness. In the strange situation, anxious-ambivalent infants are more likely to cling anxiously to their mother. If she leaves, they cry; when she returns, they may be indifferent or hostile. As adults, anxious-ambivalent individuals are less trusting, and therefore more possessive and jealous. They may break up repeatedly with the same person. When discussing conflicts, they get emotional and often angry (Cassidy, 2000; Simpson et al., 1996). By contrast, friends who support each others' freedom and acknowledge each others' perspectives usually have a satisfying relationship.

dismissive attachment
an avoidant relationship style marked by distrust of others

fearful attachment
an avoidant relationship style marked by a fear of rejection

People with negative views of others exhibit either the **dismissing** or the **fearful attachment** style; the two styles share the characteristic of *avoidance*. Although internally aroused, avoidant infants reveal little distress during separation or clinging on reunion. As adults, avoidant people tend to be less invested in relationships and more likely to leave them. They also are more likely to engage in one-night stands of sex without love. Examples of the two styles might be "I want to keep my options open" (dismissing) and "I am uncomfortable getting close to others" (fearful).

STORY BEHIND THE RESEARCH

Kim Bartholomew
Simon Fraser University

My interest in adult attachment stems from an obvious, but perplexing, observation. On the one hand, people are highly motivated to form satisfying intimate relationships. And yet, despite this motivation, the goal of finding and maintaining the perfect (or at least good enough) intimate relationship all too often proves elusive. I have looked to attachment theory as a theoretical framework for understanding the range of difficulties people experience in their intimate relationships. My research has focused on how adult attachment orientations, as assessed through semi-structured interviews, may affect functioning in close relationships. During the course of a longitudinal study of attachment processes in young established couples, I became acutely aware of the high levels of abuse in some relationships and the surprisingly high stability of most of these relationships. Through this work and through an association with Donald Dutton, a family violence researcher at U.B.C., my students and I became interested in violent relationships. Working with both clinical and community samples, we have applied an attachment perspective to understanding the dynamics of abusive relationships and the difficulty many individuals experience leaving abusive relationships. We have observed that individuals who lack confidence in the acceptance and responsiveness of their partners are prone to experience high levels of attachment anxiety, leading them (in some cases) to act in aggressive, seemingly counterproductive, ways in an attempt to gain proximity to their partners. In our most recent line of research, we are investigating attachment, childhood socialization, and partner abuse in gay men.

Some researchers attribute these varying attachment styles, which have been observed across 62 cultures (Schmitt et al., 2004), to parental responsiveness. Cindy Hazan (2004) sums up the idea: "Early attachment experiences form the basis for *internal working models* or characteristic ways of thinking about relationships." Thus, sensitive, responsive mothers—mothers who engender a sense of basic trust in the world's reliability—typically have securely attached infants, observed Mary Ainsworth (1979) and Erik Erikson (1963). In fact, one study of 100 Israeli grandmother-daughter-granddaughter threesomes found intergenerational consistency of attachment styles (Besser & Priel, 2005). And youths who have experienced nurturing and involved parenting teams tend later to have warm and supportive relationships with their romantic partners (Conger et al., 2000). Other researchers believe attachment styles may reflect inherited temperament (Harris, 1998). Teens who are prone to anger and anxiety tend to have, as young adults, more fragile relationships (Donnellan et al., 2005). Regardless, early attachment styles do seem to lay a foundation for future relationships.

POSITIVE ILLUSIONS

Is it better for your partner to see you for who you really are or do you want your partner to glamorize you and look past your faults? Research by John Holmes, Sandra Murray, and Dale Griffin (1996, 1997, 2000) suggests that couples are happier if they glamorize their partner seeing them even more positively than their partners see themselves. It seems that turning your partner's faults into virtues strengthens and solidifies a relationship. For example, in one study they had people describe how often they argued with their partner—knowing that most people would say they argued little. They then had people read a made up article alleging that if couples don't argue then this indicates that they are unable to address their differences, and unlikely to stay together in the long run. Compared to those who did not read this article, those who did remembered having more arguments and reinterpreted their partner's behaviour so that the "fault" of not arguing actually was a virtue. Just as self-serving biases (see Chapter 2) may allow us to maintain positive views of ourselves, positive illusions about our relationship partners may allow us to maintain positive views of our relationships.

Positive views of ourselves may actually underlie our positive illusions about our relationships. People with low self-esteem are less likely to have positive illusions about their partners than people with high self-esteem and the lack of illusions among low self-esteem people fuels their doubts and insecurities about their relationships (Murray, Holmes & Griffin, 2000; Murray, Holmes, Griffin, Bellavia & Rose, 2001; Murray, Rose, Bellavia, Holmes & Kusche, 2002). Such doubts can lead to behaviour that undermines the relationship as a breakdown in trust occurs. Thus a healthy dose of positive illusions seems to be an antidote to worries and anxiety that can undermine relationships.

EQUITY

If each partner in a relationship pursues his or her personal desires willy-nilly, the relationship will die. Therefore, our society teaches us to exchange rewards by what Elaine Hatfield, William Walster, and Ellen Berscheid (1978) have called an **equity** principle of attraction: What you and your partner get out of a relationship should be proportional to what you each put into it. If two people receive equal outcomes, they should contribute equally; otherwise one or the other will feel it is unfair. If both feel their outcomes correspond to the assets and efforts each contributes, then both perceive equity.

equity
a condition in which the outcomes people receive from a relationship are proportional to what they contribute to it. Note: Equitable outcomes needn't always be equal outcomes.

Strangers and casual acquaintances maintain equity by exchanging benefits: You lend me your class notes; later, I'll lend you mine. I invite you to my party; you invite me to yours. Those in an enduring relationship, including roommates and those in love, do not feel bound to trade similar benefits—notes for notes, parties for parties (Berg, 1984). They feel freer to maintain equity by exchanging a variety of benefits ("When you drop by to lend me your notes, why don't you stay for dinner?") and eventually to stop keeping track of who owes whom.

Long-term equity

Is it crass to suppose that friendship and love are rooted in an equitable exchange of rewards? Don't we sometimes give in response to a loved one's need, without expecting any sort of return? Indeed, those involved in an equitable, long-term relationship are unconcerned with short-term equity. Margaret Clark and Judson Mills (1979, 1993; Clark, 1984, 1986) argue that people even take pains to *avoid* calculating any exchange benefits. When we help a good friend, we do not want instant repayment. If someone invites us for dinner, we wait before reciprocating, lest the person attribute the motive for our return invitation to be merely paying off a social debt. True friends tune into

"Love is the most subtle kind of self-interest."
Holbrook Johnson

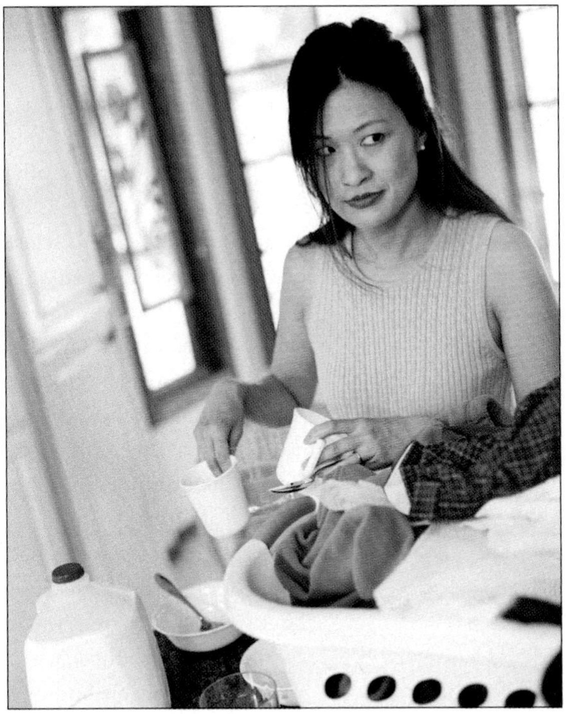

Do women still do the majority of household tasks? Although domestic responsibilities may be more evenly balanced between genders, perceived inequality can result in marital distress and dissatisfaction.

one another's needs even when reciprocation is impossible (Clark et al., 1986, 1989). One clue that an acquaintance is becoming such a friend is the person's sharing when sharing is unexpected (Miller et al., 1989). Similarly, happily married people tend *not* to keep score of how much they are giving and getting (Buunk & Van Yperen, 1991).

In a series of experiments Clark and Mills confirmed that *not* being calculating is a mark of friendship. Tit-for-tat exchanges boosted people's liking when the relationship was relatively formal but *diminished* liking when the two sought friendship. Clark and Mills surmise that marriage contracts in which each partner specifies what is expected from the other are more likely to undermine than enhance love. Only when the other's positive behaviour is voluntary can we attribute it to love.

Still, the long-term equity principle explains why people usually bring equal assets to romantic relationships. Recall that often they are matched for attractiveness, status, and so forth. If they are mismatched in one area, such as attractiveness, they tend to be mismatched in some other area, such as status. But in total assets, they are an equitable match. No one says, and few even think, "I'll trade you my good looks for your big income." But especially in relationships that last, equity is the rule.

Perceived equity and satisfaction

Those in an equitable relationship are more content (Fletcher et al., 1987; Hatfield et al., 1985; Van Yperen & Buunk, 1990). Those who perceive their relationship as *in*equitable feel discomfort: The one who has the better deal may feel guilty and the one who senses a raw deal may feel strong irritation. (Given the self-serving bias—most husbands perceive themselves as contributing more housework than their wives credit them for—the person who is "overbenefited" is less sensitive to the inequity.)

Robert Schafer and Patricia Keith (1980) surveyed several hundred married couples of all ages, noting those who felt their marriages were somewhat unfair because one spouse contributed too little to the cooking, housekeeping, parenting, or providing. Inequity took its toll: Those who perceived inequity also felt more distressed and depressed. During the child-rearing years, when wives often feel underbenefited and husbands overbenefited, marital satisfaction tends to dip. During the honeymoon and empty-nest stages, spouses are more likely to perceive equity and to feel satisfaction with their marriages (Feeney et al., 1994). When both partners freely give and receive, and make decisions together, the odds of sustained, satisfying love are good.

Perceived inequity triggers marital distress, agree Nancy Grote and Margaret Clark (2001) from their tracking of married couples over time. But they also report that the traffic between inequity and distress runs both ways: Marital distress exacerbates the perception of unfairness (Figure 11–8).

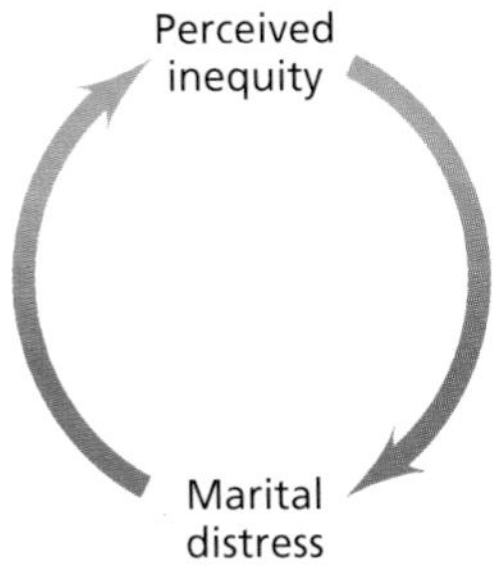

FIGURE 11–8

Perceived inequities trigger marital distress, which fosters the perception of inequities. (Adapted from Grote & Clark, 2001)

SELF-DISCLOSURE

Deep, companionate relationships are intimate. They enable us to be known as we truly are and feel accepted. We discover this exquisite experience in a good marriage or a close friendship—a relationship where trust displaces anxiety and where we are therefore free to open ourselves without fear of losing the other's affection (Holmes & Rempel, 1989). Such relationships are characterized by what the late Sidney Jourard called **self-disclosure** (Derlega et al., 1993). As a relationship grows, self-disclosing partners reveal more and more of themselves to one another; their knowledge of one another penetrates to deeper and deeper levels.

self-disclosure revealing intimate aspects of oneself to others

Research studies find that most of us enjoy such intimacy. We feel pleased when a normally reserved person says that something about us "made me feel like opening up" and share confidential information (Archer & Cook, 1986; D. Taylor et al., 1981). It's gratifying to be singled out for another's disclosure. Not only do we like those who disclose, we also disclose to those whom we like. And after disclosing to them, we like them more (Collins & Miller, 1994). Lacking opportunities for intimacy, we experience the pain of loneliness (Berg & Peplau, 1982; Solano et al., 1982).

Experiments have probed both the *causes* and the *effects* of self-disclosure. When are people most willing to disclose intimate information concerning "what you like and don't like about yourself" or "what you're most ashamed and most proud of"? And what effects do such revelations have on those who reveal and receive them?

disclosure reciprocity the tendency for one person's intimacy of self-disclosure to match that of a conversational partner

The most reliable finding is the **disclosure reciprocity** effect: Disclosure begets disclosure (Berg, 1987; Miller, 1990; Reis & Shaver, 1988). We reveal more to those who have been open with us. But intimacy is seldom instant. (If it is, the person may seem indiscreet and unstable.) Appropriate intimacy progresses like a dance: I reveal a little, you reveal a little—but not too much. You then reveal more, and I reciprocate.

For those in love, deepening intimacy is exciting. "Rising intimacy will create a strong sense of passion," note Roy Baumeister and Ellen Bratslavsky (1999). This helps explain why those who remarry after the loss of a spouse tend to begin the new marriage with an increased frequency of sex, and why passion often rides highest when intimacy is restored following severe conflict.

Some people—most of them women—are especially skilled "openers"—they easily elicit intimate disclosures from others, even from those who normally don't reveal very much of themselves (Miller et al., 1983; Pegalis et al., 1994; Shaffer et al., 1996). Such people tend to be good listeners. During conversation they maintain attentive facial expressions and appear to be comfortably enjoying themselves (Purvis et al., 1984). They may also express interest by uttering supportive phrases while their conversational partner is speaking. They are what psychologist Carl Rogers (1980) called "growth-promoting" listeners—people who are *genuine* in revealing their own feelings, who are *accepting* of others' feelings, and who are *empathic,* sensitive, reflective listeners.

> *"What is a Friend? I will tell you. It is a person with whom you dare to be yourself."*
>
> Frank Crane, *A Definition of Friendship*

What are the effects of such self-disclosure? Jourard (1964) argued that dropping our masks, letting ourselves be known as we are, nurtures love. He presumed that it is gratifying to open up to another and then to receive the trust another implies by being open with us. For example, having an intimate friend with whom we can discuss threats to our self-image seems to help us survive such stresses (Swann & Predmore, 1985). A true friendship is a special relationship that helps us cope with our other relationships. "When

I am with my friend," reflected the Roman playwright Seneca, "methinks I am alone, and as much at liberty to speak anything as to think it." At its best, marriage is such a friendship, sealed by commitment.

Intimate self-disclosure is one of companionate love's delights. Dating and married couples who most reveal themselves to one another express more satisfaction with their relationship and are more likely to endure in it (Berg & McQuinn, 1986; Hendrick et al., 1988; Sprecher, 1987). In a study of newlywed couples that were all equally in love, those who most deeply and accurately knew each other were most likely to enjoy enduring love (Neff & Karney, 2005). Married partners who most strongly agree that "I try to share my most intimate thoughts and feelings with my partner" tend to have the most satisfying marriages (Sanderson & Cantor, 2001).

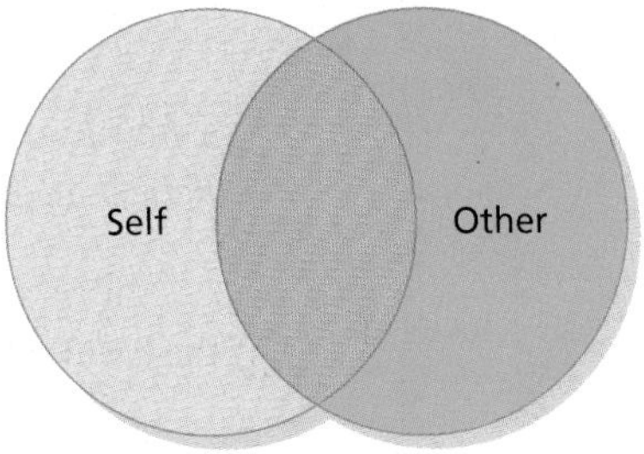

FIGURE 11–9

Love: An overlapping of selves—you become part of me, I part of you.

From A. L. Weber and J. H. Harvey, *Perspective on Close Relationships.* Published by Allyn & Bacon, Boston, MA. © 1994 by Pearson Education. Reprinted by permission of the publisher. (From Aron & Aron, 1994)

Researchers have also found that women are often more willing to disclose their fears and weaknesses than are men (Cunningham, 1981). As feminist writer Kate Millett (1975) put it, "Women express, men repress." Nevertheless, men today, particularly men with egalitarian gender-role attitudes, seem increasingly willing to reveal intimate feelings and to enjoy the satisfactions that accompany a relationship of mutual trust and self-disclosure. And that, say Arthur Aron and Elaine Aron (1994), is the essence of love—two selves connecting, disclosing, and identifying with one another; two selves, each retaining their individuality, yet sharing activities, delighting in similarities, and mutually supporting (Figure 11–9).

That being so, might we cultivate closeness by experiences that mirror the escalating closeness of budding friendships? The Arons and their collaborators (1997) wondered. So they paired volunteer students for 45 minutes with another student whom they didn't know. For the first 15 minutes, they shared thoughts on a list of personal, but low-intimacy topics such as, "When did you last sing to yourself?" The next 15 minutes were spent on more intimate topics such as, "What is your most treasured memory?" The last 15 minutes invited even more self-disclosure, with questions such as: "Complete this sentence: 'I wish I had someone with whom I could share . . .'" and "When did you last cry in front of another person? By yourself?"

Compared to control participants who spent the 45 minutes in small talk ("What was your high school like?" "What is your favourite holiday?"), those who experienced the escalating self-disclosure ended the hour feeling remarkably close to their conversation partners—in fact, "closer than the closest relationship in the lives of 30 percent of similar students," reported the researchers. These relationships surely were not yet marked by the loyalty and commitment of true friendship. Nevertheless, the experiment provides a striking demonstration of how readily a sense of closeness to others can grow, given open self-disclosure.

SUMMING UP: WHAT ENABLES CLOSE RELATIONSHIPS?

From infancy to old age, attachments are central to human life. Secure attachments, as in an enduring marriage, mark happy lives.

Companionate love is most likely to endure when both partners feel the partnership is equitable, with both perceiving themselves receiving from the relationship in proportion to what they contribute to it. One reward of companionate love is the opportunity for intimate self-disclosure; a state achieved gradually as each partner reciprocates the other's increasing openness.

HOW DO RELATIONSHIPS END?

Often love dies. What factors predict marital dissolution? How do couples typically detach or renew their relationships?

In 1971, a man wrote a love poem to his bride, slipped it into a bottle, and dropped it into the Pacific Ocean. A decade later, a jogger found it on a Guam beach:

> If, by the time this letter reaches you, I am old and grey, I know that our love will be as fresh as it is today. It may take a week or it may take years for this note to find you. . . . If this should never reach you, it will still be written in my heart that I will go to extreme means to prove my love for you. Your husband, Bob.

The woman to whom the love note was addressed was reached by phone. When the note was read to her she burst out laughing. And the more she heard, the harder she laughed. "We're divorced," she finally said, and slammed down the phone.

So it often goes. Comparing their unsatisfying relationship with the support and affection they imagine is available elsewhere, people are divorcing more often—at double the 1960 rate. Roughly 40 percent of Canadian marriages now end in divorce. Enduring relationships are rooted in enduring love and satisfaction, but also in inattention to possible alternative partners, fear of the costs of termination, and a sense of moral obligation (Adams & Jones, 1997; Miller, 1997). As economic and social barriers to divorce weakened during the 1960s and 1970s, thanks partly to women's increasing employment, divorce rates rose. "We are living longer, but loving more briefly," quips Os Guiness (1993, p. 309).

Britain's royal House of Windsor knows well the hazards of modern marriage. The fairy-tale marriages of Princess Margaret, Princess Anne, Prince Charles, and Prince Andrew all crumbled, smiles replaced with stony stares. Shortly after her 1986 marriage to Prince Andrew, Sarah Ferguson gushed, "I love his wit, his charm, his looks. I worship him." Andrew reciprocated her euphoria: "She is the best thing in my life." Six years later, Andrew, having decided her friends were "philistines," and Sarah, having derided Andrew's boorish behaviour as "terribly gauche," called it quits (*Time,* 1992).

DIVORCE

Divorce rates have varied widely by country, ranging from 0.01 percent of the population annually in Bolivia, the Philippines, and Spain to 4.7 percent in the world's most divorce-prone country, the United States. To predict a culture's divorce rates, it helps to know its values (Triandis, 1994). Individualistic cultures (where love is a feeling and people ask, "What does my heart say?") have more divorce than do communal cultures (where love entails obligation and people ask, "What will other people say?"). Individualists marry "for as long as we both shall love," collectivists more often for life. Individualists expect more passion and personal fulfillment in a marriage, which puts greater pressure on the relationship (Dion & Dion, 1993). "Keeping romance alive" was rated as important to a good marriage by 78 percent of American women surveyed and 29 percent of Japanese women (*American Enterprise,* 1992).

Even in Western society, however, those who enter relationships with a long-term orientation and an intention to persist do experience healthier, less turbulent, and more durable partnerships (Arriaga, 2001; Arriaga & Agnew, 2001). Those whose commitment to a union outlasts the desires that gave birth to it will endure times of conflict and unhappiness. One national survey found that 86 percent of those who were unhappily married but who stayed with the marriage were, when reinterviewed five years later, now mostly "very" or "quite" happy with their marriages (Popenoe, 2002). By contrast, "narcissists"—those more focused on their own desires and image—enter relationships with less commitment and less likelihood of long-term relational success (Campbell & Foster, 2002).

Risk of divorce also depends on who marries whom (Fergusson et al., 1984; Myers, 2000; Tzeng, 1992). People usually stay married if they

- Married after age 20
- Both grew up in stable, two-parent homes
- Dated for a long while before marriage
- Are well and similarly educated
- Enjoy a stable income from a good job
- Live in a small town or on a farm
- Did not cohabit or become pregnant before marriage
- Are religiously committed
- Are of similar age, faith, and education

None of these predictors, by itself, is essential to a stable marriage. But if none of these things is true for someone, marital breakdown is an almost sure bet. If all are true, they are *very* likely to stay together until death. The English perhaps had it right, several centuries ago, when presuming that the temporary intoxication of passionate love was a foolish basis for permanent marital decisions. Better, they felt, to choose a mate based on stable friendship and compatible backgrounds, interests, habits, and values (Stone, 1977).

> *"Passionate love is in many ways an altered state of consciousness. . . . In many states today, there are laws that a person must not be in an intoxicated condition when marrying. . . . But passionate love is a kind of intoxication."*
>
> Roy Baumeister, *Meanings of Life*, 1991

THE DETACHMENT PROCESS

Severing bonds produces a predictable sequence of agitated preoccupation with the lost partner, followed by deep sadness and, eventually, the beginnings of emotional detachment and a return to normal living (Hazan & Shaver, 1994). Even newly separated couples who have long ago ceased feeling affection are often surprised at their desire to be near the former partner. Deep and long-standing attachments seldom break quickly; detaching is a process, not an event.

Among dating couples, the closer and longer the relationship and the fewer the available alternatives, the more painful the breakup (Simpson, 1987). Surprisingly, Roy Baumeister and Sara Wotman (1992) report that, months or years later, people recall more pain over spurning someone's love than over having been spurned. Their distress arises from guilt over hurting someone, from upset over the heartbroken lover's persistence, or from uncertainty over how to respond. Among married couples, breakup has additional costs: shocked parents and friends, guilt over broken vows, anguish over reduced household income, and possibly restricted parental rights. Still, each year millions of couples

"Don't you understand? I love you! I need you! I want to spend the rest of my vacation with you!"

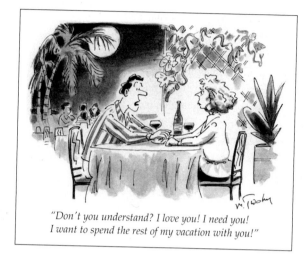

are willing to pay such costs to extricate themselves from what they perceive as the greater costs of continuing a painful, unrewarding relationship. Such costs include, in one study of 328 married couples, a tenfold increase in depression symptoms when a marriage is marked by discord rather than satisfaction (O'Leary et al., 1994).

When relationships suffer, those without better alternatives or who feel invested in a relationship (through time, energy, mutual friendships, possessions, and perhaps children) will seek alternatives to the relationship. Caryl Rusbult and her colleagues (1986, 1987) have explored three ways of coping with a failing relationship. Some people exhibit *loyalty*—by waiting for conditions to improve. The problems are too painful to speak of and the risks of separation are too great, so the loyal partner perseveres, hoping the good old days will return. Others (especially men) exhibit *neglect;* they ignore the partner and allow the relationship to deteriorate. When painful dissatisfactions are ignored, an insidious emotional uncoupling ensues as the partners talk less and begin redefining their lives without each other. Still others will *voice* their concerns and take active steps to improve the relationship by discussing problems, seeking advice, and attempting to change. Voice is particularly likely for people who see themselves as independent (unique and separate from others). People who see themselves as interdependent (more connected to others), are more likely to react with loyalty (Sinclair & Fehr, 2005). Each of these responses is constructive, especially compared to exiting or neglecting the relationship, but represent very different ways of coping with relationship stress.

Study after study—in fact, 115 studies of 45 000 couples—reveal that unhappy couples disagree, command, criticize, and put down. Happy couples more often agree, approve, assent, and laugh (Karney & Bradbury, 1995; Noller & Fitzpatrick, 1990). After observing 2000 couples, John Gottman (1994) noted that healthy marriages were not necessarily devoid of conflict. Rather, they were marked by an ability to reconcile differences and to overbalance criticism with affection. In successful marriages, positive interactions (smiling, touching, complimenting, laughing) outnumbered negative interactions (sarcasm, disapproval, insults) by at least a 5 to 1 ratio.

It's not distress and arguments that predict divorce, add Ted Huston and colleagues (2001) from their following of newlyweds through time. (Most newlyweds experience conflict.) Rather, it's coldness, disillusionment, and hopelessness that predict a dim marital future. This is especially so, observed William Swann and his associates (2003, 2006), when inhibited men are coupled with critical women.

Successful couples have learned, sometimes aided by communication training, to restrain the cancerous putdowns and gut-level fire-with-fire reactions, to fight fair (by stating feelings without insulting), and to depersonalize conflict with comments like, "I know it's not your fault" (Markman et al., 1988; Notarius & Markman, 1993; Yovetich & Rusbult, 1994). Would unhappy relationships get better if the partners agreed to *act* more as happy couples do—by complaining and criticizing less? By affirming and agreeing more? By setting time aside to voice their concerns? By having fun together daily? As attitudes trail behaviours, do affections trail actions?

Joan Kellerman, James Lewis, and James Laird (1989) wondered. They knew that among couples passionately in love, eye gazing is typically prolonged and mutual (Rubin, 1973). Would intimate eye gazing similarly stir feelings between those not in love (much as 45 minutes of escalating self-disclosure evoked feelings of closeness among those unacquainted students)? To find out, they asked unacquainted male-female pairs to gaze intently for two minutes either at one another's hands or in one another's eyes. When they separated, the eye gazers reported a tingle of attraction and affection toward each other. Simulating love had begun to stir it.

By enacting and expressing love, researcher Robert Sternberg (1988) believes the passion of initial romance can evolve into enduring love:

> "Living happily ever after" need not be a myth, but if it is to be a reality, the happiness must be based upon different configurations of mutual feelings at various times in a relationship. Couples who expect their passion to last forever, or their intimacy to remain unchallenged, are in for disappointment. . . . We must constantly work at understanding, building, and rebuilding our loving relationships. Relationships are constructions, and they decay over time if they are not maintained and improved. We cannot expect a relationship simply to take care of itself, any more than we can expect that of a building. Rather, we must take responsibility for making our relationships the best they can be.

SUMMING UP: HOW DO RELATIONSHIPS END?

Often love does not endure. As divorce rates rose in the twentieth century, researchers discerned predictors of marital dissolution. Onc predictor is an individualistic culture that values feelings over commitment; other factors include the couple's age, education, values, and similarity. Researchers are also identifying the process through which couples either detach or rebuild their relationships. And they are identifying the positive and nondefensive communication styles that mark healthy, stable marriages.

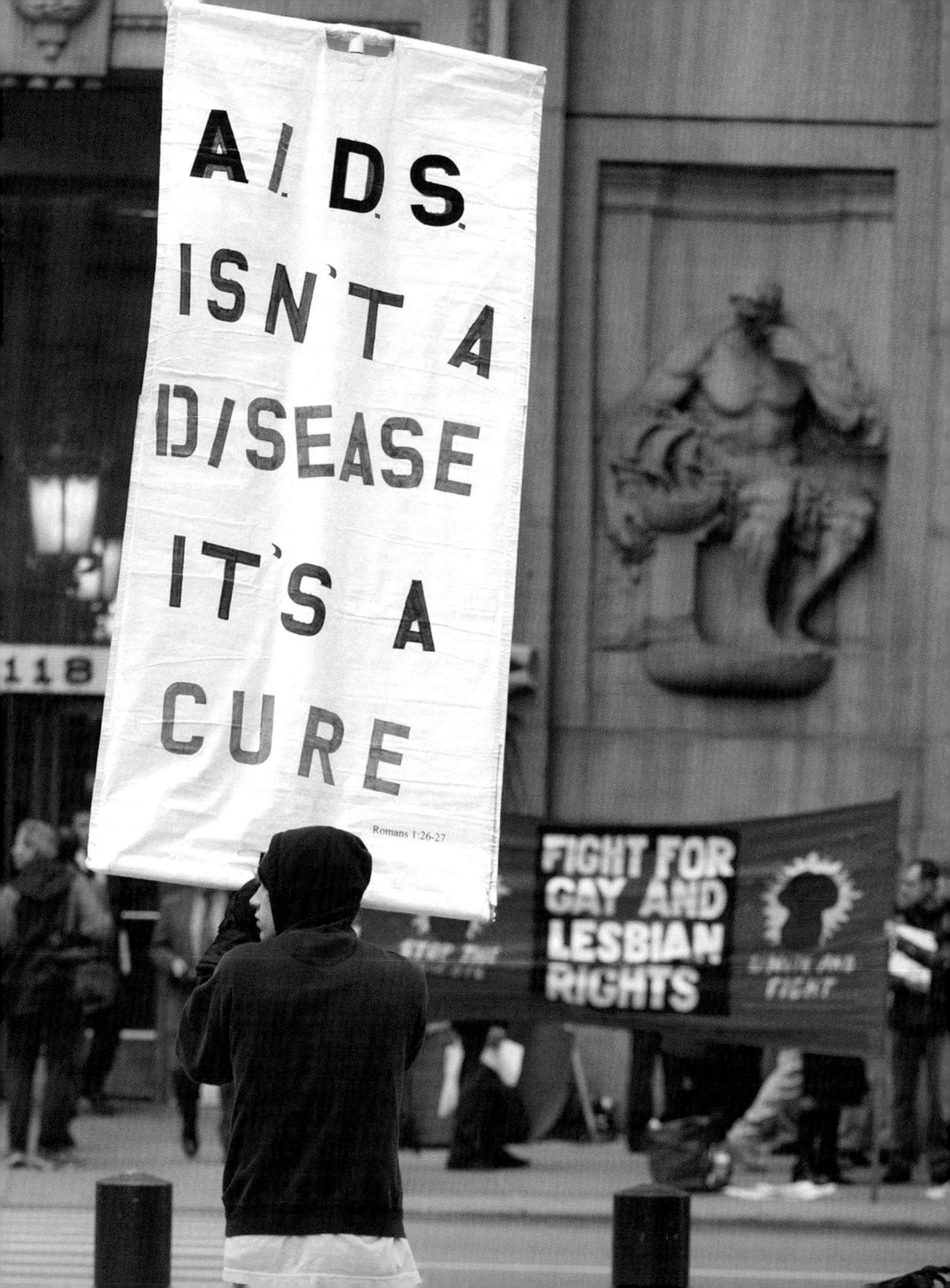
A.I.D.S.
ISN'T A
DISEASE
IT'S A
CURE
Romans 1:26-27
FIGHT FOR
GAY AND
LESBIAN
RIGHTS
118

CHAPTER TWELVE

Prejudice: Disliking Others

It was 30 degrees below zero and after midnight on January 28, 2000, in Saskatoon when Darrell Night recalls being picked up by the police outside a friend's apartment. He admits that he was intoxicated that night, but he tells a chilling story: Police took him to an isolated area on the outskirts of town, opened the car door, and said, "Get the f—— out of here, you f——ing Indian." Many were disinclined to believe Night's story, but its credibility was enhanced when the frozen bodies of two other Native men were found in the same isolated location (*Toronto Sun*, February 20, 2000).

Are such acts of prejudice and discrimination common in Canada, or do multicultural values blunt the impact of prejudice? Sadly, prejudice is an all-too-common feature of the Canadian landscape. In 2003, the Ontario Human Rights Commission reported that racial profiling was a commonly occurring practice in Ontario. Blacks, Latinos, Natives, and Middle Easterners commonly receive greater scrutiny from law enforcement and customs officers. In one study in Kingston, Ontario, police officers were 3.4 times more likely to stop Blacks and 1.4 times more likely to stop Natives than Whites, and this occurred even when the officers knew their stops would be evaluated for evidence of racial profiling (CBC Web site, May 27, 2005).

THE NATURE AND POWER OF PREJUDICE

How is "prejudice" distinct from "stereotyping," "discrimination," "racism," and "sexism"? Are stereotypes necessarily false or malicious? What forms does prejudice assume today?

WHAT IS PREJUDICE?

prejudice a negative prejudgment of a group and its individual members

stereotype a belief about the personal attributes of a group of people. Stereotypes can be overgeneralized, inaccurate, and resistant to new information.

Prejudice, stereotyping, discrimination, racism, sexism: The terms often overlap. Let's clarify them. Each of the situations just described involved a negative evaluation of some group. And that is the essence of **prejudice**: *a negative prejudgment of a group and its individual members.* (Some prejudice definitions include *positive* prejudgments as well, but nearly all uses of "prejudice" refer to *negative* tendencies—or what Gordon Allport termed in his classic, *The Nature of Prejudice,* "an antipathy based upon a faulty and inflexible generalization" [1954, p. 9].) Prejudice biases us against a person based solely on our identifying the person with a particular group.

Prejudice is an attitude. As we saw in Chapter 4, an attitude is a distinct combination of feelings, inclinations to act, and beliefs. This combination is the ABC of attitudes: *a*ffect (feelings), *b*ehaviour tendency (inclination to act), and *c*ognition (beliefs). A prejudiced person might *dislike* those different from self and *behave* in a discriminatory manner, *believing* them ignorant and dangerous. Like many attitudes, prejudice is complex, and may include a component of patronizing affection that serves to keep the target disadvantaged.

The negative evaluations that mark prejudice can stem from emotional associations, from the need to justify behaviour, or from negative beliefs, called **stereotypes**. To stereotype is to generalize. To simplify the world, we generalize: The British are reserved; Italians are outgoing. Professors are absentminded; Serbs are cruel. Here are some widely shared stereotypes:

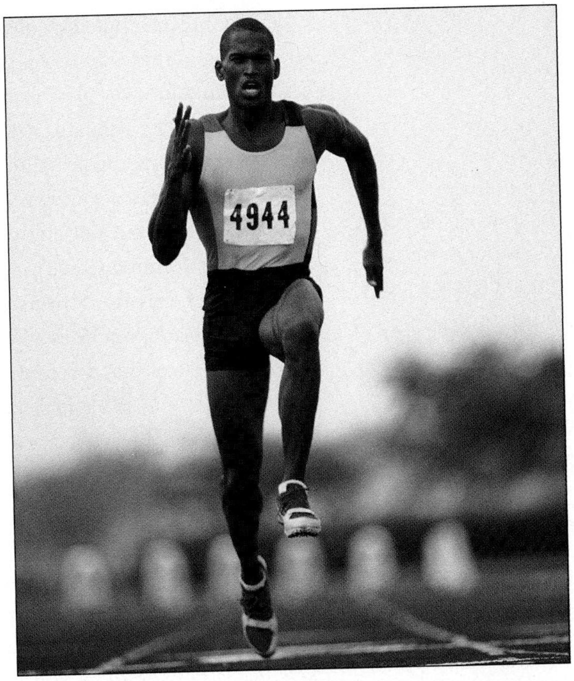

Stereotypes sometimes reflect reality. Persons with sub-Saharan African ancestry comprise 12 percent of the world's people and in 2000 held the top 15 world running records, ranging from 100 metres to the marathon (DiPietro, 2000). Even when describing reality with more or less accuracy, however, stereotypes do not explain causation.

- During the 1980s and early 1990s, women who assumed the title of "Ms." were seen as more assertive and ambitious than those who called themselves "Miss" or "Mrs." (Dion, 1987; Dion & Cota, 1991; Dion & Schuller, 1991). Now that "Ms." is more commonplace, the stereotype has shifted. Married women who keep their own surname are seen as assertive and ambitious (Crawford et al., 1998; Etaugh et al., 1999).
- In 19 nations, older adults are seen as likeable but less strong and active than younger adults (Williams, 1993).
- Public opinion surveys reveal that Europeans have definite ideas about other Europeans. They see Germans as relatively hard-working, the French as pleasure-loving, the British as cool and unexcitable, Italians as amorous, and the Dutch as reliable. (Coming from Willem Koomen and Michiel Bähler, 1996, at the University of Amsterdam, these findings one expects to be reliable.)
- Europeans also view southern Europeans as more emotional and less efficient than northern Europeans (Linssen & Hagendoorn, 1994). The stereotype of the southerner as more expressive even holds within countries: James Pennebaker and his colleagues (1996) report that across 20 northern hemisphere countries (but not in six southern hemisphere countries), southerners within a country are perceived as more expressive than northerners.

Such generalizations can be more or less true (and are not always negative). Old people are less active. Southern countries in the northern hemisphere do have higher rates of violence. People living in the south in these countries do report being more expressive than those in the northern regions of their country. "Stereotypes," note Lee Jussim, Clark McCauley, and Yueh-Ting Lee (1995), "may be positive or negative, accurate or inaccurate." An accurate stereotype may even be desirable. We call it "sensitivity to diversity" or "cultural awareness in a multicultural world." To stereotype the British as more concerned about punctuality than are Mexicans is to understand what to expect and how to act with minimal friction in each culture.

Familiar stereotypes: "Heaven is a place with an American house, Chinese food, British police, a German car, and French art. Hell is a place with a Japanese house, Chinese police, British food, German art, and a French car."

Anonymous, as reported by Yueh-Ting Lee (1996)

A problem with stereotypes arises when they are *overgeneralized* or just plain wrong. To presume that most First Nations people need treatment for alcoholism is to overgeneralize, because it just isn't so. Another problem arises when people attribute negatively evaluated differences to biology, ignoring toxic social forces. People may see that women are less likely than men to become engineers or chief executive officers, but they often do not see the underlying causes that prevent women from succeeding in these fields. People are quick to judge that women do not have the math or leadership ability to succeed in these fields, but the evidence suggests otherwise (Eagly et al., 1995; Hyde et al., 1990; Kimball, 1989). The barriers that actually prevent women's success, such as unfair evaluations and self-fulfilling prophecies, are much harder for people to recognize.

Prejudice is a negative *attitude;* **discrimination** is negative *behaviour.* Discriminatory behaviour often, but not always, has its source in prejudicial attitudes (Dovidio et al., 1996). As Chapter 4 emphasized, however, attitudes and behaviour are often loosely linked, partly because our behaviour reflects more than our inner convictions. Prejudiced attitudes need not breed hostile acts, nor does all oppression spring from prejudice. **Racism** and **sexism** are institutional practices that discriminate, even when there is no prejudicial intent. If word-of-mouth hiring practices in an all-male business have the effect of excluding potential female employees, the practice could be called sexist—even if an employer intended no discrimination.

discrimination unjustifiable negative behaviour toward a group or its members

racism (1) an individual's prejudicial attitudes and discriminatory behaviour toward people of a given race, or (2) institutional practices (even if not motivated by prejudice) that subordinate people of a given race

sexism (1) an individual's prejudicial attitudes and discriminatory behaviour toward people of a given sex, or (2) institutional practices (even if not motivated by prejudice) that subordinate people of a given sex

PREJUDICE: SUBTLE AND OVERT

The attitude of prejudice, like other attitudes, can be measured by asking people a number of straightforward questions, such as "Is it true that Blacks have gotten more economically than they deserve?" (McConahay, 1986) or "Is it true that the government and news media have been showing more concern about the treatment of women than is warranted by women's actual experiences?" (Swim et al., 1995). Such measures of people's prejudice have been collected for more than 75 years, and an interesting pattern has emerged. For most social groups, overt expressions of prejudice have decreased. For example, national surveys suggest that outright prejudice is less common then it was 30 years ago. Kalin and Barry (1995) note that despite some remaining prejudice toward members of ethnic groups, Canadians are genuinely motivated to develop a truly multicultural society.

Does that mean that prejudice is no longer a serious social problem? Unfortunately, after many experiments, it has become clear that such an optimistic view is not warranted. Although overt expression of prejudice has decreased, subtle forms of prejudice are still widespread. It appears that prejudice may have gone underground.

Subtle forms of prejudice

Recall from Chapter 4 that when White students indicate racial attitudes and men indicate their sympathy for women's rights while hooked up to a supposed lie detector, they admit to prejudice. Other experiments have assessed people's *behaviour* toward Blacks and Whites. As we will see in Module A, Whites are equally helpful to any person in need—except when the needy person is remote (say, a wrong-number caller with an apparent Black accent who needs a message relayed). Likewise, when asked to use electric shocks to "teach" a task, White people give no more (if anything less) shock to a Black than to a White person—except when they are angered or when the recipient can't retaliate or know who did it (Crosby et al., 1980; Rogers & Prentice-Dunn, 1981).

Thus, prejudiced attitudes and discriminatory behaviour surface when they can hide behind the screen of some other motive. In France, Britain, Germany, Australia, and the Netherlands, subtle prejudice (exaggerating ethnic differences, feeling less admiration and affection for immigrant minorities, rejecting them for supposedly nonracial reasons) is replacing blatant prejudice (Pedersen & Walker, 1997; Pettigrew, 1998). Some researchers call such subtle prejudice "modern racism" or "cultural racism." Modern prejudice often appears subtly, in our preferences for what is familiar, similar, and comfortable (Dovidio et al., 1992; Esses et al., 1993a).

On paper-and-pencil questionnaires, Janet Swim and her co-researchers (1995, 1997) have found a subtle ("modern") sexism that parallels subtle ("modern") racism. Both forms appear in denials of discrimination and in antagonism toward efforts to promote equality (as in "Blacks are getting too demanding in their push for equal rights").

We can also detect bias in behaviour. That's what a research team led by Ian Ayres (1991) did. Team members visited 90 Chicago-area car dealers, using a uniform strategy to negotiate the lowest price on a new car that cost the dealer about $11,000. White males were given a final price that averaged $11,362; White females were given an average price of $11,504; Black males were given an average price of $11,783; and Black females were given an average price of $12,237.

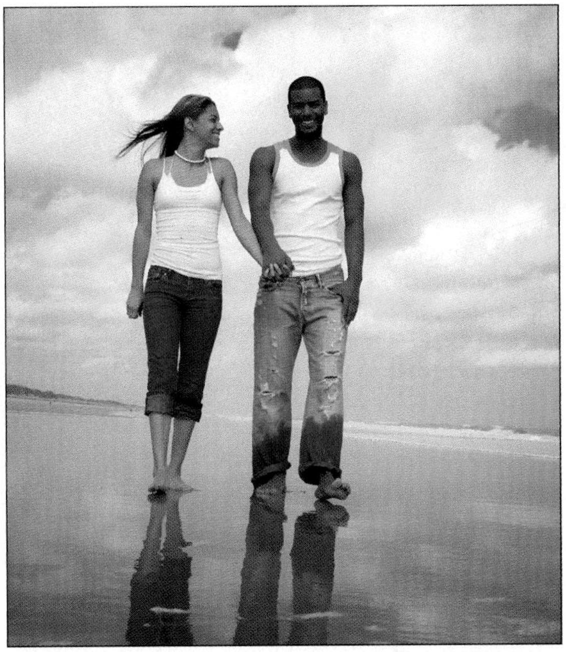

Although prejudice dies last in socially intimate contacts, interracial marriage has increased in most countries.

John Dovidio, Kerry Kawakami, and Samuel Gaertner (2002) had White students interact with a White or a Black confederate. They found that the students' responses on racism scales predicted racial bias in what they said in the interaction. But their automatic emotional reactions to Blacks predicted their nonverbal behaviour.

Automatic prejudice

This sort of modern prejudice illustrates again our dual attitude system (Chapter 2). We can have differing explicit (conscious) and implicit (automatic) attitudes toward the same target. Thus we may retain from childhood a habitual, automatic fear or dislike of people for whom we now express respect and appreciation. Although explicit attitudes may change dramatically with education, implicit attitudes may linger, changing only as we form new habits through practice (Kawakami et al., 2000).

A raft of experiments (Banaji & Bhaskar, 2000; Bargh & Chartrand, 1999; Fazio et al., 1995; Greenwald et al., 2000; and Wittenbrink et al., 1997) have confirmed the phenomenon of automatic stereotyping and prejudice. These studies briefly flash words or faces that "prime" (automatically activate) stereotypes of some racial, gender, or age group. Without their awareness, the participants' activated stereotypes may then bias their behaviour. Having been primed with images associated with Blacks, for example, they may then react with more hostility to an experimenter's annoying request. In clever experiments by Anthony Greenwald and his colleagues (1998, 2000), 9 in 10 White people took longer to identify pleasant words (such as *peace* and *paradise*) as "good" when associated with Black rather than White faces. The participants, mind you, typically expressed little or no prejudice, only an unconscious, unintended response. Moreover, report Kurt Hugenberg and Galen Bodenhausen (2003), the more strongly people exhibit such implicit prejudice, the readier they are to perceive anger in Black faces (Figure 12–1).

"Many [people] have confessed to me . . . that even though in their minds they no longer feel prejudice towards Blacks, they still feel squeamish when they shake hands with a Black. These feelings are left over from what they learned in their families as children."

Thomas Pettigrew (1987, p. 20)

FIGURE 12–1

Facing prejudice.

Where does the anger disappear? Kurt Hugenberg and Galen Bodenhausen showed university students a movie of faces morphing from angry to happy. Those who had scored as most prejudiced (on an implicit racial attitudes test) perceived anger lingering more in ambiguous Black than White faces.

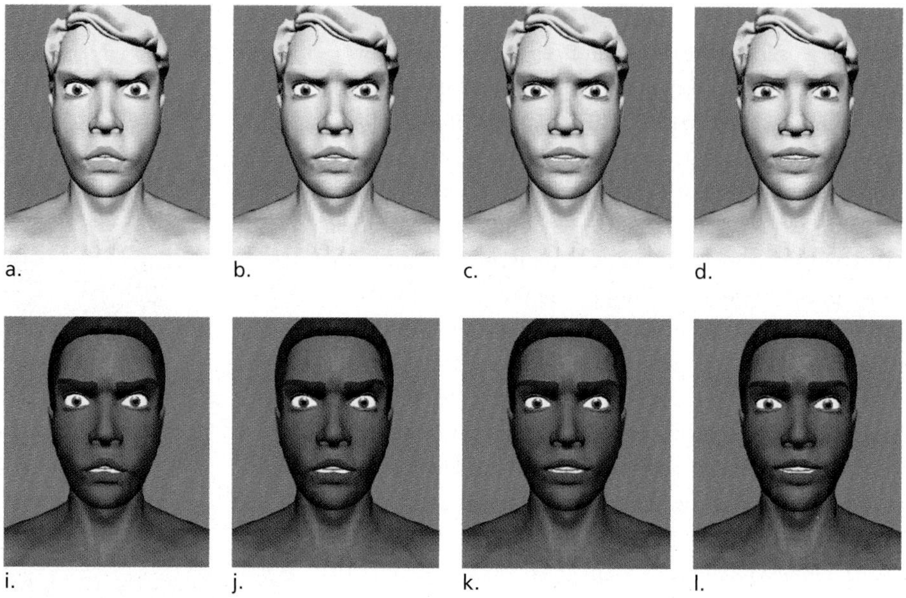

In separate experiments, Joshua Correll and his coworkers (2002, 2006) and Anthony Greenwald and his coworkers (2003) invited people to press buttons quickly to "shoot" or "not shoot" men who suddenly appeared on-screen holding either a gun or a harmless object such as a flashlight or bottle. The participants (both Blacks and Whites, in one of the studies) more often mistakenly shot targets who were Black. In a related series of studies, Keith Payne (2001), and Charles Judd and colleagues (2004), found that when primed with a Black rather than White face, people think guns: they more quickly recognize a gun and they more often mistake tools, such as a wrench, for a gun. These studies help explain why Amadou Diallo (a Black immigrant in New York City) was shot 41 times by police officers for removing his wallet from his back pocket.

Automatic prejudice. When Joshua Correll and his colleagues invited people to react quickly to individuals holding either a gun or a harmless object, race influenced perceptions and reactions.

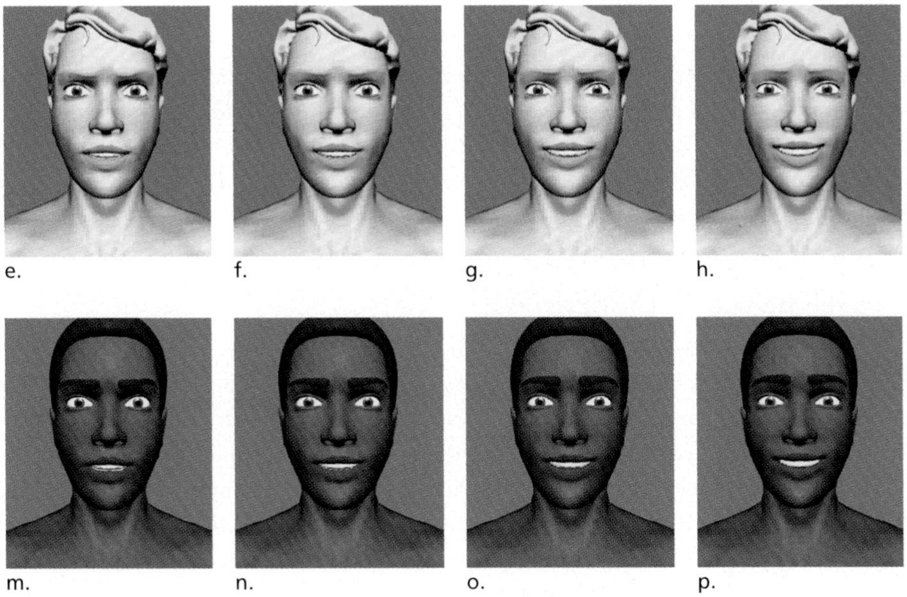

It also appears that different brain regions are involved in automatic and overt stereotyping (Correll et al., 2006; Cunningham et al., 2004; Eberhardt, 2005). Pictures of outgroups that elicit the most disgust (such as drug addicts and the homeless) elicit more amygdala than frontal cortex activity (Harris & Fiske, 2006). These findings suggest that automatic prejudices involve primitive regions of the brain associated with fear, such as the amygdala, whereas overt prejudice is more closely associated with the frontal cortex, which enables conscious thinking.

Even the social scientists who study prejudice seem vulnerable to it, note Anthony Greenwald and Eric Schuh (1994). They analyzed biases in authors' citations of social science articles by people with selected non-Jewish names (Erickson, McBride, and so forth) and Jewish names (Goldstein, Siegel, and so forth). Their analysis of nearly 30 000 citations, including 17 000 citations of prejudice research, found something remarkable: Compared with Jewish authors, non-Jewish authors had 40 percent higher odds of citing non-Jewish names. (Greenwald and Schuh could not determine whether Jewish authors were overciting their Jewish colleagues, non-Jewish authors were overciting their non-Jewish colleagues, or both.)

SUMMING UP: THE NATURE AND POWER OF PREJUDICE

Prejudice is a negative prejudgment of a group and its individual members. Stereotypes are beliefs about the personal attributes of a group of people and they can be overgeneralized, inaccurate, and resistant to new information. Discrimination is unjustifiable negative behaviour toward a group or its members. Prejudice takes many forms including racism and sexism and can occur subtly and even automatically.

SOCIAL SOURCES OF PREJUDICE

As we have emphasized throughout this book, the social situations we encounter are powerful forces that shape our attitudes and behaviours. The formation of prejudice is no exception to this general rule. Unequal status and conflict between groups, the desire to see our own groups positively, conformity pressures, and fears and hostilities can all fuel the formation of prejudice.

GENDER ROLES AND PREJUDICE

gender role
a set of behaviour expectations (norms) for males and females

Culture, as we noted earlier, is what's shared by a large group and transmitted across generations—ideas, attitudes, behaviours, and traditions. We can see the shaping power of culture in ideas about how men and women should behave—and in the scorn that they endure when violating expectations (Kite, 2001). In countries everywhere, girls spend more time helping with housework and child care, while boys spend more time in unsupervised play (Edwards, 1991). Even in contemporary, dual-career, North American marriages, men do most of the household repairs and women arrange the child care (Bianchi et al., 2000; Biernat & Wortman, 1991).

Do you ever present one self to members of your own sex and a different self to members of the other sex?

Gender socialization, it has been said, gives girls "roots" and boys "wings." In Caldecott Award children's books over the last half-century, girls have four times more often than boys been shown using household objects (such as broom, sewing needle, or pots and pans), and boys have five times more often than girls been shown using production objects (such as pitchfork, plough, or gun) (Crabb & Bielawski, 1994). The adult result: "Everywhere," reports the United Nations (1991), women do most household work. And "everywhere, cooking and dishwashing are the least shared household chores." Such behaviour expectations for males and females define **gender roles**.

"That was a fine report, Barbara. But since the sexes speak different languages, I probably didn't understand a word of it."

In the last half-century—a thin slice of our long history—gender roles have begun to change. In 1938, one in five approved "of a married woman earning money in business or industry if she has a husband capable of supporting her." By 1980 the percentage of women in the full-time workforce had steadily increased to 32 percent and by 1997 to 39 percent (Statistics Canada, 1997). A similar influx of women in the workforce has occurred in Australia, Great Britain, and the U.S. Since 1975, increasing numbers of women have been training to become lawyers, doctors and engineers—though gains in engineering have been modest. Can such differences in gender roles lead to gender stereotyping and sexism? Let's examine these concepts.

Gender stereotypes

From research on stereotypes, two conclusions are indisputable: Strong gender stereotypes exist, and, as often happens, members of the stereotyped group accept the stereotypes (Wood, Conway, Pushkar & Dugas, 2005). Men and women agree that you *can* judge the book by its sexual cover. In one survey, Mary Jackman and Mary Senter (1981) found that only 22 percent of men thought the two sexes equally "emotional." Of the remaining 78 percent, those who believed females were more emotional outnumbered those who thought males were by 15 to 1. And what did the women believe? To within 1 percentage point, their responses were identical.

Consider, too, a study by Natalie Porter, Florence Geis, and Joyce Jennings Walstedt (1983). They showed students pictures of "a group of graduate students working as a team on a research project" (Figure 12–2). Then they gave them a test of "first impressions," asking them to guess who contributed most to the group. Ignoring the woman at the head of the table, each of the men in Figure 12–2 received more of the leadership choices than all three women combined! This stereotype of men as leaders was true not only of women as well as men but also of feminists as well as nonfeminists. Newer research reveals that behaviours associated with leadership are perceived less favourably when enacted by a woman (Eagly & Karau, 2000). Assertiveness can seem less becoming in a woman than in a man (making it harder for women to become and succeed as leaders). How pervasive are gender stereotypes? Very pervasive.

Canadian husbands do 67 percent of the maintenance and repairs around the home, but only 27 percent of the meal preparation and cleanup, and only 23 percent of the housecleaning.

Statistics Canada, 1998

"All the pursuits of men are the pursuits of women also, and in all of them a woman is only a lesser man."

Plato, *Republic*

FIGURE 12–2

Which one of these people would you guess is the group's strongest contributor? When shown this picture, college students usually guessed one of the two men, although those shown photos of same-sex groups most commonly guessed the person at the head of the table.

"Women are wonderful primarily because they are [perceived as] so nice. [Men are] perceived as superior to women in agentic [competitive, dominant] attributes that are viewed as equipping people for success in paid work, especially in male-dominated occupations."

Alice Eagly (1994)

Remember that stereotypes are generalizations about a group of people and may be true, false, or overgeneralized from a kernel of truth. (They may also be self-fulfilling.) The average man and woman do differ somewhat in social connectedness, empathy, social power, aggressiveness, and sexual initiative (though not in intelligence). Do we then conclude that gender stereotypes are accurate? Sometimes stereotypes exaggerate differences. But not always, observed Janet Swim (1994). She found that stereotypes of men's and women's restlessness, nonverbal sensitivity, aggressiveness, and so forth were reasonable approximations of actual gender differences. Moreover, such stereotypes have persisted across time and culture. Averaging data from 27 countries, John Williams and his colleagues (1999, 2000) found that folks everywhere perceive women as more agreeable, men as more outgoing. The persistence and omnipresence of gender stereotypes leads some evolutionary psychologists to believe they reflect innate, stable reality (Lueptow et al., 1995).

Stereotypes (beliefs) are not prejudices (attitudes). Stereotypes may support prejudice. Yet one might believe, without prejudice, that men and women are "different yet equal." Let us therefore see how researchers probe for gender prejudice.

Sexism: Benevolent and hostile

Judging from what people tell survey researchers, attitudes toward women are quite positive. Alice Eagly and her associates (1991) and Geoffrey Haddock and Mark Zanna (1994) report that people don't respond to women with gut-level negative emotions as they do to certain other groups. Most people like women more than men. They perceive women as more understanding, kind, and helpful. A *favourable* stereotype, which Eagly (1994) dubs the *women-are-wonderful effect*, results in a favourable attitude.

But gender attitudes often are ambivalent, report Peter Glick, Susan Fiske, and their colleagues (1996, 2000, 2001) from their surveys of 15 000 people in 19 nations. They frequently mix a *benevolent sexism* ("Women have a superior moral sensibility") with *hostile sexism* ("Once a man commits, she puts him on a tight leash").

Stereotypes about men also come in contrasting pairs. Peter Glick and his colleagues (2004) report ambivalent sexism toward men with benevolent attitudes of men as powerful and hostile attitudes that characterize men as immoral. People who endorse benevolent sexism toward men also tend to endorse benevolent sexism toward men. These complimentary ambivalent sexist views of men and women may arise from the strong motive to justify the status quo in gender relations (Jost & Kay, 2005; Kay, Lau & Spencer, 2008).

Gender discrimination

There is good news for those who are upset by gender bias. One heavily publicized finding of prejudice against women came from a 1968 study in which Philip Goldberg gave women several short articles and asked them to judge the value of each. Sometimes a given article was attributed to a male author (for example, John T. McKay) and sometimes to a female author (for example, Joan T. McKay). In general, the articles received lower ratings when attributed to a female. The historic mark of oppression—self-deprecation—surfaced clearly: Women were prejudiced against women.

"And just why do we always call my income the second income?"
VIETOR

Gender prejudice gets expressed subtly.

Eager to demonstrate the subtle reality of gender prejudice, Myers obtained Goldberg's materials and repeated the experiment for my own students' benefit. They (women and men) showed no such tendency to deprecate women's work. So Janet Swim, Eugene Borgida, Geoffrey Maruyama, and David Myers (1989) searched the literature and corresponded with investigators to learn all we could about studies of gender bias in the evaluation of men's and women's work. To our surprise, the biases that occasionally surfaced were as often against men as women. But the most common result across 104 studies involving almost 20 000 people was *no difference*. On most comparisons, judgments of someone's work were unaffected by whether the work was attributed to a female or a male. Summarizing other studies of people's evaluations of women and men as leaders, professors, and so forth, Alice Eagly (1994) says, "Experiments have not demonstrated any *overall* tendency to devalue women's work."

Question: *"Misogyny" is the hatred of women. What is the corresponding word for the hatred of men?* **Answer:** *In most dictionaries, no such word exists.*

Is gender bias fast becoming extinct in Western countries? Has the women's movement nearly completed its work? As with racial prejudice, blatant gender prejudice is dying, but subtle bias lives. The bogus-pipeline method, for example, exposes bias. As we noted in Chapter 4, men who believe an experimenter can read their true attitudes with a sensitive lie detector express less sympathy toward women's rights.

In the world beyond democratic Western countries, gender discrimination looms even larger:

- Two-thirds of the world's unschooled children are girls (United Nations, 1991).
- In Saudi Arabia, women are forbidden to drive (Beyer, 1990).
- Around the world, people tend to prefer having baby boys. In the United States in 1941, 38 percent of expectant parents said they preferred a boy if they could only have one child; 24 percent preferred a girl; and 23 percent said they didn't care. In 2003,

the answers were virtually unchanged with 38 percent still preferring a boy (Lyons, 2003; Simmons, 2000). With the widespread use of ultrasound to determine the sex of a fetus and the growing availability of abortion, these preferences are affecting the number of boys and girls. The 2000 China census revealed 119 newborn boys for every 100 girls (Walfish, 2001). The 2001 India census reported that Punjab Province had 126 newborn boys for every 100 girls (Dugger, 2001). The net result is tens of millions of "missing women."

To conclude, overt prejudice against people of colour and against women is far less common today than it was four decades ago. The same is true of prejudice against gays and lesbians. Nevertheless, techniques that are sensitive to subtle prejudice still detect widespread bias. And in parts of the world, gender prejudice is literally deadly. Therefore, we need to look carefully and closely at the social, emotional, and cognitive sources of prejudice.

SOCIAL INEQUALITIES: JUSTIFYING THE STATUS QUO

A principle to remember: *Unequal status breeds prejudice.* Masters view slaves as lazy, irresponsible, lacking ambition—as having just those traits that justify the slavery. Historians debate the forces that create unequal status. But once these inequalities exist, prejudice helps justify the economic and social superiority of those who have wealth and power. You tell us the economic relationship between two groups and we'll predict the intergroup attitudes. Stereotypes rationalize unequal status (Yzerbyt et al., 1997).

Examples abound. Until recently, prejudice everywhere in the world was greatest in regions where slavery was practised. Nineteenth-century European politicians and writers justified

Racial prejudice often begins during times of conflict, as during the Second World War when Japanese Canadians were sent to internment camps.

imperial expansion by describing exploited colonized people as "inferior," "requiring protection," and a "burden" to be borne (G. W. Allport, 1958, pp. 204–205). Four decades ago, sociologist Helen Mayer Hacker (1951) noted how stereotypes of Blacks and women helped rationalize the inferior status of each: Many people thought both groups were mentally slow, emotional and primitive, and "contented" with their subordinate role. Blacks were "inferior"; women were "weak." Blacks were all right in their place; women's place was in the home.

"Prejudice is never easy unless it can pass itself off for reason."

William Hazlitt, 1778–1830, "On Prejudice"

As this hints, Peter Glick and Susan Fiske's distinction between "hostile" and "benevolent" sexism extends to other prejudices. We see other groups as competent or as likeable, but usually not as both. We *respect* the competence of those high in status and *like* those who agreeably accept a lower status. In the United States, report Fiske and her colleagues (1999), Asians, Jews, Germans, nontraditional women, and assertive Blacks and gay men tend to be respected but not liked so well. Traditionally subordinate Blacks, traditional women, feminine gay men, and people with disabilities tend to be seen as less competent but liked for their emotional, spiritual, artistic, or athletic qualities.

In times of conflict, attitudes adjust easily to behaviour. People often view enemies as subhuman and depersonalize them with labels. During the Second World War, the Japanese people became "the Japs." After the war was over, they became "the intelligent, hardworking Japanese." Attitudes are amazingly adaptable. As we have noted in previous chapters, cruel acts breed cruel attitudes.

"It is human nature to hate those whom we have injured."

Tacitus, *Agricola*

Gender stereotypes, too, help rationalize gender roles. After studying these stereotypes worldwide, John Williams and Deborah Best (1990b) noted that if women provide most of the care to young children, it is reassuring to think women are naturally nurturant. If males run the businesses, hunt, and fight wars, it is comforting to suppose that men are aggressive, independent, and adventurous. In experiments, people perceive members of unknown groups as having traits that suit their roles (Hoffman & Hurst, 1990).

Aaron Kay, John Jost and their colleagues (Jost & Kay, 2005; Kay, Jost & Young, 2005; Kay et al., 2007) argue that the motive to see the system as just, fair, and benevolent lies behind these complimentary stereotypes. They argue that by seeing strengths and weaknesses in all group differences and positive and negative outcomes for all groups, that differences in power and opportunities are glossed over and allow people to see the social system in a positive light.

Individual differences in personality also seem to predict how much people justify the status quo. Those high in **social dominance orientation** tend to view people in terms of hierarchies. They like their social groups to be high status, that is, they like to be on the top of the hierarchy. Being in a dominant high-status position also tends to promote this orientation (Guimond et al., 2003). Jim Sidanius, Felicia Pratto, and their colleagues (Pratto et al., 1994; Sidanius et al., 1996; Sidanius & Pratto, 1999) argue that this desire to be on top leads people high in social dominance to embrace prejudice and to support political positions that justify prejudice. Indeed, people high in social dominance orientation often support policies that maintain hierarchies such as tax cuts for the well-off and oppose policies that undermine hierarchy, such as affirmative action. People high in social dominance orientation also prefer professions, such as politics and business, which increase their status and maintain hierarchies. They avoid jobs, such as social work, that undermine hierarchies. Status may breed prejudice, but some people seek it out and try to maintain this status more than others.

social dominance orientation a motivation to have one's group be dominant over other social groups

SOCIALIZATION

Prejudice springs from unequal status, and from other social sources, including our acquired values and attitudes. The influence of family socialization appears in children's prejudices. Even children's automatic racial attitudes reflect their parents' explicit prejudice (Sinclair et al., 2004).

The authoritarian personality

In the 1940s, University of California Berkeley researchers—two of whom had fled Nazi Germany—set out on an urgent research mission: to uncover the psychological roots of an anti-Semitism so poisonous that it caused the slaughter of millions of Jews and turned many millions of Europeans into indifferent spectators. In studies of American adults, Theodor Adorno and his colleagues (1950) discovered that hostility toward Jews often coexisted with hostility toward other minorities. Prejudice appeared to be less an attitude specific to one group than a way of thinking about those who are different. Moreover, these judgmental, **ethnocentric** people shared authoritarian tendencies—intolerance for weakness, a punitive attitude, and a submissive respect for their ingroup's authorities, as reflected in their agreement with such statements as, "Obedience and respect for authority are the most important virtues children should learn."

ethnocentric believing in the superiority of one's own ethnic and cultural group, and having a corresponding disdain for all other groups

As children, authoritarian people often faced harsh discipline. This supposedly led them to repress their hostilities and impulses and to "project" them onto outgroups. The insecurity of authoritarian children seemed to predispose them toward an excessive concern with power and status and an inflexible right-wrong way of thinking that made ambiguity difficult to tolerate. Such people therefore tended to be submissive to those with power over them and aggressive or punitive toward those beneath them.

Scholars criticized the research for focusing on right-wing authoritarianism and overlooking dogmatic authoritarianism of the left. Still, its main conclusion has survived: Authoritarian tendencies, sometimes reflected in ethnic tensions, surge during threatening times of economic recession and social upheaval (Doty et al., 1991; Sales, 1973). In contemporary Russia, individuals scoring high in authoritarianism have tended to support a return to Marxist-Leninist ideology and to oppose democratic reform (McFarland et al., 1992, 1996).

Moreover, contemporary studies of right-wing authoritarians by University of Manitoba psychologist Bob Altemeyer (1988, 1992) confirm that there *are* individuals whose fears and hostilities surface as prejudice. Their feelings of moral superiority may go hand in hand with brutality toward perceived inferiors.

Different forms of prejudice—toward Blacks, gays and lesbians, women, old people, fat people, AIDS victims, the homeless—*do* tend to coexist in the same individuals (Bierly, 1985; Crandall, 1994; Peterson et al., 1993; Snyder & Ickes, 1985). As Altemeyer concludes, right-wing authoritarians tend to be "equal opportunity bigots."

Particularly striking are people high in social dominance orientation and authoritarian personality. Altemeyer (2004) reports that these "Double Highs" are, not surprisingly, "among the most prejudiced persons in our society." What is perhaps most surprising and more troubling is that they seem to display the worst qualities of each type of personality, striving for status often in manipulative ways while being dogmatic and ethnocentric. Altemeyer argues that although these people are relatively rare, they are predisposed to be leaders of hate groups.

Although authoritarianism and social dominance can co-exist, it appears they have different ideological bases and different functions. Authoritarianism appears more related to concern with security and control, whereas social dominance orientation appears more related to one's group status (Cohrs et al., 2005). They can function together to form a toxic environment in groups, however. Leanne Son Hing, from the University of Guelph and her colleagues (Son Hing, Bobocel, Zanna & McBride, 2007) examined combinations of authoritarian and high social dominance leaders and followers. They found that high social dominance orientation leaders who had high authoritarian followers were more likely than any other combination to throw ethics out the window in the blind pursuit of profit.

Religion and prejudice

Those who benefit from social inequalities while avowing that "all are created equal" need to justify keeping things the way they are. What could be a more powerful justification than to believe God has ordained the existing social order? For all sorts of cruel deeds, noted William James, "Piety is the mask" (1902, p. 264).

In almost every country, leaders invoke religion to sanctify the present order. The use of religion to support injustice helps explain a consistent pair of findings concerning Christianity, North America's dominant religion: (1) Church members express more racial prejudice than nonmembers, and (2) those professing traditional or fundamentalist Christian beliefs express more prejudice than those professing less traditional beliefs (Altemeyer & Hunsberger, 1992; Batson et al., 1993; Woodberry & Smith, 1998).

Knowing the correlation between two variables—religion and prejudice—tells us nothing about their causal connection. There might be no connection at all. Perhaps people with less education are both more fundamentalist and more prejudiced. Perhaps prejudice causes religion, by leading people to create religious ideas to support their prejudices. Or perhaps religion causes prejudice, by leading people to believe that because all individuals possess free will, impoverished minorities have themselves to blame for their status.

If indeed religion causes prejudice, then more religious church members should also be more prejudiced. But three other findings consistently indicate otherwise:

- Among church members, faithful church attenders were, in 24 out of 26 comparisons, *less* prejudiced than occasional attenders (Batson & Ventis, 1982).
- Gordon Allport and Michael Ross (1967) found that those for whom religion is an end in itself (those who agree, for example, with the statement, "My religious beliefs are what really lie behind my whole approach to life") express *less* prejudice than those for whom religion is more a means to other ends (who agree, "A primary reason for my interest in religion is that my church is a congenial social activity"). And those who score highest on Gallup's "spiritual commitment" index are more welcoming of a person of another race moving in next door (Gallup & Jones, 1992).
- Protestant ministers and Roman Catholic priests give more support to human rights than do laypeople (Fichter, 1968; Hadden, 1969). In Germany, 45 percent of clergy in 1934 had aligned themselves with the Confessing Church, which was organized to oppose the Nazi regime (Reed, 1989).

"We have just enough religion to make us hate, but not enough to make us love one another."

Jonathan Swift, "Thoughts on Various Subjects," 1706

What, then, is the relationship between religion and prejudice? The answer we get depends on *how* we ask the question. If we define religiousness as church membership or willingness to agree at least superficially with traditional beliefs, then the more religious people are the more racially prejudiced. Bigots often rationalize bigotry with religion. If we assess depth of religious commitment in any of several other ways, however, then the very devout are less prejudiced—hence the religious roots of the modern civil rights movement, among whose leaders were many ministers and priests. As Gordon Allport concluded, "The role of religion is paradoxical. It makes prejudice and it unmakes prejudice" (1958, p. 413).

Conformity

Once established, prejudice is maintained largely by inertia. If prejudice is socially accepted, many people will follow the path of least resistance and conform to the fashion. They will act not so much out of a need to hate as out of a need to be liked and accepted.

Thomas Pettigrew's (1958) studies of Whites in South Africa and the American South revealed that, during the 1950s, those who conformed most to other social norms were also most prejudiced; those who were less conforming mirrored less of the surrounding prejudice.

Conformity also maintains gender prejudice. "If we have come to think that the nursery and the kitchen are the natural sphere of a woman," wrote George Bernard Shaw in an 1891 essay, "we have done so exactly as English children come to think that a cage is the natural sphere of a parrot—because they have never seen one anywhere else." Children who *have* seen women elsewhere—children of employed women—have less stereotyped views of men and women (Hoffman, 1977).

In all these findings, there is a message of hope. If prejudice is not deeply ingrained in personality, then as fashions change and new norms evolve, prejudice can diminish. And so it has.

INSTITUTIONAL SUPPORTS

Schools reinforce dominant cultural attitudes. One analysis of stories in 134 children's readers written before 1970 found that male characters outnumbered female characters three to one (Women on Words and Images, 1972). Who was portrayed as showing initiative, bravery, and competence? Note the answer in this excerpt from the classic *Dick and Jane* children's reader: Jane, sprawled out on the sidewalk, her roller skates beside her, listens as Mark explains to his mother:

> "She cannot skate," said Mark.
> "I can help her.
> "I want to help her.
> "Look at her, Mother.
> "Just look at her.
> "She's just like a girl.
> "She gives up."

Not until the 1970s, when changing ideas about males and females brought new perceptions of such portrayals, was this blatant (to us) stereotyping widely noticed and changed.

Institutional supports for prejudice often go unnoticed. Usually, they are not deliberate attempts to oppress a group. More often, they simply reflect cultural assumptions, as when the one "flesh"-coloured crayon in the Crayola box was pinkish white.

What contemporary examples of institutionalized biases still go unnoticed? Here is one that most of us failed to notice, although it was right before our eyes: By examining 1750 photographs of people in magazines and newspapers, Dane Archer and his associates (1983) discovered that about two-thirds of the average male photo, but less than half of the average female photo, was devoted to the face. As Archer widened his search, he discovered that such "face-ism" is common. He found it in the periodicals of 11 other countries, in 920 portraits gathered from the artwork of six centuries, and in the amateur drawings of students. Georgia Nigro and her colleagues (1988) confirmed the face-ism phenomenon in more magazines, including *Ms.*

The researchers suspect that the visual prominence given the faces of men and the bodies of women both reflects and perpetuates gender bias. In research in Germany, Norbert Schwarz and Eva Kurz (1989) confirmed that people whose faces are prominent in photos seem more intelligent and ambitious.

SUMMING UP: SOCIAL SOURCES OF PREJUDICE

Social sources of prejudice abound. One important source of prejudice is inequalities in society. People are motivated to the status quo and develop complementary stereotypes that serve this end. Another important source of prejudice is the roles into which we are socialized. Of particular importance are gender roles in society, as they are an important factor in the way men and women are seen. How we are socialized by our parents and friends also has an important influence on our level of prejudice.

MOTIVATIONAL SOURCES OF PREJUDICE

Prejudice may be bred by social situations, but motivation underlies both the hostilities of prejudice and the desire to be unbiased. Frustration can feed prejudice, as can the desire

"And now at this point in the meeting I'd like to shift the blame away from me and onto someone else."

Scapegoats provide an outlet for frustrations and hostilities.

to see one's group as superior, and the desire to see the world as just. But at times, people are also motivated to avoid prejudice.

FRUSTRATION AND AGGRESSION: THE SCAPEGOAT THEORY

As we saw in Chapter 10, pain and frustration (the blocking of a goal) often evoke hostility. When the cause of our frustration is intimidating or vague, we often redirect our hostility. This phenomenon of "displaced aggression" may have contributed to the lynchings of Blacks in the southern United States after their Civil War. Between 1882 and 1930, there were more lynchings in years when cotton prices were low and economic frustration was therefore presumably high (Hepworth & West, 1988; Hovland & Sears, 1940). Ethnic peace is easier to maintain during prosperous times.

Targets for this displaced aggression vary. Following their defeat in the First World War and their country's subsequent economic chaos, many Germans saw Jews as villains. Long before Hitler came to power, one German leader explained: "The Jew is just convenient. . . . If there were no Jews, the anti-Semites would have to invent them" (quoted by G. W. Allport, 1958, p. 325). In earlier centuries people vented their fear and hostility on witches, whom they sometimes burned or drowned in public. Passions provoke prejudice.

> *"Whoever is dissatisfied with himself is continually ready for revenge."*
>
> Nietzsche, *The Gay Science*, 1882–1887

One source of frustration is competition. When two groups compete for jobs, housing, or social prestige, one group's goal fulfillment can become the other group's frustration. Thus the **realistic group conflict theory** suggests that prejudice arises when groups compete for scarce resources (Esses et al., 1998). A corresponding ecological principle, Gause's law, states that maximum competition will exist between species with identical needs.

realistic group conflict theory the theory that prejudice arises from competition between groups for scarce resources

In Canada, opposition to immigration since 1975 has gone up and down with the unemployment rate (Palmer, 1996). In Western Europe, for example, some people agree, "Over the last five years people like yourself have been economically worse off than most [name of country's minority group]." These frustrated people express relatively high levels of blatant prejudice (Pettigrew & Meertens, 1995). When interests clash, prejudice—for some people—pays.

SOCIAL IDENTITY THEORY: FEELING SUPERIOR TO OTHERS

Humans are a group-bound species. Our ancestral history prepares us to feed and protect ourselves—to live—in groups. Humans cheer for their groups, kill for their groups, die for their groups. Not surprisingly, we also define ourselves by our groups, note Australian social psychologists John Turner (1981, 1987, 1991, 2001), Michael Hogg (1992, 1996, 2003), and their colleagues. Self-concept—our sense of who we are—contains not just a *personal identity* (our sense of our personal attributes and attitudes) but a **social identity**. Fiona identifies herself as a woman, an Aussie, a Labourite, a University of New South Wales student, a member of the MacDonald family. We carry such social identities like playing cards, playing them when appropriate.

social identity the "we" aspect of our self-concept; the part of our answer to "Who am I?" that comes from our group

Working with the late British social psychologist Henri Tajfel [pronounced TOSH-fel], Turner proposed social identity theory. Turner and Tajfel observed the following:

- *We categorize:* We find it useful to put people, ourselves included, into categories. To label someone as a Hindu, a Scot, or a bus driver is a shorthand way of saying some other things about the person.
- *We identify:* We associate ourselves with certain groups (our **ingroups**), and gain self-esteem by doing so.
- *We compare:* We contrast our groups with other groups (**outgroups**), with a favourable bias toward our own group.

ingroup "us"—a group of people who share a sense of belonging, a feeling of common identity

outgroup "them"—a group that people perceive as distinctively different from or apart from their ingroup

We evaluate ourselves partly by our group memberships. Having a sense of "we-ness" strengthens our self-concepts. It *feels* good. We seek not only *respect* for ourselves but *pride* in our groups (Smith & Tyler, 1997). Moreover, seeing our groups as superior helps us feel even better. It's as if we all think, "I am an X [name your group]. X is good. Therefore, I am good."

Lacking a positive personal identity, people often seek self-esteem by identifying with a group. Thus, many youths find pride, power, and identity in gang affiliations. Many superpatriots define themselves by their national identities (Staub, 1997). And many people at loose ends find identity in their associations with new religious movements, self-help groups, or fraternal clubs (Figure 12–3).

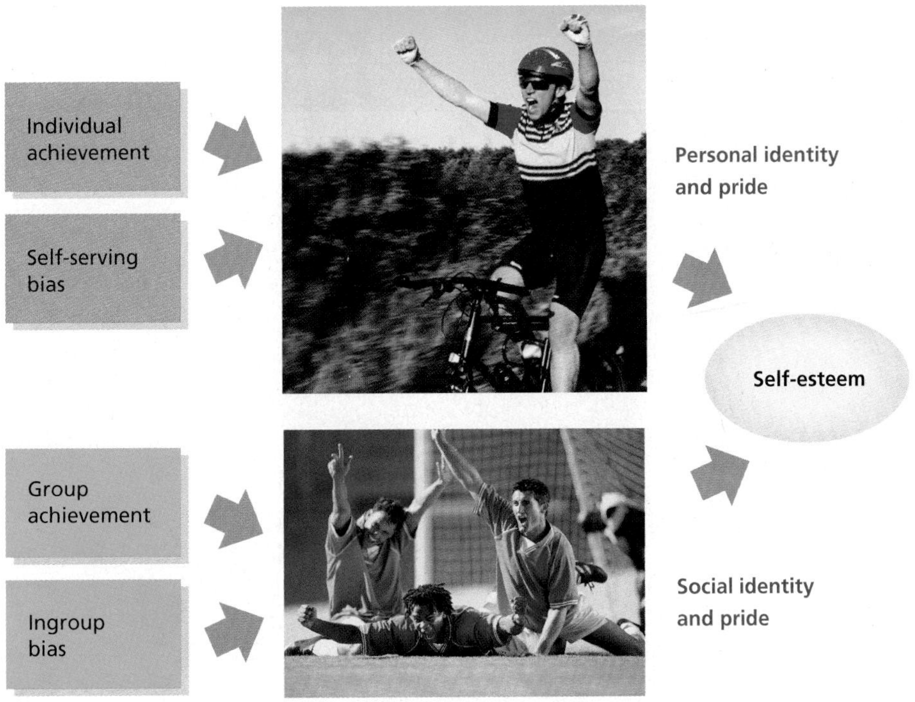

FIGURE 12–3

Personal identity and social identity together feed self-esteem.

Ingroup bias

The group definition of who you are—your race, religion, gender, academic major—implies a definition of who you are not. The circle that includes "us" (the ingroup) excludes "them" (the outgroup). Thus, the mere experience of being formed into groups may promote **ingroup bias**. Ask children, "Which are better, the children in your school or the children at [another school nearby]?" Virtually all will say their own school has the better children. For adults, too, the closer to home, the better things seem. More than 80 percent of both Whites and Blacks say race relations are generally good in their neighbourhoods, but fewer than 60 percent see relations as generally good in the country as a whole (Sack & Elder, 2000). Merely sharing a birthday with someone creates enough of a bond to evoke heightened cooperation in a laboratory experiment (Miller et al., 1998).

ingroup bias
the tendency to favour one's own group

"There is a tendency to define one's own group positively in order to evaluate oneself positively."

John C. Turner (1984)

Ingroup bias is one more example of the human quest for a positive self-concept (Chapter 2). We are so group conscious that given any excuse to think of ourselves as a group we will do so—and will then exhibit ingroup bias. Cluster people into groups defined by nothing more than their driver's licence number's last digit, and they'll feel a certain kinship with their number mates. In a series of experiments, Tajfel and Michael Billig (1974; Tajfel, 1970, 1981, 1982) discovered how little it takes to provoke favouritism toward *us* and unfairness toward *them*. In one study, Tajfel and Billig had British teenagers evaluate modern abstract paintings and then told them that they and some others had favoured the art of Paul Klee over that of Wassily Kandinsky. Finally, without ever meeting the other members of their group, the teens divided some money among members of both groups. They gave more money to people in their group rather than the other group, even though they had no idea who these people were or what their group membership meant.

In Rwanda, ingroup bias lay behind the murder of half the minority Tutsi population and led to a huge refugee exodus when the majority Hutus were defeated.

In many experiments, defining groups even in such a trivial way produced ingroup favouritism. David Wilder (1981) summarized the typical result: "When given the opportunity to divide 15 points [worth money], subjects generally award 9 or 10 points to their own group and 5 or 6 points to the other group." This bias occurs with both sexes and with people of all ages and nationalities, though especially with people from individualist cultures (Gudykunst, 1989). (People in communal cultures identify more with all their peers and so treat everyone more the same.)

We also are more prone to ingroup bias when our group is small and lower in status relative to the outgroup (Ellemers et al., 1997; Mullen et al., 1992). When we're part of a small group surrounded by a larger group, we are also conscious of our group membership; when our ingroup is the majority, we think less about it. To be a foreign student, to be gay or lesbian, or to be of a minority race or gender at some social gathering is to feel one's social identity more keenly and to react accordingly.

Even forming conspicuous groups on *no* logical basis—say, merely by composing groups X and Y with the flip of a coin—will produce some ingroup bias (Billig & Tajfel, 1973; Brewer & Silver, 1978; Locksley et al., 1980). In Kurt Vonnegut's novel *Slapstick*, computers gave everyone a new middle name; all "Daffodil-11s" then felt unity with one another and distance from "Raspberry-13s." The self-serving bias (Chapter 2) rides again, enabling people to achieve a more positive social identity: "We" are better than "they," even when "we" and "they" are defined randomly!

"Nationality is a sense of belonging and a sense of place—a pleasure in your history, in the peculiarities of your people's behaviour, in the music and the familiar sounds of the world around you. I don't think a particular culture is better. I just think it's a culture you are more at home with."

Bill Wilson, Scottish Nationalist Party activist, 2003

Because of our social identifications, we conform to our group norms. We sacrifice ourselves for team, family, nation. We may dislike outgroups. The more important our social identity and the more strongly attached we feel to a group, the more we react prejudicially to threats from another group (Crocker & Luhtanen, 1990; Hinkle et al., 1992). Israeli historian and former Jerusalem deputy mayor Meron Benvenisti (1988) reported that among Jerusalem's Jews and Arabs, social identity is so central to self-concept that it constantly reminds them of who they are not. Thus, on the integrated street where he lived, his own children—to his dismay—"have not acquired a single Arab friend."

When our group has been successful, we can also make ourselves feel better by identifying more strongly with it. When queried after their football team's victory, students frequently report "*We* won." When questioned after their team's defeat, students are more likely to say, "*They* lost." Basking in the reflected glory of a successful ingroup is strongest among those who have just experienced an ego blow, such as learning they did poorly on a "creativity test"

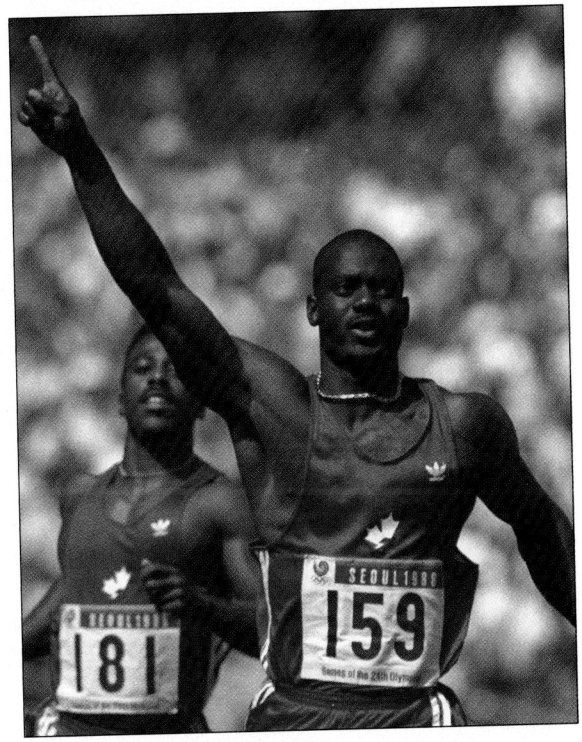

Basking in reflected glory. After Jamaican-Canadian sprinter Ben Johnson won the Olympic 100-metre race, Canadian media described this victory by a "Canadian." After Johnson's gold medal was taken away due to steroid use, Canadian media then emphasized his "Jamaican" identity (Stelzl & Seligman, 2004).

"Uh-oh! They seem to have loved it!"

Something favoured by an "outgroup" may be cast in a negative light.

(Cialdini et al., 1976). We can also bask in the reflected glory of a friend's achievement—except when the friend outperforms us on something pertinent to our identity (Tesser et al., 1988). If you think of yourself as an outstanding psychology student, you will likely take more pleasure in a friend's excellence in mathematics.

Ingroup bias is the favouring of one's own group. Such favouritism could reflect (1) liking for the ingroup, (2) dislike for the outgroup, or (3) both. If both, loyalty to one's group should produce a devaluing of other groups. Is that true? Does ethnic pride cause prejudice? Does a strong feminist identity lead feminists to dislike nonfeminists? Does loyalty to a particular fraternity or sorority lead its members to deprecate independents and members of other fraternities and sororities?

Experiments support both explanations. Outgroup stereotypes prosper when people feel keenly their ingroup identity, such as when they are with other ingroup members (Wilder & Shapiro, 1991). At a club meeting, we sense most strongly our differences from those in another club. When anticipating bias against our group, we more strongly disparage the outgroup (Vivian & Berkowitz, 1993).

STORY BEHIND THE RESEARCH

Victoria Esses
University of Western Ontario

I grew up in Toronto and watched it evolve from a very homogeneous city to one of the most ethnically diverse cities in the world. This planted the seed for my later interest in studying intergroup attitudes. I began to study intergroup attitudes as a postdoctoral fellow at the University of Waterloo in the late 1980s, conducting research on the effects of mood on the expression of ethnic stereotypes, and the role of values, stereotypes, and emotions in determining intergroup attitudes. Since then, my interest in this topic has moved in several different directions. One important direction is the investigation of attitudes toward immigrants and immigration, which again came out of my experiences in Toronto. It struck me that immigrants seemed to be the target of considerable prejudice and discrimination, even among people who were themselves immigrants only a generation or two ago. In addition, it seemed that people justified their negative attitudes and behaviour toward immigrants on the basis of competition for resources, such as jobs. This led to my current research on the role of group competition in determining prejudice and discrimination toward immigrants. I feel fortunate to be able to work in an area in which I can apply theory and research in social psychology to important social issues.

Yet ingroup bias results as much or more from perceiving that one's own group is good (Brewer, 1979) as from a sense that other groups are bad (Rosenbaum & Holtz, 1985). So it seems that positive feelings for our own groups need not be mirrored by equally strong negative feelings for outgroups. Devotion to one's own race, religion, and social group sometimes does predispose a person to devalue other races, religions, and social groups. But the sequence is not automatic. Indeed, a multicultural rather than a colour-blind perspective does not lead to sharper perception of group differences, note Christopher Wolsko and others (2000) from their research with university students. But some of the stereotypes bred by multiculturalism are favourable to the outgroup. For psychological and social health, they say, we need to acknowledge simultaneously our individual uniqueness, our group identity, and our common humanity.

Father, Mother, and Me, sister and Auntie say All the people like us are We, and every one else is They. And They live over the sea, While We live over the way. But would you believe it? They look upon We As only a sort of They!

Rudyard Kipling, 1926 (quoted by Mullen, 1991)

Need for status, self-regard, and belonging

Status is relative: To perceive ourselves as having status, we need people below us. Thus one psychological benefit of prejudice, or of any status system, is a feeling of superiority. Most of us can recall a time when we took secret satisfaction in another's failure—perhaps seeing a brother or sister punished or a classmate failing a test. In Europe and North America, prejudice is often greater among those low or slipping on the socioeconomic ladder and among those whose positive self-image is being threatened (Lemyre & Smith, 1985; Pettigrew et al., 1998; Thompson & Crocker, 1985). In one study, members of lower-status sororities were more disparaging of other sororities than were members of higher-status sororities (Crocker et al., 1987). Perhaps people whose status is secure have less need to feel superior.

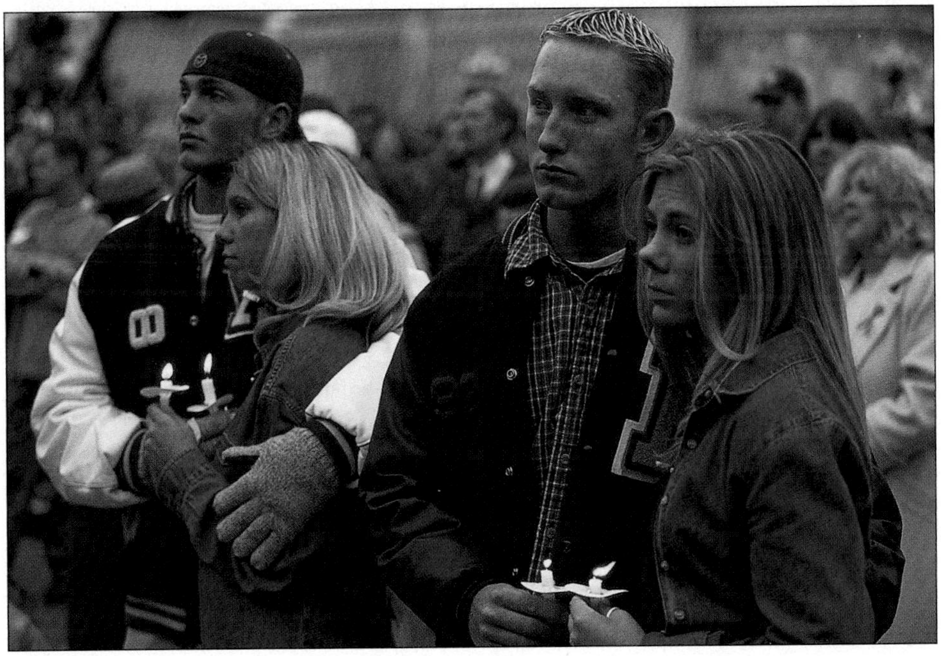

The curse of cliques? Did the tendency of high school students to form ingroups and disparage outgroups—jocks, preppies, goths, geeks—contribute to a tribal atmosphere that helped form the context for recent school massacres, here at Colorado's Columbine High School, or elsewhere?

In study after study, thinking about your own mortality—by writing a short essay on dying and the emotions aroused by thinking about death—also provokes enough insecurity to intensify ingroup favouritism and outgroup prejudice (Greenberg et al., 1990, 1994; Harmon-Jones et al., 1996; Schimel et al. 1999; Solomon et al., 2000). Among Whites, thinking about death can even promote liking for racists who argue for their group's superiority (Greenberg et al., in press). With death on their minds, people exhibit "terror management" by derogating those who further arouse their anxiety by challenging their worldviews. When people are already feeling vulnerable about their mortality, prejudice helps bolster a threatened belief system. The news is not all bad, however. Thinking about death can also lead people to pursue communal feelings such as togetherness and altruism (McGregor et al., 2001).

"By exciting emulation and comparisons of superiority, you lay the foundation of lasting mischief; you make brothers and sisters hate each other."

Samuel Johnson, quoted in James Boswell's *Life of Samuel Johnson*, 1791

All this suggests that a man who doubts his own strength and independence might, by proclaiming women to be pitifully weak and dependent, boost his masculine image. Indeed, when Joel Grube, Randy Kleinhesselink, and Kathleen Kearney (1982) had Washington State University men view young women's videotaped job interviews, men with low self-acceptance disliked strong, nontraditional women. Men with high self-acceptance preferred them. Similarly, James Meindl and Melvin Lerner (1984) found that a humiliating experience—accidentally knocking over a stack of someone's important computer cards—provoked English-speaking Canadian students to express increased hostility toward French-speaking Canadians. Experiments confirm the connection between self-image and prejudice: Affirm people and they will evaluate an outgroup more positively; threaten their self-esteem and they will restore it by denigrating an outgroup (Fein & Spencer, 1997; Spencer et al., 1998).

A despised outgroup serves yet another need: the need to belong to an ingroup. As we will see in Module A, the perception of a common enemy unites a group. School spirit is seldom so strong as when the game is with the archrival. The sense of comradeship among workers is often highest when they all feel a common antagonism toward management. To solidify the Nazi hold over Germany, Hitler used the "Jewish menace." Despised outgroups can strengthen the ingroup. When the need to belong is met, people become more accepting of outgroups, report Mario Mikulincer and Phillip Shaver (2001). They subliminally primed some Israeli students with words that fostered a sense of belonging (*love, support, hug*) and others with neutral words. The students then read an essay that was supposedly written either by a fellow Jewish student or an Arab student. When primed with neutral words, the Israeli students evaluated the supposed Israeli student's essay as superior to the supposed Arab student's essay. When primed with a sense of belonging, this bias disappeared.

"It's not enough that we succeed. Cats must also fail."

MOTIVATION TO SEE THE WORLD AS JUST

In a series of experiments conducted at the Universities of Waterloo and Kentucky, Melvin Lerner and his colleagues

(Lerner & Miller, 1978; Lerner, 1980) discovered that merely *observing* another innocent person being victimized is enough to make the victim seem less worthy. Imagine that you, along with some others, are participating in one of Lerner's studies—supposedly on the perception of emotional cues (Lerner & Simmons, 1966). One of the participants, a confederate, is selected by lottery to perform a memory task. This person receives painful shocks whenever she gives a wrong answer. You and the others note her emotional responses.

After watching the victim receive these apparently painful shocks, the experimenter asks you to evaluate her. How would you respond? With compassionate sympathy? We might expect so. As Ralph Waldo Emerson wrote, "The martyr cannot be dishonoured." On the contrary, the experiments revealed that martyrs can be dishonoured. When observers were powerless to alter the victim's fate, they often rejected and devalued the victim. Juvenal, the Roman satirist, anticipated these results: "The Roman mob follows after Fortune . . . and hates those who have been condemned."

Linda Carli and her colleagues (1989, 1999) report that this **just-world phenomenon** colours our impressions of rape victims. Carli had people read detailed descriptions of interactions between a man and a woman. For example, a woman and her boss meet for dinner, go to his home, and each have a glass of wine. Some read a scenario that has a happy ending: "Then he led me to the couch. He held my hand and asked me to marry him." In hindsight, people find the ending unsurprising and admire the man's and woman's character traits. Others read the same scenario with a different ending: "But then he became very rough and pushed me onto the couch. He held me down on the couch and raped me." Given this ending, people see it as inevitable and blame the woman for behaviour that seems faultless in the first scenario.

just-world phenomenon
the tendency of people to believe the world is just and that people therefore get what they deserve and deserve what they get

Lerner (1980) noted that such disparaging of hapless victims results from the human need to believe that, "I am a just person living in a just world, a world where people get what they deserve." From early childhood, he argues, we are taught that good is rewarded and evil punished. Hard work and virtue pay dividends; laziness and immorality do not. From this it is

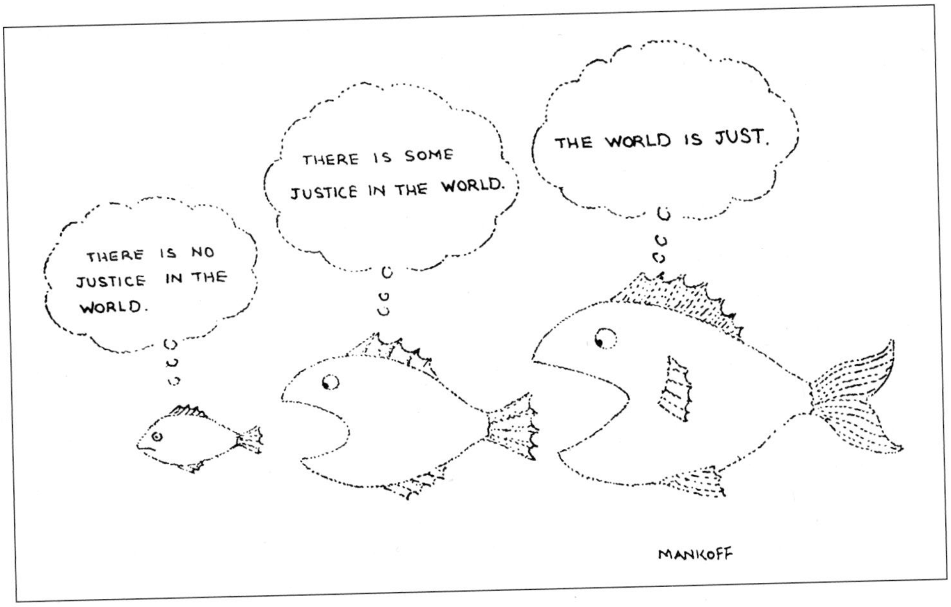

The just-world phenomenon.

but a short leap to assuming that those who flourish must be good and those who suffer must deserve their fate.

Recently Carolyn Hafer from Brock University and her colleagues (Hafer, 2000; Hafer & Begue, 2005; Hafer & Olson, 2003) have provided compelling evidence that an innocent victim threatens people's sense of justice. In one study, for example, students either watched a boy describe how he had been beaten and robbed while he was travelling in North America or not. Those who watched the innocent victim describe his assault were especially slow at reading words related to justice in much the same way that spider phobics are slow to read words about spiders. People seemed afraid to think about justice when confronted with an innocent victim. In a later study they demonstrated that watching the same video led students to distance themselves from the victim—they said they weren't like him—and the more they distanced themselves from him the more they derogated him.

Research on the motive to see the world as just suggests that this motive is so strong that it can lead people to ignore gross injustice and instead see no injustice at all. Those who assume a just world believe that rape victims must have behaved seductively (Borgida & Brekke, 1985), that battered spouses must have provoked their beatings (Summers & Feldman, 1984), that poor people don't deserve better (Furnham & Gunter, 1984), and that sick people are responsible for their illnesses (Gruman & Sloan, 1983). Such beliefs enable successful people to reassure themselves that they, too, deserve what they have. The wealthy and healthy can see their own good fortune, and others' misfortune, as justly deserved. Linking good fortune with virtue and misfortune with moral failure enables the fortunate to feel pride and to avoid responsibility for the unfortunate.

People loathe a loser even when the loser's misfortune quite obviously stems from mere bad luck. People *know* that gambling outcomes are just good or bad luck and should not affect their evaluations of the gambler. Still, they can't resist playing Monday-morning quarterback—judging people by their results. Ignoring the fact that reasonable decisions can bring bad results, they judge losers as less competent (Baron & Hershey, 1988). Lawyers and stock market speculators may similarly judge themselves by their outcomes, becoming smug after successes and self-reproachful after failures. Talent and initiative are not unrelated to success. But the just-world assumption discounts the uncontrollable factors that can derail one's best efforts.

MOTIVATION TO AVOID PREJUDICE

Motivations not only lead people to be prejudiced, they also lead people to avoid prejudice. Although most of us don't want to be prejudiced, a prejudice habit lingers. Patricia Devine and her colleagues (1989, 2000) report that people low and high in prejudice sometimes have similar automatic prejudicial responses. Try as we might to suppress unwanted thoughts—thoughts about food, thoughts about romance with a friend's partner, judgmental thoughts about another group—they sometimes refuse to go away (Macrae et al., 1994; Wegner & Erber, 1992). This is especially so for older adults, who lose some of their ability to inhibit unwanted thoughts and therefore to suppress old stereotypes (von Hippel et al., 2000). The result for all of us: Unwanted (dissonant) thoughts and feelings often persist. Breaking the prejudice habit is not easy.

In real life, encountering a minority person may trigger a similar knee-jerk stereotype. Those with accepting and those with disapproving attitudes toward homosexuals may both feel uncomfortable sitting with a gay male on a bus seat (Monteith, 1993). Encountering an unfamiliar Black male, people—even those who pride themselves on not being prejudiced—may respond warily. In one experiment by E. J. Vanman and colleagues (1990), White people viewed slides of White and Black people, imagined themselves interacting with them, and rated their probable liking of the person. Although the participants saw themselves liking the Black more than the White persons, their facial muscles told a different story. Instruments revealed that when a Black face appeared, there tended to be more activity in frowning than smiling muscles. An emotion processing centre in the brain also becomes more active as a person views an unfamiliar person of another race (Hart et al., 2000).

On a brighter note, researchers who study stereotyping contend that prejudicial reactions are not inevitable (Crandall & Eshelman, 2003; Kunda & Spencer, 2003). The motivation to avoid prejudice can lead people to modify their thoughts and actions. Aware of the gap between how they should feel and how they do feel, self-conscious people will feel guilt and try to inhibit their prejudicial response (Bodenhausen & Macrae, 1998; Macrae et al., 1998; Zuwerink et al., 1996). Even automatic prejudices subside when people's motivation to avoid prejudice is internal (because prejudice is wrong) rather than external (because they don't want others to think badly of them).

The moral: Overcoming what Devine calls "the prejudice habit" isn't easy. If you find yourself reacting with knee-jerk presumptions or feelings, don't despair; that's not unusual. It's what you do with that awareness that matters. Do you let those feelings hijack your behaviour? Or do you compensate by monitoring and correcting your behaviour in future situations?

SUMMING UP: MOTIVATIONAL SOURCES OF PREJUDICE

People's motivations impact prejudice. Frustration breeds hostility, which people sometimes vent on scapegoats and sometimes express more directly against competing groups.

People also are motivated to view themselves and their groups as superior to other groups. Even trivial group memberships lead people to favour their group over others. A threat to self-image heightens such ingroup favouritism, as does the need to belong.

The motive to see the world as just can also powerfully shape people's views of others. If a group faces a difficult plight this motive can lead people to believe that members of the group deserve that plight. On a more positive note, the motivation to avoid prejudice can lead people to break the prejudice habit.

COGNITIVE SOURCES OF PREJUDICE

To understand stereotyping and prejudice, it also helps to remember how our minds work. How do the ways in which we think about the world, and simplify it, influence our stereotypes? And how do our stereotypes affect our judgments?

CATEGORIZATION

Prejudice arises not only from social and motivational influences but also at times from cool calculation. The same processes that allow people to simplify and make sense of the world, also at times lead people to make prejudicial evaluations of others. One way we simplify our environment is to "categorize"—to organize the world by clustering objects into groups. A biologist classifies plants and animals. A human classifies people. Having done so, we think about them more easily. If persons in a group are similar, knowing their group can provide useful information with minimal effort (Macrae et al., 1994). Customs inspectors and airplane antihijack personnel are therefore given "profiles" of suspicious individuals (Kraut & Poe, 1980).

We find it especially easy and efficient to rely on stereotypes when

- pressed for time (Kaplan et al., 1993),
- preoccupied (Gilbert & Hixon, 1991),
- tired (Bodenhausen, 1990),
- emotionally aroused (Esses et al., 1993b; Stroessner & Mackie, 1993), and
- too young to appreciate diversity (Biernat, 1991).

Ethnicity and sex are, in our current world, powerful ways of categorizing people. Imagine Tom, a 45-year-old, Black real estate agent in New Brunswick. We suspect that your image of "Black male" predominates over the categories "middle-aged," "businessperson," and "easterner."

Experiments expose our spontaneous categorization of people by race. Much as we organize what is actually a colour continuum into what we perceive as distinct colours, so we cannot resist categorizing people into groups. We label people of widely varying ancestry as simply "Black" or "White," as if such categories were black and white. When subjects view different people making statements, they often forget who said what, yet remember the race of the person who made each statement (Hewstone et al., 1991; Stroessner et al., 1990; Taylor et al., 1978). By itself, such categorization is not prejudice, but it does provide a foundation for prejudice.

In fact, it's necessary for prejudice. Social identity theory implies that those who feel their social identity keenly will concern themselves with correctly categorizing people as *us* or *them.* To test this prediction, Jim Blascovich, Natalie Wyer, Laura Swart, and Jeffrey Kibler (1997) compared racially prejudiced people (who feel their racial identity keenly) with nonprejudiced people—who proved equally speedy at classifying white, black, and grey ovals. But how much time did each group take to categorize *people* by race? Especially when shown faces whose race was somewhat ambiguous (Figure 12–4), prejudiced people took longer, with more apparent concern for classifying people as us (one's own race) or them (another race).

FIGURE 12–4

Racial categorization.

Quickly: What race is this person? Less prejudiced people respond more quickly, with less apparent concern with possibly misclassifying someone (as if thinking, who cares?).

Perceived similarities and differences

Picture the following objects: apples, chairs, pencils.

There is a strong tendency to see objects within a group as being more uniform than they really are. Were your apples all red? Your chairs all straight-backed? Your pencils all yellow? Once we classify two days in the same month, they seem more alike, temperature-wise, than the same interval across months. People guess the eight-day average temperature difference between, say, November 15 and 23 to be less than the eight-day difference between November 30 and December 8 (Krueger & Clement, 1994).

It's the same with people. Once we assign people to groups—athletes, drama majors, math professors—we are likely to exaggerate the similarities within groups and the differences between them (S. E. Taylor, 1981; Wilder, 1978). Mere division into groups can create an **outgroup homogeneity effect**—a sense that *they* are "all alike" and different from "us" and "our" group (Ostrom & Sedikides, 1992). Because we generally like people we think are similar to us and dislike those we perceive as different, the natural result is ingroup bias (Byrne & Wong, 1962; Rokeach & Mezei, 1966; Stein et al., 1965).

outgroup homogeneity effect perception of outgroup members as more similar to one another than are ingroup members. Thus "they are alike; we are diverse."

The mere fact of a group decision can also lead outsiders to overestimate a group's unanimity. If a conservative wins a national election by a slim majority, observers infer "the people have turned conservative." If a liberal won by a similarly slim margin, voter attitudes would hardly have differed, but observers would now attribute a "liberal mood" to the country. Whether a decision is made by majority rule or by a designated group executive, people usually presume that it reflects the entire group's attitudes, observe Scott Allison and his coworkers (1985 to 1996). When the Onex Corporation tried to take over Air Canada, Buzz Hargrove, then-president of the Canadian Auto Workers (CAW), sided with Onex. The media reported that the CAW was behind Onex, even though it was clear that many union members felt otherwise.

When the group is our own, we are more likely to see diversity:

- Many non-Europeans see the Swiss as a fairly homogeneous people. But to the people of Switzerland, the Swiss are diverse, encompassing French-, German-, and Italian-speaking groups.
- Those in a minority tend to feel more shared identity than those in the majority (Haslam & Oakes, 1995; Ryan, 1996). Nevertheless, those in the minority are especially likely to see important differences between their own subgroup and other subgroups, while those in the majority tend to lump all minority group members together (Huddy & Virtanen, 1995).
- Sorority sisters perceive the members of any other sorority as less diverse than the mix in their own (Park & Rothbart, 1982). And business majors and engineering majors overestimate the uniformity of the other group's traits and attitudes (Judd et al., 1991).

In general, the greater our familiarity with a social group, the more we see its diversity (Brown & Wootton-Millward, 1993; Linville et al., 1989). The less our familiarity, the more we stereotype. Also, the smaller and less powerful the group, the more we stereotype (Fiske, 1993; Mullen & Hu, 1989). To those in power, we pay attention.

"Women are more like each other than men [are]."

Lord (not Lady) Chesterfield

Perhaps you have noticed: *They*—the members of any racial group other than your own—even *look* alike. Many of us can recall embarrassing ourselves by confusing two people of another racial group, prompting the person we've misnamed to say, "You think we all look alike." Experiments by John Brigham, June Chance, Alvin Goldstein, and Roy Malpass in the United States and by Hayden Ellis in Scotland reveal that people of other races do in fact *seem* to look more alike than do people of one's own race (Brigham & Williamson, 1979; Chance & Goldstein, 1981; Ellis, 1981). When White students are shown faces of a few White and a few Black individuals and then asked to pick these individuals out of a photographic lineup, they show an **own-race bias**. They more accurately recognize the White faces than the Black, and they often falsely recognize Black faces

own-race bias the tendency for people to more accurately recognize faces of their own race

The term "own-race bias" is a misnomer in the case of Anglo and Hispanic identifications. Most Hispanic people are classified as Caucasians.

Follow-up research also reveals an "own-age bias": People more accurately recognize people similar to their own age

(Wright & Stroud, 2002).

never before seen. Testing of a split-brain patient, which allows the two brain hemispheres to be tested separately, revealed that the right hemisphere exhibits superior recognition of own-race faces (Turk et al., 2005).

But are members of some races just easier to identify than others? Apparently not. As Figure 12–5 illustrates, Blacks more easily recognize another Black than they do a White (Bothwell et al., 1989), and Latinos more readily recognize another Latino whom they saw a couple of hours earlier than they do a White (Platz & Hosch, 1988).

It's true outside the laboratory as well, as Daniel Wright and his colleagues (2001) found after either a Black or a White researcher approached Black and White people in South African and English shopping malls. When later asked to identify the researcher from lineups, people better recognized those of their own race. Follow-up research also reveals an "own-age bias:" People more accurately recognize people similar to their own age (Wright & Stroud, 2002). It's not that we cannot perceive differences among faces of another race. Rather, when looking at a face from another racial group we often attend, first, to race ("that man is Black") rather than to individual features. When viewing someone of our own race, we are less race conscious and more attentive to individual details (Levin, 2000).

DISTINCTIVENESS

Other ways we perceive our worlds also breed stereotypes. Distinctive people and vivid or extreme occurrences often capture attention and distort judgments.

Distinctive people

Have you ever found yourself in a situation where you were the only person present of your sex, race, or nationality? If so, your difference from the others probably made you more noticeable and the object of more attention. A Black in an otherwise White group, a man in an otherwise female group, or a woman in an otherwise male group seems more prominent and influential

FIGURE 12–5

The own-race bias.

White subjects more accurately recognize the faces of Whites than of Blacks; Black subjects more accurately recognize the faces of Blacks than of Whites. (From P. G. Devine and R. S. Malpass, 1985)

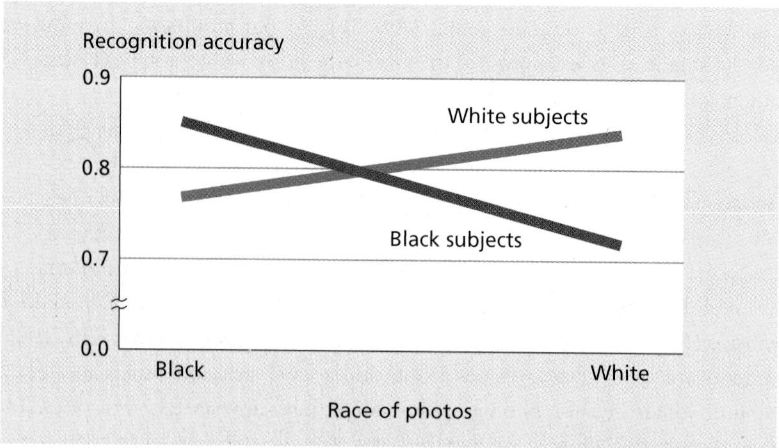

and to have exaggerated good and bad qualities (Crocker & McGraw, 1984; S. E. Taylor et al., 1979). This occurs because when someone in a group is made salient (conspicuous), we tend to see that person as causing whatever happens (Taylor & Fiske, 1978). If we are positioned to look at Joe, an average group member, Joe will seem to have a greater than average influence on the group. People who capture our attention seem more responsible for what happens.

Have you noticed that people also define you by your most distinctive traits and behaviours? Tell people about someone who is a skydiver and a tennis player, report Lori Nelson and Dale Miller (1997), and they will think of the person as a skydiver. Asked to choose a gift book for the person, they will pick a skydiving book over a tennis book. A person who has both a pet snake and a pet dog is seen more as a snake owner than a dog owner. People also take note of those who violate expectations (Bettencourt et al., 1997). "Like a flower blooming in winter, intellect is more readily noticed where it is not expected," reflected Stephen Carter (1993, p. 54) on his experience as a Black intellectual. Such perceived distinctiveness makes it easier for highly capable job applicants from low-status groups to get noticed, though they also must work harder to prove their abilities are genuine (Biernat & Kobrynowicz, 1997).

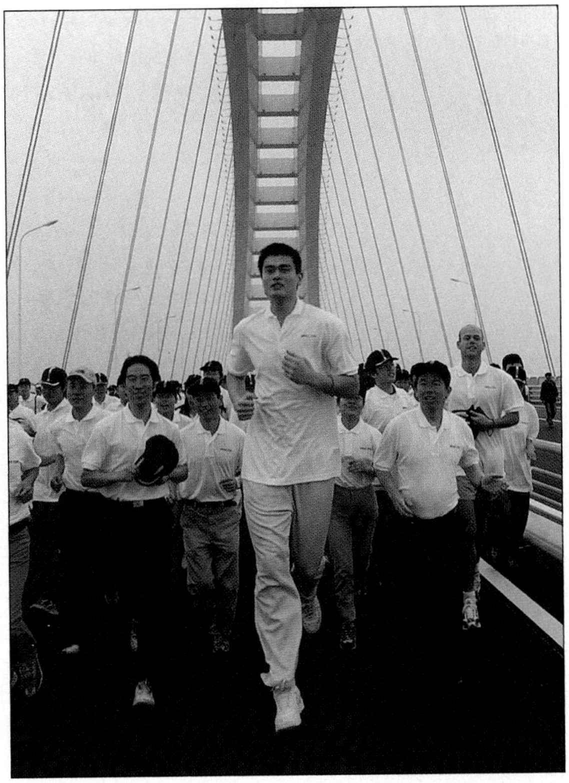

Distinctive people, such as Houston Rockets 7′6″ player Yao Ming, draw attention.

Ellen Langer and Lois Imber (1980) cleverly demonstrated the attention paid distinctive people. They asked Harvard students to watch a video of a man reading. The students paid closer attention when they were led to think he was out of the ordinary—a cancer patient, a homosexual, or a millionaire. They detected characteristics that other viewers ignored, and their evaluation of him was more extreme. Those who thought the man a cancer patient noticed distinctive facial characteristics and bodily movements and thus perceived him as much more "different from most people" than did the other viewers. The extra attention we pay to distinctive people creates an illusion that they differ more from others than they really do. If people thought you had the IQ of a genius, they would probably notice things about you that otherwise would pass unnoticed.

Distinctiveness feeds self-consciousness

When surrounded by Whites, Blacks sometimes detect people reacting to their distinctiveness. Many report being stared or glared at, being subject to insensitive comments, and receiving bad service (Swim et al., 1998). Sometimes we misperceive others as reacting to our distinctiveness. At Dartmouth College, researchers Robert Kleck and Angelo Strenta (1980) discovered this when they led college women to feel disfigured. The women thought the purpose of the experiment was to assess how someone would react to a facial scar created with theatrical makeup; the scar was on the right cheek, running from the ear to the mouth. Actually, the purpose was to see how the women themselves, when made to feel deviant, would perceive others' behaviour

Self-consciousness about being different affects how we interpret others' behaviour.

toward them. After applying the makeup, the experimenter gave each woman a small hand mirror so she could see the authentic-looking scar. When she put the mirror down, he then applied some "moisturizer" to "keep the makeup from cracking." What the "moisturizer" really did was remove the scar.

The scene that followed was poignant. A young woman, feeling terribly self-conscious about her supposedly disfigured face, talked with another woman who sees no such disfigurement and knows nothing of what has gone on before. If you have ever felt similarly self-conscious—perhaps about a physical handicap, acne, even just a bad hair day—then perhaps you can sympathize with the self-conscious woman. Compared with women who were led to believe their conversational partners merely thought they had an allergy, the "disfigured" women became acutely sensitive to how their partners were looking at them. They rated their partners as more tense, distant, and patronizing. In fact, observers who later analyzed videotapes of how the partners treated "disfigured" persons could find no such differences in treatment. Self-conscious about being different, the "disfigured" women misinterpreted mannerisms and comments they would otherwise not have noticed.

Self-conscious interactions between a majority and minority person can therefore feel tense even when both are well intentioned (Devine et al., 1996). Tom, who is known to be gay, meets Bill, who is straight. Tolerant Bill wants to respond without prejudice. But feeling unsure of himself, he holds back a bit. Tom, expecting negative attitudes from most people, misreads Bill's hesitancy as hostility and responds with a seeming chip on his shoulder.

Anyone can experience this phenomenon. Majority group members (Manitoba White people in one study) often have beliefs—"meta-stereotypes"—about how minorities stereotype them (Vorauer et al., 1998). Even relatively unprejudiced Canadian Whites, Israeli Jews, or American Christians may sense that outgroup minorities stereotype them as prejudiced, arrogant, or patronizing. If George worries that Gamal perceives him as "your typical educated racist," he may be on guard when talking with Gamal.

Stigma consciousness

People vary in *stigma consciousness*—in how likely they are to expect that others will stereotype them. Gays and lesbians, for example, differ in how much they suppose others "interpret all my behaviours" in terms of their sexual orientation (Pinel, 1999). Seeing oneself as a victim of pervasive prejudice has its ups and downs (Branscombe et al., 1999; Dion, 1998). The downside is that those who perceive themselves as frequent victims live with the stress of stereotype threats and presumed antagonism and therefore experience lower well-being. While living in Europe, stigma-conscious Americans—people who perceive Europeans as resenting Americans—live more fretfully than those who feel accepted.

The upside is that perceptions of prejudice buffer individual self-esteem. If someone is nasty, "Well, it's not directed at me personally." Moreover, perceived prejudice and discrimination enhance our feelings of social identity and prepare us to join in collective social action.

Vivid cases

Our minds also use distinctive cases as a shortcut to judging groups. Are Blacks good athletes? "Well, there's Lenox Lewis and Marion Jones and Jerome Iginla. Yeah, I'd say so." Note the thought processes at work here: Given limited experience with a particular social group, we recall examples of it and generalize from those (Sherman, 1996). Moreover, encountering exemplars of negative stereotypes (a hostile Black person in one recent experiment) can prime such stereotypes, leading people to minimize contact with the group (Hendersen-King & Nisbett, 1996). Such generalizing from single cases can cause problems. Vivid instances, though more available in memory, are seldom representative of the larger group. Exceptional athletes, though distinctive and memorable, are not the best basis for judging the distribution of athletic talent among an entire group.

Those in a numerical minority, being more conspicuous, also may be numerically overestimated by the majority. What proportion of your country's population would you say is Muslim? People in non-Muslim countries often overestimate this proportion. (In Canada, for example, less than 1 percent have declared themselves as Muslim in the 1991 Census.) Or consider a 1990 Gallup poll report that the average American estimated 32 percent of the U.S. population was Black and 21 percent Hispanic (Gates, 1993). The U.S. Census Bureau figures were 12 and 9 percent.

Myron Rothbart and his colleagues (1978) showed how distinctive cases also fuel stereotypes. They had University of Oregon students view 50 slides, each of which stated the man's height. For one group of students, 10 of the men were slightly over 6 feet (up to 6 feet, 4 inches). For other students, these 10 men were well over 6 feet (up to 6 feet, 11 inches). When asked later how many of the men were over 6 feet, those given the moderately tall examples recalled 5 percent too many. Those given the extremely tall examples recalled 50 percent too many. In a follow-up experiment, students read descriptions of the actions of 50 men, 10 of whom had committed either nonviolent crimes, such as forgery, or violent crimes, such as rape. Of those shown the list with the violent crimes, most overestimated the number of criminal acts.

The attention-getting power of distinctive, extreme cases helps explain why middle-class people so greatly exaggerate the dissimilarities between themselves and the underclass. Contrary to stereotypes of "welfare queens" driving Cadillacs, people living in poverty generally share the aspirations of the middle class and would rather provide for themselves than accept public assistance (Cook & Curtin, 1987). Moreover, the less we know about a group, the more we are influenced by a few vivid cases (Quattrone & Jones, 1980).

Distinctive events

illusory correlation
a false impression that two variables correlate (see Chapter 3)

Stereotypes assume a correlation between group membership and individuals' characteristics ("Italians are emotional," "Jews are shrewd," "Accountants are perfectionists"). Even under the best of conditions, our attentiveness to unusual occurrences can create **illusory correlations**. Because we are sensitive to distinctive events, the co-occurrence of two such events is especially noticeable—more noticeable than each of the times the unusual events do not occur together.

David Hamilton and Robert Gifford (1976) demonstrated illusory correlation in a clever experiment. They showed students slides on which various people, members of "Group A" or "Group B," were said to have done something desirable or undesirable. For example, "John, a member of Group A, visited a sick friend in the hospital." Twice as many statements described members of Group A as Group B, but both groups did nine desirable acts for every four undesirable behaviours. Since both Group B and the undesirable acts were less frequent, their co-occurrence—for example, "Allen, a member of Group B, dented the fender of a parked car and didn't leave his name"—was an unusual combination that caught people's attention. The students therefore overestimated the frequency with which the "minority" group (B) acted undesirably and judged Group B more harshly.

Remember, Group B members actually committed undesirable acts in the same proportion as Group A members. Moreover, the students had no pre-existing biases for or against Group B, and they received the information more systematically than daily experience ever offers it. Although researchers debate why it happens, they agree that illusory correlation occurs and provides yet another source for the formation of racial stereotypes (Berndsen et al., 2002).

The mass media reflect and feed this phenomenon. When a self-described homosexual murders someone, homosexuality often gets mentioned. When a heterosexual murders someone, the person's sexual orientation is seldom mentioned. Likewise, when ex–mental patients Mark Chapman and John Hinckley, Jr., shot John Lennon and U.S. President Reagan, respectively, the assailants' mental histories commanded attention. Assassins and mental hospitalization are both relatively infrequent, making the combination especially newsworthy. Such reporting adds to the illusion of a large correlation between (1) violent tendencies and (2) homosexuality or mental hospitalization.

Unlike the students who judged Groups A and B, we often have pre-existing biases. David Hamilton's further research with Terrence Rose (1980) reveals that our pre-existing stereotypes can lead us to "see" correlations that aren't there. The researchers had University of California Santa Barbara students read sentences in which various adjectives described the members of different occupational groups ("Doug, an accountant, is timid and thoughtful"). In actuality, each occupation was described equally often by each adjective; accountants, doctors, and salespeople were equally often timid, wealthy, and talkative. The students, however, *thought* they had more often read descriptions of timid accountants, wealthy doctors, and talkative salespeople. Their stereotyping led them to perceive correlations that weren't there, thus helping to perpetuate the stereotypes. To believe is to see.

ATTRIBUTIONS

fundamental attribution error
see Chapter 3

In explaining others' actions, we frequently commit the **fundamental attribution error**. We attribute their behaviour so much to their inner dispositions that we discount important

situational forces. The error occurs partly because our attention focuses on the person, not on the situation. A person's race or sex is vivid and attention-getting; the situational forces working on that person are usually less visible. Slavery was often overlooked as an explanation for slave behaviour; the behaviour was instead attributed to the slaves' own nature. Until recently, the same was true of how we explained the perceived differences between women and men. Because gender-role constraints were hard to see, we attributed men's and women's behaviour solely to their innate dispositions. The more people assume that human traits are fixed dispositions, the stronger are their stereotypes (Levy et al., 1998).

Group-serving bias

Thomas Pettigrew (1979, 1980) argues that attribution errors can bias people's explanations of group members' behaviours. We grant members of our own group the benefit of the doubt: "She donated because she has a good heart; he refused because he had to under the circumstances." When explaining acts by members of other groups, we more often assume the worst: "He donated to gain favour; she refused because she's selfish." Hence, as we noted earlier in this chapter, the shove that Whites perceive as mere "horsing around" when done by another White becomes a "violent gesture" when done by a Black (Duncan, 1976).

Positive behaviour by outgroup members is more often dismissed. It may be seen as a "special case" ("He is certainly bright and hardworking—not at all like other Hispanics"), as owing to luck or some special advantage ("She probably got admitted just because her med school had to fill its quota for women applicants"), as demanded by the situation ("Under the circumstances, what could the cheap Scot do but pay the whole cheque?"), or as attributable to extra effort ("Jewish students get better grades because they're so compulsive"). Disadvantaged groups exhibit less of this **group-serving bias** (Fletcher & Ward, 1989; Hewstone & Ward, 1985; Jackson et al., 1993).

group-serving bias explaining away outgroup members' positive behaviours; also attributing negative behaviours to their dispositions (while excusing such behaviour by one's own group)

The group-serving bias can subtly colour our language. A team of University of Padova (Italy) researchers led by Anne Maass (1995, 1996, 1998) has found that positive behaviours by another ingroup member are often described as general dispositions (for example, "Lucy is helpful"). When performed by an outgroup member, the same behaviour is often described as a specific, isolated act ("Maria opened the door for the man with the cane"). With negative behaviour, the specificity reverses: "Joe shoved her" vs. "Juan was aggressive." Maass calls this group-serving bias the *linguistic intergroup bias.*

Earlier we noted that blaming the victim can justify the blamer's own superior status (Table 12–1). Blaming occurs as people attribute an outgroup's failures to its members' flawed dispositions, notes Miles Hewstone (1990): "They fail because they're stupid; we fail because

TABLE 12–1 How self-enhancing social identities support stereotypes

	Ingroup	Outgroup
Attitude	Favouritism	Denigration
Perceptions	Heterogeneity (we differ)	Homogeneity (they're alike)
Attributions for negative behaviour	To situations	To dispositions

we didn't try." If women, Blacks, or Jews have been abused, they must somehow have brought it on themselves. When the British made a group of German civilians walk through the Bergen-Belsen concentration camp at the close of the Second World War, one German responded: "What terrible criminals these prisoners must have been to receive such treatment."

SUMMING UP: COGNITIVE SOURCES OF PREJUDICE

A fresh look at prejudice in recent research shows how the stereotyping that underlies prejudice is a by-product of our thinking—our ways of simplifying the world. First, clustering people into categories exaggerates the uniformity within a group and the differences between groups. Second, a distinctive individual, such as a lone minority person, has a compelling quality. Such persons make us aware of differences that would otherwise go unnoticed. The occurrence of two distinctive events—perhaps a minority person committing an unusual crime—helps create an *illusory correlation* between people and behaviour. Third, attributing others' behaviour to their dispositions can lead to the group-serving bias: assigning outgroup members' negative behavior to their natural character while explaining away their positive behaviours.

WHAT ARE THE CONSEQUENCES OF PREJUDICE?

Beyond the causes of prejudice, it is important to examine its consequences. Stereotypes can be self-perpetuating—their existence can prevent their change. Stereotypes can also create their own reality. Even if they are initially untrue, their existence can make them become true. The negative allegations of prejudice can also undermine people's performance and affect how people interpret discrimination.

SELF-PERPETUATING STEREOTYPES

Prejudice is prejudgment. Prejudgments are inevitable: None of us is a dispassionate bookkeeper of social happenings, tallying evidence for and against our biases. Our prejudgments guide our attention, our interpretations, and our memories. For example, once we judge an item as belonging to a category such as a particular race or sex, our memory for it shifts toward the features we associate with that category. Johanne Huart and his colleagues (2005) demonstrated this by showing Belgian university students a computer generated face that was a blend of 70 percent of the features of the typical male and 30 percent female (or vice versa). Later, those shown the 70 percent of the features of a typical male recalled seeing a male (as you might expect), but also misrecalled the face as being more typically male than it actually was.

> *"Labels act like shrieking sirens, deafening us to all finer discriminations that we might otherwise perceive."*
>
> Gordon Allport, *The Nature of Prejudice*, 1954

Prejudgments also guide our interpretations. Whenever a member of a group behaves as expected, we duly note the fact; our prior belief is confirmed. When a member of a group behaves inconsistently with our expectation, we may explain away the behaviour as due to special circumstances (Crocker et al., 1983). The contrast to a stereotype can also make someone seem exceptional. Telling someone that "Maria played hockey" and others that "Mark played hockey" may make Maria seem more athletic than Mark (Biernat, 2003). Stereotypes therefore influence how we construe someone's behaviour (Kunda & Sherman-Williams, 1993; Sanbonmatsu et al., 1994; Stangor & McMillan, 1992).

Perhaps you, too, can recall a time when, try as you might, you could not overcome someone's opinion of you, a time when no matter what you did you were misinterpreted. Misinterpretations are likely when someone *expects* an unpleasant encounter with you (Wilder & Shapiro, 1989). William Ickes and his colleagues (1982) demonstrated this in an experiment with pairs of university-age men. Upon arrival, the experimenters falsely forewarned one member of each pair that the other subject was "one of the unfriendliest people I've talked to lately." The two were then introduced and left alone together for five minutes. Students in another condition were led to think the other subject was exceptionally friendly.

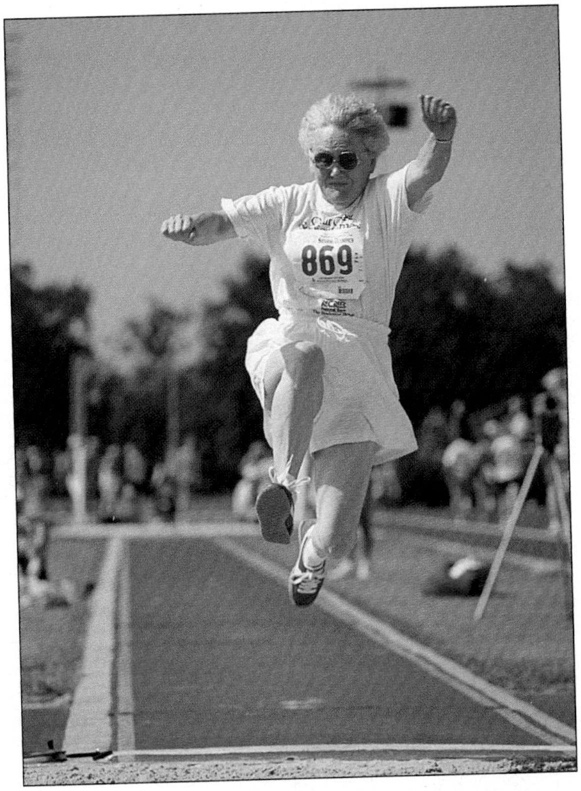

When people violate our stereotypes, we salvage the stereotype by splitting off a new subgroup stereotype, such as "senior Olympians."

Those in both conditions were friendly to the new acquaintance. In fact, those who expected him to be *un*friendly went out of their way to be friendly, and their smiles and other friendly behaviours elicited a warm response. But unlike the positively biased students, those expecting an unfriendly person attributed this reciprocal friendliness to their own "kid-gloves" treatment of him. They afterwards expressed more mistrust and dislike for the person and rated his behaviour as less friendly. Despite their partner's actual friendliness, the negative bias induced these students to "see" hostilities lurking beneath his "forced smiles." As researcher David Hamilton (1981) quipped, "I wouldn't have seen it if I hadn't believed it!"

We do notice information that is strikingly inconsistent with a stereotype, but even this information has less impact than might be expected. When we focus on an atypical example, we can salvage the stereotype by splitting off a new category (Brewer, 1988; Hewstone, 1994; Kunda & Oleson, 1995, 1997). The positive image that British schoolchildren form of their friendly school police officers (whom they perceive as a special category) doesn't improve their image of police officers in general (Hewstone et al., 1992). This **subtyping**—putting people who deviate into a different class of people—helps maintain the stereotype that police officers are unfriendly and dangerous (Figure 12-6). A different way to accommodate the inconsistent information is to recognize that the stereotype does not apply for everyone in the category. Homeowners who have desirable Black neighbours can form a new and different stereotype of "professional, middle-class Blacks." This **subgrouping**—forming a subgroup stereotype—tends to lead to modest change in the stereotype as the stereotype becomes more differentiated (Richards & Hewstone, 2001). Subtypes are exceptions to the group; subgroups are acknowledged as a part of the overall group.

subtyping accommodating groups of individuals who deviate from one's stereotype by thinking of them as a special category of people with different properties

subgrouping accommodating groups of individuals who deviate from one's stereotype by forming a new stereotype about this subset of the group

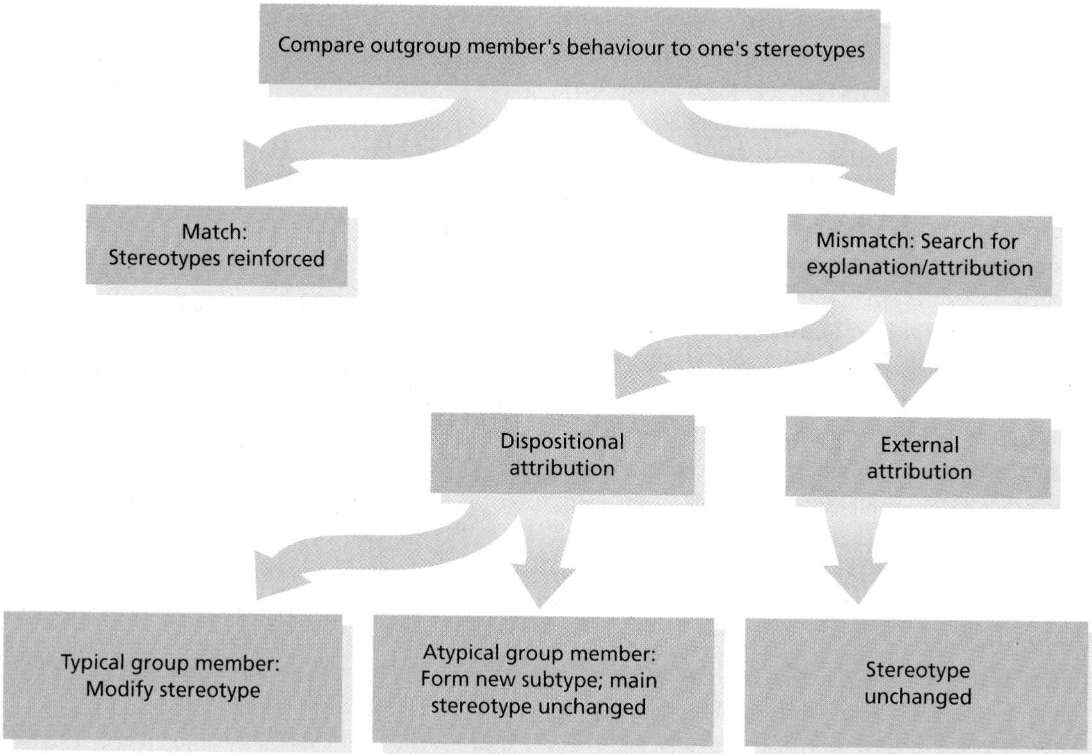

FIGURE 12–6

Attribution and stereotype change.

When someone's behaviour doesn't fit our stereotype, we can change the stereotype, split off a subtype, or attribute the behaviour to the peculiar situation. (After Hewstone, 1989 and Wilder et al., 1996)

DISCRIMINATION'S IMPACT: THE SELF-FULFILLING PROPHECY

Attitudes may coincide with the social hierarchy not only as a rationalization for it but also because discrimination affects its victims. "One's reputation," wrote Gordon Allport, "cannot be hammered, hammered, hammered into one's head without doing something to one's character" (1958, p. 139). If we could snap our fingers and end all discrimination, it would be naive then to say, "The tough times are all over, folks! You can now put on suits or dresses and be attaché-carrying executives and professionals." When the oppression ends, its effects linger, like a societal hangover.

In *The Nature of Prejudice*, Allport catalogued 15 possible effects of victimization. Allport believed these reactions were reducible to two basic types—those that involve blaming oneself (withdrawal, self-hate, aggression against one's own group) and those that involve blaming external causes (fighting back, suspiciousness, increased group pride). If the net results are negative—say, higher rates of crime—people can use them to justify the discrimination that helps maintain them: "If we let those people in our nice neighbourhood, property values will plummet."

Does discrimination affect its victims in this way? We must be careful not to overstate the point. The soul and style of Black culture is for many a proud heritage, not just a response to victimization (Jones, 1983). Thus, while White youth are learning to de-emphasize ethnic differences and avoid stereotypes, Black youth "are increasingly taking pride in their ethnicity and positively valuing ethnic differences," report Charles Judd and his co-researchers (1995).

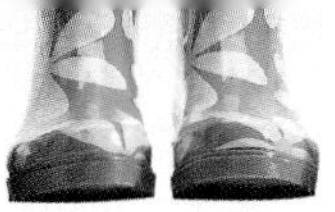

Nevertheless, social beliefs *can* be self-confirming, as demonstrated in a clever pair of experiments by Carl Word, Mark Zanna, and Joel Cooper (1974). In the first experiment, Princeton University White men interviewed White and Black research assistants posing as job applicants. When the applicant was Black, the interviewers sat farther away, ended the interview 25 percent sooner, and made 50 percent more speech errors than when the applicant was White. Imagine being interviewed by someone who sat at a distance, stammered, and ended the interview rather quickly. Would it affect your performance or your feelings about the interviewer?

To find out, the researchers conducted a second experiment in which trained interviewers treated students as the interviewers in the first experiment had treated either the White or Black applicants. When videotapes of the interviews were later rated, those who were treated like the Blacks in the first experiment seemed more nervous and less effective. Moreover, the interviewees could themselves sense a difference; those treated as were the Blacks judged their interviewers to be less adequate and less friendly. The experimenters concluded part of "the 'problem' of black performance resides . . . within the interaction setting itself." As with other self-fulfilling prophecies (recall Chapter 3) prejudice affects its targets.

"It is understandable that the suppressed people should develop an intense hostility towards a culture whose existence they make possible by their work, but in whose wealth they have too small a share."

Sigmund Freud, *The Future of an Illusion*, 1927

"If we foresee evil in our fellow man, we tend to provoke it; if good, we elicit it."

Gordon Allport, The *Nature of Prejudice*, 1958

STEREOTYPE THREAT

Placed in a situation in which others expect you to perform poorly, your anxiety may cause you to confirm the belief. One of the authors is a short guy in his late 50s. When he joins a pickup basketball game with bigger, younger players, he often suspects that they expect him to be a detriment to their team and that tends to undermine his confidence and performance. Claude Steele and his colleagues call this phenomenon **stereotype threat**—a self-confirming apprehension that one will be evaluated based on a negative stereotype (Steele, 1997; Steele, Spencer & Aronson, 2002).

stereotype threat a disruptive concern, when facing a negative stereotype, that one will be evaluated based on a negative stereotype. Unlike self-fulfilling prophecies that hammer one's reputation into one's self-concept, stereotype threat situations have immediate effects.

In several experiments, Steven Spencer, Claude Steele, and Diane Quinn (1999) gave a very difficult math test to men and women students who had similar math backgrounds. When told that there were *no* gender differences on the test and no evaluation of any group stereotype, the women's performance consistently equalled the men's. Told that there *was* a gender difference, the women dramatically confirmed the stereotype (Figure 12–7). Frustrated by the extremely difficult items, they apparently felt added apprehension, which undermined their performances.

The media can provoke stereotype threat. Paul Davies and his colleagues (2002) had women and men watch a series of commercials expecting that they would be tested for their memory of details. For half the participants, the commercials contained only neutral stimuli; for the other half, some of the commercials contained images of "airheaded" women. After seeing the stereotypic images, women not only performed worse than men on a math test, they also reported less interest in obtaining a math or science major or entering a math or science career.

"Math class is tough!"

"Teen Talk" Barbie Doll (later removed from the market)

Might racial stereotypes be similarly self-fulfilling? Steele and Joshua Aronson (1995) confirmed that they are when giving difficult verbal abilities tests to Whites and Blacks. Blacks

FIGURE 12–7

Stereotype threat and women's math performance.

Steven Spencer, Claude Steele, and Diane Quinn (1999) gave equally capable men and women a difficult math test. When participants were led to believe there were gender differences on the test, women scored lower than men. When the threat of confirming the stereotype was removed (when gender differences were not expected), women did just as well as men.

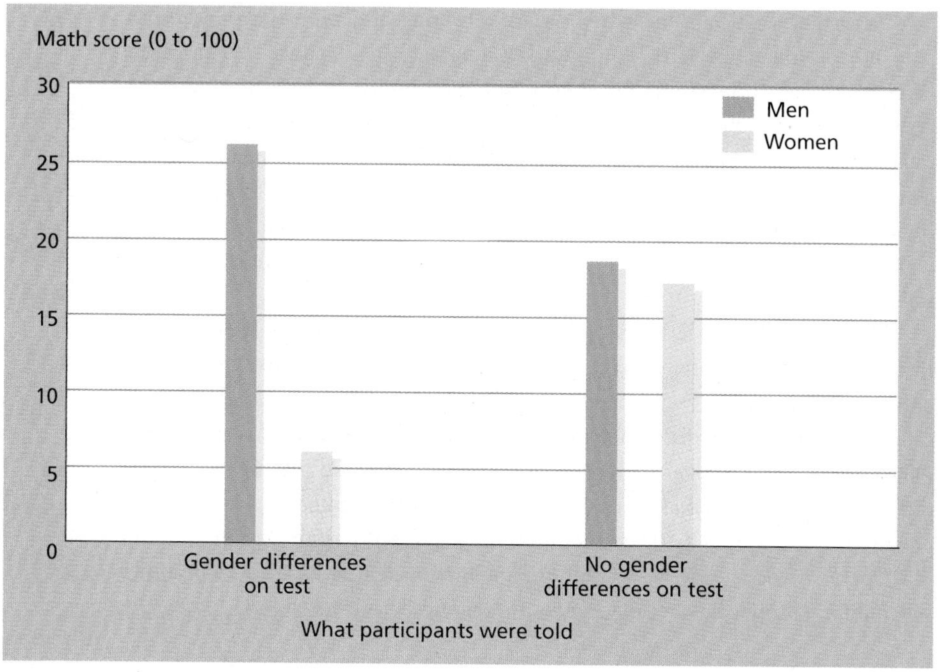

underperformed Whites only when taking the tests under conditions high in stereotype threat. Jeff Stone and his colleagues (1999) report that stereotype threat affects athletic performance, too. Blacks did worse than usual when a golf task was framed as a test of "sports intelligence," and Whites did worse when it was a test of "natural athletic ability." "When people are reminded of a negative stereotype about themselves—'White men can't jump' or 'Black men can't think'—it can adversely affect performance," Stone (2000) surmised.

If you tell students they are at risk of failure (as is often suggested by minority support programs), the stereotype may erode their performance, says Steele (1997), and cause them to "disidentify" with school and seek self-esteem elsewhere (Figure 12–8). Indeed, as Black students move from grade 8 to grade 10, there is a weakening connection between their school performance and self-esteem (Osborne, 1995). Moreover, students led to think they have benefited from gender- or race-based preferences in gaining admission to a college or an academic group tend to underperform those who are led to feel competent (Brown et al., 2000). Better, therefore, to challenge students to believe in their potential, observes Steele. In another of his research team's experiments, Black students responded well to criticism of their writing when also told, "I wouldn't go to the trouble of giving you this feedback if I didn't think, based on what I've read in your letter, that you are capable of meeting the higher standard that I mentioned" (Cohen et al., 1999).

But how does stereotype threat undermine performance? Toni Schmader and her colleagues (Schmader, Johns & Forbes, 2008) have identified three distinct ways that stereotype threat interferes with performance. One rout is emotional: stereotype threat causes stress and this stress interferes with functioning in the prefrontal cortex of the brain which plays an important role in complex problem solving. A second rout is cognitive: Stereotype threat is distracting causing people to actively monitor their performance. The effort it takes to monitor

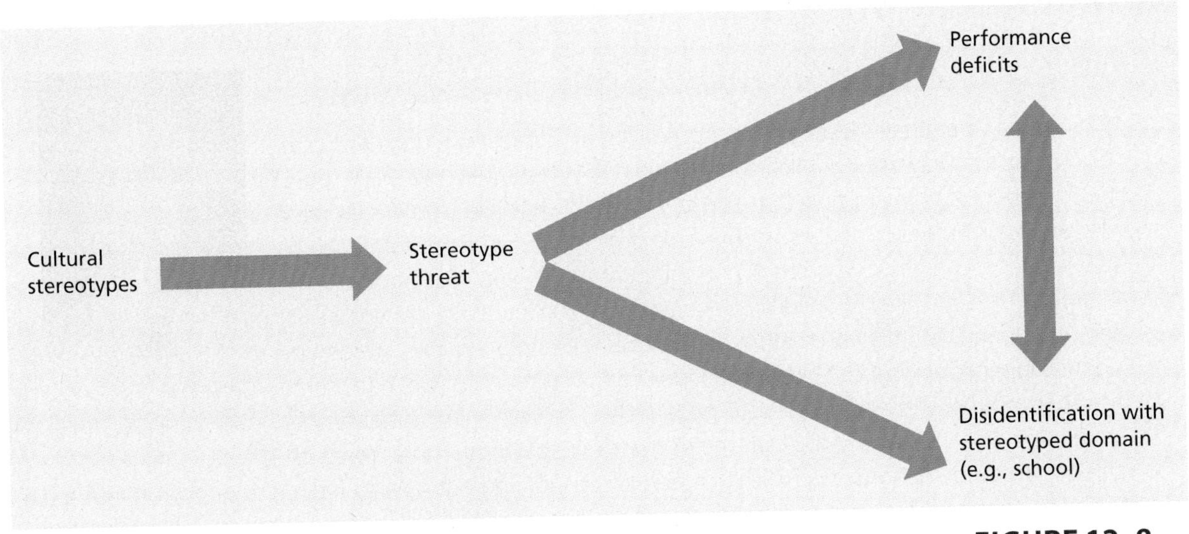

FIGURE 12–8
Threat from facing a negative stereotype can produce performance deficits and disidentification.

one's performance in this way increases mental demands and decreases working memory (Croizet et al., 2004; Schmader & Johns, 2003; Steele et al., 2002). The third route is motivational: people try to suppress negative thoughts and feelings that they may be fulfilling the stereotype and the energy this requires also impairs performance (Logel et al., 2008).

If stereotype threats can disrupt performance, could *positive* stereotypes enhance it? Margaret Shih, Todd Pittinsky, and Nalini Ambady (1999) confirmed this possibility. When Asian-American females were asked biographical questions that reminded them of their gender identity before taking a math test, their performance plunged (compared to a control group). When similarly reminded of their Asian identity, their performance rose. Negative stereotypes disrupt performance and positive stereotypes, it seems, facilitate performance.

DO STEREOTYPES BIAS JUDGMENTS OF INDIVIDUALS?

Yes, stereotypes bias judgments, but here is good news: *People often evaluate individuals more positively than the groups they compose* (Miller & Felicio, 1990). Anne Locksley, Eugene Borgida, and Nancy Brekke have found that once someone knows a person, "Stereotypes may have minimal, if any, impact on judgments about that person" (Borgida et al., 1981; Locksley et al., 1980, 1982). They discovered this by giving university students anecdotal information about recent incidents in the life of "Nancy." In a supposed transcript of a telephone conversation, Nancy told a friend how she responded to three different situations (for example, being harassed by a seedy character while shopping). Some of the students read transcripts portraying Nancy responding assertively (telling the seedy character to leave); others read a report of passive responses (simply ignoring the character until he finally drifts away). Still other students received the same information, except that the person was named "Paul" instead of Nancy. A day later the students predicted how Nancy (or Paul) would respond to other situations.

Did knowing the person's sex have any effect on these predictions? None at all. Expectations of the person's assertiveness were influenced solely by what the students had learned about that individual the day before. Even their judgments of

"There are no good women climbers. Women climbers either aren't good climbers or they aren't real women."

Anonymous climber
(cited by Rothbart & Lewis, 1988)

STORY BEHIND THE RESEARCH

Claude Steele
Stanford University

During a committee meeting on campus diversity at the University of Michigan in the late 1980s, I noticed an interesting fact: at every level of entering SAT score, minority students were getting lower college grades than their non-minority counterparts. Soon, Steven Spencer, Joshua Aronson, and I found that this was a national phenomenon; it happened at most colleges and it happened to other groups whose abilities were negatively stereotyped, such as women in advanced math classes. This underperformance wasn't caused by group differences in preparation. It happened at all levels of preparation (as measured by SATs).

Eventually, we produced this underperformance in the laboratory by simply having motivated people perform a difficult task in a domain where their group was negatively stereotyped. We also found that we could eliminate this underperformance by making the same task irrelevant to the stereotype, by removing the "stereotype threat," as we had come to call it. This latter finding spawned more research: figuring out how to reduce stereotype threat and its ill effects. Through this work, we have gained an appreciation for two big things: first, the importance of life context in shaping psychological functioning, and second, the importance of social identities like age, race, and gender in shaping that context.

masculinity and femininity were unaffected by knowing the person's sex. Gender stereotypes had been left on the shelf; the students evaluated Nancy and Paul as individuals.

An important principle discussed in Chapter 3 explains that finding. Given (1) general (base-rate) information about a group and (2) trivial but vivid information about a particular group member, the vivid information usually overwhelms the effect of the general information. This is especially so when the person doesn't fit our image of the typical group member (Fein & Hilton, 1992; Lord et al., 1991). For example, imagine yourself being told how *most* people in an experiment actually behaved and then viewing a brief interview with one of the supposed subjects. Would you react like the typical viewer—by guessing the person's behaviour from the interview, ignoring the base-rate information on how most people actually behaved?

People often believe such stereotypes, yet ignore them when given vivid, anecdotal information. Thus, many people believe "politicians are crooks" but "our MP Mr. Jones has integrity." (No wonder people have such a low opinion of politicians yet usually re-elect their own representatives.)

These findings resolve a puzzling set of findings considered early in this chapter. We know that gender stereotypes (1) are strong yet (2) have little effect on people's judgments of work attributed to a man or a woman. Now we see why. People may have strong gender stereotypes yet ignore them when judging a particular individual.

Strong stereotypes matter

Strong and seemingly relevant stereotypes do, however, colour our judgments of individuals as well as groups. When Thomas Nelson, Monica Biernat, and Melvin Manis (1990) had students

estimate the heights of individually pictured men and women, they judged the individual men as taller—even when their heights were equal, even when they were told that in this sample sex didn't predict height, and even when they were offered cash rewards for accuracy.

In a follow-up study, Nelson, Michele Acker, and Manis (1996) showed university students photos of other students from the university's engineering and nursing schools, along with descriptions of each student's interests. Even when informed that the sample contained an equal number of males and females from each school, the same description was judged more likely to come from a nursing student when attached to a female face. Thus, even when a strong gender stereotype is known to be irrelevant, it has an irresistible force.

Stereotypes bias interpretations and memories

Stereotypes also colour how we interpret events, note David Dunning and David Sherman (1997). If told, "some felt the politician's statements were untrue," people will infer the politician was lying. If told, "some felt the physicist's statements were untrue," they infer only that the physicist was mistaken. When told two people had an altercation, people perceive it as a fist fight if told it involved two lumberjacks, but as a verbal spat if told it involved two marriage counsellors. A person concerned about her physical condition seems vain if she is a model but health conscious if a triathelete. Indeed, subjects will often later "recognize" false descriptions of an event that fit their stereotype-influenced interpretations. As a prison guides and constrains its inmates, conclude Dunning and Sherman, the "cognitive prison" of our stereotypes guides and constrains our impressions.

Sometimes we make judgments, or begin interacting with someone, with little to go on but our stereotype. In such cases stereotypes can strongly bias our interpretations and memories of people. For example, Charles Bond and his colleagues (1988) found that, after getting to know their patients, White psychiatric nurses equally often put Black and White patients in physical restraints. But they restrained *incoming* Black patients more often than their White counterparts. With little else to go on, stereotypes mattered.

Such bias can also operate more subtly. In an experiment by John Darley and Paget Gross (1983), students viewed a videotape of a grade-four girl, Hannah. The tape depicted her either in a depressed urban neighbourhood, supposedly the child of lower-class parents, or in an affluent suburban setting, the child of professional parents. Asked to guess Hannah's ability level in various subjects, both groups of viewers refused to use Hannah's class background to prejudge her ability level; each group rated her ability level at her grade level. Other students also viewed a second videotape, showing Hannah taking an oral achievement test in which she got some questions right and some wrong.

Those who had previously been introduced to upper-class Hannah judged her answers as showing high ability and later recalled her getting most questions right; those who had met lower-class Hannah judged her ability as below grade level and recalled her missing almost half the questions. But remember: The second videotape was *identical* for both groups. So we see that when stereotypes are strong and the information about someone is ambiguous (unlike the cases of Nancy and Paul), stereotypes can *subtly* bias our judgments of individuals.

Finally, we evaluate people more extremely when their behaviour violates our stereotypes (Bettencourt et al., 1997). A woman who rebukes someone cutting in front of her in a movie line ("Shouldn't you go to the end of the line?") may seem more assertive than a man who

STORY BEHIND THE RESEARCH

Ziva Kunda had long been interested in how people's motives and desires coloured their judgment. Her earlier work suggested that people attempted to be rational, and drew their desired conclusions only if they could justify them. However, they often did not realize that their justifications could be biased by their motives—when constructing justifications, people search selectively for those beliefs that lend support to their desired conclusion. If they could successfully recruit such beliefs, they could draw their desired conclusion, not realizing that they may also possess other beliefs that argue against it. It occurred to Lisa Sinclair and Ziva that a negative group stereotype may sometimes provide a handy justification for disparaging a group member whom one is motivated to discredit. People may be motivated to discredit anyone who has criticized them, but may be better able to justify disparaging a woman or a member or a visible minority than disparaging a White man. As a result, people may view a woman or a Black man who criticizes them more negatively than they view a White man who delivers the same criticism.

Ziva Kunda
University of Waterloo

reacts similarly (Manis et al., 1988). Are your ratings of your professors affected by such processes? A series of studies (Kunda & Sinclair, 1999; Sinclair & Kunda, 1999; Sinclair & Kunda, 2000) by University of Winnipeg professor Lisa Sinclair and University of Waterloo professor Ziva Kunda suggests that they might very well be. They analyzed students' evaluations of their professors and found that when students get good grades they tend to like their professors, and this is true whether their professors are men or women. When students get bad grades, however, they are especially harsh on female professors.

Kunda and Sinclair have found similar findings in a series of laboratory studies. After completing a test of leadership ability while being watched by a "manager" in an adjacent room, participants were praised or criticized on their performance by the manager. When they were praised the participants liked both the male and the female manager, but when they were criticized they evaluated the female manager much more negatively. In another study, they found similar results with White and Black male managers (see Figure 12–9).

SUMMING UP: WHAT ARE THE CONSEQUENCES OF PREJUDICE?

Prejudice and stereotyping have important consequences when judging unknown individuals and when deciding policies regarding whole groups. Once formed, stereotypes tend to perpetuate themselves and resist change. They also create their own realities through self-fulfilling prophecies. Prejudice can also undermine people's performances through stereotype threat, by making them apprehensive that others will view them stereotypically. Stereotypes also predispose how we perceive people and interpret events.

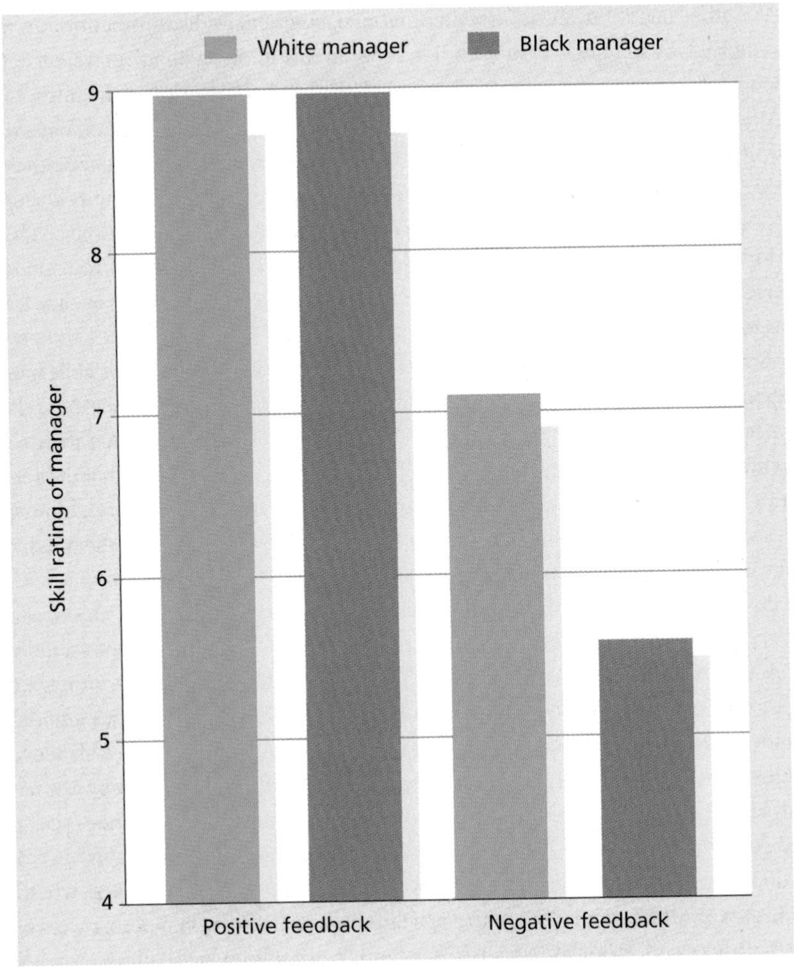

FIGURE 12-9

Harsher evaluation of a stereotyped target.

When University of Waterloo students received positive feedback from a "manager," his race did not matter, but when they received negative feedback, they saw a Black manager as less competent than a White manager. (Data from Sinclair & Kunda 1999)

REACTIONS TO PREJUDICE AND STEREOTYPING

Over the last 15 years, numerous studies have begun to investigate "the other side of prejudice"—that is, how people cope with prejudiced evaluation by others. So far we have examined the social, emotional, and cognitive sources of prejudice and stereotyping, but prejudice also has consequences. People who experience discrimination know these consequences all too well, but they do not always acknowledge them.

Despite the fact that people are reluctant to acknowledge experiencing personal discrimination, they understand that there are times when they are being discriminated against, and this understanding has costs and benefits. On the one hand, if people come to believe that others will be prejudiced against them, they can lose a sense of control over their environment. In general, the more that people believe they experience discrimination, the more anxious and depressed they are (Branscombe et al., 1999). Believing that one experiences pervasive prejudice is a downer.

On the other hand, however, believing that one experiences discrimination can also protect self-esteem. Crocker and Major (1989) first noted this in reviewing the level of self-esteem of a number of groups in society. Recall from Chapter 2 that we often form our views of ourselves from how we are viewed by others. Applying this theory to groups that experience prejudice, it seems that these groups would have lower self-esteem, but in general they do not. Negatively valued ethnic groups, the physically handicapped, and the facially disfigured all have self-esteem as high as or higher than those who do not face these challenges. What would account for these robust feelings of self-esteem? Crocker and Major argue that one way such groups protect their self-esteem is by attributing the negative evaluations they face in specific situations to prejudice.

The first studies to test these ideas were conducted by Ken Dion and his colleagues at the University of Toronto (Dion, 1975; Dion & Earn, 1975). In one study (Dion, 1975), Dion had women receive either a few or a lot of tickets from confederates who were either male or female. When women received only a few tickets from the male confederates, they attributed the males' actions to prejudice, but they did not do so when the confederates were female. These groundbreaking studies demonstrate that people who face prejudice are vigilant to the possibility that others may discriminate against them.

But do such attributions protect self-esteem? A number of studies by Crocker, Major, and their colleagues suggest that they do (Major, Quinton & McCoy, 2002). In one study (Crocker, Voekl, Testa & Major, 1991), the researchers gave Blacks and Whites positive or negative feedback from a fellow student who either listened to their performance in an adjacent room (and could not see them because blinds separating the rooms were drawn) or listened to and watched their performance with the blinds open. When Blacks were negatively evaluated with the blinds closed, their self-esteem suffered, but when the blinds were open they appeared to be protected from the negative feedback and their self-esteem was unaffected.

So, do perceptions help or hurt? The answer seems to be that it depends on whether these perceptions are chronic or in response to a specific situation. Those who perceive chronic prejudice in their lives suffer, but in response to a specific negative event, believing that the event was due to prejudice can protect one's self-esteem.

PERCEPTION OF DISCRIMINATION

Most women know that gender bias exists. They believe that sex discrimination affects most working women, as shown by the lower salaries for women and especially for jobs, such as child care, that are filled mostly by women. Garbage haulers (mostly men) make more than preschool teachers (mostly women). Curiously, however, Faye Crosby and her colleagues (1989) have repeatedly found that most women deny feeling personally discriminated against. Discrimination, they believe, is something *other* women face. Their employers are not villainous. They are doing better than the average woman. Hearing no complaints, managers—even in discriminatory organizations—can persuade themselves that justice prevails.

Similar denials of *personal* disadvantage, while perceiving discrimination against one's *group,* occur among unemployed people, out-of-the-closet lesbians, and Canadian minorities (Dion & Kawakami, 1996; Taylor et al., 1990). This *personal/group discrimination discrepancy,* as Donald Taylor and his colleagues (1990) label the phenomenon, enables individuals to maintain a perception of control over their performance and relationships (see Figure 12–10). (Curiously however, personal/group discrepancy extends to nondiscriminatory events. People also see others as more likely than themselves to be affected by, say, an economic recession, rising health costs, and better physical fitness facilities—Moghaddam et al., 1997).

It is not only the concerns of those who have traditionally faced prejudice but also the concerns of those who have not that make social interactions difficult. Jacquie Vorauer from the University of Manitoba and her colleagues (Vorauer, Main & O'Connell, 1998; Vorauer, Hunter, Main & Roy, 2000) have examined the concerns that members of dominant groups have about the stereotypes that others have of them—meta-stereotypes (a stereotype about stereotypes). They found that at the University of Manitoba White students have very clear ideas about the stereotypes that First Nations Canadians may have about them. They are concerned that First Nations people may view them as prejudiced, unfair, selfish, arrogant, phony, etc.

In a series of studies they led White students to believe that they would be interacting with First Nations Canadians. The more that students expected to be perceived in terms of the meta-stereotype, the more they anticipated experiencing negative emotions in the interaction. Interestingly, highly prejudiced White students expected to be perceived in terms of the meta-stereotype more than less prejudiced students. These meta-stereotypes were more important in predicting their reaction to the situation than the students' level of prejudice itself.

Vorauer along with Nicole Shelton and Jennier Richeson (Shelton, Richeson & Vorauer, 2006) have described how these processes affect inter-ethnic interactions. They find that concerns about being seen in a stereotypic way leads to awkward interactions (Shelton & Richeson, 2006) and decreased executive functioning among White students (Trawalter & Richeson, 2006). Overcoming these obstacles seems to be an essential step in promoting better relationships across groups.

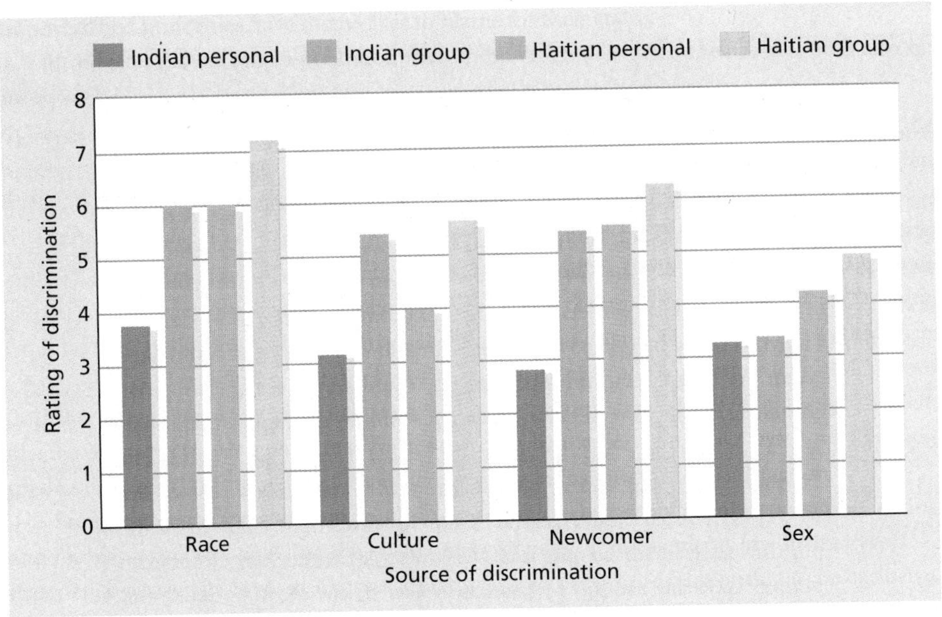

FIGURE 12–10

The personal/group discrimination discrepancy.

People report experiencing very little discrimination personally, but they do perceive discrimination against their group. (Taylor et al., 1990)

STORY BEHIND THE RESEARCH

Don Taylor
McGill University

We were on a mission to get mainstream social psychology to broaden its individualistic emphasis and recognize intergroup relations as a central topic. Systemic discrimination was a key preoccupation for us and being the "white male" I would often ask female and visible minority students to describe their experiences with discrimination. I began to notice a theme to their responses, which took the form—"Well, I personally have never faced discrimination, but my group is unfairly treated in the following ways."

We were embarking on a large field study involving visible minority immigrants to Canada from all walks of life, and wanted to gauge the extent to which they felt discriminated against. We decided to ask participants to rate, in two separate questions, the extent to which their group, and they personally as a member of their group, had been discriminated against.

The personal/group discrimination discrepancy was born. Respondents consistently rated discrimination directed at their group to be higher than discrimination directed at themselves personally, as a member of that group.

The methodological implications were immediate and obvious. Any attempt to gauge societal prejudice and discrimination would produce very different conclusions depending on the focus of the question, personal or group. A group-based question would portray society as relatively prejudiced, whereas a question about personal discrimination would give the impression that society was relatively free from bigotry.

The bigger challenge, of course, is to explain the personal/group discrimination discrepancy. Perhaps one of you will take it up.

SUMMING UP: REACTIONS TO PREJUDICE AND STEREOTYPING

Reactions to experiencing prejudice and discrimination are varied. On one hand, blaming poor performance on prejudice can be a way to protect self-esteem. On the other hand, people are reluctant to acknowledge that they individually experience prejudice. Targets of prejudice are thus often vigilant to the possibility of being discriminated against but also are motivated to deny that such discrimination actually occurs.

MODULES

SOCIAL PSYCHOLOGY APPLIED

Throughout this book, we have aimed to link laboratory to life by relating social psychology's principles and findings to everyday happenings. We now conclude by recollecting a number of these big ideas and applying them in four practical contexts. Module A, "Social Psychology in Conflict and Peacemaking," considers how social conflicts develop and how they can be justly and amicably resolved. Module B, "Social Psychology in the Clinic," applies social psychology to evaluating and promoting mental and physical health. Module C, "Social Psychology in Court," explores social thinking and social influences on jurors and juries. Module D, "Social Psychology and the Sustainable Future," asks what social psychological principles might contribute to help avert an ecological holocaust, triggered by increasing population, consumption, and global warming.

MODULE A

Social Psychology in Conflict and Peacemaking

What creates conflict?
Social dilemmas
Perceived injustice
Misperception

How can peace be achieved?
Bargaining
Mediation
Arbitration
Conciliation

There is a speech that has been spoken in many languages by the leaders of many countries. It goes like this: "The intentions of our country are entirely peaceful. Yet, we are also aware that other nations, with their new weapons, threaten us. Thus we must defend ourselves against attack. By so doing, we shall protect our way of life and preserve the peace" (Richardson, 1960). Almost every nation claims concern only for peace but, mistrusting other nations, arms itself in self-defence. The result is a world that spends US$2 billion per day on arms and armies while hundreds of millions die of malnutrition and untreated disease.

The elements of such **conflict** (a perceived incompatibility of actions or goals) are similar at many levels, whether we examine conflict between nations in an arms race, religious factions disputing points of doctrine, corporate executives and workers disputing salaries, to a bickering married couple. Whether their perceptions are accurate or inaccurate, people in conflict sense that one side's gain is the other's loss. "We want peace and security." "So do we, but you threaten us." "We want more pay." "We can't afford to give it to you." "I'd like the music off." "I'd like it on." Sometimes the result is that everybody loses, as when a salary cap impasse between owners and players caused the 2005 National Hockey League season to be cancelled.

conflict
a perceived incompatibility of actions or goals

A relationship or an organization without conflict is probably apathetic. Conflict signifies involvement, commitment, and caring. If understood, if recognized, it can stimulate renewed and improved human relations. Without conflict, people seldom face and resolve their problems.

Peace, in its most positive sense, is more than the suppression of open conflict, more than a fragile superficial calm. Peace is the outcome of a creatively managed conflict. Peace is the parties reconciling their perceived differences and reach genuine accord. "We got our increased pay. You got your increased profit. Now we're helping each other achieve our aspirations." Peace, says peace researcher Royce Anderson (2004), "is a condition in which individuals, families, groups, communities, and/or nations experience low levels of violence and engage in mutually harmonious relationships."

WHAT CREATES CONFLICT?

Social-psychological studies have identified several ingredients. What's striking (and what simplifies our task) is that these ingredients are common to all levels of social conflict, whether interpersonal, intergroup, or international.

SOCIAL DILEMMAS

Several of the problems that most threaten our human future—nuclear arms, global warming, overpopulation, natural resource depletion—arise as various parties pursue their self-interest, ironically, to their collective detriment. Anyone can think, "It would cost me lots to buy expensive pollution controls. Besides, by itself my pollution is trivial." Many others reason similarly, and the result is unclean air and water.

In some societies individuals benefit by having many children who, they assume, can assist with the family tasks and provide security in the parents' old age. But when most families have many children, the result is the collective devastation of overpopulation. Choices that are individually rewarding become collectively punishing. We therefore have an urgent dilemma: How can we reconcile individuals' well-being, including their right to pursue their personal interests, with communal well-being?

To isolate and illustrate this dilemma, social psychologists have used laboratory games that expose the heart of many real social conflicts. By showing us how well-meaning people become

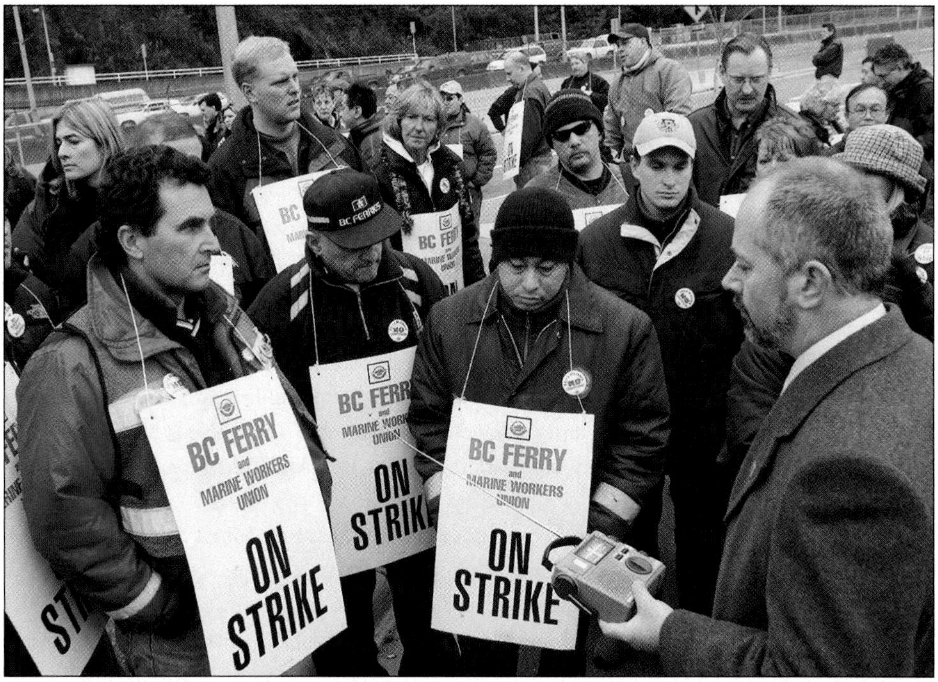

Although workers and management often cooperate in their work, they also can experience conflict, which is most evident during a strike.

trapped in mutually destructive behaviour, they illuminate some fascinating, yet troubling, paradoxes of human existence. "Social psychologists who study conflict are in much the same position as the astronomers," notes conflict researcher Morton Deutsch (1999). "We cannot conduct true experiments with large-scale social events. But we can identify the conceptual similarities between the large scale and the small, as the astronomers have between the planets and Newton's apple. That is why the games people play as subjects in our laboratory may advance our understanding of war, peace, and social justice."

social trap
a situation in which the conflicting parties, by each rationally pursuing its self-interest, become caught in mutually destructive behaviour. Examples include the Prisoner's Dilemma and the Tragedy of the Commons.

We will consider two laboratory games that are each an example of a **social trap**: the Prisoners' Dilemma and the Tragedy of the Commons.

The Prisoners' Dilemma

This dilemma derives from an anecdote concerning two suspects questioned separately by the Crown attorney (Rapoport, 1960). They are jointly guilty; however, the Crown has only enough evidence to convict them of a lesser offence. So the Crown creates an incentive for each to confess privately:

> If Prisoner A confesses and Prisoner B doesn't, the Crown will grant the confessor immunity to A, and will use the confession to convict B of a maximum offence (and vice versa if B confesses and A doesn't).
>
> If both confess, each will receive a moderate sentence.
>
> If neither confesses, each will be convicted of a lesser crime and receive a light sentence.

The matrix of Figure A–1 summarizes the choices. If you were a prisoner faced with such a dilemma, with no chance to talk to the other prisoner, would you confess?

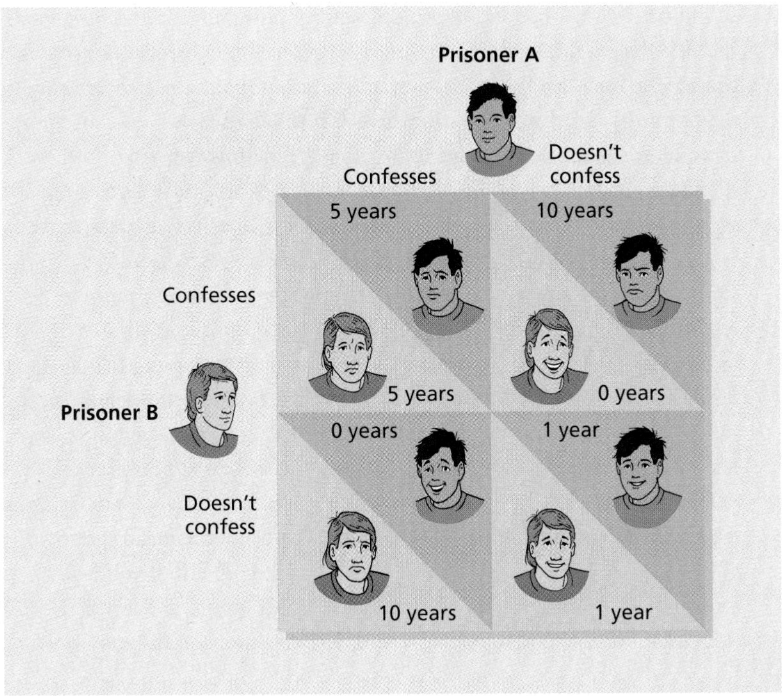

FIGURE A–1

The Prisoners' Dilemma.

In each box, the number above the diagonal is prisoner A's outcome. Thus, if both prisoners confess, both get five years. If neither confesses, each gets a year. If one confesses, that prisoner is set free in exchange for evidence used to convict the other of a crime bringing a 10-year sentence. If you were one of the prisoners, would you confess?

Many people say they would confess to be granted immunity, even though mutual non-confession elicits lighter sentences than mutual confession. Perhaps this is because (as shown in the matrix of Figure A–1) no matter what the other prisoner decides, each is better off confessing than being convicted individually. If the other also confesses, the sentence is moderate rather than severe. If the other does not confess, one goes free.

In some 2000 studies (Dawes, 1991), university students have faced variations of the Prisoners' Dilemma with the choices being to defect or cooperate, and the outcome not being prison terms but chips, money, or course points. As Figure A–2 illustrates, on any given decision, a person is better off defecting (because such behaviour exploits the other's cooperation or protects against the other's exploitation). However—and here's the rub—by not cooperating, both parties end up far worse off than if they had trusted each other and thus had gained a joint profit. This dilemma often traps each one in a maddening predicament in which both realize they *could* mutually profit. But, unable to communicate and mistrusting one another, become "locked in" to not cooperating.

"When multiplied by 2, a national policy of Peace Through Strength leads inevitably to an arms race."

George Levinger (1987)

The Tragedy of the Commons

Many social dilemmas involve more than two parties. Global warming stems from widespread deforestation and from the carbon dioxide emitted by the world's cars, furnaces, and coal-fired power plants. Each gas-guzzling SUV contributes infinitesimally to the problem, and the harm each does is diffused over many people. To model such social predicaments, researchers have developed laboratory dilemmas that involve multiple people.

FIGURE A–2

Laboratory version of the Prisoners' Dilemma.

The numbers represent some reward, such as money. In each box, the number above the diagonal lines is the outcome for person A. Unlike the Prisoners' Dilemma (a one-shot decision), most laboratory versions involve repeated plays.

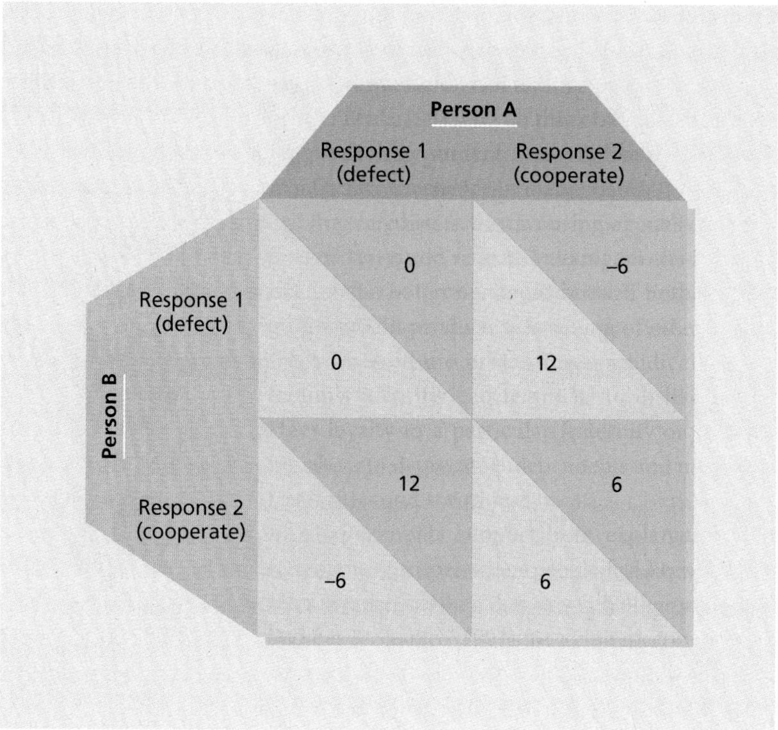

A metaphor for the insidious nature of social dilemmas is what ecologist Garrett Hardin (1968) called the "tragedy of the commons." He derived the name from the centrally located pasture area in old English towns.

In today's world the "commons" can be air, water, whales, cookies, or any shared and limited resource. If all use the resource in moderation, it may replenish itself as rapidly as it's harvested. The grass will grow, the whales will reproduce, and the cookie jar gets restocked. If not,

STORY BEHIND THE RESEARCH

I am brash enough to believe that laboratory studies of conflict can illumine our understanding of the dynamics of war, peace, and social justice. From small groups to nations, the social processes appear similar. Thus social psychologists who study conflict are in much the same position as the astronomers. We cannot conduct true experiments with large-scale social events. But we can identify the conceptual similarities between the large scale and the small, as the astronomers have between the planets and Newton's apple. By experimenting with small-scale social situations, we may thus be able to understand, predict, and influence large-scale social processes. That is why the games people play as subjects in our laboratory may advance our understanding of war, peace, and social justice.

Morton Deutsch
Columbia University

there occurs a tragedy of the commons. Imagine 100 farmers surrounding a commons capable of sustaining 100 cows. When each grazes one cow, the common feeding ground is optimally used. But then someone reasons, "If I put a second cow in the pasture, I'll double my output, minus the mere 1 percent overgrazing." So this farmer adds a second cow. So do each of the other farmers. The inevitable result? The Tragedy of the Commons—a grassless mud field.

Many real predicaments parallel this story. Internet congestion occurs as unregulated individuals, seeking to maximize their own gain, surf the Web, filling its pipelines with graphical information (Huberman & Lukose, 1997). Likewise, environmental pollution is the sum of many minor pollutions, each of which benefits the individual polluters much more than they could benefit themselves (and the environment) if they stopped polluting. We litter public places—dorm lounges, parks, zoos—while keeping our personal spaces clean. And we deplete our natural resources because the immediate personal benefits of, say, taking a long, hot shower outweigh the seemingly inconsequential costs. Whalers knew others would exploit the whales if they didn't and that taking a few whales would hardly diminish the species. Therein lay the tragedy. Everybody's business (conservation) became nobody's business.

Is such individualism unique to Western societies? Individualistic Kaori Sato (1987) gave students in a more collective culture, Japan, opportunities to harvest—for actual money—trees from a simulated forest. When the students shared equally the costs of planting the forest, the result was like those in Western cultures. More than half the trees were harvested before they had grown to the most profitable size.

Sato's forest reminds us of the cookie jars in our homes. What we *should* have done is conserve cookies during the interval between weekly restockings, so that each day we could each munch two or three. Lacking regulation and fearing that other family members would soon deplete the resource, what we actually did was maximize our individual cookie consumption by downing one after the other. The result: Within 24 hours the cookie glut would often end, the jar sitting empty for the rest of the week.

When resources are not partitioned, people often consume more than they realize (Herlocker et al., 1997). As a bowl of mashed potatoes starts passing around a table of 10, it is likely that more people will scoop out a disproportionate share than when a platter of 10 chicken drumsticks is passed.

The Prisoners' Dilemma and the Tragedy of the Commons games have several similar features. First, both tempt people to explain their own behaviour situationally ("I had to protect myself against exploitation by my opponent") and to explain their partners' behaviour dispositionally ("she was greedy," "he was untrustworthy"). Most never realize that their counterparts are viewing them with the same fundamental attribution error (Hine & Gifford, 1996). People with self-inflating, self-focused narcissistic tendencies are especially unlikely to display empathy for others' perspectives (Campbell et al., 2005).

Second, motives often change. At first, people are eager to make some easy money, then to minimize their losses, and finally to save face and avoid defeat (Brockner et al., 1982; Teger, 1980). These shifting motives can make it harder to negotiate a solution. Early on, mediators can focus on proposing resolutions that maximize the benefits to both sides. As time progresses, however, solutions must increasingly address not only the substantive issues, but they must let all parties enter an agreement with the sense that they have prevented important losses and avoided defeat.

non-zero-sum games games in which outcomes need not sum to zero. With cooperation, both can win; with competition, both can lose. (Also called *mixed-motive situations.*)

Third, most real-life conflicts, like the Prisoners' Dilemma and the Tragedy of the Commons, are **non-zero-sum games**. The two sides' profits and losses need not add up to zero. Both can win; both can lose. Each game pits the immediate interests of individuals against the well-being of the group. Each is a diabolical social trap that shows how, even when individuals behave "rationally," harm can result. No malicious person planned for Los Angeles to be smothered in smog, for the horrendous destruction of the Bosnian conflict, or for the earth's atmosphere to be warmed by a blanket of carbon dioxide.

Not all self-serving behaviour leads to collective doom. In a plentiful commons—as in the world of the eighteenth-century capitalist economist Adam Smith (1976, p. 18)—individuals who seek to maximize their own profit may also give the community what it needs: "It is not from the benevolence of the butcher, the brewer, or the baker, that we expect our dinner," he observed, "but from their regard to their own interest."

Resolving social dilemmas

In those situations that are indeed social traps, how can we induce people to cooperate for their mutual betterment? Research with the laboratory dilemmas reveals several ways (Gifford & Hine, 1997).

Regulation

If taxes were entirely voluntary, how many would pay their full share? Surely, many would not, which is why modern societies do not depend on charity to pay for social and military security. We also develop rules to safeguard our common good. Fishing and hunting have long been regulated by local seasons and limits; at the global level, an International Whaling Commission sets an agreed-upon "harvest" that enables whales to regenerate.

When after eight years of war, more than a million casualties, and ruined economies, Iran and Iraq finally laid down their arms, the border over which they had fought was exactly the same as when they started.

STEVE BENSON reprinted by permission of United Feature Syndicate, Inc.

In everyday life, however, regulation has costs—cost of administering and enforcing the regulations, cost of diminished personal freedom. A volatile political question thus arises: At what point does a regulation's cost exceed its benefits?

Small is beautiful

There is another way to resolve social dilemmas: Make the group small. In small commons, each person feels more responsible and effective (Kerr, 1989). As a group grows larger, people more often think "I couldn't have made a difference anyway"—a common excuse for noncooperation (Kerr & Kaufman-Gilliland, 1997). In small groups, people also feel more identified with a group's success. Anything else that enhances group identity will also increase cooperation. Even just a few minutes of discussion or just believing that one shares similarities with others in the group can increase "we feeling," and cooperation (Brewer, 1987; Orbell et al., 1988).

"For that which is common to the greatest number has the least care bestowed upon it."

Aristotle

In small rather than large groups, individuals are also more likely to take no more than their equal share of available resources (Allison et al., 1992). On the Puget Sound Island where one of the authors grew up, the small neighbourhood shared a communal water supply. On hot summer days when the reservoir ran low, a light came on, signalling the community's 15 families to conserve. Recognizing their responsibility to one another, and feeling as if conservation really mattered, each family conserved. Never did the reservoir run dry.

In a much larger commons—say, a city—voluntary conservation is less successful. Because the harm one does diffuses across many others, each individual can rationalize away personal accountability. Some political theorists and social psychologists therefore argue that, where feasible, the commons should be divided into smaller territories (Edney, 1980). In his 1902 *Mutual Aid*, the Russian revolutionary Pyotr Kropotkin set down a vision of small communities rather than central government making consensus decisions for the benefit of all (Gould, 1988).

Appeals to altruistic norms

In Chapter 9, we described how increasing people's feelings of responsibility for others boosts altruism. Can we therefore assume that appeals to altruistic motives will prompt people to act for the common good?

The evidence is mixed. On the one hand, it seems that just *knowing* the dire consequences of noncooperation has little effect. In laboratory games, people realize that their self-serving choices are mutually destructive, yet they continue to make them. Outside the laboratory, warnings of doom and appeals to conserve have brought little response. Pleas to carpool, conserve water, even to refrain from littering, often go unheeded. In the summer of 2003 the town of Guelph, which is near Steven Spencer's home, had a ban on lawn sprinkling, yet driving through town he would estimate that 80 percent of the lawns remained green. *Knowing* the good does not necessarily lead to doing the good.

Still, most people do adhere to norms of social responsibility, reciprocity, equity, and keeping one's commitments (Kerr, 1992). The problem is how to tap such feelings. One such way is by defining situations in ways that imply cooperative norms. Lee Ross and Andrew Ward (1996) invited Stanford dormitory advisers to nominate male students who they thought especially likely to cooperate and to defect while playing a prisoner's dilemma game. In reality the two groups of students were equally likely to cooperate. What dramatically affected

To change behaviour, many cities have changed the payoff matrix. Fast carpool-only lanes increase the benefits of carpooling and the costs of driving alone.

cooperation was whether the researchers labelled the simulation the "Wall Street Game" (in which case one-third of the participants cooperated) or the "Community Game" (with two-thirds cooperating).

"Never in the field of human conflict was so much owed by so many to so few."

Sir Winston Churchill, House of Commons, August 20, 1940

Communication can also tap altruistic norms. When permitted to communicate, participants in laboratory games frequently appeal to the social-responsibility norm: "If you defect on the rest of us, you're going to have to live with it for the rest of your life" (Dawes et al., 1977). Noting this, researcher Robyn Dawes (1980) and his associates gave people a short sermon about group benefits, exploitation, and ethics. Then the people played a dilemma game. The appeal worked: People were convinced to forgo immediate personal gain for the common good.

Could such appeals work in large-scale dilemmas? Jeffery Scott Mio and his colleagues (1993) found that, after reading about the commons dilemma (as you have), theatre patrons littered less than patrons who read about voting. Moreover, when cooperation obviously serves the public good, one can usefully appeal to the social-responsibility norm (Lynn & Oldenquist, 1986). When, for example, people believe public transportation can save time, they will be more likely to use it if they also believe it reduces pollution (Van Vugt et al., 1996). In the struggle for civil rights, many marchers willingly agreed, for the sake of the larger group, to suffer harassment, beatings, and jail. In wartime, people make great personal sacrifices for the good of their group. As Winston Churchill said of the Battle of Britain, the actions of the Royal Air Force pilots were genuinely altruistic: A great many people owed a great deal to those who flew into battle knowing there was a high probability they would not return (Levinson, 1950).

To summarize, we can minimize destructive entrapment in social dilemmas by establishing rules that regulate self-serving behaviour, by keeping groups small, and by invoking altruistic norms.

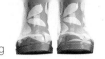

PERCEIVED INJUSTICE

"That's unfair!" "What a rip off!" "We deserve better!" Such comments typify conflicts bred by perceived injustice. But what is "justice"? According to some social-psychological theorists, people perceive justice as **equity**—the distribution of rewards in proportion to individuals' contributions (Walster et al., 1978). If you and I have a relationship (employer-employee, teacher-student, husband-wife, colleague-colleague), it is equitable if

equity
a condition in which the outcomes people receive from a relationship are proportional to what they contribute to it. Note: Equitable outcomes needn't always be equal outcomes.

$$\frac{\text{My outcomes}}{\text{My outputs}} = \frac{\text{Your outcomes}}{\text{Your outputs}}$$

If you contribute more and benefit less than I do, you will feel exploited and irritated; I may feel exploitative and guilty. Chances are, though, that you more than I will be sensitive to the inequity (Greenberg, 1986; Messick & Sentis, 1979).

We may agree with the equity principle's definition of justice yet disagree on whether our relationship is equitable. If two people are colleagues, what will each consider a relevant input? The one who is older may favour basing pay on seniority, the other on current productivity. Given such a disagreement, whose definition is likely to prevail? More often than not, those with social power convince themselves and others that they deserve what they're getting (Mikula, 1984). This has been called a "golden" rule: Whoever has the gold makes the rules.

Knowing that one's group has overbenefited can trigger collective guilt, much as individuals can feel guilt when receiving what's undeserved. To restore a sense of justice, such collective guilt can motivate an apology or an offer of compensation (Mallet & Swim, 2003). However, the exploiter can also relieve guilt by devaluing others' inputs. As we described in Chapter 12, those who inflict harm may blame the victim and thus maintain their belief in a just world.

"Do unto others 20% better than you would expect them to do unto you, to correct for subjective error."

Linus Pauling (1962)

And how do those who are exploited react? Elaine Hatfield, William Walster, and Ellen Berscheid (1978) detected three possibilities. They can accept and justify their inferior position ("We're poor; it's what we deserve, but we're happy"). They can demand compensation, perhaps by harassing, embarrassing, even cheating their exploiter. If all else fails, they may try to restore equity by retaliating.

An interesting implication of equity theory—an implication that has been confirmed experimentally—is that the more competent and worthy people feel (the more they value their inputs), the more they will feel underbenefited and thus eager to retaliate (Ross et al., 1971). Intense social protests generally come from those who believe themselves worthy of more than they are receiving. See Table A–1.

Critics argue that equity is not the only conceivable definition of justice. (Pause a moment: Can you imagine any other?) Edward Sampson (1975) says equity theorists wrongly assume that the economic principles that guide Western, capitalist nations are universal. Some noncapitalist cultures define justice not as equity but as **equality** or **need-based distribution**: "From each according to his abilities, to each according to his needs" (Karl Marx). When rewards are distributed to those within one's group, people socialized under the influence of collectivist cultures, such as China and India, likewise favour need or equality more than do individualistic Westerners (Hui et al., 1991; Leung & Bond, 1984; Murphy-Berman et al., 1984).

equality
the equal distribution of rewards to all individuals

need-based distribution
the distribution of rewards based on need for those rewards

On what basis *should* rewards be distributed? Need? Equality? Merit? Some combination of these? Political philosopher John Rawls (1971) invites us to consider a future in which

TABLE A–1 Gallup polls reveal increased perceptions of gender inequality

All things considered, who has a better life in this country—men or women?

	1972	1993
Men	29%	60%
Women	35	21
Same	30	15
No opinion	6	5

Source: Roper Center for Public Opinion Research, 1997.

"Solutions to the distribution problem are nontrivial. Children fight, colleagues complain, group members resign, tempers flare, and nations battle over issues of fairness. As parents, employers, teachers, and presidents know, the most frequent response to an allocation decision is 'not fair.'"

Arnold Kahn & William Gaeddert (1985)

our own place on the economic ladder was unknown. Which standard of justice would we prefer? Gregory Mitchell and his colleagues (1993) report that university students want enough priority placed on equality to meet their own needs, should they find themselves at the bottom.

MISPERCEPTION

Recall that conflict is a *perceived* incompatibility of actions or goals. Many conflicts contain but a small core of truly incompatible goals; the bigger problem is the misperceptions of the other's motives and goals. As referred to in Chapter 8, the Eagles and the Rattlers did indeed have some genuinely incompatible aims. But their perceptions subjectively magnified their differences (Figure A–3).

In earlier chapters we considered the seeds of such misperception. The *self-serving bias* leads individuals and groups to accept credit for their good deeds and shuck responsibility for bad deeds, without according others the same benefit of the doubt. A tendency to *self-justify* further inclines people to deny the wrong of their evil acts that cannot be shucked off. Thanks to the *fundamental attribution error,* each side sees the other's hostility as reflecting an evil disposition. One then filters the information and interprets it to fit one's *preconceptions.* Groups frequently *polarize* these self-serving, self-justifying, biasing tendencies. One symptom of *groupthink* is the tendency to perceive one's own group as moral and strong, the opposition as evil and weak. Terrorist acts that are despicable brutality to most people are "holy war" to others. Indeed, the mere fact of being in a group triggers an *ingroup bias.* And negative *stereotypes,* once formed, are often resistant to contradictory evidence.

So it should not surprise us, though it should sober us, to discover that people in conflict form distorted images of one another. Ervin Staub and Daniel Bar-Tal (2003) argue that groups in intractable conflict almost always:

- see their own goals as supremely important
- take pride in their own group and devalue the outgroup
- believe themselves victimized
- elevate patriotism, solidarity, and loyalty to the group's needs
- celebrate self-sacrifice and suppress criticism

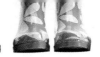

Although one side to a conflict may indeed be acting with greater moral virtue, the point is that ways of thinking about the enemy are fairly predictable.

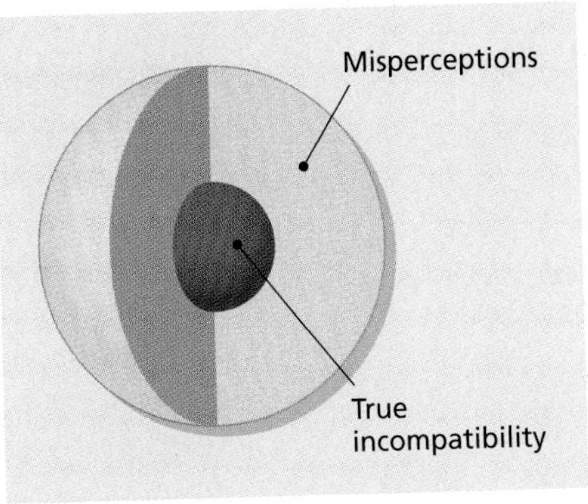

FIGURE A–3

Many conflicts contain a core of truly incompatible goals surrounded by a larger exterior of misperceptions.

Simplistic thinking

When tension rises—as happens during an international crisis—rational thinking becomes more difficult (Janis, 1989). Views of the enemy become more simplistic and stereotyped, and seat-of-the-pants judgments become more likely. Experiments by Peter Carnevale and Tahira Probst (1998) show that even the mere expectation of conflict can serve to freeze thinking and impede creative problem solving.

Researchers have also analyzed political rhetoric preceding the outset of major wars, surprise military attacks, regional conflicts, and revolutions (Conway et al., 2001). In nearly every case, attacking leaders displayed increasingly simplistic we-are-good/they-are-bad thinking immediately prior to their aggressive actions, but shifts away from simplistic rhetoric typically proceeded major peace agreements.

Shifting perceptions

If misperceptions accompany conflict, then they should appear and disappear as conflicts wax and wane. And they do, with startling ease. The same processes that create the enemy's image can reverse that image when the enemy becomes an ally. Thus the "bloodthirsty, cruel, treacherous, buck-toothed little Japs" of the Second World War (who were deemed so dangerous that even Canadian citizens of Japanese descent were sent to internment camps) soon became our "intelligent, hardworking, self-disciplined, resourceful allies." Our Second World War allies, the Russians, then became the "warlike, treacherous" ones.

The Germans, who after two world wars were hated, then admired, and then again hated, were once again admired—apparently no longer plagued by what earlier was presumed to be cruelty in their national character. So long as Iraq was attacking Iran, even while using chemical weapons and massacring its own Kurds, many nations supported it. Our enemy's enemy is our friend. When Iraq ended its war with Iran and invaded oil-rich Kuwait, Iraq's behaviour suddenly became "barbaric." Clearly, images of our enemies not only justify our actions but also change with amazing ease.

The extent of misperceptions during conflict provides a chilling reminder that people need not be insane or abnormally evil to form these distorted images of their antagonists. When in conflict with another nation, another group, or simply a roommate or parent, we readily develop misperceptions that allow us to perceive our own motives and actions as wholly good and the other's as totally evil. Our antagonists usually form a mirror-image perception of us.

So, trapped in a social dilemma, competing for scarce resources, or perceiving injustice, the conflict continues until something enables both parties to peel away their misperceptions and work at reconciling their actual differences. Good advice, then, is when in conflict do not assume that the other fails to share your values and morality. Rather, compare perceptions, assuming that the other is likely perceiving the situation differently.

SUMMING UP: WHAT CREATES CONFLICT?

Whenever two people, two groups, or two nations interact, their perceived needs and goals may conflict. Many social problems arise as people pursue individual self-interest, to their collective detriment. Two laboratory games, the Prisoners' Dilemma and the Tragedy of the Commons, capture this clash of individual versus communal well-being. In real life, as in laboratory experiments, we can avoid such traps by establishing rules that regulate self-serving behaviour; by keeping social groups small so people feel responsibility for one another; and by invoking altruistic norms.

Conflicts also arise when people feel unjustly treated. According to equity theory, people define justice as the distribution of rewards in proportion to one's contributions. Conflicts occur when people disagree on the extent of their contributions and thus on the equity of their outcomes.

Conflicts frequently contain a small core of truly incompatible goals, surrounded by a thick layer of misperceptions of the adversary's motives and goals.

HOW CAN PEACE BE ACHIEVED?

Conflicting parties have other ways to resolve their differences. When husband and wife, or labour and management, or nation X and nation Y disagree, they can **bargain** with one another directly. They can ask a third party to **mediate** by making suggestions and facilitating their negotiations. Or they can **arbitrate** by submitting their disagreement to someone who will study the issues and impose a settlement.

bargaining seeking an agreement through direct negotiation between parties to a conflict

mediation an attempt by a neutral third party to resolve a conflict by facilitating communication and offering suggestions

arbitration resolution of a conflict by a neutral third party who studies both sides and imposes a settlement

BARGAINING

If we want to buy or sell a new car, are we better off adopting a tough bargaining stance—opening with an extreme offer so that splitting the difference will yield a favourable result? Or are we better off beginning with a sincere "good-faith" offer?

Experiments suggest no simple answer. On the one hand, those who demand more will often get more. Robert Cialdini, Leonard Bickman, and John Cacioppo (1979) provide a typical result: In a control condition, they approached various Chevrolet dealers and asked the price of a new Monte Carlo sports coupe with designated options. In an experimental condition, they approached other dealers and first struck a tougher bargaining stance, asking for and rejecting a price on a *different* car ("I need a lower price than that. That's a lot"). When they then asked the price of the Monte Carlo, exactly as in the control condition, they received offers that averaged some $200 lower.

Tough bargaining may lower the other party's expectations, making the other side willing to settle for less (Yukl, 1974). But toughness can sometimes backfire. Many a conflict is not over a pie of fixed size but over a pie that shrinks if the conflict continues. Yet often negotiators fail to realize their common interests, and about 20 percent of the time negotiate "lose-lose" agreements that are mutually costly (Thompson & Hrebec, 1996).

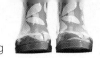

One lose-lose scenario is simply a time delay. When a strike is prolonged, both labour and management lose. Being tough is another potential lose-lose scenario. If the other party responds with an equally tough stance, both may be locked into positions from which neither can back down without losing face. The nurse's strike in Quebec in the summer of 1999 had some of these features. Premier Lucien Bouchard had announced before the strike that he would not give a raise greater than 5 percent over three years, and the nurses announced they would not accept such a deal. After such statements it is difficult for either side to compromise and reach an agreement.

MEDIATION

A third-party mediator may offer suggestions that enable conflicting parties to make concessions and still save face (Pruitt, 1998). If my concession can be attributed to a mediator, who is gaining an equal concession from my antagonist, then neither of us will be viewed as caving in to the other's demands.

Turning win-lose into win-win

Mediators also help resolve conflicts by facilitating constructive communication. Their first task is to help the parties rethink the conflict and gain information about other's interests (Thompson, 1998). Typically, people on both sides have a competitive "win-lose" orientation: They are successful if their opponent is unhappy with the result, and unsuccessful if their opponent is pleased (Thompson et al., 1995). The mediator aims to replace this win-lose orientation with a cooperative "win-win" orientation, by prodding them to set aside their conflicting demands and instead to think about each other's underlying needs, interests, and goals. In experiments, Leigh Thompson (1990) found that, with experience, negotiators become better able to make mutually beneficial tradeoffs and thus to achieve win-win resolutions.

A classic story of such a resolution concerns the two sisters who quarrelled over an orange (Follett, 1940). Finally they compromised and split the orange in half, whereupon one sister squeezed her half for juice while the other used the peel to make a cake. In a series of compelling experiments, Dean Pruitt and his associates induced bargainers to search for **integrative agreements**. If the sisters had agreed to split the orange, giving one sister all the juice and the other all the peel, they would have hit on such an agreement, one that integrates both parties' interests (Kimmel et al., 1980; Pruitt & Lewis, 1975, 1977). Compared to compromises, in which each party sacrifices something important, integrative agreements are more enduring. Because they are mutually rewarding, they also lead to better ongoing relationships (Pruitt, 1986).

integrative agreements win-win agreements that reconcile both parties' interests to their mutual benefit

Unravelling misperceptions with controlled communications

Communication often helps reduce self-fulfilling misperceptions. Perhaps you can recall experiences similar to that of this university student:

> Often, after a prolonged period of little communication, I perceive Martha's silence as a sign of her dislike for me. She, in turn, thinks that my quietness is a result of my being mad at her. My silence induces her silence, which makes me even more silent . . . until this snowballing effect is broken by some

> occurrence that makes it necessary for us to interact. And the communication then unravels all the misinterpretations we had made about one another.

The outcome of such conflicts often depends on *how* people communicate their feelings to one another. Roger Knudson and his colleagues (1980) invited married couples to come to the psychology laboratory and relive, through role playing, one of their past conflicts. Before, during, and after their conversation (which often generated as much emotion as the actual previous conflict), the couples were closely observed and questioned. Couples who evaded the issue—by failing to make their positions clear or failing to acknowledge their spouse's position—left with the illusion that they were more in harmony and agreement than they really were. Often, they came to believe they now agreed more when actually they agreed less. In contrast, those who engaged the issue—by making their positions clear and by taking one another's views into account—achieved more actual agreement and gained more accurate information about one another's perceptions. That helps explain why couples who communicate their concerns directly and openly are usually happily married (Grush & Glidden, 1987).

Such findings have triggered new programs that train couples and children how to manage conflicts constructively (Horowitz & Boardman, 1994). If managed constructively, conflict provides opportunities for reconciliation and more genuine harmony. Psychologists Ian Gotlib and Catherine Colby (1988) offer advice on how to avoid destructive quarrels and how to have good quarrels (see Table A–2). Children, for example, learn that conflict is normal, that people can learn to get along with those who are different, that most disputes can be resolved with two winners, and that nonviolent communication strategies are an alternative to a world of bullies and victims. This "violence prevention curriculum . . . is not about passivity," notes Deborah Prothrow-Stith (1991, p. 183). "It is about using anger not to hurt oneself or one's peers, but to change the world."

TABLE A–2 How to fight constructively

Do Not	Do
• apologize prematurely.	• fight privately away from children.
• evade the argument, give the silent treatment, or walk out on it.	• clearly define the issue and repeat the other's arguments in your own words.
• use your intimate knowledge of the other person to hit below the belt and humiliate.	• divulge your positive and negative feelings.
• bring in unrelated issues.	• welcome feedback about your behaviour.
• feign agreement while harbouring resentment.	• clarify where you agree and disagree and what matters most to each of you.
• tell the other party how she or he is feeling.	• ask questions that help the other find words to express the concern.
• attack indirectly by criticizing someone or something the other person values.	• wait for spontaneous explosions to subside, without retaliating.
• undermine the other by intensifying their insecurity or threatening disaster.	• offer positive suggestions for mutual improvement.

David Johnson and Roger Johnson (1995, 2000, 2003) put children from grades one to nine through about a dozen hours of conflict resolution training in six schools, with very heartening results. Before the training, most students were involved in daily conflicts—put-downs and teasing, playground turn-taking conflicts, conflicts over possessions—conflicts that nearly also resulted in a winner and a loser. After training, the children more often found win-win solutions, better mediated friends' conflicts, and retained and applied their new skills in and out of school throughout the school year. When implemented with a whole student body, the result is a more peaceful student community and increased academic achievement.

"[There is] a psychological barrier between us, a barrier of suspicion, a barrier of rejection; a barrier of fear, of deception, a barrier of hallucination. . . ."

President Anwar al-Sadat, to the Israeli Knesset, 1977

Conflict researchers report that a key factor is *trust* (Ross & Ward, 1995). If you believe the other person is well intentioned, you are then more likely to divulge your needs and concerns. Lacking such trust, you may fear that being open will give the other party information that might be used against you.

When the two parties mistrust each other and communicate unproductively, a third-party mediator—a marriage counsellor, a labour mediator, a diplomat—sometimes helps. Often the mediator is someone trusted by both sides. In the 1980s it took an Algerian Muslim to mediate the conflict between Iran and Iraq, and the Pope to resolve a geographical dispute between Argentina and Chile (Carnevale & Choi, 2000).

After coaxing the conflicting parties to rethink their perceived win-lose conflict, the mediator often has each party identify and rank its goals. When goals are compatible, the ranking procedure makes it easier for each to concede on less important goals so that both achieve their chief goals (Erickson et al., 1974; Schulz & Pruitt, 1978). South Africa achieved internal peace when White and Black South Africans granted each other's top priorities—replacing apartheid with majority rule and safeguarding the security, welfare, and rights of Whites (Kelman, 1998).

Communication facilitators work to break down barriers, as in this diversity training exercise for teenagers.

Once labour and management both believe that management's goal of higher productivity and profit is compatible with labour's goal of better wages and working conditions, they can begin to work for an integrative win-win solution. If workers will forgo benefits that are moderately beneficial to them but very costly to management (perhaps company-provided dental care), and if management will forgo moderately valuable arrangements that workers very much resent (perhaps inflexibility of working hours), then both sides may gain (Ross & Ward, 1995). Rather than seeing itself as making a concession, each side can see the negotiation as an effort to exchange bargaining chips for things more valued.

When the parties then convene to communicate directly, they are usually *not* set loose in the hope that, eyeball to eyeball, the conflict will resolve itself. In the midst of a threatening, stressful conflict, emotions often disrupt the ability to understand the other party's point of view. Communication may become most difficult just when it is most needed (Tetlock, 1985).

The mediator will therefore often structure the encounter to help each party understand and feel understood by the other. The mediator may ask the conflicting parties to restrict their arguments to statements of fact, including statements of how they feel and how they respond when the other acts in a given way: "I enjoy having music on. When you play it loud, I find it hard to concentrate. That makes me crabby." Also, the mediator may ask people to reverse roles and argue the other's position. (Experiments show that inducing empathy decreases stereotyping and increases cooperation—Batson & Moran, 1999; Galinsky & Muskowitz, 2000.) Or the mediator may have them restate one another's positions before replying with their own: "It annoys you when I play my music and you're trying to study."

Neutral third parties may also suggest mutually agreeable proposals that would be dismissed—"reactively devalued"—if offered by either side. The very same proposal that is seen as a cheap trick when presented by the opposition is often seen as an interesting suggestion when presented by the mediator. Even good proposals are greeted with suspicion when presented by the opposition. Likewise, people will often reactively devalue a concession offered by an adversary ("they must not value it"); the same concession may seem less like a token gesture when suggested by a third party.

These peacemaking principles, based partly on laboratory experiments, partly on practical experience, have helped mediate both international and industrial conflicts (Blake & Mouton, 1962, 1979; Fisher, 1994; Wehr, 1979). Social psychologist have conducted workshops that promote healing and reconciliation bringing together influential Arabs and Israelis, Pakistanis and Indians, and Tutsi and Hutus in Rwanda (Kelman, 1997; Staub & Pearlman, 2004; 2005a, b). Using methods such as those we've considered, these researchers counter misperceptions and have participants creatively seek solutions for their common good. Isolated, the participants are free to speak directly to their adversaries without fear of their constituents' second-guessing what they are saying. The result? Those from both sides typically come to understand the other's perspective and how the other side responds to their own group's actions.

ARBITRATION

Some conflicts are so intractable, the underlying interests so divergent, that a mutually satisfactory resolution is unattainable. Bosnian Serbs and Muslims could not both have jurisdiction over the same homelands. In a divorce dispute over custody of a child, both parents cannot

enjoy full custody. In these and many other cases (disputes over tenants' repair bills, athletes' wages, and national territories), a third-party mediator may—or may not—help resolve the conflict.

If not, the parties may turn to *arbitration* by having the mediator or another third party *impose* a settlement. Disputants usually prefer to settle their differences without arbitration, so they retain control over the outcome. Neil McGillicuddy and others (1987) observed this preference in an experiment involving disputants coming to one arbitration centre. When people knew they would face an arbitrated settlement if mediation failed, they tried harder to resolve the problem, exhibited less hostility, and thus were more likely to reach agreement.

> *"In the research on the effects of mediation one finding stands out: The worse the state of the parties' relationship is with one another, the dimmer the prospects that mediation will be successful."*
>
> Kenneth Kressel & Dean Pruitt (1985)

In cases where differences seem large and irreconcilable, the prospect of arbitration may have an opposite effect (Pruitt, 1986). The disputants may freeze their positions, hoping to gain an advantage when the arbitrator chooses a compromise. To combat this tendency, some disputes, such as those involving salaries of individual baseball players, are settled with "final-offer arbitration" in which the third party chooses one of the two final offers. Final-offer arbitration motivates each party to make a reasonable proposal.

Typically, however, the final offer is not as reasonable as it would be if each party, free of self-serving bias, saw its own proposal through others' eyes. Negotiation researchers report that most disputants are made stubborn by "optimistic overconfidence" (Kahneman & Tversky, 1995). Successful mediation is hindered when, as often happens, both parties believe they have a two-thirds chance of winning a final-offer arbitration (Bazerman, 1986, 1990).

CONCILIATION

Sometimes tension and suspicion run so high that communication, much less resolution, becomes all but impossible. Each party may threaten, coerce, or retaliate against the other. Unfortunately, such acts tend to be reciprocated, thus escalating the conflict. So, would a strategy of appeasing the other party by being unconditionally cooperative produce a satisfying result? Often not. In laboratory games, those who are 100 percent cooperative often get exploited. Politically, a one-sided pacifism is out of the question.

Social psychologist Charles Osgood (1962, 1980) advocated a third alternative—one that is conciliatory, rather than retaliatory, yet strong enough to discourage exploitation. Osgood called it "graduated and reciprocated initiatives in tension reduction," nicknamed **GRIT**.

> **GRIT**
> acronym for "graduated and reciprocated initiatives in tension reduction"—a strategy designed to de-escalate international tensions

GRIT requires one side to initiate a few small de-escalatory actions, after *announcing a conciliatory intent.* The initiator states its desire to reduce tension, declares each conciliatory act prior to making it, and invites the adversary to reciprocate. Such announcements create a framework that helps the adversary correctly interpret what otherwise might be seen as weak or tricky actions. They also bring public pressure on the adversary to follow the reciprocity norm.

Next, the initiator establishes credibility and genuineness by carrying out, exactly as announced, several verifiable *conciliatory acts.* This intensifies the pressure to reciprocate. Making conciliatory acts diverse—perhaps offering medical information, closing a military base, and lifting a trade ban—keeps the initiator from making a significant sacrifice in any one area

"Don't worry, dear—it's just a *peace* offensive."

People perceive that they respond more favorably to conciliation, but that others might be responsive to coercion.

BALOO reprinted by permission of Cartoon Features Syndicate.

and leaves the adversary freer to choose its own means of reciprocation. If the adversary reciprocates voluntarily, its own conciliatory behaviour may soften its attitudes.

GRIT *is* conciliatory. But it is not "surrender on the installment plan." The remaining aspects of the plan protect each side's self-interest by *maintaining retaliatory capability.* The initial conciliatory steps entail some small risk but do not jeopardize either one's security; rather, they are calculated to begin edging both sides down the tension ladder. If one side takes an aggressive action, the other side reciprocates in kind, making it clear it will not tolerate exploitation. Yet the reciprocal act is not an overresponse that would re-escalate the conflict. If the adversary offers its own conciliatory acts, these, too, are matched or even slightly exceeded.

Does GRIT really work? In laboratory dilemma games a successful strategy has proved to be simple "tit-for-tat," which begins with a cooperative opening play and thereafter matches the other party's last response (Axelrod & Dion, 1988; Parks & Rumble, 2001; Van Lange & Visser, 1999). Although initially friendly, tit-for-tat immediately punishes noncooperation but also immediately forgives wayward opponents who again cooperate. In a lengthy series of experiments, Svenn Lindskold and his associates (1976 to 1988) have tested other aspects of the GRIT strategy. Lindskold (1978) reports that his own and others' studies provide "strong support for the various steps in the GRIT proposal." In laboratory games, announcing cooperative intent *does* boost cooperation. Repeated conciliatory acts *do* breed greater trust (although self-serving biases often make one's own acts seem more conciliatory and less hostile than those of the adversary). Maintaining an equality of power *does* protect against exploitation.

"I am not suggesting that principles of individual behaviour can be applied to the behaviour of nations in any direct, simpleminded fashion. What I am trying to suggest is that such principles may provide us with hunches about internation behaviour that can be tested against experience in the larger arena."

Charles E. Osgood (1966)

Applications in the real world

Peace-creating strategies have been tried outside the laboratory, with promising results. One of the best examples of such a strategy was Lester B. Pearson's handling of the Suez Canal crisis. In the summer of 1956 Egyptian president Gamal Abdal Nasser declared that the Egyptian government was taking control of the Suez Canal. He hoped to raise money from tolls charged to ships going through the canal to finance the Aswan High Dam on the Nile River. A company controlled by British and French interests had previously controlled the canal. England and France were taken aback by the announcement and were worried that Egyptian control of the canal might eventually restrict the flow of goods (particularly oil) to Western Europe. In October 1956, these worries led England, France, and their ally Israel to invade the canal zone. They gained control of the area but were roundly criticized in international circles, precipitating a major international crisis. Would the Soviet Union come to Egypt's aid? Would the world powers stumble into another war? International outrage forced Britain, France, and Israel to withdraw from the canal zone, and Anthony Eden, the British foreign minister, to resign.

Into this pressure cooker of a situation stepped Lester B. Pearson, then the foreign minister of Canada. He formulated a plan where concessions were made to both Egypt and Britain, as well as France, and Israel. In exchange, United Nations peacekeeping troops were sent into the canal zone to ensure that the plan would be implemented. Egypt was allowed to collect tolls on ships going through the canal to finance the building of the Aswan High Dam. Britain and France were assured that the canal would remain open and trade would not be restricted to Western Europe. Israel was given shipping rights that they had not previously enjoyed.

Lester B. Pearson received international acclaim (and the Nobel Peace Prize in 1957) for his role in handling the crisis. He, of course, went on to become prime minister of Canada.

Might conciliatory efforts also help reduce tension between individuals? There is every reason to expect so. When a relationship is strained and communication nonexistent, it sometimes takes only a conciliatory gesture—a soft answer, a warm smile, a gentle touch—for both parties to begin easing down the tension ladder, to a rung where contact, cooperation, and communication again become possible.

SUMMING UP: HOW CAN PEACE BE ACHIEVED?

Although conflicts are readily kindled and fuelled by social dilemmas, and misperceptions, some equally powerful forces, such as bargaining, mediation, arbitration and conciliation, can transform hostility into harmony.

Conflicting parties can also seek to resolve their differences by bargaining either directly or through a third-party mediator.

Third-party mediators can help by prodding the antagonists to replace their competitive win-lose view of their conflict with a more cooperative win-win orientation. Mediators can also structure communications that will peel away misperceptions and increase mutual understanding and trust.

When a negotiated settlement is not reached, the conflicting parties may defer the outcome to an arbitrator, who either dictates a settlement or selects one of the two final offers.

Sometimes tensions run so high that genuine communication is impossible. In such cases, small conciliatory gestures by one party may elicit reciprocal conciliatory acts by the other party. One such conciliatory strategy, GRIT (graduated and reciprocated initiatives in tension reduction), aims to alleviate tense international situations. Those who mediate tense labour-management and international conflicts sometimes use another peacemaking strategy. They instruct the participants, as this chapter instructed you, in the dynamics of conflict and peacemaking in the hope that understanding can help us establish and enjoy peaceful, rewarding relationships.

MODULE B

Social Psychology in the Clinic

If you are a typical university student, you may occasionally feel mildly depressed—dissatisfied with your life, discouraged about the future, sad, lacking appetite and energy, unable

to concentrate, perhaps even wondering if life is worth living. Maybe disappointing grades have seemed to jeopardize your career goals. Perhaps the breakup of a relationship has left you in despair. At such times, you may fall into self-focused brooding that only worsens your feelings. For some 10 percent of men and nearly twice that many women, life's down times are not just temporary blue moods but one or more major depressive episodes that last for weeks without any obvious cause.

Among the many thriving areas of applied social psychology is one that relates social psychology's concepts to depression; to other problems such as loneliness, anxiety, and physical illness; and to happiness and well-being. This bridge-building research between social psychology and **clinical psychology** seeks answers to four important questions: (1) As laypeople or as professional psychologists, how can we improve our judgments and predictions about others? (2) How do the ways in which we think about self and others fuel problems such as depression, loneliness, anxiety, and ill health? (3) How might people reverse these maladaptive thought patterns? (4) What part do close, supportive relationships play in health and happiness?

clinical psychology the study, assessment, and treatment of people with psychological difficulties

WHAT INFLUENCES THE ACCURACY OF CLINICAL JUDGMENTS?

Do the influences on our social judgment (discussed in Chapters 2 through 4) also affect clinicians' judgments of clients? If so, what biases should clinicians and their clients be wary of?

A parole board talks with a convicted rapist and ponders whether to release him. A clinical psychologist ponders whether her patient is seriously suicidal. A physician notes a patient's symptoms and decides whether to recommend an invasive test. A school social worker ponders whether a child's overheard threat was a macho joke, a onetime outburst, or a signal indicating a potential school assassin.

Such clinical judgments are also *social* judgments, and thus vulnerable to illusory correlations, overconfidence bred by hindsight, and self-confirming diagnoses (Garb, 2005; Maddux, 1993). Let's see why alerting mental health workers to how people form impressions (and *mis*-impressions) might help avert serious misjudgments.

ILLUSORY CORRELATIONS

As we note in Chapter 3, it is tempting to see correlations where none exist. If we expect two things to be associated—if, for example, we believe that premonitions predict events—it's easy to perceive illusory correlations. Even when shown random data, we may notice and remember instances when premonitions and events are coincidentally related, and soon forget all the instances when premonitions aren't borne out and when events happen without a prior premonition.

> *"To free a man of error is to give, not to take away. Knowledge that a thing is false is a truth."*
>
> Arthur Schopenhauer, 1788–1860

Clinicians, like all of us, may perceive illusory correlations. If expecting particular responses to Rorschach inkblots to be more common among people with paranoid delusions, they may, in reflecting on their experience, believe they have witnessed such associations. To discover when such a perception is an illusory correlation, psychological science offers a simple method: Have one clinician administer and interpret the test. Have another clinician assess the same person's symptoms. Repeat this process with many people. The proof of the pudding is in the eating: Are test outcomes in fact correlated with reported symptoms? Some tests are indeed predictive. Others, such as the Rorschach inkblots and the Draw-a-Person test, have correlations far weaker than their users suppose (Lilienfeld et al., 2000, 2005).

Why, then, do clinicians continue to express confidence in uninformative or ambiguous tests? Pioneering experiments by Loren Chapman and Jean Chapman (1969, 1971) help us see why. They invited both university students and professional clinicians to study some test performances and diagnoses. If the students or clinicians *expected* a particular association they generally *perceived* it, regardless of whether the data were supportive. For example, clinicians who believed that suspicious people draw peculiar eyes on the Draw-a-Person test perceived such a relationship—even when shown cases in which suspicious people drew peculiar eyes *less* often than nonsuspicious people. Believing that a relationship existed between two things, they were more likely to notice confirming instances.

In fairness to clinicians, illusory thinking also occurs among political analysts, historians, sportscasters, personnel directors, stockbrokers, and many other professionals, including research psychologists. As researchers we have often been blind to the shortcomings of our theoretical analyses. We so eagerly presume that our idea of truth is *the* truth that, no matter how hard we try, we cannot see our own errors. This is evident in the editorial review process that precedes any research publication. Over the years we have read dozens of reviews of our own manuscripts and have been reviewers for dozens of others. Our experience is that it is far easier to spot someone else's sloppy thinking than to perceive one's own.

"No one can see his own errors."

Psalms 19:12

HINDSIGHT AND OVERCONFIDENCE

If someone we know commits suicide, how do we react? One common reaction is to think that we, or those close to the person, should have been able to predict and therefore to prevent the suicide: "We should have known!" In hindsight, we can see the suicidal signs and the pleas for help. One experiment gave people a description of a depressed person. Some participants were told that the person subsequently committed suicide. Compared to those not informed of the suicide, those who were became more likely to say they "would have expected" it (Goggin & Range, 1985). Moreover, those told of the suicide viewed the victim's family more negatively. After a tragedy, an I-should-have-known-it-all-along phenomenon can leave family, friends, and therapists feeling guilty.

David Rosenhan (1973) and seven associates provided a striking example of potential error in after-the-fact explanations. To test mental health workers' clinical insights, they each made an appointment with a different mental hospital admissions office and complained of "hearing voices." Apart from giving false names and vocations, they reported their life histories and emotional states honestly and exhibited no further symptoms. Most were diagnosed as schizophrenic and remained hospitalized for two to three weeks. Hospital clinicians then searched for early incidents in the pseudo-patients' life histories and hospital behaviour that "confirmed" and "explained" the diagnosis. Rosenhan tells of one pseudo-patient who truthfully explained to the interviewer that he

> had a close relationship with his mother but was rather remote from his father during his early childhood. During adolescence and beyond, however, his father became a close friend, while his relationship with his mother cooled. His present relationship with his wife was characteristically close and warm. Apart from occasional angry exchanges, friction was minimal. The children had rarely been spanked.

The interviewer, "knowing" the person suffered from schizophrenia, explained the problem this way:

> This white 39-year-old male . . . manifests a long history of considerable ambivalence in close relationships, which begins in early childhood. A warm relationship with his mother cools during his adolescence. A distant relationship to his father is described as becoming very intense. Affective stability is absent. His attempts to control emotionality with his wife and children are punctuated by angry outbursts and, in the case of the children, spankings. And while he says that he has several good friends, one senses considerable ambivalence embedded in those relationships also.

Rosenhan later told some staff members (who had heard about his controversial experiment but doubted such mistakes could occur in their hospital) that during the next three months one or more pseudo-patients would seek admission to their hospital. After the three months, he asked the staff to guess which of the 193 patients admitted during that time were really pseudo-patients. Of the 193 new patients, 41 were accused by at least one staff member of being pseudo-patients. Actually, there were none.

SELF-CONFIRMING DIAGNOSES

So far we've seen that mental health workers sometimes perceive illusory correlations and that hindsight explanations are often questionable. A third problem with clinical judgment is that people may also supply information that fulfills clinicians' expectations. To get a feel for how this phenomenon might be tested experimentally, imagine yourself on a blind date with someone who has been told that you are an uninhibited, outgoing person. To see whether this is true, your date slips questions into the conversation, such as "Have you ever done anything crazy in front of other people?" As you answer such questions, will you reveal a different "you" than if your date had been told you were shy and retiring?

In a clever series of experiments, Mark Snyder (1984), in collaboration with William Swann and others, gave interviewers some hypotheses to test concerning individuals' traits. Snyder and Swann found that people often test for a trait by looking for information that confirms it. As in the above blind-date example, if people are trying to find out if someone is an extrovert, they often solicit instances of extroversion ("What would you do if you wanted to liven things up at a party?"). Testing for introversion, they are more likely to ask, "What factors make it hard for you to really open up to people?" In response, those probed for extroversion seem more sociable, and those probed for introversion seem more shy. Our assumptions and expectations about another help create the kind of person we see.

Russell Fazio and his colleagues (1981) reproduced this finding and also discovered that those asked the "extroverted questions" later perceived themselves as actually more outgoing than those asked the introverted questions. Moreover, they really became noticeably more outgoing. An accomplice of the experimenter later met each participant in a waiting room and 70 percent of the time correctly guessed from the person's behaviour which condition the person had come from.

Confirmation bias also appears when people evaluate themselves. Consider for a moment: Are you happy with your social life? Ziva Kunda and colleagues (1993) put this question to students at the University of Waterloo and elsewhere. The students searched their memories for confirming instances and thus ended up feeling happier than students asked, "Are you unhappy with your social life?" Seek and you shall find.

In other experiments, Snyder and his colleagues (1982) tried to get people to search for behaviours that would *disconfirm* the trait they were testing. In one experiment, they told the interviewers, "It is relevant and informative to find out ways in which the person . . . may not be like the stereotype." In another experiment Snyder (1981a) offered "$25 to the person who develops the set of questions that tell the most about . . . the interviewee." Still, confirmation bias persisted: People resisted choosing "introverted" questions when testing for extroversion.

"As is your sort of mind,
So is your sort of search:
You'll find
What you desire."

Robert Browning, 1812–1889

On the basis of Snyder's experiments, can you see why the behaviours of people undergoing psychotherapy come to fit their therapists' theories (Whitman et al., 1963)? When Harold Renaud and Floyd Estess (1961) conducted life-history interviews of 100 healthy, successful adult men, they were startled to discover that their subjects' childhood experiences were loaded with "traumatic events," tense relations with certain people, and bad decisions by their parents—the very factors usually used to explain psychiatric problems. When Freudian therapists go fishing for traumas in early childhood experiences, they often find their hunches confirmed. Thus, surmises Snyder (1981a):

> The psychiatrist who believes (erroneously) that adult gay males had bad childhood relationships with their mothers may meticulously probe for recalled (or fabricated) signs of tension between their gay clients and their mothers, but neglect to so carefully interrogate their heterosexual clients about their maternal relationships. No doubt, any individual could recall some friction with his or her mother, however minor or isolated the incidents.

IMPLICATIONS FOR BETTER CLINICAL PRACTICE

Professional clinicians are "vulnerable to insidious errors and biases," concluded James Maddux (1993). They

- are frequently the victims of illusory correlation
- are too readily convinced of their own after-the-fact analyses

- often fail to appreciate that erroneous diagnoses can be self-confirming
- often overestimate the predictive powers of their clinical intuition

The implications for mental health workers are easily stated: Be mindful that clients' verbal agreement with what you say does not prove its validity. Beware of the tendency to see relationships that you expect to see or that are supported by striking examples readily available in your memory. Rely on your notes more than your memory. Recognize that hindsight is seductive: It can lead you to feel overconfident and sometimes to judge yourself too harshly for not having foreseen outcomes. Guard against the tendency to ask questions that assume your preconceptions are correct; consider opposing ideas and test them, too (Garb, 1994).

"One thing I have learned in a long life: that all our science, measured against reality, is primitive and childlike—and yet it is the most precious thing we have."

Albert Einstein, in B. Hoffman & H. Dukes, *Albert Einstein: Creator and Rebel*, 1973

SUMMING UP: WHAT INFLUENCES THE ACCURACY OF CLINICAL JUDGMENTS?

As psychiatrists and clinical psychologists diagnose and treat their clients, they may perceive illusory correlations. Hindsight explanations of people's difficulties are sometimes too easy. Indeed, after-the-fact explaining can breed overconfidence in clinical judgment. When interacting with clients, erroneous diagnoses are sometimes self-confirming, because interviewers tend to seek and recall information that verifies what they are looking for.

Research on the errors that so easily creep into intuitive judgments illustrates the need for rigorous testing of intuitive conclusions. The scientific method cannot answer all questions and is itself vulnerable to bias. Thankfully, however, it can help us sift truth from falsehood.

WHAT COGNITIVE PROCESSES ACCOMPANY BEHAVIOUR PROBLEMS?

One of psychology's most intriguing research frontiers concerns the cognitive processes that accompany psychological disorders. What are the memories, attributions, and expectations of depressed, lonely, shy, or illness-prone people?

DEPRESSION

People who feel depressed tend to think negatively. They view life through dark-coloured glasses. With seriously depressed people—those who are feeling worthless, lethargic, uninterested in friends and family, and unable to sleep or eat normally—the negative thinking is self-defeating. Their intensely pessimistic outlook leads them to magnify every bad experience and minimize every good one. As one depressed young woman reported, "The real me is worthless and inadequate. I can't move forward with my work because I become frozen with doubt" (Burns, 1980, p. 29).

Distortion or realism?

Are all depressed people unrealistically negative? To find out, Lauren Alloy and Lyn Abramson (1979) studied university students who were either mildly depressed or not depressed. They had the students press a button, and observe the button controlled a light coming on. Surprisingly, the depressed students were quite accurate in estimating their degree of control. It was the nondepressives whose judgments were distorted; they exaggerated the extent of their control. Despite their self-preoccupation, mildly depressed people also are more attuned to others' feelings (Harkness et al., 2005).

depressive realism the tendency of mildly depressed people to make accurate rather than self-serving judgments, attributions, and predictions

This surprising phenomenon of **depressive realism**, nicknamed the "sadder-but-wiser effect," shows up in various judgments of one's control or skill (Ackermann & DeRubeis, 1991; Alloy et al., 1990). Shelley Taylor (1989, p. 214) explains:

> Normal people exaggerate how competent and well liked they are. Depressed people do not. Normal people remember their past behaviour with a rosy glow. Depressed people [unless severely depressed] are more evenhanded in recalling their successes and failures. Normal people describe themselves primarily positively. Depressed people describe both their positive and negative qualities. Normal people take credit for successful outcomes and tend to deny responsibility for failure. Depressed people accept responsibility for both success and failure. Normal people exaggerate the control they have over what goes on around them. Depressed people are less vulnerable to the illusion of control. Normal people believe to an unrealistic degree that the future holds a bounty of good things and few bad things. Depressed people are more realistic in their perceptions of the future. In fact, on virtually every point on which normal people show enhanced self-regard, illusions of control, and unrealistic visions of the future, depressed people fail to show the same biases. "Sadder but wiser" does indeed appear to apply to depression.

explanatory style one's habitual way of explaining life events. A negative, pessimistic, depressive explanatory style attributes failures to stable, global, and internal causes.

Underlying the thinking of depressed people are their attributions of responsibility. Consider: If you fail an exam and blame yourself, you may conclude that you are stupid or lazy; consequently, you may feel depressed. If you attribute the failure to an unfair exam or to other circumstances beyond your control, you may feel angry. In over 100 studies involving 15 000 subjects, depressed people have been more likely than nondepressed people to exhibit a negative **explanatory style** (Peterson & Steen, 2002; Sweeney et al., 1986) As shown in Figure B–1, this explanatory style attributes failure and setbacks to causes that are *stable* ("It's going to last forever"), *global* ("It's going to affect everything I do"), and *internal* ("It's all my fault"). The result of this pessimistic, overgeneralized, self-blaming thinking, say Abramson and her colleagues (1989), is a depressing sense of hopelessness.

> *"Life is the art of being well deceived."*
>
> William Hazlitt, 1778–1830

Is negative thinking a cause or a result of depression?

The cognitive accompaniments of depression raise a chicken-and-egg question: Do depressed moods cause negative thinking, or does negative thinking cause depression?

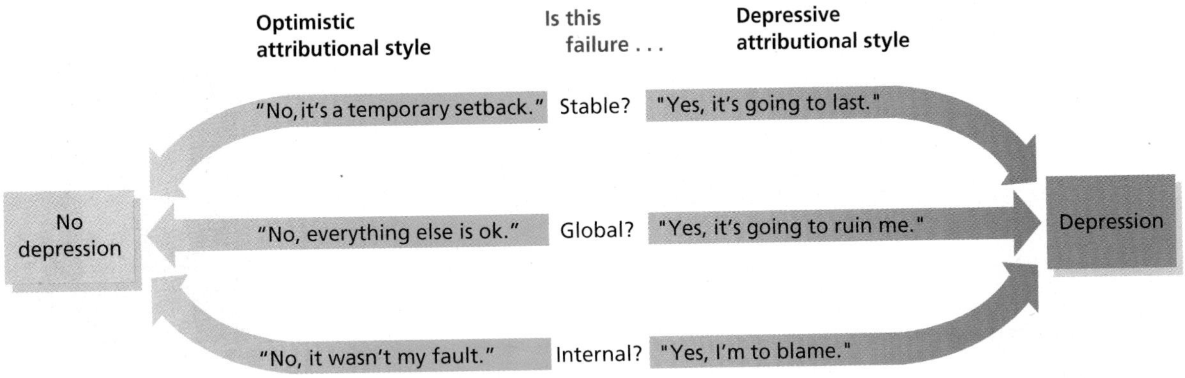
Optimistic attributional style
Is this failure . . .
Depressive attributional style
"No, it's a temporary setback."
Stable?
"Yes, it's going to last."
No depression
"No, everything else is ok."
Global?
"Yes, it's going to ruin me."
Depression
"No, it wasn't my fault."
Internal?
"Yes, I'm to blame."

FIGURE B–1

Depressive explanatory style.

Depression is linked with a negative, pessimistic way of explaining and interpreting failures.

Depressed moods cause negative thinking

As we saw in Chapter 3, our moods definitely colour our thinking. When we *feel* happy, we *think* happy. We see and recall a good world. But let our mood turn gloomy and our thoughts switch on to a different track. Off come the rose-coloured glasses; on come the dark glasses. Now the bad mood primes our recollections of negative events (Bower, 1987; Johnson & Magaro, 1987). Our relationships seem to sour, our self-image takes a dive, our hopes for the future dim, people's behaviour seems more sinister (Brown & Taylor, 1986; Mayer & Salovey, 1987). As depression increases, memories and expectations plummet; when depression lifts, thinking brightens (Barnett & Gotlib, 1988; Kuiper & Higgins, 1985). As an example, *currently* depressed people recall their parents as having been rejecting and punitive. But *formerly* depressed people recall their parents in the same positive terms as do never-depressed people (Lewinsohn & Rosenbaum, 1987). Thus, when you hear depressed people trashing their parents, remember: Moods modify memory.

By studying basketball fans, Edward Hirt and his colleagues (1992) demonstrated that even a temporary bad mood can darken our thinking. After the fans were either depressed by watching their team lose or elated by a victory, the researchers asked them to predict the team's future performance, and their own. After a loss, people offered bleaker assessments not only of the team's future but also of their own likely performance at throwing darts, solving anagrams, and getting a date. When things aren't going our way, it may seem as though they never will.

A depressed mood also affects behaviour. The person who is depressed tends to be withdrawn, glum, and quick to complain. Stephen Strack and James Coyne (1983) found that depressed people were realistic in thinking that others didn't appreciate their behaviour; their pessimism and bad moods can even trigger social rejection (Carver et al., 1994). Depressed behaviour can also trigger reciprocal depression in others. College students who have depressed roommates tend to become a little depressed themselves (Burchill & Stiles, 1988; Joiner, 1994; Sanislow et al., 1989). In dating couples, too, depression is often contagious (Katz et al., 1999).

Depressed people are therefore at risk for being divorced, fired, or socially shunned, thus magnifying their depression (Coyne et al., 1991; Gotlib & Lee, 1989; Sacco & Dunn, 1990). They may also seek out those whose unfavourable views of them verify, and further magnify, their low self-images (Lineham, 1997; Swann et al., 1991). One experiment gave people a choice between reading a favourable assessment of their personality by one graduate student or an unfavourable assessment by another student. Eighty-two percent of depressed people elected to

STORY BEHIND THE RESEARCH

Shelley Taylor
UCLA

Some years ago, I was conducting interviews with people who had cancer for a study on adjustment to intensely stressful events. I was surprised to learn that, for some people, the cancer experience actually seemed to have brought benefits, as well as the expected liabilities. Many people told me that they thought they were better people for the experience, they felt they were better adjusted to cancer than other people, they believed that they could exert control over their cancer in the future, and they believed their futures would be cancer-free, even when we knew from their medical histories that their cancers were likely to recur.

As a result, I became fascinated by how people can construe even the worst of situations as good, and I've studied these "positive illusions" ever since. Through our research, we learned quickly that you don't have to experience a trauma to demonstrate positive illusions. Most people, including the majority of university students, think of themselves as somewhat better than average, as more in control of the circumstances around them than may actually be true, and as likely to experience more positive future outcomes in life than may be realistic. These illusions are not a sign of maladjustment, quite the contrary. Good mental health may depend on the ability to see things as somewhat better than they are and to find benefits even when things seem most bleak.

see the unfavourable feedback, whereas only 25 percent of high-self-esteem people made that choice (Giesler et al., 1996).

We can see, then, that being depressed has cognitive and behavioural effects. Does it also work the other way? Does depression have cognitive *origins*?

Negative thinking causes depressed moods

Depression is natural when experiencing severe stress—losing a job, getting divorced or rejected, or suffering any experience that disrupts our sense of who we are and why we are worthy human beings (Hamilton et al., 1993; Kendler et al., 1993). The brooding that comes with this short-term depression can be adaptive. Insights gained during times of depressed inactivity may later result in better strategies for interacting with the world. But depression-prone people respond to bad events with self-focused rumination and self-blame (Mor & Winquist, 2002; Pyszczynski et al., 1991; Wood et al., 1990a, 1990b). Their self-esteem fluctuates more rapidly up with boosts and down with threats (Butler et al., 1994).

Why are some people so affected by even *minor* stresses? Evidence suggests that when stress-induced rumination is filtered through a negative explanatory style, the frequent outcome is depression (Robins & Alloy, 2003). Colin Sacks and Daphne Bugental (1987) asked some young women to get acquainted with a stranger who sometimes acted cold and unfriendly, creating an awkward social situation. Unlike optimistic women, those with a pessimistic explanatory style—who characteristically offer stable, global, and internal attributions for bad events—reacted to the social failure by feeling depressed. Moreover, they then behaved more antagonistically toward the next people they met. Their negative thinking led to a negative mood response, which then led to negative behaviour. Such depressive rumination is more common among women, reports Susan Nolen-Hoeksema (2003). When trouble strikes, men tend to act, women tend to think—and often to "overthink," she reports.

Outside the laboratory, studies of children, teenagers, and adults confirm that those with the pessimistic explanatory style are more likely to become depressed when bad things happen. One study monitored university students every six weeks for two-and-a-half years (Alloy et al., 1999). Only 1 percent of those who began college with optimistic thinking styles had a first depressive episode, but 17 percent of those with pessimistic thinking styles did. "A recipe for severe depression is preexisting pessimism encountering failure," notes Martin Seligman (1991, p. 78). Moreover, patients who end therapy no longer feeling depressed but still with a negative explanatory style tend to relapse as bad events occur (Seligman, 1992). If those with a more optimistic explanatory style relapse, they often recover quickly (Metalsky et al., 1993; Needles & Abramson, 1990).

Researcher Peter Lewinsohn and his colleagues (1985) have assembled these findings into a coherent psychological understanding of depression. In their view, the negative self-image, attributions, and expectations of a depressed person are an essential link in a vicious cycle that is triggered by negative experience—perhaps academic or vocational failure, or family conflict, or social rejection (Figure B–2). In those vulnerable to depression, such stresses trigger brooding, self-focused, self-blaming thoughts (Pyszczynski et al, 1991; Wood et al., 1990a, 1990b). Such ruminations create a depressed mood that drastically alters the way a person thinks and acts, which then fuels further negative experiences, self-blame, and depressed mood. In experiments, mildly depressed people's moods brighten when a task diverts their attention to something external (Nix et al., 1995). (Happiness seems best pursued by focusing not on oneself but beyond oneself.) Depression is therefore *both* a cause and a consequence of negative cognitions.

Martin Seligman (1991, 1998, 2002) believes that self-focus and self-blame help explain the near-epidemic levels of depression in the Western world today. In North America, for example, young adults today are three times as likely as their grandparents to have suffered depression—despite their grandparents' experiencing a lower standard of living and greater hardship (Cross-National Collaborative Group, 1992; Swindle et al., 2000). Seligman believes that the decline of religion and family, plus the growth of individualism, breeds hopelessness and self-blame when things don't go well. Failed courses, careers, and marriages produce despair when we stand alone, with nothing and no one to fall back on. If, as a macho *Fortune* ad declared, you can "make it on your own," on "your own drive, your own guts, your own energy, your own ambition," then whose fault is it if you don't make it? In nonwestern cultures, where close-knit relationships and cooperation are the norm, major depression is less common and less tied to guilt and self-blame over perceived failure. In Japan, for example, depressed people instead tend to report feeling shame over letting down their family or coworkers (Draguns, 1990).

These insights into the thinking style linked with depression have prompted social psychologists to study thinking patterns associated with other problems. How do those who are

FIGURE B–2
The vicious cycle of depression.

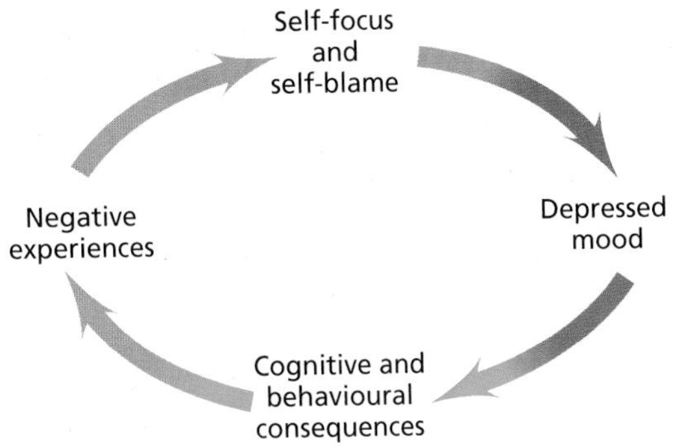

STORY BEHIND THE RESEARCH

My dual background in social and personality psychology often leads me to topics at the intersection of the two fields; for example, how do personality impressions develop in social contexts? Several speculations about the topic arose from the inclusion of discussion groups in some of my undergraduate courses. When students met several times to work on a task, one thing became clear: First impressions don't always rule. For certain personality types, the first impression they make on other group members does not necessarily match the group's final impression of them. So my graduate students and I designed a series of studies to follow one type of individual whose bad first impression improves over type, namely, the shy person. We also studied another type of individual whose good shiny first impression gradually darkens, namely the self-enhancer. The moral of this scientific story: Social perceptions are a constantly shifting product of the context, the time frame, and the target's actual personality.

Del Paulhus
University of British Columbia

plagued with excessive anxiety, shyness, or substance abuse view themselves? How well do they recall their successes and their failures? To what do they attribute their ups and downs? Where is their attention focused—on themselves or on others?

ANXIETY AND SHYNESS

Shyness is a form of social anxiety characterized by self-consciousness and worry about what others think (Anderson & Harvey, 1988; Asendorpf, 1987; Carver & Scheier, 1986). Being interviewed for a much-wanted job, dating someone for the first time, stepping into a roomful of strangers, performing before an important audience, or giving a speech (one of the most common phobias) can make almost anyone feel anxious. But some people feel anxious in almost any situation in which they might be evaluated, such as having a casual lunch with a coworker. For these people, anxiety is more a trait than a temporary state.

Doubting our ability in social situations

What causes us to feel anxious in social situations? Why are some people shackled in the prison of their own social anxiety? Barry Schlenker and Mark Leary (1982b, 1985; Leary & Kowalski, 1995) answer those questions by applying self-presentation theory. As you may recall from Chapters 2 and 4, self-presentation theory assumes that we are eager to present ourselves in ways that make a good impression. The implications for social anxiety are straightforward: *We feel anxious when we are motivated to impress others but doubt our ability to do so.* This simple principle helps explain a variety of research findings, each of which may ring true in your own experience. We feel most anxious when we are

- with powerful, high-status people—people whose impressions of us matter
- in an evaluative context, as when making a first impression on the parents of one's fiancé

- self-conscious (as shy people often are) and our attention is focused on ourselves and how we are coming across
- focused on something central to our self-image, as when a university professor presents ideas before peers at a professional convention
- in novel or unstructured situations, such as a first school dance or first formal dinner, where we are unsure of the social rules

For most people, the natural tendency in all such situations is to be cautiously self-protective: to talk less; to avoid topics that reveal one's ignorance; to be guarded about oneself; to be unassertive, agreeable, and smiling. Ironically, such anxious concern with making a good impression often makes a bad impression (Broome & Wegner, 1994; Meleshko & Alden, 1993). With time, however, shy people often become well liked. Consider a series of interesting studies conducted by Del Paulhus (Paulhus, 1998; Paulhus & Morgan, 1997) at the University of British Columbia. Unlike in other studies, he examined how people perceive each other over time. In the short run they found results consistent with previous research—self-enhancing people were evaluated positively and shy people were evaluated negatively. After seven meetings, however, this pattern reversed—the egotistical self-enhancers got on people's nerves, but the modesty, sensitivity, and discretion of shy people eventually led people to like them.

Overpersonalizing situations

Compared with unshy people, shy, self-conscious people (whose numbers include many adolescents) see incidental events as somehow related to themselves (Fenigstein, 1984, Fenigstein & Vanable, 1992). Shown someone they think is interviewing them live (actually a videotaped interviewer), they perceive the interviewer as less accepting and interested in them (Pozo et al., 1991). Shy, anxious people overpersonalize situations, a tendency that breeds anxious concern and, in extreme cases, paranoia.

To reduce social anxiety, some people turn to alcohol. Alcohol lowers anxiety as it reduces self-consciousness (Hull & Young, 1983). Thus, chronically self-conscious people are especially likely to drink following a failure. If recovering from alcoholism, they are more likely than those low in self-consciousness to relapse when they again experience stress or failure.

Alcohol can also reduce anxiety by restricting people's ability to think about their internal states. Claude Steele and Robert Josephs (1990) have called this effect of alcohol "alcohol myopia." In their research, Steele and Josephs have shown that when people are drunk they can only focus on the most salient cues in their environment. So, if anxious people are drinking at a rowdy party they are likely to focus on the party and thus be unable to focus on their anxiety. On the other hand, if they are drinking alone in a quiet room they will be more likely to focus on their anxiety (as there is little else to focus on) and become more anxious. This may be one reason that people often drink primarily in social situations.

Alcohol myopia can also lead to serious health consequences, as Queen's University professor Tara McDonald and University of Waterloo professors Mark Zanna and Geoff Fong (1995) have shown. They had students at a local pub answer a survey about drinking and driving either when they arrived at the pub (i.e., when they were sober) or at the end of the night after they had had quite a bit to drink. They either asked people their attitudes about drinking and driving or about drinking and driving only a short distance. They found that the way they asked the question made no difference for sober students, but the students who were intoxicated were less negative about drinking and driving only a short distance than about drinking and driving in general (see Figure B–3). It seems that alcohol myopia made these students focus on the cue that it was only a short distance, and they were unable to retrieve their belief that drinking and driving was dangerous. This same effect of alcohol—a narrowing of attention—can lead people to engage in dangerous social behaviours such as drinking and driving, and having unprotected casual sex (MacDonald et al., 2000a, 2000b).

SUMMING UP: WHAT COGNITIVE PROCESSES ACCOMPANY BEHAVIOUR PROBLEMS?

Social psychologists are actively exploring the attributions and expectations of depressed, lonely, socially anxious, and physically ill people. Depressed people have a negative explanatory style, interpreting negative events as being stable, global, and internally caused. Despite their more negative judgments, mildly depressed people in laboratory tests tend to be surprisingly realistic. Depression can be a vicious circle in which negative thoughts elicit self-defeating behaviours and vice versa.

Most people experience anxiety in situations where they are being evaluated, but shy individuals are extremely prone to anxiety even in friendly, casual situations. This can be another vicious circle in which anxious feelings elicit awkward, off-putting behaviour.

HEALTH PSYCHOLOGY: SOCIAL PSYCHOLOGY AND ILLNESS

In the industrialized world, at least half of all deaths are linked with behaviour—with consuming cigarettes, alcohol, drugs, and harmful foods; with reactions to stress; with lack of exercise

FIGURE B–3

When people are intoxicated, they can only focus on a very limited amount of information, an effect called alcohol myopia. If people focus on cues that lower their inhibition, such as the short distance home, then they may be more likely to drink and drive. (MacDonald, Fong & Zanna, 1995)

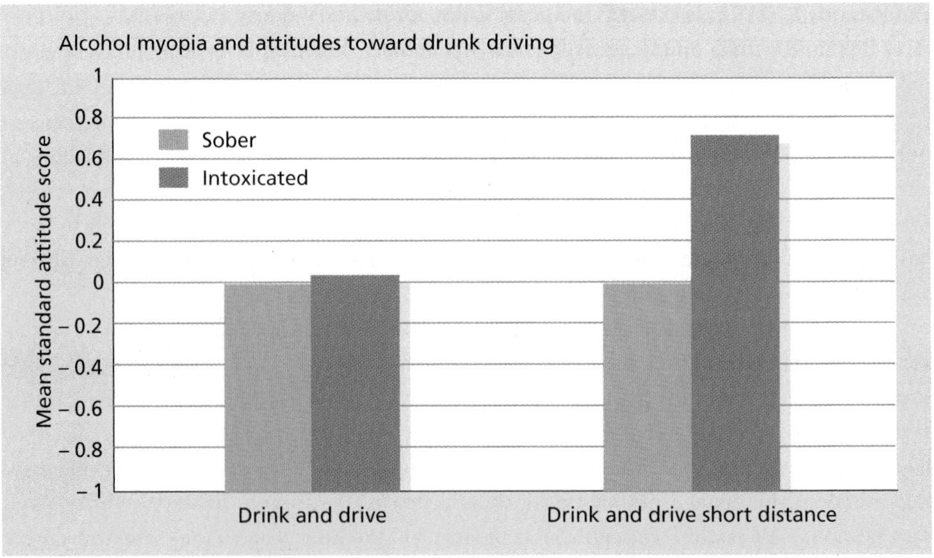

and not following a doctor's orders. Efforts to study and change these behavioural contributions to illness helped create a new interdisciplinary field called **behavioural medicine**. Psychology's contribution to this interdisciplinary science is its new subfield, **health psychology**. Its numbers include many of the estimated 3500 psychologists now working in Canadian and U.S. medical schools (Michaelson, 1993). Health psychologists study how people respond to illness symptoms and how emotions and explanations influence health.

behavioural medicine an interdisciplinary field that integrates and applies behavioural and medical knowledge about health and disease

health psychology the study of the psychological roots of health and illness. It provides psychology's contribution to behavioural medicine.

REACTIONS TO ILLNESS

How do people decide whether they are ill? How do they explain their symptoms? What influences their willingness to seek and follow treatment?

Noticing symptoms

Chances are you have recently experienced at least one of these physical complaints: headache, stomach ache, nasal congestion, sore muscles, ringing in the ears, excess perspiration, cold hands, racing heart, dizziness, stiff joints, and diarrhea or constipation (Pennebaker, 1982). Such symptoms require interpretation. Are they meaningless? Or are you coming down with something that requires medical attention? Hardly a week goes by without our playing doctor by self-diagnosing the significance of some symptom.

Noticing and interpreting our body's signals is like noticing and interpreting how our car is running. Unless the signals are loud and clear, we often miss them. Most of us cannot tell whether a car needs an oil change merely by listening to its engine. Similarly, most of us are not astute judges of our heart rate, blood-sugar level, or blood pressure. People guess their blood pressure based on how they feel, which often is unrelated to their actual blood pressure (Baumann & Leventhal, 1985). Furthermore, the early signs of many illnesses, including cancer and heart disease, are subtle and easy to miss.

Explaining symptoms: Am I sick?

With more serious aches and pains, the questions become more specific—and more critical. Does the small cyst match our idea of a malignant lump? Is the stomach ache bad enough to be appendicitis? Is the pain in the chest area merely—as many heart attack victims suppose—a muscle spasm? Indeed, half or more of heart attack victims die without having sought medical help (Friedman & DiMatteo, 1989).What factors influence how we explain symptoms?

Once we notice symptoms, we tend to interpret them according to familiar disease schemas (Bishop, 1991). In medical schools, this can have amusing results. As part of their training, medical students learn the symptoms associated with various diseases. Because they also experience various symptoms, they sometimes attribute their symptoms to recently learned disease schemas. ("Maybe this wheeze is the beginning of pneumonia.") As you may have discovered, psychology students are prone to this same effect as they read about psychological disorders.

Socially constructed disorders

The commonness and ambiguity of mild symptoms open the door to social suggestion. Might people socially construct an everyday ailment? Might people form the idea that their everyday

"When a man can't explain a woman's actions, the first thing he thinks about is the condition of her uterus."

Clare Boothe Luce, *Slam the Door Softly*, 1970

symptoms match those of an ailment they've heard about, and then use it to explain such symptoms? Researchers Pamela Kato and Diane Ruble (1992) maintain that this helps explain why many women believe they are more depressed, tense, and irritable during the two or three days before menstruation.

Is the so-called premenstrual syndrome (PMS) a social constructed disorder? As we saw in Chapter 4, illusory correlations occur when people notice and remember instances that confirm their belief—and do not notice instances that contradict them. Thus, a woman who feels tense the day before her period is due may attribute the tension to PMS. But if the woman feels similarly tense a week later, or does not feel tense the day her next period is about to start, she may be less likely to notice and remember these disconfirming instances.

Many researchers now believe that some women do indeed experience not only menstrual discomfort but also premenstrual tension (Hurt et al., 1992; Richardson, 1990). Thus, the American Psychiatric Association included a severe form of PMS (called *premenstrual dysphoric disorder*) in *DSM-IV*. They did so despite objections and evidence from several researchers and from the Psychiatric Association's Committee on Women, which maintain that women's menstrual cycle problems should not be pathologized as a psychiatric disorder (DeAngelis, 1993).

Several studies have engaged Canadian and Australian women in keeping daily mood diaries (Hardie, 1997; and see Figure B–4). Although many women *recall* feeling out of sorts just before their last period, their own day-to-day self-reports often reveal little emotional fluctuation across the menstrual cycle. Moreover, women who *say* they suffer PMS don't differ in mood fluctuations from those who don't. In one study, those who reported severe premenstrual symptoms differed only slightly from other women in actual day-to-day reports throughout their menstrual cycles (Gallant et al., 1992). And contrary to the presumptions of some

FIGURE B–4

Menstruation, actual mood, and recalled mood.

Cathy McFarland and her colleagues (1989) found that Ontario women's daily mood reports did not vary across their menstrual cycle. Yet they recalled that their moods were generally worse just before and during menstruation and better at other times of the cycle.

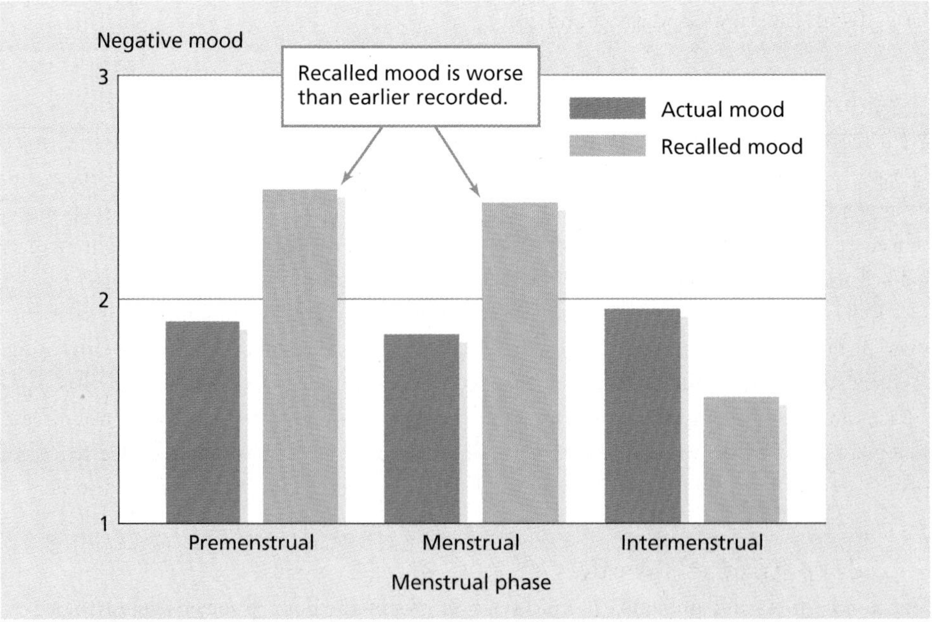

employers, women's physical and mental skills do not fluctuate noticeably with their menstrual cycles. Leta Hollingworth discovered this in her 1914 doctoral dissertation (using women's daily reports rather than their recollections). Many others since then have confirmed her finding (Rosenberg, 1984; Sommer, 1992).

Moreover, PMS complaints vary with culture but not with any known biological differences among women. All this is just what one would expect from a socially constructed disorder, say critics (Richardson, 1993; Rodin, 1992; Usher, 1992). With so many everyday symptoms on PMS checklists—lethargy, sadness, irritability, headaches, insomnia (or sleepiness), disinterest in sex (or heightened interest in sex)—"who wouldn't have 'PMS'?" asked Carol Tavris (1992).

Do I need treatment?

Once people notice a symptom and interpret it as possibly serious, several factors influence their decision to seek medical care. People more often seek treatment if they believe their symptoms have a physical rather than a psychological cause (Bishop, 1987). They may delay seeking help, however, if they feel embarrassed, if they think the likely benefits of medical attention won't justify the cost and inconvenience, or if they want to avoid a possibly devastating diagnosis.

Numerous studies have found a gender difference in decisions to seek medical treatment: Women report more symptoms, use more prescription and nonprescription drugs, and visit physicians 40 percent more often. Women also visit psychotherapists 50 percent more often than men. Women also visit psychotherapists 50 percent more often (Olfson & Pincus, 1994).

Are women more often sick? Apparently not. In fact, men may be more disease-prone. Among other problems, men have higher rates of hypertension, ulcers, and cancer, as well as shorter life expectancies. So why are women more likely to see a doctor? Perhaps women are more attentive to their internal states. Perhaps they are less reluctant to admit "weakness" and seek help (Bishop, 1984). Or perhaps women simply feel freer to make time for a doctor's appointment (Marcus & Siegel, 1982).

Patients are more willing to follow treatment instructions when they have a warm relationship with their doctor, when they help plan their treatment, and when options are framed attractively. People are more likely to elect an operation when given "a 40-percent chance of surviving" than when given "a 60-percent chance of not surviving" (Rothman & Salovey, 1997; Wilson et al., 1987). Such "gain-framed" messages also persuade more people to use sunscreen, eschew cigarettes, and get HIV tests (Detweiler et al., 1999; Salovey et al., 2002; Schneider et al., 2000). Better to tell people that "sunscreen maintains healthy, young-looking skin" than to tell them that "not using sunscreen decreases your chances of healthy, young-looking skin."

EMOTIONS AND ILLNESS

Do our emotions predict our susceptibility to heart disease, stroke, cancer, and other ailments (Figure B–5)? Consider the following.

Heart disease has been linked with a competitive, impatient, and—the aspect that matters—*anger-prone* personality (Matthews, 1988; Williams, 1993). Under stress, reactive, anger-prone "Type A" people secrete more of the stress hormones believed to accelerate the buildup of plaque on the walls of the heart's arteries.

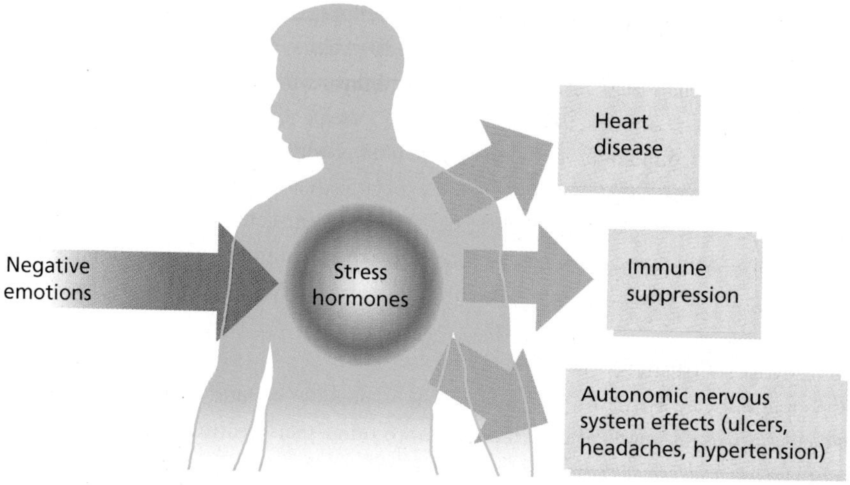

FIGURE B–5
Stress-caused negative emotions may have various effects on health. This is especially so for depressed or anger-prone people.

Depression also increases the risk of various ailments. Mildly depressed people are more vulnerable to heart disease, even after controlling for differences in smoking and other disease-related factors (Anda et al., 1993). The year after a heart attack, depressed people have a doubled risk of further heart problems (Frasure-Smith et al., 1995, 1999, 2005). The toxicity of negative emotions contributes to the high rate of depression and anxiety among chronically ill people (Cohen & Rodriguez, 1995).

George Valliant (1997) witnessed the effect of distress when he followed a group of male university graduates from mid-life into old age. Of those whom at age 52 he classified as "squares" (having never abused alcohol, used tranquilizers, or seen a psychiatrist), only 5 percent had died by age 75. Of those classified as "distressed" (who had abused alcohol and either used tranquilizers or seen a psychiatrist), 38 percent had died.

Optimism and health

Stories abound of people who take a sudden turn for the worse when something makes them lose hope, or who suddenly improve when hope is renewed. As cancer attacks the liver of nine-year-old Jeff, his doctors fear the worst. But Jeff remains optimistic. He is determined to grow up to be a cancer research scientist. One day Jeff is elated. A specialist who has taken a long-distance interest in his case is planning to stop off while on a cross-country trip. There is so much Jeff wants to tell the doctor and to show him from the diary he has kept since he got sick. On the anticipated day, fog blankets his city. The doctor's plane is diverted to another city, from which the doctor flies on to his final destination. Hearing the news, Jeff cries quietly. The next morning, pneumonia and fever have developed, and Jeff lies listless. By evening he is in a coma. The next afternoon he dies (Visintainer & Seligman, 1983).

Understanding the links between attitudes and disease requires more than dramatic true stories. If hopelessness coincides with cancer we are left to wonder: Does cancer breed hopelessness, or does hopelessness also hinder resistance to cancer? To resolve this chicken-and-egg riddle, researchers have (1) experimentally created hopelessness by subjecting organisms to uncontrollable stresses and (2) correlated the hopeless explanatory style with future illnesses.

Stress and illness

The clearest indication of the effects of hopelessness—what Chapter 2 labels *learned helplessness*—comes from experiments that subject animals to mild but uncontrollable electric shocks, loud noises, or crowding. Such experiences do not *cause* diseases such as cancer, but they do lower the body's resistance. Rats injected with live cancer cells more often develop and die of tumours if they also receive inescapable shocks than if they receive escapable shocks or no shocks. Moreover, compared to juvenile rats given controllable shocks, those given uncontrollable shocks are twice as likely in adulthood to develop tumours if given cancer cells and another round of shocks (Visintainer & Seligman, 1985). Animals that have learned helplessness react more passively, and blood tests reveal a weakened immune response.

It's a big leap from rats to humans. But a growing body of evidence reveals that people who undergo highly stressful experiences become more vulnerable to disease (Segerstrom & Miller, 2004). Sustained stress suppresses the immune system, leaving us more vulnerable to infections and malignancy (Cohen, 2002, 2004). The death of a spouse, the stress of a space flight landing, even the strain of an exam week have all been associated with depressed immune defences (Jemmott & Locke, 1984).

Consider:

- A temporary stress magnified the severity of symptoms experienced by volunteers who were knowingly infected with a cold virus (Dixon, 1986).
- Newlywed couples who became angry while discussing problems suffered more immune system suppression the next day (Kiecolt-Glaser et al., 1993).
- A large Swedish study found that, compared with unstressed workers, those with a history of workplace stress had 5.5 times greater risk of colon cancer (Courtney et al., 1993). The cancer difference was not attributable to differences in age, smoking, drinking, or physical traits.

The Delany sisters, both over 100, attributed their longevity to a positive outlook on life.

- Compared to nonprocrastinating students, carefree procrastinators reported lower stress and illness early in a semester but higher stress and illness late in the term. Overall, the self-defeating procrastinators also were sicker and got lower grades (Tice & Baumeister, 1997).

Explanatory style and illness

If uncontrollable stress affects health, depresses immune functioning, and generates a passive, hopeless resignation, then will people who exhibit such pessimism be more vulnerable to illness? Several studies have confirmed that a pessimistic style of explaining bad events (saying, "It's going to last, it's going to undermine everything, and it's my fault") makes illness more likely. Christopher Peterson and Martin Seligman (1987) studied the press quotations of 94 members of baseball's Hall of Fame and gauged how often they offered pessimistic (stable, global, internal) explanations for bad events, such as losing big games. Those who routinely did so tended to die at somewhat younger ages. Optimists—who offered stable, global, and internal explanations for *good* events—usually outlived the pessimists.

Other studies have followed lives through time. In one, Harvard graduates who expressed the most optimism in 1946 were the healthiest when restudied 34 years later. In another, Catholic nuns who expressed the most positive feelings at an average age of 22 outlived their more dour counterparts by an average seven years over the ensuing half century and more (Danner et al., 2001). It is important to note, however, that healthy behaviours—exercise, good nutrition, not drinking to excess—are an essential contributor to the longevity of many optimists (Peterson & Bossio, 2000).

From their own studies, researchers Howard Tennen and Glenn Affleck (1987) agree that a positive, hopeful explanatory style is generally good medicine. But they also remind us that every silver lining has a cloud. Optimists may see themselves as invulnerable and thus fail to take sensible precautions; for example, those who smoke hazardous high-tar cigarettes optimistically underestimate the risks involved (Segerstrom et al., 1993). And when things go wrong in a big way—when the optimist encounters a devastating illness—adversity can be shattering. Optimism is good for health. But remember: Even optimists have a mortality rate of 100 percent.

SUMMING UP: HEALTH PSYCHOLOGY: SOCIAL PSYCHOLOGY AND ILLNESS

The mushrooming field of health psychology is exploring how people decide they are ill, how they explain their symptoms, and when they seek and follow treatment. It also is exploring the effects of negative emotions and the links among illness, stress, and a pessimistic explanatory style.

HOW DO SOCIAL RELATIONSHIPS SUPPORT HEALTH AND WELL-BEING?

There is one other major topic in the social psychology of mental and physical well-being. Supportive close relationships—feeling liked, affirmed, and encouraged by intimate friends and family—predict both health and happiness.

Our relationships are fraught with stress. "Hell is others," wrote Jean-Paul Sartre. When Peter Warr and Roy Payne (1982) asked a representative sample of British adults what, if anything, had emotionally strained them the day before, "family" was their most frequent answer. And stress, as we have seen, aggravates health problems such as coronary heart disease, hypertension, and suppression of our disease-fighting immune system.

Still, on balance, close relationships contribute less to illness than to health and happiness. Asked what prompted yesterday's times of pleasure, the same British sample, by an even larger margin, again answered "family." Close relationships provide our greatest heartaches, but also our greatest joys.

CLOSE RELATIONSHIPS AND HEALTH

Eight extensive investigations, each interviewing thousands of people across several years, have reached a common conclusion: Close relationships predict health (Berkman, 1995; Ryff & Singer, 2000). Health risks are greater among lonely people, who often experience more stress, sleep less well, and commit suicide more often (Cacioppo et al., 2002a, 2002b, 2003). Compared with those with few social ties, those who have close relationships with friends, kin, or other members of close-knit religious or community organizations are less likely to die prematurely. Outgoing, affectionate, relationship-oriented people not only have more friends, they are less susceptible to cold viruses with which an experimenter injects them (see Figure B–6, Cohen et al., 1997, 2003).

Married couples also tend to live healthier, longer lives than their unmarried counterparts. One major study found that people, regardless of age, sex, race, and income, tend to be healthier if married (National Center for Health Statistics, 2004). Indeed social support from a spouse is a potent resource for coping (Marin, Holtzman, DeLongis & Robinson, 2007). Married folks

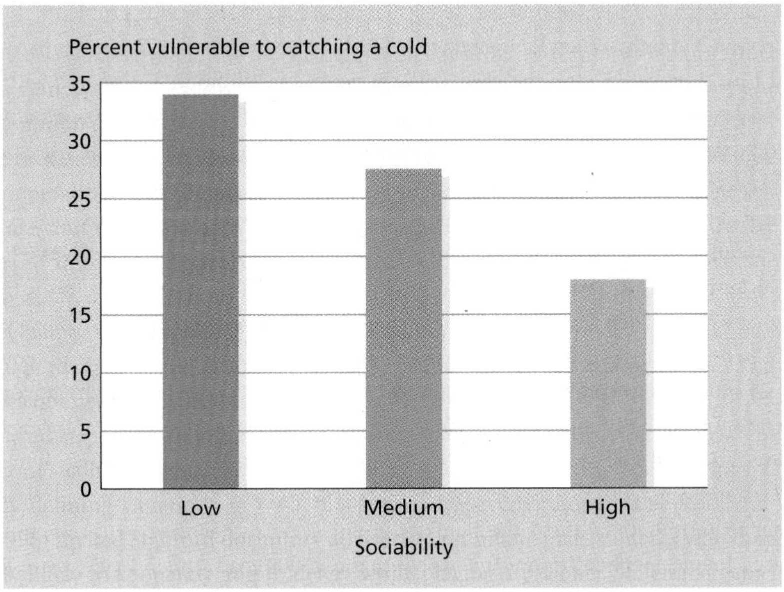

FIGURE B–6
Rate of colds by sociability.
After a cold virus injection, highly sociable people were less vulnerable to catching colds. (From Cohen et al., 2003)

experience less pain from headaches and backaches, suffer less stress, and drink and smoke less. Moreover, in one five-year study of 423 elderly married couples, those who *gave* the most social support (from rides and errands for friends and neighbours to emotional support of their spouse) enjoyed greater longevity, even after controlling for age, sex, initial health, and economic status (Brown et al., 2003). Especially among women, suggests a Finnish study that tracked more than 700 people's illnesses, it is better to give social support than to only receive it (Väänänen et al., 2005).

Moreover, losing social ties heightens the risk of disease:

- A Finnish study of 96 000 widowed people found their risk of death doubled in the week following their partner's death (Kaprio et al., 1987).
- An American National Academy of Sciences study reveals that those who are recently widowed become more vulnerable to disease and death (Dohrenwend et al., 1982).
- A study of 30 000 men revealed that when a marriage ends, men drink and smoke more and eat fewer vegetables and more fried foods (Eng et al., 2001).

Confiding and health

So there is a link between social support and health. But why? Perhaps those who enjoy close relationships eat better, exercise more, and smoke and drink less. Perhaps a supportive network helps us evaluate and overcome stressful events (Taylor et al., 1997). In more than 80 studies, social support has been linked with better functioning cardiovascular and immune systems (Uchino et al., 1996). Thus, when we are wounded by someone's dislike or the loss of a job, a friend's advice, help, and reassurance may indeed be good medicine (Cutrona, 1986; Rook, 1987). Even when the problem isn't mentioned, friends provide us with distraction and a sense that, come what may, we're accepted, liked, and respected.

With someone we consider a close friend, we may confide painful feelings. In one study, James Pennebaker and Robin O'Heeron (1984) contacted the surviving spouses of suicide or car accident victims. Those who bore their grief alone had more health problems than those who expressed it openly. When Pennebaker (1990) surveyed more than 700 university women, he found 1 in 12 reported a traumatic sexual experience in childhood. Compared with women who had experienced nonsexual traumas, such as parental death or divorce, the sexually abused women reported more headaches, stomach ailments, and other health problems, *especially if they had kept their history of abuse secret.*

To isolate the confiding, confessional side of close relationships, Pennebaker asked the bereaved spouses to share what upsetting events had been weighing on their minds. Those they first asked to describe a trivial event were physically tense. They stayed tense until they confided their troubles. Then they relaxed. Writing about personal traumas in a diary also seems to help. When volunteers in another experiment did so, they had fewer health problems during the next six months. One participant explained, "Although I have not talked with anyone about what I wrote, I was finally able to deal with it, work through the pain instead of trying to block it out. Now it doesn't hurt to think about it." Even if it's only "talking to my diary," it helps to be able to confide (King, 2001).

Other experiments confirm the benefits of engaging rather than suppressing stressful experiences. In one, Stephen Lepore and his colleagues (2000) had students view a stressful slide show and video on the Holocaust and either talk about it immediately afterwards or not. Two days later, those who talked were experiencing less stress and fewer intrusive thoughts. Even mentally revisiting a recent problem that was still "stressing you out"—vividly recalling the incident and associated feelings—served to boost active coping and mood (Rivkin & Taylor, 1999).

Poverty, inequality, and health

We have seen connections between health and the feelings of control that accompany a positive explanatory style. And we have seen connections between health and social support. Feelings of control and support together with health care and nutrition factors help explain why economic status correlates with longevity. Recall from Chapter 1 the study of old grave markers in Glasgow, Scotland: Those with the costliest, highest pillars (indicating affluence) tended to have lived the longest (Carroll et al., 1994). Still today, in Scotland, Canada, and the United States, poorer people are at greater risk for premature death. Poverty predicts perishing. Being wealthy predicts being healthy.

The correlation between poverty and ill health could run either way. Bad health isn't good for one's income. But most evidence indicates that the causal arrow runs from poverty toward ill health (Sapolsky, 2005). So how *does* poverty "get under the skin"? The answers include (a) reduced access to quality health care, (b) unhealthier lifestyles (smoking is much more common among less educated and lower-income people), and, to a striking extent, (c) increased stress. To be poor is to be at risk for increased stress, negative emotions, and a toxic environment (Adler & Snibbe, 2003; Chen, 2004; Gallo & Matthews, 2003). To be poor is to more often be sleep-deprived after working a second job, earning paycheques that don't cover the bills, commuting on crowded public transit, living in a high-pollution area, and doing hard labour that's controlled by someone else. Even among primates, those with the least control—at the bottom of the social pecking order—are most vulnerable when exposed to a cold-like virus (Cohen et al., 1997). Poverty and its associated stresses help explain the lower life expectancy of disadvantaged minorities. In the United States, for example, at birth the average White person has a life expectancy of 78 years, the average Black person 73 years (CDC, 2005). Poverty also helps explain a curious but oft-reported correlation between intelligence and health. Edinburgh University researcher Ian Deary (2005) and his colleagues observed this correlation after stumbling across data from an intelligence test administered on June 1, 1932, to virtually all Scots born in 1921. When they searched Scotland's death records, they found, as have researchers in other countries since, that "whether you live to collect your old-age pension depends in part on your IQ at age 11. You just can't keep a good predictor down." Partly, the low-intelligence risk factor—which is roughly equivalent to that of obesity or high blood pressure, he reports—is due to the low-IQ persons having been less likely to cease smoking after its risks became known, and therefore more likely to die of lung cancer. Poverty-related stresses and lack of control also contribute, he notes. People also die younger in regions with great income inequality (Kawachi et al., 1999; Lynch et al., 1998; Marmot & Wilkinson, 1999). Gaps between the rich and poor are greater in Britain and the Canada and people in these countries have lower life expectancies than people in Japan and Sweden. Where inequality has grown over the last decade, as in Eastern Europe and Russia, life expectancy has been at the falling end of the teeter-totter.

Is inequality merely an indicator of poverty? The mixed evidence indicates that poverty matters but that inequality matters, too. John Lynch and his colleagues (1998, 2000) report that people at every income level are at greater risk of early death if they live in a community with great income inequality. It's not just being poor, it's also *feeling* poor, relative to one's surroundings, which proves toxic. And that, Robert Sapolsky (2005) suggests, helps explain why the United States, which has the greatest income inequality of Westernized nations, simultaneously ranks number 1 in the world on health care expenditures and number 29 on life expectancy.

Inequality may also lead to a more inefficient health care system. Not only does the U.S. rank low on life expectancy, when you look at any number of specific outcomes it is clear that the U.S. mix of private and public funding is much less efficient than the Canadian system of publicly funded health care (Woodhammer & Himmelstein, 1991). Canada spends far less on health care than the U.S., but the care received by and the subsequent health of Canadians is noticeably better than the typical person in the U.S. This health care advantage is especially large for those with the lowest incomes, but extends to all income levels.

CLOSE RELATIONSHIPS AND HAPPINESS

Confiding painful feelings is good not only for the body but for the soul as well. That's the conclusion of studies showing that people are happier when supported by a network of friends and family.

"Woe to him who is alone when he falls and has not another to lift him up."

Ecclesiastes 4:10b

Some studies, summarized in Chapter 2, compare people in a competitive, individualistic culture, such as that of Canada, Australia, and the United States, with those in collectivist cultures, such as those of Japan and many developing countries. Individualistic cultures offer independence, privacy, and pride in personal achievements. The tighter social bonds of collectivist cultures offer protection from loneliness, alienation, divorce, and stress-related diseases.

Friendships and happiness

Other studies compare individuals with few or many close relationships. Being attached to friends with whom we can share intimate thoughts has two effects, observed the seventeenth-century philosopher Francis Bacon. "It redoubleth joys, and cutteth griefs in half." So it seems from answers to a question asked in one large-scale survey (Burt, 1986): "Looking over the last six months, who are the people with whom you discussed matters important to you?" Compared to those who could not name a single person with whom they had such interactions those who named five or more such friends were 60 percent more likely to feel "very happy."

Other findings confirm the importance of social networks. Across the lifespan, friendships foster self-esteem and well-being (Hartup & Stevens, 1997). For example,

- The happiest university students are those who feel satisfied with their love life (Emmons et al., 1983).
- Those who enjoy close relationships cope better with various stresses, including bereavement, rape, job loss, and illness (Abbey & Andrews, 1985; Perlman & Rook, 1987).
- Among 800 alumni of one university surveyed by Wesley Perkins, those who preferred having very close friends and a close marriage to having a high income and occupational success were twice as likely as their former classmates to describe themselves as "fairly" or "very" happy (Perkins, 1991). When asked, "What is necessary for your

happiness?" or "What is it that makes your life meaningful?" most people mention—before anything else—satisfying close relationships with family, friends, or romantic partners (Berscheid, 1985; Berscheid & Peplau, 1983). Happiness hits close to home.

"The sun looks down on nothing half so good as a household laughing together over a meal."

C. S. Lewis, "Membership," 1949

Marital attachment and happiness

For more than 9 in 10 people worldwide, one eventual example of a close relationship is marriage. Does marriage correlate positively with happiness? Or is there more happiness in the pleasure-seeking single life than in the "bondage," "chains," and "yoke" of marriage?

A mountain of data reveal that most people are happier attached than unattached. Survey after survey of many tens of thousands of Europeans and North Americans has produced a consistent result: Compared to those single or widowed, and especially compared to those divorced or separated, married people report being happier and more satisfied with life (Gove et al., 1990; Inglehart, 1990). In Canada, married people are more satisfied with their lives than people who have never been married, who are more satisfied than people who have been widowed or divorced (Tepperman & Curtis, 1995). This marriage-happiness link occurs across ethnic groups (Parker et al., 1995). Moreover, satisfaction with marriage predicts overall happiness much better than does satisfaction with job, finances, or community (Lane, 1998). And among the nonmarried, rates of suicide and depression run higher (Stack, 1992; and see Figure B–7). Indeed, there are few stronger predictors of happiness than a close, nurturing, equitable, intimate, lifelong companionship with one's best friend.

Is marriage, as is so often supposed, more strongly associated with men's happiness than women's? Given women's greater contribution to household work and to supportive nurturing,

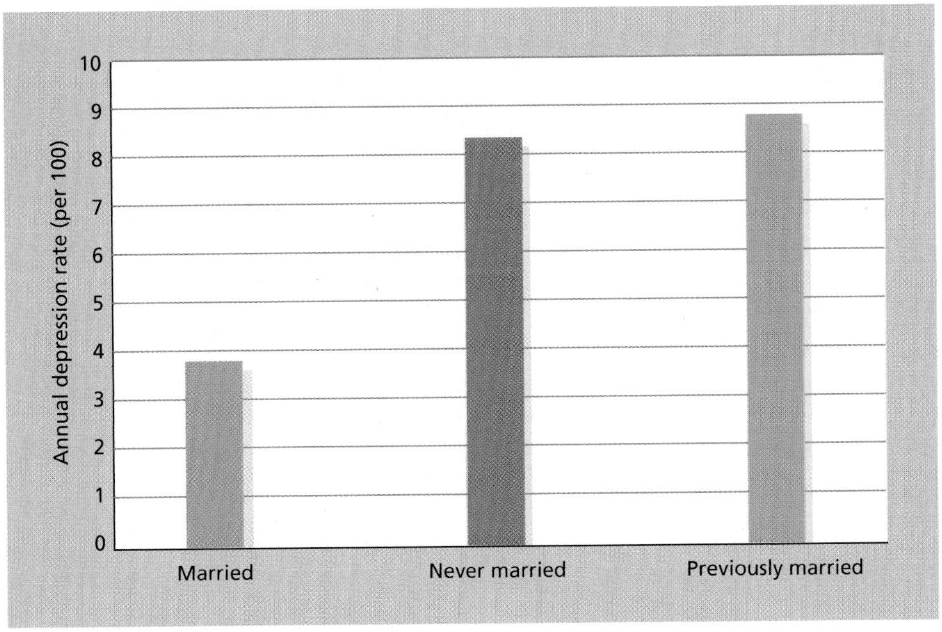

FIGURE B–7

Marital status and depression.

A Statistics Canada survey of treatment for depression found depression rates more than two times greater among adults not married. (Data from Statistics Canada, 1996)

we might expect so. The married vs. never-married happiness gap, however, is only slightly greater among men than women. In European surveys, and in a statistical digest of 93 other studies, this happiness gap is virtually identical for men and women (Inglehart, 1990; Wood et al., 1989). Although a bad marriage is often more depressing to a woman than to a man, the myth that single women are happier than married women can be laid to rest. Throughout the Western world, married people of both sexes report more happiness than those never married, divorced, or separated.

More important than being married, however, is the marriage's quality. People who say their marriage is satisfying—who find themselves still in love with their partner—rarely report being unhappy, discontented with life, or depressed. Fortunately, most married people *do* declare their marriages happy ones. In one large survey, almost two-thirds say their marriages are "very happy." Three out of four say their spouses are their best friends. Four out of five people say they would marry the same people again. The consequence? Most such people feel quite happy with life as a whole.

Why are married people generally happier? Does marriage promote happiness? Or is it the other way around—does happiness promote marriage? Are happy people more appealing as marriage partners? Do grouchy or depressed people more often stay single or suffer divorce? Certainly, happy people are more fun to be with. They are also more outgoing, trusting, compassionate, and focused on others (Myers, 1993). Unhappy people, as we have noted, are more often socially rejected. Depression often triggers marital stress, which deepens the depression (Davila et al., 1997). So, positive, happy people more readily form happy relationships.

But "the prevailing opinion of researchers," reports University of Oslo sociologist Arne Mastekaasa (1995), is that the marriage-happiness connection is "mainly due" to the beneficial effects of marriage. Put on your thinking cap: If the happiest people marry sooner and more often, then as people age (and progressively less happy people move into marriage), the average happiness of both married and never-married people should decline. (The older, less happy newlyweds would pull down the average happiness of married people, and the unmarried group would be more and more left with the unhappy people.) But the data do not support this prediction. This suggests that marital intimacy does—for most people—pay emotional dividends. One team that followed 1380 adults over 15 years concurs (Horwitz et al., 1997). The tendency for married people to be less depressed occurs even after controlling for premarital happiness.

Marriage enhances happiness for at least two reasons. First, married people are more likely to enjoy an enduring, supportive, intimate relationship, and are less likely to suffer loneliness. No wonder male medical students in a study by Robert Coombs survived medical school with less stress and anxiety if married (Coombs, 1991). A good marriage gives each partner a dependable companion, a lover, a friend.

There is a second, more prosaic, reason why marriage promotes happiness, or at least buffers us from misery. Marriage offers the roles of spouse and parent, which can provide additional sources of self-esteem (Crosby, 1987). True, multiple roles can multiply stress. Our circuits can and do overload. Yet each also provides rewards, status, avenues to enrichment, escape from stress faced in other parts of one's life. A self with many identities is like a mansion with many rooms. When fire struck one wing of Windsor Castle most of the castle still remained for royals and tourists to enjoy. When our personal identity stands on several legs, it, too, holds up under the loss of any one. If we mess up at work, well, we can tell ourselves we're still good husbands and fathers, and in the final analysis, these parts of us are what matter most.

SUMMING UP: HOW DO SOCIAL RELATIONSHIPS SUPPORT HEALTH AND WELL-BEING?

Health and happiness are influenced not only by social cognition but also by social relations. People who enjoy close, supportive relationships are at less risk for illness and premature death. Such relationships assist people's coping with stress, especially when they enable people to confide their intimate emotions.

Close relationships also foster happiness. People who have intimate, long-term attachments with friends and family members cope better with loss and report greater happiness. Compared to unmarried adults, those married, for example, are much more likely to report being very happy, and are less at risk for depression. This appears due both to the greater social success of happy people and to the well-being engendered by a supportive life companion.

MODULE C

Social Psychology in Court

On January 31, 1969, Gail Miller set out in –42 degree weather for her job as a nursing assistant at the Saskatoon City Hospital. She never made it. She was found later that day lying face down in a snow bank, lifeless. She had been brutally beaten, raped, and stabbed. A trail of evidence (blood, a knife handle, a boot, and a wallet) led to a building not far away. There, visiting an acquaintance with two of his travelling companions, was a 16-year-old drifter named David Milgaard.

Milgaard was questioned and denied any involvement in the murder. His companions, when questioned, backed his alibi, but after extensive questioning (and deprivation from the drugs they were addicted to) changed their story. One companion said he could not account for Milgaard's whereabouts and the other said that she saw Milgaard commit the murder. The police felt they had their man. Milgaard was tried, convicted, and sentenced to life in prison.

Unbeknownst to the police, another man, Larry Fisher, was living in the same building where David Milgaard had stayed that fateful night. As he confessed in 1970, he had committed a series of rapes in Saskatoon that winter, and as DNA testing later demonstrated, he was the man that killed Gail Miller. David Milgaard spent 23 years in prison for a crime he did not commit. How could the criminal justice system fail him in such a fundamental way? The case raised other questions as well; all examined in social psychological experiments:

- There were no true eyewitnesses to this crime. But, how influential was the eyewitness testimony? What makes a credible witness?
- Milgaard was a drifter and seen as a hippie. Can jurors ignore, as they should, their prejudices and the defendant's appearance and social status?
- How well do jurors comprehend important information, such as statistical probabilities involved in DNA blood tests?

Such questions fascinate lawyers, judges, and defendants. And they are questions to which social psychology can suggest answers, as most law schools have recognized when they hire professors of "law and social science."

We can think of a courtroom as a miniature social world, one that magnifies everyday social processes with major consequences for those involved. In criminal cases, psychological factors may influence decisions involving arrest, interrogation, prosecution, plea bargaining, sentencing, and parole. Of criminal cases disposed of in Canadian courts, three in four never come to trial (Statistics Canada, 1996). Much of the trial lawyer's work therefore "is not persuasion in the courtroom but bargaining in the conference room" (Saks & Hastie, 1978, pp. 119–120). Even in the conference room, decisions are made based on speculation about what a jury or judge might do.

So, whether a case reaches a jury verdict or not, the social dynamics of the courtroom matter. Let's therefore consider two sets of factors that have been heavily researched: (1) features of the courtroom drama that can influence jurors' judgments of a defendant and (2) characteristics of both the jurors and their deliberations.

HOW RELIABLE IS EYEWITNESS TESTIMONY?

As the courtroom drama unfolds, jurors hear testimony, form impressions of the defendant, listen to instructions from the judge, and render a verdict. Let's take these steps one at a time, starting with eyewitness testimony.

HOW PERSUASIVE IS EYEWITNESS TESTIMONY?

In Chapter 3, we noted that anecdotes and personal testimonies, being vivid and concrete, can be powerfully persuasive, often more so than information that is logically compelling but abstract. There's no better way to end an argument than to say, "I saw it with my own eyes!"

Elizabeth Loftus (1974, 1979) found that those who had "seen" were indeed believed, even when their testimony was shown to be useless. When students were presented with a hypothetical robbery-murder case with circumstantial evidence but no eyewitness testimony, only 18 percent voted for conviction. Other students received the same information but with the addition of a single eyewitness. Now, knowing that someone had declared, "That's the one!" 72 percent voted for conviction. For a third group, the defence attorney discredited this testimony (the witness had 20/400 vision and was not wearing glasses). Did this discrediting reduce the effect of the testimony? In this case, not much: 68 percent still voted for conviction.

Later experiments revealed that discrediting may reduce somewhat the number of guilty votes (Whitley, 1987). But unless contradicted by another eyewitness (Leippe, 1985), a vivid eyewitness account is difficult to erase from jurors' minds. That helps explain why, compared to criminal cases lacking eyewitness testimony, those that have eyewitness testimony are more likely to produce convictions (Visher, 1987).

Can't jurors spot erroneous testimony? To find out, Gary Wells, R. C. L. Lindsay, and their colleagues staged hundreds of eyewitnessed thefts of a University of Alberta calculator. Afterwards, they asked each eyewitness to identify the culprit from a photo lineup. Other people, acting as jurors, observed the eyewitnesses being questioned and then evaluated their testimony. Are incorrect eyewitnesses believed less often than those who are accurate? As it happened, both correct and incorrect eyewitnesses were believed 80 percent of the time (Wells et al., 1979). This led the researchers to speculate that "human observers have absolutely no ability to discern eyewitnesses who have mistakenly identified an innocent person" (Wells et al., 1980).

Eyewitness recall of detail is sometimes impressive. When John Yuille and Judith Cutshall (1986) studied accounts of a midafternoon murder on a busy Burnaby, British Columbia, street, they found that eyewitnesses' recall for detail was 80 percent accurate.

In a follow-up experiment, Lindsay, Wells, and Carolyn Rumpel (1981) staged the theft under conditions that sometimes allowed witnesses a good, long look at the thief and sometimes didn't. The jurors believed the witnesses more when conditions were good. But even when conditions were so poor that two-thirds of the witnesses had actually misidentified an innocent person, 62 percent of the jurors still usually believed the witnesses.

Wells and Michael Leippe (1981) also have found that jurors are more skeptical of eyewitnesses whose memory for trivial details is poor—though these tend to be the most *accurate* witnesses. Jurors think a witness who can remember that there were three pictures hanging in the room must have "really been paying attention" (Bell & Loftus, 1988, 1989). Actually, those who pay attention to details are *less* likely to pay attention to the culprit's face.

WHEN EYES DECEIVE

David Milgaard is not the only person who has been falsely accused of a crime. Stories abound of innocent people who have wasted years in prison because of the testimony of eyewitnesses who were sincerely wrong (Brandon & Davies, 1973). Yet there are tens of thousands of cases each year that depend on eyewitness testimony, so even dozens of such cases would not prove that eyewitness accounts are unreliable. To assess the accuracy of eyewitness recollections, we need to learn their overall rates of "hits" and "misses." One way to gather such information is to stage crimes comparable to those in everyday life and then solicit eyewitness reports.

This has now been done many times, sometimes with disconcerting results. For example, in one study, 141 students witnessed an "assault" on a professor. Seven weeks later, when Robert Buckhout (1974) asked them to identify the assailant from a group of six photographs, 60 percent chose an innocent person. No wonder eyewitnesses to actual crimes sometimes disagree about what they saw. Later studies have confirmed that eyewitnesses often are more confident than correct. For example, Brian Bornstein and Douglas Zickafoose (1999) found that students felt, on average, 74 percent sure of their later recollections of a classroom visitor, but were only 55 percent correct.

Of course, some witnesses are more confident than others. And Wells and his colleagues report that it's the confident witnesses jurors find most believable. So it is disconcerting that unless conditions are very favourable, as when the culprit is very distinctive-looking, the certainty of witnesses bears only a modest relation to their accuracy (Lüüs & Wells, 1994; Sporer et al., 1995). Intuitive confidence does correlate somewhat with accuracy, especially among people who make positive identifications. Yet some people—whether right or wrong—chronically express themselves more assertively. And that, says Michael Leippe (1994), explains why mistaken eyewitnesses are so often persuasive.

This finding would surely come as a surprise to many judges. In most cases the law is such that judges are supposed to take a witness's certainty of his or her testimony into account. One panel of judges even declared that among the factors to be considered in determining accuracy is "the level of certainty demonstrated by the witness" (Wells & Murray, 1983). If judges and juries take this to heart they will often be swayed by certain but wrong testimony.

"Certitude is not the test of certainty."

Oliver Wendell Holmes, Collected Legal Papers

Errors sneak into our perceptions and our memories because our minds are not videotape machines. People are quite good at recognizing a pictured face when later shown the same picture alongside a new face. But University of Stirling face researcher Vicki Bruce (1998) was surprised to discover that subtle differences in views, expression, or lighting "are hard for human vision to deal with." We construct our memories, based partly on what we perceived at the time and partly on our expectations, beliefs, and current knowledge (Figure C–1).

The strong emotions that accompany witnessed crimes and traumas may further corrupt eyewitness memories. Charles Morgan and his colleagues (2004) documented the effects of stress on memory with more than 500 soldiers at survival schools—mock prisoner of war camps that were training the soldiers to withstand deprivation of food and sleep, combined with intense, confrontational interrogation. A day after release from the camp, when the soldiers were asked to identify their intimidating interrogators from a 15-person lineup, only 30 percent could do so, although 62 percent could recall a low-stress interrogator. Thus, conclude the researchers, "contrary to popular conception that most people would never forget the face of a clearly seen individual who had physically confronted them and threatened them for more than 30 minutes, [many] were unable to correctly identify the perpetrator."

FIGURE C–1
Sometimes believing is seeing.
Cultural expectations affect perceiving, remembering, and reporting. In a 1947 experiment on rumour transmission, Gordon Allport and Leo Postman showed people this picture of a White man holding a razor blade and then had them tell a second person about it, who then told a third person, and so on. After six tellings, the razor blade in the White man's hand usually shifted to the Black man's. (Allport, G. W. and L. Postman, 1947, 1975. Figure from *The Psychology of Rumor* by Gordon W. Allport and Leo Postman, copyright © 1947 and renewed 1975 by Holt, Rinehart and Winston, reproduced by permission of the publisher. Illustration by Graphic Presentation Services.)

THE MISINFORMATION EFFECT

Elizabeth Loftus and her associates (1978) provided a dramatic demonstration of memory construction. They showed students 30 slides depicting successive stages of an automobile-pedestrian accident. One critical slide showed a red Datsun stopped at a stop sign or a yield sign. Afterwards they asked half the students, among other questions, "Did another car pass the red Datsun while it was stopped at the stop sign?" They asked the other half the same question but with the words "stop sign" replaced by "yield sign." Later, all viewed both slides in Figure C–2 and recalled which one they had previously seen. Those earlier asked the question consistent with what they had seen were 75 percent correct. Those previously asked the misleading question were only 41 percent correct; more often than not, they *denied* seeing what they had actually seen and instead "remembered" the picture they had never seen!

In other studies of this **misinformation effect** (remembering wrong information), Loftus (1979a, 1979b, 2001) found that after suggestive questions witnesses may believe that a red light was actually green or that a robber had a moustache when he didn't. When questioning eyewitnesses, police and attorneys commonly ask questions framed by their own understanding of what happened. So it is troubling to discover how easily witnesses incorporate misleading information into their memories, especially when they believe the questioner is well informed and when suggestive questions are repeated (Smith & Ellsworth, 1987; Zaragoza & Mitchell, 1996).

misinformation effect witnessing an event, receiving misleading information about it, and then incorporating the "misinformation" into one's memory of the event

It also is troubling to realize that false memories feel and look like real memories. Thus, they can be as persuasive as real memories—convincingly sincere, yet sincerely wrong. This is true of young children (who are especially susceptible to misinformation) as well as adults. Stephen Ceci and Maggie Bruck (1993a, 1993b) demonstrated children's suggestibility by asking children, once a week for 10 weeks, to "Think real hard, and tell me if this ever happened to you." For example, "Can you remember going to the hospital with the mousetrap on your

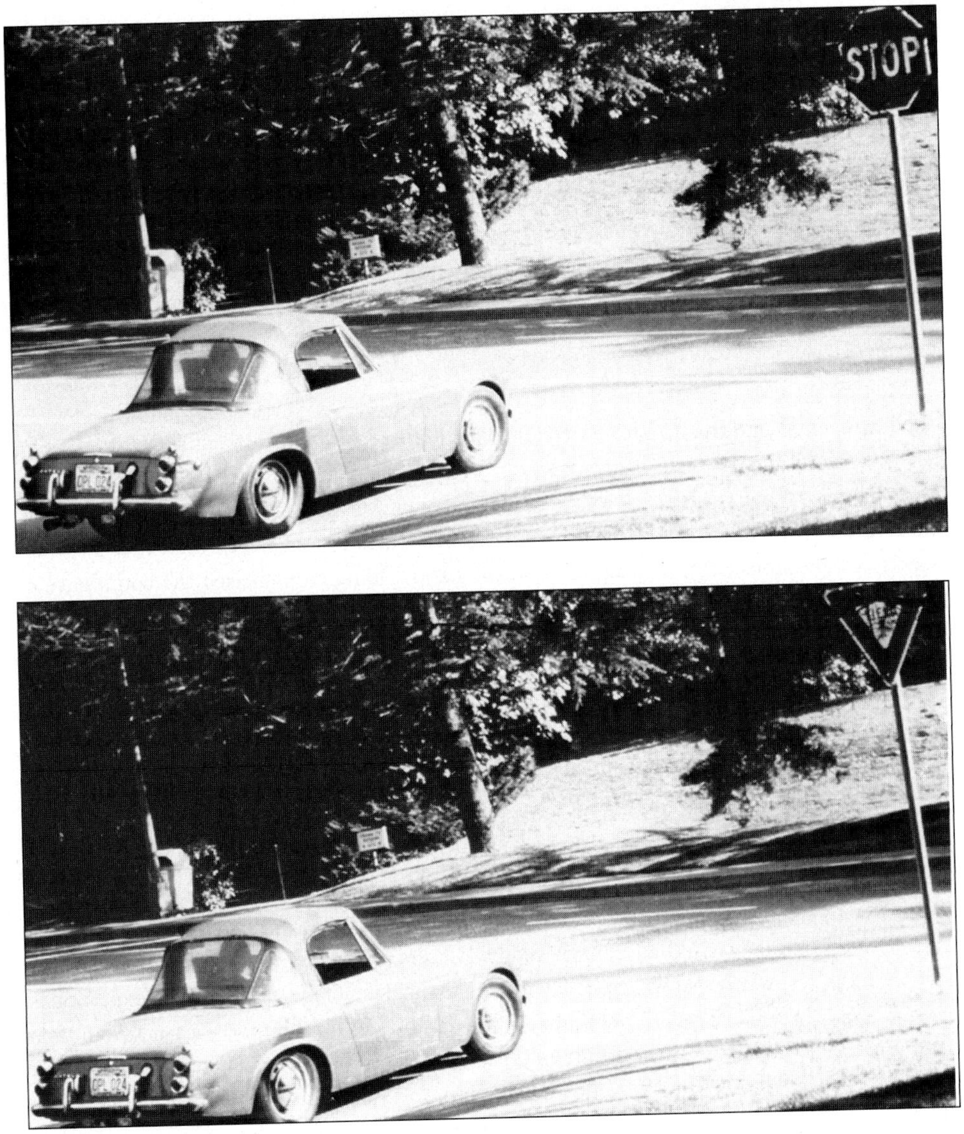

FIGURE C–2

The misinformation effect.

When shown one of these two pictures and then asked a question suggesting the sign from the other photo, most people later "remembered" seeing the sign they had never actually seen. (From Loftus, Miller & Burns, 1978. Photos courtesy of Elizabeth Loftus)

finger." Remarkably, when then interviewed by a new adult who asked the same question, 58 percent of preschoolers produced false and often detailed stories about the fictitious event. One boy explained that his brother had pushed him into a basement woodpile, where his finger got stuck in the trap. "And then we went to the hospital, and my mommy, daddy, and Colin drove me there, to the hospital in our van, because it was far away. And the doctor put a bandage on this finger."

Given such vivid stories, professional psychologists were often fooled. They could not reliably separate real from false memories—nor could the children. Told the incident never actually happened, some protested. "But it really did happen. I remember it!" For Bruck and Ceci (1999, 2004), such findings raise the possibility of false accusations, as in alleged child sex abuse cases where children's memories may have been contaminated by repeated suggestive questioning and where there is no corroborating evidence. Given suggestive interview questions, Bruck and Ceci report, most preschoolers and many older children will produce false reports such as seeing a thief steal food in their daycare centre.

Even among university students, imagining childhood events, such as breaking a window with their hand or having a nurse remove a skin sample, led one-fourth to recall that the imagined event actually happened (Garry et al., 1996; Mazzoni & Memom, 2003). This "imagination inflation" happens partly because visualizing something activates similar areas in the brain as does actually experiencing it (Gonsalves et al., 2004).

RETELLING

Retelling events commits people to their recollections, accurate or not. An accurate retelling helps them later resist misleading suggestions (Bregman & McAllister, 1982). Other times, the more we retell a story, the more we convince ourselves of a falsehood. Wells, Ferguson, and Lindsay (1981) demonstrated this by having eyewitnesses to a staged theft rehearse their answers to questions before taking the witness stand. Doing so increased the confidence of those who were wrong, and thus made jurors who heard their false testimony more likely to convict the innocent person.

In Chapter 4, we noted that we often adjust what we say to please our listeners and, having done so, come to believe the altered message. Imagine witnessing an argument that erupts into a fight in which one person injures the other. Afterwards, the injured party sues. Before the trial a smooth lawyer for one of the two parties interviews you. Might you slightly adjust your testimony, giving a version of the fight that supports this lawyer's client? If you did so, might your later recollections in court be similarly slanted?

Blair Sheppard and Neil Vidmar (1980) report that the answer to both questions is yes. At the University of Western Ontario, they had some students serve as witnesses to a fight and others as lawyers and judges. When interviewed by lawyers for the defendant, the witnesses later gave the judge testimony that was more favourable to the defendant. In a follow-up experiment, Vidmar and Nancy Laird (1983) noted that witnesses did not omit important facts from their testimony; they just changed their tone of voice and choice of words depending on whether they thought they were a witness for the defendant or for the plaintiff. Even this was enough to bias the impressions of those who heard the testimony. So it's not only suggestive questions that can distort eyewitness recollections but also their own retellings, which may be subtly adjusted to suit their audience.

FEEDBACK TO WITNESSES

> *Eyewitness to a crime on viewing a lineup:* "Oh, my God . . . I don't know . . . It's one of those two . . . but I don't know . . . Oh, man . . . the guy a little bit taller than number two . . . It's one of those two, but I don't know . . ."
> *Months later at trial:* "You were positive it was number two? It wasn't a maybe?"
> *Eyewitness's answer:* "There was no maybe about it . . . I was absolutely positive." (*Missouri v. Hutching,* 1994, reported by Wells & Bradfield, 1998).

STORY BEHIND THE RESEARCH

Gary L. Wells
Iowa State University

The legal system has always struck me as relying heavily on doctrine and precedent in making assumptions. What attracted me to social psychology was the possibility of scientifically testing many of these assumptions. Consider the assumption that eyewitnesses to crimes can report reliably on events they have observed. Using staged crimes, I have shown that eyewitnesses can be highly inaccurate and yet sincerely confident. This research reveals that people's confidence in the accuracy of their memories reflects social and personality factors rather than the quality of their memories. One exciting development from this research is that I have been able to devise ways to improve eyewitness accuracy. This shows that social psychologists can do more than identify problems, we can also develop solutions.

What explains witnesses misrecalling their original uncertainty? Gary Wells and Amy Bradfield (1998) wondered. Past research has shown that one's confidence gains a boost from learning that another witness has fingered the same person, from being asked the same question repeatedly, and from preparing for cross-examination (Lüüs & Wells, 1994; Shaw, 1996; Wells et al., 1981). Might the lineup interviewer's feedback also influence not just confidence but—the I-knew-it-all-along phenomenon rides again—recollections of earlier confidence?

To find out, Wells and Bradfield conducted two experiments in which 352 university students viewed a grainy security camera video of a man entering a store. Moments later, off camera, he murders a security guard. They then viewed the photo spread from the actual criminal case, minus the gunman's photo, and were asked to identify the gunman. All 352 students made a false identification, following which the experimenter gave confirming feedback ("Good. You identified the actual suspect"), disconfirming feedback ("Actually, the suspect was number ____"), or no feedback. Finally, all were later asked, "At the time that you identified the person in the photo spread, how certain were you that the person you identified from the photos was the gunman that you saw in the video?" (from 1, not at all certain, to 7, totally certain).

The experiment produced two striking results: First, the effect of the experimenter's casual comment was huge. In the confirming feedback condition, 58 percent of the eyewitnesses rated their certainty as 6 or 7 when making their initial judgment—four times the 14 percent who said the same in the no-feedback condition and eleven times the 5 percent in the disconfirming condition. We shouldn't be surprised that witnesses' post-feedback confidence would be raised by confirming feedback, but these were ratings of their remembered *pre*-feedback confidence.

It wasn't obvious to the subjects that those judgments would be affected. For the second rather amazing finding is that when asked if the feedback had influenced their answer, 58 percent said no. Moreover, as a group those who felt uninfluenced were no less so than those who said they were (Figure C–3).

The lesson here runs deeper than jury research. Once again we see why we need social psychological research. As social psychologists have so often found—recall Milgram's obedience

FIGURE C–3

Recalled certainty of eyewitnesses after receiving confirming or disconfirming feedback (Experiment 2).

Note that participants who said feedback did not influence them were influenced no less. (Data from Wells & Bradfield, 1998)

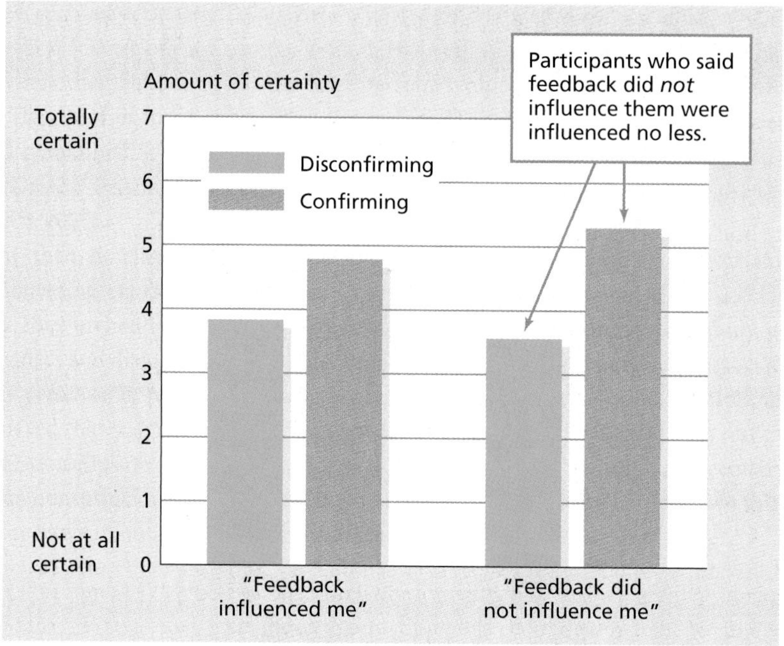

experiments—simply asking people how they would act, or asking what explains their actions, sometimes gives us wrong answers. Benjamin Franklin was right: "There are three things extremely hard, Steel, a Diamond, and to know one's self." And that is why we need to do not only surveys that ask people to explain themselves, but experiments in which we see what they actually do.

REDUCING ERROR

Given these error-prone tendencies, what constructive steps can be taken to increase the accuracy of eyewitnesses and jurors? Experts have several ideas.

Train police interviewers

When Ronald Fisher and his coworkers (1987, 1989) examined tape-recorded interviews of eyewitnesses conducted by experienced Florida police detectives, they found a typical pattern. Following an open-ended beginning ("Tell me what you recall"), the detectives would occasionally interrupt with follow-up questions, including questions eliciting terse answers ("How tall was he?").

Fisher and Edward Geiselman (1992) say interviews should begin by allowing eyewitnesses to offer their own unprompted recollections. The recollections will be most complete if the interviewer jogs the memory by first guiding people to reconstruct the setting. Have them visualize the scene and what they were thinking and feeling at the time. Even showing pictures of the setting—of, say, the store checkout lane with a clerk standing where she was

robbed—can promote accurate recall (Cutler & Penrod, 1988). After giving witnesses ample, uninterrupted time to report everything that comes to mind, the interviewer then jogs their memory with evocative questions ("Was there anything unusual about the voice? Was there anything unusual about the person's appearance or clothing?").

When Fisher and his colleagues (1989, 1994) trained detectives to question in this way, the information they elicited from eyewitnesses increased 50 percent without increasing the false memory rate. In response to such results, most police agencies in North America and Britain have adopted this "cognitive interview" procedure (Geiselman, 1996). Many agencies now include the procedure in their training program, including the witness interviewing manual distributed to all police officers in England and Wales (Bower, 1997). (The procedure also shows promise for enhancing information gathered in oral histories and medical surveys.)

"While the rules of evidence and other safeguards provide protection in the courtroom, they are absent in the backroom of the precinct station."

Ernest Hilgard & Elizabeth Loftus (1979)

Interviewers on memory reconnaissance missions must be careful to keep their questions free of hidden assumptions. Loftus and Guido Zanni (1975) found that questions such as "Did you see the broken headlight?" triggered twice as many "memories" of nonexistent events as did questions without the hidden assumption: "Did you see a broken headlight?"

Flooding eyewitnesses with an array of mugshots also reduces accuracy in later identifying the culprit (Brigham & Cairns, 1988). Errors are especially likely when the witness has to stop, think, and analytically compare faces. Verbally describing a robber's face disrupts later recognition of it from a photographic lineup. Some researchers think this "verbal overshadowing" occurs because one's memory for the face accommodates the verbal depiction; others believe that the word-based description replaces the unconscious perception, or makes it inaccessible (Fallshore & Schooler, 1995; Meissner et al., 2001; Schooler, 2002).

Accurate identifications tend to be automatic and effortless. The right face just pops out (Dunning & Stern, 1994). In recent studies by David Dunning and Scott Perretta (2002), eyewitnesses who make their identifications in less than 10 to 12 seconds were nearly 90 percent accurate; those taking longer were roughly 50 percent accurate. Although other studies challenge a neat 10- to 12-second rule, they confirm that quicker identifications are generally more accurate (Weber et al., 2004). For example, when Tim Valentine and his colleagues (2003) analyzed 640 eyewitness viewing they, too, found that nearly 9 in 10 "fast" identifications were for the actual suspect, but fewer than 4 in 10 slower identifications were accurate. Younger eyewitnesses, and those who had viewed the culprit for more than a minute, were also more accurate than older eyewitnesses and those who had less than a minute's exposure.

Minimize false lineup identifications

The case of Ron Shatford illustrates how the composition of a police lineup can promote misidentification (Doob & Kirshenbaum, 1973). After a suburban Toronto department store robbery, the cashier involved could only recall that the culprit was not wearing a tie and was "very neatly dressed and rather good looking." When police put the good-looking Shatford in a lineup with 11 unattractive men, all of whom wore ties, the cashier readily identified him as the culprit. Only after he had served 15 months of a long sentence did another person confess, allowing Shatford to be retried and found not guilty.

Gary Wells (1984, 1993, 2005) reports that one way to reduce misidentifications is to remind witnesses that the person they saw may or may not be in the lineup. Alternatively, give eyewitnesses a "blank" lineup that contains no suspects and screen out those who make false identifications. Those who do not make such errors turn out to be more accurate when they later face the actual lineup.

Dozens of studies in Europe, North America, Australia, and South Africa show that mistakes also subside when witnesses simply make individual yes or no judgments in response to a *sequence* of people (Lindsay & Wells, 1985; Meissner et al., 2005, Steblay et al., 2001). A simultaneous lineup tempts people to pick the person who, among the lineup members, most resembles the perpetrator. Witnesses viewing just one suspect at a time are just as likely to make accurate identifications and much less likely to make false ones. If witnesses view a group of photos or people simultaneously, they are more likely to choose whoever most resembles the culprit.

These no-cost procedures make police lineups more like good experiments. They contain a *control group* (a no-suspect lineup or a lineup in which mock witnesses try to guess the suspect based merely on a general description). They have an experimenter who is *blind* to the hypotheses (an officer who doesn't know which person is the suspect). Questions are *scripted and neutral,* so they don't subtly demand a particular response (the procedure doesn't imply the culprit *is* in the lineup). And they prohibit confidence-inflating post-lineup comments ("you got him") prior to trial testimony. Such procedures greatly reduce the natural human confirmation bias (having an idea and seeking confirming evidence). Lineups can also now be effectively administered by computers (MacLin et al., 2005).

Although procedures such as double-blind testing are common in psychological science, they are still uncommon in criminal procedures (Wells & Olson, 2003). But their time may be coming. Police could use a new procedure developed by Queen's University researchers Sean Pryke, Rod Lindsay, and their colleagues (2004). They invited students to identify a prior class visitor from multiple lineups that separately presented face, body, and voice samples. Their findings: An eyewitness who consistently identified the same suspect—by face, by body, and by voice—was nearly always an accurate eyewitness.

Educate jurors

Do jurors evaluate eyewitness testimony rationally? Do they intuitively understand how the circumstances of a lineup determine its reliability? Do they know whether to take an eyewitness's self-confidence into account? Do they realize how memory can be influenced by earlier misleading questions, by stress at the time of the incident, by the interval between the event and the questioning, by whether the suspect is the same or a different race, by whether recall of other details is sharp or hazy? Studies in Canada, Great Britain, and the United States reveal that jurors discount most of these factors, all of which are known to influence eyewitness testimony (Cutler et al., 1988; Devenport et al., 2002; Noon & Hollin, 1987; Wells & Turtle, 1987; Yarmey, 2003a, 2003b).

To educate jurors, experts are now frequently asked (usually by defence attorneys) to testify about eyewitness testimony. Their aim is to offer jurors the sort of information you have been reading, to help them evaluate the testimony of both prosecution and defence witnesses. Table C–1 above, drawn from a survey of 64 experts on eyewitness testimony, lists the most agreed-upon phenomena.

TABLE C–1 **Influences on eyewitness testimony**

Phenomenon	Eyewitness Experts Agreeing*
Question wording. An eyewitness's testimony about an event can be affected by how the questions put to that eyewitness are worded.	98%
Lineup instructions. Police instructions can affect an eyewitness's willingness to make an identification.	98%
Confidence malleability. An eyewitness's confidence can be influenced by factors that are unrelated to identification accuracy.	95%
Mug-shot-induced bias. Exposure to mug shots of a suspect increases the likelihood that the witness will later choose that suspect in a lineup.	95%
Postevent information. Eyewitnesses' testimony about an event often reflects not only what they actually saw but information they obtained later on.	94%
Attitudes and expectations. An eyewitness's perception and memory of an event may be affected by his or her attitudes and expectations.	92%
Cross-race bias. Eyewitnesses are more accurate when identifying members of their own race than members of other races.	90%
Accuracy versus confidence. An eyewitness's confidence is not a good predictor of his or her identification accuracy.	87%

*"This phenomenon is reliable enough for psychologists to present it in courtroom testimony."

Source: From S. M. Kassin, V. A. Tubb, H. M. Hosch & A. Memon (2001). "On the 'General Acceptance' of Eyewitness Testimony Research: A New Survey of the Experts." *American Psychologist*, 56, pp. 405–416. Copyright 2001 by the American Psychological Association. Reprinted by permission.

Taught the conditions under which eyewitness accounts *are* trustworthy, jurors become more likely to trust such testimony (Cutler et al., 1989; Wells, 1986). Moreover, attorneys and judges are recognizing the importance of some of these factors when deciding when to ask for or permit suppression of lineup evidence (Stinson et al., 1996, 1997).

SUMMING UP: HOW RELIABLE IS EYEWITNESS TESTIMONY?

In hundreds of experiments, social psychologists have found that the accuracy of eyewitness testimony can be impaired by a host of factors in the ways people form judgments and memories. Some eyewitnesses express themselves more assertively than others. The assertive witness is more likely to be believed, although assertiveness is actually a trait of the witness and not of the certainty of the information. The human eye is not a video camera; it is vulnerable to variations in light, angle, and other changes that impair recognition of a face.

As the sequence of events in a crime is told repeatedly, errors may creep in and become embraced by the witness as part of the true account. To reduce such errors, interviewers are advised to let the witness tell what he or she remembers without interruption, and to encourage the witness to visualize the scene of the incident and the emotional state the witness was in when the incident occurred. Educating jurors about the pitfalls of eyewitness testimony can improve the way testimony is received and, ultimately, the accuracy of the verdict.

WHAT INFLUENCES THE INDIVIDUAL JUROR AND THE JURY AS A GROUP?

Verdicts depend on what happens in the courtroom—the eyewitness testimonies, the defendant's characteristics, the judge's instructions. But verdicts also depend on how the individual jurors process information and how the members of the jury influence one another.

JURORS AS INDIVIDUALS

To gain insight into how jurors process information, Nancy Pennington and Reid Hastie (1993) have studied the thought processes of mock jurors, sampled from courthouse jury pools, while viewing re-enactments of actual trials. In making their decisions, jurors first construct a story that makes sense of all the evidence. After observing one murder trial, some jurors concluded that a quarrel made the defendant angry, triggering him to get a knife, search for the decedent, and stab him to death. Others surmised that the frightened defendant picked up a knife that he used to defend himself when he later encountered the decedent. When the jurors begin deliberating, they are often surprised to discover that others have constructed different stories. This implies—and research confirms—that jurors are persuaded when attorneys present evidence like a narrative story. In felony cases—where the conviction rate can be as high as 80 percent—the Crown case follows a story structure more often than the defence case.

Next the jurors must grasp the judge's instructions concerning the available verdict categories. For these instructions to be effective, jurors must first understand them. Study after study has found that many people do not understand the standard legalese of judicial instructions. Depending on the type of case, a jury may be told that the standard of proof is a "preponderance of the evidence," "clear and convincing evidence," or "beyond a reasonable doubt." Such statements may have one meaning for the legal community and different meanings in the minds of jurors (Kagehiro, 1990).

After observing actual cases and later interviewing the jurors, Stephen Adler (1994) found "lots of sincere, serious people who—for a variety of reasons—were missing key points, focusing on irrelevant issues, succumbing to barely recognized prejudices, failing to see through the cheapest appeals to sympathy or hate, and generally botching the job."

Jurors may be further confused if the criteria change as proceedings move from the trial phase that determines guilt or innocence into the penalty phase (Luginbuhl, 1992). In some cases, for example, jurors are to convict only if there is "proof beyond a reasonable doubt." But a "preponderance of the evidence" is sufficient when judging whether mitigating circumstances, such as an abusive childhood, should lighten the sentence.

Finally, jurors must compare their explanation with the verdict categories. When using the judge's definition of, say, justifiable self-defence, jurors must decide whether "pinned against a wall" matches their understanding of the required circumstance "unable to escape." Often a judge's abstract, jargon-filled definition of verdict categories loses in the competition with the jurors' own mental images of these crimes. Vicki Smith (1991) reports that, regardless of the judge's definition, if a defendant's actions match jurors' images of "vandalism," "assault," or "robbery," they will find the person guilty.

People also have a hard time comprehending statistics and scientific information when it is presented as evidence. When Larry Fisher was finally tried for Gail Miller's murder in 1999, the jury was presented with evidence that there was only one chance in 950 trillion that the DNA from the sperm found on Gail Miller's clothes belonged to anyone other than Larry Fisher. This evidence by all rational accounts should have ruled David Milgaard out as a suspect in the case. These sorts of statistics, however, are difficult to comprehend and jurors often have trouble figuring out exactly what they mean. Perhaps aware of jurors' fragile understanding of such statistical principles, Fisher's lawyer tried to argue that despite the DNA evidence there was still a good chance that David Milgaard was the person who really raped and murdered Gail Miller. In this instance the jury was able to see through the lawyer's erroneous argument. Unfortunately, juries are not always able to do so. The more typical finding is that juries do not pay enough attention to statistical evidence.

Gary Wells (1992) reports that even when people (including experienced trial judges) understand naked statistical probabilities, they may be unpersuaded. The numbers, it seems, must be supported by a convincing story. Thus, reports Wells, one Toronto mother lost a paternity suit seeking child support from her child's alleged father despite a blood test showing a 99.8 percent probability that the man was her child's father. She lost after the man took the stand and persuasively denied the allegation.

Understanding how jurors misconstrue judicial instructions and statistical information is a first step toward better decisions. A next step might be giving jurors access to transcripts rather than forcing them to rely on their memories in processing complex information (Bourgeois et al., 1993). A further step is devising and testing clearer, more effective ways to present information—a task on which several social psychologists are currently at work. For example, when a judge quantifies the required standard of proof (as, say, 51, 71, or 91 percent certainty) jurors understand and respond appropriately (Kagehiro, 1990).

And surely there must be a simpler way to tell jurors, as required in Illinois death penalty cases, not to impose the death sentence in murder cases when there are justifying circumstances: "If you do not unanimously find from your consideration of all the evidence that there are no mitigating factors sufficient to preclude imposition of a death sentence, then you should sign the verdict requiring the court to impose a sentence other than death" (Diamond, 1993). Given jury instructions rewritten into simple language, jurors are less susceptible to the judge's biases (Halverson et al., 1997).

Phoebe Ellsworth and Robert Mauro (1998) sum up the dismal conclusions of jury researchers: "Legal instructions are typically delivered in a manner likely to frustrate the most conscientious attempts at understanding. . . . The language is technical and . . . no attempt is made either to assess jurors' mistaken preconceptions about the law or to provide any kind of useful education."

THE JURY AS A GROUP

Imagine a jury that, having finished a trial, has entered the jury room to begin its deliberations. Researchers Harry Kalven and Hans Zeisel (1966) reported that chances are about 2 in 3 that the jurors will initially *not* agree on a verdict. Yet, after discussion, 95 percent emerge with a consensus. Obviously, group influence has occurred.

Thousands of times a year small groups sampled from the people called for jury duty convene to seek a group decision (Kagehiro, 1990). Are they subject to the social influences that mould other decision groups—to patterns of majority and minority influence, to group polarization, to groupthink? Let's start with a simple question: If we knew the jurors' initial leanings, could we predict their verdict?

The law prohibits observation of actual juries. So researchers simulate the jury process by presenting a case to mock juries and having them deliberate as a real jury would. In a series of such studies James Davis, Robert Holt, Norbert Kerr, and Garold Stasser tested various mathematical schemes for predicting group decisions, including decisions by mock juries (Davis et al., 1975, 1977, 1989; Kerr et al., 1976). Will some mathematical combination of initial decisions predict the final group decision? Davis and his colleagues found that the scheme that predicts best varies according to the nature of the case. But in several experiments, a "two-thirds-majority" scheme fared best: The group verdict was usually the alternative favoured by at least two-thirds of the jurors at the outset. Without such a majority, a hung jury was likely.

Likewise, in Kalven and Zeisel's survey of juries, 9 in 10 reached the verdict favoured by the majority on the first ballot. Although you might fantasize about someday being the courageous lone juror who sways the majority, the fact is it seldom happens.

Minority influence

Seldom, yet sometimes, what was initially a minority prevails. A typical 12-person jury is like a typical small university class: The three quietest people rarely talk and the three most vocal people contribute more than half the talking (Hastie et al., 1983). If jurors who favoured a particular verdict are vocal and persist in their views, they are more likely to eventually prevail. From the research on minority influence we know that jurors in the minority will be most persuasive when they are consistent, persistent, and self-confident. This is especially so if they can begin to trigger some defections from the majority (Gordijn et al., 2002; Kerr, 1981).

Group polarization

Jury deliberation shifts people's opinions in other intriguing ways as well. In experiments, deliberation often magnifies initial sentiments. For example, Robert Bray and Audrey Noble (1978) had University of Kentucky students listen to a 30-minute tape of a murder trial. Then, assuming the defendant was found guilty, they recommended a prison sentence. Groups of high authoritarians initially recommended strong punishments (56 years) and after deliberation were even more punitive (68 years). The low-authoritarian groups were initially more lenient (38 years) and after deliberation became more so (29 years).

Confirmation that group polarization can occur in juries comes from an ambitious study in which Reid Hastie, Steven Penrod, and Nancy Pennington (1983) put together 69 twelve-person juries from Massachusetts citizens on jury duty. Each jury was shown a re-enactment of an actual murder case, with roles played by an experienced judge and actual attorneys. Then they were given unlimited time to deliberate the case in a jury room. As Figure C–4 shows, the evidence was incriminating: Four out of five jurors voted guilty before deliberation, but felt unsure enough that a weak verdict of manslaughter was their most popular preference. After deliberation, nearly all agreed the accused was guilty, and most now preferred a stronger verdict—second-degree murder. Through deliberation, their initial leanings had grown stronger.

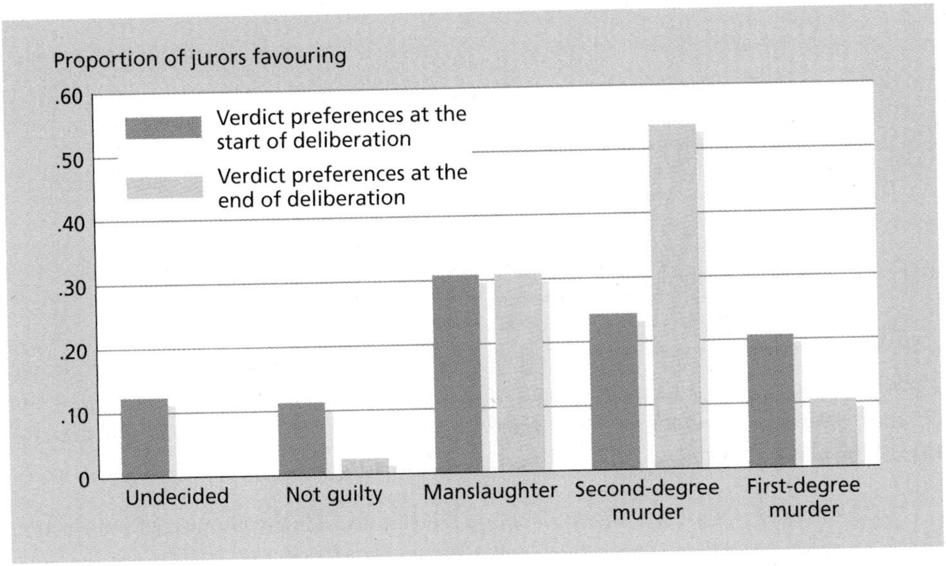

FIGURE C–4

Group polarization in juries.

In highly realistic simulations of a murder trial, 828 Massachusetts jurors stated their initial verdict preferences, and then deliberated the case for periods ranging from three hours to five days. Deliberation strengthened initial tendencies, which favoured the prosecution. (From Hastie et al., 1983)

Leniency

In many experiments, one other curious effect of deliberation has surfaced: Especially when the evidence is not highly incriminating, as it was in the experiment just described, deliberating jurors often become more lenient (MacCoun & Kerr, 1988). This qualifies the "two-thirds-majority-rules" finding, for if even a bare majority initially favours *acquittal,* it usually will prevail (Stasser et al., 1981). Moreover, a minority that favours acquittal stands a better chance of prevailing than one that favours conviction (Tindale et al., 1990).

Once again, a survey of actual juries confirms the laboratory results. Kalven and Zeisel (1966) report that in those cases where the majority does not prevail, it usually shifts to acquittal. When a judge disagrees with the jury's decision, it is usually because the jury acquits someone the judge would have convicted.

> *"It is better that ten guilty persons escape than one innocent suffer."*
>
> William Blackstone, 1769

Might "informational influence" (stemming from others' persuasive arguments) account for the increased leniency? The "innocent-unless-proved-guilty" and "proof-beyond-a-reasonable-doubt" rules put the burden of proof on those who favour conviction. Perhaps this makes evidence of the defendant's innocence more persuasive. Or perhaps "normative influence" creates the leniency effect, as jurors who view themselves as fair-minded confront other jurors who are even more concerned with protecting a possibly innocent defendant.

SUMMING UP: WHAT INFLUENCES THE INDIVIDUAL JUROR AND THE JURY AS A GROUP?

Social psychologists are interested in not only the interactions among witnesses, judges, and juries, but also what happens within and between individual jurors. One major concern is jurors' ability to comprehend evidence, especially when it involves statistics indicating the probability that a given person committed the crime.

Juries are groups and they are swayed by the same influences that bear upon other types of groups, including that opposing views may become more entrenched and polarized. In addition, especially when evidence is not highly incriminating, deliberation may make jurors more lenient than they originally were.

WHAT DO SIMULATED JURIES TELL US ABOUT REAL JURIES?

Perhaps while reading this chapter, you have wondered what some critics (Tapp, 1980; Vidmar, 1979) have wondered: Isn't there an enormous gulf between college students discussing a hypothetical case and real jurors deliberating a real person's fate?

Indeed there is. It is one thing to ponder a pretend decision given minimal information and quite another to agonize over the complexities and profound consequences of an actual case. So Reid Hastie, Martin Kaplan, James Davis, Eugene Borgida, and others have asked their participants, who sometimes are drawn from actual juror pools, to view enactments of actual trials. The enactments are so realistic that sometimes participants forget the trial they are watching on television is staged (Thompson et al., 1981).

Researchers also defend the laboratory simulations, by noting that the laboratory offers a practical, inexpensive method for studying important issues under controlled conditions (Bray & Kerr, 1982; Dillehay & Nietzel, 1980). What is more, as researchers have begun testing them in more realistic situations, findings from the laboratory studies have often held up quite well. No one contends that the simplified world of the jury experiment mirrors the complex world of the real courtroom. Rather, the experiments help us formulate theories with which we interpret the complex world.

Come to think of it, are these jury simulations any different from social psychology's other experiments, all of which create simplified versions of complex realities? By varying just one or two factors at a time in this simulated reality, the experimenter pinpoints how changes in one or two aspects can affect us. And that is the essence of social psychology's experimental method.

SUMMING UP: WHAT DO SIMULATED JURIES TELL US ABOUT REAL JURIES?

Simulated juries are not real juries, so we must be cautious in generalizing research findings to actual courtrooms. Yet, like all experiments in social psychology, laboratory jury experiments help us formulate theories and principles that we can use to interpret the more complex world of everyday life.

MODULE D

Social Psychology and the Sustainable Future[1]

Life is good. Today the average North American enjoys luxuries unknown even to royalty in centuries past: hot showers, flush toilets, central air-conditioning, microwave ovens, jet travel, wintertime fresh fruit, big-screen digital television, email,

[1]Parts of this module are adapted from *The American Paradox: Spiritual Hunger in an Age of Plenty* (by David G. Myers, Yale University Press, 2000), where further information about materialism and about wealth, inequality, and well-being may be found.

and Post-it notes. But on the horizon, beyond the sunny skies of comfort and convenience, dark clouds of an environmental disaster are gathering. In scientific gatherings hosted by the United Nations, Britain's Royal Society, and the U.S. National Academy of Sciences, a consensus has emerged: Increasing population and increasing consumption have combined to overshoot the earth's ecological carrying capacity (Figure D–1).

AN ENVIRONMENTAL CALL TO ACTION

Although these are, materially, the best of times for many people on earth, humanity is creating a climate change that may, if human behaviour does not change, become a weapon of mass destruction.

In 1950 the earth carried 2.5 billion people and 50 million cars. Today it has 6.6 billion people and 500 million cars, and economic growth in developing countries is putting millions more cars on the road (N. Myers, 2000). In addition to being a waste-disposal problem, cars burn gasoline. This combustion, along with the burning of coal and oil to generate electricity and heat buildings, produces an excess of carbon dioxide, which—along with other greenhouse gases from agricultural and industrial sources—contributes to global warming.

There is now strong evidence that significant global warming is occurring, reports a joint statement by the National Academy of Sciences and 10 other nations' science academies, including Canada's (2005): "The threat of climate change is clear and increasing." The five warmest years on record have occurred since 1998 (WMO, 2005). Ocean temperatures are rising. Glaciers are retreating and the polar icecaps are thinning. The sea level is rising. Permafrost is thawing. "The consequences of the past century's temperature increase," notes *Science* editor Donald Kennedy (2006), "are becoming dramatically apparent in the increased frequency of extreme weather events." With the changing climate, hurricanes, heat waves, droughts and

FIGURE D–1

The ecological overshoot.

The human demand for things such as land, timber, fish, and fuels is increasingly exceeding the earth's regenerative capacity. (www.footprintnetwork.org, 2006)

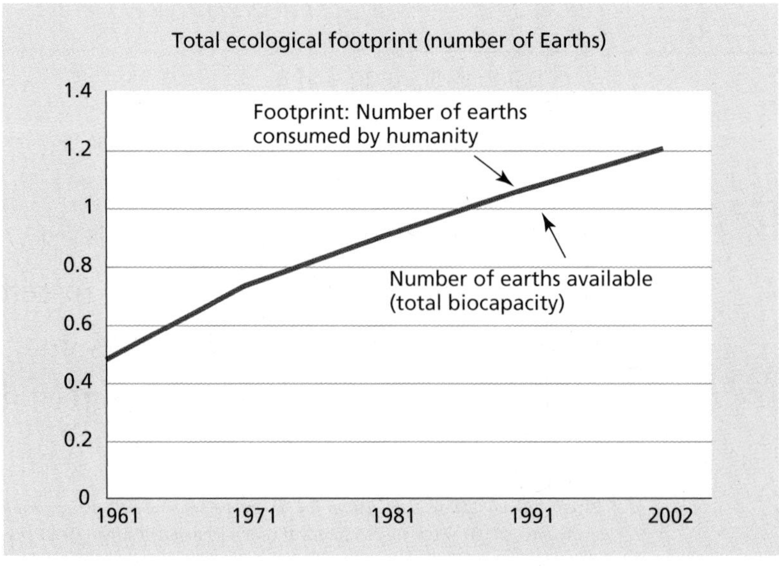

Does the convenience of a ready-made beverage justify the resources consumed idling in line?

floods are becoming more common and extreme weather-related insurance payouts are increasing (Rohter, 2004). As precipitation falls more as rain, and less as snow, the likely result will be more floods in rainy seasons and less melting snow and glaciers for rivers during dry seasons. It's a national security issue, say some: Terrorist bombs and global warming are both weapons of mass destruction.

Global warming is causing not only climate change itself but also environmental destruction. Trees and shrubs are invading the North American tundra, crowding out tundra species. Similarly, plants and animals are gradually migrating toward the poles and toward higher elevations, interfering with polar and alpine ecosystems. Semiarid agricultural and grazing lands, notably those in sub-Saharan Africa, are gradually turning into desert.

In addition to these global warming-linked effects, ecosystems around the world are in danger because of human exploitation. As the earth's population increases, the demand increases for resources to produce basic human necessities (food, clothing, shelter) as well as luxuries. Most of the world's original forest cover has been taken down, and what remains in the tropics is being cleared for agriculture, livestock grazing, logging, and settlements. With deforestation come soil erosion, diminished absorption of greenhouse gases, greater extremes of rainfall and temperature resulting in periodic floods and droughts, and the devastation of many animal species. A growing population's appetite for fish, together with ecosystem destruction, has also led to decreasing annual catches in 11 of 15 major oceanic fishing areas and in 7 of 10 major fish species (Karavellas, 2000; McGinn, 1998). In part because of overfishing, stocks of wild salmon, Atlantic cod, haddock, herring, and other species have suffered major depletion.

With consumption and population both destined to increase (despite falling birth rates—see Figure D–2), further pollution, global warming, and environmental destruction seem inevitable. The simple, stubborn fact is that the earth cannot

"Climate change is the most severe problem that we are facing today—more severe even than the threat of terrorism."

Britain's chief science adviser, David King, 2004

"One day fairly soon we will all go belly up like guppies in a neglected fishbowl. I suggest an epitaph for the whole planet: . . . 'We could have saved it, but we were to darn cheap and lazy.'"

Kurt Vonnegut, "Notes from My Bed of Gloom," 1990

FIGURE D–2

World population growth.

(Population Reference Bureau, 2006)

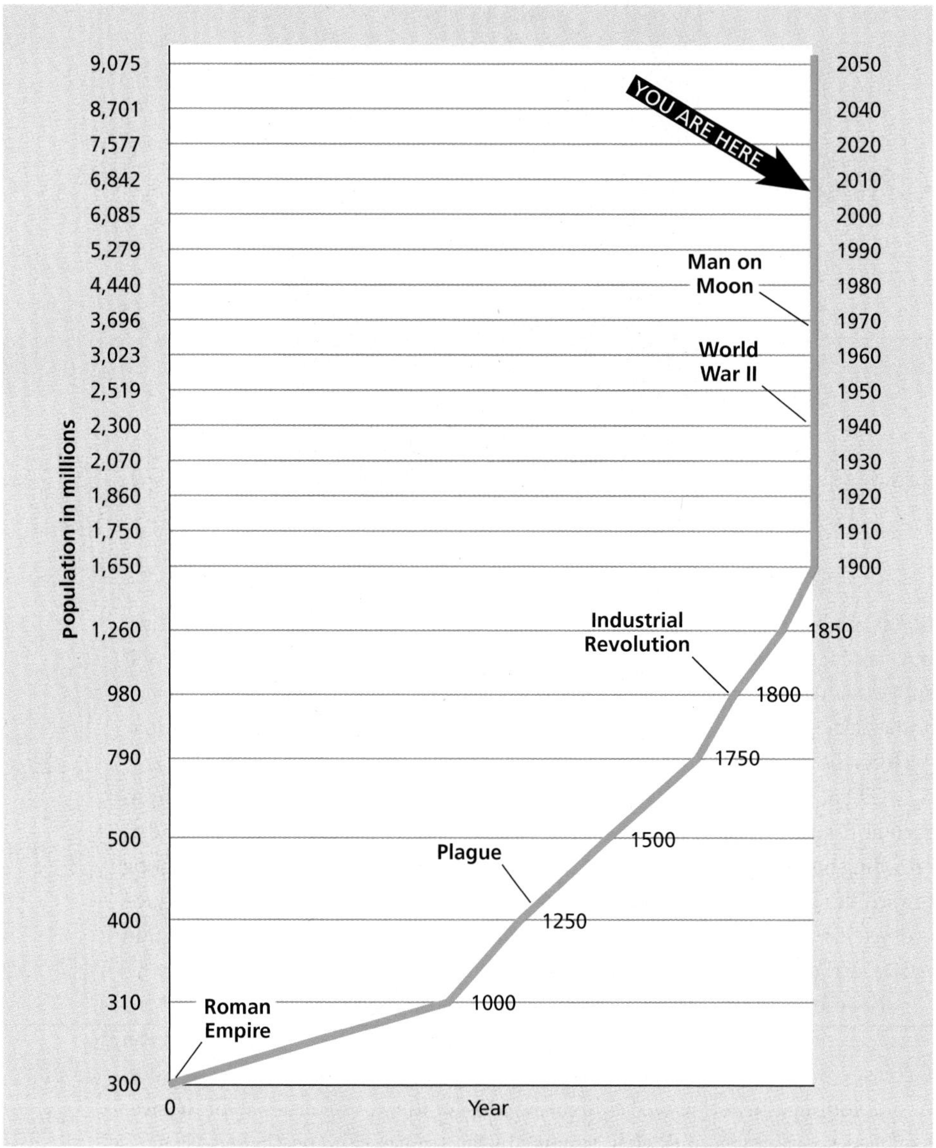

indefinitely support developed countries' current rate of consumption, much less the projected increase in consumption as less-developed countries attain higher living standards. Thus, the need for more sustainable consumption has taken on "urgency and global significance" (Heap & Kent, 2000). For the human species to survive and flourish, some things must change.

ENABLING SUSTAINABLE LIVING

Although increasing population and consumption have overshot the world's carrying capacity, new technologies together with reduced consumption may enable sustainable living.

Close, supportive relationships are a key element in well-being.

What shall we do? Eat, drink, and be merry for tomorrow is doom? Behave as have so many participants in Prisoners' Dilemma games, by pursuing self-interest to our collective detriment? ("Heck, on a global scale, my consumption is infinitesimal; it makes my life comfortable and costs the world practically nothing.") Wring our hands and vow never to bring children into a hurting world?

Those more optimistic about the future see two routes to sustainable lifestyles: (a) increasing technological efficiency and agricultural productivity, and (b) moderating consumption and decreasing population.

NEW TECHNOLOGIES

One component in a sustainable future is improved eco-technologies. Today's new refrigerators consume half the energy of those sold a decade ago (Heap & Comim, 2005). We have replaced many incandescent bulbs with energy-saving fluorescent bulbs, replaced printed and delivered letters and catalogues with email and e-commerce, and replaced many commuter kilometres driven with telecommuting.

There is also good news about cars. To begin with, today's middle-aged adults drive cars that get twice the mileage and produce a twentieth of the pollution of the ones they drove as teenagers. For the future, we have hybrid cars, which conserve gasoline by using an electric power cell; and flex-fuel cars, which can run on ethanol produced from a variety of vegetable sources such as soybeans, or on a mixture of ethanol and gasoline.

Plausible future technologies include diodes that emit light for 20 years without bulbs; ultrasound washing machines that consume no water, heat, or soap; reusable and compostable plastics; cars running on fuel cells that combine hydrogen and oxygen and produce water exhaust; lightweight materials stronger than steel; and roofs and roads that double as solar energy collectors (N. Myers, 2000).

Given the speed of innovation (who could have imagined today's world a century ago?), the future will surely bring solutions that we aren't yet imagining. Surely, say the optimists, the future will bring increased material well-being for more people requiring many fewer raw materials and much less polluting waste.

REDUCING CONSUMPTION

The second component of a sustainable future is the control of consumption. Instead of more people consuming and polluting more, a stable population will need to consume and pollute less.

Thanks to family planning efforts, the world's population growth rate has decelerated, especially in developed nations. Even in less-developed countries, when food security has improved and women have become educated and empowered, birth rates have fallen. But if birth rates everywhere instantly fell to a replacement level of 2.1 children per woman, the lingering momentum of population growth, fed by the bulge of younger humans, would continue for years to come.

Given that humans have already overshot the earth's carrying capacity, individual consumption must also moderate. With our material appetites continually swelling—as more people seek personal computers, air conditioning, jet travel—what can be done to moderate consumption by those who can afford to overconsume?

One way is through public policies that harness the motivating power of incentives. As a general rule, we get less of what we tax, and more of what we reward. Many cities are using tax monies to build bike lanes and subsidize improved mass transportation, thus encouraging alternatives to cars. On jammed highways, many regions have created high-occupancy vehicle lanes that reward carpooling and penalize driving solo. Gregg Esterbrook (2004) notes that if the United States had raised its gasoline tax by 50 cents a decade ago, as was proposed, the country would now have smaller, more fuel-efficient cars (as do Europeans, with their higher petrol taxes) and would therefore import less oil. This, in turn, would have led to lower oil consumption, less global warming, lower gas prices, and a smaller trade deficit weighing down the economy. A higher gas tax would have similar effects in Canada too.

Robert Frank (1999), an economist well-versed in social psychology, suggests how a socially responsible market economy might reward achievement while promoting more sustainable consumption. His proposal is simple: Tax people not on what they earn but on what they spend—which is their earnings minus their savings and their charity. The tax could be made progressive with ample exemptions for dependants and higher tax rates for the big spenders. Frank argues that a progressive consumption tax (beginning, say, with a 20-percent tax rate on annual consumption beyond $40,000 for a family of four and rising to 70 percent for consumption over $500,000) promises to moderate consumption. Such tax would encourage savings and investment while increasing the price on nonessential luxury goods. Public policy could also give business and industry more incentives for conserving and penalties for consuming.

Support for such policies will require a shift in public consciousness not unlike that occurring during the 1960s civil rights movement and the 1970s women's movement. As the earth's atmosphere heats up and petroleum and other fossil fuels become scarce, such a shift is inevitable, eventually. Is there any hope that, before a crisis arises, human priorities might shift from accumulating money to finding meaning, and from aggressive consumption to nurturing connections? The British government's plan for achieving sustainable development includes an emphasis on promoting personal well-being and social health. Perhaps social psychology can help point the way to greater well-being, by documenting *materialism*, by informing people that *economic growth does not automatically improve human morale*, and by helping people understand *why materialism and money fail to satisfy*.

SUMMING UP: AN ENVIRONMENTAL CALL TO ACTION

Humanity can prepare for a sustainable future by increasing technological efficiency. We can also create incentives and change actions and attitudes to control population and moderate consumption. Attending to concepts in social psychology that address our attitudes and our behaviours may help accomplish those objectives. Rapid cultural change has happened in the last 40 years, and there is hope that in response to the global crisis it can happen again.

THE SOCIAL PSYCHOLOGY OF MATERIALISM AND WEALTH

What might social psychology contribute to our understanding of changing materialism? To what extent do money and consumption buy happiness? And why do materialism and economic growth not bring enduringly greater satisfaction?

Does money buy happiness? Few of us would agree. But ask a different question—"Would a little more money make you a little happier?"—and most of us will say yes. There is, we believe, some connection between wealth and well-being. That belief feeds what Juliet Schor (1998) calls the "cycle of work and spend"—working more to buy more.

INCREASED MATERIALISM

Although the earth asks that we live more lightly upon it, materialism has surged. According to one Gallup poll (1990), 1 in 2 women, 2 in 3 men, and 4 in 5 people earning more than $75,000 a year in the U.S. would like to be rich—although, considering that half the world's people live on less than $2 a day, an income of $75,000 means they are already fabulously rich (Shah, 2005). Think of it as today's American dream: life, liberty, and the purchase of happiness.

Such materialism surged during the 1970s and 1980s. The most dramatic evidence comes from a largescale annual survey of nearly a quarter million students entering university. The proportion considering it "very important or essential" that they become "very well off financially" rose from 39 percent in 1970 to 74 percent in 2005. Those proportions virtually flipped with those who considered it very important to "develop a meaningful philosophy of life." Materialism was up, spirituality down.

What a change in values! Among 19 listed objectives, new university students in most recent years have ranked becoming "very well off financially" number 1. That outranks not only developing a life philosophy but also "becoming an authority in my own field," "helping others in difficulty," and "raising a family."

WEALTH AND WELL-BEING

Does consumption indeed enable "the good life?" Does being well off produce—or at least correlate with—psychological well-being? Would people be happier if they could exchange a simple lifestyle for one with palatial surroundings, Alps ski vacations, and executive-class travel? Would they be happier if they won a publishers' sweepstake and could choose from its suggested indulgences: a 13-metre yacht, deluxe motor home, designer wardrobe, luxury car, and private housekeeper? Social psychological theory and evidence offer some answers.

"Whoever said money can't buy happiness isn't spending it right."

Lexus advertisement

We can observe the traffic between wealth and well-being by asking, first, if rich nations are happier. There is, indeed, some correlation between national wealth and well-being (measured as self-reported happiness and life satisfaction). The Scandinavians have been mostly prosperous and satisfied; the Bulgarians are neither. But 1990s data revealed that once nations reached about $10 000 GNP per person, which was roughly the economic level of Ireland before its recent economic surge, higher levels of national wealth were not predictive of increased well-being. Better to be Irish than Bulgarian. But happiness was about the same whether one was an average Irish person or an average Belgian, Canadian, or Norwegian (with more than double the Irish purchasing power) (Inglehart, 1990).

We can ask, second, whether within any given nation, rich people are happier. In poor countries—where low income more often threatens basic human needs—being relatively well off does predict greater well-being (Argyle, 1999). In affluent countries, where most can afford life's necessities, affluence still matters—partly because people with more money perceive more control in their lives (Johnson & Krueger, 2006). But compared with poor countries, income matters little. Once a comfortable income level is reached, more and more money provides diminishing long-term returns. World values researcher Ronald Inglehart (1990, p. 242) therefore found the income-happiness correlation to be "surprisingly weak."

Even the superrich—for example, those on *Forbes 100* list—have reported only slightly greater happiness than average (Diener et al., 1985). And even winning a major lottery seems not to enduringly elevate well-being (Brickman et al., 1978). Such jolts of joy have "a short half-life," notes Richard Ryan.

We can ask, third, whether, over time, a culture's happiness rises with its affluence. Does our collective well-being float upward with a rising economic tide? Apparently not. Compared to their grandparents, today's young adults have grown up with much more affluence, slightly less happiness, and at greater risk of depression and assorted social pathologies (Klerman & Wiessman, 1989; Seligman, 1989).

"I always in the back of my mind figured a lot of money will buy you a little bit of happiness. But it's not really true."

Google billionaire co-founder Sergey Brin, 2006

It is hard to avoid a startling conclusion: Our becoming much better off over the last four decades has not been accompanied by one iota of increased subjective well-being. The same is true of the European countries, Japan, and the U.S., reports Richard Easterlin (1995). In Britain, for example, great increases in the percent of households with cars, central heating, and telephones have not been accompanied by increased happiness. After a decade of extraordinary economic growth in China—from few owning a phone and 40 percent owning a colour television to most people now having such things—Gallup surveys revealed a decreasing proportion of people satisfied "with the way things are going in your life today" (Burkholder, 2005). The findings are startling because they challenge modern materialism: *Economic growth in affluent countries has provided no apparent boost to human morale.*

WHY MATERIALISM FAILS TO SATISFY

It is striking that economic growth in affluent countries has failed to satisfy. It is further striking that individuals who strive most for wealth tend to live with lower well-being, a finding that "comes through very strongly in every culture I've looked at," reports Richard Ryan (1999). Seek extrinsic goals—wealth, beauty, popularity—and you may find anxiety, depression, and psychosomatic ills (Eckersley, 2005; Sheldon et al., 2004). Those who instead strive for intrinsic goals such as "intimacy, personal growth, and contribution to the community" experience a higher quality of life, concludes Tim Kasser (2000, 2002).

Pause a moment and think: What is the single most personally satisfying event that you experienced in the last month? Ken Sheldon and his colleagues (2001) put that question (and similar questions about the last week and semester) to samples of university students. Then they asked them to rate the extent to which 10 different needs were met by the satisfying event. The students rated self-esteem, relatedness (feeling connected with others), and autonomy (feeling in control) as the three emotional needs that most strongly accompanied the satisfying event. At the bottom of the list of factors predicting satisfaction was money and luxury.

People who identify themselves with expensive possessions experience fewer positive moods, report Emily Solberg, Ed Diener, and Michael Robinson (2003). Such materialists tend to report a relatively large gap between what they want and what they have, and to enjoy fewer close, fulfilling relationships. Especially unhappy are those who desire money to overcome self-doubt and to surpass others, rather than to enhance family security, enjoy freedom, and be charitable (Srivastava et al., 2001). Diener and Martin Seligman (2002) also report that *very* happy university students are marked not by their money but by their "rich and satisfying close relationships." The challenge for healthy nations, then, is to foster improving standards of living without encouraging a materialism and consumerism that displaces the deep need to belong.

"Why do you spend your money for that which is not bread, and your labor for that which does not satisfy?"

Isaiah 55:2

But why should this be so? Why are we not happier after getting that beautiful home and new car? And how do yesterday's luxuries—CD sound systems, colour television, personal computers—so quickly become today's necessities and tomorrow's relics? Two principles drive this psychology of consumption.

Our human capacity for adaptation

The **adaptation-level phenomenon** is our tendency to judge our experience (for example, of sounds, temperatures, or income) relative to a neutral level defined by our prior experience. We adjust our neutral levels—the points at which sounds seem neither loud nor soft, temperatures neither hot nor cold, events neither pleasant nor unpleasant—on the basis of our experience. We then notice and react to up or down changes from those levels.

adaptation-level phenomenon
the tendency to adapt to a given level of stimulation and thus to notice and react to changes from that level

Thus, as our achievements rise above past levels, we feel successful and satisfied. As our social prestige, income, or in-home technology improves, we feel pleasure. Before long, however, we adapt. What once felt good registers as neutral, and what formerly felt neutral now feels like deprivation.

"O.K., if you can't see your way to giving me a pay raise, how about giving Parkerson a pay cut?"

Social comparisons foster feelings.

Would it ever, then, be possible to create a social paradise? Donald Campbell (1975) answered no: If you woke up tomorrow to your utopia—perhaps a world with no bills, no ills, someone who loves you unreservedly—you would feel euphoric, for a time. Yet before long, you would recalibrate your adaptation level and again sometimes feel gratified (when achievements surpass expectations), sometimes feel deprived (when they fall below), and sometimes feel neutral.

To be sure, adaptation to some events, such as the death of a spouse, may be incomplete, as the sense of loss lingers (Diener et al., 2006). Yet, as Chapter 2 explained, we generally underestimate our adaptive capacity. People have difficulty predicting the intensity and duration of their future positive and negative emotions, a phenomenon called "impact bias" (Wilson & Gilbert, 2003). The elation from getting what we want—riches, top exam scores, the Toronto Blue Jays winning the World Series—evaporates more rapidly than we expect. We also sometimes "miswant." When first-year university students predicted their satisfaction with various housing possibilities shortly before entering their school's housing lottery, they focused on physical features. "I'll be happiest in a beautiful and well-located dorm," many students seemed to think. But they were wrong. When contacted a year later, it was the social features, such as a sense of community, that predicted happiness, reports Elizabeth Dunn of the University of British Columbia and her colleagues (2003). Likewise, Leaf Van Boven and Thomas Gilovich (2003) report from surveys and experiments that positive *experiences* (often social experiences) leave us happier. The best things in life are not things.

Our wanting to compare

Much of life revolves around social comparison, a point made by the old joke about two hikers who meet a bear. One reaches into his backpack and pulls out a pair of sneakers. "Why bother putting those on?" asks the other. "You can't outrun a bear." "I don't have to outrun the bear," answers the first. "I just have to outrun you."

Similarly, happiness is relative to our comparisons with others, especially with others within our own groups (Lyubomirsky, 2001; Zagefka & Brown, 2005). Whether we feel good or bad depends on with whom we're comparing ourselves. We are slow-witted or clumsy only when others are smart or agile. Let one professional athlete sign a contract for $15 million a year and an $8-million-a-year teammate may now feel less satisfied. "Our poverty became a reality. Not because of our having less, but by our neighbours having more," recalled Will Campbell in *Brother to a Dragonfly*.

Further feeding our luxury fever is the tendency to compare upward: As we climb the ladder of success or affluence, we mostly compare ourselves with peers who are at or above our current level, not with those who have less. People living in communities where a few residents are very wealthy tend to feel less satisfied as they compare upward.

The rich-poor gap has grown, observes Michael Hagerty (2000), and this helps explain why rising affluence has not produced increased happiness. Rising income inequality, notes Hagerty, makes for more people who have rich neighbours. Television's modelling of the lifestyles of the wealthy also serves to accentuate feelings of "relative deprivation" and desires for more (Schor, 1998).

The adaptation-level and social comparison phenomena give us pause. They imply that the quest for happiness through material achievement requires continually expanding affluence. But the good news is that adaptation to simpler lives can also happen. If we shrink our consumption by choice or by necessity, we will initially feel a pinch, but it will pass. "Weeping may tarry for the night, but joy comes with the morning," reflected the Psalmist. Indeed, thanks to our capacity to adapt and to adjust comparisons, the emotional impact of significant life events—losing a job or even a disabling accident—dissipates sooner than most people suppose (Gilbert et al., 1998).

TOWARD SUSTAINABILITY AND SURVIVAL

As individuals and as a global society, we face difficult social and political issues. How might a democratic society induce people to adopt values that emphasize happiness over materialism? How might a market economy mix incentives for prosperity with restraints that preserve a habitable planet? To what extent can we depend on technological innovations, such as alternative energy sources, to reduce our ecological footprint? And in the meantime, to what extent does the superordinate goal of preserving the earth for our grandchildren call us each to limit our own liberties—our freedom to drive, burn, and dump whatever we wish?

"All our wants, beyond those which a very moderate income will supply, are purely imaginary."

Henry St. John, *Letter to Swift*, 1719

A shift to postmaterialist values will gain momentum as people, governments, and corporations take these steps:

- Face the implications of population and consumption growth for pollution, climate change, and habitat and environmental destruction
- Realize that materialist values make for *less* happy lives
- Identify and promote the things in life that matter more than economic growth.

"If the world is to change for the better it must have a change in human consciousness," said Czech poet-president Vaclav Havel (1990). We must discover "a deeper sense of responsibility toward the world, which means responsibility toward something higher than self." If people came to believe that stacks of unplayed CDs, closets full of seldom-worn clothes, and garages with luxury cars do not define the good life, then might a shift in consciousness become possible? Instead of being an indicator of social status, might conspicuous consumption become gauche?

Social psychology's contribution to a sustainable future will come partly through its consciousness-transforming insights into adaptation and social comparison. These insights also come from experiences that lower people's comparison standards and thereby cool luxury fever and renew contentment. In two such experiments, Marshall Dermer and his colleagues (1979) put university women through some imaginative exercises in deprivation. After viewing depictions of

"However great the discrepancies between men's lots, there is always a certain balance of joy and sorrow which equalizes all."

La Rochefoucauld, *Maxims*, 1665

how grim life was in 1900, or after imagining and then writing about being burned and disfigured, the women expressed greater satisfaction with their own lives.

In another experiment, Jennifer Crocker and Lisa Gallo (1985) found that people who five times completed the sentence "I'm glad I'm not a . . ." afterwards felt less depressed and more satisfied with their lives than did those who had completed sentences beginning "I wish I were a . . .". Realizing that others have it worse helps us count our blessings. "I cried because I had no shoes," says a Persian proverb, "until I met a man who had no feet." *Downward* social comparison facilitates contentment.

Social psychology also contributes to a sustainable and survivable future through its explorations of the good life. If materialism does not enhance quality of life, what does?

- *Close, supportive relationships.* As we saw in Chapter 11, our deep need to belong is satisfied by close, supportive relationships. Those supported by intimate friendships or a committed marriage are much likelier to declare themselves "very happy."
- *Faith communities* and other voluntary organizations are often a source of such connections, as well as of meaning and hope. That helps explain a finding from one large-scale survey of 42 000 North Americans since 1972: only 26 percent of those rarely or never attending religious services declared themselves very happy, but 47 percent of those attending multiple times weekly declared the same.
- *Positive thinking habits.* Optimism, self-esteem, perceived control, and extroversion also mark happy experiences and happy lives.
- *Flow.* Work and leisure experiences that engage one's skills mark happy lives. Between the anxiety of being overwhelmed and stressed, and the apathy of being underwhelmed and bored, notes Mihaly Csikszentmihalyi (1990, 1999), lies a zone in which people experience *flow,* an optimal state in which, absorbed in an activity, we lose consciousness of self and time. When their experience is sampled using electronic pagers, people report greatest enjoyment not when mindlessly passive, but when unselfconsciously absorbed in a mindful challenge. In fact, the *less* expensive (and generally more involving) a leisure activity, the *happier* people are while doing it. Most people are happier gardening than power boating, talking to friends than watching TV. Low consumption recreations prove most satisfying.

That is good news indeed. Those things that make for the genuinely good life—close relationships, social networks based on belief, positive thinking, engaging activity—are enduringly sustainable. And that is an idea close to the heart of Jigme Singye Wangchuk, King of Bhutan. "Gross national happiness is more important than gross national product," he believes. Writing from the Centre of Bhutan Studies in Bhutan, Sander Tideman (2003) explains: "Gross National Happiness . . . aims to promote real progress and sustainability by measuring the quality of life, rather than the mere sum of production and consumption." Now other nations, too, are assessing national quality of life.

SUMMING UP: THE SOCIAL PSYCHOLOGY OF MATERIALISM AND WEALTH

To judge from the expressed values of college and university students and the "luxury fever" that marked late-twentieth-century North America, today's Canadians and Americans—and to a lesser extent people in other Western countries—live in a highly materialistic age.

Does wealth indeed advance well-being? People in rich nations report greater happiness and life satisfaction than those in poor nations (though with diminishing returns as one moves from moderately to very wealthy countries). Rich people within a country are somewhat happier than working-class people, though again more and more money provides diminishing returns (as evident in studies of the super rich and of lottery winners). Does economic growth over time make people happier? Not at all, it seems from the slight decline in self-reported happiness and the increasing rate of depression during the post-1960 years of increasing affluence.

Two principles help explain why materialism fails to satisfy: the adaptation-level phenomenon and social comparison. When incomes and consumption rise, we soon adapt. And comparing with others we may find our relative position unchanged.

To build a sustainable and satisfying future, we can individually seek and, as a society promote close relationships, social networks based on belief, positive thinking habits, and engaging activity.

GLOSSARY

A

acceptance conformity that involves both acting and believing in accord with social pressure.

adaptation-level phenomenon the tendency to adapt to a given level of stimulation and thus to notice and react to changes from that level.

aggression physical or verbal behaviour intended to hurt someone. In laboratory experiments, this might mean delivering electric shocks or saying something likely to hurt another's feelings. By this social psychological definition, one can be socially assertive without being aggressive.

altruism a motive to increase another's welfare without conscious regard for one's self-interests.

analytical reasoning reasoning that emphasizes the proper use of rules and that contradictory statements cannot be true.

arbitration resolution of a conflict by a neutral third party who studies both sides and imposes a settlement.

attitude a favourable or unfavourable evaluative reaction toward something or someone, exhibited in one's beliefs, feelings, or intended behaviour.

attitude inoculation exposing people to weak attacks on their attitudes so that when stronger attacks come, they will have refutations available.

attractiveness having qualities that appeal to an audience. An appealing communicator (often someone similar to the audience) is most persuasive on matters of subjective preference.

attribution theory the theory of how people explain others' behaviour—for example, by attributing it either to internal dispositions (enduring traits, motives, and attitudes) or to external situations.

autokinetic phenomenon self (*auto*) motion (*kinetic*). The apparent movement of a stationary point of light in the dark. Perhaps you have experienced this when thinking you have spotted a moving satellite in the sky, only to realize later that it was merely an isolated star.

automatic processing "implicit" or intuitive thinking that is effortless, habitual, and without awareness.

availability heuristic a cognitive rule that judges the likelihood of things in terms of their availability in memory. If instances of something come readily to mind, we presume it to be commonplace.

B

bargaining seeking an agreement through direct negotiation between parties to a conflict.

behavioural confirmation a type of self-fulfilling prophecy whereby people's social expectations lead them to act in ways that cause others to confirm their expectations.

behavioural medicine an interdisciplinary field that integrates and applies behavioural and medical knowledge about health and disease.

belief perseverance persistence of one's initial conceptions, as when the basis for one's belief is discredited but an explanation of why the belief might be true survives.

bogus pipeline a procedure that fools people into disclosing their attitudes. Participants are first convinced that a machine can use their psychological responses to measure their private attitudes. Then they are asked to predict the machine's reading, thus revealing their attitudes.

bystander effect the finding that a person is less likely to provide help when there are other bystanders.

C

catharsis emotional release. The catharsis view of aggression is that aggressive drive is reduced when one "releases" aggressive energy, either by acting aggressively or by fantasizing aggression.

central route to persuasion occurs when interested people focus on the arguments and respond with favourable thoughts.

channel of communication the way the message is delivered—whether face to face, in writing, on film, or in some other way.

clinical psychology the study, assessment, and treatment of people with psychological difficulties.

coactors a group of people working simultaneously and individually on a noncompetitive task.

cognitive dissonance tension that arises when one is simultaneously aware of two inconsistent cognitions. For example, dissonance may occur when we realize that we have, with little justification, acted contrary to our attitudes or made a decision favouring one alternative despite reasons favouring another.

cohesiveness a "we feeling"—the extent to which members of a group are bound together, such as by attraction for one another.

collectivism giving priority to the goals of one's groups (often one's extended family or work group) and defining one's identity accordingly.

companionate love the affection we feel for those with whom our lives are deeply intertwined.

complementarity the popularly supposed tendency, in a relationship between two people, for each to complete what is missing in the other.

compliance conformity that involves publicly acting in accord with social pressure while privately disagreeing.

confederate an accomplice of the experimenter.

confirmation bias a tendency to search for information that confirms one's preconceptions.

conflict a perceived incompatibility of actions or goals.

conformity a change in behaviour or belief to accord with others.

controlled processing "explicit" thinking that is deliberate, reflective, and conscious.

correlational research the study of the naturally occurring relationships among variables.

counterfactual thinking imagining alternative scenarios and outcomes that might have happened, but didn't.

credibility a credible communicator is perceived as both expert and trustworthy.

cult (also called New Religious movement) a group typically characterized by (1) the distinctive ritual of its devotion to a god or a person, (2) isolation from the surrounding "evil" culture, and (3) a charismatic leader. (A sect, by contrast, is a spinoff from a major religion.)

culture the enduring behaviours, ideas, attitudes, and traditions shared by a large group of people and transmitted from one generation to the next.

D

deindividuation loss of self-awareness and evaluation apprehension; occurs in group situations that foster anonymity and draw attention away from the individual.

demand characteristics cues in an experiment that tell the participant what behaviour is expected.

dependent variable the variable being measured, so called because it may depend on manipulations of the independent variable.

depressive realism the tendency of mildly depressed people to make accurate rather than self-serving judgments, attributions, and predictions.

disclosure reciprocity the tendency for one person's intimacy of self-disclosure to match that of a conversational partner.

discrimination unjustifiable negative behaviour toward a group or its members.

dismissive attachment an avoidant relationship style marked by distrust of others.

displacement the redirection of aggression to a target other than the source of the frustration. Generally, the new target is a safer or more socially acceptable target.

dispositional attribution attributing behaviour to the person's disposition and traits.

door-in-the-face technique a strategy for gaining a concession. After someone first turns down a large request (the door-in-the-face), the same requester counteroffers with a more reasonable request.

dual attitudes differing implicit (automatic) and explicit (consciously controlled) attitudes toward the same object. Verbalized explicit attitudes may change with education and persuasion; implicit attitudes change slowly, with practice that forms new habits.

E

egoism a motive (supposedly underlying all behaviour) to increase one's own welfare. The opposite of *altruism*, which aims to increase another's welfare.

empathy the vicarious experience of another's feelings; putting oneself in another's shoes.

equality the equal distribution of rewards to all individuals.

equity a condition in which the outcomes people receive from a relationship are proportional to what they contribute to it. Note: Equitable outcomes needn't always be equal outcomes.

ethnocentrism believing in the superiority of one's own ethnic and cultural group, and having a corresponding disdain for all other groups.

evaluation apprehension concern for how others are evaluating us.

evolutionary psychology the study of the evolution of behaviour using principles of natural selection.

experimental realism degree to which an experiment absorbs and involves its participants.

experimental research studies that seek clues to cause-effect relationships by manipulating one or more factors (independent variables) while controlling others (holding them constant).

explanatory style one's habitual way of explaining life events. A negative, pessimistic, depressive explanatory style attributes failures to stable, global, and internal causes.

F

false consensus effect the tendency to overestimate the commonality of one's opinions and one's undesirable or unsuccessful behaviours.

false uniqueness effect the tendency to underestimate the commonality of one's abilities and one's desirable or successful behaviours.

fearful attachment an avoidant relationship style marked by a fear of rejection.

field research research done in natural, real-life settings outside the laboratory.

foot-in-the-door phenomenon the tendency for people who have first agreed to a small request to comply later with a larger request.

free riders people who benefit from the group but give little in return.

frustration the blocking of goal-directed behaviour.

frustration–aggression theory the theory that frustration triggers a readiness to aggress.

fundamental attribution error the tendency for observers to underestimate situational influences and overestimate dispositional influences on others' behaviour. (Also called *correspondence bias*, because we so often see behaviour as corresponding to a disposition.)

G

gender role a set of behaviour expectations (norms) for males and females.

GRIT acronym for "graduated and reciprocated initiatives in tension reduction"—a strategy designed to de-escalate international tensions.

group two or more people who, for longer than a few moments, interact with and influence one another and perceive one another as "us."

group polarization group-produced enhancement of members' pre-existing tendencies; a strengthening of the members' *average* tendency, not a split within the group.

group-serving bias explaining away outgroup members' positive behaviours; also attributing negative behaviours to their dispositions (while excusing such behaviour by one's own group).

groupthink "The mode of thinking that persons engage in when concurrence-seeking becomes so dominant in a cohesive in-group that it tends to override realistic appraisal of alternative courses of action." —Irving Janis (1971).

H

health psychology the study of the psychological roots of health and illness. It provides psychology's contribution to behavioural medicine.

heuristics a thinking strategy that enables quick, efficient judgments.

hindsight bias the tendency to exaggerate, after learning an outcome, one's ability to have foreseen how something turned out. Also known as the *I-knew-it-all-along phenomenon*.

holistic reasoning reasoning that emphasizes considering all possible influences and balancing competing forces.

hostile aggression aggression driven by anger and performed as an end in itself.

hypothesis a testable proposition that describes a relationship that may exist between events.

I

illusion of control perception of uncontrollable events as subject to one's control or as more controllable than they are.

illusory correlation (1) Perception of a relationship where none exists, or perception of a stronger relationship than actually exists. (2) A false impression that two variables correlate.

impact bias overestimating the enduring impact of emotion-causing events.

independent variable the experimental factor that a researcher manipulates.

individualism the concept of giving priority to one's goals over group goals and defining one's identity in terms of personal attributes rather than group identifications.

informational influence conformity that results from accepting evidence about reality provided by other people.

informed consent an ethical principle requiring that research participants be told enough to enable them to choose whether they wish to participate.

ingratiation the use of strategies such as flattery, by which people seek to gain another's favour.

ingroup "us"—a group of people who share a sense of belonging, a feeling of common identity.

ingroup bias the tendency to favour one's own group.

instinctive behaviour an innate, unlearned behaviour pattern exhibited by all members of a species.

instrumental aggression aggression that is a means to some other end.

insufficient justification effect reduction of dissonance by internally justifying one's behaviour when external justification is "insufficient."

integrative agreements win-win agreements that reconcile both parties' interests to their mutual benefit.

interaction the effect of one factor (such as biology) depends on another factor (such as environment).

J

just-world phenomenon the tendency of people to believe the world is just and that people therefore get what they deserve and deserve what they get.

K

kin selection the idea that evolution has selected altruism toward one's close relatives to enhance the survival of mutually shared genes.

L

leadership the process by which certain group members motivate and guide the group.

learned helplessness the hopelessness and resignation learned when a human or animal perceives no control over repeated bad events.

low-ball technique a tactic for getting people to agree to something. People who agree to an initial request will often still comply when the requester ups the ante. People who receive only the costly request are less likely to comply with it.

M

matching phenomenon the tendency for men and women to choose as partners those who are a "good match" in attractiveness and other traits.

mediation an attempt by a neutral third party to resolve a conflict by facilitating communication and offering suggestions.

mere-exposure effect the tendency for novel stimuli to be liked more or rated more positively after the rater has been repeatedly exposed to them.

mirror-image perceptions reciprocal views of one another often held by parties in conflict; for example, each may view itself as moral and peace-loving and the other as evil and aggressive.

misattribution mistakenly attributing a behaviour to the wrong cause.

misinformation effect (1) incorporating "misinformation" into one's memory of the event, after witnessing an event and receiving misleading information about it. (2) Witnessing an event, receiving misleading information about it, and then incorporating the "misinformation" into one's memory of the event.

moral exclusion the perception of certain individuals or groups as outside the boundary within which one applies moral values and rules of fairness. Moral *inclusion* is regarding others as within one's circle of moral concern.

mundane realism degree to which an experiment is superficially similar to everyday situations.

N

natural selection the evolutionary process by which nature selects traits that best enable organisms to survive and reproduce in particular environmental niches.

naturalistic fallacy the error of defining what is good in terms of what is observable. For example: What's typical is normal; what's normal is good.

need for cognition the motivation to think and analyze. Assessed by agreement with items such as "the notion of thinking abstractly is appealing to me" and disagreement with items such as "I only think as hard as I have to."

need to belong a motivation to bond with others in relationships that provide ongoing, positive interactions.

need-based distribution the distribution of rewards based on need for those rewards.

non-zero-sum games games in which outcomes need not sum to zero. With cooperation, both can win; with competition, both can lose. (Also called *mixed-motive situations.*)

normative influence conformity based on a person's desire to fulfill others' expectations, often to gain acceptance.

norms rules for accepted and expected behaviour. Norms prescribe "proper" behaviour. (In a different sense of the word, norms also describe what most others do—what is *normal.*)

O

obedience acting in accord with a direct order.

outgroup "them"—a group that people perceive as distinctively different from or apart from their ingroup.

outgroup homogeneity effect perception of outgroup members as more similar to one another than are ingroup members. Thus "they are alike; we are diverse."

overconfidence phenomenon the tendency to be more confident than correct—to overestimate the accuracy of one's beliefs.

overjustification effect the result of bribing people to do what they already like doing; they may then see their action as externally controlled rather than intrinsically appealing.

own-race bias the tendency for people to more accurately recognize faces of their own race.

P

passionate love a state of intense longing for union with another. Passionate lovers are absorbed in one another, feel ecstatic at attaining their partner's love, and are disconsolate on losing it.

peripheral route to persuasion occurs when people are influenced by incidental cues, such as a speaker's attractiveness.

persuasion the process by which a message induces change in beliefs, attitudes, or behaviours.

physical-attractiveness stereotype the presumption that physically attractive people possess other socially desirable traits as well: What is beautiful is good.

pluralistic ignorance a false impression of how other people are thinking, feeling, or responding.

possible selves images of what we dream of or dread becoming in the future.

prejudice a negative prejudgment of a group and its individual members.

preoccupied attachment attachments marked by a sense of one's own unworthiness and anxiety, ambivalence, and possessiveness.

primacy effect other things being equal, information presented first usually has the most influence.

priming activating particular associations in memory.

prosocial behaviour positive, constructive, helpful social behaviour; the opposite of antisocial behaviour.

proximity geographical nearness. Proximity (more precisely, "functional distance") powerfully predicts liking.

R

racism (1) an individual's prejudicial attitudes and discriminatory behaviour toward people of a given race, or (2) institutional practices (even if not motivated by prejudice) that subordinate people of a given race.

random assignment the process of assigning participants to the conditions of an experiment such that all persons have the same chance of being in a given condition. (Note the distinction between random *assignment* in experiments and random *sampling* in surveys. Random assignment helps us infer cause and effect. Random sampling helps us generalize to a population.)

random sample survey procedure in which every person in the population being studied has an equal chance of inclusion.

reactance (1) a motive to protect or restore one's sense of freedom. Reactance arises when someone threatens our freedom of action. (2) The desire to assert one's sense of freedom.

realistic group conflict theory the theory that prejudice arises from competition between groups for scarce resources.

recency effect information presented last sometimes has the most influence. Recency effects are less common than primacy effects.

reciprocity norm an expectation that people will help, not hurt, those who have helped them.

regression toward the average the statistical tendency for extreme scores or extreme behaviour to return toward one's average.

relative deprivation the perception that one is less well off than others to whom one compares oneself.

representativeness heuristic the tendency to presume, sometimes despite contrary odds, that someone or something belongs to a particular group if resembling (representing) a typical member.

reward theory of attraction the theory that we like those whose behaviour is rewarding to us or whom we associate with rewarding events.

role a set of norms that define how people in a given social position ought to behave.

S

secure attachment attachments rooted in trust and marked by intimacy.

self-affirmation theory a theory that people often experience self-image threat after engaging in an undesirable behaviour, they compensate for this threat by affirming another aspect of the self. Threaten people's self-concept in one domain, and they will compensate either by refocusing or by doing good deeds in some other domain.

self-awareness a self-conscious state in which attention focuses on oneself. It makes people more sensitive to their own attitudes and dispositions.

self-concept a person's answers to the question "Who am I?"

self-disclosure revealing intimate aspects of oneself to others.

self-esteem a person's overall self-evaluation or sense of self-worth.

self-fulfilling prophecy a belief that leads to its own fulfillment.

self-handicapping protecting one's self-image with behaviours that create a handy excuse for later failure.

self-monitoring being attuned to the way one presents oneself in social situations and adjusting one's performance to create the desired impression.

self-perception theory the theory that when unsure of our attitudes, we infer them much as would someone observing us—by looking at our behaviour and the circumstances under which it occurs.

self-presentation the act of expressing oneself and behaving in ways designed to create a favourable impression or an impression that corresponds to one's ideals.

self-reference effect the tendency to process efficiently and remember well information related to oneself.

self-schema beliefs about self that organize and guide the processing of self-relevant information.

self-serving attributions a form of self-serving bias; the tendency to attribute positive outcomes to oneself and negative outcomes to other factors.

self-serving bias the tendency to perceive oneself favourably.

sexism (1) an individual's prejudicial attitudes and discriminatory behaviour toward people of a given sex, or (2) institutional practices (even if not motivated by prejudice) that subordinate people of a given sex.

situational attribution attributing behaviour to the environment.

sleeper effect a delayed impact of a message; occurs when we remember the message but forget the reason for discounting it.

social comparison evaluating one's abilities and opinions by comparing oneself to others.

social dominance orientation a motivation to have one's group be dominant over other social groups.

social-exchange theory the theory that human interactions are transactions that aim to maximize one's rewards and minimize one's costs.

social facilitation (1) original meaning—the tendency of people to perform simple or well-learned tasks better when others are present; (2) current meaning—the strengthening of dominant (prevalent, likely) responses owing to the presence of others.

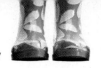

social identity the "we" aspect of our self-concept. The part of our answer to "Who am I?" that comes from our group memberships. Examples: "I am Australian." "I am Catholic."

social learning theory the theory that we learn social behaviour by observing and imitating and by being rewarded and punished.

social loafing the tendency for people to exert less effort when they pool their efforts toward a common goal than when they are individually accountable.

social neuroscience an integration of biological and social perspectives that explores the neural and psychological bases of social and emotional behaviours.

social psychology the scientific study of how people think about, influence, and relate to one another.

social representations socially shared beliefs. Widely held ideas and values, including our assumptions and cultural ideologies. Our social representations help us make sense of our world.

social script culturally provided mental instructions for how to act in various situations.

social-responsibility norm an expectation that people will help those dependent upon them.

social trap a situation in which the conflicting parties, by each rationally pursuing its self-interest, become caught in mutually destructive behaviour. Examples include the Prisoners' Dilemma and the Tragedy of the Commons.

stereotype a belief about the personal attributes of a group of people. Stereotypes can be overgeneralized, inaccurate, and resistant to new information.

stereotype threat a disruptive concern, when facing a negative stereotype, that one will be evaluated based on a negative stereotype. Unlike self-fulfilling prophecies that hammer one's reputation into one's self-concept, stereotype threat situations have immediate effects.

subgrouping accommodating groups of individuals who deviate from one's stereotype by forming a new stereotype about this subset of the group.

subtyping accommodating groups of individuals who deviate from one's stereotype by thinking of them as a special category of people with different properties.

superordinate goal a shared goal that necessitates cooperative effort; a goal that overrides people's differences from one another.

T

temporal comparison a comparison between how the self is viewed now and how the self was viewed in the past or how the self is expected to be viewed in the future.

theory an integrated set of principles that explain and predict observed events.

two-factor theory of emotion arousal × its label = emotion.

two-step flow of communication the process by which media influence often occurs through opinion leaders, who in turn influence others.

U

upward social comparison comparing with others who are better, or better off, may trigger feelings of relative deprivation.

REFERENCES

Abbey, A. (1987). Misperceptions of friendly behavior as sexual interest: A survey of naturally occurring incidents. *Psychology of Women Quarterly*, 11, 173-194. (p. 93)

Abbey, A. (1991). Acquaintance rape and alcohol consumption on college campuses: How are they linked? *Journal of American College Health, 39*(4), 165-165.

Abbey, A. (1991). Misperception as an antecedent of acquaintance rape: A consequence of ambiguity in communication between women and men. In A. Parrot (Ed.), *Acquaintance rape*. New York: Wiley. (p. 93)

Abbey, A., & Andrews, F. M. (1985). Modeling the psychological determinants of life quality. *Social Indicators Research*, 16, 1-34. (p. 506)

Abelson, R. (1972). Are attitudes necessary? In B. T. King & E. McGinnies (Eds.), *Attitudes, conflict and social change*. New York: Academic Press. (p. 113)

Abrams, D. (1991). AIDS: What young people believe and what they do. Paper presented at the British Association for the Advancement of Science conference. (p. 59)

Abrams, D., Wetherell, M., Cochrane, S., Hogg, M. A., & Turner, J. C. (1990). Knowing what to think by knowing who you are: Self-categorization and the nature of norm formation, conformity and group polarization. *British Journal of Social Psychology*, 29, 97-119. (p. 237)

Abramson, L. Y., Metalsky, G. I., & Alloy, L. B. (1989). Hopelessness depression: A theory-based subtype. *Psychological Review*, 96, 358-372. (p. 490)

Ackermann, R., & DeRubeis, R. J. (1991). Is depressive realism real? *Clinical Psychology Review*, 11, 565-584. (p. 490)

Adair, J. G., Dushenko, T. W., & Lindsay, R. C. L. (1985). Ethical regulations and their impact on research practice. *American Psychologist*, 40, 59-72. (p. 26)

Adams, D. (Ed.) (1991). The Seville statement on violence: Preparing the ground for the constructing of peace. *UNESCO*. (p. 338)

Adams, G. (2005). The cultural grounding of personal relationship: Enemyship in North American and West African worlds. *Journal of Personality and Social Psychology*, ***88***, 948. (p. 280)

Adams, J. M., & Jones, W. H. (1997). The conceptualization of marital commitment: An integrative analysis. *Journal of Personality and Social Psychology*, 72, 1177-1196. (p. 410)

Aderman, D., & Berkowitz, L. (1983). Self-concern and the unwillingness to be helpful. *Social Psychology Quarterly*, 46, 293-301. (p. 300)

Adler, N. E., & Snibbe, A. C. (2003). The role of psychosocial processes in explaining the gradient between socioeconomic status and health. *Current Directions in Psychological Science*, ***12***, 119. (p. 505)

Adler, R. P., Lesser, G. S., Meringoff, L. K., Robertson, T. S., & Ward, S. (1980). *The effects of television advertising on children*. Lexington, Mass.: Lexington Books. (p. 177)

Adorno, T., Frenkel-Brunswik, E., Levinson, D., & Sanford, R. N. (1950). *The authoritarian personality*. New York: Harper. (p. 428)

Agnew, G. A., & Carron, A. V. (1994). Crowd effects and the home advantage. *International Journal of Sport Psychology*, 25, 53-62. (p. 220)

Aiello, J. R., Thompson, D. E., & Brodzinsky, D. M. (1983). How funny is crowding anyway? Effects of room size, group size, and the introduction of humor. *Basic and Applied Social Psychology*, 4, 193-207. (p. 220)

Ainsworth, M. D. S. (1973). The development of infant-mother attachment. In B. Caldwell & H. Ricciuti (Eds.), *Review of child development research* (Vol. 3). Chicago: University of Chicago Press. (p. 404)

Ainsworth, M. D. S. (1979). Infant-mother attachment. *American Psychologist*, 34, 932-937. (p. 404)

Ajzen, I. (1982). On behaving in accordance with one's attitudes. In M. P. Zanna, E. T. Higgins, & C. P. Herman (Eds.). *Consistency in social behavior: The Ontario Symposium*, vol. 2. Hillside, NJ: Erlbaum. (p. 115)

Ajzen, I., & Fishbein, M. (1977). Attitude-behavior relations: A theoretical analysis and review of empirical research. *Psychological Bulletin*, 84, 888-918. (p. 115)

Ajzen, I., & Timko, C. (1986). Correspondence between health attitudes and behavior. *Basic and Applied Social Psychology*, 7, 259-276. (p. 116)

Albarrac'n, D., Gillette, J. C., Earl, A. N., Glasman, L. R., Durantini, M. R., & Ho, M. (2005). A test of major assumptions about behavior change: A comprehensive look at the effects of passive and active HIV-prevention interventions since the beginning of the epidemic. *Psychological Bulletin*, ***131***, 856. (p. 162)

Albarracin, D., Johnson, B. T., Fishbein, M., & Muellerleile, P. A. (2001). Theories of reasoned action and planned behavior as models of condom use: A meta-analysis. *Psychological Bulletin*, 127, 142-161. (p. 116)

Allee, W. C., & Masure, R. M. (1936). A comparison of maze behavior in paired and isolated shell-parakeets (Melopsittacus undulatus Shaw) in a two-alley problem box. *Journal of Comparative Psychology*, 22, 131-155. (p. 218)

Allen, V. L., & Levine, J. M. (1969). Consensus and conformity. *Journal of Experimental Social Psychology*, 5, 389-399. (p. 202)

Allison, S. T., & Messick, D. M. (1985). The group attribution error. *Journal of Experimental Social Psychology*, 21, 563-579. (p. 443)

Allison, S. T., & Messick, D. M. (1987). From individual inputs to group outputs, and back again: Group processes and inferences about members. In C. Hendrick (Ed.), *Group processes: Review of personality and social psychology*, Vol. 8. Newbury Park, Ca.: Sage. (p. 443)

Allison, S. T., Beggan, J. K., McDonald, R. A., & Rettew, M. L. (1995). The belief in majority determination of group decision outcomes. *Basic and Applied Social Psychology*, 16, 367-382. (p. 443)

Allison, S. T., Jordan, M. R., & Yeatts, C. E. (1992). A cluster-analytic approach toward identifying the structure and content of human decision making. *Human Relations*, 45, 49-72. (p. 443)

Allison, S. T., Mackie, D. M., & Messick, D. M. (1996). Outcome biases in social perception: Implications for dispositional inference, attitude change, stereotyping, and social behavior. *Advances in*

Experimental Social Psychology, 28, 53-93. (p. 443)

Allison, S. T., Mackie, D. M., Muller, M. M., & Worth, L. T. (1993). Sequential correspondence biases and perceptions of change: The Castro studies revisited. *Personality and Social Psychology Bulletin*, 19, 151-157. (p. 95)

Allison, S. T., McQueen, L. R., & Schaerfl, L. M. (1992). Social decision making processes and the equal partitionment of shared resources. *Journal of Experimental Social Psychology*, 28, 23-42. (p. 87)

Allison, S. T., Messick, D. M., & Goethals, G. R. (1989). On being better but not smarter than others: The Muhammad Ali effect. *Social Cognition*, 7, 275-296. (p. 58)

Allison, S. T., Worth, L. T., & King, M. W. C. (1990). Group decisions as social inference heuristics. *Journal of Personality and Social Psychology*, 58, 801-811. (p. 443)

Alloy, L. B., & Abramson, L. Y. (1979). Judgment of contingency in depressed and nondepressed students: Sadder but wiser? *Journal of Experimental Psychology*: General, 108, 441-485. (p. 490)

Alloy, L. B., Albright, J. S., Abramson, L. Y., & Dykman, B. M. (1990). Depressive realism and nondepressive optimistic illusions: The role of the self. In R. E. Ingram (Ed.), *Contemporary psychological approaches to depression: Theory, research and treatment*. New York: Plenum. (p. 490)

Allport, F. H. (1920). The influence of the group upon association and thought. *Journal of Experimental Psychology*, 3, 159-182. (p. 217)

Allport, G. (1954). *The nature of prejudice*. Cambridge, Mass.: Addison-Wesley. (p. 282)

Allport, G. W. (1958). *The nature of prejudice* (abridged). Garden City, NY: Anchor Books. (p. 427)

Allport, G. W., & Ross, J. M. (1967). Personal religious orientation and prejudice. *Journal of Personality and Social Psychology*, 5, 432-443. (p. 429)

Altemeyer, B. (1988). *Enemies of freedom: Understanding right-wing authoritarianism*. San Francisco: Jossey-Bass. (p. 428)

Altemeyer, B. (1992). Six studies of right-wing authoritarianism among American state legislators. Unpublished manuscript, University of Manitoba. (p. 428)

Altemeyer, B. (2004). Highly dominating, highly authoritarian personalities. *Journal of Social Psychology,* ***144***, 421. (p. 428)

Altemeyer, B., & Hunsberger, B. (1992). Authoritarianism, religious fundamentalism, quest, and prejudice. *International Journal for the Psychology of Religion*, 2, 113-133. (p. 429)

Alwin, D. F., Cohen, R. L., & Newcomb, T. M. (1991). *Political attitudes over the life span: The Bennington women after fifty years*. Madison, WI: University of Wisconsin Press. (p. 166)

Amato, P. R. (1986). Emotional arousal and helping behavior in a real-life emergency. *Journal of Applied Social Psychology*, 16, 633-641. (p. 309)

American Enterprise (1992, January/February). *Women, men, marriages & ministers*, 106. (p. 410)

American Psychological Association (1993). Violence and youth: Psychology's response. Vol I: *Summary report of the American Psychological Association Commission on Violence and Youth*. Washington DC: Public Interest Directorate, American Psychological Association. (p. 336)

Anda, R., Williamson, D., Jones, D., Macera, C., Eaker, E., Glassman, A., & Marks, J. (1993). Depressed affect, hopelessness, and the risk of ischemic heart disease in a cohort of U.S. adults. *Epidemiology*, 4, 285-294. (p. 500)

Andersen, S. M. (1998). Service Learning: A National Strategy for Youth Development. *A Position Paper issued by the Task Force on Education Policy*. Washington, DC: Institute for Communitarian Policy Studies, George Washington University. (p. 297)

Anderson, C. A. (1982). Inoculation and counter-explanation: Debiasing techniques in the perseverance of social theories. *Social Cognition*, 1, 126-139. (p. 78)

Anderson, C. A. (1999). Attributional style, depression, and loneliness: A cross-cultural comparison of American and Chinese students. *Personality and Social Psychology Bulletin*, **25**, 482-499. (p. 69)

Anderson, C. A. (2003). Video games and aggressive behavior. In D. Ravitch and J. P. Viteritti (Eds.), *Kids stuff: Marking violence and vulgarity in the popular culture. Baltimore*, MD: Johns Hopkins University Press. (p. 361)

Anderson, C. A. (2004). An update on the effects of violent video games. *Journal of Adolescence*, 27, 113-122. (p. 361)

Anderson, C. A., & Bushman, B. J. (1997). External validity of "trivial" experiments: The case of laboratory aggression. *Review of General Psychology*, 1, 19-41. (p. 364)

Anderson, C. A., & Bushman, B. J. (2002). Media violence and the American public revisited. *American Psychologist*, 57, 448-450. (p. 357)

Anderson, C. A., & Harvey, R. J. (1988). Discriminating between problems in living: An examination of measures of depression, loneliness, shyness, and social anxiety. *Journal of Social and Clinical Psychology*, 6, 482-491. (p. 494)

Anderson, C. A., & Sechler, E. S. (1986). Effects of explanation and counterexplanation on the development and use of social theories. *Journal of Personality and Social Psychology*, 50, 24-34. (p. 78)

Anderson, C. A., Carnagey, N. L., & Eubanks, J. (2003). Exposure to violent media: The effects of songs with violent lyrics on aggressive thoughts and feelings. *Journal of Personality and Social Psychology*, 84, 960-971. (p. 358)

Anderson, C. A., Carnagey, N. L., Flanagan, M., Benjamin, A. J., Jr., Eubanks, J., & Valentine, J. C. (2004). Violent video games: Specific effects of violent content on aggressive thoughts and behavior. In M. P. Zanna (Ed.), *Advances in experimental social psychology, vol. 36*. (pp. 199-249). San Diego, CA, US: Elsevier Academic Press. (p. 362)

Anderson, C. A., Deuser, W. E., & DeNeve, K. M. (1995). Hot temperatures, hostile affect, hostile cognition, and arousal: Tests of a general model of affective aggression. *Personality and Social Psychology Bulletin*, 21, 434-448. (p. 347)

Anderson, C. A., Lepper, M. R., & Ross, L. (1980). Perseverance of social theories: The role of explanation in the persistence of discredited information. *Journal of Personality and Social Psychology*, 39, 1037-1049. (p. 77)

Anderson, C., Keltner, D., & John, O. P. (2003). Emotional convergence between people over time. *Journal of Personality and Social Psychology*, 84, 1054-1068. (p. 389)

Anderson, C.A., Benjamin, A.J., Jr., & Bartholow, B.D. (1998). Does the gun pull the trigger? Automatic priming effects of weapon pictures and weapon names. *Psychological Science*, 9, 308-314. (p. 349)

Anderson, R. (2004). A definition of peace. *Peace and Conflict: Journal of Peace Psychology. Special Issue: Assessing Cultures of Peace,* ***10***, 101-116. (p. 465)

Anthony, D. B., Holmes, J. G., & Wood, J. V. (2007). Social acceptance and self-esteem: Tuning the sociometer to interpersonal value. *Journal of Personality and Social Psychology,* ***92***, 1024. (p. 46)

Archer, D., & Gartner, R. (1976). Violent acts and violent times: A comparative approach to postwar homicide rates. *American Sociological Review*, 41, 937-963. (p. 367)

Archer, D., Iritani, B., Kimes, D. B., & Barrios, M. (1983). Face-ism: Five studies of sex differences in facial prominence. *Journal of Personality and Social Psychology*, 45, 725-735. (p. 431)

Archer, J. (1991). The influence of testosterone on human aggression. *British Journal of Psychology*, 82, 1-28. (p. 337)

Archer, J., & Coyne, S. M. (2005). An integrated review of indirect, relational, and social aggression. *Personality and Social Psychology Review,* **9**, 212.

Archer, R. L., & Cook, C. E. (1986). Personalistic self-disclosure and attraction: Basis for relationship or scarce resource. *Social Psychology Quarterly*, 49, 268-272. (p. 408)

Arendt, H. (1963). Eichmann in Jerusalem: A report on the banality of evil. New York: Viking Press. (p. 199)

Argyle, M. (1999). Causes and correlates of happiness. In D. Kahneman, E. Diener, and N. Schwartz (Eds.), *Foundations of hedonic psychology: Scientific perspectives on enjoyment and suffering*. New York: Russell Sage Foundation. (p. 534)

Argyle, M., & Henderson M. (1985). *The anatomy of relationships*. London: Heinemann. (p. 262)

Argyle, M., Shimoda, K., & Little, B. (1978). Variance due to persons and situations in England and Japan. *British Journal of Social and Clinical Psychology*, 17, 335-337. (p. 292)

Arkes, H. R. (1990). Some practical judgment/decision making research. Paper presented at the American Psychological Association convention. (p. 161)

Arkin, R. M., & Baumgardner, A. H. (1985). Self-handicapping. In J. H. Harvey & C. Weary (Eds.), *Attribution: Basic issues and applications*. New York: Academic Press. (p. 68)

Arkin, R. M., & Maruyama, G. M. (1979). Attribution, affect, and college exam performance. *Journal of Educational Psychology*, 71, 85-93. (p. 56)

Arkin, R. M., Appleman, A., & Burger, J. M. (1980). Social anxiety, self-presentation, and the self-serving bias in causal attribution. *Journal of Personality and Social Psychology*, 38, 23-35. (p. 375)

Arkin, R. M., Cooper, H., & Kolditz, T. (1980). A statistical review of the literature concerning the self-serving attribution bias in interpersonal influence situations. *Journal of Personality*, 48, 435-448. (p. 56)

Arkin, R. M., Lake, E. A., & Baumgardner, A. H. (1986). Shyness and self-presentation. In W. H. Jones, J. M. Cheek, & S. R. Briggs (Eds.), *Shyness: Perspectives on research and treatment*. New York: Plenum. (p. 67)

Armor, D. A., & Taylor, S. E. (1996). Situated optimism: Specific outcome expectancies and self-regulation. In M. P. Zanna (ed.), *Advances in experimental social psychology*, vol. 30. San Diego: Academic Press. (p. 59)

Arms, R. L., Russell, G. W., & Sandilands, M. L. (1979). Effects on the hostility of spectators of viewing aggressive sports. *Social Psychology Quarterly*, 42, 275-279. (p. 367)

Arnett, J. J. (2000). Optimistic bias in adolescent and adult smokers and nonsmokers. *Addictive Behaviors*, 25, 625-632. (p. 165)

Aron, A., & Aron, E. (1989). *The heart of social psychology*, 2nd ed. Lexington, MA: Lexington Books. (p. 186)

Aron, A., & Aron, E.N. (1994). Love. In A.L. Weber & J.H. Harvey (Eds.) *Perspective on close relationships.* Boston: Allyn & Bacon (p. 409)

Aron, A., Dutton, D. G., Aron, E. N., & Iverson, A. (1989). Experiences of falling in love. *Journal of Social and Personal Relationships*, 6, 243-257. (p. 391)

Aron, A., Fisher, H., Mashek, D. J., Strong, G., Li, H., & Brown, L. L. (2005). Reward, motivation, and emotion systems associated with early-stage intense romantic love. *Journal of Neurophysiology, 94*(1), 327. (p. 399)

Aron, A., Melinat, E., Aron, E. N., Vallone, R. D., & Bator, R. J. (1997). The experimental generation of interpersonal closeness: A procedure and some preliminary findings. *Personality and Social Psychology Bulletin*, 23, 363-377. (p. 409)

Aron, A., Norman, C. C., Aron, E. N., McKenna, C., & Heyman, R. E. (2000). Couples' shared participation in novel and arousing activities and experienced relationship quality. *Journal of Personality and Social Psychology*, 78, 273-284. (p. 399)

Aronson E. (1992). Stateways can change folkways. In R. M. Baird & S. E. Rosenbaum (Eds.), *Bigotry, prejudice, and hatred: Definitions, causes and solutions*, pp. 185-201. (p. 125)

Aronson, E. (1988). *The social animal*. New York: Freeman. (p. 394)

Aronson, E. (1997). Bring the family, address to American Psychological Society annual convention, reported in *APS Observer*, July/August, pp. 17, 34, 35. (p. 156)

Aronson, E., & Linder, D. (1965). Gain and loss of esteem as determinants of interpersonal attractiveness. *Journal of Experimental Social Psychology*, 1, 156-171. (p. 393)

Aronson, E., & Mettee, D. R. (1974). Affective reactions to appraisal from others. *Foundations of interpersonal attraction*. New York: Academic Press. (p. 393)

Aronson, E., & Mills, J. (1959). The effect of severity of initiation on liking for a group. *Journal of Abnormal and Social Psychology*, 59, 177-181. (p. 170)

Aronson, E., Brewer, M., & Carlsmith, J. M. (1985). Experimentation in social psychology. In G. Lindzey & E. Aronson (Eds.), *Handbook of social psychology*, vol. 1. Hillsdale, N.J.: Erlbaum. (p. 29)

Aronson, E., Turner, J. A., & Carlsmith, J. M. (1963). Communicator credibility and communicator discrepancy as determinants of opinion change. *Journal of Abnormal and Social Psychology*, 67, 31-36. (p. 156)

Arriaga, X. B. (2001). The ups and downs of dating: Fluctuations in satisfaction in newly formed romantic relationships. *Journal of Personality and Social Psychology,* ***80***, 754. (p. 411)

Arriaga, X. B., & Agnew, C. R. (2001). Being committed: Affective, cognitive, and conative components of relationship commitment. *Personality and Social Psychology Bulletin,* ***27***, 1190. (p. 411)

Asch, S. E. (1946). Forming impressions of personality. *Journal of Abnormal and Social Psychology*, 41, 258-290. (p. 159)

Asch, S. E. (1955, November). Opinions and social pressure. *Scientific American*, 31-35. (p. 187)

Asendorpf, J. B. (1987). Videotape reconstruction of emotions and cognitions related to shyness. *Journal of Personality and Social Psychology*, 53, 541-549. (p. 494)

Ash, R. (1999). *The top 10 of everything 2000*. New York: DK Publishing. (p. 333)

Asher, J. (1987, April). Born to be shy? *Psychology Today*, pp. 56-64. (p. 336)

Astin, A. W. (1972). *Four critical years*. San Francisco: Jossey-Bass. (p. 163)

Averill, J. R. (1983). Studies on anger and aggression: Implications for theories of emotion. *American Psychologist*, 38, 1145-1160. (p. 339)

Axelrod, R., & Dion, D. (1988). The further evolution of cooperation. *Science*, 242, 1385-1390. (p. 482)

Axsom, D., Yates, S., & Chaiken, S. (1987). Audience response as a heuristic cue in persuasion. *Journal of Personality and Social Psychology*, 53, 30-40. (p. 167)

Ayres, I. (1991). Fair driving: Gender and race discrimination in retail car negotiations. *Harvard Law Review*, 104, 817-872. (p. 419)

Ayres, I., & Nalebuff, B. (2003, April 15). Charity begins at Schedule A. *New York Times* (www.nytimes.com). (p. 326)

Azrin, N. H. (1967, May). Pain and aggression. *Psychology Today*, pp. 27-33. (p. 345)

Baars, B. J., & McGovern, K. (1994). *How not to start a scientific revolution*. US: American Psychological Association. (p. 73)

Babad, E., Bernieri, F., & Rosenthal, R. (1991). Students as judges of teachers' verbal and nonverbal behavior. *American Educational Research Journal*, 28, 211-234. (p. 104)

Babad, E., Hills, M., & O'Driscoll, M. (1992). Factors influencing wishful thinking and predictions of election outcomes. *Basic and Applied Social Psychology*, 13, 461-476. (p. 60)

Bachman, J. G., Johnston, L. D., O'Malley, P. M., & Humphrey, R. N. (1988). Explaining the recent decline in marijuana use: Differentiating the effects of perceived risks, disapproval, and general lifestyle factors. *Journal of Health and Social Behavior*, 29, 92-112. (p. 149)

Bailenson, J. N., & Yee, N. (2005). Digital chameleons: Automatic assimilation of nonverbal gestures in immersive virtual environments. *Psychological Science*, ***16***, 814. (p. 152)

Baize, H. R., Jr., & Schroeder, J. E. (1995). Personality and mate selection in personal ads: Evolutionary preferences in a public mate selection process. *Journal of Social Behavior and Personality*, 10, 517-536. (p. 381)

Baker, L. A., & Emery, R. E. (1993). When every relationship is above average: Perceptions and expectations of divorce at the time of marriage. *Law and Human Behavior*, 17, 439-450. (p. 59)

Baldwin, M. W., & Carrell, S. E., & Lopez, D. F. (1989). Priming relationship schemas: My advisor and the Pope are watching me from the back of my head. *Journal of Experimental Social Psychology*, 26, 435-454. (p. 33)

Baldwin, M. W., Keelan, J. P. R., Fehr, B., Enns, V., Koh-Rangarajoo, E. (1996). Social-cognitive conceptualization of attachment working models: Availability and accessibility effects. *Journal of Personality and Social Psychology*, 71, 94-109. (p. 404)

Balkan, L. (1970). *Les effects du bilinguisme francais-anglais sur les aptitudes intellectuelles*. Brussells, Belgium: Aimav. (p. 289)

Banaji, M. R. & Bhaskar, R. (2000). Implicit stereotypes and memory: The bounded rationality of social beliefs. In D. L. Schacter & E. Scarry (Eds.), *Memory, brain, and belief*. Cambridge, MA: Harvard University Press. (p. 419)

Bandura, A. (1979). The social learning perspective: Mechanisms of aggression. In H. Toch (Ed.), *Psychology of crime and criminal justice*. New York: Holt, Rinehart & Winston. (p. 343)

Bandura, A. (1997). *Self-efficacy: The exercise of control*. New York: Freeman. (p. 342)

Bandura, A., & Bussey, K. (2004). On broadening the cognitive, motivational, and sociostructural scope of theorizing about gender development and functioning: Comment on Martin, Ruble, and Szkrybalo (2002). *Psychological Bulletin*, ***130***, 691. (p. 267)

Bandura, A., & Walters, R. H. (1959). *Adolescent aggression*. New York: Ronald Press. (p. 343)

Bandura, A., & Walters, R. H. (1963). *Social learning and personality development*. New York: Holt, Rinehart and Winston. (p. 357)

Bandura, A., Ross, D., & Ross, S. A. (1961). Transmission of aggression through imitation of aggressive models. *Journal of Abnormal and Social Psychology*, 63, 575-582. (p. 342)

Banks, S. M., Salovey, P., Greener, S., Rothman, A. J., Moyer, A., Beauvais, J., & Epel, E. (1995). The effects of message framing on mammography utilization. *Health Psychology*, 14, 178-184. (p. 155)

Barash, D. (1979). *The whisperings within*. New York: Harper & Row. (pp. 305)

Barash, D. P. (2003). *The survival game: How game theory explains cooperation and competition*. New York: Henry Holt. (p. 257)

Bargh, J. A., & Chartrand, T. L. (1999). The unbearable automaticity of being. *American Psychologist*, 54, 462-479. (p. 38)

Bargh, J. A., & Raymond, P. (1995). The naive misuse of power: Nonconscious sources of sexual harassment. *Journal of Social Issues. Special Issue: Gender Stereotyping, Sexual Harassment, and the Law, 51*(1), 85-96. (p. 93)

Barnes, R. D., Ickes, W., & Kidd, R. F. (1979). Effects of the perceived intentionality and stability of another's dependency on helping behavior. *Personality and Social Psychology Bulletin*, 5, 367-372. (p. 304)

Barnett, M. A., King, L. M., Howard, J. A., & Melton, E. M. (1980). Experiencing negative affect about self or other: Effects on helping behavior in children and adults. Paper presented at the Midwestern Psychological Association convention. (p. 301)

Barnett, P. A., & Gotlib, I. H. (1988). Psychosocial functioning and depression: Distinguishing among antecedents, concomitants, and consequences. *Psychological Bulletin*, 104, 97-126. (p. 491)

Baron J., & Hershey, J. C. (1988). Outcome bias in decision evaluation. *Journal of Personality and Social Psychology*, 54, 569-579. (p. 440)

Baron, L., & Straus, M. A. (1984). Sexual stratification, pornography, and rape in the United States. In N. M. Malamuth & E. Donnerstein (Eds.), *Pornography and sexual aggression*. New York: Academic Press. (p. 352)

Baron, R. A. (1977). *Human aggression*. New York: Plenum Press. (p. 368)

Baron, R. S. (1986). Distraction-conflict theory: Progress and problems. In L.

Berkowitz (Ed.), *Advances in experimental social psychology*, Orlando, Fla.: Academic Press. (p. 221)

Baron, R. S. (2000). Arousal, capacity, and intense indoctrination. *Personality and Social Psychology Review*, 4, 238-254. (p. 172)

Baron, R. S., Hoppe, S. I., Kao, C. F., Brunsman, B., Linneweh, B., & Rogers, D. (1996). Social corroboration and opinion extremity. *Journal of Experimental Social Psychology*, 32, 537-560. (p. 273)

Baron, R. S., Kerr, N. L., & Miller, N. (1992). *Group process, group decision, group action*. Pacific Grove, CA: Brooks/Cole. (p. 341)

Barongan, C., & Hall, G. C. N. (1995). The influence of misogynous rap music on sexual aggression against women. *Psychology of Women Quarterly*, 19, 195-207. (p. 359)

Barry, D. (1998). *Dave Barry Turns 50*. New York: Crown. (p. 57)

Bartholomew, K., & Horowitz, L. (1991). Attachment styles among young adults: A test of a four-category model. *Journal of Personality and Social Psychology*, 61, 226-244. (p. 404)

Bartholow, B. D., & Heinz, A. (2006). Alcohol and aggression without consumption: Alcohol cues, aggressive thoughts, and hostile perception bias. *Psychological Science, **17***, 30. (p. 336)

Bartholow, B. D., Anderson, C. A., Carnagey, N. L., & Benjamin, A. J., Jr. (2005). Interactive effects of life experience and situational cues on aggression: The weapons priming effect in hunters and nonhunters. *Journal of Experimental Social Psychology, **41***, 48. (p. 362)

Bartholow, B. D., Bushman, B. J., & Sestir, M. A. (2006). Chronic violent video game exposure and desensitization to violence: Behavioral and event-related brain potential data. *Journal of Experimental Social Psychology, **42***, 532. (p. 362)

Bassili, J. N. (1995). Response latency and the accessibility of voting intentions: What contributes to accessibility and how it affects vote choice. *Personality and Social Psychology Bulletin*, 21, 686-695. (p. 116)

Bassili, J. N. (2003). The minority slowness effect: Subtle inhibitions in the expression of views not shared by others. *Journal of Personality and Social Psychology*, 84, 261-276. (p. 251)

Bassili, J. N., & Roy, J. P. (1998). On the representation of strong and weak attitudes about policy in memory. *Political Psychology*, 19, 669-681. (p. 112)

Batson, C. D. (1983). Sociobiology and the role of religion in promoting prosocial behavior: An alternative view. *Journal of Personality and Social Psychology*, 45, 1380-1385. (p. 325)

Batson, C. D. (1999a). Behind the scenes. In D. G. Myers, *Social psychology*, 6th edition. New York: McGraw-Hill. (p. 311)

Batson, C. D. (1999b). Addressing the altruism question experimentally. Paper presented at a Templeton Foundation/Fetzer Institute Symposium on Empathy, Altruism, and Agape, Cambridge, Mass. (p. 311)

Batson, C. D. (2001). Addressing the altruism question experimentally. In S. G. Post, L. B. Underwood, J. P. Schloss, & W. B. Hurlbut (Eds.), *Altruism and altruistic love: Science, philosophy, and religion in dialogue*. New York: Oxford University Press. (p. 308)

Batson, C. D. (2006). "Not all self-interest after all": Economics of empathy-induced altruism. In D. De Cremer, M. Zeelenberg & J. K. Murnighan (Eds.), Social psychology and economics. (pp. 281-299). Mahwah, NJ, US: Lawrence Erlbaum Associates Publishers. (p. 63)

Batson, C. D., & Moran, T. (1999). Empathy-induced altruism in a prisoner's dilemma. *European Journal of Social Psychology*, 29, 909-924. (p. 113)

Batson, C. D., & Ventis, W. L. (1982). *The religious experience: A social psychological perspective*. New York: Oxford University Press. (p. 429)

Batson, C. D., & Weeks, J. L. (1996). Mood effects of unsuccessful helping: Another test of the empathy-altruism hypothesis. *Personality and Social Psychology Bulletin*, 22, 148-157. (p. 310)

Batson, C. D., Coke, J. S., Jasnoski, M. L., & Hanson, M. (1978). Buying kindness: Effect of an extrinsic incentive for helping on perceived altruism. *Personality and Social Psychology Bulletin*, 4, 86-91. (p. 320)

Batson, C. D., Duncan, B. D., Ackerman, P., Buckley, T., & Birch, K. (1981). Is empathic emotion a source of altruistic motivation? *Journal of Personality and Social Psychology*, 40, 290-302. (p. 310)

Batson, C. D., Harris, A. C., McCaul, K. D., Davis, M., & Schmidt, T. (1979). Compassion or compliance: Alternative dispositional attributions for one's helping behavior. *Social Psychology Quarterly*, 42, 405-409. (p. 327)

Batson, C. D., Kobrynowicz, D., Dinnerstein, J. L., Kampf, H. C., & Wilson, A. D. (1997). In a very different voice: Unmasking moral hypocrisy. *Journal of Personality and Social Psychology*, 72, 1335-1348. (p. 113)

Batson, C. D., Schoenrade, P., & Ventis, W. L. (1993). *Religion and the individual: A social-psychological perspective*. New York: Oxford University Press. (p. 429)

Batson, C. D., Thompson, E. R., Seuferling, G., Whitney, H., & Strongman, J. A. (1999). Moral hypocrisy: Appearing moral to oneself without being so. *Journal of Personality and Social Psychology*, 77, 525-537. (p. 117)

Baumann, L. J., & Leventhal, H. (1985). "I can tell when my blood pressure is up, can't I?" *Health Psychology*, 4, 203-218. (p. 497)

Baumeister, R. (2005). Rejected and alone. *The Psychologist, **18***, 732. (p. 258)

Baumeister, R. F. (1996). Self-regulation and ego threat: Motivated cognition, self deception, and destructive goal setting. In P. M. Gollwitzer, & J. A. Bargh (Eds.), *The psychology of action: Linking cognition and motivation to behavior.* (27-47). New York, NY, US: Guilford Press. (p. 47)

Baumeister, R. F., & Bratslavsky, E. (1999). Passion, intimacy, and time: Passionate love as a function of change in intimacy. *Personality and Social Psychology Review*, 3, 49-67. (p. 408)

Baumeister, R. F., & Exline, J. J. (2000). Self-control, morality, and human strength. *Journal of Social and Clinical Psychology*, 19, 29-42. (p. 52)

Baumeister, R. F., & Ilko, S. A. (1995). Shallow gratitude: Public and private acknowledgement of external help in accounts of success. *Basic and Applied Social Psychology*, 16, 191-209. (p. 67)

Baumeister, R. F., & Leary, M. R. (1995). The need to belong: Desire for interpersonal attachment as a fundamental human motivation. *Psychological Bulletin*, 117, 495-527. (p. 46)

Baumeister, R. F., & Scher, S. J. (1988). Self-defeating behavior patterns among normal individuals: Review and analysis of common self-destructive tendencies. *Psychological Bulletin*, 104, 3-22. (p. 67)

Baumeister, R. F., & Wotman, S. R. (1992). *Breaking hearts: The two sides of unrequited love.* New York: Guilford. (p. 411)

Baumeister, R. F., Bratslavsky, E., Muraven, M., & Tice, D. M. (1998). Ego depletion: Is the active self a limited resource? *Journal of Personality and Social Psychology*, in press. (p. 52)

Baumeister, R. F., Campbell, J. D., Krueger, J. I., & Vohs, K. D. (2003). Does high self-esteem cause better performance, interpersonal success, happiness, or healthier lifestyles? *Psychological Science in the Public Interest*, 4 (1), 1-44. (p. 47)

Baumeister, R. F., Chesner, S. P., Senders, P. S., & Tice, D. M. (1988). Who's in charge here? Group leaders do lend help in emergencies. *Personality and Social Psychology Bulletin*, 14, 17-22. (p. 96)

Baumeister, R. F., Twenge, J. M., & Nuss, C. K. (2002). Effects of social exclusion on cognitive processes: Anticipated aloneness reduces intelligent thought. *Journal of Personality and Social Psychology*, 83, 817-827. (p. 373)

Baumgardner, A. H. (1991). Claiming depressive symptoms as a self-handicap: A protective self-presentation strategy. *Basic and Applied Social Psychology*, 12, 97-113. (p. 68)

Baumgardner, A. H., & Brownlee, E. A. (1987). Strategic failure in social interaction: Evidence for expectancy disconfirmation process. *Journal of Personality and Social Psychology*, 52, 525-535. (p. 68)

Baumhart, R. (1968). *An honest profit.* New York: Holt, Rinehart & Winston. (p. 57)

Baxter, T. L., & Goldberg, L. R. (1987). Perceived behavioral consistency underlying trait attributions to oneself and another: An extension of the actor-observer effect. *Personality and Social Psychology Bulletin*, 13, 437-447. (p. 100)

Bayer, E. (1929). Beitrage zur zeikomponenten theorie des hungers. *Zeitschrift fur Psychologie*, 112, 1-54. (p. 217)

Bazerman, M. H. (1986, June). Why negotiations go wrong. *Psychology Today*, pp. 54-58. (p. 481)

Bazerman, M. H. (1990). *Judgment in managerial decision making*, 2nd ed. New York: Wiley. (p. 481)

Beaman, A. L., & Klentz, B. (1983). The supposed physical attractiveness bias against supporters of the women's movement: A meta-analysis. *Personality and Social Psychology Bulletin*, 9, 544-550. (p. 386)

Beaman, A. L., Klentz, B., Diener, E., & Svanum, S. (1979). Self-awareness and transgression in children: Two field studies. *Journal of Personality and Social Psychology*, 37, 1835-1846. (p. 231)

Beauregard, K. S., & Dunning, D. (1998). Turning up the contrast: Self-enhancement motives prompt egocentric contrast effects in social judgments. *Journal of Personality and Social Psychology*. (p. 63)

Beauvois, J. L., & Dubois, N. (1988). The norm of internality in the explanation of psychological events. *European Journal of Social Psychology*, 18, 299-316. (p. 101)

Beck, A. J., Kline, S. A., & Greenfeld, L. A. (1988). Survey of youth in custody, 1987. U.S. Department of Justice, *Bureau of Justice Statistics Special Report.* (p. 343)

Bell, B. E., & Loftus, E. F. (1988). Degree of detail of eyewitness testimony and mock juror judgments. *Journal of Applied Social Psychology*, 18, 1171-1192. (p. 512)

Bell, B. E., & Loftus, E. F. (1989). Trivial persuasion in the courtroom: The power of (a few) minor details. *Journal of Personality and Social Psychology*, 56, 669-679. (p. 512)

Bell, P. A. (1980). Effects of heat, noise, and provocation on retaliatory evaluative behavior. *Journal of Social Psychology*, 110, 97-100. (p. 346)

Belson, W. A. (1978). *Television violence and the adolescent boy.* Westmead, England: Saxon House, Teakfield Ltd. (p. 356)

Bem, D. J. (1972). Self-perception theory. In L. Berkowitz (Ed.), *Advances in experimental social psychology.* Vol. 6. New York: Academic Press. (p. 132)

Bem, D. J., & McConnell, H. K. (1970). Testing the self-perception explanation of dissonance phenomena: On the salience of premanipulation attitudes. *Journal of Personality and Social Psychology*, 14, 23-31. (p. 79)

Bennett, R. (1991, February). *Pornography and extrafamilial child sexual abuse: Examining the relationship.* Unpublished manuscript, Los Angeles Police Department Sexually Exploited Child Unit. (p. 353)

Bennis, W. (1984). Transformative power and leadership. In T. J. Sergiovani & J. E. Corbally (Eds.), *Leadership and organizational culture.* Urbana: University of Illinois Press. (p. 249)

Benvenisti, M. (1988, October 16). Growing up in Jerusalem. *New York Times Magazine*, pp. 34-37. (p. 435)

Ben-Zeev, S. (1997). The influence of bilingualism on cognitive strategy and cognitive development. *Child Development*, 48, 1009-1018. (p. 289)

Berg, J. H. (1984). Development of friendship between roommates. *Journal of Personality and Social Psychology*, 46, 346-356. (p. 397)

Berg, J. H. (1987). Responsiveness and self-disclosure. In V. J. Derlega & J. H. Berg (Eds.), *Self-disclosure: Theory, research, and therapy.* New York: Plenum. (p. 408)

Berg, J. H., & McQuinn, R. D. (1986). Attraction and exchange in continuing and noncontinuing dating relationships. *Journal of Personality and Social Psychology*, 50, 942-952. (p. 397)

Berg, J. H., & Peplau, L. A. (1982). Loneliness: The relationship of self-disclosure and androgyny. *Personality and Social Psychology Bulletin*, 8, 624-630. (p. 408)

Berglas, S., & Jones, E. E. (1978). Drug choice as a self-handicapping strategy in response to noncontingent success. *Journal of Personality and Social Psychology*, 36, 405-417. (p. 67)

Berkman, L. F. (1995). The role of social relations in health promotion. *Psychosomatic Medicine*, 57, 245-254. (p. 503)

Berkowitz, L. (1954). Group standards, cohesiveness, and productivity. *Human Relations*, 7, 509-519. (p. 203)

Berkowitz, L. (1968, September). Impulse, aggression and the gun. *Psychology Today*, pp. 18-22. (p. 348)

Berkowitz, L. (1972). Social norms, feelings, and other factors affecting helping and altruism. In L. Berkowitz (Ed.), *Advances in experimental social psychology* (Vol. 6). New York: Academic Press. (b) (p. 304)

Berkowitz, L. (1978). Whatever happened to the frustration-aggression hypothesis? *American Behavioral Scientists*, 21, 691-708. (p. 339)

Berkowitz, L. (1981, June). How guns control us. *Psychology Today*, pp. 11-12. (p. 348)

Berkowitz, L. (1983). Aversively stimulated aggression: Some parallels and differences in research with animals and humans. *American Psychologist*, 38, 1135-1144. (p. 345)

Berkowitz, L. (1984). Some effects of thoughts on anti- and prosocial influences of media events: A cognitive-neoassociation analysis, *Psychological Bulletin*, 95, 410-427. (p. 359)

Berkowitz, L. (1987). Mood, self-awareness, and willingness to help. *Journal of Personality and Social Psychology*, 52, 721-729. (p. 302)

Berkowitz, L. (1989). Frustration-aggression hypothesis: Examination and reformulation. *Psychological Bulletin*, 106, 59-73. (p. 339)

Berkowitz, L. (1995). A career on aggression. In G. G. Brannigan & M. R. Merrens (eds.), *The social psychologists: Research adventures*. New York: McGraw-Hill. (p. 348)

Berkowitz, L., & Geen, R. G. (1966). Film violence and the cue properties of available targets. *Journal of Personality and Social Psychology*, 3, 525-530. (p. 357)

Berkowitz, L., & LePage, A. (1967). Weapons as aggression-eliciting stimuli. *Journal of Personality and Social Psychology*, 7, 202-207. (p. 349)

Berndsen, M., Spears, R., Pligt, J. V. D., & McGarty, C. (2002). Illusory correlation and stereotype formation: Making sense of group differences and cognitive biases. In C. McGarty, V. Y. Yzerbyt & R. Spears (Eds.), *Stereotypes as explanations: The formation of meaningful beliefs about social groups*. (pp. 90-110). New York, NY, US: Cambridge University Press. (p. 448)

Bernhardt, P. C. (1997). Influences of serotonin and testosterone in aggression and dominance: Convergence with social psychology. *Current Directions in Psychology*, 6, 44-48. (p. 337)

Bernhardt, P. C., Dabbs, J. M., Jr., Fielden, J. A., & Lutter, C. D. (1998). Testosterone changes during vicarious experiences of winning and losing among fans at sporting events. *Physiology & Behavior*, **65**, 59. (p. 337)

Berns, G. S., Chappelow, J., Zink, C. F., Pagnoni, G., Martin-Skurski, M. E., & Richards, J. (2005). Neurobiological correlates of social conformity and independence during mental rotation. *Biological Psychiatry*, **58**, 245. (p. 207)

Berscheid, E. (1981). An overviewof the psychological effects of physical attractiveness and some comments upon the psychological effects of knowledge of the effects of physical attractiveness. In W. Lucker, K. Ribbens, & J. A. McNamera (Eds.), *Logical aspects of facial form (craniofacial growth series)*. Ann Arbor: University of Michigan Press. (p. 382)

Berscheid, E. (1985). Interpersonal attraction. In G. Lindzey & E. Aronson (Eds.), *The handbook of social psychology*. New York: Random House. (p. 507)

Berscheid, E. (1999). The greening of relationship science. *American Psychologist*, 54, 260-266. (p. 99)

Berscheid, E., & Peplau, L. A. (1983). The emerging science of relationships. In Kelley, H. H., Berscheid, E., Christensen, A., Harvey, J. H., Huston, T. L., Levinger, G., McClintock, E., Peplau, L. A. & Peterson, D. R. (Eds.), *Close relationships*. New York: Freeman. (p. 507)

Berscheid, E., & Walster (Hatfield), E. (1978). *Interpersonal attraction*. Reading, Mass.: Addison-Wesley. (p. 391)

Berscheid, E., Boye, D., & Walster (Hatfield), E. (1968). Retaliation as a means of restoring equity. *Journal of Personality and Social Psychology*, 10, 370-376. (p. 124)

Berscheid, E., Dion, K., Walster (Hatfield), E., & Walster, G. W. (1971). Physical attractiveness and dating choice: A test of the matching hypothesis. *Journal of Experimental Social Psychology*, 7, 173-189. (p. 380)

Berscheid, E., Graziano, W., Monson, T., & Dermer, M. (1976). Outcome dependency: Attention, attribution, and attraction. *Journal of Personality and Social Psychology*, 34, 978-989. (p. 376)

Berscheid, E., Snyder, M., & Omoto, A. M. (1989). Issues in studying close relationships: Conceptualizing and measuring closeness. In C. Hendrick (Ed.), *Review of personality and social psychology*, Vol. 10. Newbury Park, Ca.: Sage. (p. 401)

Berscheid, E., Walster, G. W., & Hatfield (was Walster), E. (1969). Effects of accuracy and positivity of evaluation on liking for the evaluator. Unpublished manuscript. Summarized by E. Berscheid and E. Walster (Hatfield) (1978), *Interpersonal attraction*. Reading, Mass.: Addison-Wesley. (p. 391)

Bettencourt, A., & Dorr, N. (1997). Collective self-esteem as a mediator of the relationship between allocentrism and subjective well-being. *Personality and Social Psychology Bulletin*, 23, 955-965. (p. 445)

Bettencourt, B. A., Dill, K. E., Greathouse, S. A., Charlton, K., & Mulholland, A. (1997). Evaluations of ingroup and outgroup members: The role of category-based expectancy violation. *Journal of Experimental Social Psychology*, 33, 244-275. (p. 457)

Beyer, L. (1990, Fall issue on women). Life behind the veil. *Time*, p. 37. (p. 425)

Bianchi, S. M., Milkie, M. A., Sayer, L. C., & Robinson, J. P. (2000). Is anyone doing the housework? Trends in the gender division of household labor. *Social Forces*, 79, 191-228. (p. 422)

Bickersteth, P., & Das, J. P. (1981). Syllogistic reasoning among school children from Canada and Sierra Leone. *International Journal of Psychology*, 16, 1-11. (p. 273)

Bickman, L. (1975). Bystander intervention in a crime: The effect of a mass-media campaign. *Journal of Applied Social Psychology*, 5, 296-302. (p. 323)

Bickman, L. (1979). Interpersonal influence and the reporting of a crime. *Personality and Social Psychology Bulletin*, 5, 32-35. (p. 323)

Bickman, L., & Green, S. K. (1977). Situational cues and crime reporting: Do signs make a difference? *Journal of Applied Social Psychology*, 7, 1-18. (p. 323)

Bierbrauer, G. (1979). Why did he do it? Attribution of obedience and the phenomenon of dispositional bias. *European Journal of Social Psychology*, 9, 67-84. (p. 198)

Bierhoff, H. W., Klein, R., & Kramp, P. (1991). Evidence for the altruistic personality from data on accident research. *Journal of Personality*, 59, 263-280. (p. 322)

Bierly, M. M. (1985). Prejudice toward contemporary outgroups as a generalized attitude. *Journal of Applied Social Psychology*, 15, 189-199. (p. 428)

Biernat, M. (1991). Gender stereotypes and the relationship between masculinity and femininity: A developmental analysis. *Journal of Personality and Social Psychology*, 61, 351-365. (p. 442)

Biernat, M., & Kobrynowicz, D. (1997). Gender- and race-based standards of competence: Lower minimum standards but higher ability standards for devalued groups. *Journal of Personality and Social Psychology*, 72, 544-557. (p. 445)

Biernat, M., & Wortman, C. B. (1991). Sharing of home responsibilities between professionally employed women and their husbands. *Journal of Personality and Social Psychology*, 60, 844-860. (p. 422)

Biernat, M., Vescio, T. K., & Green, M. L. (1996). Selective self-stereotyping. *Journal of Personality and Social Psychology*, 71, 1194-1209. (p. 65)

Biernat, M., Vescio, T. K., & Theno, S. A. (1996). Violating American values: A "Value congruence" approach to understanding outgroup attitudes. *Journal of Experimental Social Psychology*, 32, 387-410. (p. 389)

Billig, M., & Tajfel, H. (1973). Social categorization and similarity in intergroup behaviour. *European Journal of Social Psychology*, 3, 27-52. (p. 435)

Biner, P. M. (1991). Effects of lighting-induced arousal on the magnitude of goal valence. *Personality and Social Psychology Bulletin*, 17, 219-226. (p. 347)

Bingenheimer, J. B., Brennan, R. T., & Earls, F. J. (2005). Firearm violence exposure and serious violent behavior. *Science*, ***308***, 1323. (p. 344)

Binham, R. (1980, March-April). Trivers in Jamaica. *Science* 80, pp. 57-67. (p. 306)

Bird, C. E. (1999). Gender, household labor, and psychological distress: The impact of the amount and division of housework. *Journal of Health & Social Behavior*, 40, 32-45. (p. 58)

Bishop, G. D. (1984). Gender, role, and illness behavior in a military population. *Health Psychology*, 3, 519-534. (p. 499)

Bishop, G. D. (1987). Lay conceptions of physical symptoms. *Journal of Applied Social Psychology*, 17, 127-146. (p. 499)

Bishop, G. D. (1991). Understanding the understanding of illness: Lay disease representations. In J. A. Skelton & R. T. Croyle (Eds.), *Mental representation in health and illness*. New York: Springer-Verlag. (p. 497)

Blackburn, R. T., Pellino, G. R., Boberg, A., & O'Connell, C. (1980). Are instructional improvement programs off target? *Current Issues in Higher Education*, 1, 31-48. (p. 65)

Blake, R. R., & Mouton, J. S. (1962). The intergroup dynamics of win-lose conflict and problem-solving collaboration in union-management relations. In M. Sherif (Ed.), *Intergroup relations and leadership*. New York: Wiley. (p. 480)

Blake, R. R., & Mouton, J. S. (1979). Intergroup problem solving in organizations: From theory to practice. In W. G. Austin and S. Worchel (Eds.), *The social psychology of intergroup relations*. Monterey, Calif.: Brooks/Cole. (p. 284)

Blanchard, F. A., & Cook, S. W. (1976). Effects of helping a less competent member of a cooperating interracial group on the development of interpersonal attraction. *Journal of Personality and Social Psychology*, 34, 1245-1255. (p. 126)

Blank, H., Fischer, V., & Erdfelder, E. (2003). Hindsight bias in political elections. *Memory*, 11, 491-504. (p. 80)

Blascovich, J., Wyer, N. A., Swart, L. A., & Kibler, J. L. (1997). Racism and racial categorization. *Journal of Personality and Social Psychology*, 72, 1364-1372. (p. 422)

Blass, T. (1990). *Psychological approaches to the Holocaust: Review and evaluation.* Paper presented to the American Psychological Association convention. (p. 209)

Blass, T. (1991). Understanding behavior in the Milgram obedience experiment: The role of personality, situations, and their interactions. *Journal of Personality and Social Psychology*, 60, 398-413. (p. 209)

Blass, T. (1996). Stanley Milgram: A life of inventiveness and controversy. In G. A. Kimble, C. A. Boneau, & M. Wertheimer (eds.). *Portraits of pioneers in psychology*, Vol. II. Washington, D.C.: American Psychological Association. (p. 191)

Block J., & Funder, D. C. (1986). Social roles and social perception: Individual differences in attribution and error. *Journal of Personality and Social Psychology*, 51, 1200-1207. (p. 97)

Bodenhausen, G. V. (1990). Stereotypes as judgmental heuristics: Evidence of circadian variations in discrimination. *Psychological Science*, 1, 319-322. (p. 442)

Bodenhausen, G. V. (1993). Emotions, arousal, and stereotypic judgments: A heuristic model of affect and stereotyping. In D. M. Mackie & D. L. Hamilton (eds.), *Affect, cognition, and stereotyping: Interactive processes in group perception*. San Diego, CA: Academic Press. (p. 153)

Bodenhausen, G. V., & Macrae, C. N. (1998). Stereotype activation and inhibition. In R. S. Wyer, Jr., *Stereotype activation and inhibition: Advances in social cognition*, vol. 11. Mahwah, NJ: Erlbaum. (p. 441)

Bodenhausen, G. V., Sheppard, L. A., & Kramer, G. F. (1994). Negative affect and social judgment: The differential impact of anger and sadness. *European Journal of Social Psychology*, 24, 45-62. (p. 91)

Boggiano, A. K., & Ruble, D. N. (1985). Children's responses to evaluative feedback. In R. Schwarzer (Ed.), *Self-related cognitions in anxiety and motivation.* Hillsdale, N.J.: Erlbaum. (p. 136)

Boggiano, A. K., Barrett, M., Weiher, A. W., McClelland, G. H., & Lusk, C. M. (1987). Use of the maximal-operant principle to motivate children's intrinsic interest. *Journal of Personality and Social Psychology*, 53, 866-879. (p. 135)

Boggiano, A. K., Harackiewicz, J. M., Bessette, J. M., & Main, D. S. (1985). Increasing children's interest through performance-contingent reward. *Social Cognition*, 3, 400-411. (p. 135)

Bohner, G., Bless, H., Schwarz, N., & Strack, F. (1988). What triggers causal attributions? The impact of valence and subjective probability. *European Journal of Social Psychology*, 18, 335-345. (p. 93)

Boldt, E. D. (1976). Acquiescence and conventionality in a communal society. *Journal of Cross Cultural Psychology*, 7, 21-36. (p. 203)

Bond, C. F., Jr., DiCandia, C. G., & MacKinnon, J. R. (1988). Responses to violence in a psychiatric setting: The role of patient's race. *Personality and Social Psychology Bulletin*, 14, 448-458. (p. 457)

Bond, C.F., Jr., & Titus, L.J. (1983). Social facilitation: A meta-analysis of 241 studies. *Psychologial Bulletin*, 94, 265-292. (p. 219)

Bond, M. H. (2004). Culture and aggression: From context to coercion. *Personality and Social Psychology Review*, 8, 62-78. (p. 280)

Bond, R., & Smith, P. B. (1996). Culture and conformity: A meta-analysis of studies using Asch's (1952b, 1956) line judgment task. *Psychological Bulletin*, 119, 111-137. (p. 278)

Boninger, D. S., Gleicher, F., & Strathman, A. (1994). Counterfactual thinking: From what might have been to what may be. *Journal of Personality and Social Psychology*, 67, 297-307. (p. 87)

Bono, J. E., & Judge, T. A. (2004). Personality and transformational and transactional leadership: A meta-analysis. *Journal of Applied Psychology*, ***89***, 901. (p. 250)

Borgida, E. (1981). Legal reform of rape laws. In L. Bickman (Ed.), *Applied social psychology annual*. Vol. 2. Beverly Hills, Calif.: Sage Publications, pp. 211-241. (p. 455)

Borgida, E., & Brekke, N. (1985). Psycholegal research on rape trials. In A. W. Burgess (Ed.), *Rape and sexual assault: A research handbook*. New York: Garland. (p. 440)

Borkenau, P., & Liebler, A. (1993). Consensus and self-other agreement for trait inferences from minimal information. *Journal of Personality. Special Issue: Viewpoints on Personality: Consensus, Self-Other Agreement, and Accuracy in Personality Judgment, 61*(4), 477. (p. 83)

Bornstein, B. H., & Zicafoose, D. J. (1999). "I know I know it, I know I saw it": The stability of the confidence-accuracy relationship across domains. *Journal of Experimental Psychology: Applied*, 5, 76-88. (p. 513)

Bornstein, R. F. (1989). Exposure and affect: Overview and meta-analysis of research, 1968-1987. *Psychological Bulletin*, 106, 265-289. (p. 376)

Bornstein, R. F., & D'Agostino, P. R. (1992). Stimulus recognition and the mere exposure effect. *Journal of Personality and Social Psychology*, 63, 545-552. (p. 377)

Bossard, J. H. S. (1932). Residential propinquity as a factor in marriage selection. *American Journal of Sociology*, 38, 219-224. (p. 375)

Bothwell, R. K., Brigham, J. C., & Malpass, R. S. (1989). Cross-racial identification. *Personality and Social Psychology Bulletin*, 15, 19-25. (p. 444)

Botvin, G. J., Schinke, S., & Orlandi, M. A. (1995). School-based health promotion: Substance abuse and sexual behavior. *Applied & Preventive Psychology*, 4, 167-184. (p. 176)

Botwin, M. D., Buss, D. M., & Shackelford, T. K. (1997). Personality and mate preferences: Five factors in mate selection and marital satisfaction. *Journal of Personality*, 65, 107-136. (p. 390)

Bourgeois, M. J., Horowitz, I. A., & Lee, L. F. (1993). Effects of technicality and access to trial transcripts on verdicts and information processing in a civil trial. *Personality and Social Psychology Bulletin*, 19, 219-226. (p. 523)

Bowen, E. (1988, April 4). What ever became of Honest Abe? *Time*. (p. 6)

Bower, G. H. (1987). Commentary on mood and memory. *Behavioral Research and Therapy*, 25, 443-455. (p. 91)

Bowlby, J. (1980). *Loss, sadness and depression*. Vol. III of Attachment and loss. London: Basic Books. (p. 403)

Boyatzis, C. J., Matillo, G. M., & Nesbitt, K. M. (1995). Effects of the "Mighty Morphin Power Rangers" on children's aggression with peers. *Child Study Journal*, 25, 45-55. (p. 27)

Bradley, W., & Mannell, R. C. (1984). Sensitivity of intrinsic motivation to reward procedure instructions. *Personality and Social Psychology Bulletin*, 10, 426-431. (p. 136)

Brandon, R., & Davies, C. (1973). *Wrongful imprisonment: Mistaken convictions and their consequences*. Hamden, Conn.: Archon Books. (p. 513)

Branscombe, N. R., Schmitt, M. T., & Harvey, R. D. (1999). Perceiving pervasive discrimination among African Americans: Implications for group identification and well-being. *Journal of Personality and Social Psychology*, 77, 135-149. (p. 447)

Brauer, M., Judd, C. M., & Gliner, M. D. (1995). The effects of repeated expressions on attitude polarization during group discussions. *Journal of Personality and Social Psychology*, 68, 1014-1029. (p. 237)

Brauer, M., Judd, C. M., & Jacquelin, V. (2001). The communication of social stereotypes: The effects of group discussion and information distribution on stereotypic appraisals. *Journal of Personality and Social Psychology, **81***, 463. (p. 234)

Bray, R. M., & Kerr, N. L. (1982). Methodological considerations in the study of the psychology of the courtroom. In N. L. Kerr & R. M. Bray (Eds.), *The psychology of the courtroom*. Orlando, Fla.: Academic Press. (p. 526)

Bray, R. M., & Noble, A. M. (1978). Authoritarianism and decisions of mock juries: Evidence of jury bias and group polarization. *Journal of Personality and Social Psychology*, 36, 1424-1430. (p. 524)

Breckler, S. J., & Wiggins, E. C. (1989). Affect versus evaluation in the structure of attitudes. *Journal of Experimental Social Psychology*, 25, 253-271. (p. 112)

Bregman, N. J., & McAllister, H. A. (1982). Eyewitness testimony: The role of commitment in increasing reliability. *Social Psychology Quarterly*, 45, 181-184. (p. 516)

Brehm, J. W. (1956). Post-decision changes in desirability of alternatives. *Journal of Abnormal Social Psychology*, 52, 384-389. (p. 132)

Brehm, S., & Brehm, J. W. (1981). *Psychological reactance: A theory of freedom and control*. New York: Academic Press. (p. 210)

Brenner, S. N., & Molander, E. A. (1977). Is the ethics of business changing? *Harvard Business Review*, January-February, pp. 57-71. (p. 57)

Brewer, M. B. (1979). In-group bias in the minimal intergroup situation: A cognitive-motivational analysis. *Psychological Bulletin*, 86, 307-324. (p. 437)

Brewer, M. B. (1987). Collective decisions. *Social Science*, 72, 140-143. (p. 471)

Brewer, M. B. (1988). A dual process model of impression formation. In T. Srull & R. Wyer (Eds.), *Advances in social cognition*, Vol. 1. Hillsdale, N.J.: Erlbaum. (p. 451)

Brewer, M. B., & Silver, M. (1978). In-group bias as a function of task characteristics. *European Journal of Social Psychology*, 8, 393-400. (p. 435)

Brickman, P. (1978). Is it real? In J. Harvey, W. Ickes, & R. Kidd (Eds.), *New directions in attribution research*. Vol. 2. Hillsdale, N.J.: Erlbaum. (p. 265)

Brickman, P., Coates, D. & Janoff-Bulman, R. J. (1978). Lottery winners and accident victims: Is happiness relative? *Journal of Personality and Social Psychology*, 36, 917-927. (p. 534)

Briere, N. M. & Vallerand, R. J. (1990). Effect of private self-consciousness and success outcome on causal dimensions. *Journal of Social Psychology*, 130, 325-332. (p. 56)

Brigham, J. C., & Cairns, D. L. (1988). The effect of mugshot inspections on eyewitness identification accuracy. *Journal of Applied Social Psychology*, 18, 1394-1410. (p. 519)

Brigham, J. C., & Williamson, N. L. (1979). Cross-racial recognition and age: When you're over 60, do they still all look alike? *Personality and Social Psychology Bulletin*, 5, 218-222. (p. 433)

Brock, T. C. (1965). Communicator-recipient similarity and decision change. *Journal of Personality and Social Psychology*, 1, 650-654. (p. 152)

Brockner, J., Rubin, J. Z., Fine, J., Hamilton, T. P., Thomas, B., & Turetsky, B. (1982). Factors affecting entrapment in escalating conflicts: The importance of timing. *Journal of Research in Personality*, 16, 247-266. (p. 467)

Broome, A., & Wegner, D. M. (1994). *Some positive effects of releasing socially anxious people from the need to please*. Paper presented to the American Psychological Society convention. (p. 495)

Brown, D. E. (1991). *Human universals*. New York: McGraw-Hill. (p. 256)

Brown, D. E. (2000). Human universals and their implications. In N. Roughley (Ed.), *Being humans: Anthropological universality and particularity in transdisciplinary perspectives.* New York: Walter de Gruyter. (p. 256)

Brown, H. J., Jr. (1990). *P.S. I love you.* Nashville, TN: Rutledge Hill. (p. 58)

Brown, J. D. (1986). Evaluations of self and others: Self-enhancement biases in social judgments. *Social Cognition*, 4, 353-376. (p. 288)

Brown, J. D., & Dutton, K. A. (1994). *From the top down: Self-esteem and self-evaluation.* Unpublished manuscript, University of Washington. (p. 51)

Brown, J. D., & Taylor, S. E. (1986). Affect and the processing of personal information: Evidence for mood-activated self-schemata. *Journal of Experimental Social Psychology*, 22, 436-452. (p. 91)

Brown, J. D., Novick, N. J., Lord, K. A., & Richards, J. M. (1992). When Gulliver travels: Social context, psychological closeness, and self-appraisals. *Journal of Personality and Social Psychology*, 62, 717-727. (p. 386)

Brown, R. & Hewstone, M. (2005). An integrative theory of intergroup contact. *Advances in Experimental Social Psychology*, 37, 255-343. (p. 282)

Brown, R. (1965). *Social psychology.* New York: Free Press. (p. 262)

Brown, R. (1973). *A first language: The early stages.* Cambridge, MA: Harvard University Press. (p. 289)

Brown, R. (1987). Theory of politeness: An exemplary case. Paper presented to the Society of Experimental Social Psychology meeting. Cited by R. O. Kroker & L. A. Wood, 1992, Are the rules of address universal? IV: Comparison of Chinese, Korean, Greek, and German usage. *Journal of Cross-Cultural Psychology*, 23, 148-162. (p. 262)

Brown, R. P., Charnsangavej, T., Keough, K. A., Newman, M. L., & Rentfrom, P. J. (2000). Putting the "affirm" into affirmative action: Preferential selection and academic performance. *Journal of Personality and Social Psychology*, 79, 736-747. (p. 454)

Brown, R., & Hewstone, M. (2005). An integrative theory of intergroup contact. In M. P. Zanna (Ed.), *Advances in experimental social psychology, vol. 37.* (pp. 255-343). San Diego, CA, US: Elsevier Academic Press.

Brown, R., & Wootton-Millward, L. (1993). Perceptions of group homogeneity during group formation and change. *Social Cognition*, 11, 126-149. (p. 443)

Brown, R., Maras, P., Masser, B., Vivian, J., & Hewstone, M. (2001). Life on the ocean wave: Testing some intergroup hypotheses in a naturalistic setting. *Group Processes and Intergroup Relations*, 4, 81-97. (p. 338)

Brown, R., Vivian, J., & Hewstone, M. (1999). Changing attitudes through intergroup contact: The effects of group membership salience. *European Journal of Social Psychology*, 29, 741-764. (p. 282)

Brown, S. L., Nesse, R. M., Vinokur, A. D., & Smith, D. M. (2003). Providing social support may be more beneficial than receiving it. *Psychological Science*, 14, 320-327. (p. 504)

Brown, V. R., & Paulus, P. B. (2002). Making group brainstorming more effective: Recommendations from an associative memory perspective. *Current Directions in Psychological Science*, 11, 208-212. (p. 247)

Browning, C. (1992). *Ordinary men: Reserve police battalion 101 and the final solution in Poland.* New York: HarperCollins. (p. 199)

Bruce, V. (1998). Fleeting images of shade: Identifying people caught on video. *The Psychologist*, ***11***, 331-337. (p. 513)

Bryan, J. H., & Test, M. A. (1967). Models and helping: Naturalistic studies in aiding behavior. *Journal of Personality and Social Psychology*, 6, 400-407. (p. 319)

Buckhout, R. (1974, December). Eyewitness testimony. *Scientific American*, pp. 23-31. (p. 513)

Buehler, R., & Griffin, D. (2003). Planning, personality, and prediction: The role of future focus in optimistic time predictions. *Organizational Behavior and Human Decision Processes, 92*(1-2), 80. (p. 83)

Buehler, R., Griffin, D., & Ross, M. (1994). Exploring the "planning fallacy": When people underestimate their task completion times. *Journal of Personality and Social Psychology*, 67, 366-381. (p. 83)

Buehler, R., Griffin, D., & Ross, M. (2002). Inside the planning fallacy: The causes and consequences of optimistic time predictions. In T. Gilovich, D. Griffin & D. Kahneman (Eds.), *Heuristics and biases: The psychology of intuitive judgment.* (p. 250-270). New York, NY, US: Cambridge University Press. (p. 83)

Buehler, R., Messervey, D., & Griffin, D. (2005). Collaborative planning and prediction: Does group discussion affect optimistic biases in time estimation? *Organizational Behavior and Human Decision Processes, 97*(1), 47. (p. 83)

Burchill, S. A. L., & Stiles, W. B. (1988). Interactions of depressed college students with their roommates: Not necessarily negative. *Journal of Personality and Social Psychology*, 55, 410-419. (p. 491)

Bureau of the Census (1993, May 4). Voting survey, reported by Associated Press.

Burger, J. M. (1987). Increased performance with increased personal control: A self-presentation interpretation. *Journal of Experimental Social Psychology*, 23, 350-360. (p. 248)

Burger, J. M. (1991). Changes in attributions over time: The ephemeral fundamental attribution error. *Social Cognition*, 9, 182-193. (p. 99)

Burger, J. M., & Burns, L. (1988). The illusion of unique invulnerability and the use of effective contraception. *Personality and Social Psychology Bulletin*, 14, 264-270. (p. 59)

Burger, J. M., & Pavelich, J. L. (1994). Attributions for presidential elections: The situational shift over time. *Basic and Applied Social Psychology*, 15, 359-371. (p. 99)

Burger, J. M., Messian, N., Patel, S., del Prade, A., & Anderson, C. (2004). What a coincidence! The effects of incidental similarity on compliance. *Personality and Social Psychology Bulletin*, 30, 35-43. (p. 202)

Burgess, R. L., & Huston, T. L. (Eds.) (1979). *Social exchange in developing relationships.* New York: Academic Press. (p. 394)

Burkholder, R. (2003, February 14). Unwilling coalition? Majorities in Britain, Canada oppose military action in Iraq. *Gallup Poll Tuesday Briefing* (www.gallup.com/poll). (p. 144)

Burn, S. M. (1992). Locus of control, attributions, and helplessness in the homeless. *Journal of Applied Social Psychology*, 22, 1161-1174. (p. 53)

Burns, D. D. (1980). *Feeling good: The new mood therapy.* New York: Signet. (p. 489)

Burnstein, E., & Vinokur, A. (1977). Persuasive argumentation and social comparison as determinants of attitude polarization. *Journal of Experimental Social Psychology*, 13, 315-332. (p. 236)

Burnstein, E., & Worchel, P. (1962). Arbitrariness of frustration and its consequences for aggression in a social situation. *Journal of Personality*, 30, 528-540. (p. 339)

Burnstein, E., Crandall, R., & Kitayama, S. (1994). Some neo-Darwinian decision rules for altruism: Weighing cues for inclusive fitness as a function of the biological importance of the decision. *Journal of Personality and Social Psychology*, 67, 773-789. (p. 306)

Burr, W. R. (1973). *Theory construction and the sociology of the family*. New York: Wiley. (p. 375)

Burros, M. (1988, February 24). Women: Out of the house but not out of the kitchen. *New York Times*. (p. 58)

Burson, K. A., Larrick, R. P., & Klayman, J. (2006). Skilled or unskilled, but still unaware of it: How perceptions of difficulty drive miscalibration in relative comparisons. *Journal of Personality and Social Psychology, 90*(1), 60. (p. 82)

Burt, R. S. (1986). Strangers, friends and happiness. *GSS Technical Report No. 72*. Chicago: National Opinion Research Center, University of Chicago. (p. 506)

Bushman, B. J. (1993). Human aggression while under the influence of alcohol and other drugs: An integrative research review. *Current Directions in Psychological Science*, 2, 148-152. (p. 336)

Bushman, B. J. (1995). Moderating role of trait aggressiveness in the effects of violent media on aggression. *Journal of Personality and Social Psychology*, 69, 950-960. (p. 358)

Bushman, B. J. (1998). Priming effects of media violence on the accessibility of aggressive constructs in memory. *Personality and Social Psychology Bulletin*, 24, 537-545. (p. 360)

Bushman, B. J. (2002). Does venting anger feed or extinguish the flame? Catharsis, rumination, distraction, anger, and aggressive responding. *Personality and Social Psychology Bulletin*, 28, 724-731. (pp. 366)

Bushman, B. J., & Anderson, C. A. (2001). Media violence and the American public: Scientific facts versus media misinformation. *American Psychologist*, 56, 477-489. (p. 357)

Bushman, B. J., & Baumeister, R. (1998). Threatened egotism, narcissism, self-esteem, and direct and displaced aggression: Does self-love or self-hate lead to violence? *Journal of Personality and Social Psychology*, 75, 219-229. (p. 47)

Bushman, B. J., & Cooper, H. M. (1990). Effects of alcohol on human aggression: An integrative research review. *Psychological Bulletin*, 107, 341-354. (p. 336)

Bushman, B. J., & Geen, R. G. (1990). Role of cognitive-emotional mediators and individual differences in the effects of media violence on aggression. *Journal of Personality and Social Psychology*, 58, 156-163. (p. 359)

Bushman, B. J., Baumeister, R. F., & Phillips, C. M. (2000). Do people aggress to improve their mood? Catharsis beliefs, affect regulation opportunity, and aggressive responding. *Journal of Personality and Social Psychology*. (p. 367)

Bushman, B. J., Baumeister, R. F., & Stack, A. D. (1999). Catharsis, aggression, and persuasive influence: Self-fulfilling or self-defeating prophecies? *Journal of Personality and Social Psychology*, 76, 367-376. (p. 367)

Bushman, B. J., Bonacci, A. M., Pedersen, W. C., Vasquez, E. A., & Miller, N. (2005). Chewing on it can chew you up: Effects of rumination on triggered displaced aggression. *Journal of Personality and Social Psychology*, **88**, 969. (p. 347)

Buss, D. M. (1984). Toward a psychology of person-environment (PE) correlation: The role of spouse selection. *Journal of Personality and Social Psychology*, 47, 361-377. (p. 390)

Buss, D. M. (1985). Human mate selection. *American Scientist*, 73, 47-51. (p. 390)

Buston, P. M., & Emlen. S. T. (2003). Cognitive processes underlying human mate choice: The relationship between self-perception and mate preference in Western society. *Proceedings of the National Academy of Science*, **100**, 8805–8810. (p. 388)

Butcher, S. H. (1951). *Aristotle's theory of poetry and fine art*. New York: Dover Publications. (p. 366)

Butler, A. C., Hokanson, J. E., & Flynn, H. A. (1994). A comparison of self-esteem lability and low trait self-esteem as vulnerability factors for depression. *Journal of Personality and Social Psychology*, 66, 166-177. (p. 492)

Butler, J. L., & Baumeister, R. F. (1998). The trouble with friendly faces: Skilled performance with a supportive audience. *Journal of Personality and Social Psychology*, 75, 1213-1230. (p. 220)

Buunk, B. P., & van der Eijnden, R. J. J. M. (1997). Perceived prevalence, perceived superiority, and relationship satisfaction: Most relationships are good, but ours is the best. *Personality and Social Psychology Bulletin*, 23, 219-228. (p. 65)

Buunk, B. P., & Van Yperen, N. W. (1991). Referential comparisons, relational comparisons, and exchange orientation: Their relation to marital satisfaction. *Personality and Social Psychology Bulletin*, 17, 709-717. (p. 407)

Bylsma, W. H., & Major, B. (1994). Social comparisons and contentment. *Psychology of Women Quarterly*, 18, 241-249. (p. 341)

Byrne, D. (1971). *The attraction paradigm*. New York: Academic Press. (pp. 388)

Byrne, D., & Clore, G. L. (1970). A reinforcement model of evaluative responses. *Personality: An International Journal*, 1, 103-128. (p. 395)

Byrne, D., & Wong, T. J. (1962). Racial prejudice, interpersonal attraction, and assumed dissimilarity of attitudes. *Journal of Abnormal and Social Psychology*, 65, 246-253. (p. 443)

Bytwerk, R. L. (1976). Julius Streicher and the impact of Der Stürmer. *Wiener Library Bulletin*, 29, 41-46. (p. 144)

Bytwerk, R. L., & Brooks, R. D. (1980). *Julius Streicher and the rhetorical foundations of the holocaust*. Paper presented to the Central States Speech Association convention. (p. 156)

Cacioppo, J. T., Hawkley, L. C. Crawford, L. E., Ernst, J. M., Burlseon, M. H., Kowalewski, R. B., Malarkey, W. B., Van Cauter, E., & Bernstson, G. G. (2002b). Loneliness and health: Potential mechanisms. *Psychosomatic Medicine*, 64, 407-417. (p. 503)

Cacioppo, J. T., Hawkley, L. C., & Bernstson, G. G. (2003). The anatomy of loneliness. *Current Directions in Psychological Science*, 12, 71-74. (p. 503)

Cacioppo, J. T., Hawkley, L. C., Bernstson, G. G., Ernst, J. M., Gibbs, A. C., Stickgold, R., & Hobson, J. A. (2002a). Do lonely days invade the nights? Potential social modulation of sleep efficiency.

Psychological Science, 13, 384-387. (p. 503)

Cacioppo, J. T., Petty, R. E., & Morris, K. J. (1983). Effects of need for cognition on message evaluation, recall, and persuasion. *Journal of Personality and Social Psychology*, 45, 805-818. (p. 153)

Cacioppo, J. T., Petty, R. E., Feinstein, J. A., & Jarvis, W. B. G. (1996). Dispositional differences in cognitive motivation: The life and times of individuals varying in need for cognition. *Psychological Bulletin*, 119, 197-253. (p. 153)

Cacioppo, J. T., Uchino, B. N., Crites, S. L., Snydersmith, M. A., Smith, G., Berntson, G. G., & Lang, P. J. (1991). Relationship between facial expressiveness and sympathetic activation in emotion: A critical review, with emphasis on modeling underlying mechanisms and individual differences. *Journal of Personality and Social Psychology*, 62, 110-128. (p. 134)

Campbell, D. T. (1975). On the conflicts between biological and social evolution and between psychology and oral tradition. *American Psychologist*, 30, 1103-1126. (b) (p. 12)

Campbell, D. T. (1975). The conflict between social and biological evolution and the concept of original sin. *Zygon*, 10, 234-249. (a) (p. 305)

Campbell, W. K., & Foster, C. A. (2002). Narcissism and commitment in romantic relationships: An investment model analysis. *Personality and Social Psychology Bulletin, **28***, 484. (p. 411)

Campbell, W. K., & Sedikides, C. (1999). Self-threat magnifies the self-serving bias: A meta-analytic integration. *Review of General Psychology*, 3, 23-43. (p. 55)

Campbell, W. K., Bush, C. P., Brunell, A. B., & Shelton, J. (2005). Understanding the social costs of narcissism: The case of the Tragedy of the Commons. *Personality and Social Psychology Bulletin, **31***, 1358. (p. 469)

Canadian Centre on Substance Abuse (1997). *Canadian Profile: Alcohol, Tobacco, & Other Drugs*. Ottawa: Canadian Centre on Substance Abuse. (p. 210)

Cantril, H., & Bumstead, C. H. (1960). Reflections on the human venture. New York: New York University Press. (p. 251)

Caputo, D., & Dunning, D. (2005). What you don't know: The role played by errors of omission in imperfect self-assessments. *Journal of Experimental Social Psychology, 41*(5), 488. (p. 82)

Carducci, B. J., Cosby, P. C., & Ward, D. D. (1978). Sexual arousal and interpersonal evaluations. *Journal of Experimental Social Psychology*, 14, 449-457. (p. 399)

Carli, L. L. (1999). Cognitive reconstruction, hindsight, and reactions to victims and perpetrators. *Personality and Social Psychology Bulletin*, 25, 966-979. (p. 439)

Carli, L. L., & Leonard, J. B. (1989). The effect of hindsight on victim derogation. *Journal of Social and Clinical Psychology*, 8, 331-343. (p. 439)

Carlo, G., Eisenberg, N., Troyer, D., Switzer, G., & Speer, A. L. (1991). The altruistic personality: In what contexts is it apparent? *Journal of Personality and Social Psychology*, 61, 450-458. (p. 322)

Carlsmith, J. M., & Gross, A. E. (1969). Some effects of guilt on compliance. *Journal of Personality and Social Psychology*, 11, 232-239. (p. 299)

Carlsmith, J. M., Ellsworth, P., & Whiteside, J. (1968). Guilt, confession and compliance. Unpublished manuscript, Stanford University. Cited by J. L. Freeman, D. O. Sears, & J. M. Carlsmith in *Social psychology*. Englewood Cliffs, N.J.: Prentice-Hall, 1970, pp. 275-276. (p. 300)

Carlson, J., & Hatfield, E. (1992). *The psychology of emotion*. Fort Worth, TX: Holt, Rinehart & Winston. (p. 402)

Carlson, J., & Miller, N. (1987). Explanation of the relation between negative mood and helping. *Psychological Bulletin*, 102, 91-108. (p. 300)

Carlson, M., Charlin, V., & Miller, N. (1988). Positive mood and helping behavior: A test of six hypotheses. *Journal of Personality and Social Psychology*, 55, 211-229. (p. 301)

Carlson, M., Marcus-Newhall, A., & Miller, N. (1990). Effects of situational aggression cues: A quantitative review. *Journal of Personality and Social Psychology*, 58, 622-633. (p. 339)

Carlston, D. E., & Shovar, N. (1983). Effects of performance attributions on others' perceptions of the attributor. *Journal of Personality and Social Psychology*, 44, 515-525. (p. 69)

Carlston, D. E., & Skowronski, J. J. (2005). Linking versus thinking: Evidence for the different associative and attributional bases of spontaneous trait transference and spontaneous trait inference. *Journal of Personality and Social Psychology, 89*(6), 884. (p. 76)

Carnevale, P. J., & Choi, D-W. (2000). Culture in the mediation of international disputes. *International Journal of Psychology*, 35, 105-110. (p. 479)

Carroll, D., Davey Smith, G., & Bennett, P. (1994, March). Health and socio-economic status. *The Psychologist*, pp. 122-125. (pp. 21)

Carter, S. & Snow, C. (2004). *Helping singles enter better marriages using predictive models of marital success.* Paper presented at the annual meeting of the American Psychological Society, May 2004. (p. 389)

Carter, S. L. (1993). *Reflections of an affirmative action baby*. New York: Basic Books. (p. 445)

Cartwright, D. S. (1975). The nature of gangs. In D. S. Cartwright, B. Tomson, & H. Schwartz (Eds.), *Gang delinquency*. Monterey, Calif.: Brooks/Cole. (p. 235)

Carvallo, M., & Gabriel, S. (2006). No man is an island: The need to belong and dismissing avoidant attachment style. *Personality and Social Psychology Bulletin*, **32**, 697-709. (p. 372)

Carver, C. S., & Scheier, M. F. (1978). Self-focusing effects of dispositional self-consciousness, mirror presence, and audience presence. *Journal of Personality and Social Psychology*, 36, 324-332. (p. 100)

Carver, C. S., & Scheier, M. F. (1981). *Attention and self-regulation*. New York: Springer-Verlag. (p. 117)

Carver, C. S., & Scheier, M. F. (1986). Analyzing shyness: A specific application of broader self-regulatory principles. In W. H. Jones, J. M. Cheek, & S. R. Briggs (Eds.), *Shyness: Perspectives on research and treatment*. New York: Plenum. (p. 494)

Carver, C. S., Kus, L. A., & Scheier, M. F. (1994). Effect of good versus bad mood and optimistic versus pessimistic outlook on social acceptance versus rejection. *Journal of Social and Clinical Psychology*, 13, 138-151. (p. 491)

Cash, T. F., & Janda, L. H. (1984, December). The eye of the beholder. *Psychology Today*, pp. 46-52. (p. 382)

Caspi, A., & Herbener, E. S. (1990). Continuity and change: Assortative marriage and the consistency of personality in adulthood. *Journal of Personality and Social Psychology*, 58, 250-258. (p. 388)

Caspi, A., Harrington, H., Milne, B., Amell, J. W., Theodore, R. F., & Moffitt, T. E.

(2003). Children's behavioral styles at age 3 are linked to their adult personality traits at age 26. *Journal of Personality, 71*, 495-513. (p. 259)

Cassidy, J. (2000). Adult romantic attachments: A developmental perspective on individual differences. *Review of General Psychology*, 4, 111-131. (p. 404)

Catalano, R., Novaco, R., & McConnell, W. (1997). A model of the net effect of job loss on violence. *Journal of Personality and Social Psychology*, 72, 1440-1447. (p. 339)

Ceci, S. J., & Bruck, M. (1993). Child witnesses: Translating research into policy. *Social Policy Report* (Society for Research in Child Development), 7(3), 1-30. (p. 514)

Ceci, S. J., & Bruck, M. (1993). Suggestibility of the child witness: A historical review and synthesis. *Psychological Bulletin*, 113, 403-439. (p. 514)

Centerwall, B. S. (1989). Exposure to television as a risk factor for violence. *American Journal of Epidemiology*, 129, 643-652. (p. 357)

Chaiken, S. (1979). Communicator physical attractiveness and persuasion. *Journal of Personality and Social Psychology*, 37, 1387-1397. (p. 151)

Chaiken, S. (1980). Heuristic versus systematic information processing and the use of source versus message cues in persuasion. *Journal of Personality and Social Psychology*, 39, 752-766. (p. 153)

Chaiken, S., & Eagly, A. H. (1978). Communication modality as a determinant of message persuasiveness and message comprehensibility. *Journal of Personality and Social Psychology*, 34, 605-614. (p. 164)

Chaiken, S., & Eagly, A. H. (1983). Communication modality as a determinant of persuasion: The role of communicator salience. *Journal of Personality and Social Psychology*, 45, 241-256. (p. 164)

Chaiken, S., & Maheswaran, D. (1994). Neuristic processing can bias systematic processing: Effects of source credibility, argument ambiguity, and task importance on attitude judgment. *Journal of Personality and Social Psychology*, 66, 460-473. (p. 147)

Chaiken, S., Pomerantz, E. M., & Giner-Sorolla, R. (1995). Structural consistency and attitude strength. In R. E. Petty and J. A. Krosnick (eds.), *Attitude strength: antecedents and consequences*. Hillsdale, NJ: Erlbaum. (p. 117)

Chambers, J. R., & Windschitl, P. D. (2004). Biases in social comparative judgments: The role of nonmotivated factors in above-average and comparative-optimism effects. *Psychological Bulletin, **130**,* 813. (p. 63)

Chance, J. E., & Goldstein, A. G. (1981). Depth of processing in response to own and other-race faces. *Personality and Social Psychology Bulletin*, 7, 475-480. (p. 443)

Chapman, L. J., & Chapman, J. P. (1969). Genesis of popular but erroneous psychodiagnostic observations. *Journal of Abnormal Psychology*, 74, 272-280. (p. 486)

Chapman, L. J., & Chapman, J. P. (1971, November). Test results are what you think they are. *Psychology Today*, pp. 18-22, 106-107. (p. 486)

Chartrand, T. L., & Bargh, J. A. (1999). The chameleon effect: The perception-behavior link and social interaction. *Journal of Personality and Social Psychology*, 76, 893-910. (p. 185)

Check, J., & Malamuth, N. (1984). Can there be positive effects of participation in pornography experiments? *Journal of Sex Research*, 20, 14-31. (p. 353)

Chen, E., Langer, D. A., Raphaelson, Y. E., & Matthews, K. A. (2004). Socioeconomic status and health in adolescents: The role of stress interpretations. *Child Development, **75**,* 1039. (p. 505)

Chen, F. F., & Kenrick, D. T. (2002). Repulsion or attraction? Group membership and assumed attitude similarity. *Journal of Personality and Social Psychology*, 83, 111-125. (p. 389)

Chen, S. C. (1937). Social modification of the activity of ants in nest-building. *Physiological Zoology*, 10, 420-436. (p. 217)

Cherlin, A. J., Chase-Lansdale, P. L., & McRae, C. (1998). Effects of parental divorce on mental health throughout the life course. *American Sociological Review*, 63, 239-249. (p. 343)

Choi, I., & Choi, Y. (2002). Culture and self-concept flexibility. *Personality & Social Psychology Bulletin*, 28, 1508-1517. (p. 268)

Choi, I., & Nisbett, R. E. (1998). Situational salience and cultural differences in the correspondence bias and actor-observer bias. *Personality and Social Psychology Bulletin*, 24, 949-960. (p. 270)

Choi, I., Nisbett, R. E., & Norenzayan, A. (1999). Causal attribution across cultures: Variation and universality. *Psychological Bulletin*, 125, 47-63. (p. 270)

Chomsky, N. (1959). Review of B. F. Skinner's verbal behavior. *Language*, 35, 26-58. (p. 189)

Christensen, L. (1988). Deception in psychological research: When is its use justified? *Personality and Social Psychology Bulletin*, 14, 664-675. (p. 31)

Chua-Eoan, H. (1997, April 7). Imprisoned by his own passions. *Time*, pp. 40-42. (p. 170)

Church, G. J. (1986, January 6). China. *Time*, pp. 6-19. (p. 279)

Cialdini, R. B. (1984). *Influence: How and why people agree to things*. New York: William Morrow. (p. 132)

Cialdini, R. B. (1988). *Influence: Science and practice*. Glenview, Il.: Scott, Foresman/Little, Brown. (p. 123)

Cialdini, R. B. (1991). Altruism or egoism? That is (still) the question. *Psychological Inquiry*, 2, 124-126. (p. 310)

Cialdini, R. B. (1995). A full-cycle approach to social psychology. In G. G. Brannigan & M. R. Merrens (eds.), *The social psychologists: Research adventures*. New York: McGraw-Hill. (p. 324)

Cialdini, R. B., & Schroeder, D. A. (1976). Increasing compliance by legitimizing paltry contributions: When even a penny helps. *Journal of Personality and Social Psychology*, 34, 599-604. (p. 324)

Cialdini, R. B., Bickman, L., & Cacioppo, J. T. (1979). An example of consumeristic social psychology: Bargaining tough in the new car showroom. *Journal of Applied Social Psychology*, 9, 115-126. (p. 476)

Cialdini, R. B., Borden, R. J., Thorne, A., Walker, M. R., Freeman, S., & Sloan, L. R. (1976). Basking in reflected glory: Three (football) field studies. *Journal of Personality and Social Psychology*, 39, 406-415. (p. 436)

Cialdini, R. B., Brown, S. L., Lewis, B. P., Luce, C., & Neuberg, S. L. (1997). Reinterpreting the empathy-altruism relationship: When one into one equals oneness. *Journal of Personality and Social Psychology*, 73, 481-494. (p. 310)

Cialdini, R. B., Cacioppo, J. T., Bassett, R., & Miller, J. A. (1978). Lowball procedure for producing compliance: Commitment then cost. *Journal of Personality and Social Psychology*, 36, 463-476. (p. 122)

Cialdini, R. B., Demaine, L. J., Barrett, D. W., Sagarin, B. J., & Rhoads, K. L. V. (2003). The poison parasite defense: A strategy for sapping a stronger opponent's persuasive strength. Unpublished manuscript, Arizona State University. (p. 176)

Cialdini, R. B., Kenrick, D. T., & Baumann, D. J. (1981). Effects of mood on prosocial behavior in children and adults. In N. Eisenberg-Berg (Ed.), *The development of prosocial behavior*. New York: Academic Press. (p. 300)

Cialdini, R. B., Vincent, J. E., Lewis, S. K., Catalan, J., Wheeler, D., & Danby, B. L. (1975). Reciprocal concessions procedure for inducing compliance: The door-in-the-face technique. *Journal of Personality and Social Psychology*, 31, 206-215. (p. 324)

Cicerello, A., & Sheehan, E. P. (1995). Personal advertisements: A content analysis. *Journal of Social Behavior and Personality*, 10, 751-756. (p. 381)

Cioffi, D., & Garner, R. (1998). The effect of response options on decisions and subsequent behavior: Sometimes inaction is better. *Personality and Social Psychology Bulletin*, 24, 463-472. (p. 327)

Clark, M. S. (1984). Record keeping in two types of relationships. *Journal of Personality and Social Psychology*, 47, 549-557. (p. 406)

Clark, M. S. (1986). Evidence for the effectiveness of manipulations of desire for communal versus exchange relationships. *Personality and Social Psychology Bulletin*, 12, 414-425. (p. 406)

Clark, M. S., & Bennett, M. E. (1992). Research on relationships: Implications for mental health. In D. Ruble, P. Costanzo (ed.), *The social psychology of mental health*. New York: Guilford. (p. 46)

Clark, M. S., & Mills, J. (1979). Interpersonal attraction in exchange and communal relationships. *Journal of Personality and Social Psychology*, 37, 12-24. (p. 406)

Clark, M. S., & Mills, J. (1993). The difference between communal and exchange relationships: What it is and is not. *Personality and Social Psychology Bulletin*, 19, 684-691. (p. 406)

Clark, M. S., Mills, J., & Corcoran, D. (1989). Keeping track of needs and inputs of friends and strangers. *Personality and Social Psychology Bulletin*, 15, 533-542. (p. 407)

Clark, M. S., Mills, J., & Powell, M. C. (1986). Keeping track of needs in communal and exchange relationships. *Journal of Personality and Social Psychology*, 51, 333-338. (p. 407)

Clark, R. D., III (1995). A few parallels between group polarization and minority influence. In S. Moscovici, H. Mucchi-Faina, & A. Maass (eds.), *Minority influence*. Chicago: Nelson-Hall. (p. 252)

Clark, R. D., III, & Maass, S. A. (1988). The role of social categorization and perceived source credibility in minority influence. *European Journal of Social Psychology*, 18, 381-394. (p. 202)

Clarke, A. C. (1952). An examination of the operation of residual propinquity as a factor in mate selection. *American Sociological Review*, 27, 17-22. (p. 375)

Cleghorn, J. (2000). Beyond the bottom line: Redefining philanthropy in the 21st Century. *Ketchum Leaders in Philanthropy Series*. Canadian Centre for Philanthropy Toronto. (p. 308)

Cleghorn, R. (1980, October 31). ABC News, meet the Literary Digest. *Detroit Free Press*. (p. 24)

Clifford, M. M., & Walster, E. H. (1973). The effect of physical attractiveness on teacher expectation. *Sociology of Education*, 46, 248-258. (p. 381)

Cline, V. B., Croft, R. G., & Courrier, S. (1973). Desensitization of children to television violence. *Journal of Personality and Social Psychology*, 27, 360-365. (p. 359)

Clore, G. L., Wiggins, N. H., & Itkin, G. (1975). Gain and loss in attraction: Attributions from nonverbal behavior. *Journal of Personality and Social Psychology*, 31, 706-712. (p. 393)

Coates, B., Pusser, H. E., & Goodman, I. (1976). The influence of "Sesame Street" and "Mister Rogers' Neighborhood" on children's social behavior in the preschool. *Child Development*, 47, 138-144. (p. 327)

Codol, J. P. (1976). On the so-called superior conformity of the self behavior: Twenty experimental investigations. *European Journal of Social Psychology*, 5, 457-501. (p. 65)

Cohen, B., Waugh, G., & Place, K. (1989). At the movies: An unobtrusive study of arousal attraction. *Journal of Social Psychology*, 129, 691-693. (p. 399)

Cohen, D. (1998). Culture, social organization, and patterns of violence. *Journal of Personality and Social Psychology*, 75, 408-419. (p. 280)

Cohen, D., & Gunz, A. (2002). As seen by the other. . .: Perspectives on the self in the memories and emotional perceptions of Easterners and Westerners. *Psychological Science*, 13, 55-59. (p. 276)

Cohen, D., & Nisbett, R. E. (1997). Field experiments examining the culture of honor: The role of institutions in perpetuating norms about violence. *Personality and Social Psychology Bulletin*, 23, 1188-1199. (p. 280)

Cohen, D., Nisbett, R. E., Bowdle, B. F., & Schwarz, N. (1996). Insult, aggression, and the southern culture of honor: An "Experimental Ethnography." *Journal of Personality and Social Psychology*, 70, 945-960. (p. 280)

Cohen, G. L., Steele, C. M., & Ross, L. D. (1999). The mentor's dilemma: Providing critical feedback across the racial divide. *Personality and Social Psychology Bulletin*, 25, 1302-1318. (p. 454)

Cohen, M., & Davis, N. (1981). Medication errors: Causes and prevention. Philadelphia: G. F. Stickley Co. Cited by R. B. Cialdini (1989). *Agents of influence: Bunglers, smugglers, and sleuths*. Paper presented at the American Psychological Association convention. (p. 193)

Cohen, S. (1980). Training to understand TV advertising: Effects and some policy implications. Paper presented at the American Psychological Association convention. (p. 178)

Cohen, S. (2002). Psychosocial stress, social networks, and susceptibility to infection. In H. G. Koenig, & H. J. Cohen (Eds.), *The link between religion and health: Psychoneuroimmunology and the faith factor.* (pp. 101-123). New York, NY, US: Oxford University Press. (p. 501)

Cohen, S. (2004). Social relationships and health. *American Psychologist.Special Issue: Awards Issue 2004, **59***, 676. (p. 501)

Cohen, S., & Rodriguez, M. S. (1995). Pathways linking affective disturbances and physical disorders. *Health Psychology*, 14, 374-380. (p. 500)

Cohen, S., Doyle, W. J., Skoner, D. P., Rabin, B. S., & Gwaltney, J. M., Jr. (1997). Social ties and susceptibility to the common cold. *Journal of the American Medical Association*, 277, 1940-1944. (p. 503)

Cohen, S., Doyle, W. J., Turner, R., Alper, C. M., & Skoner, D. P. (2003). Sociability and susceptibility to the common cold. *Psychological Science*, 14, 389-395. (p. 503)

Cohrs, J. C., Moschner, B., Maes, J., & Kielmann, S. (2005). The motivational bases of right-wing authoritarianism and social dominance orientation: Relations to values and attitudes in the aftermath of September 11, 2001. *Personality and Social Psychology Bulletin, **31***, 1425. (p. 429)

Coleman, L. M., Jussim, L., & Abraham, J. (1987). Students' reactions to teachers' evaluations: The unique impact of negative feedback. *Journal of Applied Social Psychology*, 17, 1051-1070. (p. 392)

Collins, N. L., & Miller, L. C. (1994). Self-disclosure and liking: A meta-analytic review. *Psychological Bulletin*, 116, 457-475. (p. 408)

Collins, R. L. (1996). For better or worse: The impact of upward social comparison on self-evaluations. *Psychological Bulletin*, 119, 51-69. (p. 340)

Colman, A. M. (1991). Crowd psychology in South African murder trials. *American Psychologist*, 46, 1071-1079. See also, A. M. Colman (1991), Psychological evidence in South African murder trials. *The Psychologist*, 14, 482-486.

Comer, D. R. (1995). A model of social loafing in real work group. *Human Relations*, 48, 647-667. (p. 226)

Conger, R. D., Cui, M., Bryant, C. M., & Elder, G. H. (2000). Competence in early adult romantic relationships: A developmental perspective on family influences. *Journal of Personality and Social Psychology*, 79, 224-237. (p. 405)

Conway, F., & Siegelman, J. (1979). *Snapping: America's epidemic of sudden personality change.* New York: Delta Books. (p. 171)

Conway, L. G., III, & Schaller, M. (2005). When authorities' commands backfire: Attributions about consensus and effects on deviant decision making. *Journal of Personality and Social Psychology, **89***, 311.

Conway, M., & Ross, M. (1985). Remembering one's own past: The construction of personal histories. In R. Sorrentino & E. T. Higgins (Eds.) *Handbook of motivation and cognition.* New York: Guilford. (p. 80)

Conway, M., & Ross, M. (1986). Remembering one's own past: The construction of personal histories. In R. Sorrentino & E. T. Higgins (Eds.), *Handbook of motivation and cognition.* New York: Guilford. (p. 80)

Cook, S. W. (1984). Cooperative interaction in multiethnic contexts. In N. Miller & M. B. Brewer (eds.), *Groups in contact: The psychology of desegregation.* Orlando, FL: Academic Press. (p. 286)

Cook, T. D., & Curtin, T. R. (1987). The mainstream and the underclass: Why are the differences so salient and the similarities so unobtrusive? In J. C. Masters & W. P. Smith (Eds.), *Social comparison, social justice, and relative deprivation: Theoretical, empirical, and policy perspectives.* Hillsdale, N.J.: Erlbaum. (p. 447)

Cook, T. D., & Flay, B. R. (1978). The persistence of experimentally induced attitude change. In L. Berkowitz (Ed.), *Advances in experimental social psychology.* Vol. 11. New York: Academic Press. (p. 149)

Cooley, C. H. (1902). *Human nature and the social order.* New York: Schocken Books. (p. 45)

Coombs, R. H. (1991, January). Marital status and personal well-being: A literature review. *Family Relations*, 40, 97-102. (p. 508)

Cooper, H. (1983). Teacher expectation effects. In L. Bickman (Ed.), *Applied social psychology annual*, Vol. 4. Beverly Hills, Ca.: Sage. (p. 104)

Cooper, J. (1999). Unwanted consequences and the self: In search of the motivation for dissonance reduction. In (Eds.) E. Harmon-Jones, J. Mills. *Cognitive dissonance: Progress on a pivotal theory in social psychology.* Science conference series. (pp. 149-173). Washington, DC, US: American Psychological Association. (p. 129)

Correll, J., Park, B., Judd, C. M., & Wittenbrink, B. (2002). The police officer's dilemma: Using ethnicity to disambiguate potentially threatening individuals. *Journal of Personality and Social Psychology*, 83, 1314-1329. (p. 420)

Correll, J., Urland, G. R., & Ito, T. A. (2006). Event-related potentials and the decision to shoot: The role of threat perception and cognitive control. *Journal of Experimental Social Psychology, **42***, 120-128. (p. 420)

Costanzo, M. (1998). *Just revenge.* New York: St. Martins. (p. 334)

Cota, A. A., & Dion, K. L. (1986). Salience of gender and sex composition of ad hoc groups: An experimental test of distinctiveness theory. *Journal of Personality and Social Psychology*, 50, 770-776. (p. 212)

Cottrell, N. B., Wack, D. L., Sekerak, G. J., & Rittle, R. M. (1968). Social facilitation of dominant responses by the presence of an audience and the mere presence of others. *Journal of Personality and Social Psychology*, 9, 245-250. (p. 221)

Courneya, K. S. (1995). Understanding readiness for regular physical activity in older individuals: An application of the theory of planned behavior. *Health Psychology*, 14, 80-87. (p. 116)

Courneya, K. S., & Carron, A. V. (1992). The home advantage in sport competitions: A literature review. *Journal of Sport and Exercise Psychology*, 14, 13-27.

Court, J. H. (1985). Sex and violence: A ripple effect. In N. M. Malamuth & E. Donnerstein (Eds.), *Pornography and sexual aggression.* New York: Academic Press. (p. 352)

Courtney, J. G., Longnecker, M. P., Theorell, T., & de Verdier, M. G. (1993). *Stressful life events and the risk of colorectal cancer.* Epidemiology, 4, 407-414. (p. 501)

Coyne, J. C., Burchill, S. A. L., & Stiles, W. B. (1991). In C. R. Snyder & D. O. Forsyth (Eds.), *Handbook of social and clinical psychology: The health perspective.* New York: Pergamon. (p. 491)

Crabb, P. B., & Bielawski, D. (1994). The social representation of material culture and gender in children's books. *Sex Roles*, 30, 69-79. (p. 120)

Crandall, C. S. (1988). Social contagion of binge eating. *Journal of Personality and Social Psychology*, 55, 588-598. (p. 203)

Crandall, C. S. (1994). Prejudice against fat people: Ideology and self-interest. *Journal of Personality and Social Psychology*, 66, 882-894. (p. 428)

Crandall, C. S., & Eshleman, A. (2003). A justification-suppression model of the expression and experience of prejudice. *Psychological Bulletin*, 129, 414-446. (p. 441)

Crawford Solberg, E., Diener, E., Wirtz, D., Lucas, R. E., & Oishi, S. (2002). Wanting, having, and satisfaction: Examining the role of desire discrepancies in satisfaction with income. *Journal of Personality and Social Psychology, **83***, 725.

Crawford, M., Stark, A. C., & Renner, C. H. (1998). The meaning of Ms.: Social assimilation of a gender concept. *Psychology of Women Quarterly*, 22, 197-208. (p. 417)

Crawford, T. J. (1974). Sermons on racial tolerance and the parish neighborhood context. *Journal of Applied Social Psychology, **4***, 1. (p. 160)

Crocker, J. (1981). Judgment of covariation by social perceivers. *Psychological Bulletin*, 90, 272-292. (p. 88)

Crocker, J., & Gallo, L. (1985). *The self-enhancing effect of downward comparison.* Paper presented at the American Psychological Association convention. (p. 538)

Crocker, J., & Luhtanen, R. (1990). Collective self-esteem and ingroup bias. *Journal of Personality and Social Psychology*, 58, 60-67. (p. 435)

Crocker, J., & Major, B. (1989). Social stigma and self-esteem: The self-protective properties of stigma. *Psychological Review*, 96, 608-630. (p. 460)

Crocker, J., & McGraw, K. M. (1984). What's good for the goose is not good for the gander: Solo status as an obstacle to occupational achievement for males and females. *American Behavioral Scientist*, 27, 357-370. (p. 445)

Crocker, J., & Park, L. E. (2004). The costly pursuit of self-esteem. *Psychological Bulletin*, 130, 392-414. (p. 149)

Crocker, J., & Wolfe, C. (2001). Contingencies of self-worth. *Psychological Review.* (p. 51)

Crocker, J., Hannah, D. B., & Weber, R. (1983). Personal memory and causal attributions. *Journal of Personality and Social Psychology*, 44, 55-56. (p. 450)

Crocker, J., Luhtanen, R. K., & Sommers, S. R. (2005). Contingencies of self-worth: Progress and prospects. *European Review of Social Psychology,* **15**, 133. (p. 49)

Crocker, J., Thompson, L. L., McGraw, K. M., & Ingerman, C. (1987). Downward comparison, prejudice, and evaluations of others: Effects of self-esteem and threat. *Journal of Personality and Social Psychology*, 52, 907-916. (p. 437)

Crocker, J., Voelkl, K., Testa, M., & Major, B. (1991). Social stigma: The affective consequences of attributional ambiguity. *Journal of Personality and Social Psychology*, 60, 218-228. (p. 460)

Croizet, J. C., Despres, G., Gauzins, M. E., Huguet, P., Leyens, J. P., & Meot, A. (2004). Stereotype threat undermines intellectual performance by triggering a disruptive mental load. *Personality and Social Psychology Bulletin*, 30, 721-731. (p. 455)

Cropley, A. J., & Cardey, R. M. (1975). Contact with the dominant culture and cognitive competence in Canadian Indians and Whites. *Canadian Journal of Behavioural Science*, 7, 328-338. (p. 273)

Crosby, F. J. (Ed.) (1987). *Spouse, parent, worker: On gender and multiple roles.* New Haven, CT: Yale University Press. (p. 508)

Crosby, F., Bromley, S., & Saxe, L. (1980). Recent unobtrusive studies of black and white discrimination and prejudice: A literature review. *Psychological Bulletin*, 87, 546-563. (p. 418)

Crosby, F., Pufall, A., Snyder, R. C., O'Connell, M., & Whalen, P. (1989). The denial of personal disadvantage among you, me, and all the other ostriches. In M. Crawford & M. Gentry (Eds.), *Gender and thought*. New York: Springer-Verlag. (p. 460)

Cross, P. (1977). Not can but will college teaching be improved? *New Directions for Higher Education*, Spring, No. 17, pp. 1-15. (p. 65)

Cross, S. E., Liao, M-H., & Josephs, R. (1992). *A cross-cultural test of the self-evaluation maintenance model.* Paper presented at the American Psychological Association convention. (p. 268)

Cross-National Collaborative Group (1992). The changing rate of major depression. *Journal of the American Medical Association*, 268, 3098-3105. (p. 493)

Crowley, G. (1996, June 3). The biology of beauty. *Newsweek*, pp. 61-69. (p. 379)

Croxton, J. S., & Miller, A. G. (1987). Behavioral disconfirmation and the observer bias. *Journal of Social Behavior and Personality*, 2, 145-152. (p. 10)

Croxton, J. S., & Morrow, N. (1984). Memory biases in the reconstruction of interpersonal encounters. *Journal of Social and Clinical Psychology*, 2, 348-354. (p. 79)

Croxton, J. S., Eddy, T., & Morrow, N. (1984). Memory biases in the reconstruction of interpersonal encounters. *Journal of Social & Clinical Psychology, 2*(4), 348.

Csikszentmihalyi, M. (1990). *Flow: The psychology of optimal experience.* New York: Harper & Row. (p. 538)

Csikszentmihalyi, M. (1999). If we are so rich, why aren't we happy? *American Psychologist*, 54, 821-827. (p. 538)

Cunningham, J. D. (1981). Self-disclosure intimacy: Sex, sex-of-target, cross-national, and generational differences. *Personality and Social Psychology Bulletin*, 7, 314-319. (p. 409)

Cunningham, M. R., Shaffer, D. R., Barbee, A. P., Wolff, P. L., & Kelley, D. J. (1990). Separate processes in the relation of elation and depression to helping: Social versus personal concerns. *Journal of Experimental Social Psychology*, 26, 13-33. (p. 302)

Cunningham, W. A., Raye, C. L., & Johnson, M. K. (2004). Implicit and explicit evaluation: FMRI correlates of valence, emotional intensity, and control in the processing of attitudes. *Journal of Cognitive Neuroscience. Special Issue: Social Cognitive Neuroscience,* **16**, 1717. (p. 421)

Curtis, S. (1977). *Genie: A psycholinguistic study of a modern-day "wild child."* New York: Academic Press. (p. 289)

Cutler, B. L., & Penrod, S. D. (1988). Context reinstatement and eyewitness identification. In G. M. Davies & D. M. Thomson (Eds.), *Context reinstatement and eyewitness identification*. New York: Wiley. (a) (p. 518)

Cutler, B. L., & Penrod, S. D. (1988). Improving the reliability of eyewitness identification: Lineup construction and presentation. *Journal of Applied Psychology*, 73, 281-290. (b) (p. 520)

Cutler, B. L., Penrod, S. D., & Dexter, H. R. (1989). The eyewitness, the expert psychologist and the jury. *Law and Human Behavior*, 13, 311-332. (p. 521)

Cutrona, C. E. (1986). Behavioral manifestations of social support: A microanalytic investigation. *Journal of Personality and Social Psychology*, 51, 201-208. (p. 504)

Dabbs, J. M., & Janis, I. L. (1965). Why does eating while reading facilitate opinion change? An experimental inquiry. *Journal of Experimental Social Psychology*, 1, 133-144. (p. 153)

Dabbs, J. M., Jr. (1992). Testosterone measurements in social and clinical psychology. *Journal of Social and Clinical Psychology*, 11, 302-321. (p. 337)

Dabbs, J. M., Jr., & Hargrove, M. F. (1998). Age, testosterone, and behavior among female prison inmates. *Psychosomatic Medicine*, in press. (p. 337)

Dabbs, J. M., Jr., & Morris, R. (1990). Testosterone, social class, and antisocial behavior in a sample of 4,462 men. *Psychological Science*, 1, 209-211. (p. 337)

Dabbs, J. M., Jr., Carr, T. S., Frady, R. L., & Riad, J. K. (1995). Testosterone, crime, and misbehavior among 692 male prison inmates. *Personality and Individual Differences*, 18, 627-633. (p. 337)

Dabbs, J. M., Jr., Karpas, A. E., Dyomina, N., Juechter, J., & Roberts, A. (2002). Experimental raising or lowering of testosterone level affects mood in normal men and women. *Social Behavior and Personality*, ***30***, 795. (p. 337)

Dabbs, J. M., Jr., Riad, J. K., & Chance, S. E. (2001). Testosterone and ruthless homicide. *Personality and Individual Differences*, ***31***, 599. (p. 337)

Dabbs, J. M., Jr., Strong, R., & Milun, R. (1998). Exploring the mind of testosterone: A beeper study. *Journal of Research in Personality*, in press. (p. 337)

Damon, W. (1995). *Greater Expectations: Overcoming the Culture of Indulgence in America's Homes and Schools.* New York: Free Press. (p. 22)

Danner, D. D., Snowdon, D. A., & Friesen, W. V. (2001). Positive emotions in early life and longevity: Findings from the Nun Study. *Journal of Personality and Social Psychology*, 80, 804-813. (p. 502)

Darley, J. M. (1995). Book review essay. *Political Psychology*, in press. (p. 321)

Darley, J. M., & Batson, C. D. (1973). From Jerusalem to Jericho: A study of situational and dispositional variables in helping behavior. *Journal of Personality and Social Psychology*, 27, 100-108. (p. 319)

Darley, J. M., & Berscheid, E. (1967). Increased liking as a result of the anticipation of personal contact. *Human Relations*, 20, 29-40. (p. 376)

Darley, J. M., & Gross, P. H. (1983). A hypothesis-confirming bias in labelling effects. *Journal of Personality and Social Psychology*, 44, 20-33. (p. 457)

Darley, J. M., & Latané, B. (1968). Bystander intervention in emergencies: Diffusion of responsibility. *Journal of Personality and Social Psychology*, 8, 377-383. (p. 312)

Darley, J. M., Teger, A. I., & Lewis, L. D. (1973). Do groups always inhibit individuals' response to potential emergencies? *Journal of Personality and Social Psychology*, 26, 395-399. (p. 318)

Darley, S., & Cooper, J. (1972). Cognitive consequences of forced noncompliance. *Journal of Personality and Social Psychology*, 24, 321-326. (p. 179)

Darwin, C. (1859/1988). *The origin of species*. Vol. 15 of The Works of Charles Darwin, edited by P. H. Barrett & R. B. Freeman. New York: New York University Press. (p. 257)

Das, E. H. H. J., de Wit, J. B. F., & Stroebe, W. (2003). Fear appeals motivate acceptance of action recommendations: Evidence for a positive bias in the processing of persuasive messages. *Personality and Social Psychology Bulletin*, 29, 650-664. (p. 155)

Dashiell, J. F. (1930). An experimental analysis of some group effects. *Journal of Abnormal and Social Psychology*, 25, 190-199. (p. 217)

Davidson, R. J., Putnam, K. M., & Larson, C. L. (2000). Dysfunction in the neural circuitry of emotion regulation-A possible prelude to violence. *Science*, 289, 591-594. (p. 335)

Davie, M. (1986). *The Titanic: The full story of a tragedy*. London: Collins. (p. 241)

Davies, P. G., Spencer, S. J., Quinn, D. M., & Gerhardstein, R. (2002). Consuming images: How television commercials that elicit stereotype threat can restrain women academically and professionally. *Personality and Social Psychology Bulletin*, 28, 1615-1628. (p. 453)

Davila, J., Bradbury, T. N., Cohan, C. L., & Tochluk, S. (1997). Marital functioning and depressive symptoms: Evidence for a stress generation model. *Journal of Personality and Social Psychology*, 73, 849-861. (p. 508)

Davis, C. G., Lehman, D. R., Silver, R. C., Wortman, C. B., & Ellard, J. H. (1996). Self-blame following a traumatic event: The role of perceived avoidability. *Personality and Social Psychology Bulletin*, 22, 557-567. (p. 88)

Davis, C. G., Lehman, D. R., Wortman, C. B., Silver, R. C., & Thompson, S. C. (1995). The undoing of traumatic life events. *Personality and Social Psychology Bulletin*, 21, 109-124. (p. 88)

Davis, J. H., Kameda, T., Parks, C., Stasson, M., & Zimmerman, S. (1989). Some social mechanics of group decision making: The distribution of opinion, polling sequence, and implications for consensus. *Journal of Personality and Social Psychology*, 57, 1000-1012. (p. 524)

Davis, J. H., Kerr, N. L., Atkin, R. S., Holt, R., & Meek, D. (1975). The decision processes of 6- and 12-person mock juries assigned unanimous and two-thirds majority rules. *Journal of Personality and Social Psychology*, 32, 1-14. (p. 524)

Davis, J. H., Kerr, N. L., Strasser, G., Meek, D., & Holt, R. (1977). Victim consequences, sentence severity, and decision process in mock juries. *Organizational Behavior and Human Performance*, 18, 346-365. (p. 524)

Davis, J. H., Stasson, M. F., Parks, C. D., Hulbert, L., Kameda, T., Zimmerman, S. K., & Ono, K. (1993). Quantitative decisions by groups and individuals: Voting procedures and monetary awards by mock civil juries. *Journal of Experimental Social Psychology*, 29, 326-346. (p. 175)

Davis, K. E. (1985, February). Near and dear: Friendship and love compared. *Psychology Today*, pp. 22-30. (p. 403)

Davis, K. E., & Jones, E. E. (1960). Changes in interpersonal perception as a means of reducing cognitive dissonance. *Journal of Abnormal and Social Psychology*, 61, 402-410. (p. 124)

Davis, L., & Greenlees, C. (1992). *Social loafing revisited: Factors that mitigate-and reverse-performance loss.* Paper presented at the Southwestern Psychological Association convention. (p. 226)

Davis, M. H. (1979). *The case for attributional egotism.* Paper presented at the American Psychological Association convention. (p. 56)

Davis, M. H., & Stephan, W. G. (1980). Attributions for exam performance. *Journal of Applied Social Psychology*, 10, 235-248. (p. 56)

Dawes, R. (1998, October). The social usefulness of self-esteem: A skeptical view. *Harvard Mental Health Letter*, pp. 4-5. (p. 47)

Dawes, R. M. (1980). Social dilemmas. *Annual Review of Psychology*, 31, 169-193. (p. 472)

Dawes, R. M. (1980). You can't systematize human judgment: Dyslexia. In R. A. Shweder (Ed.), *New directions for methodology of social and behavioral science: Fallible judgment in behavioral research.* San Francisco: Jossey-Bass. (p. 109)

Dawes, R. M. (1990). The potential nonfalsity of the false consensus effect. In R. M. Hogarth (Ed.), *Insights in decision making: A tribute to Hillel J. Einhorn.* Chicago: University of Chicago Press. (p. 61)

Dawes, R. M. (1991). Social dilemmas, economic self-interest, and evolutionary theory. In D. R. Brown & J. E. Keith Smith (Eds.), *Frontiers of mathematical psychology: Essays in honor of Clyde Coombs*. New York: Springer-Verlag. (p. 467)

Dawes, R. M. (1994). *House of cards: Psychology and psychotherapy built on myth*. New York: Free Press. (p. 22)

Dawes, R. M. (1998). Behavioral decision making and judgment. In D. T. Gilbert, S. T. Fiske & G. Lindzey (Eds.), *The handbook of social psychology*, vols. 1 and 2 (4th ed.). (pp. 497-548). New York, NY, US: McGraw-Hill.

Dawes, R. M., McTavish, J., & Shaklee, H. (1977). Behavior, communication, and assumptions about other people's behavior in a commons dilemma situation. *Journal of Personality and Social Psychology*, 35, 1-11. (p. 472)

Dawkins, R. (1976). *The selfish gene*. New York: Oxford University Press. (pp. 305)

de Hoogh, A. H. B., den Hartog, D. N., Koopman, P. L., Thierry, H., van den Berg, Peter T., van der Weide, Joost G., et al. (2004). Charismatic leadership, environmental dynamism, and performance. *European Journal of Work and Organizational Psychology*, ***13***, 447. (p. 249)

de Vries, N. K., & van Knippenberg, A. (1987). Biased and unbiased self-evaluations of ability: The effects of further testing. *British Journal of Social Psychology*, 26, 9-15. (p. 69)

DeAngelis, T. (1993, September). Controversial diagnosis is voted into latest DSM. *Monitor*, pp. 32-33. (p. 498)

Deary, I. J. (2005). Intelligence, health and death. *The Psychologist*, ***18***, 610. (p. 505)

DeBruine, L. M. (2002). Facial resemblance enhances trust. *Proceedings of the Royal Society of London*, 269, 1307-1312. (p. 320)

DeBruine, L. M. (2004). Resemblance to self increases the appeal of child faces to both men and women. *Evolution and Human Behavior*, ***25***, 142. (p. 378)

Deci, E. L., & Ryan, R. M. (1985). *Intrinsic motivation and self-determination in human behavior*. New York: Plenum. (p. 137)

Deci, E. L., & Ryan, R. M. (1987). The support of autonomy and the control of behavior. *Journal of Personality and Social Psychology*, 53, 1024-1037. (p. 53)

Deci, E. L., & Ryan, R. M. (1991). A motivational approach to self: Integration in personality. In R. Dienstbier (Ed.) Vol. 38. *Perspectives on motivation* (pp. 237-288), Lincoln, NE: University of Nebraska Press. Nebraska Symposium on Motivation. (p. 135)

Deci, E. L., & Ryan, R. M. (1997). *Behaviorists in search of the null: Revisiting the undermining of intrinsic motivation by extrinsic rewards*. Unpublished manuscript, University of Rochester. (p. 135)

Delgado, J. (1973). In M. Pines, *The brain changers*. New York: Harcourt Brace Jovanovich. (p. 118)

della Cava, M. R. (2003, April 2). Iraq gets sympathetic press around the world. *USA Today* (www.usatoday.com). (p. 144)

Dembroski, T. M., Lasater, T. M., & Ramirez, A. (1978). Communicator similarity, fear arousing communications, and compliance with health care recommendations. *Journal of Applied Social Psychology*, 8, 254-269. (p. 152)

Dengerink, H. A., & Myers, J. D. (1977). Three effects of failure and depression on subsequent aggression. *Journal of Personality and Social Psychology*, 35, 88-96. (p. 347)

DePaulo, B. M., Charlton, K., Cooper, H., Lindsay, J. J., & Muhlenbruck, L. (1997). The accuracy-confidence correlation in the detection of deception. *Personality and Social Psychology Review*, 1, 346-357. (p. 82)

Derlega, V., Metts, S., Petronio, S., & Margulis, S. T. (1993). *Self-disclosure*. Newbury Park, CA: Sage. (p. 408)

Dermer, M., & Pyszczynski, T. A. (1978). Effects of erotica upon men's loving and liking responses for women they love. *Journal of Personality and Social Psychology*, 36, 1302-1309. (p. 399)

Dermer, M., Cohen, S. J., Jacobsen, E., & Anderson, E. A. (1979). Evaluative judgments of aspects of life as a function of vicarious exposure to hedonic extremes. *Journal of Personality and Social Psychology*, 37, 247-260. (p. 537)

Desforges, D. M., Lord, C. G., Pugh, M. A., Sia, T. L., Scarberry, N. C., & Ratcliff, C. D. (1997). Role of group representativeness in the generalization part of the contact hypothesis. *Basic and Applied Social Psychology*, 19, 183-204. (p. 285)

Deutsch, F. M., & Saxon, S. E. (1998). The double standard of praise and criticism for mothers and fathers. *Psychology of Women Quarterly*, 22, 665-683. (p. 261)

Deutsch, M. (1990). Psychological roots of moral exclusion. *Journal of Social Issues*, 46, 21-25. (p. 325)

Deutsch, M. (1999). Behind the scenes. In D. G. Myers, *Social psychology*, 6th edition. New York: McGraw-Hill, 519. (p. 466)

Deutsch, M., & Gerard, H. B. (1955). A study of normative and informational social influence upon individual judgment. *Journal of Abnormal and Social Psychology*, 51, 629-636. (p. 204)

Devine, P. G. (1989). Stereotypes and prejudice: Their automatic and controlled components. *Journal of Personality and Social Psychology*, 56, 5-18. (p. 440)

Devine, P. G., Evett, S. R., & Vasquez-Suson, K. A. (1996). Exploring the interpersonal dynamics of intergroup contact. In R. Sorrentino & E. T. Higgins (eds.), *Handbook of motivation and cognition: The interpersonal content*, vol. 3. New York: Guilford. (p. 446)

Devine, P. G., Plant, E. A., & Buswell, B. N. (2000). Breaking the prejudice habit: Progress and obstacles. In S. Oskamp (Ed.), *Reducing prejudice and discrimination*. Mahwah, N.J.: Erlbaum, 2000. (p. 440)

Diamond, S. S. (1993). Instructing on death: Psychologists, juries, and judges. *American Psychologist*, 48, 423-434. (p. 523)

Diekman, A. B., McDonald, M., & Gardner, W. L. (2000). Love means never having to be careful: The relationship between reading romance novels and safe sex behavior. *Psychology of Women Quarterly*, 24, 179-188. (p. 86)

Diekmann, K. A., Samuels, S. M., Ross, L., & Bazerman, M. H. (1997). Self-interest and fairness in problems of resource allocation: Allocators versus recipients. *Journal of Personality and Social Psychology*, 72, 1061-1074. (p. 56)

Diener, E. & Seligman, M. E. P. (2002). Very happy people. *Psychological Science*, 13, 81-84. (p. 535)

Diener, E. (1976). Effects of prior destructive behavior, anonymity, and group presence on deindividuation and aggression. *Journal of Personality and Social Psychology*, 33, 497-507. (p. 229)

Diener, E. (1979). Deindividuation, self-awareness, and disinhibition. *Journal of Personality and Social Psychology*, 37, 1160-1171. (p. 231)

Diener, E. (1980). Deindividuation: The absence of self-awareness and self-regulation in group members. In P. Paulus (Ed.), *The psychology of group influence*. Hillsdale, N.J.: Erlbaum. (p. 231)

Diener, E., & Crandall, R. (1979). An evaluation of the Jamaican anticrime program. *Journal of Applied Social Psychology*, 9, 135-146. (p. 369)

Diener, E., & Wallbom, M. (1976). Effects of self-awareness on antinormative behavior. *Journal of Research in Personality*, 10, 107-111. (p. 117)

Diener, E., Horwitz, J., & Emmons, R. A. (1985). Happiness of the very wealthy. *Social Indicators*, 16, 263-274. (p. 534)

Diener, E., Lucas, R. E., & Scollon, C. N. (2006). Beyond the hedonic treadmill: Revising the adaptation theory of well-being. *American Psychologist, **61***, 305. (p. 536)

Dienstbier, R. A., Roesch, S. C., Mizumoto, A., Hemenover, S. H., Lott, R. C., & Carlo, G. (1998). Effects of weapons on guilt judgments and sentencing recommendations for criminals. *Basic and Applied Social Psychology*, 20, 93-102. (p. 349)

Dijksterhuis, A., Chartrand, T. L., & Aarts, H. (2007). Effects of priming and perception on social behavior and goal pursuit. In J. A. Bargh (Ed.), *Social psychology and the unconscious: The automaticity of higher mental processes.* (pp. 51-131). New York, NY, US: Psychology Press. (p. 41)

Dijksterhuis, A., Smith, P. K., van Baaren, R. B., & Wigboldus, D. H. J. (2005). The unconscious consumer: Effects of environment on consumer behavior. *Journal of Consumer Psychology, **15***, 193-202. (p. 147)

Dillehay, R. C., & Nietzel, M. T. (1980). Constructing a science of jury behavior. In L. Wheeler (Ed.), *Review of personality and social psychology* (Vol. 1). Beverly Hills, Calif.: Sage Publications. (p. 526)

Dion, K. K. (1972). Physical attractiveness and evaluations of children's transgressions. *Journal of Personality and Social Psychology*, 24, 207-213. (p. 381)

Dion, K. K. (1973). Young children's stereotyping of facial attractiveness. *Developmental Psychology*, 9, 183-188. (p. 381)

Dion, K. K. (1979). Physical attractiveness and interpersonal attraction. In M. Cook & G. Wilson (Eds.), *Love and attraction.* New York: Pergamon Press. (p. 381)

Dion, K. K., & Berscheid, E. (1974). Physical attractiveness and peer perception among children. *Sociometry*, 37, 1-12. (p. 381)

Dion, K. K., & Dion, K. L. (1985). Personality, gender, and the phenomenology of romantic love. In P. R. Shaver (Ed.), *Review of personality and social psychology*, vol. 6. Beverly Hills, Ca.: Sage. (p. 400)

Dion, K. K., & Dion, K. L. (1993). Individualistic and collectivistic perspectives on gender and the cultural context of love and intimacy. *Journal of Social Issues*, 49, 53-69. (p. 410)

Dion, K. K., & Dion, K. L. (1996). Cultural perspectives on romantic love. *Personal Relationships*, 3, 5-17. (p. 402)

Dion, K. K., & Stein, S. (1978). Physical attractiveness and interpersonal influence. *Journal of Experimental Social Psychology*, 14, 97-109. (p. 151)

Dion, K. L. (1975). Women's reactions to discrimination from members of the same or opposite sex. *Journal of Research in Personality*, 9, 294-306. (p. 460)

Dion, K. L. (1985). Responses to perceived discrimination and relative deprivation. In J. M. Olson, C. P. Herman, & M. P. Zanna (Eds.), *Relative deprivation and social comparison: The Ontario symposium*, vol. 4. Hillsdale, N.J.: Erlbaum. (p. 341)

Dion, K. L. (1987). What's in a title? The Ms. stereotype and images of women's titles of address. *Psychology of Women Quarterly*, 11, 21-36. (p. 417)

Dion, K. L. (1998). The social psychology of perceived prejudice and discrimination. *Colloquium presentation*, Carleton University. (p. 447)

Dion, K. L., & Cota, A. A. (1991). The Ms. stereotype: Its domain and the role of explicitness in title preference. *Psychology of Women Quarterly*, 15, 403-410. (p. 417)

Dion, K. L., & Dion, K. K. (1988). Romantic love: Individual and cultural perspectives. In R. J. Sternberg & M. L. Barnes (Eds.), *The psychology of love.* New Haven, Conn.: Yale University Press. (p. 402)

Dion, K. L., & Earn, B. M. (1975). The phenomenology of being a target of prejudice. *Journal of Personality and Social Psychology*, 32, 944-950. (p. 460)

Dion, K. L., & Kawakami, K. (1996). *Canadian Journal of Behavioural Science*, 28, 203-213. (p. 460)

Dion, K. L., & Schuller, R. A. (1991). The Ms. stereotype: Its generality and its relation to managerial and marital status stereotypes. *Canadian Journal of Behavioural Science*, 23, 25-40. (p. 417)

Dion, K. L., Dion, K. K., & Keelan, J. P. (1990). Appearance anxiety as a dimension of social-evaluative anxiety: Exploring the ugly duckling syndrome. *Contemporary Social Psychology*, 14(4), 220-224. (p. 379)

Dishion, T. J., McCord, J., & Poulin, F. (1999). When interventions harm: Peer groups and problem behavior. *American Psychologist*, 54, 755-764. (p. 235)

Dixon, B. (1986, April). Dangerous thoughts: How we think and feel can make us sick. *Science* 86, pp. 63-66. (p. 501)

Dohrenwend, B., Pearlin, L., Clayton, P., Hamburg, B., Dohrenwend, B. P., Riley, M., & Rose, R. (1982). Report on stress and life events. In G. R. Elliott & C. Eisdorfer (Eds.), *Stress and human health: Analysis and implications of research* (A study by the Institute of Medicine/ National Academy of Sciences). New York: Springer. (p. 504)

Dolinski, D. (2000). On inferring one's beliefs from one's attempt and consequences for subsequent compliance. *Journal of Personality and Social Psychology*, 78, 260-272. (p. 328)

Dolinski, D., & Nawrat, R. (1998). "Fear-then-relief" procedure for producing compliance: Beware when the danger is over. *Journal of Experimental Social Psychology*, 34, 27-50. (p. 301)

Dollard, J., Doob, L., Miller, N., Mowrer, O. H., & Sears, R. R. (1939). *Frustration and aggression.* New Haven, Conn.: Yale University Press. (p. 338)

Dolnik, L., Case, T. I., & Williams, K. D. (2003). Stealing thunder as a courtroom tactic revisited: Processes and boundaries. *Law and Human Behavior, **27***, 267. (p. 166)

Donnerstein, E. (1980). Aggressive erotica and violence against women. *Journal of Personality and Social Psychology*, 39, 269-277. (p. 353)

Donnerstein, E. (1998). *Why do we have those new ratings on television.* Invited address to the National Institute on the Teaching of Psychology. (p. 355)

Donnerstein, E., Linz, D., & Penrod, S. (1987). *The question of pornography.* London: Free Press. (p. 351)

Doob, A. N., & Kirshenbaum, H. M. (1973). Bias in police lineups-partial remembering. *Journal of Police Science and Administration*, 1, 287-293. (p. 519)

Doob, A. N., & McLaughlin, D. S. (1989). Ask and you shall be given: Request size and donations to a good cause. *Journal of Applied Social Psychology*, 19, 1049-1056. (p. 325)

Doob, A. N., & Roberts, J. (1988). Public attitudes toward sentencing in Canada. In N. Walker & M. Hough (Eds.), *Sentencing and the public*. London: Gower. (p. 86)

Doty, R. M., Peterson, B. E., & Winter, D. G. (1991). Threat and authoritarianism in the United States, 1978-1987. *Journal of Personality and Social Psychology*, 61, 629-640. (p. 428)

Douglas, K. M., & McGarty, C. (2001). Identifiability and self-presentation: Computer-mediated communication and intergroup interaction. *British Journal of Social Psychology*, 40, 399-416. (p. 229)

Dovidio, J. F. (1991). The empathy-altruism hypothesis: Paradigm and promise. *Psychological Inquiry*, 2, 126-128. (p. 311)

Dovidio, J. F., Allen, J. L., & Schroeder, D. A. (1990). Specificity of empathy-induced helping: Evidence for altruistic motivation. *Journal of Personality and Social Psychology*, 59, 249-260. (p. 310)

Dovidio, J. F., Gaertner, S. L., Anastasio, P. A., & Sanitioso, R. (1992). Cognitive and motivational bases of bias: Implications of aversive racism for attitudes toward Hispanics. In S. Knouse, P. Rosenfeld, & A. Culbertson (Eds.), *Hispanics in the workplace*. Newbury Park, CA: Sage. (p. 419)

Dovidio, J. R., Brigham, J. C., Johnson, B. T., & Gaertner, S. L. (1996). Stereotyping, prejudice, and discrimination: Another look. In N. Macrae, M. Hewstone, & C. Stangor (eds.), *Stereotypes and stereotyping*. New York: Guilford. (p. 418)

Drabman, R. S., & Thomas, M. H. (1974). Does media violence increase children's toleration of real-life aggression? *Developmental Psychology*, 10, 418-421. (p. 359)

Drabman, R. S., & Thomas, M. H. (1975). Does TV violence breed indifference? *Journal of Communications*, 25(4), 86-89. (p. 359)

Drabman, R. S., & Thomas, M. H. (1976). Does watching violence on television cause apathy? *Pediatrics*, 57, 329-331. (p. 359)

Draguns, J. G. (1990). *Normal and abnormal behavior in cross-cultural perspective: Specifying the nature of their relationship.* Nebraska Symposium on Motivation 1989, 37, 235-277. (p. 493)

Driedger, L. (1975). In search of cultural identity factors: A comparison of ethnic students. *Canadian Review of Sociology and Anthropology*, 12, 150-161. (p. 287)

Driskell, J. E., & Mullen, B. (1990). Status, expectations, and behavior: A meta-analytic review and test of the theory. *Personality and Social Psychology Bulletin*, 16, 541-553. (p. 203)

Dryer, D. C., & Horowitz, L. M. (1997). When do opposites attract? Interpersonal complementarity versus similarity. *Journal of Personality and Social Psychology*, 72, 592-603. (p. 390)

Duclos, S. E., Laird, J. D., Schneider, E., Sexter, M., Stern, L., & Van Lighten, O. (1989). Emotion-specific effects of facial expressions and postures on emotional experience. *Journal of Personality and Social Psychology*, 57, 100-108. (p. 134)

Duffy, M. (2003, June 9). Weapons of mass disappearance. *Time*, pp. 28-33. (p. 144)

Dugger, C. W. (2001, April 22). Abortion in India spurred by sex text skew the ratio against girls. *The New York Times*. Late edition, p. 12. (p. 426)

Dunn, E. W., Wilson, T. D., & Gilbert, D. T. (2003). Location, location, location: The misprediction of satisfaction in housing lotteries. *Personality and Social Psychology Bulletin*, **29**, 1421. (p. 536)

Dunning, D. (1995). Trait importance and modifiability as factors influencing self-assessment and self-enhancement motives. *Personality and Social Psychology Bulletin*, 21, 1297-1306. (p. 63)

Dunning, D. (1999). A newer look: Motivated social cognition and the schematic representation of social concepts. *Psychological Inquiry*, 10, 1-11. (p. 55)

Dunning, D. (2005). *Self-insight: Roadblocks and detours on the path to knowing thyself.* New York, NY, US: Psychology Press. (p. 83)

Dunning, D., & Hayes, A. F. (1996). Evidence for egocentric comparison in social judgment. *Journal of Personality and Social Psychology*, 71, 213-229. (p. 51)

Dunning, D., & Perretta, S. (2002). Automaticity and eyewitness accuracy: A 10- to 12-second rule for distinguishing accurate from inaccurate positive identifications. *Journal of Applied Psychology*, 87, 951-962. (p. 519)

Dunning, D., & Sherman, D. A. (1997). Stereotypes and tacit inference. *Journal of Personality and Social Psychology*, 73, 459-471. (p. 457)

Dunning, D., & Stern, L. B. (1994). Distinguishing accurate from inaccurate eyewitness identifications via inquiries about decision processes. *Journal of Personality and Social Psychology*, 67, 818-835. (p. 519)

Dunning, D., Griffin, D. W., Milojkovic, J. D., & Ross, L. (1990). The overconfidence effect in social prediction. *Journal of Personality and Social Psychology*, 58, 568-581. (p. 81)

Dunning, D., Meyerowitz, J. A., & Holzberg, A. D. (1989). Ambiguity and self-evaluation. *Journal of Personality and Social Psychology*, 57, 1082-1090. (p. 58)

Dunning, D., Perie, M., & Story, A. L. (1991). Self-serving prototypes of social categories. *Journal of Personality and Social Psychology*, 61, 957-968. (p. 58)

Dutton, D. (2005). Once upon a time. *Washington Post*, Sunday, May 8.

Dutton, D. G., & Aron, A. (1989). Romantic attraction and generalized liking for others who are sources of conflict-based arousal. *Canadian Journal of Behavioural Science*, 21, 246-257. (p. 399)

Dutton, D. G., & Aron, A. P. (1974). Some evidence for heightened sexual attraction under conditions of high anxiety. *Journal of Personality and Social Psychology*, 30, 510-517. (p. 399)

Duval, S., & Wicklund, R. A. (1972). *A theory of objective self-awareness*. New York: Academic Press. (p. 99)

Duval, S., Duval, V. H., & Neely, R. (1979). Self-focus, felt responsibility, and helping behavior. *Journal of Personality and Social Psychology*, 37, 1769-1778. (p. 323)

Eagly, A. (1994). *Are people prejudiced against women?* Donald Campbell Award invited address, American Psychological Association convention. (p. 424)

Eagly, A. H., & Chaiken, S. (1993). *The psychology of attitudes*. San Diego: Harcourt Brace Jovanovich. (p. 146)

Eagly, A. H., & Chaiken, S. (1998). Attitude structure and function. In D. Gilbert, S. Fiske, and G. Lindzey (Eds.), *The handbook of social psychology*, 4th edition. New York: McGraw-Hill. (p. 146)

Eagly, A. H., & Crowley, M. (1986). Gender and helping behavior: A meta-analytic review of the social psychological literature. *Psychological Bulletin*, 100, 283-308. (p. 322)

Eagly, A. H., & Karau, S. J. (2000). *Few women at the top: Is prejudice a cause?* Unpublished manuscript, Northwestern University. (p. 423)

Eagly, A. H., Ashmore, R. D., Makhijani, M. G., & Longo, L. C. (1991). What is beautiful is good, but . . .: A meta-analytic review of research on the physical attractiveness stereotype. *Psychological Bulletin*, 110, 109-128. (p. 381)

Eagly, A. H., Karau, S. J., & Makhijani, M. G. (1995). Gender and the effectiveness of leaders: A meta-analysis. *Psychological Bulletin*, 117, 125-145. (p. 418)

Eagly, A. H., Wood, W., & Chaiken, S. (1978). Casual inferences about communicators and their effect on opinion change. *Journal of Personality and Social Psychology*, 36, 424-435. (p. 150)

Easterlin, R. (1995). Will raising the incomes of all increase the happiness of all? *Journal of Economic Behavior and Organization*, 27, 35-47. (p. 534)

Eastwick, P. W., & Finkel, E. J. (2008). Sex differences in mate preferences revisited: Do people know what they initially desire in a romantic partner? *Journal of Personality and Social Psychology,* ***94***, 245. (p. 380)

Eaton, J., & Struthers, C. W. (2006). The reduction of psychological aggression across varied interpersonal contexts through repentance and forgiveness. *Aggressive Behavior,* ***32***, 195. (p. 339)

Ebbesen, E. B., Duncan, B., & Konecni, V. J. (1975). Effects of content of verbal aggression on future verbal aggression: A field experiment. *Journal of Experimental Social Psychology*, 11, 192-204. (p. 367)

Eberhardt, J. L., Goff, P. A., Purdie, V. J., & Davies, P. G. (2004). Seeing black: Race, crime, and visual processing. *Journal of Personality and Social Psychology,* ***87***, 876.

Economist (1991, July 6). *War in Europe.* p. 11. (p. 260)

Edney, J. J. (1980). The commons problem: Alternative perspectives. *American Psychologist*, 35, 131-150. (p. 471)

Edwards, C. P. (1991). Behavioral sex differences in children of diverse cultures: The case of nurturance to infants. In M. Pereira & L. Fairbanks (Eds.), *Juveniles: Comparative socio-ecology.* Oxford: Oxford University Press. (p. 422)

Edwards, K. (1990). The interplay of affect and cognition in attitude formation and change. *Journal of Personality and Social Psychology*, 59, 202-216. (p. 153)

Ehrlinger, J., Gilovich, T., & Ross, L. (2005). Peering into the bias blind spot: Peoples assessments of bias in themselves and others. *Personality and Social Psychology Bulletin,* ***31***, 680. (p. 58)

Eibach, R. P., Libby, L. K., & Gilovich, T. D. (2003). When change in the self is mistaken for change in the world. *Journal of Personality and Social Psychology*, 84, 917-931. (p. 61)

Eisenberg, N., Fabes, R. A., Schaller, M., Miller, P., Carlo, G., Poulin, R., Shea, C., & Shell, R. (1991). Personality and socialization correlates of vicarious emotional responding. *Journal of Personality and Social Psychology*, 61, 459-470. (p. 322)

Eisenberger, N. I., Lieberman, M. D., & Williams, K. D. (2003). Does rejection hurt? An fMRI study of social exclusion. *Science*, 302, 290-292. (p. 136)

Eisenberger, R. & Shanock, L. (2003). Rewards, intrinsic motivation, and creativity: A case study of conceptual and methodological isolation. *Creativity Research Journal,* ***15***, 121-130.

Eisenberger, R., & Armeli, S. (2001). Can salient reward increase creative performance without reducing intrinsic creative interest? *Journal of Personality and Social Psychology*, 72, 652-660. (p. 136)

Eisenberger, R., & Cameron, J. (1999). Detrimental effects of reward: Reality or myth? *American Psychologist*, 51, 1153-1166. (p. 136)

Eisenberger, R., Rhoades, L. (2001). Incremental effects of reward on creativity. *Journal of Personality and Social Psychology*, **81**, 728-741. (p. 136)

Eisenberger, R., Rhoades, L., & Cameron, J. (1999). Does pay for performance increase or decrease perceived self-determination and intrinsic motivation. *Journal of Personality and Social Psychology*, **77**, 1026-1040. (p. 136)

Eiser, J. R., Sutton, S. R., & Wober, M. (1979). Smoking, seat-belts, and beliefs about health. *Addictive Behaviors*, 4, 331-338. (p. 129)

Ekman, P. (1994). Strong evidence for universals in facial expressions: A reply to Russell's mistaken critique. *Psychological Bulletin*, 115, 268-287. (p. 275)

Ekman, P., & Friesen, W. V. (1975). *Unmasking the face.* Englewood Cliffs, NJ: Prentice-Hall. (p. 375)

Ekman, P., Friesen, W. V., O'Sullivan, M., Chan, A., Diacoyanni-Tarlatzis, I., Heider, K., Krause, R., LeCompte, W. A., Pitcairn, T., Ricci-Bitti, P. E., Scherer, K., Tomita, M., & Tzavaras, A. (1987). Universals and cultural differences in the judgments of facial expressions of emotion. *Journal of Personality and Social Psychology*, 53, 712-717. (p. 275)

Elder, G. H., Jr. (1969). Appearance and education in marriage mobility. *American Sociological Review*, 34, 519-533. (p. 381)

Eldersveld, S. J., & Dodge, R. W. (1954). Personal contact or mail propaganda? An experiment in voting turnout and attitude change. In D. Katz, D. Cartwright, S. Eldersveld, & A. M. Lee (Eds.), *Public opinion and propaganda.* New York: Dryden Press. (p. 162)

Elfendbein, H. A., & Ambady, N. (2002). On the universality and cultural specificity of emotion recognition: A meta-analysis. *Psychological Bulletin*, 128, 203-235. (p. 275)

Ellemers, N., Van Rijswijk, W., Roefs, M., & Simons, C. (1997). Bias in intergroup perceptions: Balancing group identity with social reality. *Personality and Social Psychology Bulletin*, 23, 186-198. (p. 435)

Ellis, H. D. (1981). Theoretical aspects of face recognition. In G. H. Davies, H. D. Ellis, & J. Shepherd (Eds.), *Perceiving and remembering faces.* London: Academic Press. (p. 443)

Ellison, P. A., Govern, J. M., Petri, H. L., & Figler, M. H. (1995). Anonymity and aggressive driving behavior: A field study. *Journal of Social Behavior and Personality*, 10, 265-272. (p. 229)

Ellsworth, P. C., & Mauro, R. (1998). Psychology and law. In D. Gilbert, S. T. Fiske, & G. Lindzey (eds.), *Handbook of social psychology*, 4th ed. New York: McGraw-Hill. (p. 523)

Elms, A. C. (1995). Obedience in retrospect. *Journal of Social Issues*, 51, 21-31. (p. 191)

Emmons, R. A., Larsen, R. J., Levine, S., & Diener, E. (1983). *Factors predicting satisfaction judgments: A comparative examination.* Paper presented at the Midwestern Psychological Association. (p. 506)

Emswiller, T., Deaux, K., & Willits, J. E. (1971). Similarity, sex, and requests for small favors. *Journal of Applied Social Psychology*, 1, 284-291. (p. 320)

Eng, P. M., Kawachi, I., Fitzmaurice, G., & Rimm, E. B. (2001). Effects of marital transitions on changes in dietary and other health behaviors in men. Paper presented to the American Psychosomatic Society meeting. (p. 504)

Engemann, K. M., & Owyang, M. T. (2005). So much for that merit raise: the link between wages and appearance. *The Regional Economist*, April, 2005.

Ennis, B. J., & Verrilli, D. B., Jr. (1989). Motion for leave to file brief amicus curiae and brief of Society for the Scientific Study of Religion, American Sociological Association, and others. U.S. Supreme Court Case No. 88-1600, *Holy Spirit Association for the Unification of World Christianity, et al., v. David Molko and Tracy Leal.* On petition for write of certiorari to the Supreme Court of California. Washington, DC: Jenner & Block, 21 Dupont Circle NW. (p. 173)

Ennis, R., & Zanna, M. P. (1991). *Hockey assault: Constitutive versus normative violations.* Paper presented at the Canadian Psychological Association convention. (p. 342)

Epley, N., & Dunning, D. (2000). Feeling 'holier than thou': Are self-serving assessments produced by errors in self- or other prediction? *Journal of Personality and Social Psychology*, 79, 861-875. (p. 41)

Epley, N., & Gilovich, T. (1999). Just going along: Nonconscious priming and conformity to social pressure. *Journal of Experimental Social Psychology, 35*(6). (p. 73)

Epstein, S. (1980). The stability of behavior: II. Implications for psychological research. *American Psychologist*, 35, 790-806. (p. 209)

Erickson, B., Holmes, J. G., Frey, R., Walker, L., & Thibaut, J. (1974). Functions of a third party in the resolution of conflict: The role of a judge in pretrial conferences. *Journal of Personality and Social Psychology*, 30, 296-306. (p. 479)

Erickson, B., Lind, E. A. Johnson, B. C., & O'Barr, W. M. (1978). Speech style and impression formation in a court setting: The effects of powerful and powerless speech. *Journal of Experimental Social Psychology*, 14, 266-279. (p. 149)

Erikson, E. H. (1963). *Childhood and society.* New York: Norton. (p. 405)

Eron, L. D. (1987). The development of aggressive behavior from the perspective of a developing behaviorism. *American Psychologist*, 42, 425-442. (p. 356)

Eron, L. D., & Huesmann, L. R. (1980). Adolescent aggression and television. *Annals of the New York Academy of Sciences*, 347, 319-331. (p. 356)

Eron, L. D., & Huesmann, L. R. (1984). The control of aggressive behavior by changes in attitudes, values, and the conditions of learning. In R. J. Blanchard & C. Blanchard (Eds.), *Advances in the study of aggression*, vol. 1. Orlando, Fla.: Academic Press. (p. 369)

Eron, L. D., & Huesmann, L. R. (1985). The role of television in the development of prosocial and antisocial behavior. In D. Olweus, M. Radke-Yarrow, and J. Block (Eds.), *Development of antisocial and prosocial behavior.* Orlando, Fla.: Academic Press. (p. 356)

Escobar-Chaves, L. S., Tortolero, S. R., Markham, C. M., Low, B. J., Eitel, P., & Thickstun, P. (2005). Impact of the media on adolescent sexual attitudes and behaviors. *Pediatrics*, **116**, 303-326. (p. 360)

Esser, J. K. (1998, February-March). Alive and well after 25 years. A review of groupthink research. *Organizational Behavior and Human Decision Processes*, 73, 116-141. (p. 243)

Esses, V. M. (1989). Mood as a moderator of acceptance of interpersonal feedback. *Journal of Personality and Social Psychology*, 57, 769-781. (p. 91)

Esses, V. M., Haddock, G., & Zanna, M. P. (1993a). Values, stereotypes, and emotions as determinants of intergroup attitudes. In D. Mackie & D. Hamilton (Eds.), *Affect, cognition and stereotyping: Interactive processes in intergroup perception.* San Diego, CA: Academic Press. (p. 419)

Esses, V. M., Haddock, G., & Zanna, M. P. (1993b). The role of mood in the expression of intergroup stereotypes. In M. P. Zanna & J. M. Olson (eds.), *The psychology of prejudice: The Ontario symposium*, vol. 7. Hillsdale, NJ: Erlbaum. (p. 442)

Esses, V. M., Jackson, L. M., & Armstrong, T. L. (1998). Intergroup competition and attitudes toward immigrants and immigration: An instrumental model of group conflict. *Journal of Social Issues*, 54, 699-724. (p. 432)

Etaugh, C. E., Bridges, J. S., Cummings-Hill, M., & Cohen, J. (1999). "Names can never hurt me": The effects of surname use on perceptions of married women. *Psychology of Women Quarterly*, 23, 819-823. (p. 417)

Evans, G. W. (1979). Behavioral and physiological consequences of crowding in humans. *Journal of Applied Social Psychology*, 9, 27-46. (p. 220)

Evans, R. I., Smith, C. K., & Raines, B. E. (1984). Deterring cigarette smoking in adolescents: A psycho-social-behavioral analysis of an intervention strategy. In A. Baum, J. Singer, & S. Taylor (Eds.), *Handbook of psychology and health: Social psychological aspects of health*, vol. 4, Hillsdale, N.J.: Erlbaum. (p. 176)

Fabrigar, L. R., & Petty, R. E. (1999). The role of the affective and cognitive bases of attitudes in susceptibility to affectively and cognitively based persuasion. *Personality and Social Psychology Bulletin*, 25, 363-381. (p. 153)

Fabrigar, L. R., Priester, J. R., Petty, R. E., & Wegener, D. T. (1998). The impact of attitude accessibility on elaboration of persuasive messages. *Personality and Social Psychology Bulletin*, 24, 339-352. (p. 167)

Falbo, T., Poston, D. L., Jr., Triscari, R. S., & Zhang, X. (1997). Self-enhancing illusions among Chinese schoolchildren. *Journal of Cross-Cultural Psychology*, 28, 172-191. (p. 69)

Fallshore, M., & Schooler, J. W. (1995). Verbal vulnerability of perceptual expertise. *Journal of Experimental Psychology: Learning, Memory, and Cognition*, 21, 1608-1623. (p. 519)

Farquhar, J. W., Maccoby, N., Wood, P. D., Alexander, J. K., Breitrose, H., Brown, B. W., Jr., Haskell, W. L., McAlister, A. L., Meyer, A. J., Nash, J. D., & Stern, M. P. (1977, June 4). Community education for cardiovascular health. *Lancet*, 1192-1195. (p. 162)

Farrell, M. A. (2005). The effect of a market-oriented organisational culture on sales-force behaviour and attitudes. *Journal of Strategic Marketing*, ***13***, 261. (p. 177)

Farwell, L., & Weiner, B. (2000). Bleeding hearts and the heartless: Popular perceptions of liberal and conservative ideologies. *Personality and Social Psychology Bulletin*, 26, 845-852. (p. 272)

Faulkner, S. L., & Williams, K. D. (1996). *A study of social loafing in industry.* Paper presented to the Midwestern Psychological Association convention. (p. 225)

Fazio, R. (1987). Self-perception theory: A current perspective. In M. P. Zanna, J. M. Olson, & C. P. Herman (Eds.), *Social influence: The Ontario symposium*, vol. 5. Hillsdale, N.J.: Erlbaum. (p. 140)

Fazio, R. H., & Zanna, M. P. (1981). Direct experience and attitude-behavior consistency. In L. Berkowitz (Ed.), *Advances in experimental social psychology*, Vol. 14. New York: Academic Press. (p. 117)

Fazio, R. H., Jackson, J. R., Dunton, B. C., & Williams, C. J. (1995). Variability in automatic activation as an unobtrusive measure of racial attitudes: A bona fide pipeline? *Journal of Personality and Social Psychology*, 69, 1013-1027. (p. 419)

Fazio, R. H., Zanna, M. P., & Cooper, J. (1977). Dissonance versus self-perception: An integrative view of each theory's proper domain of application. *Journal of Experimental Social Psychology*, 13, 464-479. (p. 140)

Fazio, R. H., Zanna, M. P., & Cooper, J. (1979). On the relationship of data to theory: A reply to Ronis and Greenwald. *Journal of Experimental Social Psychology*, 15, 70-76. (p. 140)

Feather, N. T. (1983). Causal attributions for good and bad outcomes in achievement and affiliation situations. *Australian Journal of Psychology*, 35, 37-48. (b) (p. 69)

Feeney, J. A. (1996). Attachment, caregiving, and marital satisfaction. *Personal Relationships*, 3, 401-416. (p. 404)

Feeney, J. A., & Noller, P. (1990). Attachment style as a predictor of adult romantic relationships. *Journal of Personality and Social Psychology*, 58, 281-291. (p. 404)

Feeney, J., Peterson, C., & Noller, P. (1994). Equity and marital satisfaction over the family life cycle. *Personality Relationships*, 1, 83-99. (p. 407)

Feierabend, I., & Feierabend, R. (1968, May). Conflict, crisis, and collision: A study of international stability. *Psychology Today*, pp. 26-32, 69-70. (p. 340)

Feierabend, I., & Feierabend, R. (1972). Systemic conditions of political aggression: An application of frustration-aggression theory. In I. K. Feierabend, R. L. Feierabend, & T. R. Gurr (Eds.), *Anger, violence, and politics: Theories and research*. Englewood Cliffs, N.J.: Prentice Hall. (p. 340)

Fein, S., & Hilton, J. L. (1992). Attitudes toward groups and behavioral intentions toward individual group members: The impact of nondiagnostic information. *Journal of Experimental Social Psychology*, 28, 101-124. (p. 456)

Fein, S., & Spencer, S. J. (1997). Prejudice as self-image maintenance: Affirming the self through derogating others. *Journal of Personality and Social Psychology*, 73, 31-44. (p. 63)

Feingold, A. (1988). Matching for attractiveness in romantic partners and same-sex friends: A meta-analysis and theoretical critique. *Psychological Bulletin*, 104, 226-235. (p. 380)

Feingold, A. (1990). Gender differences in effects of physical attractiveness on romantic attraction: A comparison across five research paradigms. *Journal of Personality and Social Psychology*, 59, 981-993. (p. 379)

Feingold, A. (1991). Sex differences in the effects of similarity and physical attractiveness on opposite-sex attraction. *Basic and Applied Social Psychology*, 12, 357-367. (p. 379)

Feingold, A. (1992). Gender differences in mate selection preferences: A test of the parental investment model. *Psychological Bulletin*, 112, 125-139. (p. 381)

Feldman, R. S., & Prohaska, T. (1979). The student as Pygmalion: Effect of student expectation on the teacher. *Journal of Educational Psychology*, 71, 485-493. (p. 104)

Feldman, R. S., & Theiss, A. J. (1982). The teacher and student as Pygmalions: Joint effects of teacher and student expectations. *Journal of Educational Psychology*, 74, 217-223. (p. 104)

Felson, R. B. (2000). A social psychological approach to interpersonal aggression. In V. B. Van Hasselt, & M. Hersen (Eds.), *Aggression and violence: An introductory text.* (pp. 9-22). Needham Heights, MA, US: Allyn & Bacon. (p. 334)

Fenigstein, A. (1984). Self-consciousness and the overperception of self as a target. *Journal of Personality and Social Psychology*, 47, 860-870. (p. 51)

Fergusson, D. M., Horwood, L. J., & Shannon, F. T. (1984). A proportional hazards model of family breakdown. *Journal of Marriage and the Family*, 46, 539-549. (p. 411)

Feshbach, N. D. (1980). *The child as "psychologist" and "economist": Two curricula.* Paper presented at the American Psychological Association convention. (p. 177)

Festinger, L. (1954). A theory of social comparison processes. *Human Relations*, 7, 117-140. (p. 237)

Festinger, L. (1957). *A theory of cognitive dissonance.* Stanford: Stanford University Press. (p. 128)

Festinger, L. (1987). *Reflections on cognitive dissonance theory: 30 years later.* Paper presented at the American Psychological Association convention. (p. 244)

Festinger, L., & Carlsmith, J. M. (1959). Cognitive consequences of forced compliance. *Journal of Abnormal and Social Psychology*, 58, 203-210. (p. 129)

Festinger, L., & Maccoby, N. (1964). On resistance to persuasive communications. *Journal of Abnormal and Social Psychology*, 68, 359-366. (p. 166)

Festinger, L., Pepitone, A., & Newcomb, T. (1952). Some consequences of deindividuation in a group. *Journal of Abnormal and Social Psychology*, 47, 382-389. (p. 228)

Feynman, R. (1967). *The character of physical law.* Cambridge, Mass.: MIT Press. (p. 137)

Fichter, J. (1968). *America's forgotten priests: What are they saying?* New York: Harper. (p. 429)

Fiebert, M. S. (1990). Men, women and housework: The Roshomon effect. *Men's Studies Review*, 8, 6. (p. 58)

Fiedler, F. E. (1987, September). When to lead, when to stand back. *Psychology Today*, pp. 26-27. (p. 248)

Fineberg, H. V. (1988). Education to prevent AIDS: Prospects and obstacles. *Science*, 239, 592-596. (p. 156)

Fischhoff, B. (1982). Debiasing. In D. Kahneman, P. Slovic, & A. Tversky (Eds.), *Judgment under uncertainty: Heuristics and biases.* New York: Cambridge University Press. (p. 85)

Fischhoff, B., & Bar-Hillel, M. (1984). Diagnosticity and the base rate effect. *Memory and Cognition*, 12, 402-410. (p. 85)

Fishbein, D., & Thelen, M. H. (1981). *Husband-wife similarity and marital satisfaction: A different approach.* Paper presented at the Midwestern Psychological Association convention. (a) (p. 390)

Fishbein, D., & Thelen, M. H. (1981). Psychological factors in mate selection and marital satisfaction: A review (Ms. 2374). *Catalog of Selected Documents in Psychology*, 11, 84. (b) (p. 390)

Fishbein, M., & Ajzen, I. (1974). Attitudes toward objects as predictive of single and multiple behavioral criteria. *Psychological Review*, 81, 59-74. (p. 115)

Fisher, H. (1994, April). The nature of romantic love. Journal of NIH Research, pp. 59-64. (p. 401)

Fisher, R. J. (1994). Generic principles for resolving intergroup conflict. *Journal of Social Issues*, 50, 47-66. (p. 480)

Fisher, R. P., & Geiselman, R. E. (1992). *Memory-enhancing techniques for investigative interviewing: The cognitive interview*. Springfield, IL: Charles C Thomas. (p. 518)

Fisher, R. P., Geiselman, R. E., & Amador, M. (1989). Field test of the cognitive interview: Enhancing the recollection of actual victims and witnesses of crime. *Journal of Applied Psychology*, 74, 722-727. (p. 518)

Fisher, R. P., Geiselman, R. E., & Raymond, D. S. (1987). Critical analysis of police interview techniques. *Journal of Police Science and Administration*, 15, 177-185. (p. 518)

Fisher, R. P., McCauley, M. R., & Geiselman, R. E. (1994). Improving eyewitness testimony with the Cognitive Interview. In D. F. Ross, J. D. Read, & M. P. Toglia (eds.), *Adult eyewitness testimony: Current trends and developments*. Cambridge, England: Cambridge University Press. (p. 519)

Fiske, A. P., Kitayama, S., Markus, H. R., & Nisbett, R. E. (1998). The cultural matrix of social psychology. In D. Gilbert, S. Fiske, and G. Lindzey (eds.), *The handbook of social psychology*, 4th edition. Hillsdale, NJ: Erlbaum. (p. 259)

Fiske, S. T. (1992). Thinking is for doing: Portraits of social cognition from Daguerrotype to Laserphoto. *Journal of Personality and Social Psychology*, 63, 877-889. (p. 109)

Fiske, S. T., & Ruscher, J. B. (1993). Negative interdependence and prejudice: Whence the affect? In D. Mackie & D. Hamilton (Eds.), *Affect, cognition and stereotyping: Interactive processes in intergroup perception*. San Diego, CA: Academic Press. (p. 443)

Fiske, S. T., Harris, L. T., & Cuddy, A. J. C. (2004). Why ordinary people torture enemy prisoners. *Science,* ***306***, 1482. (p. 12)

Fiske, S. T., Xu, J., Cuddy, A. C., & Glick, P. (1999). (Dis)respecting versus (Dis)liking: Status and interdependence predict ambivalent stereotypes of competence and warmth. *Journal of Social Issues*, 55, 473-489. (p. 427)

Fitzpatrick, A. R., & Eagly, A. H. (1981). Anticipatory belief polarization as a function of the expertise of a discussion partner. *Personality and Social Psychology Bulletin*, 1, 636-642. (p. 237)

Fitzsimons, G. M., & Bargh, J. A. (2004). Automatic self-regulation. In R. F. Baumeister, & K. D. Vohs (Eds.), *Handbook of self-regulation: Research, theory, and applications.* (pp. 151-170). New York, NY, US: Guilford Press. (p. 52)

Flay, B. R., Ryan, K. B., Best, J. A., Brown, K. S., Kersell, M. W., d'Avernas, J. R., & Zanna, M. P. (1985). Are social-psychological smoking prevention programs effective? The Waterloo study. *Journal of Behavioral Medicine*, 8, 37-59. (p. 176)

Fletcher, G. J. O., & Ward, C. (1989). Attribution theory and processes: A cross-cultural perspective. In M. H. Bond (Ed.), *The cross-cultural challenge to social psychology*. Newbury Park, Ca.: Sage. (p. 449)

Fletcher, G. J. O., Danilovics, P., Fernandez, G., Peterson, D., & Reeder, G. D. (1986). Attributional complexity: An individual differences measure. *Journal of Personality and Social Psychology*, 51, 875-884. (p. 103)

Fletcher, G. J. O., Fincham, F. D., Cramer, L., & Heron, N. (1987). The role of attributions in the development of dating relationships. *Journal of Personality and Social Psychology*, 53, 481-489. (p. 407)

Fletcher, G. J. O., Simpson, J. A., Thomas, G., & Giles, L. (1999). Ideals in intimate relationships. *Journal of Personality and Social Psychology*, 76, 72-89. (p. 396)

Fletcher, G. J. O., Tither, J. M., O'Loughlin, C., Friesen, M., & Overall, N. (2004). Warm and homely or cold and beautiful? Sex differences in trading off traits in mate selection. *Personality and Social Psychology Bulletin,* ***30***, 659. (p. 379)

Foa, U. G., & Foa, E. B. (1975). *Resource theory of social exchange*. Morristown, N.J.: General Learning Press. (p. 297)

Fogelman, E. (1994). *Conscience and courage: Rescuers of Jews during the Holocaust.* New York: Doubleday Anchor. (p. 325)

Follett, M. P. (1940). Constructive conflict. In H. C. Metcalf & L. Urwick (Eds.), *Dynamic administration: The collected papers of Mary Parker Follett.* New York: Harper. (p. 477)

Forgas, J. P., & Moylan, S. (1987). After the movies: Transient mood and social judgments. *Personality and Social Psychology Bulletin*, 13, 467-477. (p. 90)

Forgas, J. P., Bower, G. H., & Krantz, S. E. (1984). The influence of mood on perceptions of social interactions. *Journal of Experimental Social Psychology*, 20, 497-513. (p. 91)

Form, W. H., & Nosow, S. (1958). *Community in disaster*. New York: Harper. (p. 306)

Forsyth, D. R., Berger, R. E., & Mitchell, T. (1981). The effects of self-serving vs. other-serving claims of responsibility on attraction and attribution in groups. *Social Psychology Quarterly*, 44, 59-64. (p. 69)

Foss, R. D. (1978). *The role of social influence in blood donation.* Paper presented at the American Psychological Association convention. (p. 323)

Frank, J. (1974). *Persuasion and healing: A comparative study of psychotherapy*. New York: Schocken. (p. 173)

Frank, J. D. (1982). Therapeutic components shared by all psychotherapies. In J. H. Harvey, & M. M. Parks (Eds.), *Psychotherapy research and behavior change*, Vol. 1 (pp. 9-37). Washington, DC, US: American Psychological Association. (p. 173)

Frank, M. G., & Gilovich, T. (1989). Effect of memory perspective on retrospective causal attributions. *Journal of Personality and Social Psychology*, 57, 399-403. (p. 98)

Frank, R. (1999). *Luxury fever: Why money fails to satisfy in an era of excess*. New York: The Free Press. (p. 532)

Frasure-Smith, N., Lesperance, F., & Talajic, M. (1995). The impact of negative emotions on prognosis following myocardial infarction: Is it more than depression? *Health Psychology*, 14, 388-398. (p. 500)

Freedman, J. L., & Fraser, S. C. (1966). Compliance without pressure: The foot-in-the-door technique. *Journal of Personality and Social Psychology*, 4, 195-202. (p. 122)

Freedman, J. L., & Sears, D. O. (1965). Warning, distraction, and resistance to influence. *Journal of Personality and Social Psychology*, 1, 262-266. (p. 166)

Freedman, J. L., Birsky, J., & Cavoukian, A. (1980). Environmental determinants of behavioral contagion: Density and number. *Basic and Applied Social Psychology*, 1, 155-161. (p. 220)

Freedman, J. L., Cunningham, J. A., & Krismer, K. (1992). Inferred values and the reverse-incentive effect in induced compliance. *Journal of Personality and Social Psychology*, 62, 357-368. (p. 136)

Freedman, J. S. (1965). Long-term behavioral effects of cognitive dissonance. *Journal of Experimental Social Psychology*, 1, 145-155. (p. 125)

Freeman, M. A. (1997). Demographic correlates of individualism and collectivism: A study of social values in Sri Lanka. *Journal of Cross-Cultural Psychology*, 28, 321-341. (p. 267)

French, J. R. P. (1968). The conceptualization and the measurement of mental health in terms of self-identity theory. In S. B. Sells (Ed.), *The definition and measurement of mental health*. Washington, D.C.: Department of Health, Education, and Welfare. (Cited by M. Rosenberg, 1979, *Conceiving the self*. New York: Basic Books.) (p. 57)

Friedman, H. S., & DiMatteo, M. R. (1989). *Health psychology*. Englewood Cliffs, NJ: Prentice-Hall. (p. 497)

Friedman, H. S., Riggio, R. E., & Casella, D. F. (1988). Nonverbal skill, personal charisma, and initial attraction. *Personality and Social Psychology Bulletin*, 14, 203-211. (p. 390)

Friedman, T. L. (2003, June 4). Because we could. *New York Times* (www.nytimes.com). (p. 144)

Friedrich, J. (1996). On seeing oneself as less self-serving than others: The ultimate self-serving bias? *Teaching of Psychology*, 23, 107-109. (p. 65)

Friedrich, L. K., & Stein, A. H. (1973). Aggressive and prosocial television programs and the natural behavior of preschool children. *Monographs of the Society of Research in Child Development*, 38 (4, Serial No. 151). (p. 327)

Friedrich, L. K., & Stein, A. H. (1975). Prosocial television and young children: The effects of verbal labeling and role playing on learning and behavior. *Child Development*, 46, 27-38. (p. 327)

Frieze, I. H., Olson, J. E., & Russell, J. (1991). Attractiveness and income for men and women in management. *Journal of Applied Social Psychology*, 21, 1039-1057. (p. 382)

Froming, W. J., Walker, G. R., & Lopyan, K. J. (1982). Public and private self-awareness: When personal attitudes conflict with societal expectations. *Journal of Experimental Social Psychology*, 18, 476-487. (p. 117)

Fuller, S. R., & Aldag, R. J. (1998). Organizational Tonypandy: Lessons from a quarter century of the groupthink phenomenon. *Organizational Behavior and Human Decision Processes*, in press. (p. 243)

Fultz, J., Batson, C. D., Fortenbach, V. A., McCarthy, P. M., & Varney, L. L. (1986). Social evaluation and the empathy-altruism hypothesis. *Journal of Personality and Social Psychology*, 50, 761-769. (p. 310)

Funder, D. C. (1987). Errors and mistakes: Evaluating the accuracy of social judgment. *Psychological Bulletin*, 101, 75-90. (p. 108)

Furnham, A. (1982). Explanations for unemployment in Britain. *European Journal of Social Psychology*, 12, 335-352. (p. 101)

Furnham, A., & Gunter, B. (1984). Just world beliefs and attitudes towards the poor. *British Journal of Social Psychology*, 23, 265-269. (p. 440)

Gabrenya, W. K., Jr., Wang, Y.-E., & Latané, B. (1985). Social loafing on an optimizing task: Cross-cultural differences among Chinese and Americans. *Journal of Cross-Cultural Psychology*, 16, 223-242. (p. 279)

Gaebelein, J. W., & Mander, A. (1978). Consequences for targets of aggression as a function of aggressor and instigator roles: Three experiments. *Personality and Social Psychology Bulletin*, 4, 465-468. (p. 363)

Gaertner, L., Sedikides, C., & Graetz, K. (1999). In search of self-definition: Motivational primacy of the individual self, motivational primacy of the collective self, or contextual primacy? *Journal of Personality and Social Psychology*, 76, 5-18. (p. 268)

Gaertner, S. L., Dovidio, J. F., Anastasio, P. A., Bachman, B. A., & Rust, M. C. (1993). The Common Ingroup Identity Model: Recategorization and the reduction of intergroup bias. In W. Stroebe & M. Hewstone (eds.), *European Review of Social Psychology*, vol. 4. London: Wiley. (p. 284)

Gaertner, S. L., Dovidio, J. F., Nier, J. A., Ward, C. M., & Banker, B. S. (1998). Across cultural divides: The value of superordinate identity. In D. Prentice & D. Miller (eds.), *Cultural divides: The social psychology of intergroup contact*. New York: Russell Sage Foundation. (p. 284)

Galanter, M. (1989). *Cults: Faith, healing, and coercion*. New York: Oxford University Press. (p. 173)

Galanter, M. (1990). Cults and zealous self-help movements: A psychiatric perspective. *American Journal of Psychiatry*, 147, 543-551. (p. 173)

Galinsky, A. D., & Moskowitz, G. B. (2000). Perspective-taking: Decreasing stereotype expression, stereotype accessibility, and in-group favoritism. *Journal of Personality and Social Psychology*, 78, 708-724. (p. 480)

Galizio, M., & Hendrick, C. (1972). Effect of musical accompaniment on attitude: The guitar as a prop for persuasion. *Journal of Applied Social Psychology*, 2, 350-359. (p. 153)

Gallant, S. J., Popiel, D. A., Hoffman, D. M., Chakraborty, P. K., and Hamilton, J. A. (1992). Using daily ratings to confirm premenstrual syndrome/late luteal phase disorder. Part I. Effects of demand characteristics and expectations. *Psychosomatic Medicine*, 54, 149-166. (p. 498)

Gallo, L. C., & Matthews, K. A. (2003). Understanding the association between socioeconomic status and physical health: Do negative emotions play a role? *Psychological Bulletin*, **129**, 10. (p. 505)

Gallup Organization (1990). April 19-22 survey reported in *American Enterprise*, September/October, 1990, p. 92. (p. 533)

Gallup Organization (2003, June 10). American public opinion about Iraq. Gallup Poll News Service (www.gallup.com/poll/focus/sr030610.asp). (p. 144)

Gallup, G. H. (1972). *The Gallup Poll: Public opinion 1935-1971*. (Vol. 3). New York: Random House, pp. 551, 1716. (p. 355)

Gallup, G. H., Jr., & Jones, T. (1992). *The saints among us*. Harrisburg, PA: Morehouse. (p. 429)

Gallupe, R. B., Cooper, W. H., Grise, M. L., & Bastianutti, L. M. (1994). Blocking electronic brainstorms. *Journal of Applied Psychology*, 79, 77-86. (p. 246)

Gangestad, S. W., & Thornhill, R. (1997). Human sexual selection and developmental stability. In J. A. Simpson & D. T. Kenrick (eds.), *Evolutionary social psychology*. Mahway, NJ: Erlbaum. (p. 383)

Gangestad, S. W., Simpson, J. A., Cousins, A. J., Garver-Apgar, C. E., & Christensen, P. N. (2004). Women's preferences for male behavioral displays change across the menstrual cycle. *Psychological Science, **15***, 203. (p. 384)

Garb, H. N. (1994). Judgment research: Implications for clinical practice and testimony in court. *Applied and Preventive Psychology*, 3, 173-183. (p. 489)

Garb, H. N. (2005). Clinical judgment and decision making. *Annual Review of Clinical Psychology, **1***, 67. (p. 485)

Garcia-Marques, T., Mackie, D. M., Claypool, H. M., & Garcia-Marques, L. (2004). Positivity can cue familiarity. *Personality and Social Psychology Bulletin, **30***, 585. (p. 377)

Gardner, M. (1997, July/August). Heaven's Gate: The UFO cult of Bo and Peep. *Skeptical Inquirer*, pp. 15-17. (p. 170)

Garry, M., Manning, C. G., Loftus, E. F., & Sherman, S. J. (1996). Imagination inflation: Imagining a childhood event inflates confidence that it occurred. *Psychonomic Bulletin & Review, **3***, 208.

Garry, M., Manning, C. G., Loftus, E. F., & Sherman, S. J. (1996). Imagination inflation: Imagining a childhood event inflates confidence that it occurred. *Psychonomic Bulletin & Review*, 3, 208-214. (p. 78)

Gastorf, J. W., Suls, J., & Sanders, G. S. (1980). Type A coronary-prone behavior pattern and social facilitation. *Journal of Personality and Social Psychology*, 8, 773-780. (p. 221)

Gates, D. (1993, March 29). White male paranoia. *Newsweek*, pp. 48-53. (p. 447)

Gates, M. F., & Allee, W. C. (1933). Conditioned behavior of isolated and grouped cockroaches on a simple maze. *Journal of Comparative Psychology*, 15, 331-358. (p. 218)

Gavanski, I., & Hoffman, C. (1987). Awareness of influences on one's own judgments: The roles of covariation detection and attention to the judgment process. *Journal of Personality and Social Psychology*, 52, 453-463. (p. 43)

Gavanski, I., & Wells, G. L. (1989). Counterfactual processing of normal and exceptional events. *Journal of Experimental Social Psychology*, 35, 314-325. (p. 87)

Gawande, A. (2002). *Complications: A surgeon's notes on an imperfect science.* New York: Metropolitan Books, Holt and Company. (p. 57)

Gazzaniga, M. (1985). *The social brain: Discovering the networks of the mind.* New York: Basic Books. (p. 118)

Geen, R. G. (1998). Aggression and antisocial behavior. In D. Gilbert, S. Fiske, & G. Lindzey (eds.), *Handbook of social psychology*, 4th ed. New York: McGraw-Hill. (p. 337)

Geen, R. G., & Gange, J. J. (1983). Social facilitation: Drive theory and beyond. In H. H. Blumberg, A. P. Hare, V. Kent, & M. Davies (Eds.), *Small groups and social interaction*, Vol. 1. London: Wiley. (p. 219)

Geen, R. G., & Quanty, M. B. (1977). The catharsis of aggression: An evaluation of a hypothesis. In L. Berkowitz (Ed.), *Advances in experimental social psychology* (Vol. 10). New York: Academic Press. (p. 367)

Geen, R. G., & Thomas, S. L. (1986). The immediate effects of media violence on behavior. *Journal of Social Issues*, 42(3), 7-28. (p. 359)

Geiselman, R. E. (1996, May 14). *On the use and efficacy of the cognitive interview: Commentary on Memon & Stevenage on witness memory.* Psycoloquy.96.7.11. witnessmemory.2.geiselman (from psyc@phoenix. princeton.edu@ukacr1.bitnet). (p. 519)

Gelinas, D. J. (1995). Dissociative identity disorder and the trauma paradigm. In L. M. Cohen, J. N. Berzoff & M. R. Elin (Eds.), *Dissociative identity disorder: Theoretical and treatment controversies.* (pp. 175-222). Lanham, MD, US: Jason Aronson. (p. 93)

Genesee, F. (1978). Scholastic effects of French immersion: An overview after ten years. *Interchange*, 9, 20-29. (p. 289)

Gentile, D. A., & Anderson, C. A. (2003). Violent video games: The newest media violence hazard. In D. A. Gentile (Ed.), *Media violence and children.* Westport, CT: Ablex. (p. 361)

Gentile, D. A., Lynch, P. J., Linder, J. R., & Walsh, D. A. (2004). The effects of violent video game habits on adolescent hostility, aggressive behaviors, and school performance. *Journal of Adolescence, **27***, 5. (p. 357)

Gerard, H. B. (1994). A retrospective review of Festinger's A theory of cognitive dissonance. *Contemporary Psychology*, 39, 1013-1017. (p. 113)

Gerard, H. B. (1999). A social psychologist examines his past and looks to the future. In A. Rodrigues, & R. V. Levine (Eds.), *Reflections on 100 years of experimental social psychology.* (pp. 47-81). New York, NY, US: Basic Books. (p. 206)

Gerard, H. B., & Mathewson, G. C. (1966). The effects of severity of initiation on liking for a group: A replication. *Journal of Experimental Social Psychology*, 2, 278-287. (p. 170)

Gerard, H. B., Wilhelmy, R. A., & Conolley, E. S. (1968). Conformity and group size. *Journal of Personality and Social Psychology*, 8, 79-82. (p. 201)

Gerbner, G. (1994). The politics of media violence: Some reflections. In C. Hamelink & O. Linne (eds.), *Mass communication research: On problems and policies.* Norwood, NJ: Ablex. (p. 355)

Gerbner, G., Gross, L., Signorielli, N., Morgan, M., & Jackson-Beeck, M. (1979). The demonstration of power: Violence profile No. 10. *Journal of Communication*, 29, 177-196. (p. 360)

Gergen, K. E. (1982). *Toward transformation in social knowledge.* New York: Springer-Verlag. (p. 328)

Gerrig, R. J. & Prentice, D. A. (1991, September). The representation of fictional information. *Psychological Science*, 2, 336-340. (p. 86)

Gerstenfeld, P. B., Grant, D. R., & Chiang, C. (2003). Hate online: A content analysis of extremist Internet sites. *Analyses of Social Issues and Public Policy (ASAP), **3***, 29. (p. 235)

Gibbons, F. X. (1978). Sexual standards and reactions to pornography: Enhancing behavioral consistency through self-focused attention. *Journal of Personality and Social Psychology*, 36, 976-987. (p. 117)

Gibbons, F. X., & Wicklund, R. A. (1982). Self-focused attention and helping behavior. *Journal of Personality and Social Psychology*, 43, 462-474. (p. 300)

Gibbons, F. X., Eggleston, T. J., & Benthin, A. C. (1997). Cognitive reactions to smoking relapse: The reciprocal relation between dissonance and self-esteem. *Journal of Personality and Social Psychology*, 72, 184-195. (p. 129)

Gibson, B., & Sanbonmatsu, D. M. (2004). Optimism, pessimism, and gambling: The downside of optimism. *Personality and Social Psychology Bulletin*, 30, 149-160. (p. 59)

Giesler, R. B., Josephs, R. A., & Swann, W. B., Jr. (1996). Self-verification in clinical depression: The desire for negative evaluation. *Journal of Abnormal Psychology*, 105, 358-368. (p. 492)

Gifford, R., & Hine, D. W. (1997). Toward cooperation in commons dilemmas. *Canadian Journal of Behavioural Science*, 29, 167-179. (p. 470)

Gigone, D., & Hastie, R. (1993). The common knowledge effect: Information sharing and group judgment. *Journal of Personality and Social Psychology*, 65, 959-974. (p. 236)

Gilbert, D. T., & Ebert, J. E. J. (2002). Decisions and revisions: The affective forecasting of escapable outcomes. Unpublished manuscript, Harvard University. (p. 42)

Gilbert, D. T., & Hixon, J. G. (1991). The trouble of thinking: Activation and application of stereotypic beliefs. *Journal of Personality and Social Psychology*, 60, 509-517. (p. 442)

Gilbert, D. T., & Jones, E. E. (1986). Perceiver-induced constraint: Interpretations of self-generated reality. *Journal of Personality and Social Psychology*, 50, 269-280. (p. 96)

Gilbert, D. T., & Malone, P. S. (1995). The correspondence bias. *Psychological Bulletin*, 117, 21-38. (p. 94)

Gilbert, D. T., & Wilson, T. D. (2000). Miswanting: Some problems in the forecasting of future affective states. In J. Forgas (Ed.), *Feeling and thinking: The role of affect in social cognition*. Cambridge: Cambridge University Press. (p. 42)

Gilbert, D. T., Krull, D. S., & Malone, P. S. (1990). Unbelieving the unbelievable: Some problems in the rejection of false information. *Journal of Personality and Social Psychology*, 59, 601-613. (p. 174)

Gilbert, D. T., Lieberman, M. D., Morewedge, C. K., & Wilson, T. D. (2004). The peculiar longevity of things not so bad. *Psychological Science*, 15, 14-19. (p. 43)

Gilbert, D. T., McNulty, S. E., Giuliano, T. A., & Benson, J. E. (1992). Blurry words and fuzzy deeds: The attribution of obscure behavior. *Journal of Personality and Social Psychology*, 62, 18-25. (p. 100)

Gilbert, D. T., Pinel, E. C., Wilson, T. D., Blumberg, S. J., & Wheatley, T. P. (1998). Immune neglect: A source of durability bias in affective forecasting. *Journal of Personality and Social Psychology*, 75, 617-638. (p. 42)

Gilmor, T. M., & Reid, D. W. (1979). Locus of control and causal attribution for positive and negative outcomes on university examinations. *Journal of Research in Personality*, 13, 154-160. (p. 56)

Gilovich, T., & Douglas, C. (1986). Biased evaluations of randomly determined gambling outcomes. *Journal of Experimental Social Psychology*, 22, 228-241. (p. 89)

Gilovich, T., & Eibach, R. (2001). The fundamental attribution error where it really counts. *Psychological Inquiry, 12*(1), 23. (p. 102)

Gilovich, T., & Medvec, V. H. (1994). The temporal pattern to the experience of regret. *Journal of Personality and Social Psychology*, 67, 357-365. (p. 88)

Gilovich, T., Kerr, M., & Medvec, V. H. (1993). Effect of temporal perspective on subjective confidence. *Journal of Personality and Social Psychology*, 64, 552-560. (p. 83)

Gilovich, T., Savitsky, K., & Medvec, V. H. (1997). *The illusion of transparency: Biased assessments of others' ability to read our emotional states*. Unpublished manuscript, Cornell University. (p. 313)

Gilovich, T., Wang, R. F., Regan, D., & Nishina, S. (2003). Regrets of action and inaction across cultures. *Journal of Cross-Cultural Psychology*, 34, 61-71. (p. 88)

Ginsburg, B., & Allee, W. C. (1942). Some effects of conditioning on social dominance and subordination in inbred strains of mice. *Physiological Zoology*, 15, 485-506. (p. 342)

Gladue, B. A., Boechler, M., & McCaul, K. D. (1989). Hormonal response to competition in human males. *Aggressive Behavior*, 15, 409-422. (p. 337)

Glass, D. C. (1964). Changes in liking as a means of reducing cognitive discrepancies between self-esteem and aggression. *Journal of Personality*, 32, 531-549. (p. 124)

Gleason, M. E. J., Masumi, I., Bolger, N., & Shrout, P. E. (2003). Daily supportive equity in close relationships. *Personality and Social Psychology Bulletin*, ***29***, 1036-1045. (p. 297)

Glenn, N. D. (1980). Aging and attitudinal stability. In O. G. Brim, Jr., & J. Kagan (Eds.), *Constancy and change in human development*. Cambridge, Mass.: Harvard University Press. (p. 166)

Glenn, N. D. (1981). *Personal communication*. (p. 166)

Glick, P., & Fiske, S. T. (1996). The ambivalent sexism inventory: Differentiating hostile and benevolent sexism. *Journal of Personality and Social Psychology*, 70, 491-512. (p. 424)

Glick, P., Fiske, S. J. & 29 others (2000). Beyond prejudice as simple antipathy: Hostile and benevolent sexism across cultures. *Journal of Personality and Social Psychology*, 79, 763-775. (p. 424)

Glick, P., Lameiras, M., Fiske, S. T., Eckes, T., Masser, B., Volpato, C., et al. (2004). Bad but bold: Ambivalent attitudes toward men predict gender inequality in 16 nations. *Journal of Personality and Social Psychology,* ***86***, 713. (p. 424)

Goethals, G. R., & Zanna, M. P. (1979). The role of social comparison in choice shifts. *Journal of Personality and Social Psychology*, 37, 1469-1476. (p. 238)

Goethals, G. R., Messick, D. M., & Allison, S. T. (1991). The uniqueness bias: Studies of constructive social comparison. In J. Suls & T. A. Wills (Eds.), *Social comparison: Contemporary theory and research*. Hillsdale, NJ: Erlbaum. (p. 61)

Goggin, W. C., & Range, L. M. (1985). The disadvantages of hindsight in the perception of suicide. *Journal of Social and Clinical Psychology*, 3, 232-237. (p. 486)

Goldhagen, D. J. (1996). *Hitler's willing executioners*. New York: Knopf. (p. 144)

Goldman, W., & Lewis, P. (1977). Beautiful is good: Evidence that the physically attractive are more socially skillful. *Journal of Experimental Social Psychology*, 13, 125-130. (p. 382)

Goldsmith, C. (2003, March 25). World media turn wary eye on U.S. *Wall Street Journal*, p. A12. (p. 144)

Goldstein, A. P. (1994). Delinquent gangs. In A. P. Goldstein, B. Harootunian, and J. C. Conoley (Eds.), *Student aggression: Prevention, control, and replacement*. New York: Guilford. (p. 364)

Goldstein, A. P., & Glick, B. (1994). Aggression replacement training: Curriculum and evaluation. *Simulation and Gaming*, 25, 9-26. (p. 368)

Goldstein, J. H., & Arms, R. L. (1971). Effects of observing athletic contests on hostility. *Sociometry*, 34, 83-90. (p. 367)

Gonsalves, B., Reber, P. J., Gitelman, D. R., Parrish, T. B., Mesulam, M., & Paller, K. A. (2004). Neural evidence that vivid imagining can lead to false remembering. *Psychological Science*, ***15***, 655. (p. 516)

Goodhart, D. E. (1986). The effects of positive and negative thinking on performance in an achievement situation. *Journal of Personality and Social Psychology*, 51, 117-124. (p. 60)

Gordijn, E. H., De Vries, N. K., & De Dreu, C. K. W. (2002). Minority influence on focal and related attitudes: Change in size, attributions and information processing. *Personality and Social Psychology Bulletin*, **28**, 1315. (p. 524)

Gordon, R. A. (1996). Impact of ingratiation on judgments and evaluations: A meta-analytic investigation. *Journal of Personality and Social Psychology*, 71, 54-70. (p. 392)

Gordon, R., & Mentzel, R. K. (1990). Sympathy and altruism in response to disasters. *Journal of Social Psychology*, 130, 309-316. (p. 309)

Gortmaker, S. L., Must, A., Perrin, J. M., Sobol, A. M., & Dietz, W. H. (1993). Social and economic consequences of overweight in adolescence and young adulthood. *New England Journal of Medicine*, 329, 1008-1012. (p. 26)

Gotlib, I. H., & Colby, C. A. (1988). How to have a good quarrel. In P. Marsh (Ed.), *Eye to eye: How people interact*. Topsfield, MA: Salem House. (p. 478)

Gotlib, I. H., & Lee, C. M. (1989). The social functioning of depressed patients: A longitudinal assessment. *Journal of Social and Clinical Psychology*, 8, 223-237. (p. 491)

Gottlieb, J., & Carver, C. S. (1980). Anticipation of future interaction and the bystander effect. *Journal of Experimental Social Psychology*, 16, 253-260. (p. 323)

Gottman, J. (with N. Silver) (1994). *Why marriages succeed or fail*. New York: Simon & Schuster. (p. 412)

Gould, M. S., & Shaffer, D. (1986). The impact of suicide in television movies: Evidence of imitation. *New England Journal of Medicine*, 315, 690-694. (p. 186)

Gould, R., Brounstein, P. J., & Sigall, H. (1977). Attributing ability to an opponent: Public aggrandizement and private denigration. *Sociometry*, 40, 254-261. (p. 66)

Gould, S. J. (1988, July). Kropotkin was no crackpot. Natural History, pp. 12-21. (p. 471)

Gouldner, A. W. (1960). The norm of reciprocity: A preliminary statement. *American Sociological Review*, 25, 161-178. (p. 302)

Gove, W. R., Style, C. B., & Hughes, M. (1990). The effect of marriage on the well-being of adults: A theoretical analysis. *Journal of Family Issues*, 11, 4-35. (p. 507)

Grammer, K., & Thornhill, R. (1994). Human facial attractiveness and sexual selection: The role of symmetry and averageness. *Journal of Comparative Psychology*, 108, 233-242. (p. 383)

Gray, C., Russell, P., & Blockley, S. (1991). The effects upon helping behaviour of wearing pro-gay identification. *British Journal of Social Psychology*, 30, 171-178. (p. 320)

Gray, J. D., & Silver, R. C. (1990). Opposite sides of the same coin: Former spouses' divergent perspectives in coping with their divorce. *Journal of Personality and Social Psychology*, 59, 1180-1191. (p. 55)

Graziano, W. G., Jensen-Campbell, L. A., & Finch, J. F. (1997). The self as a mediator between personality and adjustment. *Journal of Personality and Social Psychology*, 73, 392-404. (p. 52)

Green, M. C., Strange, J. J., & Brock, T. C. (Eds.) (2002). *Narrative impact: Social and cognitive foundations*. Mahwah, NJ: Erlbaum. (p. 86)

Greenberg, J. (1986). Differential intolerance for inequity from organizational and individual agents. *Journal of Applied Social Psychology*, 16, 191-196. (p. 473)

Greenberg, J., Pyszczynski, T., Solomon, S., Rosenblatt, A., Veeder, M., Kirkland, S., & Lyon, D. (1990). Evidence for terror management theory II: The effects of mortality salience on reactions to those who threaten or bolster the cultural worldview. *Journal of Personality and Social Psychology*, 58, 308-318. (p. 438)

Greenberg, J., Pyszczynski, T., Solomon, S., Simon, L., & Breus, M. (1994). Role of consciousness and accessibility of death-related thoughts in mortality salience effects. *Journal of Personality and Social Psychology*, 67, 627-637. (p. 438)

Greenberg, J., Schimel, J., & Martins, A. (in press). *Motivation and Emotion*. (p. 438)

Greenberg, J., Solomon, S., & Pyszczynski, T. (1997). Terror management theory of self-esteem and cultural worldviews: Empirical assessments and conceptual refinements. *Advances in Experimental Social Psychology*, 29, in press. (p. 64)

Greenwald, A. G. (1975). On the inconclusiveness of crucial cognitive tests of dissonance versus self-perception theories. *Journal of Experimental Social Psychology*, 11, 490-499. (p. 137)

Greenwald, A. G. (1980). The totalitarian ego: Fabrication and revision of personal history. *American Psychologist*, 35, 603-618. (p. 80)

Greenwald, A. G., & Banaji, M. R. (1995). Implicit social cognition: Attitudes, self-esteem, and stereotypes. *Psychological Review*, 102, 4-27. (p. 38)

Greenwald, A. G., & Schuh, E. S. (1994). An ethnic bias in scientific citations. *European Journal of Social Psychology*, 24, 623-639. (p. 421)

Greenwald, A. G., Banaji, M. R., Rudman, L. A., Farnham, S. D., Nosek, B. A., & Mellott, D. S. (2002). A unified theory of implicit attitudes, stereotypes, self-esteem, and self-concept. *Psychological Bulletin*, 109, 3-25. (p. 115)

Greenwald, A. G., Banaji, M. R., Rudman, L. A., Farnham, S. D., Nosek, B. A., & Rosier, M. (2000). Prologue to a unified theory of attitudes, stereotypes, and self-concept. In J. P. Forgas (Ed.), *Feeling and thinking: The role of affect in social cognition and behavior*. New York: Cambridge University Press. (p. 419)

Greenwald, A. G., McGhee, D. E., Schwartz, J. L. K. (1998). Measuring individual differences in implicit cognition: The implicit association test. *Journal of Personality and Social Psychology*, 74, 1464-1480. (p. 419)

Greenwald, A. G., Nosek, B. A., & Banaji, M. R. (2003). Understanding and using the implicit association test: I. An improved scoring algorithm. *Journal of Personality and Social Psychology*, 85, 197-216. (p. 115)

Griffin, B. Q., Combs, A. L., Land, M. L., & Combs, N. N. (1983). Attribution of success and failure in college performance. *Journal of Psychology*, 114, 259-266. (p. 56)

Griffin, D., & Buehler, R. (1993). Role of construal processes in conformity and dissent. *Journal of Personality and Social Psychology*, **65**, 657.

Griffitt, W. (1970). Environmental effects on interpersonal affective behavior. Ambient effective temperature and attraction. *Journal of Personality and Social Psychology*, 15, 240-244. (p. 346)

Griffitt, W., & Veitch, R. (1971). Hot and crowded: Influences of population density and temperature on interpersonal

affective behavior. *Journal of Personality and Social Psychology*, 17, 92-98. (p. 346)
Griffitt, W., & Veitch, R. (1974). Preacquaintance attitude similarity and attraction revisited: Ten days in a fallout shelter. *Sociometry*, 37, 163-173. (p. 388)
Groenenboom, A., Wilke, H. A. M., & Wit, A. P. (2001). Will we be working together again? The impact of future interdependence on group members' task motivation. *European Journal of Social Psychology, **31***, 369. (p. 226)
Gross, A. E., & Crofton, C. (1977). What is good is beautiful. *Sociometry*, 40, 85-90. (p. 386)
Gross, J. T. (2001). *Fear: Anti-Semitism in Poland after Auschwitz*. New York: Random House. (p. 333)
Grote, N. K., & Clark, M. S. (2001). Perceiving unfairness in the family: Cause or consequence of marital distress? *Journal of Personality and Social Psychology, **80***, 281. (p. 407)
Grove, J. R., Hanrahan, S. J., & McInman, A. (1991). Success/failure bias in attributions across involvement categories in sport. *Personality and Social Psychology Bulletin*, 17, 93-97. (p. 55)
Grube, J. W., Kleinhesselink, R. R., & Kearney, K. A. (1982). Male self-acceptance and attraction toward women. *Personality and Social Psychology Bulletin*, 8, 107-112. (p. 438)
Gruder, C. L., Cook, T. D., Hennigan, K. M., Flay, B., Alessis, C., & Kalamaj, J. (1978). Empirical tests of the absolute sleeper effect predicted from the discounting cue hypothesis. *Journal of Personality and Social Psychology*, 36, 1061-1074. (p. 149)
Gruman, J. C., & Sloan, R. P. (1983). Disease as justice: Perceptions of the victims of physical illness. *Basic and Applied Social Psychology*, 4, 39-46. (p. 440)
Grunberger, R. (1971). *The 12-year-Reich: A social history of Nazi Germany 1933-1945*. New York: Holt, Rinehart & Winston. (p. 126)
Grush, J. E. (1980). Impact of candidate expenditures, regionality, and prior outcomes on the 1976 Democratic presidential primaries. *Journal of Personality and Social Psychology*, 38, 337-347. (p. 161)
Grush, J. E., & Glidden, M. V. (1987). *Power and satisfaction among distressed and nondistressed couples*. Paper presented at the Midwestern Psychological Association convention. (p. 478)
Guay, F., Mageau, G. A., & Vallerand, R. J. (2003). On the hierarchical structure of self-determined motivation: A test of top-down, bottom-up, reciprocal, and horizontal effects. *Personality & Social Psychology Bulletin*, 29(8), 992-1004. (p. 53)
Gudykunst, W. B. (1989). Culture and intergroup processes. In M. H. Bond (Ed.), *The cross-cultural challenge to social psychology*. Newbury Park, Ca.: Sage. (p. 435)
Gueguen, N. & Jacob, C. (2001). Fundraising on the Web: The effect of an electronic foot-in-the-door on donation. *CyberPsychology and Behavior*, **4**, 705-709. (p. 122)
Guerin, B. (1993). *Social facilitation*. Paris: Cambridge University Press. (p. 219)
Guerin, B. (1994). What do people think about the risks of driving? Implications for traffic safety interventions. *Journal of Applied Social Psychology*, 24, 994-1021. (p. 57)
Guerin, B., & Innes, J. M. (1982). Social facilitation and social monitoring: A new look at Zajonc's mere presence hypothesis. *British Journal of Social Psychology*, 21, 7-18. (p. 221)
Guimond, S., Dambrun, N., Michinov, N., & Duarte, S. (2003). Does social dominance generate prejudice? Integrating individual and contextual determinants of intergroup cognitions. *Journal of Personality and Social Psychology*, 84, 697-721. (p. 427)
Guiness, O. (1993). *The American hour: A time of reckoning and the once and future role of faith*. New York: Free Press. (p. 410)
Gupta, U., & Singh, P. (1982). Exploratory study of love and liking and type of marriages. Indian *Journal of Applied Psychology*, 19, 92-97. (p. 402)
Gutierres, S. E., Kenrick, D. T., & Partch, J. J. (1999). Beauty, dominance, and the mating game: Contrast effects in self-assessment reflect gender differences in mate selection. Journal of *Personality and Social Psychology*, 25, 1126-1134. (p. 386)

Hacker, H. M. (1951). Women as a minority group. *Social Forces*, 30, 60-69. (p. 427)
Hackman, J. R. (1986). The design of work teams. In J. Lorsch (Ed.), *Handbook of organizational behavior*. Englewood Cliffs, N.J.: Prentice-Hall. (p. 226)
Hadden, J. K. (1969). *The gathering storm in the churches*. Garden City, NY: Doubleday. (p. 429)
Haddock, G, & Zanna, M.P. (1994). Preferring "housewives" to "feminists." *Psychology of Women Quarterly*, 18, 25-52. (p. 424)
Hafer, C. L., & Bègue, L. (2005). Experimental research on just-world theory: Problems, developments, and future challenges. *Psychological Bulletin, **131***, 128.
Hafer, C. L., Reynolds, K. L., & Obertynski, M. A. (1996). Message comprehensibility and persuasion: Effects of complex language in counterattitudinal appeals of laypeople. *Social Cognition*, 14, 317-337. (p. 167)
Hagerty, M. R. (2000). Social comparisons of income in one's community: Evidence from national surveys of income and happiness. *Journal of Personality and Social Psychology*, 78, 764-771. (p. 537)
Hagiwara, S. (1983). Role of self-based and sample-based consensus estimates as mediators of responsibility judgments for automobile accidents. *Japanese Psychological Research*, 25, 16-28. (p. 69)
Haidt, J. (2003). The moral emotions. In R. J. Davidson (Ed.). H*andbook of affective sciences*. Oxford: Oxford University Press. (p. 319)
Hall, T. (1985, June 25). The unconverted: Smoking of cigarettes seems to be becoming a lower-class habit. *Wall Street Journal*, pp. 1, 25. (p. 80)
Hallahan, M., Lee, F., & Herzog, T. (1997). It's not just whether you win or lose, it's also where you play the game: A naturalistic, cross-cultural examination of the positivity bias. *Journal of Cross-Cultural Psychology*, 28, 768-778. (p. 69)
Halverson, A. M., Hallahan, M., Hart, A. J., & Rosenthal, R. (1997). Reducing the biasing effects of judges' nonverbal behavior with simplified jury instruction. *Journal of Applied Psychology*, 82, 590-598.(p. 523)
Hamberger, J., & Hewstone, M. (1997). Inter-ethnic contact as a predictor of blatant and subtle prejudice: Tests of a model in four West European nations. *British Journal of Social Psychology*, 36, 173-190. (p. 282)
Hamblin, R. L., Buckholdt, D., Bushell, D., Ellis, D., & Feritor, D. (1969). Changing the game from get the teacher to learn. *Transaction*, January, pp. 20-25, 28-31. (p. 368)
Hamilton, D. L. (1981). Illusory correlation as a basis for stereotyping. In D. L.

Hamilton (Ed.), *Cognitive processes in stereotyping and intergroup behavior.* Hillsdale, N.J.: Erlbaum. (p. 451)

Hamilton, D. L., & Gifford, R. K. (1976). Illusory correlation in interpersonal perception: A cognitive basis of stereotypic judgments. *Journal of Experimental Social Psychology*, 12, 392-407. (p. 448)

Hamilton, D. L., & Rose, T. L. (1980). Illusory correlation and the maintenance of stereotypic beliefs. *Journal of Personality and Social Psychology*, 39, 832-845. (p. 448)

Hamilton, V. L., Hoffman, W. S., Broman, C. L., & Rauma, D. (1993). Unemployment, distress, and coping: A panel study of autoworkers. *Journal of Personality and Social Psychology*, 65, 234-247. (p. 492)

Hampson, R. B. (1984). Adolescent prosocial behavior: Peer-group and situational factors associated with helping. *Journal of Personality and Social Psychology*, 46, 153-162. (p. 322)

Hardie, E. A. (1997). Prevalence and predictors of cyclic and noncyclic affective change. *Psychology of Women Quarterly*, 21, 299-314. (p. 498)

Hardin, G. (1968). The tragedy of the commons. *Science*, 162, 1243-1248. (p. 468)

Hardy, C., & Latané, B. (1986). Social loafing on a cheering task. *Social Science*, 71, 165-172. (p. 224)

Haritos-Fatouros, M. (1988). The official torturer: A learning model for obedience to the authority of violence. *Journal of Applied Social Psychology*, 18, 1107-1120. (p. 196)

Harkins, S. G. (1981). *Effects of task difficulty and task responsibility on social loafing.* Presentation to the First International Conference on Social Processes in Small Groups, Kill Devil Hills, North Carolina. (p. 224)

Harkins, S. G., & Jackson, J. M. (1985). The role of evaluation in eliminating social loafing. *Personality and Social Psychology Bulletin*, 11, 457-465. (p. 224)

Harkins, S. G., & Petty, R. E. (1981). Effects of source magnification of cognitive effort on attitudes: An information-processing view. *Journal of Personality and Social Psychology*, 40, 401-413. (p. 166)

Harkins, S. G., & Petty, R. E. (1982). Effects of task difficulty and task uniqueness on social loafing. *Journal of Personality and Social Psychology*, 43, 1214-1229. (p. 226)

Harkins, S. G., & Petty, R. E. (1987). Information utility and the multiple source effect. *Journal of Personality and Social Psychology*, 52, 260-268. (p. 167)

Harkins, S. G., & Szymanski, K. (1989). Social loafing and group evaluation. *Journal of Personality and Social Psychology*, 56, 934-941. (p. 226)

Harkins, S. G., Latane, B., & Williams, K. (1980). Social loafing: Allocating effort or taking it easy? *Journal of Experimental Social Psychology*, 16, 457-465. (p. 223)

Harkness, K. L., Sabbagh, M. A., Jacobson, J. A., Chowdrey, N. K., & Chen, T. (2005). Enhanced accuracy of mental state decoding in dysphoric college students. *Cognition & Emotion, **19***, 999. (p. 490)

Harmon-Jones, E., & Allen, J. J. B. (2001). The role of affect in the mere exposure effect: Evidence from psychophysiological and individual differences approaches. *Personality and Social Psychology Bulletin*, 27, 889-898. (p. 377)

Harmon-Jones, E., Brehm, J. W., Greenberg, J., Simon, L., & Nelson, D. E. (1996). Evidence that the production of aversive conse-quences is not necessary to create cognitive dissonance. *Journal of Personality and Social Psychology*, 70, 5-16. (p. 139)

Harrel, W. A. (1994). Effects of blind pedestrians on motorists. *Journal of Social Psychology*, 134, 529-539. (p. 304)

Harris, J. R. (1998). *The nurture assumption.* New York: Free Press. (p. 405)

Harris, L. T., & Fiske, S. T. (2006). Dehumanizing the lowest of the low: Neuroimaging responses to extreme out-groups. *Psychological Science, **17***, 847. (p. 421)

Harris, M. J., & Rosenthal, R. (1985). Mediation of interpersonal expectancy effects: 31 meta-analyses. *Psychological Bulletin*, 97, 363-386. (p. 104)

Harris, M. J., & Rosenthal, R. (1986). Four factors in the mediation of teacher expectancy effects. In R. S. Feldman (Ed.), *The social psychology of education.* New York: Cambridge University Press. (p. 104)

Harrison, A. A. (1977). Mere exposure. In L. Berkowitz (Ed.), *Advances in experimental social psychology* (Vol. 10). New York: Academic Press, pp. 39-83. (p. 377)

Hart, A. J., Whalen, P. J., Shin, L. M., & others. (2000, August). Differential response in the human amygdala to racial outgroup vs. ingroup face stimuli. Neuroreport: For Rapid Communication of *Neuroscience Research*, 11, 2351-2355. (p. 441)

Hartup, W. W., & Stevens, N. (1997). Friendships and adaptation in the life course. *Psychological Bulletin*, 121, 355-370. (p. 506)

Harvey, J. H., Town, J. P., & Yarkin, K. L. (1981). How fundamental is the fundamental attribution error? *Journal of Personality and Social Psychology*, 40, 346-349. (p. 100)

Haselton, M. G., & Nettle, D. (2006). The paranoid optimist: An integrative evolutionary model of cognitive biases. *Personality and Social Psychology Review, **10***, 47. (p. 59)

Haslam, S. A., & Oakes, P. J. (1995). How context-independent is the group homogeneity effect? A response to Bartsch and Judd. *European Journal of Social Psychology*, 25, 469-475. (p. 443)

Hastie, R., Penrod, S. D., & Pennington, N. (1983). *Inside the jury.* Cambridge, Mass.: Harvard University Press. (p. 524)

Hatfield (Walster), E., Aronson, V., Abrahams, D., & Rottman, L. (1966). Importance of physical attractiveness in dating behavior. *Journal of Personality and Social Psychology*, 4, 508-516. (p. 379)

Hatfield (was Walster), E., Walster, G. W., & Berscheid, E. (1978). *Equity: Theory and research.* Boston: Allyn and Bacon. (p. 395)

Hatfield, E. (1988). Passionate and compassionate love. In R. J. Sternberg & M. L. Barnes (Eds.), *The psychology of love.* New Haven, Conn.: Yale University Press. (p. 398)

Hatfield, E., & Sprecher, S. (1986). *Mirror, mirror: The importance of looks in everyday life.* Albany, N.Y.: SUNY Press. (p. 403)

Hatfield, E., Cacioppo, J. T., & Rapson, R. (1992). The logic of emotion: Emotional contagion. In M. S. Clark (Ed.), *Review of personality and social psychology.* Newbury Park, CA: Sage. (p. 134)

Hatfield, E., Traupmann, J., Sprecher, S., Utne, M., & Hay, J. (1985). Equity and intimate relations: Recent research. In W. Ickes (Ed.), *Compatible and incompatible relationships.* New York: Springer-Verlag. (p. 407)

Haugtvedt, C. P., & Wegener, D. T. (1994). Message order effects in persuasion: An attitude strength perspective. *Journal of Consumer Research*, 21, 205-218. (p. 160)

Havel, V. (1990). *Disturbing the peace.* New York: Knopf. (p. 537)

Hazan, C., & Shaver, P. R. (1994). Attachment as an organizational framework for research on close relationships. *Psychological Inquiry*, 5, 1-22. (p. 411)

Hazan, C., Gur-Yaish, N., & Campa, M. (2004). What does it mean to be attached? In W. S. Rholes, & J. A. Simpson (Eds.). *Adult attachment: Theory, research, and clinical implications.* (pp. 55-85). New York, NY, US: Guilford Publications.

Headey, B., & Wearing, A. (1987). The sense of relative superiority-central to well-being. *Social Indicators Research*, 20, 497-516. (p. 57)

Heap, B., & Kent, J. (Eds.) (2000). *Towards sustainable consumption: A European perspective.* London: The Royal Society. (p. 530)

Hearold, S. (1986). A synthesis of 1043 effects of television on social behavior. In G. Comstock (Ed.), *Public communication and behavior*, Vol. 1. Orlando, Fl.: Academic Press. (p. 326)

Heatherton, T. F. & Vohs, K. D. (2000). Personality processes and individual differences-interpersonal evaluations following threats to self: role of self-esteem. *Journal of Personality and Social Psychology*, 78, 725-736. (p. 47)

Hedge, A., & Yousif, Y. H. (1992). Effects of urban size, urgency, and cost on helpfulness: A cross-cultural comparison between the United Kingdom and the Sudan. *Journal of Cross-Cultural Psychology*, 23, 107-115. (p. 306)

Heider, F. (1958). *The psychology of interpersonal relations.* New York: Wiley. (p. 94)

Heine, S. J., & Lehman, D. R. (1995). Cultural variation in unrealistic optimism: Does the West feel more invulnerable than the East? *Journal of Personality and Social Psychology*, 68, 595-607. (p. 69)

Heine, S. J., & Lehman, D. R. (1997). The cultural construction of self-enhancement: An examination of group-serving biases. *Journal of Personality and Social Psychology*, 72, 1268-1283. (p. 69)

Heine, S. J., Lehman, D. R., Markus, H. R., & Kitayama, S. (1999). Is there a universal need for positive self-regard? *Psychological Review*, 106, 766-794. (p. 267)

Hellman, P. (1980). *Avenue of the righteous of nations.* New York: Atheneum. (p. 296)

Helmrich, R. L. (1997, May). Managing human error in aviation. *Scientific American*, pp. 62-67. (p. 244)

Hemsley, G. D., & Doob, A. N. (1978). The effect of looking behavior on perceptions of a communicator's credibility. *Journal of Applied Social Psychology*, 8, 136-144. (p. 150)

Hendersen-King, E. I., & Nisbett, R. E. (1996). Anti-black prejudice as a function of exposure to the negative behavior of a single black person. *Journal of Personality and Social Psychology*, 71, 654-664. (p. 447)

Hendrick, C., & Hendrick, S. (1993). *Romantic love.* Newbury Park, CA: Sage. (p. 397)

Hendrick, C., & Hendrick, S. S. (2003). Romantic love: Measuring cupid's arrow. In S. J. Lopez, & C. R. Snyder (Eds.), *Positive psychological assessment: A handbook of models and measures.* (pp. 235-249). Washington, DC, US: American Psychological Association. doi:10.1037/10612-015. (p. 397)

Hendrick, S. S., & Hendrick, C. (1995). Gender differences and similarities in sex and love. *Personal Relationships*, 2, 55-65. (p. 400)

Hendrick, S. S., Hendrick, C., & Adler, N. L. (1988). Romantic relationships: Love, satisfaction, and staying together. *Journal of Personality and Social Psychology*, 54, 980-988. (p. 409)

Hennigan, K. M., Del Rosario, M. L., Health, L., Cook, T. D., Wharton, J. D., & Calder, B. J. (1982). Impact of the introduction of television on crime in the United States: Empirical findings and theoretical implications. *Journal of Personality and Social Psychology*, 42, 461-477. (p. 341)

Henslin, M. (1967). Craps and magic. *American Journal of Sociology*, 73, 316-330. (p. 89)

Hepworth, J. T., & West, S. G. (1988). Lynchings and the economy: A time-series reanalysis of Hovland and Sears (1940). *Journal of Personality and Social Psychology*, 55, 239-247. (p. 432)

Herek, G. (1993). Interpersonal contact and heterosexuals' attitudes toward gay men: Results from a national survey. *Journal of Sex Research*, 30, 239-244. (p. 282)

Herlocker, C. E., Allison, S. T., Foubert, J. D., & Beggan, J. K. (1997). Intended and unintended overconsumption of physical, spatial, and temporal resources. *Journal of Personality and Social Psychology*, 73, 992-1004. (p. 469)

Hewstone, M. (1990). The 'ultimate attribution error'? A review of the literature on intergroup causal attribution. *European Journal of Social Psychology*, 20, 311-335. (p. 449)

Hewstone, M. (1994). Revision and change of stereotypic beliefs: In search of the elusive subtyping model. In S. Stroebe & M. Hewstone (eds.), *European review of social psychology*, vol. 5. Chichester, England: Wiley. (p. 451)

Hewstone, M. (1996). Contact and categorization: Social psychological interventions to change intergroup relations. In N. Macrae, C. Stangor, & M. Hewstone (eds.), *Foundations of stereotypes and stereotyping.* New York: Guilford. (p. 286)

Hewstone, M., & Fincham, F. (1996). Attribution theory and research: Basic issues and applications. In M. Hewstone, W. Stroebe, and G. M. Stephenson (eds.), *Introduction to social psychology: A European perspective.* Oxford, UK: Blackwell. (p. 93)

Hewstone, M., & Ward, C. (1985). Ethnocentrism and causal attribution in southeast Asia. *Journal of Personality and Social Psychology*, 48, 614-623. (p. 449)

Hewstone, M., Hantzi, A., & Johnston, L. (1991). Social categorisation and person memory: The pervasiveness of race as an organizing principle. *European Journal of Social Psychology*, 21, 517-528. (p. 442)

Hewstone, M., Hopkins, N., & Routh, D. A. (1992). Cognitive models of stereotype change: Generalization and subtyping in young people's views of the police. *European Journal of Social Psychology*, 22, 219-234. (p. 451)

Higbee, K. L., Millard, R. J., & Folkman, J. R. (1982). Social psychology research during the 1970s: Predominance of experimentation and college students. *Personality and Social Psychology Bulletin*, 8, 180-183. (p. 26)

Higgins, E. T., & Bargh, J. A. (1987). Social cognition and social perception. *Annual Review of Psychology*, 38, 369-425. (p. 50)

Higgins, E. T., & McCann, C. D. (1984). Social encoding and subsequent attitudes, impressions and memory: "Context-driven" and motivational aspects of processing. *Journal of Personality and Social Psychology*, 47, 26-39. (p. 121)

Higgins, E. T., & Rholes, W. S. (1978). Saying is believing: Effects of message modification on memory and liking for the person described. *Journal of Experimental Social Psychology*, 14, 363-378. (p. 121)

Hill, T., Smith, N. D., & Lewicki, P. (1989). The development of self-image bias: A real-world demonstration. *Personality and Social Psychology Bulletin*, 15, 205-211. (p. 58)

Hilmert, C. J., Kulik, J. A., & Christenfeld, N. J. S. (2006). Positive and negative opinion modeling: The influence of another's similarity and dissimilarity. *Journal of Personality and Social Psychology,* ***90***, 440. (p. 203)

Hilton, J. L., & von Hippel, W. (1990). The role of consistency in the judgment of stereotype-relevant behaviors. *Personality and Social Psychology Bulletin*, 16, 430-448. (p. 74)

Hine, D. W., & Gifford, R. (1996). Attributions about self and others in commons dilemmas. *European Journal of Social Psychology*, 26, 429-445. (p. 469)

Hinkle, S., Brown, R., & Ely, P. G. (1992). Social identity theory processes: Some limitations and limiting conditions. *Revista de Psicologia Social*, 99-111. (p. 435)

Hinsz, V. B. (1990). Cognitive and consensus processes in group recognition memory performance. *Journal of Personality and Social Psychology*, 59, 705-718. (p. 246)

Hinsz, V. B., Tindale, R. S., & Vollrath, D. A. (1997). The emerging conceptualization of groups as information processors. *Psychological Bulletin*, 121, 43-64. (p. 236)

Hirschman, R. S., & Leventhal, H. (1989). Preventing smoking behavior in school children: An initial test of a cognitive-development program. *Journal of Applied Social Psychology*, 19, 559-583. (p. 176)

Hirt, E. R. (1990). Do I see only what I expect? Evidence for an expectancy-guided retrieval model. *Journal of Personality and Social Psychology*, 58, 937-951. (p. 78)

Hirt, E. R., & Markman, K. D. (1995). Multiple explanation: A consider-an-alternative strategy for debiasing judgments. *Journal of Personality and Social Psychology*, 69, 1069-1088. (p. 78)

Hirt, E. R., Zillmann, D., Erickson, G. A., & Kennedy, C. (1992). Costs and benefits of allegiance: Changes in fans' self-ascribed competencies after team victory versus defeat. *Journal of Personality and Social Psychology*, 63, 724-738. (p. 491)

Hobden, K. L., & Olson, J. M. (1994). From jest to antipathy: Disparagement humor as a source of dissonance-motivated attitude change. *Basic and Applied Social Psychology*, 15, 239-249. (p. 130)

Hodges, B. H., & Geyer, A. L. (2006). A nonconformist account of the Asch experiments: Values, pragmatics, and moral dilemmas. *Personality and Social Psychology Review,* ***10***, 2. (p. 187)

Hodson, G., & Olson, J. M. (2005). Testing the generality of the name letter effect: Name initials and everyday attitudes. *Personality and Social Psychology Bulletin,* ***31***, 1099. (p. 378)

Hoffman, C., & Hurst, N. (1990). Gender stereotypes: Perception or rationalization? *Journal of Personality and Social Psychology*, 58, 197-208. (p. 427)

Hoffman, L. W. (1977). Changes in family roles, socialization, and sex differences. *American Psychologist*, 32, 644-657. (p. 430)

Hoffman, M. A., Hill, C. E., Holmes, Stacey E., & Freitas, G. F. (2005). Supervisor perspective on the process and outcome of giving easy, difficult, or no feedback to supervisees. *Journal of Counseling Psychology*, **52**, 3-13. (p. 115)

Hoffman, M. L. (1981). Is altruism part of human nature? *Journal of Personality and Social Psychology*, 40, 121-137. (p. 309)

Hofling, C. K., Brotzman, E., Dairymple, S., Graves, N., & Pierce, C. M. (1966). An experimental study in nurse-physician relationships. *Journal of Nervous and Mental Disease*, 143, 171-180. (p. 193)

Hogan, R., Curphy, G. J., & Hogan, J. (1994). What we know about leadership: Effectiveness and personality. *American Psychologist*, 49, 493-504. (p. 249)

Hogg, M. A. (1992). *The social psychology of group cohesiveness: From attraction to social identity*. London: Harvester Wheatsheaf. (p. 432)

Hogg, M. A. (1996). Intragroup processes, group structure and social identity. In W. P. Robinson (ed.), *Social groups and identies: Developing the legacy of Henri Tajfel.* Oxford: Butterworth Heinemann. (p. 432)

Hogg, M. A. (2003). Social identity. In M. R. Leary & J. P. Tangey (Eds.), *Handbook of self and identity*. New York: Guilford Press. (p. 432)

Hogg, M. A., & Hains, S. C. (1998). Friendship and group identification: A new look at the role of cohesiveness in groupthink. *European Journal of Social Psychology,* ***28***, 323. (p. 243)

Hogg, M. A., Turner, J. C., & Davidson, B. (1990). Polarized norms and social frames of reference: A test of the self-categorization theory of group polarization. *Basic and Applied Social Psychology*, 11, 77-100. (p. 237)

Holland, R. W., Hendriks, M., & Aarts, H. (2005). Smells like clean spirit: Nonconscious effects of scent on cognition and behavior. *Psychological Science, 16*(9), 689. (p. 73)

Holland, R. W., Meertens, R. M., & Van Vugt, M. (2002). Dissonance on the road: Self-esteem as a moderator of internal and external self-justification strategies. *Personality and Social Psychology Bulletin*, 28, 1712-1724. (p. 138)

Holmberg, D., & Holmes, J. G. (1994). Reconstruction of relationship memories: A mental models approach. In N. Schwarz & S. Sudman (Eds.), *Autobiographical memory and the validity of retrospective reports.* New York: Springer-Verlag. (p. 80)

Holmes, J. G., & Rempel, J. K. (1989). Trust in close relationships. In C. Hendrick (Ed.), *Review of personality and social psychology*, Vol. 10. Newbury Park, Ca.: Sage. (p. 408)

Holmes, J. G., Miller, D. T., & Lerner, M. J. (1997). *Committing altruism under the cloak of self-interest: The exchange fiction.* Unpublished manuscript, University of Waterloo. (p. 297)

Holtzworth, A., & Jacobson, N. S. (1988). An attributional approach to marital dysfunction and therapy. In J. E. Maddux, C. D. Stoltenberg, & R. Rosenwein (Eds.), *Social processes in clinical and counseling psychology*. New York: Springer-Verlag. (p. 93)

Holtzworth-Munroe, A., & Jacobson, N. S. (1985). Causal attributions of married couples: When do they search for causes? What do they conclude when they do? *Journal of Personality and Social Psychology, 48*(6), 1398. doi:10.1037/0022-3514.48.6.1398. (p. 93)

Holtzworth-Munroe, A., & Jacobson, N. S. (1988). Toward a methodology for coding spontaneous causal attributions: Preliminary results with married couples.

Journal of Social & Clinical Psychology, 7(2-3), 101.

Hoorens, V. (1993). Self-enhancement and superiority biases in social comparison. In W. Stroebe & M. Hewstone (Eds.), *European review of social psychology*, vol. 4. Chichester: Wiley. (p. 57)

Hoorens, V. (1995). Self-favoring biases, self-presentation and the self-other asymmetry in social comparison. *Journal of Personality*, 63, 793-819. (p. 57)

Hoorens, V., Nuttin, J. M., Herman, I. E., & Pavakanun, U. (1990). Mastery pleasure versus mere ownership: A quasi-experimental cross-cultural and cross-alphabetical test of the name letter effect. *European Journal of Social Psychology*, 20, 181-205. (p. 377)

Hormuth, S. E. (1986). Lack of effort as a result of self-focused attention: An attributional ambiguity analysis. *European Journal of Social Psychology*, 16, 181-192. (p. 68)

Hornstein, H. (1976). *Cruelty and kindness.* Englewood Cliffs, N.J.: Prentice-Hall. (p. 335)

Horowitz, S. V., & Boardman, S. K. (1994). Managing conflict: Policy and research implications. *Journal of Social Issues*, 50, 197-211. (p. 478)

Horwitz, A. V., White, H. R., Howell-White, S. (1997). Becoming married and mental health: A longitudinal study of a cohort of young adults. *Journal of Marriage and the Family*, 58, 895-907. (p. 508)

House, R. J., & Singh, J. V. (1987). Organizational behavior: Some new directions for I/O psychology. *Annual Review of Psychology*, 38, 669-718. (p. 249)

Houston, V., & Bull, R. (1994). Do people avoid sitting next to someone who is facially disfigured? *European Journal of Social Psychology*, 24, 279-284. (p. 381)

Hovland, C. I., & Sears, R. (1940). Minor studies of aggression: Correlation of lynchings with economic indices. *Journal of Psychology*, 9, 301-310. (p. 432)

Hovland, C. I., Lumsdaine, A. A., & Sheffield, F. D. (1949). *Experiments on mass communication. Studies in social psychology in World War II* (Vol. III). Princeton, N.J.: Princeton University Press. (p. 145)

Howard, D. J. (1997). Familiar phrases as peripheral persuasion cues. *Journal of Experimental Social Psychology*, 33, 231-243. (p. 147)

Huart, J., Corneille, O., & Becquart, E. (2005). Face-based categorization, context-based categorization, and distortions in the recollection of gender ambiguous faces. *Journal of Experimental Social Psychology, **41***, 598. (p. 450)

Huberman, B., & Lukose, R. (1997). Social dilemmas and internet congestion. *Science*, 277, 535-537. (p. 469)

Huddy, L., & Virtanen, S. (1995). Subgroup differentiation and subgroup bias among Latinos as a function of familiarity and positive distinctiveness. *Journal of Personality and Social Psychology*, 68, 97-108. (p. 443)

Huesmann, L. R., Lagerspetz, K., & Eron, L. D. (1984). Intervening variables in the TV violence-aggression relation: Evidence from two countries. *Developmental Psychology*, 20, 746-775. (p. 356)

Huesmann, L. R., Moise-Titus, J., Podolski, C-L., & Eron, L. D. (2003). Longitudinal relations between children's exposure to TV violence and their aggressive and violent behavior in young adulthood: 1977-1992. *Developmental Psychology*, 39, 201-222. (p. 336)

Hugenberg, K. & Bodenhausen, G. V. (2003). Facing prejudice: Implicit prejudice and the perception of facial threat. *Psychological Science*, 14, 640-643. (p. 419)

Hui, C. H., Triandis, H. C., & Yee, C. (1991). Cultural differences in reward allocation: Is collectivism the explanation? *British Journal of Social Psychology*, 30, 145-157. (p. 473)

Hull, J. G., & Young, R. D. (1983). The self-awareness-reducing effects of alcohol consumption: Evidence and implications. In J. Suls & A. G. Greenwald (Eds.), *Psychological perspectives on the self*, Vol. 2. Hillsdale, N.J.: Erlbaum. (p. 232)

Hunt, P. J., & Hillery, J. M. (1973). Social facilitation in a location setting: An examination of the effects over learning trials. *Journal of Experimental Social Psychology*, 9, 563-571. (p. 219)

Hunter, J. D. (2002, June 21-22). "To change the world." Paper presented to the Board of Directors of The Trinity Forum, Denver, Colorado. (p. 144)

Huo, Y. J., Smith, H. J., Tyler, T. R., & Lind, E. A. (1996). Superordinate identification, subgroup identification, and justice concerns: Is separatism the problem; is assimilation the answer? *Psychological Science*, 7, 40-45. (p. 286)

Hurt, S. W., Schnurr, P. P., Severino, S. K., Freeman, E. W., Gise, L. H., Rivera-Tovar, A., & Steege, J. F. (1992). Late luteal phase dysphoric disorder in 670 women evaluated for premenstrual complaints. *American Journal of Psychiatry*, 149, 525-530. (p. 498)

Huston, A. C., Donnerstein, E., Fairchild, H., Feshbach, N. D., Katz, P. A., & Murray, J. P. (1992). *Big world, small screen: The role of television in American society.* Lincoln, NE: University of Nebraska Press. (p. 355)

Huston, T. L. (1973). Ambiguity of acceptance, social desirability, and dating choice. *Journal of Experimental Social Psychology*, 9, 32-42. (p. 380)

Huston, T. L., & Chorost, A. F. (1994). Behavioral buffers on the effect of negativity on marital satisfaction: A longitudinal study. *Personal Relationships*, 1, 223-239. (p. 401)

Huston, T. L., Niehuis, S., & Smith, S. E. (2001). The early marital roots of conjugal distress and divorce. *Current Directions in Psychological Science*, 10, 116-119. (p. 412)

Hutnik, N. (1985). Aspects of identity in a multi-ethnic society. *New Community*, 12, 298-309. (p. 287)

Hyde, J. S., Fennema, E. H., &Lamon, S. J. (1990). Gender differences in mathematics performance: A meta-analysis. *Psychological Bulletin*, 107. (p. 418)

Hyman, I. E., Jr., Husband, T. H., & Billings, F. J. (1995). False memories of childhood experiences. *Applied Cognitive Psychology*, 9, 181-197. (p. 78)

Hyman, R. (1981). Cold reading: How to convince strangers that you know all about them. In K. Frazier (Ed.), *Paranormal borderlands of science*. Buffalo, NY: Prometheus Books.

Ianco-Worrall, A. D. (1972). Bilingualism and cognitive development. *Child Development*, 43, 1390-1400. (p. 289)

Ickes, B. (1980). *On disconfirming our perceptions of others.* Paper presented at the American Psychological Association convention. (p. 270)

Ickes, W., Layden, M. A., & Barnes, R. D. (1978). Objective self-awareness and individuation: An empirical link. *Journal of Personality*, 46, 146-161. (p. 232)

Ickes, W., Patterson, M. L., Rajecki, D. W., & Tanford, S. (1982). Behavioral and cognitive consequences of reciprocal versus compensatory responses to preinteraction expectancies. *Social Cognition*, 1, 160-190. (p. 209)

Ickes, W., Snyder, M., & Garcia, S. (1997). Personality influences on the choice of situations. In R. Hogan, J. Johnson, & S. Briggs (eds.), *Handbook of personality psychology*. San Diego: Academic Press. (p. 292)

Imai, Y. (1994). Effects of influencing attempts on the perceptions of powerholders and the powerless. *Journal of Social Behavior and Personality*, 9, 455-468. (p. 56)

Ingham, A. G., Levinger, G., Graves, J., & Peckham, V. (1974). The Ringelmann effect: Studies of group size and group performance. *Journal of Experimental Social Psychology*, 10, 371-384. (p. 223)

Inglehart, M. R., Markus, H., & Brown, D. R. (1989). The effects of possible selves on academic achievement-a panel study. In J. P. Forgas & J. M. Innes (Eds.), Recent advances in social psychology: *An international perspective*. North-Holland: Elsevier Science Publishers. (p. 51)

Inglehart, R. (1990). *Culture shift in advanced industrial society*. Princeton, NJ: Princeton University Press. (p. 507)

Inglehart, R. F., & C.Welzel. (2005). "Liberalism, Postmaterialism and the Growth of Freedom." *International Review of Sociology*, **15**, 81-108. (p. 54)

Insko, C. A., Nacoste, R. W., & Moe, J. L. (1983). Belief congruence and racial discrimination: Review of the evidence and critical evaluation. *European Journal of Social Psychology*, 13, 153-174. (p. 389)

Isen, A. M., & Means, B. (1983). The influence of positive affect on decision-making strategy. *Social Cognition*, 2, 28-31. (p. 90)

Isen, A. M., Clark, M., & Schwartz, M. F. (1976). Duration of the effect of good mood on helping: Footprints on the sands of time. *Journal of Personality and Social Psychology*, 34, 385-393. (p. 301)

Isen, A. M., Horn, N., & Rosenhan, D. L. (1973). Effects of success and failure on children's generosity. *Journal of Personality and Social Psychology*, 27, 239-247. (p. 302)

Isozaki, M. (1984). The effect of discussion on polarization of judgments. *Japanese Psychological Research*, 26, 187-193. (p. 234)

Ito, T. A., Miller, N., & Pollock, V. E. (1996). Alcohol and aggression: A meta-analysis on the moderating effects of inhibitory cues, triggering events, and self-focused attention. *Psychological Bulletin*, 120, 60-82. (p. 336)

Izard, C. E. (1977). *Human emotions*. New York: Plenum Press. (p. 275)

Izard, C. E. (1994). Innate and universal facial expressions: Evidence from developmental and cross-cultural research. *Psychological Bulletin*, 115, 288-299. (p. 275)

Jackman, M. R., & Senter, M. S. (1981). Beliefs about race, gender, and social class different, therefore unequal: Beliefs about trait differences between groups of unequal status. In D. J. Treiman & R. V. Robinson (Eds.), *Research in stratification and mobility* (Vol. 2). Greenwich, CT: JAI Press. (p. 423)

Jackson, J. M., & Latané, B. (1981). All alone in front of all those people: Stage fright as a function of number and type of co-performers and audience. *Journal of Personality and Social Psychology*, 40, 73-85. (p. 220)

Jackson, L. A., Hunter, J. E., & Hodge, C. N. (1995). Physical attractiveness and intellectual competence: A meta-analytic review. *Social Psychology Quarterly*, in press. (p. 381)

Jackson, L. A., Sullivan, L. A., & Hodge, C. N. (1993). Stereotype effects on attributions, predictions, and evaluations: No two social judgments are quite alike. *Journal of Personality and Social Psychology*, 65, 69-84. (p. 449)

Jacobs, R. C., & Campbell, D. T. (1961). The perpetuation of an arbitrary tradition through several generations of a laboratory microculture. *Journal of Abnormal and Social Psychology*, 62, 649-658. (p. 184)

Jacoby, S. (1986, December). When opposites attract. *Reader's Digest*, pp. 95-98. (p. 390)

Jain, U. (1990). Social perspectives on causal attribution. In G. Misra (Ed.), *Applied social psychology in India*. New Delhi: Sage. (p. 69)

James, W. (1890, reprinted 1950). *The principles of psychology*, vol. 2. New York: Dover Publications. (p. 134)

James, W. (1902, reprinted 1958). *The varieties of religious experience*. New York: Mentor Books. (p. 429)

Jamieson, D. W., Lydon, J. E., Stewart, G., & Zanna, M. P. (1987). Pygmalion revisited: New evidence for student expectancy effects in the classroom. *Journal of Educational Psychology*, 79, 461-466. (p. 105)

Janis, I. (1989). *Crucial decisions: Leadership in policymaking and crisis management*. New York: Free Press. (p. 475)

Janis, I. L. (1971, November). Groupthink. *Psychology Today*, pp. 43-46. (p. 240)

Janis, I. L. (1982). Counteracting the adverse effects of concurrence-seeking in policy-planning groups: Theory and research perspectives. In H. Brandstatter, J. H. Davis, & G. Stocker-Kreichgauer (Eds.), *Group decision making*. New York: Academic Press. (p. 240)

Janis, I. L., Kaye, D., & Kirschner, P. (1965). Facilitating effects of eating while reading on responsiveness to persuasive communications. *Journal of Personality and Social Psychology*, 1, 181-186. (p. 153)

Jankowiak, W. R., & Fischer, E. F. (1992). A cross-cultural perspective on romantic love. *Ethnology*, 31, 149-155. (p. 400)

Jelalian, E., & Miller, A. G. (1984). The perseverance of beliefs: Conceptual perspectives and research developments. *Journal of Social and Clinical Psychology*, 2, 25-56. (p. 77)

Jellison, J. M., & Green, J. (1981). A self-presentation approach to the fundamental attribution error: The norm of internality. *Journal of Personality and Social Psychology*, 40, 643-649. (p. 272)

Jemmott, J. B., III., & Locke, S. E. (1984). Psychosocial factors, immunologic mediation, and human susceptibility to infectious diseases: How much do we know? *Psychological Bulletin*, 95, 78-108. (p. 501)

Jennings, D. L., Amabile, T. M., & Ross, L. (1982). Informal covariation assessment: Data-based vs theory-based judgments. In D. Kahneman, P. Slovic, & A. Tversky (Eds.), *Judgment under uncertainty: Heuristics and biases*. New York: Cambridge University Press. (p. 88)

Jetten, J., Hornsey, M. J., & Adarves-Yorno, I. (2006). When group members admit to being conformist: The role of relative intragroup status in conformity self-reports. *Personality and Social Psychology Bulletin*, **32**, 162. (p. 203)

Ji, L., Nisbett, R. E., & Su, Y. (2001). Culture, change, and prediction. *Psychological Science*, 12, 450-456. (p. 273)

Jobs, S. (2005). *You've got to find what you love*. Address given at the Stanford University commencement exercises. (p. 37)

John, O. P., & Srivastava, S. (1999). The Big Five trait taxonomy: History, measurement, and theoretical perspectives. In L. A. Pervin & O. P. John (Eds.), *Handbook of personality: Theory and research*. New York: Guilford. (p. 262)

Johnson, B. T., & Eagly, A. H. (1990). Involvement and persuasion: Types, traditions, and the evidence. *Psychological Bulletin*, 107, 375-384. (p. 167)

Johnson, C. B., Stockdale, M. S., & Saal, F. E. (1991). Persistence of men's misperceptions of friendly cues across a variety of interpersonal encounters. *Psychology of Women Quarterly*, 15, 463-475. (p. 93)

Johnson, D. J., & Rusbult, C. E. (1989). Resisting temptation: Devaluation of alternative partners as a means of maintaining commitment in close relationships. *Journal of Personality and Social Psychology*, 57, 967-980. (p. 387)

Johnson, D. W., & Johnson, R. T. (1995). Teaching students to be peacemakers: Results of five years of research. Peace and Conflict: *Journal of Peace Psychology*, 1, 417-438. (p. 479)

Johnson, E. J., & Tversky, A. (1983). Affect, generalization, and the perception of risk. *Journal of Personality and Social Psychology*, 45, 20-31. (p. 90)

Johnson, J. D., Jackson, L. A., & Gatto, L. (1995). Violent attitudes and deferred academic aspirations: Deleterious effects of exposure to rap music. *Basic and Applied Social Psychology*, 16, 27-41. (p. 359)

Johnson, J. G., Cohen, P., Smailes, E. M., Kasen, S. & Brook, J. S. (2002). Television viewing and aggressive behavior during adolescence and adulthood. *Science,* **295**, 2468-2471. (p. 357)

Johnson, J. T., Jemmott, J. B., III, & Pettigrew, T. F. (1984). Causal attribution and dispositional inference: Evidence of inconsistent judgments. *Journal of Experimental Social Psychology*, 20, 567-585. (p. 100)

Johnson, J., & Newport, E. L. (1991). Critical period effects on universal properties of language: The status of subjacency in the acquisition of a second language. *Cognition*, 39, 215-258. (p. 289)

Johnson, J., Shenkman, K. D., Newport, E. L., & Medin, D. L. (1996). Indeterminacy in the grammar of adult language learners. *Journal of Memory and Language*, 35, 335-352. (p. 289)

Johnson, M. H., & Magaro, P. A. (1987). Effects of mood and severity on memory processes in depression and mania. *Psychological Bulletin*, 101, 28-40. (p. 91)

Johnson, R. D., & Downing, L. J. (1979). Deindividuation and valence of cues: Effects of prosocial and antisocial behavior. *Journal of Personality and Social Psychology*, 37, 1532-1538. (p. 230)

Johnson, R. W., Kelly, R. J., & LeBlanc, B. A. (1995). Motivational basis of dissonance: Aversive consequences or inconsistency. *Personality and Social Psychology Bulletin*, 21, 850-855. (p. 139)

Johnson, W., & Krueger, R. F. (2006). How money buys happiness: Genetic and environmental processes linking finances and life satisfaction. *Journal of Personality and Social Psychology,* **90**, 680. (p. 534)

Johnston, L., O'Malley, P. M., & Bachman, J. G. (1996). *National survey results on drug use from the Monitoring the Future study, 1975-1995*. Rockville, Md.: National Institute on Drug Abuse, U.S. Dept. of Health and Human Services, Public Health Service, National Institutes of Health, Washington, D.C. (p. 355)

Joiner, T. E., Jr. (1994). Contagious depression: Existence, specificity to depressed symptoms, and the role of reassurance seeking. *Journal of Personality and Social Psychology*, 67, 287-296. (p. 491)

Joiner, T. E., Jr. (1999). The clustering and contagion of suicide. *Current Directions in Psychological Science*, 8, 89-92. (p. 186)

Jonas, K. (1992). Modelling and suicide: A test of the Werther effect. *British Journal of Social Psychology*, 31, 295-306. (p. 186)

Jones, E. E. (1964). *Ingratiation*. New York: Appleton-Century-Crofts. (p. 392)

Jones, E. E. (1976). How do people perceive the causes of behavior? *American Scientist*, 64, 300-305. (p. 98)

Jones, E. E., & Davis, K. E. (1965). From acts to dispositions: The attribution process in person perception. In L. Berkowitz (Ed.), *Advances in experimental social psychology* (Vol. 2). New York: Academic Press. (p. 94)

Jones, E. E., & Harris, V. A. (1967). The attribution of attitudes. *Journal of Experimental Social Psychology*, 3, 2-24. (p. 95)

Jones, E. E., & Nisbett, R. E. (1971). *The actor and the observer: Divergent perceptions of the cases of behavior*. Morristown, N.J.: General Learning Press. (p. 98)

Jones, E. E., Rock, L., Shaver, K. G., Goethals, G. R., & Ward, L. M. (1968). Pattern of performance and ability attribution: An unexpected primacy effect. *Journal of Personality and Social Psychology*, 10, 317-340. (p. 159)

Jones, J. M. (1983). The concept of race in social psychology: From color to culture. In L. Wheeler & P. Shaver (Eds.), *Review of personality and social psychology*, Vol. 4. Beverly Hills, Ca.: Sage. (p. 452)

Jones, J. M. (1988). *Piercing the veil: Bicultural strategies for coping with prejudice and racism*. Invited address at the national conference, "Opening Doors: An Appraisal of Race Relations in America," University of Alabama, June 11. (p. 389)

Jones, J. T., & Cunningham, J. D. (1996). Attachment styles and other predictors of relationship satisfaction in dating couples. *Personal Relationships*, 3, 387-399. (p. 404)

Jones, J. T., Pelham, B. W., & Mirenberg, M. C. (2002). Name letter preferences are not merely mere exposure: Implicit egotism as self-regulation. *Journal of Experimental Social Psychology*, 38, 170-177. (p. 378)

Jones, J. T., Pelham, B. W., Carvallo, M., & Mirenberg, M. C. (2004). How do I love thee? let me count the Js: Implicit egotism and interpersonal attraction. *Journal of Personality and Social Psychology,* **87**, 665. (p. 378)

Jones, R. A., & Brehm, J. W. (1970). Persuasiveness of one- and two-sided communications as a function of awareness there are two sides. *Journal of Experimental Social Psychology*, 6, 47-56. (p. 158)

Jones, W. H., Carpenter, B. N., & Quintana, D. (1985). Personality and interpersonal predictors of loneliness in two cultures. *Journal of Personality and Social Psychology*, 48, 1503-1511. (p. 31)

Jordan, C. H., Spencer, S. J., & Zanna, M. P. (2005). Types of high self-esteem and prejudice: How implicit self-esteem relates to ethnic discrimination among high explicit self-esteem individuals. *Personality & Social Psychology Bulletin*, 31(5), 693-702. (p. 48)

Jordan, C. H., Spencer, S. J., Zanna, M. P., Hoshino-Browne, E., & Correll, J. (2003). Secure and defensive high self-esteem. *Journal of Personality and Social Psychology*, 85, 969-978. (p. 48)

Josephson, W. L. (1987). Television violence and children's aggression: Testing the priming, social script, and disinhibition predictions. *Journal of Personality and Social Psychology*, 53, 882-890. (p. 359)

Jost, J. T., & Kay, A. C. (2005). Exposure to benevolent sexism and complementary gender stereotypes: Consequences for specific and diffuse forms of system justification. *Journal of Personality and Social Psychology*, ***88***, 498. (p. 424)

Jourard, S. M. (1964), *The transparent self.* Princeton, N.J.: Van Nostrand. (p. 408)

Jourden, F. J., & Heath, C. (1996). The evaluation gap in performance perceptions: Illusory perceptions of groups and individuals. *Journal of Applied Psychology*, 81, 369-379. (p. 65)

Judd, C. M., Blair, I. V., & Chapleau, K. M. (2004). Automatic stereotypes vs. automatic prejudice: Sorting out the possibilities in the Payne (2001) weapon paradigm. *Journal of Experimental Social Psychology*, 40, 75-81. (p. 420)

Judd, C. M., Park, B., Ryan, C. S., Brauer, M., & Kraus, S. (1995). Stereotypes and ethnocentrism: Diverging interethnic perceptions of African American and White American youth. *Journal of Personality and Social Psychology*, 69, 460-481. (p. 452)

Judd, C. M., Ryan, C. S., & Park, B. (1991). Accuracy in the judgment of in-group and out-group variability. *Journal of Personality and Social Psychology*, 61, 366-379. (p. 443)

Jussim, L. (1986). Self-fulfilling prophecies: A theoretical and integrative review. *Psychological Review*, 93, 429-445. (p. 104)

Jussim, L. (2005). Accuracy in social perception: Criticisms, controversies, criteria, components, and cognitive processes. In M. P. Zanna (Ed.), *Advances in experimental social psychology, vol. 37.* (pp. 1-93). San Diego, CA, US: Elsevier Academic Press. (p. 12)

Jussim, L., McCauley, C. R., & Lee, Y-T. (1995). Introduction: Why study stereotype accuracy and inaccuracy? In Y. T. Lee, L. Jussim, & C. R. McCauley (eds.), *Stereotypes accuracy: Toward appreciating group differences.* Washington, DC: American Psychological Association. (p. 417)

Kagan, J. (1989). Temperamental contributions to social behavior. *American Psychologist*, 44, 668-674. (p. 336)

Kagehiro, D. K. (1990). Defining the standard of proof in jury instructions. *Psychological Science*, 1, 194-200. (p. 522)

Kahan, T. L., & Johnson, M. K. (1992). Self effects in memory for person information. *Social Cognition*, 10, 30-50. (p. 50)

Kahle, L. R., & Berman, J. (1979). Attitudes cause behaviors: A cross-lagged panel analysis. *Journal of Personality and Social Psychology*, 37, 315-321. (p. 115)

Kahn, M. W. (1951). The effect of severe defeat at various age levels on the aggressive behavior of mice. *Journal of Genetic Psychology*, 79, 117-130. (p. 342)

Kahneman, D., & Miller, D. T. (1986). Norm theory: Comparing reality to its alternatives. *Psychological Review*, 93, 75-88. (p. 87)

Kahneman, D., & Snell, J. (1992). Predicting a changing taste: Do people know what they will like? *Journal of Behavioral Decision Making*, 5, 187-200. (p. 377)

Kahneman, D., & Tversky, A. (1979). Intuitive prediction: Biases and corrective procedures. *Management Science*, 12, 313-327. (p. 81)

Kahneman, D., & Tversky, A. (1995). Conflict resolution: A cognitive perspective. In K. Arrow, R. Mnookin, L. Ross, A. Tversky, & R. Wilson (eds.), *Barriers to the negotiated resolution of conflict.* New York: Norton. (p. 481)

Kalick, S. M. (1977). Plastic surgery, physical appearance, and person perception. Unpublished doctoral dissertation, Harvard University. Cited by E. Berscheid in, *An overview of the psychological effects of physical attractiveness and some comments upon the psychological effects of knowledge of the effects of physical attractiveness.* In W. Lucker, K. Ribbens, & J. A. McNamera (Eds.), Logical aspects of facial form (craniofacial growth series). Ann Arbor: University of Michigan Press, 1981. (p. 382)

Kalin R., & Berry, J. W., (1982). The social ecology of ethnic attitudes in Canada. Canadian *Journal of Behavioural Science*, 14, 97-109. (p. 282)

Kalin, R., & Berry, J. W. (1995). Ethnic and civic self-identity in Canada: Analyses of 1974 and 1991 national surveys. *Canadian Ethnic Studies*, 27, 1-15. (p. 49)

Kalven, H., Jr., & Zeisel, H. (1966). *The American jury*. Chicago: University of Chicago Press. (p. 523)

Kameda, T., & Sugimori, S. (1993). Psychological entrapment in group decision making: An assigned decision rule and a groupthink phenomenon. *Journal of Personality and Social Psychology*, 65, 282-292. (p. 251)

Kammer, D. (1982). Differences in trait ascriptions to self and friend: Unconfounding intensity from variability. *Psychological Reports*, 51, 99-102. (p. 100)

Kanagawa, C., Cross, S. E., & Markus, H. R. (2001). "Who am I?" The cultural psychology of the conceptual self. *Personality and Social Psychology Bulletin*, 27, 90-103. (p. 267)

Kandel, D. B. (1978). Similarity in real-life adolescent friendship pairs. *Journal of Personality and Social Psychology*, 36, 306-312. (p. 390)

Kanekar, S., & Nazareth, A. (1988). Attributed rape victim's fault as a function of her attractiveness, physical hurt, and emotional disturbance. *Social Behaviour*, 3, 37-40. (p. 93)

Kaplan, M. F. (1989). Task, situational, and personal determinants of influence processes in group decision making. In E. J. Lawler (Ed.), *Advances in group processes* (vol. 6). Greenwich, CT: JAI Press. (p. 238)

Kaplan, M. F., Wanshula, L. T., & Zanna, M. P. (1993). Time pressure and information integration in social judgment: The effect of need for structure. In O. Svenson & J. Maule (Eds.), *Time pressure and stress in human judgment and decision making.* Cambridge: Cambridge University Press. (p. 442)

Kaprio, J., Koskenvuo, M., & Rita, H. (1987). Mortality after bereavement: A propsective study of 95,647 widowed persons. *American Journal of Public Health*, 77, 283-287. (p. 504)

Karau, S. J., & Williams, K. D. (1993). Social loafing: A meta-analytic review and theoretical integration. *Journal of Personality and Social Psychology*, 65, 681-706. (p. 224)

Karau, S. J., & Williams, K. D. (1997). The effects of group cohesiveness on social loafing and social compensation. *Group Dynamics: Theory, Research, and Practice*, ***1***, 156-168. (p. 226)

Karavellas, D. (2000). Sustainable consumption and fisheries. In B. Heap and J. Kent (Eds.), *Towards sustainable consumption: A European perspective*. London: The Royal Society. (p. 529)

Karney, B. R., & Bradbury, T. N. (1995). The longitudinal course of marital quality and stability: A review of theory, method, and research. *Psychological Bulletin*, 118, 3-34. (p. 412)

Kashima, E. S., & Kashima, Y. (1998). Culture and language: the case of cultural dimensions and personal pronoun use. *Journal of Cross-Cultural Psychology*, 29, 461-486. (p. 267)

Kashima, Y., & Kashima, E. S. (2003). Individualism, GNP, climate, and pronoun drop: Is individualism determined by affluence and climate, or does language use play a role? *Journal of Cross-Cultural Psychology*, 34, 125-134. (p. 267)

Kasser, T. (2000). Two versions of the American dream: Which goals and values make for a high quality of life? In E. Diener and D. Rahtz (Eds.), *Advances in quality of life: Theory and research*. Dordrecth, Netherlands: Kluwer. (p. 535)

Kasser, T., & Ahuvia, A. (2002). Materialistic values and well-being in business students. *European Journal of Social Psychology, **32***, 137. (p. 535)

Kasser, T., & Sheldon, K. M. (2000). Of wealth and death: Materialism, mortality salience, and consumption behavior. *Psychological Science, **11***, 348.

Kassin, S. M., Goldstein, C. C., & Savitsky, K. (2003). Behavioral confirmation in the interrogation room: On the dangers of presuming guilt. *Law and Human Behavior, 27*(2), 187. (p. 105)

Kato, P. S., & Ruble, D. N. (1992). Toward an understanding of women's experi-ence of menstrual cycle symptoms. In V. Adesso, D. Reddy, & R. Fleming (Eds.), *Psychological perspectives on women's health*. Washington, DC: Hemisphere. (p. 498)

Katz, A. M., & Hill, R. (1958). Residential propinquity and marital selection: A review of theory, method, and fact. *Marriage and Family Living*, 20, 237-335. (p. 375)

Katz, E. (1957). The two-step flow of communication: An up-to-date report on a hypothesis. *Public Opinion Quarterly*, 21, 61-78. (p. 163)

Katz, J., Beach, S. R. H., & Joiner, T. E., Jr. (1999). Contagious depression in dating couples. *Journal of Social and Clinical Psychology*, 18, 1-13. (p. 491)

Katzev, R., & Wang, T. (1994). Can commitment change behavior? A case study of environmental actions. *Journal of Social Behavior and Personality*, 9, 13-26. (p. 205)

Katzev, R., Edelsack, L., Steinmetz, G., & Walker, T. (1978). The effect of reprimanding transgressions on subsequent helping behavior: Two field experiments. *Personality and Social Psychology Bulletin*, 4, 126-129. (p. 324)

Kaufman, J., & Zigler, E. (1987). Do abused children become abusive parents? *American Journal of Orthopsychiatry*, 57, 186-192. (p. 343)

Kaufmann, H., & Kooman, A. (1967). Predicted compliance in obedience situations as a function of implied instructional variables. *Psychonomic Science*, 7, 205-206. (p. 189)

Kawakami, K., & Dion, K. L. (1993). The impact of salient self-identities on relative deprivation and action intentions. *European Journal of Social Psychology*, 23, 525-540. (p. 341)

Kawakami, K., Dovidio, J. F., Moll, J., Hermsen, S., & Russin, A. (2000). Just say no (to stereotyping): Effects of training in the negation of stereotypic associations on stereotype activation. *Journal of Personality and Social Psychology*, 78, 871-888. (p. 419)

Kay, A. C., Jost, J. T., & Young, S. (2005). Victim derogation and victim enhancement as alternate routes to system justification. *Psychological Science, **16***, 240. (p. 427)

Kay, A. C., Jost, J. T., Mandisodza, A. N., Sherman, S. J., Petrocelli, J. V., & Johnson, A. L. (2007). Panglossian ideology in the service of system justification: How complementary stereotypes help us to rationalize inequality. In M. P. Zanna (Ed.), *2005 Society of Experimental Social Psychology Conference, 2005*, San Diego, CA, US (pp. 305-358). San Diego, CA, US: Elsevier Academic Press. (p. 427)

Keating, J. P., & Brock, T. C. (1974). Acceptance of persuasion and the inhibition of counterargumentation under various distraction tasks. *Journal of Experimental Social Psychology*, 10, 301-309. (p. 166)

Keelan, J. P., Dion, K. K., & Dion, K. L. (1998). Attachment style and relationship satisfaction: Test of a self-disclosure explanation. *Canadian Journal of Behavioural Science*, 30, 24-35. (p. 404)

Keller, E., & Berry, J. L. (2003). *The influentials*. NewYork: Simon & Schuster. (p. 163)

Kellerman, J., Lewis, J., & Laird, J. D. (1989). Looking and loving: The effects of mutual gaze on feelings of romantic love. *Journal of Research in Personality*, 23, 145-161. (p. 413)

Kellermann, A. L. & 9 others (1993). Gun ownership as a risk factor for homicide in the home. *New England Journal of Medicine*, 329, 1984-1991. (p. 350)

Kellermann, A. L. (1997). Comment: Gunsmoke-changing public attitudes toward smoking and firearms. *American Journal of Public Health*, 87, 910-912. (p. 350)

Kelley, H. H. (1973). The process of causal attribution. *American Psychologist*, 28, 107-128. (p. 94)

Kelley, H. H., & Stahelski, A. J. (1970). The social interaction basis of cooperators' and competitors' beliefs about others. *Journal of Personality and Social Psychology*, 16, 66-91. (p. 105)

Kelley, K., Dawson, L., & Musialowski, D. M. (1989). Three faces of sexual explicitness: The good, the bad, and the useful. In D. Zillmann & J. Bryant (Eds.), *Pornography: Research advances and policy considerations*. Hillsdale, NJ: Erlbaum. (p. 367)

Kelman, H. C. (1997). Group processes in the resolution of international conflicts: Experiences from the Israeli-Palestinian case. *American Psychologist*, 52, 212-220. (p. 480)

Kelman, H. C. (1998). *Building a sustainable peace: The limits of pragmatism in the Israeli-Palestinian negotiations*. Address to the American Psychological Association convention. (p. 479)

Kendler, K. S., Neale, M., Kessler, R., Heath, A., & Eaves, L. (1993). A twin study of recent life events and difficulties. *Archives of General Psychiatry*, 50, 789-796. (p. 492)

Kennedy, D. (2006). *State of the planet*. Washington, D.C.: The American Association for the Advancement of Science. (p. 528)

Kenny, D. A. (1994). *Interpersonal perception: A social relations analysis*. Storrs, CT: Guilford Press. (p. 41)

Kenny, D. A., & Acitelli, L. K. (2001). Accuracy and bias in the perception of the partner in a close relationship. *Journal of Personality and Social Psychology*, 80, 439-448. (p. 389)

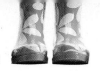

Kenny, D. A., & Nasby, W. (1980). Splitting the reciprocity correlation. *Journal of Personality and Social Psychology*, 38, 249-256. (p. 391)

Kenrick, D. T., & Gutierres, S. E. (1980). Contrast effects and judgments of physical attractiveness: When beauty becomes a social problem. *Journal of Personality and Social Psychology*, 38, 131-140. (p. 385)

Kenrick, D. T., & MacFarlane, S. W. (1986). Ambient temperature and horn-honking: A field study of the heat/ aggression relationship. *Environment and Behavior*, 18, 179-191. (p. 346)

Kenrick, D. T., & Trost, M. R. (1987). A biosocial theory of heterosexual relationships. In K. Kelly (Ed.), *Females, males, and sexuality*. Albany: State University of New York Press. (p. 402)

Kenrick, D. T., Gutierres, S. E., & Goldberg, L. L. (1989). Influence of popular erotica on judgments of strangers and mates. *Journal of Experimental Social Psychology*, 25, 159-167. (p. 385)

Kernis, M. H. (2003). High self-esteem: A differentiated perspective. In E. C. Chang & L. J. Sanna (Eds.), *Virtue, vice, and personality: The complexity of behavior*. Washington, DC: APA Books. (p. 49)

Kerr, N. L. (1981). Effects of prior juror experience on juror behavior. *Basic and Applied Social Psychology, **2***, 175. (p. 524)

Kerr, N. L. (1983). Motivation losses in small groups: A social dilemma analysis. *Journal of Personality and Social Psychology*, 45, 819-828. (p. 226)

Kerr, N. L. (1989). Illusions of efficacy: The effects of group size on perceived efficacy in social dilemmas. *Journal of Experimental Social Psychology*, 25, 287-313. (p. 471)

Kerr, N. L. (1992). Norms in social dilemmas. In D. Schroeder (Ed.), *Social dilemmas: Psychological perspectives*. New York: Praeger. (p. 471)

Kerr, N. L., & Bruun, S. E. (1981). Ringelmann revisted: Alternative explanations for the social loafing effect. *Personality and Social Psychology Bulletin*, 7, 224-231. (p. 224)

Kerr, N. L., & Bruun, S. E. (1983). Dispensibility of member effort and group motivation losses: Free-rider effects. *Journal of Personality and Social Psychology*, 44, 78-94. (p. 226)

Kerr, N. L., & Kaufman-Gilliland, C. M. (1997). ". . and besides, I probably couldn't have made a difference anyway": Justification of social dilemma defection via perceived self-inefficacy. *Journal of Experimental Social Psychology*, 33, 211-230. (p. 471)

Kerr, N. L., & MacCoun, R. J. (1985). The effects of jury size and polling method on the process and product of jury deliberation. *Journal of Personality and Social Psychology*, 48, 349-363. (p. 205)

Kerr, N. L., Atkin, R. S., Stasser, G., Meek, D., Holt, R. W., & Davis, J. H. (1976). Guilt beyond a reasonable doubt: Effects of concept definition and assigned decision rule on the judgments of mock jurors. *Journal of Personality and Social Psychology*, 34, 282-294. (p. 524)

Kidd, J. B., & Morgan, J. R. (1969). A predictive information system for management. *Operational Research Quarterly*, 20, 149-170. (p. 65)

Kiecolt-Glaser, J. K., Malarkey, W. B., Chee, M., Newton, T., Cacioppo, J. T., Mao, H-Y., & Glaser, R. (1993). Negative behavior during marital conflict is associated with immunological down-regulation. *Psychosomatic Medicine*, 55, 395-409. (p. 501)

Kiesler, C. A. (1971). *The psychology of commitment: Experiments linking behavior to belief*. New York: Academic Press. (p. 175)

Kihlstrom, J. F., & Cantor, N. (1984). Mental representations of the self. In L. Berkowitz (Ed.), *Advances in experimental social psychology*, vol. 17. New York: Academic Press. (p. 50)

Kim, H., & Markus, H. R. (1999). Deviance of uniqueness, harmony or conformity? A cultural analysis. *Journal of Personality and Social Psychology*, 77, 785-800. (p. 268)

Kimball, M. M. (1989). A new perspective on women's math achievement. *Psychological Bulletin*, 105, 198-214. (p. 418)

Kimmel, M. J., Pruitt, D. G., Magenau, J. M., Konar-Goldband, E., & Carnevale, P. J. D. (1980). Effects of trust, aspiration, and gender on negotiation tactics. *Journal of Personality and Social Psychology*, 38, 9-22. (p. 477)

Kinder, D. R., & Sears, D. O. (1985). Public opinion and political action. In G. Lindzey & E. Aronson (Eds.), *The handbook of social psychology*, 3rd ed. New York: Random House. (p. 75)

King, L. A. (2001). The health benefits of writing about life goals. *Personality and Social Psychology Bulletin*, 27, 798-807. (p. 504)

Kingdon, J. W. (1967). Politicans' beliefs about voters. *The American Political Science Review*, 61, 137-145. (p. 55)

Kinnier, R. T., & Metha, A. T. (1989). Regrets and priorities at three stages of life. *Counseling and Values*, 33, 182-193. (p. 88)

Kitayama, S. (1999). Behind the scenes. In D. G. Myers, *Social psychology*, 6th edition. New York: McGraw-Hill. (p. 169)

Kitayama, S., & Karasawa, M. (1997). Implicit self-esteem in Japan: Name letters and birthday numbers. *Personality and Social Psychology Bulletin*, 23, 736-742. (p. 377)

Kitayama, S., & Markus, H. R. (1995). Culture and self: Implications for internationalizing psychology. In N. R. Godlberger & J. B. Veroff (eds.), *The culture and psychology reader*. New York: New York University Press. (p. 267)

Kitayama, S., & Markus, H. R. (2000). The pursuit of happiness and the realization of sympathy: Cultural patterns of self, social relations, and well-being. In E. Diener & E. M. Suh (Eds.), *Subjective well-being across cultures*. Cambridge, Mass.: MIT Press. (p. 269)

Kitayama, S., Ishii, K., Imada, T., Takemura, K., & Ramaswamy, J. (2006). Voluntary settlement and the spirit of independence: Evidence from Japan's "northern frontier." *Journal of Personality and Social Psychology, **91***, 369. (p. 280)

Kite, M. E. (2001). Changing times, changing gender roles: Who do we want women and men to be? In R. K. Unger (Ed.), *Handbook of the psychology of women and gender*. New York: Wiley. (p. 422)

Klaas, E. T. (1978). Psychological effects of immoral actions: The experimental evidence. *Psychological Bulletin*, 85, 756-771. (p. 121)

Kleck, R. E., & Strenta, A. (1980). Perceptions of the impact of negatively valued physical characteristics on social interaction. *Journal of Personality and Social Psychology*, 39, 861-873. (p. 445)

Klein, J. G. (1991). Negative effects in impression formation: A test in the political arena. *Personality and Social Psychology Bulletin*, 17, 412-418. (p. 391)

Klein, S. B., Cosmides, L., Murray, E. R., & Tooby, J. (2004). On the acquisition of knowledge about personality traits: Does learning about the self engage different mechanisms than learning about others. *Social Cognition, **22**,* 367. (p. 69)

Klein, W. M., & Kunda, Z. (1992). Motivated person perception: Constructing justifications for desired beliefs. *Journal of Experimental Social Psychology*, 28, 145-168. (p. 376)

Kleinke, C. L. (1977). Compliance to requests made by gazing and touching experimenters in field settings. *Journal of Experimental Social Psychology*, 13, 218-223. (p. 192)

Kleinsmith, J., Kasser, T., & McAndrew, F. T. (2006). Guns, testosterone, and aggression: An experimental test of a mediational hypothesis. *Psychological Science, **17***, 568. (p. 337)

Klentz, B., Beaman, A. L., Mapelli, S. D., & Ullrich, J. R. (1987). Perceived physical attractiveness of supporters and nonsupporters of the women's movement: An attitude-similarity-mediated error (AS-ME). *Personality and Social Psychology Bulletin*, 13, 513-523. (p. 386)

Klerman, G. L., & Weissman, M. M. (1989). Increasing rates of depression. *Journal of the American Medical Association*, 261, 2229-2235. (p. 534)

Klineberg, O. (1938). Emotional expression in Chinese literature. *Journal of Abnormal and Social Psychology*, 33, 517-520. (p. 275)

Klopfer, P. H. (1958). Influence of social interaction on learning rates in birds. *Science*, 128, 903. (p. 218)

Knight, G. P., Johnson, L. G., Carlo, G., & Eisenberg, N. (1994). A multiplicative model of the dispositional antecedents of a prosocial behavior: Predicting more of the people more of the time. *Journal of Personality and Social Psychology*, 66, 178-183. (p. 309)

Knight, J. A., & Vallacher, R. R. (1981). Interpersonal engagement in social perception: The consequences of getting into the action. *Journal of Personality and Social Psychology*, 40, 990-999. (p. 376)

Knight, P. A., & Weiss, H. M. (1980). *Benefits of suffering: Communicator suffering, benefiting, and influence.* Paper presented at the American Psychological Association convention. (p. 150)

Knowles, E. S. (1983). Social physics and the effects of others: Tests of the effects of audience size and distance on social judgment and behavior. *Journal of Personality and Social Psychology*, 45, 1263-1279. (p. 220)

Knox, R. E., & Inkster, J. A. (1968). Postdecision dissonance at post-time. *Journal of Personality and Social Psychology*, 8, 319-323. (p. 132)

Knudson, R. M., Sommers, A. A., & Golding, S. L. (1980). Interpersonal perception and mode of resolution in marital conflict. *Journal of Personality and Social Psychology*, 38, 751-763. (p. 478)

Koehler, D. J. (1991). Explanation, imagination, and confidence in judgment. *Psychological Bulletin*, 110, 499-519. (p. 85)

Koehler, D. J., & Poon, C. S. K. (2006). Self-predictions overweight strength of current intentions. *Journal of Experimental Social Psychology, 42*(4), 517. (p. 83)

Koestner, R. F. (1993). *False consensus effects for the 1992 Canadian referendum.* Paper presented at the American Psychological Association. (p. 60)

Koestner, R., & Wheeler, L. (1988). Self-presentation in personal advertisements: The influence of implicit notions of attraction and role expectations. *Journal of Social and Personal Relationships*, 5, 149-160. (p. 381)

Koezuka, N., Koo, M., Allison, K. R., Adlaf, E. M., Dwyer, J. J. M., Faulkner, G., et al. (2006). The relationship between sedentary activities and physical inactivity among adolescents: Results from the Canadian community health survey. *Journal of Adolescent Health,* **39**, 515. (p. 360)

Koole, S. L., Dijksterhuis, A., & van Knippenberg, A. (2001). What's in a name? Implicit self-esteem and the automatic self. *Journal of Personality and Social Psychology*, 80, 669-685. (p. 378)

Koomen, W., & Bahler, M. (1996). National stereotypes: Common representations and ingroup favouritism. *European Journal of Social Psychology*, 26, 325-331. (p. 417)

Koomen, W., & Dijker, A. J. (1997). Ingroup and outgroup stereotypes and selective processing. *European Journal of Social Psychology*, 27, 589-601. (p. 261)

Koop, C. E. (1987). Report of the Surgeon General's workshop on pornography and public health. *American Psychologist*, 42, 944-945. (p. 353)

Koop, C. E. (1997, June 22). Quoted by J. Fisher and J. Schwartz, Trying to snuff out the tobacco culture. *Washington Post*, pp. A1, A3. (p. 112)

Koriat, A., Lichtenstein, S., & Fischhoff, B. (1980). Reasons for confidence. *Journal of Experimental Social Psychology: Human Learning and Memory*, 6, 107-118. (p. 85)

Korn, J. H., & Nicks, S. D. (1993). *The rise and decline of deception in social psychology.* Poster (Paper?) presented at the American Psychological Society convention. (p. 29)

Krackow, A., & Blass, T. (1995). When nurses obey or defy inappropriate physician orders: Attributional differences. *Journal of Social Behavior and Personality*, 10, 585-594. (p. 193)

Kraus, S. J. (1995). Attitudes and the prediction of behavior: A meta-analysis of the empirical literature. *Personality and Social Psychology Bulletin*, 21, 58-75. (p. 114)

Kraut, R. E. (1973). Effects of social labeling on giving to charity. *Journal of Experimental Social Psychology*, 9, 551-562. (p. 325)

Kraut, R. E., & Poe, D. (1980). Behavioral roots of person perception: The deception judgments of customs inspectors and laymen. *Journal of Personality and Social Psychology*, 39, 784-798. (p. 442)

Kravitz, D. A., & Martin, B. (1986). Ringelmann rediscovered: The original article. *Journal of Personality and Social Psychology*, 50, 936-941. (p. 223)

Krebs, D. (1970). Altruism-An examination of the concept and a review of the literature. *Psychological Bulletin*, 73, 258-302. (p. 297)

Krebs, D. (1975). Empathy and altruism. *Journal of Personality and Social Psychology*, 32, 1134-1146. (p. 299)

Krebs, D. L. (1998). The evolution of moral behaviors. In C. Crawford & D. L. Krebs (Eds.), *Handbook of evolutionary psychology: Ideas, issues, and applications.* Mahwah, N.J.: Erlbaum. (p. 306)

Krisberg, K. (2004). Successful 'truth' anti-smoking campaign in funding jeopardy: New commission works to save campaign. *Nation's Health, **34**,* (4). (p. 152)

Kroger, R. O., & Wood, L. A. (1992). Are the rules of address universal? IV: Comparison of Chinese, Korean, Greek, and German usage. *Journal of Cross-Cultural Psychology*, 23, 148-162. (p. 262)

Krosnick, J. A., & Alwin, D. F. (1989). Aging and susceptibility to attitude change.

Journal of Personality and Social Psychology, 57, 416-425. (p. 165)
Krosnick, J. A., & Schuman, H. (1988). Attitude intensity, importance, and certainty and susceptibility to response effects. *Journal of Personality and Social Psychology*, 54, 940-952. (p. 25)
Krueger, A. B., & Maleckova, J. (2003), Education, poverty and terrorism: Is there a causal connection? *Journal of Economic Perspectives*, ***17***, 119-144. (p. 340)
Krueger, J. (1996). Personal beliefs and cultural stereotypes about racial characteristics. *Journal of Personality and Social Psychology*, 71, 536-548. (p. 61)
Krueger, J. I., & Funder, D. C. (2003a). Towards a balanced social psychology: Causes, consequences and cures for the problem-seeking approach to social behavior and cognition. *Behavior and Brain Sciences,* **27**, 313-349. (p. 108)
Krueger, J. I., & Funder, D. C. (2003b). Social psychology: A field in search of a center—Response. *Behavior and Brain Sciences,* **27**, 361-376. (p. 108)
Krueger, J., & Clement, R. W. (1994). Memory-based judgments about multiple categories: A revision and extension of Tajfel's accentuation theory. *Journal of Personality and Social Psychology*, 67, 35-47. (p. 442)
Krueger, J., & Clement, R. W. (1997). Estimates of social consensus by majorities and minorities: The case for social projection. *Personality and Social Psychology Review*, 1, 299-313. (p. 60)
Kruger, J., & Dunning, D. (1999). Unskilled and unaware of it: How difficulties in recognizing one's own incompetence lead to inflated self-assessments. *Journal of Personality and Social Psychology*, 77, 1121-1134. (p. 82)
Kruger, J., & Evans, M. (2004). If you don't want to be late, enumerate: Unpacking reduces the planning fallacy. *Journal of Experimental Social Psychology, 40*(5), 586. (p. 85)
Kruger, J., & Gilovich, T. (1999). "Naive cynicism" in everyday theories of responsibility assessment: On biased assumptions of bias. *Journal of Personality and Social Psychology*, 76, 743-753. (p. 55)
Kruger, J., Epley, N., Parker, J., & Ng, Z. (2005). Egocentrism over e-mail: Can we communicate as well as we think? *Journal of Personality and Social Psychology, 89*(6), 925. (p. 88)
Kruglanski, A. W., & Ajzen, I. (1983). Bias and error in human judgment. *European Journal of Social Psychology*, 13, 1-44. (p. 108)
Kruglanski, A. W., & Fishman, S. (2006). Terrorism between "syndrome" and "tool." *Current Directions in Psychological Science,* ***15***, 45. (p. 333)
Kruglanski, A. W., & Fishman, S. (2006). The psychology of terrorism: "syndrome" versus "tool" perspectives. *Terrorism & Political Violence,* ***18***, 193-215.
Kruglanski, A. W., & Webster, D. M. (1991). Group members' reactions to opinion deviates and conformists at varying degrees of proximity to decision deadline and of environmental noise. *Journal of Personality and Social Psychology*, 61, 212-225. (p. 251)
Kruglanski, A. W., Webster, D. M., & Klem, A. (1993). Motivated resistance and openness to persuasion in the presence or absence of prior information. *Journal of Personality and Social Psychology*, 65, 861-876. (p. 168)
Krugman, P. (2003, February 18). Behind the great divide. *New York Times* (www.nytimes.com). (p. 144)
Kubany, E. S., Bauer, G. B., Pangilinan, M. E., Muroka, M. Y., & Enriquez, V. G. (1995). Impact of labeled anger and blame in intimate relationships. *Journal of Cross-Cultural Psychology*, 26, 65-83. (p. 368)
Kuiper, N. A., & Higgins, E. T. (1985). Social cognition and depression: A general integrative perspective. *Social Cognition*, 3, 1-15. (p. 491)
Kuiper, N. A., & Rogers, T. B. (1979). Encoding of personal information: Self-other differences. *Journal of Personality and Social Psychology*, 37, 499-514. (p. 50)
Kunda, Z. & Spencer, S. J. (2003). When do stereotypes come to mind and when do they color judgment? A goal-based theoretical framework for stereotype activation and application. *Psychological Bulletin*, 129, 522-544. (p. 441)
Kunda, Z. (1990). The case for motivated reasoning. *Psychological Bulletin*, 108, 480-498. (p. 55)
Kunda, Z., & Oleson, K. C. (1995). Maintaining stereotypes in the face of disconfirmation: Constructing grounds for subtyping deviants. *Journal of Personality and Social Psychology*, 68, 565-579. (p. 451)
Kunda, Z., & Oleson, K. C. (1997). When exceptions prove the rule: How extremity of deviance determines the impact of deviant examples on stereotypes. *Journal of Personality and Social Psychology*, 72, 965-979. (p. 451)
Kunda, Z., & Sherman-Williams, B. (1993). Stereotypes and the construal of individuating information. *Personality and Social Psychology Bulletin*, 19, 90-99. (p. 451)
Kunda, Z., & Sinclair, L. (1999). Motivated reasoning with stereotypes: Activation, application, and inhibition. *Psychological Inquiry*, 10, 12-22. (p. 458)
Kunda, Z., Fong, G. T., Sanitioso, R., & Reber, E. (1993). Directional questions direct self-conceptions. *Journal of Experimental Social Psychology*, 29, 63-86. (p. 488)
Kunst-Wilson, W. R., & Zajonc, R. B. (1980). Affective discrimination of stimuli that cannot be recognized. *Science*, 207, 557-558. (p. 377)

LaFromboise, T., Coleman, H. L. K., & Gerton, J. (1993). Psychological impact of biculturalism: Evidence and theory. *Psychological Bulletin*, 114, 395-412. (p. 287)
Lagerspetz, K. (1979). Modification of aggressiveness in mice. In S. Feshbach & A. Fraczek (Eds.), *Aggression and behavior change*. New York: Praeger. (p. 336)
Lagerspetz, K. M. J., Bjorkqvist, K., Berts, M., & King, E. (1982). Group aggression among school children in three schools. *Scandinavian Journal of Psychology*, 23, 45-52. (p. 364)
Laird, J. D. (1974). Self-attribution of emotion: The effects of expressive behavior on the quality of emotional experience. *Journal of Personality and Social Psychology*, 29, 475-486. (p. 134)
Laird, J. D. (1984). The real role of facial response in the experience of emotion: A reply to Tourangeau and Ellsworth, and others. *Journal of Personality and Social Psychology*, 47, 909-917. (p. 134)
Lakin, J. L., & Chartrand, T. L. (2003). Using nonconscious behavioral mimicry to create affiliation and rapport. *Psychological Science*, 14, 334-339. (p. 388)
Lalancette, M-F., & Standing, L. (1990). Asch fails again. *Social Behavior and Personality*, 18, 7-12. (p. 278)
Lalonde, R. N. (1992). The dynamics of group differentiation in the face of defeat.

Personality and Social Psychology Bulletin, 18, 336-342. (p. 55)
Lam, K. C. H., Buehler, R., McFarland, C., Ross, M., & Cheung, I. (2005). Cultural differences in affective forecasting: The role of focalism. *Personality and Social Psychology Bulletin, **31**,* 1296. (p. 43)
Lamal, P. A. (1979). College student common beliefs about psychology. *Teaching of Psychology*, 6, 155-158. (p. 78)
Lambert, W. E. (1992). Challenging established views on social issues: The power and limitations of research. *American Psychologist*, 47, 533-542. (p. 289)
Lambert, W. E., & Taylor, D. M. (1984). Language and the education of ethnic minority children in Canada. In R. J. Samuda, J. W. Berry, & M. Laferriere (Eds.), *Multiculturalism in Canada.* Toronto: Allyn & Bacon. (p. 289)
Lambert, W. E., & Tucker, G. R. (1972). *Bilingual education of children: The St. Lambert experiment.* Rowley, MA: Newbury House. (p. 289)
Landers, A. (1969, April 8). Syndicated newspaper column. April 8, 1969. Cited by L. Berkowitz in The case for bottling up rage. *Psychology Today*, September, 1973, pp. 24-31. (p. 366)
Landers, A. (1985, August). Is affection more important than sex? *Reader's Digest*, pp. 44-46. (p. 24)
Lane, R. E. (1998). Searching for lost companions in the groves of the market. In D. Kahneman, E. Diener, & N. Schwarz (eds.), *Understanding well-being: Scientific perspectives on enjoyment and suffering.* New York: Russell Sage Foundation, in press. (p. 507)
Langer, E. J. (1977). The psychology of chance. *Journal for the Theory of Social Behavior*, 7, 185-208. (p. 89)
Langer, E. J., & Imber, L. (1980). The role of mindlessness in the perception of deviance. *Journal of Personality and Social Psychology*, 39, 360-367. (p. 445)
Langer, E. J., & Rodin, J. (1976). The effects of choice and enhanced personal responsibility for the aged: A field experiment in an institutional setting. *Journal of Personality and Social Psychology*, 334, 191-198. (p. 52)
Langer, E. J., & Roth, J. (1975). Heads I win, tails it's chance: The illusion of control as a function of the sequence of outcomes in a purely chance task. *Journal of Personality and Social Psychology*, 32, 951-955. (p. 159)
Langlois, J. H., & Roggman, L. A. (1990). Attractive faces are only average. *Psychological Science*, 1, 115-121. (p. 383)
Langlois, J. H., Kalakanis, L., Rubenstein, A. J., Larson, A., Hallam, M., & Smoot, M. (2000). Maxims or myths of beauty? A meta-analytic and theoretical review. *Psychological Bulletin*, 126, 390-423. (p. 382)
Langlois, J. H., Roggman, L. A., & Musselman, L. (1994). What is average and what is not average about attractive faces? *Psychological Science*, 5, 214-220. (p. 383)
Langlois, J. H., Roggman, L. A., Casey, R. J., Ritter, J. M., Rieser-Danner, L. A., & Jenkins, V. Y. (1987). Infant preferences for attractive faces: Rudiments of a stereotype? *Developmental Psychology*, 23, 363-369. (p. 381)
Langlois, J., Kalakanis, L., Rubenstein, A., Larson, A., Hallam, M., & Smoot, M. (1996). *Maxims and myths of beauty: A meta-analytic and theoretical review.* Paper presented to the American Psychological Society convention. (p. 382)
Larsen, K. (1974). Conformity in the Asch experiment. *Journal of Social Psychology*, 94, 303-304. (p. 278)
Larsen, K. S. (1990). The Asch conformity experiment: Replication and transhistorical comparisons. *Journal of Social Behavior and Personality*, 5(4), 163-168. (p. 278)
Larsen, R. J., & Diener, E. (1987). Affect intensity as an individual difference characteristic: A review. *Journal of Research in Personality*, 21, 1-39. (p. 336)
Larson, J. R., Jr., Foster-Fishman, P. G., & Keys, C. B. (1994). Discussion of shared and unshared information in decision-making groups. *Journal of Personality and Social Psychology*, 67, 446-461. (p. 236)
Larsson, K. (1956). *Conditioning and sexual behavior in the male albino rat.* Stockholm: Almqvist & Wiksell. (p. 217)
Larwood, L. (1978). Swine flu: A field study of self-serving biases. *Journal of Applied Social Psychology*, 18, 283-289. (p. 57)
Larwood, L., & Whittaker, W. (1977). Managerial myopia: Self-serving biases in organizational planning. *Journal of Applied Psychology*, 62, 194-198. (p. 65)
Lassiter, G. D., & Dudley, K. A. (1991). The a priori value of basic research: The case of videotaped confessions. *Journal of Social Behavior and Personality*, 6, 7-16. (p. 99)
Lassiter, G. D., & Irvine, A. A. (1986). Videotaped confessions: The impact of camera point of view on judgments of coercion. *Journal of Applied Social Psychology*, 16, 268-276. (p. 99)
Lassiter, G. D., & Munhall, P. J. (2001). The genius effect: Evidence for a nonmotivational interpretation. *Journal of Experimental Social Psychology*, 37, 349-355. (p. 57)
Latané, B., & Dabbs, J. M., Jr. (1975). Sex, group size and helping in three cities. *Sociometry*, 38, 180-194. (p. 312)
Latané, B., & Darley, J. M. (1968). Group inhibition of bystander intervention in emergencies. *Journal of Personality and Social Psychology*, 10, 215-221. (p. 313)
Latané, B., & Darley, J. M. (1970). *The unresponsive bystander: Why doesn't he help?* New York: Appleton-Century-Crofts. (p. 312)
Latané, B., & Nida, S. (1981). Ten years of research on group size and helping. *Psychological Bulletin*, 89, 308-324. (p. 312)
Latané, B., & Rodin, J. (1969). A lady in distress: Inhibiting effects of friends and strangers on bystander intervention. *Journal of Experimental Social Psychology*, 5, 189-202. (p. 314)
Latané, B., Williams, K., & Harkins. S. (1979). Many hands make light the work: The causes and consequences of social loafing. *Journal of Personality and Social Psychology*, 37, 822-832. (p. 223)
Lau, G. P., Kay, A. C., & Spencer, S. J. (2008). Loving those who justify inequality: The effects of system threat on attraction to women who embody benevolent sexist ideals. *Psychological Science, **19**,* 20.
Laughlin, P. R. (1996). Group decision making and collective induction. In E. H. Witte & J. H. Davis (Eds.), *Understanding group behavior: Consensual action by small groups.* Mahwah, NJ: Erlbaum. (p. 245)
Laughlin, P. R., & Adamopoulos, J. (1980). Social combination processes and individual learning for six-person cooperative groups on an intellective task. *Journal of Personality and Social Psychology*, 38, 941-947. (p. 245)
Laughlin, P. R., Zander, M. L., Knievel, E. M., & Tan, T. K. (2003). Groups perform better than the best individuals on letters-to-numbers problems: Informative equations and effective strategies. *Journal*

of Personality and Social Psychology, 85, 684-694. (p. 245)

Laumann, E. O., Gagnon, J. H., Michael, R. T., & Michaels, S. (1994). *The social organization of sexuality: Sexual practices in the United States*. Chicago: University of Chicago Press. (p. 94)

Leary, M. (1994). *Self-presentation: Impression management and interpersonal behavior*. Pacific Grove, CA: Brooks/Cole. (p. 128)

Leary, M. R. (1998). The social and psychological importance of self-esteem. In R. M. Kowalski & M. R. Leary (Eds.), *The social psychology of emotional and behavioral problems*. Washington, D.C.: American Psychological Association. (p. 22)

Leary, M. R. (2004). The function of self-esteem in terror management theory and sociometer theory: Comment on Pyszczynski et al. (2004). *Psychological Bulletin*, ***130***, 478. (p. 68)

Leary, M. R., & Downs, D. L. (1995). Interpersonal functions of the self-esteem motive: The self-esteem system as a sociometer. In M. Kernis (ed.), *Efficacy, agency, and self-esteem*. New York: Plenum. (p. 45)

Leary, M. R., & Kowalski, R. M. (1995). *Social anxiety*. New York: Guilford. (p. 494)

Leary, M. R., Tambor, E. S., Terdal, S. K., & Downs, D. L. (1995). Self-esteem as an interpersonal monitor: The sociometer hypothesis. *Journal of Personality and Social Psychology*, ***68***, 518.

LeDoux, J. (1994, June). Emotion, memory and the brain. *Scientific American*, pp. 50-57. (p. 38)

LeDoux, J. (1996). *The emotional brain: The mysterious underpinnings of emotional life*. New York: Simon & Schuster. (p. 38)

Lee, F., Hallahan, M., & Herzog, T. (1996). Explaining real-life events: How culture and domain shape attributions. *Personality and Social Psychology Bulletin*, 22, 732-741. (p. 272)

Lee, J. A. (1988). Love-styles. In R. J. Sternberg & M. L. Barnes (Eds.), *The psychology of love*. New Haven, CT: Yale University Press. (p. 397)

Lee, R. Y-P., & Bond, M. H. (1996). *How friendship develops out of personality and values: A study of interpersonal attraction in Chinese culture*. Unpublished manuscript, Chinese University of Hong Kong. (p. 388)

Lee, Y-T., & Seligman, M. E. P. (1997). Are Americans more optimistic than the Chinese? *Personality and Social Psychology Bulletin*, 23, 32-40. (p. 69)

Lefebvre, L. M. (1979). Causal attributions for basketball outcomes by players and coaches. *Psychological Belgica*, 19, 109-115. (p. 69)

Lehman, D. R., Krosnick, J. A., West, R. L., & Fan, L. (1992). The focus of judgment effect: A question wording effect due to hypothesis confirmation bias. *Personality and Social Psychology Bulletin*, 18, 690-699. (p. 25)

Lehman, D. R., Lempert, R. O., & Nisbett, R. E. (1988). The effects of graduate training on reasoning: Formal discipline and thinking about everyday-life events. *American Psychologist*, 43, 431-442. (p. 109)

Leippe, M. R. (1985). The influence of eyewitness nonidentification on mock-jurors. *Journal of Applied Social Psychology*, 15, 656-672. (p. 512)

Leippe, M. R. (1994). The appraisal of eyewitness testimony. In D. F. Ross, J. D. Read, & M. P. Toglia (Eds.), *Adult eyewitness testimony: Current trends and developments*. New York: Cambridge. (p. 513)

Leippe, M. R., & Eisenstadt, D. (1994). Generalization of dissonance reduction: Decreasing prejudice through induced compliance. *Journal of Personality and Social Psychology*, 67, 395-413. (p. 130)

Leippe, M. R., & Elkin, R. A. (1987). *Dissonance reduction strategies and accountability to self and others: Ruminations and some initial research*. Presentation to the Fifth International Conference on Affect, Motivation, and Cognition, Nags Head Conference Center. (p. 130)

Lemyre, L., & Smith, P. M. (1985). Intergroup discrimination and self-esteem in the minimal group paradigm. *Journal of Personality and Social Psychology*, 49, 660-670. (p. 437)

Leon, D. (1969). The Kibbutz: A new way of life. London: Pergamon Press. Cited by B. Latan?, K. Williams, & S. Harkins (1979), Many hands make light the work: The causes and consequences of social loafing. *Journal of Personality and Social Psychology*, 1979, 37, 822-832. (p. 226)

Lepore, S. J., Ragan, J. D., & Jones, S. (2000). Talking facilitates cognitive-emotional processes of adaptation to an acute stressor. *Journal of Personality and Social Psychology*, 78, 499-508. (p. 504)

Lepper, M. R., & Greene, D. (Eds.) (1979). *The hidden costs of reward*. Hillsdale, N.J.: Erlbaum. (p. 135)

Lerner, M. J. (1980). *The belief in a just world: A fundamental delusion*. New York: Plenum. (p. 439)

Lerner, M. J., & Miller, D. T. (1978). Just world research and the attribution process: Looking back and ahead. *Psychological Bulletin*, 85, 1030-1051. (p. 439)

Lerner, M. J., & Simmons, C. H. (1966). Observer's reaction to the "innocent victim": Compassion or rejection? *Journal of Personality and Social Psychology*, 4, 203-210. (p. 439)

Lerner, M. J., Somers, D. G., Reid, D., Chiriboga, D., & Tierney, M. (1991). Adult children as caregivers: Egocentric biases in judgments of sibling contributions. *The Gerontologist*, 31, 746-755. (p. 57)

Leung, K., & Bond, M. H. (1984). The impact of cultural collectivism on reward allocation. *Journal of Personality and Social Psychology*, 47, 793-804. (p. 473)

Leung, K., & Bond, M. H. (2004). Social axioms: A model of social beliefs in multi-cultural perspective. *Advances in Experimental Social Psychology*, in press. (p. 262)

Leventhal, H. (1970). Findings and theory in the study of fear communications. In L. Berkowitz (Ed.), *Advances in experimental social psychology* (Vol. 5). New York: Academic Press. (p. 154)

Levin, D. T. (2000). Race as a visual feature: Using visual search and perceptual discrimination tasks to understand face categories and the cross-race recognition deficit. *Journal of Experimental Psychology: General*, 129, 559-574. (p. 444)

Levine, G. M., Halberstadt, J. B., & Goldstone, R. L. (1996). Reasoning and the weighting of attributes in attitude judgments. *Journal of Personality and Social Psychology*, 70, 230-240. (p. 44)

Levine, J. M. (1989). Reaction to opinion deviance in small groups. In P. Paulus (Ed.), *Psychology of group influence: New perspectives*. Hillsdale, N.J.: Erlbaum. (p. 251)

Levine, J. M., & Moreland, R. L. (1985). Innovation and socialization in small groups. In S. Moscovici, G. Mugny, & E. Van Avermaet (Eds.), *Perspectives on minority influence*. Cambridge: Cambridge University Press. (p. 252)

Levine, R. (2003). *The power of persuasion: How we're bought and sold*. New York: Wiley. (p. 57)

Levine, R. V. (2001). Cross-cultural differences in helping strangers. *Journal of Cross-Cultural Psychology*, 32, 543-560. (p. 316)

Levine, R. V. (2003). The kindness of strangers. *American Scientist*, 91, 226-233. (p. 316)

LeVine, R. V., Martinez, T. S., Brase, G., & Sorenson, K. (1994). Helping in 36 U.S. cities. *Journal of Personality and Social Psychology*, 67, 69-82. (p. 316)

Levy, S. R., Stroessner, S. J., & Dweck, C. S. (1998). Stereotype formation and endorsement: The role of implicit theories. *Journal of Personality and Social Psychology*, 74, 1421-1436. (p. 449)

Levy-Leboyer, C. (1988). Success and failure in applying psychology. *American Psychologist*, 43, 779-785. (p. 154)

Lewandowsky, S., Stritzke, W. G. K., Oberauer, K., & Morales, M. (2005). Memory for fact, fiction, and misinformation: The Iraq War 2003. *Psychological Science, 16*(3), 190. (p. 77)

Lewicki, P. (1985). Nonconscious biasing effects of single instances on subsequent judgments. *Journal of Personality and Social Psychology*, 48, 563-574. (p. 395)

Lewin, K. (1936). *A dynamic theory of personality*. New York: McGraw-Hill. (p. 209)

Lewinsohn, P. M., & Rosenbaum, M. (1987). Recall of parental behavior by acute depressives, remitted depressives, and nondepressives. *Journal of Personality and Social Psychology*, 52, 611-619. (p. 491)

Lewinsohn, P. M., Hoberman, H., Teri, L., & Hautziner, M. (1985). An integrative theory of depression. In S. Reiss & R. Bootzin (Eds.), *Theoretical issues in behavior therapy*. New York: Academic Press. (p. 493)

Lewis, C. S. (1974). *The horse and his boy*. New York: Collier Books. (p. 131)

Lewis, D. O. (1998). *Guilty by reason of insanity*. London: Arrow. (p. 335)

Leyens, J. P., Camino, L., Parke, R. D., & Berkowitz, L. (1975). Effects of movie violence on aggression in a field setting as a function of group dominance and cohesion. *Journal of Personality and Social Psychology*, 32, 346-360. (p. 357)

Liberman, A., & Chaiken, S. (1992). Defensive processing of personally relevant health messages. *Personality and Social Psychology Bulletin*, 18, 669-679. (p. 156)

Lichtenstein, S., & Fischhoff, B. (1980). Training for calibration. *Organizational Behavior and Human Performance*, 26, 149-171. (p. 85)

Lieberman, M. D., Ochsner, K. N., Gilbert, D. T., & Schacter, D. L. (2001). Do amnesics exhibit cognitive dissonance reduction? The role of explicit memory and attention in attitude change. *Psychological Science*, 12, 135-140. (p. 139)

Liebrand, W. B. G., Messick, D. M., & Wolters, F. J. M. (1986). Why we are fairer than others: A cross-cultural replication and extension. *Journal of Experimental Social Psychology*, 22, 590-604. (p. 69)

Lilienfeld, S. O., Fowler, K. A., Lohr, J. M., & Lynn, S. J. (2005). Pseudoscience, nonscience, and nonsense in clinical psychology: Dangers and remedies. In R. H. Wright, & N. A. Cummings (Eds.), *Destructive trends in mental health: The well-intentioned path to harm.* (pp. 187-218). New York, NY, US: Routledge. (p. 486)

Lilienfeld, S. O., Lohr, J. M., & Morier, D. (2001). The teaching of courses in the science and pseudoscience of psychology: Useful resources. *Teaching of Psychology*, ***28***, 182. (p. 486)

Lindsay, R. C. L., & Wells, G. L. (1985). Improving eyewitness identifications from lineups: Simultaneous versus sequential lineup presentation. *Journal of Applied Psychology*, 70, 556-564. (p. 520)

Lindsay, R. C. L., Wells, G. L., & Rumpel, C. H. (1981). Can people detect eyewitness-identification accuracy within and across situations? *Journal of Applied Psychology*, 66, 79-89. (p. 512)

Lindskold, S. (1978). Trust development, the GRIT proposal, and the effects of conciliatory acts on conflict and cooperation. *Psychological Bulletin*, 85, 772-793. (p. 482)

Lindskold, S., & Collins, M. G. (1978). Inducing cooperation by groups and individuals. *Journal of Conflict Resolution*, 22, 679-690. (p. 482)

Lindskold, S., & Finch, M. L. (1981). Styles of announcing conciliation. *Journal of Conflict Resolution*, 25, 145-155. (p. 482)

Lindskold, S., & Han, G. (1988). GRIT as a foundation for integrative bargaining. *Personality and Social Psychology Bulletin*, 14, 335-345. (p. 482)

Lindskold, S., Bennett, R., & Wayner, M. (1976). Retaliation level as a foundation for subsequent conciliation. *Behavioral Science*, 21, 13-18. (p. 482)

Lindskold, S., Betz, B., & Walters, P. S. (1986). Transforming competitive or cooperative climate. *Journal of Conflict Resolution*, 30, 99-114. (p. 482)

Lindskold, S., Han, G., & Betz, B. (1986). Repeated persuasion in interpersonal conflict. *Journal of Personality and Social Psychology*, 51, 1183-1188. (b) (p. 482)

Lindskold, S., Han, G., & Betz, B. (1986). The essential elements of communication in the GRIT strategy. *Personality and Social Psychology Bulletin*, 12, 179-186. (a) (p. 482)

Lindskold, S., Walters, P. S., Koutsourais, H., & Shayo, R. (1981). *Cooperators, competitors, and response to GRIT*. Unpublished manuscript, Ohio University. (p. 482)

Lineham, M. M. (1997). Self-verification and drug abusers: Implications for treatment. *Psychological Science*, 8, 181-184. (p. 491)

Linssen, H., & Hagendoorn, L. (1994). Social and geographical factors in the explanation of the content of European nationality stereotypes. *British Journal of Social Psychology*, 33, 165-182. (p. 417)

Linville, P. W., Gischer, W. G., & Salovey, P. (1989). Perceived distributions of the characteristics of in-group and out-group members: Empirical evidence and a computer simulation. *Journal of Personality and Social Psychology*, 57, 165-188. (p. 443)

Lipsitz, A., Kallmeyer, K., Ferguson, M., & Abas, A. (1989). Counting on blood donors: Increasing the impact of reminder calls. *Journal of Applied Social Psychology*, 19, 1057-1067. (p. 122)

Little, A., & Perrett, D. (2002). Putting beauty back in the eye of the beholder. *The Psychologist*, 15, 28-32. (p. 383)

Livingston, R. W. (2001). What you see is what you get: Systematic variability in perceptual-based social judgment. *Personality and Social Psychology Bulletin*, ***27***, 1086. (p. 382)

Locke, E. A., & Latham, G. P. (1990). Work motivation and satisfaction: Light at the end of the tunnel. *Psychological Science*, 1, 240-246. (p. 248)

Locke, K. D., & Horowitz, L. M. (1990). Satisfaction in interpersonal interactions as a function of similarity in level of dysphoria. *Journal of Personality and Social Psychology*, 58, 823-831. (p. 390)

Locksley, A., Borgida, E., Brekke, N., & Hepburn, C. (1980). Sex stereotypes and social judgment. *Journal of Personality and Social Psychology*, 39, 821-831. (p. 435)

Locksley, A., Hepburn, C., & Ortiz, V. (1982). Social stereotypes and judgments of individuals: An instance of the base-rate fallacy. *Journal of Experimental Social Psychology*, 18, 23-42. (p. 455)

Lockwood, P., & Kunda, Z. (1997). Superstars and me: Predicting the impact of role models on the self. *Journal of Personality and Social Psychology*, 73, 91-103. (p. 45)

Lockwood, P., Dolderman, D., Sadler, P., & Gerchak, E. (2004). Feeling better about doing worse: Social comparisons within romantic relationships. *Journal of Personality and Social Psychology, **87***, 80. (p. 46)

Lockwood, P., Marshall, T. C., & Sadler, P. (2005). Promoting success or preventing failure: Cultural differences in motivation by positive and negative role models. *Personality and Social Psychology Bulletin, **31***, 379. (p. 269)

Loewenstein, G., & Schkade, D. (1999). Wouldn't it be nice? Predicting future feelings. In D. Kahneman, E. Diener, & N. Schwarz (Eds.), *Understanding well-being: Scientific perspectives on enjoyment and suffering*. New York: Russell Sage Foundation, pp. 85-105. (p. 42)

Lofland, J., & Stark, R. (1965). Becoming a worldsaver: A theory of conversion to a deviant perspective. *American Sociological Review*, 30, 862-864. (p. 172)

Loftin, C., McDowall, D., Wiersema, B., & Cottey, T. J. (1991). Effects of restrictive licensing of handguns on homicide and suicide in the District of Columbia. *New England Journal of Medicine*, 325, 1615-1620. (p. 349)

Loftus, E. F. (1974, December). Reconstructing memory: The incredible eyewitness. *Psychology Today*, pp. 117-119. (p. 512)

Loftus, E. F. (1979). *Eyewitness testimony*. Cambridge, Mass.: Harvard University Press. (a) (p. 512)

Loftus, E. F. (1979). The malleability of human memory. *American Scientist*, 67, 312-320. (b) (p. 512)

Loftus, E. F. (2001, November). Imagining the past. *The Psychologist*, 14, 584-587. (p. 514)

Loftus, E. F. (2003). Make-believe memories. *American Psychologist, 58*(11), 867. (p. 78)

Loftus, E. F., & Pickrell, J. (1995). The formation of false memories. *Psychiatric Annals*, 25, 720-725. (p. 78)

Loftus, E. F., & Zanni, G. (1975). Eyewitness testimony: The influence of the wording in a question. *Bulletin of the Psychonomic Society*, 5, 86-88. (p. 519)

Loftus, E. F., Miller, D. G., & Burns, H. J. (1978). Semantic integration of verbal information into a visual memory. *Journal of Experimental Social Psychology: Human Learning and Memory*, 4, 19-31. (p. 514)

Logel, C. E. R., Walton, G., Spencer, S. J., von Hippel, W., Bell, A., & Iserman, E. (2009). Interacting with sexist men triggers social identity threat among female engineers. *Journal of Personality and Social Psychology*, in press.

Lombardo, J. P., Weiss, R. F., & Buchanan, W. (1972). Reinforcing and attracting functions of yielding. *Journal of Personality and Social Psychology*, 21, 359-368. (p. 396)

London, P. (1970). The rescuers: Motivational hypotheses about Christians who saved Jews from the Nazis. In J. Macaulay & L. Berkowitz (Eds.), *Altruism and helping behavior*. New York: Academic Press. (p. 326)

Lonner, W. J. (1989). The introductory psychology text and cross-cultural psychology: Beyond Ekman, Whorf, and biased I.Q. tests. In D. Keats, D. R. Munro & L. Mann (Eds.), *Heterogeneity in cross-cultural psychology*. (p. 261)

Lord, C. G., Lepper, M. R., & Preston, E. (1984). Considering the opposite: A corrective strategy for social judgment. *Journal of Personality and Social Psychology*, 47, 1231-1243. (p. 77)

Lord, C. G., Ross, L., & Lepper, M. (1979). Biased assimilation and attitude polarization: The effects of prior theories on subsequently considered evidence. *Journal of Personality and Social Psychology*, 37, 2098-2109. (p. 74)

Lord, C.G., Desforges, D.M., Ramsey, S.L., Trezza, G.R., & Lepper, M.R. (1991). Typicality effects in attitude-behavior consistency: Efffects of category discrimination and category knowledge. *Journal of Experimental Social Psychology*, 27, 550-575. (p. 456)

Lord, W. (1955). *A Night to Remember*. New York: Holt. (p. 240)

Lortie-Lussier, M., Lemieux, S., Godbout, L. (1989). Reports of a public manifestation: Their impact according to minority influence theory. *Journal of Social Psychology*, 129, 285-295. (p. 248)

Lott, A. J., & Lott, B. E. (1961). Group cohesiveness, communication level, and conformity. *Journal of Abnormal and Social Psychology*, 62, 408-412. (p. 203)

Lott, A. J., & Lott, B. E. (1974). The role of reward in the formation of positive interpersonal attitudes. In T. Huston (ed.), *Foundations of interpersonal attraction*. New York: Academic Press. (p. 395)

Louis, W., & Taylor, D. M. (2001). When the survival of language is at stake: The future of Inuttitut in Arctic Quebec. *Journal of Language and Social Psychology*, 20, 111-143. (p. 289)

Lovett, F. (1997). Thinking about values (report of December 13, 1996 Wall Street Journal national survey). *The Responsive Community*, 7(2), 87. (p. 57)

Lowenstein, D. (2000 May 20). Interview. *The World*. www.cnn.com/TRANSCRIPTS/0005/20/stc.00.html. (p. 362)

Lueptow, L. B., Garovich, L., & Lueptow, M. B. (1995). The persistence of gender stereotypes in the face of changing sex roles: Evidence contrary to the sociocultural model. *Ethology and Sociobiology*, 16, 509-530. (p. 424)

Luginbuhl, J. (1992). Comprehension of judges' instructions in the penalty phase of a capital trial: Focus on mitigating circumstances. *Law and Human Behavior*, 16, 203-218. (p. 522)

Lumsdaine, A. A., & Janis, I. L. (1953). Resistance to "counter-propaganda" produced by one-sided and two-sided "propaganda" presentations. *Public Opinion Quarterly*, 17, 311-318. (p. 158)

Lumsden, A., Zanna, M. P., & Darley, J. M. (1980). *When a newscaster presents counter-additional information: Education or propaganda?* Paper presented to the Canadian Psychological Association annual convention. (p. 145)

Lüüs, C. A. E., & Wells, G. L. (1994). Eyewitness identification confidence. In D. F.

Ross, J. D. Read, & M. P. Toglia (eds.), *Adult eyewitness testimony: Current trends and developments.* Cambridge, England: Cambridge University Press. (p. 513)

Lydon, J. E., Meana, M., Sepinwall, D., Richards, N., & Mayman, S. (1999). The commitment calibration hypothesis: When do people devalue attractive alternatives? *Personality and Social Psychology Bulletin*, 25, 152-161. (p. 387)

Lydon, J., & Dunkel-Schetter, C. (1994). Seeing is committing: A longitudinal study of bolstering commitment in amniocenesis patients. *Personality and Social Psychology Bulletin*, 20, 218-227. (p. 192)

Lykken, D. T. (1997). The American crime factory. *Psychological Inquiry*, 8, 261-270. (p. 235)

Lykken, D. T., & Tellegen, A. (1993). Is human mating adventitious or the result of lawful choice? A twin study of mate selection. *Journal of Personality and Social Psychology*, 65, 56-68. (p. 375)

Lynch, B. S., & Bonnie, R. J. (1994). Toward a youth-centered prevention policy. In B. S. Lynch and R. J. Bonnie (eds.), *Growing up tobacco free: Preventing nicotine addiction in children and youths.* Washington, DC: National Academy Press. (p. 42)

Lynn, M., & Oldenquist, A. (1986). Egoistic and nonegoistic motives in social dilemmas. *American Psychologist*, 41, 529-534. (p. 472)

Lyons, L. (2003, September 23). Oh, boy: Americans still prefer sons. *Gallup Poll Tuesday Briefing* (www.gallup.com). (p. 426)

Lyubomirsky, S. (2001). Why are some people happier than others? The role of cognitive and motivational processes in well-being. *American Psychologist*, 56, 239-249. (p. 536)

Ma, V., & Schoeneman, T. J. (1997). Individualism versus collectivism: A comparison of Kenyan and American self-concepts. *Basic and Applied Social Psychology*, 19, 261-273. (p. 267)

Maass, A. (1998). Personal communication from Universita degli Studi di Padova. (p. 252)

Maass, A., & Clark, R. D., III (1984). Hidden impact of minorities: Fifteen years of minority influence research. *Psychological Bulletin*, 95, 428-450. (p. 252)

Maass, A., & Clark, R. D., III (1986). Conversion theory and simultaneous majority/minority influence: Can reactance offer an alternative explanation? *European Journal of Social Psychology*, 16, 305-309. (p. 252)

Maass, A., Ceccarelli, R., & Rudin, S. (1996). Linguistic intergroup bias: Evidence for in-group-protective motivation. *Journal of Personality and Social Psychology*, 71, 512-526. (p. 449)

Maass, A., Milesi, A., Zabbini, S., & Stahlberg, D. (1995). Linguistic intergroup bias: Differential expectancies or in-group protection? *Journal of Personality and Social Psychology*, 68, 116-126. (p. 449)

Maass, A., Montalcini, F., & Biciotti, E. (1998). On the (dis-)confirmability of stereotypic attributes. *European Journal of Social Psychology*, 28, 383-402. (p. 449)

Maass, A., Volparo, C., & Mucchi-Faina, A. (1996). Social influence and the verifiability of the issue under discussion: Attitudinal versus objective items. *British Journal of Social Psychology*, 35, 15-26. (p. 252)

Maccoby, N. (1980). Promoting positive health behaviors in adults. In L. A. Bond & J. C. Rosen (Eds.), *Competence and coping during adulthood.* Hanover, N.H.: University Press of New England. (p. 162)

Maccoby, N., & Alexander, J. (1980). Use of media in lifestyle programs. In P. O. Davidson & S. M. Davidson (Eds.). *Behavioral medicine: Changing health lifestyles.* New York: Brunner/Mazel. (p. 162)

MacCoun, R. J., & Kerr, N. L. (1988). Asymmetric influence in mock jury deliberation: Jurors' bias for leniency. *Journal of Personality and Social Psychology*, 54, 21-33. (p. 525)

MacDonald, G., & Leary, M. R. (2005). Why does social exclusion hurt? The relationship between social and physical pain. *Psychological Bulletin*, ***131***, 202.

MacDonald, T. K., & Ross, M. (1997). *Assessing the accuracy of predictions about dating relationships: How and why do lovers' predictions differ from those made by observers?* Unpublished manuscript, University of Lethbridge. (p. 41)

Mack, D., & Rainey, D. (1990). Female applicants' grooming and personnel selection. *Journal of Social Behavior and Personality*, 5, 399-407. (p. 382)

Mackay, M., Tiplady, B., & Scholey, A. B. (2002). Interactions between alcohol and caffeine in relation to psychomotor speed and accuracy. *Human Psychopharmacology: Clinical and Experimental*, **17**, 151-156.

MacLeod, C., & Campbell, L. (1992). Memory accessibility and probability judgments: An experimental evaluation of the availability heuristic. *Journal of Personality and Social Psychology*, 63, 890-902. (p. 86)

MacLin, O. H., Zimmerman, L. A., & Malpass, R. S. (2005). PC Eyewitness and the sequential superiority effect: Computer-based lineup administration. *Law and Human Behavior*, ***29***, 303. (p. 520)

MacNamara, J. (1973). Nurseries, streets and classrooms. *Modern Language Journal*, 57, 250-254. (p. 289)

Macrae, C. N., & Johnston, L. (1998). Help, I need somebody: Automatic action and inaction. *Social Cognition*, 16, 400-417. (p. 38)

Macrae, C. N., Bodenhausen, G. V., & Milne, A. B. (1998). Saying no to unwanted thoughts: Self-focus and the regulation of mental life. *Journal of Personality and Social Psychology*, in press. (p. 441)

Macrae, C. N., Bodenhausen, G. V., Milne, A. B., & Jetten, J. (1994). Out of mind but back in sight: Stereotypes on the rebound. *Journal of Personality and Social Psychology*, 67, 808-817. (p. 440)

Macrae, C. N., Stangor, C., & Milne, A. B. (1994). Activating social stereotypes: A functional analysis. *Journal of Experimental Social Psychology*, 30, 370-389. (p. 442)

Maddux, J. E. (1993). The mythology of psychopathology: A social cognitive view of deviance, difference, and disorder. *The General Psychologist*, 29(2), 34-45. (p. 485)

Maddux, J. E., & Rogers, R. W. (1983). Protection motivation and self-efficacy: A revised theory of fear appeals and attitude change. *Journal of Experimental Social Psychology*, 19, 469-479. (p. 156)

Madon, S., Jussim, L., & Eccles, J. (1997). In search of the powerful self-fulfilling prophecy. *Journal of Personality and Social Psychology*, 72, 791-809. (p. 104)

Maio, G. R., & Olson, J. M. (1990). Involvement and persuasion: Evidence for different types of involvement. *Canadian Journal of Behavioural Science*, 27, 64-78. (p. 167)

Maio, G. R., Bell, D., & Esses, V. M. (1996). Ambivalence in persuasion: The processing of messages about immigrant groups.

Journal of Experimental Social Psychology, 32, 513-536. (p. 157)

Major, B., Quinton, W. J., & McCoy, S. K. (2002). Antecedents and consequences of attributions to discrimination: Theoretical and empirical advances. In M. P. Zanna (Ed.). *Advances in experimental social psychology* (Vol. 34) (pp. 251-330). San Diego: Academic Press. (p. 460)

Malamuth, N. M., & Check, J. V. P. (1981). The effects of media exposure on acceptance of violence against women: A field experiment. *Journal of Research in Personality*, 15, 436-446. (p. 351)

Malamuth, N. M., & Check, J. V. P. (1984). Debriefing effectiveness following exposure to pornographic rape depictions. *Journal of Sex Research*, 20, 1-13. (p. 353)

Malamuth, N. M., Haber, S., Feshbach, S., & others. (1980, March). *Journal of Research in Personality*, 14, 121-137. (p. 351)

Malkiel, B. G. (1985). *A random walk down Wall Street*, 4th ed. New York: W. W. Norton. (p. 83)

Malkiel, B. G. (1995, June). Returns from investing in equity mutual funds 1971 to 1991. *Journal of Finance*, pp. 549-572. (p. 83)

Mallet, R. K., & Swim, J. K. (2003). Collective guilt in the United States: Predicting support for social policies that alleviate social injustice. In N. Branscombe & B. Doosje (Eds.), *Collective guilt: International perspectives*. New York: Cambridge University Press. (p. 473)

Mandel, D. R., & Lehman, D. R. (1996). Counterfactual thinking and ascriptions of cause and preventability. *Journal of Personality and Social Psychology*, 71, 450-463. (p. 88)

Manis, M., Nelson, T. E., & Shedler, J. (1988). Stereotypes and social judgment: Extremity, assimilation, and contrast. *Journal of Personality and Social Psychology*, 55, 28-36. (p. 458)

Mann, L. (1981). The baiting crowd in episodes of threatened suicide. *Journal of Personality and Social Psychology*, 41, 703-709. (p. 228)

Marcus, A. C., & Siegel, J. M. (1982). Sex differences in the use of physician services: A preliminary test of the fixed role hypothesis. *Journal of Health and Social Behavior*, 23, 186-197. (p. 499)

Marcus, S. (1974). Review of Obedience to authority. *New York Times Book Review*, January 13, pp. 1-2. (p. 191)

Marcus-Newhall, A., Pedersen, W. C., Carlson, M., & Miller, N. (2000). Displaced aggression is alive and well: A meta-analytic review. *Journal of Personality and Social Psychology*, 78, 670-689. (p. 339)

Marigold, D. C., Holmes, J. G., & Ross, M. (2007). More than words: Reframing compliments from romantic partners fosters security in low self-esteem individuals. *Journal of Personality and Social Psychology*, **92**, 232. (p. 392)

Marin, T. J., Holtzman, S., DeLongis, A., & Robinson, L. (2007). Coping and the response of others. *Journal of Social and Personal Relationships*, **24**, 951. (p. 503)

Markman, H. J., Floyd, F. J., Stanley, S. M., & Storaasli, R. D. (1988). Prevention of marital distress: A longitudinal investigation. *Journal of Consulting and Clinical Psychology*, 56, 210-217. (p. 412)

Marks, G., & Miller, N. (1987). Ten years of research on the false-consensus effect: An empirical and theoretical review. *Psychological Bulletin*, 102, 72-90. (p. 60)

Markus, H. R., & Kitayama, S. (1994). A collective fear of the collective: Implications for selves and theories of selves. *Personality and Social Psychology Bulletin*, 20, 568-579. (p. 182)

Markus, H., & Kitayama, S. (1991). Culture and the self: Implications for cognition, emotion, and motivation. *Psychological Review*, 98, 224-253. (p. 69)

Markus, H., & Nurius, P. (1986). Possible selves. *American Psychologist*, 41, 954-969. (p. 51)

Markus, H., & Wurf, E. (1987). The dynamic self-concept: A social psychological perspective. *Annual Review of Psychology*, 38, 299-337. (p. 50)

Marsh, H. W., & Parker, J. W. (1984). Determinants of student self-concept: Is it better to be a relatively large fish in a small pond even if you don't learn to swim as well? *Journal of Personality and Social Psychology*, 47, 213-231. (p. 46)

Marsh, H. W., Hau, K. T., & Kong, C. K. (2000). Multilevel causal ordering of academic self-concept and achievement: Influence of language of instruction (English compared with Chinese) for Hong Kong students. *American Educational Research Journal*, 39, 727-763. (p. 289)

Marshall, L. (Ed.) 1912. *Sinking of the Titanic and great sea disasters*. Philadelphia, PA: Universal Book and Bible House. (p. 241)

Marshall, R. (1997). Variances in levels of individualism across two cultures and three social classes. *Journal of Cross-Cultural Psychology*, 28, 490-495. (p. 267)

Marshall, W. L. (1989). Pornography and sex offenders. In D. Zillmann & J. Bryant (Eds.), *Pornography: Research advances and policy considerations*. Hillsdale, NJ: Erlbaum. (p. 352)

Martin, L. L., & Erber, R. (2005). Can social psychology impart any wisdom to the world? *Psychological Inquiry, 16*(4), 151. (p. 108)

Martin, R. (1996). Minority influence and argument generation. *British Journal of Social Psychology*, 35, 91-103. (p. 251)

Martino, S. C., Collins, R. L., Kanouse, D. E., Elliott, M., & Berry, S. H. (2005). Social cognitive processes mediating the relationship between exposure to television's sexual content and adolescents' sexual behavior. *Journal of Personality and Social Psychology*, **89**, 914-924. (p. 360)

Marvelle, K., & Green, S. (1980). Physical attractiveness and sex bias in hiring decisions for two types of jobs. *Journal of the National Association of Women Deans, Administrators, and Counselors*, 44(1), 3-6. (p. 382)

Marx, G. (1960). *Groucho and me*. New York: Dell. (p. 54)

Maslow, A. H., & Mintz, N. L. (1956). Effects of esthetic surroundings: I. Initial effects of three esthetic conditions upon perceiving "energy" and "well-being" in faces. *Journal of Psychology*, 41, 247-254. (p. 395)

Mastekaasa, A. (1995). Age variations in the suicide rates and self-reported subjective well-being of married and never married persons. *Journal of Community & Applied Social Psychology*, 5, 21-39. (p. 508)

Masuda, T., & Kitayama, S. (2004). Perceiver-induced constraint and attitude attribution in Japan and the US: A case for the cultural dependence of the correspondence bias. *Journal of Experimental Social Psychology*, **40**, 409. (p. 272)

Matheson, K., Cole, B., & Majka, K. (2003). Dissidence from within: Examining the effects of intergroup context on group members' reactions to attitudinal opposition. *Journal of Experimental Social Psychology*, **39**, 161. (p. 206)

Mathews, K., Shepherd, J. & Sivarajasingham, V. (2007). Violence related injury and the price of beer in England and Wales. *Applied Economics*, **38**, 661-670.

Matsuda, T., Ellsworth, P. C., Mesquita, B., Leu, J., Tanida, S., & Van de Veerdonk, E. (2008). Placing the face in context: Cultural differences in the perception of facial emotion. *Journal of Personality and Social Psychology*, **94**, 365. (p. 276)

Matsumoto, D. (1994). *People: Psychology from a cultural perspective.* Pacific Grove, CA: Brooks/Cole. (p. 288)

Matsumoto, D., & Ekman, P. (1989). American Japanese cultural differences in intensity ratings of facial expressions of emotion. *Motivation and Emotion*, 13, 143-157. (p. 276)

Matsumoto, D., Kudoh, T., Scherer, K., & Wallbott, H. (1988). Antecedents of and reactions to emotions in the United States and Japan. *Journal of Cross-Cultural Psychology*, 19, 267-286. (p. 276)

Matthews, K. A. (1988). CHD and Type A behaviors: Update on and alternative to the Booth-Kewley and Friedman quantitative review. *Psychological Bulletin*, 104, 373-380. (p. 499)

Maxwell, G. M. (1985). Behaviour of lovers: Measuring the closeness of relationships. *Journal of Personality and Social Psychology*, 2, 215-238. (p. 403)

Mayer, J. D., & Salovey, P. (1987). Personality moderates the interaction of mood and cognition. In K. Fiedler & J. Forgas (Eds.), *Affect, cognition, and social behavior.* Toronto: Hogrefe. (p. 91)

Mayton, D. M., II, Diessner, R., & Granby, C. D. (1996). Nonviolence and human values: Empirical support for theoretical relations. *Peace and Conflict: Journal of Peace Psychology*, 2, 245-253. (p. 287)

Mazzoni, G., & Memon, A. (2003). Imagination can create false autobiographical memories. *Psychological Science*, ***14***, 186. (p. 516)

McAlister, A., Perry, C., Killen, J., Slinkard, L. A., & Maccoby, N. (1980). Pilot study of smoking, alcohol and drug abuse prevention. *American Journal of Public Health*, 70, 719-721. (p. 176)

McAndrew, F. T. (1981). Pattern of performance and attributions of ability and gender. *Journal of Personality and Social Psychology*, 7, 583-587. (p. 159)

McAneny, L. (1994, June). Alcohol in America: Number of drinkers holding steady, but drinking less. *Gallup Poll Monthly*, pp. 14-19. (p. 350)

McCann, C. D., & Hancock, R. D. (1983). Self-monitoring in communicative interactions: Social cognitive consequences of goal-directed message modification. *Journal of Experimental Social Psychology*, 19, 109-121. (p. 68)

McCarrey, M., Edwards, H. P., & Rozario, W. (1982). Ego-relevant feedback, affect, and self-serving attributional bias. *Personality and Social Psychology Bulletin*, 8, 189-194. (p. 63)

McCarthy, J. F., & Kelly, B. R. (1978). Aggression, performance variables, and anger self-report in ice hockey players. *Journal of Psychology*, 99, 97-101. (b) (p. 342)

McCarthy, J. F., & Kelly, B. R. (1978). Aggressive behavior and its effect on performance over time in ice hockey athletes: An archival study. *International Journal of Sport Psychology*, 9, 90-96. (a) (p. 342)

McCauley, C. (1989). The nature of social influence in groupthink: Compliance and internalization. *Journal of Personality and Social Psychology*, 57, 250-260. (p. 242)

McCauley, C. (2004). Psychological issues in understanding terrorism and the response to terrorism. In C. E. Stout (Ed.), *Psychology of terrorism: Coping with the continuing threat, condensed edition.* (pp. 33-65). Westport, CT, US: Praeger Publishers/Greenwood Publishing Group. (p. 339)

McClure, J. (1998). Discounting causes of behavior: Are two reasons better than one? *Journal of Personality and Social Psychology*, 74, 7-20. (p. 95)

McConahay, J. B. (1986). Modern racism, ambivalence, and the Modern Racism Scale. In J. F. Dovidio & S. L. Gaertner (Eds.). *Prejudice, discrimination, and racism* (pp. 91-125). San Diego, CA: Academic Press. (p. 418)

McCrae, R. R., & Costa, P. T., Jr. (1999). A five-factor theory of personality. In L. A. Pervin & O. P. John (Eds.), *Handbook of personality: Theory and research.* New York: Guilford. (p. 262)

McCullough, J. L., & Ostrom, T. M. (1974). Repetition of highly similar messages and attitude change. *Journal of Applied Psychology*, 59, 395-397. (p. 379)

McDonald, T. K., Zanna, M. P., & Fong, G. T. (1995). Decision making in altered states: Effects of alcohol on attitudes toward drinking and driving. *Journal of Personality and Social Psychology*, 68, 973-985. (p. 495)

McFarland, C., & Ross, M. (1987). *Personality and Social Psychology Bulletin,* 13, 228-238. (p. 79)

McFarland, S. G., Ageyev, V. S., & Abalakina-Paap, M. A. (1992). Authoritarianism in the former Soviet Union. *Journal of Personality and Social Psychology*, 63, 1004-1010. (p. 428)

McFarland, S. G., Ageyev, V. S., & Djintcharadze, N. (1996). Russian authoritarianism two years after communism. *Personality and Social Psychology Bulletin*, 22, 210-217. (p. 428)

McGillicuddy, N. B., Welton, G. L., & Pruitt, D. G. (1987). Third-party intervention: A field experiment comparing three different models. *Journal of Personality and Social Psychology*, 53, 104-112. (p. 481)

McGinn, A. P. (1998, June 20). *Hidden forces mask crisis in world fisheries.* Worldwatch Institute (www.worldwatch.org). (p. 529)

McGlone, M. S., & Tofighbakhsh, J. (2000). Birds of a feather flock conjointly (?): Rhyme as reason in aphorisms. *Psychological Science*, 11, 424-428. (p. 161)

McGlynn, R. P., Tubbs, D. D., & Holzhausen, K. G. (1995). Hypothesis generation in groups constrained by evidence. *Journal of Experimental Social Psychology*, 31, 64-81. (p. 246)

McGrath, J. E. (1984). *Groups: Interaction and performance.* Englewood Cliffs, N.J.: Prentice-Hall. (p. 216)

McGregor, I., & Jordan, C. H. (2007). The mask of zeal: Low implicit self-esteem, threat, and defensive extremism. *Self & Identity*, **6**, 223-237. (p. 49)

McGregor, I., & Marigold, D. C. (2003). Defensive zeal and the uncertain self: What makes you so sure? *Journal of Personality & Social Psychology,* 85(5), 838-852. (p. 49)

McGregor, I., Nail, P. R., Marigold, D. C., & Kang, S. (2005). Defensive pride and consensus: Strength in imaginary numbers. *Journal of Personality and Social Psychology*, ***89***, 978. (p. 49)

McGregor, I., Newby-Clark, I. R., & Zanna, M. P. (1998). Epistemic discomfort is moderated by simultaneous accessibility of inconsistent elements. In E. Harmon-Jones and J. Mills (eds.), *Cognitive dissonance theory 40 years later: A revival with revisions and controversies.* Washington,

DC: American Psychological Association. (p. 139)

McGregor, I., Zanna, M. P., Holmes, J. G., & Spencer, S. J. (2001). Conviction in the face of uncertainty: Going to extremes and being oneself. *Journal of Personality and Social Psychology*, 80, 472-478. (p. 438)

McGuire, W. J. (1964). Inducing resistance to persuasion: Some contemporary approaches. In L. Berkowitz (Ed.), *Advances in experimental social psychology* (Vol. 1). New York: Academic Press. (p. 175)

McGuire, W. J., & Padawer-Singer, A. (1978). Trait salience in the spontaneous self-concept. *Journal of Personality and Social Psychology*, 33, 743-754. (p. 212)

McGuire, W. J., McGuire, C. V., & Winton, W. (1979). Effects of household sex composition on the salience of one's gender in the spontaneous self-concept. *Journal of Experimental Social Psychology*, 15, 77-90. (p. 212)

McGuire, W. J., McGuire, C. V., Child, P., & Fujioka, T. (1978). Salience of ethnicity in the spontaneous self-concept as a function of one's ethnic distinctiveness in the social environment. *Journal of Personality and Social Psychology*, 36, 511-520. (p. 213)

McKelvie, S. J. (1995). Bias in the estimated frequency of names. *Perceptual and Motor Skills*, 81, 1331-1338. (p. 86)

McKelvie, S. J. (1997). The availability heuristic: Effects of fame and gender on the estimated frequency of male and female names. *Journal of Social Psychology*, 137, 63-78. (p. 86)

McKenna, F. P., & Myers, L. B. (1997). Illusory self-assessments-Can they be reduced? *British Journal of Psychology*, 88, 39-51. (p. 57)

McKenna, K. Y. A., & Bargh, J. A. (1998). Coming out in the age of the Internet: Identity demarginalization through virtual group participation. *Journal of Personality and Social Psychology*, 75, 681-694. (p. 235)

McKenna, K. Y. A., & Bargh, J. A. (2000). Plan 9 from cyberspace: The implications of the Internet for personality and social psychology. *Personality and Social Psychology Review*, 4, 57-75. (p. 235)

McKenzie-Mohr, D., & Zanna, M. P. (1990). Treating women as sexual objects: Look to the (gender schematic) male who has viewed pornography. *Personality and Social Psychology Bulletin*, 16, 296-308. (p. 367)

McLaughlin, J. (1977). Second-language learning in children. *Psychological Bulletin*, 84, 438-459. (p. 289)

McMillen, D. L., & Austin, J. B. (1971). Effect of positive feedback on compliance following transgression. *Psychonomic Science*, 24, 59-61. (p. 299)

McMillen, D. L., Sanders, D. Y., & Solomon, G. S. (1977). Self-esteem, attentiveness, and helping behavior. *Journal of Personality and Social Psychology*, 3, 257-261. (p. 301)

McPherson, M., Smith-Lovin, L., & Cook, J. M. (2001). Birds of a feather: Homophily in social networks. *Annual Review of Sociology, **27***, 415.

Mead, G. H. (1934). *Mind, self, and society*. Chicago: University of Chicago Press. (p. 45)

Medalia, N. Z., & Larsen, O. N. (1958). Diffusion and belief in collective delusion: The Seattle windshield pitting epidemic. *American Sociological Review*, 23, 180-186. (p. 185)

Medvec, V. H., & Savitsky, K. (1997). When doing better means feeling worse: The effects of categorical cutoff points on counterfactual thinking and satisfaction. *Journal of Personality and Social Psychology*, 72, 1284-1296. (p. 87)

Medvec, V. H., Madey, S. F., & Gilovich, T. (1995). When less is more: Counterfactual thinking and satisfaction among Olympic medalists. *Journal of Personality and Social Psychology*, 69, 603-610. (p. 87)

Meech, P., & Kilborn, R. (1992). Media and identity in a stateless nation: The case of Scotland. Media. *Culture and Society*, 14, 245-259. (p. 49)

Mehl, M. R., & Pennebaker, J. W. (2003). The sounds of social life: A psychometric analysis of students' daily social environments and natural conversations. *Journal of Personality and Social Psychology*, 84, 857-870. (p. 8)

Mehlman, P. T. & 7 others (1994). Low CSF 5-HIAA concentrations and severe aggression and impaired impulse control in nonhuman primates. *American Journal of Psychiatry*, 151, 1485-1491. (p. 337)

Meindl, J. R., & Lerner, M. J. (1984). Exacerbation of extreme responses to an out-group. *Journal of Personality and Social Psychology*, 47, 71-84. (p. 438)

Meissner, C. A., Brigham, J. C., & Kelley, C. M. (2001). The influence of retrieval processes in verbal overshadowing. *Memory and Cognition*, 29, 176-186. (p. 519)

Meissner, C. A., Tredoux, C. G., Parker, J. F., & MacLin, O. H. (2005). Eyewitness decisions in simultaneous and sequential lineups: A dual-process signal detection theory analysis. *Memory & Cognition, **33***, 783. (p. 520)

Meleshko, K. G. A., & Alden, L. E. (1993). Anxiety and self-disclosure: Toward a motivational model. *Journal of Personality and Social Psychology*, 64, 1000-1009. (p. 495)

Merikle, P. M., Smilek, D., & Eastwood, J. D. (2001). Perception without awareness: Perspectives from cognitive psychology. *Cognition. Special Issue: The Cognitive Neuroscience of Consciousness, 79*(1-2), 115. (p. 73)

Merton, R. K. (1948). The self-fulfilling prophecy. *Antioch Review*, 8, 193-210. (p. 103)

Merton, R. K., & Kitt, A. S. (1950). Contributions to the theory of reference group behavior. In R. K. Merton & P. F. Lazarsfeld (Eds.), *Continuities in social research: Studies in the scope and method of the American soldier*. Glencoe, Ill.: Free Press. (p. 341)

Messick, D. M., & Sentis, K. P. (1979). Fairness and preference. *Journal of Experimental Social Psychology*, 15, 418-434. (p. 473)

Metalsky, G. I., Joiner, T. E., Jr., Hardin, T. S., & Abramson, L. Y. (1993). Depressive reactions to failure in a naturalistic setting: A test of the hopelessness and self-esteem theories of depression. *Journal of Abnormal Psychology*, 102, 101-109. (p. 493)

Meyers, S. A., & Berscheid, E. (1997). The language of love: The difference a preposition makes. *Personality and Social Psychology Bulletin*, 23, 347-362. (p. 398)

Michaels, J. W., Blommel, J. M., Brocato, R. M., Linkous, R. A., & Rowe, J. S. (1982). Social facilitation and inhibition in a natural setting. *Replications in Social Psychology*, 2, 21-24. (p. 219)

Mickelson, K. D., Kessler, R. C., & Shaver, P. R. (1997). Adult attachment in a nationally representative sample. *Journal of Personality and Social Psychology*, 73, 1092-1106. (p. 404)

Mikula, G. (1984). Justice and fairness in interpersonal relations: Thoughts and suggestions. In H. Taijfel (Ed.), *The social dimension: European developments in social psychology*, Vol. 1, Cambridge: Cambridge University Press. (p. 473)

Mikulincer, M., & Shaver, P. R. (2001). Attachment theory and intergroup bias: Evidence that priming the secure base schema attenuates negative reactions to out-groups. *Journal of Personality and Social Psychology*, 81, 97-115. (p. 438)

Mikulincer, M., Florian, V., & Hirschberger, G. (2003). The existential function of close relationships: Introducing death into the science of love. *Personality and Social Psychology Review*, 7, 20-40. (p. 372)

Milgram, A. (2000). My personal view of Stanley Milgram. In T. Blass (Ed.), *Obedience to authority: Current perspectives on the Milgram paradigm*. Mahwah, N.J.: Erlbaum. (p. 189)

Milgram, S. (1961, December). Nationality and conformity. *Scientific American*, December, pp. 45-51. (p. 278)

Milgram, S. (1963). Behavioral study of obedience. *Journal of Abnormal and Social Psychology*, 67, 371-378. (p. 189)

Milgram, S. (1965). Some conditions of obedience and disobedience to authority. *Human Relations*, 18, 57-76. (p. 188)

Milgram, S. (1974). *Obedience to authority*. New York: Harper and Row. (p. 5)

Milgram, S., Bickman, L., & Berkowitz, L. (1969). Note on the drawing power of crowds of different size. *Journal of Personality and Social Psychology*, 13, 79-82. (p. 201)

Millar, M. G., & Millar, K. U. (1996). The effects of direct and indirect experience on affective and cognitive responses and the attitude-behavior relation. *Journal of Experimental Social Psychology*, 32, 561-579. (p. 117)

Millar, M. G., & Tesser, A. (1992). The role of beliefs and feelings in guiding behavior: The mismatch model. In L. Martin & A. Tesser (Eds.), *The construction of social judgment*. Hillsdale NJ: Erlbaum. (p. 44)

Miller, A. G. (1986). *The obedience experiments: A case study of controversy in social science*. New York: Praeger. (p. 190)

Miller, A. G., Ashton, W., & Mishal, M. (1990). Beliefs concerning the features of constrained behavior: A basis for the fundamental attribution error. *Journal of Personality and Social Psychology*, 59, 635-650. (p. 95)

Miller, A. G., Gillen, G., Schenker, C., & Radlove, S. (1973). *Perception of obedience to authority*. Proceedings of the 81st annual convention of the American Psychological Association, 8, 127-128. (p. 198)

Miller, C. E., & Anderson, P. D. (1979). Group decision rules and the rejection of deviates. *Social Psychology Quarterly*, 42, 354-363. (p. 206)

Miller, C. T., & Felicio, D. M. (1990). Person-positivity bias: Are individuals liked better than groups? *Journal of Experimental Social Psychology*, 26, 408-420. (p. 304)

Miller, D. T., & McFarland, C. (1987). Pluralistic ignorance: When similarity is interpreted as dissimilarity. *Journal of Personality and Social Psychology*, 53, 298-305. (p. 237)

Miller, D. T., Downs, J. S., & Prentice, D. A. (1998). Minimal conditions for the creation of a unit relationship: The social bond between birthdaymates. *European Journal of Social Psychology*. (p. 434)

Miller, J. G. (1984). Culture and the development of everyday social explanation. *Journal of Personality and Social Psychology*, 46, 961-978. (p. 157)

Miller, K. I., & Monge, P. R. (1986). Participation, satisfaction, and productivity: A meta-analytic review. *Academy of Management Journal*, 29, 727-753. (p. 53)

Miller, L. (2004). Psychotherapeutic interventions for survivors of terrorism. *American Journal of Psychotherapy, **58***, 1. (p. 194)

Miller, L. C. (1990). Intimacy and liking: Mutual influence and the role of unique relationships. *Journal of Personality and Social Psychology*, 59, 50-60. (p. 408)

Miller, L. C., Berg, J. H., & Archer, R. L. (1983). Openers: Individuals who elicit intimate self-disclosure. *Journal of Personality and Social Psychology*, 44, 1234-1244. (p. 408)

Miller, L. C., Berg, J. H., & Rugs, D. (1989). *Selectivity and sharing: Needs and norms in developing friendships*. Unpublished manuscript, Scripps College. (p. 407)

Miller, L. E., & Grush, J. E. (1986). Individual differences in attitudinal versus normative determination of behavior. *Journal of Experimental Social Psychology*, 22, 190-202. (p. 117)

Miller, N., & Campbell, D. T. (1959). Recency and primacy in persuasion as a function of the timing of speeches and measurements. *Journal of Abnormal and Social Psychology*, 59, 1-9. (p. 159)

Miller, N., & Marks, G. (1982). Assumed similarity between self and other: Effect of expectation of future interaction with that other. *Social Psychology Quarterly*, 45, 100-105. (p. 376)

Miller, N., Maruyama, G., Beaber, R. J., & Valone, K. (1976). Speed of speech and persuasion. *Journal of Personality and Social Psychology*, 34, 615-624. (p. 150)

Miller, P. A., & Eisenberg, N. (1988). The relation of empathy to aggressive and externalizing/antisocial behavior. *Psychological Bulletin*, 103, 324-344. (p. 309)

Miller, P. J. E., & Rempel, J. K. (2004). Trust and partner-enhancing attributions in close relationships. *Personality and Social Psychology Bulletin, **30***, 695. (p. 404)

Miller, R. L., Brickman, P., & Bolen, D. (1975). Attribution versus persuasion as a means for modifying behavior. *Journal of Personality and Social Psychology*, 31, 430-441. (p. 106)

Miller, R. S. (1997). Inattentive and contented: Relationship commitment and attention to alternatives. *Journal of Personality and Social Psychology*, 73, 758-766. (p. 410)

Miller, R. S., & Schlenker, B. R. (1985). Egotism in group members: Public and private attributions of responsibility for group performance. *Social Psychology Quarterly*, 48, 85-89. (p. 69)

Millett, K. (1975). The shame is over. *Ms.*, January, pp. 26-29. (p. 409)

Mio, J. S., Thompson, S. C., & Givens, G. H. (1993). The commons dilemma as a metaphor: Memory, influence, and implications for environmental conservation. *Metaphor and Symbolic Activity*, 8, 23-42. (p. 472)

Mischel, W. (1968). *Personality and assessment*. New York: Wiley. (p. 208)

Mita, T. H., Dermer, M., & Knight, J. (1977). Reversed facial images and the mere-exposure hypothesis. *Journal of Personality and Social Psychology*, 35, 597-601. (p. 377)

Mitchell, G., Tetlock, P. E., Mellers, B. A., & Ordonez, L. D. (1993). Judgments of social justice: Compromises between equality and efficiency. *Journal of*

Personality and Social Psychology, 65, 629-639. (p. 474)

Mitchell, T. R., & Thompson, L. (1994). A theory of temporal adjustments of the evaluation of events: Rosy prospection and rosy retrospection. In C. Stubbart, J. Porac, & J. Meindl (Eds.), *Advances in managerial cognition and organizational information processing*. Greenwich, CT: JAI Press. (p. 79)

Mitchell, T. R., Thompson, L., Peterson, E., & Cronk, R. (1997). Temporal adjustments in the evaluation of events: The "rosy view." *Journal of Experimental Social Psychology*, 33, 421-448. (p. 79)

Moffitt, T., Caspi, A., Sugden, K., Taylor, A., Craig, I. W., Harrington, H., McClay, J., Mill, J., Martin, J., Braithwaite, A., Poulton, R. (2003). Influence of life stress on depression: Moderation by a polymorphism in the 5-HTT gene. *Science*, 301, 386-389. (p. 336)

Moghaddam, F. M., Stolkin, A. J., & Hutcheson, L. S. (1997). A generalized personal/group discrepancy: Testing the domain specificity of a perceived higher effect of events on one's group than on oneself. *Personality and Social Psychology Bulletin*, 23, 743-750. (p. 461)

Monin, B., & Norton, M. I. (2003). Perceptions of a fluid consensus: Uniqueness bias, false consensus, false polarization, and pluralistic ignorance in water conservation crisis. *Personality and Social Psychology*, 29, 559-567. (p. 60)

Monson, T. C., & Snyder, M. (1977). Actors, observers, and the attribution process: Toward a reconceptualization. *Journal of Experimental Social Psychology*, 13, 89-111. (p. 100)

Monson, T. C., Hesley, J. W., & Chernick, L. (1982). Specifying when personality traits can and cannot predict behavior: An alternative to abandoning the attempt to predict single-act criteria. *Journal of Personality and Social Psychology*, 43, 385-399. (p. 209)

Monteith, M. J. (1993). Self-regulation of prejudiced responses: Implications for progress in prejudice-reduction efforts. *Journal of Personality and Social Psychology*, 65, 469-485. (p. 440)

Montoya, R. M., & Horton, R. S. (2004). On the importance of cognitive evaluation as a determinant of interpersonal attraction. *Journal of Personality and Social Psychology*, ***86***, 696. (p. 388)

Moody, K. (1980). Growing up on television: The TV effect. New York: Times Books. (p. 177)

Moore, D. L., & Baron, R. S. (1983). Social facilitation: A physiological analysis. In J. T. Cacioppo & R. Petty (Eds.), *Social psychophysiology*. New York: Guilford Press. (p. 219)

Moore, D. W. (2003, March 18). Public approves of Bush ultimatum by more than 2-to-1 margin. Gallup News Service (www.gallup.com). (p. 144)

Mor, N., & Winquist, J. (2002). Self-focused attention and negative affect: A meta-analysis. *Psychological Bulletin*, ***128***, 638. (p. 492)

Moreland, R. L., & Zajonc, R. B. (1977). Is stimulus recognition a necessary condition for the occurrence of exposure effects? *Journal of Personality and Social Psychology*, 35, 191-199. (p. 377)

Morgan, C. A., III, Hazlett, G., Doran, A., Garrett, S., Hoyt, G., Thomas, P., et al. (2004). Accuracy of eyewitness memory for persons encountered during exposure to highly intense stress. *International Journal of Law and Psychiatry*, ***27***, 265. (p. 513)

Morier, D., & Seroy, C. (1994). The effect of interpersonal expectancies on men's self-presentation of gender role attitudes to women. *Sex Roles*, 31, 493-504. (p. 120)

Morris, M. W., & Peng, K. (1994). Culture and cause: American and Chinese attributions for social and physical events. *Journal of Personality and Social Psychology*, 67, 949-971. (p. 270)

Morris, W. N., & Miller, R. S. (1975). The effects of consensus-breaking and consensus-preempting partners on reduction of conformity. *Journal of Experimental Social Psychology*, 11, 215-223. (p. 202)

Morrow, L. (1983, August 1). All the hazards and threats of success. *Time*, pp. 20-25. (p. 182)

Moscovici, S. (1985). Social influence and conformity. In G. Lindzey & E. Aronson (Eds.), *The handbook of social psychology*, 3rd ed. Hillsdale, N.J.: Erlbaum. (p. 251)

Moscovici, S. (1988). Notes towards a description of social representations. *European Journal of Social Psychology*, 18, 211-250. (p. 12)

Moscovici, S., & Zavalloni, M. (1969). The group as a polarizer of attitudes. *Journal of Personality and Social Psychology*, 12, 124-135. (p. 234)

Moscovici, S., Lage, S., & Naffrechoux, M. (1969). Influence of a consistent minority on the responses of a majority in a color perception task. *Sociometry*, 32, 365-380. (p. 251)

Moyer, K. E. (1976). *The psychobiology of aggression*. New York: Harper & Row. (p. 335)

Moyer, K. E. (1983). The physiology of motivation: Aggression as a model. In C. J. Scheier & A. M. Rogers (Eds.), *G. Stanley Hall Lecture Series* (Vol. 3). Washington, DC: American Psychological Association. (p. 335)

Moynihan, D. P. (1979). Social science and the courts. *Public Interest*, 54, 12-31. (p. 12)

Mucchi-Faina, A., Maass, A., & Volpato, C. (1991). Social influence: The role of originality. *European Journal of Social Psychology*, 21, 183-197. (p. 251)

Muehlenhard, C. L. (1988). Misinterpreted dating behaviors and the risk of date rape. *Journal of Social and Clinical Psychology*, 6, 20-37. (p. 93)

Mueller, C. W., Donnerstein, E., & Hallam, J. (1983). Violent films and prosocial behavior. *Personality and Social Psychology Bulletin*, 9, 83-89. (p. 359)

Mullen, B. (1986). Atrocity as a function of lynch mob composition: A self-attention perspective. *Personality and Social Psychology Bulletin*, 12, 187-197. (a) (p. 364)

Mullen, B. (1986). Stuttering, audience size, and the other-total ratio: A self-attention perspective. *Journal of Applied Social Psychology*, 16, 139-149. (b) (p. 220)

Mullen, B., & Baumeister, R. F. (1987). Group effects on self-attention and performance: Social loafing, social facilitation, and social impairment. In C. Hendrick (Ed.), *Group processes and intergroup relations: Review of personality and social psychology*, Vol. 9. Newbury Park, Ca.: Sage. (p. 221)

Mullen, B., & Copper, C. (1994). The relation between group cohesiveness and performance: An integration. *Psychological Bulletin*, 115, 210-227. (p. 240)

Mullen, B., & Goethals, G. R. (1990). Social projection, actual consensus and valence. British *Journal of Social Psychology*, 29, 279-282. (p. 60)

Mullen, B., & Hu, L. (1989). Perceptions of ingroup and outgroup variability: A meta-analytic integration. *Basic and*

Applied Social Psychology, 10, 233-252. (p. 443)

Mullen, B., & Riordan, C. A. (1988). Self-serving attributions for performance in naturalistic settings: A meta-analytic review. *Journal of Applied Social Psychology*, 18, 3-22. (p. 55)

Mullen, B., Brown, R., & Smith, C. (1992). Ingroup bias as a function of salience, relevance, and status: An integration. *European Journal of Social Psychology*, 22, 103-122. (p. 435)

Mullen, B., Bryant, B., & Driskell, J. E. (1997). Presence of others and arousal: An integration. *Group Dynamics: Theory, Research, and Practice*, 1, 52-64. (p. 218)

Mullen, B., Salas, E., & Driskell, J. E. (1989). Salience, motivation, and artifact as contributions to the relation between participation rate and leadership. *Journal of Experimental Social Psychology*, 25, 545-559. (p. 252)

Muller, S., & Johnson, B. T. (1990). *Fear and persuasion: A linear relationship?* Paper presented to the Eastern Psychological Association convention. (p. 154)

Mullin, C. R., & Linz, D. (1995). Desensitization and resensitization to violence against women: Effects of exposure to sexually violent films on judgments of domestic violence victims. *Journal of Personality and Social Psychology*, 69, 449-459. (p. 351)

Munro, G. D., Ditto, P. H., Lockhart, L. K., Fagerlin, A., Gready, M., & Peterson, E. (1997). *Biased assimilation of sociopolitcal arguments: Evaluating the 1996 U.S. Presidential debate.* Unpublished manuscript, Hope College. (p. 75)

Muraven, M., Tice, D. M., & Baumeister, R. F. (1998). Self-control as a limited resource: Regulatory depletion patterns. *Journal of Personality and Social Psychology*, 74, 774-790. (p. 52)

Murphy, C. M., & O'Farrell, T. J. (1996). Marital violence among alcoholics. *Current Directions in Psychological Science*, 5, 183-187. (p. 336)

Murphy-Berman, V., & Sharma, R. (1986). Testing the assumptions of attribution theory in India. *Journal of Social Psychology*, 126, 607-616. (p. 69)

Murphy-Berman, V., Berman, J. J., Singh, P., Pachauri, A., & Kumar, P. (1984). Factors affecting allocation to needy and meritorious recipients: A cross-cultural comparison. *Journal of Personality and Social Psychology*, 46, 1267-1272. (p. 473)

Murray, J. P., & Kippax, S. (1979). From the early window to the late night show: International trends in the study of television's impact on children and adults. In L. Berkowitz (Ed.), *Advances in experimental social psychology*, vol. 12. New York: Academic Press. (p. 355)

Murray, S. L., & Holmes, J. G. (1997). A leap of faith? Positive illusions in romantic relationships. *Personality and Social Psychology Bulletin*, 23, 586-604. (p. 394)

Murray, S. L., Gellavia, G. M., Rose, P., & Griffin, D. W. (2003). Once hurt, twice hurtful: How perceived regard regulates daily marital interactions. *Journal of Personality and Social Psychology*, 84, 126-147. (p. 106)

Murray, S. L., Holmes, J. G., & Griffin, D. W. (1996). The benefits of positive illusions: Idealization and the construction of satisfaction in close relationships. *Journal of Personality and Social Psychology*, 70, 79-98. (p. 394)

Murray, S. L., Holmes, J. G., & Griffin, D. W. (1996). The self-fulfilling nature of positive illusions in romantic relationships: Love is not blind, but prescient. *Journal of Personality and Social Psychology*, 71, 1155-1180. (p. 105)

Murray, S. L., Holmes, J. G., & Griffin, D. W. (2000). Self-esteem and the quest for felt security: How perceived regard regulates attachment processes. *Journal of Personality and Social Psychology*, 78, 478-498. (p. 406)

Murray, S. L., Holmes, J. G., Gellavia, G., Griffin, D. W., & Dolderman, D. (2002). Kindred spirits? The benefits of egocentrism in close relationships. *Journal of Personality and Social Psychology*, 82, 563-581. (p. 389)

Murray, S. L., Holmes, J. G., MacDonald, G., & Ellsworth, P. C. (1998). Through the looking glass darkly? When self-doubts turn into relationship insecurities. *Journal of Personality and Social Psychology*, 75, 1459-1480. (p. 48)

Murray, S. L., Rose, P., Bellavia, G. M., Holmes, J. G., & Kusche, A. G. (2002). When rejection stings: How self-esteem constrains relationship-enhancement processes. *Journal of Personality and Social Psychology*, 83, 556-573. (p. 406)

Murray, S. L., Rose, P., Holmes, J. G., Derrick, J., Podchaski, E. J., Bellavia, G., et al. (2005). Putting the partner within reach: A dyadic perspective on felt security in close relationships. *Journal of Personality and Social Psychology*, **88**, 327. (p. 393)

Murray, S.L., Holmes, J.G., Griffin, D.W., Bellavia, G., & Rose, P. (2001). The mismeasure of love: How self-doubt contaminates relationship beliefs. *Personality and Social Psychology Bulletin*, 27, 423-436. (p. 406)

Murstein, B. L. (1986). Paths to marriage. Newbury Park, Ca.: Sage. (p. 380)

Muson, G. (1978). Teenage violence and the telly. *Psychology Today*, March, pp. 50-54. (p. 356)

Mussweiler, T. (2006). Doing is for thinking! Stereotype activation by stereotypic movements. *Psychological Science*, **17**, 17-21. (p. 135)

Myers, D. G. (1993). *The pursuit of happiness.* New York: Avon. (p. 90)

Myers, D. G. (2000). *The American paradox: Spiritual hunger in an age of plenty.* New Haven, Conn.: Yale University Press. (p. 411)

Myers, D. G., & Bishop, G. D. (1970). Discussion effects on racial attitudes. *Science*, 169, 778-789. (p. 235)

Myers, D. G., & Scanzoni, L. D. (2005). *What God has joined together? A Christian case for gay marriage.* San Francisco: Harper San Francisco. (p. 145)

Myers, N. (2000). Sustainable consumption: The meta-problem. In B. Heap & J. Kent (Eds.), *Towards sustainable consumption: A European perspective.* London: The Royal Society. (p. 528)

Nadler, A., & Fisher, J. D. (1986). The role of threat to self-esteem and perceived control in recipient reaction to help: Theory development and empirical validation. In L. Berkowitz (Ed.), *Advances in experimental social psychology*, vol. 19. Orlando, FL: Academic Press. (p. 303)

Nadler, A., Goldberg, M., & Jaffe, Y. (1982). Effect of self-differentiation and anonymity in group on deindividuation. *Journal of Personality and Social Psychology*, 42, 1127-1136. (p. 232)

Nagar, D., & Pandey, J. (1987). Affect and performance on cognitive task as a function of crowding and noise. *Journal of Applied Social Psychology*, 17, 147-157. (p. 220)

Nail, P. R., MacDonald, G., & Levy, D. A. (2000). Proposal of a four-dimensional

model of social response. *Psychological Bulletin*, 126, 454-470. (p. 183)

National Television *Violence Study* (1997). Thousand Oaks, CA: Sage. (p. 355)

Needles, D. J., & Abramson, L. Y. (1990). Positive life events, attributional style, and hopefulness: Testing a model of recovery from depression. *Journal of Abnormal Psychology*, 99, 156-165. (p. 493)

Neff, L. A., & Karney, B. R. (2005). To know you is to love you: The implications of global adoration and specific accuracy for marital relationships. *Journal of Personality and Social Psychology,* ***88***, 480. (p. 409)

Nelson, L. D., & Morrison, E. L. (2005). The symptoms of resource scarcity: Judgments of food and finances influence preferences for potential partners. *Psychological Science,* ***16***, 167. (p. 383)

Nelson, L. J., & Miller, D. T. (1997). The distinctiveness effect in social categorization: You are what makes you unusual. *Psychological Science*, in press. (p. 445)

Nelson, L., & LeBoeuf, R. (2002). Why do men overperceive women's sexual intent? False consensus vs. evolutionary explanations. Paper presented to the annual meeting of the Society for Personality and Social Psychology. (p. 93)

Nelson, T. E., Acker, M., & Manis, M. (1996). Irrepressible stereotypes. *Journal of Experimental Social Psychology*, 32, 13-38. (p. 457)

Nelson, T. E., Biernat, M. R., & Manis, M. (1990). Everyday base rates (sex stereotypes): Potent and resilient. *Journal of Personality and Social Psychology*, 59, 664-675. (p. 456)

Nemeth, C. (1979). The role of an active minority in intergroup relations. In W. G. Austin and S. Worchel (Eds.), *The social psychology of intergroup relations*. Monterey, Calif.: Brooks/Cole. (p. 251)

Nemeth, C. J. (1999). Behind the scenes. In D. G. Myers, *Social psychology*, 6th edition. New York: McGraw-Hill. (p. 253)

Nemeth, C. J., Connell, J. B., Rogers, J. D., & Brown, K. S. (2001). Improving decision making by means of dissent. *Journal of Applied Social Psychology,* ***31***, 48. (p. 244)

Nemeth, C., & Chiles, C. (1988). Modelling courage: The role of dissent in fostering independence. *European Journal of Social Psychology*, 18, 275-280. (p. 202)

Nemeth, C., & Wachtler, J. (1974). Creating the perceptions of consistency and confidence: A necessary condition for minority influence. *Sociometry*, 37, 529-540. (p. 252)

Nemeth, C., Brown, K., & Rogers, J. (2001). Devil's advocate versus authentic dissent: Stimulating quantity and quality. *European Journal of Social Psychology,* ***31***, 707. (p. 244)

Neumann, R., & Strack, F. (2000). Approach and avoidance: The influence of proprioceptive and exteroceptive cues on encoding of affective information. *Journal of Personality and Social Psychology*, 79, 39-48. (p. 185)

Newcomb, T. M. (1961). *The acquaintance process*. New York: Holt, Rinehart and Winston. (p. 375)

Newman, A. (2001, February 4). Rotten teeth and dead babies. New York Times Magazine (www.nytimes.com). (p. 154)

Newman, H. M., & Langer, E. J. (1981). Post-divorce adaptation and the attribution of responsibility. *Sex Roles*, 7, 223-231. (p. 64)

Newman, L. S. (1993). How individualists interpret behavior: Idiocentrism and spontaneous trait inference. *Social Cognition*, 11, 243-269. (p. 272)

Newport, F., Moore, D. W., Jones, J. M., & Saad, L. (2003, March 21). Special release: American opinion on the war. *Gallup Poll Tuesday Briefing* (www.gallup.com/poll/tb/goverpubli/s0030325.asp). (p. 144)

Nias, D. K. B. (1979). Marital choice: Matching or complementation? In M. Cook and G. Wilson (Eds.), *Love and attraction*. Oxford: Pergamon. (p. 390)

Nichols, J. (2003, February 9). Man overdoses online as chatters watch him die. *Grand Rapids Press*, p. A20. (p. 314)

Nicholson, N., Cole, S. G., & Rocklin, T. (1985). Conformity in the Asch situation: A comparison between contemporary British and U. S. university students. *British Journal of Social Psychology*, 24, 59-63. (p. 278)

Niemi, R. G., Mueller, J., & Smith, T. W. (1989). *Trends in public opinion: A compendium of survey data*. New York: Greenwood Press. (p. 366)

Nigro, G. N., Hill, D. E., Gelbein, M. E., & Clark, C. L. (1988). Changes in the facial prominence of women and men over the last decade. *Psychology of Women Quarterly*, 12, 225-235. (p. 431)

Nisbett, R. (2003). *The geography of thought: How Asians and Westerners think differently . . . and why*. New York: Free Press. (p. 267)

Nisbett, R. E. (1990). Evolutionary psychology, biology, and cultural evolution. *Motivation and Emotion*, 14, 255-263. (p. 344)

Nisbett, R. E. (1993). Violence and U.S. regional culture. *American Psychologist*, 48, 441-449. (p. 344)

Nisbett, R. E., & Ross, L. (1980). *Human inference: Strategies and shortcomings of social judgment*. Englewood Cliffs, N.J.: Prentice-Hall. (p. 108)

Nisbett, R. E., & Ross, L. (1991). *The person and the situation*. New York: McGraw-Hill. (p. 248)

Nisbett, R. E., & Schachter, S. (1966). Cognitive manipulation of pain. *Journal of Experimental Social Psychology*, 2, 227-236. (p. 40)

Nisbett, R. E., Fong, G. T., Lehman, D. R., & Cheng, P. W. (1987). Teaching reasoning. *Science*, 238, 625-631. (p. 109)

Nisbett, R. E., Peng, K., Choi, I., & Norenzayan, A. (2001). Culture and systems of thought: Holistic versus analytic cognition. *Psychological Review*, 108, 291-310. (p. 273)

Nix, G., Watson, C., Pyszczynski, T., & Greenberg, J. (1995). Reducing depressive affect through external focus of attention. *Journal of Social and Clinical Psychology*, 14, 36-52. (p. 493)

Nolan, S. A., Flynn, C., & Garber, J. (2003). Prospective relations between rejection and depression in young adolescents. *Journal of Personality and Social Psychology*, 85, 745-755. (p. 372)

Noller, P., & Fitzpatrick, M. A. (1990). Marital communication in the eighties. *Journal of Marriage and the Family*, 52, 832-843. (p. 412)

Noon, E., & Hollin, C. R. (1987). Lay knowledge of eyewitness behaviour: A British survey. *Applied Cognitive Psychology*, 1, 143-153. (p. 520)

Norem, J. K., & Cantor, N. (1986). Defensive pessimism: Harnessing anxiety as motivation. *Journal of Personality and Social Psychology*, 51, 1208-1217. (p. 60)

Norenzayan, A., & Heine, S. J. (2005). Psychological universals: What are they and how can we know? *Psychological Bulletin,* ***131***, 763. (p. 261)

Norenzayan, A., Nisbett, R. E., & Choi, I. (2002). Cultural similarities and differences in social inference: Evidence from behavioral predictions and lay theories of behavior. *Personality and Social Psychology Bulletin*, 28, 109-120. (p. 272)

Notarius, C., & Markman, H. J. (1993). *We can work it out*. New York: Putnam. (p. 412)

Nuttin, J. M., Jr. (1987). Affective consequences of mere ownership: The name letter effect in twelve European languages. *European Journal of Social Psychology*, 17, 318-402. (p. 377)

O'Dea, T. F. (1968). Sects and cults. In D. L. Sills (Ed.), *International encyclopedia of the social sciences* (Vol. 14). New York: Macmillan. (p. 172)

O'Leary, K. D., Christian, J. L., & Mendell, N. R. (1994). A closer look at the link between marital discord and depressive symptomatology. *Journal of Social and Clinical Psychology*, 13, 33-41. (p. 412)

Oaten, M., & Cheng, K. (2006). Improved self-control: The benefits of a regular program of academic study. *Basic and Applied Social Psychology, **28***, 1. (p. 52)

Oddone-Paolucci, E., Genuis, M., & Violato, C. (2000). A meta-analysis of the published research on the effects of pornography. In C. Violata (Ed.), *The changing family and child development*. Aldershot, England: Ashgate Publishing. (p. 351)

Ohbuchi, K., & Kambara, T. (1985). Attacker's intent and awareness of outcome, impression management, and retaliation. *Journal of Experimental Social Psychology*, 21, 321-330. (p. 347)

Olfson, M., & Pincus, H. A. (1994). Outpatient therapy in the United States: II. Patterns of utilization. *American Journal of Psychiatry*, 151, 1289-1294. (p. 499)

Oliner, S. P., & Oliner, P. M. (1988). *The altruistic personality: Rescuers of Jews in Nazi Europe*. New York: The Free Press. (p. 326)

Olson, I. R., & Marshuetz, C. (2005). Facial attractiveness is appraised in a glance. *Emotion, **5***, 498.

Olson, J. M., & Cal, A. V. (1984). Source credibility, attitudes, and the recall of past behaviours. *European Journal of Social Psychology*, 14, 203-210. (p. 149)

Olson, J. M., & Zanna, M. P. (1981). *Promoting physical activity: A social psychological perspective*. Report prepared for the Ministry of Culture and Recreation, Sports and Fitness Branch, 77 Bloor St. West, 8th Floor, Toronto, Ontario M7A 2R9, November. (p. 112)

Olson, J. M., Roese, N. J., & Zanna, M. P. (1996). Expectancies. In E. T. Higgins & A. W. Kruglanski (eds.), *Social psychology: Handbook of basic principles*. New York: Guilford Press, in press. (p. 105)

Olweus, D. (1979). Stability of aggressive reaction patterns in males: A review. *Psychological Bulletin*, 86, 852-875. (p. 336)

Olweus, D., Mattsson, A., Schalling, D., & Low, H. (1988). Circulating testosterone levels and aggression in adolescent males: A causal analysis. *Psychosomatic Medicine*, 50, 261-272. (p. 337)

Orbell, J. M., van de Kragt, A. J. C., & Dawes, R. M. (1988). Explaining discussion-induced cooperation. *Journal of Personality and Social Psychology*, 54, 811-819. (p. 471)

Orive, R. (1984). Group similarity, public self-awareness, and opinion extremity: A social projection explanation of deindividuation effects. *Journal of Personality and Social Psychology*, 47, 727-737. (p. 231)

Ornstein, R. (1991). *The evolution of consciousness: Of Darwin, Freud, and cranial fire: The origins of the way we think*. New York: Prentice-Hall. (p. 122)

Osbeck, L. M., Moghaddam, F. M., & Perreault, S. (1996). Similarity and attraction among majority and minority groups in a multicultural context. *International Journal of Intercultural Relations*, 20, 1-10. (p. 389)

Osberg, T. M., & Shrauger, J. S. (1986). Self-prediction: Exploring the parameters of accuracy. *Journal of Personality and Social Psychology*, 51, 1044-1057. (p. 41)

Osberg, T. M., & Shrauger, J. S. (1990). The role of self-prediction in psychological assessment. In J. N. Butcher & C. D. Spielberger (Eds.), *Advances in Personality Assessment*, vol. 8. Hillsdale, NJ: Erlbaum. (p. 41)

Osborne, J. W. (1995). Academics, self-esteem, and race: A look at the underlying assumptions of the disidentification hypothesis. *Personality and Social Psychology Bulletin*, 21, 449-455. (p. 454)

Osgood, C. E. (1962). An alternative to war or surrender. Urbana, Ill.: University of Illinois Press. (p. 481)

Osgood, C. E. (1980). *GRIT: A strategy for survival in mankind's nuclear age?* Paper presented at the Pugwash Conference on New Directions in Disarmament, Racine, Wis. (p. 481)

Oskamp, S. (1991). *Curbside recycling: Knowledge, attitudes, and behavior*. Paper presented at the Society for Experimental Social Psychology meeting, Columbus, Ohio. (p. 116)

Osterhouse, R. A., & Brock, T. C. (1970). Distraction increases yielding to propaganda by inhibiting counterarguing. *Journal of Personality and Social Psychology*, 15, 344-358. (p. 166)

Ostrom, T. M., & Sedikides, C. (1992). Outgroup homogeneity effects in natural and minimal groups. *Psychological Bulletin*, 112, 536-552. (p. 443)

Oyserman, D., Coon, H. M., & Kemmelmeier, M. (2002a). Rethinking individualism and collectivism: Evaluation of theoretical assumptions and meta-analyses. *Psychological Bulletin*, 128, 3-72. (p. 267)

Oyserman, D., Kemmelmeier, M., & Coon, H. M. (2002b). Cultural psychology, a new look: Reply to Bond (2002), Fiske (2002), Kitayama (2002), and Miller (2002). *Psychological Bulletin*, 128, 110-117. (p. 267)

Padgett, V. R. (1989). *Predicting organizational violence: An application of 11 powerful principles of obedience*. Paper presented at the American Psychological Association Convention. (p. 192)

Pallak, M. S., Mueller, M., Dollar, K., & Pallak, J. (1972). Effect of commitment on responsiveness to an extreme consonant communication. *Journal of Personality and Social Psychology*, 23, 429-436. (p. 157)

Palmer, D. L. (1996). Determinants of Canadian attitudes toward immigration: More than just racism? *Canadian Journal of Behavioural Science*, 28, 180-192. (p. 432)

Palmer, E. L., & Dorr, A. (Eds.) (1980). *Children and the faces of television: Teaching, violence, selling*. New York: Academic Press. (p. 177)

Paloutzian, R. (1979). *Pro-ecology behavior: Three field experiments on litter pickup*. Paper presented at the Western Psychological Association convention. (p. 161)

Pandey, J., Sinha, Y., Prakash, A., & Tripathi, R. C. (1982). Right-left political ideologies and attribution of the causes of poverty. *European Journal of Social Psychology*, 12, 327-331. (p. 101)

Papastamou, S., & Mugny, G. (1990). Synchronic consistency and psychologization in minority influence. *European Journal of Social Psychology*, 20, 85-98. (p. 251)

Pape, R. (2003). *Dying to Win: The Strategic Logic of Suicide Terrorism*. New York: Random House. (p. 333)

Park, B., & Rothbart, M. (1982). Perception of out-group homogeneity and levels of social categorization: Memory for the subordinate attributes of in-group and out-group members. *Journal of Personality and Social Psychology*, 42, 1051-1068. (p. 443)

Parke, R. D., Berkowitz, L., Leyens, J. P., West, S. G., & Sebastian, J. (1977). Some effects of violent and nonviolent movies on the behavior of juvenile delinquents. In L. Berkowitz (Ed.), *Advances in experimental social psychology* (Vol. 10). New York: Academic Press. (p. 357)

Parker, K. D., Ortega, S. T., & VanLaningham, J. (1995). Life satisfaction, self-esteem, and personal happiness among Mexican and African Americans. *Sociological Spectrum*, 15, 131-145. (p. 507)

Parks, C. D., & Rumble, A. C. (2001). Elements of reciprocity and social value orientation. *Personality and Social Psychology Bulletin*, 27, 1301-1309. (p. 482)

Pascarella, E. T., & Terenzini, P. T. (1991). *How collects affects students: Findings and insights from twenty years of research*. San Francisco: Jossey-Bass. (p. 235)

Patterson, G. R., Chamberlain, P., & Reid, J. B. (1982). A comparative evaluation of parent training procedures. *Behavior Therapy*, 13, 638-650. (p. 343)

Patterson, G. R., Littman, R. A., & Bricker, W. (1967). Assertive behavior in children: A step toward a theory of aggression. *Monographs of the Society of Research in Child Development* (Serial No. 113), 32, 5. (p. 342)

Paulhus, D. (1982). Individual differences, self-presentation, and cognitive dissonance: Their concurrent operation in forced compliance. *Journal of Personality and Social Psychology*, 43, 838-852. (p. 128)

Paulhus, D. L. (1998). Interpersonal and intrapsychic adaptiveness of trait self-enhancement: A mixed blessing? *Journal of Personality and Social Psychology*, 74, 1197-1208. (p. 495)

Paulhus, D. L., & Lim, D. T. K. (1994). Arousal and evaluative extremity in social judgments: A dynamic complexity model. *European Journal of Social Psychology*, 24, 89-99. (p. 91)

Paulhus, D. L., & Morgan, K. L. (1997). Perceptions of intelligence in leaderless groups: The dynamic effects of shyness and acquaintance. *Journal of Personality and Social Psychology*, 72, 581-591. (p. 495)

Paulus, P. B. (1998). Developing consensus about groupthink after all these years. *Organizational Behavior and Human Decision Processes*, in press. (p. 244)

Paulus, P. B. Brown, V., & Ortega, A. H. (1997). Group creativity. In R. E. Purser and A. Montuori (eds.), *Social creativity*, vol. 2. Cresskill, NJ: Hampton Press. (p. 246)

Paulus, P. B., Larey, T. S., & Dzindolet, M. T. (1998). Creativity in groups and teams. In M. Turner (ed.), *Groups at work: Advances in theory and research*. Hillsdale, NJ: Erlbaum. (p. 246)

Paulus, P. B., Larey, T. S., & Ortega, A. H. (1995). Performance and perceptions of brainstormers in an organizational setting. *Basic and Applied Social Psychology*, 17, 249-265. (p. 246)

Payne, B. K. (2001). Prejudice and perception: The role of automatic and controlled processes in misperceiving a weapon. *Journal of Personality and Social Psychology*, 81, 181-192. (p. 420)

Pearl, E., & Lambert, E. (1962). The relation of bilingualism to intelligence. *Psychological Monographs*, 546. (p. 289)

Pedersen, A., & Walker, I. (1997). Prejudice against Australian Aborigines: Old-fashioned and modern forms. *European Journal of Social Psychology*, 27, 561-587. (p. 419)

Pedersen, W. C., Gonzales, C., & Miller, N. (2000). The moderating effect of trivial triggering provocation on displaced aggression. *Journal of Personality and Social Psychology*, 78, 913-927. (p. 339)

Pegalis, L. J., Shaffer, D. R., Bazzini, D. G., & Greenier, K. (1994). On the ability to elicit self-disclosure: Are there gender-based and contextual limitations on the opener effect? *Personality and Social Psychology Bulletin*, 20, 412-420. (p. 408)

Pelham, B. W., Mirenberg, M. C., & Jones, J. T. (2002). Why Susie sells seashells by the seashore. Implicit egotism and major life decisions. *Journal of Personality and Social Psychology*, 82, 469-487. (p. 378)

Peng, K., & Nisbett, R. E. (1999). Dialectical responses to questions about dialectical thinking. *American Psychologist*, 55, 1067-1068. (p. 273)

Pennebaker, J. (1990). *Opening up: The healing power of confiding in others*. New York: William Morrow. (p. 504)

Pennebaker, J. W. (1982). *The psychology of physical symptoms*. New York: Springer-Verlag. (p. 497)

Pennebaker, J. W., & O'Heeron, R. C. (1984). Confiding in others and illness rate among spouses of suicide and accidental death victims. *Journal of Abnormal Psychology*, 93, 473-476. (p. 504)

Pennebaker, J. W., Rime, B., & Sproul, G. (1996). Stereotypes of emotional expressiveness of northerners and southerners: A cross-cultural test of Montesquieu's hypotheses. *Journal of Personality and Social Psychology*, 70, 372-380. (p. 417)

Pennington, N., & Hastie, R. (1993). The story model for juror decision making. In R. Hastie (ed.), *Inside the juror: The psychology of juror decision making*. New York: Cambridge University Press. (p. 522)

Penton-Voak, I. S., Perrett, D. I., & Peirce, J. W. (2001). *Computer graphic studies of the role of facial similarity in judgements of attractiveness*. New Brunswick, NJ, US: Transaction Publishers. (p. 383)

Peplau, L. A., & Gordon, S. L. (1985). Women and men in love: Gender differences in close heterosexual relationships. In V. E. O'Leary, R. K. Unger, & B. S. Wallston (Eds.), *Women, gender, and social psychology*. Hillsdale, N.J.: Erlbaum. (p. 400)

Pereira, J. (2003, January 10). Just how far does First Amendment protection go? *Wall Street Journal*, pp. B1, B3. (p. 361)

Perkins, H. W. (1991). Religious commitment, Yuppie values, and well-being in post-collegiate life. *Review of Religious Research*, 32, 244-251. (p. 506)

Perlman, D., & Rook, K. S. (1987). Social support, social deficits, and the family: Toward the enhancement of well-being. In S. Oskamp (Ed.), *Family processes and problems: Social psychological aspects*. Newbury Park, CA: Sage. (p. 506)

Perloff, L. S. (1987). Social comparison and illusions of invulnerability. In C. R. Snyder & C. R. Ford (Eds.), *Coping with negative life events: Clinical and social psychological perspectives.* New York: Plenum. (p. 59)

Perls, F. S. (1973). Ego, hunger and aggression: The beginning of Gestalt therapy. Random House, 1969. Cited by Berkowitz in The case for bottling up rage. *Psychology Today*, July, pp. 24-30. (p. 366)

Perrin, S., & Spencer, C. (1981). Independence or conformity in the Asch experiment as a reflection of cultural or situational factors. *British Journal of Social Psychology*, 20, 205-209. (p. 278)

Persico, N., Postelwaite, A., & Silverman, D. (2004). The effect of adolescent experience on labor market outcomes: The case of height. *Journal of Political Economy,* **112**, 1019-1053. (p. 382)

Persky, S. & Blascovich, J. (2007). Immersive virtual environments versus traditional platforms: Effects of violent and nonviolent video game play. *Media Psychology,* **10**, 135-156.

Pessin, J., & Husband, R. W. (1933). Effects of social stimulation on human maze learning. *Journal of Abnormal and Social Psychology*, 28, 148-154. (p. 218)

Peterson, B.E., Doty, R.M., & Winter, D.G. (1993). Authoritarianism and attitudes toward contemporary social issues. *Personality and Social Psychology Bulletin*, 17, 174-184. (p. 428)

Peterson, C., & Bossio, L. M. (2000). Optimism and physical well-being. In E. C. Chang (Ed.), *Optimism and pessimism.* Washington, D.C.: APA Books. (p. 502)

Peterson, C., & Seligman, M. E. P. (1987). Explanatory style and illness. *Journal of Personality*, 55, 237-265. (p. 502)

Peterson, C., Schwartz, S. M., & Seligman, M. E. P. (1981). Self-blame and depression symptoms. *Journal of Personality and Social Psychology*, 41, 253-259. (p. 64)

Peterson, J. L., & Zill, N. (1981). Television viewing in the United States and children's intellectual, social, and emotional development. *Television and Children*, 2(2), 21-28. (p. 360)

Peterson, R. S., & Nemeth, C. J. (1996). Focus versus flexibility: Majority and minority influence can both improve performance. *Personality and Social Psychology Bulletin*, 22, 14-23. (p. 251)

Peto, R., Lopez, A. D., Boreham, J., Thun, M., & Heath, C., Jr. (1992). Mortality from tobacco in developed countries: Indirect estimation from national vital statistics. *Lancet*, 339, 1268-1278. (p. 111)

Pettigrew, T. F. (1958). Personality and socio-cultural factors in intergroup attitudes: A cross-national comparison. *Journal of Conflict Resolution*, 2, 29-42. (p. 430)

Pettigrew, T. F. (1979). The ultimate attribution error: Extending Allport's cognitive analysis of prejudice. *Personality and Social Psychology Bulletin*, 55, 461-476. (p. 449)

Pettigrew, T. F. (1980). Prejudice. In S. Thernstrom et al. (Eds.), *Harvard encyclopedia of American ethnic groups.* Cambridge, Mass.: Harvard University Press. (p. 449)

Pettigrew, T. F. (1997). Generalized intergroup contact effects on prejudice. *Personality and Social Psychology Bulletin*, 23, 173-185. (p. 282)

Pettigrew, T. F. (1998). Intergroup contact theory. *Annual Review of Psychology*, in press. (p. 282)

Pettigrew, T. F. (2003). Peoples under threat: Americans, Arabs, and Israelis. *Peace and Conflict: Journal of Peace Psychology,* **9**, 69. (p. 340)

Pettigrew, T. F., & Meertens, R. W. (1995). Subtle and blatant prejudice in western Europe. *European Journal of Social Psychology*, 25, 57-76. (p. 432)

Pettigrew, T. F., & Tropp, L. R. (2006). A meta-analytic test of intergroup contact theory. *Journal of Personality and Social Psychology,* **90**, 751. (p. 282)

Petty, R. E., & Cacioppo, J. T. (1979). Effects of forewarning of persuasive intent and involvement on cognitive response and persuasion. *Personality and Social Psychology Bulletin*, 5, 173-176. (a) (p. 157)

Petty, R. E., & Cacioppo, J. T. (1986). *Communication and persuasion: Central and peripheral routes to attitude change.* New York: Springer-Verlag. (p. 146)

Petty, R. E., & Wegener, D. T. (1998). Attitude change: Multiple roles for persuasion variables. In D. Gilbert, S. Fiske, & G. Lindzey (eds), *Handbook of social psychology*, 4th edition. New York: McGraw-Hill. (p. 158)

Petty, R. E., & Wegener, D. T. (1999). The elaboration likelihood model: Current status and controversies. In S. Chaiken & Y. Trope (Eds.). *Dual-process theories in social psychology* (pp. 41-72). New York: Guilford. (p. 146)

Petty, R. E., Cacioppo, J. T., & Goldman, R. (1981). Personal involvement as a determinant of argument-based persuasion. *Journal of Personality and Social Psychology*, 41, 847-855. (p. 153)

Petty, R. E., Haugtvedt, C. P., & Smith, S. M. (1995). Elaboration as a determinant of attitude strength: Creating attitudes that are persistent, resistant, and predictive of behavior. In R. E. Petty & J. A. Krosnick (Eds.), *Attitude strength: Antecedents and consequences.* Hillsdale, NJ: Erlbaum. (p. 147)

Petty, R. E., Schumann, D. W., Richman, S. A., & Strathman, A. J. (1993). Positive mood and persuasion: Different roles for affect under high and low elaboration conditions. *Journal of Personality and Social Psychology*, 64, 5-20. (p. 153)

Petty, R. E., Wegener, D. T., & Fabrigar, L. R. (1997). Attitudes and attitude change. *Annual Review of Psychology*, 48, 609-647. (p. 140)

Pew (2003). Views of a changing world 2003. The Pew Global Attitudes Project. Washington, DC: Pew Research Center for the People and the Press (http://people-press.org/reports/pdf/185.pdf). (p. 144)

Phillips, D. P. (1985). Natural experiments on the effects of mass media violence on fatal aggression: Strengths and weaknesses of a new approach. In L. Berkowitz (Ed.), *Advances in experimental social psychology*, Vol. 19. Orlando, Fla.: Academic Press. (p. 185)

Phillips, D. P., Carstensen, L. L., & Paight, D. J. (1989). Effects of mass media news stories on suicide, with new evidence on the role of story content. In D. R. Pfeffer (Ed.), *Suicide among youth: Perspectives on risk and prevention.* Washington, DC: American Psychiatric Press. (p. 185)

Phinney, J. S. (1990). Ethnic identity in adolescents and adults: Review of research. *Psychological Bulletin*, 108, 499-514. (p. 287)

Piliavin, I. M., Rodin, J., & Piliavin, J. A. (1969). Good Samaritanism: An underground phenomenon. *Journal of Personality and Social Psychology*, 13, 289-299. (p. 316)

Piliavin, J. A. (2003). Doing well by doing good: Benefits for the benefactor. In C. L. M. Keyes, & J. Haidt (Eds.), *Flourishing: Positive psychology and the life well-lived.* 227-247. (p. 297)

Piliavin, J. A., Evans, D. E., & Callero, P. (1982). Learning to "Give to unnamed strangers": The process of commitment to regular blood donation. In E. Staub, D. Bar-Tal, J. Karylowski, & J. Reykawski (Eds.), *The development and maintenance of prosocial behavior: International perspectives*. New York: Plenum. (p. 297)

Pincus, J. H. (2001). *Base instincts: What makes killers kill?* New York: W. W. Norton & Co., Inc. (p. 335)

Pinel, E. C. (1999). Stigma consciousness: The psychological legacy of social stereotypes. *Journal of Personality and Social Psychology*, 76, 114-128. (p. 447)

Pinker, S. (2002). *The blank slate*. New York: Viking. (p. 257)

Platow, M. J., Haslam, S. A., Both, A., Chew, I., Cuddon, M., Goharpey, N., et al. (2005). "It's not funny if they're laughing": Self-categorization, social influence, and responses to canned laughter. *Journal of Experimental Social Psychology, **41***, 542-550.

Platz, S. J., & Hosch, H. M. (1988). Cross-racial/ethnic eyewitness identification: A field study. *Journal of Applied Social Psychology*, 18, 972-984. (p. 444)

Pliner, P., Hart, H., Kohl, J., & Saari, D. (1974). Compliance without pressure: Some further data on the foot-in-the-door technique. *Journal of Experimental Social Psychology*, 10, 17-22. (p. 122)

Poniewozik, J. (2003, November 24). All the news that fits your reality. *Time*, p. 90. (p. 74)

Popenoe, D. (2002). *Seven Secrets to a Happy Marriage*. New York: Ladies Home Journal. (p. 411)

Porter, N., Geis, F. L., & Jennings (Walstedt), J. (1983). Are women invisible as leaders? *Sex Roles*, 9, 1035-1049. (p. 423)

Postmes, T., & Spears, R. (1998). Deindividuation and antinormative behavior: A meta-analysis. *Psychological Bulletin*, 123, 238-259. (p. 231)

Potter, T., Corneille, O., Ruys, K. I., & Rhodes, G. (2007). "Just another pretty face": A multidimensional scaling approach to face attractiveness and variability. *Psychonomic Bulletin & Review, **14***, 368.

Powell, J. (1989). *Happiness is an inside job*. Valencia, CA: Tabor. (p. 54)

Pozo, C., Carver, C. S., Wellens, A. R., & Scheier, M. F. (1991). Social anxiety and social perception: Construing others' reactions to the self. *Personality and Social Psychology Bulletin*, 17, 355-362. (p. 495)

Pratkanis, A. R., & Turner, M. E. (1996). The procactive removal of discriminatory barriers: Affirmative action as effective help. *Journal of Social Issues*, 52, 111-132. (p. 303)

Pratkanis, A. R., Greenwald, A. G., Leippe, M. R., & Baumgardner, M. H. (1988). In search of reliable persuasion effects: III. The sleeper effect is dead. Long live the sleeper effect. *Journal of Personality and Social Psychology*, 54, 203-218. (p. 149)

Pratto, F., Sidanius, J., Stallworth, L. M., & Malle, B. F. (1994). Social dominance orientation: A personality variable predicting social and political attitudes. *Journal of Personality and Social Psychology*, 67, 741-763. (p. 427)

Prentice-Dunn, S., & Rogers, R. W. (1980). Effects of deindividuating situational cues and aggressive models on subjective deindividuation and aggression. *Journal of Personality and Social Psychology*, 39, 104-113. (p. 231)

Prentice-Dunn, S., & Rogers, R. W. (1989). Deindividuation and the self-regulation of behavior. In P. B. Paulus (Ed.), *Psychology of group influence*, 2nd ed. Hillsdale, N.J.: Erlbaum. (p. 231)

Presson, P. K., & Benassi, V. A. (1996). Illusion of control: A meta-analytic review. *Journal of Social Behavior and Personality*, 11, 493-510. (p. 89)

Price, G. H., Dabbs, J. M., Jr., Clower, B. J., & Resin, R. P. (1974). *At first glance-Or, is physical attractiveness more than skin deep?* Paper presented at the Eastern Psychological Association convention. Cited by K. L. Dion & K. K. Dion (1979). Personality and behavioral correlates of romantic love. In M. Cook & G. Wilson (Eds.), *Love and attraction*. Oxford: Pergamon. (p. 387)

Prislin, R., & Pool, G. J. (1996). Behavior, consequences, and the self: Is all well that ends well? *Personality and Social Psychology Bulletin*, 22, 933-948. (p. 139)

Pritchard, I. L. (1998). *The effects of rap music: On aggressive attitudes toward women*. Master's thesis, Humboldt State University. (p. 359)

Prohaska, V. (1994). "I know I'll get an A": Confident overestimation of final course grades. *Teaching of Psychology*, 21, 141-143. (p. 59)

Pronin, E., & Ross, L. (2006). Temporal differences in trait self-ascription: When the self is seen as an other. *Journal of Personality and Social Psychology, 90*(2), 197. (p. 99)

Pronin, E., Gilovich, T., & Ross, L. (2004). Objectivity in the eye of the beholder: Divergent perceptions of bias in self versus others. *Psychological Review, 111*(3), 781. (p. 102)

Pronin, E., Kruger, J., Savitsky, K., & Ross, L. (2001). You don't know me, but I know you: The illusion of asymmetric insight. *Journal of Personality and Social Psychology*, 81, 639-656. (p. 57)

Pronin, E., Lin, D. Y., & Ross, L. (2002). The bias blind spot: Perceptions of bias in self versus others. *Personality and Social Psychology Bulletin*, 28, 369-381. (p. 58)

Prothrow-Stith, D. (with M. Wiessman) (1991). *Deadly consequences*. New York: HarperCollins. (p. 478)

Pruitt, D. G. (1986, July). Trends in the scientific study of negotiation. Negotiation Journal, pp. 237-244. (p. 481)

Pruitt, D. G. (1998). Social conflict. In D. Gilbert, S. T. Fiske, & G. Lindzey (eds.), *Handbook of social psychology*, 4th ed. New York: McGraw-Hill. (p. 477)

Pruitt, D. G., & Kimmel, M. J. (1977). Twenty years of experimental gaming: Critique, synthesis, and suggestions for the future. *Annual Review of Psychology*, 28, 363-392. (p. 477)

Pruitt, D. G., & Lewis, S. A. (1975). Development of integrative solutions in bilateral negotiation. *Journal of Personality and Social Psychology*, 31, 621-633. (p. 477)

Pruitt, D. G., & Lewis, S. A. (1977). The psychology of integrative bargaining. In D. Druckman (Ed.), *Negotiations: A social-psychological analysis*. New York: Halsted. (p. 477)

Pruitt, D. G., & Rubin, J. Z. (1986). *Social conflict*. San Francisco: Random House. (p. 477)

Pryke, S., Lindsay, R. C. L., Dysart, J. E., & Dupuis, P. (2004). Multiple independent identification decisions: A method of calibrating eyewitness identifications. *Journal of Applied Psychology, 89*(1), 73. doi:10.1037/0021-9010.89.1.73. (p. 520)

Pryor, J. B. & Reeder, G. D. (1993). *The social psychology of HIV infection*. Hillsdale, NJ: Erlbaum. (p. 59)

Pryor, J. B., DeSouza, E. R., Fitness, J., Hutz, C., Kumpf, M., Lubbert, K., et al. (1997). Gender differences in the interpretation of social-sexual behavior: A cross-cultural

perspective on sexual harassment. *Journal of Cross-Cultural Psychology, 28*(5), 509.
Pryor, J. B., DeSouza, E. R., Fitness, J., Hutz, C., Kumpf, M., Lubbert, K., Pesonen, O., & Erber, M. W. (1997). Gender differences in the interpretation of social-sexual behavior: A cross-cultural perspective on sexual harassment. *Journal of Cross-Cultural Psychology*, 28, 509-534. (p. 93)
Public Opinion (1984, August/September). *Vanity Fare*, p. 22. (p. 57)
Purvis, J. A., Dabbs, J. M., Jr., & Hopper, C. H. (1984). The "opener": Skilled user of facial expression and speech pattern. *Personality and Social Psychology Bulletin*, 10, 61-66. (p. 408)
Putnam, R. (2000). *Bowling alone*. New York: Simon & Schuster. (p. 328)
Pyszczynski, T., & Greenberg, J. (1981). Determinants of reduction in intended effort as a strategy for coping with anticipated failure. *Journal of Research in Personality*, 17, 412-422. (p. 68)
Pyszczynski, T., Hamilton, J. C., Greenberg, J., & Becker, S. E. (1991). Self-awareness and psychological dysfunction. In C. R. Snyder & D. O. Forsyth (Eds.), *Handbook of social and clinical psychology: The health perspective*. New York: Pergamon. (p. 492)

Quartz, S. R., & Sejnowski, T. J. (2002). *Liars, lovers, and heroes: What the new brain science reveals about how we become who we are*. New York: Morrow. (p. 291)
Quattrone, G. A. (1982). Behavioral consequences of attributional bias. *Social Cognition*, 1, 358-378. (p. 100)
Quattrone, G. A., & Jones, E. E. (1980). The perception of variability within in-groups and out-groups: Implications for the law of small numbers. *Journal of Personality and Social Psychology*, 38, 141-152. (p. 447)

Raine, A. (1993). *The psychopathology of crime: Criminal behavior as a clinical disorder*. San Diego, CA: Academic Press. (p. 336)
Raine, A., Lencz, T., Bihrle, S., LaCasse, L., & Colletti, P. (2000). Reduced prefrontal gray matter volume and reduced autonomic activity in antisocial personality disorder. *Archives of General Psychiatry*, 57, 119-127. (p. 335)
Raine, A., Stoddard, J., Bihrle, S., & Buchsbaum, M. (1998). Prefrontal glucose deficits in murderers lacking psychosocial deprivation. *Neuropsychiatry, Neuropsychology, & Behavioral Neurology*, 11, 1-7. (p. 335)
Rank, S. G., & Jacobson, C. K. (1977). Hospital nurses' compliance with medication overdose orders: A failure to replicate. *Journal of Health and Social Behavior*, 18, 188-193. (p. 193)
Rapoport, A. (1960). *Fights, games, and debates*. Ann Arbor: University of Michigan Press. (p. 466)
Rawls, J. (1971). *A theory of justice*. Cambridge, MA: Belknap Press of Harvard University Press. (p. 473)
Reed, D. (1989, November 25). Video collection documents Christian resistance to Hitler. Associated Press release in *Grand Rapids Press*, pp. B4, B5. (p. 429)
Reeder, G. D., Fletcher, G. J., & Furman (1989). The role of observers' expectations in attitude attribution. *Journal of Experimental Social Psychology*, 25, 168-188. (p. 100)
Reese, N. J., & Olson, J. M. (1993). The structure of counterfactual thought. *Personality and Social Psychology Bulletin*, 19, 312-319. (p. 88)
Regan, D. T., & Cheng, J. B. (1973). Distraction and attitude change: A resolution. *Journal of Experimental Social Psychology*, 9, 138-147. (p. 166)
Regan, D. T., & Fazio, R. (1977). On the consistency between attitudes and behavior: Look to the method of attitude formation. *Journal of Experimental Social Psychology*, 13, 28-45. (p. 117)
Regan, D. T., Williams, M., & Sparling, S. (1972). Voluntary expiation of guilt: A field experiment. *Journal of Personality and Social Psychology*, 24, 42-45. (p. 300)
Regan, P. C. (1998). What if you can't get what you want? Willingness to compromise ideal mate selection standards as a function of sex, mate value, and relationship context. *Personality and Social Psychology Bulletin*, 24, 1294-1303. (p. 396)
Reid, P., & Finchilescu, G. (1995). The disempowering effects of media violence against women on college women. *Psychology of Women Quarterly*, 19, 397-411. (p. 360)
Reifman, A. S., Larrick, R. P., & Fein, S. (1991). Temper and temperature on the diamond: The heat-aggression relationship in major league baseball. *Personality and Social Psychology Bulletin*, 17, 580-585. (p. 346)
Reis, H. T., & Shaver, P. (1988). Intimacy as an interpersonal process. In S. Duck (Ed.), *Handbook of personal relationships: Theory, relationships and interventions*. Chichester, England: Wiley. (p. 408)
Reis, H. T., Nezlek, J., & Wheeler, L. (1980). Physical attractiveness in social interaction. *Journal of Personality and Social Psychology*, 38, 604-617. (p. 379)
Reis, H. T., Wheeler, L., Spiegel, N., Kernis, M. H., Nezlek, J., & Perri, M. (1982). Physical attractiveness in social interaction: II. Why does appearance affect social experience? *Journal of Personality and Social Psychology*, 43, 979-996. (p. 379)
Renaud, H., & Estess, F. (1961). Life history interviews with one hundred normal American males: "Pathogenecity" of childhood. *American Journal of Orthopsychiatry*, 31, 786-802. (p. 488)
Rhine, R. J., & Severance, L. J. (1970). Ego-involvement, discrepancy, source credibility, and attitude change. *Journal of Personality and Social Psychology*, 16, 175-190. (p. 157)
Rhodes, G. (2006). The evolutionary psychology of facial beauty. *Annual Review of Psychology, 57*, 199. (p. 383)
Rhodes, G., Sumich, A., & Byatt, G. (1999). Are average facial configurations attractive only because of their symmetry. *Psychological Science*, 10, 52-58. (p. 383)
Rhodes, N., & Wood, W. (1992). Self-esteem and intelligence affect influenceability: The mediating role of message reception. *Psychological Bulletin*, 111, 156-171. (p. 164)
Rhodewalt, F. (1987). *Is self-handicapping an effective self-protective attributional strategy?* Paper presented at the American Psychological Association convention. (p. 67)
Rhodewalt, F., Saltzman, A. T., & Wittmer J. (1984). Self-handicapping among competitive athletes: The role of practice in self-esteem protection. *Basic and Applied Social Psychology*, 5, 197-209. (p. 67)
Rholes, W. S., Newman, L. S., & Ruble, D. N. (1990). Understanding self and other: Developmental and motivational aspects of perceiving persons in terms of invariant dispositions. In E. T. Higgins & R. M. Sorrentino (Eds.), *Handbook of motivation and cognition: Foundations of social*

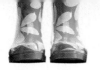

behavior, Vol. 2. New York: Guilford. (p. 272)

Rice, B. (1985, September). Performance review: The job nobody likes. *Psychology Today*, pp. 30-36. (p. 56)

Rice, M. E., & Grusec, J. E. (1975). Saying and doing: Effects on observer performance. *Journal of Personality and Social Psychology*, 32, 584-593. (p. 319)

Richards, Z., & Hewstone, M. (2001). Subtyping and subgrouping: Processes for the prevention and promotion of stereotype change. *Personality and Social Psychology Review*, 5, 52-73. (p. 451)

Richardson, J. T. E. (1990). Questionnaire studies of paramenstrual symptoms. *Psychology of Women Quarterly*, 14, 15-42. (p. 498)

Richardson, J. T. E. (1993). *The premenstrual syndrome: A brief history*. Paper presented to the Annual Conference of the British Psychological Society. (p. 499)

Richardson, L. F. (1960). Generalized foreign policy. *British Journal of Psychology Monographs Supplements*, 23. Cited by A. Rapoport in *Fights, games, and debates*. Ann Arbor: University of Michigan Press, 1960, p. 15. (p. 464)

Ridge, R. D., & Reber, J. S. (2002). "I think she's attracted to me": The effect of men's beliefs on women's behavior in a job interview scenario. *Basic and Applied Social Psychology*, 24, 1-14. (p. 106)

Riess, M., Rosenfeld, P., Melburg, V., & Tedeschi, J. T. (1981). Self-serving attributions: Biased private perceptions and distorted public descriptions. *Journal of Personality and Social Psychology*, 41, 224-231. (p. 68)

Riggs, J. M. (1992). Self-handicapping and achievement. In A. K. Boggiano & T. S. Pittman (Eds.), *Achievement and motivation: A social-developmental perspective*. New York: Cambridge University Press. (p. 68)

Riordan, C. A. (1980). *Effects of admission of influence on attributions and attraction*. Paper presented at the American Psychological Association convention. (p. 396)

Rivkin, I. D., & Taylor, S. E. (1999). The effects of mental simulation on coping with controllable stressful events. *Personality and Social Psychology Bulletin*, 25, 1451-1462. (p. 505)

Robberson, M. R., & Rogers, R. W. (1988). Beyond fear appeals: Negative and positive persuasive appeals to health and self-esteem. *Journal of Applied Social Psychology*, 18, 277-287. (p. 154)

Robertson, I. (1987). Sociology. New York: Worth Publishers. (p. 260)

Robins, R. W., Spranca, M. D., & Mendelsohn, G. A. (1996). The actor-observer effect revisited: Effects of individual differences and repeated social interactions on actor and observer attributions. *Journal of Personality and Social Psychology*, 71, 375-389. (p. 100)

Robinson, M. S., & Alloy, L. B. (2003). Negative cognitive styles and stress-reactive rumination interact to predict depression: A prospective study. *Cognitive Therapy and Research*, **27**, 275.

Robinson, T. N., Wilde, M. L., Navracruz, L. C., Haydel, F., & Varady, A. (2001). Effects of reducing children's television and video game use on aggressive behavior. *Archives of Pediatric and Adolescent Medicine*, 155, 17-23. (p. 369)

Rochat, F. (1993). *How did they resist authority? Protecting refugees in Le Chambon during World War II*. Paper presented at the American Psychological Association convention. (p. 196)

Rochat, F., & Modigliani, A. (1995). The ordinary quality of resistance: From Milgram's laboratory to the village of Le Chambon. *Journal of Social Issues*, 51, 195-210. (p. 196)

Rodin, M. (1992). The social construction of premenstrual syndrome. *Social Science and Medicine*, 35, 49-56. (p. 499)

Roese, N. J. (1997). The functional basis of counterfactual thinking. *Journal of Personality and Social Psychology*, 66, 805-818. (p. 88)

Roese, N. L., & Olson, J. M. (1994). Attitude importance as a function of repeated attitude expression. *Journal of Experimental Social Psychology*, 66, 805-818. (p. 140)

Roger, L. H., Cortes, D. E., & Malgady, R. B. (1991). Acculturation and mental health status among Hispanics: Convergence and new directions for research. *American Psychologist*, 46, 585-597. (p. 287)

Rogers, C. R. (1958). Reinhold Niebuhr's The self and the dramas of history: A criticism. *Pastoral Psychology*, 9, 15-17. (p. 54)

Rogers, C. R. (1980). *A way of being*. Boston: Houghton Mifflin. (p. 408)

Rogers, R. W., & Prentice-Dunn, S. (1981). Deindividuation and anger-mediated interracial aggression: Unmasking regressive racism. *Journal of Personality and Social Psychology*, 41, 63-73. (p. 418)

Rohrer, J. H., Baron, S. H., Hoffman, E. L., & Swander, D. V. (1954). The stability of autokinetic judgments. *Journal of Abnormal and Social Psychology*, 49, 595-597. (p. 184)

Rokeach, M. (1968). *Beliefs, attitudes, and values*. San Francisco: Jossey-Bass. (p. 389)

Rokeach, M., & Mezei, L. (1966). Race and shared beliefs as factors in social choice. *Science*, 151, 167-172. (p. 443)

Romer, D., Gruder, D. L., & Lizzadro, T. (1986). A person-situation approach to altruistic behavior. *Journal of Personality and Social Psychology*, 51, 1001-1012. (p. 322)

Rook, K. S. (1987). Social support versus companionship: Effects on life stress, loneliness, and evaluations by others. *Journal of Personality and Social Psychology*, 52, 1132-1147. (p. 504)

Rosenbaum, M. E., & Holtz, R. (1985). The minimal intergroup discrimination effect: Out-group derogation, not in-group favorability. Paper presented at the American Psychological Association convention. (p. 437)

Rosenberg, L. A. (1961). Group size, prior experience and conformity. *Journal of Abnormal and Social Psychology*, 63, 436-437. (p. 201)

Rosenberg, R. (1984). Leta Hollingworth: Toward a sexless intelligence. In M. Lewin (Ed.), *In the shadow of the past: Psychology portrays the sexes*. New York: Columbia University Press. (p. 499)

Rosenblatt, A., & Greenberg, J. (1988). Depression and interpersonal attraction: The role of perceived similarity. *Journal of Personality and Social Psychology*, 55, 112-119. (p. 390)

Rosenblatt, R. (1994, April 24). The buck stops somewhere else. *Detroit Free Press Magazine*, pp. 6-13. (p. 112)

Rosenfeld, D., Folger, R., & Adelman, H. F. (1980). When rewards reflect competence: A qualification of the overjustification effect. *Journal of Personality and Social Psychology*, 39, 368-376. (p. 136)

Rosenhan, D. L. (1970). The natural socialization of altruistic autonomy. In J. Macaulay & L. Berkowitz (Eds.) *Altruism and helping behavior*. New York: Academic Press. (p. 326)

Rosenhan, D. L. (1973). On being sane in insane places. *Science*, 179, 250-258. (p. 486)

Rosenthal, D. A., & Feldman, S. S. (1992). The nature and stability of ethnic identity in Chinese youth: Effects of length of residence in two cultural contexts. *Journal of Cross-Cultural Psychology*, 23, 214-227. (p. 287)

Rosenthal, R. (1985). From unconscious experimenter bias to teacher expectancy effects. In J. B. Dusek, V. C. Hall, & W. J. Meyer (Eds.), *Teacher expectancies.* Hillsdale, N.J.: Erlbaum. (p. 103)

Rosenthal, R. (1991). Teacher expectancy effects: A brief update 25 years after the Pygmalion experiment. *Journal of Research in Education*, 1, 3-12. (p. 104)

Rosenthal, R. (2002). Covert communication in classrooms, clinics, courtrooms, and cubicles. *American Psychologist, 57*(11), 839. (p. 104)

Rosenthal, R. (2003). Covert communication in laboratories, classrooms, and the truly real world. *Current Directions in Psychological Science, 12*(5), 151. (p. 105)

Rosenthal, R., & Jacobson, L. (1968). *Pygmalion in the classroom: Teacher expectation and pupils' intellectual development.* New York: Holt, Rinehart & Winston. (p. 104)

Ross, L. (1977). The intuitive psychologist and his shortcomings: Distortions in the attribution process. In L. Berkowitz (Ed.), *Advances in experimental social psychology* (Vol. 10). New York: Academic Press. (p. 95)

Ross, L. (1981). The "intuitive scientist" formulation and its developmental implications. In J. H. Havell & L. Ross (Eds.), *Social cognitive development: Frontiers and possible futures.* Cambridge, England: Cambridge University Press. (p. 36)

Ross, L., & Anderson, C. A. (1982). Shortcomings in the attribution process: On the origins and maintenance of erroneous social assessments. In D. Kahneman, P. Slovic, & A. Tversky (Eds.), *Judgment under uncertainty: Heuristics and biases.* New York: Cambridge University Press. (p. 76)

Ross, L., & Ward, A. (1995). Psychological barriers to dispute resolution. In M. P. Zanna (ed.), *Advances in experimental social psychology*, vol. 27. San Diego: Academic Press. (p. 479)

Ross, L., & Ward, A. (1996). Naive realism in everyday life: Implications for social conflict and misunderstanding. In T. Brown, E. Reed, & E. Turiel (Eds.), *Values and knowledge.* Hillsdale, NJ: Erlbaum. (p. 471)

Ross, L., Amabile, T. M., & Steinmetz, J. L. (1977). Social roles, social control, and biases in social-perception processes. *Journal of Personality and Social Psychology*, 35, 485-494. (p. 96)

Ross, M. & Wilson, A. E. (2002). It feels like yesterday: Self-esteem, valence of personal past experiences, and judgments of subjective distance. *Journal of Personality and Social Psychology*, 82, 792-803. (p. 61)

Ross, M., & Buehler, R. (1994). *Creative remembering. In U. Neisser & R. Fivush (eds.), The remembering self.* New York: Cambridge University Press. (p. 78)

Ross, M., & Fletcher, G. J. O. (1985). Attribution and social perception. In G. Lindzey & E. Aronson (Eds.), *The Handbook of Social Psychology*, 3rd ed. New York: Random House. (p. 91)

Ross, M., & Newby-Clark, I. R. (1998). Construing the past and future. *Social Cognition*, 16, 133-150. (p. 81)

Ross, M., & Sicoly, F. (1979). Egocentric biases in availability and attribution. *Journal of Personality and Social Psychology*, 37, 322-336. (p. 58)

Ross, M., McFarland, C., & Fletcher, G. J. O. (1981). The effect of attitude on the recall of personal histories. *Journal of Personality and Social Psychology*, 40, 627-634. (p. 80)

Ross, M., Thibaut, J., & Evenbeck, S. (1971). Some determinants of the intensity of social protest. *Journal of Experimental Social Psychology*, 7, 401-418. (p. 473)

Ross, M., Xun, W. Q. E., & Wilson, A. E. (2002). Language and the bicultural self. *Personality and Social Psychology Bulletin*, 28, 1040-1050. (p. 288)

Roszell, P., Kennedy, D., & Grabb, E. (1990). Physical attractiveness and income attainment among Canadians. *Journal of Psychology*, 123, 547-559. (p. 382)

Rotenberg, K. J., Gruman, J. A., & Ariganello, M. (2002). Behavioral confirmation of the loneliness stereotype. *Basic and Applied Social Psychology*, 24, 81-89. (p. 106)

Rothbart, M., & Birrell, P. (1977). Attitude and perception of faces. *Journal of Research Personality*, 11, 209-215. (p. 75)

Rothbart, M., & Taylor, M. (1992). Social categories and social reality. In G. R. Semin & K. Fielder (eds.), *Language, interaction and social cognition.* London: Sage. (p. 213)

Rothbart, M., Fulero, S., Jensen, C., Howard, J., & Birrell, P. (1978). From individual to group impressions: Availability heuristics in stereotype formation. *Journal of Experimental Social Psychology*, 14, 237-255. (p. 447)

Rothman, A. J., & Salovey, P. (1997). Shaping perceptions to motivate healthy behavior: The role of message framing. *Psychological Bulletin*, 121, 3-19. (p. 499)

Rotton, J., & Frey, J. (1985). Air pollution, weather, and violent crimes: Concomitant time-series analysis of archival data. *Journal of Personality and Social Psychology*, 49, 1207-1220. (p. 346)

Rotundo, M., Nguyen, D-H., & Sackett, P. R. (2001). A meta-analytic review of gender differences in perceptions of sexual harassment. *Journal of Applied Psychology*, 86, 914-922. (p. 93)

Rowe, D. C., Almeida, D. M., & Jacobson, K. C. (1999). School context and genetic influences on aggression in adolescence. *Psychological Science*, 10, 277-280. (p. 336)

Rowe, D. C., Vazsonyi, A. T., & Flannery, D. J. (1994). No more than skin deep: Ethnic and racial similarity in developmental process. *Psychological Review*, 101, 396-413. (p. 31)

Ruback, R. B., Carr, T. S., & Hoper, C. H. (1986). Perceived control in prison: Its relation to reported crowding, stress, and symptoms. *Journal of Applied Social Psychology*, 16, 375-386. (p. 53)

Rubin, J. Z. (1986). *Can we negotiate with terrorists: Some answers from psychology.* Paper presented at the American Psychological Association convention. (p. 342)

Rubin, Z. (1973). *Liking and loving: An invitation to social psychology.* New York: Holt, Rinehart and Winston. (p. 413)

Rudolph, U., Roesch, S. C., Greitemeyer, T., & Weiner, B. (2004). A meta-analytic review of help giving and aggression from an attributional perspective: Contributions to a general theory of motivation. *Cognition & Emotion, **18**,* 815. (p. 304)

Ruiter, R. A. C., Kok, G., Verplanken, B., & Brug, J. (2001). Evoked fear and effects of appeals on attitudes to performing breast self-examination: An information-processing perspective. *Health Education Research*, 16, 307-319. (p. 155)

Rule, B. G., Taylor, B. R., & Dobbs, A. R. (1987). Priming ffects of heat on aggressive thoughts. *Social Cognition*, 5, 131-143. (p. 346)

Rusbult, C. E., Johnson, D. J., & Morrow, G. D. (1986). Impact of couple patterns of problem solving on distress and non-distress in dating relationships. *Journal of Personality and Social Psychology*, 50, 744-753. (p. 412)

Rusbult, C. E., Morrow, G. D., & Johnson, D. J. (1987). Self-esteem and problem-solving behaviour in close relationships. *British Journal of Social Psychology*, 26, 293-303. (p. 412)

Rushton, J. P. (1975). Generosity in children: Immediate and long-term effects of modeling, preaching, and moral judgment. *Journal of Personality and Social Psychology*, 31, 459-466. (p. 319)

Rushton, J. P. (1991). Is altruism innate? *Psychological Inquiry*, 2, 141-143. (p. 306)

Rushton, J. P., & Campbell, A. C. (1977). Modeling, vicarious reinforcement and extraversion on blood donating in adults: Immediate and long-term effects. *European Journal of Social Psychology*, 7, 297-306. (p. 319)

Rushton, J. P., Brainerd, C. J., & Pressley, M. (1983). Behavioral development and construct validity: The principle of aggregation. *Psychological Bulletin*, 94, 18-38. (p. 209)

Rushton, J. P., Chrisjohn, R. D., & Fekken, G. C. (1981). The altruistic personality and the self-report altruism scale. *Personality and Individual Differences*, 2, 293-302. (p. 322)

Rushton, J. P., Fulker, D. W., Neale, M. C., Nias, D. K. B., & Eysenck, H. J. (1986). Altruism and aggression: The heritability of individual differences. *Journal of Personality and Social Psychology*, 50, 1192-1198. (p. 336)

Rushton, J. P., Russell, R. J. H., & Wells, P. A. (1984). Genetic similarity theory: Beyond kin selection. *Behavior Genetics*, 14, 179-193. (p. 305)

Russell, G. W. (1983). Psychological issues in sports aggression. In J. H. Goldstein (Ed.), *Sports violence*. New York: Springer-Verlag. (p. 367)

Russell, J. A. (1994). Is there universal recognition of emotion from facial expression? A review of the cross-cultural studies. *Psychological Bulletin*, 115, 102-141. (p. 275)

Russell, J. A. (1995). Facial expressions of emotion: What lies beyond minimal universality? *Psychological Bulletin*, 118, 379-391. (p. 275)

Rutkowski, G. K., Gruder, C. L., & Romer, D. (1983). Group cohesiveness, social norms, and bystander intervention. *Journal of Personality and Social Psychology*, 44, 545-552. (p. 318)

Ruvolo, A., & Markus, H. (1992). Possible selves and performance: The power of self-relevant imagery. *Social Cognition*, 9, 95-124. (p. 52)

Ruzzene, M., & Noller, P. (1986). Feedback motivation and reactions to personality interpretations that differ in favorability and accuracy. *Journal of Personality and Social Psychology*, 51, 1293-1299. (p. 69)

Ryan, C. S. (1996). Accuracy of Black and White college students' in-group and out-group stereotypes. *Personality and Social psychology Bulletin*, 22, 1114-1127. (p. 443)

Ryan, R. (1999, February 2). Quoted by A. Kohn, In pursuit of affluence, at a high price. *New York Times* (via www.nytimes.com). (p. 535)

Ryckman, R. M., Robbins, M. A., Kaczor, L. M., & Gold, J. A. (1989). Male and female raters' stereotyping of male and female physiques. *Personality and Social Psychology Bulletin*, 15, 244-251. (p. 26)

Ryff, C. D., & Singer, B. (2000). Interpersonal flourishing: A positive health agenda for the new millennium. *Personality and Social Psychology Review*, 4, 30-44. (p. 503)

Saal, F. E., Johnson, C. B., & Weber, N. (1989). Friendly or sexy? It may depend on whom you ask. *Psychology of Women Quarterly*, 13, 263-276. (p. 93)

Sabini, J., & Silver, M. (1982). *Moralities of everyday life*. New York: Oxford University Press. (p. 198)

Sacco, W. P., & Dunn, V. K. (1990). Effect of actor depression on observer attributions: Existence and impact of negative attributions toward the depressed. *Journal of Personality and Social Psychology*, 59, 517-524. (p. 491)

Sack, K., & Elder, J. (2000, July 11). Poll finds optimistic outlook but enduring racial division. *New York Times* (www.nytimes.com). (p. 434)

Sacks, C. H., & Bugental, D. P. (1987). Attributions as moderators of affective and behavioral responses to social failure. *Journal of Personality and Social Psychology*, 53, 939-947. (p. 492)

Sagarin, B. J., Cialdini, R. B., Rice, W. E., & Serna, S. B. (2002). Dispelling the illusion of invulnerability: The motivations and mechanisms of resistance to persuasion. *Journal of Personality and Social Psychology*, 83, 526-541. (p. 174)

Sagarin, B. J., Rhoads, K. v L., & Cialdini, R. B. (1998). Deceiver's distrust: Denigration as a consequence of undiscovered deception. *Personality and Social Psychology Bulletin*, 24, 1167-1176. (p. 60)

Saks, M. J., & Hastie, R. (1978). *Social psychology in court*. New York: Van Nostrand Reinhold. (p. 511)

Sakurai, M. M. (1975). Small group cohesiveness and detrimental conformity. *Sociometry*, 38, 340-357. (p. 203)

Sales, S. M. (1972). Economic threat as a determinant of conversion rates in authoritarian and nonauthoritarian churches. *Journal of Personality and Social Psychology*, 23, 420-428. (p. 172)

Sales, S. M. (1973). Threat as a factor in authoritarianism: An analysis of archival data. *Journal of Personality & Social Psychology*, 28, 44-57. (p. 428)

Salovey, P., Mayer, J. D., & Rosenhan, D. L. (1991). Mood and healing: Mood as a motivator of helping and helping as a regulator of mood. In M. S. Clark (Ed.), *Prosocial behavior*. Newbury Park, CA: Sage. (p. 301)

Saltzstein, H. D., & Sandberg, L. (1979). Indirect social influence: Change in judgmental processor anticipatory conformity. *Journal of Experimental Social Psychology*, 15, 209-216. (p. 204)

Sampson, E. E. (1975). On justice as equality. *Journal of Social Issues*, 31(3), 45-64. (p. 473)

Sanbonmatsu, D. M., & Fazio, R. H. (1990). The role of attitudes in memory-based decision making. *Journal of Personality and Social Psychology*, 59, 614-622. (p. 112)

Sanbonmatsu, D. M., Akimoto, S. A., & Biggs, E. (1993). Overestimating causality: Attributional effects of confirmatory processing. *Journal of Personality and Social Psychology*, 65, 892-903. (p. 83)

Sanbonmatsu, D. M., Akimoto, S. A., & Gibson, B. D. (1994). Stereotype-based blocking in social explanation. *Personality and Social Psychology Bulletin*, 20, 71-81. (p. 451)

Sande, G. N., Goethals, G. R., & Radloff, C. E. (1988). Perceiving one's own traits and others': The multifaceted self. *Journal of Personality and Social Psychology*, 54, 13-20. (p. 100)

Sanders, G. S. (1981). Driven by distraction: An integrative review of social facilitation and theory and research. *Journal of Experimental Social Psychology*, 17, 227-251. (a) (p. 221)

Sanders, G. S. (1981). Toward a comprehensive account of social facilitation: Distraction/conflict does not mean theoretical conflict. *Journal of Experimental Social Psychology*, 17, 262-265. (b) (p. 221)

Sanders, G. S., & Baron, R. S. (1977). Is social comparison irrelevant for producing choice shifts? *Journal of Experimental Social Psychology*, 13, 303-314. (p. 238)

Sanders, G. S., Baron, R. S., & Moore, D. L. (1978). Distraction and social comparison as mediators of social facilitation effects. *Journal of Experimental Social Psychology*, 14, 291-303. (p. 221)

Sanderson, C. A., & Cantor, N. (2001). The association of intimacy goals and marital satisfaction: A test of four mediational hypotheses. *Personality and Social Psychology Bulletin, 27*, 1567. (p. 409)

Sanislow, C. A., III, Perkins, D. V., & Balogh, D. W. (1989). Mood induction, interpersonal perceptions, and rejection in the roommates of depressed, nondepressed-disturbed, and normal college students. *Journal of Social and Clinical Psychology*, 8, 345-358. (p. 491)

Sanitioso, R., Kunda, Z., & Fong, G. T. (1990). Motivated recruitment of autobiographical memories. *Journal of Personality and Social Psychology*, 59, 229-241. (p. 63)

Sansone, C. (1986). A question of competence: The effects of competence and task feedback on intrinsic interest. *Journal of Personality and Social Psychology*, 51, 918-931. (p. 136)

Sapolsky, R. M. (2005). The influence of social hierarchy on primate health. *Science*, **308**, 648. (p. 505)

Sartre, J-P. (1946/1948). *Anti-Semite and Jew*. New York: Shocken Books. (p. 4)

Sato, K. (1987). Distribution of the cost of maintaining common resources. *Journal of Experimental Social Psychology*, 23, 19-31. (p. 469)

Saucier, D. A., & Miller, C. T. (2003). The persuasiveness of racial arguments as a subtle measure of racism. *Personality and Social Psychology Bulletin*, 29, 1303-1315. (p. 74)

Savitsky, K., Medvec, V. H., & Gilovich, T. (1997). Remembering and regretting: The Zeigarnik effect and the cognitive availability of regrettable actions and inactions. *Personality and Social Psychology Bulletin*, 23, 248-257. (p. 88)

Schachter, S. (1951). Deviation, rejection and communication. *Journal of Abnormal and Social Psychology*, 46, 190-207. (p. 206)

Schachter, S., & Singer, J. E. (1962). Cognitive, social and physiological determinants of emotional state. *Psychological Review*, 69, 379-399. (p. 347)

Schafer, R. B., & Keith, P. M. (1980). Equity and depression among married couples. *Social Psychology Quarterly*, 43, 430-435. (p. 407)

Schaffner, P. E. (1985). Specious learning about reward and punishment. *Journal of Personality and Social Psychology*, 48, 1377-1386. (p. 89)

Schaffner, P. E., Wandersman, A., & Stang D. (1981). Candidate name exposure and voting: Two field studies. *Basic and Applied Social Psychology*, 2, 195-203. (p. 379)

Schaller, M., & Cialdini, R. B. (1988). The economics of empathic helping: Support for a mood management motive. *Journal of Experimental Social Psychology*, 24, 163-181. (p. 310)

Schaller, M., & Cialdini, R. B. (1990). Happiness, sadness, and helping:A motivational integration. In E. T. Higgins, & R. M. Sorrentino (Eds.). *Handbook of motivation and cognition: Foundations of social behavior*. Vol. 2. (pp. 265-296). New York, NY, USA: The Guilford Press. (p. 301)

Schein, E. H. (1956). The Chinese indoctrination program for prisoners of war: A study of attempted brainwashing. *Psychiatry*, 19, 149-172. (p. 127)

Scherer, K. (1997). The role of culture in emotion-antecedent appraisal. *Journal of Personality and Social Psychology*, 73, 902-922. (p. 276)

Schiffenbauer, A., & Schiavo, R. S. (1976). Physical distance and attraction: An intensification effect. *Journal of Experimental Social Psychology*, 12, 274-282. (p. 220)

Schimel, J., Arndt, J., Pyszczynski, T., & Greenberg, J. (2001). Being accepted for who we are: Evidence that social validation of the intrinsic self reduces general defensiveness. *Journal of Personality and Social Psychology*, 80, 35-52. (p. 49)

Schimel, J., Pyszczynski, T., Greenberg, J., O'Mahen, H., & Arndt, J. (2000). Running from the shadow: Psychological distancing from others to deny characteristics people fear in themselves. *Journal of Personality and Social Psychology, 78*, 446. (p. 390)

Schimel, J., Simon, L., Greenberg, J., Pyszczynski, T., Solomon, S., & Waxmonsky, J. (1999). Stereotypes and terror management: Evidence that mortality salience enhances stereotypic thinking and preferences. *Journal of Personality and Social Psychology*, 77, 905-926. (p. 438)

Schimmack, U., Oishi, S., & Diener, E. (2005). Individualism: A valid and important dimension of cultural differences between nations. *Personality and Social Psychology Review,* **9**, 17. (p. 267)

Schkade, D. A., & Kahneman, D. (1998). Does living in California make people happy? A focusing illusion in judgments of life satisfaction. *Psychological Science*, 9, 340-346. (p. 43)

Schlenker, B. R. (1974). Social psychology and science. *Journal of Personality and Social Psychology*, 29, 1-15. (p. 12)

Schlenker, B. R. (1976). *Egocentric perceptions in cooperative groups: A conceptualization and research review*. Final Report, Office of Naval Research Grant NR 170-797. (p. 64)

Schlenker, B. R., & Leary, M. R. (1982). Social anxiety and self-presentation: A conceptualization and model. *Psychological Bulletin*, 92, 641-669. (b) (p. 69)

Schlenker, B. R., & Leary, M. R. (1985). Social anxiety and communication about the self. *Journal of Language and Social Psychology*, 4, 171-192. (p. 494)

Schlenker, B. R., & Miller, R. S. (1977). Egocentrism in groups: Self-serving biases or logical information processing? *Journal of Personality and Social Psychology*, 35, 755-764. (b) (p. 64)

Schlenker, B. R., & Miller, R. S. (1977). Group cohesiveness as a determinant of egocentric perceptions in cooperative groups. *Human Relations*, 30, 1039-1055. (a) (p. 64)

Schlenker, B. R., & Weigold, M. F. (1992). Interpersonal processes involving impression regulation and management. *Annual Review of Psychology*, 43, 133-168. (p. 68)

Schlesinger, A., Jr. (1991, July 8). The cult of ethnicity, good and bad. *Time*, p. 21. (p. 256)

Schmader, T., & Johns, M. (2003). Converging evidence that stereotype threat reduces working memory capacity. *Journal of Personality and Social Psychology*, 85, 440-451. (p. 455)

Schmader, T., Johns, M., & Forbes, C. (2008). An integrated process model of stereotype threat effects on performance. *Psychological Review, **115***, 336. (p. 454)

Schmitt, D. P., Alcalay, L., Allensworth, M., Allik, J., Ault, L., Austers, I., et al. (2004). Patterns and universals of adult romantic attachment across 62 cultural regions: Are models of self and of other pancultural constructs? *Journal of Cross-Cultural Psychology, **35***, 367. (p. 405)

Schneider, M. E., Major, B., Luhtanen, R., & Crocker, J. (1996). Social stigma and the potential costs of assumptive help. *Personality and Social Psychology Bulletin*, 22, 201-209. (p. 303)

Schoeneman, T. J. (1994). Individualism. In V. S. Ramachandran (Ed.), *Encyclopedia of Human Behavior*. San Diego: Academic Press. (p. 267)

Schooler, J. W. (2002). Verbalization produces a transfer inappropriate processing shift. *Applied Cognitive Psychology*, 16, 989-997. (p. 519)

Schor, J. B. (1998). *The overworked American*. New York: Basic Books. (p. 533)

Schroeder, D. A., Dovidio, J. F., Sibicky, M. E., Matthews, L. L., & Allen, J. L. (1988). Empathic concern and helping behavior: Egoism or altruism. *Journal of Experimental Social Psychology*, 24, 333-353. (p. 310)

Schulz, J.W., & Pruitt, D.G. (1978). The effects of mutual concern on joint welfare. *Journal of Experimental Social Psychology*, 14, 480-92. (p. 479)

Schuman, H., & Kalton, G. (1985). Survey methods. In G. Lindzey & E. Aronson (Eds.), *Handbook of social psychology*, Vol. 1. Hillsdale, N.J.: Erlbaum. (p. 25)

Schuman, H., & Ludwig, J. (1983). The norm of even-handedness in surveys as in life. *American Sociological Review*, 48, 112-120. (p. 24)

Schuman, H., & Scott, J. (1989). Generations and collective memories. *American Sociological Review*, 54, 359-381. (p. 166)

Schutte, J. W., & Hosch, H. M. (1997). Gender differences in sexual assault verdicts. *Journal of Social Behavior and Personality*, 12, 759-772. (p. 93)

Schwartz, S. H., & Gottlieb, A. (1981). Participants' post-experimental reactions and the ethics of bystander research. *Journal of Experimental Social Psychology*, 17, 396-407. (p. 318)

Schwarz, N., & Kurz, E. (1989). What's in a picture? The impact of face-ism on trait attribution. *European Journal of Social Psychology*, 19, 311-316. (p. 431)

Schwarz, N., Bless, H., & Bohner, G. (1991). Mood and persuasion: Affective states influence the processing of persuasive communications. In M. Zanna (Ed.), *Advances in experimental social psychology*, vol. 24. New York: Academic Press. (p. 153)

Schwarz, N., Strack, F., Hilton, D. J., & Naderer, G. (1991). Base rates, representativeness, and the logic of conversation: The contextual relevance of "irrelevant" information. *Social Cognition.Special Issue: Social Cognition and Communication: Human Judgment in its Social Context, 9*(1), 67.

Schwarz, N., Strack, F., Kommer, D., & Wagner, D. (1987). Soccer, rooms, and the quality of your life: Mood effects on judgments of satisfaction with life in general and with specific domains. *Journal of Applied Social Psychology*, 17, 69-79. (p. 90)

Schweitzer, K., Zillmann, D., Weaver, J. B., & Luttrell, E. S. (1992, Spring). Perception of threatening events in the emotional aftermath of a televised college football game. *Journal of Broadcasting and Electronic Media*, pp. 75-82. (p. 90)

Scott, J. P., & Marston, M. V. (1953). Nonadaptive behavior resulting from a series of defeats in fighting mice. *Journal of Abnormal and Social Psychology*, 48, 417-428. (p. 342)

Sears, D. O. (1979). *Life stage effects upon attitude change, especially among the elderly*. Manuscript prepared for Workshop on the Elderly of the Future, Committee on Aging, National Research Council, Annapolis, Md., May 3-5. (p. 165)

Sears, D. O. (1986). College sophomores in the laboratory: Influences of a narrow data base on social psychology's view of human nature. *Journal of Personality and Social Psychology*, 51, 515-530. (p. 165)

Sedikides, C. (1993). Assessment, enhancement, and verification determinants of the self-evaluation process. *Journal of Personality and Social Psychology*, 65, 317-338. (p. 63)

Segal, H. A. (1954). Initial psychiatric findings of recently repatriated prisoners of war. *American Journal of Psychiatry*, 61, 358-363. (p. 127)

Segal, N. L. (1984). Cooperation, competition, and altruism within twin sets: A reappraisal. *Ethology and Sociobiology*, 5, 163-177. (p. 305)

Segal, N. L., & Hershberger, S. L. (1999). Cooperation and competition between twins: Findings from a Prisoner's Dilemma game. *Evolution and Human Behavior*, 20, 29-51. (p. 305)

Segerstrom, S. C., & Miller, G. E. (2004). Psychological stress and the human immune system: A meta-analytic study of 30 years of inquiry. *Psychological Bulletin, **130***, 601. (p. 501)

Segerstrom, S. C., McCarthy, W. J., Caskey, N. H., Gross, T. M., & Jarvik, M. E. (1993). Optimistic bias among cigarette smokers. *Journal of Applied Social Psychology*, 23, 1606-1618. (p. 502)

Seligman, C., Fazio, R. H., & Zanna, M. P. (1980). Effects of salience of extrinsic rewards on liking and loving. *Journal of Personality and Social Psychology*, 38, 453-460. (p. 392)

Seligman, M. (1994). *What you can change and what you can't*. New York: Knopf. (p. 22)

Seligman, M. E. P. (1975). *Helplessness: On depression, development and death*. San Francisco: W. H. Freeman. (p. 52)

Seligman, M. E. P. (1989). Explanatory style: Predicting depression, achievement, and health. In M. D. Yapko (Ed.), *Brief therapy approaches to treating anxiety and depression*. New York: Brunner/Mazel. (p. 534)

Seligman, M. E. P. (1991). *Learned optimism*. New York: Knopf. (p. 52)

Sengupta, S. (2003, May 27). Congo war toll soars as U.N. pleads for aid. New York Times (www.nytimes.com). (p. 332)

Sentyrz, S. M., & Bushman, B. J. (1997). *Mirror, mirror on the wall, who's the thinnest one of all? Effects of self-awareness on consumption of fatty, reduced-fat, and fat-free products.* Unpublished manuscript, Iowa State University. (p. 231)

Seta, C. E., & Seta, J. J. (1992). Increments and decrements in mean arterial pressure levels as a function of audience composition: An averaging and summation analysis. *Personality and Social Psychology Bulletin*, 18, 173-181. (p. 221)

Seta, J. J. (1982). The impact of comparison processes on coactors' task performance. *Journal of Personality and Social Psychology*, 42, 281-291. (p. 221)

Shackelford, T. K., & Larsen, R. J. (1997). Facial asymmetry as an indicator of psychological, emotional, and physiological distress. *Journal of Personality and Social Psychology*, 72, 456-466. (p. 383)

Shaffer, D. R., Pegalis, L. J., & Bazzini, D. G. (1996). When boy meets girls (revisited): Gender, gender-role orientation, and prospect of future interaction as determinants of self-disclosure among same- and opposite-sex acquaintances. *Personality and Social Psychology Bulletin*, 22, 495-506. (p. 408)

Shah, J. Y. (2005). The automatic pursuit and management of goals. *Current Directions in Psychological Science, **14**,* 10. (p. 533)

Sharpe, D., Adair, J. G., & Roese, N. J. (1992). Twenty years of deception research: A decline in subjects' trust? *Personality and Social Psychology Bulletin*, 18, 585-590. (p. 31)

Shaver, P. R., & Hazan, C. (1993). Adult romantic attachment: Theory and evidence. In D. Perlman & W. Jones (Eds.), *Advances in personal relationships*, vol. 4. Greenwich, CT: JAI. (p. 404)

Shaver, P. R., & Hazan, C. (1994). Attachment. In A. L. Weber & J. H. Harvey (eds.), Perspectives on close relationships. Boston: Allyn & Bacon. (p. 404)

Shaver, P., Hazan, C., & Bradshaw, D. (1988). Love as attachment: The integration of three behavioral systems. In R. J. Sternberg & M. L. Barnes (Eds.), *The psychology of love*. New Haven: Yale University Press. (p. 404)

Shaw, J. S., III (1996). Increases in eyewitness confidence resulting from postevent questioning. *Journal of Experimental Psychology: Applied*, 2, 126-146. (p. 517)

Shaw, M. E. (1981). *Group dynamics: The psychology of small group behavior*. New York: McGraw-Hill. (p. 216)

Sheese, B. E., & Graziano, W. G. (2005). Deciding to defect: The effects of video-game violence on cooperative behavior. *Psychological Science, **16**,* 354. (p. 362)

Sheldon, K. M., Elliot, A. J., Youngmee, K., & Kasser, T. (2001). What is satisfying about satisfying events? Testing 10 candidate psychological needs. *Journal of Personality and Social Psychology*, 80, 325-339. (p. 535)

Sheldon, K. M., Ryan, R. M., Deci, E. L., & Kasser, T. (2004). The independent effects of goal contents and motives on well-being: It's both what you pursue and why you pursue it. *Personality and Social Psychology Bulletin, **30**,* 475. (p. 535)

Shell, R. M., & Eisenberg, N. (1992). A developmental model of recipients' reactions to aid. *Psychological Bulletin*, 111, 413-433. (p. 303)

Sheppard, B. H., & Vidmar, N. (1980). Adversary pretrial procedures and testimonial evidence: Effects of lawyer's role and machiavelian-ism. *Journal of Personality and Social Psychology*, 39, 320-322. (p. 516)

Shepperd, J. A., & Arkin, R. M. (1991). Behavioral other-enhancement: Strategically obscuring the link between performance and evaluation. *Journal of Personality and Social Psychology*, 60, 79-88. (p. 67)

Shepperd, J. A., & Taylor, K. M. (1999). Ascribing advantages to social comparison targets. *Basic and Applied Social Psychology*, 21, 103-117. (p. 226)

Shepperd, J. A., & Wright, R. A. (1989). Individual contributions to a collective effort: An incentive analysis. *Personality and Social Psychology Bulletin*, 15, 141-149. (p. 226)

Shepperd, J. A., Helweg-Larsen, M., & Ortega, L. (2003). Are comparative risk judgments consistent across time and events? *Personality and Social Psychology Bulletin, **29**,* 1169

Shepperd, J. A., Oullette, J. A., & Fernandez, J. K. (1996). Abandoning unrealistic optimism: Performance estimates and the temporal proximity of self-relevant feedback. *Journal of Personality and Social Psychology*, 70, 844-855. (p. 59)

Sherif, M. (1935). A study of some social factors in perception. *Archives of Psychology*, No. 187. (p. 183)

Sherif, M. (1937). An experimental approach to the study of attitudes. *Sociometry*, 1, 90-98. (p. 183)

Sherif, M. (1966). *In common predicament: Social psychology of intergroup conflict and cooperation*. Boston: Houghton Mifflin. (p. 283)

Sherman, J. W. (1996). Development and mental representation of stereotypes. *Journal of Personality and Social Psychology*, 70, 1126-1141. (p. 447)

Sherman, S. J., Cialdini, R. B., Schwartzman, D. F., & Reynolds, K. D. (1985). Imagining can heighten or lower the perceived likelihood of contracting a disease: The mediating effect of ease of imagery. *Personality and Social Psychology Bulletin*, 11, 118-127. (p. 86)

Sherman, S. J., Presson, C. C., Chassin, L., Bensenberg, M., Corty, E., & Olshavsky, R. (1983). Smoking intentions in adolescents: Direct experience and predictability. *Personality and Social Psychology Bulletin*, 8, 376-383. (p. 117)

Shih, M., Pittinsky, T. L., & Ambady, N. (1999). Stereotype susceptibility: Identity salience and shifts in quantitative performance. *Psychological Science*, 10, 80-83. (p. 455)

Shipman, P. (2003). We are all African. *American Scientist*, **91**, 496. (p. 257)

Short, J. F., Jr. (Ed.) (1969). *Gang delinquency and delinquent subcultures*. New York: Harper & Row. (p. 344)

Shostak, M. (1981). *Nisa: The life and words of a !Kung woman*. Cambridge, MA: Harvard University Press. (p. 401)

Shotland, R. L. (1989). A model of the causes of date rape in developing and close relationships. In C. Hendrick (Ed.), *Review of personality and social psychology*, Vol. 10. Beverly Hills: Sage. (p. 93)

Shotland, R. L., & Stebbins, C. A. (1983). Emergency and cost as determinants of helping behavior and the slow accumulation of social psychological knowledge. *Social Psychology Quarterly*, 46, 36-46. (p. 304)

Shotland, R. L., & Straw, M. K. (1976). Bystander response to an assault: When a man attacks a woman. *Journal of Personality and Social Psychology*, 34, 990-999. (p. 315)

Showers, C., & Ruben, C. (1987). *Distinguishing pessimism from depression: Negative expectations and positive coping mechanisms*. Paper presented at the

American Psychological Association convention. (p. 60)

Shrauger, J. S. (1975). Responses to evaluation as a function of initial self-perceptions. *Psychological Bulletin*, 82, 581-596. (p. 392)

Shrauger, J. S. (1983). *The accuracy of self-prediction: How good are we and why?* Paper presented at the Midwestern Psychological Association convention. (p. 40)

Sidanius, J., & Pratto, F. (1999). *Social Dominance: An Intergroup Theory of Social Hierarchy and Oppression*. New York: Cambridge University Press. (p. 427)

Sidanius, J., Pratto, F., & Bobo, L. (1996). Racism, conservatism, affirmative action, and intellectual sophistication: A matter of principled conservatism or group dominance? *Journal of Personality and Social Psychology*, 70, 476-490. (p. 427)

Sieff, E. M., Dawes, R. M., & Loewenstein, G. F. (1999). Anticipated versus actual responses to HIV test results. *American Journal of Psychology*, 112, 297-311. (p. 42)

Sigall, H. (1970). Effects of competence and consensual validation on a communicator's liking for the audience. *Journal of Personality and Social Psychology*, 16, 252-258. (p. 396)

Sigall, H., & Page, R. (1971). Current stereotypes: A little fading, a little faking. *Journal of Personality and Social Psychology*, 18, 247-255. (p. 115)

Silke, A. (2003). Deindividuation, anonymity, and violence: Findings from Northern Ireland. *Journal of Social Psychology*, 143, 493-499. (p. 230)

Silver, M., & Geller, D. (1978). On the irrelevance of evil: The organization and individual action. *Journal of Social Issues*, 34, 125-136. (p. 198)

Simmons, W. W. (2000, December). When it comes to having children, Americans still prefer boys. *The Gallup Poll Monthly*, pp. 63-64. (p. 426)

Simon, H. A. (1957). *Models of man: Social and rational*. New York: Wiley. (p. 108)

Simon, P. (1996, April 17). American provincials. Christian Century, pp. 421-422. (p. 25)

Simonton, D. K. (1994). *Greatness: Who makes history and why*. New York: Guilford. (p. 250)

Simpson, J. A. (1987). The dissolution of romantic relationships: Factors involved in relationship stability and emotional distress. *Journal of Personality and Social Psychology*, 53, 683-692. (p. 372)

Simpson, J. A., Campbell, B., & Berscheid, E. (1986). The association between romantic love and marriage: Kephart (1967) twice revisited. *Personality and Social Psychology Bulletin*, 12, 363-372. (p. 402)

Simpson, J. A., Gangestad, S. W., & Lerma, M. (1990). Perception of physical attractiveness: Mechanisms involved in the maintenance of romantic relationships. *Journal of Personality and Social Psychology*, 59, 1192-1201. (p. 387)

Simpson, J. A., Rholes, W. S., & Nelligan, J. S. (1992). Support seeking and support giving within couples in an anxiety-provoking situation: The role of attachment styles. *Journal of Personality and Social Psychology*, 62, 434-446. (p. 404)

Simpson, J. A., Rholes, W. S., & Phillips, D. (1996). Conflict in close relationships: An attachment perspective. *Journal of Personality and Social Psychology*, 71, 899-914. (p. 404)

Sinclair, L., & Fehr, B. (2005). Voice versus loyalty: Self-construals and responses to dissatisfaction in romantic relationships. *Journal of Experimental Social Psychology*, ***41***, 298. (p. 412)

Sinclair, L., & Kunda, Z. (1999). Reactions to a Black professional: Motivated inhibition and activation of conflicting stereotypes. *Journal of Personality and Social Psychology*, 77, 885-904. (p. 458)

Sinclair, L., & Kunda, Z. (2000). Motivated stereotyping of women: She's fine if she praised me but incompetent if she criticized me. *Personality and Social Psychology Bulletin*, 26, 1329-1342. (p. 458)

Sinclair, S., Dunn, L. & Lowery, B. (2005). The influence of parental racial attitudes on children's automatic racial prejudice, *Journal of Experimental Social Psychology*, **41**, 283-289.

Singer, M. (1979). *Cults and cult members*. Address to the American Psychological Association convention. (a) (p. 172)

Singer, M. (1979, July-August). Interviewed by M. Freeman. Of cults and communication: A conversation with Margaret Singer. *APA Monitor*, pp. 6-7. (b) (p. 171)

Singh, R., & Ho, S. J. (2000). Attitudes and attraction: A new test of the attraction, repulsion and similarity-dissimilarity asymmetry hypotheses. *British Journal of Social Psychology*, 39, 197-211. (p. 389)

Singh, R., & Teoh, J. B. P. (1999). Attitudes and attraction: A test of two hypotheses for the similarity-dissimilarity asymmetry. *British Journal of Social Psychology*, 38, 427-443. (p. 389)

Sittser, G. L. (1994, April). Long night's journey into light. *Second Opinion*, pp. 10-15. (p. 88)

Sivard, R. L. (1996). *World military and social expenditures 1996*, 16th edition. Washington, DC: World Priorities. (p. 332)

Six, B., & Eckes, T. (1996). Metaanalysen in der Einstellungs-Verhaltens-Forschung. *Zeitschrift fur Sozialpsychologie*, pp. 7-17. (p. 116)

Skaalvik, E. M., & Hagtvet, K. A. (1990). Academic achievement and self-concept: An analysis of causal predominance in a developmental perspective. *Journal of Personality and Social Psychology*, 58, 292-307. (p. 22)

Skinner, B. F. (1971). *Beyond freedom and dignity*. New York: Knopf. (p. 298)

Skitka, L. J., & Tetlock, P. E. (1993). Providing public assistance: Cognitive and motivational processes underlying liberal and conservative policy preferences. *Journal of Personality and Social Psychology*, 65, 1205-1223. (p. 304)

Skov, R. B., & Sherman, S. J. (1986). Information-gathering processes: Diagnosticity, hypothesis-confirmatory strategies, and perceived hypothesis confirmation. *Journal of Experimental Social Psychology*, 22, 93-121. (p. 84)

Skurnik, I., Yoon, C., Park, D. C., & Schwarz, N. (2005). How warnings about false claims become recommendations. *Journal of Consumer Research*, ***31***, 713. (p. 161)

Sloan, J. H., Kellerman, A. L., Reay, D. T., Ferris, J. A., Koepsell, T., Rivara, F. P., Rice, C., Gray, L., & LoGerfo, J. (1988). Handgun regulations, crime, assaults, and homicide: A tale of two cities. *New England Journal of Medicine*, 319, 1256-1261. (p. 349)

Slovic, P. (1972). From Shakespeare to Simon: Speculations-and some evidence-about man's ability to process information. *Oregon Research Institute Research Bulletin*, 12(2). (p. 107)

Smith, A. (1976). *The wealth of nations*. Book 1. Chicago: University of Chicago Press. (Originally published, 1776.) (p. 470)

Smith, D. E., Gier, J. A., & Willis, F. N. (1982). Interpersonal touch and compliance with a marketing request. *Basic and Applied Social Psychology*, 3, 35-38. (p. 192)

Smith, H. (1976) *The Russians.* New York: Balantine Books. Cited by B. Latane, K. Williams, and S. Harkins in, Many hands make light the work. *Journal of Personality and Social Psychology*, 1979, 37, 822-832. (p. 279)

Smith, H. J., & Tyler, T. R. (1997). Choosing the right pond: The impact of group membership on self-esteem and group-oriented behavior. *Journal of Experimental Social Psychology*, 33, 146-170. (p. 433)

Smith, M. B. (1978). Psychology and values. *Journal of Social Issues*, 34, 181-199. (p. 13)

Smith, P. B., & Tayeb, M. (1989). Organizational structure and processes. In M. Bond (Ed.), *The cross-cultural challenge to social psychology*. Newbury Park, Ca.: Sage. (p. 249)

Smith, V. L. (1991). Prototypes in the courtroom: Lay representations of legal concepts. *Journal of Personality and Social Psychology*, 61, 857-872. (p. 522)

Smith, V. L., & Ellsworth, P. C. (1987). The social psychology of eyewitness accuracy: Misleading questions and communicator expertise. *Journal of Applied Psychology*, 72, 294-300. (p. 514)

Snyder, C. R. (1978). The "illusion" of uniqueness. *Journal of Humanistic Psychology*, 18, 33-41. (p. 57)

Snyder, C. R. (1980). The uniqueness mystique. *Psychology Today*, March, pp. 86-90. (p. 212)

Snyder, C. R., & Fromkin, H. L. (1980). *Uniqueness; The human pursuit of difference.* New York: Plenum. (p. 212)

Snyder, C. R., & Higgins, R. L. (1988). Excuses: Their effective role in the negotiation of reality. *Psychological Bulletin*, 104, 23-35. (p. 64)

Snyder, M. (1981). Seek, and ye shall find: Testing hypotheses about other people. In E. T. Higgins, C. P. Herman, & M. P. Zanna (Eds.), *Social cognition: The Ontario symposium on personality and social psychology.* Hillsdale, N.J.: Erlbaum. (a) (p. 488)

Snyder, M. (1983). The influence of individuals on situations: Implications for understanding the links between personality and social behavior. *Journal of Personality*, 51, 497-516. (p. 292)

Snyder, M. (1984). When belief creates reality. In L. Berkowitz (Ed.), *Advances in experimental social psychology*, Vol. 18. New York: Academic Press. (p. 106)

Snyder, M. (1987). *Public appearances/ private realities: The psychology of self-monitoring.* New York: Freeman. (p. 68)

Snyder, M., & Haugen, J. A. (1994). Why does behavioral confirmation occur? A functional perspective on the role of the perceiver. *Journal of Experimental Social Psychology*, 30, 218-246. (p. 27)

Snyder, M., & Haugen, J. A. (1995). Why does behavioral confirmation occur? A functional perspective on the role of the target. *Personality and Social Psychology Bulletin*, 21, 963-974. (p. 27)

Snyder, M., & Ickes, W. (1985). Personality and social behavior. In G. Lindzey & E. Aronson (Eds.), *Handbook of social psychology* (3rd ed.). New York: Random House. (p. 292)

Snyder, M., & Swann, W. B., Jr. (1976). When actions reflect attitudes: The politics of impression management. *Journal of Personality and Social Psychology*, 34, 1034-1042. (p. 116)

Snyder, M., Campbell, B., & Preston, E. (1982). Testing hypotheses about human nature: Assessing the accuracy of social stereotypes. *Social Cognition*, 1, 256-272. (p. 488)

Snyder, M., Grether, J., & Keller, K. (1974). Staring and compliance: A field experiment on hitch-hiking. *Journal of Applied Social Psychology*, 4, 165-170. (p. 323)

Snyder, M., Tanke, E. D., & Berscheid, E. (1977). Social perception and interpersonal behavior: On the self-fulfilling nature of social stereotypes. *Journal of Personality and Social Psychology*, 35, 656-666. (b) (p. 106)

Sober, E., & Wilson, D. S. (1998). *Unto others: The evolution and psychology of unselfish behavior.* Cambridge, Mass.: Harvard University Press. (p. 306)

Solano, C. H., Batten, P. G., & Parish, E. A. (1982). Loneliness and patterns of self-disclosure. *Journal of Personality and Social Psychology*, 43, 524-531. (p. 408)

Solberg, E. C., Diener, E., & Robinson, M. D. (2003). Why are materialists less satisfied? In T. Kasser & A. D. Kanner (Eds.), *Psychology and consumer culture: The struggle for a good life in a materialistic world.* Washington, DC: APA Books. (p. 535)

Solomon, H., & Solomon, L. Z. (1978). *Effects of anonymity on helping in emergency situations.* Paper presented at the Eastern Psychological Association convention. (p. 323)

Solomon, H., Solomon, L. Z., Arnone, M. M., Maur, B. J., Reda, R. M., & Rother, E. O. (1981). Anonymity and helping. *Journal Social Psychology*, 113, 37-43. (p. 323)

Solomon, L. Z., Solomon, H., & Stone, R. (1978). Helping as a function of number of bystanders and ambiguity of emergency. *Personality and Social Psychology Bulletin*, 4, 318-321. (p. 316)

Solomon, S., Greenberg, J., & Pyszczynski, T. (2000). Pride and prejudice: Fear of death and social behavior. *Current Directions in Psychological Science*, 9, 200-203. (p. 438)

Sommer, B. (1992). Cognitive performance and the menstrual cycle. In J. T. Richardson (Ed.), *Cognition and the menstrual cycle: Research, theory, and culture.* New York: Springer-Verlag. (p. 499)

Son Hing, L. S., Bobocel, D. R., Zanna, M. P., & McBride, M. V. (2007). Authoritarian dynamics and unethical decision making: High social dominance orientation leaders and high right-wing authoritarianism followers. *Journal of Personality and Social Psychology,* **92**, 67. (p. 429)

Sorrentino, R. M., Bobocel, D. R., Gitta, M. Z., Olsen, J. M., & Hewitt, E. C. (1988). Uncertainty orientation and persuasion: Individual differences in the effects of personal relevance on social judgments. *Journal of Personality and Social Psychology*, 55, 357-371. (p. 168)

Sparrell, J. A., & Shrauger, J. S. (1984). *Self-confidence and optimism in self-prediction.* Paper presented at the American Psychological Association convention. (p. 59)

Spector, P. E. (1986). Perceived control by employees: A meta-analysis of studies concerning autonomy and participation at work. *Human Relations*, 39, 1005-1016. (p. 248)

Speer, A. (1971). *Inside the Third Reich: Memoirs.* (P. Winston & C. Winston. trans.). New York: Avon Books. (p. 242)

Spencer, S. J., & Fein, S., & Wolfe, C. T., & Fong, C., & Dunn, M. A. (1998). Automatic activation of stereotypes: The role of self-image threat. *Personality and Social Psychology Bulletin*, 24, 1139-1152. (p. 438)

Spencer, S. J., Steele, C. M., & Quinn, D. M. (1999). Stereotype threat and women's math performance. *Journal of Experimental Social Psychology*, 35, 4-28. (p. 453)

Spencer-Rodgers, J., Peng, K., Wang, L., & Hou, Y. (2004). Dialectical self-esteem and east-west differences in psychological well-being. *Personality and Social Psychology Bulletin*, **30**, 1416. (p. 269)

Spiegel, H. W. (1971). *The growth of economic thought*. Durham, N.C.: Duke University Press. (p. 59)

Spitz, H. H. (1999). Beleaguered Pygmalion: A history of the controversy over claims that teacher expectancy raises intelligence. *Intelligence*, 27, 199-234. (p. 104)

Spivak, J. (1979, June 6). *Wall Street Journal*. (p. 279)

Sporer, S. L., Penrod, S., Read, D., & Cutler, B. (1995). Choosing, confidence, and accuracy: A meta-analysis of the confidence-accuracy relation in eyewitness identification studies. *Psychological Bulletin*, 118, 315-327. (p. 513)

Sprecher, S. (1987). The effects of self-disclosure given and received on affection for an intimate partner and stability of the relationship. *Journal of Personality and Social Psychology*, 4, 115-127. (p. 409)

Sprecher, S., Aron, A., Hatfield, E., Cortese, A., Potapova, E., & Levitskaya, A. (1994). Love: American style, Russian style, and Japanese style. *Personal Relationships*, 1, 349-369. (p. 379)

Srivastava, A., Locke, E. A., & Bartol, K. M. (2001). Money and subjective well-being: It's not the money, it's the motives. *Journal of Personality and Social Psychology*, 80, 959-971. (p. 535)

Stack, S. (1992). Marriage, family, religion, and suicide. In R. Maris, A. Berman, J. Maltsberg, and R. Yufits (eds.), *Assessment and prediction of suicide*. New York: Guilford. (p. 507)

Stam, H., Lubeck, I., Radtke, H. L. (1998). Repopulating social psychology texts: Disembodied "subjects" and embodied subjectivety. In Bayer, B. M., Shotter, J., (Eds.) *Reconstructing the psychological subject: Bodies, practices and technologies. Inquiries in social construction*. (pp. 153-186). London, England UK: Sage Publications, Inc. (p. 190)

Stangor, C., & McMillan, D. (1992). Memory for expectancy-congruent and expectancy-incongruent information: A review of the social and social developmental literatures. *Psychological Bulletin*, 111, 42-61. (p. 451)

Stark, R., & Bainbridge, W. S. (1980). Networks of faith: Interpersonal bonds and recruitment of cults and sects. *American Journal of Sociology*, 85, 1376-1395. (p. 172)

Stasser, G. (1991). Pooling of unshared information during group discussion. In S. Worchel, W. Wood, & J. Simpson (Eds.), *Group process and productivity*. Beverly Hills, CA: Sage. (p. 236)

Stasser, G., Kerr, N. L., & Bray, R. M. (1981). The social psychology of jury deliberations: Structure, process, and product. In N. L. Kerr & R. M. Bray (Eds.), *The psychology of the courtroom*. New York: Academic Press. (p. 525)

Statistics Canada (1997). The Justice Data Factfinder. *Juristat: Canadian Centre for Justice Statistics*, 17, number 13. (p. 422)

Staub, E. (1978). *Positive social behavior and morality: Social and personal influences*, vol. 1. Hillsdale, NJ: Erlbaum. (p. 298)

Staub, E. (1989). *The roots of evil: The origins of genocide and other group violence*. Cambridge: Cambridge University Press. (p. 196)

Staub, E. (1990). Moral exclusion: Personal goal theory, and extreme destructiveness. *Journal of Social Issues*, 46, 47-64. (p. 325)

Staub, E. (1991). Altruistic and moral motivations for helping and their translation into action. *Psychological Inquiry*, 2, 150-153. (p. 311)

Staub, E. (1991). Psychological and cultural origins of extreme destructiveness and extreme altruism. In W. Kurtines & J. Gewirtz (Eds.), *The handbook of moral behavior and development*. Hillsdale, NJ: Erlbaum. (p. 326)

Staub, E. (1996). Altruism and aggression in children and youth: Origins and cures. In R. Feldman (Ed.), *The psychology of adversity*. Amherst, MA: University of Massachusetts Press. (p. 343)

Staub, E. (1997). Blind versus constructive patriotism: Moving from embeddedness in the group to critical loyalty and action. In D. Bar-Tal and E. Staub (Eds.), *Patriotism in the lives of individuals and nations*. Chicago: Nelson-Hall. (p. 433)

Staub, E. (1997). *Halting and preventing collective violence: The role of bystanders*. Background paper for symposium organized by the Friends of Raoul Wallenberg, Stockholm, June 13-16. (p. 318)

Staub, E. (1999). The origins and prevention of genocide, mass killing, and other collective violence. *Peace and Conflict*, 5, 303-336. (p. 332)

Staub, E. (2004). Justice, healing, and reconciliation: How the people's courts in Rwanda can promote them. *Peace and Conflict: Journal of Peace Psychology*, ***10***, 25.

Staub, E. (2005). Hotel Rwanda: Goodness in the midst of evil. *PsycCRITIQUES*, *50*(15). (p. 480)

Staub, E., Pearlman, L. A., Gubin, A., & Hagengimana, A. (2005). Healing, reconciliation, forgiving and the prevention of violence after genocide or mass killing: An intervention and its experimental evaluation in Rwanda. *Journal of Social & Clinical Psychology*, ***24***, 297. (p. 480)

Steblay, N., Dysart, J. E., Fulero, S., & Lindsay, R. C. L. (2001). Eyewitness accuracy rates in sequential and simultaneous lineup presentations: A meta-analytic comparison. *Law and Human Behavior*, 25, 459-473. (p. 520)

Steele, C. M. (1988). The psychology of self-affirmation: Sustaining the integrity of the self. In L. Berkowitz (Ed.), *Advances in experimental social psychology*, Vol. 21. Orlando, Fl.: Academic Press. (p. 138)

Steele, C. M. (1997). A threat in the air: How stereotypes shape intellectual identity and performance. *American Psychologist*, 52, 613-629. (p. 453)

Steele, C. M., & Aronson, J. (1995). Stereotype threat and the intellectual test performance of African Americans. *Journal of Personality and Social Psychology*, 69, 797-811. (p. 453)

Steele, C. M., & Josephs, R. A. (1990). Alcohol myopia: Its prized and dangerous effects. *American Psychologist*, 45, 921-933. (p. 495)

Steele, C. M., & Southwick, L. (1985). Alcohol and social behavior I: The psychology of drunken excess. *Journal of Personality and Social Psychology*, 48, 18-34. (p. 336)

Steele, C. M., Southwick, L. L., & Critchlow, B. (1981). Dissonance and alcohol: Drinking your troubles away. *Journal of Personality and Social Psychology*, 41, 831-846. (p. 139)

Steele, C. M., Spencer, S. J., & Lynch, M. (1993). Self-image resilience and dissonance: The role of affirmational resources. *Journal of Personality and Social Psychology*, 64, 885-896. (p. 138)

Steele, C. M., Spencer, S. J., Aronson, J. (2002). Contending with group image: The psychology of stereotype and social identity threat. In Zanna, M. P. (Ed.), *Advances in experimental social psychology*, 34, 379-440. San Diego, CA: Academic Press, Inc. (p. 453)

Stein, A. H., & Friedrich, L. K. (1972). Television content and young children's behavior. In J. P. Murray, E. A. Rubinstein, & G. A. Comstock (Eds.), *Television and social learning*. Washington, D.C.: Government Printing Office. (p. 327)

Stein, D. D., Hardyck, J. A., & Smith, M. B. (1965). Race and belief: An open and shut case. *Journal of Personality and Social Psychology*, 1, 281-289. (p. 443)

Stephan, W. G., Berscheid, E., & Walster, E. (1971). Sexual arousal and heterosexual perception. *Journal of Personality and Social Psychology*, 20, 93-101. (p. 399)

Stern, J. (1999, November 8). Babe tube. *Time*, pp. 133-135. (p. 355)

Sternberg, R. J. (2003). A duplex theory of hate and its development and its application to terrorism, massacres, and genocide. *Review of General Psychology*, 7, 299-328. (p. 332)

Sternberg, R. J., & Grajek, S. (1984). The nature of love. *Journal of Personality and Social Psychology*, 47, 312-329. (p. 403)

Stinson, V., Devenport, J. L., Cutler, B. L., & Kravitz, D. A. (1997). How effective is the motion-to-suppress safeguard? Judges' perceptions of the suggestiveness and fairness of biased lineup procedures. *Journal of Personality and Social Psychology*, 82, 211-220. (p. 521)

Stinson, V., Devenport, J. L., Cutler, B. L., & Kravitz, D. A. (1996). How effective is the presence-of-counsel safeguard? Attorney perceptions of suggestiveness, fairness, and correctability of biased lineup procedures. *Journal of Applied Psychology*, 81, 64-75. (p. 521)

Stone, A. A., Hedges, S. M., Neale, J. M., & Satin, M. S. (1985). Prospective and cross-sectional mood reports offer no evidence of a "blue Monday" phenomenon. *Journal of Personality and Social Psychology*, 49, 129-134. (p. 40)

Stone, A. L., & Glass, C. R. (1986). Cognitive distortion of social feedback in depression. *Journal of Social and Clinical Psychology*, 4, 179-188. (p. 90)

Stone, J. (2000, November 6). Quoted by Sharon Begley, The stereotype trap. *Newsweek*. (p. 454)

Stone, J., Lynch, C. I., Sjomeling, M., & Darley, J. M. (1999). Stereotype threat effects on Black and White athletic performance. *Journal of Personality and Social Psychology*, 77, 1213-1227. (p. 140)

Stone, L. (1977). *The family, sex and marriage in England, 1500-1800*. New York: Harper & Row. (p. 411)

Stoner, J. A. F. (1961). A comparison of individual and group decisions involving risk. Unpublished master's thesis, Massachusetts Institute of Technology, 1961. Cited by D. G. Marquis in, Individual responsibility and group decisions involving risk. *Industrial Management Review*, 3, 8-23. (p. 232)

Storms, M. D., & Thomas, G. C. (1977). Reactions to physical closeness. *Journal of Personality and Social Psychology*, 35, 412-418. (p. 220)

Stouffer, S. A., Suchman, E. A., DeVinney, L. C., Star, S. A., & Williams, R. M., Jr. (1949). *The American soldier: Adjustment during army life* (Vol. 1.). Princeton, N.J.: Princeton University Press. (p. 341)

Strachman, A., & Schimel, J. (2006). Terror management and close relationships: Evidence that mortality salience reduces commitment among partners with different worldviews. *Journal of Social and Personal Relationships*, **23**, 965. (p. 372)

Strack, F., & Deutsch, R. (2004). Reflective and impulsive determinants of social behavior. *Personality and Social Psychology Review*, in press. (p. 38)

Strack, S., & Coyne, J. C. (1983). Social confirmation of dysphoria: Shared and private reactions to depression. *Journal of Personality and Social Psychology*, 44, 798-806. (p. 491)

Straus, M. A., & Gelles, R. J. (1980). *Behind closed doors: Violence in the American family*. New York: Anchor/Doubleday. (p. 343)

Stroebe, W., & Diehl, M. (1994). Productivity loss in idea-generating groups. In W. Stroebe & M. Hewstone (Eds.), *European review of social psychology*, vol. 5. Chichester: Wiley. (p. 246)

Stroebe, W., Insko, C. A., Thompson, V. D., & Layton, B. D. (1971). Effects of physical attractiveness, attitude similarity, and sex on various aspects of interpersonal attraction. *Journal of Personality and Social Psychology*, 18, 79-91. (p. 380)

Stroessner, S. J., & Mackie, D. M. (1993). Affect and perceived group variability: Implications for stereotyping and prejudice. In D. M. Mackie & D. L. Hamilton (Eds.), *Affect, cognition, and stereotyping: Interactive processes in group perception*. San Diego, CA: Academic Press. (p. 442)

Stroessner, S. J., Hamilton, D. L., & Lepore, L. (1990). *Intergroup categorization and intragroup differentiation: Ingroup-outgroup differences*. Paper presented at the American Psychological Association convention. (p. 442)

Strong, S. R. (1978). Social psychological approach to psychotherapy research. In S. L. Garfield & A. E. Bergin (Eds.), *Handbook of psychotherapy and behavior change*, 2nd ed. New York: Wiley. (p. 173)

Suedfeld, P. (2000). Reverberations of the Holocaust fifty years later: Psychology's contributions to understanding persecution and genocide. *Canadian Psychology*, 41, 1-9. (p. 318)

Suls, J., Wan, C. K., & Sanders, G. S. (1988). False consensus and false uniqueness in estimating the prevalence of health-protective behaviors. *Journal of Applied Social Psychology*, 18, 66-79. (p. 61)

Summers, G., & Feldman, N. S. (1984). Blaming the victim versus blaming the perpetrator: An attributional analysis of spouse abuse. *Journal of Social and Clinical Psychology*, 2, 339-347. (p. 440)

Sundstrom, E., De Meuse, K. P., & Futrell, D. (1990). Work teams: Applications and effectiveness. *American Psychologist*, 45, 120-133. (p. 248)

Sunstein, C. R. (2001). *Republic.com*. Princeton, NJ: Princeton University Press. (p. 235)

Sussman, N. M. (2000). The dynamic nature of cultural identity throughout cultural transitions: Why home is not so sweet. *Personality and Social Psychology Review*, 4, 355-373. (p. 264)

Svenson, O. (1981). Are we all less risky and more skillful than our fellow drivers? *Acta Psychologica*, 47, 143-148. (p. 57)

Swain, M. (1974). French immersion programs across Canada. *The Canadian Modern Language Review*, 31, 117-128. (p. 289)

Swann, W. B., Jr. (1984). Quest for accuracy in person perception: A matter of pragmatics. *Psychological Review*, 91, 457-475. (p. 108)

Swann, W. B., Jr. (1996). *Self-traps: The elusive quest for higher self-esteem*. New York: Freeman. (p. 63)

Swann, W. B., Jr. (1997). The trouble with change: Self-verification and allegiance to the self. *Psychological Science*, 8, 177-180. (p. 63)

Swann, W. B., Jr., & Gill, M. J. (1997). Confidence and accuracy in person perception: Do we know what we think we know about our relationship partners? *Journal of Personality and Social Psychology*, 73, 747-757. (p. 82)

Swann, W. B., Jr., & Predmore, S. C. (1985). Intimates as agents of social support: Sources of consolation or despair? *Journal of Personality and Social Psychology*, 49, 1609-1617. (p. 408)

Swann, W. B., Jr., & Read, S. J. (1981). Acquiring self-knowledge: The search for feedback that fits. *Journal of Personality and Social Psychology*, 41, 1119-1128. (p. 84)

Swann, W. B., Jr., Milton, L. P., & Polzer, J. T. (2000). Should we create a niche or fall in line? Identity negotiation and small group effectiveness. *Journal of Personality and Social Psychology*, 79, 238-250. (p. 84)

Swann, W. B., Jr., Rentfrow, P. J., & Gosling, S. D. (2003). The precarious couple effect: Verbally inhibited men + critical, disinhibited women = bad chemistry. *Journal of Personality and Social Psychology*, 85, 1095-1106. (p. 412)

Swann, W. B., Jr., Sellers, J. G., & McClarty, K. L. (2006). Tempting today, troubling tomorrow: The roots of the precarious couple effect. *Personality and Social Psychology Bulletin*, ***32***, 93. (p. 412)

Swann, W. B., Jr., Stein-Seroussi, A., & Giesler, R. B. (1992). Why people self-verify. *Journal of Personality and Social Psychology*, 62, 392-401. (p. 84)

Swann, W. B., Jr., Stein-Seroussi, A., & McNulty, S. E. (1992). Outcasts in a white lie society. The enigmatic worlds of people with negative self-conceptions. *Journal of Personality and Social Psychology*, 62, 618-624. (p. 84)

Swann, W. B., Jr., Wenzlaff, R. M., Krull, D. S., & Pelham, B. W. (1991). Seeking truth, reaping despair: Depression, self-verification and selection of relationship partners. *Journal of Abnormal Psychology*, 101, 293-306. (p. 84)

Swap, W. C. (1977). Interpersonal attraction and repeated exposure to rewarders and punishers. *Personality and Social Psychology Bulletin*, 3, 248-251. (p. 377)

Swedish Information Service (1980). *Social change in Sweden*, September, No. 19, p. 5. (Published by the Swedish Consulate General, 825 Third Avenue, New York, N.Y. 10022.) (p. 369)

Sweeney, J. (1973). An experimental investigation of the free rider problem. *Social Science Research*, 2, 277-292. (p. 224)

Sweeney, P. D., Anderson, K., & Bailey, S. (1986). Attributional style in depression: A meta-analytic review. *Journal of Personality and Social Psychology*, 50, 947-991. (p. 490)

Swim, J. K. (1994). Perceived versus meta-analytic effect sizes: An assessment of the accuracy of gender stereotypes. *Journal of Personality and Social Psychology*, 66, 21-36. (p. 424)

Swim, J. K., & Cohen, L. L. (1997). Overt, covert, and subtle sexism. *Psychology of Women Quarterly*, 21, 103-118. (p. 419)

Swim, J. K., & Hyers, L. L. (1998). Excuse me—What did you just say?!: Women's public and private reactions to sexist remarks. *Journal of Experimental Social Psychology*, in press. (p. 197)

Swim, J. K., Aikin, J. K., Hall, W. S., & Hunter, B. A. (1995). Sexism and racism: Old-fashioned and modern prejudices. *Journal of Personality and Social Psychology*, 68, 199-214. (p. 418)

Swim, J. K., Cohen, L. L., & Hyers, L. L. (1998). Experiencing everyday prejudice and discrimination. In J. K. Swim & C. Stangor (Eds.), *Prejudice: The target's perspective*. San Diego: Academic Press. (p. 445)

Symons, C. S., & Johnson, B. T. (1997). The self-reference effect in memory: A meta-analysis. *Psychological Bulletin*, 121, 371-394. (p. 50)

Tafarodi, R. W., Lo, C., Yamaguchi, S., Lee, W. W-S., & Katsura, H. (2004). The inner self in three countries. *Journal of Cross-Cultural Psychology*, 35, 97-117. (p. 268)

Tajfel, H. (1970, November). Experiments in intergroup discrimination. *Scientific American*, pp. 96-102. (p. 434)

Tajfel, H. (1981). *Human groups and social categories: Studies in social psychology*. London: Cambridge University Press. (p. 434)

Tajfel, H. (1982). Social psychology of intergroup relations. *Annual Review of Psychology*, 33, 1-39. (p. 434)

Tajfel, H., & Billig, M. (1974). Familiarity and categorization in intergroup behavior. *Journal of Experimental Social Psychology*, 10, 159-170. (p. 434)

Takooshian, H., & Bodinger, H. (1982). Bystander indifference to street crime. In L. Savitz & N. Johnston (Eds.), *Contemporary criminology*. New York: Wiley. (p. 315)

Tang, S-H., & Hall, V. C. (1994). The overjustification effect: A meta-analysis. *Applied Cognitive Psychology*, in press. (p. 136)

Taubes, G. (1992). Violence epidemiologists tests of hazards of gun ownership. *Science*, 258, 213-215. (p. 350)

Tavris, C. (1992). *The mismeasure of woman*. New York: Simon & Schuster. (p. 499)

Taylor, D. G., Sheatsley, P. B., & Greeley, A. M. (1978). Attitudes toward racial integration. *Scientific American*, 238(6), 42-49. (p. 442)

Taylor, D. M., & Doria, J. R. (1981). Self-serving and group-serving bias in attribution. *Journal of Social Psychology*, 113, 201-211. (p. 65)

Taylor, D. M., Wright, S. C., Moghaddam, F. M., & Lalonde, R. N. (1990). The personal/group discrimination discrepancy: Perceiving my group, but not myself, to be a target for discrimination. *Personality and Social Psychology Bulletin*, 16, 254-262. (p. 460)

Taylor, S. E. (1979). Remarks at symposium on social psychology and medicine, American Psychological Association convention. (p. 445)

Taylor, S. E. (1981). A categorization approach to stereotyping. In D. L. Hamilton (Ed.), *Cognitive processes in stereotyping and intergroup behavior*. Hillsdale, N.J.: Erlbaum. (p. 443)

Taylor, S. E. (1989). *Positive illusions: Creative self-deception and the healthy mind*. New York: Basic Books. (p. 490)

Taylor, S. E., & Fiske, S. T. (1978). Salience, attention, and attribution: Top of the head phenomena. In L. Berkowitz (Ed.), *Advances in experimental social psychology* (Vol. 11). New York: Academic Press. (p. 445)

Taylor, S. E., Lerner, J. S., Sherman, D. K., Sage, R. M., & McDowell, N. K. (2003). Are self-enhancing cognitions associated with healthy or unhealthy biological profiles? *Journal of Personality and Social Psychology, **85***, 605. (p. 64)

Taylor, S. E., Repetti, R. L., & Seeman, T. (1997). Health psychology: What is an unhealthy environment and how does it get under the skin? *Annual Review of Psychology*, 48, 411-447. (p. 504)

Taylor, S. P., & Chermack, S. T. (1993). Alcohol, drugs and human physical aggression. *Journal of Studies on Alcohol*, Supplement No. 11, 78-88. (p. 336)

Taylor, S. P., & Pisano, R. (1971). Physical aggression as a function of frustration and physical attack. *Journal of Social Psychology*, 84, 261-267. (p. 347)

Tedeschi, J. T., Nesler, M., & Taylor, E. (1987). *Misattribution and the bogus pipeline: A test of dissonance and impression management theories.* Paper presented at the American Psychological Association convention. (p. 128)

Teger, A. I. (1980). *Too much invested to quit.* New York: Pergamon Press. (p. 469)

Teigen, K. H., Evensen, P. C., Samoilow, D. K., & Vatne, K. B. (1999). Good luck and bad luck: How to tell the difference. *European Journal of Social Psychology*, 29, 981-1010. (p. 88)

Tennen, H., & Affleck, G. (1987). The costs and benefits of optimistic explanations and dispositional optimism. *Journal of Personality*, 55, 377-393. (p. 502)

Tennov, D. (1979). *Love and limerence: The experience of being in love.* New York: Stein and Day, p. 22. (p. 301)

Tepperman & Curtis (1995). A life satisfaction scale. *Social Indicators Research*, 35, 255-270. (p. 507)

Tesser, A. (1988). Toward a self-evaluation maintenance model of social behavior. In L. Berkowitz (Ed.), *Advances in experimental social psychology*, Vol. 21. San Diego, Ca.: Academic Press. (p. 46)

Tesser, A., Martin, L., & Mendolia, M. (1995). The impact of thought on attitude extremity and attitude-behavior consistency. In R. E. Petty and J. A Krosnick (Eds.), *Attitude strength: Antecedents and consequences.* Hillsdale, NJ: Erlbaum. (p. 237)

Tesser, A., Millar, M., & Moore, J. (1988). Some affective consequences of social comparison and reflection processes: The pain and pleasure of being close. *Journal of Personality and Social Psychology*, 54, 49-61. (p. 436)

Tetlock, P. E. (1985). Integrative complexity of American and Soviet foreign policy rhetoric: A time-series analysis. *Journal of Personality and Social Psychology*, 49, 1565-1585. (p. 480)

Tetlock, P. E. (1998). Close-call counterfactuals and belief-system defenses: I was not almost wrong but I was almost right. *Journal of Personality and Social Psychology*, 75, 639-652. (p. 84)

Tetlock, P. E. (1999). Theory-driven reasoning about plausible pasts and probable futures in world politics: Are we prisoners of our preconceptions? *American Journal of Political Science*, 43, 335-366. (p. 84)

Tetlock, P. E., Peterson, R. S., McGuire, C., Chang, S., & Feld, P. (1992). Assessing political group dynamics: A test of the groupthink model. *Journal of Personality and Social Psychology*, 63, 403-425. (p. 243)

Thomas, G. C., & Batson, C. D. (1981). Effect of helping under normative pressure on self-perceived altruism. *Social Psychology Quarterly*, 44, 127-131. (p. 327)

Thomas, G. C., Batson, C. D., & Coke, J. S. (1981). Do Good Samaritans discourage helpfulness? Self-perceived altruism after exposure to highly helpful others. *Journal of Personality and Social Psychology*, 40, 194-200. (p. 327)

Thompson, L. (1990a). An examination of naive and experienced negotiators. *Journal of Personality and Social Psychology*, 59, 82-90. (p. 477)

Thompson, L. (1990b). The influence of experience on negotiation performance. *Journal of Experimental Social Psychology*, 26, 528-544. (p. 477)

Thompson, L. (1998). *The mind and heart of the negotiator.* Upper Saddle River, NJ: Prentice-Hall. (p. 477)

Thompson, L. L., & Crocker, J. (1985). Prejudice following threat to the self-concept. Effects of performance expectations and attributions. Unpublished manuscript, Northwestern University. (p. 437)

Thompson, L., & Hrebec, D. (1996). Lose-lose agreements in interdependent decision making. *Psychological Bulletin*, 120, 396-409. (p. 476)

Thompson, L., Valley, K. L., & Kramer, R. M. (1995). The bittersweet feeling of success: An examination of social perception in negotiation. *Journal of Experimental Social Psychology*, 31, 467-492. (p. 477)

Thompson, W. C., Cowan, C. L., & Rosenhan, D. L. (1980). Focus of attention mediates the impact of negative affect on altruism. *Journal of Personality and Social Psychology*, 38, 291-300. (p. 300)

Thompson, W. C., Fong, G. T., & Rosenhan, D. L. (1981). Inadmissible evidence and juror verdicts. *Journal of Personality and Social Psychology*, 40, 453-463. (p. 526)

Thornton, B., & Maurice, J. (1997). Physique contrast effect: Adverse impact of idealized body images for women. *Sex Roles*, 37, 433-439. (p. 386)

Tice, D. M., & Baumeister, R. F. (1997). Longitudinal study of procrastination, performance, stress, and health: The costs and benefits of dawdling. *Psychological Science*, 8, 454-458. (p. 502)

Tice, D. M., Butler, J. L., Muraven, M. B., & Stillwell, A. M. (1995). When modesty prevails: Differential favorability of self-presentation to friends and strangers. *Journal of Personality and Social Psychology*, 69, 1120-1138. (p. 68)

Tideman, S. G. (2004). *Provisional Report on Conference on Gross National Happiness, February 18-20, 2004, Bhutan.* Bussum the Netherlands: Gross General Happiness.org.

Timko, C., & Moos, R. H. (1989). Choice, control, and adaptation among elderly residents of sheltered care settings. *Journal of Applied Social Psychology*, 19, 636-655. (p. 53)

Tindale, R. S., Davis, J. H., Vollrath, D. A., Nagao, D. H., & Hinsz, V. B. (1990). Asymmetrical social influence in freely interacting groups: A test of three models. *Journal of Personality and Social Psychology*, 58, 438-449. (p. 525)

Tomorrow, T. (2003, April 30). Passive tense verbs deployed before large audience; stories remain unclear. (www240.pair.com/tomtom/pages/ja/ja_fr.html) (p. 144)

Toronto News (1977, July 26). (p. 55)

Torrence, E. P., Gowan, J. C., Wu, J. M., & Alioti, N. C. (1970). Creative functioning of monolingual and bilingual children in Singapore. *Journal of Educational Psychology*, 61, 72-75. (p. 289)

Totterdell, P., Kellett, S., Briner, R. B., & Teuchmann, K. (1998). Evidence of mood linkage in work groups. *Journal of Personality and Social Psychology*, 74, 1504-1515. (p. 184)

Traut-Mattausch, E., Schulz-Hardt, S., Greitemeyer, T., & Frey, D. (2004). Expectancy confirmation in spite of disconfirming evidence: The case of price increases due to the introduction of the euro. *European Journal of Social Psychology, 34*(6), 739. (p. 77)

Travis, L. E. (1925). The effect of a small audience upon eye-hand coordination. *Journal of Abnormal and Social Psychology*, 20, 142-146. (p. 217)

Triandis, H. C. (1982). *Incongruence between intentions and behavior: A review*. Paper presented at the American Psychological Association convention. (p. 114)

Triandis, H. C. (1994). *Culture and social behavior*. New York: McGraw-Hill. (p. 152)

Triandis, H. C. (2000). Culture and conflict. *International Journal of Psychology*, 55, 145-152. (p. 269)

Triandis, H. C., Bontempo, R., Villareal, M. J., Asai, M., & Lucca, N. (1988). Individualism and collectivism: Cross-cultural perspectives on self-ingroup relationships. *Journal of Personality and Social Psychology*, 54, 323-338. (p. 402)

Trolier, T. K., & Hamilton, D. L. (1986). Variables influencing judgments of correlational relations. *Journal of Personality and Social Psychology*, 50, 879-888. (p. 88)

Tropp, L. R., & Pettigrew, T. F. (2005). Differential relationships between intergroup contact and affective and cognitive dimensions of prejudice. *Personality and Social Psychology Bulletin*, ***31***, 1145. (p. 282)

Tropp, L. R., & Pettigrew, T. F. (2005). Relationships between intergroup contact and prejudice among minority and majority status groups. *Psychological Science*, ***16***, 951. (p. 282)

Trost, M. R., Maass, A., & Kenrick, D. T. (1992). Minority influence: Personal relevance biases cognitive processes and reverses private acceptance. *Journal of Experimental Social Psychology*, 28, 234-254. (p. 251)

Trottier, K., Polivy, J., & Herman, C. P. (2007). Effects of exposure to thin and overweight peers: Evidence of social comparison in restrained and unrestrained eaters. *Journal of Social & Clinical Psychology*, ***26***, 155. (p. 46)

Turk, D. J., Handy, T. C., & Gazzaniga, M. S. (2005). Can perceptual expertise account for the own-race bias in face recognition? A split-brain study. *Cognitive Neuropsychology*, ***22***, 877. (p. 444)

Turner, C. W., Hesse, B. W., & Peterson-Lewis, S. (1986). Naturalistic studies of the long-term effects of television violence. *Journal of Social Issues*, 42(3), 51-74. (p. 356)

Turner, J. C. (1981). The experimental social psychology of intergroup behaviour. In J. Turner & H. Giles (eds.), *Intergroup behaviour*. Oxford, England: Blackwell. (p. 432)

Turner, J. C. (1987). *Rediscovering the social group: A self-categorization theory*. New York: Basil Blackwell. (p. 216)

Turner, J. C. (1991). *Social influence*. Milton Keynes, England: Open University Press. (p. 432)

Turner, J. C., & Haslam, S. A. (2001). Social identity, organizations, and leadership. In M. E. Turner (Ed.), Groups at work: *Theory and research*. Mahwah, NJ: Erlbaum. (p. 432)

Turner, M. E., & Pratkanis, A. R. (1993). Effects of preferential and meritorious selection on performance: An examination of intuitive and self-handicapping perspectives. *Personality and Social Psychology Bulletin*, 19, 47-58. (p. 68)

Turner, M. E., & Pratkanis, A. R. (1994). Social identity maintenance prescriptions for preventing groupthink: Reducing identity protection and enhancing intellectual conflict. *International Journal of Conflict Management*, 5, 254-270. (p. 241)

Turner, M. E., Pratkanis, A. R., Probasco, P., & Leve, C. (1992). Threat cohesion, and group effectiveness: Testing a social identity maintenance perspective on groupthink. *Journal of Personality and Social Psychology*, 63, 781-796. (p. 241)

Turner, N., Barling, J., Epitropaki, O., Butcher, V., & Milner, C. (2002). Transformational leadership and moral reasoning. *Journal of Applied Psychology*, ***87***, 304. (p. 250)

TV Guide (1977, January 26), pp. 5-10. (p. 356)

Tverksy, A., & Kahneman, D. (1974). Judgment under uncertainty: Heuristics and biases. *Science*, 185, 1123-1131. (p. 88)

Tversky, A., & Kahneman, D. (1973). Availability: A neuristic for judging frequency and probability. *Cognitive Psychology*, 5, 207-302. (p. 86)

Tversky, A., & Kahneman, D. (1983). Extensional versus intuitive reasoning: The conjunction fallacy in probability judgment. *Psychological Review*, 90, 293-315. (p. 86)

Twenge, J. M., Baumeister, R. F., Tice, D. M., & Stucke, T. S. (2001). If you can't join them, beat them: Effects of social exclusion on aggressive behavior. *Journal of Personality and Social Psychology*, 81, 1058-1069. (p. 373)

Twenge, J. M., Catanese, K. R., & Baumeister, R. F. (2002). Social exclusion causes self-defeating behavior. *Journal of Personality and Social Psychology*, 83, 606-615. (p. 373)

Tyler, T. R., & Lind, E. A. (1990). Intrinsic versus community-based justice models: When does group membership matter? *Journal of Social Issues*, 46, 83-94. (p. 325)

Tzeng, M. (1992). The effects of socioeconomic heterogamy and changes on marital dissolution for first marriages. *Journal of Marriage and the Family*, 54, 609-619. (p. 411)

Uchino, B. N., Cacioppo, J. T., & Kiecolt-Glaser, J. K. (1996). The relationship between social support and physiological processes: A review with emphasis on underlying mechanisms and implications for health. *Psychological Bulletin*, 119, 488-531. (p. 504)

Uleman, J. S. (1989). A framework for thinking intentionally about unintended thoughts. In J. S. Uleman & J. A. Bargh (Eds.), *Unintended thought: The limits of awareness, intention, and control*. New York: Guilford. (p. 94)

Unger, R. K. (1979). *Whom does helping help?* Paper presented at the Eastern Psychological Association convention, April. (p. 297)

United Nations (1991). *The world's women 1970-1990: Trends and statistics*. New York: United Nations. (p. 120)

Usher, J. M. (1992). Research and theory related to female reproduction: Implications for clinical psychology. *British Journal of Clinical Psychology*, 31, 129-151. (p. 499)

Väänänen, A., Buunk, B. P., Kivimäki, M., Pentti, J., & Vahtera, J. (2005). When it is better to give than to receive: Long-term health effects of perceived reciprocity in support exchange. *Journal of Personality and Social Psychology*, ***89***, 176. (p. 504)

Vaillant, G. E. (1977). *Adaptation to life*. Boston: Little, Brown. (p. 79)

Valentine, T., Pickering, A., & Darling, S. (2003). Characteristics of eyewitness identification that predict the outcome of real lineups. *Applied Cognitive Psychology, 17*, 969. (p. 519)

Valliant, G. E. (1997). *Report on distress and longevity.* Paper presented to the American Psychiatric Association convention. (p. 500)

Vallone, R. P., Griffin, D. W., Lin, S., & Ross, L. (1990). Overconfident prediction of future actions and outcomes by self and others. *Journal of Personality and Social Psychology*, 58, 582-592. (p. 83)

Vallone, R. P., Ross, L., & Lepper, M. R. (1985). The hostile media phenomenon: Biased perception and perceptions of media bias in coverage of the "Beirut Massacre." *Journal of Personality and Social Psychology*, 49, 577-585. (p. 74)

van Baaren, R. B., Holland, R. W., Karremans, R. W., & van Knippenberg, A. (2003b). Mimicry and interpersonal closeness. Unpublished manuscript, University of Nijmegen. (p. 388)

van Baaren, R. B., Holland, R. W., Kawakami, K., & van Knippenberg, A. (2004). Mimicry and prosocial behavior. *Psychological Science, **15***, 71. (p. 185)

van Baaren, R. B., Holland, R. W., Steenaert, B., & van Knippenberg, A. (2003a). Mimicry for money: Behavioral consequences of imitation. *Journal of Experimental Social Psychology*, **39**, 393-398. (p. 388)

Van Boven, L., & Gilovich, T. (2003). To do or to have? That is the question. *Journal of Personality and Social Psychology, **85***, 1193. (p. 536)

Van Boven, L., & Loewenstein, G. (2003). Social projection of transient drive states. *Personality and Social Psychology Bulletin*, 29, 1159-1168. (p. 60)

Van Lange, P. A. M. (1991). Being better but not smarter than others: The Muhammad Ali effect at work in interpersonal situations. *Personality and Social Psychology Bulletin*, 17, 689-693. (p. 58)

Van Lange, P. A. M., & Visser, K. (1999). Locomotion in social dilemmas: How people adapt to cooperative, tit-for-tat, and noncooperative partners. *Journal of Personality and Social Psychology*, 77, 762-773. (p. 482)

Van Lange, P. A. M., Taris, T. W., & Vonk, R. (1997). Dilemmas of academic practice: perceptions of superiority among social psychologists. *European Journal of Social Psychology*, 27, 675-685. (p. 58)

Van Vugt, M., Van Lange, P. A. M., & Meertens, R. M. (1996). Commuting by car or public transportation? A social dilemma analysis of travel mode judgements. *European Journal of Social Psychology*, 26, 373-395. (p. 472)

Van Yperen, N. W., & Buunk, B. P. (1990). A longitudinal study of equity and satisfaction in intimate relationships. *European Journal of Social Psychology*, 20, 287-309. (p. 407)

Vancouver, J. B., Rubin, B., & Kerr, N. L. (1991). Sex composition of groups and member motivation III: Motivational losses at a feminine task. *Basic and Applied Social Psychology*, 12, 133-144. (p. 226)

Vanderslice, V. J., Rice, R. W., & Julian, J. W. (1987). The effects of participation in decision-making on worker satisfaction and productivity: An organizational simulation. *Journal of Applied Social Psychology*, 17, 158-170. (p. 248)

Vanman, E. J., Paul, B. Y., Kaplan, D. L., & Miller, N. (1990). Facial electromyography differentiates racial bias in imagined cooperative settings. *Psychophysiology*, 27, 563. (p. 441)

Vasquez, E. A., Denson, T. F., Pedersen, W. C., Stenstrom, D. M., & Miller, N. (2005). The moderating effect of trigger intensity on triggered displaced aggression. *Journal of Experimental Social Psychology, **41***, 61. (p. 339)

Vaughan, K. B., & Lanzetta, J. T. (1981). The effect of modification of expressive displays on vicarious emotional arousal. *Journal of Experimental Social Psychology*, 17, 16-30. (p. 134)

Veysey, B. M., & Messner, S. F. (1999). Further testing of social disorganization theory: An elaboration of Sampson and Groves's "Community structure and crime." *Journal of Research in Crime and Delinquency*, 36, 156-174. (p. 235)

Vidmar, N., & Laird, N. M. (1983). Adversary social roles: Their effects on witnesses' communication of evidence and the assessments of adjudicators. *Journal of Personality and Social Psychology*, 44, 888-898. (p. 516)

Vignoles, V. L., Chryssochoou, X., & Breakwell, G. M. (2000). The distinctiveness principle: Identity, meaning, and the bounds of cultural relativity. *Personality and Social Psychology Review, **4***, 337. (p. 212)

Visher, C. A. (1987). Juror decision making: The importance of evidence. *Law and Human Behavior*, 11, 1-17. (p. 512)

Visintainer, M. A., & Seligman, M. E. (1983, July/August). The hope factor. *American Health*, pp. 59-61. (p. 500)

Visintainer, M. A., & Seligman, M. E. P. (1985). Tumor rejection and early experience of uncontrollable shock in the rat. Unpublished manuscript, University of Pennsylvania. See also, M. A. Visintainer et al. (1982). Tumor rejection in rats after inescapable versus escapable shock. *Science*, 216, 437-439. (p. 501)

Visser, P. S., & Krosnick, J. A. (1998). Development of attitude strength over the life cycle: Surge and decline. *Journal of Personality and Social Psychology, **75***, 1389. (p. 166)

Vitelli, R. (1988). The crisis issue assessed: An empirical analysis. *Basic and Applied Social Psychology*, 9, 301-309. (p. 29)

Vivian, J. E., & Berkowitz, N. H. (1993). Anticipated outgroup evaluations and intergroup bias. *European Journal of Social Psychology*, 23, 513-524. (p. 436)

Vivian, J., Hewstone, M., & Brown, R. (1997). Intergroup contact: Theoretical and empirical developments. In R. Ben-Ari & Y. Rich (eds.), *Enhancing education in heterogeneous schools: Theory and application*. Ramat-Gan: Bar-Ilan University Press. (p. 285)

Vohs, K. D., Baumeister, R. F., & Ciarocco, N. J. (2005). Self-regulation and self-presentation: Regulatory resource depletion impairs impression management and effortful self-presentation depletes regulatory resources. *Journal of Personality and Social Psychology, **88***, 632. (p. 68)

von Hippel, W., Silver, L. A., & Lynch, M. B. (2000). Stereotyping against your will: The role of inhibitory ability in stereotyping and prejudice among the elderly. *Personality and Social Psychology Bulletin*, 26, 523-532. (p. 440)

Vorauer, J. D., & Miller, D. T. (1997). Failure to recognize the effect of implicit social influence on the presentation of self. *Journal of Personality and Social Psychology*, 73, 281-295. (p. 35)

Vorauer, J. D., & Ratner, R. K. (1996). Who's going to make the first move? Pluralistic ignorance as an impediment to relationsip formation. *Journal of Social and Personal Relationships*, 13, 483-506. (p. 237)

Vorauer, J. D., Hunter, A. J., Main, K. J., & Roy, S. A. (2000). Meta-stereotype activation: Evidence from indirect measures for specific evaluative concerns experienced by members of dominant groups in intergroup interaction. *Journal of Personality and Social Psychology*, 78, 690-707. (p. 461)

Vorauer, J. D., Main, K. J., & O'Connell, G. B. (1998). How do individuals expect to be viewed by members of lower status groups? Content and implications of meta-stereotypes. *Journal of Personality and Social Psychology*, 75, 917-937. (p. 446)

Wagner, R. V. (2006). Terrorism: A peace psychological analysis. *Journal of Social Issues, **62***, 155. (p. 339)

Wagner, U., Hewstone, M., & Machleit, U. (1989). Contact and prejudice between Germans and Turks: A correlational study. *Human Relations*, 42, 561-574. (p. 282)

Wagstaff, G. F. (1983). Attitudes to poverty, the Protestant ethic, and political affiliation: A preliminary investigation. *Social Behavior and Personality*, 11, 45-47. (p. 101)

Walker, M., Harriman, S., & Costello, S. (1980). The influence of appearance on compliance with a request. *Journal of Social Psychology*, 112, 159-160. (p. 203)

Walker, R. (2004). The hidden (in plain sight) persuaders. *New York Times Magazine*, December 5, 2004. (p. 162)

Wallace, D. S., Paulson, R. M., Lord, C. G., & Bond, C. F., Jr. (2004). Which behaviors do attitudes predict? Meta-analyzing the effects of social pressure and perceived difficulty. Unpublished manuscript, Fayetteville State University. (p. 116)

Wallace, M. *New York Times*, November 25, 1969. (p. 194)

Waller, J. (2002). *Becoming evil: How ordinary people commit genocide and mass killing*. Oxford: Oxford University Press. (p. 199)

Walster (Hatfield), E. (1965). The effect of self-esteem on romantic liking. *Journal of Experimental Social Psychology*, 1, 184-197. (p. 392)

Walster (Hatfield), E., & Festinger, L. (1962). The effectiveness of "overheard" persuasive communications. *Journal of Abnormal and Social Psychology*, 65, 395-402. (p. 150)

Walster (Hatfield), E., Aronson, V., Abrahams, D., & Rottman, L. (1966). Importance of physical attractiveness in dating behavior. *Journal of Personality and Social Psychology*, 4, 508-516. (p. 379)

Walster (Hatfield), E., Walster, G. W., & Berscheid, E. (1978). *Equity: Theory and research*. Boston: Allyn and Bacon. (p. 395)

Ward, W. C., & Jenkins, H. M. (1965). The display of information and the judgment of contingency. *Canadian Journal of Psychology*, 19, 231-241. (p. 88)

Warnick, D. H., & Sanders, G. S. (1980). The effects of group discussion on eyewitness accuracy. *Journal of Applied Social Psychology*, 10, 249-259. (p. 246)

Warr, P., & Payne, R. (1982). Experiences of strain and pleasure among British adults. *Social Science and Medicine*, 16, 1691-1697. (p. 503)

Wason, P. C. (1960). On the failure to eliminate hypotheses in a conceptual task. *Quarterly Journal of Experimental Psychology*, 12, 129-140. (p. 84)

Watson, D. (1982, November). The actor and the observer: How are their perceptions of causality divergent? *Psychological Bulletin*, 92, 682-700. (p. 270)

Watson, R. I., Jr. (1973). Investigation into deindividuation using a cross-cultural survey technique. *Journal of Personality and Social Psychology*, 25, 342-345. (p. 229)

Watts, W. A. (1967). Relative persistence of opinion change induced by active compared to passive participation. *Journal of Personality and Social Psychology*, 5, 4-15. (p. 117)

Weary, G., & Edwards, J. A. (1994). Social cognition and clinical psychology: Anxiety, depression, and the processing of social information. In R. Wyer & T. Srull (eds.), *Handbook of social cognition*, vol. 2. Hillsdale, NJ: Erlbaum. (p. 90)

Weary, G., Harvey, J. H., Schwieger, P., Olson, C. T., Perloff, R., & Pritchard, S. (1982). Self-presentation and the moderation of self-serving biases. *Social Cognition*, 1, 140-159. (p. 68)

Weber, N., Brewer, N., Wells, G. L., Semmler, C., & Keast, A. (2004). Eyewitness identification accuracy and response latency: The unruly 10-12-second rule. *Journal of Experimental Psychology: Applied, **10***, 139. (p. 519)

Webster, D. M. (1993). Motivated augmentation and reduction of the overattribution bias. *Journal of Personality and Social Psychology*, 65, 261-271. (p. 100)

Wegner, D. M. (2002). *The illusion of conscious will*. Cambridge, MA: MIT Press. (p. 40)

Wegner, D. M., & Erber, R. (1992). The hyperaccessibility of suppressed thoughts. *Journal of Personality and Social Psychology*, 63, 903-912. (p. 440)

Wehr, P. (1979). *Conflict regulation*. Boulder, Colo.: Westview Press. (p. 480)

Weiner, B. (1981). *The emotional consequences of causal ascriptions*. Unpublished manuscript, UCLA. (p. 339)

Weiner, B. (1985). "Spontaneous" causal thinking. *Psychological Bulletin*, 97, 74-84. (p. 93)

Weiner, B. (1985). An attributional theory of achievement motivation and emotion. *Psychological Review, 92*(4), 548.

Weiner, B. (1995). *Judgments of responsibility: A foundation for a theory of social conduct*. New York: Guilford. (p. 93)

Weinstein, N. D. (1980). Unrealistic optimism about future life events. *Journal of Personality and Social Psychology*, 39, 806-820. (p. 59)

Weinstein, N. D. (1982). Unrealistic optimism about susceptibility to health problems. *Journal of Behavioral Medicine*, 5, 441-460. (p. 59)

Weiss, J., & Brown, P. (1976). *Self-insight error in the explanation of mood*. Unpublished manuscript, Harvard University. (p. 40)

Wells, G. L. (1984). The psychology of lineup identifications. *Journal of Applied Social Psychology*, 14, 89-103. (p. 519)

Wells, G. L. (1986). Expert psychological testimony: Empirical and conceptual analyses of effects. *Law and Human Behavior*, 10, 83-95. (p. 521)

Wells, G. L. (1992). Naked statistical evidence of liability: Is subjective probability enough? *Journal of Personality and Social Psychology*, 62, 739-752. (p. 523)

Wells, G. L. (1993). What do we know about eyewitness identification? *American Psychologist*, 48, 553-571. (p. 519)

Wells, G. L. (2005). Helping experimental psychology affect legal policy. In N. Brewer, & K. D. Williams (Eds.), *Psychology and law: An empirical perspective*. (483-500). New York, NY, US: Guilford Press.

Wells, G. L., & Bradfield, A. L. (1998). "Good, you identified the suspect": Feedback to eyewitnesses distorts their reports of the witnessing experience. *Journal of Applied Psychology*, in press. (p. 516)

Wells, G. L., & Leippe, M. R. (1981). How do triers of fact enter the accuracy of eyewitness identification? Memory for peripheral detail can be misleading. *Journal of Applied Psychology*, 66, 682-687. (p. 512)

Wells, G. L., & Murray, D. M. (1983). What can psychology say about the Neil v. Biggers criteria for judging eyewitness accuracy? *Journal of Applied Psychology*, 68, 347-362. (p. 513)

Wells, G. L., & Petty, R. E. (1980). The effects of overt head movements on persuasion: Compatibility and incompatibility of responses. *Basic and Applied Social Psychology*, 1, 219-230. (p. 134)

Wells, G. L., & Turtle, J. W. (1987). Eyewitness testimony research: Current knowledge and emergent controversies. *Canadian Journal of Behavioral Science*, 19, 363-388. (p. 520)

Wells, G. L., Ferguson, T. J., & Lindsay, R. C. L. (1981). The tractability of eyewitness confidence and its implications for triers of fact. *Journal of Applied Psychology*, 66, 688-696. (p. 517)

Wells, G. L., Lindsay, R. C. L., & Ferguson, T. (1979). Accuracy, confidence, and juror perceptions in eyewitness identification. *Journal of Applied Psychology*, 64, 440-448. (p. 512)

Wells, G. L., Lindsay, R. C. L., & Tousignant, J. P. (1980). Effects of expert psychological advice on human performance in judging the validity of eyewitness testimony. *Law and Human Behavior*, 4, 275-285. (p. 512)

Wener, R., Frazier, W., & Farbstein, J. (1987, June). Building better jails. *Psychology Today*, pp. 40-49. (p. 53)

Wenzlaff, R. M., & Prohaska, M. L. (1989). When misery prefers company: Depression, attributions, and responses to others' moods. *Journal of Experimental Social Psychology*, 25, 220-233. (p. 390)

Werner, C. M., Stoll, R., Birch, P., & White, P. H. (2002). Clinical validation and cognitive elaboration: Signs that encourage sustained recycling. *Basic and Applied Social Psychology*, 24, 185-203. (p. 157)

Weyant, J. M. (1984). Applying social psychology to induce charitable donations. *Journal of Applied Social Psychology*, 14, 441-447. (p. 325)

Weyant, J. M., & Smith, S. L. (1987). Getting more by asking for less: The effects of request size on donations of charity. *Journal of Applied Social Psychology*, 17, 392-400. (p. 325)

White, G. L., & Kight, T. D. (1984). Misattribution of arousal and attraction: Effects of salience of explanations for arousal. *Journal of Experimental Social Psychology*, 20, 55-64. (p. 399)

White, H. R., Brick, J., & Hansell, S. (1993). A longitudinal investigation of alcohol use and aggression in adolescence. *Journal of Studies on Alcohol*, Supplement No. 11, 62-77. (p. 336)

White, J. A., & Plous, S. (1995). Self-enhancement and social responsibility: On caring more, but doing less, than others. *Journal of Applied Social Psychology*, 25, 1297-1318. (p. 58)

White, K., & Lehman, D. R. (2005). Culture and social comparison seeking: The role of self-motives. *Personality and Social Psychology Bulletin, 31*, 232. (p. 269)

White, M. J., & Gerstein, L. H. (1987). Helping: The influence of anticipated social sanctions and self-monitoring. *Journal of Personality*, 55, 41-54. (p. 322)

Whitley, B. E., Jr. (1987). The effects of discredited eyewitness testimony: A meta-analysis. *Journal of Social Psychology*, 127, 209-214. (p. 512)

Whitley, B. E., Jr., & Frieze, I. H. (1985). Children's causal attributions for success and failure in achievement settings: A meta-analysis. *Journal of Educational Psychology*, 77, 608-616. (p. 55)

Whittaker, J. O., & Meade, R. D. (1967). Social pressure in the modification and distortion of judgment: A cross-cultural study. *International Journal of Psychology*, 2, 109-113. (p. 278)

Whorf, B. L. (1956). Science and linguistics. In J. B. Carrol (Ed.), *Language, thought, and reality: Selected writings of Benjamin Lee Whorf*. Cambridge, MA: MIT Press. (p. 288)

Whyte, G. (1993). Escalating commitment in individual and group decision making: A prospect theory approach. *Organizational Behavior and Human Decision Processes*, 54, 430-455. (p. 234)

Widom, C. S. (1989). Does violence beget violence? A critical examination of the literature. *Psychological Bulletin*, 106, 3-28. (p. 343)

Wiebe, D. J. (2003). Homicide and suicide risks associated with firearms in the home: A national case-control study. *Annals of Emergency Medicine* **41**, 771-782. (p. 350)

Wiegman, O. (1985). Two politicians in a realistic experiment: Attraction, discrepancy, intensity of delivery, and attitude change. *Journal of Applied Social Psychology*, 15, 673-686. (p. 149)

Wiesel, E. (1985, April 6). The brave Christians who saved Jews from the Nazis. *TV Guide*, pp. 4-6. (p. 296)

Wilder, D. A. (1977). Perception of groups, size of opposition, and social influence. *Journal of Experimental Social Psychology*, 13, 253-268. (p. 201)

Wilder, D. A. (1978). Perceiving persons as a group: Effect on attributions of causality and beliefs. *Social Psychology*, 41, 13-23. (p. 443)

Wilder, D. A. (1981). Perceiving persons as a group: Categorization and intergroup relations. In. D. L. Hamilton (Ed.). *Cognitive processes in stereotyping and intergroup behavior.* Hillsdale, N.J.: Lawrence Erlbaum. (p. 435)

Wilder, D. A. (1990). Some determinants of the persuasive power of in-groups and out-groups: Organization of information and attribution of independence. *Journal of Personality and Social Psychology*, 59, 1202-1213. (p. 152)

Wilder, D. A., & Shapiro, P. (1991). Facilitation of outgroup stereotypes by enhanced ingroup identity. *Journal of Experimental Social Psychology*, 27, 431-452. (p. 436)

Wilder, D. A., & Shapiro, P. N. (1989). Role of competition-induced anxiety in limiting the beneficial impact of positive behavior by out-group members. *Journal of Personality and Social Psychology*, 56, 60-69. (p. 451)

Wilkes, J. (1987, June). Murder in mind. *Psychology Today*, pp. 27-32. (p. 334)

Wilkinson, G. S. (1990, February). Food sharing in vampire bats. *Scientific American*, 262, 76-82. (p. 306)

Williams, D. K., Bourgeois, M. J., & Croyle, R. T. (1993). The effects of stealing thunder in criminal and civil trials. *Law and Human Behavior*, 17, 597-609. (p. 158)

Williams, J. E. (1993). Young adults' views of aging: A nineteen nation study. In M. I. Winkler (ed.), Documentos: Conferencia del XXIV Congreso Interamericano de Psicologia. (101-123) Santiago, *Chile:*

Sociedad Interamericana de Psicologia. (p. 417)

Williams, J. E., & Best, D. L. (1990b). *Sex and psyche: Gender and self viewed cross-culturally.* Newbury Park, CA: Sage. (p. 427)

Williams, J. E., Satterwhite, R. C., & Best, D. L. (1999). Pancultural gender stereotypes revisited: The Five Factor model. *Sex Roles,* 40, 513-525. (p. 424)

Williams, J. E., Satterwhite, R. C., & Best, D. L. (2000). Five-factor gender stereotypes in 27 countries. Paper presented at the XV Congress of the International Association for Cross-Cultural Psychology, Pultusk, Poland. (p. 424)

Williams, K. D. (2002). *Ostracism: The power of silence.* New York: Guilford. (p. 10)

Williams, K. D., & Karau, S. J. (1991). Social loafing and social compensation: The effects of expectations of coworker performance. *Journal of Personality and Social Psychology,* 61, 570-581. (p. 226)

Williams, K. D., & Zadro, L. (2001). Ostracism: On being ignored, excluded and rejected. In M. Leary (Ed.), *Interpersonal rejection.* New York: Oxford. (p. 10)

Williams, K. D., Cheung, C. K. T., & Choi, W. (2000). Cyberostracism: Effects of being ignored over the Internet. *Journal of Personality and Social Psychology,* 79, 748-762. (p. 373)

Williams, K. D., Harkins, S., & Latané, B. (1981). Identifiability as a deterrent to social loafing: Two cheering experiments. *Journal of Personality and Social Psychology,* 40, 303-311. (p. 225)

Williams, K. D., Nida, S. A., Baca, L. D., & Latané, B. (1989). Social loafing and swimming: Effects of identifiability on individual and relay performance of intercollegiate swimmers. *Basic and Applied Social Psychology,* 10, 73-81. (p. 225)

Williams, R. (1993). *Anger kills.* New York: Times Books. (p. 499)

Williams, T. M. (Ed.) (1986). *The impact of television: A natural experiment in three communities.* Orlando, FL: Academic Press. (p. 357)

Williamson, G. M., & Clark, M. S. (1989). Providing help and desired relationship type as determinants of changes in moods and self-evaluations. *Journal of Personality and Social Psychology,* 56, 722-734. (p. 300)

Willis, F. N., & Hamm, H. K. (1980). The use of interpersonal touch in securing compliance. *Journal of Nonverbal Behavior,* 5, 49-55. (p. 192)

Wills, T. A. (1981). Downward comparison principles in social psychology. *Psychological Bulletin,* 90, 245-271. (p. 63)

Wilson, A. E. & Ross, M. (2001). From chump to champ: People's appraisals of their earlier and present selves. *Journal of Personality and Social Psychology,* 80, 572-584. (p. 61)

Wilson, D. K., Kaplan, R. M., & Schneiderman, L. J. (1987). Framing of decisions and selections of alternatives in health care. *Social Behaviour,* 2, 51-59. (p. 499)

Wilson, E. O. (1978). *On human nature.* Cambridge, MA: Harvard University Press. (p. 306)

Wilson, J. P., & Petruska, R. (1984). Motivation, model attributes, and prosocial behavior. *Journal of Personality and Social Psychology,* 46, 458-468. (p. 322)

Wilson, R. C., Gaft, J. G., Dienst, E. R., Wood, L., & Bavry, J. L. (1975). *College professors and their impact on students.* New York: Wiley. (p. 163)

Wilson, R. S., & Matheny, A. P., Jr. (1986). Behavior-genetics research in infant temperament: The Louisville twin study. In R. Plomin & J. Dunn (Eds.), *The study of temperament: Changes, continuities, and challenges.* Hillsdale, N.J.: Erlbaum. (p. 336)

Wilson, T. D. (1985). Strangers to ourselves: The origins and accuracy of beliefs about one's own mental states. In J. H. Harvey & G. Weary (Eds.), *Attribution in contemporary psychology.* New York: Academic Press. (p. 43)

Wilson, T. D. (2002). *Strangers to ourselves: Discovering the adaptive unconscious.* Cambridge, MA: Harvard University Press. (p. 43)

Wilson, T. D., & Gilbert, D. T. (2003). Affective forecasting. *Advances in Experimental Social Psychology,* 35, 346-413. (p. 42)

Wilson, T. D., Dunn, D. S., Kraft, D., & Lisle, D. J. (1989). Introspection, attitude change, and attitude-behavior consistency: The disruptive effects of explaining why we feel the way we do. In L. Berkowitz (Eds.), *Advances in experimental social psychology,* Vol. 22. San Diego, Ca.: Academic Press. (p. 43)

Wilson, T. D., Laser, P. S., & Stone, J. I. (1982). Judging the predictors of one's mood: Accuracy and the use of shared theories. *Journal of Experimental Social Psychology,* 18, 537-556. (p. 40)

Wilson, T. D., Lindsey, S., & Schooler, T. Y. (2000). A model of dual attitudes. *Psychological Review,* 107, 101-126. (p. 44)

Wilson, T. D., Lisle, D. J., Schooler, J. W., Hodges, S. D., Klaaren, K. J., & LaFleur, S. J. (1993). Introspecting about reasons can reduce post-choice satisfaction. *Personality and Social Psychology Bulletin,* 19, 331-339. (p. 44)

Wilson, W. R. (1979). Feeling more than we can know: Exposure effects without learning. *Journal of Personality and Social Psychology,* 37, 811-821. (p. 377)

Winsler, A., Diaz, R. M., Espinosa, L., & Rodriguez, J. L. (1999). When learning a second language does not mean losing the first: Bilingual language development in low-income, Spanish-speaking children attending bilingual preschool. *Child Development,* 70, 349-362. (p. 289)

Winter, F. W. (1973). A laboratory experiment of individual attitude response to advertising exposure. *Journal of Marketing Research,* 10, 130-140. (p. 379)

Wisman, A., & Koole, S. L. (2003). Hiding in the crowd: Can mortality salience promote affiliation with others who oppose one's worldviews? *Journal of Personality and Social Psychology,* 84, 511-526. (p. 372)

Wittenbrink, B., Judd, C. M., & Park, B. (1997). Evidence for racial prejudice at the implicit level and its relationship with questionnaire measures. *Journal of Personality and Social Psychology,* 72, 262-274. (p. 419)

Wixon, D. R., & Laird, J. D. (1976). Awareness and attitude change in the forced-compliance paradigm: The importance of when. *Journal of Personality and Social Psychology,* 34, 376-384. (p. 79)

Wojciszke, B., Bazinska, R., & Jaworski, M. (1998). On the dominance of moral categories in impression formation. *Personality and Social Psychology Bulletin,* 24, 1251-1263. (p. 396)

Wolsko, C., Park, B., Judd, C. M., & Wittenbrink, B. (2000). Framing interethnic ideology: Effects of multicultural and color blind perspectives on judgments of groups and individuals. *Journal of Personality and Social Psychology,* 78, 635-654. (p. 437)

Women on Words and Images (1972). *Dick and Jane as victims: Sex stereotyping in children's readers.* Princeton: Women on Words and Images. Cited by C. Tavris & C. Offir (1977) in *The longest war: Sex differences in perspective.* New York: Harcourt Brace Jovanovich, p. 177. (p. 430)

Wood, J. V. (1989). Theory and research concerning social comparisons of personal attributes. *Psychological Bulletin,* 106, 231-248. (p. 340)

Wood, J. V., Heimpel, S. A., & Michela, J. L. (2003). Savoring versus dampening: Self-esteem differences in regulating positive affect. *Journal of Personality and Social Psychology, **85***, 566. (p. 63)

Wood, J. V., Heimpel, S. A., Newby-Clark, I. R., & Ross, M. (2005). Snatching defeat from the jaws of victory: Self-esteem differences in the experience and anticipation of success. *Journal of Personality and Social Psychology, **89***, 764. (p. 47)

Wood, J. V., Saltzberg, J. A., & Goldsamt, L. A. (1990). Does affect induce self-focused attention? *Journal of Personality and Social Psychology*, 58, 899-908. (p. 300)

Wood, J. V., Saltzberg, J. A., Neale, J. M., Stone, A. A., & Rachmiel, T. B. (1990). Self-focused attention, coping responses, and distressed mood in everyday life. *Journal of Personality and Social Psychology*, 58, 1027-1036. (p. 492)

Wood, W., Conway, M., Pushkar, D., & Dugas, M. J. (2005). People's perceptions of women's and men's worry about life issues: Worrying about love, accomplishment, or money? *Sex Roles, **53***, 545. (p. 423)

Wood, W., Rhodes, N., & Whelan, M. (1989). Sex differences in positive well-being: A consideration of emotional style and marital status. *Psychological Bulletin*, 106, 249-264. (p. 508)

Woodberry, R. D., & Smith, C. S. (1998). Fundamentalism et al: Conservative Protestants in America. *Annual Review of Sociology*, 24, 25-56. (p. 429)

Woodzicka, J. A., & LaFrance, M. (2001). Real versus imagined gender harassment. *Journal of Social Issues*, 57(1), 15-30. (p. 41)

Worchel, S., & Brown, E. H. (1984). The role of plausibility in influencing environmental attributions. *Journal of Experimental Social Psychology*, 20, 86-96. (p. 220)

Worchel, S., & Norvell, N. (1980). Effect of perceived environmental conditions during cooperation on intergroup attraction. *Journal of Personality and Social Psychology*, 38, 764-772. (p. 285)

Worchel, S., Andreoli, V. A., & Folger, R. (1977). Intergroup cooperation and intergroup attraction: The effect of previous interaction and outcome of combined effort. *Journal of Experimental Social Psychology*, 13, 131-140. (p. 285)

Worchel, S., Axsom, D., Ferris, F., Samah, G., & Schweitzer, S. (1978). Deterrents of the effect of intergroup cooperation on intergroup attraction. *Journal of Conflict Resolution*, 22, 429-439. (p. 285)

Worchel, S., Jenner, S. M., & Hebl, M. R. (1998). Changing the guard: How origin of new leader and disposition of ex-leader affect group performance and perceptions. *Small Group Research, **29***, 436. (p. 226)

Word, C. O., Zanna, M. P., & Cooper, J. (1974). The nonverbal mediation of self-fulfilling prophecies in interracial interaction. *Journal of Experimental Social Psychology*, 10, 109-120. (p. 453)

Workman, E. A., & Williams, R. L. (1980). Effects of extrinsic rewards on intrinsic motivation in the classroom. *Journal of School Psychology*, 18, 141-147. (p. 136)

Worringham, C. J., & Messick, D. M. (1983). Social facilitation of running: An unobtrusive study. *Journal of Social Psychology*, 121, 23-29. (p. 221)

Wright, D. B., & Stroud, J. N. (2002). Age differences in lineup identification accuracy: People are better with their own age. *Law and Human Behavior*, 26, 641-654. (p. 444)

Wright, D. B., Boyd, C. E., & Tredoux, C. G. (2001). A field study of own-race bias in South Africa and England. *Psychology, Public Policy, & Law*, 7, 119-133. (p. 444)

Wright, E. F., Lüüs, C. A., & Christie, S. D. (1990). Does group discussion facilitate the use of consensus information in making causal attributions? *Journal of Personality and Social Psychology*, 59, 261-269. (p. 246)

Wright, R. (1995, March 13). The biology of violence. *New Yorker*, pp. 69-77. (p. 337)

Wright, R. (2000). *Non-zero: The logic of human destiny.* New York: Vintage Books.

Wright, S. C., & Taylor, D. M. (1995). Identity and the language of the classroom: Investigating the impact of heritage versus second language instruction on personal and collective self-esteem. *Journal of Educational Psychology*, 87, 241-252. (p. 290)

Wright, S. C., Aron, A., McLaughlin-Volpe, T., & Ropp, S. A. (1997). The extended contact effect: Knowledge of cross-group friendships and prejudice. *Journal of Personality and Social Psychology*, 73, 73-90. (p. 285)

Wright, S. C., Taylor, D. M., & Macarthur, J. (2000). Subtractive bilingualism and the survival of the Inuit language: Heritage- versus second-language education. *Journal of Educational Psychology*, 92, 63-84. (p. 290)

Wu, C., & Shaffer, D. R. (1987). Susceptibility to persuasive appeals as a function of source credibility and prior experience with the attitude object. *Journal of Personality and Social Psychology*, 52, 677-688. (p. 117)

Wu, D. Y. H., & Tseng, W. S. (1985). Introduction: the characteristics of chinese culture. In D. Y. H. Wu and W. S. Tseng (Eds.), *Chinese culture and mental health.* San Diego, Ca.: Academic Press. (p. 69)

Wylie, R. C. (1979). *The self-concept (Vol. 2): Theory and research on selected topics.* Lincoln, Neb.: University of Nebraska Press. (p. 57)

Yarmey, A. D. (2003a). Eyewitness identification: Guidelines and recommendations for identification procedures in the United States and in Canada. *Canadian Psychology*, 44, 181-189. (p. 520)

Yarmey, A. D. (2003b). Eyewitnesses. In D. Carson and R. Bull, *Handbook of psychology in legal contexts*, 2nd ed. Chichester, England: Wiley. (p. 520)

Ybarra, O. (1999). Misanthropic person memory when the need to self-enhance is absent. *Personality and Social Psychology Bulletin*, 25, 261-269. (p. 48)

Yinon, Y., Sharon, I., Gonen, Y., & Adam, R. (1982). Escape from responsibility and help in emergencies among persons alone or within groups. *European Journal of Social Psychology*, 12, 301-305. (p. 318)

Young, W. R. (1977, February). There's a girl on the tracks! *Reader's Digest*, pp. 91-95. (p. 296)

Younger, J. C., Walker, L., & Arrowood, J. A. (1977). Postdecision dissonance at the fair. *Personality and Social Psychology Bulletin*, 3, 284-287. (p. 132)

Yousif, Y., & Korte, C. (1995). Urbanization, culture, and helpfulness. *Journal of Cross-Cultural Psychology*, 26, 474-489. (p. 316)

Yovetich, N. A., & Rusbult, C. E. (1994). Accommodative behavior in close relationships: Exploring transformation of motivation. *Journal of Experimental Social Psychology*, 30, 138-164. (p. 412)

Yuchtman (Yaar), E. (1976). Effects of social-psychological factors on subjective economic welfare. In B. Strumpel (Ed.), *Economic means for human needs.* Ann Arbor: Institute for Social Research, University of Michigan. (p. 340)

Yukl, G. (1974). Effects of the opponent's initial offer, concession magnitude, and concession frequency on bargaining behavior. *Journal of Personality and Social Psychology*, 30, 323-335. (p. 476)

Yzerbyt, V. Y., & Leyens, J-P. (1991). Requesting information to form an impression: The influence of valence and confirmatory status. *Journal of Experimental Social Psychology*, 27, 337-356. (p. 391)

Yzerbyt, V., Rocher, S., & Schadron, G. (1997). Stereotypes as explanations: A subjective essentialistic view of group perception. In R. Spears, P. J. Oakes, N. Ellemers, & S. A. Haslam (Eds.), *The social psychology of stereotyping and group life.* Oxford: Blackwell. (p. 426)

Zagefka, H., & Brown, R. (2005). Comparisons and perceived deprivation in ethnic minority settings. *Personality and Social Psychology Bulletin, **31***, 467. (p. 536)

Zajonc, R. B. (1965). Social facilitation. *Science*, 149, 269-274. (p. 218)

Zajonc, R. B. (1998). Emotions. In D. Gilbert, S. T. Fiske, & G. Lindzey (Eds.), *Handbook of social psychology*, 4th ed. New York: McGraw-Hill. (p. 377)

Zajonc, R. B. (2000). *Massacres: Mass murders in the name of moral imperatives.* Unpublished manuscript, Stanford University. (p. 364)

Zanna, M. P. (1993). Message receptivity: A new look at the old problem of open- vs. closed-mindedness. In A. Mitchell (Ed.), *Advertising: Exposure, memory and choice.* Hillsdale, NJ: Erlbaum. (p. 156)

Zanna, M. P., & Cooper, J. (1974). Dissonance and the pill: An attributional approach to studying the arousal properties of dissonance. *Journal of Personality and Social Psychology*, 29, 703-709. (p. 137)

Zanna, M. P., & Olson, J. M. (1982). Individual differences in attitudinal relations. In M. P. Zanna, E. T. Higgins, & C. P. Herman, (Eds.) *Consistency in social behavior: The Ontario symposium*, Vol. 2. Hillsdale, N.J.: Erlbaum. (p. 68)

Zanna, M. P., & Pack, S. J. (1975). On the self-fulfilling nature of apparent sex differences in behavior. *Journal of Experimental Social Psychology*, 11, 583-591. (p. 120)

Zanna, M. P., Crosby, F., & Loewenstein, G. (1987). Male reference groups and discontent among female professionals. In B. A. Gutek & L. Larwood (Eds.), *Women's career development.* Newbury Park, Ca.: Sage. (p. 341)

Zanna, M. P., Olson, J. M., & Fazio, R. H. (1981). Self-perception and attitude-behavior consistency. *Personality and Social Psychology Bulletin*, 7, 252-256. (p. 117)

Zaragoza, M. S., & Mitchell, K. J. (1996). Repeated exposure to suggestion and the creation of false memories. *Psychological Science*, 7, 294-300. (p. 514)

Zebrowitz, L. A., Collins, M. A., & Dutta, R. (1998). The relationship between appearance and personality across the life span. *Personality and Social Psychology Bulletin*, 24, 736-749. (p. 386)

Zebrowitz, L. A., Olson, K., & Hoffman, K. (1993). Stability of babyfaceness and attractiveness across the life span. *Journal of Personality and Social Psychology*, 64, 453-466. (p. 386)

Zebrowitz-McArthur, L. (1988). Person perception in cross-cultural perspective. In M. H. Bond (Ed.), *The cross-cultural challenge to social psychology.* Newbury Park, Ca.: Sage. (p. 272)

Zillmann, D. (1988). Cognition-excitation interdependencies in aggressive behavior. *Aggressive Behavior*, 14, 51-64. (p. 347)

Zillmann, D. (1989). Effects of prolonged consumption of pornography. In D. Zillmann & J. Bryant (Eds.), *Pornography: Research advances and policy considerations.* Hillsdale, NJ: Erlbaum. (p. 348)

Zillmann, D., & Paulus, P. B. (1993). Spectators: Reactions to sports events and effects on athletic performance. In R. N. Singer, N. Murphey, & L. K. Tennant (Eds.), *Handbook of research on sport psychology.* New York: Macmillan. (p. 219)

Zillmann, D., & Weaver, J. B., III. (1999). Effects of prolonged exposure to gratuitous media violence on provoked and unprovoked hostile behavior. *Journal of Applied Social Psychology*, 29, 145-165. (p. 357)

Zimbardo, P. G. (1970). The human choice: Individuation, reason, and order versus deindividuation, impulse, and chaos. In W. J. Arnold & D. Levine (Eds.), *Nebraska symposium on motivation, 1969.* Lincoln: University of Nebraska Press. (p. 228)

Zimbardo, P. G. (1971). *The psychological power and pathology of imprisonment.* A statement prepared for the U.S. House of Representatives Committee on the Judiciary, Subcommittee No. 3: Hearings on Prison Reform, San Francisco, Calif., October 25. (p. 119)

Zimbardo, P. G. (1972). *The Stanford prison experiment.* A slide/tape presentation produced by Philip G. Zimbardo, Inc., P. O. Box 4395, Stanford, Calif. 94305. (p. 119)

Zimbardo, P. G., Ebbesen, E. B., & Maslach, C. (1977). *Influencing attitudes and changing behavior.* Reading, Mass.: Addison-Wesley. (p. 231)

Zucker, G. S., & Weiner, B. (1993). Conservatism and perceptions of poverty: An attributional analysis. *Journal of Applied Social Psychology*, 23, 925-943. (p. 101)

Zuckerman, E. W., & Jost, J. T. (2001). What makes you think you're so popular? Self-evaluation maintenance and the subjective side of the "friendship paradox." *Social Psychology Quarterly*, 64, 207-223. (p. 46)

Zuwerink, J. R., Monteith, M. J., Devine, P. G., & Cook, D. A. (1996). Prejudice toward blacks: With and without compunction? *Basic and Applied Social Psychology*, 18, 131-150. (p. 441)

ACKNOWLEDGEMENTS

Chapter 2

Figure 2–1, p. 37, From Markus & S. Kitayama, 1991, "Culture and the self: Implications for cognition, emotion, and motivation," *Psychological Review,* 98, pp. 224–253. Copyright 1991 by the American Psychological Association. Reprinted by permission.

Figure 2–2, p. 39, Adapted from *Journal of Experimental Social Psychology,* 26, M. W. Baldwin, S. E. Carrell, and D. F. Lopez, "Priming relationship schemas: My advisor and the Pope are watching me from the back of my head," pp. 435–454, 1989, with permission of Elsevier.

Figure 2–3, p. 45, Adapted from P. Lockwood and Z. Kunda, "Superstars and me: Predicting the impact of role models on the self," *Journal of Personality and Social Psychology,* 73, 1997, pp. 91–103. Copyright © 1997 by the American Psychological Association. Adapted with permission.

Figure 2–4, p. 48, From T.F. Heatherton & K.D. Vohs, 2000, *Journal of Personality and Social Psychology, 78,* pp. 725–736. Copyright 2000 by the American Psychological Association. Reprinted by permission.

Figure 2–6, p. 62, Adapted from A. Wilson & M. Ross, (2001). "From chump to champ: People's appraisals of their earlier and present selves," *Journal of Personality and Social Psychology,* 80, 572–584. (p. 36) Copyright 2001 by the American Psychological Association. Reprinted with permission.

Chapter 3

Figure 3–2, p. 76, © Bettmann/CORBIS Images.

Figure 3–3, p. 91, From J.P. Forgas, G.H. Bower, and S.E. Kranz, 1984, "The influence of mood on perceptions of social interactions," *Journal of Experimental Social Psychology,* 20. Reprinted with permission from Elsevier.

Figure 3–5, p. 96, Data from Jones & Harris, 1967.

Figure 3–7, p. 102, © Esbin-Anderson/Image Works.

Chapter 4

Figure 4–1, p. 116, © Kevin P. Casey/CORBIS.

Figure 4–3, p. 133, (all) © Colin Young-Wolff/PhotoEdit.

Figure 4–5, p. 139, M. P. Zanna, and J. Cooper, "Dissonance and the pill: An attributional approach to studying the arousal properties of dissonance," *Journal of Personality and Social Psychology*, 29, 1974, pp. 703–709. Copyright © 1974 by the American Psychological Association. Adapted with permission.

Chapter 5

Figure 5–1, p. 146, From W. J. McGuire, "An information-processing model of advertising effectiveness," in *Behavioral and Management Sciences in Marketing,* edited by H. L. Davis and A. J. Silk, 1978. Copyright © 1978. Reprinted by permission of John Wiley & Sons, Inc.

Figure 5–9, p. 167, Adapted from L. R. Fabrigar, J. R. Priester, R. E. Petty, and D. T. Wegener, "The impact of attitude accessibility on elaboration of persuasive messages," *Personality and Social Psychology Bulletin*, 24, 1998, pp. 339–352. Reprinted by permission of Sage Publications.

Chapter 6

Figure 6–3, p. 190, From the Milgram Obedience Experiment, in S. Milgram, 1965, "Some Conditions of Obedience and Disobedience to Authority," *Human Relations,* 18, pp. 57–76. Reprinted by permission.

Figure 6–4, p. 201, © James A. Sugar/CORBIS Images.

Figure 6–6, p. 208, Adapted from D. Griffin, D, and R. Buehler, R, "Role of construal process in conformity and dissent," *Journal of Personality and Social Psychology*, 65, 1993, pp. 657–669. Copyright © 1993 by the American Psychological Association. Adapted with permission.

Chapter 7

Figure 7–2, p. 223, Courtesy Alan G. Ingham.

Figure 7–3, p. 224, From Williams, Jackson, and Karau, 1991, in *Social Dilemmas: Perspectives on Individuals and Groups*, D. A. Schroeder, ed. © 1992 by Praeger Publishers. Reproduced with permission of Greenwood Publishing Group, Inc., Westport, CT.

Figure 7–4, p. 225, (Top) © CORBIS/R-F Website (Bottom) © David Young-Wolff/PhotoEdit.

Figure 7–5, p. 229, © Bettmann/CORBIS Images.

Chapter 8

Figure 8–4, p. 268. From S. Kitayama, S. Duffy, T. Hawamura, & J. Larsen, 2003, "Perceiving an Object and its Context in Different Cultures: A Cultural Look at New Look," *Psychological Science,* 14, pp. 201–206. Reprinted by permission.

Figure 8–5, p. 268, From H. Markus and S. Kitayama, "Culture and the Self: Implications for Cognition, Emotion, and Motivation," *Psychological Review*, 98, 1991, pp. 224–253. Copyright 1991 by the American Psychological Association. Reprinted with permission.

Figure 8–6, p. 276, Ekman, P. (1973). *Darwin and Facial Expressions: A Century of Research in Review*. New York: Academic Press.

Chapter 9

Figure 9–2, p. 304, From M. A. Whatley, J. M. Webster, R. H. Smith, and A. Rhodes, 1991. "The Effect of a Favor on Public and Private Compliance: How Internalized is the Norm of Reciprocity?" *Basic and Applied Social Psychology*, 21, pp. 251–259. Reprinted with permission of Lawrence Erlbaum Associates.

Figure 9–3, p. 309, From C. D. Batson, J. Fultz, and P. A. Schoenrade, "Distress and empathy: Two qualitatively distinct vicarious emotions with different motivational consequences," *Journal of Personality*, 55: 1, Spring 1987, Adapted from R.V. Levine, 2003. "The kindness of strangers," American Scientist, 91, 226–233.

Figure 9–7, p. 321, Courtesy Lisa LeBruine.

Chapter 10

Figure 10–4, p. 350, Data is adapted from Statistics Canada Uniform Crime Report, 1996. Reprinted by permission.

Chapter 11

Figure 11–1, p. 374, Eisenberger, N. I., Lieberman, M. D., and Williams, K. D. (2003). "Does rejection hurt? An MRI study of social exclusion." *Science, 302*, pp. 290–292. © 2003 American Association for the Advancement of Science.

Figure 11–2, p. 384, Braun, C., Gruendl, M., Marberger, C., and Scherber, C., 2001, *Beautycheck—Causes and Consequences of Human Facial Attractiveness* as presented at the German Students Award 2000/2001.

Figure 11–3, p. 387, Adapted from J. E. Lydon, M. Meana, D. Sepinwall, N. Richards, N., and S. Mayman, "The commitment calibration hypothesis: When do people devalue attractive alternatives?" *Personality and Social Psychology Bulletin*, 25, 1999, pp. 152–161. Reprinted by permission of Sage Publications.

Figure 11–4, p. 395, (all) Dr. Pawel Lewicki, University of Tulsa, Oklahoma.

Figure 11–6, p. 400, Image courtesy of Lucy L. Brown.

Figure 11–9, p. 409, From A. L. Weber and J. H. Harvey, *Perspective on Close Relationships*. Published by Allyn and Bacon, Boston, MA. © 1994 by Pearson Education. Reprinted by permission of the publisher (From Aron & Aron, 1994.).

Chapter 12

Figure 12–1, pp. 420 and 421, (All) Figure created using stimuli from K. Hugenberg and G. V. Hodenhausen, 2000, "Facing Prejudice: Implicit Prejudice and the Perception of Facial Threat," *Psychological Science, 6*, pp. 640–643. Used with permission of authors. Photos courtesy Kurt Hugenberg, 2000, "Facing Prejudice: Implicit Prejudice and the Perception of Facial Threat," *Psychological Science*, 6, pp. 640–643. Used with permission of authors.

Figure 12–2, p. 423, © Courtesy Dr. Natalie Porter.

Figure 12–3, p. 433, (Top) © Brand X/ PhotoDisc/Getty Images; (Bottom) © Digital Vision/PhotoDisc/Getty Images.

Figure 12–4, p. 442, courtesy James Blascovich.

Figure 12–5, p. 444, From P. G. Devine and R. S. Malpass, 1985, "Orienting Strategies in Differential Face Recognition," *Personality and Social Psychology Bulletin*, 11, pp. 33–40. Reprinted by permission of Sage Publications, Inc.

Figure 12–6, p. 452, Adapted from D. A. Wilder, A. F. Simon, and M. Faith, "Enhancing the impact of counterstereotypic information: Dispositional attributions for deviance," *Journal of Personality and Social Psychology*, 71 (2), 1996, p. 277. Copyright © 1996 by the American Psychological Association. Adapted by permission.

Figure 12–10, p. 461, From Taylor et al., 1990, "The personal/group discrimination discrepancy: Perceiving my group, but not myself, to be a target for discrimination," *Personality and Social Psychology Bulletin*, 16, pp. 254–262.

Module B

Figure B–3, p. 496, Adapted from T. K. MacDonald, M. P. Zanna, and G. T. Fong, "Decision making in altered states: Effects of alcohol on attitudes toward drinking and driving," *Journal of Personality and Social Psychology*, 68, 1995, pp. 973–985. Copyright © 1995 by the American Psychological Association. Adapted with permission.

Module C

Figure C–2, p. 515, (Both) Courtesy Elizabeth Loftus.

Module D

Figure D–2, p. 530, Reprinted by permission of the Population Reference Bureau.

Photo Credits

Chapter 1

Page 2, © PhotoDisc/Getty Images, page 5, The Canadian Press (Jonathan Hayward), page 14 (top), © Steven Spencer, page 14 (bottom), Courtesy Fathali M. Moghaddam, page 21 © Corrance/Still Digital, page 27, © Mary Kate Denny/ PhotoEdit, page 30, © PA/The Canadian Press (Owen Humphreys).

Chapter 2

Page 34, © PhotoDisc/Getty Images, page 42, © AP/Gene Blythe/Wide World Photos, page 47, © Michael Newman/ PhotoEdit, page 56, Courtesy Mike Ross, page 60, © Larry Dale Gordon/Getty Images, page 65, © PhotoDisc/Getty Images, page 69, © Tibor Bognar/ CORBIS Images.

Chapter 3

Page 70, © David J. Phillip/Pool/Reuters/ CORBIS, page 75, © CP/Ian Barrett, page 77, © PhotoDisc/Getty Images, page 80, © PhotoDisc/Getty Images, page 82, Courtesy of Robert Buehler, page 87, © Mark Tomalty/Masterfile, page 90, © PhotoDisc/Getty Images, page 92, Courtesy of Professor Joseph P. Forgas, page 93, © Ellen Senisi/Image Works, page 96, © Everett Collection, page 101, © St. Catherines Standard/Bob Tymczyszyne, page 106, Image Source/ Punchstock.

Chapter 4

Page 110, © Henrischmit/Dreamstime, page 112, © CP/Paul Chiasson, page 113, Courtesy James T. Olson, page 119, ©Associated Press, page 120, © Philip Zimbardo, page 121, Courtesy Mark Zanna, page 123, © CP/David Lewis/ istockphoto, page 124, © CP/Kevin Frayer, page 126, © Chris Bernard/ istockphoto, page 129, Courtesy Leon Festinger, page 131, © Brand X Pictures/ Jupiter Images, page 133, Courtesy Fritz Strack, page 135, F. Bernieri, J. Davis, R. Rosenthal, & C. Knee (1994).

Chapter 5

Page 142, © Topham/Image Works, page 144, Courtesy Children's Defence Fund, page 153, CP/Robert Laberge/Getty Images for NASCAR, page 155, © Health Canada, page 161, © Time Life Pictures/ Getty Images, page 165, courtesy Shelly Chaiken, page 173, © Kate Brooks/CORBIS Images, page 175, © Rachel Epstein/ Image Works, page 179, © Dagmar Heymans/istockphoto.

Chapter 6

Page 180, © Nikada/istockphoto, page 187, © William Vandevert, page 192, Stanley Milgram, 1965, from the film *Obedience*, distributed by the Pennsylvania State University, PCR, page 193, © AP/Wide World Photos, page 195, © Benny Gool/ Capetown Independent Newspaper, page 196, Courtesy Alexandra Milgram, page 197, © Winnipeg Free Press/Marc Gallant, page 201, © James A. Sugar/CORBIS Images, page 204, © AP/Wide World Photos, page 207, © Shaun Best/Reuters/ CORBIS, page 209, © Zia Soleil/Getty, page 211, ©Kathy Wynn/Dreamstime.

com, page 213, © Michael Newman/PhotoEdit.

Chapter 7

Page 214, © Jacob Wackerhausen/istockphoto, page 218, Bob Winsett, Corbis Images, page 220, © Mike Okoniewski, page 226, © Jamie Squire, Getty Images, page 227, Courtesy the Department of National Defence, page 230, © AP/Wide World Photos, page 236, © Tom Brakefield/Stock Connection, page 239, © Kobal Collection, page 243, © The Canadian Press/Frank Gunn, page 245, © Meyer Bruce/CORBIS Images, page 246, Courtesy Daniel Kahneman, page 249, © Mark Richards/PhotoEdit.

Chapter 8

Page 254, © Junghee Choi/istockphoto, page 260, © Steven Spencer, page 262, © Fujifotos/ImageWorks, page 265, (left) © Ralph Bower/Vancouver Sun, (right) © CP/Victoria Times Colonist, page 271, (left) Courtesy Dr. Hazel Rose Marcus, Stanford University, (right) Courtesy Mel Manis, page 272, © Alexander Hafemann/istockphoto, page 281, CORBIS, page 283, Bonnie Jacobs/istockphoto, page 285, Brand X Pictures/Getty Images, page 286, CORBIS.

Chapter 9

Page 294, © Darryl Brooks/Dreamstime, page 298, Courtesy Dennis Krebs, page 307, Courtesy Mark Schaller, page 310, © The Canadian Press/Tom Hanson, page 314, © Mark Zemnick, page 315, © CORBIS Sygma, page 316, © The McGraw-Hill Companies, Inc./Christopher Kerrigan, photographer, page 326, © CP/Hans Deryk.

Chapter 10

Page 330, Digital Vision/Getty Images, page 335, © Poodles Rock/CORBIS, page 337, © Jeff Share/Black Star, page 342, © O. Buriel/Photo Researchers, page 343, © Albert Bandura, page 346, © AP/Wide World Photos, page 348, © CP/Chuck Stoody, page 350, © Brandon Sun/Colin Corneau, page 352, © Kingston Whig Standard/Jack Chiang, page 358, Courtesy Jacques-Phillippe Leyens, page 364, © Gus van Dyk, Pilanesberg.

Chapter 11

Page 370, Brand X Pictures/Getty Images, page 373, © Digital Vision/Getty Images, page 376, PhotoDisc/Getty Images, page 383, Courtesy Ellen Berscheid, University of Minnesota, page 386, (Left) © Rick Smolan/Stock Boston, (Centre Left) © Paul Lau, (Centre Right) © Catherine Karnow/Woodfin Camp, (Right) © Marc Romanelli/Getty Images, page 388, © Granger Collection, page 391, © Jerome Sessini/inVisu/CORBIS, page 397, © Joe Polillio, page 401, Courtesy James M. Jones, page 405, Courtesy Kim Bartholemew, page 407, © Bananastock/Maxximages.com.

Chapter 12

Page 414, © Tim Boyle/Getty Images, page 417, © Digital Vision/Getty Images, page 419, © Martin Purmensky/Dreamstime, page 420, (Both) J. Correll, B. Park, C. M. Judd, and B. Wittenbrink, 2002, "The police officer's dilemma: Using ethnicity to disambiguate potentially threatening individuals," *Journal of Personality and Social Psychology*, 83, 1316, Fig. 1. Images courtesy Josh Correll, page 426, CP Photo, 1999, National Archives of Canada/Tak Toyota, page 434, © CP/Ryan Remiorz, page 435, © AP/Wide World Photos, page 436, Courtesy Victoria Esses, page 437, © 1999 Allan Tannenbaum, page 445, © AP/Wide World Photos, page 451, © Bob Daemmrich/Stock Boston, page 456, Courtesy Dr. Claude Steele, page 458, Courtesy Paul Thagard, page 462, Courtesy Don Taylor.

Module A

Page 464, Courtesy Steven Spencer, page 466, © CP/Chuck Stoody, page 472, © Joseph Sohm, ChromoSohm/CORBIS Images, page 479, © Mark Antman/Image Works.

Module B

Page 484, Courtesy Steven Spencer, page 492, Courtesy Shelley Taylor, page 494, Courtesy Del Paulhus, page 501, © Jacques Chenet/Getty Images.

Module C

Page 510, Courtesy Steven Spencer, page 517, Courtesy Gary Wells.

Module D

Page 527, GNU and Creative Commons, page 529, © Ilene MacDonald/Alamy, page 531, © Kayte M. Deioma/PhotoEdit.

SUBJECT INDEX

A

B

D

E

F

G

N

O

P

R

NAME INDEX

A

B

C

D

E

F

I

J

K

L

M

N

O

P

Q

R

S

X

Y

Z

T

U

V

W